The
Warner
Guide to
UK &
US Hit
Singles

The
Warner
Guide to
UK &
US Hit
Singles

Compiled by
Dave McAleer

CARLTON

LITTLE
BROWN

A CARLTON/LITTLE, BROWN BOOK

First published in Great Britain in 1994 by Little, Brown and Company

ISBN: 0-316-91076-7

A CIP catalogue record for this book is available from the British Library.

Little, Brown and Company (UK) Ltd
Brettenham House
Lancaster Place
London WC2E 7EN.

Project Editor: Honor Head
Project Art Director: Bobbie Colgate Stone
Editor: Tony Brown
Design: Simon Wilder
Production: Sarah Schuman

Printed and bound in Great Britain by Mackays

All photographs supplied by London Features International

Author's Acknowledgements:
The Billboard Chart information is copyright ©1954/91 by BPI Communications used courtesy
of Billboard. Billboard ® is a registered trademark of BPI Communications.

The Billboard Chart information is copyright © 1991/92/93 by BPI Communications and
Soundscan, Inc. used courtesy of Billboard. Billboard ® is a registered trademark of BPI
Communications.

UK Chart information 1954 -1963 courtesy of *NME.*
UK Chart information 1964 -1983 © *Music Week*
UK Chart information 1983 -1990 © BPI. Compiled by Gallup.
UK Chart information 1990 - 1993 © CIN. Compiled by Gallup.

Contents

The complete Top 20 US and UK charts from 1954 to the present day. Also detailed are artists' first and last hit; peak position of the previous month; the record label; weeks in the chart; instant UK/US chart comparison and whether the record achieved gold or platinum status.

Chart facts, artist gossip and commentary on the general developments in the music industry specific to each month.

Alphabetical listing of all artists who had a Top 20, nationality of artist, and chart entry dates of hits.

Alphabetical listing by song title giving artist to enable quick and easy cross-referencing.

Johnny Mathis

Most of the world's top recording artists in the forty-year period between 1954 and 1993 hailed from either America or Britain. These two countries set the majority of musical trends, that kept pop record buyers entertained around the globe.

The major musical happening during the period was undoubtedly the growth of rock. It evolved out of late 1940s R&B and C&W music and was spread world-wide in the mid-1950s by Bill Haley and Elvis Presley. In the 1960s, The Beatles and other British bands, weaned on American rock'n'roll and R&B, gave it a new lease of life. Rock then diversified into scores of successful sub-genres, making many more American and British recording artists international household names.

These forty years have seen many changes including the rise in popularity of female singers, black artists, and performers from outside the USA. Among the few things of which you could be certain during the period was that an endless stream of teen idols would come and go, that there would always be room for a good "novelty", and that the moral majority would, from time to time, attack the lyrics of rock and R&B records.

The aim of this book is to try and put the 10,000 most successful records of the rock era into some kind of perspective. The transatlantic chart careers of every American or British hit can be checked in the easy-to-follow, fact-packed charts. At a glance you can see all the similarities and indeed differences between the tastes of America and Britain, the most important and influential countries in the world of music.

HOW THIS BOOK WORKS The chart positions used for compiling the monthly Top 20s were those accepted at the time as the most accurate. In America, Billboard's chart positions have been used throughout, while in Britain, data for the first ten years is taken from the most popularly used chart at the time printed in the *New Musical Express (NME)*, and from 1964 onwards from the chart carried in the industry's trade magazine, *Record Retailer* which later became *Music Week*.

If a single's title was spelt differently in the USA and Britain, it is listed on the chart as it was spelt in that country. However, in the index it can be found under the American spelling.

The gold record designation (G) used on the charts indicates that the record sold over a million copies in that country. Gold records only started being certified in the USA in 1958, and even then some companies (including Motown) did not believe in certifying sales figures. Therefore some educated guesses have had to be made in this area. Also platinum (P) certification for two million sellers only started in 1976, records that previously sold over that amount (and there were many), only carry a (G) designation.

Equivalent American or British chart positions are not included if there is a gap of three years of more between the two chart entries, since this would give a false impression of the record's success at the time. Also, when two artists have more than one hit together, e.g. Marvin Gaye & Tammi Terrell, the first and last hit designations refer to the actual duo, and not the first named artist as in all other cases.

CHART FILES The Top 20 UK and US charts are compiled by means of a complex and comprehensive system which considers not only a record's weekly chart positions and peak position, but also the number of weeks it spent on the Top 10 and Top 20, its weeks at No. 1 (if applicable) and its performance on other major charts.

Apart from normal chart features these Top 20s also show:
(a) The total number of weeks a record spent in the country's Top 20 during that chart run.
(b) The record's equivalent position in the UK/US, if within three years either way.
(c) Whether it was the artist's (or the first named artist in the case of duos) first (F) or most recent (L) Top 20 entry in that country.
(d) Whether it sold a million (G) or two million copies (P) in that country.

LISTING BY ARTIST'S NAME This easy-to-check index lists an artist's hits in alphabetical order and shows the month the hit entered this book's UK and US Top 20. Therefore, it is a simple matter to check the charts concerned for more information about the record. This index also shows the nationality of the act concerned and indicates if the record was a re-issue or re-mix of a previous Top 20 hit (*), or whether the act was a shared hit (❖). If it was a shared hit, the main entry is under the artist first named on the label but the song is also listed under the second or other names.

LISTING BY SONG TITLE An alphabetical listing of all the song titles in this book with the artist's name.

The chart below is based on a points system which takes in to consideration a record's weekly Top 20 position, its peak position and weeks in Top 10 and Top 20. If a record has been re-issued or re-mixed then points are added together. If a record has been re-recorded it is counted separately.

US Top 100 Singles 1954-93

Pos	Title	Artist
1	The Twist	Chubby Checker
2	I Will Always Love You	Whitney Houston
3	End Of The Road	Boyz II Men
4	Hound Dog/Don't Be Cruel	Elvis Presley
5	Little Things Mean A Lot	Kitty Kallen
6	Cherry Pink And Apple Blossom White	Perez Prado
7	Singing The Blues	Guy Mitchell
8	Wanted	Perry Como
9	Physical	Olivia Newton-John
10	Mack The Knife	Bobby Darin
11	You Light Up My Life	Debby Boone
12	Rock Around The Clock	Bill Haley & His Comets
13	Oh! My Pa-Pa	Eddie Fisher
14	Hey There	Rosemary Clooney
15	Sh-Boom	Crew-Cuts
16	Hey Jude	Beatles
17	Bette Davis Eyes	Kim Carnes
18	Monster Mash	Bobby 'Boris' Pickett & The Crypt Kickers
19	Endless Love	Diana Ross & Lionel Richie
20	Heartbreak Hotel	Elvis Presley
21	Dreamlover	Mariah Carey
22	Theme From 'A Summer Place'	Percy Faith
23	That's The Way Love Goes	Janet Jackson
24	(I Can't Help) Falling In Love With You	UB40
25	All Shook Up	Elvis Presley
26	Mr Sandman	Chordettes
27	Sixteen Tons	Tennessee Ernie Ford
28	Every Breath You Take	Police
29	Jump	Kris Kross
30	Night Fever	Bee Gees
31	Teddy Bear	Elvis Presley

Whitney Houston   **Bee Gees**

Pos	Title	Artist
32	Love Letters In The Sand	Pat Boone
33	Eye Of The Tiger	Survivor
34	The Yellow Rose Of Texas	Mitch Miller
35	Jailhouse Rock	Elvis Presley
36	The Wayward Wind	Gogi Grant
37	Le Freak	Chic
38	Informer	Snow
39	Shadow Dancing	Andy Gibb
40	Sincerely	McGuire Sisters
41	Tonight's The Night (Gonna Be Alright)	Rod Stewart
42	Tossin' And Turnin'	Bobby Lewis
43	Baby Got Back	Sir Mix-A-Lot
44	The Ballad Of Davy Crockett	Bill Hayes
45	Flashdance...What A Feeling	Irene Cara

Pos	Title	Artist
46	I Love Rock 'n' Roll	Joan Jett & The Blackhearts
47	Love Me Tender	Elvis Presley
48	Autumn Leaves	Roger Williams
49	I Want To Hold Your Hand	Beatles
50	Say Say Say	Paul McCartney & Michael Jackson
51	Call Me	Blondie
52	Bohemian Rhapsody	Queen
53	Ebony And Ivory	Paul McCartney & Stevie Wonder
54	I'm A Believer	Monkees
55	Memories Are Made Of This	Dean Martin
56	I Heard It Through The Grapevine	Marvin Gaye
57	Lisbon Antigua	Nelson Riddle
58	Lady	Kenny Rogers
59	Billie Jean	Michael Jackson
60	I Need You Now	Eddie Fisher
61	(Everything I Do) I Do It For You	Bryan Adams
62	Centerfold	J. Geils Band
63	It's All In The Game	Tommy Edwards
64	Aquarius/Let The Sunshine In	Fifth Dimension
65	Black Or White	Michael Jackson
66	My Sharona	Knack
67	Save The Best For Last	Vanessa Williams
68	I Just Want To Be Your Everything	Andy Gibb
69	Joy To The World	Three Dog Night
70	(Just Like) Starting Over	John Lennon
71	The First Time Ever I Saw Your Face	Roberta Flack
72	This Ole House	Rosemary Clooney
73	Make Love To Me!	Jo Stafford
74	Are You Lonesome Tonight?	Elvis Presley
75	At The Hop	Danny & The Juniors
76	The Poor People Of Paris	Les Baxter
77	Best Of My Love	Emotions
78	Secret Love	Doris Day
79	Tammy	Debbie Reynolds
80	Bridge Over Troubled Water	Simon & Garfunkel
81	How Deep Is Your Love	Bee Gees
82	Stayin' Alive	Bee Gees
83	When Doves Cry	Prince
84	It's Now Or Never	Elvis Presley
85	Another One Bites The Dust	Queen
86	I'd Do Anything For Love (But I Won't Do That)	Meat Loaf*
87	I'll Be There	Jackson Five
88	Maggie May/Reason To Believe	Rod Stewart
89	All Night Long (All Night)	Lionel Richie
90	Like A Virgin	Madonna
91	Upside Down	Diana Ross
92	Freak Me	Silk
93	Raindrops Keep Fallin' On My Head	B.J. Thomas
94	Love Is A Many-Splendored Thing	Four Aces
95	Silly Love Songs	Wings
96	Nel Blu Dipinto Di Blu (Volare)	Domenico Modugno
97	I Can't Stop Loving You	Ray Charles
98	Alone Again (Naturally)	Gilbert O'Sullivan
99	Bad Girls	Donna Summer
100	Love Is Blue	Paul Mauriat

*Still charting at end of survey

Pos	Title	Artist
1	Rock Around The Clock	Bill Haley & His Comets
2	Relax	Frankie Goes To Hollywood
3	Bohemian Rhapsody	Queen
4	You've Lost That Lovin' Feeling	Righteous Brothers
5	Holiday	Madonna
6	(Everything I Do) I Do It For You	Bryan Adams
7	Sailing	Rod Stewart
8	Do They Know It's Christmas	Band Aid
9	Take My Breath Away	Berlin
10	Albatross	Fleetwood Mac
11	Let's Twist Again	Chubby Checker
12	Reet Petite	Jackie Wilson
13	I Will Survive	Gloria Gaynor
14	Young Girl	Gary Puckett & The Union Gap

Madonna   *John Travolta*

Pos	Title	Artist
15	He Ain't Heavy, He's My Brother	Hollies
16	Secret Love	Doris Day
17	Imagine	John Lennon
18	You To Me Are Everything	Real Thing
19	Cara Mia	David Whitfield
20	Space Oddity	David Bowie
21	Mary's Boy Child	Harry Belafonte
22	Give Me Your Word	Tennessee Ernie Ford
23	All Right Now	Free
24	Leader Of The Pack	Shangri-Las
25	When I Fall In Love	Nat 'King' Cole
26	Rose Marie	Slim Whitman
27	Young At Heart	Bluebells
28	She Loves You	Beatles
29	I Heard It Through The Grapevine	Marvin Gaye
30	Crazy For You	Madonna
31	Oh Mein Papa	Eddie Calvert
32	Blue Monday	New Order
33	A Whiter Shade Of Pale	Procol Harum
34	Diana	Paul Anka
35	Here In My Heart	Al Martino
36	I Will Always Love You	Whitney Houston
37	When A Man Loves A Woman	Percy Sledge
38	You're The One That I Want	John Travolta & Olivia Newton-John
39	Unchained Melody	Righteous Brothers
40	In The Air Tonight	Phil Collins
41	Y.M.C.A.	Village People
42	Reach Out I'll Be There	Four Tops
43	Wonderful Land	Shadows
44	I Remember You	Frank Ifield
45	Happy Xmas (War Is Over)	John Lennon/Plastic Ono Band
46	Sugar Sugar	Archies
47	All I Have To Do Is Dream/Claudette	Everly Brothers
48	It's Now Or Never	Elvis Presley
49	Cathy's Clown	Everly Brothers
50	Two Tribes	Frankie Goes To Hollywood
51	Mull Of Kintyre/Girls' School	Wings

Pos	Title	Artist
52	I'll Be Home	Pat Boone
53	Heartbreak Hotel	Elvis Presley
54	Hey Jude	Beatles
55	Last Christmas/Everything She Wants	Wham!
56	Magic Moments	Perry Como
57	Just Walkin' In The Rain	Johnnie Ray
58	Who's Sorry Now	Connie Francis
59	Whatever Will Be Will Be	Doris Day
60	Rivers Of Babylon/Brown Girl In The Ring	Boney M
61	Side Saddle	Russ Conway
62	Stay	Shakespears Sister
63	Can't Get By Without You	Real Thing
64	All Shook Up	Elvis Presley
65	Young Love	Tab Hunter
66	Living Doll	Cliff Richard
67	What Do You Want To Make Those Eyes At Me For	Emile Ford & The Checkmates
68	Have You Seen Her	Chi-Lites
69	The Israelites	Desmond Dekker & The Aces
70	Tears	Ken Dodd
71	Baby Love	Supremes
72	Rhythm Is A Dancer	Snap
73	Hold My Hand	Don Cornell
74	Green Green Grass Of Home	Tom Jones
75	Let's Dance	Chris Montez
76	Cherry Pink And Apple Blossom White	Eddie Calvert
77	Telstar	Tornados
78	Drive	Cars
79	Carolina Moon/Stupid Cupid	Connie Francis
80	I'd Do Anything For Love (But I Won't Do That)	Meat Loaf*
81	I See The Moon	Stargazers
82	The Last Waltz	Engelbert Humperdinck
83	In The Summertime	Mungo Jerry
84	I Want You Back	Jackson Five
85	Apache	Shadows
86	Softly Softly	Ruby Murray
87	Two Little Boys	Rolf Harris
88	From Me To You	Beatles
89	House Of The Rising Sun	Animals
90	The Wonder Of You	Elvis Presley
91	Release Me	Engelbert Humperdinck

Cliff Richard   *Jackson Five*

Pos	Title	Artist
92	Merry Xmas Everybody	Slade
93	Ride On Time	Black Box
94	It Must Be Love	Madness
95	Those Were The Days	Mary Hopkin
96	A Woman In Love	Frankie Laine
97	Distant Drums	Jim Reeves
98	Summer Nights	John Travolta & Olivia Newton-John
99	Travellin' Light	Cliff Richard
100	No Other Love	Ronnie Hilton

Top All Time Singles Artists In The US

Pos	Name	First Hit	Last Hit
1	Elvis Presley	1956	77
2	Beatles	1964	82
3	Stevie Wonder	1963	87
4	Michael Jackson	1971	93
5	Elton John	1971	92
6	Madonna	1984	93
7	Rolling Stones	1964	89

Rolling Stones

Pos	Name	First Hit	Last Hit
8	Paul McCartney/ Wings	1971	86
9	Supremes	1964	72
10	Bee Gees	1967	89
11	Chicago	1970	90
12	Whitney Houston	1985	93
13	Prince	1980	93
14	Daryl Hall & John Oates	1976	90
15	Janet Jackson	1986	93
16	Marvin Gaye	1963	82
17	Olivia Newton-John	1973	85
18	Aretha Franklin	1967	89
19	Rod Stewart	1971	93
20	Ricky Nelson	1957	72
21	Beach Boys	1962	88
22	Temptations	1964	73
23	Four Seasons	1962	76
24	Neil Diamond	1966	82
25	Pat Boone	1955	62
26	Phil Collins	1981	90
27	Connie Francis	1958	63
28	Diana Ross	1970	85
29	Donna Summer	1975	89
30	Carpenters	1970	81
31	Billy Joel	1978	93
32	Everly Brothers	1957	62
33	Lionel Richie	1981	87
34	Paul Anka	1957	75
35	Kenny Rogers	1968	84
36	Jackson Five/ Jacksons	1969	84
37	Brenda Lee	1960	66
38	Mariah Carey	1990	93
39	Three Dog Night	1969	74
40	George Michael	1985	92
41	Barbra Streisand	1964	81
42	Dionne Warwick	1964	87
43	Perry Como	1955	70
44	Duran Duran	1983	93
45	Huey Lewis & The News	1982	91
46	Bobby Vinton	1962	74
47	Eagles	1972	80
48	Ray Charles	1959	67
49	Barry Manilow	1974	84
50	Cher	1965	91
51	Herman's Hermits	1964	67
52	Bryan Adams	1983	92
53	Foreigner	1977	88
54	Chubby Checker	1960	64
55	Bobby Darin	1958	66
56	Kool & The Gang	1974	87
57	Four Tops	1964	81
58	Paula Abdul	1989	92
59	Linda Ronstadt	1975	90
60	Neil Sedaka	1959	80
61	Platters	1955	67
62	Commodores	1975	85
63	Fleetwood Mac	1976	88
64	Gladys Knight & The Pips	1961	88
65	Bob Seger & The Silver Bullet Band	1969	87
66	John Cougar Mellencamp	1981	91
67	Brook Benton	1959	70
68	Richard Marx	1987	92
69	Simon & Garfunkel	1965	75
70	Gloria Estefan	1986	91
71	Smokey Robinson & The Miracles	1961	76
72	Fats Domino	1955	61
73	Nat 'King' Cole	1955	63
74	Bruce Springsteen	1980	92
75	Heart	1976	90
76	Roy Orbison	1960	89
77	John Lennon	1969	84
78	Dave Clark Five	1964	67
79	Bobby Brown	1988	93
80	Frank Sinatra	1955	67
81	Eddie Fisher	1954	56
82	Creedence Clearwater Revival	1968	71
83	Bon Jovi	1986	93
84	Spinners	1970	80
85	Pointer Sisters	1973	85
86	Sam Cooke	1957	65
87	Johnny Rivers	1964	77
88	Fifth Dimension	1967	72
89	New Kids On The Block	1988	92
90	KC & The Sunshine Band	1975	80
91	Genesis	1980	92
92	Dion	1960	68
93	Michael Bolton	1985	92
94	Air Supply	1980	85
95	Monkees	1966	86
96	John Denver	1971	76
97	Cyndi Lauper	1984	89
98	James Brown	1963	86
99	Andy Gibb	1977	81
100	Billy Ocean	1984	88

Charts based on a points system which takes into consideration a Records Weekly top 20 position, its peak position and weeks in top 10 and top 20. If a record has been re-issued or re-mixed then points are added together. If a record has been re-recorded it is counted separately.

*Still charting at end of survey

Top All Time Singles Artists In The UK

Pos	Name	First Hit	Last Hit
1	Elvis Presley	1956	80
2	Cliff Richard	1958	93
3	Beatles	1963	82
4	Madonna	1984	93
5	Michael Jackson	1972	93
6	Rod Stewart	1971	93
7	David Bowie	1969	93
8	Queen	1974	91
9	Paul McCartney/ Wings	1971	93
10	Rolling Stones	1963	86
11	Abba	1974	92
12	Elton John	1971	92
13	Status Quo	1968	90
14	Stevie Wonder	1966	88
15	Lonnie Donegan	1956	62
16	Shadows	1960	80
17	Slade	1971	84
18	Everly Brothers	1957	65
19	Hollies	1963	88
20	Bee Gees	1967	91
21	Shakin' Stevens	1980	90
22	Tom Jones	1965	93
23	Frank Sinatra	1955	86
24	Kylie Minogue	1988	92
25	Diana Ross	1970	93
26	Pat Boone	1955	62
27	UB40	1980	93
28	Madness	1979	92
29	Pet Shop Boys	1985	93
30	Roy Orbison	1960	66
31	T. Rex	1970	91
32	Perry Como	1956	73
33	Supremes	1964	72
34	Kinks	1964	83
35	Adam Faith	1959	64
36	Phil Collins	1981	93
37	Connie Francis	1958	62
38	Electric Light Orchestra	1972	83
39	Hot Chocolate	1970	87
40	Manfred Mann	1964	73
41	Duran Duran	1981	93
42	Whitney Houston	1985	93
43	Frankie Vaughan	1955	67
44	Beach Boys	1964	87
45	Petula Clark	1955	88
46	Frankie Laine	1955	59
47	Police	1979	84
48	Olivia Newton-John	1971	90
49	Blondie	1978	82
50	Gary Glitter	1972	84
51	Shirley Bassey	1957	73
52	Four Tops	1966	88
53	Bill Haley	1955	74
54	U2	1983	93
55	Erasure	1986	92
56	Prince	1984	93
57	Showaddywaddy	1974	79
58	Who	1965	81
59	Mud	1973	76
60	Donna Summer	1976	89
61	Wham!	1982	86
62	Dean Martin	1955	69
63	Herman's Hermits	1964	70
64	George Michael	1984	92
65	Sweet	1971	78
66	Cilla Black	1964	71
67	Billy Fury	1959	65
68	Dusty Springfield	1963	89
69	David Whitfield	1955	58
70	Jason Donovan	1988	91
71	Jacksons/Jackson Five	1970	88
72	Jam	1977	82
73	Roxy Music	1972	82
74	John Lennon	1969	84
75	Boney M	1977	92
76	Engelbert Humperdinck	1967	72
77	David Essex	1973	83
78	Gene Pitney	1963	68
79	Duane Eddy	1958	86
80	Depeche Mode	1981	93
81	Bay City Rollers	1971	77
82	Iron Maiden	1982	93
83	Johnnie Ray	1955	57
84	10cc	1972	78
85	Spandau Ballet	1980	86
86	Bananarama	1982	91
87	Nat 'King' Cole	1955	91
88	Kim Wilde	1981	93
89	Leo Sayer	1973	83
90	Andy Williams	1957	74
91	Stylistics	1972	76
92	Guy Mitchell	1956	60
93	Searchers	1963	66
94	Winifred Atwell	1955	59
95	Bobby Darin	1958	66
96	Sandie Shaw	1964	69
97	Jim Reeves	1960	70
98	Fleetwood Mac	1968	88
99	New Kids On The Block	1989	91
100	A-Ha	1985	93

David Bowie

50s

Little Richard

Dean Martin

Left: *Elvis Presley*

The record business was growing and thriving long before rock'n'roll (r'n'r) hit the pop chart. Many of the century's most respected recording artists reached their peaks in the early 1950s, and scores of outstanding pop songs were first heard in those years. The sales of singles by song stylists such as Perry Como, Doris Day and Eddie Fisher were staggering, and performers like Johnnie Ray and Frankie Laine created the type of fan hysteria normally associated with later idols.

Bill Haley and the Comets

11

50s

By the beginning of 1954, few in the record industry foresaw the arrival of r'n'r, and none could have imagined the impact that it would have on the musical status quo. When the first r'n'r records appeared on the pop chart, the music was simply regarded as a "novelty" or a "passing fad". History, however, shows that r'n'r, which evolved from the collision between rhythm & blues, country & western and pop in the first half of the decade, had grown into the biggest force in transatlantic popular music by the late 1950s.

At the dawn of the "fabulous fifties", R&B's popularity had been confined to the USA's African American population. By 1952, hip white teenagers were discovering it, and soon its influence was being felt in both C&W and pop music. Several white acts, including Bill Haley and His Comets, incorporated the R&B beat into their music helping to form the hybrid known as "rock'n'roll". In the mid-1950s, sanitized cover versions of R&B hits flooded the pop charts on both sides of the Atlantic. Soon the public tired of pale imitations and insisted on the "real thing" – be it tagged R&B or rock'n'roll (which was then basically commercial R&B under another name). Fats Domino, Pat Boone, Frankie Lymon and The Teenagers, Chuck Berry, The Platters and Little Richard were among the first rock'n'roll stars to emerge. The floodgates really opened for rock'n'rollers in 1956, when Elvis Presley re-wrote all the record books. He was soon followed by such great original artists as Gene Vincent, Carl Perkins, Buddy Holly, the Everly Brothers, Jerry Lee Lewis and also scores of less talented would-be rock'n'roll heroes.

R&B music was still the source of most rock'n'roll in 1957, but thanks to the input of country & western, rockabilly and pop performers, rock'n'roll was now evolving in its own right. By 1959, rock'n'roll had softened and even the term itself was used more sparingly.

By the end of the fifties, Elvis was in the US Army, Little Richard had retired and Chuck Berry and The Platters had been charged with immoral offences. Alan Freed, rock'n'roll's greatest mentor and top radio DJ, had been sacked, Jerry Lee Lewis was in disgrace for marrying a minor and Buddy Holly was dead – all-in-all, rock'n'roll was in a pretty bad way. R&B, however, continued to be exciting and the new rock'n'roll-based and gospel-laced sound, which helped put a record 44 R&B singles in the US Top 20 in 1959, was to greatly influence many records in the swinging and soulful sixties.

Frankie Lymon and The Teenagers

Ricky Nelson

The Four Aces

Top UK Artists in US 1954-59
1 Laurie London
2 Frank Weir
3 Chris Barber Jazz Band
4 Russ Hamilton
5 Lonnie Donegan
6 David Whitfield
7 Frank Chacksfield
8 Reg Owen
9 Eddie Calvert
10 Cyril Stapleton

Lonnie Donegan

Top Singles Artists in the US 1954-1959

1	Elvis Presley	(US)	RCA
2	Pat Boone	(US)	Dot
3	Perry Como	(US)	RCA
4	Ricky Nelson	(US)	Verve/Imperial
5	Platters	(US)	Mercury
6	Eddie Fisher	(US)	RCA
7	Everly Brothers	(US)	Cadence
8	Fats Domino	(US)	Imperial
9	Nat 'King' Cole	(US)	Capitol
10	Paul Anka	(Can)	ABC Paramount
11	Four Aces	(US)	Decca
12	Frankie Avalon	(US)	Chancellor
13	Bill Haley & His Comets	(US)	Decca
14	Crew-Cuts	(Can)	Mercury
15	McGuire Sisters	(US)	Coral
16	Patti Page	(US)	Mercury
17	Frank Sinatra	(US)	Capitol
18	Four Lads	(US)	Columbia
19	Coasters	(US)	Atco
20	Bobby Darin	(US)	Atco

Top US Singles 1954-59

1	Hound Dog/Don't Be Cruel	Elvis Presley
2	Little Things Mean A Lot	Kitty Kallen
3	Cherry Pink And Apple Blossom White	Perez Prado
4	Singing The Blues	Guy Mitchell
5	Wanted	Perry Como
6	Mack The Knife	Bobby Darin
7	Rock Around The Clock	Bill Haley & His Comets
8	Oh! My Pa-Pa	Eddie Fisher
9	Hey There	Rosemary Clooney
10	Sh-Boom	Crew-Cuts

Top Singles Artists in the UK 1954-1959

1	Elvis Presley	(US)	HMV/RCA
2	Lonnie Donegan	(UK)	Decca/Pye Nixa
3	Pat Boone	(US)	London American
4	Frankie Laine	(US)	Philips
5	Bill Haley & His Comets	(US)	Brunswick
6	David Whitfield	(UK)	Decca
7	Perry Como	(US)	HMV/RCA
8	Johnnie Ray	(US)	Philips
9	Dean Martin	(US)	Capitol
10	Frank Sinatra	(US)	Capitol
11	Frankie Vaughan	(UK)	Philips
12	Winifred Atwell	(UK)	Decca
13	Ruby Murray	(UK)	Columbia
14	Guy Mitchell	(US)	Philips
15	Everly Brothers	(US)	London American
16	Doris Day	(US)	Philips
17	Ronnie Hilton	(UK)	HMV
18	Dickie Valentine	(UK)	Decca
19	Connie Francis	(US)	MGM
20	Tommy Steele	(UK)	Decca

Top UK Singles 1954-59

1	Rock Around The Clock	Bill Haley and His Comets
2	Secret Love	Doris Day
3	Cara Mia	David Whitfield
4	Mary's Boy Child	Harry Belafonte
5	Give Me Your Word	Tennessee Ernie Ford
6	Rose Marie	Slim Whitman
7	Oh Mein Papa	Eddie Calvert
8	Diana	Paul Anka
9	All I Have To Do Is Dream/ Claudette	Everly Brothers
10	I'll Be Home	Pat Boone

The McGuire Sisters

Paul Anka

The Drifters

UK 1954

JAN-MAR

◆ Swiss song 'Oh Mein Papa' (aka 'Oh! My Pa-Pa') was the top transatlantic hit. In the USA Eddie Fisher's vocal topped the chart with British-based trumpeter Eddie Calvert's version runner-up. In Britain the roles were reversed.

◆ American songwriter Joe Darion had a hot winter with his compositions 'Changing Partners' (Patti Page, Kay Starr, Bing Crosby) and 'Ricochet' (Teresa Brewer, Joan Regan) hitting on both sides of the Atlantic.

◆ Even though 'I Saw Mommy Kissing Santa Claus' was written by Englishman, Tommie Connor, the Christmas novelty was not released in Britain until a year after 13-year-old Jimmy Boyd had topped the US chart with the song. It then charted for both Boyd and Britain's top female vocal group, The Beverley Sisters.

January 1954

This Mnth	Prev Mnth	Title	Artist	Label	Wks 20	(US Pos)	
1	12	Oh Mein Papa	Eddie Calvert	Columbia	21	(9)	F
2	1	Answer Me	Frankie Laine	Philips	17		
3	4	Let's Have A Party	Winifred Atwell	Philips	9		
4	3	Swedish Rhapsody	Mantovani	Decca	18		
5	15	Cloud Lucky Seven	Guy Mitchell	Philips	15		
6	-	Blowing Wild	Frankie Laine	Philips	12		
7	-	Rags To Riches	David Whitfield	Decca	11		
8	6	Chika Boom	Guy Mitchell	Philips	15		
9	2	Answer Me	David Whitfield	Decca	14		
10	18	Ricochet	Joan Regan	Decca	5		F
11	10	Poppa Piccolino	Diana Decker	Columbia	10		F L
12	-	Happy Wanderer	Obernkirchen Children's Choir	Parlophone	26		F L
13	-	That's Amore	Dean Martin	Capitol	11	(2)	
14	11	Crying In The Chapel	Lee Lawrence	Decca	6		F
15	-	The Creep	Ken Mackintosh	HMV	2		F
16	7	Swedish Rhapsody	Ray Martin	Columbia	4		L
17	8	I Saw Mommy Kissing Santa Claus	Beverley Sisters	Philips	5		F
18	5	I Saw Mommy Kissing Santa Claus	Jimmy Boyd	Columbia	6	(1)	F L
19	-	Oh! My Pa-Pa	Eddie Fisher	HMV	3	(1)	
20	16	Dragnet	Ray Anthony	Capitol	2	(3)	F L

February 1954

This Mnth	Prev Mnth	Title	Artist	Label	Wks 20	(US Pos)	
1	1	Oh Mein Papa	Eddie Calvert	Columbia	21	(9)	F
2	6	Blowing Wild	Frankie Laine	Philips	12		
3	5	Cloud Lucky Seven	Guy Mitchell	Philips	15		
4	13	That's Amore	Dean Martin	Capitol	11	(2)	
5	7	Rags To Riches	David Whitfield	Decca	11		
6	-	Tennessee Wig Walk	Bonnie Lou	Parlophone	10		F L
7	12	Happy Wanderer	Obernkirchen Children's Choir	Parlophone	26		F L
8	-	Man	Rosemary Clooney	Philips	5		
9	2	Answer Me	Frankie Laine	Philips	17		
10	4	Swedish Rhapsody	Mantovani	Decca	18		
11	-	Skin Deep	Ted Heath	Decca	3		
12	8	Chika Boom	Guy Mitchell	Philips	15		
13	-	Don't Laugh At Me	Norman Wisdom	Columbia	15		F
14	-	The Book	David Whitfield	Decca	15		
15	-	I See The Moon	Stargazers	Decca	15		
16	-	Ebb Tide	Frank Chacksfield	Decca	2	(2)	
17	-	Woman (Uh-Huh)	Jose Ferrer	Philips	4	(18)	F L
18	19	Oh! My Pa-Pa	Eddie Fisher	HMV	3	(1)	
19	-	Cuff Of My Shirt	Guy Mitchell	Philips	3		
20	-	Sippin' Soda	Guy Mitchell	Philips	1		

March 1954

This Mnth	Prev Mnth	Title	Artist	Label	Wks 20	(US Pos)	
1	15	I See The Moon	Stargazers	Decca	15		
2	1	Oh Mein Papa	Eddie Calvert	Columbia	21	(9)	F
3	7	Happy Wanderer	Obernkirchen Children's Choir	Parlophone	26		F L
4	6	Tennessee Wig Walk	Bonnie Lou	Parlophone	10		F L
5	13	Don't Laugh At Me	Norman Wisdom	Columbia	15		F
6	4	That's Amore	Dean Martin	Capitol	11	(2)	
7	14	The Book	David Whitfield	Decca	15		
8	2	Blowing Wild	Frankie Laine	Philips	12		
9	3	Cloud Lucky Seven	Guy Mitchell	Philips	15		
10	-	Changing Partners	Kay Starr	Capitol	14	(13)	
11	17	Woman (Uh-Huh)	Jose Ferrer	Philips	4	(18)	F L
12	-	Bell Bottom Blues	Alma Cogan	HMV	9		F
13	-	Skin Deep	Duke Ellington	Philips	2		F L
14	5	Rags To Riches	David Whitfield	Decca	11		
15	-	Changing Partners	Bing Crosby	Brunswick	3	(17)	
16	-	Granada	Frankie Laine	Philips	2		
17	8	Man	Rosemary Clooney	Philips	5		
18	19	Cuff Of My Shirt	Guy Mitchell	Philips	3		
19	-	Moonlight Serenade	Glenn Miller	HMV	1		F
20	-	From Here To Eternity	Frank Sinatra	Capitol	9		

January 1954

This Mnth	Prev Mnth	Title	Artist	Label	Wks 20	(UK Pos)	
1	10	Oh! My Pa-Pa	Eddie Fisher	RCA	19	(9)	
2	1	Rags To Riches	Tony Bennett	Columbia	24		
3	2	That's Amore	Dean Martin	Capitol	22	(2)	
4	5	Changing Partners	Patti Page	Mercury	19		
5	12	Stranger In Paradise	Tony Bennett	Columbia	19	(1)	
6	4	Ricochet	Teresa Brewer	Coral	19	(18)	
7	14	Stranger In Paradise	Four Aces	Decca	16	(6)	
8	3	Ebb Tide	Frank Chacksfield	London	23	(9)	
9	-	The Gang That Sang 'Heart Of My Heart'	Four Aces	Decca	15		
10	11	Oh, Mein Papa	Eddie Calvert	Essex	9	(1)	F
11	-	Stranger In Paradise	Tony Martin	RCA	9	(6)	
12	-	Secret Love	Doris Day	Columbia	20	(1)	
13	8	Eh Cumpari	Julius La Rosa	Cadence	20		
14	17	Changing Partners	Kay Starr	Capitol	9	(4)	
15	-	What Is Was, Was Football	Andy Griffith	Capitol	6		F L
16	6	You You You	Ames Brothers	RCA	8		
17	7	Vaya Con Dios	Les Paul & Mary Ford	Capitol	7	(7)	
18	16	You Alone	Perry Como	RCA	12		
19	9	Santa Baby	Eartha Kitt	RCA	5		
20	-	Till We Two Are One	Georgie Shaw	Decca	12		F L

February 1954

This Mnth	Prev Mnth	Title	Artist	Label	Wks 20	(UK Pos)	
1	1	Oh! My Pa-Pa	Eddie Fisher	RCA	19	(9)	
2	12	Secret Love	Doris Day	Columbia	20	(1)	
3	3	That's Amore	Dean Martin	Capitol	22	(2)	
4	5	Stranger In Paradise	Tony Bennett	Columbia	19	(1)	
5	4	Changing Partners	Patti Page	Mercury	19		
6	7	Stranger In Paradise	Four Aces	Decca	16	(6)	
7	-	Make Love To Me!	Jo Stafford	Columbia	20	(8)	
8	9	The Gang That Sang 'Heart Of My Heart'	Four Aces	Decca	15		
9	-	From The Vine Came The Grape	Gaylords	Mercury	12		
10	20	Till We Two Are One	Georgie Shaw	Decca	12		F L
11	2	Rags To Riches	Tony Bennett	Columbia	24		
12	-	Till Then	Hilltoppers	Dot	11		
13	-	I Get So Lonely	Four Knights	Capitol	21	(5)	L
14	11	Stranger In Paradise	Tony Martin	RCA	9	(6)	
15	6	Ricochet	Teresa Brewer	Coral	19	(18)	
16	-	At The Darktown Strutters' Ball	Lou Monte	RCA	7		F
17	-	Young-At-Heart	Frank Sinatra	Capitol	21	(12)	
18	-	From The Vine Came The Grape	Hilltoppers	Dot	11		
19	15	What Is Was, Was Football	Andy Griffith	Capitol	6		F L
20	-	Woman (Uh-Huh)	Jose Ferrer	Columbia	4	(7)	F L

March 1954

This Mnth	Prev Mnth	Title	Artist	Label	Wks 20	(UK Pos)	
1	7	Make Love To Me!	Jo Stafford	Columbia	20	(8)	
2	2	Secret Love	Doris Day	Columbia	20	(1)	
3	13	I Get So Lonely	Four Knights	Capitol	21	(5)	L
4	1	Oh! My Pa-Pa	Eddie Fisher	RCA	19	(9)	
5	17	Young-At-Heart	Frank Sinatra	Capitol	21	(12)	
6	3	That's Amore	Dean Martin	Capitol	22	(2)	
7	-	Cross Over The Bridge	Patti Page	Mercury	18	(13)	
8	4	Stranger In Paradise	Tony Bennett	Columbia	19	(1)	
9	-	Wanted	Perry Como	RCA	21	(4)	
10	5	Changing Partners	Patti Page	Mercury	19		
11	9	From The Vine Came The Grape	Gaylords	Mercury	12		
12	10	Till We Two Are One	Georgie Shaw	Decca	12		F L
13	-	Answer Me, My Love	Nat 'King' Cole	Capitol	18		
14	16	At The Darktown Strutters' Ball	Lou Monte	RCA	7		F
15	18	From The Vine Came The Grape	Hilltoppers	Dot	11		
16	12	Till Then	Hilltoppers	Dot	11		
17	8	The Gang That Sang 'Heart Of My Heart'	Four Aces	Decca	15		
18	-	Somebody Bad Stole De Wedding Bell	Eartha Kitt	RCA	4		L
19	6	Stranger In Paradise	Four Aces	Decca	16	(6)	
20	-	Cuddle Me	Ronnie Gaylord	Mercury	12		F L

◆ DJ Alan 'Moondog' Freed was first heard on America's east coast when tapes of his Cleveland rock'n'roll radio show were aired on WNJR, Newark.

▲ Trucker Elvis Presley recorded 'I'll Never Stand In Your Way' and 'Casual Love Affair' at a "make your own record" service at Sun Records, Memphis.

◆ Atlantic Records veteran R&B performer Joe Turner recorded the rock'n'roll standard, 'Shake, Rattle & Roll' which Bill Haley & The Comets would turn into the first transatlantic rock'n'roll hit.

UK 1954

APR-JUNE

◆ A children's choir from the German town of Obernkirchen had one of the year's top sellers. America, too, loved the 'The Happy Wanderer', which charted in the US by Henri Rene and Britain's Frank Weir.

▲ British songstress Petula Clark made her UK chart debut with the French song, 'The Little Shoemaker'. This foot-tapping composition also gave The Gaylords their biggest American hit.

◆ American heart-throbs Frankie Laine, Guy Mitchell and Johnnie Ray had British hits with records that failed in their homeland. Among these was Ray's No. 1 'Such A Night', banned by the BBC for being too suggestive.

April 1954

This Mnth	Prev Mnth	Title	Artist	Label	Wks 20	(US Pos)	
1	1	I See The Moon	Stargazers	Decca	15		
2	3	Happy Wanderer	Obernkirchen Children's Choir	Parlophone	26		F L
3	-	Secret Love	Doris Day	Philips	29	(1)	
4	10	Changing Partners	Kay Starr	Capitol	14	(13)	
5	5	Don't Laugh At Me	Norman Wisdom	Columbia	15		F
6	12	Bell Bottom Blues	Alma Cogan	HMV	9		F
7	2	Oh Mein Papa	Eddie Calvert	Columbia	21	(9)	F
8	-	Such A Night	Johnnie Ray	Philips	18		
9	7	The Book	David Whitfield	Decca	15		
10	-	The Kid's Last Fight	Frankie Laine	Philips	10		
11	-	Bimbo	Ruby Wright	Parlophone	5		F
12	4	Tennessee Wig Walk	Bonnie Lou	Parlophone	10		F L
13	15	Changing Partners	Bing Crosby	Brunswick	3	(17)	
14	6	That's Amore	Dean Martin	Capitol	11	(2)	
15	-	Dime And A Dollar	Guy Mitchell	Philips	5		
16	16	Granada	Frankie Laine	Philips	2		
17	-	Tenderly	Nat 'King' Cole	Capitol	1		
18	18	Cuff Of My Shirt	Guy Mitchell	Philips	3		
19	-	Friends And Neighbours	Billy Cotton & His Band	Decca	12		L
20	-	Happy Wanderer	Stargazers	Decca	1		

May 1954

This Mnth	Prev Mnth	Title	Artist	Label	Wks 20	(US Pos)	
1	3	Secret Love	Doris Day	Philips	29	(1)	
2	8	Such A Night	Johnnie Ray	Philips	18		
3	2	Happy Wanderer	Obernkirchen Children's Choir	Parlophone	26		F L
4	10	The Kid's Last Fight	Frankie Laine	Philips	10		
5	4	Changing Partners	Kay Starr	Capitol	14	(13)	
6	1	I See The Moon	Stargazers	Decca	15		
7	19	Friends And Neighbours	Billy Cotton & His Band	Decca	12		L
8	5	Don't Laugh At Me	Norman Wisdom	Columbia	15		F
9	-	Someone Else's Roses	Joan Regan	Decca	8		
10	-	Heart Of My Heart	Max Bygraves	HMV	8		
11	15	Dime And A Dollar	Guy Mitchell	Philips	5		
12	11	Bimbo	Ruby Wright	Parlophone	5		F
13	6	Bell Bottom Blues	Alma Cogan	HMV	9		F
14	9	The Book	David Whitfield	Decca	15		
15	-	Make Love To Me!	Jo Stafford	Philips	1	(1)	
16	7	Oh Mein Papa	Eddie Calvert	Columbia	21	(9)	F
17	-	Cross Over The Bridge	Patti Page	Oriole	8	(3)	L
18	-	Deadwood Stage	Doris Day	Columbia	7		
19	-	Shadow Waltz	Mantovani	Decca	5		
20	-	Heartless	Frankie Vaughan	HMV	5		

June 1954

This Mnth	Prev Mnth	Title	Artist	Label	Wks 20	(US Pos)	
1	1	Secret Love	Doris Day	Philips	29	(1)	
2	2	Such A Night	Johnnie Ray	Philips	18		
3	7	Friends And Neighbours	Billy Cotton & His Band	Decca	12		L
4	3	Happy Wanderer	Obernkirchen Children's Choir	Parlophone	26		F L
5	9	Someone Else's Roses	Joan Regan	Decca	8		
6	-	I Get So Lonely	Four Knights	Capitol	11	(3)	F L
7	-	Wanted	Perry Como	HMV	15	(1)	
8	10	Heart Of My Heart	Max Bygraves	HMV	8		
9	4	The Kid's Last Fight	Frankie Laine	Philips	10		
10	5	Changing Partners	Kay Starr	Capitol	14	(13)	
11	-	Cara Mia	David Whitfield	Decca	25	(10)	
12	-	Wanted	Al Martino	Capitol	15		
13	14	The Book	David Whitfield	Decca	15		
14	-	The Little Shoemaker	Petula Clark	Polygon	10		F
15	-	Idle Gossip	Perry Como	HMV	15		
16	11	Dime And A Dollar	Guy Mitchell	Philips	5		
17	17	Cross Over The Bridge	Patti Page	Oriole	8	(3)	L
18	-	The Happy Wanderer	Frank Weir	Decca	3	(4)	F
19	18	Deadwood Stage	Doris Day	Columbia	7		
20	-	Friends And Neighbours	Max Bygraves & The Tanner Sisters	HMV	3		

April 1954

This Mnth	Prev Mnth	Title	Artist	Label	Wks 20	(UK Pos)	
1	9	Wanted	Perry Como	RCA	21	(4)	
2	1	Make Love To Me!	Jo Stafford	Columbia	20	(8)	
3	7	Cross Over The Bridge	Patti Page	Mercury	18	(13)	
4	3	I Get So Lonely	Four Knights	Capitol	21	(5)	L
5	2	Secret Love	Doris Day	Columbia	20	(1)	
6	5	Young-At-Heart	Frank Sinatra	Capitol	21	(12)	
7	13	Answer Me, My Love	Nat 'King' Cole	Capitol	18		
8	-	A Girl, A Girl	Eddie Fisher	RCA	11		
9	-	Here	Tony Martin	RCA	15		L
10	-	There'll Be No Teardrops Tonight	Tony Bennett	Columbia	6		
11	11	From The Vine Came The Grape	Gaylords	Mercury	12		
12	-	The Man With The Banjo	Ames Brothers	RCA	13		
13	4	Oh! My Pa-Pa	Eddie Fisher	RCA	19	(9)	
14	15	From The Vine Came The Grape	Hilltoppers	Dot	11		
15	20	Cuddle Me	Ronnie Gaylord	Mercury	12		F L
16	-	Little Things Mean A Lot	Kitty Kallen	Decca	25	(1)	F
17	6	That's Amore	Dean Martin	Capitol	22	(2)	
18	8	Stranger In Paradise	Tony Bennett	Columbia	19	(1)	
19	-	Anema E Core	Eddie Fisher	RCA	4		
20	-	Man Upstairs	Kay Starr	Capitol	16		

May 1954

This Mnth	Prev Mnth	Title	Artist	Label	Wks 20	(UK Pos)	
1	1	Wanted	Perry Como	RCA	21	(4)	
2	6	Young-At-Heart	Frank Sinatra	Capitol	21	(12)	
3	2	Make Love To Me!	Jo Stafford	Columbia	20	(8)	
4	4	I Get So Lonely	Four Knights	Capitol	21	(5)	L
5	3	Cross Over The Bridge	Patti Page	Mercury	18	(13)	
6	16	Little Things Mean A Lot	Kitty Kallen	Decca	25	(1)	F
7	7	Answer Me, My Love	Nat 'King' Cole	Capitol	18		
8	-	If You Love Me (Really Love Me)	Kay Starr	Capitol	17		
9	12	The Man With The Banjo	Ames Brothers	RCA	13		
10	20	Man Upstairs	Kay Starr	Capitol	16		
11	9	Here	Tony Martin	RCA	15		L
12	8	A Girl, A Girl	Eddie Fisher	RCA	11		
13	-	The Happy Wanderer	Frank Weir	London	17		F L
14	-	Jilted	Teresa Brewer	Coral	7		
15	5	Secret Love	Doris Day	Columbia	20	(1)	
16	-	Three Coins In The Fountain	Four Aces	Decca	16	(5)	
17	-	The Happy Wanderer	Henri Rene	RCA	12		F L
18	15	Cuddle Me	Ronnie Gaylord	Mercury	12		F L
19	-	Poor Butterfly	Hilltoppers	Dot	4		
20	10	There'll Be No Teardrops Tonight	Tony Bennett	Columbia	6		

June 1954

This Mnth	Prev Mnth	Title	Artist	Label	Wks 20	(UK Pos)	
1	6	Little Things Mean A Lot	Kitty Kallen	Decca	25	(1)	F
2	16	Three Coins In The Fountain	Four Aces	Decca	16	(5)	
3	1	Wanted	Perry Como	RCA	21	(4)	
4	13	The Happy Wanderer	Frank Weir	London	17		F L
5	-	Hernando's Hideaway	Archie Bleyer	Cadence	16		F L
6	8	If You Love Me (Really Love Me)	Kay Starr	Capitol	17		
7	2	Young-At-Heart	Frank Sinatra	Capitol	21	(12)	
8	7	Answer Me, My Love	Nat 'King' Cole	Capitol	18		
9	10	Man Upstairs	Kay Starr	Capitol	16		
10	4	I Get So Lonely	Four Knights	Capitol	21	(5)	L
11	11	Here	Tony Martin	RCA	15		L
12	5	Cross Over The Bridge	Patti Page	Mercury	18	(13)	
13	-	Three Coins In The Fountain	Frank Sinatra	Capitol	10	(1)	
14	9	The Man With The Banjo	Ames Brothers	RCA	13		
15	17	The Happy Wanderer	Henri Rene	RCA	12		F L
16	-	I Understand Just How You Feel	Four Tunes	Jubilee	13		L
17	-	Crazy 'Bout You, Baby	Crew-Cuts	Mercury	14		F
18	3	Make Love To Me!	Jo Stafford	Columbia	20	(8)	
19	-	Isle Of Capri	Gaylords	Mercury	6		
20	-	Steam Heat	Patti Page	Mercury	2		

◆ Bill Haley & The Comets recorded 'Rock Around The Clock' (originally released in March by Sonny Dae & The Knights). It was initially only a minor US hit.

◆ Mercury Records became the first label to stop supplying 78 rpm records to radio stations.

◆ As *Billboard* announced "Teenagers Demand Music With A Beat", 'Gee' by The Crows (considered by many to be the first rock'n' roll record) entered the pop and R&B charts.

◆ Alan Freed's first stage show outside Cleveland attracted 10,000 fans to Newark to watch an all-star R&B line-up which included Muddy Waters, The Clovers, Charles Brown and The Harptones.

UK 1954 JULY-SEPT

British balladeer David Whitfield had his biggest hit, 'Cara Mia'. It not only topped the UK chart but also reached the US Top 10, earning him a gold disc.

▲ Many US pop acts covered R&B hits: The McGuire Sisters (above) scored with The Spaniels' 'Goodnight, Sweetheart, Goodnight', June Valli's 'I Understand' joined the original by The Four Tunes on the American chart, and Canadian quartet The Crew-Cuts had a US No. 1 with The Chords' scat smash, 'Sh-Boom'. The latter becoming the first rock-related hit in Britain.

◆ The British singles chart was extended to a Top 20 from a Top 12.

July 1954

This Mnth	Prev Mnth	Title	Artist	Label	Wks 20	(US Pos)	
1	11	Cara Mia	David Whitfield	Decca	25	(10)	
2	1	Secret Love	Doris Day	Philips	29	(1)	
3	-	Little Things Mean A Lot	Kitty Kallen	Brunswick	23	(1)	F L
4	15	Idle Gossip	Perry Como	HMV	15		
5	12	Wanted	Al Martino	Capitol	15		
6	7	Wanted	Perry Como	HMV	15	(1)	
7	2	Such A Night	Johnnie Ray	Philips	18		
8	14	The Little Shoemaker	Petula Clark	Polygon	10		F
9	6	I Get So Lonely	Four Knights	Capitol	11	(3)	F L
10	3	Friends And Neighbours	Billy Cotton & His Band	Decca	12		L
11	-	Three Coins In The Fountain	Frank Sinatra	Capitol	19	(7)	
12	4	Happy Wanderer	Obernkirchen Children's Choir	Parlophone	26		F L
13		The Story Of Three Loves	Winifred Atwell	Decca	9		
14	-	Three Coins In The Fountain	Four Aces	Brunswick	6	(2)	F
15	5	Someone Else's Roses	Joan Regan	Decca	8		
16	8	Heart Of My Heart	Max Bygraves	HMV	8		
17	-	Young-At-Heart	Frank Sinatra	Capitol	1	(2)	F
18	-	Never Never Land	Frank Weir	Decca	13		
19	-	Charleston	Winifred Atwell	Decca	8		
20	-	The Little Shoemaker	Frank Weir	Decca	4		

August 1954

This Mnth	Prev Mnth	Title	Artist	Label	Wks 20	(US Pos)	
1	1	Cara Mia	David Whitfield	Decca	25	(10)	
2	3	Little Things Mean A Lot	Kitty Kallen	Brunswick	23	(1)	F L
3	11	Three Coins In The Fountain	Frank Sinatra	Capitol	19	(7)	
4	4	Idle Gossip	Perry Como	HMV	15		
5	2	Secret Love	Doris Day	Philips	29	(1)	
6	5	Wanted	Al Martino	Capitol	15		
7	14	Three Coins In The Fountain	Four Aces	Brunswick	6	(2)	F
8	6	Wanted	Perry Como	HMV	15	(1)	
9	-	My Friend	Frankie Laine	Philips	15		
10	13	The Story Of Three Loves	Winifred Atwell	Decca	9		
11	8	The Little Shoemaker	Petula Clark	Polygon	10		F
12	9	I Get So Lonely	Four Knights	Capitol	11	(3)	F L
13	-	Black Hills Of Dakota	Doris Day	Philips	7		
14	-	Little Things Mean A Lot	Alma Cogan	HMV	5		
15	7	Such A Night	Johnnie Ray	Philips	18		
16	18	Never Never Land	Frank Weir	Decca	13		
17	-	Midnight	Eddie Calvert	Columbia	7		
18	-	Three Coins In The Fountain	Tony Brent	Columbia	6		
19	-	Destiny	Johnnie Ray	Columbia	4		
20	19	Charleston	Winifred Atwell	Decca	8		

September 1954

This Mnth	Prev Mnth	Title	Artist	Label	Wks 20	(US Pos)	
1	3	Three Coins In The Fountain	Frank Sinatra	Capitol	19	(7)	
2	1	Cara Mia	David Whitfield	Decca	25	(10)	
3	2	Little Things Mean A Lot	Kitty Kallen	Brunswick	23	(1)	F L
4	9	My Friend	Frankie Laine	Philips	15		
5	-	Hold My Hand	Don Cornell	Vogue	21	(5)	F
6	4	Idle Gossip	Perry Como	HMV	15		
7	5	Secret Love	Doris Day	Philips	29	(1)	
8	-	Smile	Nat 'King' Cole	Capitol	14	(14)	
9	13	Black Hills Of Dakota	Doris Day	Philips	7		
10	-	Gilly Gilly Ossenfeffer Katzenellen Bogen By The Sea	Max Bygraves	HMV	8		
11	-	West Of Zanzibar	Anthony Steel & The Radio Revellers	Polygon	6		F L
12	6	Wanted	Al Martino	Capitol	15		
13	10	The Story Of Three Loves	Winifred Atwell	Decca	9		
14	14	Little Things Mean A Lot	Alma Cogan	HMV	5		
15	8	Wanted	Perry Como	HMV	15	(1)	
16	-	Story Of Tina	Ronnie Harris	Columbia	2		F
17	-	Some Day	Frankie Laine	Columbia	3	(18)	
18	16	Never Never Land	Frank Weir	Decca	13		
19	-	Dixieland	Winifred Atwell	Decca	4		
20	-	Little Things Mean A Lot	Jimmy Young	Decca	2		

July 1954

This Mnth	Prev Mnth	Title	Artist	Label	Wks 20	(UK Pos)	
1	1	Little Things Mean A Lot	Kitty Kallen	Decca	25	(1)	F
2	5	Hernando's Hideaway	Archie Bleyer	Cadence	16		F L
3	2	Three Coins In The Fountain	Four Aces	Decca	16	(5)	
4	4	The Happy Wanderer	Frank Weir	London	17		F L
5	-	Sh-Boom	Crew-Cuts	Mercury	21	(12)	
6	6	If You Love Me (Really Love Me)	Kay Starr	Capitol	17		
7	-	The Little Shoemaker	Gaylords	Mercury	18		L
8	13	Three Coins In The Fountain	Frank Sinatra	Capitol	10	(1)	
9	16	I Understand Just How You Feel	Four Tunes	Jubilee	13		L
10	3	Wanted	Perry Como	RCA	21	(4)	
11	-	Sh-Boom	Chords	Cat	11		F L
12	17	Crazy 'Bout You, Baby	Crew-Cuts	Mercury	14		F
13	-	Goodnight, Sweetheart, Goodnight	McGuire Sisters	Coral	10		F
14	15	The Happy Wanderer	Henri Rene	RCA	12		F L
15	9	Man Upstairs	Kay Starr	Capitol	16		
16	-	Hey There	Rosemary Clooney	Columbia	23	(4)	
17	-	In The Chapel In The Moonlight	Kitty Kallen	Decca	12		
18	-	The Little Shoemaker	Hugo Winterhalter	RCA	7		
19	-	I Understand	June Valli	RCA	4		L
20	7	Young-At-Heart	Frank Sinatra	Capitol	21	(12)	

August 1954

This Mnth	Prev Mnth	Title	Artist	Label	Wks 20	(UK Pos)	
1	5	Sh-Boom	Crew-Cuts	Mercury	21	(12)	
2	7	The Little Shoemaker	Gaylords	Mercury	18		L
3	1	Little Things Mean A Lot	Kitty Kallen	Decca	25	(1)	F
4	16	Hey There	Rosemary Clooney	Columbia	23	(4)	
5	2	Hernando's Hideaway	Archie Bleyer	Cadence	16		F L
6	17	In The Chapel In The Moonlight	Kitty Kallen	Decca	12		
7	3	Three Coins In The Fountain	Four Aces	Decca	16	(5)	
8	13	Goodnight, Sweetheart, Goodnight	McGuire Sisters	Coral	10		F
9	-	The High And The Mighty	Les Baxter	Capitol	9		
10	-	I'm A Fool To Care	Les Paul & Mary Ford	Capitol	12		
11	-	The High And The Mighty	Leroy Holmes	MGM	11		F L
12	-	The High And The Mighty	Victor Young	Decca	11		
13	4	The Happy Wanderer	Frank Weir	London	17		F L
14	11	Sh-Boom	Chords	Cat	11		F L
15	-	This Ole House	Rosemary Clooney	Columbia	23	(1)	L
16	12	Crazy 'Bout You, Baby	Crew-Cuts	Mercury	14		F
17	18	The Little Shoemaker	Hugo Winterhalter	RCA	7		
18	9	I Understand Just How You Feel	Four Tunes	Jubilee	13		
19	-	Sway	Dean Martin	Capitol	6	(6)	
20	-	They Were Doin' The Mambo	Vaughn Monroe	RCA	12		L

September 1954

This Mnth	Prev Mnth	Title	Artist	Label	Wks 20	(UK Pos)	
1	1	Sh-Boom	Crew-Cuts	Mercury	21	(12)	
2	4	Hey There	Rosemary Clooney	Columbia	23	(4)	
3	2	The Little Shoemaker	Gaylords	Mercury	18		L
4	-	Skokiaan	Ralph Marterie	Mercury	14		L
5	15	This Ole House	Rosemary Clooney	Columbia	23	(1)	L
6	6	In The Chapel In The Moonlight	Kitty Kallen	Decca	12		
7	12	The High And The Mighty	Victor Young	Decca	11		
8	3	Little Things Mean A Lot	Kitty Kallen	Decca	25	(1)	F
9	-	Skokiaan	Four Lads	Columbia	11		
10	9	The High And The Mighty	Les Baxter	Capitol	9		
11	11	The High And The Mighty	Leroy Holmes	MGM	11		F L
12	-	I Need You Now	Eddie Fisher	RCA	21	(13)	
13	-	Shake, Rattle And Roll	Bill Haley & His Comets	Decca	20	(4)	G
14	10	I'm A Fool To Care	Les Paul & Mary Ford	Capitol	12		
15	20	They Were Doin' The Mambo	Vaughn Monroe	RCA	12		L
16	-	Hold My Hand	Don Cornell	Coral	15	(1)	
17	8	Goodnight, Sweetheart, Goodnight	McGuire Sisters	Coral	10		F
18	-	Hey There	Sammy Davis Jr.	Decca	4	(19)	F
19	-	If I Give My Heart To You	Doris Day	Columbia	15	(4)	
20	5	Hernando's Hideaway	Archie Bleyer	Cadence	16		F L

◆ The suggestive lyrics of top R&B hits, 'Honey Love' by Clyde McPhatter & The Drifters, 'Work With Me Annie', 'Sexy Ways' and 'Annie Had A Baby' by The Midnighters, and 'Shake, Rattle & Roll' by Joe Turner attracted bad publicity. Incidentally, Bill Haley's cleaned-up version of the latter became a transatlantic pop hit.

◆ Elvis Presley signed to Sun Records and released his version of R&B singer Arthur 'Big Boy' Crudup's 'That's All Right Mama' coupled with C&W performer Bill Monroe's 'Blue Moon Of Kentucky'.

◆ Alan Freed successfully took his radio programme, *Moondog Rock'n'Roll Party*, from WJW in Cleveland to WINS, New York.

UK 1954 OCT-DEC

◆American heart-throb Frankie Laine's British tour was a resounding succcess: at one particular show in Manchester he was greeted by 14,000 noisy fans.

◆ Elvis Presley, who had yet to have a UK release, was voted eighth Most Promising New C&W Singer in *Billboard's* US DJ poll – Tommy Collins took the crown.

◆ The flagging dance hall business on both sides of the Atlantic was revitalized firstly by the growth in interest in Latin American dances like the tango and mambo, and secondly by rock'n'roll. The latter was just starting to make an impression in the UK thanks to records like 'Sh-Boom' by The Crew-Cuts and 'Shake, Rattle And Roll' by Bill Haley & The Comets.

October 1954

This Mnth	Prev Mnth	Title	Artist	Label	Wks 20	(US Pos)	
1	5	Hold My Hand	Don Cornell	Vogue	21	(5)	F
2	8	Smile	Nat 'King' Cole	Capitol	14	(14)	
3	1	Three Coins In The Fountain	Frank Sinatra	Capitol	19	(7)	
4	4	My Friend	Frankie Laine	Philips	15		
5	3	Little Things Mean A Lot	Kitty Kallen	Brunswick	23	(1)	F L
6	2	Cara Mia	David Whitfield	Decca	25	(10)	
7	-	If I Give My Heart To You	Doris Day	Philips	10	(4)	
8	-	Sway	Dean Martin	Capitol	7	(15)	
9	-	My Son My Son	Vera Lynn	Decca	14		
10	-	The Story Of Tina	Al Martino	Capitol	8		
11	-	This Ole House	Rosemary Clooney	Philips	18	(1)	
12	-	This Ole House	Billie Anthony	Columbia	15		F
13	-	There Must Be A Reason	Frankie Laine	Philips	9		
14	-	Sh-Boom	Crew-Cuts	Mercury	9	(1)	F
15	10	Gilly Gilly Ossenfeffer Katzenellen Bogen By The Sea	Max Bygraves	HMV	8		
16	9	Black Hills Of Dakota	Doris Day	Philips	7		
17	7	Secret Love	Doris Day	Philips	29	(1)	
18	-	Rain Rain Rain	Frankie Laine	Philips	16		
19	-	If I Give My Heart To You	Joan Regan	Decca	11		
20	-	Make Her Mine	Nat 'King' Cole	Capitol	2		

November 1954

1	9	My Son My Son	Vera Lynn	Decca	14		
2	11	This Ole House	Rosemary Clooney	Philips	18	(1)	
3	1	Hold My Hand	Don Cornell	Vogue	21	(5)	F
4	19	If I Give My Heart To You	Joan Regan	Decca	11		
5	2	Smile	Nat 'King' Cole	Capitol	14	(14)	
6	7	If I Give My Heart To You	Doris Day	Philips	10	(4)	
7	12	This Ole House	Billie Anthony	Columbia	15		F
8	18	Rain Rain Rain	Frankie Laine	Philips	16		
9	6	Cara Mia	David Whitfield	Decca	25	(10)	
10	5	Little Things Mean A Lot	Kitty Kallen	Brunswick	23	(1)	F L
11	4	My Friend	Frankie Laine	Philips	15		
12	-	Santo Natale	David Whitfield	Decca	10		
13	-	No One But You	Billy Eckstine	MGM	17		F
14	13	There Must Be A Reason	Frankie Laine	Philips	9		
15	3	Three Coins In The Fountain	Frank Sinatra	Capitol	19	(7)	
16	14	Sh-Boom	Crew-Cuts	Mercury	9	(1)	F
17	-	I Need You Now	Eddie Fisher	HMV	10	(1)	
18	-	Let's Have Another Party	Winifred Atwell	Decca	8		
19	8	Sway	Dean Martin	Capitol	7	(15)	
20	-	Sh-Boom	Stan Freberg	Capitol	2		F L

December 1954

1	18	Let's Have Another Party	Winifred Atwell	Decca	8		
2	12	Santo Natale	David Whitfield	Decca	10		
3	29	This Ole House	Rosemary Clooney	Philips	18	(1)	
4	13	No One But You	Billy Eckstine	MGM	17		F
5	-	I Still Believe	Ronnie Hilton	HMV	14		F
6	1	My Son My Son	Vera Lynn	Decca	14		
7	3	Hold My Hand	Don Cornell	Vogue	21	(5)	F
8	8	Rain Rain Rain	Frankie Laine	Philips	16		
9	7	This Ole House	Billie Anthony	Columbia	15		F
10	4	If I Give My Heart To You	Joan Regan	Decca	11		
11	-	Heartbeat	Ruby Murray	Columbia	16		F
12	-	Let's Get Together No. 1	Big Ben Banjo Band	Columbia	4		F
13	-	Finger Of Suspicion	Dickie Valentine	Decca	15		
14	17	I Need You Now	Eddie Fisher	HMV	10	(1)	
15	-	I Can't Tell A Waltz From A Tango	Alma Cogan	HMV	11		
16	5	Smile	Nat 'King' Cole	Capitol	14	(14)	
17	-	Shake, Rattle And Roll	Bill Haley & His Comets	Brunswick	14	(7)	
18	6	If I Give My Heart To You	Doris Day	Philips	10	(4)	
19	-	Veni Vidi Vici	Ronnie Hilton	HMV	8		
20	-	Let's Have A Party	Winifred Atwell	Philips	6		

October 1954

This Mnth	Prev Mnth	Title	Artist	Label	Wks 20	(UK Pos)	
1	2	Hey There	Rosemary Clooney	Columbia	23	(4)	
2	12	I Need You Now	Eddie Fisher	RCA	21	(13)	
3	5	This Ole House	Rosemary Clooney	Columbia	23	(1)	L
4	1	Sh-Boom	Crew-Cuts	Mercury	21	(12)	
5	19	If I Give My Heart To You	Doris Day	Columbia	15	(4)	
6	4	Skokiaan	Ralph Marterie	Mercury	14		L
7	16	Hold My Hand	Don Cornell	Coral	15	(1)	
8	13	Shake, Rattle And Roll	Bill Haley & His Comets	Decca	20	(4)	G
9	9	Skokiaan	Four Lads	Columbia	11		
10	-	Cara Mia	David Whitfield	London	12	(1)	F L
11	3	The Little Shoemaker	Gaylords	Mercury	18		L
12	-	Papa Loves Mambo	Perry Como	RCA	16	(16)	
13	7	The High And The Mighty	Victor Young	Decca	11		
14	-	If I Give My Heart To You	Denise Lor	Majar	9		F L
15	15	They Were Doin' The Mambo	Vaughn Monroe	RCA	12		L
16	-	Smile	Nat 'King' Cole	Capitol	6	(2)	
17	-	Teach Me Tonight	De Castro Sisters	Abbott	17		F L
18	-	Whither Thou Goest	Les Paul & Mary Ford	Capitol	8		
19	6	In The Chapel In The Moonlight	Kitty Kallen	Decca	12		
20	-	Oop-Shoop	Crew-Cuts	Mercury	4		

November 1954

This Mnth	Prev Mnth	Title	Artist	Label	Wks 20	(UK Pos)	
1	2	I Need You Now	Eddie Fisher	RCA	21	(13)	
2	3	This Ole House	Rosemary Clooney	Columbia	23	(1)	L
3	1	Hey There	Rosemary Clooney	Columbia	23	(4)	
4	12	Papa Loves Mambo	Perry Como	RCA	16	(16)	
5	7	Hold My Hand	Don Cornell	Coral	15	(1)	
6	5	If I Give My Heart To You	Doris Day	Columbia	15	(4)	
7	-	Mr. Sandman	Chordettes	Cadence	19	(11)	F
8	17	Teach Me Tonight	De Castro Sisters	Abbott	17		F L
9	8	Shake, Rattle And Roll	Bill Haley & His Comets	Decca	20	(4)	G
10	-	Muskrat Ramble	McGuire Sisters	Coral	7		
11	6	Skokiaan	Ralph Marterie	Mercury	14		L
12	10	Cara Mia	David Whitfield	London	12	(1)	F L
13	-	Mambo Italiano	Rosemary Clooney	Columbia	8	(1)	
14	-	Count Your Blessings	Eddie Fisher	RCA	13		
15	4	Sh-Boom	Crew-Cuts	Mercury	21	(12)	
16	18	Whither Thou Goest	Les Paul & Mary Ford	Capitol	8		
17	-	(Bazoom) I Need Your Lovin'	Cheers	Capitol	5		F
18	9	Skokiaan	Four Lads	Columbia	11		
19	-	Hajji Baba	Nat 'King' Cole	Capitol	4		
20	-	Mr. Sandman	Four Aces	Decca	12	(9)	

December 1954

This Mnth	Prev Mnth	Title	Artist	Label	Wks 20	(UK Pos)	
1	7	Mr. Sandman	Chordettes	Cadence	19	(11)	F
2	1	I Need You Now	Eddie Fisher	RCA	21	(13)	
3	2	This Ole House	Rosemary Clooney	Columbia	23	(1)	L
4	8	Teach Me Tonight	De Castro Sisters	Abbott	17		F L
5	4	Papa Loves Mambo	Perry Como	RCA	16	(16)	
6	14	Count Your Blessings	Eddie Fisher	RCA	13		
7	-	Let Me Go, Lover	Joan Weber	Columbia	14	(16)	F L
8	-	The Naughty Lady Of Shady Lane	Ames Brothers	RCA	14	(6)	
9	9	Shake, Rattle And Roll	Bill Haley & His Comets	Decca	20	(4)	G
10	-	Mr. Sandman	Four Aces	Decca	12	(9)	
11	3	Hey There	Rosemary Clooney	Columbia	23	(4)	
12	5	Hold My Hand	Don Cornell	Coral	15	(1)	
13	6	If I Give My Heart To You	Doris Day	Columbia	15	(4)	
14	13	Mambo Italiano	Rosemary Clooney	Columbia	8	(1)	
15	-	Make Yourself Comfortable	Sarah Vaughan	Mercury	14		F
16	-	Dim, Dim The Lights (I Want Some Atmosphere)	Bill Haley & His Comets	Decca	12		
17	-	Hearts Of Stone	Fontane Sisters	Dot	16		F G
18	-	Let Me Go, Lover!	Teresa Brewer	Coral	9	(9)	
19	-	That's All I Want From You	Jaye P. Morgan	RCA	18		F
20	-	Hearts Of Stone	Charms	Deluxe	7		F

◆ R&B radio stations, juke box operators and trade papers agreed it was time to halt "off-color and offensive" records – The Midnighters were the main scapegoats.

◆ Many major American labels announced that they were getting more involved in R&B to "increase the number of records they sold to teenagers".

▲ The Chordettes had their first and biggest transatlantic hit with 'Mr. Sandman', one of the catchiest tunes of the era.

UK 1955
JAN-MAR

▲ Bill Haley's 'Rock Around The Clock' had a two-week chart run in Britain. In the US, it became the theme to the controversial film, *The Blackboard Jungle*.

◆ In America, 'Let Me Go Lover' by 18-year-old Joan Weber sold 500,000 copies in its first week . In Britain, eight versions battled it out, including one by Irish newcomer, Ruby Murray, who had a record five singles in the Top 20.

◆ 'Give Me Your Word', which was the B-side of Tennessee Ernie Ford's minor US success, 'River Of No Return', surprised many people by topping the British chart.

January 1955

This Mnth	Prev Mnth	Title	Artist	Label	Wks 20	(US Pos)	
1	13	Finger Of Suspicion	Dickie Valentine	Decca	15		
2	-	Mambo Italiano	Rosemary Clooney	Philips	16	(10)	
3	4	No One But You	Billy Eckstine	MGM	17		F
4	5	I Still Believe	Ronnie Hilton	HMV	14		F
5	11	Heartbeat	Ruby Murray	Columbia	16		F
6	17	Shake, Rattle And Roll	Bill Haley & His Comets	Brunswick	14	(7)	
7	-	Mr. Sandman	Dickie Valentine	Decca	12		
8	15	I Can't Tell A Waltz From A Tango	Alma Cogan	HMV	11		
9	-	Mr. Sandman	Chordettes	Columbia	9	(1)	F
10	8	Rain Rain Rain	Frankie Laine	Philips	16		
11	-	Mr. Sandman	Four Aces	Brunswick	5	(10)	
12	3	This Ole House	Rosemary Clooney	Philips	18	(1)	
13	1	Let's Have Another Party	Winifred Atwell	Decca	8		
14	2	Santo Natale	David Whitfield	Decca	10		
15	7	Hold My Hand	Don Cornell	Vogue	21	(5)	F
16	-	Give Me Your Word	Tennessee Ernie Ford	Capitol	24		F
17	-	Count Your Blessings	Bing Crosby	Brunswick	3		
18	19	Veni Vidi Vici	Ronnie Hilton	HMV	8		
19	-	Softly Softly	Ruby Murray	Columbia	23		
20	9	This Ole House	Billie Anthony	Columbia	15		F

February 1955

This Mnth	Prev Mnth	Title	Artist	Label	Wks 20	(US Pos)	
1	19	Softly Softly	Ruby Murray	Columbia	23		
2	2	Mambo Italiano	Rosemary Clooney	Philips	16	(10)	
3	1	Finger Of Suspicion	Dickie Valentine	Decca	15		
4	16	Give Me Your Word	Tennessee Ernie Ford	Capitol	24		F
5	5	Heartbeat	Ruby Murray	Columbia	16		F
6	6	Shake, Rattle And Roll	Bill Haley & His Comets	Brunswick	14	(7)	
7	-	Naughty Lady Of Shady Lane	Dean Martin	Capitol	10		
8	-	The Naughty Lady Of Shady Lane	Ames Brothers	HMV	6	(3)	F L
9	3	No One But You	Billy Eckstine	MGM	17		F
10	7	Mr. Sandman	Dickie Valentine	Decca	12		
11	-	Happy Days And Lonely Nights	Ruby Murray	Columbia	8		
12	-	Let Me Go, Lover	Teresa Brewer	Vogue/Coral	10	(8)	F
13	-	Beyond The Stars	David Whitfield	Decca	9		
14	4	I Still Believe	Ronnie Hilton	HMV	14		F
15	-	Mobile	Ray Burns	Columbia	13		F
16	-	A Blossom Fell	Dickie Valentine	Decca	10		
17	-	Happy Days And Lonely Nights	Frankie Vaughan	HMV	3		
18	-	Majorca	Petula Clark	Polygon	5		
19	-	Mambo Italiano	Dean Martin	Capitol	2		
20	-	Drinking Song	Mario Lanza	HMV	1		

March 1955

This Mnth	Prev Mnth	Title	Artist	Label	Wks 20	(US Pos)	
1	4	Give Me Your Word	Tennessee Ernie Ford	Capitol	24		F
2	1	Softly Softly	Ruby Murray	Columbia	23		
3	-	Let Me Go, Lover	Dean Martin	Capitol	9		
4	2	Mambo Italiano	Rosemary Clooney	Philips	16	(10)	
5	-	A Blossom Fell	Nat 'King' Cole	Capitol	10	(2)	
6	15	Mobile	Ray Burns	Columbia	13		F
7	7	Naughty Lady Of Shady Lane	Dean Martin	Capitol	10		
8	3	Finger Of Suspicion	Dickie Valentine	Decca	15		
9	5	Heartbeat	Ruby Murray	Columbia	16		F
10	-	Let Me Go, Lover	Ruby Murray	Columbia	7		
11	13	Beyond The Stars	David Whitfield	Decca	9		
12	12	Let Me Go, Lover	Teresa Brewer	Vogue/Coral	10	(8)	F
13	11	Happy Days And Lonely Nights	Ruby Murray	Columbia	8		
14	16	A Blossom Fell	Dickie Valentine	Decca	10		
15	-	Tomorrow	Johnny Brandon	Polygon	8		F
16	-	Wedding Bells	Eddie Fisher	HMV	11		
17	18	Majorca	Petula Clark	Polygon	5		
18	-	If Anyone Finds This I Love You	Ruby Murray	Columbia	11		
19	8	The Naughty Lady Of Shady Lane	Ames Brothers	HMV	6	(3)	F L
20	6	Shake, Rattle And Roll	Bill Haley & His Comets	Brunswick	14	(7)	

January 1955

This Mnth	Prev Mnth	Title	Artist	Label	Wks 20	(UK Pos)	
1	1	Mr. Sandman	Chordettes	Cadence	19	(11)	F
2	7	Let Me Go, Lover	Joan Weber	Columbia	14	(16)	F L
3	8	The Naughty Lady Of Shady Lane	Ames Brothers	RCA	14	(6)	
4	17	Hearts Of Stone	Fontane Sisters	Dot	16		F G
5	4	Teach Me Tonight	De Castro Sisters	Abbott	17		F L
6	18	Let Me Go, Lover!	Teresa Brewer	Coral	9	(9)	
7	3	This Ole House	Rosemary Clooney	Columbia	23	(1)	L
8	2	I Need You Now	Eddie Fisher	RCA	21	(13)	
9	15	Make Yourself Comfortable	Sarah Vaughan	Mercury	14		F
10	6	Count Your Blessings	Eddie Fisher	RCA	13		
11	10	Mr. Sandman	Four Aces	Decca	12	(9)	
12	-	Melody Of Love	Billy Vaughn	Dot	21		F G
13	19	That's All I Want From You	Jaye P. Morgan	RCA	18		F
14	16	Dim, Dim The Lights (I Want Some Atmosphere)	Bill Haley & His Comets	Decca	12		
15	-	Sincerely	McGuire Sisters	Coral	17	(14)	G
16	9	Shake, Rattle And Roll	Bill Haley & His Comets	Decca	20	(4)	G
17	-	(My Baby Don't Love Me) No More	DeJohn Sisters	Epic	9		F L
18	5	Papa Loves Mambo	Perry Como	RCA	16	(16)	
19	-	Earth Angel (Will You Be Mine)	Penguins	Dootone	11		F L
20	20	Hearts Of Stone	Charms	Deluxe	7		F

February 1955

This Mnth	Prev Mnth	Title	Artist	Label	Wks 20	(UK Pos)	
1	15	Sincerely	McGuire Sisters	Coral	17	(14)	G
2	4	Hearts Of Stone	Fontane Sisters	Dot	16		F G
3	12	Melody Of Love	Billy Vaughn	Dot	21		F G
4	2	Let Me Go, Lover	Joan Weber	Columbia	14	(16)	F L
5	13	That's All I Want From You	Jaye P. Morgan	RCA	18		F
6	-	Ko Ko Mo (I Love You So)	Perry Como	RCA	12		
7	1	Mr. Sandman	Chordettes	Cadence	19	(11)	F
8	19	Earth Angel (Will You Be Mine)	Penguins	Dootone	11		F L
9	-	Tweedle Dee	Georgia Gibbs	Mercury	17	(20)	G
10	3	The Naughty Lady Of Shady Lane	Ames Brothers	RCA	14	(6)	
11	-	Melody Of Love	David Carroll	Mercury	11		F L
12	-	Ko Ko Mo (I Love You So)	Crew-Cuts	Mercury	9		
13	-	The Crazy Otto (Medley)	Johnny Maddox	Dot	16		F L
14	9	Make Yourself Comfortable	Sarah Vaughan	Mercury	14		F
15	-	Earth Angel	Crew-Cuts	Mercury	10	(4)	
16	-	Melody Of Love	Four Aces	Decca	13		
17	17	(My Baby Don't Love Me) No More	DeJohn Sisters	Epic	9		F L
18	-	Open Up Your Heart (And Let The Sunshine In)	Cowboy Church Sunday School	Decca	16		F L
19	6	Let Me Go, Lover!	Teresa Brewer	Coral	9	(9)	
20	11	Mr. Sandman	Four Aces	Decca	12	(9)	

March 1955

This Mnth	Prev Mnth	Title	Artist	Label	Wks 20	(UK Pos)	
1	1	Sincerely	McGuire Sisters	Coral	17	(14)	G
2	13	The Crazy Otto (Medley)	Johnny Maddox	Dot	16		F L
3	3	Melody Of Love	Billy Vaughn	Dot	21		F G
4	9	Tweedle Dee	Georgia Gibbs	Mercury	17	(20)	G
5	-	The Ballad Of Davy Crockett	Bill Hayes	Cadence	20	(2)	F L
6	6	Ko Ko Mo (I Love You So)	Perry Como	RCA	12		
7	2	Hearts Of Stone	Fontane Sisters	Dot	16		F G
8	15	Earth Angel	Crew-Cuts	Mercury	10	(4)	
9	-	How Important Can It Be?	Joni James	MGM	13		
10	5	That's All I Want From You	Jaye P. Morgan	RCA	18		F
11	11	Melody Of Love	David Carroll	Mercury	11		F L
12	12	Ko Ko Mo (I Love You So)	Crew-Cuts	Mercury	9		
13	18	Open Up Your Heart (And Let The Sunshine In)	Cowboy Church Sunday School	Decca	16		F L
14	8	Earth Angel (Will You Be Mine)	Penguins	Dootone	11		F L
15	-	Ballad Of Davy Crockett	Fess Parker	Columbia	17		F
16	16	Melody Of Love	Four Aces	Decca	13		
17	-	Pledging My Love	Johnny Ace	Duke	3		F L
18	-	Darling Je Vous Aime Beaucoup	Nat 'King' Cole	Capitol	13		
19	-	Cherry Pink And Apple Blossom White	Perez Prado	RCA	22	(1)	F G
20	-	Ballad Of Davy Crockett	Tennessee Ernie Ford	Capitol	15	(3)	

◆ Alan Freed's first *Rock'n'Roll Party* with an all-star bill including Fats Domino, Joe Turner and The Drifters, attracted a record 15,000 fans. It was an all-R&B show – as yet, rock'n'roll had no stars of its own.

◆ Some jukeboxes increased their cost per play from a nickel to a dime.

◆ As 45s outsold 78s for the first time, many labels dropped the prices of 45s and increased those of 78s to hurry the demise of the latter.

◆ With the aim of slowing down the number of pop versions of R&B records, vocalist Lavern Baker appealed to Congress to legally put an end to note-for-note cover versions of original songs.

◆ A bi-weekly Top 15 album chart was introduced by *Billboard*.

UK 1955
APR-JUNE

◆ EMI launched "stereosonic sound", described as "an amazing 3D aural effect" and promoted producer George Martin to head of their Parlophone label.

◆ Latin American dance craze the mambo had its finest moment thanks to Perez Prado's transatlantic smash 'Cherry Pink And Apple Blossom White'.

◆ Sixteen months after they had simultaneously climbed the American Top 20, versions of 'Stranger In Paradise' by Tony Bennett, Tony Martin and The Four Aces also battled it out on the British chart. The song which was adapted from classical composer Borodin's 'Polovtsian Dances' came from the musical *Kismet*. The only local version to hit was by trumpeter Eddie Calvert, whose 'Oh, Mein Papa' had previously sold a million in the USA.

April 1955

This Mnth	Prev Mnth	Title	Artist	Label	Wks 20	(US Pos)	
1	1	Give Me Your Word	Tennessee Ernie Ford	Capitol	24		F
2	-	Cherry Pink And Apple Blossom White	Perez Prado	HMV	17	(1)	F
3	2	Softly Softly	Ruby Murray	Columbia	23		
4	18	If Anyone Finds This I Love You	Ruby Murray	Columbia	11		
5	16	Wedding Bells	Eddie Fisher	HMV	11		
6	-	Under The Bridges Of Paris	Dean Martin	Capitol	8		
7	-	Cherry Pink And Apple Blossom White	Eddie Calvert	Columbia	21		
8	6	Mobile	Ray Burns	Columbia	13		F
9	-	Prize Of Gold	Joan Regan	Decca	8	(55)	
10	5	A Blossom Fell	Nat 'King' Cole	Capitol	10	(2)	
11	-	Under The Bridges Of Paris	Eartha Kitt	HMV	10		F L
12	-	Stranger In Paradise	Tony Bennett	Philips	16	(2)	F
13	-	Ready Willing And Able	Doris Day	Philips	9		
14	3	Let Me Go, Lover	Dean Martin	Capitol	9		
15	-	Earth Angel	Crew-Cuts	Mercury	20	(8)	L
16	-	Stranger In Paradise	Tony Martin	HMV	13	(10)	F
17	15	Tomorrow	Johnny Brandon	Polygon	8		F
18	14	A Blossom Fell	Dickie Valentine	Decca	10		
19	-	A Blossom Fell	Ronnie Hilton	HMV	5		
20	10	Let Me Go, Lover	Ruby Murray	Columbia	7		

May 1955

This Mnth	Prev Mnth	Title	Artist	Label	Wks 20	(US Pos)	
1	12	Stranger In Paradise	Tony Bennett	Philips	16	(2)	F
2	2	Cherry Pink And Apple Blossom White	Perez Prado	HMV	17	(1)	F
3	7	Cherry Pink And Apple Blossom White	Eddie Calvert	Columbia	21		
4	1	Give Me Your Word	Tennessee Ernie Ford	Capitol	24		F
5	15	Earth Angel	Crew-Cuts	Mercury	20	(8)	L
6	16	Stranger In Paradise	Tony Martin	HMV	13	(10)	F
7	3	Softly Softly	Ruby Murray	Columbia	23		
8	-	Unchained Melody	Al Hibbler	Brunswick	17	(5)	F L
9	5	Wedding Bells	Eddie Fisher	HMV	11		
10	-	Unchained Melody	Jimmy Young	Decca	19		
11	-	If You Believe	Johnnie Ray	Philips	11		
12	4	If Anyone Finds This I Love You	Ruby Murray	Columbia	11		
13	13	Ready Willing And Able	Doris Day	Philips	9		
14	11	Under The Bridges Of Paris	Eartha Kitt	HMV	10		F L
15	-	Unchained Melody	Les Baxter	Capitol	9	(2)	F L
16	-	Melody Of Love	Ink Spots	Parlophone	4		F L
17	-	Stranger In Paradise	Four Aces	Brunswick	6	(5)	
18	6	Under The Bridges Of Paris	Dean Martin	Capitol	8		
19	-	Stranger In Paradise	Eddie Calvert	Columbia	4		
20	-	Where Will The Baby's Dimple Be	Rosemary Clooney	Philips	13		

June 1955

This Mnth	Prev Mnth	Title	Artist	Label	Wks 20	(US Pos)	
1	3	Cherry Pink And Apple Blossom...	Eddie Calvert	Columbia	21		
2	8	Unchained Melody	Al Hibbler	Brunswick	17	(5)	F L
3	10	Unchained Melody	Jimmy Young	Decca	19		
4	1	Stranger In Paradise	Tony Bennett	Philips	16	(2)	F
5	5	Earth Angel	Crew-Cuts	Mercury	20	(8)	L
6	2	Cherry Pink And Apple Blossom...	Perez Prado	HMV	17	(1)	F
7	-	Dreamboat	Alma Cogan	HMV	16		
8	6	Stranger In Paradise	Tony Martin	HMV	13	(10)	F
9	20	Where Will The Baby's Dimple Be	Rosemary Clooney	Philips	13		
10	11	If You Believe	Johnnie Ray	Philips	11		
11	17	Stranger In Paradise	Four Aces	Brunswick	6	(5)	
12	4	Give Me Your Word	Tennessee Ernie Ford	Capitol	24		F
13	15	Unchained Melody	Les Baxter	Capitol	9	(2)	F L
14	-	I Wonder	Dickie Valentine	Decca	15		
15	-	Sing It With Joe	Joe 'Mr. Piano' Henderson	Polygon	4		F
16	-	You My Love	Frank Sinatra	Capitol	7		
17	7	Softly Softly	Ruby Murray	Columbia	23		
18	-	Cool Water	Frankie Laine	Philips	22		
19	-	Crazy Otto Rag	Stargazers	Decca	3		
20	-	Stowaway	Barbara Lyon	Columbia	8		F

April 1955

This Mnth	Prev Mnth	Title	Artist	Label	Wks 20	(UK Pos)	
1	5	The Ballad Of Davy Crockett	Bill Hayes	Cadence	20	(2)	F L
2	2	The Crazy Otto (Medley)	Johnny Maddox	Dot	16		F L
3	19	Cherry Pink And Apple Blossom White	Perez Prado	RCA	22	(1)	F G
4	4	Tweedle Dee	Georgia Gibbs	Mercury	17	(20)	G
5	15	Ballad Of Davy Crockett	Fess Parker	Columbia	17		F
6	1	Sincerely	McGuire Sisters	Coral	17	(14)	G
7	-	Dance With Me Henry (Wallflower)	Georgia Gibbs	Mercury	16		L
8	3	Melody Of Love	Billy Vaughn	Dot	21		F G
9	20	Ballad Of Davy Crockett	Tennessee Ernie Ford	Capitol	15	(3)	
10	9	How Important Can It Be?	Joni James	MGM	13		
11	18	Darling Je Vous Aime Beaucoup	Nat 'King' Cole	Capitol	13		
12	-	Unchained Melody	Les Baxter	Capitol	20	(10)	F G
13	13	Open Up Your Heart (And Let The Sunshine In)	Cowboy Church Sunday School	Decca	16		F L
14	-	Unchained Melody	Al Hibbler	Decca	18	(2)	F G
15	6	Ko Ko Mo (I Love You So)	Perry Como	RCA	12		
16	16	Melody Of Love	Four Aces	Decca	13		
17	8	Earth Angel	Crew-Cuts	Mercury	10	(4)	
18	-	The Breeze And I	Caterina Valente	Decca	11	(5)	F L
19	-	Play Me Hearts And Flowers (I Wanna Cry)	Johnny Desmond	Coral	5		F
20	11	Melody Of Love	David Carroll	Mercury	11		F L

May 1955

This Mnth	Prev Mnth	Title	Artist	Label	Wks 20	(UK Pos)	
1	3	Cherry Pink And Apple Blossom...	Perez Prado	RCA	22	(1)	F G
2	12	Unchained Melody	Les Baxter	Capitol	20	(10)	F G
3	7	Dance With Me Henry (Wallflower)	Georgia Gibbs	Mercury	16		L
4	1	The Ballad Of Davy Crockett	Bill Hayes	Cadence	20	(2)	F L
5	14	Unchained Melody	Al Hibbler	Decca	18	(2)	F G
6	5	Ballad Of Davy Crockett	Fess Parker	Columbia	17		F
7	9	Ballad Of Davy Crockett	Tennessee Ernie Ford	Capitol	15	(3)	
8	2	The Crazy Otto (Medley)	Johnny Maddox	Dot	16		F L
9	-	Unchained Melody	Roy Hamilton	Epic	13		F
10	11	Darling Je Vous Aime Beaucoup	Nat 'King' Cole	Capitol	13		
11	-	Honey-Babe	Art Mooney	MGM	16		F L
12	4	Tweedle Dee	Georgia Gibbs	Mercury	17	(20)	G
13	-	Whatever Lola Wants	Sarah Vaughan	Mercury	11		
14	-	A Blossom Fell/If I May	Nat 'King' Cole	Capitol	18	(3)	G
15	18	The Breeze And I	Caterina Valente	Decca	11	(5)	F L
16	-	Don't Be Angry	Crew-Cuts	Mercury	7		
17	-	Rock Around The Clock	Bill Haley & His Comets	Decca	22	(1)	G
18	6	Sincerely	McGuire Sisters	Coral	17	(14)	G
19	8	Melody Of Love	Billy Vaughn	Dot	21		F G
20	-	Two Hearts	Pat Boone	Dot	6		F

June 1955

This Mnth	Prev Mnth	Title	Artist	Label	Wks 20	(UK Pos)	
1	1	Cherry Pink And Apple Blossom...	Perez Prado	RCA	22	(1)	F G
2	2	Unchained Melody	Les Baxter	Capitol	20	(10)	F G
3	14	A Blossom Fell/If I May	Nat 'King' Cole	Capitol	18	(3)	G
4	3	Dance With Me Henry (Wallflower)	Georgia Gibbs	Mercury	16		L
5	17	Rock Around The Clock	Bill Haley & His Comets	Decca	22	(1)	G
6	5	Unchained Melody	Al Hibbler	Decca	18	(2)	F G
7	-	Learnin' The Blues	Frank Sinatra	Capitol	18	(2)	G
8	11	Honey-Babe	Art Mooney	MGM	16		F L
9	4	The Ballad Of Davy Crockett	Bill Hayes	Cadence	20	(2)	F L
10	6	Ballad Of Davy Crockett	Fess Parker	Columbia	17		F
11	9	Unchained Melody	Roy Hamilton	Epic	13		F
12	13	Whatever Lola Wants	Sarah Vaughan	Mercury	11		
13	7	Ballad Of Davy Crockett	Tennessee Ernie Ford	Capitol	15	(3)	
14	-	It's A Sin To Tell A Lie	Somethin' Smith & The Redheads	Epic	16		F L
15	-	Something's Gotta Give	McGuire Sisters	Coral	10		
16	15	The Breeze And I	Caterina Valente	Decca	11	(5)	F L
17	-	Love Me Or Leave Me	Sammy Davis Jr.	Decca	3	(8)	
18	-	Something's Gotta Give	Sammy Davis Jr.	Decca	9	(11)	
19	16	Don't Be Angry	Crew-Cuts	Mercury	7		
20	-	Heart	Eddie Fisher	RCA	7		

◆ The Davy Crockett craze spread across America, with recordings of the theme from the Disney film, *Davy Crockett, King Of The Wild Frontier*, charting by Bill Hayes, Fess Parker and Tennessee Ernie Ford.

▲ Perry Como, who was charting with a cover version of Gene & Eunice's R&B hit, 'Ko Ko Mo (I Love You So)', signed a lucrative 12 year TV contract with NBC.

◆ American Juke Box operators announced that there was 60% more R&B records being selected than a year ago.

UK 1955

JULY–SEPT

◆ Despite its failure in the US, 'Rose Marie' (from the 1925 musical of the same name) by Florida C&W artist Slim Whitman, held the top spot in Britain for 11 successive weeks – a record he held until 1991 when it was broken by Bryan Adams.

◆ Despite the fact that 'Rock Around The Clock' topped the US charts in early July, rock'n'roll was not even mentioned in *NME* until late September, and then only in a reader's letter from the West Indies.

◆ Among the earliest R&B songs to chart in Britain were 'Earth Angel' and 'Sincerely', albeit the sanitized American pop versions by the Crew-Cuts and the McGuire Sisters respectively.

◆ The first commercial television station was launched in Britain as a rival to the BBC. There would not be a third television channel until the early 1960s.

July 1955

This Mnth	Prev Mnth	Title	Artist	Label	Wks 20	(US Pos)	
1	7	**Dreamboat**	Alma Cogan	HMV	16		
2	3	**Unchained Melody**	Jimmy Young	Decca	19		
3	2	**Unchained Melody**	Al Hibbler	Brunswick	17	(5)	F L
4	1	**Cherry Pink And Apple Blossom White**	Eddie Calvert	Columbia	21		
5	14	**I Wonder**	Dickie Valentine	Decca	15		
6	-	**Evermore**	Ruby Murray	Columbia	17		
7	18	**Cool Water**	Frankie Laine	Philips	22		
8	5	**Earth Angel**	Crew-Cuts	Mercury	20	(8)	L
9	9	**Where Will The Baby's Dimple Be**	Rosemary Clooney	Philips	13		
10	-	**Rose Marie**	Slim Whitman	London	19		F
11	4	**Stranger In Paradise**	Tony Bennett	Philips	16	(2)	F
12	-	**Every Day Of My Life**	Malcolm Vaughan	HMV	16		F
13	-	**Ev'rywhere**	David Whitfield	Decca	20		
14	20	**Stowaway**	Barbara Lyon	Columbia	8		F L
15	6	**Cherry Pink And Apple Blossom White**	Perez Prado	HMV	17	(1)	F
16	8	**Stranger In Paradise**	Tony Martin	HMV	13	(10)	F
17	-	**Strange Lady In Town**	Frankie Laine	Philips	13		
18	-	**Sincerely**	McGuire Sisters	Vogue Coral	4	(1)	
19	10	**If You Believe**	Johnnie Ray	Philips	11		
20	13	**Unchained Melody**	Les Baxter	Capitol	9	(2)	F L

August 1955

1	10	**Rose Marie**	Slim Whitman	London	19		F
2	7	**Cool Water**	Frankie Laine	Philips	22		
3	6	**Evermore**	Ruby Murray	Columbia	17		
4	1	**Dreamboat**	Alma Cogan	HMV	16		
5	13	**Ev'rywhere**	David Whitfield	Decca	20		
6	12	**Every Day Of My Life**	Malcolm Vaughan	HMV	16		F
7	-	**Learnin' The Blues**	Frank Sinatra	Capitol	13	(2)	
8	17	**Strange Lady In Town**	Frankie Laine	Philips	13		
9	2	**Unchained Melody**	Jimmy Young	Decca	19		
10	5	**I Wonder**	Dickie Valentine	Decca	15		
11	4	**Cherry Pink And Apple Blossom White**	Eddie Calvert	Columbia	21		
12	3	**Unchained Melody**	Al Hibbler	Brunswick	17	(5)	F L
13	-	**Mama**	David Whitfield	Decca	11		
14	-	**Indian Love Call**	Slim Whitman	London American	12	(10)	
15	-	**John And Julie**	Eddie Calvert	Columbia	11		
16	-	**The Breeze And I**	Caterina Valente	Polydor	14	(13)	F L
17	8	**Earth Angel**	Crew-Cuts	Mercury	20	(8)	L
18	9	**Where Will The Baby's Dimple Be**	Rosemary Clooney	Philips	13		
19	14	**Stowaway**	Barbara Lyon	Columbia	8		F L
20	-	**You My Love**	Frank Sinatra	Capitol	7		

September 1955

1	1	**Rose Marie**	Slim Whitman	London	19		F
2	7	**Learnin' The Blues**	Frank Sinatra	Capitol	13	(2)	
3	2	**Cool Water**	Frankie Laine	Philips	22		
4	5	**Ev'rywhere**	David Whitfield	Decca	20		
5	16	**The Breeze And I**	Caterina Valente	Polydor	14	(13)	F L
6	3	**Evermore**	Ruby Murray	Columbia	17		
7	8	**Strange Lady In Town**	Frankie Laine	Philips	13		
8	15	**John And Julie**	Eddie Calvert	Columbia	11		
9	6	**Every Day Of My Life**	Malcolm Vaughan	HMV	16		F
10	14	**Indian Love Call**	Slim Whitman	London American	12	(10)	
11	-	**Close The Door**	Stargazers	Decca	9		
12	-	**The Man From Laramie**	Jimmy Young	Decca	12		
13	-	**Love Me Or Leave Me**	Sammy Davis Jr.	Brunswick	6	(10)	
14	-	**Stars Shine In Your Eyes**	Ronnie Hilton	HMV	7		
15	-	**Something's Gotta Give**	Sammy Davis Jr.	Brunswick	7	(9)	F
16	-	**That's How A Love Song Was Born**	Ray Burns	Columbia	6		L
17	-	**Blue Star**	Cyril Stapleton	Decca	12		
18	13	**Mama**	David Whitfield	Decca	11		
19	4	**Dreamboat**	Alma Cogan	HMV	16		
20	-	**China Doll**	Slim Whitman	London American	2		

July 1955

This Mnth	Prev Mnth	Title	Artist	Label	Wks 20	(UK Pos)	
1	5	Rock Around The Clock	Bill Haley & His Comets	Decca	22	(1)	G
2	1	Cherry Pink And Apple Blossom White	Perez Prado	RCA	22	(1)	F G
3	3	A Blossom Fell/If I May	Nat 'King' Cole	Capitol	18	(3)	G
4	7	Learnin' The Blues	Frank Sinatra	Capitol	18	(2)	G
5	2	Unchained Melody	Les Baxter	Capitol	20	(10)	F G
6	15	Something's Gotta Give	McGuire Sisters	Coral	10		
7	8	Honey-Babe	Art Mooney	MGM	16		F L
8	-	Hard To Get	Giselle Mackenzie	X	15		F L
9	6	Unchained Melody	Al Hibbler	Decca	18	(2)	F G
10	14	It's A Sin To Tell A Lie	Somethin' Smith & The Redheads	Epic	16		F L
11	18	Something's Gotta Give	Sammy Davis Jr.	Decca	9	(11)	
12	-	Ain't That A Shame	Pat Boone	Dot	18	(7)	G
13	-	Sweet And Gentle	Alan Dale	Coral	7		F L
14	4	Dance With Me Henry (Wallflower)	Georgia Gibbs	Mercury	16		L
15	11	Unchained Melody	Roy Hamilton	Epic	13		F
16	20	Heart	Eddie Fisher	RCA	7		
17	-	The House Of Blue Lights	Chuck Miller	Mercury	10		F L
18	9	The Ballad Of Davy Crockett	Bill Hayes	Cadence	20	(2)	F L
19	-	A Story Untold	Crew-Cuts	Mercury	4		
20	-	Hummingbird	Les Paul & Mary Ford	Capitol	9		L

August 1955

This Mnth	Prev Mnth	Title	Artist	Label	Wks 20	(UK Pos)	
1	1	Rock Around The Clock	Bill Haley & His Comets	Decca	22	(1)	G
2	12	Ain't That A Shame	Pat Boone	Dot	18	(7)	G
3	4	Learnin' The Blues	Frank Sinatra	Capitol	18	(2)	G
4	3	A Blossom Fell/If I May	Nat 'King' Cole	Capitol	18	(3)	G
5	8	Hard To Get	Giselle Mackenzie	X	15		F L
6	-	The Yellow Rose Of Texas	Mitch Miller	Columbia	19	(2)	G
7	10	It's A Sin To Tell A Lie	Somethin' Smith & The Redheads	Epic	16		F L
8	-	Seventeen	Boyd Bennett & His Rockets	King	13	(16)	F L
9	20	Hummingbird	Les Paul & Mary Ford	Capitol	9		L
10	17	The House Of Blue Lights	Chuck Miller	Mercury	10		F L
11	2	Cherry Pink And Apple Blossom White	Perez Prado	RCA	22	(1)	F G
12	5	Unchained Melody	Les Baxter	Capitol	20	(10)	F G
13	-	The Yellow Rose Of Texas	Johnny Desmond	Coral	14		L
14	6	Something's Gotta Give	McGuire Sisters	Coral	10		
15	-	Domani (Tomorrow)	Julius La Rosa	Cadence	4		L
16	-	Maybellene	Chuck Berry	Chess	10		F
17	11	Something's Gotta Give	Sammy Davis Jr.	Decca	9	(11)	
18	13	Sweet And Gentle	Alan Dale	Coral	7		F L
19	-	Wake The Town And Tell The People	Les Baxter	Capitol	11		
20	-	I'll Never Stop Loving You	Doris Day	Columbia	4	(17)	

September 1955

This Mnth	Prev Mnth	Title	Artist	Label	Wks 20	(UK Pos)	
1	6	The Yellow Rose Of Texas	Mitch Miller	Columbia	19	(2)	G
2	2	Ain't That A Shame	Pat Boone	Dot	18	(7)	G
3	1	Rock Around The Clock	Bill Haley & His Comets	Decca	22	(1)	G
4	16	Maybellene	Chuck Berry	Chess	10		F
5	-	Autumn Leaves	Roger Williams	Kapp	23		F G
6	13	The Yellow Rose Of Texas	Johnny Desmond	Coral	14		L
7	8	Seventeen	Boyd Bennett & His Rockets	King	13	(16)	F L
8	-	Seventeen	Fontane Sisters	Dot	11		
9	-	Love Is A Many-Splendored Thing	Four Aces	Decca	20	(2)	G
10	-	Tina Marie	Perry Como	RCA	13	(24)	
11	19	Wake The Town And Tell The People	Les Baxter	Capitol	11		
12	3	Learnin' The Blues	Frank Sinatra	Capitol	18	(2)	G
13	5	Hard To Get	Giselle Mackenzie	X	15		F L
14	-	Gum Drop	Crew-Cuts	Mercury	7		
15	-	Moments To Remember	Four Lads	Columbia	23		G
16	-	The Longest Walk	Jaye P. Morgan	RCA	6		L
17	-	Song Of The Dreamer	Eddie Fisher	RCA	5		
18	9	Hummingbird	Les Paul & Mary Ford	Capitol	9		L
19	4	A Blossom Fell/If I May	Nat 'King' Cole	Capitol	18	(3)	G
20	-	The Bible Tells Me So	Don Cornell	Coral	12		L

◆ Rock'n'roll had its first No. 1 hit, 'Rock Around The Clock' by Bill Haley & The Comets. It was estimated that Haley would earn $500,000 in 1955 from shows alone.

◆ Pat Boone debuted in the US Top 20 with Fats Domino's R&B No. 1, 'Ain't That A Shame', as Elvis Presley's name first appeared on the C&W chart with 'Baby Let's Play House'.

▲ *Rock 'N' Roll Revue*, arguably the first rock'n'roll film, was premiered. It starred Nat 'King' Cole (above) and Joe Turner.

◆ 'Maybelline' R&B singer/songwriter Chuck Berry's debut disk, "motor-vated" into the US Top 5.

UK 1955

OCT-DEC

◆ American composer Jerry Ross died aged 29, as his compositions, 'Hernando's Hideaway' and 'Hey There', held three places in the UK Top 5.

◆ Thanks to its exposure in the hit film *The Blackboard Jungle*, 'Rock Around The Clock' by Bill Haley & The Comets became the first rock'n'roll record to top the UK chart.

◆ The price of singles in Britain went up to 5s 7d (53 cents/27p).

◆ While American Johnnie Ray wowed the audience on the UK's top TV show *Sunday Night At The London Palladium*, British balladeer David Whitfield made his third successful appearance on Ed Sullivan's top rated American TV show.

October 1955

This Mnth	Prev Mnth	Title	Artist	Label	Wks 20	(US Pos)	
1	12	The Man From Laramie	Jimmy Young	Decca	12		
2	17	Blue Star	Cyril Stapleton	Decca	12		
3	1	Rose Marie	Slim Whitman	London	19		F
4	3	Cool Water	Frankie Laine	Philips	22		
5	-	Yellow Rose Of Texas	Mitch Miller	Philips	13	(1)	F L
6	4	Ev'rywhere	David Whitfield	Decca	20		
7	5	The Breeze And I	Caterina Valente	Polydor	14	(13)	F L
8	-	Hernando's Hideaway	Johnston Brothers	Decca	13		
9	2	Learnin' The Blues	Frank Sinatra	Capitol	13	(2)	
10	11	Close The Door	Stargazers	Decca	9		
11	-	Hey There	Rosemary Clooney	Philips	11	(1)	
12	-	Rock Around The Clock	Bill Haley & His Comets	Brunswick	17	(1)	G
13	-	Hernando's Hideaway	Johnnie Ray	Philips	5	(24)	
14	-	Hey There	Johnnie Ray	Philips	9		
15	10	Indian Love Call	Slim Whitman	London American	12	(10)	
16	-	I'll Come When You Call	Ruby Murray	Columbia	7		
17	9	Every Day Of My Life	Malcolm Vaughan	HMV	16		F
18	6	Evermore	Ruby Murray	Columbia	17		
19	13	Love Me Or Leave Me	Sammy Davis Jr.	Brunswick	6	(10)	
20	-	Go On By	Alma Cogan	HMV	4		

November 1955

This Mnth	Prev Mnth	Title	Artist	Label	Wks 20	(US Pos)	
1	8	Hernando's Hideaway	Johnston Brothers	Decca	13		
2	12	Rock Around The Clock	Bill Haley & His Comets	Brunswick	17	(1)	G
3	1	The Man From Laramie	Jimmy Young	Decca	12		
4	14	Hey There	Johnnie Ray	Philips	9		
5	11	Hey There	Rosemary Clooney	Philips	11	(1)	
6	2	Blue Star	Cyril Stapleton	Decca	12		
7	5	Yellow Rose Of Texas	Mitch Miller	Philips	13	(1)	F L
8	16	I'll Come When You Call	Ruby Murray	Columbia	7		
9	-	Let's Have A Ding Dong	Winifred Atwell	Decca	10		
10	6	Ev'rywhere	David Whitfield	Decca	20		
11	-	Song Of The Dreamer	Johnnie Ray	Philips	5		
12	-	Love Is A Many Splendoured Thing	Four Aces	Brunswick	13	(1)	
13	4	Cool Water	Frankie Laine	Philips	22		
14	-	Twenty Tiny Fingers	Stargazers	Decca	11		L
15	3	Rose Marie	Slim Whitman	London	19		F
16	-	Yellow Rose Of Texas	Gary Miller	Nixa	5		F
17	7	The Breeze And I	Caterina Valente	Polydor	14	(13)	F L
18	-	Ain't That A Shame	Pat Boone	London American	9	(2)	F
19	-	Meet Me On The Corner	Max Bygraves	HMV	11		
20	-	Yellow Rose Of Texas	Ronnie Hilton	HMV	2		

December 1955

This Mnth	Prev Mnth	Title	Artist	Label	Wks 20	(US Pos)	
1	2	Rock Around The Clock	Bill Haley & His Comets	Brunswick	17	(1)	G
2	-	Christmas Alphabet	Dickie Valentine	Decca	7		
3	12	Love Is A Many Splendoured Thing	Four Aces	Brunswick	13	(1)	
4	9	Let's Have A Ding Dong	Winifred Atwell	Decca	10		
5	19	Meet Me On The Corner	Max Bygraves	HMV	11		
6	14	Twenty Tiny Fingers	Stargazers	Decca	11		L
7	7	Yellow Rose Of Texas	Mitch Miller	Philips	13	(1)	F L
8	1	Hernando's Hideaway	Johnston Brothers	Decca	13		
9	-	Suddenly There's A Valley	Petula Clark	Nixa	10		
10	18	Ain't That A Shame	Pat Boone	London American	9	(2)	F
11	-	Hawkeye	Frankie Laine	Philips	8		
12	-	When You Lose The One You Love	David Whitfield	Decca	11	(62)	
13	-	Suddenly There's A Valley	Jo Stafford	Philips	6	(21)	L
14	-	The Singing Dogs (Medley)	Singing Dogs	Nixa	4		F L
15	-	Never Do A Tango With An Eskimo	Alma Cogan	HMV	5		
16	4	Hey There	Johnnie Ray	Philips	9		
17	5	Hey There	Rosemary Clooney	Philips	11	(1)	
18	-	Suddenly There's A Valley	Lee Lawrence	Columbia	3		L
19	6	Blue Star	Cyril Stapleton	Decca	12		
20	-	On With The Motley	Harry Secombe	Philips	3		F

US 1955 OCT-DEC

October 1955

This Mnth	Prev Mnth	Title	Artist	Label	Wks 20	(UK Pos)	
1	9	Love Is A Many-Splendored Thing	Four Aces	Decca	20	(2)	G
2	1	The Yellow Rose Of Texas	Mitch Miller	Columbia	19	(2)	G
3	5	Autumn Leaves	Roger Williams	Kapp	23		F G
4	15	Moments To Remember	Four Lads	Columbia	23		G
5	2	Ain't That A Shame	Pat Boone	Dot	18	(7)	G
6	-	The Shifting Whispering Sands (Pts 1 & 2)	Billy Vaughn	Dot	13	(20)	
7	10	Tina Marie	Perry Como	RCA	13	(24)	
8	20	The Bible Tells Me So	Don Cornell	Coral	12		L
9	6	The Yellow Rose Of Texas	Johnny Desmond	Coral	14		L
10	8	Seventeen	Fontane Sisters	Dot	11		
11	-	Black Denim Trousers	Cheers	Capitol	8		L
12	-	The Shifting, Whispering Sands	Rusty Draper	Mercury	13		
13	-	Only You	Platters	Mercury	18	(5)	F G
14	-	He	Al Hibbler	Decca	20		
15	4	Maybellene	Chuck Berry	Chess	10		F
16	3	Rock Around The Clock	Bill Haley & His Comets	Decca	22	(1)	G
17	11	Wake The Town And Tell The People	Les Baxter	Capitol	11		
18	7	Seventeen	Boyd Bennett & His Rockets	King	13	(16)	F L
19	-	My Bonnie Lassie	Ames Brothers	RCA	7		
20	-	Suddenly There's A Valley	Gogi Grant	Era	9		F

November 1955

This Mnth	Prev Mnth	Title	Artist	Label	Wks 20	(UK Pos)	
1	3	Autumn Leaves	Roger Williams	Kapp	23		F G
2	1	Love Is A Many-Splendored Thing	Four Aces	Decca	20	(2)	G
3	4	Moments To Remember	Four Lads	Columbia	23		G
4	2	The Yellow Rose Of Texas	Mitch Miller	Columbia	19	(2)	G
5	13	Only You	Platters	Mercury	18	(5)	F G
6	-	Sixteen Tons	Tennessee Ernie Ford	Capitol	17	(1)	G L
7	-	I Hear You Knocking	Gale Storm	Dot	16		F G
8	12	The Shifting, Whispering Sands	Rusty Draper	Mercury	13		
9	14	He	Al Hibbler	Decca	20		
10	-	At My Front Door (Crazy Little Mama)	Pat Boone	Dot	9		
11	6	The Shifting Whispering Sands (Pts 1 & 2)	Billy Vaughn	Dot	13	(20)	
12	19	My Bonnie Lassie	Ames Brothers	RCA	7		
13	11	Black Denim Trousers	Cheers	Capitol	8		L
14	-	Forgive My Heart	Nat 'King' Cole	Capitol	5		
15	-	Love And Marriage	Frank Sinatra	Capitol	13	(3)	
16	20	Suddenly There's A Valley	Gogi Grant	Era	9		F
17	8	The Bible Tells Me So	Don Cornell	Coral	12		L
18	-	He	McGuire Sisters	Coral	10		
19	7	Tina Marie	Perry Como	RCA	13	(24)	
20	-	It's Almost Tomorrow	Dream Weavers	Decca	18	(1)	F L

December 1955

This Mnth	Prev Mnth	Title	Artist	Label	Wks 20	(UK Pos)	
1	6	Sixteen Tons	Tennessee Ernie Ford	Capitol	17	(1)	G L
2	1	Autumn Leaves	Roger Williams	Kapp	23		F G
3	7	I Hear You Knocking	Gale Storm	Dot	16		F G
4	3	Moments To Remember	Four Lads	Columbia	23		G
5	2	Love Is A Many-Splendored Thing	Four Aces	Decca	20	(2)	G
6	-	Memories Are Made Of This	Dean Martin	Capitol	17	(1)	G
7	5	Only You	Platters	Mercury	18	(5)	F G
8	9	He	Al Hibbler	Decca	20		
9	15	Love And Marriage	Frank Sinatra	Capitol	13	(3)	
10	20	It's Almost Tomorrow	Dream Weavers	Decca	18	(1)	F L
11	8	The Shifting, Whispering Sands	Rusty Draper	Mercury	13		
12	18	He	McGuire Sisters	Coral	10		
13	10	At My Front Door (Crazy Little Mama)	Pat Boone	Dot	9		
14	-	Nuttin' For Christmas	Barry Gordon	MGM	3		F G L
15	-	Band Of Gold	Don Cherry	Columbia	16	(6)	L
16	11	The Shifting Whispering Sands (Pts 1 & 2)	Billy Vaughn	Dot	13	(20)	
17	-	Only You (And You Alone)	Hilltoppers	Dot	5	(3)	
18	-	The Great Pretender	Platters	Mercury	17	(5)	G
19	4	The Yellow Rose Of Texas	Mitch Miller	Columbia	19	(2)	G
20	-	Daddy-O	Fontane Sisters	Dot	3		

◆ RCA Records paid $40,000 to sign Elvis Presley – a small fortune for an artist who had yet to have a pop hit. His final Sun single, 'I Forgot To Remember To Forget You', topped the C&W chart.

▲ Buddy Holly was signed by Decca Records. He had been a support act for both Elvis Presley and Bill Haley & The Comets when they performed in his home town, Lubbock, Texas.

◆ Rockin' R&B music got its first national TV exposure when Bo Diddley, Lavern Baker and The Five Keys appeared in a special 15 minute segment of the Ed Sullivan show.

UK 1956 JAN-MAR

◆ America's fastest seller of 1955, '16 Tons' by Tennessee Ernie Ford, which rocketed to the top in the USA in a record three weeks and sold over 600,000 copies in its first nine days, also topped the UK chart.

▲ Lonnie Donegan's 'Rock Island Line' introduced the transatlantic public to skiffle – a do-it-yourself folk/blues based music that launched a thousand British groups.

◆ George Martin had three productions simultaneously in the UK Top 20. The records being by TV personality Eamonn Andrews, Eve Boswell and (later Beatles' publisher) Dick James.

January 1956

This Mnth	Prev Mnth	Title	Artist	Label	Wks 20	(US Pos)	
1	1	Rock Around The Clock	Bill Haley & His Comets	Brunswick	17	(1)	G
2	3	Love Is A Many Splendoured Thing	Four Aces	Brunswick	13	(1)	
3	-	Rock-A-Beatin' Boogie	Bill Haley & His Comets	Brunswick	8	(23)	
4	-	Sixteen Tons	Tennessee Ernie Ford	Capitol	11	(1)	
5	-	The Ballad Of Davy Crockett	Bill Hayes	London American	9	(1)	F L
6	5	Meet Me On The Corner	Max Bygraves	HMV	11		
7	-	Love And Marriage	Frank Sinatra	Capitol	8	(6)	
8	-	The Ballad Of Davy Crockett	Tennessee Ernie Ford	Capitol	7	(6)	L
9	15	Never Do A Tango With An Eskimo	Alma Cogan	HMV	5		
10	12	When You Lose The One You Love	David Whitfield	Decca	11	(62)	
11	6	Twenty Tiny Fingers	Stargazers	Decca	11		L
12	9	Suddenly There's A Valley	Petula Clark	Nixa	10		
13	-	Rock Island Line	Lonnie Donegan	Decca	14	(8)	F
14	-	The Tender Trap	Frank Sinatra	Capitol	9	(24)	
15	-	Pickin' A Chicken	Eve Boswell	Parlophone	10		F L
16	-	Sixteen Tons	Frankie Laine	Philips	3		
17	11	Hawkeye	Frankie Laine	Philips	8		
18	-	Someone On Your Mind	Jimmy Young	Decca	5		
19	10	Ain't That A Shame	Pat Boone	London American	9	(2)	F
20	2	Christmas Alphabet	Dickie Valentine	Decca	7		

February 1956

This Mnth	Prev Mnth	Title	Artist	Label	Wks 20	(US Pos)	
1	4	Sixteen Tons	Tennessee Ernie Ford	Capitol	11	(1)	
2	14	The Tender Trap	Frank Sinatra	Capitol	9	(24)	
3	5	The Ballad Of Davy Crockett	Bill Hayes	London American	9	(1)	F L
4	-	Memories Are Made Of This	Dean Martin	Capitol	14	(1)	
5	-	Zambesi	Lou Busch	Capitol	15	(75)	F L
6	7	Love And Marriage	Frank Sinatra	Capitol	8	(6)	
7	-	Only You	Hilltoppers	London American	21	(15)	F
8	13	Rock Island Line	Lonnie Donegan	Decca	14	(8)	F
9	8	The Ballad Of Davy Crockett	Tennessee Ernie Ford	Capitol	7	(6)	L
10	-	Dreams Can Tell A Lie	Nat 'King' Cole	Capitol	9		
11	-	It's Almost Tomorrow	Dream Weavers	Brunswick	16	(8)	F L
12	3	Rock-A-Beatin' Boogie	Bill Haley & His Comets	Brunswick	8	(23)	
13	-	Rock And Roll Waltz	Kay Starr	HMV	18	(1)	L
14	-	Band Of Gold	Don Cherry	Philips	11	(5)	F L
15	-	Robin Hood	Gary Miller	Nixa	6		
16	2	Love Is A Many Splendoured Thing	Four Aces	Brunswick	13	(1)	
17	-	Robin Hood	Dick James	Parlophone	8		F
18	15	Pickin' A Chicken	Eve Boswell	Parlophone	10		F L
19	-	Memories Are Made Of This	Dave King	Decca	13		F
20	-	Young And Foolish	Edmund Hockridge	Nixa	7		F

March 1956

This Mnth	Prev Mnth	Title	Artist	Label	Wks 20	(US Pos)	
1	11	It's Almost Tomorrow	Dream Weavers	Brunswick	16	(8)	F L
2	4	Memories Are Made Of This	Dean Martin	Capitol	14	(1)	
3	13	Rock And Roll Waltz	Kay Starr	HMV	18	(1)	L
4	5	Zambesi	Lou Busch	Capitol	15	(75)	F L
5	7	Only You	Hilltoppers	London American	21	(15)	F
6	19	Memories Are Made Of This	Dave King	Decca	13		F
7	14	Band Of Gold	Don Cherry	Philips	11	(5)	F L
8	-	See You Later Alligator	Bill Haley & His Comets	Brunswick	11	(6)	
9	20	Young And Foolish	Edmund Hockridge	Nixa	7		F
10	8	Rock Island Line	Lonnie Donegan	Decca	14	(8)	F
11	-	The Great Pretender	Jimmy Parkinson	Columbia	10		F
12	-	Poor People Of Paris	Winifred Atwell	Decca	15		
13	2	The Tender Trap	Frank Sinatra	Capitol	9	(24)	
14	1	Sixteen Tons	Tennessee Ernie Ford	Capitol	11	(1)	
15	-	Chain Gang	Jimmy Young	Decca	5		
16	-	Theme From 'The Three Penny Opera'	Dick Hyman Trio	MGM	9	(10)	F L
17	10	Dreams Can Tell A Lie	Nat 'King' Cole	Capitol	9		
18	-	Zambesi	Eddie Calvert	Columbia	5		
19	-	In Old Lisbon	Frank Chacksfield	Decca	4		L
20	18	Pickin' A Chicken	Eve Boswell	Parlophone	10		F L

January 1956

This Mnth	Prev Mnth	Title	Artist	Label	Wks 20	(UK Pos)	
1	6	Memories Are Made Of This	Dean Martin	Capitol	17	(1)	G
2	1	Sixteen Tons	Tennessee Ernie Ford	Capitol	17	(1)	G L
3	18	The Great Pretender	Platters	Mercury	17	(5)	G
4	3	I Hear You Knocking	Gale Storm	Dot	16		F G
5	15	Band Of Gold	Don Cherry	Columbia	16	(6)	L
6	-	Lisbon Antigua	Nelson Riddle	Capitol	20		F G L
7	9	Love And Marriage	Frank Sinatra	Capitol	13	(3)	
8	4	Moments To Remember	Four Lads	Columbia	23		G
9	-	Rock And Roll Waltz	Kay Starr	RCA	16	(1)	G L
10	10	It's Almost Tomorrow	Dream Weavers	Decca	18	(1)	F L
11	8	He	Al Hibbler	Decca	20		
12	2	Autumn Leaves	Roger Williams	Kapp	23		F G
13	-	Dungaree Doll	Eddie Fisher	RCA	12		
14	-	Angels In The Sky	Crew-Cuts	Mercury	12		L
15	7	Only You	Platters	Mercury	18	(5)	F G
16	-	See You Later, Alligator	Bill Haley & His Comets	Decca	13	(7)	
17	-	Teenage Prayer	Gale Storm	Dot	8		
18	14	Nuttin' For Christmas	Barry Gordon	MGM	3		F G L
19	-	Are You Satisfied?	Rusty Draper	Mercury	5		
20	5	Love Is A Many-Splendored Thing	Four Aces	Decca	20	(2)	G

February 1956

This Mnth	Prev Mnth	Title	Artist	Label	Wks 20	(UK Pos)	
1	9	Rock And Roll Waltz	Kay Starr	RCA	16	(1)	G L
2	1	Memories Are Made Of This	Dean Martin	Capitol	17	(1)	G
3	3	The Great Pretender	Platters	Mercury	17	(5)	G
4	6	Lisbon Antigua	Nelson Riddle	Capitol	20		F G L
5	16	See You Later, Alligator	Bill Haley & His Comets	Decca	13	(7)	
6	2	Sixteen Tons	Tennessee Ernie Ford	Capitol	17	(1)	G L
7	-	No, Not Much!	Four Lads	Columbia	15		G
8	5	Band Of Gold	Don Cherry	Columbia	16	(6)	L
9	10	It's Almost Tomorrow	Dream Weavers	Decca	18	(1)	F L
10	13	Dungaree Doll	Eddie Fisher	RCA	12		
11	14	Angels In The Sky	Crew-Cuts	Mercury	12		L
12	-	I'll Be Home	Pat Boone	Dot	14	(1)	G
13	-	The Poor People Of Paris	Les Baxter	Capitol	17		G L
14	-	Moritat (A Theme From 'The Three Penny Opera')	Dick Hyman	MGM	11	(9)	F L
15	17	Teenage Prayer	Gale Storm	Dot	8		
16	19	Are You Satisfied?	Rusty Draper	Mercury	5		
17	-	Why Do Fools Fall In Love	Frankie Lymon & The Teenagers	Gee	15	(1)	F G
18	11	He	Al Hibbler	Decca	20		
19	4	I Hear You Knocking	Gale Storm	Dot	16		F G
20	-	Go On With The Wedding	Patti Page	Mercury	3		

March 1956

This Mnth	Prev Mnth	Title	Artist	Label	Wks 20	(UK Pos)	
1	4	Lisbon Antigua	Nelson Riddle	Capitol	20		F G L
2	13	The Poor People Of Paris	Les Baxter	Capitol	17		G L
3	1	Rock And Roll Waltz	Kay Starr	RCA	16	(1)	G L
4	7	No, Not Much!	Four Lads	Columbia	15		G
5	3	The Great Pretender	Platters	Mercury	17	(5)	G
6	12	I'll Be Home	Pat Boone	Dot	14	(1)	G
7	5	See You Later, Alligator	Bill Haley & His Comets	Decca	13	(7)	
8	17	Why Do Fools Fall In Love	Frankie Lymon & The Teenagers	Gee	15	(1)	F G
9	-	Hot Diggity (Dog Ziggity Boom)	Perry Como	RCA	17	(4)	G
10	2	Memories Are Made Of This	Dean Martin	Capitol	17	(1)	G
11	14	Moritat (... 'The Three Penny Opera')	Dick Hyman	MGM	11	(9)	F L
12	8	Band Of Gold	Don Cherry	Columbia	16	(6)	L
13	-	Blue Suede Shoes	Carl Perkins	Sun	14	(10)	F G L
14	-	Heartbreak Hotel	Elvis Presley	RCA	20	(2)	F G
15	-	A Tear Fell	Teresa Brewer	Coral	15	(2)	
16	-	A Theme From 'The Three Penny Opera' (Moritat)	Richard Hayman & Jan August	Mercury	6		L
17	9	It's Almost Tomorrow	Dream Weavers	Decca	18	(1)	F L
18	10	Dungaree Doll	Eddie Fisher	RCA	12		
19	-	Eddie My Love	Teen Queens	RPM	4		F L
20	-	Why Do Fools Fall In Love	Gale Storm	Dot	3		

US 1956
JAN-MAR

◆ Despite being described as "immoral" and "part of a plot to undermine the morals of our youth", rock'n'roll was achieving a measure of respectability, and starting to receive the media coverage its sales merited.

◆ Filming began on *Rock Around The Clock*, starring Bill Haley, The Platters and Little Richard. Meanwhile Haley's album of that name became the first rock'n'roll LP to chart.

◆ Pat Boone had four different cover records of R&B hits on the US chart – 'At My Front Door' (The Eldorados), 'Tutti Frutti' (Little Richard), 'Gee Whittakers' (Five Keys) and 'I'll Be Home' (The Flamingos).

◆ Elvis Presley and Carl Perkins achieved the supposed impossible when 'Heartbreak Hotel' and 'Blue Suede Shoes' respectively, shot up the pop, C&W and R&B charts.

UK 1956
APR-JUNE

◆ Alan Freed signed with Radio Luxembourg. According to a spokesman for Freed's radio station WINS, "Rock and roll is already big in Britain and Europe, but they don't call it that yet".

◆ In the month that Elvis and Carl Perkins debuted on the British chart and Alan Freed was first heard in Europe, the first Eurovision Song Contest was held: it was won by Lys Assia from Switzerland with a song called 'Refrains'.

◆ The British singles chart was extended to a Top 30.

◆ As Elvis Presley was first seen on the front cover of *NME*, Britain's Lonnie Donegan appeared on the cover of the noted US music magazine *Cash Box*. On returning from his American tour, Donegan left Chris Barber's Jazz band and formed his own skiffle group.

April 1956

This Mnth	Prev Mnth	Title	Artist	Label	Wks 20	(US Pos)	
1	12	Poor People Of Paris	Winifred Atwell	Decca	15		
2	1	It's Almost Tomorrow	Dream Weavers	Brunswick	16	(8)	F L
3	3	Rock And Roll Waltz	Kay Starr	HMV	18	(1)	L
4	5	Only You	Hilltoppers	London American	21	(15)	F
5	6	Memories Are Made Of This	Dave King	Decca	13		F
6	4	Zambesi	Lou Busch	Capitol	15	(75)	F L
7	2	Memories Are Made Of This	Dean Martin	Capitol	14	(1)	
8	8	See You Later Alligator	Bill Haley & His Comets	Brunswick	11	(6)	
9	16	Theme From 'The Three Penny Opera'	Dick Hyman Trio	MGM	9	(10)	F L
10	-	My September Love	David Whitfield	Decca	21		
11	11	The Great Pretender	Jimmy Parkinson	Columbia	10		F
12	-	A Tear Fell	Teresa Brewer	Vogue/Coral	15	(9)	
13	-	Willie Can	Alma Cogan	HMV	7		
14	-	No Other Love	Ronnie Hilton	HMV	13		
15	-	Theme From 'The Threepenny Opera'	Billy Vaughn	London American	5	(37)	L
16	15	Chain Gang	Jimmy Young	Decca	5		
17	18	Zambesi	Eddie Calvert	Columbia	5		
18	-	Theme From The Threepenny Opera	Louis Armstrong	Philips	7		
19	7	Band Of Gold	Don Cherry	Philips	11	(5)	F L
20	-	You Can't Be True To Two	Dave King	Decca	7		

May 1956

This Mnth	Prev Mnth	Title	Artist	Label	Wks 20	(US Pos)	
1	14	No Other Love	Ronnie Hilton	HMV	13		
2	1	Poor People Of Paris	Winifred Atwell	Decca	15		
3	12	A Tear Fell	Teresa Brewer	Vogue/Coral	15	(9)	
4	3	Rock And Roll Waltz	Kay Starr	HMV	18	(1)	L
5	10	My September Love	David Whitfield	Decca	21		
6	2	It's Almost Tomorrow	Dream Weavers	Brunswick	16	(8)	F L
7	4	Only You	Hilltoppers	London American	21	(15)	F
8	-	I'll Be Home	Pat Boone	London American	23	(6)	
9	-	Lost John/Stewball	Lonnie Donegan	Pye Nixa	14	(58)	
10	-	Main Title Theme From The Man With The Golden Arm	Billy May	Capitol	6	(49)	F L
11	18	Theme From The Threepenny Opera	Louis Armstrong	Philips	7		
12	20	You Can't Be True To Two	Dave King	Decca	7		
13	-	Heartbreak Hotel	Elvis Presley	HMV	19	(1)	F
14	-	The Happy Whistler	Don Robertson	Capitol	7	(9)	F L
15	8	See You Later Alligator	Bill Haley & His Comets	Brunswick	11	(6)	
16	5	Memories Are Made Of This	Dave King	Decca	13		F
17	7	Memories Are Made Of This	Dean Martin	Capitol	14	(1)	
18	-	Blue Suede Shoes	Carl Perkins	London American	7	(3)	F L
19	-	Mountain Greenery	Mel Torme	Vogue/Coral	17		F
20	9	Theme From 'The Three Penny Opera'	Dick Hyman Trio	MGM	9	(10)	F L

June 1956

This Mnth	Prev Mnth	Title	Artist	Label	Wks 20	(US Pos)	
1	8	I'll Be Home	Pat Boone	London American	23	(6)	
2	9	Lost John/Stewball	Lonnie Donegan	Pye Nixa	14	(58)	
3	1	No Other Love	Ronnie Hilton	HMV	13		
4	13	Heartbreak Hotel	Elvis Presley	HMV	19	(1)	F
5	3	A Tear Fell	Teresa Brewer	Vogue/Coral	15	(9)	
6	-	Hot Diggity	Perry Como	HMV	12	(2)	
7	-	The Saints Rock 'n Roll	Bill Haley & His Comets	Brunswick	22	(18)	
8	5	My September Love	David Whitfield	Decca	21		
9	-	Blue Suede Shoes	Elvis Presley	HMV	8	(20)	
10	-	Too Young To Go Steady	Nat 'King' Cole	Capitol	10		
11	14	The Happy Whistler	Don Robertson	Capitol	7	(9)	F L
12	-	Moonglow/Theme From 'Picnic'	Morris Stoloff	Brunswick	8	(2)	F L
13	2	Poor People Of Paris	Winifred Atwell	Decca	15		
14	4	Rock And Roll Waltz	Kay Starr	HMV	18	(1)	L
15	18	Blue Suede Shoes	Carl Perkins	London American	7	(3)	F L
16	7	Only You	Hilltoppers	London American	21	(15)	F
17	10	Main Title Theme From The Man With The Golden Arm	Billy May	Capitol	6	(49)	F L
18	-	Songs For Swinging Lovers (L.P.)	Frank Sinatra	Capitol	5		
19	-	Hot Diggity	Michael Holliday	Columbia	4		
20	-	Gal With The Yaller Shoes	Michael Holliday	Columbia	3		

32

April 1956

This Mnth	Prev Mnth	Title	Artist	Label	Wks 20	(UK Pos)	
1	2	The Poor People Of Paris	Les Baxter	Capitol	17		G L
2	14	Heartbreak Hotel	Elvis Presley	RCA	20	(2)	F G
3	9	Hot Diggity (Dog Ziggity Boom)	Perry Como	RCA	17	(4)	G
4	13	Blue Suede Shoes	Carl Perkins	Sun	14	(10)	F G L
5	1	Lisbon Antigua	Nelson Riddle	Capitol	20		F G L
6	8	Why Do Fools Fall In Love	Frankie Lymon & The Teenagers	Gee	15	(1)	F G
7	6	I'll Be Home	Pat Boone	Dot	14	(1)	G
8	4	No, Not Much!	Four Lads	Columbia	15		G
9	-	Rock Island Line	Lonnie Donegan	Imperial	8	(8)	F
10	15	A Tear Fell	Teresa Brewer	Coral	15	(2)	
11	3	Rock And Roll Waltz	Kay Starr	RCA	16	(1)	G L
12	-	(You've Got) The Magic Touch	Platters	Mercury	11		
13	-	Long Tall Sally	Little Richard	Specialty	9	(3)	G
14	-	Moonglow And Theme From 'Picnic'	Morris Stoloff	Decca	18	(7)	F G L
15	5	The Great Pretender	Platters	Mercury	17	(5)	G
16	11	Moritat (A Theme From 'The Three Penny Opera')	Dick Hyman	MGM	11	(9)	F L
17	-	Themes From 'The Man With The Golden Arm'	Richard Maltby	Vik	6		F L
18	-	Ivory Tower	Cathy Carr	Fraternity	14		F L
19	-	Eddie My Love	Fontane Sisters	Dot	3		L
20	-	Main Title From 'The Man With The Golden Arm'	Elmer Bernstein	Decca	6		F L

May 1956

This Mnth	Prev Mnth	Title	Artist	Label	Wks 20	(UK Pos)	
1	2	Heartbreak Hotel	Elvis Presley	RCA	20	(2)	F G
2	3	Hot Diggity (Dog Ziggity Boom)	Perry Como	RCA	17	(4)	G
3	14	Moonglow And Theme From 'Picnic'	Morris Stoloff	Decca	18	(7)	F G L
4	4	Blue Suede Shoes	Carl Perkins	Sun	14	(10)	F G L
5	1	The Poor People Of Paris	Les Baxter	Capitol	17		G L
6	12	(You've Got) The Magic Touch	Platters	Mercury	11		
7	-	Moonglow And Theme From 'Picnic'	George Cates	Coral	13		F L
8	18	Ivory Tower	Cathy Carr	Fraternity	14		F L
9	6	Why Do Fools Fall In Love	Frankie Lymon/The Teenagers	Gee	15	(1)	F G
10	13	Long Tall Sally	Little Richard	Specialty	9	(3)	G
11	-	Standing On The Corner	Four Lads	Columbia	14	(26)	
12	-	The Wayward Wind	Gogi Grant	Era	19	(9)	G L
13	-	I'm In Love Again	Fats Domino	Imperial	15	(12)	G
14	10	A Tear Fell	Teresa Brewer	Coral	15	(2)	
15	9	Rock Island Line	Lonnie Donegan	Imperial	8	(8)	F
16	5	Lisbon Antigua	Nelson Riddle	Capitol	20		F G L
17	-	The Happy Whistler	Don Robertson	Capitol	10	(8)	F L
18	-	Ivory Tower	Charms	Deluxe	7		L
19	-	I Want You To Be My Girl	Frankie Lymon/The Teenagers	Gee	6		
20	7	I'll Be Home	Pat Boone	Dot	14	(1)	G

June 1956

This Mnth	Prev Mnth	Title	Artist	Label	Wks 20	(UK Pos)	
1	12	The Wayward Wind	Gogi Grant	Era	19	(9)	G L
2	3	Moonglow And Theme From 'Picnic'	Morris Stoloff	Decca	18	(7)	F G L
3	1	Heartbreak Hotel	Elvis Presley	RCA	20	(2)	F G
4	11	Standing On The Corner	Four Lads	Columbia	14	(26)	
5	13	I'm In Love Again	Fats Domino	Imperial	15	(12)	G
6	7	Moonglow And Theme From 'Picnic'	George Cates	Coral	13		F L
7	8	Ivory Tower	Cathy Carr	Fraternity	14		F L
8	2	Hot Diggity (Dog Ziggity Boom)	Perry Como	RCA	17	(4)	G
9	-	I Want You, I Need You, I Love You	Elvis Presley	RCA	18	(14)	G
10	17	The Happy Whistler	Don Robertson	Capitol	10	(8)	F L
11	-	I Almost Lost My Mind	Pat Boone	Dot	15	(14)	G
12	-	Transfusion	Nervous Norvus	Dot	8		F L
13	6	(You've Got) The Magic Touch	Platters	Mercury	11		
14	-	On The Street Where You Live	Vic Damone	Columbia	12	(1)	L
15	-	More	Perry Como	RCA	12	(10)	
16	-	Picnic	McGuire Sisters	Coral	7		
17	4	Blue Suede Shoes	Carl Perkins	Sun	14	(10)	F G L
18	10	Long Tall Sally	Little Richard	Specialty	9	(3)	G
19	19	I Want You To Be My Girl	Frankie Lymon/The Teenagers	Gee	6		
20	-	The Church Bells May Ring	Diamonds	Mercury	4		

▲ R&B veterans Fats Domino (above) and Little Richard made their Top 10 debuts as Gene Vincent and Roy Orbison had their first Top 100 entries.

◆ A quarter of America's population watched Elvis on the *Milton Berle Show* performing 'Heartbreak Hotel', which soon passed the million sales mark. For the record, his debut album sold over 150,000 in just 10 days.

◆ CBS radio premiered America's first nationally broadcast rock'n'roll show, *Rock'n'Roll Dance Party*, hosted by Alan Freed.

◆ Columbia Records announced that they would gradually drop 78 rpm production.

UK 1956 JULY-SEPT

◆ Britain's first rock 'n' roll riots were reported, as the film *Rock Around The Clock* went on general release. The film had teenagers jiving in the aisles and, sometimes, slashing cinema seats.

▲ At a time when American artists ruled the UK charts, Frankie Lymon & The Teenagers became the first black American act to top the British hit parade.

◆ The first successful charity record in the rock era was 'All Star Hit Parade', which featured British hit-makers, including David Whitfield and Dickie Valentine, singing other artists current hits. It raised £10,000 for the National Playing Fields Association.

July 1956

This Mnth	Prev Mnth	Title	Artist	Label	Wks 20	(US Pos)	
1	1	I'll Be Home	Pat Boone	London American	23	(6)	
2	4	Heartbreak Hotel	Elvis Presley	HMV	19	(1)	F
3	-	All Star Hit Parade	Various Artists	Decca	8		F L
4	-	Why Do Fools Fall In Love	Frankie Lymon & The Teenagers	Columbia	15	(6)	F
5	-	I'm Walking Backwards For Christmas/Bluebottle Blues	Goons	Decca	8		F
6	6	Hot Diggity	Perry Como	HMV	12	(2)	
7	2	Lost John/Stewball	Lonnie Donegan	Pye Nixa	14	(58)	
8	-	Experiments With Mice	Johnny Dankworth	Parlophone	8	(61)	F
9	-	The Wayward Wind	Gogi Grant	London American	9	(1)	F L
10	7	The Saints Rock 'n Roll	Bill Haley & His Comets	Brunswick	22	(18)	
11	-	Wayward Wind	Tex Ritter	Capitol	11	(28)	F L
12	8	My September Love	David Whitfield	Decca	21		
13	-	Who Are We	Ronnie Hilton	HMV	8		
14	-	Walk Hand In Hand	Tony Martin	HMV	13	(21)	L
15	-	Whatever Will Be Will Be	Doris Day	Philips	20	(3)	
16	12	Moonglow/Theme From 'Picnic'	Morris Stoloff	Brunswick	8	(2)	F L
17	3	No Other Love	Ronnie Hilton	HMV	13		
18	18	Songs For Swinging Lovers (L.P.)	Frank Sinatra	Capitol	5		
19	5	A Tear Fell	Teresa Brewer	Vogue/Coral	15	(9)	
20	10	Too Young To Go Steady	Nat 'King' Cole	Capitol	10		

August 1956

This Mnth	Prev Mnth	Title	Artist	Label	Wks 20	(US Pos)	
1	15	Whatever Will Be Will Be	Doris Day	Philips	20	(3)	
2	4	Why Do Fools Fall In Love	Frankie Lymon/The Teenagers	Columbia	15	(6)	F
3	14	Walk Hand In Hand	Tony Martin	HMV	13	(21)	L
4	-	Sweet Old-Fashioned Girl	Teresa Brewer	Vogue/Coral	13	(12)	L
5	-	Mountain Greenery	Mel Torme	Vogue/Coral	17		F
6	2	Heartbreak Hotel	Elvis Presley	HMV	19	(1)	F
7	1	I'll Be Home	Pat Boone	London American	23	(6)	
8	11	Wayward Wind	Tex Ritter	Capitol	11	(28)	F L
9	10	The Saints Rock 'n Roll	Bill Haley & His Comets	Brunswick	22	(18)	
10	13	Who Are We	Ronnie Hilton	HMV	8		
11	-	Rockin' Through The Rye	Bill Haley & His Comets	Brunswick	19	(78)	
12	3	All Star Hit Parade	Various Artists	Decca	8		F L
13	-	Serenade	Slim Whitman	London American	8		
14	5	I'm Walking Back.../Bluebottle...	Goons	Decca	8		F
15	-	Walk Hand In Hand	Ronnie Carroll	Philips	7		F
16	9	The Wayward Wind	Gogi Grant	London American	9	(1)	F L
17	8	Experiments With Mice	Johnny Dankworth	Parlophone	8	(61)	F
18	6	Hot Diggity	Perry Como	HMV	12	(2)	
19	-	I Almost Lost My Mind	Pat Boone	London American	6	(2)	
20	-	Left Bank	Winifred Atwell	Decca	5		

September 1956

This Mnth	Prev Mnth	Title	Artist	Label	Wks 20	(US Pos)	
1	1	Whatever Will Be Will Be	Doris Day	Philips	20	(3)	
2	-	Lay Down Your Arms	Anne Shelton	Philips	13	(59)	
3	11	Rockin' Through The Rye	Bill Haley & His Comets	Brunswick	19	(78)	
4	2	Why Do Fools Fall In Love	Frankie Lymon/The Teenagers	Columbia	15	(6)	F
5	4	Sweet Old-Fashioned Girl	Teresa Brewer	Vogue/Coral	13	(12)	L
6	3	Walk Hand In Hand	Tony Martin	HMV	13	(21)	L
7	-	The Great Pretender/Only You	Platters	Mercury	10	(2)	F
8	-	Bloodnok's Rock 'n' Roll Call/ Ying Tong Song	Goons	Decca	8		
9	5	Mountain Greenery	Mel Torme	Vogue/Coral	17		F
10	9	The Saints Rock 'n Roll	Bill Haley & His Comets	Brunswick	22	(18)	
11	-	Bring A Little Water Sylvie/ Dead Or Alive	Lonnie Donegan	Pye Nixa	8		
12	-	A Woman In Love	Frankie Laine	Philips	19	(19)	
13	-	Born To Be With You	Chordettes	London American	8	(8)	
14	13	Serenade	Slim Whitman	London American	8		
15	-	Hound Dog	Elvis Presley	HMV	22	(1)	
16	-	I Want You I Need You I Love You	Elvis Presley	HMV	6	(1)	
17	6	Heartbreak Hotel	Elvis Presley	HMV	19	(1)	F
18	19	I Almost Lost My Mind	Pat Boone	London American	6	(2)	
19	-	Rock Around The Clock	Bill Haley & His Comets	Brunswick	11		
20	-	I'm In Love Again	Fats Domino	London American	5	(4)	F

34

July 1956

This Mnth	Prev Mnth	Title	Artist	Label	Wks 20	(UK Pos)	
1	1	The Wayward Wind	Gogi Grant	Era	19	(9)	G L
2	11	I Almost Lost My Mind	Pat Boone	Dot	15	(14)	G
3	9	I Want You, I Need You, I Love You	Elvis Presley	RCA	18	(14)	G
4	15	More	Perry Como	RCA	12	(10)	
5	2	Moonglow And Theme From 'Picnic'	Morris Stoloff	Decca	18	(7)	F G L
6	5	I'm In Love Again	Fats Domino	Imperial	15	(12)	G
7	-	Be-Bop-A-Lula	Gene Vincent & His Blue Caps	Capitol	14	(16)	F
8	-	Born To Be With You	Chordettes	Cadence	12	(8)	
9	14	On The Street Where You Live	Vic Damone	Columbia	12	(1)	L
10	4	Standing On The Corner	Four Lads	Columbia	14	(26)	
11	-	My Prayer	Platters	Mercury	17	(4)	G
12	-	Allegheny Moon	Patti Page	Mercury	16		
13	-	Whatever Will Be Will Be (Que Sera Sera)	Doris Day	Columbia	20	(1)	G
14	-	A Sweet Old Fashioned Girl	Teresa Brewer	Coral	11	(3)	L
15	12	Transfusion	Nervous Norvus	Dot	8		F L
16	6	Moonglow And Theme From 'Picnic'	George Cates	Coral	13		F L
17	3	Heartbreak Hotel	Elvis Presley	RCA	20	(2)	F G
18	7	Ivory Tower	Cathy Carr	Fraternity	14		F L
19	-	It Only Hurts For A Little While	Ames Brothers	RCA	11		
20	-	Stranded In The Jungle	Cadets	Modern	3		F L

August 1956

This Mnth	Prev Mnth	Title	Artist	Label	Wks 20	(UK Pos)	
1	11	My Prayer	Platters	Mercury	17	(4)	G
2	-	Hound Dog/Don't Be Cruel	Elvis Presley	RCA	23	(2)	G
3	13	Whatever Will Be Will Be (Que...)	Doris Day	Columbia	20	(1)	G
4	3	I Want You, I Need You, I Love You	Elvis Presley	RCA	18	(14)	G
5	2	I Almost Lost My Mind	Pat Boone	Dot	15	(14)	G
6	12	Allegheny Moon	Patti Page	Mercury	16		G
7	1	The Wayward Wind	Gogi Grant	Era	19	(9)	G L
8	7	Be-Bop-A-Lula	Gene Vincent & His Blue Caps	Capitol	14	(16)	F
9	-	The Flying Saucer (Parts 1 & 2)	Buchanan & Goodman	Luniverse	8		F G
10	4	More	Perry Como	RCA	12	(10)	
11	-	Canadian Sunset	Hugo Winterhalter & Eddie Heywood	RCA	19		G L
12	8	Born To Be With You	Chordettes	Cadence	12	(8)	
13	14	A Sweet Old Fashioned Girl	Teresa Brewer	Coral	11	(3)	L
14	9	On The Street Where You Live	Vic Damone	Columbia	12	(1)	L
15	5	Moonglow And Theme From 'Picnic'	Morris Stoloff	Decca	18	(7)	F G L
16	-	Theme Song From 'Song For A Summer Night'	Mitch Miller	Columbia	9		
17	6	I'm In Love Again	Fats Domino	Imperial	15	(12)	G
18	-	The Fool	Sanford Clark	Dot	12		F L
19	19	It Only Hurts For A Little While	Ames Brothers	RCA	11		
20	20	Stranded In The Jungle	Cadets	Modern	3		F L

September 1956

This Mnth	Prev Mnth	Title	Artist	Label	Wks 20	(UK Pos)	
1	2	Hound Dog/Don't Be Cruel	Elvis Presley	RCA	23	(2)	G
2	1	My Prayer	Platters	Mercury	17	(4)	G
3	3	Whatever Will Be Will Be (Que...)	Doris Day	Columbia	20	(1)	G
4	11	Canadian Sunset	Hugo Winterhalter & Eddie Heywood	RCA	19		G L
5	-	Tonight You Belong To Me	Patience & Prudence	Liberty	15	(28)	F G
6	9	The Flying Saucer (Parts 1 & 2)	Buchanan & Goodman	Luniverse	8		F G
7	6	Allegheny Moon	Patti Page	Mercury	16		G
8	-	Honky Tonk (Parts 1 & 2)	Bill Doggett	King	18		F G L
9	18	The Fool	Sanford Clark	Dot	12		F L
10	8	Be-Bop-A-Lula	Gene Vincent & His Blue Caps	Capitol	14	(16)	F
11	16	Theme From 'Song For A Summer...'	Mitch Miller	Columbia	9		
12	-	Canadian Sunset	Andy Williams	Cadence	9		F
13	4	I Want You, I Need You, I Love You	Elvis Presley	RCA	18	(14)	G
14	5	I Almost Lost My Mind	Pat Boone	Dot	15	(14)	G
15	-	Just Walking In The Rain	Johnnie Ray	Columbia	21	(1)	G
16	-	Soft Summer Breeze	Eddie Heywood	Mercury	9		F L
17	-	You Don't Know Me	Jerry Vale	Columbia	9		F L
18	7	The Wayward Wind	Gogi Grant	Era	19	(9)	G L
19	10	More	Perry Como	RCA	12	(10)	
20	13	A Sweet Old Fashioned Girl	Teresa Brewer	Coral	11	(3)	L

◆ Rock'n'roll and R&B were becoming separate entities. A multi-racial rock'n'roll show in Maryland starring Carl Perkins, The Teenagers and Chuck Berry attracted nearly 70,000 fans. Meanwhile, an R&B DJ association decided to disassociate R&B from rock'n'roll – since rock's bad publicity was affecting their business.

◆ As Pat Boone and Elvis raided the R&B archives for, 'I Almost Lost My Mind' and 'Hound Dog', R&B stars, The Platters and Fats Domino, revived pop faves, 'My Prayer' and 'Blueberry Hill'.

◆ Harry Belafonte's album **Calypso** topped the LP chart, a position it held for 31 weeks. However, aside from Belafonte's success, the prophesied calypso craze never really got off the ground.

UK 1956
OCT-DEC

▲ In the *NME* poll, Elvis was runner-up to Bill Haley as World's Most Outstanding Vocal Personality, and to Frank Sinatra (above) as World's Outstanding Singer. In the *Billboard* DJ poll he was voted Most Played Male Pop and C&W Artist.

◆ Britain had its first home-grown Top 20 rock'n'roll hit, 'Rock With The Caveman' written and performed by teenager Tommy Steele. Within three months Steele's life story was being filmed.

◆ For several weeks Bill Haley & The Comets had five singles in the UK Top 20.

October 1956

This Mnth	Prev Mnth	Title	Artist	Label	Wks 20	(US Pos)	
1	12	A Woman In Love	Frankie Laine	Philips	19	(19)	
2	2	Lay Down Your Arms	Anne Shelton	Philips	13	(59)	
3	15	Hound Dog	Elvis Presley	HMV	22	(1)	
4	1	Whatever Will Be Will Be	Doris Day	Philips	20	(3)	
5	-	Giddy-Up-A-Ding-Dong	Freddie Bell & The Bellboys	Mercury	8		F L
6	3	Rockin' Through The Rye	Bill Haley & His Comets	Brunswick	19	(78)	
7	7	The Great Pretender/Only You	Platters	Mercury	10	(2)	F
8	8	Bloodnok's Rock 'n' Roll Call/ Ying Tong Song	Goons	Decca	8		
9	11	Bring A Little Water Sylvie/ Dead Or Alive	Lonnie Donegan	Pye Nixa	8		
10	19	Rock Around The Clock	Bill Haley & His Comets	Brunswick	11		
11	-	Just Walkin' In The Rain	Johnnie Ray	Philips	18	(3)	
12	-	When Mexico Gave Up The Rumba	Mitchell Torok	Brunswick	15		F L
13	10	The Saints Rock 'n Roll	Bill Haley & His Comets	Brunswick	22	(18)	
14	-	More	Perry Como	HMV	8	(4)	
15	13	Born To Be With You	Chordettes	London American	8	(8)	
16	-	Razzle Dazzle	Bill Haley & His Comets	Brunswick	4	(15)	
17	-	See You Later Alligator	Bill Haley & His Comets	Brunswick	6	(6)	
18	4	Why Do Fools Fall In Love	Frankie Lymon & The Teenagers	Columbia	15	(6)	F
19	-	More	Jimmy Young	Decca	14		
20	5	Sweet Old-Fashioned Girl	Teresa Brewer	Vogue/Coral	13	(12)	L

November 1956

This Mnth	Prev Mnth	Title	Artist	Label	Wks 20	(US Pos)	
1	11	Just Walkin' In The Rain	Johnnie Ray	Philips	18	(3)	
2	1	A Woman In Love	Frankie Laine	Philips	19	(19)	
3	3	Hound Dog	Elvis Presley	HMV	22	(1)	
4	-	My Prayer	Platters	Mercury	10	(1)	
5	19	More	Jimmy Young	Decca	14		
6	6	Rockin' Through The Rye	Bill Haley & His Comets	Brunswick	19	(78)	
7	10	Rock Around The Clock	Bill Haley & His Comets	Brunswick	11		
8	12	When Mexico Gave Up The Rumba	Mitchell Torok	Brunswick	15		F L
9	-	Green Door	Frankie Vaughan	Philips	15		
10	2	Lay Down Your Arms	Anne Shelton	Philips	13	(59)	
11	-	Rip It Up	Bill Haley & His Comets	Brunswick	14	(25)	
12	-	Make It A Party	Winifred Atwell	Decca	10		
13	4	Whatever Will Be Will Be	Doris Day	Philips	20	(3)	
14	5	Giddy-Up-A-Ding-Dong	Freddie Bell & The Bellboys	Mercury	8		F L
15	-	St. Therese Of The Roses	Malcolm Vaughan	HMV	18		
16	-	The Green Door	Jim Lowe	London American	5	(2)	F L
17	-	Love Me As If There Were No Tomorrow	Nat 'King' Cole	Capitol	7		
18	-	Blue Moon	Elvis Presley	HMV	8	(55)	
19	14	More	Perry Como	HMV	8	(4)	
20	-	Cindy, Oh Cindy	Eddie Fisher	HMV	13	(10)	L

December 1956

This Mnth	Prev Mnth	Title	Artist	Label	Wks 20	(US Pos)	
1	1	Just Walkin' In The Rain	Johnnie Ray	Philips	18	(3)	
2	9	Green Door	Frankie Vaughan	Philips	15		
3	15	St. Therese Of The Roses	Malcolm Vaughan	HMV	18		
4	11	Rip It Up	Bill Haley & His Comets	Brunswick	14	(25)	
5	20	Cindy, Oh Cindy	Eddie Fisher	HMV	13	(10)	L
6	4	My Prayer	Platters	Mercury	10	(1)	
7	-	True Love	Bing Crosby & Grace Kelly	Capitol	23	(5)	
8	2	A Woman In Love	Frankie Laine	Philips	19	(19)	
9	12	Make It A Party	Winifred Atwell	Decca	10		
10	3	Hound Dog	Elvis Presley	HMV	22	(1)	
11	5	More	Jimmy Young	Decca	14		
12	18	Blue Moon	Elvis Presley	HMV	8	(55)	
13	8	When Mexico Gave Up The Rumba	Mitchell Torok	Brunswick	15		F L
14	-	Christmas Island	Dickie Valentine	Decca	3		
15	-	Love Me Tender	Elvis Presley	HMV	9	(1)	
16	-	Two Different Worlds	Ronnie Hilton	HMV	7		
17	-	A House With Love In It	Vera Lynn	Decca	6		
18	-	Cindy Oh Cindy	Tony Brent	Columbia	3		
19	-	Moonlight Gambler	Frankie Laine	Philips	9	(5)	
20	-	Singing The Blues	Guy Mitchell	Philips	20	(1)	

October 1956

This Mnth	Prev Mnth	Title	Artist	Label	Wks 20	(UK Pos)	
1	1	Hound Dog/Don't Be Cruel	Elvis Presley	RCA	23	(2)	G
2	8	Honky Tonk (Parts 1 & 2)	Bill Doggett	King	18		F G L
3	4	Canadian Sunset	Hugo Winterhalter & Eddie Heywood	RCA	19		G L
4	15	Just Walking In The Rain	Johnnie Ray	Columbia	21	(1)	G
5	-	The Green Door	Jim Lowe	Dot	21	(8)	F G
6	5	Tonight You Belong To Me	Patience & Prudence	Liberty	15	(28)	F G
7	3	Whatever Will Be Will Be (Que Sera Sera)	Doris Day	Columbia	20	(1)	G
8	2	My Prayer	Platters	Mercury	17	(4)	G
9	-	Friendly Persuasion/Chains Of Love	Pat Boone	Dot	13	(3)	G
10	-	Love Me Tender	Elvis Presley	RCA	18	(11)	G
11	12	Canadian Sunset	Andy Williams	Cadence	9		F
12	9	The Fool	Sanford Clark	Dot	12		F L
13	-	True Love	Bing Crosby & Grace Kelly	Capitol	19	(4)	G
14	-	Blueberry Hill	Fats Domino	Imperial	20	(6)	G
15	16	Soft Summer Breeze	Eddie Heywood	Mercury	9		F L
16	-	You'll Never Ever Know/It Isn't Right	Platters	Mercury	8	(23)	
17	7	Allegheny Moon	Patti Page	Mercury	16		G
18	-	Cindy, Oh Cindy	Vince Martin With The Tarriers	Glory	12	(26)	F L
19	-	True Love	Jane Powell	Verve	7		F L
20	17	You Don't Know Me	Jerry Vale	Columbia	9		F L

November 1956

This Mnth	Prev Mnth	Title	Artist	Label	Wks 20	(UK Pos)	
1	10	Love Me Tender	Elvis Presley	RCA	18	(11)	G
2	5	The Green Door	Jim Lowe	Dot	21	(8)	F G
3	1	Hound Dog/Don't Be Cruel	Elvis Presley	RCA	23	(2)	G
4	4	Just Walking In The Rain	Johnnie Ray	Columbia	21	(1)	G
5	-	Singing The Blues	Guy Mitchell	Columbia	19	(1)	G
6	14	Blueberry Hill	Fats Domino	Imperial	20	(6)	G
7	2	Honky Tonk (Parts 1 & 2)	Bill Doggett	King	18		F G L
8	13	True Love	Bing Crosby & Grace Kelly	Capitol	19	(4)	G
9	9	Friendly Persuasion/Chains Of Love	Pat Boone	Dot	13	(3)	G
10	3	Canadian Sunset	Hugo Winterhalter & Eddie Heywood	RCA	19		G L
11	6	Tonight You Belong To Me	Patience & Prudence	Liberty	15	(28)	F G
12	18	Cindy, Oh Cindy	Vince Martin With The Tarriers	Glory	12	(26)	F L
13	-	Hey! Jealous Lover	Frank Sinatra	Capitol	11		
14	16	You'll Never Ever Know/It Isn't Right	Platters	Mercury	8	(23)	
15	-	Cindy, Oh Cindy	Eddie Fisher	RCA	11	(5)	L
16	7	Whatever Will Be Will Be (Que...)	Doris Day	Columbia	20	(1)	G
17	19	True Love	Jane Powell	Verve	7		F L
18	-	I Walk The Line	Johnny Cash	Sun	3		F
19	-	A Rose And A Baby Ruth	George Hamilton IV	ABC Paramount	13		F G
20	-	Garden Of Eden	Joe Valino	Vik	7	(23)	F L

December 1956

This Mnth	Prev Mnth	Title	Artist	Label	Wks 20	(UK Pos)	
1	5	Singing The Blues	Guy Mitchell	Columbia	19	(1)	G
2	1	Love Me Tender	Elvis Presley	RCA	18	(11)	G
3	2	The Green Door	Jim Lowe	Dot	21	(8)	F G
4	6	Blueberry Hill	Fats Domino	Imperial	20	(6)	G
5	4	Just Walking In The Rain	Johnnie Ray	Columbia	21	(1)	G
6	8	True Love	Bing Crosby & Grace Kelly	Capitol	19	(4)	G
7	19	A Rose And A Baby Ruth	George Hamilton IV	ABC Paramount	13		F G
8	13	Hey! Jealous Lover	Frank Sinatra	Capitol	11		
9	3	Hound Dog/Don't Be Cruel	Elvis Presley	RCA	23	(2)	G
10	-	Love Me	Elvis Presley	RCA	11		
11	7	Honky Tonk (Parts 1 & 2)	Bill Doggett	King	18		F G L
12	15	Cindy, Oh Cindy	Eddie Fisher	RCA	11	(5)	L
13	-	Rock-A-Bye Your Baby With A Dixie Melody	Jerry Lewis	Decca	12	(12)	F L
14	9	Friendly Persuasion/Chains Of Love	Pat Boone	Dot	13	(3)	G
15	12	Cindy, Oh Cindy	Vince Martin With The Tarriers	Glory	12	(26)	F L
16	-	Since I Met You Baby	Ivory Joe Hunter	Atlantic	9		F L
17	20	Garden Of Eden	Joe Valino	Vik	7	(23)	F L
18	-	Gonna Get Along Without Ya Now	Patience & Prudence	Liberty	4	(22)	L
19	-	The Banana Boat Song	Tarriers	Glory	12	(15)	L
20	-	Mama From The Train	Patti Page	Mercury	5		

◆ Elvis Presley's 'Hound Dog' sold over three million while his recordbreaking 'Love Me Tender' amassed a million advance orders entering the best sellers at No. 2 (behind 'Hound Dog'). In 1956, Elvis put 17 different sides into the chart and held the top spot for six months. Presley products earned $20 million and he closed the year with 10 separate records on the US Top 100.

◆ RCA Records advised record dealers to start selling pre-recorded tapes, which they assured them would be a lucrative sideline.

◆ In October four British acts were simultaneously situated in the Top 100; They were Anne Shelton and the orchestras of Ted Heath, Bob Sharples and Cyril Stapleton.

◆ As the Presley phenomenon spread, a line of teenage lipsticks were launched, including shades such as Heartbreak Pink and Hound Dog Orange!

UK 1957 JAN-MAR

◆ The Philips label ended a record run of five successive UK chart toppers (covering a 22 week period). The artists involved were Doris Day, Anne Shelton, Frankie Laine, Johnnie Ray and Guy Mitchell.

◆ Britain launched its first pop TV shows: *Cool For Cats*, where professional dancers performed choreographed routines to current records, and the very influential *6-5 Special* which featured live artists.

◆ Bill Haley & The Comets received an amazing media welcome to Britain, where *Rock Around The Clock* had became the first million seller. However, UK interest in them quickly faded and they left with minimal press coverage, and no future recordings made the Top 20.

January 1957

This Mnth	Prev Mnth	Title	Artist	Label	Wks 20	(US Pos)	
1	20	Singing The Blues	Guy Mitchell	Philips	20	(1)	
2	-	Singing The Blues	Tommy Steele	Decca	10		
3	3	St. Therese Of The Roses	Malcolm Vaughan	HMV	18		
4	1	Just Walkin' In The Rain	Johnnie Ray	Philips	18	(3)	
5	2	Green Door	Frankie Vaughan	Philips	15		
6	7	True Love	Bing Crosby & Grace Kelly	Capitol	23	(5)	
7	5	Cindy, Oh Cindy	Eddie Fisher	HMV	13	(10)	L
8	-	Friendly Persuasion	Pat Boone	London American	17	(9)	
9	-	Garden Of Eden	Frankie Vaughan	Philips	12		
10	10	Hound Dog	Elvis Presley	HMV	22	(1)	
11	4	Rip It Up	Bill Haley & His Comets	Brunswick	14	(25)	
12	15	Love Me Tender	Elvis Presley	HMV	9	(1)	
13	-	Blueberry Hill	Fats Domino	London American	10	(3)	
14	19	Moonlight Gambler	Frankie Laine	Philips	9	(5)	
15	8	A Woman In Love	Frankie Laine	Philips	19	(19)	
16	-	Don't You Rock Me Daddy-O	Lonnie Donegan	Pye Nixa	16		
17	-	Garden Of Eden	Gary Miller	Pye Nixa	2		
18	13	When Mexico Gave Up The Rumba	Mitchell Torok	Brunswick	15		F L
19	11	More	Jimmy Young	Decca	14		
20	9	Make It A Party	Winifred Atwell	Decca	10		

February 1957

This Mnth	Prev Mnth	Title	Artist	Label	Wks 20	(US Pos)	
1	9	Garden Of Eden	Frankie Vaughan	Philips	12		
2	1	Singing The Blues	Guy Mitchell	Philips	20	(1)	
3	8	Friendly Persuasion	Pat Boone	London American	17	(9)	
4	6	True Love	Bing Crosby & Grace Kelly	Capitol	23	(5)	
5	16	Don't You Rock Me Daddy-O	Lonnie Donegan	Pye Nixa	16		
6	3	St. Therese Of The Roses	Malcolm Vaughan	HMV	18		
7	13	Blueberry Hill	Fats Domino	London American	10	(3)	
8	-	Young Love	Tab Hunter	London American	17	(1)	F
9	2	Singing The Blues	Tommy Steele	Decca	10		
10	-	Don't Forbid Me	Pat Boone	London American	14	(3)	
11	7	Cindy, Oh Cindy	Eddie Fisher	HMV	13	(10)	L
12	-	Don't Knock The Rock	Bill Haley & His Comets	Brunswick	7	(45)	
13	-	Don't You Rock Me Daddy-O	Vipers Skiffle Group	Parlophone	6		F
14	10	Hound Dog	Elvis Presley	HMV	22	(1)	
15	5	Green Door	Frankie Vaughan	Philips	15		
16	-	Rock-A-Bye Your Baby (With A Dixie Melody)	Jerry Lewis	Brunswick	5	(10)	F L
17	4	Just Walkin' In The Rain	Johnnie Ray	Philips	18	(3)	
18	11	Rip It Up	Bill Haley & His Comets	Brunswick	14	(25)	
19	-	Adoration Waltz	David Whitfield	Decca	8		
20	-	You Don't Owe Me A Thing	Johnnie Ray	Philips	10	(10)	

March 1957

This Mnth	Prev Mnth	Title	Artist	Label	Wks 20	(US Pos)	
1	8	Young Love	Tab Hunter	London American	17	(1)	F
2	10	Don't Forbid Me	Pat Boone	London American	14	(3)	
3	-	Knee Deep In The Blues	Guy Mitchell	Philips	11	(21)	
4	5	Don't You Rock Me Daddy-O	Lonnie Donegan	Pye Nixa	16		
5	2	Singing The Blues	Guy Mitchell	Philips	20	(1)	
6	-	Long Tall Sally	Little Richard	London American	14	(6)	F
7	1	Garden Of Eden	Frankie Vaughan	Philips	12		
8	4	True Love	Bing Crosby & Grace Kelly	Capitol	23	(5)	
9	-	Banana Boat Song	Harry Belafonte	HMV	14	(5)	F
10	3	Friendly Persuasion	Pat Boone	London American	17	(9)	
11	-	Banana Boat Song	Shirley Bassey	Philips	6		.F
12	19	Adoration Waltz	David Whitfield	Decca	8		
13	-	Young Love	Sonny James	Capitol	7	(2)	F L
14	12	Don't Knock The Rock	Bill Haley & His Comets	Brunswick	7	(45)	
15	7	Blueberry Hill	Fats Domino	London American	10	(3)	
16	-	The Girl Can't Help It	Little Richard	London American	10	(49)	
17	-	Wisdom Of A Fool	Norman Wisdom	Columbia	4		L
18	6	St. Therese Of The Roses	Malcolm Vaughan	HMV	18		
19	20	You Don't Owe Me A Thing	Johnnie Ray	Philips	10	(10)	
20	16	Rock-A-Bye Your Baby (With A Dixie Melody)	Jerry Lewis	Brunswick	5	(10)	F L

38

US 1957 JAN-MAR

January 1957

This Mnth	Prev Mnth	Title	Artist	Label	Wks 20	(UK Pos)	
1	1	Singing The Blues	Guy Mitchell	Columbia	19	(1)	G
2	3	The Green Door	Jim Lowe	Dot	21	(8)	F G
3	4	Blueberry Hill	Fats Domino	Imperial	20	(6)	G
4	2	Love Me Tender	Elvis Presley	RCA	18	(11)	G
5	19	The Banana Boat Song	Tarriers	Glory	12	(15)	L
6	-	Don't Forbid Me	Pat Boone	Dot	16	(2)	G
7	5	Just Walking In The Rain	Johnnie Ray	Columbia	21	(1)	G
8	6	True Love	Bing Crosby & Grace Kelly	Capitol	19	(4)	G
9	-	Moonlight Gambler	Frankie Laine	Columbia	12	(13)	G L
10	10	Love Me	Elvis Presley	RCA	11		
11	-	Young Love	Sonny James	Capitol	13	(11)	F G L
12	7	A Rose And A Baby Ruth	George Hamilton IV	ABC Paramount	13		F G
13	-	Young Love	Tab Hunter	Dot	13	(1)	F G
14	13	Rock-A-Bye Your Baby With A Dixie Melody	Jerry Lewis	Decca	12	(12)	F L
15	-	Blue Monday	Fats Domino	Imperial	10	(23)	G
16	-	Banana Boat (Day-O)	Harry Belafonte	RCA	12	(2)	G
17	12	Cindy, Oh Cindy	Eddie Fisher	RCA	11	(5)	L
18	8	Hey! Jealous Lover	Frank Sinatra	Capitol	11		
19	16	Since I Met You Baby	Ivory Joe Hunter	Atlantic	9		F L
20	-	Jamaica Farewell	Harry Belafonte	RCA	8		

February 1957

This Mnth	Prev Mnth	Title	Artist	Label	Wks 20	(UK Pos)	
1	-	Too Much	Elvis Presley	RCA	10	(6)	G
2	13	Young Love	Tab Hunter	Dot	13	(1)	F G
3	11	Young Love	Sonny James	Capitol	13	(11)	F G L
4	6	Don't Forbid Me	Pat Boone	Dot	16	(2)	G
5	1	Singing The Blues	Guy Mitchell	Columbia	19	(1)	G
6	16	Banana Boat (Day-O)	Harry Belafonte	RCA	12	(2)	G
7	5	The Banana Boat Song	Tarriers	Glory	12	(15)	L
8	9	Moonlight Gambler	Frankie Laine	Columbia	12	(13)	G L
9	15	Blue Monday	Fats Domino	Imperial	10	(23)	G
10	3	Blueberry Hill	Fats Domino	Imperial	20	(6)	G
11	-	You Don't Owe Me A Thing	Johnnie Ray	Columbia	4	(12)	L
12	-	Love Is Strange	Mickey & Sylvia	Groove	11		F L
13	2	The Green Door	Jim Lowe	Dot	21	(8)	F G
14	-	Marianne	Terry Gilkyson & The Easy Riders	Columbia	11		F G L
15	4	Love Me Tender	Elvis Presley	RCA	18	(11)	G
16	14	Rock-A-Bye Your Baby With A Dixie Melody	Jerry Lewis	Decca	12	(12)	F L
17	10	Love Me	Elvis Presley	RCA	11		
18	-	Wringle Wrangle	Fess Parker	Disneyland	3		L
19	12	A Rose And A Baby Ruth	George Hamilton IV	ABC Paramount	13		F G
20	20	Jamaica Farewell	Harry Belafonte	RCA	8		

March 1957

This Mnth	Prev Mnth	Title	Artist	Label	Wks 20	(UK Pos)	
1	2	Young Love	Tab Hunter	Dot	13	(1)	F G
2	-	Teen-Age Crush	Tommy Sands	Capitol	11		F G
3	4	Don't Forbid Me	Pat Boone	Dot	16	(2)	G
4	-	Butterfly	Charlie Gracie	Cameo	14	(12)	F G
5	1	Too Much	Elvis Presley	RCA	10	(6)	G
6	14	Marianne	Terry Gilkyson & The Easy Riders	Columbia	11		F G L
7	6	Banana Boat (Day-O)	Harry Belafonte	RCA	12	(2)	G
8	3	Young Love	Sonny James	Capitol	13	(11)	F G L
9	-	Round And Round	Perry Como	RCA	15		G
10	-	Party Doll	Buddy Knox	Roulette	14	(29)	F G
11	-	Butterfly	Andy Williams	Cadence	12	(1)	G
12	-	I'm Walkin'	Fats Domino	Imperial	10	(19)	G
13	-	Marianne	Hilltoppers	Dot	8	(20)	L
14	12	Love Is Strange	Mickey & Sylvia	Groove	11		F L
15	7	The Banana Boat Song	Tarriers	Glory	12	(15)	L
16	8	Moonlight Gambler	Frankie Laine	Columbia	12	(13)	G L
17	9	Blue Monday	Fats Domino	Imperial	10	(23)	G
18	-	Little Darlin'	Diamonds	Mercury	16	(3)	G
19	-	Come Go With Me	Dell-Vikings	Dot	17		F G
20	-	Why Baby Why	Pat Boone	Dot	10	(17)	G

▲ Parentally approved rock'n'roll star Pat Boone performed at President Eisenhower's Inaugural Ball and signed a $1 million TV deal.

◆ An Alan Freed show starring The Platters, The Teenagers and rockabilly star Buddy Knox, broke records at New York's Paramount Theater.

◆ Fats Domino scored his third successive R&B No 1 with 'I'm Walkin'' (which followed 'Blueberry Hill' and 'Blue Monday') – holding the top slot for 23 out of 24 weeks!

◆ RCA Records announced they would cease the pressing of 78 rpm records at the end of 1957.

UK 1957
APR-JUNE

▲ In April, Little Richard (above) had three singles in the UK Top 20 and 14-year-old Frankie Lymon & The Teenagers had two. The youthful group, who successfully toured Britain and topped the bill at the London Palladium, were not to chart again.

◆ Skiffle, now reaching its peak of popularity, had its first chart topper with Lonnie Donegan's adaptation of the traditional American folk song 'Cumberland Gap'.

◆ Britain's Chas McDevitt Skiffle Group reached the American Top 40 with 'Freight Train'. A cover version by Rusty Draper overtook them and made the Top 20.

April 1957

This Mnth	Prev Mnth	Title	Artist	Label	Wks 20	(US Pos)	
1	1	Young Love	Tab Hunter	London American	17	(1)	F
2	-	Cumberland Gap	Lonnie Donegan	Pye Nixa	11		
3	9	Banana Boat Song	Harry Belafonte	HMV	14	(5)	F
4	2	Don't Forbid Me	Pat Boone	London American	14	(3)	
5	6	Long Tall Sally	Little Richard	London American	14	(6)	F
6	3	Knee Deep In The Blues	Guy Mitchell	Philips	11	(21)	
7	-	Look Homeward Angel	Johnnie Ray	Philips	10	(36)	
8	4	Don't You Rock Me Daddy-O	Lonnie Donegan	Pye Nixa	16		
9	8	True Love	Bing Crosby & Grace Kelly	Capitol	23	(5)	
10	16	The Girl Can't Help It	Little Richard	London American	10	(49)	
11	-	Baby Baby	Frankie Lymon & The Teenagers	Columbia	8		L
12	-	Ninety-Nine Ways	Tab Hunter	London American	10	(12)	L
13	-	Heart	Max Bygraves	Decca	7		
14	5	Singing The Blues	Guy Mitchell	Philips	20	(1)	
15	-	Cumberland Gap	Vipers Skiffle Group	Parlophone	4		L
16	-	I'm Not A Juvenile Delinquent	Frankie Lymon & The Teenagers	Columbia	4		
17	19	You Don't Owe Me A Thing	Johnnie Ray	Philips	10	(10)	
18	-	I'll Take You Home Again Kathleen	Slim Whitman	London American	11	(93)	
19	-	When I Fall In Love	Nat 'King' Cole	Capitol	19		
20	-	Freight Train	Chas McDevitt Skiffle Group	Oriole	14	(40)	F L

May 1957

This Mnth	Prev Mnth	Title	Artist	Label	Wks 20	(US Pos)	
1	-	Rock-A-Billy	Guy Mitchell	Philips	11	(10)	
2	-	Butterfly	Andy Williams	London American	12	(4)	F
3	2	Cumberland Gap	Lonnie Donegan	Pye Nixa	11		
4	19	When I Fall In Love	Nat 'King' Cole	Capitol	19		
5	12	Ninety-Nine Ways	Tab Hunter	London American	10	(12)	L
6	11	Baby Baby	Frankie Lymon & The Teenagers	Columbia	8		L
7	-	Yes Tonight Josephine	Johnnie Ray	Philips	15		
8	3	Banana Boat Song	Harry Belafonte	HMV	14	(5)	F
9	20	Freight Train	Chas McDevitt Skiffle Group	Oriole	14	(40)	F L
10	18	I'll Take You Home Again Kathleen	Slim Whitman	London American	11	(93)	
11	-	Too Much	Elvis Presley	HMV	8	(1)	
12	1	Young Love	Tab Hunter	London American	17	(1)	F
13	7	Look Homeward Angel	Johnnie Ray	Philips	10	(36)	
14	5	Long Tall Sally	Little Richard	London American	14	(6)	F
15	-	Chapel Of The Roses	Malcolm Vaughan	HMV	7		
16	10	The Girl Can't Help It	Little Richard	London American	10	(49)	
17	-	Mr. Wonderful	Peggy Lee	Brunswick	13	(25)	F
18	-	Butterfly	Charlie Gracie	Parlophone	3	(3)	F
19	-	Butterfingers	Tommy Steele	Decca	15		
20	4	Don't Forbid Me	Pat Boone	London American	14	(3)	

June 1957

This Mnth	Prev Mnth	Title	Artist	Label	Wks 20	(US Pos)	
1	7	Yes Tonight Josephine	Johnnie Ray	Philips	15		
2	4	When I Fall In Love	Nat 'King' Cole	Capitol	19		
3	2	Butterfly	Andy Williams	London American	12	(4)	F
4	-	Gamblin' Man/Putting On The Style	Lonnie Donegan	Pye Nixa	18		
5	-	Around The World	Ronnie Hilton	HMV	15		
6	-	Around The World	Bing Crosby	Brunswick	14	(25)	
7	1	Rock-A-Billy	Guy Mitchell	Philips	11	(10)	
8	-	Little Darlin'	Diamonds	Mercury	15	(2)	F L
9	9	Freight Train	Chas McDevitt Skiffle Group	Oriole	14	(40)	F L
10	17	Mr. Wonderful	Peggy Lee	Brunswick	13	(25)	F
11	-	Around The World	Gracie Fields	Columbia	7		F L
12	-	A White Sport Coat	King Brothers	Parlophone	11		F
13	-	We Will Make Love	Russ Hamilton	Oriole	16		F
14	11	Too Much	Elvis Presley	HMV	8	(1)	
15	10	I'll Take You Home Again Kathleen	Slim Whitman	London American	11	(93)	
16	15	Chapel Of The Roses	Malcolm Vaughan	HMV	7		
17	-	All Shook Up	Elvis Presley	HMV	18	(1)	
18	-	Fabulous	Charlie Gracie	Parlophone	13	(16)	
19	-	Island In The Sun	Harry Belafonte	RCA	22	(30)	
20	3	Cumberland Gap	Lonnie Donegan	Pye Nixa	11		

April 1957

This Mnth	Prev Mnth	Title	Artist	Label	Wks 20	(UK Pos)	
1	18	Little Darlin'	Diamonds	Mercury	16	(3)	G
2	9	Round And Round	Perry Como	RCA	15		G
3	-	All Shook Up	Elvis Presley	RCA	17	(1)	G
4	10	Party Doll	Buddy Knox	Roulette	14	(29)	F G
5	19	Come Go With Me	Dell-Vikings	Dot	17		F G
6	12	I'm Walkin'	Fats Domino	Imperial	10	(19)	G
7	-	Gone	Ferlin Husky	Capitol	14		F G
8	11	Butterfly	Andy Williams	Cadence	12	(1)	G
9	20	Why Baby Why	Pat Boone	Dot	10	(17)	G
10	4	Butterfly	Charlie Gracie	Cameo	14	(12)	F G
11	2	Teen-Age Crush	Tommy Sands	Capitol	11		F G
12	-	Mama Look At Bubu	Harry Belafonte	RCA	7		L
13	-	Party Doll	Steve Lawrence	Coral	8		F
14	6	Marianne	Terry Gilkyson & The Easy Riders	Columbia	11		F G L
15	-	School Day	Chuck Berry	Chess	11	(24)	G
16	1	Young Love	Tab Hunter	Dot	13	(1)	F G
17	-	I'm Stickin' With You	Jimmy Bowen	Roulette	9		F L
18	-	I'm Sorry/He's Mine	Platters	Mercury	6	(18)	
19	-	Ninety-Nine Ways	Tab Hunter	Dot	4	(5)	L
20	-	So Rare	Jimmy Dorsey	Fraternity	21		G L

May 1957

This Mnth	Prev Mnth	Title	Artist	Label	Wks 20	(UK Pos)	
1	3	All Shook Up	Elvis Presley	RCA	17	(1)	G
2	1	Little Darlin'	Diamonds	Mercury	16	(3)	G
3	15	School Day	Chuck Berry	Chess	11	(24)	G
4	2	Round And Round	Perry Como	RCA	15		G
5	7	Gone	Ferlin Husky	Capitol	14		F G
6	5	Come Go With Me	Dell-Vikings	Dot	17		F G
7	4	Party Doll	Buddy Knox	Roulette	14	(29)	F G
8	-	A White Sport Coat (And A Pink Carnation)	Marty Robbins	Columbia	13		F G
9	20	So Rare	Jimmy Dorsey	Fraternity	21		G L
10	-	Love Letters In The Sand	Pat Boone	Dot	20	(2)	G
11	-	A Teenagers Romance/I'm Walkin'	Ricky Nelson	Verve	13		F G
12	9	Why Baby Why	Pat Boone	Dot	10	(17)	G
13	-	Dark Moon	Bonnie Guitar	Dot	7		F L
14	-	Rock-A-Billy	Guy Mitchell	Columbia	8	(1)	
15	12	Mama Look At Bubu	Harry Belafonte	RCA	7		L
16	-	Dark Moon	Gale Storm	Dot	15		L
17	6	I'm Walkin'	Fats Domino	Imperial	10	(19)	G
18	10	Butterfly	Charlie Gracie	Cameo	14	(12)	F G
19	8	Butterfly	Andy Williams	Cadence	12	(1)	G
20	18	I'm Sorry/He's Mine	Platters	Mercury	6	(18)	

June 1957

This Mnth	Prev Mnth	Title	Artist	Label	Wks 20	(UK Pos)	
1	10	Love Letters In The Sand	Pat Boone	Dot	20	(2)	G
2	11	A Teenagers Romance/I'm Walkin'	Ricky Nelson	Verve	13		F G
3	8	A White Sport Coat (And A Pink Carnation)	Marty Robbins	Columbia	13		F G
4	1	All Shook Up	Elvis Presley	RCA	17	(1)	G
5	9	So Rare	Jimmy Dorsey	Fraternity	21		G L
6	-	Bye Bye Love	Everly Brothers	Cadence	19	(6)	F G
7	3	School Day	Chuck Berry	Chess	11	(24)	G
8	16	Dark Moon	Gale Storm	Dot	15		L
9	2	Little Darlin'	Diamonds	Mercury	16	(3)	G
10	-	Searchin'/Young Blood	Coasters	Atco	19	(30)	F G
11	-	Start Movin' (In My Direction)	Sal Mineo	Epic	7	(16)	F L
12	5	Gone	Ferlin Husky	Capitol	14		F G
13	6	Come Go With Me	Dell-Vikings	Dot	17		F G
14	13	Dark Moon	Bonnie Guitar	Dot	7		F L
15	-	Four Walls	Jim Reeves	RCA	8		F
16	-	I Like Your Kind Of Love	Andy Williams	Cadence	6	(16)	
17	4	Round And Round	Perry Como	RCA	15		G
18	-	It's Not For Me To Say	Johnny Mathis	Columbia	15		F G
19	-	Old Cape Cod	Patti Page	Mercury	9		
20	-	Valley Of Tears/It's You I Love	Fats Domino	Imperial	6		

US 1957 APR-JUNE

◆ With the drop from popularity of Bill Haley & The Comets, the media on both sides of the Atlantic prophesied the speedy demise of rock'n'roll.

◆ *The Alan Freed Show* premiered on US TV. His first guests included The Dell-Vikings and Guy Mitchell, who, like label-mate Johnnie Ray, scored his last British No. 1 hit this quarter.

◆ Richard Berry & The Pharaohs unsuccessfully released Berry's composition 'Louie Louie' – which went on to become one of the most recorded songs in rock history.

◆ After his original versions of a string of hits failed to crossover, C&W star Marty Robbins graduated to the top of the pop chart with his composition, 'A White Sport Coat (And A Pink Carnation)'.

UK 1957 JULY-SEPT

◆ Elvis Presley had his first British No. 1 with 'All Shook Up'. He also headed the US singles chart with 'Teddy Bear' and the American album listings with 'Lovin' You'.

◆ John Lennon and Paul McCartney met for the first time at a Church Garden Fete as fellow Merseyside singer/songwriter Russ Hamilton earned a pot of gold for his double sided transatlantic smash, 'We Will Make Love'/'Rainbow'.

▲ Fifteen-year-old Paul Anka topped the transatlantic chart with his composition 'Diana' (written about his childhood baby-sitter), which went on to sell over a million in Britain.

July 1957

This Mnth	Prev Mnth	Title	Artist	Label	Wks 20	(US Pos)	
1	17	All Shook Up	Elvis Presley	HMV	18	(1)	
2	4	Gamblin' Man/Putting On The Style	Lonnie Donegan	Pye Nixa	18		
3	8	Little Darlin'	Diamonds	Mercury	15	(2)	F L
4	13	We Will Make Love	Russ Hamilton	Oriole	16		F
5	5	Around The World	Ronnie Hilton	HMV	15		
6	1	Yes Tonight Josephine	Johnnie Ray	Philips	15		
7	12	A White Sport Coat	King Brothers	Parlophone	11		F
8	2	When I Fall In Love	Nat 'King' Cole	Capitol	19		
9	6	Around The World	Bing Crosby	Brunswick	14	(25)	
10	-	Butterfingers	Tommy Steele	Decca	15		
11	10	Mr. Wonderful	Peggy Lee	Brunswick	13	(25)	F
12	-	Teddy Bear	Elvis Presley	HMV	18	(1)	
13	-	Love Letters In The Sand	Pat Boone	London American	21	(1)	
14	18	Fabulous	Charlie Gracie	Parlophone	13	(16)	
15	9	Freight Train	Chas McDevitt Skiffle Group	Oriole	14	(40)	F L
16	-	Lucille	Little Richard	London American	7	(21)	
17	19	Island In The Sun	Harry Belafonte	RCA	22	(30)	
18	-	Bye Bye Love	Everly Brothers	London American	13	(2)	F
19	3	Butterfly	Andy Williams	London American	12	(4)	F
20	-	I Like Your Kind Of Love	Andy Williams	London American	2	(10)	

August 1957

This Mnth	Prev Mnth	Title	Artist	Label	Wks 20	(US Pos)	
1	13	Love Letters In The Sand	Pat Boone	London American	21	(1)	
2	1	All Shook Up	Elvis Presley	HMV	18	(1)	
3	12	Teddy Bear	Elvis Presley	HMV	18	(1)	
4	17	Island In The Sun	Harry Belafonte	RCA	22	(30)	
5	2	Gamblin' Man/Putting On The Style	Lonnie Donegan	Pye Nixa	18		
6	4	We Will Make Love	Russ Hamilton	Oriole	16		F
7	3	Little Darlin'	Diamonds	Mercury	15	(2)	F L
8	18	Bye Bye Love	Everly Brothers	London American	13	(2)	F
9	-	Last Train To San Fernando	Johnny Duncan & The Blue Grass Boys	Columbia	16		F L
10	-	Diana	Paul Anka	Columbia	23	(1)	F G
11	5	Around The World	Ronnie Hilton	HMV	15		
12	-	With All My Heart	Petula Clark	Pye Nixa	16		
13	10	Butterfingers	Tommy Steele	Decca	15		
14	9	Around The World	Bing Crosby	Brunswick	14	(25)	
15	16	Lucille	Little Richard	London American	7	(21)	
16	14	Fabulous	Charlie Gracie	Parlophone	13	(16)	
17	6	Yes Tonight Josephine	Johnnie Ray	Philips	15		
18	8	When I Fall In Love	Nat 'King' Cole	Capitol	19		
19	7	A White Sport Coat	King Brothers	Parlophone	11		F
20	-	Start Movin'	Sal Mineo	Philips	6	(9)	F L

September 1957

This Mnth	Prev Mnth	Title	Artist	Label	Wks 20	(US Pos)	
1	10	Diana	Paul Anka	Columbia	23	(1)	F G
2	1	Love Letters In The Sand	Pat Boone	London American	21	(1)	
3	9	Last Train To San Fernando	Johnny Duncan & The Blue Grass Boys	Columbia	16		F L
4	4	Island In The Sun	Harry Belafonte	RCA	22	(30)	
5	12	With All My Heart	Petula Clark	Pye Nixa	16		
6	-	Water Water/Handful Of Songs	Tommy Steele	Decca	13		
7	2	All Shook Up	Elvis Presley	HMV	18	(1)	
8	-	Wanderin' Eyes/I Love You So Much It Hurts	Charlie Gracie	London American	12	(71)	L
9	-	Paralysed	Elvis Presley	HMV	9	(59)	
10	8	Bye Bye Love	Everly Brothers	London American	13	(2)	F
11	-	Tammy	Debbie Reynolds	Vogue Coral	15	(1)	F L
12	3	Teddy Bear	Elvis Presley	HMV	18	(1)	
13	5	Gamblin' Man/Putting On The Style	Lonnie Donegan	Pye Nixa	18		
14	16	Fabulous	Charlie Gracie	Parlophone	13	(16)	
15	-	Jenny Jenny	Little Richard	London American	5	(10)	
16	6	We Will Make Love	Russ Hamilton	Oriole	16		F
17	-	Stardust	Billy Ward & His Dominoes	London American	6	(14)	F L
18	-	Shiralee	Tommy Steele	Decca	3		
19	7	Little Darlin'	Diamonds	Mercury	15	(2)	F L
20	-	Build Your Love	Johnnie Ray	Philips	3	(58)	L

US 1957 JULY-SEPT

July 1957

This Mnth	Prev Mnth	Title	Artist	Label	Wks 20	(UK Pos)	
1	-	Teddy Bear	Elvis Presley	RCA	16	(3)	G
2	1	Love Letters In The Sand	Pat Boone	Dot	20	(2)	G
3	6	Bye Bye Love	Everly Brothers	Cadence	19	(6)	F G
4	5	So Rare	Jimmy Dorsey	Fraternity	21		G L
5	10	Searchin'/Young Blood	Coasters	Atco	19	(30)	F G
6	20	Valley Of Tears/It's You I Love	Fats Domino	Imperial	6		
7	18	It's Not For Me To Say	Johnny Mathis	Columbia	15		F G
8	8	Dark Moon	Gale Storm	Dot	15		L
9	-	Over The Mountain; Across The Sea	Johnnie & Joe	Chess	8		F L
10	-	Send For Me/My Personal Possession	Nat 'King' Cole	Capitol	13		
11	19	Old Cape Cod	Patti Page	Mercury	9		
12	-	Jenny, Jenny/Miss Ann	Little Richard	Specialty	8	(11)	
13	4	All Shook Up	Elvis Presley	RCA	17	(1)	G
14	3	A White Sport Coat (And A Pink Carnation)	Marty Robbins	Columbia	13		F G
15	-	Short Fat Fannie	Larry Williams	Specialty	12	(21)	F G
16	2	A Teenagers Romance/I'm Walkin'	Ricky Nelson	Verve	13		F G
17	-	I'm Gonna Sit Right Down And Write Myself A Letter	Billy Williams	Coral	11	(22)	F G L
18	16	I Like Your Kind Of Love	Andy Williams	Cadence	6	(16)	
19	-	C.C. Rider	Chuck Willis	Atlantic	5		F
20	9	Little Darlin'	Diamonds	Mercury	16	(3)	G

August 1957

This Mnth	Prev Mnth	Title	Artist	Label	Wks 20	(UK Pos)	
1	1	Teddy Bear	Elvis Presley	RCA	16	(3)	G
2	2	Love Letters In The Sand	Pat Boone	Dot	20	(2)	G
3	-	Tammy	Debbie Reynolds	Dot	19	(2)	G L
4	3	Bye Bye Love	Everly Brothers	Cadence	19	(6)	F G
5	5	Searchin'/Young Blood	Coasters	Atco	19	(30)	F G
6	4	So Rare	Jimmy Dorsey	Fraternity	21		G L
7	10	Send For Me/My Personal...	Nat 'King' Cole	Capitol	13		
8	17	I'm Gonna Sit Right Down...	Billy Williams	Coral	11	(22)	F G L
9	-	Diana	Paul Anka	ABC Paramount	15	(1)	F G
10	-	White Silver Sands	Don Rondo	Jubilee	8		F L
11	15	Short Fat Fannie	Larry Williams	Specialty	12	(21)	F G
12	-	Whispering Bells	Dell-Vikings	Dot	9		L
13	-	Rainbow	Russ Hamilton	Kapp	11		F L
14	7	It's Not For Me To Say	Johnny Mathis	Columbia	15		F G
15	-	Stardust	Billy Ward & His Dominoes	Liberty	10	(13)	
16	-	Remember You're Mine/There's A Gold Mine In The Sky	Pat Boone	Dot	11	(5)	G
17	11	Old Cape Cod	Patti Page	Mercury	9		
18	-	Whole Lot Of Shakin' Going On	Jerry Lee Lewis	Sun	13	(8)	F G
19	-	That'll Be The Day	Crickets	Brunswick	10	(1)	F G
20	-	Love Me To Pieces	Jill Corey	Columbia	2		F L

September 1957

This Mnth	Prev Mnth	Title	Artist	Label	Wks 20	(UK Pos)	
1	3	Tammy	Debbie Reynolds	Dot	19	(2)	G L
2	9	Diana	Paul Anka	ABC Paramount	15	(1)	F G
3	19	That'll Be The Day	Crickets	Brunswick	10	(1)	F G
4	18	Whole Lot Of Shakin' Going On	Jerry Lee Lewis	Sun	13	(8)	F G
5	-	Honeycomb	Jimmie Rodgers	Roulette	14	(30)	F G
6	1	Teddy Bear	Elvis Presley	RCA	16	(3)	G
7	13	Rainbow	Russ Hamilton	Kapp	11		F L
8	-	Mr. Lee	Bobbettes	Atlantic	9		F L
9	-	In The Middle Of An Island/I Am	Tony Bennett	Columbia	6		
10	5	Searchin'/Young Blood	Coasters	Atco	19	(30)	F G
11	16	Remember You're Mine/There's A...	Pat Boone	Dot	11	(5)	G
12	7	Send For Me/My Personal...	Nat 'King' Cole	Capitol	13		
13	4	Bye Bye Love	Everly Brothers	Cadence	19	(6)	F G
14	2	Love Letters In The Sand	Pat Boone	Dot	20	(2)	G
15	-	Chances Are/The Twelfth Of Never	Johnny Mathis	Columbia	19		G
16	15	Stardust	Billy Ward & His Dominoes	Liberty	10	(13)	
17	14	It's Not For Me To Say	Johnny Mathis	Columbia	15		F G
18	12	Whispering Bells	Dell-Vikings	Dot	9		L
19	-	Happy, Happy Birthday Baby	Tune Weavers	Checker	9		F L
20	11	Short Fat Fannie	Larry Williams	Specialty	12	(21)	F G

◆ 'Bye Bye Love' – rejected by 27 artists (including Elvis) earned the Everly Brothers a gold disc. It also topped the C&W listing and entered the R&B and British charts.

◆ CBS TV premiered *The Big Record* hosted by Patti Page, and *American Bandstand* debuted nationally. However, Jerry Lee Lewis' wildly outrageous performance on the Steve Allen and short-lived Alan Freed TV shows caused the biggest sensation.

◆ The *Billboard* album chart was extended to a Top 25.

◆ For the first time the top four artists on the R&B chart were all white: Paul Anka, Jimmie Rodgers, Jerry Lee Lewis and The Crickets. However, the year's top R&B record was 'Searchin''/'Young Blood', which gave The Coasters their first major hit.

UK 1957 OCT-DEC

▲ *NME* readers voted Pat Boone, World's Outstanding Male Singer, Elvis Presley, World's Outstanding Musical Personality, Doris Day (above), World's Top Female Singer and The Platters, World's Top Group.

◆ Elvis Presley had a record seven singles in the UK Top 30. In America **Elvis' Christmas Album,** which had unprecedented American advance orders, replaced his **Lovin' You** at the top.

◆ The third, and fastest, million selling single in Britain in 1957 was Harry Belafonte's 'Mary's Boy Child', it passed seven figures in less than two months.

October 1957

This Mnth	Prev Mnth	Title	Artist	Label	Wks 20	(US Pos)	
1	1	Diana	Paul Anka	Columbia	23	(1)	F G
2	2	Love Letters In The Sand	Pat Boone	London American	21	(1)	
3	11	Tammy	Debbie Reynolds	Vogue Coral	15	(1)	F L
4	4	Island In The Sun	Harry Belafonte	RCA	22	(30)	
5	-	That'll Be The Day	Crickets	Vogue Coral	12	(1)	F
6	3	Last Train To San Fernando	Johnny Duncan & The Blue Grass Boys	Columbia	16		F L
7	8	Wanderin' Eyes/I Love You So...	Charlie Gracie	London American	12	(71)	L
8	5	With All My Heart	Petula Clark	Pye Nixa	16		
9	-	Party	Elvis Presley	RCA	14		
10	6	Water Water/Handful Of Songs	Tommy Steele	Decca	13		
11	12	Teddy Bear	Elvis Presley	HMV	18	(1)	
12	-	Remember You're Mine/There's A Goldmine In The Sky	Pat Boone	London American	13	(10)	
13	7	All Shook Up	Elvis Presley	HMV	18	(1)	
14	-	Man On Fire/Wanderin' Eyes	Frankie Vaughan	Philips	11		
15	-	Whole Lotta Shakin' Goin' On	Jerry Lee Lewis	London American	7	(3)	F
16	9	Paralysed	Elvis Presley	HMV	9	(59)	
17	-	My Dixie Darling	Lonnie Donegan	Pye Nixa	8		
18	17	Stardust	Billy Ward & His Dominoes	London American	6	(14)	F L
19	15	Jenny Jenny	Little Richard	London American	5	(10)	
20	-	Call Rosie On The Phone	Guy Mitchell	Philips	3		

November 1957

This Mnth	Prev Mnth	Title	Artist	Label	Wks 20	(US Pos)	
1	5	That'll Be The Day	Crickets	Vogue Coral	12	(1)	F
2	9	Party	Elvis Presley	RCA	14		
3	3	Tammy	Debbie Reynolds	Vogue Coral	15	(1)	F L
4	12	Remember You're Mine/There's A...	Pat Boone	London American	13	(10)	
5	-	Be My Girl	Jim Dale	Parlophone	12		F L
6	1	Diana	Paul Anka	Columbia	23	(1)	F G
7	14	Man On Fire/Wanderin' Eyes	Frankie Vaughan	Philips	11		
8	-	Mary's Boy Child	Harry Belafonte	RCA	9	(12)	G
9	-	I Love You Baby	Paul Anka	Columbia	13	(97)	
10	-	Gotta Have Something In The Bank Frank	Frankie Vaughan & The Kaye Sisters	Philips	7		
11	-	Wake Up Little Susie	Everly Brothers	London American	11	(1)	
12	17	My Dixie Darling	Lonnie Donegan	Pye Nixa	8		
13	15	Whole Lotta Shakin' Goin' On	Jerry Lee Lewis	London American	7	(3)	F
14	10	Water Water/Handful Of Songs	Tommy Steele	Decca	13		
15	2	Love Letters In The Sand	Pat Boone	London American	21	(1)	
16	7	Wanderin' Eyes/I Love You So...	Charlie Gracie	London American	12	(71)	L
17	-	Santa Bring My Baby Back To Me	Elvis Presley	RCA	7		
18	8	With All My Heart	Petula Clark	Pye Nixa	16		
19	-	Alone	Petula Clark	Pye Nixa	9		
20	-	Ma He's Making Eyes At Me	Johnny Otis Show	Capitol	15		F

December 1957

This Mnth	Prev Mnth	Title	Artist	Label	Wks 20	(US Pos)	
1	8	Mary's Boy Child	Harry Belafonte	RCA	9	(12)	G
2	20	Ma He's Making Eyes At Me	Johnny Otis Show	Capitol	15		F
3	11	Wake Up Little Susie	Everly Brothers	London American	11	(1)	
4	9	I Love You Baby	Paul Anka	Columbia	13	(97)	
5	-	My Special Angel	Malcolm Vaughan	HMV	14		
6	5	Be My Girl	Jim Dale	Parlophone	12		F L
7	-	Let's Have A Ball	Winifred Atwell	Decca	5		
8	19	Alone	Petula Clark	Pye Nixa	9		
9	-	Reet Petite	Jackie Wilson	Coral	11	(62)	F
10	2	Party	Elvis Presley	RCA	14		
11	-	All The Way	Frank Sinatra	Capitol	16	(15)	
12	4	Remember You're Mine/There's A...	Pat Boone	London American	13	(10)	
13	17	Santa Bring My Baby Back To Me	Elvis Presley	RCA	7		
14	6	Diana	Paul Anka	Columbia	23	(1)	F G
15	-	Great Balls Of Fire	Jerry Lee Lewis	London American	11	(2)	
16	-	He's Got The Whole World In His Hands	Laurie London	Parlophone	7	(2)	F L
17	1	That'll Be The Day	Crickets	Vogue Coral	12	(1)	F
18	10	Gotta Have Something In The Bank...	Frankie Vaughan/Kaye Sisters	Philips	7		
19	-	April Love	Pat Boone	London American	17	(1)	
20	7	Man On Fire/Wanderin' Eyes	Frankie Vaughan	Philips	11		

October 1957

This Mnth	Prev Mnth	Title	Artist	Label	Wks 20	(UK Pos)	
1	-	Wake Up Little Susie	Everly Brothers	Cadence	13	(2)	G
2	5	Honeycomb	Jimmie Rodgers	Roulette	14	(30)	F G
3	1	Tammy	Debbie Reynolds	Dot	19	(2)	G L
4	15	Chances Are/The Twelfth Of Never	Johnny Mathis	Columbia	19		G
5	2	Diana	Paul Anka	ABC Paramount	15	(1)	F G
6	-	Jailhouse Rock	Elvis Presley	RCA	17	(1)	G
7	19	Happy, Happy Birthday Baby	Tune Weavers	Checker	9		F L
8	4	Whole Lot Of Shakin' Going On	Jerry Lee Lewis	Sun	13	(8)	F G
9	3	That'll Be The Day	Crickets	Brunswick	10	(1)	F G
10	-	Be-Bop Baby/Have I Told You Lately That I Love You	Ricky Nelson	Imperial	15		G
11	8	Mr. Lee	Bobbettes	Atlantic	9		F L
12	-	Keep A Knockin'	Little Richard	Specialty	7	(21)	
13	-	Hula Love	Buddy Knox	Roulette	7		L
14	-	Fascination	Jane Morgan	Kapp	10		F L
15	-	Lotta Lovin'/Wear My Ring	Gene Vincent & His Blue Caps	Capitol	7		L
16	11	Remember You're Mine/There's A Gold Mine In The Sky	Pat Boone	Dot	11	(5)	G
17	-	Silhouettes	Rays	Cameo	16		F G L
18	7	Rainbow	Russ Hamilton	Kapp	11		F L
19	-	You Send Me	Sam Cooke	Keen	14	(29)	F G
20	6	Teddy Bear	Elvis Presley	RCA	16	(3)	G

November 1957

This Mnth	Prev Mnth	Title	Artist	Label	Wks 20	(UK Pos)	
1	6	Jailhouse Rock	Elvis Presley	RCA	17	(1)	G
2	1	Wake Up Little Susie	Everly Brothers	Cadence	13	(2)	G
3	19	You Send Me	Sam Cooke	Keen	14	(29)	F G
4	17	Silhouettes	Rays	Cameo	16		F G L
5	10	Be-Bop Baby/Have I Told You...	Ricky Nelson	Imperial	15		G
6	4	Chances Are/The Twelfth Of Never	Johnny Mathis	Columbia	19		G
7	-	Little Bitty Pretty One	Thurston Harris	Aladdin	8		F L
8	-	My Special Angel	Bobby Helms	Decca	14	(22)	F G
9	2	Honeycomb	Jimmie Rodgers	Roulette	14	(30)	F G
10	-	April Love/When The Swallows Come Back To Capistrano	Pat Boone	Dot	17	(7)	G
11	3	Tammy	Debbie Reynolds	Dot	19	(2)	G L
12	-	Melodie D'Amour	Ames Brothers	RCA	9		
13	14	Fascination	Jane Morgan	Kapp	10		F L
14	12	Keep A Knockin'	Little Richard	Specialty	7	(21)	
15	-	Just Born/Ivy Rose	Perry Como	RCA	8		
16	5	Diana	Paul Anka	ABC Paramount	15	(1)	F G
17	7	Happy, Happy Birthday Baby	Tune Weavers	Checker	9		F L
18	-	Raunchy	Bill Justis	Phillips	11	(11)	F L
19	-	Rock & Roll Music	Chuck Berry	Chess	9		
20	-	Raunchy	Ernie Freeman	Imperial	7		F L

December 1957

This Mnth	Prev Mnth	Title	Artist	Label	Wks 20	(UK Pos)	
1	1	Jailhouse Rock	Elvis Presley	RCA	17	(1)	G
2	10	April Love/When The Swallows Come Back To Capistrano	Pat Boone	Dot	17	(7)	G
3	3	You Send Me	Sam Cooke	Keen	14	(29)	F G
4	18	Raunchy	Bill Justis	Phillips	11	(11)	F L
5	-	Peggy Sue	Buddy Holly	Coral	14	(6)	F G
6	6	Chances Are/The Twelfth Of Never	Johnny Mathis	Columbia	19		G
7	4	Silhouettes	Rays	Cameo	16		F G L
8	-	At The Hop	Danny & The Juniors	ABC Paramount	15	(3)	F G
9	-	Great Balls Of Fire	Jerry Lee Lewis	Sun	11	(1)	G
10	19	Rock & Roll Music	Chuck Berry	Chess	9		
11	2	Wake Up Little Susie	Everly Brothers	Cadence	13	(2)	G
12	-	Kisses Sweeter Than Wine	Jimmie Rodgers	Roulette	11	(7)	G
13	5	Be-Bop Baby/Have I Told You...	Ricky Nelson	Imperial	15		G
14	8	My Special Angel	Bobby Helms	Decca	14	(22)	F G
15	20	Raunchy	Ernie Freeman	Imperial	7		F L
16	7	Little Bitty Pretty One	Thurston Harris	Aladdin	8		F L
17	-	All The Way/Chicago	Frank Sinatra	Capitol	9	(3)	
18	-	Bony Moronie/You Bug Me, Baby	Larry Williams	Specialty	7	(11)	L
19	15	Just Born/Ivy Rose	Perry Como	RCA	8		
20	-	Liechtensteiner Polka	Will Glahe	London	2		F L

US 1957

OCT-DEC

◆ Early rock greats Gene Vincent and Buddy Knox had their final US Top 20 hits, and Little Richard stunned the music world by announcing he was trading rock'n'roll for religion.

◆ Thanks partly to the rise of Top 40 radio, 1957 saw the boundaries between pop, R&B and C&W become blurred. In fact, at one time, the Top 6 on the pop and R&B charts were identical.

◆ For the first time, two female-led R&B groups found themselves in the US Top 10. New York schoolgirls The Bobbettes (aged 11-15) sang about their fifth grade teacher, 'Mr. Lee', while Massachusetts family combo The Tune Weavers, had a one-off hit with their composition, 'Happy Happy Birthday Baby'.

45

UK 1958

JAN-MAR

◆ Jackie Wilson's US flop 'Reet Petite' (composed by Motown Records founder, Berry Gordy), reached the British Top 10. Amazingly, it returned to top that chart in 1986.

◆ Elvis Presley's 'Jailhouse Rock', with record advance orders of 250,000, became the first record to enter the chart at No. 1. Meanwhile, in America, 'Don't', became Presley's tenth chart topper in less than two years.

◆ Successful songwriter Hal David's collaboration with newcomer Burt Bacharach produced two successive UK No. 1s: 'The Story Of My Life' and 'Magic Moments'.

◆ Buddy Holly & The Crickets had a very successful tour of Britain, at a time when they were charting with four hits: 'Oh, Boy!', 'Peggy Sue', 'Maybe Baby' and 'Listen To Me'.

January 1958

This Mnth	Prev Mnth	Title	Artist	Label	Wks 20	(US Pos)	
1	2	Ma He's Making Eyes At Me	Johnny Otis Show	Capitol	15		F
2	15	Great Balls Of Fire	Jerry Lee Lewis	London American	11	(2)	
3	11	All The Way	Frank Sinatra	Capitol	16	(15)	
4	5	My Special Angel	Malcolm Vaughan	HMV	14		
5	9	Reet Petite	Jackie Wilson	Coral	11	(62)	F
6	-	Peggy Sue	Buddy Holly	Coral	12	(3)	F
7	-	Oh, Boy!	Crickets	Coral	12	(11)	
8	3	Wake Up Little Susie	Everly Brothers	London American	11	(1)	
9	4	I Love You Baby	Paul Anka	Columbia	13	(97)	
10	-	Kisses Sweeter Than Wine	Jimmie Rodgers	Columbia	10	(8)	F
11	-	Kisses Sweeter Than Wine	Frankie Vaughan	Philips	8		
12	19	April Love	Pat Boone	London American	17	(1)	
13	-	Jailhouse Rock	Elvis Presley	RCA	13	(1)	
14	-	The Story Of My Life	Michael Holliday	Columbia	14		
15	1	Mary's Boy Child	Harry Belafonte	RCA	9	(12)	G
16	8	Alone	Petula Clark	Pye Nixa	9		
17	-	Jack O' Diamonds	Lonnie Donegan	Pye Nixa	6		
18	14	Diana	Paul Anka	Columbia	23	(1)	F G
19	-	At The Hop	Danny & The Juniors	HMV	13	(1)	F L
20	-	Story Of My Life	Gary Miller	Pye Nixa	5		L

February 1958

This Mnth	Prev Mnth	Title	Artist	Label	Wks 20	(US Pos)	
1	14	The Story Of My Life	Michael Holliday	Columbia	14		
2	13	Jailhouse Rock	Elvis Presley	RCA	13	(1)	
3	19	At The Hop	Danny & The Juniors	HMV	13	(1)	F L
4	7	Oh, Boy!	Crickets	Coral	12	(11)	
5	-	Magic Moments	Perry Como	RCA	15	(3)	
6	3	All The Way	Frank Sinatra	Capitol	16	(15)	
7	-	Love Me Forever	Marion Ryan	Pye Nixa	10		F L
8	6	Peggy Sue	Buddy Holly	Coral	12	(3)	F
9	12	April Love	Pat Boone	London American	17	(1)	
10	-	You Are My Destiny	Paul Anka	Columbia	10	(9)	
11	2	Great Balls Of Fire	Jerry Lee Lewis	London American	11	(2)	
12	-	Bony Moronie	Larry Williams	London American	7	(14)	F L
13	1	Ma He's Making Eyes At Me	Johnny Otis Show	Capitol	15		F
14	4	My Special Angel	Malcolm Vaughan	HMV	14		
15	-	Raunchy	Bill Justis	London American	4	(2)	F L
16	10	Kisses Sweeter Than Wine	Jimmie Rodgers	Columbia	10	(8)	F
17	-	Witchcraft	Frank Sinatra	Capitol	6	(20)	
18	11	Kisses Sweeter Than Wine	Frankie Vaughan	Philips	8		
19	-	Sugartime	McGuire Sisters	Coral	3	(7)	
20	-	Mandy	Eddie Calvert	Columbia	11		L

March 1958

This Mnth	Prev Mnth	Title	Artist	Label	Wks 20	(US Pos)	
1	5	Magic Moments	Perry Como	RCA	15	(3)	
2	1	The Story Of My Life	Michael Holliday	Columbia	14		
3	2	Jailhouse Rock	Elvis Presley	RCA	13	(1)	
4	-	Don't	Elvis Presley	RCA	10	(1)	
5	3	At The Hop	Danny & The Juniors	HMV	13	(1)	F L
6	10	You Are My Destiny	Paul Anka	Columbia	10	(9)	
7	-	Nairobi	Tommy Steele	Decca	10		
8	7	Love Me Forever	Marion Ryan	Pye Nixa	10		F L
9	-	Good Golly Miss Molly	Little Richard	London American	7	(13)	
10	9	April Love	Pat Boone	London American	17	(1)	
11	4	Oh, Boy!	Crickets	Coral	12	(11)	
12	6	All The Way	Frank Sinatra	Capitol	16	(15)	
13	-	Whole Lotta Woman	Marvin Rainwater	MGM	14	(60)	F
14	-	Catch A Falling Star	Perry Como	RCA	7	(3)	
15	-	Can't Get Along Without You/ We're Not Alone	Frankie Vaughan	Philips	3		
16	-	Baby Lover	Petula Clark	Pye Nixa	4		
17	20	Mandy	Eddie Calvert	Columbia	11		L
18	-	Maybe Baby	Crickets	Coral	8	(18)	
19	-	La Dee Dah	Jackie Dennis	Decca	7		F L
20	8	Peggy Sue	Buddy Holly	Coral	12	(3)	F

January 1958

This Mnth	Prev Mnth	Title	Artist	Label	Wks 20	(UK Pos)	
1	8	At The Hop	Danny & The Juniors	ABC Paramount	15	(3)	F G
2	-	Stood Up/Waitin' In School	Ricky Nelson	Imperial	9	(27)	G
3	9	Great Balls Of Fire	Jerry Lee Lewis	Sun	11	(1)	G
4	2	April Love/When The Swallows Come Back To Capistrano	Pat Boone	Dot	17	(7)	G
5	5	Peggy Sue	Buddy Holly	Coral	14	(6)	F G
6	1	Jailhouse Rock	Elvis Presley	RCA	17	(1)	G
7	4	Raunchy	Bill Justis	Phillips	11	(11)	F L
8	12	Kisses Sweeter Than Wine	Jimmie Rodgers	Roulette	11	(7)	G
9	3	You Send Me	Sam Cooke	Keen	14	(29)	F G
10	7	Silhouettes	Rays	Cameo	16		F G L
11	-	Oh, Boy!	Crickets	Brunswick	6	(3)	
12	-	Jingle Bell Rock	Bobby Helms	Decca	2		L
13	-	The Stroll	Diamonds	Mercury	9		G
14	-	Sail Along Silvery Moon/Raunchy	Billy Vaughn	Dot	14		G
15	-	La Dee Dah	Billy & Lillie	Swan	7		F
16	-	Sugartime	McGuire Sisters	Coral	15	(14)	G
17	6	Chances Are/The Twelfth Of Never	Johnny Mathis	Columbia	19		G
18	-	Buzz-Buzz-Buzz	Hollywood Flames	Ebb	3		F L
19	-	Get A Job	Silhouettes	Ember	9		F G L
20	14	My Special Angel	Bobby Helms	Decca	14	(22)	F G

February 1958

This Mnth	Prev Mnth	Title	Artist	Label	Wks 20	(UK Pos)	
1	-	Don't/I Beg Of You	Elvis Presley	RCA	11	(2)	G
2	1	At The Hop	Danny & The Juniors	ABC Paramount	15	(3)	F G
3	19	Get A Job	Silhouettes	Ember	9		F G L
4	2	Stood Up/Waitin' In School	Ricky Nelson	Imperial	9	(27)	G
5	14	Sail Along Silvery Moon/Raunchy	Billy Vaughn	Dot	14		G
6	-	Short Shorts	Royal Teens	ABC Paramount	8		F L
7	16	Sugartime	McGuire Sisters	Coral	15	(14)	G
8	-	Catch A Falling Star/Magic Moments	Perry Como	RCA	14	(9)	G
9	13	The Stroll	Diamonds	Mercury	9		G
10	5	Peggy Sue	Buddy Holly	Coral	14	(6)	F G
11	3	Great Balls Of Fire	Jerry Lee Lewis	Sun	11	(1)	G
12	-	You Are My Destiny	Paul Anka	ABC Paramount	6	(6)	
13	-	Dede Dinah	Frankie Avalon	Chancellor	5		F
14	4	April Love/When The Swallows Come Back To Capistrano	Pat Boone	Dot	17	(7)	G
15	15	La Dee Dah	Billy & Lillie	Swan	7		F
16	-	Oh Julie	Crescendos	Nasco	8		F L
17	-	Don't Let Go	Roy Hamilton	Epic	4		
18	8	Kisses Sweeter Than Wine	Jimmie Rodgers	Roulette	11	(7)	G
19	-	A Wonderful Time Up There/It's Too Soon To Know	Pat Boone	Dot	12	(2)	G
20	-	Maybe	Chantels	End	4		F

March 1958

This Mnth	Prev Mnth	Title	Artist	Label	Wks 20	(UK Pos)	
1	1	Don't/I Beg Of You	Elvis Presley	RCA	11	(2)	G
2	-	Sweet Little Sixteen	Chuck Berry	Chess	9	(16)	G
3	19	A Wonderful Time Up There/It's Too Soon To Know	Pat Boone	Dot	12	(2)	G
4	8	Catch A Falling Star/Magic Moments	Perry Como	RCA	14	(9)	G
5	-	Tequila	Champs	Challenge	12	(5)	F G L
6	-	26 Miles	Four Preps	Capitol	10		F G
7	16	Oh Julie	Crescendos	Nasco	8		F L
8	5	Sail Along Silvery Moon/Raunchy	Billy Vaughn	Dot	14		G
9	-	Who's Sorry Now	Connie Francis	MGM	10	(1)	F G
10	3	Get A Job	Silhouettes	Ember	9		F G L
11	6	Short Shorts	Royal Teens	ABC Paramount	8		F L
12	-	Lollipop	Chordettes	Cadence	9	(6)	G
13	7	Sugartime	McGuire Sisters	Coral	15	(14)	G
14	-	The Walk	Jimmy McCracklin	Checker	5		F L
15	-	Dinner With Drac (Part 1)	John Zacherle	Cameo	3		F L
16	-	Breathless	Jerry Lee Lewis	Sun	6	(8)	L
17	2	At The Hop	Danny & The Juniors	ABC Paramount	15	(3)	F G
18	9	The Stroll	Diamonds	Mercury	9		G
19	-	Good Golly, Miss Molly	Little Richard	Specialty	3	(8)	L
20	12	You Are My Destiny	Paul Anka	ABC Paramount	6	(6)	

US 1958 JAN-MAR

▲ TV star and teen idol Ricky Nelson topped the album chart with his debut LP, **Ricky.** Incidentally his father, Ozzie, had topped the charts in 1933 and his sons, Gunnar and Matthew, did so in 1990.

◆ Dick Clark's whose *American Bandstand* had become America's most watched daytime TV show (average audience of 8.5 million), launched *The Dick Clark Saturday Night Show.*

◆ The first rock'n'roll instrumental No. 1 was 'Tequila' by West Coast session men, The Champs – who were named after the singing cowboy Gene Autry's (who owned their label) wonder horse, Champion.

UK 1958 APR-JUNE

▲ Jerry Lee Lewis' British tour was cut short when the media discovered that his bigamously married third wife was his 14-year-old second cousin.

◆ Jack Good, producer of *6-5 Special*, launched *Oh Boy!*, a TV show which first introduced the public to such acts as Cliff Richard and Billy Fury.

◆ Despite missing the American Top 40, US country stylist Marvin Rainwater topped the British chart with his rockabilly composition 'Whole Lotta Woman'.

April 1958

This Mnth	Prev Mnth	Title	Artist	Label	Wks 20	(US Pos)	
1	1	Magic Moments	Perry Como	RCA	15	(3)	
2	13	Whole Lotta Woman	Marvin Rainwater	MGM	14	(60)	F
3	7	Nairobi	Tommy Steele	Decca	10		
4	-	Swingin' Shepherd Blues	Ted Heath	Decca	10		L
5	18	Maybe Baby	Crickets	Coral	8	(18)	
6	19	La Dee Dah	Jackie Dennis	Decca	7		F L
7	-	Tequila	Champs	London American	7	(1)	F L
8	4	Don't	Elvis Presley	RCA	10	(1)	
9	-	A Wonderful Time Up There	Pat Boone	London American	14	(4)	
10	-	Who's Sorry Now	Connie Francis	MGM	20	(5)	F
11	2	The Story Of My Life	Michael Holliday	Columbia	14		
12	-	It's Too Soon To Know	Pat Boone	London American	8	(4)	
13	17	Mandy	Eddie Calvert	Columbia	11		L
14	14	Catch A Falling Star	Perry Como	RCA	7	(3)	
15	-	Breathless	Jerry Lee Lewis	London American	6	(9)	
16	9	Good Golly Miss Molly	Little Richard	London American	7	(13)	
17	-	To Be Loved	Malcolm Vaughan	HMV	8		
18	5	At The Hop	Danny & The Juniors	HMV	13	(1)	F L
19	3	Jailhouse Rock	Elvis Presley	RCA	13	(1)	
20	-	Lollipop	Chordettes	London American	5	(2)	L

May 1958

This Mnth	Prev Mnth	Title	Artist	Label	Wks 20	(US Pos)	
1	10	Who's Sorry Now	Connie Francis	MGM	20	(5)	F
2	2	Whole Lotta Woman	Marvin Rainwater	MGM	14	(60)	F
3	9	A Wonderful Time Up There	Pat Boone	London American	14	(4)	
4	-	Tom Hark	Elias & His Zigzag Jive Flutes	Columbia	12		F L
5	-	Wear My Ring Around Your Neck	Elvis Presley	RCA	7	(2)	
6	-	Lollipop	Mudlarks	Columbia	9		F
7	-	Grand Coolie Dam	Lonnie Donegan	Pye Nixa	9		
8	4	Swingin' Shepherd Blues	Ted Heath	Decca	10		L
9	20	Lollipop	Chordettes	London American	5	(2)	L
10	15	Breathless	Jerry Lee Lewis	London American	6	(9)	
11	7	Tequila	Champs	London American	7	(1)	F L
12	1	Magic Moments	Perry Como	RCA	15	(3)	
13	12	It's Too Soon To Know	Pat Boone	London American	8	(4)	
14	-	You Need Hands/ Tulips From Amsterdam	Max Bygraves	Decca	21		
15	-	On The Street Where You Live	Vic Damone	Philips	15	(8)	F L
16	-	I May Never Pass This Way Again	Robert Earl	Philips	9		F
17	-	Kewpie Doll	Perry Como	RCA	5	(12)	
18	17	To Be Loved	Malcolm Vaughan	HMV	8		
19	-	Kewpie Doll	Frankie Vaughan	Philips	9		
20	5	Maybe Baby	Crickets	Coral	8	(18)	

June 1958

This Mnth	Prev Mnth	Title	Artist	Label	Wks 20	(US Pos)	
1	1	Who's Sorry Now	Connie Francis	MGM	20	(5)	F
2	15	On The Street Where You Live	Vic Damone	Philips	15	(8)	F L
3	4	Tom Hark	Elias & His Zigzag Jive Flutes	Columbia	12		F L
4	-	Stairway Of Love	Michael Holliday	Columbia	11		
5	14	You Need Hands/ Tulips From Amsterdam	Max Bygraves	Decca	21		
6	-	All I Have To Do Is Dream/Claudette	Everly Brothers	London American	19	(1)	
7	-	Witch Doctor	Don Lang	HMV	10		L
8	3	A Wonderful Time Up There	Pat Boone	London American	14	(4)	
9	-	Army Game	TV Cast	HMV	6		F L
10	6	Lollipop	Mudlarks	Columbia	9		F
11	19	Kewpie Doll	Frankie Vaughan	Philips	9		
12	7	Grand Coolie Dam	Lonnie Donegan	Pye Nixa	9		
13	-	Twilight Time	Platters	Mercury	12	(1)	
14	-	Book Of Love	Mudlarks	Columbia	7		L
15	5	Wear My Ring Around Your Neck	Elvis Presley	RCA	7	(2)	
16	-	I May Never Pass This Way Again	Perry Como	RCA	4		
17	-	Big Man	Four Preps	Capitol	12	(6)	F L
18	17	Kewpie Doll	Perry Como	RCA	5	(12)	
19	-	Witch Doctor	David Seville	London	5	(1)	F
20	16	I May Never Pass This Way Again	Robert Earl	Philips	9		F

April 1958

This Mnth	Prev Mnth	Title	Artist	Label	Wks 20	(UK Pos)	
1	5	Tequila	Champs	Challenge	12	(5)	F G L
2	-	He's Got The Whole World (In His Hands)	Laurie London	Capitol	13	(12)	F G L
3	3	A Wonderful Time.../It's Too Soon...	Pat Boone	Dot	12	(2)	G
4	12	Lollipop	Chordettes	Cadence	9	(6)	G
5	-	Twilight Time	Platters	Mercury	13	(3)	G
6	-	Believe What You Say/ My Bucket's Got A Hole In It	Ricky Nelson	Imperial	8		G
7	4	Catch A Falling Star/Magic Moments	Perry Como	RCA	14	(9)	G
8	2	Sweet Little Sixteen	Chuck Berry	Chess	9	(16)	G
9	9	Who's Sorry Now	Connie Francis	MGM	10	(1)	F G
10	-	Book Of Love	Monotones	Argo	9		F L
11	-	Witch Doctor	David Seville	Liberty	13	(11)	F G L
12	-	Wear My Ring Around Your Neck	Elvis Presley	RCA	10	(3)	G
13	-	Don't You Just Know It	Huey (Piano) Smith & The Clowns	Ace	6		F L
14	13	Sugartime	McGuire Sisters	Coral	15	(14)	G
15	8	Sail Along Silvery Moon/Raunchy	Billy Vaughn	Dot	14		G
16	16	Breathless	Jerry Lee Lewis	Sun	6	(8)	L
17	-	Oh Lonesome Me/ I Can't Stop Lovin' You	Don Gibson	RCA	11		F L
18	1	Don't/I Beg Of You	Elvis Presley	RCA	11	(2)	G
19	-	Are You Sincere	Andy Williams	Cadence	5		
20	6	26 Miles	Four Preps	Capitol	10		F G

May 1958

This Mnth	Prev Mnth	Title	Artist	Label	Wks 20	(UK Pos)	
1	-	All I Have To Do Is Dream	Everly Brothers	Cadence	13	(1)	G
2	11	Witch Doctor	David Seville	Liberty	13	(11)	F G L
3	12	Wear My Ring Around Your Neck	Elvis Presley	RCA	10	(3)	G
4	5	Twilight Time	Platters	Mercury	13	(3)	G
5	2	He's Got The Whole World (In His...)	Laurie London	Capitol	13	(12)	F G L
6	-	Return To Me	Dean Martin	Capitol	13	(2)	
7	10	Book Of Love	Monotones	Argo	9		F L
8	-	Looking Back/Do I Like It	Nat 'King' Cole	Capitol	11		
9	1	Tequila	Champs	Challenge	12	(5)	F G L
10	17	Oh Lonesome Me/I Can't Stop...	Don Gibson	RCA	11		F L
11	-	Johnny B. Goode	Chuck Berry	Chess	8		
12	-	Kewpie Doll	Perry Como	RCA	7	(9)	
13	6	Believe What You Say/My Bucket's...	Ricky Nelson	Imperial	8		G
14	-	Chanson D'Amour (Song Of Love)	Art & Dotty Todd	Era	8		F L
15	4	Lollipop	Chordettes	Cadence	9	(6)	G
16	3	A Wonderful Time.../It's Too Soon...	Pat Boone	Dot	12	(2)	G
17	-	Sugar Moon/Cherie I Love You	Pat Boone	Dot	8	(6)	
18	-	Big Man	Four Preps	Capitol	9	(2)	G
19	-	Secretly	Jimmie Rodgers	Roulette	11		G
20	-	For Your Love	Ed Townsend	Capitol	4		F L

June 1958

This Mnth	Prev Mnth	Title	Artist	Label	Wks 20	(UK Pos)	
1	1	All I Have To Do Is Dream	Everly Brothers	Cadence	13	(1)	G
2	-	The Purple People Eater	Sheb Wooley	MGM	9	(12)	F G L
3	2	Witch Doctor	David Seville	Liberty	13	(11)	F G L
4	19	Secretly	Jimmie Rodgers	Roulette	11		G
5	6	Return To Me	Dean Martin	Capitol	13	(2)	
6	-	Do You Want To Dance	Bobby Freeman	Josie	10		F
7	8	Looking Back/Do I Like It	Nat 'King' Cole	Capitol	11		
8	18	Big Man	Four Preps	Capitol	9	(2)	G
9	4	Twilight Time	Platters	Mercury	13	(3)	G
10	-	Yakety Yak	Coasters	Atco	10	(12)	G
11	3	Wear My Ring Around Your Neck	Elvis Presley	RCA	10	(3)	G
12	-	Jennie Lee	Jan & Arnie	Arwin	6		F
13	17	Sugar Moon/Cherie I Love You	Pat Boone	Dot	8	(6)	
14	11	Johnny B. Goode	Chuck Berry	Chess	8		
15	5	He's Got The Whole World (In His...)	Laurie London	Capitol	13	(12)	F G L
16	-	Endless Sleep	Jody Reynolds	Demon	9		F L
17	14	Chanson D'Amour (Song Of Love)	Art & Dotty Todd	Era	8		F L
18	-	What Am I Living For	Chuck Willis	Atlantic	9		G L
19	7	Book Of Love	Monotones	Argo	9		F L
20	-	Patricia	Perez Prado	RCA	15	(8)	G L

◆ Chart newcomers included 14-year-old Londoner, Laurie London , with his revival of 'He's Got The Whole World In His Hands' and Connie Francis with her tenth release, 'Who's Sorry Now'.

◆ Chuck Willis died of a perforated ulcer aged 30. The ironically titled 'What Am I Living For'/'Hang Up My Rock And Roll Shoes' was the biggest hit for the turban-wearing R&B singer/songwriter known as The King of The Stroll.

◆ Riots (including stabbings, rapes, looting and drug taking) allegedly took place after an Alan Freed show, and he was charged with incitement to riot. Some states then banned Freed shows..

◆ Two records using sped-up vocal gimmicks topped the chart: David Seville's 'Witch Doctor' and cowboy actor/singer Sheb Wooley's 'The Purple People Eater'.

UK 1958

JULY-SEPT

◆ Ricky Nelson's sixth American hit, 'Poor Little Fool', was not only the first single to top *Billboard*'s newly inaugurated Hot 100 singles chart, but it also became the first of his many British hits.

◆ Cliff Richard's debut single, 'Move It' (composed by Ian Samwell from his backing group, The Drifters), only narrowly missed topping the chart.

◆ Johnny Otis' biggest American hit, 'Willie & The Hand Jive', was inspired by a digital dance started in British coffee bars and popularized on *6-5 Special*.

◆ In August, the month that both Michael Jackson and Madonna were born, George Harrison joined John Lennon and Paul McCartney's group, The Quarry Men.

July 1958

This Mnth	Prev Mnth	Title	Artist	Label	Wks 20	(US Pos)	
1	6	All I Have To Do Is Dream/Claudette	Everly Brothers	London American	19	(1)	
2	2	On The Street Where You Live	Vic Damone	Philips	15	(8)	F L
3	5	You Need Hands/ Tulips From Amsterdam	Max Bygraves	Decca	21		
4	17	Big Man	Four Preps	Capitol	12	(6)	F L
5	13	Twilight Time	Platters	Mercury	12	(1)	
6	1	Who's Sorry Now	Connie Francis	MGM	20	(5)	F
7	-	Sugar Moon	Pat Boone	London American	10	(10)	
8	14	Book Of Love	Mudlarks	Columbia	7		L
9	-	Rave On	Buddy Holly	Coral	12	(41)	
10	7	Witch Doctor	Don Lang	HMV	10		L
11	4	Stairway Of Love	Michael Holliday	Columbia	11		
12	-	Sally Don't You Grieve/ Betty, Betty, Betty	Lonnie Donegan	Pye Nixa	6		
13	-	The Purple People Eater	Sheb Wooley	MGM	6	(1)	F L
14	3	Tom Hark	Elias & His Zigzag Jive Flutes	Columbia	12		F L
15	-	Endless Sleep	Marty Wilde	Philips	12		F
16	-	I'm Sorry I Made You Cry	Connie Francis	MGM	7	(36)	
17	9	Army Game	TV Cast	HMV	6		F L
18	-	On The Street Where You Live	David Whitfield	Decca	8		L
19	-	Hard Headed Woman	Elvis Presley	RCA	8	(1)	
20	11	Kewpie Doll	Frankie Vaughan	Philips	9		

August 1958

This Mnth	Prev Mnth	Title	Artist	Label	Wks 20	(US Pos)	
1	1	All I Have To Do Is Dream/Claudette	Everly Brothers	London American	19	(1)	
2	-	When	Kalin Twins	Brunswick	16	(5)	F L
3	19	Hard Headed Woman	Elvis Presley	RCA	8	(1)	
4	-	Return To Me	Dean Martin	Capitol	16	(4)	
5	3	You Need Hands/ Tulips From Amsterdam	Max Bygraves	Decca	21		
6	15	Endless Sleep	Marty Wilde	Philips	12		F
7	4	Big Man	Four Preps	Capitol	12	(6)	F L
8	9	Rave On	Buddy Holly	Coral	12	(41)	
9	5	Twilight Time	Platters	Mercury	12	(1)	
10	-	Patricia	Perez Prado	RCA	11	(2)	L
11	7	Sugar Moon	Pat Boone	London American	10	(10)	
12	6	Who's Sorry Now	Connie Francis	MGM	20	(5)	F
13	-	Think It Over	Crickets	Coral	5	(27)	
14	2	On The Street Where You Live	Vic Damone	Philips	15	(8)	F L
15	16	I'm Sorry I Made You Cry	Connie Francis	MGM	7	(36)	
16	-	Splish Splash	Charlie Drake	Parlophone	9		F
17	12	Sally Don't You Grieve/ Betty, Betty, Betty	Lonnie Donegan	Pye Nixa	6		
18	-	Fever	Peggy Lee	Capitol	8	(8)	L
19	-	Carolina Moon/Stupid Cupid	Connie Francis	MGM	17	(14)	
20	-	Poor Little Fool	Ricky Nelson	London American	13	(1)	F

September 1958

This Mnth	Prev Mnth	Title	Artist	Label	Wks 20	(US Pos)	
1	2	When	Kalin Twins	Brunswick	16	(5)	F L
2	19	Carolina Moon/Stupid Cupid	Connie Francis	MGM	17	(14)	
3	4	Return To Me	Dean Martin	Capitol	16	(4)	
4	-	Volare	Dean Martin	Capitol	12	(15)	
5	1	All I Have To Do Is Dream/Claudette	Everly Brothers	London American	19	(1)	
6	18	Fever	Peggy Lee	Capitol	8	(8)	L
7	20	Poor Little Fool	Ricky Nelson	London American	13	(1)	F
8	6	Endless Sleep	Marty Wilde	Philips	12		F
9	16	Splish Splash	Charlie Drake	Parlophone	9		F
10	10	Patricia	Perez Prado	RCA	11	(2)	L
11	-	Volare	Domenico Modugno	Oriole	8	(1)	F L
12	-	Mad Passionate Love	Bernard Bresslaw	HMV	9		F L
13	-	Yakety Yak	Coasters	London American	7	(2)	F
14	5	You Need Hands/Tulips From...	Max Bygraves	Decca	21		
15	-	Bird Dog	Everly Brothers	London American	16	(2)	
16	3	Hard Headed Woman	Elvis Presley	RCA	8	(1)	
17	8	Rave On	Buddy Holly	Coral	12	(41)	
18	-	Trudie	Joe 'Mr. Piano' Henderson	Pye Nixa	6		L
19	-	Girl Of My Dreams	Tony Brent	Columbia	5		L
20	-	Born Too Late	Poni-Tails	HMV	10	(7)	F L

July 1958

This Mnth	Prev Mnth	Title	Artist	Label	Wks 20	(UK Pos)	
1	-	Hard Headed Woman	Elvis Presley	RCA	8	(2)	G
2	10	Yakety Yak	Coasters	Atco	10	(12)	G
3	2	The Purple People Eater	Sheb Wooley	MGM	9	(12)	F G L
4	20	Patricia	Perez Prado	RCA	15	(8)	G L
5	-	Splish Splash	Bobby Darin	Atco	10	(18)	F G
6	-	Poor Little Fool	Ricky Nelson	Imperial	12	(4)	G
7	16	Endless Sleep	Jody Reynolds	Demon	9		F L
8	4	Secretly	Jimmie Rodgers	Roulette	11		G
9	-	Rebel-'Rouser	Duane Eddy	Jamie	8	(19)	F G
10	1	All I Have To Do Is Dream	Everly Brothers	Cadence	13	(1)	G
11	-	When	Kalin Twins	Decca	10	(1)	F G
12	6	Do You Want To Dance	Bobby Freeman	Josie	10		F
13	-	For Your Precious Love	Jerry Butler & The Impressions	Abner	5		F
14	-	Guess Things Happen That Way/ Come In Stranger	Johnny Cash	Sun	4		
15	-	My True Love/Leroy	Jack Scott	Carlton	13	(9)	F G
16	5	Return To Me	Dean Martin	Capitol	13	(2)	
17	3	Witch Doctor	David Seville	Liberty	13	(11)	F G L
18	18	What Am I Living For	Chuck Willis	Atlantic	9		G L
19	-	Willie And The Hand Jive	Johnny Otis Show	Capitol	8		F L
20	7	Looking Back/Do I Like It	Nat 'King' Cole	Capitol	11		

August 1958

This Mnth	Prev Mnth	Title	Artist	Label	Wks 20	(UK Pos)	
1	6	Poor Little Fool	Ricky Nelson	Imperial	12	(4)	G
2	4	Patricia	Perez Prado	RCA	15	(8)	G L
3	15	My True Love/Leroy	Jack Scott	Carlton	13	(9)	F G
4	-	Nel Blu Dipinto Di Blu (Volare)	Domenico Modugno	Decca	13	(10)	F G L
5	11	When	Kalin Twins	Decca	10	(1)	F G
6	-	Just A Dream	Jimmy Clanton	Ace	12		F G
7	5	Splish Splash	Bobby Darin	Atco	10	(18)	F G
8	9	Rebel-'Rouser	Duane Eddy	Jamie	8	(19)	F G
9	-	Little Star	Elegants	Apt	14	(25)	F G L
10	-	Fever	Peggy Lee	Capitol	7	(5)	
11	19	Willie And The Hand Jive	Johnny Otis Show	Capitol	8		F L
12	1	Hard Headed Woman	Elvis Presley	RCA	8	(2)	G
13	-	Ginger Bread	Frankie Avalon	Chancellor	7	(30)	
14	2	Yakety Yak	Coasters	Atco	10	(12)	G
15	-	If Dreams Came True	Pat Boone	Dot	6	(16)	
16	-	Bird Dog	Everly Brothers	Cadence	13	(2)	G
17	-	Born Too Late	Poni-Tails	ABC Paramount	10	(5)	F L
18	-	Everybody Loves A Lover	Doris Day	Columbia	8	(25)	L
19	-	Western Movies	Olympics	Demon	6	(12)	F L
20	-	Left Right Out Of Your Heart	Patti Page	Mercury	2		

September 1958

This Mnth	Prev Mnth	Title	Artist	Label	Wks 20	(UK Pos)	
1	4	Nel Blu Dipinto Di Blu (Volare)	Domenico Modugno	Decca	13	(10)	F G L
2	16	Bird Dog	Everly Brothers	Cadence	13	(2)	G
3	9	Little Star	Elegants	Apt	14	(25)	F G L
4	6	Just A Dream	Jimmy Clanton	Ace	12		F G
5	-	Rock-In' Robin/Over And Over	Bobby Day	Class	13	(29)	F G L
6	-	It's All In The Game	Tommy Edwards	MGM	14	(1)	F G
7	17	Born Too Late	Poni-Tails	ABC Paramount	10	(5)	F L
8	-	Tears On My Pillow	Little Anthony & The Imperials	End	10		F G
9	2	Patricia	Perez Prado	RCA	15	(8)	G L
10	3	My True Love/Leroy	Jack Scott	Carlton	13	(9)	F G
11	1	Poor Little Fool	Ricky Nelson	Imperial	12	(4)	G
12	-	Susie Darlin'	Robin Luke	Dot	9	(23)	F G L
13	19	Western Movies	Olympics	Demon	6	(12)	F L
14	-	Devoted To You	Everly Brothers	Cadence	6		
15	-	Summertime Blues	Eddie Cochran	Liberty	7	(18)	F L
16	13	Ginger Bread	Frankie Avalon	Chancellor	7	(30)	
17	5	When	Kalin Twins	Decca	10	(1)	F G
18	-	Are You Really Mine	Jimmie Rodgers	Roulette	4		
19	-	Near You	Roger Williams	Kapp	7		
20	10	Fever	Peggy Lee	Capitol	7	(5)	

◆ An anti-rock back-lash at radio level resulted in many labels and artists softening their sound in order to get airplay (and there-fore sales).

◆ Stereo, previously considered a gimmick for sound enthusiasts, was being taken seri-ously by labels like RCA, Columbia and Atlantic who started recording stereo pop singles.

◆ Jerry Butler & The Impressions scored arguably the first soul-ful hit single with the memorable 'For Your Precious Love'. Butler and the group soon went separate ways, both having successful careers in the 1960s.

◆ Mambo King Perez Prado's 'Patricia' spear-headed the Cha Cha Cha dance craze. Astoundingly his chart topping composition also reached the UK, R&B and even C&W listings!

UK 1958 OCT-DEC

▲ *NME* poll winners included Elvis (World's Outstanding Male), Connie Francis (World's Outstanding Female), the Everly Brothers (World's Outstanding Group) and Cliff Richard (above), whose act had been labelled "crude" and "vulgar" was Favourite New Singer.

◆ Britain's first self-composed rock No. 1 was 'Hoots Mon', a sax-led instrumental by the 'Oh Boy!' house-band, Lord Rockingham's XI. The show's producer Jack Good was speculating that in the future it would be possible to tape television shows on a video machine.

◆ *Melody Maker* introduced Britain's first album chart, a Top 15.

October 1958

This Mnth	Prev Mnth	Title	Artist	Label	Wks 20	(US Pos)	
1	2	Carolina Moon/Stupid Cupid	Connie Francis	MGM	17	(14)	
2	15	Bird Dog	Everly Brothers	London American	16	(2)	
3	4	Volare	Dean Martin	Capitol	12	(15)	
4	-	King Creole	Elvis Presley	RCA	9		
5	-	Move It	Cliff Richard	Columbia	11		F
6	20	Born Too Late	Poni-Tails	HMV	10	(7)	F L
7	-	A Certain Smile	Johnny Mathis	Fontana	14	(21)	F
8	1	When	Kalin Twins	Brunswick	16	(5)	F L
9	7	Poor Little Fool	Ricky Nelson	London American	13	(1)	F
10	12	Mad Passionate Love	Bernard Bresslaw	HMV	9		F L
11	-	Come Prima	Marino Marini	Durium	13		L
12	-	It's All In The Game	Tommy Edwards	MGM	15	(1)	F L
13	3	Return To Me	Dean Martin	Capitol	16	(4)	
14	-	More Than Ever (Come Prima)	Malcolm Vaughan	HMV	13		
15	11	Volare	Domenico Modugno	Oriole	8	(1)	F L
16	-	Volare	Marino Marini	Durium	5		F
17	-	Western Movies	Olympics	HMV	7	(8)	F L
18	-	Hoots Mon	Lord Rockingham's XI	Decca	16		F
19	9	Splish Splash	Charlie Drake	Parlophone	9		F
20	6	Fever	Peggy Lee	Capitol	8	(8)	L

November 1958

This Mnth	Prev Mnth	Title	Artist	Label	Wks 20	(US Pos)	
1	12	It's All In The Game	Tommy Edwards	MGM	15	(1)	F L
2	18	Hoots Mon	Lord Rockingham's XI	Decca	16		F
3	2	Bird Dog	Everly Brothers	London American	16	(2)	
4	11	Come Prima	Marino Marini	Durium	13		L
5	7	A Certain Smile	Johnny Mathis	Fontana	14	(21)	F
6	14	More Than Ever (Come Prima)	Malcolm Vaughan	HMV	13		
7	1	Carolina Moon/Stupid Cupid	Connie Francis	MGM	17	(14)	
8	5	Move It	Cliff Richard	Columbia	11		F
9	-	Tea For Two Cha Cha	Tommy Dorsey Orchestra	Brunswick	16	(7)	F L
10	-	It's Only Make Believe	Conway Twitty	MGM	14	(1)	F
11	4	King Creole	Elvis Presley	RCA	9		
12	-	My True Love	Jack Scott	London American	8	(3)	F
13	-	Love Makes The World Go Round	Perry Como	RCA	13	(33)	
14	-	Tom Dooley	Lonnie Donegan	Pye Nixa	12		
15	6	Born Too Late	Poni-Tails	HMV	10	(7)	F L
16	-	Someday	Jodie Sands	HMV	8	(95)	F L
17	-	Someday	Ricky Nelson	London American	8		
18	3	Volare	Dean Martin	Capitol	12	(15)	
19	17	Western Movies	Olympics	HMV	7	(8)	F L
20	-	Come On Let's Go	Tommy Steele	Decca	11		

December 1958

This Mnth	Prev Mnth	Title	Artist	Label	Wks 20	(US Pos)	
1	10	It's Only Make Believe	Conway Twitty	MGM	14	(1)	F
2	2	Hoots Mon	Lord Rockingham's XI	Decca	16		F
3	14	Tom Dooley	Lonnie Donegan	Pye Nixa	12		
4	1	It's All In The Game	Tommy Edwards	MGM	15	(1)	F L
5	9	Tea For Two Cha Cha	Tommy Dorsey Orchestra	Brunswick	16	(7)	F L
6	-	Tom Dooley	Kingston Trio	Capitol	12	(1)	F L
7	13	Love Makes The World Go Round	Perry Como	RCA	13	(33)	
8	-	High Class Baby	Cliff Richard	Columbia	9		
9	6	More Than Ever (Come Prima)	Malcolm Vaughan	HMV	13		
10	5	A Certain Smile	Johnny Mathis	Fontana	14	(21)	F
11	17	Someday	Ricky Nelson	London American	8		
12	20	Come On Let's Go	Tommy Steele	Decca	11		
13	4	Come Prima	Marino Marini	Durium	13		L
14	-	The Day The Rains Came	Jane Morgan	London American	13	(21)	F L
15	-	Mary's Boy Child	Harry Belafonte	RCA	5		G
16	3	Bird Dog	Everly Brothers	London American	16	(2)	
17	-	Mandolins In The Moonlight	Perry Como	RCA	8	(47)	
18	-	More Party Pops	Russ Conway	Columbia	3		F
19	-	Real Love	Ruby Murray	Columbia	3		
20	8	Move It	Cliff Richard	Columbia	11		F

October 1958

This Mnth	Prev Mnth	Title	Artist	Label	Wks 20	(UK Pos)	
1	6	It's All In The Game	Tommy Edwards	MGM	14	(1)	F G
2	5	Rock-In' Robin/Over And Over	Bobby Day	Class	13	(29)	F G L
3	2	Bird Dog	Everly Brothers	Cadence	13	(2)	G
4	8	Tears On My Pillow	Little Anthony & The Imperials	End	10		F G
5	12	Susie Darlin'	Robin Luke	Dot	9	(23)	F G L
6	-	Tea For Two Cha Cha	Tommy Dorsey Orchestra	Decca	10	(3)	G L
7	1	Nel Blu Dipinto Di Blu (Volare)	Domenico Modugno	Decca	13	(10)	F G L
8	3	Little Star	Elegants	Apt	14	(25)	F G L
9	-	Topsy Ii	Cozy Cole	Love	11	(29)	F G L
10	-	The End	Earl Grant	Decca	11		F L
11	-	It's Only Make Believe	Conway Twitty	MGM	13	(1)	F G
12	-	Chantilly Lace	Big Bopper	Mercury	10	(12)	F L
13	-	Tom Dooley	Kingston Trio	Capitol	15	(5)	F G
14	19	Near You	Roger Williams	Kapp	7		
15	15	Summertime Blues	Eddie Cochran	Liberty	7	(18)	F L
16	-	You Cheated	Shields	Dot	4		F L
17	4	Just A Dream	Jimmy Clanton	Ace	12		F G
18	-	How Time Flies	Jerry Wallace	Challenge	4		F
19	-	To Know Him, Is To Love Him	Teddy Bears	Dore	15	(2)	F G L
20	7	Born Too Late	Poni-Tails	ABC Paramount	10	(5)	F L

November 1958

This Mnth	Prev Mnth	Title	Artist	Label	Wks 20	(UK Pos)	
1	11	It's Only Make Believe	Conway Twitty	MGM	13	(1)	F G
2	13	Tom Dooley	Kingston Trio	Capitol	15	(5)	F G
3	1	It's All In The Game	Tommy Edwards	MGM	14	(1)	F G
4	9	Topsy Ii	Cozy Cole	Love	11	(29)	F G L
5	19	To Know Him, Is To Love Him	Teddy Bears	Dore	15	(2)	F G L
6	10	The End	Earl Grant	Decca	11		F L
7	6	Tea For Two Cha Cha	Tommy Dorsey Orchestra	Decca	10	(3)	G L
8	12	Chantilly Lace	Big Bopper	Mercury	10	(12)	F L
9	-	Lonesome Town	Ricky Nelson	Imperial	14		
10	-	I Got A Feeling	Ricky Nelson	Imperial	8	(27)	
11	2	Rock-In' Robin/Over And Over	Bobby Day	Class	13	(29)	F G L
12	-	Queen Of The Hop	Bobby Darin	Atco	10	(24)	G
13	-	Beep Beep	Playmates	Roulette	11		G
14	-	I Got Stung	Elvis Presley	RCA	10	(1)	G
15	-	One Night	Elvis Presley	RCA	11	(1)	
16	5	Susie Darlin'	Robin Luke	Dot	9	(23)	F G L
17	4	Tears On My Pillow	Little Anthony & The Imperials	End	10		F G
18	3	Bird Dog	Everly Brothers	Cadence	13	(2)	G
19	-	Forget Me Not	Kalin Twins	Decca	6		L
20	-	Mexican Hat Rock	Applejacks	Cameo	5		F L

December 1958

This Mnth	Prev Mnth	Title	Artist	Label	Wks 20	(UK Pos)	
1	5	To Know Him, Is To Love Him	Teddy Bears	Dore	15	(2)	F G L
2	2	Tom Dooley	Kingston Trio	Capitol	15	(5)	F G
3	15	One Night	Elvis Presley	RCA	11	(1)	
4	-	Problems	Everly Brothers	Cadence	9	(6)	G
5	13	Beep Beep	Playmates	Roulette	11		G
6	9	Lonesome Town	Ricky Nelson	Imperial	14		
7	-	Smoke Gets In Your Eyes	Platters	Mercury	13	(1)	G
8	1	It's Only Make Believe	Conway Twitty	MGM	13	(1)	F G
9	14	I Got Stung	Elvis Presley	RCA	10	(1)	G
10	-	The Chipmunk Song	Chipmunks	Liberty	7		F G
11	-	A Lover's Question	Clyde McPhatter	Atlantic	14		G
12	-	Whole Lotta Loving	Fats Domino	Imperial	9		G
13	4	Topsy Ii	Cozy Cole	Love	11	(29)	F G L
14	12	Queen Of The Hop	Bobby Darin	Atco	10	(24)	G
15	-	Bimbombey	Jimmie Rodgers	Roulette	7		L
16	10	I Got A Feeling	Ricky Nelson	Imperial	8	(27)	
17	3	It's All In The Game	Tommy Edwards	MGM	14	(1)	F G
18	-	Gotta Travel On	Billy Grammer	Monument	12		F G L
19	-	Love Is All We Need	Tommy Edwards	MGM	5		
20	-	My Happiness	Connie Francis	MGM	11	(4)	G

US 1958
OCT-DEC

◆ Tommy Edwards' new "beat ballad" recording of his 1951 Top 20 hit, 'It's All In The Game', topped the transatlantic charts and started a rush of re-recordings.

◆ David Seville, who had earlier introduced the sped-up vocal gimmick (with 'Witch Doctor') produced/ wrote and sang all parts on 'The Chipmunk Song' by The Chipmunks, which allegedly sold a record four million copies in two months.

◆ The Kingston Trio's revival of the nine-teenth century song 'Tom Dooley' started the late 1950s folk revival. They were to have five chart topping albums in the next three years.

◆ Sales of records slipped by 15% as pur-chases of transistor radios and tape recorders increased.

53

UK 1959 JAN-MAR

◆ Unlike Elvis, British rocker Terry Dene was released from the army after only six weeks service – on medical grounds.

◆ Lonnie Donegan, whose UK hit 'Does Your Chewing Gum Lose Its Flavour' reached the American Top 3 in 1961, signed a record £10,000 recording deal.

◆ For the first time three British records simultaneously made the US Top 20: 'Petite Fleur' by Chris Barber, 'The Children's Marching Song' by Cyril Stapleton and 'Manhattan Spiritual' by Reg Owen - all instrumentals.

◆ EMI Records stopped pressing 78 rpm singles in the UK.

◆ A revival of 'Baby Face' gave the recently retired Little Richard his biggest British hit. In America it missed the Top 40.

January 1959

This Mnth	Prev Mnth	Title	Artist	Label	Wks 20	(US Pos)	
1	1	It's Only Make Believe	Conway Twitty	MGM	14	(1)	F
2	14	The Day The Rains Came	Jane Morgan	London American	13	(21)	F L
3	2	Hoots Mon	Lord Rockingham's XI	Decca	16		F
4	5	Tea For Two Cha Cha	Tommy Dorsey Orchestra	Brunswick	16	(7)	F L
5	3	Tom Dooley	Lonnie Donegan	Pye Nixa	12		
6	-	Baby Face	Little Richard	London American	10	(41)	
7	-	To Know Him, Is To Love Him	Teddy Bears	London American	11	(1)	F L
8	6	Tom Dooley	Kingston Trio	Capitol	12	(1)	F L
9	-	Kiss Me Honey Honey Kiss Me	Shirley Bassey	Philips	13		
10	7	Love Makes The World Go Round	Perry Como	RCA	13	(33)	
11	12	Come On Let's Go	Tommy Steele	Decca	11		
12	8	High Class Baby	Cliff Richard	Columbia	9		
13	-	One Night/I Got Stung	Elvis Presley	RCA	10	(4)	
14	-	As I Love You	Shirley Bassey	Philips	16		
15	17	Mandolins In The Moonlight	Perry Como	RCA	8	(47)	
16	4	It's All In The Game	Tommy Edwards	MGM	15	(1)	F L
17	-	You Always Hurt The One You Love	Connie Francis	MGM	5		
18	-	Smoke Gets In Your Eyes	Platters	Mercury	19	(1)	
19	-	Chantilly Lace	Big Bopper	Mercury	4	(6)	F L
20	-	Problems	Everly Brothers	London American	9	(2)	

February 1959

This Mnth	Prev Mnth	Title	Artist	Label	Wks 20	(US Pos)	
1	14	As I Love You	Shirley Bassey	Philips	16		
2	13	One Night/I Got Stung	Elvis Presley	RCA	10	(4)	
3	9	Kiss Me Honey Honey Kiss Me	Shirley Bassey	Philips	13		
4	18	Smoke Gets In Your Eyes	Platters	Mercury	19	(1)	
5	7	To Know Him, Is To Love Him	Teddy Bears	London American	11	(1)	F L
6	-	Does Your Chewing Gum Lose It's Flavour	Lonnie Donegan	Pye Nixa	11	(5)	
7	6	Baby Face	Little Richard	London American	10	(41)	
8	20	Problems	Everly Brothers	London American	9	(2)	
9	2	The Day The Rains Came	Jane Morgan	London American	13	(21)	F L
10	-	(All Of A Sudden) My Heart Sings	Paul Anka	Columbia	12	(15)	
11	-	A Pub With No Beer	Slim Dusty	Columbia	13		F L
12	-	Petite Fleur	Chris Barber's Jazz Band	Pye Nixa	18	(5)	F L
13	-	The Little Drummer Boy	Beverley Sisters	Decca	11		
14	-	High School Confidential	Jerry Lee Lewis	London American	4	(22)	
15	1	It's Only Make Believe	Conway Twitty	MGM	14	(1)	F
16	4	Tea For Two Cha Cha	Tommy Dorsey Orchestra	Brunswick	16	(7)	F L
17	-	My Happiness	Connie Francis	MGM	13	(2)	
18	-	Little Drummer Boy	Harry Simeone Chorale	Top Rank	4	(13)	F L
19	-	Apple Blossom Time	Rosemary June	Pye-Int	3		F L
20	-	Gigi	Billy Eckstine	Mercury	12		

March 1959

This Mnth	Prev Mnth	Title	Artist	Label	Wks 20	(US Pos)	
1	4	Smoke Gets In Your Eyes	Platters	Mercury	19	(1)	
2	1	As I Love You	Shirley Bassey	Philips	16		
3	-	Side Saddle	Russ Conway	Columbia	25		
4	11	A Pub With No Beer	Slim Dusty	Columbia	13		F L
5	12	Petite Fleur	Chris Barber's Jazz Band	Pye Nixa	18	(5)	F L
6	17	My Happiness	Connie Francis	MGM	13	(2)	
7	13	The Little Drummer Boy	Beverley Sisters	Decca	11		
8	6	Does Your Chewing Gum Lose It's Flavour	Lonnie Donegan	Pye Nixa	11	(5)	
9	-	Stagger Lee	Lloyd Price	HMV	11	(1)	F
10	10	(All Of A Sudden) My Heart Sings	Paul Anka	Columbia	12	(15)	
11	-	It Doesn't Matter Anymore	Buddy Holly	Coral	21	(13)	
12	2	One Night/I Got Stung	Elvis Presley	RCA	10	(4)	
13	20	Gigi	Billy Eckstine	Mercury	12		
14	3	Kiss Me Honey Honey Kiss Me	Shirley Bassey	Philips	13		
15	-	Tomboy	Perry Como	RCA	10	(29)	
16	8	Problems	Everly Brothers	London American	9	(2)	
17	-	C'mon Everybody	Eddie Cochran	London American	10	(35)	
18	5	To Know Him, Is To Love Him	Teddy Bears	London American	11	(1)	F L
19	-	Wonderful Secret Of Love	Robert Earl	Philips	4		L
20	18	Little Drummer Boy	Harry Simeone Chorale	Top Rank	4	(13)	F L

January 1959

This Mnth	Prev Mnth	Title	Artist	Label	Wks 20	(UK Pos)	
1	7	Smoke Gets In Your Eyes	Platters	Mercury	13	(1)	G
2	20	My Happiness	Connie Francis	MGM	11	(4)	G
3	10	The Chipmunk Song	Chipmunks	Liberty	7		F G
4	18	Gotta Travel On	Billy Grammer	Monument	12		F G L
5	11	A Lover's Question	Clyde McPhatter	Atlantic	14		G
6	1	To Know Him, Is To Love Him	Teddy Bears	Dore	15	(2)	F G L
7	12	Whole Lotta Loving	Fats Domino	Imperial	9		G
8	-	Donna	Ritchie Valens	Del-Fi	14	(29)	F G L
9	-	16 Candles	Crests	Coed	11		F G
10	3	One Night	Elvis Presley	RCA	11	(1)	
11	4	Problems	Everly Brothers	Cadence	9	(6)	G
12	-	Lonely Teardrops	Jackie Wilson	Brunswick	11		F G
13	6	Lonesome Town	Ricky Nelson	Imperial	14		
14	-	Stagger Lee	Lloyd Price	ABC Paramount	12	(7)	F G
15	2	Tom Dooley	Kingston Trio	Capitol	15	(5)	F G
16	-	Goodbye Baby	Jack Scott	Carlton	7		
17	15	Bimbombey	Jimmie Rodgers	Roulette	7		L
18	5	Beep Beep	Playmates	Roulette	11		G
19	-	Manhattan Spiritual	Reg Owen	Palette	7	(20)	F L
20	-	All American Boy	Bill Parsons	Fraternity	9	(22)	F L

February 1959

This Mnth	Prev Mnth	Title	Artist	Label	Wks 20	(UK Pos)	
1	14	Stagger Lee	Lloyd Price	ABC Paramount	12	(7)	F G
2	8	Donna	Ritchie Valens	Del-Fi	14	(29)	F G L
3	9	16 Candles	Crests	Coed	11		F G
4	20	All American Boy	Bill Parsons	Fraternity	9	(22)	F L
5	1	Smoke Gets In Your Eyes	Platters	Mercury	13	(1)	G
6	2	My Happiness	Connie Francis	MGM	11	(4)	G
7	12	Lonely Teardrops	Jackie Wilson	Brunswick	11		F G
8	4	Gotta Travel On	Billy Grammer	Monument	12		F G L
9	16	Goodbye Baby	Jack Scott	Carlton	7		
10	19	Manhattan Spiritual	Reg Owen	Palette	7	(20)	F L
11	-	Tall Paul	Annette	Disneyland	8		F
12	-	I Cried A Tear	Lavern Baker	Atlantic	9		G L
13	-	Hawaiian Wedding Song	Andy Williams	Cadence	10		
14	5	A Lover's Question	Clyde McPhatter	Atlantic	14		G
15	-	Peter Gunn	Ray Anthony	Capitol	9		L
16	-	Petite Fleur (Little Flower)	Chris Barber Jazz Band	Laurie	6	(3)	F G L
17	-	Charlie Brown	Coasters	Atco	10	(6)	G
18	-	The Children's Marching Song (Nick Nack Paddy Wack)	Cyril Stapleton	London	4		F L
19	-	(All Of A Sudden) My Heart Sings	Paul Anka	ABC Paramount	5	(10)	
20	-	The Children's Marching Song	Mitch Miller	Columbia	5		L

March 1959

This Mnth	Prev Mnth	Title	Artist	Label	Wks 20	(UK Pos)	
1	-	Venus	Frankie Avalon	Chancellor	11	(16)	G
2	17	Charlie Brown	Coasters	Atco	10	(6)	G
3	-	Alvin's Harmonica	Chipmunks	Liberty	7		G
4	1	Stagger Lee	Lloyd Price	ABC Paramount	12	(7)	F G
5	-	It's Just A Matter Of Time	Brook Benton	Mercury	9		F G
6	2	Donna	Ritchie Valens	Del-Fi	14	(29)	F G L
7	-	I've Had It	Bell Notes	Time	8		F L
8	-	Tragedy	Thomas Wayne	Fernwood	8		F L
9	16	Petite Fleur (Little Flower)	Chris Barber Jazz Band	Laurie	6	(3)	F G L
10	12	I Cried A Tear	Lavern Baker	Atlantic	9		G L
11	15	Peter Gunn	Ray Anthony	Capitol	9		L
12	-	Never Be Anyone Else But You	Ricky Nelson	Imperial	9	(14)	
13	-	Come Softly To Me	Fleetwoods	Dolphin	10	(6)	F G
14	13	Hawaiian Wedding Song	Andy Williams	Cadence	10		
15	3	16 Candles	Crests	Coed	11		F G
16	11	Tall Paul	Annette	Disneyland	8		F
17	-	Pink Shoe Laces	Dodie Stevens	Crystalette	12		F G L
18	4	All American Boy	Bill Parsons	Fraternity	9	(22)	F L
19	-	It's Late	Ricky Nelson	Imperial	6	(3)	G
20	-	Please Mr. Sun	Tommy Edwards	MGM	3		

▲ Berry Gordy, composer of several of Jackie Wilson's (above) hits including his current R&B No. 1, 'Lonely Teardrops', launched his own label Tamla with 'Come To Me' by Marv Johnson.

◆ The plane crash that killed Buddy Holly, Ritchie Valens and The Big Bopper which merited front page stories in Britain received less coverage Stateside. Interestingly, of the three stars, only Holly did not have one of his songs in the British Top 20 on the day he (and the music?) died.

UK 1959 APR-JUNE

▲ American rockers faring better in Britain included Little Richard, Eddie Cochran (above, whose 'C'mon Everybody' revisited the UK Top 20 in 1988) and the late Buddy Holly, whose 'It Doesn't Matter Anymore' topped the chart.

◆ As an anglicized version of the American TV show, *Juke Box Jury*, debuted on British TV, *Your Hit Parade* (which took a MOR-slanted look at current hits) ended its record run in America – it had started 29 years earlier on radio.

April 1959

This Mnth	Prev Mnth	Title	Artist	Label	Wks 20	(US Pos)	
1	3	Side Saddle	Russ Conway	Columbia	25		
2	11	It Doesn't Matter Anymore	Buddy Holly	Coral	21	(13)	
3	1	Smoke Gets In Your Eyes	Platters	Mercury	19	(1)	
4	5	Petite Fleur	Chris Barber's Jazz Band	Pye Nixa	18	(5)	F L
5	6	My Happiness	Connie Francis	MGM	13		
6	9	Stagger Lee	Lloyd Price	HMV	11	(1)	F
7	-	Donna	Marty Wilde	Philips	11		
8	2	As I Love You	Shirley Bassey	Philips	16		
9	13	Gigi	Billy Eckstine	Mercury	12		
10	-	Charlie Brown	Coasters	London American	11	(2)	
11	4	A Pub With No Beer	Slim Dusty	Columbia	13		F L
12	17	C'mon Everybody	Eddie Cochran	London American	10	(35)	
13	15	Tomboy	Perry Como	RCA	10	(29)	
14	7	The Little Drummer Boy	Beverley Sisters	Decca	11		
15	-	Wait For Me	Malcolm Vaughan	HMV	8		L
16	-	Sing Little Birdie	Pearl Carr & Teddy Johnson	Columbia	5		F
17	-	A Fool Such As I/ I Need Your Love Tonight	Elvis Presley	RCA	14	(2)	
18	8	Does Your Chewing Gum Lose It's Flavour	Lonnie Donegan	Pye Nixa	11	(5)	
19	-	By The Light Of The Silvery Moon	Little Richard	London American	3		
20	10	(All Of A Sudden) My Heart Sings	Paul Anka	Columbia	12	(15)	

May 1959

This Mnth	Prev Mnth	Title	Artist	Label	Wks 20	(US Pos)	
1	17	A Fool Such As I/ I Need Your Love Tonight	Elvis Presley	RCA	14	(2)	
2	2	It Doesn't Matter Anymore	Buddy Holly	Coral	21	(13)	
3	1	Side Saddle	Russ Conway	Columbia	25		
4	7	Donna	Marty Wilde	Philips	11		
5	-	It's Late	Ricky Nelson	London American	18	(9)	
6	4	Petite Fleur	Chris Barber's Jazz Band	Pye Nixa	18	(5)	F L
7	-	I've Waited So Long	Anthony Newley	Decca	13		
8	-	Come Softly To Me	Fleetwoods	London American	8	(1)	F L
9	10	Charlie Brown	Coasters	London American	11	(2)	
10	-	Come Softly To Me	Frankie Vaughan/Kaye Sisters	Philips	8		
11	-	I Go Ape	Neil Sedaka	RCA	10	(42)	F
12	-	Mean Streak	Cliff Richard	Columbia	8		
13	3	Smoke Gets In Your Eyes	Platters	Mercury	19	(1)	
14	12	C'mon Everybody	Eddie Cochran	London American	10	(35)	
15	-	Fort Worth Jail	Lonnie Donegan	Pye Nixa	4		
16	-	Roulette	Russ Conway	Columbia	18		
17	-	Guitar Boogie Shuffle	Bert Weedon	Top Rank	8		F L
18	-	May You Always	McGuire Sisters	Coral	5	(11)	L
19	-	Idle On Parade (EP)	Anthony Newley	Decca	2		F
20	6	Stagger Lee	Lloyd Price	HMV	11	(1)	F

June 1959

This Mnth	Prev Mnth	Title	Artist	Label	Wks 20	(US Pos)	
1	1	A Fool Such As I/ I Need Your Love Tonight	Elvis Presley	RCA	14	(2)	
2	16	Roulette	Russ Conway	Columbia	18		
3	2	It Doesn't Matter Anymore	Buddy Holly	Coral	21	(13)	
4	7	I've Waited So Long	Anthony Newley	Decca	13		
5	5	It's Late	Ricky Nelson	London American	18	(9)	
6	-	Dream Lover	Bobby Darin	London American	17	(2)	
7	3	Side Saddle	Russ Conway	Columbia	25		
8	-	A Teenager In Love	Marty Wilde	Philips	13		
9	17	Guitar Boogie Shuffle	Bert Weedon	Top Rank	8		F L
10	12	Mean Streak	Cliff Richard	Columbia	8		
11	11	I Go Ape	Neil Sedaka	RCA	10	(42)	F
12	-	May You Always	Joan Regan	HMV	10		L
13	6	Petite Fleur	Chris Barber's Jazz Band	Pye Nixa	18	(5)	F L
14	4	Donna	Marty Wilde	Philips	11		
15	10	Come Softly To Me	Frankie Vaughan/Kaye Sisters	Philips	8		
16	-	Peter Gunn Theme	Duane Eddy	London American	10	(27)	
17	8	Come Softly To Me	Fleetwoods	London American	8	(1)	F L
18	-	Battle Of New Orleans	Lonnie Donegan	Pye	14		
19	9	Charlie Brown	Coasters	London American	11	(2)	
20	-	A Teenager In Love	Craig Douglas	Top Rank	8		F

April 1959

This Mnth	Prev Mnth	Title	Artist	Label	Wks 20	(UK Pos)	
1	13	Come Softly To Me	Fleetwoods	Dolphin	10	(6)	F G
2	1	Venus	Frankie Avalon	Chancellor	11	(16)	G
3	17	Pink Shoe Laces	Dodie Stevens	Crystalette	12		F G L
4	-	A Fool Such As I	Elvis Presley	RCA	9	(1)	G
5	12	Never Be Anyone Else But You	Ricky Nelson	Imperial	9	(14)	
6	-	Guitar Boogie Shuffle	Virtues	Hunt	9		F L
7	-	I Need Your Love Tonight	Elvis Presley	RCA	8	(1)	
8	5	It's Just A Matter Of Time	Brook Benton	Mercury	9		F G
9	8	Tragedy	Thomas Wayne	Fernwood	8		F L
10	19	It's Late	Ricky Nelson	Imperial	6	(3)	G
11	2	Charlie Brown	Coasters	Atco	10	(6)	G
12	-	The Happy Organ	Dave 'Baby' Cortez	Clock	10		F G
13	-	Since I Don't Have You	Skyliners	Calico	6		F L
14	-	Tell Him No	Travis & Bob	Sandy	6		F L
15	-	Tijuana Jail	Kingston Trio	Capitol	5		
16	-	Sea Cruise	Frankie Ford	Ace	5		F L
17	-	Turn Me Loose	Fabian	Chancellor	8		F
18	3	Alvin's Harmonica	Chipmunks	Liberty	7		G
19	-	Sorry (I Ran All The Way Home)	Impalas	Cub	9	(28)	F G L
20	7	I've Had It	Bell Notes	Time	8		F L

May 1959

This Mnth	Prev Mnth	Title	Artist	Label	Wks 20	(UK Pos)	
1	19	Sorry (I Ran All The Way Home)	Impalas	Cub	9	(28)	F G L
2	12	The Happy Organ	Dave 'Baby' Cortez	Clock	10		F G
3	-	Kansas City	Wilbert Harrison	Fury	10		F G L
4	-	Kookie, Kookie (Lend Me Your Comb)	Edward Byrnes & Connie Stevens	Warner	8	(27)	F G L
5	4	A Fool Such As I	Elvis Presley	RCA	9	(1)	G
6	3	Pink Shoe Laces	Dodie Stevens	Crystalette	12		F G L
7	6	Guitar Boogie Shuffle	Virtues	Hunt	9		F L
8	1	Come Softly To Me	Fleetwoods	Dolphin	10	(6)	F G
9	17	Turn Me Loose	Fabian	Chancellor	8		F
10	-	A Teenager In Love	Dion & The Belmonts	Laurie	10	(28)	F G L
11	-	Dream Lover	Bobby Darin	Atco	11	(1)	G
12	-	The Battle Of New Orleans	Johnny Horton	Columbia	14	(16)	F G
13	7	I Need Your Love Tonight	Elvis Presley	RCA	8	(1)	
14	-	Quiet Village	Martin Denny	Liberty	9		F G L
15	-	Enchanted	Platters	Mercury	7		
16	14	Tell Him No	Travis & Bob	Sandy	6		F L
17	2	Venus	Frankie Avalon	Chancellor	11	(16)	G
18	-	Only You	Frank Pourcel's French Fiddles	Capitol	7		F L
19	-	Three Stars	Tommy Dee	Crest	4		F L
20	-	Take A Message To Mary	Everly Brothers	Cadence	5	(20)	

June 1959

This Mnth	Prev Mnth	Title	Artist	Label	Wks 20	(UK Pos)	
1	12	The Battle Of New Orleans	Johnny Horton	Columbia	14	(16)	F G
2	-	Personality	Lloyd Price	ABC Paramount	11	(9)	G
3	11	Dream Lover	Bobby Darin	Atco	11	(1)	G
4	3	Kansas City	Wilbert Harrison	Fury	10		F G L
5	14	Quiet Village	Martin Denny	Liberty	9		F G L
6	10	A Teenager In Love	Dion & The Belmonts	Laurie	10	(28)	F G L
7	-	Tallahassee Lassie	Freddy Cannon	Swan	8	(17)	F G
8	-	Lonely Boy	Paul Anka	ABC Paramount	12	(3)	G
9	4	Kookie, Kookie (Lend Me Your Comb)	Edward Byrnes & Connie Stevens	Warner	8	(27)	F G L
10	18	Only You	Frank Pourcel's French Fiddles	Capitol	7		F L
11	-	Along Came Jones	Coasters	Atco	6		
12	-	Lipstick On Your Collar	Connie Francis	MGM	10	(3)	G
13	-	So Fine	Fiestas	Old Town	5		F L
14	2	The Happy Organ	Dave 'Baby' Cortez	Clock	10		F G
15	-	Frankie	Connie Francis	MGM	7		
16	1	Sorry (I Ran All The Way Home)	Impalas	Cub	9	(28)	F G L
17	-	Endlessly	Brook Benton	Mercury	5	(28)	
18	-	Goodbye Jimmy, Goodbye	Kathy Linden	Felsted	4		L
19	-	Bobby Sox To Stockings	Frankie Avalon	Chancellor	7		
20	-	I'm Ready	Fats Domino	Liberty	4		

◆ Stars who appeared in Alan Freed's final film, *Go, Johnny, Go*, included Chuck Berry, the late Ritchie Valens, Jackie Wilson and Jimmy Clanton.

◆ Dodie Stevens, who started recording when she was eight, turned 'Pink Shoe Laces' into gold, while fellow 13-year-old Dolly Parton's debut disc, 'Puppy Love' went unnoticed.

◆ As Chubby Checker's first single, 'The Class' charted, Hank Ballard's original recording of 'The Twist' hit the R&B Top 20. A year later Checker closely cloned Ballard's record and made musical history.

◆ Dick Clark announced the launch of a series of *Dick Clark Caravan of Stars* – the idea was that he would select acts for the shows but would not personally appear in them.

◆ The *Billboard* album chart was extended to a Top 50 for mono LPs, and a Top 30 stereo chart was introduced.

UK 1959

JULY-SEPT

◆ As Cliff Richard scored his first No. 1 with 'Living Doll', Duane Eddy hit with his version of 'Peter Gunn Theme' – in 1986 both artists returned to the Top 10 with re-recordings of these compositions.

◆ Mantovani, who had five albums on the US Top 30 stereo album chart, became the first British-based act to top the American LP chart when **Film Encores** moved into the top slot.

◆ Early stars appearing on Jack Good's new TV series, *Boy Meets Girls*, included American hit makers Johnny Cash, Sammy Turner, Jerry Keller and The Browns.

◆ Buddy Holly's ex-group, The Crickets, backed the Everly Brothers on their latest transatlantic hit, '('Til) I Kissed You'.

◆ To avoid confusion with US hit makers The Drifters, Cliff Richard's group changed their name to The Shadows.

July 1959

This Mnth	Prev Mnth	Title	Artist	Label	Wks 20	(US Pos)	
1	6	Dream Lover	Bobby Darin	London American	17	(2)	
2	18	Battle Of New Orleans	Lonnie Donegan	Pye	14		
3	8	A Teenager In Love	Marty Wilde	Philips	13		
4	2	Roulette	Russ Conway	Columbia	18		
5	16	Peter Gunn Theme	Duane Eddy	London American	10	(27)	
6	-	Personality	Anthony Newley	Decca	9		
7	-	Living Doll	Cliff Richard	Columbia	19	(30)	
8	1	A Fool Such As I/ I Need Your Love Tonight	Elvis Presley	RCA	14	(2)	
9	-	Goodbye Jimmy, Goodbye	Ruby Murray	Columbia	11		L
10	5	It's Late	Ricky Nelson	London American	18	(9)	
11	-	Lipstick On Your Collar	Connie Francis	MGM	15	(5)	
12	4	I've Waited So Long	Anthony Newley	Decca	13		
13	7	Side Saddle	Russ Conway	Columbia	25		
14	-	Personality	Lloyd Price	HMV	7	(2)	L
15	12	May You Always	Joan Regan	HMV	10		L
16	-	Big Hunk O' Love	Elvis Presley	RCA	8	(1)	
17	3	It Doesn't Matter Anymore	Buddy Holly	Coral	21	(13)	
18	20	A Teenager In Love	Craig Douglas	Top Rank	8		F
19	-	Poor Jenny	Everly Brothers	London American	7	(22)	
20	-	I Know	Perry Como	RCA	12	(47)	

August 1959

This Mnth	Prev Mnth	Title	Artist	Label	Wks 20	(US Pos)	
1	7	Living Doll	Cliff Richard	Columbia	19	(30)	
2	1	Dream Lover	Bobby Darin	London American	17	(2)	
3	2	Battle Of New Orleans	Lonnie Donegan	Pye	14		
4	11	Lipstick On Your Collar	Connie Francis	MGM	15	(5)	
5	-	Lonely Boy	Paul Anka	Columbia	13	(1)	
6	16	Big Hunk O' Love	Elvis Presley	RCA	8	(1)	
7	3	A Teenager In Love	Marty Wilde	Philips	13		
8	4	Roulette	Russ Conway	Columbia	18		
9	-	The Heart Of A Man	Frankie Vaughan	Philips	12		
10	-	Only Sixteen	Craig Douglas	Top Rank	14		
11	-	Someone	Johnny Mathis	Fontana	13	(35)	
12	6	Personality	Anthony Newley	Decca	9		
13	-	Ragtime Cowboy Joe	Chipmunks	London American	5	(16)	L
14	20	I Know	Perry Como	RCA	12	(47)	
15	5	Peter Gunn Theme	Duane Eddy	London American	10	(27)	
16	10	It's Late	Ricky Nelson	London American	18	(9)	
17	9	Goodbye Jimmy, Goodbye	Ruby Murray	Columbia	11		L
18	-	China Tea	Russ Conway	Columbia	10		
19	-	Tallahassee Lassie	Tommy Steele	Decca	3		
20	-	Mona Lisa	Conway Twitty	MGM	12	(29)	L

September 1959

This Mnth	Prev Mnth	Title	Artist	Label	Wks 20	(US Pos)	
1	10	Only Sixteen	Craig Douglas	Top Rank	14		
2	1	Living Doll	Cliff Richard	Columbia	19	(30)	
3	5	Lonely Boy	Paul Anka	Columbia	13	(1)	
4	-	Here Comes Summer	Jerry Keller	London American	12	(14)	F L
5	18	China Tea	Russ Conway	Columbia	10		
6	4	Lipstick On Your Collar	Connie Francis	MGM	15	(5)	
7	11	Someone	Johnny Mathis	Fontana	13	(35)	
8	20	Mona Lisa	Conway Twitty	MGM	12	(29)	L
9	9	The Heart Of A Man	Frankie Vaughan	Philips	12		
10	3	Battle Of New Orleans	Lonnie Donegan	Pye	14		
11	2	Dream Lover	Bobby Darin	London American	17	(2)	
12	-	40 Miles Of Bad Road	Duane Eddy	London American	9	(9)	
13	-	('Til) I Kissed You	Everly Brothers	London American	14	(4)	
14	-	Just A Little Too Much	Ricky Nelson	London American	8	(9)	
15	-	Sal's Got A Sugar Lip	Lonnie Donegan	Pye	3		
16	14	I Know	Perry Como	RCA	12	(47)	
17	6	Big Hunk O' Love	Elvis Presley	RCA	8	(1)	
18	-	The Three Bells	Browns	RCA	11	(1)	F L
19	-	High Hopes	Frank Sinatra	Capitol	12	(30)	
20	8	Roulette	Russ Conway	Columbia	18		

July 1959

This Mnth	Prev Mnth	Title	Artist	Label	Wks 20	(UK Pos)	
1	8	Lonely Boy	Paul Anka	ABC Paramount	12	(3)	G
2	1	The Battle Of New Orleans	Johnny Horton	Columbia	14	(16)	F G
3	-	Waterloo	Stonewall Jackson	Columbia	9		F G L
4	2	Personality	Lloyd Price	ABC Paramount	11	(9)	G
5	-	Tiger	Fabian	Chancellor	8		G
6	12	Lipstick On Your Collar	Connie Francis	MGM	10	(3)	G
7	-	My Heart Is An Open Book	Carl Dobkins Jr.	Decca	11		F G L
8	3	Dream Lover	Bobby Darin	Atco	11	(1)	G
9	7	Tallahassee Lassie	Freddy Cannon	Swan	8	(17)	F G
10	19	Bobby Sox To Stockings	Frankie Avalon	Chancellor	7		
11	-	A Boy Without A Girl	Frankie Avalon	Chancellor	5		
12	-	I Only Have Eyes For You	Flamingos	End	7		F L
13	-	Forty Miles Of Bad Road	Duane Eddy	Jamie	7	(11)	
14	-	Big Hunk O' Love	Elvis Presley	RCA	9	(4)	G
15	15	Frankie	Connie Francis	MGM	7		
16	-	There Goes My Baby	Drifters	Atlantic	10		F G
17	11	Along Came Jones	Coasters	Atco	6		
18	-	M.T.A.	Kingston Trio	Capitol	4		
19	-	Just A Little Too Much	Ricky Nelson	Imperial	4	(11)	
20	-	Lavender-Blue	Sammy Turner	Big Top	8		F

August 1959

This Mnth	Prev Mnth	Title	Artist	Label	Wks 20	(UK Pos)	
1	14	Big Hunk O' Love	Elvis Presley	RCA	9	(4)	G
2	20	Lavender-Blue	Sammy Turner	Big Top	8		F
3	7	My Heart Is An Open Book	Carl Dobkins Jr.	Decca	11		F G L
4	16	There Goes My Baby	Drifters	Atlantic	10		F G
5	1	Lonely Boy	Paul Anka	ABC Paramount	12	(3)	G
6	-	What'd I Say (Pt. 1)	Ray Charles	Atlantic	7		F G
7	-	The Three Bells	Browns	RCA	12	(6)	F G
8	-	What A Difference A Day Makes	Dinah Washington	Mercury	8		F
9	-	Sea Of Love	Phil Phillips With The Twilights	Mercury	9		F G L
10	5	Tiger	Fabian	Chancellor	8		G
11	2	The Battle Of New Orleans	Johnny Horton	Columbia	14	(16)	F G
12	13	Forty Miles Of Bad Road	Duane Eddy	Jamie	7	(11)	
13	-	Sleep Walk	Santo & Johnny	Canadian American	11	(22)	F G L
14	3	Waterloo	Stonewall Jackson	Columbia	9		F G L
15	19	Just A Little Too Much	Ricky Nelson	Imperial	4	(11)	
16	-	It Was I	Skip & Flip	Brent	6		F
17	-	My Wish Came True	Elvis Presley	RCA	4		
18	-	I'm Gonna Get Married	Lloyd Price	ABC Paramount	10	(23)	G
19	-	Sweeter Than You	Ricky Nelson	Imperial	5	(19)	
20	-	I Want To Walk You Home	Fats Domino	Imperial	7	(14)	

September 1959

This Mnth	Prev Mnth	Title	Artist	Label	Wks 20	(UK Pos)	
1	13	Sleep Walk	Santo & Johnny	Canadian American	11	(22)	F G L
2	7	The Three Bells	Browns	RCA	12	(6)	F G
3	18	I'm Gonna Get Married	Lloyd Price	ABC Paramount	10	(23)	G
4	9	Sea Of Love	Phil Phillips With The Twilights	Mercury	9		F G L
5	-	('Til) I Kissed You	Everly Brothers	Cadence	11	(2)	
6	-	Red River Rock	Johnny & The Hurricanes	Warwick	10	(3)	F
7	-	Broken-Hearted Melody	Sarah Vaughan	Mercury	8	(7)	G L
8	-	Mack The Knife	Bobby Darin	Atco	19	(1)	G
9	20	I Want To Walk You Home	Fats Domino	Imperial	7	(14)	
10	-	Baby Talk	Jan & Dean	Dore	6		
11	-	Kissin' Time	Bobby Rydell	Cameo	5		F
12	-	Put Your Head On My Shoulder	Paul Anka	ABC Paramount	12	(7)	
13	-	Poison Ivy	Coasters	Atco	9	(15)	G L
14	2	Lavender-Blue	Sammy Turner	Big Top	8		F
15	6	What'd I Say (Pt. 1)	Ray Charles	Atlantic	7		F G
16	-	Teen Beat	Sandy Nelson	Original Sound	10	(9)	F G
17	4	There Goes My Baby	Drifters	Atlantic	10		F G
18	-	Just Ask Your Heart	Frankie Avalon	Chancellor	8		
19	-	Mr. Blue	Fleetwoods	Dolton	14		G
20	-	Morgen	Ivo Robic	Laurie	6	(23)	F L

◆ *Billboard* slated fears that rock'n'roll was ready for the rockin' chair', pointing out that 50% of hits were still rock-related.

▲ Soulful, gospel-influenced R&B was taking off. Examples included 'What'd I Say' by Ray Charles (above), 'There Goes My Baby' by The Drifters and 'Shout' by the Isley Brothers – all musical milestones.

◆ While he worked on his debut movie, *Hound Dog Man*, the much maligned teen idol, Fabian, had the biggest hit of his career with 'Tiger'. Incidentally, another teen star, Paul Anka, topped the chart with 'Lonely Boy' from his first film, *Girl's Town*.

UK 1959

OCT-DEC

◆ Elvis Presley (World's Outstanding Male), Connie Francis (World's Outstanding Female) and the Everly Brothers (World's Outstanding Group) were again the major winners in the *NME* Readers' Poll.

◆ Among the many other new groups in Britain were Johnny & The Moondogs (members included three Beatles) who reached the final in a TV *Star Search*.

▲ Transatlantic star Guy Mitchell, who had made his chart debut in 1950, ended the decade with the No. 1 single in America, 'Heartaches By The Number'.

October 1959

This Mnth	Prev Mnth	Title	Artist	Label	Wks 20	(US Pos)	
1	-	Mack The Knife	Bobby Darin	London American	14	(1)	
2	4	Here Comes Summer	Jerry Keller	London American	12	(14)	F L
3	13	('Til) I Kissed You	Everly Brothers	London American	14	(4)	
4	1	Only Sixteen	Craig Douglas	Top Rank	14		
5	2	Living Doll	Cliff Richard	Columbia	19	(30)	
6	18	The Three Bells	Browns	RCA	11	(1)	F L
7	-	Sea Of Love	Marty Wilde	Philips	11		
8	-	Travellin' Light	Cliff Richard	Columbia	16		
9	19	High Hopes	Frank Sinatra	Capitol	12	(30)	
10	-	Broken Hearted Melody	Sarah Vaughan	Mercury	12	(7)	F
11	8	Mona Lisa	Conway Twitty	MGM	12	(29)	L
12	7	Someone	Johnny Mathis	Fontana	13	(35)	
13	3	Lonely Boy	Paul Anka	Columbia	13	(1)	
14	5	China Tea	Russ Conway	Columbia	10		
15	14	Just A Little Too Much	Ricky Nelson	London American	8	(9)	
16	-	Red River Rock	Johnny & The Hurricanes	London American	13	(5)	F
17	12	40 Miles Of Bad Road	Duane Eddy	London American	9	(9)	
18	-	Peggy Sue Got Married	Buddy Holly	Coral	5		
19	-	Makin' Love	Floyd Robinson	RCA	7	(20)	F L
20	9	The Heart Of A Man	Frankie Vaughan	Philips	12		

November 1959

This Mnth	Prev Mnth	Title	Artist	Label	Wks 20	(US Pos)	
1	8	Travellin' Light	Cliff Richard	Columbia	16		
2	1	Mack The Knife	Bobby Darin	London American	14	(1)	
3	16	Red River Rock	Johnny & The Hurricanes	London American	13	(5)	F
4	-	What Do You Want To Make Those Eyes At Me For	Emile Ford & The Checkmates	Pye	18		F
5	3	('Til) I Kissed You	Everly Brothers	London American	14	(4)	
6	7	Sea Of Love	Marty Wilde	Philips	11		
7	-	Put Your Head On My Shoulder	Paul Anka	Columbia	10	(2)	
8	10	Broken Hearted Melody	Sarah Vaughan	Mercury	12	(7)	F
9	9	High Hopes	Frank Sinatra	Capitol	12	(30)	
10	6	The Three Bells	Browns	RCA	11	(1)	F L
11	19	Makin' Love	Floyd Robinson	RCA	7	(20)	F L
12	-	Oh! Carol	Neil Sedaka	RCA	14	(9)	
13	-	One More Sunrise (Morgen)	Dickie Valentine	Pye	7		L
14	-	Teen Beat	Sandy Nelson	Top Rank	8	(4)	F
15	-	What Do You Want	Adam Faith	Parlophone	15		F
16	2	Here Comes Summer	Jerry Keller	London American	12	(14)	F L
17	-	Mr. Blue	Mike Preston	Decca	5		F
18	-	Snow Coach	Russ Conway	Columbia	8		
19	11	Mona Lisa	Conway Twitty	MGM	12	(29)	L
20	4	Only Sixteen	Craig Douglas	Top Rank	14		

December 1959

This Mnth	Prev Mnth	Title	Artist	Label	Wks 20	(US Pos)	
1	15	What Do You Want	Adam Faith	Parlophone	15		F
2	4	What Do You Want To Make Those Eyes At Me For	Emile Ford & The Checkmates	Pye	18		F
3	12	Oh! Carol	Neil Sedaka	RCA	14	(9)	
4	1	Travellin' Light	Cliff Richard	Columbia	16		
5	-	Seven Little Girls Sitting In The Back Seat	Avons	Columbia	10		F L
6	3	Red River Rock	Johnny & The Hurricanes	London American	13	(5)	F
7	7	Put Your Head On My Shoulder	Paul Anka	Columbia	10	(2)	
8	18	Snow Coach	Russ Conway	Columbia	8		
9	-	Rawhide	Frankie Laine	Philips	13		L
10	-	More And More Party Pops	Russ Conway	Columbia	5		
11	2	Mack The Knife	Bobby Darin	London American	14	(1)	
12	-	Little White Bull	Tommy Steele	Decca	12		
13	-	Piano Party	Winifred Atwell	Decca	5		L
14	14	Teen Beat	Sandy Nelson	Top Rank	8	(4)	F
15	-	Among My Souvenirs	Connie Francis	MGM	6	(7)	
16	-	Staccato's Theme	Elmer Bernstein	Capitol	10		F L
17	-	Jingle Bell Rock	Max Bygraves	Decca	3		
18	5	('Til) I Kissed You	Everly Brothers	London American	14	(4)	
19	-	Little Donkey	Beverley Sisters	Decca	4		L
20	6	Sea Of Love	Marty Wilde	Philips	11		

US 1959 OCT-DEC

October 1959

This Mnth	Prev Mnth	Title	Artist	Label	Wks 20	(UK Pos)	
1	8	Mack The Knife	Bobby Darin	Atco	19	(1)	G
2	12	Put Your Head On My Shoulder	Paul Anka	ABC Paramount	12	(7)	
3	19	Mr. Blue	Fleetwoods	Dolton	14		G
4	16	Teen Beat	Sandy Nelson	Original Sound	10	(9)	F G
5	1	Sleep Walk	Santo & Johnny	Canadian American	11	(22)	F G L
6	5	('Til) I Kissed You	Everly Brothers	Cadence	11	(2)	
7	13	Poison Ivy	Coasters	Atco	9	(15)	G L
8	-	Lonely Street	Andy Williams	Cadence	10		
9	18	Just Ask Your Heart	Frankie Avalon	Chancellor	8		
10	2	The Three Bells	Browns	RCA	12	(6)	F G
11	-	Primrose Lane	Jerry Wallace	Challenge	11		G
12	6	Red River Rock	Johnny & The Hurricanes	Warwick	10	(3)	F
13	3	I'm Gonna Get Married	Lloyd Price	ABC Paramount	10	(23)	G
14	-	Don't You Know	Della Reese	RCA	10		F G
15	-	Deck Of Cards	Wink Martindale	Dot	9	(18)	F G L
16	-	Battle Hymn Of The Republic	Mormon Tabernacle Choir	Columbia	5		F L
17	4	Sea Of Love	Phil Phillips With The Twilights	Mercury	9		F G L
18	7	Broken-Hearted Melody	Sarah Vaughan	Mercury	8	(7)	G L
19	20	Morgen	Ivo Robic	Laurie	6	(23)	F L
20	-	The Battle Of Kookamonga	Homer & Jethro	RCA	5		F L

November 1959

This Mnth	Prev Mnth	Title	Artist	Label	Wks 20	(UK Pos)	
1	1	Mack The Knife	Bobby Darin	Atco	19	(1)	G
2	3	Mr. Blue	Fleetwoods	Dolton	14		G
3	14	Don't You Know	Della Reese	RCA	10		F G
4	2	Put Your Head On My Shoulder	Paul Anka	ABC Paramount	12	(7)	
5	-	Heartaches By The Number	Guy Mitchell	Columbia	12	(5)	G L
6	15	Deck Of Cards	Wink Martindale	Dot	9	(18)	F G L
7	8	Lonely Street	Andy Williams	Cadence	10		
8	-	So Many Ways	Brook Benton	Mercury	9		
9	-	In The Mood	Ernie Fields	Rendezvous	10	(13)	F L
10	4	Teen Beat	Sandy Nelson	Original Sound	10	(9)	F G
11	11	Primrose Lane	Jerry Wallace	Challenge	11		G
12	-	Seven Little Girls Sitting In The Back Seat	Paul Evans & The Curls	Guaranteed	7	(25)	F
13	-	We Got Love	Bobby Rydell	Cameo	9		
14	-	Danny Boy	Conway Twitty	MGM	7		
15	-	Be My Guest	Fats Domino	Imperial	5	(11)	
16	-	Oh! Carol	Neil Sedaka	RCA	8	(3)	
17	-	Misty	Johnny Mathis	Columbia	7	(12)	
18	9	Just Ask Your Heart	Frankie Avalon	Chancellor	8		
19	7	Poison Ivy	Coasters	Atco	9	(15)	G L
20	-	The Enchanted Sea	Islanders	Mayflower	3		F L

December 1959

This Mnth	Prev Mnth	Title	Artist	Label	Wks 20	(UK Pos)	
1	5	Heartaches By The Number	Guy Mitchell	Columbia	12	(5)	G L
2	1	Mack The Knife	Bobby Darin	Atco	19	(1)	G
3	-	Why	Frankie Avalon	Chancellor	10	(20)	G L
4	-	El Paso	Marty Robbins	Columbia	12	(19)	G
5	13	We Got Love	Bobby Rydell	Cameo	9		
6	-	The Big Hurt	Miss Toni Fisher	Signet	12	(30)	F L
7	-	It's Time To Cry	Paul Anka	ABC Paramount	9	(28)	
8	9	In The Mood	Ernie Fields	Rendezvous	10	(13)	F L
9	2	Mr. Blue	Fleetwoods	Dolton	14		G
10	-	Way Down Yonder In New Orleans	Freddy Cannon	Swan	9	(3)	G
11	3	Don't You Know	Della Reese	RCA	10		F G
12	8	So Many Ways	Brook Benton	Mercury	9		
13	-	Hound Dog Man	Fabian	Chancellor	7		L
14	-	Among My Souvenirs	Connie Francis	MGM	6	(11)	G
15	16	Oh! Carol	Neil Sedaka	RCA	8	(3)	
16	-	Scarlet Ribbons	Browns	RCA	5		
17	15	Be My Guest	Fats Domino	Imperial	5	(11)	
18	-	Uh! Oh! Part 2	Nutty Squirrels	Hanover	5		F L
19	-	Pretty Blue Eyes	Steve Lawrence	ABC Paramount	11		
20	14	Danny Boy	Conway Twitty	MGM	7		

◆ Bobby Darin's transatlantic No. 1 'Mack The Knife' won the Grammy for Best Record of 1959 despite being banned by some stations who felt it might encourage gang warfare.

◆ The biggest group to sing on a Top 20 record were the 375 voiced Mormon Tabernacle Choir with their stirring version of the 97-year-old American fave 'Battle Hymn Of The Republic'.

◆ The US government stepped up its probe into payola (DJs receiving payments for playing records). Rock 'n' roll's No. 1 DJ, Alan Freed, was to become the main scapegoat.

◆ RCA Records offered Sam Cooke $100,000 to sign with them. The soulful singer/songwriter who had earlier topped the chart with 'You Send Me' would receive more than twice the amount they had paid for Elvis Presley.

60s

Duane Eddy

Nancy Sinatra

The Beach Boys

By the dawn of the 1960s, raw rock'n' roll had almost been disowned by the R&B and C&W markets. Rock'n'roll, which initially looked set to overthrow popular music, had been absorbed into the mainstream, tamed and tainted by many less revolutionary styles of music, evolving into 'Teen Beat', a watered-down and clean-cut off-spring. Thankfully, R&B, which by its very nature was more vibrant and less controllable, continued to produce sounds that appealed to both black and white teenagers.

The Beatles

Elvis Presley

Top UK Artists in US 1960-69	
1	Beatles
2	Rolling Stones
3	Herman's Hermits
4	Dave Clark Five
5	Petula Clark
6	Eric Burdon & The Animals
7	Donovan
8	Peter & Gordon
9	Tom Jones
10	Bee Gees

Top US Artists in UK 1960-69	
1	Elvis Presley
2	Roy Orbison
3	Everly Brothers
4	Beach Boys
5	Supremes
6	Gene Pitney
7	Jim Reeves
8	Del Shannon
9	Brenda Lee
10	Duane Eddy

60s

Many British record buyers in the early 1960s still loved basic rock'n'roll, while others avidly collected rhythm and blues from the 1950s and 1960s. Musicians naturally tried to emulate the music they liked best, which gave birth to Merseybeat and the British R&B boom. In 1964, America too succumbed to Britain's foremost exponents of Merseybeat, The Beatles, after which many other British acts followed in their wake. The British invaders, however, were not all as original as The Beatles, and many simply revived or covered black American R&B songs, in the way that white US pop stars had ten years earlier.

Sonny and Cher

The result of this was that for a while American artists seemed to play second fiddle, but by 1966, they were back in the spotlight, albeit sharing it with their British counterparts.

By 1967, the single had relinquished its crown to the album as rock musicians began taking themselves and their music more seriously. Many experimented with their music and rock's horizons regularly widened to encompass hybrids that a while earlier would have seemed unbelievable. It was the decade of The Beatles, The Rolling Stones, Motown's hit machine, Bob Dylan and countless other performers who shaped much of the music that followed, and laid the ground-rules for rock in the last three decades of the century.

The Isleys

Musical trends were plentiful in the swinging sixties. Among them were the twist, surf music, folk, soul, bubblegum, psychedelia and numerous other, often tenuously rock related, forms of music. MOR (middle-of-the-road) music also thrived, and for every successful progressive rock band there were a handful of straight-ahead, pretension-free pop acts – many gaining a degree of popularity only dreamed of by their more adventurous and better respected brothers.

Roy Orbison

The sixties is a decade that has improved with age – without doubt an exciting musical era unlike any that had preceded it, but one that has greatly benefited from hindsight, and which has gained a reverence that, arguably, it did not fully earn.

The Shangri-Las

The Rolling Stones

The Monkees

Chubby Checker

Top Singles Artists In The US 1960-69

1	Beatles	(UK)	Capitol/Apple
2	Elvis Presley	(US)	RCA
3	Supremes	(US)	Motown
4	Four Seasons	(US)	Vee Jay/Philips
5	Beach Boys	(US)	Capitol
6	Rolling Stones	(UK)	London
7	Brenda Lee	(US)	Decca
8	Temptations	(US)	Gordy
9	Herman's Hermits	(UK)	MGM
10	Chubby Checker	(US)	Parkway
11	Connie Francis	(US)	MGM
12	Bobby Vinton	(US)	Epic
13	Ray Charles	(US)	ABC Paramount
14	Dave Clark Five	(UK)	Epic
15	Marvin Gaye	(US)	Tamla
16	Monkees	(US)	Colgems
17	Aretha Franklin	(US)	Atlantic
18	Stevie Wonder	(US)	Tamla
19	Roy Orbison	(US)	Monument
20	Dion	(US)	Laurie/Columbia

Top Singles Artists In The UK 1960-69

1	Cliff Richard	(UK)	Columbia
2	Beatles	(UK)	Parlophone/Apple
3	Elvis Presley	(US)	RCA
4	Shadows	(UK)	Columbia
5	Rolling Stones	(UK)	Decca
6	Hollies	(UK)	Parlophone
7	Manfred Mann	(UK)	HMV/Fontana
8	Roy Orbison	(US)	London American
9	Adam Faith	(UK)	Parlophone
10	Kinks	(UK)	Pye
11	Everly Brothers	(US)	London/Warner
12	Tom Jones	(UK)	Decca
13	Billy Fury	(UK)	Decca
14	Beach Boys	(US)	Capitol
15	Herman's Hermits	(UK)	Columbia
16	Cilla Black	(UK)	Parlophone
17	Engelbert Humperdinck	(UK)	Decca
18	Supremes	(US)	Tamla Motown
19	Dusty Springfield	(UK)	Philips
20	Searchers	(UK)	Pye

Top US Singles 1960-69

1	The Twist	Chubby Checker
2	Hey Jude	Beatles
3	Theme From 'A Summer Place'	Percy Faith
4	Tossin' And Turnin'	Bobby Lewis
5	I Want To Hold Your Hand	Beatles
6	I'm A Believer	Monkees
7	I Heard It Through The Grapevine	Marvin Gaye
8	Aquarius/Let The Sunshine In	Fifth Dimension
9	Are You Lonesome Tonight?	Elvis Presley
10	It's Now Or Never	Elvis Presley

The Supremes

Top UK Singles 1960-69

1	She Loves You	Beatles
2	Wonderful Land	Shadows
3	I Remember You	Frank Ifield
4	Sugar Sugar	Archies
5	It's Now Or Never	Elvis Presley
6	Cathy's Clown	Everly Brothers
7	You've Lost That Lovin' Feeling	Righteous Brothers
8	Tears	Ken Dodd
9	Green Green Grass Of Home	Tom Jones
10	Telstar	Tornados

UK 1960 JAN-MAR

◆ American rockers Eddie Cochran and Gene Vincent successfully toured the UK and Britain's Cliff Richard joined *Dick Clark Caravan Of Stars* in America.

◆ Elvis Presley set foot in Britain for the only time when changing planes in Scotland on his way back to the US from Germany to be demobbed. On his return to the US he was rushed into the studios for his first recording session in two years.

▲ British teen idol Adam Faith scored his second successive No. 1 single.

◆ *Record Retailer* introduced Britain's first Top 50 single and Top 20 album charts.

January 1960

This Mnth	Prev Mnth	Title	Artist	Label	Wks 20	(US Pos)	
1	2	What Do You Want To Make Those Eyes At Me For	Emile Ford & The Checkmates	Pye	18		F
2	1	What Do You Want	Adam Faith	Parlophone	15		F
3	3	Oh! Carol	Neil Sedaka	RCA	14	(9)	
4	16	Staccato's Theme	Elmer Bernstein	Capitol	10		F L
5	5	Seven Little Girls Sitting In The Back Seat	Avons	Columbia	10		F L
6	12	Little White Bull	Tommy Steele	Decca	12		
7	-	Starry Eyed	Michael Holliday	Columbia	9		L
8	9	Rawhide	Frankie Laine	Philips	13		L
9	-	Why	Anthony Newley	Decca	12		
10	-	Way Down Yonder In New Orleans	Freddy Cannon	Top Rank	11	(3)	
11	-	Heartaches By The Number	Guy Mitchell	Philips	9	(1)	L
12	-	Bad Boy	Marty Wilde	Philips	7	(45)	
13	6	Travellin' Light	Cliff Richard	Columbia	16		
14	-	Be My Guest	Fats Domino	London American	7	(8)	
15	-	Voice In The Wilderness	Cliff Richard	Columbia	10		
16	-	In The Mood	Ernie Fields	London American	5	(4)	F L
17	-	Some Kind-A Earthquake	Duane Eddy	London American	5	(37)	
18	15	Among My Souvenirs	Connie Francis	MGM	6	(7)	
19	-	Reveille Rock	Johnny & The Hurricanes	London American	4	(25)	
20	10	More And More Party Pops	Russ Conway	Columbia	5		

February 1960

This Mnth	Prev Mnth	Title	Artist	Label	Wks 20	(US Pos)	
1	9	Why	Anthony Newley	Decca	12		
2	15	Voice In The Wilderness	Cliff Richard	Columbia	10		
3	10	Way Down Yonder In New Orleans	Freddy Cannon	Top Rank	11	(3)	
4	-	Poor Me	Adam Faith	Parlophone	11		
5	7	Starry Eyed	Michael Holliday	Columbia	9		L
6	-	Pretty Blue Eyes	Craig Douglas	Top Rank	8		
7	-	On A Slow Boat To China	Emile Ford	Pye	9		
8	1	What Do You Want To Make Those Eyes At Me For	Emile Ford & The Checkmates	Pye	18		F
9	-	Beyond The Sea (La Mer)	Bobby Darin	London American	6	(6)	
10	11	Heartaches By The Number	Guy Mitchell	Philips	9	(1)	L
11	-	Running Bear	Johnny Preston	Mercury	12	(1)	F
12	-	Summer Set	Acker Bilk	Columbia	10		F
13	-	Misty	Johnny Mathis	Fontana	6	(12)	
14	2	What Do You Want	Adam Faith	Parlophone	15		F
15	-	Harbour Lights	Platters	Mercury	7	(8)	L
16	4	Staccato's Theme	Elmer Bernstein	Capitol	10		F L
17	6	Little White Bull	Tommy Steele	Decca	12		
18	-	You Got What It Takes	Marv Johnson	London American	10	(10)	F
19	8	Rawhide	Frankie Laine	Philips	13		L
20	3	Oh! Carol	Neil Sedaka	RCA	14	(9)	

March 1960

This Mnth	Prev Mnth	Title	Artist	Label	Wks 20	(US Pos)	
1	4	Poor Me	Adam Faith	Parlophone	11		
2	11	Running Bear	Johnny Preston	Mercury	12	(1)	F
3	-	Delaware	Perry Como	RCA	8	(22)	
4	1	Why	Anthony Newley	Decca	12		
5	7	On A Slow Boat To China	Emile Ford & The Checkmates	Pye	9		
6	18	You Got What It Takes	Marv Johnson	London American	10	(10)	F
7	-	Theme From 'A Summer Place'	Percy Faith	Philips	12	(1)	F L
8	12	Summer Set	Acker Bilk	Columbia	10		F
9	2	Voice In The Wilderness	Cliff Richard	Columbia	10		
10	-	What In The World's Come Over You	Jack Scott	Top Rank	7	(5)	L
11	3	Way Down Yonder In New Orleans	Freddy Cannon	Top Rank	11	(3)	
12	6	Pretty Blue Eyes	Craig Douglas	Top Rank	8		
13	-	Be Mine	Lance Fortune	Pye	7		F L
14	-	Fings Ain't What They Used T'be	Max Bygraves	Decca	10		
15	-	My Old Man's A Dustman	Lonnie Donegan	Pye	9		
16	-	Who Could Be Bluer	Jerry Lordan	Parlophone	5		F L
17	9	Beyond The Sea (La Mer)	Bobby Darin	London American	6	(6)	
18	-	Beatnik Fly	Johnny & The Hurricanes	London American	9	(15)	
19	-	Bonnie Came Back	Duane Eddy	London American	4	(26)	
20	-	Royal Event	Russ Conway	Columbia	3		

January 1960

This Mnth	Prev Mnth	Title	Artist	Label	Wks 20	(UK Pos)	
1	4	El Paso	Marty Robbins	Columbia	12	(19)	G
2	3	Why	Frankie Avalon	Chancellor	10	(20)	G L
3	-	Running Bear	Johnny Preston	Mercury	12	(1)	F G
4	6	The Big Hurt	Miss Toni Fisher	Signet	12	(30)	F L
5	10	Way Down Yonder In New Orleans	Freddy Cannon	Swan	9	(3)	G
6	-	Go Jimmy Go	Jimmy Clanton	Ace	8		
7	7	It's Time To Cry	Paul Anka	ABC Paramount	9	(28)	
8	19	Pretty Blue Eyes	Steve Lawrence	ABC Paramount	11		
9	14	Among My Souvenirs	Connie Francis	MGM	6	(11)	G
10	-	The Village Of St. Bernadette	Andy Williams	Cadence	7		
11	-	Teen Angel	Mark Dinning	MGM	11	(28)	F G L
12	1	Heartaches By The Number	Guy Mitchell	Columbia	12	(5)	G L
13	13	Hound Dog Man	Fabian	Chancellor	7		L
14	-	You Got What It Takes	Marv Johnson	UA	8	(5)	F
15	-	Where Or When	Dion & The Belmonts	Laurie	9		L
16	2	Mack The Knife	Bobby Darin	Atco	19	(1)	G
17	-	Sandy	Larry Hall	Strand	5		F L
18	5	We Got Love	Bobby Rydell	Cameo	9		
19	-	Not One Minute More	Della Reese	RCA	4		L
20	-	Smokie-Part 2	Bill Black's Combo	Hi	3		F

February 1960

1	11	Teen Angel	Mark Dinning	MGM	11	(28)	F G L
2	3	Running Bear	Johnny Preston	Mercury	12	(1)	F G
3	-	Handy Man	Jimmy Jones	Cub	12	(3)	F G
4	15	Where Or When	Dion & The Belmonts	Laurie	9		L
5	-	He'll Have To Go	Jim Reeves	RCA	16	(11)	G L
6	-	What In The World's Come Over You	Jack Scott	Top Rank	10	(6)	G L
7	-	Theme From 'A Summer Place'	Percy Faith	Columbia	15	(4)	G L
8	-	Lonely Blue Boy	Conway Twitty	MGM	6		L
9	-	Let It Be Me	Everly Brothers	Cadence	8	(18)	
10	1	El Paso	Marty Robbins	Columbia	12	(19)	G
11	-	Beyond The Sea	Bobby Darin	Atco	8	(8)	G
12	14	You Got What It Takes	Marv Johnson	UA	8	(5)	F
13	-	Down By The Station	Four Preps	Capitol	8		
14	6	Go Jimmy Go	Jimmy Clanton	Ace	8		
15	2	Why	Frankie Avalon	Chancellor	10	(20)	G L
16	8	Pretty Blue Eyes	Steve Lawrence	ABC Paramount	11		
17	-	Baby (You Got What It Takes)	Brook Benton & Dinah Washington	Mercury	10		G
18	-	Wild One	Bobby Rydell	Cameo	10	(12)	G
19	4	The Big Hurt	Miss Toni Fisher	Signet	12	(30)	F L
20	10	The Village Of St. Bernadette	Andy Williams	Cadence	7		

March 1960

1	7	Theme From 'A Summer Place'	Percy Faith	Columbia	15	(4)	G L
2	5	He'll Have To Go	Jim Reeves	RCA	16	(11)	G L
3	18	Wild One	Bobby Rydell	Cameo	10	(12)	G
4	3	Handy Man	Jimmy Jones	Cub	12	(3)	F G
5	17	Baby (You Got What It Takes)	Brook Benton & Dinah Washington	Mercury	10		G
6	6	What In The World's Come Over You	Jack Scott	Top Rank	10	(6)	G
7	-	Puppy Love	Paul Anka	ABC Paramount	9		G
8	-	Sweet Nothin's	Brenda Lee	Decca	11	(4)	F G
9	11	Beyond The Sea	Bobby Darin	Atco	8	(8)	G
10	-	Harbor Lights	Platters	Mercury	8	(11)	
11	1	Teen Angel	Mark Dinning	MGM	11	(28)	F G L
12	-	Forever	Little Dippers	University	6		F L
13	9	Let It Be Me	Everly Brothers	Cadence	8	(18)	
14	-	Lady Luck	Lloyd Price	ABC Paramount	7		
15	2	Running Bear	Johnny Preston	Mercury	12	(1)	F G
16	-	O Dio Mio	Annette	Vista	5		
17	-	Beatnik Fly	Johnny & The Hurricanes	Warwick	5	(8)	L
18	-	Mama	Connie Francis	MGM	5	(8)	G
19	4	Where Or When	Dion & The Belmonts	Laurie	9		F L
20	-	Midnite Special	Paul Evans	Guaranteed	4		

◆ The success of Mark Dinning's moving ballad, 'Teen Angel' (about a 16-year-old girl who was killed by a speeding locomotive) inspired many similar death-discs.

◆ The Grammy for Best Record Of 1960 went to Percy Faith's transatlantic success, 'Theme From A Summer Place', which topped the US chart for nine weeks.

◆ The Big Bopper (who was killed in the crash that took Buddy Holly's life), penned and sang background vocals on Johnny Preston's transatlantic smash 'Running Bear'.

◆ Jimmy Jones had a transatlantic smash with his own composition 'Handy Man'. He had originally recorded the song without success in 1956 with the group The Sparks Of Rhythm. The song returned to the Top 5 seventeen years later by James Taylor.

◆ The Everly Brothers initial release on Warner Brothers, their own composition 'Cathy's Clown', topped the chart on both sides of the Atlantic.

◆ Gene Vincent was injured and Eddie Cochran killed in a car crash in England. Cochran's first posthumous release, 'Three Steps To Heaven' topped the UK chart.

◆ The Silver Beetles (Beatles) toured Scotland as backing band to little heralded rocker Johnny Gentle, and appeared alongside Gerry & The Pacemakers at a gig on Merseyside.

◆ Singer/actor/songwriter Anthony Newley had his second successive UK No. 1, 'Do You Mind' – the record was also a minor US hit, as was a cover version by Andy Williams.

April 1960

This Mnth	Prev Mnth	Title	Artist	Label	Wks 20	(US Pos)	
1	15	My Old Man's A Dustman	Lonnie Donegan	Pye	9		
2	-	Fall In Love With You	Cliff Richard	Columbia	11		
3	-	Handy Man	Jimmy Jones	MGM	17	(2)	F
4	-	Do You Mind	Anthony Newley	Decca	12	(91)	
5	14	Fings Ain't What They Used T'Be	Max Bygraves	Decca	10		
6	-	Stuck On You	Elvis Presley	RCA	8	(1)	
7	7	Theme From 'A Summer Place'	Percy Faith	Philips	12	(1)	F L
8	2	Running Bear	Johnny Preston	Mercury	12	(1)	F
9	18	Beatnik Fly	Johnny & The Hurricanes	London American	9	(15)	
10	-	Someone Else's Baby	Adam Faith	Parlophone	10		
11	-	Cathy's Clown	Everly Brothers	Warner	14	(1)	
12	3	Delaware	Perry Como	RCA	8	(22)	
13	-	Wild One	Bobby Rydell	Columbia	8	(2)	F
14	6	You Got What It Takes	Marv Johnson	London American	10	(10)	F
15	-	Sweet Nothin's	Brenda Lee	Brunswick	13	(4)	F
16	10	What In The World's Come Over You	Jack Scott	Top Rank	7	(5)	L
17	-	Clementine	Bobby Darin	London American	6	(21)	
18	-	Standing On The Corner	King Brothers	Parlophone	6		
19	1	Poor Me	Adam Faith	Parlophone	11		
20	-	Footsteps	Steve Lawrence	HMV	10	(7)	F

May 1960

This Mnth	Prev Mnth	Title	Artist	Label	Wks 20	(US Pos)	
1	11	Cathy's Clown	Everly Brothers	Warner	14	(1)	
2	10	Someone Else's Baby	Adam Faith	Parlophone	10		
3	3	Handy Man	Jimmy Jones	MGM	17	(2)	F
4	4	Do You Mind	Anthony Newley	Decca	12	(91)	
5	15	Sweet Nothin's	Brenda Lee	Brunswick	13	(4)	F
6	-	Cradle Of Love	Johnny Preston	Mercury	11	(7)	
7	-	Shazam	Duane Eddy	London American	9	(45)	
8	2	Fall In Love With You	Cliff Richard	Columbia	11		
9	18	Standing On The Corner	King Brothers	Parlophone	6		
10	20	Footsteps	Steve Lawrence	HMV	10	(7)	F
11	6	Stuck On You	Elvis Presley	RCA	8	(1)	
12	-	Three Steps To Heaven	Eddie Cochran	London American	12		
13	-	Heart Of A Teenage Girl	Craig Douglas	Top Rank	5		
14	7	Theme From 'A Summer Place'	Percy Faith	Philips	12	(1)	F L
15	1	My Old Man's A Dustman	Lonnie Donegan	Pye	9		
16	-	Stairway To Heaven	Neil Sedaka	RCA	7	(9)	
17	5	Fings Ain't What They Used T'be	Max Bygraves	Decca	10		
18	-	Mama	Connie Francis	MGM	11	(8)	
19	9	Beatnik Fly	Johnny & The Hurricanes	London American	9	(15)	
20	-	Let The Little Girl Dance	Billy Bland	London American	3	(7)	F L

June 1960

This Mnth	Prev Mnth	Title	Artist	Label	Wks 20	(US Pos)	
1	1	Cathy's Clown	Everly Brothers	Warner	14	(1)	
2	6	Cradle Of Love	Johnny Preston	Mercury	11	(7)	
3	3	Handy Man	Jimmy Jones	MGM	17	(2)	F
4	12	Three Steps To Heaven	Eddie Cochran	London American	12		
5	5	Sweet Nothin's	Brenda Lee	Brunswick	13	(4)	F
6	-	Robot Man	Connie Francis	MGM	11		
7	-	I Wanna Go Home	Lonnie Donegan	Pye	9		
8	7	Shazam	Duane Eddy	London American	9	(45)	
9	18	Mama	Connie Francis	MGM	11	(8)	
10	2	Someone Else's Baby	Adam Faith	Parlophone	10		
11	-	Ain't Misbehavin'	Tommy Bruce & The Bruisers	Columbia	11		F L
12	-	Sixteen Reasons	Connie Stevens	Warner	7	(3)	F L
13	-	He'll Have To Go	Jim Reeves	RCA	6	(2)	F
14	16	Stairway To Heaven	Neil Sedaka	RCA	7	(9)	
15	10	Footsteps	Steve Lawrence	HMV	10	(7)	F
16	-	Good Timin'	Jimmy Jones	MGM	13	(3)	L
17	-	Down Yonder	Johnny & The Hurricanes	London American	5	(48)	
18	-	Lucky Five	Russ Conway	Columbia	4		
19	4	Do You Mind	Anthony Newley	Decca	12	(91)	
20	20	Let The Little Girl Dance	Billy Bland	London American	3	(7)	F L

April 1960

This Mnth	Prev Mnth	Title	Artist	Label	Wks 20	(UK Pos)	
1	1	Theme From 'A Summer Place'	Percy Faith	Columbia	15	(4)	G L
2	7	Puppy Love	Paul Anka	ABC Paramount	9		G
3	2	He'll Have To Go	Jim Reeves	RCA	16	(11)	G L
4	-	Greenfields	Brothers Four	Columbia	11	(26)	F G L
5	-	Sink The Bismarck	Johnny Horton	Columbia	10		
6	8	Sweet Nothin's	Brenda Lee	Decca	11	(4)	F G
7	3	Wild One	Bobby Rydell	Cameo	10	(12)	G
8	-	Sixteen Reasons	Connie Stevens	Warner	11	(11)	G L
9	-	Footsteps	Steve Lawrence	ABC Paramount	6	(7)	
10	18	Mama	Connie Francis	MGM	5	(8)	G
11	-	Stuck On You	Elvis Presley	RCA	11	(2)	G
12	-	I Love The Way You Love	Marv Johnson	UA	8	(28)	
13	-	White Silver Sands	Bill Black's Combo	Hi	9		G
14	-	The Old Lamplighter	Browns	RCA	8		L
15	5	Baby (You Got What It Takes)	Brook Benton & Dinah Washington	Mercury	10		G
16	10	Harbor Lights	Platters	Mercury	8	(11)	
17	-	Cradle Of Love	Johnny Preston	Mercury	9	(2)	
18	16	O Dio Mio	Annette	Vista	5		
19	-	Step By Step	Crests	Coed	6		
20	-	Night	Jackie Wilson	Brunswick	10		G

May 1960

This Mnth	Prev Mnth	Title	Artist	Label	Wks 20	(UK Pos)	
1	11	Stuck On You	Elvis Presley	RCA	11	(2)	G
2	4	Greenfields	Brothers Four	Columbia	11	(26)	F G L
3	-	Cathy's Clown	Everly Brothers	Warner	12	(1)	G
4	20	Night	Jackie Wilson	Brunswick	10		G
5	8	Sixteen Reasons	Connie Stevens	Warner	11	(11)	G L
6	17	Cradle Of Love	Johnny Preston	Mercury	9	(2)	
7	-	Good Timin'	Jimmy Jones	Cub	9	(1)	G L
8	-	Let The Little Girl Dance	Billy Bland	Old Town	8	(15)	F L
9	5	Sink The Bismarck	Johnny Horton	Columbia	10		
10	14	The Old Lamplighter	Browns	RCA	8		L
11	-	He'll Have To Stay	Jeanne Black	Capitol	7		F G L
12	-	Stairway To Heaven	Neil Sedaka	RCA	7	(12)	
13	-	Paper Roses	Anita Bryant	Carlton	9	(25)	F
14	-	Burning Bridges	Jack Scott	Top Rank	10		L
15	13	White Silver Sands	Bill Black's Combo	Hi	9		G
16	-	Cherry Pie	Skip & Flip	Brent	6		L
17	-	Love You So	Ron Holden	Donna	7		F L
18	12	I Love The Way You Love	Marv Johnson	UA	8	(28)	
19	6	Sweet Nothin's	Brenda Lee	Decca	11	(4)	F G
20	1	Theme From 'A Summer Place'	Percy Faith	Columbia	15	(4)	G L

June 1960

This Mnth	Prev Mnth	Title	Artist	Label	Wks 20	(UK Pos)	
1	3	Cathy's Clown	Everly Brothers	Warner	12	(1)	G
2	-	Everybody's Somebody's Fool	Connie Francis	MGM	12	(7)	G
3	14	Burning Bridges	Jack Scott	Top Rank	10		L
4	7	Good Timin'	Jimmy Jones	Cub	9	(1)	G L
5	13	Paper Roses	Anita Bryant	Carlton	9	(25)	F
6	-	Swingin' School	Bobby Rydell	Cameo	6		
7	17	Love You So	Ron Holden	Donna	7		F L
8	11	He'll Have To Stay	Jeanne Black	Capitol	7		F G L
9	1	Stuck On You	Elvis Presley	RCA	11	(2)	G
10	-	Alley-Oop	Hollywood Argyles	Lute	10		F G L
11	-	Because They're Young	Duane Eddy	Jamie	9	(2)	G
12	4	Night	Jackie Wilson	Brunswick	10		G
13	-	Happy-Go-Lucky-Me	Paul Evans	Guaranteed	6		L
14	-	My Home Town	Paul Anka	ABC Paramount	7		
15	-	A Rockin' Good Way	Dinah Washington & Brook Benton	Mercury	7		L
16	-	I'm Sorry	Brenda Lee	Decca	13	(10)	G
17	-	Young Emotions	Ricky Nelson	Imperial	6		
18	-	Wonderful World	Sam Cooke	Keen	7	(2)	
19	2	Greenfields	Brothers Four	Columbia	11	(26)	F G L
20	5	Sixteen Reasons	Connie Stevens	Warner	11	(11)	G L

◆ Before filming 'G.I. Blues', Elvis Presley appeared on a television special with Frank Sinatra, Dean Martin and Sammy Davis Jr. Elvis' label, RCA, announced that all singles starting with Presley's 'Stuck On You' would be issued in both mono and stereo.

▲ Tony Williams, who had sung lead on all of The Platters five million sellers, left to start a solo career. Neither Williams or The Platters achieved gold status again.

◆ Alan Freed was indicted for receiving $30,650 in payola – he pleaded not guilty. Dick Clark, however, admitted he had a financial interest in 27% of records heard on *American Bandstand*.

UK 1960 JULY-SEPT

◆ After several unsuccessful singles, Cliff Richard's backing group, The Shadows, had a No. 1 hit with 'Apache'. They also recorded one of the earliest video discs which was seen on European video juke boxes.

◆ When RCA refused to release Ray Peterson's US hit, 'Tell Laura I Love Her', EMI's cover version of the death disc by Ricky Valence rocketed to the top.

▲ Sam Cooke's current US hit, 'Wonderful World' (which he had written with Herb Alpert), was a transatlantic Top 10 hit for Herman's Hermits in in 1965, and became a major British hit by Cooke in 1986 (21 years after his death!)

July 1960

This Mnth	Prev Mnth	Title	Artist	Label	Wks 20	(US Pos)	
1	16	Good Timin'	Jimmy Jones	MGM	13	(3)	L
2	-	Please Don't Tease	Cliff Richard	Columbia	13		
3	11	Ain't Misbehavin'	Tommy Bruce & The Bruisers	Columbia	11		F L
4	-	Shakin' All Over	Johnny Kidd & The Pirates	HMV	12		F
5	-	What A Mouth	Tommy Steele	Decca	7		L
6	6	Robot Man	Connie Francis	MGM	11		
7	-	Made You	Adam Faith	Parlophone	7		
8	4	Three Steps To Heaven	Eddie Cochran	London American	12		
9	-	Angela Jones	Michael Cox	Triumph	7		F L
10	-	Look For A Star	Garry Mills	Top Rank	7	(26)	F L
11	1	Cathy's Clown	Everly Brothers	Warner	14	(1)	
12	-	When Will I Be Loved	Everly Brothers	London American	12	(8)	
13	9	Mama	Connie Francis	MGM	11	(8)	
14	-	When Johnny Comes Marching Home	Adam Faith	Parlophone	7		
15	7	I Wanna Go Home	Lonnie Donegan	Pye	9		
16	17	Down Yonder	Johnny & The Hurricanes	London American	5	(48)	
17	-	If She Should Come To You	Anthony Newley	Decca	9	(67)	
18	-	Itsy Bitsy Teenie Weenie Yellow Polka Dot Bikini	Brian Hyland	London American	9	(1)	F
19	2	Cradle Of Love	Johnny Preston	Mercury	11	(7)	
20	3	Handy Man	Jimmy Jones	MGM	17	(2)	F

August 1960

This Mnth	Prev Mnth	Title	Artist	Label	Wks 20	(US Pos)	
1	2	Please Don't Tease	Cliff Richard	Columbia	13		
2	-	Apache	Shadows	Columbia	15		F
3	-	A Mess Of Blues	Elvis Presley	RCA	14	(32)	
4	4	Shakin' All Over	Johnny Kidd & The Pirates	HMV	12		F
5	-	Because They're Young	Duane Eddy	London American	14	(4)	
6	12	When Will I Be Loved	Everly Brothers	London American	12	(8)	
7	1	Good Timin'	Jimmy Jones	MGM	13	(3)	L
8	17	If She Should Come To You	Anthony Newley	Decca	9	(67)	
9	-	Tie Me Kangaroo Down Sport	Rolf Harris	Columbia	8	(3)	F
10	18	Itsy Bitsy Teenie Weenie Yellow Polka Dot Bikini	Brian Hyland	London American	9	(1)	F
11	10	Look For A Star	Garry Mills	Top Rank	7	(26)	F L
12	-	I'm Sorry	Brenda Lee	Brunswick	8	(1)	
13	-	Paper Roses	Kaye Sisters	Philips	10		L
14	-	Girl Of My Best Friend	Elvis Presley	RCA	12		
15	3	Ain't Misbehavin'	Tommy Bruce & The Bruisers	Columbia	11		F L
16	-	As Long As He Needs Me	Shirley Bassey	Columbia	22		
17	-	Everybody's Somebody's Fool	Connie Francis	MGM	10	(1)	
18	6	Robot Man	Connie Francis	MGM	11		
19	-	Mais Oui	King Brothers	Parlophone	3		
20	14	When Johnny Comes Marching Home	Adam Faith	Parlophone	7		

September 1960

This Mnth	Prev Mnth	Title	Artist	Label	Wks 20	(US Pos)	
1	2	Apache	Shadows	Columbia	15		F
2	5	Because They're Young	Duane Eddy	London American	14	(4)	
3	-	Tell Laura I Love Her	Ricky Valance	Columbia	12		F L
4	3	A Mess Of Blues	Elvis Presley	RCA	14	(32)	
5	14	Girl Of My Best Friend	Elvis Presley	RCA	12		
6	-	Only The Lonely	Roy Orbison	London American	15	(2)	F
7	16	As Long As He Needs Me	Shirley Bassey	Columbia	22		
8	1	Please Don't Tease	Cliff Richard	Columbia	13		
9	17	Everybody's Somebody's Fool	Connie Francis	MGM	10	(1)	
10	6	When Will I Be Loved	Everly Brothers	London American	12	(8)	
11	-	How About That	Adam Faith	Parlophone	10		
12	13	Paper Roses	Kaye Sisters	Philips	10		L
13	-	Nine Times Out Of Ten	Cliff Richard	Columbia	8		
14	-	Love Is Like A Violin	Ken Dodd	Decca	7		F
15	8	If She Should Come To You	Anthony Newley	Decca	9	(67)	
16	-	Walk-Don't Run	Ventures	Top Rank	8	(2)	F
17	4	Shakin' All Over	Johnny Kidd & The Pirates	HMV	12		F
18	-	Walk Don't Run	John Barry Seven	Columbia	9		
19	12	I'm Sorry	Brenda Lee	Brunswick	8	(1)	
20	9	Tie Me Kangaroo Down Sport	Rolf Harris	Columbia	8	(3)	F

70

July 1960

This Mnth	Prev Mnth	Title	Artist	Label	Wks 20	(UK Pos)	
1	16	I'm Sorry	Brenda Lee	Decca	13	(10)	G
2	10	Alley-Oop	Hollywood Argyles	Lute	10		F G L
3	2	Everybody's Somebody's Fool	Connie Francis	MGM	12	(7)	G
4	-	Only The Lonely	Roy Orbison	Monument	10	(1)	F G
5	11	Because They're Young	Duane Eddy	Jamie	9	(2)	F
6	-	Mule Skinner Blues	Fendermen	Soma	9	(27)	F L
7	-	That's All You Gotta Do	Brenda Lee	Decca	6		
8	14	My Home Town	Paul Anka	ABC Paramount	7		
9	15	A Rockin' Good Way	Dinah Washington & Brook Benton	Mercury	7		L
10	-	When Will I Be Loved	Everly Brothers	Cadence	5	(5)	
11	-	Tell Laura I Love Her	Ray Peterson	RCA	7		F
12	-	Please Help Me, I'm Falling	Hank Locklin	RCA	10	(13)	F L
13	1	Cathy's Clown	Everly Brothers	Warner	12	(1)	G
14	-	Itsy Bitsy Teenie Weenie Yellow Polka Dot Bikini	Brian Hyland	Leader	10	(10)	F G
15	3	Burning Bridges	Jack Scott	Top Rank	10		L
16	-	Image Of A Girl	Safaris	Eldo	8		F L
17	18	Wonderful World	Sam Cooke	Keen	7	(2)	
18	-	Walkin' To New Orleans	Fats Domino	Imperial	7	(22)	
19	5	Paper Roses	Anita Bryant	Carlton	9	(25)	F
20	-	Alley-Oop	Dante & The Evergreens	Madison	5		F L

August 1960

This Mnth	Prev Mnth	Title	Artist	Label	Wks 20	(UK Pos)	
1	-	It's Now Or Never	Elvis Presley	RCA	14	(1)	G
2	14	Itsy Bitsy Teenie Weenie Yellow Polka Dot Bikini	Brian Hyland	Leader	10	(10)	F G
3	1	I'm Sorry	Brenda Lee	Decca	13	(10)	G
4	4	Only The Lonely	Roy Orbison	Monument	10	(1)	F G
5	-	Walk-Don't Run	Ventures	Dolton	12	(9)	F G
6	-	The Twist	Chubby Checker	Parkway	13	(9)	F G
7	16	Image Of A Girl	Safaris	Eldo	8		F L
8	-	Finger Poppin' Time	Hank Ballard & The Midnighters	King	10		F
9	18	Walkin' To New Orleans	Fats Domino	Imperial	7	(22)	
10	12	Please Help Me, I'm Falling	Hank Locklin	RCA	10	(13)	F L
11	11	Tell Laura I Love Her	Ray Peterson	RCA	7		F
12	-	Volare	Bobby Rydell	Cameo	8	(18)	G
13	2	Alley-Oop	Hollywood Argyles	Lute	10		F G L
14	-	Mission Bell	Donnie Brooks	Era	9		F L
15	6	Mule Skinner Blues	Fendermen	Soma	9	(27)	F L
16	-	In My Little Corner Of The World	Anita Bryant	Carlton	6		
17	3	Everybody's Somebody's Fool	Connie Francis	MGM	12	(7)	G
18	-	Feel So Fine	Johnny Preston	Mercury	5	(18)	L
19	-	(You Were Made For) All My Love	Jackie Wilson	Brunswick	4		
20	-	Dreamin'	Johnny Burnette	Liberty	7	(3)	F

September 1960

This Mnth	Prev Mnth	Title	Artist	Label	Wks 20	(UK Pos)	
1	6	The Twist	Chubby Checker	Parkway	13	(9)	F G
2	1	It's Now Or Never	Elvis Presley	RCA	14	(1)	G
3	-	My Heart Has A Mind Of Its Own	Connie Francis	MGM	12	(5)	G
4	5	Walk-Don't Run	Ventures	Dolton	12	(9)	F G
5	-	Mr. Custer	Larry Verne	Era	8		F G L
6	12	Volare	Bobby Rydell	Cameo	8	(18)	G
7	-	Chain Gang	Sam Cooke	RCA	10	(7)	G
8	-	Kiddio	Brook Benton	Mercury	8	(29)	
9	-	Theme From The Appartment	Ferrante & Teicher	UA	11		
10	-	Yogi	Ivy Three	Shell	6		F L
11	-	A Million To One	Jimmy Charles	Promo	9		F L
12	14	Mission Bell	Donnie Brooks	Era	9		F L
13	20	Dreamin'	Johnny Burnette	Liberty	7	(3)	F
14	-	So Sad (To Watch Good Love Go Bad)	Everly Brothers	Warner	8	(5)	
15	2	Itsy Bitsy Teenie Weenie Yellow...	Brian Hyland	Leader	10	(10)	F G
16	8	Finger Poppin' Time	Hank Ballard & The Midnighters	King	10		F
17	3	I'm Sorry	Brenda Lee	Decca	13	(10)	G
18	16	In My Little Corner Of The World	Anita Bryant	Carlton	6		
19	-	Save The Last Dance For Me	Drifters	Atlantic	12	(2)	G
20	-	Pineapple Princess	Annette	Vista	5		L

◆ The 33⅓ RPM single was unsuccessfully launched. It appeared that the public preferred their singles and albums to run at different speeds.

◆ The Ventures had a transatlantic hit with 'Walk, Don't Run' – a guitar instrumental which influenced the instrumental sound of many early surf music bands.

◆ Teenage chart toppers included Brenda Lee (15), Bryan Hyland (16) and Chubby Checker (19). For the record, Checker's 'The Twist' also returned to the top in 1962 and is the most successful US chart single of all time.

◆ *Billboard* reported that the average teenage girl listened to 4½ hours of pop music a day.

UK 1960 OCT-DEC

Elvis Presley's 'It's Now Or Never', which had record UK advance orders, sold over 750,000 copies in its first week and past the million mark 40 days later. Meanwhile, in America his revival of 'Are You Lonesome Tonight' became his 15th chart topping single, and **G.I. Blues** his fifth No. 1 album.

Instrumentals were big business in Britain – at times accounting for 30% of the chart. The hottest instrumental acts were The Shadows, Johnny & The Hurricanes, Duane Eddy and American session-group, The Piltdown Men.

Early rockers Roy Orbison and Johnny Burnette finally found pop success. Incidentally Orbison had penned his chart topping 'Only The Lonely' for Elvis.

October 1960

This Mnth	Prev Mnth	Title	Artist	Label	Wks 20	(US Pos)	
1	6	Only The Lonely	Roy Orbison	London American	15	(2)	F
2	3	Tell Laura I Love Her	Ricky Valance	Columbia	12		F L
3	7	As Long As He Needs Me	Shirley Bassey	Columbia	22		
4	11	How About That	Adam Faith	Parlophone	10		
5	13	Nine Times Out Of Ten	Cliff Richard	Columbia	8		
6	-	So Sad (To Watch Good Love Go Bad)	Everly Brothers	Warner	8	(7)	
7	18	Walk Don't Run	John Barry Seven	Columbia	9		
8	1	Apache	Shadows	Columbia	15		F
9	-	Chain Gang	Sam Cooke	RCA	8	(2)	F
10	-	Let's Think About Living	Bob Luman	Warner	9	(7)	F L
11	16	Walk-Don't Run	Ventures	Top Rank	8	(2)	F
12	5	Girl Of My Best Friend	Elvis Presley	RCA	12		
13	-	Dreamin'	Johnny Burnette	London American	12	(11)	F
14	-	Please Help Me, I'm Falling	Hank Locklin	RCA	7	(8)	F L
15	-	Rocking Goose	Johnny & The Hurricanes	London American	15	(60)	
16	4	A Mess Of Blues	Elvis Presley	RCA	14	(32)	
17	2	Because They're Young	Duane Eddy	London American	14	(4)	
18	-	MacDonald's Cave	Piltdown Men	Capitol	6		F
19	9	Everybody's Somebody's Fool	Connie Francis	MGM	10	(1)	
20	-	My Love For You	Johnny Mathis	Fontana	11	(47)	

November 1960

This Mnth	Prev Mnth	Title	Artist	Label	Wks 20	(US Pos)	
1	-	It's Now Or Never	Elvis Presley	RCA	14	(1)	G
2	3	As Long As He Needs Me	Shirley Bassey	Columbia	22		
3	13	Dreamin'	Johnny Burnette	London American	12	(11)	F
4	1	Only The Lonely	Roy Orbison	London American	15	(2)	F
5	15	Rocking Goose	Johnny & The Hurricanes	London American	15	(60)	
6	-	My Heart Has A Mind Of Its Own	Connie Francis	MGM	8	(1)	
7	-	Save The Last Dance For Me	Drifters	London American	14	(1)	
8	10	Let's Think About Living	Bob Luman	Warner	9	(7)	F L
9	-	Goodness Gracious Me	Peter Sellers & Sophia Loren	Parlophone	12		
10	20	My Love For You	Johnny Mathis	Fontana	11	(47)	
11	18	MacDonald's Cave	Piltdown Men	Capitol	6		F
12	-	Man Of Mystery	Shadows	Columbia	10		
13	9	Chain Gang	Sam Cooke	RCA	8	(2)	F
14	4	How About That	Adam Faith	Parlophone	10		
15	-	Mr. Custer	Charlie Drake	Parlophone	4		
16	7	Walk Don't Run	John Barry Seven	Columbia	9		
17	-	The Stranger	Shadows	Columbia	4		
18	-	Kommotion	Duane Eddy	London American	3	(78)	
19	6	So Sad (To Watch Good Love Go Bad)	Everly Brothers	Warner	8	(7)	
20	5	Nine Times Out Of Ten	Cliff Richard	Columbia	8		

December 1960

This Mnth	Prev Mnth	Title	Artist	Label	Wks 20	(US Pos)	
1	1	It's Now Or Never	Elvis Presley	RCA	14	(1)	G
2	7	Save The Last Dance For Me	Drifters	London American	14	(1)	
3	-	I Love You	Cliff Richard	Columbia	12		
4	-	Strawberry Fair	Anthony Newley	Decca	8		
5	9	Goodness Gracious Me	Peter Sellers & Sophia Loren	Parlophone	12		
6	-	Little Donkey	Nina & Frederick	Columbia	7		F
7	5	Rocking Goose	Johnny & The Hurricanes	London American	15	(60)	
8	12	Man Of Mystery	Shadows	Columbia	10		
9	-	Poetry In Motion	Johnny Tillotson	London American	13	(2)	F L
10	-	Lonely Pup (In A Christmas Shop)	Adam Faith	Parlophone	7		
11	-	Gurney Slade	Max Harris	Fontana	6		F L
12	6	My Heart Has A Mind Of Its Own	Connie Francis	MGM	8	(1)	
13	2	As Long As He Needs Me	Shirley Bassey	Columbia	22		
14	-	Perfidia	Ventures	London American	9	(15)	L
15	3	Dreamin'	Johnny Burnette	London American	12	(11)	F
16	10	My Love For You	Johnny Mathis	Fontana	11	(47)	
17	-	Blue Angel	Roy Orbison	London American	8	(9)	
18	-	Lively	Lonnie Donegan	Pye	6		
19	-	Ol' Macdonald	Frank Sinatra	Capitol	4	(25)	
20	-	Counting Teardrops	Emile Ford & The Checkmates	Pye	9		L

October 1960

This Mnth	Prev Mnth	Title	Artist	Label	Wks 20	(UK Pos)	
1	3	My Heart Has A Mind Of Its Own	Connie Francis	MGM	12	(5)	G
2	19	Save The Last Dance For Me	Drifters	Atlantic	12	(2)	G
3	7	Chain Gang	Sam Cooke	RCA	10	(7)	G
4	1	The Twist	Chubby Checker	Parkway	13	(9)	F G
5	-	I Want To Be Wanted	Brenda Lee	Decca	9		
6	-	Devil Or Angel	Bobby Vee	Liberty	9		F
7	5	Mr. Custer	Larry Verne	Era	8		F G L
8	14	So Sad (To Watch Good Love Go Bad)	Everly Brothers	Warner	8	(5)	
9	11	A Million To One	Jimmy Charles	Promo	9		F L
10	-	Let's Think About Living	Bob Luman	Warner	7	(6)	F L
11	2	It's Now Or Never	Elvis Presley	RCA	14	(1)	G
12	9	Theme From The Appartment	Ferrante & Teicher	UA	11		F
13	8	Kiddio	Brook Benton	Mercury	8	(29)	
14	-	Georgia On My Mind	Ray Charles	ABC Paramount	8	(18)	G
15	4	Walk-Don't Run	Ventures	Dolton	12	(9)	F G
16	-	You Talk Too Much	Joe Jones	Roulette	6		F L
17	-	Don't Be Cruel	Bill Black's Combo	Hi	7	(30)	
18	20	Pineapple Princess	Annette	Vista	5		L
19	-	Three Nights A Week	Fats Domino	Imperial	3		
20	-	Poetry In Motion	Johnny Tillotson	Cadence	9	(1)	F G

November 1960

This Mnth	Prev Mnth	Title	Artist	Label	Wks 20	(UK Pos)	
1	20	Poetry In Motion	Johnny Tillotson	Cadence	9	(1)	F G
2	-	Stay	Maurice Williams & The Zodiacs	Herald	8	(10)	F G L
3	14	Georgia On My Mind	Ray Charles	ABC Paramount	8	(18)	G
4	2	Save The Last Dance For Me	Drifters	Atlantic	12	(2)	
5	-	Last Date	Floyd Cramer	RCA	13		F G
6	-	Let's Go, Let's Go, Let's Go	Hank Ballard & The Midnighters	King	7		L
7	5	I Want To Be Wanted	Brenda Lee	Decca	9		
8	16	You Talk Too Much	Joe Jones	Roulette	6		F L
9	-	A Thousand Stars	Kathy Young With The Innocents	Indigo	12		F L
10	-	New Orleans	Gary U.S. Bonds	Legrand	8	(17)	F
11	-	Are You Lonesome Tonight?	Elvis Presley	RCA	12	(1)	G
12	-	North To Alaska	Johnny Horton	Columbia	14	(21)	
13	-	Alone At Last	Jackie Wilson	Brunswick	6		
14	-	Blue Angel	Roy Orbison	Monument	4	(10)	
15	17	Don't Be Cruel	Bill Black's Combo	Hi	7	(30)	
16	-	Sleep	Little Willie John	King	4		F L
17	1	My Heart Has A Mind Of Its Own	Connie Francis	MGM	12	(5)	G
18	-	He Will Break Your Heart	Jerry Butler	Vee Jay	9		
19	-	The Hucklebuck	Chubby Checker	Parkway	4		
20	6	Devil Or Angel	Bobby Vee	Liberty	9		F

December 1960

This Mnth	Prev Mnth	Title	Artist	Label	Wks 20	(UK Pos)	
1	11	Are You Lonesome Tonight?	Elvis Presley	RCA	12	(1)	G
2	5	Last Date	Floyd Cramer	RCA	13		F G
3	9	A Thousand Stars	Kathy Young/The Innocents	Indigo	12		F L
4	12	North To Alaska	Johnny Horton	Columbia	14	(21)	L
5	-	Wonderland By Night	Bert Kaempfert	Decca	13		F G
6	-	Sailor (Your Home Is The Sea)	Lolita	Kapp	10		F L
7	-	Many Tears Ago	Connie Francis	MGM	9	(12)	
8	18	He Will Break Your Heart	Jerry Butler	Vee Jay	9		
9	-	Exodus	Ferrante & Teicher	UA	14	(6)	G
10	1	Poetry In Motion	Johnny Tillotson	Cadence	9	(1)	F G
11	-	You're Sixteen	Johnny Burnette	Liberty	7	(4)	
12	2	Stay	Maurice Williams/The Zodiacs	Herald	8	(10)	F G L
13	10	New Orleans	Gary U.S. Bonds	Legrand	8	(17)	F
14	-	Lonely Teenager	Dion	Laurie	6		F
15	-	Sway	Bobby Rydell	Cameo	6	(12)	
16	6	Let's Go, Let's Go, Let's Go	Hank Ballard/The Midnighters	King	7		L
17	13	Alone At Last	Jackie Wilson	Brunswick	6		
18	-	Perfidia	Ventures	Dolton	6	(5)	
19	-	My Girl Josephine	Fats Domino	Imperial	3		
20	-	Corinna, Corinna	Ray Peterson	Dunes	7		L

▲ 'Bye Bye Baby' by Mary Wells was the first single on Motown to reach the US Hot 100.

◆ Ray Charles' versions of four standards were simultaneously situated in the US Hot 100: 'Come Rain Or Come Shine', 'Ruby', 'Hard Hearted Hannah' and the Grammy winning 'Georgia On My Mind',

◆ 'North To Alaska' hit maker Johnny Horton died in a car crash after playing Austin's Skyline club, which was the last venue C&W legend Hank Williams played. Spookily, Horton's widow had also been married to Williams.

UK 1961 JAN-MAR

◆ Trad (based on old-time New Orleans styled traditional jazz) was the latest UK music craze, with Acker Bilk, Kenny Ball and Chris Barber at the forefront of it.

▲ New transatlantic stars included the Buddy Holly-influenced 17-year-old Bobby Vee (above) and singer/songwriter Johnny Tillotson whose 'Poetry In Motion' topped the chart on both sides of the Atlantic.

◆ The Beatles played their first gig at Liverpool's Cavern Club. They were the support act to The Bluegenes (who were later successful as the Swinging Blue Jeans).

January 1961

This Mnth	Prev Mnth	Title	Artist	Label	Wks 20	(US Pos)	
1	9	Poetry In Motion	Johnny Tillotson	London American	13	(2)	F L
2	3	I Love You	Cliff Richard	Columbia	12		
3	2	Save The Last Dance For Me	Drifters	London American	14	(1)	
4	-	Portrait Of My Love	Matt Monro	Parlophone	10		F
5	1	It's Now Or Never	Elvis Presley	RCA	14	(1)	G
6	14	Perfidia	Ventures	London American	9	(15)	L
7	20	Counting Teardrops	Emile Ford & The Checkmates	Pye	9		L
8	-	Are You Lonesome Tonight?	Elvis Presley	RCA	10	(1)	
9	5	Goodness Gracious Me	Peter Sellers & Sophia Loren	Parlophone	12		
10	-	Buona Sera	Acker Bilk	Columbia	8		
11	-	Pepe	Duane Eddy	London American	8	(18)	
12	10	Lonely Pup (In A Christmas Shop)	Adam Faith	Parlophone	7		
13	-	Stay	Maurice Williams & The Zodiacs	Top Rank	6	(1)	F L
14	7	Rocking Goose	Johnny & The Hurricanes	London American	15	(60)	
15	-	Sway	Bobby Rydell	Columbia	5	(14)	
16	17	Blue Angel	Roy Orbison	London American	8	(9)	
17	4	Strawberry Fair	Anthony Newley	Decca	8		
18	8	Man Of Mystery	Shadows	Columbia	10		
19	-	You're Sixteen	Johnny Burnette	London American	8	(8)	
20	-	Sailor	Petula Clark	Pye	9		

February 1961

This Mnth	Prev Mnth	Title	Artist	Label	Wks 20	(US Pos)	
1	8	Are You Lonesome Tonight?	Elvis Presley	RCA	10	(1)	
2	20	Sailor	Petula Clark	Pye	9		
3	-	Rubber Ball	Bobby Vee	London American	7	(6)	F
4	19	You're Sixteen	Johnny Burnette	London American	8	(8)	
5	11	Pepe	Duane Eddy	London American	8	(18)	
6	4	Portrait Of My Love	Matt Monro	Parlophone	10		F
7	-	F.B.I.	Shadows	Columbia	11		
8	1	Poetry In Motion	Johnny Tillotson	London American	13	(2)	F L
9	-	Walk Right Back	Everly Brothers	Warner	11	(7)	
10	-	Sailor	Anne Shelton	Philips	5		L
11	-	Rubber Ball	Marty Wilde	Philips	4		L
12	-	Who Am I/This Is It	Adam Faith	Parlophone	9		
13	10	Buona Sera	Acker Bilk	Columbia	8		
14	-	Will You Love Me Tomorrow	Shirelles	Top Rank	9	(1)	F L
15	-	Calendar Girl	Neil Sedaka	RCA	8	(4)	
16	2	I Love You	Cliff Richard	Columbia	12		
17	-	Many Tears Ago	Connie Francis	MGM	5	(7)	
18	7	Counting Teardrops	Emile Ford & The Checkmates	Pye	9		L
19	13	Stay	Maurice Williams & The Zodiacs	Top Rank	6	(1)	F L
20	-	Riders In The Sky	Ramrods	London American	7	(30)	F L

March 1961

This Mnth	Prev Mnth	Title	Artist	Label	Wks 20	(US Pos)	
1	9	Walk Right Back	Everly Brothers	Warner	11	(7)	
2	-	Are You Sure	Allisons	Fontana	12		F L
3	-	Theme For A Dream	Cliff Richard	Columbia	9		
4	14	Will You Love Me Tomorrow	Shirelles	Top Rank	9	(1)	F L
5	-	Wooden Heart	Elvis Presley	RCA	14		
6	7	F.B.I.	Shadows	Columbia	11		
7	20	Riders In The Sky	Ramrods	London American	7	(30)	F L
8	-	My Kind Of Girl	Matt Monro	Parlophone	7	(18)	
9	2	Sailor	Petula Clark	Pye	9		
10	15	Calendar Girl	Neil Sedaka	RCA	8	(4)	
11	-	Exodus	Ferrante & Teicher	London American	10	(2)	F L
12	12	Who Am I/This Is It	Adam Faith	Parlophone	9		
13	1	Are You Lonesome Tonight?	Elvis Presley	RCA	10	(1)	
14	-	Wheels	String-A-Longs	London American	6	(3)	F L
15	-	Samantha	Kenny Ball	Pye Jazz	10		F
16	-	And The Heavens Cried	Anthony Newley	Decca	7		
17	-	Lazy River	Bobby Darin	London American	8	(14)	
18	-	Let's Jump The Broomstick	Brenda Lee	Brunswick	4		
19	-	Ja-Da	Johnny & The Hurricanes	London American	3	(86)	L
20	3	Rubber Ball	Bobby Vee	London American	7	(6)	F

74

January 1961

This Mnth	Prev Mnth	Title	Artist	Label	Wks 20	(UK Pos)	
1	5	Wonderland By Night	Bert Kaempfert	Decca	13		F G
2	9	Exodus	Ferrante & Teicher	UA	14	(6)	G
3	1	Are You Lonesome Tonight?	Elvis Presley	RCA	12	(1)	G
4	-	Will You Love Me Tomorrow	Shirelles	Scepter	12	(3)	F G
5	-	Angel Baby	Rosie & The Originals	Highland	9		F L
6	2	Last Date	Floyd Cramer	RCA	13		F G
7	-	Rubber Ball	Bobby Vee	Liberty	9	(3)	
8	-	Calcutta	Lawrence Welk	Dot	11		F G L
9	4	North To Alaska	Johnny Horton	Columbia	14	(21)	L
10	20	Corinna, Corinna	Ray Peterson	Dunes	7		L
11	3	A Thousand Stars	Kathy Young With The Innocents	Indigo	12		F L
12	-	Shop Around	Miracles	Tamla	9		F G
13	-	Calendar Girl	Neil Sedaka	RCA	8	(8)	
14	11	You're Sixteen	Johnny Burnette	Liberty	7	(4)	
15	7	Many Tears Ago	Connie Francis	MGM	9	(12)	
16	6	Sailor (Your Home Is The Sea)	Lolita	Kapp	10		F L
17	-	Emotions	Brenda Lee	Decca	6	(29)	
18	-	Wonderland By Night	Louis Prima	Dot	6		L
19	8	He Will Break Your Heart	Jerry Butler	Vee Jay	9		
20	-	Once In A While	Chimes	Tag	4		F L

February 1961

This Mnth	Prev Mnth	Title	Artist	Label	Wks 20	(UK Pos)	
1	8	Calcutta	Lawrence Welk	Dot	11		F G L
2	4	Will You Love Me Tomorrow	Shirelles	Scepter	12	(3)	F G
3	12	Shop Around	Miracles	Tamla	9		F G
4	-	Pony Time	Chubby Checker	Parkway	11		G
5	2	Exodus	Ferrante & Teicher	UA	14	(6)	G
6	13	Calendar Girl	Neil Sedaka	RCA	8	(8)	
7	-	There's A Moon Out Tonight	Capris	Old Town	7		F L
8	17	Emotions	Brenda Lee	Decca	6	(29)	
9	-	Dedicated To The One I Love	Shirelles	Scepter	11		G
10	5	Angel Baby	Rosie & The Originals	Highland	9		F L
11	-	Where The Boys Are	Connie Francis	MGM	9	(8)	G
12	1	Wonderland By Night	Bert Kaempfert	Decca	13		F G
13	-	Wings Of A Dove	Ferlin Husky	Capitol	8		L
14	-	Wheels	String-A-Longs	Warwick	8	(11)	F G L
15	-	Baby Sittin' Boogie	Buzz Clifford	Columbia	7	(14)	F L
16	-	Don't Worry	Marty Robbins	Columbia	9		
17	20	Once In A While	Chimes	Tag	4		F L
18	-	Surrender	Elvis Presley	RCA	9	(1)	G
19	-	Ebony Eyes	Everly Brothers	Warner	7	(17)	
20	-	My Empty Arms	Jackie Wilson	Brunswick	4		

March 1961

This Mnth	Prev Mnth	Title	Artist	Label	Wks 20	(UK Pos)	
1	4	Pony Time	Chubby Checker	Parkway	11		G
2	18	Surrender	Elvis Presley	RCA	9	(1)	G
3	16	Don't Worry	Marty Robbins	Columbia	9		
4	14	Wheels	String-A-Longs	Warwick	8	(11)	F G L
5	9	Dedicated To The One I Love	Shirelles	Scepter	11		G
6	11	Where The Boys Are	Connie Francis	MGM	9	(8)	G
7	-	Apache	Jorgen Ingmann	Atco	10		F L
8	19	Ebony Eyes	Everly Brothers	Warner	7	(17)	
9	15	Baby Sittin' Boogie	Buzz Clifford	Columbia	7	(14)	F L
10	-	Walk Right Back	Everly Brothers	Warner	6	(1)	
11	1	Calcutta	Lawrence Welk	Dot	11		F G L
12	-	Spanish Harlem	Ben E. King	Atco	5		F
13	-	Gee Whiz (Look At His Eyes)	Carla Thomas	Atlantic	5		F
14	-	Good Time Baby	Bobby Rydell	Cameo	5	(27)	
15	7	There's A Moon Out Tonight	Capris	Old Town	7		F L
16	-	Think Twice	Brook Benton	Mercury	5		
17	-	On The Rebound	Floyd Cramer	RCA	9	(3)	
18	-	Blue Moon	Marcels	Colpix	9	(1)	F G
19	-	You Can Have Her	Roy Hamilton	Epic	2		L
20	-	Little Boy Sad	Johnny Burnette	Liberty	3	(15)	

US 1961 JAN-MAR

◆ A doo-wop revival resulted in hits for groups like The Capris, Rosie & The Originals, The Chimes and The Marcels, whose up-date of 'Blue Moon' was a transatlantic No. 1

◆ 'Shop Around' by The Miracles became Motown's first million seller.

◆ German Orchestra leader Bert Kaempfert topped the single and album chart with 'Wonderland By Night'. Shortly afterwards he produced The Beatles, who were then performing in Germany. Kaempfert also co-wrote 'Wooden Heart', which gave Elvis a record third successive British No. 1.

◆ Frank Sinatra announced that he would soon be launching his own label, Reprise. Among the acts who joined him on the label were fellow rat-pack members Sammy Davis Jr and Dean Martin. He vowed never to release any rock'n'roll on Reprise.

UK 1961 APR-JUNE

◆ Ex-Drifter Ben E. King released 'Stand By Me' a song he had originally written for the group. It was a US Top 10 hit in both 1961 and 1986, and even topped the UK chart in 1987!

◆ Elvis Presley's 'Surrender', which like its predecessor, 'It's Now Or Never', was based on an old Italian ballad, had a record 460,000 advance orders.

◆ The first American artist to appear on new pop TV show *Thank Your Lucky Stars* was Gene Vincent. This show, more than any other, would spread the Merseybeat sound.

◆ Adam Faith (who was celebrating his 21st birthday) saw his record run of seven successive Top 5 hits end with 'Easy Going Me'.

April 1961

This Mnth	Prev Mnth	Title	Artist	Label	Wks 20	(US Pos)	
1	5	Wooden Heart	Elvis Presley	RCA	14		
2	2	Are You Sure	Allisons	Fontana	12		F L
3	17	Lazy River	Bobby Darin	London American	8	(14)	
4	-	You're Driving Me Crazy	Temperance Seven	Parlophone	12		F
5	11	Exodus	Ferrante & Teicher	London American	10	(2)	F L
6	3	Theme For A Dream	Cliff Richard	Columbia	9		
7	-	Where The Boys Are	Connie Francis	MGM	6	(4)	
8	-	Blue Moon	Marcels	Pye International	9	(1)	F L
9	1	Walk Right Back	Everly Brothers	Warner	11	(7)	
10	16	And The Heavens Cried	Anthony Newley	Decca	7		
11	-	Gee Whiz It's You	Cliff Richard	Columbia	8		
12	8	My Kind Of Girl	Matt Monro	Parlophone	7	(18)	
13	6	F.B.I.	Shadows	Columbia	11		
14	15	Samantha	Kenny Ball	Pye Jazz	10		F
15	-	Warpaint	Brook Brothers	Pye	9		F
16	-	African Waltz	Johnny Dankworth	Columbia	8		L
17	4	Will You Love Me Tomorrow	Shirelles	Top Rank	9	(1)	F L
18	-	A Hundred Pounds Of Clay	Craig Douglas	Top Rank	6		
19	-	Don't Treat Me Like A Child	Helen Shapiro	Columbia	11		F
20	-	Baby Sittin' Boogie	Buzz Clifford	Fontana	3	(6)	F L

May 1961

This Mnth	Prev Mnth	Title	Artist	Label	Wks 20	(US Pos)	
1	8	Blue Moon	Marcels	Pye International	9	(1)	F L
2	4	You're Driving Me Crazy	Temperance Seven	Parlophone	12		F
3	-	On The Rebound	Floyd Cramer	RCA	9	(4)	F L
4	-	Runaway	Del Shannon	London American	16	(1)	F
5	-	More Than I Can Say	Bobby Vee	London American	9	(61)	
6	19	Don't Treat Me Like A Child	Helen Shapiro	Columbia	11		F
7	1	Wooden Heart	Elvis Presley	RCA	14		
8	-	Theme From Dixie	Duane Eddy	London American	6	(39)	
9	-	Frightened City	Shadows	Columbia	11		
10	-	Easy Going Me	Adam Faith	Parlophone	5		
11	18	A Hundred Pounds Of Clay	Craig Douglas	Top Rank	6		
12	-	What'd I Say	Jerry Lee Lewis	London American	6	(30)	L
13	16	African Waltz	Johnny Dankworth	Columbia	8		L
14	-	You'll Never Know	Shirley Bassey	Columbia	8		
15	11	Gee Whiz It's You	Cliff Richard	Columbia	8		
16	15	Warpaint	Brook Brothers	Pye	9		F
17	3	Lazy River	Bobby Darin	London American	8	(14)	
18	-	Surrender	Elvis Presley	RCA	10	(1)	
19	-	But I Do	Clarence 'Frogman' Henry	Pye International	13	(4)	F
20	5	Exodus	Ferrante & Teicher	London American	10	(2)	F L

June 1961

This Mnth	Prev Mnth	Title	Artist	Label	Wks 20	(US Pos)	
1	4	Runaway	Del Shannon	London American	16	(1)	F
2	18	Surrender	Elvis Presley	RCA	10	(1)	
3	19	But I Do	Clarence 'Frogman' Henry	Pye International	13	(4)	F
4	9	Frightened City	Shadows	Columbia	11		
5	14	You'll Never Know	Shirley Bassey	Columbia	8		
6	-	Hello Mary Lou/Travellin' Man	Ricky Nelson	London American	15	(9)	
7	-	Halfway To Paradise	Billy Fury	Decca	18		
8	-	Have A Drink On Me	Lonnie Donegan	Pye	8		
9	-	Pasadena	Temperance Seven	Parlophone	12		
10	5	More Than I Can Say	Bobby Vee	London American	9	(61)	
11	-	Temptation	Everly Brothers	Warner	12	(27)	
12	-	Little Devil	Neil Sedaka	RCA	6	(11)	
13	3	On The Rebound	Floyd Cramer	RCA	9	(4)	F L
14	-	I've Told Every Little Star	Linda Scott	Columbia	6	(3)	F L
15	-	Running Scared	Roy Orbison	London American	9	(1)	
16	12	What'd I Say	Jerry Lee Lewis	London American	6	(30)	L
17	-	A Girl Like You	Cliff Richard	Columbia	12		
18	-	Pop Goes The Weasel	Anthony Newley	Decca	6	(85)	
19	-	Well I Ask You	Eden Kane	Decca	16		F
20	1	Blue Moon	Marcels	Pye International	9	(1)	F L

US 1961 APR-JUNE

April 1961

This Mnth	Prev Mnth	Title	Artist	Label	Wks 20	(UK Pos)	
1	18	Blue Moon	Marcels	Colpix	9	(1)	F G
2	-	Runaway	Del Shannon	Big Top	10	(1)	F G
3	7	Apache	Jorgen Ingmann	Atco	10		F L
4	17	On The Rebound	Floyd Cramer	RCA	9	(3)	
5	-	But I Do	Clarence 'Frogman' Henry	Argo	7	(3)	
6	5	Dedicated To The One I Love	Shirelles	Scepter	11		G
7	-	Mother-In-Law	Ernie K-Doe	Minit	9	(22)	F L
8	2	Surrender	Elvis Presley	RCA	9	(1)	G
9	-	Asia Minor	Kokomo	Felsted	5		F L
10	1	Pony Time	Chubby Checker	Parkway	11		G
11	-	Take Good Care Of Her	Adam Wade	Coed	8		F
12	-	Please Love Me Forever	Cathy Jean & The Roommates	Valmor	5		F L
13	-	A Hundred Pounds Of Clay	Gene McDaniels	Liberty	10		F G
14	3	Don't Worry	Marty Robbins	Columbia	9		
15	10	Walk Right Back	Everly Brothers	Warner	6	(1)	
16	-	One Mint Julep	Ray Charles	Impulse	6		
17	-	You Can Depend On Me	Brenda Lee	Decca	7		
18	-	I've Told Every Little Star	Linda Scott	Canadian American	7	(8)	F G
19	16	Think Twice	Brook Benton	Mercury	5		
20	-	Baby Blue	Echoes	Seg-Way	6		F L

May 1961

This Mnth	Prev Mnth	Title	Artist	Label	Wks 20	(UK Pos)	
1	2	Runaway	Del Shannon	Big Top	10	(1)	F G
2	7	Mother-In-Law	Ernie K-Doe	Minit	9	(22)	F L
3	13	A Hundred Pounds Of Clay	Gene McDaniels	Liberty	10		F G
4	-	Daddy's Home	Shep & The Limelites	Hull	8		F L
5	18	I've Told Every Little Star	Linda Scott	Canadian American	7	(8)	F G
6	1	Blue Moon	Marcels	Colpix	9	(1)	F G
7	-	Mama Said	Shirelles	Scepter	7		
8	-	Travelin' Man	Ricky Nelson	Imperial	12	(20)	G
9	17	You Can Depend On Me	Brenda Lee	Decca	7		
10	-	Breakin' In A Brand New Broken Heart	Connie Francis	MGM	6	(16)	
11	11	Take Good Care Of Her	Adam Wade	Coed	8		F
12	-	Portrait Of My Love	Steve Lawrence	UA	6		
13	-	Running Scared	Roy Orbison	Monument	9	(9)	G
14	16	One Mint Julep	Ray Charles	Impulse	6		
15	4	On The Rebound	Floyd Cramer	RCA	9	(3)	
16	5	But I Do	Clarence 'Frogman' Henry	Argo	7	(3)	
17	-	Hello Mary Lou	Ricky Nelson	Imperial	8	(3)	
18	-	I Feel So Bad	Elvis Presley	RCA	6	(20)	
19	-	Tragedy	Fleetwoods	Dolton	3		L
20	-	Little Devil	Neil Sedaka	RCA	3	(9)	

June 1961

This Mnth	Prev Mnth	Title	Artist	Label	Wks 20	(UK Pos)	
1	8	Travelin' Man	Ricky Nelson	Imperial	12	(20)	G
2	-	Moody River	Pat Boone	Dot	9	(14)	G
3	-	Raindrops	Dee Clark	Vee Jay	10		G L
4	-	Stand By Me	Ben E. King	Atco	7	(27)	
5	13	Running Scared	Roy Orbison	Monument	9	(9)	G
6	-	Quarter To Three	Gary U.S. Bonds	Legrand	10	(7)	G
7	-	The Writing On The Wall	Adam Wade	Coed	7		
8	18	I Feel So Bad	Elvis Presley	RCA	6	(20)	
9	-	Every Beat Of My Heart	Gladys Knight & The Pips	Vee Jay	7		F
10	-	The Boll Weevil Song	Brook Benton	Mercury	10	(28)	G
11	-	Tossin' And Turnin'	Bobby Lewis	Beltone	15		F G
12	-	Those Oldies But Goodies (Remind Me Of You)	Little Caesar & The Romans	Del-Fi	6		F L
13	-	You Always Hurt The One You Love	Clarence 'Frogman' Henry	Argo	5	(6)	L
14	7	Mama Said	Shirelles	Scepter	7		
15	-	Barbara Ann	Regents	Gee	6		F L
16	4	Daddy's Home	Shep & The Limelites	Hull	8		F L
17	17	Hello Mary Lou	Ricky Nelson	Imperial	8	(3)	
18	-	Yellow Bird	Arthur Lyman	Hi Fi	7		F L
19	3	A Hundred Pounds Of Clay	Gene McDaniels	Liberty	10		F G
20	-	Hello Walls	Faron Young	Capitol	5		F L

◆ Bob Dylan made his New York debut as opening act for blues great John Lee Hooker. Dylan also played harmonica on a recording session for Harry Belafonte.

▲ Among acts debuting on the Hot 100 were later superstars Paul Revere & The Raiders, Tony Orlando (who later had a string of hits with Dawn) and Gladys Knight & The Pips. The most successful new chart entrant, however, was singer/songwriter Del Shannon (above) whose 'Runaway' was a transatlantic topper.

◆ The album chart was extended to a Top 150 mono and Top 50 stereo LPs.

UK 1961
JULY-SEPT

◆ 'Michael', a 19th century slave song, gave American folk quintet The Highwaymen an unexpected transatlantic No. 1, despite heavy British competition from Lonnie Donegan. Incidentally, Donegan's 1959 UK hit 'Chewing Gum' was now huge in the USA.

◆ The Shadows became the first British rock act to top the UK album chart. Their boss, Cliff Richard, would be the second with his **21 Today** LP.

◆ In Liverpool, alternative pop magazine *Mersey Beat* was launched and The Beatles started playing regularly at the Cavern Club.

◆ For the first time August's top three singles were 100% British: 'You Don't Know' by 15-year-old Helen Shapiro, 'Well I Ask You' by Eden Kane and death-disc 'Johnny Remember Me' by singer/actor John Leyton.

July 1961

This Mnth	Prev Mnth	Title	Artist	Label	Wks 20	(US Pos)	
1	11	Temptation	Everly Brothers	Warner	12	(27)	
2	1	Runaway	Del Shannon	London American	16	(1)	F
3	19	Well I Ask You	Eden Kane	Decca	16		F
4	6	Hello Mary Lou/Travellin' Man	Ricky Nelson	London American	15	(9)	
5	17	A Girl Like You	Cliff Richard	Columbia	12		
6	9	Pasadena	Temperance Seven	Parlophone	12		
7	7	Halfway To Paradise	Billy Fury	Decca	18		
8	3	But I Do	Clarence 'Frogman' Henry	Pye International	13	(4)	F
9	15	Running Scared	Roy Orbison	London American	9	(1)	
10	-	You Don't Know	Helen Shapiro	Columbia	14		
11	-	You Always Hurt The One You Love	Clarence 'Frogman' Henry	Pye International	9	(12)	L
12	2	Surrender	Elvis Presley	RCA	10	(1)	
13	-	Time	Craig Douglas	Top Rank	10		
14	18	Pop Goes The Weasel	Anthony Newley	Decca	6	(85)	
15	-	Romeo	Petula Clark	Pye	11		
16	-	Moody River	Pat Boone	London American	6	(1)	
17	4	Frightened City	Shadows	Columbia	11		
18	-	Weekend	Eddie Cochran	London American	3		L
19	-	Don't You Know It	Adam Faith	Parlophone	6		
20	-	Breakin' In A Brand New Broken Heart	Connie Francis	MGM	2	(7)	

August 1961

This Mnth	Prev Mnth	Title	Artist	Label	Wks 20	(US Pos)	
1	10	You Don't Know	Helen Shapiro	Columbia	14		
2	3	Well I Ask You	Eden Kane	Decca	16		F
3	-	Johnny Remember Me	John Leyton	Top Rank	11		F
4	7	Halfway To Paradise	Billy Fury	Decca	18		
5	15	Romeo	Petula Clark	Pye	11		
6	11	You Always Hurt The One You Love	Clarence 'Frogman' Henry	Pye International	9	(12)	L
7	6	Pasadena	Temperance Seven	Parlophone	12		
8	1	Temptation	Everly Brothers	Warner	12	(27)	
9	19	Don't You Know It	Adam Faith	Parlophone	6		
10	13	Time	Craig Douglas	Top Rank	10		
11	5	A Girl Like You	Cliff Richard	Columbia	12		
12	4	Hello Mary Lou/Travellin' Man	Ricky Nelson	London American	15	(9)	
13	-	Quarter To Three	Gary U.S. Bonds	Top Rank	9	(1)	L
14	-	Reach For The Stars/ Climb Ev'ry Mountain	Shirley Bassey	Columbia	11		
15	2	Runaway	Del Shannon	London American	16	(1)	F
16	-	Climb Ev'ry Mountain	Shirley Bassey	Columbia	6		
17	-	Baby I Don't Care	Buddy Holly	Coral	6		
18	-	Marcheta	Karl Denver	Decca	7		F
19	-	That's My Home	Acker Bilk	Columbia	9		
20	-	Cupid	Sam Cooke	RCA	7	(17)	

September 1961

This Mnth	Prev Mnth	Title	Artist	Label	Wks 20	(US Pos)	
1	3	Johnny Remember Me	John Leyton	Top Rank	11		F
2	1	You Don't Know	Helen Shapiro	Columbia	14		
3	14	Reach For The Stars/ Climb Ev'ry Mountain	Shirley Bassey	Columbia	11		
4	-	Wild In The Country	Elvis Presley	RCA	8	(26)	
5	-	Kon-Tiki	Shadows	Columbia	8		
6	20	Cupid	Sam Cooke	RCA	7	(17)	
7	2	Well I Ask You	Eden Kane	Decca	16		F
8	-	Michael	Highwaymen	HMV	10	(1)	F L
9	19	That's My Home	Acker Bilk	Columbia	9		
10	5	Romeo	Petula Clark	Pye	11		
11	-	Michael Row The Boat	Lonnie Donegan	Pye	6		
12	-	Jealousy	Billy Fury	Decca	8		
13	4	Halfway To Paradise	Billy Fury	Decca	18		
14	-	Get Lost	Eden Kane	Decca	8		
15	13	Quarter To Three	Gary U.S. Bonds	Top Rank	9	(1)	L
16	-	How Many Tears	Bobby Vee	London American	5	(63)	
17	-	Together	Connie Francis	MGM	6	(6)	
18	-	Hats Off To Larry	Del Shannon	London American	8	(5)	
19	11	A Girl Like You	Cliff Richard	Columbia	12		
20	-	You'll Answer To Me	Cleo Laine	Fontana	9		F L

78

July 1961

This Mnth	Prev Mnth	Title	Artist	Label	Wks 20	(UK Pos)	
1	11	Tossin' And Turnin'	Bobby Lewis	Beltone	15		F G
2	10	The Boll Weevil Song	Brook Benton	Mercury	10	(28)	G
3	6	Quarter To Three	Gary U.S. Bonds	Legrand	10	(7)	G
4	3	Raindrops	Dee Clark	Vee Jay	10		G L
5	18	Yellow Bird	Arthur Lyman	Hi Fi	7		F L
6	-	Hats Off To Larry	Del Shannon	Big Top	8	(8)	
7	-	I Like It Like That (Pt.1)	Chris Kenner	Instant	8		F G L
8	-	Dum Dum	Brenda Lee	Decca	9	(20)	
9	9	Every Beat Of My Heart	Gladys Knight & The Pips	Vee Jay	7		F
10	-	San Antonio Rose	Floyd Cramer	RCA	7		L
11	2	Moody River	Pat Boone	Dot	9	(14)	G
12	7	The Writing On The Wall	Adam Wade	Coed	7		
13	-	Together	Connie Francis	MGM	8	(10)	
14	-	Dance On Little Girl	Paul Anka	ABC Paramount	5		
15	1	Travelin' Man	Ricky Nelson	Imperial	12	(20)	G
16	-	Let's Twist Again	Chubby Checker	Parkway	7	(1)	G
17	-	Last Night	Mar-Keys	Satellite	7		F G L
18	-	Please Stay	Drifters	Atlantic	4		
19	12	Those Oldies But Goodies (...)	Little Caesar & The Romans	Del-Fi	6		F L
20	4	Stand By Me	Ben E. King	Atco	7	(27)	

August 1961

This Mnth	Prev Mnth	Title	Artist	Label	Wks 20	(UK Pos)	
1	1	Tossin' And Turnin'	Bobby Lewis	Beltone	15		F G
2	17	Last Night	Mar-Keys	Satellite	7		F G L
3	7	I Like It Like That (Pt.1)	Chris Kenner	Instant	8		F G L
4	-	Wooden Heart	Joe Dowell	Smash	9		F G L
5	-	Michael	Highwaymen	UA	10	(1)	F G
6	-	Pretty Little Angel Eyes	Curtis Lee	Dunes	5		F L
7	8	Dum Dum	Brenda Lee	Decca	9	(20)	
8	-	You Don't Know What You Got (Until You Lose It)	Ral Donner	Gone	7	(21)	
9	16	Let's Twist Again	Chubby Checker	Parkway	7	(1)	G
10	-	School Is Out	Gary U.S. Bonds	Legrand	6		
11	13	Together	Connie Francis	MGM	8	(10)	
12	-	Don't Bet Money Honey	Linda Scott	Canadian Am.	5		
13	-	Hurt	Timi Yuro	Liberty	7		F
14	6	Hats Off To Larry	Del Shannon	Big Top	8	(8)	
15	-	I'll Be There	Damita Jo	Mercury	4		F L
16	-	Never On Sunday	Chordettes	Cadence	6		L
17	-	As If I Didn't Know	Adam Wade	Coed	4		L
18	-	Let The Four Winds Blow	Fats Domino	Imperial	3		L
19	-	I'm Gonna Knock On Your Door	Eddie Hodges	Cadence	3	(27)	F
20	-	I Fall To Pieces	Patsy Cline	Decca	3		F

September 1961

This Mnth	Prev Mnth	Title	Artist	Label	Wks 20	(UK Pos)	
1	5	Michael	Highwaymen	UA	10	(1)	F G
2	-	Take Good Care Of My Baby	Bobby Vee	Liberty	8	(1)	G
3	-	My True Story	Jive Five	Beltone	6		F L
4	-	Does Your Chewing Gum Lose It's Flavor (On The Bedpost Over Night)	Lonnie Donegan	Dot	6	(3)	L
5	-	Cryin'	Roy Orbison	Monument	10	(26)	G
6	4	Wooden Heart	Joe Dowell	Smash	9		F G L
7	8	You Don't Know What You Got (...)	Ral Donner	Gone	7	(21)	
8	-	Little Sister	Elvis Presley	RCA	7	(18)	
9	-	Who Put The Bomp (In The Bomp, Bomp, Bomp)	Barry Mann	ABC	5		F L
10	-	The Mountain's High	Dick & Deedee	Liberty	6	(25)	F G
11	-	Without You	Johnny Tillotson	Cadence	6		
12	13	Hurt	Timi Yuro	Liberty	7		F
13	1	Tossin' And Turnin'	Bobby Lewis	Beltone	15		F G
14	-	(Marie's The Name) His Latest Flame	Elvis Presley	RCA	2	(1)	
15	-	When We Get Married	Dreamlovers	Heritage	3		F L
16	-	One Track Mind	Bobby Lewis	Beltone	3		L
17	17	As If I Didn't Know	Adam Wade	Coed	4		L
18	10	School Is Out	Gary U.S. Bonds	Legrand	6		
19	12	Don't Bet Money Honey	Linda Scott	Canadian Am.	5		
20	-	A Little Bit Of Soap	Jarmels	Laurie	2		F L

▲ The Supremes (including Diana Ross), who had previously recorded as The Primettes on Lupine, released their earliest Motown single, 'Buttered Popcorn'.

◆ Among the many R&B hits charting were America's most successful single of 1961, 'Tossin' and Turnin'' by Bobby Lewis and the first hit from Stax Records, 'Last Night' by The Mar-Keys.

◆ As Chubby Checker's Grammy winning 'Let's Twist Again' hit, the twist (1960s teen dance sensation) was reported to be catching on with American adults.

UK 1961 OCT-DEC

◆ Unusually. three hits by British acts also reached the US Top 10: 'Midnight In Moscow' by Kenny Ball, 'Stranger On The Shore' by Acker Bilk and 'Let's Get Together' by 14-year-old Hayley Mills.

◆ Mantovani received five American gold albums while fellow Briton Matt Monro was voted Most Promising Artist in the *Billboard* DJ Poll.

◆ American hits from C&W stars Leroy Van Dyke, Jimmy Dean and Patsy Cline also scored in Britain, although, in the case of Cline's 'Crazy' it was 30 years later!

◆ British musician and composer John Barry was summoned to Hollywood to discuss possible film work. He is now one of the most successful film score writers of all time.

October 1961

This Mnth	Prev Mnth	Title	Artist	Label	Wks 20	(US Pos)	
1	-	Walkin' Back To Happiness	Helen Shapiro	Columbia	15	(100)	
2	8	Michael	Highwaymen	HMV	10	(1)	F L
3	-	Wild Wind	John Leyton	Top Rank	6		
4	20	You'll Answer To Me	Cleo Laine	Fontana	9		F L
5	12	Jealousy	Billy Fury	Decca	8		
6	-	Sucu-Sucu	Laurie Johnson	Pye	10		F L
7	5	Kon-Tiki	Shadows	Columbia	8		
8	18	Hats Off To Larry	Del Shannon	London American	8	(5)	
9	4	Wild In The Country	Elvis Presley	RCA	8	(26)	
10	-	When The Girl In Your Arms Is The Girl In Your Heart	Cliff Richard	Columbia	7		
11	-	Bless You	Tony Orlando	Fontana	7	(15)	F L
12	14	Get Lost	Eden Kane	Decca	8		
13	-	Mexicali Rose	Karl Denver	Decca	9		
14	1	Johnny Remember Me	John Leyton	Top Rank	11		F
15	-	You Must Have Been A Beautiful Baby	Bobby Darin	London American	8	(5)	
16	-	Granada	Frank Sinatra	Reprise	4	(64)	
17	-	Hit The Road Jack	Ray Charles	HMV	8	(1)	
18	17	Together	Connie Francis	MGM	6	(6)	
19	-	My Boomerang Won't Come Back	Charlie Drake	Parlophone	6	(21)	L
20	2	You Don't Know	Helen Shapiro	Columbia	14		

November 1961

This Mnth	Prev Mnth	Title	Artist	Label	Wks 20	(US Pos)	
1	-	His Latest Flame	Elvis Presley	RCA	8	(4)	
2	1	Walkin' Back To Happiness	Helen Shapiro	Columbia	15	(100)	
3	-	Take Good Care Of My Baby	Bobby Vee	London American	11	(1)	
4	-	Big Bad John	Jimmy Dean	Philips	11	(1)	F L
5	10	When The Girl In Your Arms Is The Girl In Your Heart	Cliff Richard	Columbia	7		
6	-	Take Five	Dave Brubeck Quartet	Fontana	10	(25)	F
7	17	Hit The Road Jack	Ray Charles	HMV	8	(1)	
8	-	The Time Has Come	Adam Faith	Parlophone	8		
9	6	Sucu-Sucu	Laurie Johnson	Pye	10		F L
10	13	Mexicali Rose	Karl Denver	Decca	9		
11	-	Tower Of Strength	Frankie Vaughan	Philips	10		
12	-	Moon River	Danny Williams	HMV	12		F
13	11	Bless You	Tony Orlando	Fontana	7	(15)	F L
14	15	You Must Have Been A Beautiful Baby	Bobby Darin	London American	8	(5)	
15	3	Wild Wind	John Leyton	Top Rank	6		
16	-	Runaround Sue	Dion	Top Rank	5	(1)	F
17	-	The Savage	Shadows	Columbia	5		
18	-	Let's Get Together	Hayley Mills	Decca	5	(8)	F L
19	-	Midnight In Moscow	Kenny Ball	Pye Jazz	11	(2)	
20	4	You'll Answer To Me	Cleo Laine	Fontana	9		F L

December 1961

This Mnth	Prev Mnth	Title	Artist	Label	Wks 20	(US Pos)	
1	11	Tower Of Strength	Frankie Vaughan	Philips	10		
2	12	Moon River	Danny Williams	HMV	12		F
3	3	Take Good Care Of My Baby	Bobby Vee	London American	11	(1)	
4	19	Midnight In Moscow	Kenny Ball	Pye Jazz	11	(2)	
5	-	Stranger On The Shore	Mr. Acker Bilk	Columbia	33	(1)	G
6	-	I'll Get By	Shirley Bassey	Columbia	6		
7	2	Walkin' Back To Happiness	Helen Shapiro	Columbia	15	(100)	
8	1	His Latest Flame	Elvis Presley	RCA	8	(4)	
9	-	Johnny Will	Pat Boone	London American	8	(35)	
10	6	Take Five	Dave Brubeck Quartet	Fontana	10	(25)	F
11	-	Let There Be Drums	Sandy Nelson	London American	9	(7)	L
12	4	Big Bad John	Jimmy Dean	Philips	11	(1)	F L
13	8	The Time Has Come	Adam Faith	Parlophone	8		
14	-	My Friend The Sea	Petula Clark	Pye	4		
15	-	So Long Baby	Del Shannon	London American	6	(28)	
16	-	Don't Bring Lulu	Dorothy Provine	Warner	6		F L
17	-	Happy Birthday, Sweet Sixteen	Neil Sedaka	RCA	11	(6)	
18	-	I Cried For You	Ricky Stevens	Columbia	4		F L
19	17	The Savage	Shadows	Columbia	5		
20	-	I'd Never Find Another You	Billy Fury	Decca	11		

October 1961

This Mnth	Prev Mnth	Title	Artist	Label	Wks 20	(UK Pos)	
1	-	Hit The Road Jack	Ray Charles	ABC Paramount	9	(4)	G
2	-	Bristol Stomp	Dovells	Parkway	11		F G
3	-	Runaround Sue	Dion	Laurie	11	(10)	G
4	5	Cryin'	Roy Orbison	Monument	10	(26)	G
5	2	Take Good Care Of My Baby	Bobby Vee	Liberty	8	(1)	G
6	-	Mexico	Bob Moore & His Orchestra	Monument	7		F L
7	-	Big Bad John	Jimmy Dean	Columbia	12	(3)	F G
8	-	Let's Get Together	Hayley Mills	Vista	7	(15)	F L
9	-	Ya Ya	Lee Dorsey	Fury	7		F
10	-	You Must Have Been A Beautiful Baby	Bobby Darin	Atco	5	(10)	
11	-	Sad Movies (Make Me Cry)	Sue Thompson	Hickory	7		F
12	-	I Love How You Love Me	Paris Sisters	Gregmark	6		F L
13	-	This Time	Troy Shondell	Liberty	10	(17)	F L
14	10	The Mountain's High	Dick & Deedee	Liberty	6	(25)	F G
15	8	Little Sister	Elvis Presley	RCA	7	(18)	
16	-	The Fly	Chubby Checker	Parkway	8		
17	-	The Way You Look Tonight	Lettermen	Capitol	6		F
18	1	Michael	Highwaymen	UA	10	(1)	F G
19	-	Tower Of Strength	Gene McDaniels	Liberty	8		
20	-	Look In My Eyes	Chantels	Carlton	4		L

November 1961

This Mnth	Prev Mnth	Title	Artist	Label	Wks 20	(UK Pos)	
1	7	Big Bad John	Jimmy Dean	Columbia	12	(3)	F G
2	3	Runaround Sue	Dion	Laurie	11	(10)	G
3	-	Fool #1	Brenda Lee	Decca	8		
4	2	Bristol Stomp	Dovells	Parkway	11		F G
5	19	Tower Of Strength	Gene McDaniels	Liberty	8		
6	13	This Time	Troy Shondell	Liberty	10	(17)	F L
7	16	The Fly	Chubby Checker	Parkway	8		
8	-	Please Mr. Postman	Marvelettes	Tamla	11		F G
9	1	Hit The Road Jack	Ray Charles	ABC Paramount	9	(4)	G
10	-	Goodbye Cruel World	James Darren	Colpix	10	(22)	F G
11	11	Sad Movies (Make Me Cry)	Sue Thompson	Hickory	7		F
12	-	You're The Reason	Bobby Edwards	Crest	5		F L
13	-	A Wonder Like You	Ricky Nelson	Imperial	4		
14	-	Heartaches	Marcels	Colpix	4		L
15	-	Crazy	Patsy Cline	Decca	5		
16	12	I Love How You Love Me	Paris Sisters	Gregmark	6		F L
17	8	Let's Get Together	Hayley Mills	Vista	7	(15)	F L
18	-	Tonight	Ferrante & Teicher	UA	6		
19	-	I Understand (Just How You Feel)	G-Clefs	Terrace	7	(16)	F L
20	9	Ya Ya	Lee Dorsey	Fury	7		F

December 1961

This Mnth	Prev Mnth	Title	Artist	Label	Wks 20	(UK Pos)	
1	8	Please Mr. Postman	Marvelettes	Tamla	11		F G
2	10	Goodbye Cruel World	James Darren	Colpix	10	(22)	F G
3	-	The Twist	Chubby Checker	Parkway	15	(14)	G
4	-	Walk On By	Leroy Van Dyke	Mercury	10	(5)	F L
5	-	Run To Him	Bobby Vee	Liberty	11	(8)	G
6	-	The Lion Sleeps Tonight	Tokens	RCA	10	(13)	G L
7	1	Big Bad John	Jimmy Dean	Columbia	12	(3)	F G
8	-	Let There Be Drums	Sandy Nelson	Imperial	7	(3)	L
9	-	Happy Birthday, Sweet Sixteen	Neil Sedaka	RCA	8	(3)	
10	18	Tonight	Ferrante & Teicher	UA	6		
11	-	Peppermint Twist (Pt. 1)	Joey Dee & The Starliters	Roulette	13	(11)	F G
12	-	Moon River	Jerry Butler	Vee Jay	5		
13	2	Runaround Sue	Dion	Laurie	11	(10)	G
14	3	Fool #1	Brenda Lee	Decca	8		
15	-	Moon River	Henry Mancini	RCA	4	(17)	F
16	15	Crazy	Patsy Cline	Decca	5		
17	19	I Understand (Just How You Feel)	G-Clefs	Terrace	7	(16)	F L
18	5	Tower Of Strength	Gene McDaniels	Liberty	8		
19	-	When I Fall In Love	Lettermen	Capitol	8		
20	-	Can't Help Falling In Love	Elvis Presley	RCA	10	(3)	G

◆ Motown, who scored their first No. 1 with 'Please Mr. Postman' by The Marvelettes, were excited about 11-year-old Steveland Judkins, whom they renamed Little Stevie Wonder.

◆ Folk singer Joan Baez debuted on the album chart as Bob Dylan recorded his debut LP. Dylan also appeared at Carnegie Hall in front of just 53 people!

◆ Phil Spector launched his own label Philles with the Top 20 hit 'There's No Other' by The Crystals. Less successful was the launching by some other labels of "Little LPs" – six track 7-inch 33 rpm records.

◆ The Beach Boys released their debut single 'Surfin'' on X Records, and performed their first gig under that name at a Ritchie Valens Memorial Show.

UK 1962
JAN-MAR

◆ The theme from Cliff Richard's film *The Young Ones* racked up 500.000 advance orders and entered the UK chart at No. 1. It went on to sell over a million in Britain. The soundtrack album also topped the chart.

◆ Decca auditioned and rejected The Beatles. Reviewing their German recorded single 'My Bonnie' *NME* said, "a group with above average ideas – worth a listen", whereas *Billboard* gave it its lowest star rating.

◆ Alexis Korner's group, Blues Incorporated (which at times included Charlie Watts, Jack Bruce, Ginger Baker, Mick Jagger and Brian Jones), played their debut gig at a club in Ealing.

◆ The *Record Mirror* became the first pop publication to include the UK Top 50 charts. The magazine became the flagship of the burgeoning British R&B boom.

January 1962

This Mnth	Prev Mnth	Title	Artist	Label	Wks 20	(US Pos)	
1	5	Stranger On The Shore	Mr. Acker Bilk	Columbia	33	(1)	G
2	20	I'd Never Find Another You	Billy Fury	Decca	11		
3	11	Let There Be Drums	Sandy Nelson	London American	9	(7)	L
4	-	The Young Ones	Cliff Richard	Columbia	13		G
5	17	Happy Birthday, Sweet Sixteen	Neil Sedaka	RCA	11	(6)	
6	-	Multiplication	Bobby Darin	London American	8	(30)	
7	-	Let's Twist Again	Chubby Checker	Columbia	18	(8)	
8	2	Moon River	Danny Williams	HMV	12		F
9	4	Midnight In Moscow	Kenny Ball	Pye Jazz	11	(2)	
10	9	Johnny Will	Pat Boone	London American	8	(35)	
11	-	Run To Him	Bobby Vee	Liberty	9	(2)	
12	-	The Twist	Chubby Checker	Columbia	5	(1)	F
13	1	Tower Of Strength	Frankie Vaughan	Philips	10		
14	-	The Lion Sleeps Tonight	Tokens	RCA	4	(1)	F L
15	-	Walk On By	Leroy Van Dyke	Mercury	9	(5)	F L
16	15	So Long Baby	Del Shannon	London American	6	(28)	
17	-	Forget Me Not	Eden Kane	Decca	9		
18	-	Language Of Love	John D. Loudermilk	RCA	4	(32)	F L
19	-	Toy Balloons	Russ Conway	Columbia	5		L
20	-	Cryin' In The Rain	Everly Brothers	Warner	9	(6)	

February 1962

This Mnth	Prev Mnth	Title	Artist	Label	Wks 20	(US Pos)	
1	4	The Young Ones	Cliff Richard	Columbia	13		G
2	7	Let's Twist Again	Chubby Checker	Columbia	18	(8)	
3	-	Rock-A-Hula-Baby	Elvis Presley	RCA	9	(23)	
4	17	Forget Me Not	Eden Kane	Decca	9		
5	15	Walk On By	Leroy Van Dyke	Mercury	9	(5)	F L
6	5	Happy Birthday, Sweet Sixteen	Neil Sedaka	RCA	11	(6)	
7	20	Cryin' In The Rain	Everly Brothers	Warner	9	(6)	
8	2	I'd Never Find Another You	Billy Fury	Decca	11		
9	1	Stranger On The Shore	Mr. Acker Bilk	Columbia	33	(1)	G
10	11	Run To Him	Bobby Vee	Liberty	9	(2)	
11	6	Multiplication	Bobby Darin	London American	8	(30)	
12	-	A Little Bitty Tear	Burl Ives	Brunswick	6	(9)	F L
13	-	Peppermint Twist	Joey Dee & The Starliters	Columbia	5	(1)	F L
14	-	Wimoweh	Karl Denver	Decca	10		
15	-	Lonesome	Adam Faith	Parlophone	4		
16	-	Can't Help Falling In Love	Elvis Presley	RCA	13	(2)	
17	-	The Comancheros	Lonnie Donegan	Pye	4		
18	-	March Of The Siamese Children	Kenny Ball	Pye Jazz	8	(88)	
19	3	Let There Be Drums	Sandy Nelson	London American	9	(7)	L
20	12	The Twist	Chubby Checker	Columbia	5	(1)	F

March 1962

This Mnth	Prev Mnth	Title	Artist	Label	Wks 20	(US Pos)	
1	18	March Of The Siamese Children	Kenny Ball	Pye Jazz	8	(88)	
2	-	Tell Me What He Said	Helen Shapiro	Columbia	10		
3	2	Let's Twist Again	Chubby Checker	Columbia	18	(8)	
4	-	Wonderful Land	Shadows	Columbia	16		
5	16	Can't Help Falling In Love	Elvis Presley	RCA	13	(2)	
6	14	Wimoweh	Karl Denver	Decca	10		
7	1	The Young Ones	Cliff Richard	Columbia	13		G
8	3	Rock-A-Hula-Baby	Elvis Presley	RCA	9	(23)	
9	9	Stranger On The Shore	Mr. Acker Bilk	Columbia	33	(1)	G
10	-	Hole In The Ground	Bernard Cribbins	Parlophone	7		F
11	-	Twistin' The Night Away	Sam Cooke	RCA	12	(9)	
12	-	Dream Baby	Roy Orbison	London American	11	(4)	
13	-	Softly As I Leave You	Matt Monro	Parlophone	8		
14	-	Hey! Baby	Bruce Channel	Mercury	9	(1)	F
15	7	Cryin' In The Rain	Everly Brothers	Warner	9	(6)	
16	-	The Wanderer	Dion	HMV	6	(2)	
17	4	Forget Me Not	Eden Kane	Decca	9		
18	12	A Little Bitty Tear	Burl Ives	Brunswick	6	(9)	F L
19	5	Walk On By	Leroy Van Dyke	Mercury	9	(5)	F L
20	-	Hey Little Girl	Del Shannon	London American	12	(38)	

January 1962

This Mnth	Prev Mnth	Title	Artist	Label	Wks 20	(UK Pos)	
1	3	The Twist	Chubby Checker	Parkway	15	(14)	G
2	11	Peppermint Twist (Pt. 1)	Joey Dee & The Starliters	Roulette	13	(11)	F G
3	6	The Lion Sleeps Tonight	Tokens	RCA	10	(13)	G L
4	20	Can't Help Falling In Love	Elvis Presley	RCA	10	(3)	G
5	-	I Know (You Don't Love Me No More)	Barbara George	AFO	8		F L
6	9	Happy Birthday, Sweet Sixteen	Neil Sedaka	RCA	8	(3)	
7	5	Run To Him	Bobby Vee	Liberty	11	(8)	G
8	4	Walk On By	Leroy Van Dyke	Mercury	10	(5)	F L
9	19	When I Fall In Love	Lettermen	Capitol	8		
10	-	Unchain My Heart	Ray Charles	ABC Paramount	6		
11	-	When The Boy In Your Arms (Is The Boy In Your Heart)	Connie Francis	MGM	6		
12	-	Norman	Sue Thompson	Hickory	9		G
13	-	Baby It's You	Shirelles	Scepter	9		
14	8	Let There Be Drums	Sandy Nelson	Imperial	7	(3)	L
15	1	Please Mr. Postman	Marvelettes	Tamla	11		F G
16	-	The Wanderer	Dion	Laurie	11	(13)	G
17	-	Town Without Pity	Gene Pitney	Musicor	4		F
18	-	A Little Bitty Tear	Burl Ives	Decca	8	(7)	F
19	2	Goodbye Cruel World	James Darren	Colpix	10	(22)	F G
20	-	Cotton Fields	Highwaymen	UA	7		L

February 1962

This Mnth	Prev Mnth	Title	Artist	Label	Wks 20	(UK Pos)	
1	-	Duke Of Earl	Gene Chandler	Vee Jay	11	(29)	F G
2	2	Peppermint Twist (Pt. 1)	Joey Dee & The Starliters	Roulette	13	(11)	F G
3	1	The Twist	Chubby Checker	Parkway	15	(14)	G
4	12	Norman	Sue Thompson	Hickory	9		G
5	16	The Wanderer	Dion	Laurie	11	(13)	G
6	4	Can't Help Falling In Love	Elvis Presley	RCA	10	(3)	G
7	-	Break It To Me Gently	Brenda Lee	Decca	9		
8	5	I Know (You Don't Love Me No More)	Barbara George	AFO	8		F L
9	-	Dear Lady Twist	Gary U.S. Bonds	Legrand	8		
10	18	A Little Bitty Tear	Burl Ives	Decca	8	(7)	F
11	13	Baby It's You	Shirelles	Scepter	9		
12	-	Cryin' In The Rain	Everly Brothers	Warner	8	(6)	
13	20	Cotton Fields	Highwaymen	UA	7		L
14	3	The Lion Sleeps Tonight	Tokens	RCA	10	(13)	G L
15	-	Hey! Baby	Bruce Channel	Smash	10	(2)	F G L
16	-	Chip Chip	Gene McDaniels	Liberty	5		L
17	-	Irresistible You	Bobby Darin	Atco	3		
18	17	Town Without Pity	Gene Pitney	Musicor	4		F
19	9	When I Fall In Love	Lettermen	Capitol	8		
20	7	Run To Him	Bobby Vee	Liberty	11	(8)	G

March 1962

This Mnth	Prev Mnth	Title	Artist	Label	Wks 20	(UK Pos)	
1	15	Hey! Baby	Bruce Channel	Smash	10	(2)	F G L
2	-	Midnight In Moscow	Kenny Ball	Kapp	9	(5)	F L
3	-	Don't Break The Heart That Loves You	Connie Francis	MGM	8	(28)	G
4	1	Duke Of Earl	Gene Chandler	Vee Jay	11	(29)	F G
5	-	Let Me In	Sensations	Argo	8		F L
6	-	What's Your Name	Don & Juan	Big Top	7		F L
7	12	Cryin' In The Rain	Everly Brothers	Warner	8	(6)	
8	-	Her Royal Majesty	James Darren	Colpix	5		
9	7	Break It To Me Gently	Brenda Lee	Decca	9		
10	5	The Wanderer	Dion	Laurie	11	(13)	G
11	-	Slow Twistin'	Chubby Checker	Parkway	10	(19)	G
12	-	Dream Baby	Roy Orbison	Monument	6	(3)	
13	-	Twistin' The Night Away	Sam Cooke	RCA	7	(4)	
14	-	Johnny Angel	Shelley Fabares	Colpix	10	(27)	F G L
15	-	Percolator (Twist)	Billy Joe & The Checkmates	Dore	5		F L
16	9	Dear Lady Twist	Gary U.S. Bonds	Legrand	8		
17	3	The Twist	Chubby Checker	Parkway	15	(14)	G
18	4	Norman	Sue Thompson	Hickory	9		G
19	16	Chip Chip	Gene McDaniels	Liberty	5		L
20	-	Good Luck Charm	Elvis Presley	RCA	10	(1)	G

US 1962
JAN-MAR

▲ The twist took off internationally. Chubby Checker signed to appear in the low-budget movie *Twist Around The Clock* (as did Dion) and Joey Dee filmed *Hey Let's Twist*. Countless artists climbed on the twist bandwagon. In America Checker's 1960 chart topper 'The Twist' returned and outsold all the competition, while in Britain his 'Let's Twist Again' reached No. 1. Checker also monopolized the US album chart with a record five LPs in the Top 12!

◆ The Radio Trade Practises Committee proposed that lyrics of pop songs be screened as too many songs dealt with sex and violence.

UK 1962 APR-JUNE

◆ British trad star Acker Bilk topped the US chart with 'Stranger On The Shore'. In the 1962 *Billboard* DJ poll he won awards for Top Instrumentalist and Top Instrumental Single.

◆ The Twist was still the bandwagon to join – even Frank Sinatra charted with 'Ev'rybody's Twistin''. Incidentally 'Twist Baby' by Owen Gray was the initial release on the newly launched Island label.

◆ The Beatles, attracted a record 900 crowd to the Cavern Club after their successful EMI audition. Meanwhile, the Dave Clark Five released their debut disc single 'That's What I Said'.

◆ *It's Trad Dad* (known as *Ring-A-Ding Rhythm* in the USA) was doing well at the box office. The film starred UK acts Helen Shapiro and Craig Douglas with Americans Chubby Checker, Del Shannon and U.S. Bonds.

April 1962

This Mnth	Prev Mnth	Title	Artist	Label	Wks 20	(US Pos)	
1	4	Wonderful Land	Shadows	Columbia	16		
2	14	Hey! Baby	Bruce Channel	Mercury	9	(1)	F
3	12	Dream Baby	Roy Orbison	London American	11	(4)	
4	-	When My Little Girl Is Smiling	Jimmy Justice	Pye	9		F
5	11	Twistin' The Night Away	Sam Cooke	RCA	12	(9)	
6	2	Tell Me What He Said	Helen Shapiro	Columbia	10		
7	20	Hey Little Girl	Del Shannon	London American	12	(38)	
8	5	Can't Help Falling In Love	Elvis Presley	RCA	13	(2)	
9	-	Never Goodbye	Karl Denver	Decca	7		
10	-	Speak To Me Pretty	Brenda Lee	Brunswick	9		
11	3	Let's Twist Again	Chubby Checker	Columbia	18	(8)	
12	6	Wimoweh	Karl Denver	Decca	10		
13	-	When My Little Girl Is Smiling	Craig Douglas	Top Rank	6		
14	-	Dr. Kildare Theme	Johnny Spence	Parlophone	5		F L
15	9	Stranger On The Shore	Mr. Acker Bilk	Columbia	33	(1)	G
16	1	March Of The Siamese Children	Kenny Ball	Pye Jazz	8	(88)	
17	-	Love Letters	Ketty Lester	London American	9	(5)	F L
18	-	Nut Rocker	B. Bumble & The Stingers	Top Rank	11	(23)	F L
19	-	Wonderful World Of The Young	Danny Williams	HMV	7		L
20	-	Ev'rybody's Twistin'	Frank Sinatra	Reprise	5	(75)	

May 1962

This Mnth	Prev Mnth	Title	Artist	Label	Wks 20	(US Pos)	
1	18	Nut Rocker	B. Bumble & The Stingers	Top Rank	11	(23)	F L
2	1	Wonderful Land	Shadows	Columbia	16		
3	17	Love Letters	Ketty Lester	London American	9	(5)	F L
4	-	Good Luck Charm	Elvis Presley	RCA	14	(1)	
5	10	Speak To Me Pretty	Brenda Lee	Brunswick	9		
6	-	I'm Looking Out The Window	Cliff Richard	Columbia	11		
7	7	Hey Little Girl	Del Shannon	London American	12	(38)	
8	4	When My Little Girl Is Smiling	Jimmy Justice	Pye	9		F
9	-	As You Like It	Adam Faith	Parlophone	10		
10	2	Hey! Baby	Bruce Channel	Mercury	9	(1)	F
11	19	Wonderful World Of The Young	Danny Williams	HMV	7		L
12	3	Dream Baby	Roy Orbison	London American	11	(4)	
13	5	Twistin' The Night Away	Sam Cooke	RCA	12	(9)	
14	-	Come Outside	Mike Sarne & Wendy Richard	Parlophone	14		F
15	-	Last Night Was Made For Love	Billy Fury	Decca	11		
16	-	The Party's Over	Lonnie Donegan	Pye	5		
17	15	Stranger On The Shore	Mr. Acker Bilk	Columbia	33	(1)	G
18	20	Ev'rybody's Twistin'	Frank Sinatra	Reprise	5	(75)	
19	-	Let's Talk About Love	Helen Shapiro	Columbia	3		
20	-	I Don't Know Why	Eden Kane	Decca	7		

June 1962

This Mnth	Prev Mnth	Title	Artist	Label	Wks 20	(US Pos)	
1	4	Good Luck Charm	Elvis Presley	RCA	14	(1)	
2	14	Come Outside	Mike Sarne & Wendy Richard	Parlophone	14		F
3	6	I'm Looking Out The Window	Cliff Richard	Columbia	11		
4	-	A Picture Of You	Joe Brown & The Bruvvers	Piccadilly	14		F
5	-	Ginny Come Lately	Brian Hyland	HMV	10	(21)	
6	15	Last Night Was Made For Love	Billy Fury	Decca	11		
7	20	I Don't Know Why	Eden Kane	Decca	7		
8	9	As You Like It	Adam Faith	Parlophone	10		
9	1	Nut Rocker	B. Bumble & The Stingers	Top Rank	11	(23)	F L
10	-	The Green Leaves Of Summer	Kenny Ball	Pye Jazz	9	(87)	
11	-	Do You Wanna Dance	Cliff Richard	Columbia	6		
12	17	Stranger On The Shore	Mr. Acker Bilk	Columbia	33	(1)	G
13	-	I Can't Stop Loving You	Ray Charles	HMV	12	(1)	
14	3	Love Letters	Ketty Lester	London American	9	(5)	F L
15	-	Theme From Dr. Kildare (Three Stars Will Shine Tonight)	Richard Chamberlain	MGM	4	(10)	F
16	-	Ain't That Funny	Jimmy Justice	Pye	8		L
17	-	A Little Love, A Little Kiss	Karl Denver	Decca	3		
18	2	Wonderful Land	Shadows	Columbia	16		
19	-	Here Comes That Feeling	Brenda Lee	Brunswick	8	(89)	
20	-	Follow That Dream E.P.	Elvis Presley	RCA	6	(15)	

US 1962 APR-JUNE

April 1962

This Mnth	Prev Mnth	Title	Artist	Label	Wks 20	(UK Pos)	
1	14	Johnny Angel	Shelley Fabares	Colpix	10	(27)	F G L
2	20	Good Luck Charm	Elvis Presley	RCA	10	(1)	G
3	11	Slow Twistin'	Chubby Checker	Parkway	10	(19)	G
4	-	Mashed Potato Time	Dee Dee Sharp	Cameo	12		F G
5	-	Young World	Rick Nelson	Imperial	7	(21)	
6	-	Love Letters	Ketty Lester	Era	7	(4)	F G L
7	-	Lover Please	Clyde McPhatter	Mercury	8		L
8	-	Soldier Boy	Shirelles	Scepter	10	(27)	G
9	3	Don't Break The Heart That Loves You	Connie Francis	MGM	8	(28)	G
10	2	Midnight In Moscow	Kenny Ball	Kapp	9	(5)	F L
11	-	Shout (Pt. 1)	Joey Dee & The Starliters	Roulette	7		
12	-	Love Me Warm And Tender	Paul Anka	RCA	5	(14)	
13	1	Hey! Baby	Bruce Channel	Smash	10	(2)	F G L
14	-	Stranger On The Shore	Acker Bilk	Atco	13	(1)	F G L
15	12	Dream Baby	Roy Orbison	Monument	6	(3)	
16	-	Dear One	Larry Finnegan	Old Town	4		F L
17	-	Twist, Twist Senora	Gary U.S. Bonds	Legrand	6		
18	13	Twistin' The Night Away	Sam Cooke	RCA	7	(4)	
19	5	Let Me In	Sensations	Argo	8		F L
20	6	What's Your Name	Don & Juan	Big Top	7		F L

May 1962

This Mnth	Prev Mnth	Title	Artist	Label	Wks 20	(UK Pos)	
1	8	Soldier Boy	Shirelles	Scepter	10	(27)	G
2	14	Stranger On The Shore	Acker Bilk	Atco	13	(1)	F G L
3	4	Mashed Potato Time	Dee Dee Sharp	Cameo	12		F G
4	1	Johnny Angel	Shelley Fabares	Colpix	10	(27)	F G L
5	-	She Cried	Jay & The Americans	UA	8		F
6	-	Old Rivers	Walter Brennan	Liberty	6		F L
7	-	P.T. 109	Jimmy Dean	Columbia	6		L
8	2	Good Luck Charm	Elvis Presley	RCA	10	(1)	G
9	-	Shout! Shout! (Knock Yourself Out)	Ernie Maresca	Seville	6		F L
10	-	Everybody Loves Me But You	Brenda Lee	Decca	6		
11	11	Shout (Pt. 1)	Joey Dee & The Starliters	Roulette	7		
12	-	Funny Way Of Laughin'	Burl Ives	Decca	5		
13	17	Twist, Twist Senora	Gary U.S. Bonds	Legrand	6		
14	3	Slow Twistin'	Chubby Checker	Parkway	10	(19)	G
15	7	Lover Please	Clyde McPhatter	Mercury	8		L
16	-	Lovers Who Wander	Dion	Laurie	7		
17	-	The One Who Really Loves You	Mary Wells	Motown	7		F
18	-	I Can't Stop Loving You	Ray Charles	ABC Paramount	12	(1)	G
19	-	Conscience	James Darren	Colpix	5	(27)	L
20	-	Uptown	Crystals	Philles	5		

June 1962

This Mnth	Prev Mnth	Title	Artist	Label	Wks 20	(UK Pos)	
1	18	I Can't Stop Loving You	Ray Charles	ABC Paramount	12	(1)	G
2	2	Stranger On The Shore	Acker Bilk	Atco	13	(1)	F G L
3	-	It Keeps Right On A-Hurtin'	Johnny Tillotson	Cadence	9		
4	-	(The Man Who Shot) Liberty Valence	Gene Pitney	Musicor	6		
5	-	Palisades Park	Freddy Cannon	Swan	9	(22)	G
6	-	The Stripper	David Rose & His Orchestra	MGM	11		F G L
7	16	Lovers Who Wander	Dion	Laurie	7		
8	-	Playboy	Marvelettes	Tamla	7		
9	-	Second Hand Love	Connie Francis	MGM	5		
10	17	The One Who Really Loves You	Mary Wells	Motown	7		F
11	1	Soldier Boy	Shirelles	Scepter	10	(27)	G
12	-	Cindy's Birthday	Johnny Crawford	Del-Fi	4		F
13	-	That's Old Fashioned (That's The Way Love Should Be)	Everly Brothers	Warner	3		L
14	3	Mashed Potato Time	Dee Dee Sharp	Cameo	12		F G
15	-	Al Di La	Emilio Pericoli	Warner	7	(23)	F L
16	-	Don't Play That Song (You Lied)	Ben E. King	Atco	4		
17	10	Everybody Loves Me But You	Brenda Lee	Decca	6		
18	-	Snap Your Fingers	Joe Henderson	Todd	6		F L
19	-	Roses Are Red (My Love)	Bobby Vinton	Epic	12	(13)	F G
20	19	Conscience	James Darren	Colpix	5	(27)	L

◆ 'Good Luck Charm', Elvis Presley's 17th US No. 1 was also his last chart topper for 7 1/2 years. Incidentally, his **Blue Hawaii** spent 20 weeks at No. 1 in the US and 18 in Britain.

◆ Latest American artists to score a transatlantic No. 1s were newcomer Bruce Channel with his composition 'Hey! Baby' and Ray Charles, then regarded as "the singer's singer", with a revival of 'I Can't Stop Loving You'.

▲ The Freewheelin' **Bob Dylan** album was released. *Billboard* said "Dylan could have a big following when he finds his own style".

UK 1962 JULY-SEPT

◆ Ringo Starr replaced drummer Pete Best in The Beatles, who recorded their Parlophone debut, 'Love Me Do'. The record, which took 17 takes, was a US No. 1 in 1964 and finally made the UK Top 10 twenty years later! Another group who were to change 1960's music, The Rolling Stones, made their live debut at the Marquee club in London.

◆ Frank Ifield scored the first of three successive No. 1s with 'I Remember You', which spent seven weeks at No. 1 in Britain and sold over a million copies.

◆ Britain's top recording act in the early rock years, Lonnie Donegan, had his last UK Top 20 entry with 'Pick A Bale of Cotton' (which, like his debut hit, 'Rock Island Line', was originally associated with US folk/blues man Leadbelly). Lonnie also launched his own TV series *Putting On The Donegan*.

July 1962

This Mnth	Prev Mnth	Title	Artist	Label	Wks 20	(US Pos)	
1	12	I Can't Stop Loving You	Ray Charles	HMV	12	(1)	
2	4	A Picture Of You	Joe Brown & The Bruvvers	Piccadilly	14		F
3	2	Come Outside	Mike Sarne & Wendy Richard	Parlophone	14		F
4	-	I Remember You	Frank Ifield	Columbia	19	(5)	F G
5	1	Good Luck Charm	Elvis Presley	RCA	14	(1)	
6	18	Here Comes That Feeling	Brenda Lee	Brunswick	8	(89)	
7	-	English Country Garden	Jimmie Rodgers	Columbia	9		L
8	5	Ginny Come Lately	Brian Hyland	HMV	10	(21)	
9	-	Don't Ever Change	Crickets	Liberty	9		L
10	-	Speedy Gonzales	Pat Boone	London American	12	(6)	
11	-	Our Favourite Melodies	Craig Douglas	Columbia	6		
12	10	The Green Leaves Of Summer	Kenny Ball	Pye Jazz	9	(87)	
13	3	I'm Looking Out The Window	Cliff Richard	Columbia	11		
14	15	Ain't That Funny	Jimmy Justice	Pye	8		L
15	6	Last Night Was Made For Love	Billy Fury	Decca	11		
16	-	Yes My Darling Daughter	Eydie Gorme	CBS	5		F
17	12	Stranger On The Shore	Mr. Acker Bilk	Columbia	33	(1)	G
18	-	Right Said Fred	Bernard Cribbins	Parlophone	6		L
19	19	Follow That Dream E.P.	Elvis Presley	RCA	6	(15)	
20	-	Ya Ya Twist	Petula Clark	Pye	5		

August 1962

This Mnth	Prev Mnth	Title	Artist	Label	Wks 20	(US Pos)	
1	4	I Remember You	Frank Ifield	Columbia	19	(5)	F G
2	10	Speedy Gonzales	Pat Boone	London American	12	(6)	
3	-	Guitar Tango	Shadows	Columbia	10		
4	-	Things	Bobby Darin	London American	12	(3)	
5	1	I Can't Stop Loving You	Ray Charles	HMV	12	(1)	
6	-	Roses Are Red	Ronnie Carroll	Philips	11		
7	2	A Picture Of You	Joe Brown & The Bruvvers	Piccadilly	14		F
8	9	Don't Ever Change	Crickets	Liberty	9		L
9	-	Once Upon A Dream	Billy Fury	Decca	8		
10	-	Little Miss Lonely	Helen Shapiro	Columbia	7		L
11	-	Let There Be Love	Nat 'King' Cole	Capitol	7		
12	-	Breaking Up Is Hard To Do	Neil Sedaka	RCA	11	(1)	
13	-	Sealed With A Kiss	Brian Hyland	HMV	8	(3)	
14	6	Here Comes That Feeling	Brenda Lee	Brunswick	8	(89)	
15	3	Come Outside	Mike Sarne & Wendy Richard	Parlophone	14		F
16	17	Right Said Fred	Bernard Cribbins	Parlophone	6		L
17	-	Roses Are Red (My Love)	Bobby Vinton	Columbia	4	(1)	F
18	-	Vacation	Connie Francis	MGM	4	(9)	L
19	7	English Country Garden	Jimmie Rodgers	Columbia	9		L
20	-	So Do I	Kenny Ball	Pye Jazz	3		

September 1962

This Mnth	Prev Mnth	Title	Artist	Label	Wks 20	(US Pos)	
1	-	She's Not You	Elvis Presley	RCA	11	(5)	
2	1	I Remember You	Frank Ifield	Columbia	19	(5)	F G
3	6	Roses Are Red	Ronnie Carroll	Philips	11		
4	-	It'll Be Me	Cliff Richard	Columbia	8		
5	4	Things	Bobby Darin	London American	12	(3)	
6	13	Sealed With A Kiss	Brian Hyland	HMV	8	(3)	
7	12	Breaking Up Is Hard To Do	Neil Sedaka	RCA	11	(1)	
8	-	Telstar	Tornados	Decca	19	(1)	F
9	2	Speedy Gonzales	Pat Boone	London American	12	(6)	
10	3	Guitar Tango	Shadows	Columbia	10		
11	-	Don't That Beat All	Adam Faith	Parlophone	8		
12	-	Sheila	Tommy Roe	HMV	11	(1)	F
13	-	The Loco-Motion	Little Eva	London American	12	(1)	F
14	-	Ballad Of Paladin	Duane Eddy	RCA	7	(33)	
15	9	Once Upon A Dream	Billy Fury	Decca	8		
16	-	Pick A Bale Of Cotton	Lonnie Donegan	Pye	5		L
17	-	Main Title Theme From 'Man With The Golden Arm'	Jet Harris	Decca	6		F
18	-	You Don't Know Me	Ray Charles	HMV	8	(2)	
19	-	Will I What	Mike Sarne with Billie Davis	Parlophone	5		L
20	-	It Might As Well Rain Until September	Carole King	London American	9	(22)	F

86

July 1962

This Mnth	Prev Mnth	Title	Artist	Label	Wks 20	(UK Pos)	
1	19	Roses Are Red (My Love)	Bobby Vinton	Epic	12	(13)	F G
2	6	The Stripper	David Rose & His Orchestra	MGM	11		F G L
3	1	I Can't Stop Loving You	Ray Charles	ABC Paramount	12	(1)	G
4	-	The Wah-Watusi	Orlons	Cameo	9		F G
5	-	Sealed With A Kiss	Brian Hyland	ABC Paramount	8	(5)	G
6	-	Wolverton Mountain	Claude King	Columbia	10		F G L
7	5	Palisades Park	Freddy Cannon	Swan	9	(22)	G
8	-	Johnny Get Angry	Joanie Sommers	Warner	7	(28)	F L
9	-	Gravy (For My Mashed Potatoes)	Dee Dee Sharp	Cameo	5		
10	15	Al Di La	Emilio Pericoli	Warner	7	(23)	F L
11	3	It Keeps Right On A-Hurtin'	Johnny Tillotson	Cadence	9		
12	-	Speedy Gonzales	Pat Boone	Dot	7	(2)	L
13	-	Breaking Up Is Hard To Do	Neil Sedaka	RCA	9	(7)	G
14	18	Snap Your Fingers	Joe Henderson	Todd	6		F L
15	-	Ahab, The Arab	Ray Stevens	Mercury	8		F
16	-	Theme From Doctor Kildare (Three Stars Will Shine Tonight)	Richard Chamberlain	MGM	7	(11)	F
17	8	Playboy	Marvelettes	Tamla	7		
18	-	Dancin' Party	Chubby Checker	Parkway	4	(17)	
19	-	I'll Never Dance Again	Bobby Rydell	Cameo	4		
20	12	Cindy's Birthday	Johnny Crawford	Del-Fi	4		F

August 1962

This Mnth	Prev Mnth	Title	Artist	Label	Wks 20	(UK Pos)	
1	13	Breaking Up Is Hard To Do	Neil Sedaka	RCA	9	(7)	G
2	1	Roses Are Red (My Love)	Bobby Vinton	Epic	12	(13)	F G
3	-	The Loco-Motion	Little Eva	Dimension	10	(2)	F G
4	4	The Wah-Watusi	Orlons	Cameo	9		F G
5	15	Ahab, The Arab	Ray Stevens	Mercury	8		F
6	-	Things	Bobby Darin	Atco	6	(3)	
7	5	Sealed With A Kiss	Brian Hyland	ABC Paramount	8	(5)	G
8	-	You Don't Know Me	Ray Charles	ABC Paramount	6	(6)	
9	12	Speedy Gonzales	Pat Boone	Dot	7	(2)	L
10	-	You'll Lose A Good Thing	Barbara Lynn	Jamie	5		F L
11	-	Little Diane	Dion	Laurie	5		
12	2	The Stripper	David Rose & His Orchestra	MGM	11		F G L
13	6	Wolverton Mountain	Claude King	Columbia	10		F G L
14	-	Party Lights	Claudine Clark	Chancellor	6		F L
15	-	Sheila	Tommy Roe	ABC Paramount	9	(2)	F G
16	-	She's Not You	Elvis Presley	RCA	7	(1)	
17	3	I Can't Stop Loving You	Ray Charles	ABC Paramount	12	(1)	G
18	16	Theme From Doctor Kildare (Three Stars Will Shine Tonight)	Richard Chamberlain	MGM	7	(11)	F
19	-	Vacation	Connie Francis	MGM	4	(13)	
20	8	Johnny Get Angry	Joanie Sommers	Warner	7	(28)	F L

September 1962

This Mnth	Prev Mnth	Title	Artist	Label	Wks 20	(UK Pos)	
1	15	Sheila	Tommy Roe	ABC Paramount	9	(2)	F G
2	-	Ramblin' Rose	Nat 'King' Cole	Capitol	10	(4)	G
3	3	The Loco-Motion	Little Eva	Dimension	10	(2)	F G
4	-	Sherry	Four Seasons	Vee Jay	10	(7)	F G
5	16	She's Not You	Elvis Presley	RCA	7	(1)	
6	-	Teenage Idol	Ricky Nelson	Imperial	6		
7	-	Green Onions	Booker T. & The M.G.'s	Stax	8	(7)	F G
8	8	You Don't Know Me	Ray Charles	ABC Paramount	6	(6)	
9	-	You Belong To Me	Duprees	Coed	6		F
10	-	Patches	Dickey Lee	Smash	9		F
11	14	Party Lights	Claudine Clark	Chancellor	6		F L
12	-	Let's Dance	Chris Montez	Monogram	7	(2)	F G
13	-	Rinky Dink	Dave 'Baby' Cortez	Chess	4		L
14	-	You Beat Me To The Punch	Mary Wells	Motown	5		
15	-	Alley Cat	Bent Fabric	Atco	5		F G L
16	6	Things	Bobby Darin	Atco	6	(3)	
17	-	Monster Mash	Bobby 'Boris' Pickett & The Crypt Kickers	Garpax	9	(3)	F G L
18	1	Breaking Up Is Hard To Do	Neil Sedaka	RCA	9	(7)	G
19	19	Vacation	Connie Francis	MGM	4	(13)	
20	2	Roses Are Red (My Love)	Bobby Vinton	Epic	12	(13)	F G

◆ As the Four Seasons and Bobby Vinton had the first of their many hits, fellow chart debutantes Chris Montez and Booker T. & The M.G.'s hit with 'Let's Dance' and 'Green Onions' respectively. The former single was a British Top 20 hit in 1962 and 1972 and the latter finally made the UK chart in 1979.

▲ The twist still ruled but many new dance crazes surfaced Stateside, including the successful Mashed Potato, Watusi, Popeye and Locomotion, the latter popularized by Little Eva.

◆ Singles sold at 98c and albums were $3.98 (mono) and $4.98 (stereo).

UK 1962 OCT-DEC

◆ As 'Return To Sender' gave Elvis Presley his 50th British hit and his 12th No. 1, his biggest 1950s rival Pat Boone visited the Top 20 for the last time.

▲ Big winners at the *NME* poll were Elvis, Brenda Lee and The Everly Brothers, with The Beatles being voted 8th most popular British group.

◆ The first British group to top the American charts were instrumental combo The Tornados with 'Telstar'. The record's producer/composer, Joe Meek, earlier turned down a chance to work with The Beatles.

October 1962

This Mnth	Prev Mnth	Title	Artist	Label	Wks 20	(US Pos)	
1	8	Telstar	Tornados	Decca	19	(1)	F
2	12	Sheila	Tommy Roe	HMV	11	(1)	F
3	13	The Loco-Motion	Little Eva	London American	12	(1)	F
4	20	It Might As Well Rain Until September	Carole King	London American	9	(22)	F
5	1	She's Not You	Elvis Presley	RCA	11	(5)	
6	-	Ramblin' Rose	Nat 'King' Cole	Capitol	10	(2)	
7	18	You Don't Know Me	Ray Charles	HMV	8	(2)	
8	4	It'll Be Me	Cliff Richard	Columbia	8		
9	-	What Now My Love	Shirley Bassey	Columbia	8		
10	-	Venus In Blue Jeans	Mark Wynter	Pye	9		F
11	2	I Remember You	Frank Ifield	Columbia	19	(5)	F G
12	11	Don't That Beat All	Adam Faith	Parlophone	8		
13	-	Let's Dance	Chris Montez	London American	13	(4)	F
14	-	Sherry	Four Seasons	Stateside	10	(1)	F
15	-	Lonely	Acker Bilk	Columbia	5		
16	3	Roses Are Red	Ronnie Carroll	Philips	11		
17	-	Swiss Maid	Del Shannon	London American	12	(64)	
18	-	Lovesick Blues	Frank Ifield	Columbia	14	(44)	
19	5	Things	Bobby Darin	London American	12	(3)	
20	-	It Started All Over Again	Brenda Lee	Brunswick	3	(29)	

November 1962

This Mnth	Prev Mnth	Title	Artist	Label	Wks 20	(US Pos)	
1	18	Lovesick Blues	Frank Ifield	Columbia	14	(44)	
2	13	Let's Dance	Chris Montez	London American	13	(4)	F
3	1	Telstar	Tornados	Decca	19	(1)	F
4	17	Swiss Maid	Del Shannon	London American	12	(64)	
5	10	Venus In Blue Jeans	Mark Wynter	Pye	9		F
6	3	The Loco-Motion	Little Eva	London American	12	(1)	F
7	-	Bobby's Girl	Susan Maughan	Philips	12		F L
8	14	Sherry	Four Seasons	Stateside	10	(1)	F
9	-	Devil Woman	Marty Robbins	CBS	10	(16)	L
10	6	Ramblin' Rose	Nat 'King' Cole	Capitol	10	(2)	
11	-	No One Can Make My Sunshine Smile	Everly Brothers	Warner	7		
12	4	It Might As Well Rain Until September	Carole King	London American	9	(22)	F
13	2	Sheila	Tommy Roe	HMV	11	(1)	F
14	-	Dance With The Guitar Man	Duane Eddy	RCA	11	(12)	
15	-	Sun Arise	Rolf Harris	Columbia	11	(61)	
16	-	Oh Lonesome Me	Craig Douglas	Decca	4		L
17	9	What Now My Love	Shirley Bassey	Columbia	8		
18	-	Return To Sender	Elvis Presley	RCA	11	(2)	
19	-	A Forever Kind Of Love	Bobby Vee	Liberty	5		
20	-	Kid Galahad E.P.	Elvis Presley	RCA	3		

December 1962

This Mnth	Prev Mnth	Title	Artist	Label	Wks 20	(US Pos)	
1	18	Return To Sender	Elvis Presley	RCA	11	(2)	
2	1	Lovesick Blues	Frank Ifield	Columbia	14	(44)	
3	15	Sun Arise	Rolf Harris	Columbia	11	(61)	
4	-	The Next Time	Cliff Richard	Columbia	12		
5	14	Dance With The Guitar Man	Duane Eddy	RCA	11	(12)	
6	2	Let's Dance	Chris Montez	London American	13	(4)	F
7	7	Bobby's Girl	Susan Maughan	Philips	12		F L
8	4	Swiss Maid	Del Shannon	London American	12	(64)	
9	-	Rockin' Around The Christmas Tree	Brenda Lee	Brunswick	4	(14)	
10	3	Telstar	Tornados	Decca	19	(1)	F
11	-	Dance On	Shadows	Columbia	10		
12	-	Bachelor Boy	Cliff Richard	Columbia	12	(99)	
13	-	It Only Took A Minute	Joe Brown & The Bruvvers	Piccadilly	8		
14	9	Devil Woman	Marty Robbins	CBS	10	(16)	L
15	-	The Main Attraction	Pat Boone	London American	5		L
16	8	Sherry	Four Seasons	Stateside	10	(1)	F
17	-	Your Cheatin' Heart	Ray Charles	HMV	4	(29)	
18	-	Up On The Roof	Kenny Lynch	HMV	7		F
19	5	Venus In Blue Jeans	Mark Wynter	Pye	9		F
20	19	A Forever Kind Of Love	Bobby Vee	Liberty	5		

US 1962 OCT-DEC

October 1962

This Mnth	Prev Mnth	Title	Artist	Label	Wks 20	(UK Pos)	
1	17	Monster Mash	Bobby 'Boris' Pickett & The Crypt Kickers	Garpax	9	(3)	F G L
2	4	Sherry	Four Seasons	Vee Jay	10	(7)	F G
3	2	Ramblin' Rose	Nat 'King' Cole	Capitol	10	(4)	G
4	10	Patches	Dickey Lee	Smash	9		F
5	-	Do You Love Me	Contours	Gordy	8		F G
6	-	I Remember You	Frank Ifield	Vee Jay	5	(1)	F L
7	12	Let's Dance	Chris Montez	Monogram	7	(2)	F G
8	7	Green Onions	Booker T. & The M.G.'s	Stax	8	(7)	F G
9	-	He's A Rebel	Crystals	UA	10	(19)	G
10	-	Only Love Can Break A Heart	Gene Pitney	Musicor	8		G
11	-	Venus In Blue Jeans	Jimmy Clanton	Ace	7		L
12	-	If I Had A Hammer	Peter, Paul & Mary	Warner	5		F
13	-	All Alone Am I	Brenda Lee	Decca	9	(11)	G
14	14	You Beat Me To The Punch	Mary Wells	Motown	5		
15	-	Surfin' Safari	Beach Boys	Capitol	3		F
16	1	Sheila	Tommy Roe	ABC Paramount	9	(2)	F G
17	-	Popeye (The Hitchhiker)	Chubby Checker	Parkway	5		
18	-	Gina	Johnny Mathis	Columbia	7		
19	-	Rain Rain Go Away	Bobby Vinton	Epic	4		
20	15	Alley Cat	Bent Fabric	Atco	5		F G L

November 1962

This Mnth	Prev Mnth	Title	Artist	Label	Wks 20	(UK Pos)	
1	-	Big Girls Don't Cry	Four Seasons	Vee Jay	13	(14)	G
2	9	He's A Rebel	Crystals	UA	10	(19)	G
3	13	All Alone Am I	Brenda Lee	Decca	9	(11)	G
4	-	Return To Sender	Elvis Presley	RCA	12	(1)	G
5	-	Next Door To An Angel	Neil Sedaka	RCA	6	(24)	
6	18	Gina	Johnny Mathis	Columbia	7		
7	10	Only Love Can Break A Heart	Gene Pitney	Musicor	8		G
8	-	Limbo Rock	Chubby Checker	Parkway	14	(29)	G
9	1	Monster Mash	Bobby 'Boris' Pickett & The Crypt Kickers	Garpax	9	(3)	F G L
10	5	Do You Love Me	Contours	Gordy	8		F G
11	-	Bobby's Girl	Marcie Blane	Seville	11		F G L
12	-	The Cha Cha Cha	Bobby Rydell	Cameo	6		
13	-	Don't Hang Up	Orlons	Cameo	8		
14	-	Close To Cathy	Mike Clifford	UA	5		F L
15	-	Nothing Can Change This Love	Sam Cooke	RCA	3		
16	17	Popeye (The Hitchhiker)	Chubby Checker	Parkway	5		
17	-	Ride	Dee Dee Sharp	Cameo	6		
18	2	Sherry	Four Seasons	Vee Jay	10	(7)	F G
19	-	The Lonely Bull	Herb Alpert	A&M	9		F
20	-	James (Hold The Ladder Steady)	Sue Thompson	Hickory	3		L

December 1962

This Mnth	Prev Mnth	Title	Artist	Label	Wks 20	(UK Pos)	
1	1	Big Girls Don't Cry	Four Seasons	Vee Jay	13	(14)	G
2	4	Return To Sender	Elvis Presley	RCA	12	(1)	G
3	11	Bobby's Girl	Marcie Blane	Seville	11		F G L
4	8	Limbo Rock	Chubby Checker	Parkway	14	(29)	G
5	-	Telstar	Tornados	London	11	(1)	F G L
6	13	Don't Hang Up	Orlons	Cameo	8		
7	19	The Lonely Bull	Herb Alpert	A&M	9		F
8	-	Release Me	Little Esther Phillips	Lenox	7		F
9	17	Ride	Dee Dee Sharp	Cameo	6		
10	-	Go Away Little Girl	Steve Lawrence	Columbia	12		G L
11	-	You Are My Sunshine	Ray Charles	ABC Paramount	5		
12	-	Keep Your Hands Off My Baby	Little Eva	Dimension	6		
13	3	All Alone Am I	Brenda Lee	Decca	9	(11)	G
14	-	Love Came To Me	Dion	Laurie	4		
15	2	He's A Rebel	Crystals	UA	10	(19)	G
16	-	Hotel Happiness	Brook Benton	Mercury	7		
17	-	Rumors	Johnny Crawford	Del-Fi	4		L
18	-	Dear Lonely Hearts	Nat 'King' Cole	Capitol	4		
19	-	Zip-A-Dee Doo-Dah	Bob B. Soxx & The Blue Jeans	Philles	6		F L
20	-	(Dance With The) Guitar Man	Duane Eddy	RCA	3	(4)	L

◆ Bobby 'Boris' Pickett's debut hit 'Monster Mash' was to reappear in the Top 20 eleven years later, and similarly the million selling 'Do You Love Me' by newcomers The Contours returned to the US Top 20 in 1988!

◆ Alan Freed pleaded guilty to payola charges. He was fined $300 and put on six months probation. Rock pioneer Freed died a forgotten man two years later.

◆ Notable chart newcomers included Peter, Paul & Mary (whose eponymous debut album hit No. 1), the Beach Boys and Herb Alpert, whose 'The Lonely Bull' was recorded in his garage at a cost of $65.

◆ "Hot Country Singles" was the new name of the C&W chart in *Billboard*.

UK 1963

JAN-MAR

◆ The Beatles second single 'Please Please Me' topped the chart. It put Merseybeat on the musical map and launched the Beat Boom. In America it was rush released but failed to click.

◆ Rock instrumentals reached new heights in February when records by (ex-Shadows) Jet Harris & Tony Meehan, The Tornados and The Shadows took the top three spots.

◆ The Scopitone video juke box was launched – it cost 5p a play to see acts like Craig Douglas and The Mudlarks – it proved to be a five minute wonder.

◆ As Cliff Richard's film *Summer Holiday* went on release, two songs from it 'The Next Time' and 'Bachelor Boy' reached the Top 5 – with combined sales topping a million. The soundtrack album topped the UK chart for 14 weeks.

January 1963

This Mnth	Prev Mnth	Title	Artist	Label	Wks 20	(US Pos)	
1	11	Dance On	Shadows	Columbia	10		
2	1	Return To Sender	Elvis Presley	RCA	11	(2)	
3	4	The Next Time	Cliff Richard	Columbia	12		
4	12	Bachelor Boy	Cliff Richard	Columbia	12	(99)	
5	5	Dance With The Guitar Man	Duane Eddy	RCA	11	(12)	
6	-	Like I Do	Maureen Evans	Oriole	9		F L
7	3	Sun Arise	Rolf Harris	Columbia	11	(61)	
8	2	Lovesick Blues	Frank Ifield	Columbia	14	(44)	
9	-	Globetrotter	Tornados	Decca	8		
10	-	Diamonds	Jet Harris & Tony Meehan	Decca	10		F
11	-	Go Away Little Girl	Mark Wynter	Pye	7		
12	18	Up On The Roof	Kenny Lynch	HMV	7		F
13	10	Telstar	Tornados	Decca	19	(1)	F
14	-	Coming Home Baby	Mel Tormé	London American	4	(36)	L
15	13	It Only Took A Minute	Joe Brown & The Bruvvers	Piccadilly	8		
16	7	Bobby's Girl	Susan Maughan	Philips	12		F L
17	-	Don't You Think It's Time	Mike Berry	HMV	7		F
18	6	Let's Dance	Chris Montez	London American	13	(4)	F
19	-	Little Town Flirt	Del Shannon	London American	8	(12)	
20	-	Desafinado	Stan Getz & Charlie Byrd	HMV	5	(15)	F L

February 1963

This Mnth	Prev Mnth	Title	Artist	Label	Wks 20	(US Pos)	
1	10	Diamonds	Jet Harris & Tony Meehan	Decca	10		F
2	-	Wayward Wind	Frank Ifield	Columbia	10		
3	19	Little Town Flirt	Del Shannon	London American	8	(12)	
4	-	Please Please Me	Beatles	Parlophone	10	(3)	F
5	9	Globetrotter	Tornados	Decca	8		
6	4	Bachelor Boy	Cliff Richard	Columbia	12	(99)	
7	-	Loop De Loop	Frankie Vaughan	Philips	8		
8	17	Don't You Think It's Time	Mike Berry	HMV	7		F
9	-	The Night Has A Thousand Eyes	Bobby Vee	Liberty	8	(3)	L
10	-	All Alone Am I	Brenda Lee	Brunswick	7	(3)	
11	-	Island Of Dreams	Springfields	Philips	12		F
12	6	Like I Do	Maureen Evans	Oriole	9		F L
13	1	Dance On	Shadows	Columbia	10		
14	3	The Next Time	Cliff Richard	Columbia	12		
15	-	Sukiyaki	Kenny Ball	Pye Jazz	5		
16	-	Walk Right In	Rooftop Singers	Fontana	5	(1)	F L
17	-	That's What Love Will Do	Joe Brown & The Bruvvers	Piccadilly	9		L
18	-	Big Girls Don't Cry	Four Seasons	Stateside	5	(1)	
19	2	Return To Sender	Elvis Presley	RCA	11	(2)	
20	-	Summer Holiday	Cliff Richard	Columbia	11		

March 1963

This Mnth	Prev Mnth	Title	Artist	Label	Wks 20	(US Pos)	
1	20	Summer Holiday	Cliff Richard	Columbia	11		
2	4	Please Please Me	Beatles	Parlophone	10	(3)	F
3	-	Like I've Never Been Gone	Billy Fury	Decca	10		
4	17	That's What Love Will Do	Joe Brown & The Bruvvers	Piccadilly	9		L
5	9	The Night Has A Thousand Eyes	Bobby Vee	Liberty	8	(3)	L
6	-	Foot Tapper	Shadows	Columbia	9		
7	11	Island Of Dreams	Springfields	Philips	12		F
8	2	Wayward Wind	Frank Ifield	Columbia	10		
9	-	Charmaine	Bachelors	Decca	9		F
10	-	One Broken Heart For Sale	Elvis Presley	RCA	5	(11)	
11	7	Loop De Loop	Frankie Vaughan	Philips	8		
12	-	Hey Paula	Paul & Paula	Philips	7	(1)	F
13	-	From A Jack To A King	Ned Miller	London American	12	(6)	F L
14	-	Tell Him	Billie Davis	Decca	5		F L
15	1	Diamonds	Jet Harris & Tony Meehan	Decca	10		F
16	-	Say Wonderful Things	Ronnie Carroll	Philips	8	(91)	L
17	-	Rhythm Of The Rain	Cascades	Warner	10	(3)	F L
18	-	How Do You Do It?	Gerry & The Pacemakers	Columbia	11	(9)	F
19	-	Brown Eyed Handsome Man	Buddy Holly	Coral	10		
20	16	Walk Right In	Rooftop Singers	Fontana	5	(1)	F L

January 1963

This Mnth	Prev Mnth	Title	Artist	Label	Wks 20	(UK Pos)	
1	10	Go Away Little Girl	Steve Lawrence	Columbia	12		G L
2	5	Telstar	Tornados	London	11	(1)	F G L
3	4	Limbo Rock	Chubby Checker	Parkway	14	(29)	G
4	-	Tell Him	Exciters	UA	7		F L
5	16	Hotel Happiness	Brook Benton	Mercury	7		
6	-	The Night Has A Thousand Eyes	Bobby Vee	Liberty	8	(3)	G
7	-	My Dad	Paul Peterson	Colpix	7		L
8	-	Pepino The Italian Mouse	Lou Monte	Reprise	5		L
9	-	Two Lovers	Mary Wells	Motown	7		
10	19	Zip-A-Dee Doo-Dah	Bob B. Soxx & The Blue Jeans	Philles	6		F L
11	-	Walk Right In	Rooftop Singers	Vanguard	9	(11)	F G
12	-	Hey Paula	Paul & Paula	Philips	10	(11)	F G
13	1	Big Girls Don't Cry	Four Seasons	Vee Jay	13	(14)	G
14	-	It's Up To You	Rick Nelson	Imperial	6	(25)	
15	3	Bobby's Girl	Marcie Blane	Seville	11		F G L
16	-	Up On The Roof	Drifters	Atlantic	7	(29)	
17	2	Return To Sender	Elvis Presley	RCA	12	(1)	G
18	-	I Saw Linda Yesterday	Dickey Lee	Smash	5		
19	11	You Are My Sunshine	Ray Charles	ABC Paramount	5		
20	-	Loop De Loop	Johnny Thunder	Diamond	7		F L

February 1963

This Mnth	Prev Mnth	Title	Artist	Label	Wks 20	(UK Pos)	
1	12	Hey Paula	Paul & Paula	Philips	10	(11)	F G
2	11	Walk Right In	Rooftop Singers	Vanguard	9	(11)	F G
3	-	Ruby Baby	Dion	Columbia	8		
4	-	Walk Like A Man	Four Seasons	Vee Jay	9	(12)	G
5	6	The Night Has A Thousand Eyes	Bobby Vee	Liberty	8	(3)	G
6	-	You've Really Got A Hold On Me	Miracles	Tamla	7		
7	20	Loop De Loop	Johnny Thunder	Diamond	7		F L
8	-	Rhythm Of The Rain	Cascades	Valiant	11	(4)	F G L
9	-	From A Jack To A King	Ned Miller	Fabor	6	(2)	F L
10	16	Up On The Roof	Drifters	Atlantic	7	(29)	
11	1	Go Away Little Girl	Steve Lawrence	Columbia	12		G L
12	-	He's Sure The Boy I Love	Crystals	Philles	4		
13	-	You're The Reason I'm Living	Bobby Darin	Capitol	10		
14	14	It's Up To You	Rick Nelson	Imperial	6	(25)	
15	4	Tell Him	Exciters	UA	7		F L
16	-	Half Heaven-Half Heartache	Gene Pitney	Musicor	6		
17	9	Two Lovers	Mary Wells	Motown	7		
18	-	Wild Weekend	Rebels	Swan	6		F L
19	-	Little Town Flirt	Del Shannon	Big Top	3	(4)	
20	-	Blame It On The Bossa Nova	Eydie Gormé	Columbia	8		F L

March 1963

This Mnth	Prev Mnth	Title	Artist	Label	Wks 20	(UK Pos)	
1	4	Walk Like A Man	Four Seasons	Vee Jay	9	(12)	G
2	-	Our Day Will Come	Ruby & The Romantics	Kapp	8	(26)	F G
3	13	You're The Reason I'm Living	Bobby Darin	Capitol	10		
4	8	Rhythm Of The Rain	Cascades	Valiant	11	(4)	F G L
5	-	The End Of The World	Skeeter Davis	RCA	9	(20)	F G
6	3	Ruby Baby	Dion	Columbia	8		
7	20	Blame It On The Bossa Nova	Eydie Gormé	Columbia	8		F L
8	1	Hey Paula	Paul & Paula	Philips	10	(11)	F G
9	-	What Will My Mary Say	Johnny Mathis	Columbia	7		
10	-	He's So Fine	Chiffons	Laurie	11	(11)	F G
11	-	In Dreams	Roy Orbison	Monument	8	(5)	
12	18	Wild Weekend	Rebels	Swan	6		F L
13	-	South Street	Orlons	Cameo	7		G
14	-	One Broken Heart For Sale	Elvis Presley	RCA	5	(8)	
15	-	Our Winter Love	Bill Pursell	Columbia	6		F L
16	2	Walk Right In	Rooftop Singers	Vanguard	9	(11)	F G
17	-	Mama Didn't Lie	Jan Bradley	Chess	6		F L
18	9	From A Jack To A King	Ned Miller	Fabor	6	(2)	F L
19	-	Send Me Some Lovin'	Sam Cooke	RCA	5		
20	-	Baby Workout	Jackie Wilson	Brunswick	7		

▲ Plane crash victim, Patsy Cline's funeral was attended by 25,000 people. Over 30 years later her albums still sold in enormous quantities on both sides of the Atlantic.

◆ Many folk singers protested because Pete Seeger and The Weavers were politically blacklisted by ABC TV's *Hootenanny*. Incidentally, the top transatlantic folk hit was 'Walk Right In' by The Rooftop Singers, who included ex Weaver Erik Darling.

◆ In March, the Top 4 US albums were all by humorists: Alan Sherman (two entries), Frank Fontaine and Vaughn Meader.

◆ The Beatles' manager Brian Epstein also looked after Billy J. Kramer & The Dakotas who had two successive No. 1s and Gerry & The Pacemakers who achieved three.

◆ Early examples of R&B covers in the "Beat Boom" included Freddie & The Dreamers' 'If You Gotta Make a Fool Of Somebody' and The Rolling Stones' version of Chuck Berry's 'Come On'. The late Buddy Holly hit the Top 5 with revivals of Chuck's 'Brown Eyed Handsome Man' and Bo Diddley's eponymous song, while in America The Beach Boys turned Berry's 'Sweet Little 16' into 'Surfin' USA' and Lonnie Mack charted with Chuck's 'Memphis'.

◆ Even though Cliff Richard sang his British chart topper, 'Summer Holiday', on Ed Sullivan's American TV show, it failed to click Stateside.

April 1963

This Mnth	Prev Mnth	Title	Artist	Label	Wks 20	(US Pos)	
1	18	How Do You Do It?	Gerry & The Pacemakers	Columbia	11	(9)	F
2	13	From A Jack To A King	Ned Miller	London American	12	(6)	F L
3	6	Foot Tapper	Shadows	Columbia	9		
4	19	Brown Eyed Handsome Man	Buddy Holly	Coral	10		
5	17	Rhythm Of The Rain	Cascades	Warner	10	(3)	F L
6	-	Say I Won't Be There	Springfields	Philips	8		L
7	16	Say Wonderful Things	Ronnie Carroll	Philips	8	(91)	L
8	1	Summer Holiday	Cliff Richard	Columbia	11		
9	-	The Folk Singer	Tommy Roe	HMV	7	(84)	
10	-	Nobody's Darlin' But Mine	Frank Ifield	Columbia	8		
11	-	From Me To You	Beatles	Parlophone	15	(41)	
12	3	Like I've Never Been Gone	Billy Fury	Decca	10		
13	-	In Dreams	Roy Orbison	London American	13	(7)	
14	9	Charmaine	Bachelors	Decca	9		F
15	-	Walk Like A Man	Four Seasons	Stateside	6	(1)	
16	-	Can't Get Used To Losing You	Andy Williams	CBS	10	(2)	
17	7	Island Of Dreams	Springfields	Philips	12		F
18	-	Robot	Tornados	Decca	5		
19	4	That's What Love Will Do	Joe Brown & The Bruvvers	Piccadilly	9		L
20	-	Let's Turkey Trot	Little Eva	London American	6	(20)	

May 1963

1	11	From Me To You	Beatles	Parlophone	15	(41)	
2	-	Scarlett O'Hara	Jet Harris & Tony Meehan	Decca	11		
3	16	Can't Get Used To Losing You	Andy Williams	CBS	10	(2)	
4	1	How Do You Do It?	Gerry & The Pacemakers	Columbia	11	(9)	F
5	13	In Dreams	Roy Orbison	London American	13	(7)	
6	10	Nobody's Darlin' But Mine	Frank Ifield	Columbia	8		
7	-	Do You Want To Know A Secret	Billy J. Kramer & The Dakotas	Parlophone	10		F
8	-	Two Kinds Of Teardrops	Del Shannon	London American	8	(50)	
9	-	Lucky Lips	Cliff Richard	Columbia	9	(62)	
10	2	From A Jack To A King	Ned Miller	London American	12	(6)	F L
11	-	Losing You	Brenda Lee	Brunswick	9	(6)	
12	6	Say I Won't Be There	Springfields	Philips	8		L
13	-	He's So Fine	Chiffons	Stateside	5	(1)	F
14	-	Deck Of Cards	Wink Martindale	London American	15		L
15	-	When Will You Say I Love You	Billy Fury	Decca	7		
16	-	Young Lovers	Paul & Paula	Philips	6	(6)	L
17	5	Rhythm Of The Rain	Cascades	Warner	10	(3)	F L
18	-	Take These Chains From My Heart	Ray Charles	HMV	13	(8)	
19	4	Brown Eyed Handsome Man	Buddy Holly	Coral	10		
20	9	The Folk Singer	Tommy Roe	HMV	7	(84)	

June 1963

1	-	I Like It	Gerry & The Pacemakers	Columbia	12	(17)	
2	7	Do You Want To Know A Secret	Billy J. Kramer & The Dakotas	Parlophone	10		F
3	1	From Me To You	Beatles	Parlophone	15	(41)	
4	18	Take These Chains From My Heart	Ray Charles	HMV	13	(8)	
5	-	If You Gotta Make A Fool Of Somebody	Freddie & The Dreamers	Columbia	9		F
6	-	Atlantis	Shadows	Columbia	11		
7	15	When Will You Say I Love You	Billy Fury	Decca	7		
8	14	Deck Of Cards	Wink Martindale	London American	15		L
9	2	Scarlett O'Hara	Jet Harris & Tony Meehan	Decca	11		
10	9	Lucky Lips	Cliff Richard	Columbia	9	(62)	
11	-	Falling	Roy Orbison	London American	8	(22)	
12	5	In Dreams	Roy Orbison	London American	13	(7)	
13	-	Bo Diddley	Buddy Holly	Coral	8		
14	8	Two Kinds Of Teardrops	Del Shannon	London American	8	(50)	
15	16	Young Lovers	Paul & Paula	Philips	6	(6)	L
16	-	Da Doo Ron Ron	Crystals	London American	10	(3)	
17	-	The Ice Cream Man	Tornados	Decca	4		L
18	-	It's My Party	Lesley Gore	Mercury	8	(1)	F
19	-	Forget Him	Bobby Rydell	Cameo Parkway	9	(4)	L
20	-	Confessin'	Frank Ifield	Columbia	11	(58)	

US 1963 APR-JUNE

April 1963

This Mnth	Prev Mnth	Title	Artist	Label	Wks 20	(UK Pos)	
1	10	He's So Fine	Chiffons	Laurie	11	(11)	F G
2	-	Can't Get Used To Losing You	Andy Williams	Columbia	9	(3)	G
3	20	Baby Workout	Jackie Wilson	Brunswick	7		
4	13	South Street	Orlons	Cameo	7		G
5	-	Puff The Magic Dragon	Peter, Paul & Mary	Warner	10		G
6	-	I Will Follow Him	Little Peggy March	RCA	9		F G L
7	5	The End Of The World	Skeeter Davis	RCA	9	(20)	F G
8	-	Young Lovers	Paul & Paula	Philips	5	(12)	L
9	2	Our Day Will Come	Ruby & The Romantics	Kapp	8	(26)	F G
10	-	Pipeline	Chantays	Dot	8	(16)	F L
11	-	Don't Say Nothin' (Bad About My Baby)	Cookies	Dimension	5		L
12	-	Do The Bird	Dee Dee Sharp	Cameo	5		L
13	11	In Dreams	Roy Orbison	Monument	8	(5)	
14	-	On Broadway	Drifters	Atlantic	4		
15	4	Rhythm Of The Rain	Cascades	Valiant	11	(4)	F G L
16	-	Watermelon Man	Mongo Santamaria	Battle	4		F L
17	3	You're The Reason I'm Living	Bobby Darin	Capitol	10		
18	15	Our Winter Love	Bill Pursell	Columbia	6		F L
19	-	Mecca	Gene Pitney	Musicor	5		
20	-	Surfin' U.S.A.	Beach Boys	Capitol	10	(28)	G

May 1963

This Mnth	Prev Mnth	Title	Artist	Label	Wks 20	(UK Pos)	
1	6	I Will Follow Him	Little Peggy March	RCA	9		F G L
2	-	If You Wanna Be Happy	Jimmy Soul	SPQR	9		F G L
3	5	Puff The Magic Dragon	Peter, Paul & Mary	Warner	10		G
4	20	Surfin' U.S.A.	Beach Boys	Capitol	10	(28)	G
5	-	Foolish Little Girl	Shirelles	Scepter	7		L
6	10	Pipeline	Chantays	Dot	8	(16)	F L
7	2	Can't Get Used To Losing You	Andy Williams	Columbia	9	(3)	G
8	-	Losing You	Brenda Lee	Decca	7	(12)	
9	-	Reverend Mr. Black	Kingston Trio	Capitol	6		L
10	1	He's So Fine	Chiffons	Laurie	11	(11)	F G
11	-	Take These Chains From My Heart	Ray Charles	ABC Paramount	6	(4)	
12	-	Two Faces Have I	Lou Christie	Roulette	7		F
13	-	I Love You Because	Al Martino	Capitol	7		F
14	19	Mecca	Gene Pitney	Musicor	5		
15	14	On Broadway	Drifters	Atlantic	4		
16	11	Don't Say Nothin' (Bad About My Baby)	Cookies	Dimension	5		L
17	-	Hot Pastrami	Dartells	Dot	6		F L
18	-	Another Saturday Night	Sam Cooke	RCA	5	(25)	
19	3	Baby Workout	Jackie Wilson	Brunswick	7		
20	-	Charms	Bobby Vee	Liberty	4		

June 1963

This Mnth	Prev Mnth	Title	Artist	Label	Wks 20	(UK Pos)	
1	-	It's My Party	Lesley Gore	Mercury	9	(9)	F G
2	-	Sukiyaki	Kyu Sakamoto	Capitol	11	(8)	F G L
3	-	You Can't Sit Down	Dovells	Parkway	9		L
4	-	Da Doo Ron Ron	Crystals	Philles	8	(4)	G
5	13	I Love You Because	Al Martino	Capitol	7		F
6	-	Those Lazy-Hazy-Crazy Days Of Summer	Nat 'King' Cole	Capitol	7		
7	-	Hello Stranger	Barbara Lewis	Atlantic	7		F
8	-	Blue On Blue	Bobby Vinton	Epic	8		
9	-	Still	Bill Anderson	Decca	7		F L
10	2	If You Wanna Be Happy	Jimmy Soul	SPQR	9		F G L
11	12	Two Faces Have I	Lou Christie	Roulette	7		F
12	4	Surfin' U.S.A.	Beach Boys	Capitol	10	(28)	G
13	-	18 Yellow Roses	Bobby Darin	Capitol	4		
14	-	One Fine Day	Chiffons	Laurie	6		
15	8	Losing You	Brenda Lee	Decca	7	(12)	
16	-	Birdland	Chubby Checker	Parkway	3		
17	-	Easier Said Than Done	Essex	Roulette	9		F G
18	18	Another Saturday Night	Sam Cooke	RCA	5	(25)	
19	1	I Will Follow Him	Little Peggy March	RCA	9		F G L
20	17	Hot Pastrami	Dartells	Dot	6		F L

▲ Del Shannon charted with a cover of The Beatles UK No. 1, 'From Me To You', and Bobby Rydell's (above) last major hit, 'Forget Him', was produced in Britain by its composer Tony Hatch.

◆ Headliners at the first Monterey Folk Festival included Bob Dylan, Joan Baez and Peter, Paul & Mary.

◆ Fifteen-year-old Little Peggy March topped the US chart with 'I Will Follow Him' and 17-year-old Lesley Gore had a No. 1 with the Quincy Jones produced 'It's My Party'. The most surprising chart topper was Kyu Sakamoto's 'Sukiyaki' - the only Japanese record ever to achieve this.

UK 1963 JULY-SEPT

▲ The Beatles debut LP **Please Please Me** topped the chart for 30 weeks and the single 'She Loves You', which had record advance orders and sold over a million in the UK, cemented their position as Britain's top group.

◆ *Ready Steady Go* was launched – it was the British pop TV show which best reflected the times. Early guests included the Rolling Stones.

◆ US R&B songs scoring by British groups included 'Sweets For My Sweet' (Searchers), 'Twist & Shout' (The Beatles, Brian Poole & The Tremeloes) and 'Do You Love Me' (Brian Poole & The Tremeloes, Dave Clark Five).

July 1963

This Mnth	Prev Mnth	Title	Artist	Label	Wks 20	(US Pos)	
1	20	Confessin'	Frank Ifield	Columbia	11	(58)	
2	1	I Like It	Gerry & The Pacemakers	Columbia	12	(17)	
3	6	Atlantis	Shadows	Columbia	11		
4	-	Devil In Disguise	Elvis Presley	RCA	8	(3)	
5	16	Da Doo Ron Ron	Crystals	London American	10	(3)	
6	4	Take These Chains From My Heart	Ray Charles	HMV	13	(8)	
7	-	Sweets For My Sweet	Searchers	Pye	10		F
8	8	Deck Of Cards	Wink Martindale	London American	15		L
9	-	Welcome To My World	Jim Reeves	RCA	9		
10	18	It's My Party	Lesley Gore	Mercury	8	(1)	F
11	-	Twist And Shout	Brian Poole & The Tremeloes	Decca	9		F
12	13	Bo Diddley	Buddy Holly	Coral	8		
13	5	If You Gotta Make A Fool Of Somebody	Freddie & The Dreamers	Columbia	9		F
14	3	From Me To You	Beatles	Parlophone	15	(41)	
15	11	Falling	Roy Orbison	London American	8	(22)	
16	-	Twist And Shout E.P.	Beatles	Parlophone	15	(2)	
17	-	Sukiyaki	Kyu Sakamoto	HMV	9	(1)	F L
18	2	Do You Want To Know A Secret	Billy J. Kramer & The Dakotas	Parlophone	10		F
19	19	Forget Him	Bobby Rydell	Cameo Parkway	9	(4)	L
20	-	You Can Never Stop Me Loving You	Kenny Lynch	HMV	6		L

August 1963

This Mnth	Prev Mnth	Title	Artist	Label	Wks 20	(US Pos)	
1	7	Sweets For My Sweet	Searchers	Pye	10		F
2	1	Confessin'	Frank Ifield	Columbia	11	(58)	
3	16	Twist And Shout E.P.	Beatles	Parlophone	15	(2)	
4	-	Bad To Me	Billy J. Kramer & The Dakotas	Parlophone	10	(9)	
5	11	Twist And Shout	Brian Poole & The Tremeloes	Decca	9		F
6	-	In Summer	Billy Fury	Decca	8		
7	4	Devil In Disguise	Elvis Presley	RCA	8	(3)	
8	-	Wipe Out	Surfaris	London American	8	(2)	F L
9	-	I'm Telling You Now	Freddie & The Dreamers	Columbia	7	(1)	
10	-	Theme From 'The Legion's Last Patrol'	Ken Thorne & His Orchestra	HMV	10		F L
11	5	Da Doo Ron Ron	Crystals	London American	10	(3)	
12	17	Sukiyaki	Kyu Sakamoto	HMV	9	(1)	F L
13	-	I'll Never Get Over You	Johnny Kidd & The Pirates	HMV	10		L
14	-	It's All In The Game	Cliff Richard	Columbia	9	(25)	
15	3	Atlantis	Shadows	Columbia	11		
16	-	You Don't Have To Be A Baby To Cry	Caravelles	Decca	7	(3)	F L
17	2	I Like It	Gerry & The Pacemakers	Columbia	12	(17)	
18	-	She Loves You	Beatles	Parlophone	24	(1)	G
19	6	Take These Chains From My Heart	Ray Charles	HMV	13	(8)	
20	20	You Can Never Stop Me Loving You	Kenny Lynch	HMV	6		L

September 1963

This Mnth	Prev Mnth	Title	Artist	Label	Wks 20	(US Pos)	
1	18	She Loves You	Beatles	Parlophone	24	(1)	G
2	14	It's All In The Game	Cliff Richard	Columbia	9	(25)	
3	4	Bad To Me	Billy J. Kramer & The Dakotas	Parlophone	10	(9)	
4	-	I Want To Stay Here	Steve Lawrence & Eydie Gormé	CBS	8	(28)	L
5	13	I'll Never Get Over You	Johnny Kidd & The Pirates	HMV	10		L
6	9	I'm Telling You Now	Freddie & The Dreamers	Columbia	7	(1)	
7	-	Just Like Eddie	Heinz	Decca	10		F
8	16	You Don't Have To Be A Baby To Cry	Caravelles	Decca	7	(3)	F L
9	-	Applejack	Jet Harris & Tony Meehan	Decca	8		L
10	-	Do You Love Me	Brian Poole & The Tremeloes	Decca	11		
11	10	Theme From 'The Legion's Last Patrol'	Ken Thorne & His Orchestra	HMV	10		F L
12	8	Wipe Out	Surfaris	London American	8	(2)	F L
13	-	Then He Kissed Me	Crystals	London American	10	(6)	
14	-	If I Had A Hammer	Trini Lopez	Reprise	10	(3)	F L
15	1	Sweets For My Sweet	Searchers	Pye	10		F
16	-	Still	Karl Denver	Decca	6		L
17	3	Twist And Shout E.P.	Beatles	Parlophone	15	(2)	
18	-	Dance On	Kathy Kirby	Decca	5		F
19	-	Shindig	Shadows	Columbia	7		
20	-	Wishing	Buddy Holly	Coral	5		L

July 1963

This Mnth	Prev Mnth	Title	Artist	Label	Wks 20	(UK Pos)	
1	17	Easier Said Than Done	Essex	Roulette	9		F G
2	-	Surf City	Jan & Dean	Liberty	10	(24)	G
3	-	So Much In Love	Tymes	Parkway	9	(17)	F G
4	-	Tie Me Kangaroo Down, Sport	Rolf Harris	Epic	7	(7)	F L
5	-	Memphis	Lonnie Mack	Fraternity	8		F L
6	2	Sukiyaki	Kyu Sakamoto	Capitol	11	(8)	F G L
7	-	Fingertips (Pt. 2)	Stevie Wonder	Tamla	10		F G
8	-	Wipe Out	Surfaris	Dot	9	(8)	F G
9	8	Blue On Blue	Bobby Vinton	Epic	8		
10	14	One Fine Day	Chiffons	Laurie	6		
11	7	Hello Stranger	Barbara Lewis	Atlantic	7		F
12	-	Pride And Joy	Marvin Gaye	Tamla	6		F
13	-	(You're The) Devil In Disguise	Elvis Presley	RCA	8	(2)	G
14	1	It's My Party	Lesley Gore	Mercury	9	(9)	F G
15	-	Not Me	Orlons	Cameo	5		
16	-	Blowin' In The Wind	Peter, Paul & Mary	Warner	8	(14)	G
17	-	Just One Look	Doris Troy	Atlantic	6		F L
18	-	On Top Of Spaghetti	Tom Glazer & The Do-Re-Mi Children's Chorus	Kapp	3		F L
19	3	You Can't Sit Down	Dovells	Parkway	9		L
20	6	Those Lazy-Hazy-Crazy Days Of Summer	Nat 'King' Cole	Capitol	7		

August 1963

This Mnth	Prev Mnth	Title	Artist	Label	Wks 20	(UK Pos)	
1	7	Fingertips (Pt. 2)	Stevie Wonder	Tamla	10		F G
2	16	Blowin' In The Wind	Peter, Paul & Mary	Warner	8	(14)	G
3	-	Judy's Turn To Cry	Lesley Gore	Mercury	7		
4	-	Candy Girl	Four Seasons	Vee Jay	8		
5	13	(You're The) Devil In Disguise	Elvis Presley	RCA	8	(2)	G
6	8	Wipe Out	Surfaris	Dot	9	(8)	F G
7	3	So Much In Love	Tymes	Parkway	9	(17)	F G
8	-	Hello Mudduh, Hello Fadduh	Allan Sherman	Warner	8	(17)	F L
9	-	More	Kai Winding	Verve	6		F L
10	-	My Boyfriend's Back	Angels	Smash	10	(28)	G L
11	2	Surf City	Jan & Dean	Liberty	10	(24)	G
12	1	Easier Said Than Done	Essex	Roulette	9		F G
13	-	Mockingbird	Inez Foxx	Symbol	6		F L
14	-	If I Had A Hammer	Trini Lopez	Reprise	8	(4)	F G
15	-	Denise	Randy & The Rainbows	Rust	5		F L
16	4	Tie Me Kangaroo Down, Sport	Rolf Harris	Epic	7	(7)	F L
17	17	Just One Look	Doris Troy	Atlantic	6		F L
18	5	Memphis	Lonnie Mack	Fraternity	8		F L
19	-	Danke Schoen	Wayne Newton	Capitol	4		F
20	-	Hopeless	Andy Williams	Columbia	4		

September 1963

This Mnth	Prev Mnth	Title	Artist	Label	Wks 20	(UK Pos)	
1	-	Blue Velvet	Bobby Vinton	Epic	10		G
2	10	My Boyfriend's Back	Angels	Smash	10	(28)	G L
3	14	If I Had A Hammer	Trini Lopez	Reprise	8	(4)	F G
4	-	Heat Wave	Martha & The Vandellas	Gordy	9		F G
5	8	Hello Mudduh, Hello Fadduh	Allan Sherman	Warner	8	(17)	F L
6	-	Then He Kissed Me	Crystals	Philles	8	(2)	L
7	-	Sally, Go 'Round The Roses	Jaynetts	Tuff	7		F L
8	-	Surfer Girl	Beach Boys	Capitol	9		
9	-	The Monkey Time	Major Lance	Okeh	6		F
10	-	Mickey's Monkey	Miracles	Tamla	5		
11	-	Cry Baby	Garnet Mimms & The Enchanters	UA	8		F L
12	13	Mockingbird	Inez Foxx	Symbol	6		F L
13	-	Wonderful! Wonderful!	Tymes	Parkway	5		
14	-	Be My Baby	Ronettes	Philles	9	(3)	F G L
15	-	Hey, Girl	Freddie Scott	Colpix	5		F L
16	4	Candy Girl	Four Seasons	Vee Jay	8		
17	-	A Walkin' Miracle	Essex	Roulette	3		L
18	-	Frankie And Johnny	Sam Cooke	RCA	4	(24)	
19	2	Blowin' In The Wind	Peter, Paul & Mary	Warner	8	(14)	G
20	15	Denise	Randy & The Rainbows	Rust	5		F L

◆ Little Stevie Wonder became the first artist to simultaneously top both the single and album chart with 'Fingertips (Pt. 2)' and **The 12 year old Genius** respectively.

◆ Bob Dylan, Joan Baez and Peter, Paul & Mary, who headlined the Newport Folk Festival, joined 200,000 civil rights demonstrators in Washington.

◆ The album **Introducing The Beatles** went unnoticed at a time when 'Tie Me Kangaroo Down Sport' by Rolf Harris was the biggest British recorded hit.

◆ The Top 150 album chart now included both mono and stereo LPs.

◆ The Monkey was the biggest of the current dance crazes, with hits coming from Major Lance ('The Monkey Time') and The Miracles ('Mickey's Monkey').

UK 1963

OCT-DEC

◆ As the year ended, The Beatles had five records in the Top 20 singles (including 2 EPs and an album) and the top two albums. The LP **With The Beatles** entered at No. 1 as did 'I Want To Hold Your Hand', which smashed all UK sales records, selling a million copies in three days. A big US launch was planned for early 1964.

◆ For the first time, British acts, The Beatles and Cliff Richard (who had been voted Most Promising Male Singer in the top US teen magazine, *16*), won awards in the World section of the *NME* readers poll.

◆ After a string of successful singles, folk/pop trio The Springfields split up and singer Dusty Springfield instantly scored a solo hit with 'I Only Want To Be With You'.

October 1963

This Mnth	Prev Mnth	Title	Artist	Label	Wks 20	(US Pos)	
1	10	Do You Love Me	Brian Poole & The Tremeloes	Decca	11		
2	13	Then He Kissed Me	Crystals	London American	10	(6)	
3	1	She Loves You	Beatles	Parlophone	24	(1)	G
4	14	If I Had A Hammer	Trini Lopez	Reprise	10	(3)	F L
5	-	Blue Bayou	Roy Orbison	London American	10	(29)	
6	-	The First Time	Adam Faith	Parlophone	8		
7	-	You'll Never Walk Alone	Gerry & The Pacemakers	Columbia	15	(48)	
8	19	Shindig	Shadows	Columbia	7		
9	-	I (Who Have Nothing)	Shirley Bassey	Columbia	9		
10	9	Applejack	Jet Harris & Tony Meehan	Decca	8		L
11	17	Twist And Shout E.P.	Beatles	Parlophone	15	(2)	
12	2	It's All In The Game	Cliff Richard	Columbia	9	(25)	
13	7	Just Like Eddie	Heinz	Decca	10		F
14	-	Hello Little Girl	Fourmost	Parlophone	6		F
15	4	I Want To Stay Here	Steve Lawrence & Eydie Gormé	CBS	8	(28)	L
16	-	Ain't Gonna Kiss Ya (E.P.)	Searchers	Pye	4		
17	-	Searchin'	Hollies	Parlophone	4		F
18	-	Everybody	Tommy Roe	HMV	4	(3)	
19	-	Memphis Tennessee	Chuck Berry	Pye International	7		
20	-	Be My Baby	Ronettes	London American	7	(2)	F

November 1963

This Mnth	Prev Mnth	Title	Artist	Label	Wks 20	(US Pos)	
1	3	She Loves You	Beatles	Parlophone	24	(1)	G
2	7	You'll Never Walk Alone	Gerry & The Pacemakers	Columbia	15	(48)	
3	-	Sugar And Spice	Searchers	Pye	7	(44)	
4	20	Be My Baby	Ronettes	London American	7	(2)	F
5	9	I (Who Have Nothing)	Shirley Bassey	Columbia	9		
6	5	Blue Bayou	Roy Orbison	London American	10	(29)	
7	-	Don't Talk To Him	Cliff Richard	Columbia	10		
8	-	Secret Love	Kathy Kirby	Decca	12		
9	19	Memphis Tennessee	Chuck Berry	Pye International	7		
10	1	Do You Love Me	Brian Poole & The Tremeloes	Decca	11		
11	-	I'll Keep You Satisfied	Billy J. Kramer & The Dakotas	Parlophone	6	(30)	
12	-	You Were Made For Me	Freddie & The Dreamers	Columbia	11	(21)	
13	2	Then He Kissed Me	Crystals	London American	10	(6)	
14	-	Maria Elena	Los Indios Tabajaras	RCA	12	(6)	F L
15	-	Fools Rush In	Rick Nelson	London American	5	(12)	
16	6	The First Time	Adam Faith	Parlophone	8		
17	4	If I Had A Hammer	Trini Lopez	Reprise	10	(3)	F L
18	-	Blowin' In The Wind	Peter, Paul & Mary	Warner	5	(2)	F
19	-	It's Almost Tomorrow	Mark Wynter	Pye	6		L
20	-	I Only Want To Be With You	Dusty Springfield	Philips	14	(12)	F

December 1963

This Mnth	Prev Mnth	Title	Artist	Label	Wks 20	(US Pos)	
1	-	I Want To Hold Your Hand	Beatles	Parlophone	13	(1)	G
2	1	She Loves You	Beatles	Parlophone	24	(1)	G
3	8	Secret Love	Kathy Kirby	Decca	12		
4	-	Glad All Over	Dave Clark Five	Columbia	14	(6)	F
5	12	You Were Made For Me	Freddie & The Dreamers	Columbia	11	(21)	
6	7	Don't Talk To Him	Cliff Richard	Columbia	10		
7	20	I Only Want To Be With You	Dusty Springfield	Philips	14	(12)	F
8	-	Dominique	Singing Nun	Philips	8	(1)	F L
9	14	Maria Elena	Los Indios Tabajaras	RCA	12	(6)	F L
10	-	Twenty Four Hours From Tulsa	Gene Pitney	UA	13	(17)	F
11	11	I'll Keep You Satisfied	Billy J. Kramer & The Dakotas	Parlophone	6	(30)	
12	2	You'll Never Walk Alone	Gerry & The Pacemakers	Columbia	15	(48)	
13	-	Geronimo	Shadows	Columbia	6		
14	-	With The Beatles L.P.	Beatles	Parlophone	5		
15	-	Swinging On A Star	Big Dee Irwin	Colpix	10	(38)	F L
16	-	I Wanna Be Your Man	Rolling Stones	Decca	8		
17	19	It's Almost Tomorrow	Mark Wynter	Pye	6		L
18	-	All I Want For Christmas Is A Beatle	Dora Bryan	Fontana	3		F L
19	4	Be My Baby	Ronettes	London American	7	(2)	F
20	-	Beatles Hits E.P.	Beatles	Parlophone	5		

October 1963

This Mnth	Prev Mnth	Title	Artist	Label	Wks 20	(UK Pos)	
1	-	Sugar Shack	Jimmy Gilmer & The Fireballs	Dot	12		F G
2	14	Be My Baby	Ronettes	Philles	9	(3)	F G L
3	1	Blue Velvet	Bobby Vinton	Epic	10		G
4	-	Busted	Ray Charles	ABC Paramount	7	(20)	
5	11	Cry Baby	Garnet Mimms & The Enchanters	UA	8		F L
6	7	Sally, Go 'Round The Roses	Jaynetts	Tuff	7		F L
7	-	Mean Woman Blues	Roy Orbison	Monument	8	(14)	
8	-	Donna The Prima Donna	Dion	Columbia	7		
9	2	My Boyfriend's Back	Angels	Smash	10	(28)	G L
10	-	Honolulu Lulu	Jan & Dean	Liberty	5		
11	-	Deep Purple	Nino Tempo & April Stevens	Atco	9	(20)	F G
12	-	Don't Think Twice It's All Right	Peter, Paul & Mary	Warner	4		
13	4	Heat Wave	Martha & The Vandellas	Gordy	9		F G
14	-	That Sunday, That Summer	Nat 'King' Cole	Capitol	5		L
15	13	Wonderful! Wonderful!	Tymes	Parkway	5		
16	-	I Can't Stay Mad At You	Skeeter Davis	RCA	6		L
17	6	Then He Kissed Me	Crystals	Philles	8	(2)	L
18	-	Washington Square	Village Stompers	Epic	9		F L
19	-	Talk To Me	Sunny & The Sunglows	Tear Drop	5		F L
20	10	Mickey's Monkey	Miracles	Tamla	5		

November 1963

This Mnth	Prev Mnth	Title	Artist	Label	Wks 20	(UK Pos)	
1	1	Sugar Shack	Jimmy Gilmer & The Fireballs	Dot	12		F G
2	18	Washington Square	Village Stompers	Epic	9		F L
3	11	Deep Purple	Nino Tempo & April Stevens	Atco	9	(20)	F G
4	-	I'm Leaving It Up To You	Dale & Grace	Montel	10		F G
5	-	It's All Right	Impressions	ABC Paramount	8		
6	-	She's A Fool	Lesley Gore	Mercury	9		
7	-	Maria Elena	Los Indios Tabajaras	RCA	6	(7)	F L
8	-	Bossa Nova Baby	Elvis Presley	RCA	4	(11)	
9	-	Everybody	Tommy Roe	ABC Paramount	8	(13)	
10	7	Mean Woman Blues	Roy Orbison	Monument	8	(14)	
11	16	I Can't Stay Mad At You	Skeeter Davis	RCA	6		L
12	-	Dominique	Singing Nun (Soeur Sourire)	Philips	11	(3)	F G L
13	-	Fools Rush In	Rick Nelson	Decca	6	(12)	
14	-	(Down At) Papa Joe's	Dixiebelles	SS7	5		F
15	8	Donna The Prima Donna	Dion	Columbia	7		
16	-	500 Miles Away From Home	Bobby Bare	RCA	4		L
17	-	Walking The Dog	Rufus Thomas	ABC	6		F L
18	4	Busted	Ray Charles	ABC Paramount	7	(20)	
19	-	Hey Little Girl	Major Lance	Okeh	4		
20	-	Little Red Rooster	Sam Cooke	RCA	5		

December 1963

This Mnth	Prev Mnth	Title	Artist	Label	Wks 20	(UK Pos)	
1	12	Dominique	Singing Nun (Soeur Sourire)	Philips	11	(3)	F G L
2	-	Louie Louie	Kingsmen	Wand	9	(26)	F G
3	-	You Don't Have To Be A Baby To Cry	Caravelles	Smash	7	(6)	F L
4	-	Since I Fell For You	Lenny Welch	Cadence	10		F L
5	4	I'm Leaving It Up To You	Dale & Grace	Montel	10		F G
6	-	Be True To Your School	Beach Boys	Capitol	7		
7	9	Everybody	Tommy Roe	ABC Paramount	8	(13)	
8	-	There I've Said It Again	Bobby Vinton	Epic	10		G
9	-	Drip Drop	Dion	Columbia	6		
10	6	She's A Fool	Lesley Gore	Mercury	9		
11	-	Popsicles And Icicles	Murmaids	Chattahoochee	9		F L
12	17	Walking The Dog	Rufus Thomas	ABC	6		F L
13	-	Talk Back Trembling Lips	Johnny Tillotson	MGM	6		L
14	1	Sugar Shack	Jimmy Gilmer & The Fireballs	Dot	12		F G
15	-	Loddy Lo	Chubby Checker	Parkway	4		
16	-	Forget Him	Bobby Rydell	Cameo	8	(15)	L
17	20	Little Red Rooster	Sam Cooke	RCA	5		
18	2	Washington Square	Village Stompers	Epic	9		F L
19	-	Wonderful Summer	Robin Ward	Dot	5		F L
20	-	Quicksand	Martha & The Vandellas	Gordy	4		

US 1963 OCT-DEC

◆ Soul music reached new heights thanks to hits from Garnett Mimms, The Impressions, Sam Cooke and Rufus Thomas.

▲ The year when the coffee house folk circuit boomed, came to an end with Grammy winners Peter, Paul & Mary (above) holding the top two places on the album chart, and Bob Dylan selling out Carnegie Hall.

◆ Belgian Nun, Soeur Sourire, topped the single and album chart as the country mourned President Kennedy. A budget priced JFK memorial album sold a reported four million copies in six days.

UK 1964 JAN-MAR

◆ *Top Of The Pops* was launched. The TV show based on the Top 20 chart is still running thirty years later. Soon afterwards the first pirate radio station Radio Caroline started broadcasting from a ship in the North Sea.

▲ The Dave Clark Five's (above) 'Bits And Pieces' had 250,000 advance orders and The Beatles 'Can't Buy Me Love' piled up record UK advance orders of over a million.

◆ For the first time the British Top 10 was made up of local artists, with Brian Epstein's first female signing, Cilla Black, leading the field.

January 1964

This Mnth	Prev Mnth	Title	Artist	Label	Wks 20	(US Pos)	
1	4	Glad All Over	Dave Clark Five	Columbia	14	(6)	F
2	1	I Want To Hold Your Hand	Beatles	Parlophone	13	(1)	G
3	7	I Only Want To Be With You	Dusty Springfield	Philips	14	(12)	F
4	-	Hippy Hippy Shake	Swinging Blue Jeans	HMV	10	(24)	F
5	2	She Loves You	Beatles	Parlophone	24	(1)	G
6	10	Twenty Four Hours From Tulsa	Gene Pitney	UA	13	(17)	F
7	15	Swinging On A Star	Big Dee Irwin	Colpix	10	(38)	F L
8	5	You Were Made For Me	Freddie & The Dreamers	Columbia	11	(21)	
9	8	Dominique	Singing Nun	Philips	8	(1)	F L
10	-	Stay	Hollies	Parlophone	7		
11	3	Secret Love	Kathy Kirby	Decca	12		
12	9	Maria Elena	Los Indios Tabajaras	RCA	12	(6)	F L
13	16	I Wanna Be Your Man	Rolling Stones	Decca	8		
14	-	Kiss Me Quick	Elvis Presley	RCA	6	(34)	
15	-	We Are In Love	Adam Faith	Parlophone	6		
16	6	Don't Talk To Him	Cliff Richard	Columbia	10		
17	-	As Usual	Brenda Lee	Brunswick	10	(12)	
18	-	Needles And Pins	Searchers	Pye	9	(13)	
19	13	Geronimo	Shadows	Columbia	6		
20	-	I'm The One	Gerry & The Pacemakers	Columbia	9	(82)	

February 1964

This Mnth	Prev Mnth	Title	Artist	Label	Wks 20	(US Pos)	
1	18	Needles And Pins	Searchers	Pye	9	(13)	
2	20	I'm The One	Gerry & The Pacemakers	Columbia	9	(82)	
3	4	Hippy Hippy Shake	Swinging Blue Jeans	HMV	10	(24)	F
4	-	Diane	Bachelors	Decca	11	(10)	
5	1	Glad All Over	Dave Clark Five	Columbia	14	(6)	F
6	17	As Usual	Brenda Lee	Brunswick	10	(12)	
7	-	5-4-3-2-1	Manfred Mann	HMV	7		F
8	-	Don't Blame Me	Frank Ifield	Columbia	7		L
9	-	Anyone Who Had A Heart	Cilla Black	Parlophone	11		F
10	-	I Think Of You	Merseybeats	Fontana	11		F
11	6	Twenty Four Hours From Tulsa	Gene Pitney	UA	13	(17)	F
12	2	I Want To Hold Your Hand	Beatles	Parlophone	13	(1)	G
13	-	Baby I Love You	Ronettes	London American	7	(24)	L
14	3	I Only Want To Be With You	Dusty Springfield	Philips	14	(12)	F
15	-	I'm The Lonely One	Cliff Richard	Columbia	4	(92)	
16	10	Stay	Hollies	Parlophone	7		
17	-	Bits And Pieces	Dave Clark Five	Columbia	9	(4)	
18	-	Candy Man	Brian Poole & The Tremeloes	Decca	6		
19	-	For You	Rick Nelson	Brunswick	4	(6)	L
20	7	Swinging On A Star	Big Dee Irwin	Colpix	10	(38)	F L

March 1964

This Mnth	Prev Mnth	Title	Artist	Label	Wks 20	(US Pos)	
1	9	Anyone Who Had A Heart	Cilla Black	Parlophone	11		F
2	17	Bits And Pieces	Dave Clark Five	Columbia	9	(4)	
3	-	Little Children	Billy J. Kramer & The Dakotas	Parlophone	9	(7)	
4	-	Not Fade Away	Rolling Stones	Decca	9	(48)	
5	4	Diane	Bachelors	Decca	11	(10)	
6	-	Just One Look	Hollies	Parlophone	9	(44)	
7	10	I Think Of You	Merseybeats	Fontana	11		F
8	-	Boys Cry	Eden Kane	Fontana	7		L
9	1	Needles And Pins	Searchers	Pye	9	(13)	
10	-	I Love You Because	Jim Reeves	RCA	26		
11	18	Candy Man	Brian Poole & The Tremeloes	Decca	6		
12	-	Let Me Go, Lover	Kathy Kirby	Decca	6		
13	-	That Girl Belongs To Yesterday	Gene Pitney	UA	7	(49)	
14	2	I'm The One	Gerry & The Pacemakers	Columbia	9	(82)	
15	-	Stay Awhile	Dusty Springfield	Philips	6	(38)	
16	-	Over You	Freddie & The Dreamers	Columbia	5		
17	6	As Usual	Brenda Lee	Brunswick	10	(12)	
18	-	Can't Buy Me Love	Beatles	Parlophone	9	(1)	G
19	7	5-4-3-2-1	Manfred Mann	HMV	7		F
20	-	Theme For Young Lovers	Shadows	Columbia	6		

US 1964 JAN-MAR

January 1964

This Mnth	Prev Mnth	Title	Artist	Label	Wks 20	(UK Pos)	
1	8	There I've Said It Again	Bobby Vinton	Epic	10		G
2	2	Louie Louie	Kingsmen	Wand	9	(26)	F G
3	11	Popsicles And Icicles	Murmaids	Chattahoochee	9		F L
4	16	Forget Him	Bobby Rydell	Cameo	8	(15)	L
5	1	Dominique	Singing Nun (Soeur Sourire)	Philips	11	(3)	F G L
6	-	Surfin' Bird	Trashmen	Garrett	7		F L
7	4	Since I Fell For You	Lenny Welch	Cadence	10		F L
8	-	The Nitty Gritty	Shirley Ellis	Congress	5		F
9	-	Midnight Mary	Joey Powers	Amy	5		F L
10	-	Drag City	Jan & Dean	Liberty	5		
11	-	As Usual	Brenda Lee	Decca	6	(5)	
12	13	Talk Back Trembling Lips	Johnny Tillotson	MGM	6		L
13	-	Hey Little Cobra	Rip Chords	Columbia	7		F L
14	-	Out Of Limits	Marketts	Warner	7		F G
15	-	Whispering	Nino Tempo & April Stevens	Atco	6	(20)	L
16	20	Quicksand	Martha & The Vandellas	Gordy	4		
17	-	Um, Um, Um, Um, Um, Um	Major Lance	Okeh	8	(40)	
18	-	I Want To Hold Your Hand	Beatles	Capitol	13	(1)	F G
19	3	You Don't Have To Be A Baby To Cry	Caravelles	Smash	7	(6)	F L
20	-	Wives And Lovers	Jack Jones	Kapp	4		F

February 1964

This Mnth	Prev Mnth	Title	Artist	Label	Wks 20	(UK Pos)	
1	18	I Want To Hold Your Hand	Beatles	Capitol	13	(1)	F G
2	-	You Don't Own Me	Lesley Gore	Mercury	8		G
3	17	Um, Um, Um, Um, Um, Um	Major Lance	Okeh	8	(40)	
4	-	She Loves You	Beatles	Swan	12	(1)	G
5	14	Out Of Limits	Marketts	Warner	7		F G
6	13	Hey Little Cobra	Rip Chords	Columbia	7		F L
7	-	Java	Al Hirt	RCA	9		F
8	-	For You	Rick Nelson	Decca	6	(14)	
9	-	Dawn (Go Away)	Four Seasons	Philips	8		
10	-	Anyone Who Had A Heart	Dionne Warwick	Scepter	6	(42)	F
11	6	Surfin' Bird	Trashmen	Garrett	7		F L
12	-	What Kind Of Fool (Do You Think I Am)	Tams	ABC	5		F L
13	-	California Sun	Rivieras	Riviera	6		F L
14	-	Talking About My Baby	Impressions	ABC Paramount	5		
15	1	There I've Said It Again	Bobby Vinton	Epic	10		G
16	-	Stop And Think It Over	Dale & Grace	Montel	5		L
17	-	Navy Blue	Diane Renay	20th Century	6		F L
18	-	A Fool Never Learns	Andy Williams	Columbia	5	(40)	
19	-	Please Please Me	Beatles	Vee Jay	8	(1)	G
20	-	See The Funny Little Clown	Bobby Goldsboro	UA	5		F

March 1964

This Mnth	Prev Mnth	Title	Artist	Label	Wks 20	(UK Pos)	
1	1	I Want To Hold Your Hand	Beatles	Capitol	13	(1)	F G
2	4	She Loves You	Beatles	Swan	12	(1)	G
3	19	Please Please Me	Beatles	Vee Jay	8	(1)	G
4	9	Dawn (Go Away)	Four Seasons	Philips	8		
5	-	Fun, Fun, Fun	Beach Boys	Capitol	7		
6	7	Java	Al Hirt	RCA	9		F
7	17	Navy Blue	Diane Renay	20th Century	6		F L
8	-	I Love You More And More Every Day	Al Martino	Capitol	5		
9	13	California Sun	Rivieras	Riviera	6		F L
10	-	Twist And Shout	Beatles	Tollie	9	(4)	G
11	-	Hello, Dolly!	Louis Armstrong	Kapp	16	(4)	F G L
12	20	See The Funny Little Clown	Bobby Goldsboro	UA	5		F
13	-	Kissin' Cousins	Elvis Presley	RCA	4	(10)	
14	-	Hi-Heel Sneakers	Tommy Tucker	Checker	4	(23)	F L
15	-	Good News	Sam Cooke	RCA	4		
16	16	Stop And Think It Over	Dale & Grace	Montel	5		L
17	-	My Heart Belongs To Only You	Bobby Vinton	Epic	4		
18	-	Glad All Over	Dave Clark Five	Epic	9	(1)	F
19	-	Suspicion	Terry Stafford	Crusader	9	(31)	F G L
20	-	I Only Want To Be With You	Dusty Springfield	Philips	4	(4)	F

◆ No one has had so many American hits in so short a time as The Beatles. Although unknown on New Year's Day, they had the top four singles and top two albums as March closed, and accounted for 60% of all records sold in the USA. A record breaking 73 million people watched their TV debut on the *Ed Sullivan Show* and their US tour was a resounding success.

◆ Other British acts scoring early in the British invasion included The Dave Clark Five, The Searchers, The Swinging Blue Jeans and Dusty Springfield.

◆ The first Country album chart showed Johnny Cash's **Ring Of Fire** at No. 1.

99

UK 1964

APR-JUNE

◆ Early rock'n'roll enjoyed a UK revival in 1964 with successful tours by Carl Perkins, Little Richard, Bill Haley and Chuck Berry whose 'No Particular Place To Go' became his first transatlantic Top 10 hit.

◆ The Rolling Stones' eponymous debut album knocked The Beatles off the top after 51 consecutive weeks at the top.

◆ Peter & Gordon's 'World Without Love' was the eighth Lennon & McCartney song to top the UK chart in 14 months, and their fifth in the USA in less than five months.

◆ Mary Wells last recording for Motown, 'My Guy', gave the label their first major transatlantic hit.

April 1964

This Mnth	Prev Mnth	Title	Artist	Label	Wks 20	(US Pos)	
1	18	Can't Buy Me Love	Beatles	Parlophone	9	(1)	G
2	-	I Believe	Bachelors	Decca	11	(33)	
3	3	Little Children	Billy J. Kramer & The Dakotas	Parlophone	9	(7)	
4	-	A World Without Love	Peter & Gordon	Columbia	9	(1)	F
5	10	I Love You Because	Jim Reeves	RCA	26		
6	6	Just One Look	Hollies	Parlophone	9	(44)	
7	4	Not Fade Away	Rolling Stones	Decca	9	(48)	
8	-	Tell Me When	Applejacks	Decca	8		F
9	13	That Girl Belongs To Yesterday	Gene Pitney	UA	7	(49)	
10	-	My Boy Lollipop	Millie	Fontana	10	(2)	F L
11	2	Bits And Pieces	Dave Clark Five	Columbia	9	(4)	
12	1	Anyone Who Had A Heart	Cilla Black	Parlophone	11		F
13	5	Diane	Bachelors	Decca	11	(10)	
14	-	Good Golly Miss Molly	Swinging Blue Jeans	HMV	5	(43)	
15	-	Move Over Darling	Doris Day	CBS	8		L
16	-	Everything's Alright	Mojos	Decca	6		F L
17	20	Theme For Young Lovers	Shadows	Columbia	6		
18	-	Don't Throw Your Love Away	Searchers	Pye	8	(16)	
19	-	Mockingbird Hill	Migil Five	Pye	6		F L
20	-	Viva Las Vegas	Elvis Presley	RCA	4	(29)	

May 1964

This Mnth	Prev Mnth	Title	Artist	Label	Wks 20	(US Pos)	
1	18	Don't Throw Your Love Away	Searchers	Pye	8	(16)	
2	10	My Boy Lollipop	Millie	Fontana	10	(2)	F L
3	-	Juliet	Four Pennies	Philips	10		F
4	2	I Believe	Bachelors	Decca	11	(33)	
5	4	A World Without Love	Peter & Gordon	Columbia	9	(1)	F
6	-	Don't Let The Sun Catch You Crying	Gerry & The Pacemakers	Columbia	6	(4)	
7	5	I Love You Because	Jim Reeves	RCA	26		
8	-	It's Over	Roy Orbison	London American	14	(9)	
9	-	A Little Loving	Fourmost	Parlophone	8		L
10	-	Walk On By	Dionne Warwick	Pye International	9	(6)	F
11	-	Constantly	Cliff Richard	Columbia	8		
12	-	You're My World	Cilla Black	Parlophone	10	(26)	
13	1	Can't Buy Me Love	Beatles	Parlophone	9	(1)	G
14	15	Move Over Darling	Doris Day	CBS	8		L
15	19	Mockingbird Hill	Migil Five	Pye	6		F L
16	-	Don't Turn Around	Merseybeats	Fontana	5		
17	-	The Rise & Fall Of Flingel Bunt	Shadows	Columbia	8		
18	16	Everything's Alright	Mojos	Decca	6		F L
19	-	I Will	Billy Fury	Decca	6		
20	-	Hubble Bubble Toil And Trouble	Manfred Mann	HMV	4		

June 1964

This Mnth	Prev Mnth	Title	Artist	Label	Wks 20	(US Pos)	
1	12	You're My World	Cilla Black	Parlophone	10	(26)	
2	8	It's Over	Roy Orbison	London American	14	(9)	
3	-	Someone Someone	Brian Poole & The Tremeloes	Decca	11	(97)	
4	-	No Particular Place To Go	Chuck Berry	Pye International	7	(10)	
5	-	Here I Go Again	Hollies	Parlophone	7		
6	-	My Guy	Mary Wells	Stateside	8	(1)	F
7	17	The Rise & Fall Of Flingel Bunt	Shadows	Columbia	8		
8	11	Constantly	Cliff Richard	Columbia	8		
9	3	Juliet	Four Pennies	Philips	10		F
10	-	Shout	Lulu	Decca	7	(94)	F
11	-	Hello, Dolly!	Louis Armstrong	London American	8	(1)	
12	-	Can't You See That She's Mine	Dave Clark Five	Columbia	6	(4)	
13	7	I Love You Because	Jim Reeves	RCA	26		
14	-	Ramona	Bachelors	Decca	8		
15	10	Walk On By	Dionne Warwick	Pye International	9	(6)	F
16	9	A Little Loving	Fourmost	Parlophone	8		L
17	2	My Boy Lollipop	Millie	Fontana	10	(2)	F L
18	-	You're No Good	Swinging Blue Jeans	HMV	8	(97)	L
19	-	Nobody I Know	Peter & Gordon	Columbia	5	(12)	
20	-	Non Ho L'Eta Per Amarti	Gigliola Cinquetti	Decca	4		F

US 1964 APR-JUNE

April 1964

This Mnth	Prev Mnth	Title	Artist	Label	Wks 20	(UK Pos)	
1	-	Can't Buy Me Love	Beatles	Capitol	7	(1)	G
2	10	Twist And Shout	Beatles	Tollie	9	(4)	G
3	19	Suspicion	Terry Stafford	Crusader	9	(31)	F G L
4	11	Hello, Dolly!	Louis Armstrong	Kapp	16	(4)	F G L
5	18	Glad All Over	Dave Clark Five	Epic	9	(1)	F
6	-	Shoop Shoop Song (It's In His Kiss)	Betty Everett	Vee Jay	7	(34)	F
7	2	She Loves You	Beatles	Swan	12	(1)	G
8	-	Don't Let The Rain Come Down (Crooked Little Man)	Serendipity Singers	Philips	9		F L
9	-	Do You Want To Know A Secret	Beatles	Vee Jay	8		G
10	-	The Way You Do The Things You Do	Temptations	Gordy	6		F
11	1	I Want To Hold Your Hand	Beatles	Capitol	13	(1)	F G
12	3	Please Please Me	Beatles	Vee Jay	8	(1)	G
13	-	Needles And Pins	Searchers	Kapp	5	(1)	F
14	-	Dead Man's Curve	Jan & Dean	Liberty	7		
15	-	Bits And Pieces	Dave Clark Five	Epic	7	(2)	
16	17	My Heart Belongs To Only You	Bobby Vinton	Epic	4		
17	-	My Guy	Mary Wells	Motown	11	(5)	
18	-	You're A Wonderful One	Marvin Gaye	Tamla	5		
19	-	That's The Way Boys Are	Lesley Gore	Mercury	4		
20	14	Hi-Heel Sneakers	Tommy Tucker	Checker	4	(23)	F L

May 1964

This Mnth	Prev Mnth	Title	Artist	Label	Wks 20	(UK Pos)	
1	4	Hello, Dolly!	Louis Armstrong	Kapp	16	(4)	F G L
2	17	My Guy	Mary Wells	Motown	11	(5)	G
3	15	Bits And Pieces	Dave Clark Five	Epic	7	(2)	
4	-	Love Me Do	Beatles	Tollie	9	(27)	G
5	9	Do You Want To Know A Secret	Beatles	Vee Jay	8		G
6	-	Ronnie	Four Seasons	Philips	6		
7	1	Can't Buy Me Love	Beatles	Capitol	7	(1)	G
8	14	Dead Man's Curve	Jan & Dean	Liberty	7		
9	-	It's Over	Roy Orbison	Monument	6	(1)	
10	8	Don't Let The Rain Come Down (Crooked Little Man)	Serendipity Singers	Philips	9		F L
11	-	Chapel Of Love	Dixie Cups	Red Bird	9	(22)	F G
12	-	Love Me With All Your Heart	Ray Charles Singers	Command	8		F L
13	-	(Just Like) Romeo & Juliet	Reflections	Golden World	5		F L
14	-	White On White	Danny Williams	UA	5		F L
15	-	Little Children	Billy J. Kramer & The Dakotas	Imperial	9	(1)	F
16	3	Suspicion	Terry Stafford	Crusader	9	(31)	F G L
17	2	Twist And Shout	Beatles	Tollie	9	(4)	G
18	-	A World Without Love	Peter & Gordon	Capitol	8	(1)	F G
19	-	Shangri-La	Robert Maxwell, His Harp & His Orchestra	Decca	4		F L
20	-	Walk On By	Dionne Warwick	Scepter	8	(9)	

June 1964

This Mnth	Prev Mnth	Title	Artist	Label	Wks 20	(UK Pos)	
1	11	Chapel Of Love	Dixie Cups	Red Bird	9	(22)	F G
2	18	A World Without Love	Peter & Gordon	Capitol	8	(1)	F G
3	12	Love Me With All Your Heart	Ray Charles Singers	Command	8		F L
4	4	Love Me Do	Beatles	Tollie	9	(27)	G
5	20	Walk On By	Dionne Warwick	Scepter	8	(9)	
6	-	I Get Around	Beach Boys	Capitol	12	(7)	G
7	-	People	Barbra Streisand	Columbia	9		F
8	2	My Guy	Mary Wells	Motown	11	(5)	G
9	15	Little Children	Billy J. Kramer & The Dakotas	Imperial	9	(1)	F
10	-	My Boy Lollipop	Millie Small	Smash	7	(2)	F G L
11	1	Hello, Dolly!	Louis Armstrong	Kapp	16	(4)	F G L
12	-	Diane	Bachelors	London	5	(1)	F
13	-	Don't Let The Sun Catch You Crying	Gerry & The Pacemakers	Laurie	7	(6)	F
14	-	Memphis	Johnny Rivers	Imperial	8		F G
15	13	(Just Like) Romeo & Juliet	Reflections	Golden World	5		F L
16	-	Tell Me Why	Bobby Vinton	Epic	4		
17	-	Every Little Bit Hurts	Brenda Holloway	Tamla	4		F L
18	-	Bad To Me	Billy J. Kramer & The Dakotas	Imperial	5	(1)	L
19	-	P.S. I Love You	Beatles	Tollie	4		
20	-	Do You Love Me	Dave Clark Five	Epic	4	(30)	

◆ 'Can't Buy Me Love' by The Beatles amassed record advance orders of over two million and hit the top in a record two weeks (as did **The Beatles Second Album**), giving them the first five places on the chart. At times, they had a record 13 different singles in the Hot 100. **Meet The Beatles** became the biggest selling album to date and was one of three Beatles LPs in the Top 4.

▲ Following in The Beatles footsteps, The Searchers, Dave Clark Five, Peter & Gordon (above) and the Rolling Stones performed in the USA.

UK 1964 JULY-SEPT

◆ The Beatles' film *A Hard Day's Night* was given a royal premiere. In Britain, the soundtrack album had a record 250,000 advance orders, while in America it became the fastest selling album ever, moving a million copies in four days.

◆ The death of US country singer Jim Reeves (the top selling solo artist in Britain in 1964) resulted in a record eight of his albums simultaneously making the Top 20.

▲ As 60s superstars The Kinks (above) and Herman's Hermits debuted on the UK chart, the High Numbers (Who), Joe Cocker and Rod Stewart released unsuccessful singles.

July 1964

This Mnth	Prev Mnth	Title	Artist	Label	Wks 20	(US Pos)	
1	-	House Of The Rising Sun	Animals	Columbia	7	(1)	F
2	-	Hold Me	P.J. Proby	Decca	8	(70)	F
3	2	It's Over	Roy Orbison	London American	14	(9)	
4	-	It's All Over Now	Rolling Stones	Decca	11	(26)	
5	-	I Won't Forget You	Jim Reeves	RCA	19	(93)	
6	3	Someone Someone	Brian Poole & The Tremeloes	Decca	11	(97)	
7	18	You're No Good	Swinging Blue Jeans	HMV	8	(97)	L
8	14	Ramona	Bachelors	Decca	8		
9	-	A Hard Day's Night	Beatles	Parlophone	11	(1)	
10	11	Hello, Dolly!	Louis Armstrong	London American	8	(1)	
11	-	I Just Don't Know What To Do With Myself	Dusty Springfield	Philips	9		
12	-	On The Beach	Cliff Richard	Columbia	8		
13	-	Kissin' Cousins	Elvis Presley	RCA	6	(12)	
14	6	My Guy	Mary Wells	Stateside	8	(1)	F
15	19	Nobody I Know	Peter & Gordon	Columbia	5	(12)	
16	12	Can't You See That She's Mine	Dave Clark Five	Columbia	6	(4)	
17	1	You're My World	Cilla Black	Parlophone	10	(26)	
18	-	Call Up The Groups	Barron Knights	Columbia	9		F
19	10	Shout	Lulu	Decca	7	(94)	F
20	-	Do Wah Diddy Diddy	Manfred Mann	HMV	10	(1)	

August 1964

This Mnth	Prev Mnth	Title	Artist	Label	Wks 20	(US Pos)	
1	9	A Hard Day's Night	Beatles	Parlophone	11	(1)	
2	20	Do Wah Diddy Diddy	Manfred Mann	HMV	10	(1)	
3	18	Call Up The Groups	Barron Knights	Columbia	9		F
4	4	It's All Over Now	Rolling Stones	Decca	11	(26)	
5	5	I Won't Forget You	Jim Reeves	RCA	19	(93)	
6	-	Tobacco Road	Nashville Teens	Decca	8	(14)	F
7	11	I Just Don't Know What To Do With Myself	Dusty Springfield	Philips	9		
8	-	I Get Around	Beach Boys	Capitol	8	(1)	F
9	12	On The Beach	Cliff Richard	Columbia	8		
10	-	Have I The Right?	Honeycombs	Pye	11	(5)	F
11	-	It's Only Make Believe	Billy Fury	Decca	5		
12	1	House Of The Rising Sun	Animals	Columbia	7	(1)	F
13	-	From A Window	Billy J. Kramer & The Dakotas	Parlophone	4	(23)	
14	-	Someday We're Gonna Love Again	Searchers	Pye	5	(34)	
15	2	Hold Me	P.J. Proby	Decca	8	(70)	F
16	-	It's For You	Cilla Black	Parlophone	6	(79)	
17	-	Wishin' And Hopin'	Merseybeats	Fontana	6		
18	-	You Really Got Me	Kinks	Pye	9	(7)	F
19	-	I Found Out The Hard Way	Four Pennies	Philips	3		
20	3	It's Over	Roy Orbison	London American	14	(9)	

September 1964

This Mnth	Prev Mnth	Title	Artist	Label	Wks 20	(US Pos)	
1	10	Have I The Right?	Honeycombs	Pye	11	(5)	F
2	18	You Really Got Me	Kinks	Pye	9	(7)	F
3	5	I Won't Forget You	Jim Reeves	RCA	19	(93)	
4	-	I Wouldn't Trade You For The World	Bachelors	Decca	11	(69)	
5	-	The Crying Game	Dave Berry	Decca	7		
6	-	I'm Into Something Good	Herman's Hermits	Columbia	10	(13)	F
7	-	Rag Doll	Four Seasons	Philips	9	(1)	
8	2	Do Wah Diddy Diddy	Manfred Mann	HMV	10	(1)	
9	-	As Tears Go By	Marianne Faithfull	Decca	10	(22)	F
10	1	A Hard Day's Night	Beatles	Parlophone	11	(1)	
12	-	Where Did Our Love Go	Supremes	Stateside	10	(1)	F
13	-	She's Not There	Zombies	Decca	6	(2)	F L
14	16	It's For You	Cilla Black	Parlophone	6	(79)	
15	-	Such A Night	Elvis Presley	RCA	5	(16)	
16	-	The Wedding	Julie Rogers	Mercury	13	(10)	F L
17	8	I Get Around	Beach Boys	Capitol	8	(1)	F
18	-	Oh Pretty Woman	Roy Orbison	London American	12	(1)	
19	4	It's All Over Now	Rolling Stones	Decca	11	(26)	
20	-	Everybody Loves Somebody	Dean Martin	Reprise	7	(1)	

July 1964

This Mnth	Prev Mnth	Title	Artist	Label	Wks 20	(UK Pos)	
1	6	I Get Around	Beach Boys	Capitol	12	(7)	G
2	14	Memphis	Johnny Rivers	Imperial	8		F G
3	-	Rag Doll	Four Seasons	Philips	10	(2)	G
4	-	Can't You See That She's Mine	Dave Clark Five	Epic	7	(10)	
5	13	Don't Let The Sun Catch You Crying	Gerry & The Pacemakers	Laurie	7	(6)	F
6	10	My Boy Lollipop	Millie Small	Smash	7	(2)	F G L
7	-	The Girl From Ipanema	Stan Getz/Astrud Gilberto	Verve	7	(29)	L
8	7	People	Barbra Streisand	Columbia	9		F
9	-	The Little Old Lady (From Pasadena)	Jan & Dean	Liberty	7		
10	-	Dang Me	Roger Miller	Smash	6		F
11	-	Good Times	Sam Cooke	RCA	5		
12	2	A World Without Love	Peter & Gordon	Capitol	8	(1)	F G
13	18	Bad To Me	Billy J. Kramer & The Dakotas	Imperial	5	(1)	L
14	-	Keep On Pushing	Impressions	ABC Paramount	5		
15	-	No Particular Place To Go	Chuck Berry	Chess	4	(3)	
16	1	Chapel Of Love	Dixie Cups	Red Bird	9	(22)	F G
17	-	Wishin' And Hopin'	Dusty Springfield	Philips	7		
18	-	A Hard Day's Night	Beatles	Capitol	10	(1)	G
19	-	Everybody Loves Somebody	Dean Martin	Reprise	11	(11)	G
20	-	Try It Baby	Marvin Gaye	Tamla	5		

August 1964

This Mnth	Prev Mnth	Title	Artist	Label	Wks 20	(UK Pos)	
1	-	Where Did Our Love Go	Supremes	Motown	11	(3)	F G
2	18	A Hard Day's Night	Beatles	Capitol	10	(1)	G
3	19	Everybody Loves Somebody	Dean Martin	Reprise	11	(11)	G
4	-	Under The Boardwalk	Drifters	Atlantic	9	(45)	
5	17	Wishin' And Hopin'	Dusty Springfield	Philips	7		
6	3	Rag Doll	Four Seasons	Philips	10	(2)	G
7	9	The Little Old Lady (From Pasadena)	Jan & Dean	Liberty	7		
8	-	C'mon And Swim	Bobby Freeman	Autumn	6		L
9	-	House Of The Rising Sun	Animals	MGM	9	(1)	F G
10	1	I Get Around	Beach Boys	Capitol	12	(7)	G
11	-	I Wanna Love Him So Bad	Jelly Beans	Red Bird	5		F L
12	-	Because	Dave Clark Five	Epic	7		G
13	-	Walk-Don't Run '64	Ventures	Dolton	5		
14	10	Dang Me	Roger Miller	Smash	6		F
15	-	How Do You Do It?	Gerry & The Pacemakers	Laurie	5	(1)	
16	-	People Say	Dixie Cups	Red Bird	5		
17	-	(You Don't Know) How Glad I Am	Nancy Wilson	Capitol	4		F L
18	2	Memphis	Johnny Rivers	Imperial	8		F G
19	-	Nobody I Know	Peter & Gordon	Capitol	4	(10)	
20	4	Can't You See That She's Mine	Dave Clark Five	Epic	7	(10)	

September 1964

This Mnth	Prev Mnth	Title	Artist	Label	Wks 20	(UK Pos)	
1	9	House Of The Rising Sun	Animals	MGM	9	(1)	F G
2	1	Where Did Our Love Go	Supremes	Motown	11	(3)	F G
3	-	Bread And Butter	Newbeats	Hickory	8	(15)	F G
4	-	G.T.O.	Ronny & The Daytonas	Mala	8		F L
5	3	Everybody Loves Somebody	Dean Martin	Reprise	11	(11)	G
6	12	Because	Dave Clark Five	Epic	7		G
7	-	Remember (Walkin' In The Sand)	Shangri-Las	Red Bird	8	(14)	F
8	-	Oh Pretty Woman	Roy Orbison	Monument	11	(1)	G
9	2	A Hard Day's Night	Beatles	Capitol	10	(1)	G
10	8	C'mon And Swim	Bobby Freeman	Autumn	6		L
11	-	Do Wah Diddy Diddy	Manfred Mann	Ascot	10	(1)	F G
12	-	Maybelline	Johnny Rivers	Imperial	4		
13	-	Haunted House	Gene Simmons	Hi	6		F L
14	-	Dancing In The Street	Martha & The Vandellas	Gordy	8	(4)	G
15	4	Under The Boardwalk	Drifters	Atlantic	9	(45)	
16	-	Selfish One	Jackie Ross	Chess	4		F L
17	-	And I Love Her	Beatles	Capitol	4		
18	-	It Hurts To Be In Love	Gene Pitney	Musicor	6	(36)	
19	15	How Do You Do It?	Gerry & The Pacemakers	Laurie	5	(1)	
20	-	Save It For Me	Four Seasons	Philips	4		

US 1964
JULY-SEPT

◆ Japan was now the third biggest record market behind the USA and UK.

◆ British group The Animals, whose four minute single 'House Of The Rising Sun' gave them a transatlantic topper, were given the red carpet treatment when they arrived in New York.

◆ 'I Get Around' and 'Where Did Our Love Go', the first chart toppers by The Beach Boys and Supremes respectively, also gave them their first British hits.

◆ British producer Jack Good (of 6-5 Special and Oh Boy! fame) launched US TV show Shindig. The initial show featured appearances from Sam Cooke and The Righteous Brothers.

◆ On Independence Day 1964, five of the American Top 10 singles were by British artists.

UK 1964 OCT-DEC

◆ A survey showed UK record sales were up 18% on 1963.

◆ The Beach Boys, who had a successful UK visit, ended the year topping the US album listings with **Beach Boys Concert.**

◆ The Drifters' 11th and last US Top 20 entry 'Saturday Night At The Movies' cracked the British Top 3 in 1972, whereas 'Leader Of The Pack' by The Shangri-Las was a major UK hit in 1965, 1972 and 1976.

▲ 'Oh Pretty Woman' by Roy Orbison (above), was the only American record to top the transatlantic charts since 'I Can't Stop Loving You' by Ray Charles in 1962.

October 1964

This Mnth	Prev Mnth	Title	Artist	Label	Wks 20	(US Pos)	
1	17	Oh Pretty Woman	Roy Orbison	London American	12	(1)	
2	11	Where Did Our Love Go	Supremes	Stateside	10	(1)	F
3	6	I'm Into Something Good	Herman's Hermits	Columbia	10	(13)	F
4	15	The Wedding	Julie Rogers	Mercury	13	(10)	F L
5	7	Rag Doll	Four Seasons	Philips	9	(1)	
6	-	When You Walk In The Room	Searchers	Pye	8	(35)	
7	4	I Wouldn't Trade You For The World	Bachelors	Decca	11	(69)	
8	3	I Won't Forget You	Jim Reeves	RCA	19	(93)	
9	-	(There's) Always Something There To Remind Me	Sandie Shaw	Pye	5	(52)	F
10	-	I'm Crying	Animals	Columbia	6	(19)	
11	-	We're Through	Hollies	Parlophone	7		
12	-	Walk Away	Matt Monro	Parlophone	11	(23)	
13	-	Together	P.J. Proby	Decca	6		
14	19	Everybody Loves Somebody	Dean Martin	Reprise	7	(1)	
15	9	As Tears Go By	Marianne Faithfull	Decca	10	(22)	F
16	-	The Twelfth Of Never	Cliff Richard	Columbia	6		
17	1	Have I The Right?	Honeycombs	Pye	11	(5)	F
18	-	How Soon	Henry Mancini & His Orchestra	RCA	4		L
19	-	One Way Love	Cliff Bennett & The Rebel Rousers	Parlophone	4		F
20	2	You Really Got Me	Kinks	Pye	9	(7)	F

November 1964

This Mnth	Prev Mnth	Title	Artist	Label	Wks 20	(US Pos)	
1	-	Baby Love	Supremes	Stateside	10	(1)	
2	1	Oh Pretty Woman	Roy Orbison	London American	12	(1)	
3	-	Sha La La	Manfred Mann	HMV	7	(12)	
4	-	He's In Town	Rockin' Berries	Piccadilly	7		F
5	-	All Day And All Of The Night	Kinks	Pye	9	(7)	
6	12	Walk Away	Matt Monro	Parlophone	11	(23)	
7	-	Um Um Um Um Um Um	Wayne Fontana & The Mindbenders	Fontana	7		F
8	4	The Wedding	Julie Rogers	Mercury	13	(10)	F L
9	6	When You Walk In The Room	Searchers	Pye	8	(35)	
10	-	Tokyo Melody	Helmut Zacharias Orchestra	Polydor	6		F L
11	-	There's A Heartache Following Me	Jim Reeves	RCA	10		
12	16	The Twelfth Of Never	Cliff Richard	Columbia	6		
13	-	Google Eye	Nashville Teens	Decca	3		L
14	-	Don't Bring Me Down	Pretty Things	Fontana	5		F
15	-	I'm Gonna Be Strong	Gene Pitney	Stateside	10	(9)	
16	9	(There's) Always Something There...	Sandie Shaw	Pye	5	(52)	F
17	-	Little Red Rooster	Rolling Stones	Decca	8		
18	2	Where Did Our Love Go	Supremes	Stateside	10	(1)	F
19	19	One Way Love	Cliff Bennettt/Rebel Rousers	Parlophone	4		F
20	-	Remember (Walkin' In The Sand)	Shangri-Las	Red Bird	3	(5)	F

December 1964

This Mnth	Prev Mnth	Title	Artist	Label	Wks 20	(US Pos)	
1	-	I Feel Fine	Beatles	Parlophone	10	(1)	G
2	15	I'm Gonna Be Strong	Gene Pitney	Stateside	10	(9)	
3	-	Downtown	Petula Clark	Pye	12	(1)	
4	17	Little Red Rooster	Rolling Stones	Decca	8		
5	-	Walk Tall	Val Doonican	Decca	10		F
6	-	Pretty Paper	Roy Orbison	London American	6	(15)	
7	1	Baby Love	Supremes	Stateside	10	(1)	
8	-	I Understand	Freddie & The Dreamers	Columbia	8	(36)	L
9	11	There's A Heartache Following Me	Jim Reeves	RCA	10		
10	5	All Day And All Of The Night	Kinks	Pye	9	(7)	
11	-	No Arms Could Ever Hold You	Bachelors	Decca	7	(27)	
12	10	Tokyo Melody	Helmut Zacharias Orchestra	Polydor	6		F L
13	-	Losing You	Dusty Springfield	Philips	5	(91)	
14	7	Um Um Um Um Um Um	Wayne Fontana/Mindbenders	Fontana	7		F
15	-	I Could Easily Fall	Cliff Richard	Columbia	8		
16	-	Message To Martha (Kentucky Bluebird)	Adam Faith	Parlophone	6		L
17	4	He's In Town	Rockin' Berries	Piccadilly	7		F
18	-	Somewhere	P.J. Proby	Liberty	8	(91)	
19	-	Blue Christmas	Elvis Presley	RCA	3		
20	-	Terry	Twinkle	Decca	9		F L

October 1964

This Mnth	Prev Mnth	Title	Artist	Label	Wks 20	(UK Pos)	
1	11	Do Wah Diddy Diddy	Manfred Mann	Ascot	10	(1)	F G
2	14	Dancing In The Street	Martha & The Vandellas	Gordy	8	(4)	G
3	8	Oh Pretty Woman	Roy Orbison	Monument	11	(1)	G
4	-	We'll Sing In The Sunshine	Gale Garnett	RCA	9		F L
5	-	Last Kiss	J. Frank Wilson & The Cavaliers	Josie	10		F G L
6	-	A Summer Song	Chad & Jeremy	World Artists	6		F
7	7	Remember (Walkin' In The Sand)	Shangri-Las	Red Bird	8	(14)	F
8	18	It Hurts To Be In Love	Gene Pitney	Musicor	6	(36)	
9	-	Let It Be Me	Jerry Butler & Betty Everett	Vee Jay	7		
10	3	Bread And Butter	Newbeats	Hickory	8	(15)	F G
11	-	Baby Love	Supremes	Motown	10	(1)	G
12	-	When I Grow Up (To Be A Man)	Beach Boys	Capitol	5	(27)	
13	4	G.T.O.	Ronny & The Daytonas	Mala	8		F L
14	-	Little Honda	Hondells	Mercury	5		F L
15	-	Chug-A-Lug	Roger Miller	Smash	5		
16	-	Have I The Right?	Honeycombs	Interphon	7	(1)	F L
17	-	Baby I Need Your Loving	Four Tops	Motown	5		F
18	-	Funny	Joe Hinton	Back Beat	4		F L
19	-	The Door Is Still Open To My Heart	Dean Martin	Reprise	5	(42)	
20	1	House Of The Rising Sun	Animals	MGM	9	(1)	F G

November 1964

This Mnth	Prev Mnth	Title	Artist	Label	Wks 20	(UK Pos)	
1	11	Baby Love	Supremes	Motown	10	(1)	G
2	-	Leader Of The Pack	Shangri-Las	Red Bird	9	(11)	G
3	-	Come A Little Bit Closer	Jay & The Americans	UA	7		
4	5	Last Kiss	J. Frank Wilson & The Cavaliers	Josie	10		F G L
5	16	Have I The Right?	Honeycombs	Interphon	7	(1)	F L
6	-	She's Not There	Zombies	Parrot	9	(12)	F G
7	-	Ringo	Lorne Greene	RCA	9	(22)	F G L
8	19	The Door Is Still Open To My Heart	Dean Martin	Reprise	5	(42)	
9	1	Do Wah Diddy Diddy	Manfred Mann	Ascot	10	(1)	F G
10	-	You Really Got Me	Kinks	Reprise	8	(1)	F
11	9	Let It Be Me	Jerry Butler & Betty Everett	Vee Jay	7		
12	3	Oh Pretty Woman	Roy Orbison	Monument	11	(1)	G
13	-	Time Is On My Side	Rolling Stones	London	8		F
14	-	Mr. Lonely	Bobby Vinton	Epic	11		G
15	-	I'm Gonna Be Strong	Gene Pitney	Musicor	7	(2)	
16	4	We'll Sing In The Sunshine	Gale Garnett	RCA	9		F L
17	15	Chug-A-Lug	Roger Miller	Smash	5		
18	-	Ask Me	Elvis Presley	RCA	4		
19	-	Mountain Of Love	Johnny Rivers	Imperial	6		
20	14	Little Honda	Hondells	Mercury	5		F L

December 1964

This Mnth	Prev Mnth	Title	Artist	Label	Wks 20	(UK Pos)	
1	14	Mr. Lonely	Bobby Vinton	Epic	11		G
2	-	Come See About Me	Supremes	Motown	11	(27)	G
3	6	She's Not There	Zombies	Parrot	9	(12)	F G
4	7	Ringo	Lorne Greene	RCA	9	(22)	F G L
5	13	Time Is On My Side	Rolling Stones	London	8		F
6	-	I Feel Fine	Beatles	Capitol	8	(1)	G
7	-	Dance, Dance, Dance	Beach Boys	Capitol	5	(24)	
8	10	You Really Got Me	Kinks	Reprise	8	(1)	F
9	15	I'm Gonna Be Strong	Gene Pitney	Musicor	7	(2)	
10	-	Goin' Out Of My Head	Little Anthony & The Imperials	DCP	9		
11	19	Mountain Of Love	Johnny Rivers	Imperial	6		
12	1	Baby Love	Supremes	Motown	10	(1)	G
13	2	Leader Of The Pack	Shangri-Las	Red Bird	9	(11)	G
14	-	I'm Into Something Good	Herman's Hermits	MGM	6	(1)	F
15	-	She's A Woman	Beatles	Capitol	6		
16	-	The Jerk	Larks	Money	7		F L
17	-	Sha La La	Manfred Mann	Ascot	7	(3)	
18	18	Ask Me	Elvis Presley	RCA	4		
19	-	The Wedding	Julie Rogers	Mercury	5	(3)	F L
20	-	Love Potion Number Nine	Searchers	Kapp	8		L

US 1964

OCT-DEC

◆ Fifteen thousand fans paid their last respects to soul singer/songwriter Sam Cooke who was shot and killed by a motel proprietor.

◆ Debuting in the US Top 20 were British acts Chad & Jeremy (who remained virtually unknown in their homeland) and The Rolling Stones, whose appearance on the *Ed Sullivan Show* made Ed Sullivan vow to never have them back (he relented later).

◆ The Beatles achieved a staggering 30 tracks in the US singles chart in 1964 (including six No. 1s). They ended the year topping the transatlantic charts with 'I Feel Fine'.

◆ The Rolling Stones' first American Top 20 hit 'Time Is On My Side' was not released as a single in Britain, and their British chart topper, 'Little Red Rooster', was never an American single. Both songs were covers of US R&B hits.

105

UK 1965 JAN-MAR

◆ Eric Clapton quit The Yardbirds (whose line-up included Jimmy Page) and was replaced by Jeff Beck.

◆ Folk rivals Bob Dylan and Donovan debuted on the UK singles chart in the same week. Interestingly, sales of singles were down 25% compared to January 1964.

◆ An all-star Motown package tour played to half empty houses. Incidentally, The Temptations' US chart topper, 'My Girl', finally hit in the UK in 1992. Fellow American, P.J. Proby, who was faring far better, was banned by the BBC, a major theatre chain and American show *Shindig*, after splitting his trousers on stage.

◆ David Bowie's group, The Mannish Boys (named, as were the Rolling Stones, after a Muddy Waters' song), signed to Parlophone and released their debut single, 'I Pity The Fool' (a cover of Bobby Bland's R&B success).

January 1965

This Mnth	Prev Mnth	Title	Artist	Label	Wks 20	(US Pos)	
1	-	Yeh Yeh	Georgie Fame	Columbia	8	(21)	F
2	1	I Feel Fine	Beatles	Parlophone	10	(1)	G
3	20	Terry	Twinkle	Decca	9		F L
4	-	Girl Don't Come	Sandie Shaw	Pye	9	(42)	
5	-	Go Now!	Moody Blues	Decca	9	(10)	F
6	3	Downtown	Petula Clark	Pye	12	(1)	
7	5	Walk Tall	Val Doonican	Decca	10		F
8	18	Somewhere	P.J. Proby	Liberty	8	(91)	
9	15	I Could Easily Fall	Cliff Richard	Columbia	8		
10	2	I'm Gonna Be Strong	Gene Pitney	Stateside	10	(9)	
11	-	Cast Your Fate To The Wind	Sounds Orchestral	Piccadilly	10	(10)	F L
12	-	Ferry Across The Mersey	Gerry & The Pacemakers	Columbia	7	(6)	
13	11	No Arms Could Ever Hold You	Bachelors	Decca	7	(27)	
14	8	I Understand	Freddie & The Dreamers	Columbia	8	(36)	L
15	-	You've Lost That Lovin' Feelin'	Cilla Black	Parlophone	5		
16	-	Come Tomorrow	Manfred Mann	HMV	7	(50)	
17	-	What Have They Done To The Rain	Searchers	Pye	6	(29)	
18	-	Baby Please Don't Go	Them	Decca	6		F
19	16	Message To Martha (Kentucky Bluebird)	Adam Faith	Parlophone	6		L
20	-	You've Lost That Lovin' Feelin'	Righteous Brothers	London American	7	(1)	F

February 1965

This Mnth	Prev Mnth	Title	Artist	Label	Wks 20	(US Pos)	
1	20	You've Lost That Lovin' Feelin'	Righteous Brothers	London American	7	(1)	F
2	-	Tired Of Waiting For You	Kinks	Pye	7	(6)	
3	-	Keep Searchin' (We'll Follow The Sun)	Del Shannon	Stateside	8	(9)	L
4	-	I'll Never Find Another You	Seekers	Columbia	11	(4)	F
5	16	Come Tomorrow	Manfred Mann	HMV	7	(50)	
6	-	The Special Years	Val Doonican	Decca	8		
7	5	Go Now!	Moody Blues	Decca	9	(10)	F
8	-	Game Of Love	Wayne Fontana & The Mindbenders	Fontana	7	(1)	
9	-	Don't Let Me Be Misunderstood	Animals	Columbia	7	(15)	
10	11	Cast Your Fate To The Wind	Sounds Orchestral	Piccadilly	10	(10)	F L
11	15	You've Lost That Lovin' Feelin'	Cilla Black	Parlophone	5		
12	-	Funny How Love Can Be	Ivy League	Piccadilly	6		F
13	18	Baby Please Don't Go	Them	Decca	6		F
14	-	It Hurts So Much	Jim Reeves	RCA	6		
15	12	Ferry Across The Mersey	Gerry & The Pacemakers	Columbia	7	(6)	
16	-	Leader Of The Pack	Shangri-Las	Red Bird	4	(1)	
17	1	Yeh Yeh	Georgie Fame	Columbia	8	(21)	F
18	4	Girl Don't Come	Sandie Shaw	Pye	9	(42)	
19	3	Terry	Twinkle	Decca	9		F L
20	-	Yes I Will	Hollies	Parlophone	7		

March 1965

This Mnth	Prev Mnth	Title	Artist	Label	Wks 20	(US Pos)	
1	-	It's Not Unusual	Tom Jones	Decca	9	(10)	F
2	4	I'll Never Find Another You	Seekers	Columbia	11	(4)	F
3	-	Silhouettes	Herman's Hermits	Columbia	9	(5)	
4	-	Come And Stay With Me	Marianne Faithfull	Decca	7	(26)	
5	-	The Last Time	Rolling Stones	Decca	9	(9)	
6	-	I'll Stop At Nothing	Sandie Shaw	Pye	7	(97)	
7	-	I Must Be Seeing Things	Gene Pitney	Stateside	6	(31)	
8	8	Game Of Love	Wayne Fontana & The Mindbenders	Fontana	7	(1)	
9	9	Don't Let Me Be Misunderstood	Animals	Columbia	7	(15)	
10	20	Yes I Will	Hollies	Parlophone	7		
11	-	Goodbye My Love	Searchers	Pye	5	(52)	
12	6	The Special Years	Val Doonican	Decca	8		
13	12	Funny How Love Can Be	Ivy League	Piccadilly	6		F
14	-	I Apologise	P.J. Proby	Liberty	5		
15	-	Goodnight	Roy Orbison	London American	5	(21)	
16	14	It Hurts So Much	Jim Reeves	RCA	6		
17	2	Tired Of Waiting For You	Kinks	Pye	7	(6)	
18	-	Concrete And Clay	Unit 4 Plus 2	Decca	9	(28)	F
19	-	Honey I Need	Pretty Things	Fontana	3		L
20	-	The Minute You're Gone	Cliff Richard	Columbia	9		

January 1965

This Mnth	Prev Mnth	Title	Artist	Label	Wks 20	(UK Pos)	
1	2	Come See About Me	Supremes	Motown	11	(27)	G
2	6	I Feel Fine	Beatles	Capitol	8	(1)	G
3	20	Love Potion Number Nine	Searchers	Kapp	8		L
4	-	Downtown	Petula Clark	Warner	11	(2)	F G
5	-	You've Lost That Lovin' Feelin'	Righteous Brothers	Philles	12	(1)	F G
6	1	Mr. Lonely	Bobby Vinton	Epic	11		G
7	16	The Jerk	Larks	Money	7		F L
8	10	Goin' Out Of My Head	Little Anthony & The Imperials	DCP	9		
9	-	Keep Searchin' (We'll Follow The Sun)	Del Shannon	Amy	7	(3)	L
10	-	How Sweet It Is To Be Loved By You	Marvin Gaye	Tamla	7	(49)	
11	15	She's A Woman	Beatles	Capitol	6		
12	-	Amen	Impressions	ABC Paramount	5		
13	-	The Name Game	Shirley Ellis	Congress	8		
14	-	Hold What You've Got	Joe Tex	Dial	6		F
15	19	The Wedding	Julie Rogers	Mercury	5	(3)	F L
16	17	Sha La La	Manfred Mann	Ascot	7	(3)	
17	3	She's Not There	Zombies	Parrot	9	(12)	F G
18	-	Thou Shalt Not Steal	Dick & Deedee	Warner	3		L
19	-	Willow Weep For Me	Chad & Jeremy	World Artists	4		
20	-	Any Way You Want It	Dave Clark Five	Epic	6	(25)	

February 1965

This Mnth	Prev Mnth	Title	Artist	Label	Wks 20	(UK Pos)	
1	5	You've Lost That Lovin' Feelin'	Righteous Brothers	Philles	12	(1)	F G
2	-	This Diamond Ring	Gary Lewis & The Playboys	Liberty	9		F G
3	4	Downtown	Petula Clark	Warner	11	(2)	F G
4	-	My Girl	Temptations	Gordy	10	(2)	G
5	13	The Name Game	Shirley Ellis	Congress	8		
6	-	Shake	Sam Cooke	RCA	5		L
7	-	The Jolly Green Giant	Kingsmen	Wand	7		L
8	-	All Day And All Of The Night	Kinks	Reprise	6	(2)	
9	-	I Go To Pieces	Peter & Gordon	Capitol	5		
10	-	Bye, Bye, Baby (Baby Goodbye)	Four Seasons	Philips	5		
11	14	Hold What You've Got	Joe Tex	Dial	6		F
12	-	Tell Her No	Zombies	Parrot	6	(42)	
13	-	The Boy From New York City	Ad Libs	Blue Cat	5		F L
14	-	Let's Lock The Door (And Throw Away The Key)	Jay & The Americans	UA	5		
15	3	Love Potion Number Nine	Searchers	Kapp	8		L
16	-	The "In" Crowd	Dobie Gray	Charger	3	(25)	F
17	-	Twine Time	Alvin Cash & The Crawlers	Mar-V-Lus	5		F L
18	10	How Sweet It Is To Be Loved By You	Marvin Gaye	Tamla	7	(49)	
19	-	King Of The Road	Roger Miller	Smash	9	(1)	G
20	-	Laugh, Laugh	Beau Brummels	Autumn	4		F

March 1965

This Mnth	Prev Mnth	Title	Artist	Label	Wks 20	(UK Pos)	
1	-	Eight Days A Week	Beatles	Capitol	8		G
2	-	Stop! In The Name Of Love	Supremes	Motown	9	(6)	G
3	4	My Girl	Temptations	Gordy	10	(2)	G
4	-	The Birds And The Bees	Jewel Akens	Era	8	(29)	F L
5	19	King Of The Road	Roger Miller	Smash	9	(1)	G
6	2	This Diamond Ring	Gary Lewis & The Playboys	Liberty	9		F G
7	-	Ferry Across The Mersey	Gerry & The Pacemakers	Laurie	7	(8)	L
8	-	Can't You Hear My Heartbeat	Herman's Hermits	MGM	8		G
9	-	Goldfinger	Shirley Bassey	UA	6	(21)	F L
10	7	The Jolly Green Giant	Kingsmen	Wand	7		L
11	-	Red Roses For A Blue Lady	Bert Kaempfert	Decca	7		L
12	1	You've Lost That Lovin' Feelin'	Righteous Brothers	Philles	12	(1)	F G
13	-	Shotgun	Jr. Walker & The All Stars	Soul	8		F
14	-	Hurt So Bad	Little Anthony & The Imperials	DCP	5		
15	12	Tell Her No	Zombies	Parrot	6	(42)	
16	3	Downtown	Petula Clark	Warner	11	(2)	F G
17	13	The Boy From New York City	Ad Libs	Blue Cat	5		F L
18	-	Little Things	Bobby Goldsboro	UA	4		
19	-	Come Home	Dave Clark Five	Epic	3	(16)	
20	-	People Get Ready	Impressions	ABC Paramount	2		

◆ America's first successful answers to the British group invasion were Gary Lewis & The Playboys and The Beau Brummels. Increasing such acts' chances, was the fact that American immigration authorities drastically cut the number of work permits given to UK groups.

◆ TV show *Hullabaloo* debuted with films of UK acts Gerry & The Pacemakers and The Zombies in the initial show. At the same time, top US DJ Murray The K said "Outside of The Beatles, British bands can't carry a show by themselves".

◆ The latest British record to top the transatlantic charts, 'Downtown' by Petula Clark, won the Grammy for Best Rock'n'Roll Record.

UK 1965 APR-JUNE

◆ Bob Dylan concluded a very successful tour of Britain (the subject of the film *Don't Look Back*) where his album **Bringing It All Back Home** followed **Freewheelin'** at No. 1.

◆ The *NME* Poll winner's concert was a Who's Who of British groups including: The Beatles, Rolling Stones, The Kinks, Herman's Hermits, Freddie & The Dreamers, Moody Blues, The Searchers, The Animals and The Mindbenders.

◆ When it was announced The Beatles would receive MBEs from the Queen, many previous holders returned theirs.

◆ Elvis Presley and The Everly Brothers made major chart comebacks with 'Crying In The Chapel' (recorded in 1960) and 'The Price Of Love' respectively.

April 1965

This Mnth	Prev Mnth	Title	Artist	Label	Wks 20	(US Pos)	
1	20	The Minute You're Gone	Cliff Richard	Columbia	9		
2	-	For Your Love	Yardbirds	Columbia	7	(6)	F
3	18	Concrete And Clay	Unit 4 Plus 2	Decca	9	(28)	F
4	-	Catch The Wind	Donovan	Pye	8	(23)	F
5	5	The Last Time	Rolling Stones	Decca	9	(9)	
6	-	Here Comes The Night	Them	Decca	8	(24)	L
7	-	Times They Are A-Changin'	Bob Dylan	CBS	7		F
8	-	I Can't Explain	Who	Brunswick	7	(93)	F
9	-	Stop! In The Name Of Love	Supremes	Tamla Motown	6	(1)	
10	1	It's Not Unusual	Tom Jones	Decca	9	(10)	F
11	3	Silhouettes	Herman's Hermits	Columbia	9	(5)	
12	-	Ticket To Ride	Beatles	Parlophone	9	(1)	
13	11	Goodbye My Love	Searchers	Pye	5	(52)	
14	-	Little Things	Dave Berry	Decca	6		
15	4	Come And Stay With Me	Marianne Faithfull	Decca	7	(26)	
16	-	I'll Be There	Gerry & The Pacemakers	Columbia	4	(14)	L
17	-	You're Breakin' My Heart	Keely Smith	Reprise	5		F L
18	-	Everybody's Gonna Be Happy	Kinks	Pye	3		
19	2	I'll Never Find Another You	Seekers	Columbia	11	(4)	F
20	-	Pop Go The Workers	Barron Knights	Columbia	8		

May 1965

This Mnth	Prev Mnth	Title	Artist	Label	Wks 20	(US Pos)	
1	12	Ticket To Ride	Beatles	Parlophone	9	(1)	
2	-	King Of The Road	Roger Miller	Philips	9	(4)	F
3	-	True Love Ways	Peter & Gordon	Columbia	10	(14)	
4	-	A World Of Our Own	Seekers	Columbia	11	(19)	
5	-	Where Are You Now (My Love)	Jackie Trent	Pye	7		F L
6	20	Pop Go The Workers	Barron Knights	Columbia	8		
7	-	Bring It On Home To Me	Animals	Columbia	8	(32)	
8	6	Here Comes The Night	Them	Decca	8	(24)	L
9	1	The Minute You're Gone	Cliff Richard	Columbia	9		
10	-	Wonderful World	Herman's Hermits	Columbia	7	(4)	
11	-	Oh No Not My Baby	Manfred Mann	HMV	5		
12	-	Subterranean Homesick Blues	Bob Dylan	CBS	6	(39)	
13	-	This Little Bird	Marianne Faithfull	Decca	7	(32)	
14	4	Catch The Wind	Donovan	Pye	8	(23)	F
15	-	Long Live Love	Sandie Shaw	Pye	9		
16	14	Little Things	Dave Berry	Decca	6		
17	9	Stop! In The Name Of Love	Supremes	Tamla Motown	6	(1)	
18	3	Concrete And Clay	Unit 4 Plus 2	Decca	9	(28)	F
19	-	Poor Man's Son	Rockin' Berries	Piccadilly	7		L
20	-	The Clapping Song	Shirley Ellis	London American	8	(8)	F L

June 1965

This Mnth	Prev Mnth	Title	Artist	Label	Wks 20	(US Pos)	
1	15	Long Live Love	Sandie Shaw	Pye	9		
2	-	Crying In The Chapel	Elvis Presley	RCA	11	(3)	
3	-	The Price Of Love	Everly Brothers	Warner	10		
4	-	Trains And Boats And Planes	Burt Bacharach	London American	7		F L
5	19	Poor Man's Son	Rockin' Berries	Piccadilly	7		L
6	4	A World Of Our Own	Seekers	Columbia	11	(19)	
7	20	The Clapping Song	Shirley Ellis	London American	8	(8)	F L
8	-	I'm Alive	Hollies	Parlophone	10		
9	13	This Little Bird	Marianne Faithfull	Decca	7	(32)	
10	-	Marie	Bachelors	Decca	6	(15)	
11	5	Where Are You Now (My Love)	Jackie Trent	Pye	7		F L
12	3	True Love Ways	Peter & Gordon	Columbia	10	(14)	
13	-	Colours	Donovan	Pye	6	(61)	
14	-	Set Me Free	Kinks	Pye	6	(23)	
15	-	You've Never Been In Love Like This Before	Unit 4 Plus 2	Decca	5	(95)	L
16	1	Ticket To Ride	Beatles	Parlophone	9	(1)	
17	-	Anyway Anyhow Anywhere	Who	Brunswick	6		
18	-	Trains And Boats And Planes	Billy J. Kramer & The Dakotas	Parlophone	4	(47)	L
19	2	King Of The Road	Roger Miller	Philips	9	(4)	F
20	-	Looking Through The Eyes Of Love	Gene Pitney	Stateside	8	(28)	

April 1965

This Mnth	Prev Mnth	Title	Artist	Label	Wks 20	(UK Pos)	
1	-	I'm Telling You Now	Freddie & The Dreamers	Tower	7	(3)	F G
2	2	Stop! In The Name Of Love	Supremes	Motown	9	(6)	G
3	13	Shotgun	Jr. Walker & The All Stars	Soul	8		F
4	8	Can't You Hear My Heartbeat	Herman's Hermits	MGM	8		G
5	-	Game Of Love	Wayne Fontana & The Mindbenders	Fontana	8	(2)	F G L
6	-	I Know A Place	Petula Clark	Warner	7	(17)	
7	-	Nowhere To Run	Martha & The Vandellas	Gordy	5	(26)	
8	4	The Birds And The Bees	Jewel Akens	Era	8	(29)	F L
9	-	Tired Of Waiting For You	Kinks	Reprise	6	(1)	
10	5	King Of The Road	Roger Miller	Smash	9	(1)	G
11	-	Mrs. Brown You've Got A Lovely Daughter	Herman's Hermits	MGM	10		G
12	1	Eight Days A Week	Beatles	Capitol	8		G
13	-	The Clapping Song	Shirley Ellis	Congress	5	(6)	L
14	-	Go Now!	Moody Blues	London	6	(1)	F
15	-	Red Roses For A Blue Lady	Vic Dana	Dolton	5		F L
16	-	I'll Never Find Another You	Seekers	Capitol	9	(1)	F
17	9	Goldfinger	Shirley Bassey	UA	6	(21)	F L
18	-	Do You Wanna Dance?	Beach Boys	Capitol	4		
19	-	The Race Is On	Jack Jones	Kapp	3		L
20	-	The Last Time	Rolling Stones	London	5	(1)	

May 1965

This Mnth	Prev Mnth	Title	Artist	Label	Wks 20	(UK Pos)	
1	11	Mrs. Brown You've Got A Lovely Daughter	Herman's Hermits	MGM	10		G
2	-	Count Me In	Gary Lewis & The Playboys	Liberty	7		
3	-	Ticket To Ride	Beatles	Capitol	9	(1)	G
4	16	I'll Never Find Another You	Seekers	Capitol	9	(1)	F
5	-	Silhouettes	Herman's Hermits	MGM	9	(3)	
6	6	I Know A Place	Petula Clark	Warner	7	(17)	
7	5	Game Of Love	Wayne Fontana/Mindbenders	Fontana	8	(2)	F G L
8	-	Help Me, Rhonda	Beach Boys	Capitol	8	(27)	G
9	-	Wooly Bully	Sam The Sham & The Pharaohs	MGM	12	(11)	F G
10	-	Just Once In My Life	Righteous Brothers	Philles	7		
11	-	Cast Your Fate To The Wind	Sounds Orchestral	Parkway	6	(5)	F L
12	-	Back In My Arms Again	Supremes	Motown	8	(40)	G
13	-	I'll Be Doggone	Marvin Gaye	Tamla	6		
14	1	I'm Telling You Now	Freddie & The Dreamers	Tower	7	(3)	F G
15	-	Baby The Rain Must Fall	Glenn Yarbrough	RCA	5		F L
16	-	Crying In The Chapel	Elvis Presley	RCA	10	(1)	G
17	20	The Last Time	Rolling Stones	London	5	(1)	
18	9	Tired Of Waiting For You	Kinks	Reprise	6	(1)	
19	-	It's Not Unusual	Tom Jones	Parrot	6	(1)	F
20	-	One Kiss For Old Time's Sake	Ronnie Dove	Diamond	4		

June 1965

This Mnth	Prev Mnth	Title	Artist	Label	Wks 20	(UK Pos)	
1	9	Wooly Bully	Sam The Sham & The Pharaohs	MGM	12	(11)	F G
2	-	I Can't Help Myself	Four Tops	Motown	11	(10)	G
3	16	Crying In The Chapel	Elvis Presley	RCA	10	(1)	G
4	12	Back In My Arms Again	Supremes	Motown	8	(40)	G
5	8	Help Me, Rhonda	Beach Boys	Capitol	8	(27)	G
6	-	Mr. Tambourine Man	Byrds	Columbia	9	(1)	F G
7	-	Wonderful World	Herman's Hermits	MGM	6	(7)	
8	3	Ticket To Ride	Beatles	Capitol	9	(1)	G
9	-	Engine Engine #9	Roger Miller	Smash	4	(33)	
10	-	Just A Little	Beau Brummels	Autumn	6		L
11	-	For Your Love	Yardbirds	Epic	7	(2)	F
12	1	Mrs. Brown You've Got A Lovely Daughter	Herman's Hermits	MGM	10		G
13	-	Hush, Hush Sweet Charlotte	Patti Page	Columbia	5		L
14	19	It's Not Unusual	Tom Jones	Parrot	6	(1)	F
15	-	(I Can't Get No) Satisfaction	Rolling Stones	London	10	(1)	G
16	-	Seventh Son	Johnny Rivers	Imperial	7		
17	-	Last Chance To Turn Around	Gene Pitney	Musicor	4		
18	4	I'll Never Find Another You	Seekers	Capitol	9	(1)	F
19	-	She's About A Mover	Sir Douglas Quintet	Tribe	4	(15)	F L
20	-	A Walk In The Black Forest	Horst Jankowski	Mercury	5	(3)	F L

US 1965
APR-JUNE

◆ In early May, the first British invasion reached its peak as British recordings held nine of the Top 10 chart places.

▲ Manchester bands Herman's Hermits (above), Freddie & The Dreamers and Wayne Fontana & The Mindbenders all topped the chart. Freddie (who at one time had four singles in the Hot 100) reached No. 1 with the two-year-old 'I'm Telling You Now', while the US-only release, 'Mrs Brown You've Got A Lovely Daughter' by Herman's Hemits, accumulated 600,000 advance orders and entered the Hot 100 at a record high position of 12 (in May they had two hits in the Top 5).

UK 1965 JULY-SEPT

◆ The Beatles' film *Help* and The Dave Clark Five's *Catch Us If You Can* (AKA *Having A Wild Weekend*) went on release.

▲ The Righteous Brother's revival of 'Unchained Melody' became a transatlantic success. It would repeat that feat in 1990.

◆ Appearing at the National Jazz & Blues Festival at Richmond were such artists as The Spencer Davis Group, Manfred Mann, Rod Stewart, The Who and The Yardbirds.

◆ After a long absence, US groups started to chart again in Britain, with newcomers, The Byrds, Sam The Sham & The Pharaohs and The Walker Brothers, leading the way.

July 1965

This Mnth	Prev Mnth	Title	Artist	Label	Wks 20	(US Pos)	
1	8	I'm Alive	Hollies	Parlophone	10		
2	-	Heart Full Of Soul	Yardbirds	Columbia	9	(9)	
3	2	Crying In The Chapel	Elvis Presley	RCA	11	(3)	
4	-	Mr. Tambourine Man	Byrds	CBS	9	(1)	F
5	20	Looking Through The Eyes Of Love	Gene Pitney	Stateside	8	(28)	
6	-	To Know You Is To Love You	Peter & Gordon	Columbia	6	(24)	
7	-	Tossing And Turning	Ivy League	Piccadilly	8		L
8	3	The Price Of Love	Everly Brothers	Warner	10		
9	-	Leave A Little Love	Lulu	Decca	5		
10	13	Colours	Donovan	Pye	6	(61)	
11	-	In The Middle Of Nowhere	Dusty Springfield	Philips	6		
12	17	Anyway Anyhow Anywhere	Who	Brunswick	6		
13	-	You've Got Your Troubles	Fortunes	Decca	9	(7)	F
14	-	There But For Fortune	Joan Baez	Fontana	7	(50)	F
15	4	Trains And Boats And Planes	Burt Bacharach	London American	7		F L
16	1	Long Live Love	Sandie Shaw	Pye	9		
17	-	Wooly Bully	Sam The Sham & The Pharaohs	MGM	6	(2)	F L
18	-	On My Word	Cliff Richard	Columbia	5		
19	14	Set Me Free	Kinks	Pye	6	(23)	
20	-	We Gotta Get Out Of This Place	Animals	Columbia	8	(13)	

August 1965

This Mnth	Prev Mnth	Title	Artist	Label	Wks 20	(US Pos)	
1	-	Help!	Beatles	Parlophone	10	(1)	
2	20	We Gotta Get Out Of This Place	Animals	Columbia	8	(13)	
3	13	You've Got Your Troubles	Fortunes	Decca	9	(7)	F
4	4	Mr. Tambourine Man	Byrds	CBS	9	(1)	F
5	-	Catch Us If You Can	Dave Clark Five	Columbia	6	(4)	
6	-	Everyone's Gone To The Moon	Jonathan King	Decca	7	(17)	F
7	-	A Walk In The Black Forest	Horst Jankowski	Mercury	12	(12)	F L
8	7	Tossing And Turning	Ivy League	Piccadilly	8		L
9	14	There But For Fortune	Joan Baez	Fontana	7	(50)	F
10	-	I Got You Babe	Sonny & Cher	Atlantic	9	(1)	F
11	-	Zorba's Dance	Marcello Minerbi	Durium	10		F L
12	-	Summer Nights	Marianne Faithfull	Decca	5	(24)	L
13	-	In Thoughts Of You	Billy Fury	Decca	5		L
14	2	Heart Full Of Soul	Yardbirds	Columbia	9	(9)	
15	-	All I Really Want To Do	Byrds	CBS	5	(40)	
16	-	With These Hands	Tom Jones	Decca	4	(27)	
17	17	Wooly Bully	Sam The Sham & The Pharaohs	MGM	6	(2)	F L
18	11	In The Middle Of Nowhere	Dusty Springfield	Philips	6		
19	-	Don't Make My Baby Blue	Shadows	Columbia	5		
20	-	He's Got No Love	Searchers	Pye	5	(79)	

September 1965

This Mnth	Prev Mnth	Title	Artist	Label	Wks 20	(US Pos)	
1	-	(I Can't Get No) Satisfaction	Rolling Stones	Decca	10	(1)	
2	-	Make It Easy On Yourself	Walker Brothers	Philips	10	(16)	
3	10	I Got You Babe	Sonny & Cher	Atlantic	9	(1)	F
4	7	A Walk In The Black Forest	Horst Jankowski	Mercury	12	(12)	F L
5	-	Like A Rolling Stone	Bob Dylan	CBS	8	(2)	
6	1	Help!	Beatles	Parlophone	10	(1)	
7	11	Zorba's Dance	Marcello Minerbi	Durium	10		F L
8	-	Look Through Any Window	Hollies	Parlophone	8	(32)	
9	15	All I Really Want To Do	Byrds	CBS	5	(40)	
10	-	Tears	Ken Dodd	Columbia	21		G
11	-	Laugh At Me	Sonny	Atlantic	6	(10)	F L
12	-	All I Really Want To Do	Cher	Liberty	5	(15)	F
13	-	That's The Way	Honeycombs	Pye	7		L
14	-	What's New Pussycat?	Tom Jones	Decca	5	(3)	
15	6	Everyone's Gone To The Moon	Jonathan King	Decca	7	(17)	F
16	-	Eve Of Destruction	Barry McGuire	RCA	10	(1)	F L
17	-	Unchained Melody	Righteous Brothers	London American	3	(4)	
18	-	See My Friend	Kinks	Pye	4		
19	-	Il Silenzio	Nini Rosso	Durium	7		F L
20	-	Just A Little Bit Better	Herman's Hermits	Columbia	5	(7)	

US 1965 JULY-SEPT

July 1965

This Mnth	Prev Mnth	Title	Artist	Label	Wks 20	(UK Pos)	
1	15	(I Can't Get No) Satisfaction	Rolling Stones	London	10	(1)	G
2	2	I Can't Help Myself	Four Tops	Motown	11	(10)	G
3	-	Yes, I'm Ready	Barbara Mason	Artic	7		F L
4	-	Cara Mia	Jay & The Americans	UA	8		
5	6	Mr. Tambourine Man	Byrds	Columbia	9	(1)	F G
6	16	Seventh Son	Johnny Rivers	Imperial	7		
7	-	I'm Henry VIII I Am	Herman's Hermits	MGM	8		G
8	-	What The World Needs Now Is Love	Jackie DeShannon	Imperial	7		F
9	-	What's New Pussycat?	Tom Jones	Parrot	8	(11)	
10	-	You Turn Me On	Ian Whitcomb	Tower	6		F L
11	1	Wooly Bully	Sam The Sham & The Pharaohs	MGM	12	(11)	F G
12	7	Wonderful World	Herman's Hermits	MGM	6	(7)	
13	11	For Your Love	Yardbirds	Epic	7	(2)	F
14	-	(Such An) Easy Question	Elvis Presley	RCA	4		
15	20	A Walk In The Black Forest	Horst Jankowski	Mercury	5	(3)	F L
16	-	Save Your Heart For Me	Gary Lewis & The Playboys	Liberty	7		
17	-	I Like It Like That	Dave Clark Five	Epic	4		
18	3	Crying In The Chapel	Elvis Presley	RCA	10	(1)	G
19	-	Too Many Rivers	Brenda Lee	Decca	3	(22)	
20	-	Laurie (Strange Things Happen)	Dickey Lee	TCF Hall	3		L

August 1965

This Mnth	Prev Mnth	Title	Artist	Label	Wks 20	(UK Pos)	
1	-	I Got You Babe	Sonny & Cher	Atco	8	(1)	F G
2	16	Save Your Heart For Me	Gary Lewis & The Playboys	Liberty	7		
3	1	(I Can't Get No) Satisfaction	Rolling Stones	London	10	(1)	G
4	-	Unchained Melody	Righteous Brothers	Philles	8	(14)	
5	7	I'm Henry VIII I Am	Herman's Hermits	MGM	8		G
6	-	It's The Same Old Song	Four Tops	Motown	7	(34)	
7	-	California Girls	Beach Boys	Capitol	7	(26)	
8	9	What's New Pussycat?	Tom Jones	Parrot	8	(11)	
9	-	Help!	Beatles	Capitol	9	(1)	G
10	-	Don't Just Stand There	Patty Duke	UA	5		F L
11	-	Down In The Boondocks	Billy Joe Royal	Columbia	6	(38)	F
12	-	Baby, I'm Yours	Barbara Lewis	Atlantic	5		
13	-	Hold Me Thrill Me Kiss Me	Mel Carter	Imperial	7		F L
14	17	I Like It Like That	Dave Clark Five	Epic	4		
15	-	Like A Rolling Stone	Bob Dylan	Columbia	7	(4)	F G
16	-	Papa's Got A Brand New Bag	James Brown	King	6	(25)	
17	-	I Want Candy	Strangeloves	Bang	4		F L
18	3	Yes, I'm Ready	Barbara Mason	Artic	7		F L
19	4	Cara Mia	Jay & The Americans	UA	8		
20	-	All I Really Want To Do	Cher	Imperial	4	(9)	F

September 1965

This Mnth	Prev Mnth	Title	Artist	Label	Wks 20	(UK Pos)	
1	9	Help!	Beatles	Capitol	9	(1)	G
2	15	Like A Rolling Stone	Bob Dylan	Columbia	7	(4)	F G
3	-	Eve Of Destruction	Barry McGuire	Dunhill	8	(3)	F G L
4	-	You Were On My Mind	We Five	A&M	9		F L
5	4	Unchained Melody	Righteous Brothers	Philles	8	(14)	
6	-	The "In" Crowd	Ramsey Lewis Trio	Argo	8		F
7	-	It Ain't Me Babe	Turtles	White Whale	5		F
8	1	I Got You Babe	Sonny & Cher	Atco	8	(1)	F G
9	-	Hang On Sloopy	McCoys	Bang	9	(5)	F G
10	7	California Girls	Beach Boys	Capitol	7	(26)	
11	-	Catch Us If You Can	Dave Clark Five	Epic	6	(5)	
12	16	Papa's Got A Brand New Bag	James Brown	King	6	(25)	
13	-	Heart Full Of Soul	Yardbirds	Epic	5	(2)	
14	6	It's The Same Old Song	Four Tops	Motown	7	(34)	
15	13	Hold Me Thrill Me Kiss Me	Mel Carter	Imperial	7		F L
16	-	Laugh At Me	Sonny	Atco	5	(9)	F L
17	-	You've Got Your Troubles	Fortunes	Press	6	(2)	F
18	-	Nothing But Heartaches	Supremes	Motown	4		
19	-	Action	Freddy Cannon	Warner	3		L
20	11	Down In The Boondocks	Billy Joe Royal	Columbia	6	(38)	F

◆ The Beatles third US tour was staggeringly successful. Their performance in front of 56,000 fans at the Shea Stadium was filmed for a TV special. During their tour they met Elvis for the only time as, coincidentally, did Herman's Hermits.

◆ Both The Rolling Stones 'Satisfaction' and The Beatles' 'Yesterday' were first issued as singles in the States, with both topping the chart. The latter, which was finally a UK hit for them in 1976, became the most recorded and most played song of all time.

◆ With Bob Dylan (whose new electric folk/rock sound was greeted with boos at the Newport Folk Festival) rivalling Lennon & McCartney as the most respected composer, and with Sonny & Cher and The Byrds being the most talked about new acts on both sides of the Atlantic – America was fast regaining the ground it had lost to Britain.

◆ Two British records which sold over a million in the UK but failed to even chart Stateside were: 'Tears' by Ken Dodd and 'The Carnival Is Over' by The Seekers.

◆ Elvis Presley's original bass player, Bill Black, died. Elvis, by the way, was again voted Top Male singer in the *NME* poll, with Dusty Springfield and The Beatles winning the other top awards.

◆ As The Stones scored their fifth successive UK No. 1 with 'Get Off Of My Cloud', Motown (America's top label in 1965) act The Supremes notched up their sixth American topper, 'I Hear A Symphony'.

◆ Decca Records released Marc Bolan's debut disc, 'The Wizard'. The label also recorded the first solo tracks by Van Morrison, whose group, Them, had temporarily disbanded.

October 1965

This Mnth	Prev Mnth	Title	Artist	Label	Wks 20	(US Pos)	
1	10	Tears	Ken Dodd	Columbia	21		G
2	-	If You Gotta Go Go Now	Manfred Mann	HMV	8		
3	16	Eve Of Destruction	Barry McGuire	RCA	10	(1)	F L
4	-	Almost There	Andy Williams	CBS	10	(67)	
5	2	Make It Easy On Yourself	Walker Brothers	Philips	10	(16)	
6	-	Hang On Sloopy	McCoys	Immediate	9	(1)	F L
7	8	Look Through Any Window	Hollies	Parlophone	8	(32)	
8	19	Il Silenzio	Nini Rosso	Durium	7		F L
9	1	(I Can't Get No) Satisfaction	Rolling Stones	Decca	10	(1)	
10	-	Message Understood	Sandie Shaw	Pye	5		
11	-	Baby Don't Go	Sonny & Cher	Reprise	5	(8)	
12	4	A Walk In The Black Forest	Horst Jankowski	Mercury	12	(12)	F L
13	-	Some Of Your Lovin'	Dusty Springfield	Philips	6		
14	-	Evil Hearted You/Still I'm Sad	Yardbirds	Columbia	6		
15	5	Like A Rolling Stone	Bob Dylan	CBS	8	(2)	
16	-	It's Good News Week	Hedgehoppers Anonymous	Decca	6	(48)	F L
17	-	In The Midnight Hour	Wilson Pickett	Atlantic	4	(21)	F
18	-	What Cha Gonna Do About It	Small Faces	Decca	5		F
19	-	Yesterday Man	Chris Andrews	Decca	11	(94)	F
20	-	Here It Comes Again	Fortunes	Decca	7	(27)	

November 1965

This Mnth	Prev Mnth	Title	Artist	Label	Wks 20	(US Pos)	
1	-	Get Off Of My Cloud	Rolling Stones	Decca	8	(1)	
2	1	Tears	Ken Dodd	Columbia	21		G
3	19	Yesterday Man	Chris Andrews	Decca	11	(94)	F
4	-	The Carnival Is Over	Seekers	Columbia	14		G
5	20	Here It Comes Again	Fortunes	Decca	7	(27)	
6	14	Evil Hearted You/Still I'm Sad	Yardbirds	Columbia	6		
7	-	It's My Life	Animals	Columbia	6	(23)	
8	16	It's Good News Week	Hedgehoppers Anonymous	Decca	6	(48)	F L
9	-	Yesterday	Matt Monro	Parlophone	7		L
10	-	My Generation	Who	Brunswick	10	(74)	
11	4	Almost There	Andy Williams	CBS	10	(67)	
12	-	1-2-3	Len Barry	Brunswick	11	(2)	F
13	-	Positively 4th Street	Bob Dylan	CBS	9	(7)	
14	-	Love Is Strange	Everly Brothers	Warner	4		L
15	3	Eve Of Destruction	Barry McGuire	RCA	10	(1)	F L
16	-	Wind Me Up (Let Me Go)	Cliff Richard	Columbia	12		
17	-	A Lovers Concerto	Toys	Stateside	9	(2)	F L
18	6	Hang On Sloopy	McCoys	Immediate	9	(1)	F L
19	2	If You Gotta Go Go Now	Manfred Mann	HMV	8		
20	-	Princess In Rags	Gene Pitney	Stateside	8	(37)	

December 1965

This Mnth	Prev Mnth	Title	Artist	Label	Wks 20	(US Pos)	
1	4	The Carnival Is Over	Seekers	Columbia	14		G
2	16	Wind Me Up (Let Me Go)	Cliff Richard	Columbia	12		
3	10	My Generation	Who	Brunswick	10	(74)	
4	12	1-2-3	Len Barry	Brunswick	11	(2)	F
5	-	Day Tripper/We Can Work it Out	Beatles	Parlophone	10	(5)	G
6	2	Tears	Ken Dodd	Columbia	21		G
7	-	The River	Ken Dodd	Columbia	11		
8	17	A Lovers Concerto	Toys	Stateside	9	(2)	F L
9	-	Maria	P.J. Proby	Liberty	6		L
10	20	Princess In Rags	Gene Pitney	Stateside	8	(37)	
11	1	Get Off Of My Cloud	Rolling Stones	Decca	8	(1)	
12	-	My Ship Is Coming In	Walker Brothers	Philips	10	(63)	
13	13	Positively 4th Street	Bob Dylan	CBS	9	(7)	
14	-	Let's Hang On!	Four Seasons	Philips	11	(3)	
15	-	Rescue Me	Fontella Bass	Chess	7	(4)	F L
16	3	Yesterday Man	Chris Andrews	Decca	11	(94)	F
17	-	Don't Bring Me Your Heartaches	Paul & Barry Ryan	Decca	4		F
18	7	It's My Life	Animals	Columbia	6	(23)	
19	-	To Whom It Concerns	Chris Andrews	Decca	5		L
20	-	Tell Me Why	Elvis Presley	RCA	4	(33)	

October 1965

This Mnth	Prev Mnth	Title	Artist	Label	Wks 20	(UK Pos)	
1	-	Yesterday	Beatles	Capitol	8	(8)	G
2	-	Treat Her Right	Roy Head	Back Beat	7	(30)	F L
3	9	Hang On Sloopy	McCoys	Bang	9	(5)	F G
4	-	Keep On Dancing	Gentrys	MGM	7		F L
5	-	A Lovers Concerto	Toys	Dynovoice	8	(5)	F G
6	6	The "in" Crowd	Ramsey Lewis Trio	Argo	8		F
7	3	Eve Of Destruction	Barry McGuire	Dunhill	8	(3)	F G L
8	-	Just A Little Bit Better	Herman's Hermits	MGM	4	(15)	
9	-	Baby Don't Go	Sonny & Cher	Reprise	5	(11)	
10	-	Get Off Of My Cloud	Rolling Stones	London	9	(1)	
11	-	Do You Believe In Magic	Lovin' Spoonful	Kama Sutra	5		F
12	-	Everybody Loves A Clown	Gary Lewis & The Playboys	Liberty	6		
13	11	Catch Us If You Can	Dave Clark Five	Epic	6	(5)	
14	17	You've Got Your Troubles	Fortunes	Press	6	(2)	F
15	4	You Were On My Mind	We Five	A&M	9		F L
16	-	You're The One	Vogues	Co & Ce	6		F
17	-	I'm Yours	Elvis Presley	RCA	4		
18	-	Positively 4th Street	Bob Dylan	Columbia	5	(8)	
19	-	Liar, Liar	Castaways	Soma	6		F L
20	-	Some Enchanted Evening	Jay & The Americans	UA	5		

November 1965

This Mnth	Prev Mnth	Title	Artist	Label	Wks 20	(UK Pos)	
1	10	Get Off Of My Cloud	Rolling Stones	London	9	(1)	
2	-	1-2-3	Len Barry	Decca	9	(3)	F L
3	-	I Hear A Symphony	Supremes	Motown	8	(39)	G
4	5	A Lovers Concerto	Toys	Dynovoice	8	(5)	F G
5	-	Rescue Me	Fontella Bass	Checker	8	(11)	F L
6	-	Let's Hang On!	Four Seasons	Philips	12	(4)	
7	-	A Taste Of Honey	Herb Alpert	A&M	8		
8	-	Turn! Turn! Turn!	Byrds	Columbia	10	(26)	G
9	16	You're The One	Vogues	Co & Ce	6		F
10	-	Ain't That Peculiar	Marvin Gaye	Tamla	7		
11	12	Everybody Loves A Clown	Gary Lewis & The Playboys	Liberty	6		
12	1	Yesterday	Beatles	Capitol	8	(8)	G
13	18	Positively 4th Street	Bob Dylan	Columbia	5	(8)	
14	-	Make Me Your Baby	Barbara Lewis	Atlantic	4		L
15	-	You've Got To Hide Your Love Away	Silkie	Fontana	4	(28)	F L
16	4	Keep On Dancing	Gentrys	MGM	7		F L
17	-	I Got You (I Feel Good)	James Brown	King	9	(29)	G
18	-	I Knew You When	Billy Joe Royal	Columbia	4		
19	-	Run, Baby Run (Back Into My Arms)	Newbeats	Hickory	5	(10)	L
20	-	But You're Mine	Sonny & Cher	Atco	4	(17)	

December 1965

This Mnth	Prev Mnth	Title	Artist	Label	Wks 20	(UK Pos)	
1	8	Turn! Turn! Turn!	Byrds	Columbia	10	(26)	G
2	6	Let's Hang On!	Four Seasons	Philips	12	(4)	
3	17	I Got You (I Feel Good)	James Brown	King	9	(29)	G
4	-	Over And Over	Dave Clark Five	Epic	8	(45)	
5	3	I Hear A Symphony	Supremes	Motown	8	(39)	G
6	-	I Can Never Go Home Anymore	Shangri-Las	Red Bird	6		L
7	-	Make The World Go Away	Eddy Arnold	RCA	7	(8)	F L
8	2	1-2-3	Len Barry	Decca	9	(3)	F L
9	-	England Swings	Roger Miller	Smash	6	(13)	L
10	-	Fever	McCoys	Bang	7	(44)	L
11	7	A Taste Of Honey	Herb Alpert	A&M	8		
12	-	I Will	Dean Martin	Reprise	5		L
13	5	Rescue Me	Fontella Bass	Checker	8	(11)	F L
14	-	Hang On Sloopy	Ramsey Lewis Trio	Cadet	4		
15	-	The Sounds Of Silence	Simon & Garfunkel	Columbia	8		F G
16	-	Ebb Tide	Righteous Brothers	Philles	6	(48)	
17	-	Don't Think Twice	Wonder Who?	Philips	4		
18	10	Ain't That Peculiar	Marvin Gaye	Tamla	7		
19	1	Get Off Of My Cloud	Rolling Stones	London	9	(1)	
20	-	We Can Work It Out	Beatles	Capitol	9	(1)	G

US
1965
OCT-DEC

◆ In the last week of the year there were eight American artists in the UK Top 20, and only two British acts in the equivalent US chart, and they were the groups that had started the invasion: The Beatles and The Dave Clark Five. Unusually, Clark's chart topping revival of 'Over & Over' was ignored in his homeland.

◆ The Grateful Dead and Jefferson Airplane headlined the first rock show at the Fillmore in San Francisco.

▲ Soul music made its presence felt on both sides of the Atlantic thanks to hits from James Brown (above), Wilson Pickett, Fontella Bass, Marvin Gaye and The Four Tops.

113

UK 1966
JAN-MAR

◆ The Beatles double sider, 'Day Tripper'/ 'We Can Work It Out', sold 750,000 copies in five days in Britain. The group also scored their eighth and last No. 1 EP with 'Yesterday', and Lennon & McCartney's Grammy winning composition, 'Michelle' hit the top by The Overlanders. Also John Lennon made his now infamous remark about The Beatles currently being more popular than Jesus.

▲ American soul music continued to thrive. Stevie Wonder (above) had his first UK hit, 'Uptight'. James Brown had the whole of *Ready Steady Go* devoted to him, and Wilson Pickett and Mary Wells also had successful appearances on that TV show.

January 1966

This Mnth	Prev Mnth	Title	Artist	Label	Wks 20	(US Pos)	
1	5	Day Tripper/We Can Work it Out	Beatles	Parlophone	10	(1)	G
2	-	Keep On Runnin'	Spencer Davis Group	Fontana	10	(76)	F
3	12	My Ship Is Coming In	Walker Brothers	Philips	10	(63)	
4	2	Wind Me Up (Let Me Go)	Cliff Richard	Columbia	12		
5	7	The River	Ken Dodd	Columbia	11		
6	1	The Carnival Is Over	Seekers	Columbia	14		G
7	14	Let's Hang On!	Four Seasons	Philips	11	(3)	
8	-	Till The End Of The Day	Kinks	Pye	8	(50)	
9	6	Tears	Ken Dodd	Columbia	21		G
10	-	Spanish Flea	Herb Alpert	Pye International	12	(27)	F
11	-	A Must To Avoid	Herman's Hermits	Columbia	7	(8)	
12	4	1-2-3	Len Barry	Brunswick	11	(2)	F
13	-	Merrie Gentle Pops	Barron Knights	Columbia	5		
14	-	Michelle	Overlanders	Pye	6		F L
15	3	My Generation	Who	Brunswick	10	(74)	
16	15	Rescue Me	Fontella Bass	Chess	7	(4)	F L
17	-	My Girl	Otis Redding	Atlantic	7		F
18	-	A Hard Day's Night	Peter Sellers	Parlophone	4		L
19	8	A Lovers Concerto	Toys	Stateside	9	(2)	F L
20	19	To Whom It Concerns	Chris Andrews	Decca	5		L

February 1966

This Mnth	Prev Mnth	Title	Artist	Label	Wks 20	(US Pos)	
1	-	You Were On My Mind	Crispian St. Peters	Decca	8	(36)	F
2	10	Spanish Flea	Herb Alpert	Pye International	12	(27)	F
3	-	These Boots Are Made For Walkin'	Nancy Sinatra	Reprise	10	(1)	F
4	-	Love's Just A Broken Heart	Cilla Black	Parlophone	6		
5	-	A Groovy Kind Of Love	Mindbenders	Fontana	10	(2)	F
6	14	Michelle	Overlanders	Pye	6		F L
7	2	Keep On Runnin'	Spencer Davis Group	Fontana	10	(76)	F
8	-	19th Nervous Breakdown	Rolling Stones	Decca	7	(2)	
9	11	A Must To Avoid	Herman's Hermits	Columbia	7	(8)	
10	-	Mirror Mirror	Pinkerton's Assorted Colours	Decca	4		F L
11	-	Tomorrow	Sandie Shaw	Pye	5		
12	-	Like A Baby	Len Barry	Brunswick	4	(27)	L
13	-	Girl	St. Louis Union	Decca	5		F L
14	-	My Love	Petula Clark	Pye	6	(1)	
15	1	Day Tripper/We Can Work it Out	Beatles	Parlophone	10	(1)	G
16	17	My Girl	Otis Redding	Atlantic	7		F
17	7	Let's Hang On!	Four Seasons	Philips	11	(3)	
18	-	Sha La La La Lee	Small Faces	Decca	8		
19	3	My Ship Is Coming In	Walker Brothers	Philips	10	(63)	
20	-	Michelle	David & Jonathan	Columbia	4	(18)	F

March 1966

This Mnth	Prev Mnth	Title	Artist	Label	Wks 20	(US Pos)	
1	5	A Groovy Kind Of Love	Mindbenders	Fontana	10	(2)	F
2	18	Sha La La La Lee	Small Faces	Decca	8		
3	-	Barbara Ann	Beach Boys	Capitol	8	(2)	
4	3	These Boots Are Made For Walkin'	Nancy Sinatra	Reprise	10	(1)	F
5	-	Backstage	Gene Pitney	Stateside	6	(25)	
6	-	I Can't Let Go	Hollies	Parlophone	6	(42)	
7	-	The Sun Ain't Gonna Shine Anymore	Walker Brothers	Philips	7	(13)	
8	8	19th Nervous Breakdown	Rolling Stones	Decca	7	(2)	
9	14	My Love	Petula Clark	Pye	6	(1)	
10	2	Spanish Flea	Herb Alpert	Pye International	12	(27)	F
11	-	Make The World Go Away	Eddy Arnold	RCA	10	(6)	F L
12	-	Shapes Of Things	Yardbirds	Columbia	7	(11)	
13	-	Lightnin' Strikes	Lou Christie	MGM	5	(1)	F
14	-	Dedicated Follower Of Fashion	Kinks	Pye	8	(36)	
15	-	Inside-Looking Out	Animals	Decca	4	(34)	
16	1	You Were On My Mind	Crispian St. Peters	Decca	8	(36)	F
17	11	Tomorrow	Sandie Shaw	Pye	5		
18	-	What Now My Love	Sonny & Cher	Atlantic	5	(14)	
19	-	Elusive Butterfly	Bob Lind	Fontana	5	(5)	F L
20	-	This Golden Ring	Fortunes	Decca	2	(82)	

January 1966

This Mnth	Prev Mnth	Title	Artist	Label	Wks 20	(UK Pos)	
1	20	We Can Work It Out	Beatles	Capitol	9	(1)	G
2	15	The Sounds Of Silence	Simon & Garfunkel	Columbia	8		F G
3	-	She's Just My Style	Gary Lewis & The Playboys	Liberty	7		
4	-	Five O'Clock World	Vogues	Co & Ce	9		
5	-	Day Tripper	Beatles	Capitol	5	(1)	G
6	16	Ebb Tide	Righteous Brothers	Philles	6	(48)	
7	-	No Matter What Shape (Your Stomach's In)	T-Bones	Liberty	8		F L
8	-	Flowers On The Wall	Statler Brothers	Columbia	5		F L
9	-	As Tears Go By	Rolling Stones	London	5		
10	-	A Must To Avoid	Herman's Hermits	MGM	6	(6)	
11	-	The Men In My Little Girl's Life	Mike Douglas	Epic	5		F L
12	4	Over And Over	Dave Clark Five	Epic	8	(45)	
13	3	I Got You (I Feel Good)	James Brown	King	9	(29)	G
14	1	Turn! Turn! Turn!	Byrds	Columbia	10	(26)	G
15	2	Let's Hang On!	Four Seasons	Philips	12	(4)	
16	10	Fever	McCoys	Bang	7	(44)	L
17	-	You Didn't Have To Be So Nice	Lovin' Spoonful	Kama Sutra	4		
18	-	Barbara Ann	Beach Boys	Capitol	6	(3)	G
19	-	Just Like Me	Paul Revere & The Raiders	Columbia	5		F
20	-	The Duck	Jackie Lee	Mirwood	5		F L

February 1966

This Mnth	Prev Mnth	Title	Artist	Label	Wks 20	(UK Pos)	
1	-	Lightnin' Strikes	Lou Christie	MGM	8	(11)	G
2	-	My Love	Petula Clark	Warner	8	(4)	G
3	-	Uptight (Everything's Alright)	Stevie Wonder	Tamla	6	(14)	G
4	18	Barbara Ann	Beach Boys	Capitol	6	(3)	G
5	-	My World Is Empty Without You	Supremes	Motown	6		
6	-	Crying Time	Ray Charles	ABC Paramount	6	(50)	
7	7	No Matter What Shape (Your Stomach's In)	T-Bones	Liberty	8		F L
8	-	These Boots Are Made For Walkin'	Nancy Sinatra	Reprise	10	(1)	F G
9	1	We Can Work It Out	Beatles	Capitol	9	(1)	G
10	-	Don't Mess With Bill	Marvelettes	Tamla	6		
11	-	Zorba The Greek	Herb Alpert & Tijuana Brass	A&M	4		
12	4	Five O'Clock World	Vogues	Co & Ce	9		
13	-	The Ballad Of The Green Berets	SSgt. Barry Sadler	RCA	11	(24)	F G L
14	-	Going To A Go-Go	Miracles	Tamla	2	(44)	
15	-	A Well Respected Man	Kinks	Reprise	5		
16	11	The Men In My Little Girl's Life	Mike Douglas	Epic	5		F L
17	-	California Dreamin'	Mamas & The Papas	Dunhill	10	(23)	F G
18	-	Working My Way Back To You	Four Seasons	Philips	4	(50)	
19	3	She's Just My Style	Gary Lewis & The Playboys	Liberty	7		
20	-	Jenny Take A Ride!	Mitch Ryder & The Detroit Wheels	New Voice	4	(33)	F

March 1966

This Mnth	Prev Mnth	Title	Artist	Label	Wks 20	(UK Pos)	
1	13	The Ballad Of The Green Berets	SSgt. Barry Sadler	RCA	11	(24)	F G L
2	8	These Boots Are Made For Walkin'	Nancy Sinatra	Reprise	10	(1)	F G
3	-	19th Nervous Breakdown	Rolling Stones	London	8	(2)	G
4	-	Listen People	Herman's Hermits	MGM	6		
5	17	California Dreamin'	Mamas & The Papas	Dunhill	10	(23)	F G
6	-	Elusive Butterfly	Bob Lind	World Pacific	7	(5)	F L
7	-	Nowhere Man	Beatles	Capitol	7		G
8	-	Homeward Bound	Simon & Garfunkel	Columbia	7	(9)	
9	1	Lightnin' Strikes	Lou Christie	MGM	8	(11)	G
10	-	I Fought The Law	Bobby Fuller Four	Mustang	5		F L
11	-	Daydream	Lovin' Spoonful	Kama Sutra	8	(2)	G
12	-	Love Makes The World Go Round	Deon Jackson	Carla	4		F L
13	18	Working My Way Back To You	Four Seasons	Philips	4	(50)	
14	-	The Cheater	Bob Kuban & The In-Men	Musicland	4		F L
15	2	My Love	Petula Clark	Warner	8	(4)	G
16	3	Uptight (Everything's Alright)	Stevie Wonder	Tamla	6	(14)	G
17	-	(You're My) Soul And Inspiration	Righteous Brothers	Verve	10	(15)	G
18	5	My World Is Empty Without You	Supremes	Motown	6		
19	-	634-5789	Wilson Pickett	Atlantic	4	(36)	F
20	-	I'm So Lonesome I Could Cry	B.J. Thomas	Scepter	8		F

US 1966 JAN-MAR

◆ The first hippy boutique, the Psychedelic Shop, opened in San Francisco, and the earliest youth culture magazine, *Crawdaddy*, was launched in New York.

◆ At a time when video tape recorders were only rich people's toys, CBS announced they were developing a metal disc containing music and pictures (that could be seen on a TV) for the mass market.

◆ Guests on the final *Shindig* TV show included The Kinks and The Who. Its rival, *Hullabaloo*, came off air soon afterwards. Also closing (for the first time) was Liverpool's Cavern Club, made famous by The Beatles.

◆ Vietnam veteran, Staff Sergeant Barry Sadler, not only topped the single chart with his patriotic self-composed debut disc, 'The Ballad Of The Green Berets', but also had a No. 1 album with **Ballads Of The Green Berets**.

UK 1966
APR-JUNE

◆ The Beatles played their last UK date, alongside the Stones and The Who, at the *NME* poll winner's concert. They started their final World tour by returning to Hamburg.

◆ Indian instrument the sitar which George Harrison had played on The Beatles' **Rubber Soul** album, was now used by the Stones on their transatlantic topper, 'Paint It Black'.

◆ American trio The Walker Brothers (who had scored two successive No. 1s) applied to become British Citizens, soon after British duo Chad & Jeremy had requested US citizenship.

◆ The British album chart was extended to 30 places.

◆ Frank Sinatra scored the only solo transatlantic chart topper of his career with Bert Kaempfert's composition 'Strangers In The Night'.

April 1966

This Mnth	Prev Mnth	Title	Artist	Label	Wks 20	(US Pos)	
1	-	Somebody Help Me	Spencer Davis Group	Fontana	7	(47)	
2	-	Hold Tight	Dave Dee, Dozy, Beaky, Mick & Tich	Fontana	10		F
3	-	The Sound Of Silence	Bachelors	Decca	9		
4	-	Elusive Butterfly	Val Doonican	Decca	8		
5	7	The Sun Ain't Gonna Shine Anymore	Walker Brothers	Philips	7	(13)	
6	-	Substitute	Who	Reaction	9		
7	19	Elusive Butterfly	Bob Lind	Fontana	5	(5)	F L
8	-	You Don't Have To Say You Love Me	Dusty Springfield	Philips	10	(4)	
9	14	Dedicated Follower Of Fashion	Kinks	Pye	8	(36)	
10	11	Make The World Go Away	Eddy Arnold	RCA	10	(6)	F L
11	-	Bang Bang (My Baby Shot Me Down)	Cher	Liberty	8	(2)	
12	12	Shapes Of Things	Yardbirds	Columbia	7	(11)	
13	6	I Can't Let Go	Hollies	Parlophone	6	(42)	
14	-	I Put A Spell On You	Alan Price Set	Decca	5	(80)	F
15	-	Alfie	Cilla Black	Parlophone	7	(95)	
16	-	Pied Piper	Crispian St. Peters	Decca	8	(4)	L
17	-	Someday One Day	Seekers	Columbia	6		
18	2	Sha La La La Lee	Small Faces	Decca	8		
19	3	Barbara Ann	Beach Boys	Capitol	8	(2)	
20	-	Pretty Flamingo	Manfred Mann	HMV	7	(29)	

May 1966

This Mnth	Prev Mnth	Title	Artist	Label	Wks 20	(US Pos)	
1	20	Pretty Flamingo	Manfred Mann	HMV	7	(29)	
2	-	Sloop John B	Beach Boys	Capitol	9	(3)	
3	-	Daydream	Lovin' Spoonful	Pye International	8	(2)	F
4	8	You Don't Have To Say You Love Me	Dusty Springfield	Philips	10	(4)	
5	16	Pied Piper	Crispian St. Peters	Decca	8	(4)	L
6	11	Bang Bang (My Baby Shot Me Down)	Cher	Liberty	8	(2)	
7	-	Wild Thing	Troggs	Fontana	8	(1)	F
8	-	Shotgun Wedding	Roy 'C'	Island	6		F
9	2	Hold Tight	Dave Dee, Dozy, Beaky, Mick & Tich	Fontana	10		F
10	-	Sorrow	Merseys	Fontana	8		L
11	-	Paint It, Black	Rolling Stones	Decca	7	(1)	
12	-	Homeward Bound	Simon & Garfunkel	CBS	7	(5)	F
13	3	The Sound Of Silence	Bachelors	Decca	9		
14	-	Strangers In The Night	Frank Sinatra	Reprise	13	(1)	
15	15	Alfie	Cilla Black	Parlophone	7	(95)	
16	-	Rainy Day Women Nos. 12 & 35	Bob Dylan	CBS	5	(2)	
17	-	Monday Monday	Mamas & The Papas	RCA	10	(1)	F
18	-	Hey Girl	Small Faces	Decca	5		
19	-	Promises	Ken Dodd	Columbia	8		
20	1	Somebody Help Me	Spencer Davis Group	Fontana	7	(47)	

June 1966

This Mnth	Prev Mnth	Title	Artist	Label	Wks 20	(US Pos)	
1	14	Strangers In The Night	Frank Sinatra	Reprise	13	(1)	
2	17	Monday Monday	Mamas & The Papas	RCA	10	(1)	F
3	10	Sorrow	Merseys	Fontana	8		L
4	11	Paint It, Black	Rolling Stones	Decca	7	(1)	
5	-	When A Man Loves A Woman	Percy Sledge	Atlantic	9	(1)	F
6	7	Wild Thing	Troggs	Fontana	8	(1)	F
7	-	Don't Bring Me Down	Animals	Decca	6	(12)	
8	19	Promises	Ken Dodd	Columbia	8		
9	2	Sloop John B	Beach Boys	Capitol	9	(3)	
10	-	Paperback Writer	Beatles	Parlophone	7	(1)	
11	16	Rainy Day Women Nos. 12 & 35	Bob Dylan	CBS	5	(2)	
12	-	Over Under Sideways Down	Yardbirds	Columbia	5	(13)	L
13	18	Hey Girl	Small Faces	Decca	5		
14	-	Don't Answer Me	Cilla Black	Parlophone	6		
15	-	Sunny Afternoon	Kinks	Pye	9	(14)	
16	-	Nothing Comes Easy	Sandie Shaw	Pye	4		
17	-	River Deep Mountain High	Ike & Tina Turner	London American	9	(88)	F
18	8	Shotgun Wedding	Roy 'C'	Island	6		F
19	1	Pretty Flamingo	Manfred Mann	HMV	7	(29)	
20	-	Nobody Needs Your Love	Gene Pitney	Stateside	9		

April 1966

This Mnth	Prev Mnth	Title	Artist	Label	Wks 20	(UK Pos)	
1	17	(You're My) Soul And Inspiration	Righteous Brothers	Verve	10	(15)	G
2	11	Daydream	Lovin' Spoonful	Kama Sutra	8	(2)	G
3	-	Bang Bang (My Baby Shot Me Down)	Cher	Imperial	8	(3)	
4	-	Secret Agent Man	Johnny Rivers	Imperial	7		
5	-	Time Won't Let Me	Outsiders	Capitol	7		F
6	3	19th Nervous Breakdown	Rolling Stones	London	8	(2)	G
7	20	I'm So Lonesome I Could Cry	B.J. Thomas	Scepter	8		F
8	1	The Ballad Of The Green Berets	SSgt. Barry Sadler	RCA	11	(24)	F G L
9	-	Good Lovin'	Young Rascals	Atlantic	9		F G
10	7	Nowhere Man	Beatles	Capitol	7		G
11	-	Kicks	Paul Revere & The Raiders	Columbia	9		
12	-	Sloop John B	Beach Boys	Capitol	7	(2)	
13	5	California Dreamin'	Mamas & The Papas	Dunhill	10	(23)	F G
14	-	Sure Gonna Miss Her	Gary Lewis & The Playboys	Liberty	4		
15	-	Monday Monday	Mamas & The Papas	Dunhill	8	(3)	G
16	8	Homeward Bound	Simon & Garfunkel	Columbia	7	(9)	
17	-	A Sign Of The Times	Petula Clark	Warner	3	(49)	
18	-	This Old Heart Of Mine	Isley Brothers	Tamla	4	(3)	
19	2	These Boots Are Made For Walkin'	Nancy Sinatra	Reprise	10	(1)	F G
20	-	Leaning On The Lamp Post	Herman's Hermits	MGM	5		

May 1966

This Mnth	Prev Mnth	Title	Artist	Label	Wks 20	(UK Pos)	
1	15	Monday Monday	Mamas & The Papas	Dunhill	8	(3)	G
2	9	Good Lovin'	Young Rascals	Atlantic	9		F G
3	-	Rainy Day Women #12 & 35	Bob Dylan	Columbia	7	(7)	
4	11	Kicks	Paul Revere & The Raiders	Columbia	9		
5	-	When A Man Loves A Woman	Percy Sledge	Atlantic	8	(4)	F G
6	12	Sloop John B	Beach Boys	Capitol	7	(2)	
7	-	A Groovy Kind Of Love	Mindbenders	Fontana	8	(2)	F G L
8	1	(You're My) Soul And Inspiration	Righteous Brothers	Verve	10	(15)	G
9	-	Message To Michael	Dionne Warwick	Scepter	6		
10	-	How Does That Grab You Darlin'	Nancy Sinatra	Reprise	4	(19)	
11	-	Gloria	Shadows Of Knight	Dunwich	6		F L
12	-	Love Is Like An Itching In My Heart	Supremes	Motown	5		
13	20	Leaning On The Lamp Post	Herman's Hermits	MGM	5		
14	4	Secret Agent Man	Johnny Rivers	Imperial	7		
15	-	Paint It ,Black	Rolling Stones	London	9	(1)	G
16	-	I Am A Rock	Simon & Garfunkel	Columbia	8	(17)	
17	-	Did You Ever Have To Make Up Your Mind	Lovin' Spoonful	Kama Sutra	7		
18	-	The Sun Ain't Gonna Shine (Anymore)	Walker Brothers	Smash	4	(1)	F L
19	-	Shapes Of Things	Yardbirds	Epic	4	(3)	
20	-	Eight Miles High	Byrds	Columbia	3	(24)	L

June 1966

This Mnth	Prev Mnth	Title	Artist	Label	Wks 20	(UK Pos)	
1	15	Paint It, Black	Rolling Stones	London	9	(1)	G
2	17	Did You Ever Have To Make Up Your Mind	Lovin' Spoonful	Kama Sutra	7		
3	16	I Am A Rock	Simon & Garfunkel	Columbia	8	(17)	
4	5	When A Man Loves A Woman	Percy Sledge	Atlantic	8	(4)	F G
5	-	Strangers In The Night	Frank Sinatra	Reprise	8	(1)	G
6	7	A Groovy Kind Of Love	Mindbenders	Fontana	8	(2)	F G L
7	-	Barefootin'	Robert Parker	Nola	7	(24)	F L
8	-	Green Grass	Gary Lewis & The Playboys	Liberty	5		
9	-	Sweet Talkin' Guy	Chiffons	Laurie	6	(4)	L
10	-	Cool Jerk	Capitols	Karen	8		F L
11	1	Monday Monday	Mamas & The Papas	Dunhill	8	(3)	G
12	-	It's A Man's Man's Man's World	James Brown	King	5	(13)	
13	-	Red Rubber Ball	Cyrkle	Columbia	8		F G
14	-	Oh How Happy	Shades Of Blue	Impact	6		F L
15	-	Paperback Writer	Beatles	Capitol	8	(1)	G
16	-	You Don't Have To Say You Love Me	Dusty Springfield	Philips	8	(1)	
17	-	Opus 17 (Don't You Worry 'Bout Me)	Four Seasons	Philips	5	(20)	
18	3	Rainy Day Women #12 & 35	Bob Dylan	Columbia	7	(7)	
19	12	Love Is Like An Itching In My Heart	Supremes	Motown	5		
20	-	The More I See You	Chris Montez	A&M	3	(3)	L

◆ Percy Sledge's transatlantic smash, 'When A Man Loves A Woman', helped put "The Muscle Shoals Sound" on the music map. It also returned to the UK Top 5 in 1987.

▲ Among the most successful new transatlantic artists were trend-setting American acts: The Lovin' Spoonful, Simon & Garfunkel (above) and The Mamas & The Papas.

◆ After losing The Righteous Brothers to MGM, Phil Spector released his most ambitious and expensive ($22,000) production, 'River Deep Mountain High' by Ike & Tina Turner, which was only successful in the UK.

UK 1966 JULY-SEPT

◆ Stars of the National Jazz & Blues Festival included The Who, The Small Faces, The Move, and the newly formed Cream.

◆ Dusty Springfield launched her own TV series, *Dusty*, and had her only chart topper. 'You Don't Have To Say You Love Me' (also her biggest solo US hit).

◆ The *NME* announced "The British Beat Boom is over". They pointed out there were now more American records on the US chart than British, and that sales of UK records in America were dropping. *NME* concluded, "Whatever happens, Britain has made her mark upon the world of pop, America now accepts us as a force to be reckoned with – the dark days when British hits in American were regarded as flukes are over".

July 1966

This Mnth	Prev Mnth	Title	Artist	Label	Wks 20	(US Pos)	
1	15	Sunny Afternoon	Kinks	Pye	9	(14)	
2	17	River Deep Mountain High	Ike & Tina Turner	London American	9	(88)	F
3	20	Nobody Needs Your Love	Gene Pitney	Stateside	9		
4	-	Get Away	Georgie Fame	Columbia	7	(70)	
5	1	Strangers In The Night	Frank Sinatra	Reprise	13	(1)	
6	-	Bus Stop	Hollies	Parlophone	7	(5)	
7	10	Paperback Writer	Beatles	Parlophone	7	(1)	
8	-	Out Of Time	Chris Farlowe	Immediate	8		F L
9	-	Black Is Black	Los Bravos	Decca	9	(4)	F
10	-	Hideaway	Dave Dee, Dozy, Beaky, Mick & Tich	Fontana	6		
11	-	I Couldn't Live Without Your Love	Petula Clark	Pye	7	(9)	
12	14	Don't Answer Me	Cilla Black	Parlophone	6		
13	5	When A Man Loves A Woman	Percy Sledge	Atlantic	9	(1)	F
14	-	Love Letters	Elvis Presley	RCA	7	(19)	
15	2	Monday Monday	Mamas & The Papas	RCA	10	(1)	F
16	-	With A Girl Like You	Troggs	Fontana	8	(29)	
17	-	The More I See You	Chris Montez	Pye International	9	(16)	
18	-	Goin' Back	Dusty Springfield	Philips	6		
19	-	Lana	Roy Orbison	London American	5		
20	7	Don't Bring Me Down	Animals	Decca	6	(12)	

August 1966

This Mnth	Prev Mnth	Title	Artist	Label	Wks 20	(US Pos)	
1	16	With A Girl Like You	Troggs	Fontana	8	(29)	
2	9	Black Is Black	Los Bravos	Decca	9	(4)	F
3	17	The More I See You	Chris Montez	Pye International	9	(16)	
4	-	Mama	Dave Berry	Decca	10		L
5	-	God Only Knows	Beach Boys	Capitol	9	(39)	
6	8	Out Of Time	Chris Farlowe	Immediate	8		F L
7	-	Yellow Submarine/Eleanor Rigby	Beatles	Parlophone	9	(2)	
8	-	Visions	Cliff Richard	Columbia	8		
9	-	Summer In The City	Lovin' Spoonful	Kama Sutra	7	(1)	L
10	14	Love Letters	Elvis Presley	RCA	7	(19)	
11	11	I Couldn't Live Without Your Love	Petula Clark	Pye	7	(9)	
12	-	Hi-Lili-Hi-Lo	Alan Price Set	Decca	7		
13	-	They're Coming To Take Me Away Ha-Haaa!	Napoleon XIV	Warner	6	(3)	F L
14	4	Get Away	Georgie Fame	Columbia	7	(70)	
15	1	Sunny Afternoon	Kinks	Pye	9	(14)	
16	18	Goin' Back	Dusty Springfield	Philips	6		
17	-	Lovers Of The World Unite	David & Jonathan	Columbia	7		L
18	-	I Saw Her Again	Mamas & The Papas	RCA	6	(5)	
19	-	I Want You	Bob Dylan	CBS	5	(20)	
20	-	All Or Nothing	Small Faces	Decca	8		

September 1966

This Mnth	Prev Mnth	Title	Artist	Label	Wks 20	(US Pos)	
1	20	All Or Nothing	Small Faces	Decca	8		
2	7	Yellow Submarine/Eleanor Rigby	Beatles	Parlophone	9	(2)	
3	5	God Only Knows	Beach Boys	Capitol	9	(39)	
4	-	Too Soon To Know	Roy Orbison	London American	10	(68)	
5	-	Distant Drums	Jim Reeves	RCA	19	(45)	
6	13	They're Coming To Take Me Away Ha-Haaa!	Napoleon XIV	Warner	6	(3)	F L
7	17	Lovers Of The World Unite	David & Jonathan	Columbia	7		L
8	4	Mama	Dave Berry	Decca	10		L
9	-	Working In The Coal Mine	Lee Dorsey	Stateside	6	(8)	F
10	-	Got To Get You Into My Life	Cliff Bennett & The Rebel Rousers	Parlophone	5		L
11	-	Just Like A Woman	Manfred Mann	Fontana	6		
12	1	With A Girl Like You	Troggs	Fontana	8	(29)	
13	-	I'm A Boy	Who	Reaction	10		
14	8	Visions	Cliff Richard	Columbia	8		
15	-	Little Man	Sonny & Cher	Atlantic	6	(21)	
16	-	You Can't Hurry Love	Supremes	Tamla Motown	8	(1)	
17	18	I Saw Her Again	Mamas & The Papas	RCA	6	(5)	
18	12	Hi-Lili-Hi-Lo	Alan Price Set	Decca	7		
19	9	Summer In The City	Lovin' Spoonful	Kama Sutra	7	(1)	L
20	-	When I Come Home	Spencer Davis Group	Fontana	4		

118

July 1966

This Mnth	Prev Mnth	Title	Artist	Label	Wks 20	(UK Pos)	
1	-	Hanky Panky	Tommy James & The Shondells	Roulette	8	(38)	F G
2	15	Paperback Writer	Beatles	Capitol	8	(1)	G
3	13	Red Rubber Ball	Cyrkle	Columbia	8	(2)	F G
4	-	Wild Thing	Troggs	Fontana/Atco	8	(2)	F G
5	16	You Don't Have To Say You Love Me	Dusty Springfield	Philips	8	(1)	
6	5	Strangers In The Night	Frank Sinatra	Reprise	8	(1)	G
7	-	Lil' Red Riding Hood	Sam The Sham & The Pharaohs	MGM	9	(46)	G L
8	-	Hungry	Paul Revere & The Raiders	Columbia	6		
9	-	Little Girl	Syndicate Of Sound	Bell	4		F L
10	-	The Pied Piper	Crispian St. Peters	Jamie	6	(5)	F L
11	-	I Saw Her Again	Mamas & The Papas	Dunhill	6	(11)	
12	-	Along Comes Mary	Association	Valiant	4		F
13	1	Paint It, Black	Rolling Stones	London	9	(1)	G
14	10	Cool Jerk	Capitols	Karen	8		F L
15	-	Sweet Pea	Tommy Roe	ABC Paramount	7		G
16	-	Dirty Water	Standells	Tower	4		F L
17	-	Ain't Too Proud To Beg	Temptations	Gordy	5	(21)	
18	-	Don't Bring Me Down	Animals	MGM	5	(6)	
19	-	Somewhere, My Love	Ray Conniff & The Singers	Columbia	5		F L
20	3	I Am A Rock	Simon & Garfunkel	Columbia	8	(17)	

August 1966

This Mnth	Prev Mnth	Title	Artist	Label	Wks 20	(UK Pos)	
1	-	Summer In The City	Lovin' Spoonful	Kama Sutra	8	(8)	G
2	7	Lil' Red Riding Hood	Sam The Sham & The Pharaohs	MGM	9	(46)	G L
3	4	Wild Thing	Troggs	Fontana/Atco	8	(2)	F G
4	-	Sunny	Bobby Hebb	Philips	8	(12)	F G L
5	-	They're Coming To Take Me Away Ha-Haaa!	Napoleon XIV	Warner	4	(4)	F L
6	10	The Pied Piper	Crispian St. Peters	Jamie	6	(5)	F L
7	-	See You In September	Happenings	B.T.Puppy	8		F
8	-	Mothers Little Helper	Rolling Stones	London	6		
9	-	I Couldn't Live Without Your Love	Petula Clark	Warner	7	(6)	
10	15	Sweet Pea	Tommy Roe	ABC Paramount	7		G
11	11	I Saw Her Again	Mamas & The Papas	Dunhill	6	(11)	
12	-	Sunshine Superman	Donovan	Epic	9	(2)	F G
13	19	Somewhere, My Love	Ray Conniff & The Singers	Columbia	5		F L
14	-	Blowin' In The Wind	Stevie Wonder	Tamla	5	(36)	
15	-	Over Under Sideways Down	Yardbirds	Epic	4	(10)	L
16	1	Hanky Panky	Tommy James & The Shondells	Roulette	8	(38)	F G
17	-	This Door Swings Both Ways	Herman's Hermits	MGM	4	(18)	
18	-	Sweet Dreams	Tommy McLain	MSL	4		F L
19	-	Summertime	Billy Stewart	Chess	4	(39)	F L
20	-	My Heart's Symphony	Gary Lewis & The Playboys	Liberty	4	(36)	

September 1966

This Mnth	Prev Mnth	Title	Artist	Label	Wks 20	(UK Pos)	
1	-	You Can't Hurry Love	Supremes	Motown	9	(3)	G
2	12	Sunshine Superman	Donovan	Epic	9	(2)	F G
3	-	Yellow Submarine	Beatles	Capitol	7	(1)	G
4	7	See You In September	Happenings	B.T.Puppy	8		F
5	-	Bus Stop	Hollies	Imperial	6	(5)	F
6	-	Wouldn't It Be Nice	Beach Boys	Capitol	5	(58)	
7	-	Cherish	Association	Valiant	8		G
8	-	Land Of 1,000 Dances	Wilson Pickett	Atlantic	5	(22)	
9	4	Sunny	Bobby Hebb	Philips	8	(12)	F G L
10	1	Summer In The City	Lovin' Spoonful	Kama Sutra	8	(8)	G
11	-	Guantanamera	Sandpipers	A&M	5	(7)	F
12	-	Working In The Coal Mine	Lee Dorsey	Amy	5	(8)	L
13	-	Beauty Is Only Skin Deep	Temptations	Gordy	6	(18)	G
14	-	Born A Woman	Sandy Posey	MGM	7	(24)	F
15	19	Summertime	Billy Stewart	Chess	4	(39)	F L
16	-	Black Is Black	Los Bravos	Parrot	6	(2)	F L
17	-	Eleanor Rigby	Beatles	Capitol	3	(1)	
18	14	Blowin' In The Wind	Stevie Wonder	Tamla	5	(36)	
19	-	96 Tears	? (Question Mark) & The Mysterians	Cameo	11	(37)	F G L
20	-	Sunny Afternoon	Kinks	Reprise	4	(1)	

◆ John Lennon's comment that The Beatles were more popular than Jesus, resulted in demonstrations during their third and last US tour. Their last ever show was, ironically, in San Francisco – the town that replaced Liverpool and Manchester as rock's trend-setting centre.

▲ Among the acts debuting in the Top 20 were Tommy James & The Shondells ('Hanky Panky' was first released in 1964), The Association, The Happenings and British superstars Donovan (above), and The Hollies.

UK
1966
OCT–DEC

◆ In the year that tape cassettes and tape cartridges were introduced commercially, sales of singles dropped 17% (they had fallen 15% in 1965), and album sales increased by 6%, after a 1965 rise of 13%.

◆ The UK album chart was further extended to a Top 40.

◆ The Beach Boys were mobbed when they arrived for a British tour. They ousted The Beatles as World's Top Group in the *NME* poll, and their transatlantic No. 1, 'Good Vibrations', showed how good pop records could be.

◆ John Lennon, who met Yoko Ono at an art exhibition, worked on his first solo film, *How I Won The War*, and Paul McCartney penned the music for the film *The Family Way* starring Hayley Mills. They reunited as the year closed to start work on **Sergeant Pepper.**

October 1966

This Mnth	Prev Mnth	Title	Artist	Label	Wks 20	(US Pos)	
1	5	Distant Drums	Jim Reeves	RCA	19	(45)	
2	-	Bend It	Dave Dee, Dozy, Beaky, Mick & Tich	Fontana	9		
3	13	I'm A Boy	Who	Reaction	10		
4	-	Winchester Cathedral	New Vaudeville Band	Fontana	9	(1)	F
5	16	You Can't Hurry Love	Supremes	Tamla Motown	8	(1)	
6	-	Have You Seen Your Mother, Baby, Standing In The Shadow	Rolling Stones	Decca	6	(9)	
7	-	Guantanamera	Sandpipers	Pye International	9	(9)	F L
8	15	Little Man	Sonny & Cher	Atlantic	6	(21)	
9	-	All I See Is You	Dusty Springfield	Philips	7	(20)	
10	-	I Can't Control Myself	Troggs	Page One	9	(43)	
11	-	Walk With Me	Seekers	Columbia	6		
12	4	Too Soon To Know	Roy Orbison	London American	10	(68)	
13	-	Reach Out I'll Be There	Four Tops	Tamla Motown	10	(1)	F
14	-	Stop Stop Stop	Hollies	Parlophone	8	(7)	
15	-	Sunny	Georgie Fame	Columbia	4		
16	-	Sunny	Bobby Hebb	Philips	3	(2)	F L
17	1	All Or Nothing	Small Faces	Decca	8		
18	-	Another Tear Falls	Walker Brothers	Philips	3		
19	-	No Milk Today	Herman's Hermits	Columbia	7	(35)	
20	2	Yellow Submarine/Eleanor Rigby	Beatles	Parlophone	9	(2)	

November 1966

This Mnth	Prev Mnth	Title	Artist	Label	Wks 20	(US Pos)	
1	13	Reach Out I'll Be There	Four Tops	Tamla Motown	10	(1)	F
2	14	Stop Stop Stop	Hollies	Parlophone	8	(7)	
3	-	Semi-Detached Surburban Mr.James	Manfred Mann	Fontana	8		
4	-	High Time	Paul Jones	HMV	8		F
5	-	Good Vibrations	Beach Boys	Capitol	11	(1)	
6	10	I Can't Control Myself	Troggs	Page One	9	(43)	
7	1	Distant Drums	Jim Reeves	RCA	19	(45)	
8	-	Gimme Some Loving	Spencer Davis Group	Fontana	7	(7)	
9	-	If I Were A Carpenter	Bobby Darin	Atlantic	7	(8)	L
10	19	No Milk Today	Herman's Hermits	Columbia	7	(35)	
11	4	Winchester Cathedral	New Vaudeville Band	Fontana	9	(1)	F
12	-	Holy Cow	Lee Dorsey	Stateside	8	(23)	L
13	7	Guantanamera	Sandpipers	Pye International	9	(9)	F L
14	-	Green Green Grass Of Home	Tom Jones	Decca	15	(11)	G
15	-	Time Drags By	Cliff Richard	Columbia	4		
16	-	A Fool Am I	Cilla Black	Parlophone	4		
17	2	Bend It	Dave Dee, Dozy, Beaky etc.	Fontana	9		
18	-	What Would I Be	Val Doonican	Decca	11		
19	-	I've Got You Under My Skin	Four Seasons	Philips	5	(9)	
20	-	Help Me Girl	Eric Burdon & The Animals	Decca	4	(29)	

December 1966

This Mnth	Prev Mnth	Title	Artist	Label	Wks 20	(US Pos)	
1	14	Green Green Grass Of Home	Tom Jones	Decca	15	(11)	G
2	18	What Would I Be	Val Doonican	Decca	11		
3	5	Good Vibrations	Beach Boys	Capitol	11	(1)	
4	-	Morningtown Ride	Seekers	Columbia	10	(44)	
5	-	Friday On My Mind	Easybeats	UA	9	(16)	F
6	-	My Mind's Eye	Small Faces	Decca	6		
7	-	Dead End Street	Kinks	Pye	9	(73)	
8	8	Gimme Some Loving	Spencer Davis Group	Fontana	7	(7)	
9	-	What Becomes Of The Brokenhearted	Jimmy Ruffin	Tamla Motown	7	(7)	F
10	3	Semi-Detached Surburban Mr.James	Manfred Mann	Fontana	8		
11	-	Sunshine Superman	Donovan	Pye	7	(1)	
12	12	Holy Cow	Lee Dorsey	Stateside	8	(23)	L
13	-	Just One Smile	Gene Pitney	Stateside	6	(64)	
14	-	You Keep Me Hangin' On	Supremes	Tamla Motown	7	(1)	
15	-	Save Me	Dave Dee, Dozy, Beaky, Mick & Tich	Fontana	7		
16	7	Distant Drums	Jim Reeves	RCA	19	(45)	
17	-	If Every Day Was Like Christmas	Elvis Presley	RCA	4		
18	1	Reach Out I'll Be There	Four Tops	Tamla Motown	10	(1)	F
19	4	High Time	Paul Jones	HMV	8		F
20	-	There Won't Be Many Coming Home	Roy Orbison	London American	3		L

October 1966

This Mnth	Prev Mnth	Title	Artist	Label	Wks 20	(UK Pos)	
1	-	Reach Out I'll Be There	Four Tops	Motown	9	(1)	G
2	19	96 Tears	? (Question Mark) & The Mysterians	Cameo	11	(37)	F G L
3	7	Cherish	Association	Valiant	8		G
4	-	Last Train To Clarksville	Monkees	Colgems	10	(23)	F G
5	-	Psychotic Reaction	Count Five	Double Shot	5		F L
6	-	Walk Away Renee	Left Banke	Smash	7		F
7	-	What Becomes Of The Brokenhearted	Jimmy Ruffin	Soul	9	(8)	F
8	-	Cherry Cherry	Neil Diamond	Bang	6		F
9	1	You Can't Hurry Love	Supremes	Motown	9	(3)	G
10	16	Black Is Black	Los Bravos	Parrot	6	(2)	F L
11	13	Beauty Is Only Skin Deep	Temptations	Gordy	6	(18)	G
12	-	Poor Side Of Town	Johnny Rivers	Imperial	10		G
13	-	I've Got You Under My Skin	Four Seasons	Philips	5	(12)	
14	-	Dandy	Herman's Hermits	MGM	6		
15	-	See See Rider	Eric Burdon & The Animals	MGM	5		
16	-	Hooray For Hazel	Tommy Roe	ABC	7		
17	-	Have You Seen Your Mother Baby Standing In The Shadow?	Rolling Stones	London	5	(5)	
18	-	If I Were A Carpenter	Bobby Darin	Atlantic	7	(9)	L
19	5	Bus Stop	Hollies	Imperial	6	(5)	F
20	2	Sunshine Superman	Donovan	Epic	9	(2)	F G

November 1966

This Mnth	Prev Mnth	Title	Artist	Label	Wks 20	(UK Pos)	
1	4	Last Train To Clarksville	Monkees	Colgems	10	(23)	F G
2	12	Poor Side Of Town	Johnny Rivers	Imperial	10		G
3	2	96 Tears	? (Question Mark)/Mysterians	Cameo	11	(37)	F G L
4	-	Good Vibrations	Beach Boys	Capitol	10	(1)	G
5	-	You Keep Me Hangin' On	Supremes	Motown	8	(8)	G
6	-	Winchester Cathedral	New Vaudeville Band	Fontana	11	(4)	F G L
7	-	I'm Your Puppet	James & Bobby Purify	Bell	7	(12)	F L
8	-	Devil With A Blue Dress On & Good Golly Miss Molly	Mitch Ryder & The Detroit Wheels	New Voice	11		
9	18	If I Were A Carpenter	Bobby Darin	Atlantic	7	(9)	L
10	1	Reach Out I'll Be There	Four Tops	Motown	9	(1)	G
11	14	Dandy	Herman's Hermits	MGM	6		
12	16	Hooray For Hazel	Tommy Roe	ABC	7		
13	-	Love Is A Hurtin' Thing	Lou Rawls	Capitol	5		F
14	-	Born Free	Roger Williams	Kapp	9		L
15	-	Rain On The Roof	Lovin' Spoonful	Kama Sutra	5		
16	6	Walk Away Renee	Left Banke	Smash	7		F
17	-	Lady Godiva	Peter & Gordon	Capitol	6	(16)	
18	7	What Becomes Of The Broken...	Jimmy Ruffin	Soul	9	(8)	F
19	17	Have You Seen Your Mother Baby...	Rolling Stones	London	5	(5)	
20	-	Coming On Strong	Brenda Lee	Decca	5		L

December 1966

This Mnth	Prev Mnth	Title	Artist	Label	Wks 20	(UK Pos)	
1	6	Winchester Cathedral	New Vaudeville Band	Fontana	11	(4)	F G L
2	-	Mellow Yellow	Donovan	Epic	8	(8)	G
3	4	Good Vibrations	Beach Boys	Capitol	10	(1)	G
4	8	Devil With A Blue Dress On &	Mitch Ryder/The Detroit Wheels	New Voice	11		
5	5	You Keep Me Hangin' On	Supremes	Motown	8	(8)	G
6	-	That's Life	Frank Sinatra	Reprise	8	(46)	
7	-	I'm A Believer	Monkees	Colgems	12	(1)	G
8	14	Born Free	Roger Williams	Kapp	9		L
9	-	Sugar Town	Nancy Sinatra	Reprise	8	(8)	G
10	17	Lady Godiva	Peter & Gordon	Capitol	6	(16)	
11	-	A Place In The Sun	Stevie Wonder	Tamla	5	(20)	
12	-	(I Know) I'm Losing You	Temptations	Gordy	6	(19)	
13	-	Snoopy Vs. The Red Baron	Royal Guardsmen	Laurie	9	(8)	F G
14	-	Whispers (Gettin' Louder)	Jackie Wilson	Brunswick	4		
15	-	I'm Ready For Love	Martha & The Vandellas	Gordy	4	(29)	
16	-	Stop Stop Stop	Hollies	Imperial	5	(2)	
17	7	I'm Your Puppet	James & Bobby Purify	Bell	7	(12)	F L
18	-	Tell It Like It Is	Aaron Neville	Par-Lo	9		F G
19	-	A Hazy Shade Of Winter	Simon & Garfunkel	Columbia	4		
20	2	Poor Side Of Town	Johnny Rivers	Imperial	10		G

◆ In 1966 a third of the records sold were LPs. Labels, were therefore actively seeking artists with album, as well as single sales potential.

◆ The year's last Top 20 included 10 American groups and only one British – The New Vaudeville Band, whose novelty, 'Winchester Cathedral', won the Grammy for Best Rock'n'Roll Record!

◆ Hottest new act was The Monkees, a quartet of actors/singers assembled for a Beatles-esque TV series. Their first two singles and debut album topped the chart. Incidentally, fellow chart newcomer, Neil Diamond, penned their hit 'I'm A Believer'.

◆ Over 10,000 records were released in 1966, and the value of record and tape sales in the USA rose to $650 million. Ten years earlier, when rock was starting to roll, 6,000 records were issued with sales totalling $250 million.

UK 1967 JAN-MAR

▲ Tom Jones had his biggest UK hit with 'Green Green Grass Of Home'. Engelbert Humperdinck (above) – who shared Jones' manager – also struck UK gold (and made the US Top 20) with a revival of another US country hit, 'Release Me'.

◆ Pink Floyd, The Jimi Hendrix Experience, Cream and The Monkees debuted on the UK chart. The latters' TV show was successful in Britain, catapulting them to the top of the charts.

◆ Joe Meek, one of Britain's best-known producers, committed suicide. He had written and produced the first British hit to top the US charts in the 1960s, 'Telstar' by The Tornados.

January 1967

This Mnth	Prev Mnth	Title	Artist	Label	Wks 20	(US Pos)	
1	1	Green Green Grass Of Home	Tom Jones	Decca	15	(11)	G
2	4	Morningtown Ride	Seekers	Columbia	10	(44)	
3	-	Happy Jack	Who	Reaction	7	(24)	
4	11	Sunshine Superman	Donovan	Pye	7	(1)	
5	-	I'm A Believer	Monkees	RCA	10	(1)	F
6	-	In The Country	Cliff Richard	Columbia	6		
7	15	Save Me	Dave Dee, Dozy, Beaky, Mick & Tich	Fontana	7		
8	-	Matthew And Son	Cat Stevens	Deram	7		F
9	-	Any Way That You Want Me	Troggs	Page One	5		
10	-	Night Of Fear	Move	Deram	7		F
11	7	Dead End Street	Kinks	Pye	9	(73)	
12	2	What Would I Be	Val Doonican	Decca	11		
13	-	Sittin' In The Park	Georgie Fame	Columbia	7		
14	14	You Keep Me Hangin' On	Supremes	Tamla Motown	7	(1)	
15	-	Pamela Pamela	Wayne Fontana	Fontana	6		L
16	-	Standing In The Shadows Of Love	Four Tops	Tamla Motown	4	(6)	
17	-	I Feel Free	Cream	Reaction	4		F
18	-	Hey Joe	Jimi Hendrix Experience	Polydor	5		F
19	3	Good Vibrations	Beach Boys	Capitol	11	(1)	
20	5	Friday On My Mind	Easybeats	UA	9	(16)	F

February 1967

This Mnth	Prev Mnth	Title	Artist	Label	Wks 20	(US Pos)	
1	5	I'm A Believer	Monkees	RCA	10	(1)	F
2	-	Let's Spend The Night Together/ Ruby Tuesday	Rolling Stones	Decca	7	(1)	
3	-	I've Been A Bad Bad Boy	Paul Jones	HMV	6		L
4	-	This Is My Song	Petula Clark	Pye	10	(3)	
5	8	Matthew And Son	Cat Stevens	Deram	7		F
6	10	Night Of Fear	Move	Deram	7		F
7	-	Release Me	Engelbert Humperdinck	Decca	15	(4)	F G
8	1	Green Green Grass Of Home	Tom Jones	Decca	15	(11)	G
9	-	Sugar Town	Nancy Sinatra	Reprise	5	(5)	
10	18	Hey Joe	Jimi Hendrix Experience	Polydor	5		F
11	-	Snoopy Vs The Red Baron	Royal Guardsmen	Stateside	8	(2)	F L
12	-	Peek-A-Boo	New Vaudeville Band	Fontana	7	(72)	
13	-	I Won't Come In While He's There	Jim Reeves	RCA	5		
14	-	Here Comes My Baby	Tremeloes	CBS	7	(13)	F
15	16	Standing In The Shadows Of Love	Four Tops	Tamla Motown	4	(6)	
16	-	I'm A Man	Spencer Davis Group	Fontana	3	(10)	L
17	-	Let Me Cry On Your Shoulder	Ken Dodd	Columbia	3		
18	-	Penny Lane/Strawberry Fields Forever	Beatles	Parlophone	8	(1)	
19	-	Mellow Yellow	Donovan	Pye	5	(2)	
20	17	I Feel Free	Cream	Reaction	4		F

March 1967

This Mnth	Prev Mnth	Title	Artist	Label	Wks 20	(US Pos)	
1	7	Release Me	Engelbert Humperdinck	Decca	15	(4)	F G
2	18	Penny Lane/Strawberry Fields...	Beatles	Parlophone	8	(1)	
3	4	This Is My Song	Petula Clark	Pye	10	(3)	
4	-	Edelweiss	Vince Hill	Columbia	11		
5	14	Here Comes My Baby	Tremeloes	CBS	7	(13)	F
6	-	On A Carousel	Hollies	Parlophone	7	(11)	
7	-	There's A Kind Of Hush	Herman's Hermits	Columbia	7	(4)	
8	-	Georgy Girl	Seekers	Columbia	7	(2)	
9	-	Detroit City	Tom Jones	Decca	6	(27)	
10	11	Snoopy Vs The Red Baron	Royal Guardsmen	Stateside	8	(2)	F L
11	19	Mellow Yellow	Donovan	Pye	5	(2)	
12	12	Peek-A-Boo	New Vaudeville Band	Fontana	7	(72)	
13	-	This Is My Song	Harry Secombe	Philips	9		L
14	1	I'm A Believer	Monkees	RCA	10	(1)	F
15	-	Give It To Me	Troggs	Page One	4		
16	-	Simon Smith & His Amazing Dancing Bear	Alan Price Set	Decca	7		
17	-	I Was Kaiser Bill's Batman	Whistling Jack Smith	Deram	7	(20)	F L
18	-	Memories Are Made Of This	Val Doonican	Decca	5		
19	13	I Won't Come In While He's There	Jim Reeves	RCA	5		
20	2	Let's Spend The Night.../Ruby...	Rolling Stones	Decca	7	(1)	

January 1967

This Mnth	Prev Mnth	Title	Artist	Label	Wks 20	(UK Pos)	
1	7	I'm A Believer	Monkees	Colgems	12	(1)	G
2	13	Snoopy Vs. The Red Baron	Royal Guardsmen	Laurie	9	(8)	F G
3	18	Tell It Like It Is	Aaron Neville	Par-Lo	9		F G
4	-	Good Thing	Paul Revere & The Raiders	Columbia	7		
5	-	Words Of Love	Mamas & The Papas	Dunhill	7	(47)	
6	-	Standing In The Shadows Of Love	Four Tops	Motown	7	(6)	G
7	9	Sugar Town	Nancy Sinatra	Reprise	8	(8)	G
8	-	Georgy Girl	Seekers	Capitol	10	(3)	G L
9	1	Winchester Cathedral	New Vaudeville Band	Fontana	11	(4)	F G L
10	-	Tell It To The Rain	Four Seasons	Philips	4	(37)	
11	-	Coming Home Soldier	Bobby Vinton	Epic	6		
12	-	Nashville Cats	Lovin' Spoonful	Kama Sutra	4	(46)	
13	6	That's Life	Frank Sinatra	Reprise	8	(46)	
14	2	Mellow Yellow	Donovan	Epic	8	(8)	G
15	-	(We Ain't Got) Nothin' Yet	Blues Magoos	Mercury	7		F L
16	-	Kind Of A Drag	Buckinghams	USA	9		F G
17	-	98.6	Keith	Mercury	6	(24)	F L
18	-	Single Girl	Sandy Posey	MGM	4	(15)	
19	-	Talk Talk	Music Machine	Original Sound	4		F L
20	4	Devil With A Blue Dress On & Good Golly Miss Molly	Mitch Ryder & The Detroit Wheels	New Voice	11		

February 1967

This Mnth	Prev Mnth	Title	Artist	Label	Wks 20	(UK Pos)	
1	1	I'm A Believer	Monkees	Colgems	12	(1)	G
2	16	Kind Of A Drag	Buckinghams	USA	9		F G
3	8	Georgy Girl	Seekers	Capitol	10	(3)	G L
4	-	Ruby Tuesday	Rolling Stones	London	9	(3)	G
5	15	(We Ain't Got) Nothin' Yet	Blues Magoos	Mercury	7		F L
6	17	98.6	Keith	Mercury	6	(24)	F L
7	-	Love Is Here And Now You're Gone	Supremes	Motown	8	(17)	G
8	3	Tell It Like It Is	Aaron Neville	Par-Lo	9		F G
9	-	The Beat Goes On	Sonny & Cher	Atco	6	(29)	
10	2	Snoopy Vs. The Red Baron	Royal Guardsmen	Laurie	9	(8)	F G
11	-	Green Green Grass Of Home	Tom Jones	Parrot	5	(1)	
12	-	Gimme Some Lovin'	Spencer Davis Group	UA	6	(2)	F
13	-	Then You Can Tell Me Goodbye	Casinos	Fraternity	7	(28)	F L
14	-	Stand By Me	Spyder Turner	MGM	5		F L
15	-	I Had Too Much To Dream (Last Night)	Electric Prunes	Reprise	6		F L
16	5	Words Of Love	Mamas & The Papas	Dunhill	7	(47)	
17	-	Mercy, Mercy, Mercy	Cannonball Adderley	Capitol	4		F L
18	4	Good Thing	Paul Revere & The Raiders	Columbia	7		
19	6	Standing In The Shadows Of Love	Four Tops	Motown	7	(6)	G
20	-	Baby I Need Your Lovin'	Johnny Rivers	Imperial	8		

March 1967

This Mnth	Prev Mnth	Title	Artist	Label	Wks 20	(UK Pos)	
1	20	Baby I Need Your Lovin'	Johnny Rivers	Imperial	8		
2	7	Love Is Here And Now You're Gone	Supremes	Motown	8	(17)	G
3	4	Ruby Tuesday	Rolling Stones	London	9	(3)	G
4	-	Sock It To Me-Baby!	Mitch Ryder & Detroit Wheels	New Voice	7		L
5	-	Penny Lane	Beatles	Capitol	6	(2)	G
6	-	Happy Together	Turtles	White Whale	10	(12)	G
7	13	Then You Can Tell Me Goodbye	Casinos	Fraternity	7	(28)	F L
8	-	Dedicated To The One I Love	Mamas & The Papas	Dunhill	8	(2)	
9	-	My Cup Runneth Over	Ed Ames	RCA	6		F
10	2	Kind Of A Drag	Buckinghams	USA	9		F G
11	-	There's A Kind Of Hush	Herman's Hermits	MGM	6	(7)	G
12	-	For What It's Worth (Stop, Hey What's That Sound)	Buffalo Springfield	Atco	8		F L
13	12	Gimme Some Lovin'	Spencer Davis Group	UA	6	(2)	F
14	-	Strawberry Fields Forever	Beatles	Capitol	5	(2)	G
15	9	The Beat Goes On	Sonny & Cher	Atco	6	(29)	
16	17	Mercy, Mercy, Mercy	Cannonball Adderley	Capitol	4		F L
17	3	Georgy Girl	Seekers	Capitol	10	(3)	G L
18	-	The Hunter Gets Captured By The Game	Marvelettes	Tamla	3		
19	1	I'm A Believer	Monkees	Colgems	12	(1)	G
20	-	I Think We're Alone Now	Tommy James & The Shondells	Roulette	10		

US 1967
JAN-MAR

◆ Reprise Records paid $50,000 for the American rights to the Jimi Hendrix Experience, whom they called "The greatest talent since The Rolling Stones".

◆ The first Human Be-In took place in San Francisco. This free festival, whose headliners included Grateful Dead and Jefferson Airplane, attracted 20,000 people.

◆ As The Spencer Davis Group debuted in the Top 20 with 'Gimme Some Loving', their 18-year-old vocalist Stevie Winwood announced he was leaving to form Traffic.

◆ Amazingly, Paul Revere & The Raiders and Johnny Rivers, who continued to add to their impressive US hit tallies, never charted across the Atlantic.

UK 1967 APR-JUNE

◆ The Beatles' album **Sergeant Pepper's Lonely Hearts Club Band**, which had been five months in the making, was released to much critical acclaim – it helped shape the future of pop and rock music. The group also broke new ground when they sang 'All You Need is Love' on the internationally linked-up TV show, *Our World*.

◆ In 1966 both Nancy and Frank Sinatra had scored transatlantic No. 1 hits, a feat they repeated as a duet with 'Somethin' Stupid'.

▲ The Monkees, who continued adding to their transatlantic toppers, had a very successful British live debut at Wembley.

April 1967

This Mnth	Prev Mnth	Title	Artist	Label	Wks 20	(US Pos)	
1	-	Somethin' Stupid	Nancy & Frank Sinatra	Reprise	11	(1)	
2	-	Puppet On A String	Sandie Shaw	Pye	13		
3	1	Release Me	Engelbert Humperdinck	Decca	15	(4)	F G
4	13	This Is My Song	Harry Secombe	Philips	9		L
5	-	A Little Bit Me, A Little Bit You	Monkees	RCA	8	(2)	
6	16	Simon Smith & His Amazing Dancing Bear	Alan Price Set	Decca	7		
7	17	I Was Kaiser Bill's Batman	Whistling Jack Smith	Deram	7	(20)	F L
8	-	Ha Ha Said The Clown	Manfred Mann	Fontana	7		
9	4	Edelweiss	Vince Hill	Columbia	11		
10	-	It's All Over	Cliff Richard	Columbia	6		
11	-	Purple Haze	Jimi Hendrix Experience	Track	8	(65)	
12	2	Penny Lane/Strawberry Fields Forever	Beatles	Parlophone	8	(1)	
13	8	Georgy Girl	Seekers	Columbia	7	(2)	
14	-	Bernadette	Four Tops	Tamla Motown	5	(4)	
15	3	This Is My Song	Petula Clark	Pye	10	(3)	
16	-	I'm Gonna Get Me A Gun	Cat Stevens	Deram	5		
17	18	Memories Are Made Of This	Val Doonican	Decca	5		
18	-	Happy Together	Turtles	London American	6	(1)	F
19	-	I Can Hear The Grass Grow	Move	Deram	6		
20	-	Touch Me Touch Me	Dave Dee, Dozy, Beaky, Mick & Tich	Fontana	3		

May 1967

This Mnth	Prev Mnth	Title	Artist	Label	Wks 20	(US Pos)	
1	2	Puppet On A String	Sandie Shaw	Pye	13		
2	-	Dedicated To The One I Love	Mamas & The Papas	RCA	10	(2)	
3	1	Somethin' Stupid	Nancy & Frank Sinatra	Reprise	11	(1)	
4	-	Silence Is Golden	Tremeloes	CBS	10	(11)	
5	-	The Boat That I Row	Lulu	Columbia	6		
6	-	Pictures Of Lily	Who	Track	6	(51)	
7	-	Funny Familiar Forgotten Feeling	Tom Jones	Decca	7	(49)	
8	11	Purple Haze	Jimi Hendrix Experience	Track	8	(65)	
9	-	Seven Drunken Nights	Dubliners	Major Minor	9		F
10	5	A Little Bit Me, A Little Bit You	Monkees	RCA	8	(2)	
11	19	I Can Hear The Grass Grow	Move	Deram	6		
12	-	Waterloo Sunset	Kinks	Pye	7		
13	-	Then I Kissed Her	Beach Boys	Capitol	8		
14	8	Ha Ha Said The Clown	Manfred Mann	Fontana	7		
15	-	Hi-Ho Silver Lining	Jeff Beck	Columbia	5		F
16	16	I'm Gonna Get Me A Gun	Cat Stevens	Deram	5		
17	-	The Wind Cries Mary	Jimi Hendrix Experience	Track	5		
18	3	Release Me	Engelbert Humperdinck	Decca	15	(4)	F G
19	-	New York Mining Disaster 1941	Bee Gees	Polydor	5	(14)	F
20	18	Happy Together	Turtles	London American	6	(1)	F

June 1967

This Mnth	Prev Mnth	Title	Artist	Label	Wks 20	(US Pos)	
1	-	A Whiter Shade Of Pale	Procol Harum	Deram	11	(5)	F
2	4	Silence Is Golden	Tremeloes	CBS	10	(11)	
3	12	Waterloo Sunset	Kinks	Pye	7		
4	-	There Goes My Everything	Engelbert Humperdinck	Decca	13	(20)	
5	-	The Happening	Supremes	Tamla Motown	8	(1)	
6	13	Then I Kissed Her	Beach Boys	Capitol	8		
7	2	Dedicated To The One I Love	Mamas & The Papas	RCA	10	(2)	
8	-	Sweet Soul Music	Arthur Conley	Atlantic	9	(2)	F L
9	-	Carrie-Anne	Hollies	Parlophone	8	(9)	
10	17	The Wind Cries Mary	Jimi Hendrix Experience	Track	5		
11	-	Okay!	Dave Dee, Dozy, Beaky, Mick & Tich	Fontana	6		
12	-	Finchley Central	New Vaudeville Band	Fontana	6		L
13	9	Seven Drunken Nights	Dubliners	Major Minor	9		F
14	6	Pictures Of Lily	Who	Track	6	(51)	
15	-	Paper Sun	Traffic	Island	5	(94)	F
16	1	Puppet On A String	Sandie Shaw	Pye	13		
17	-	Roses Of Picardy	Vince Hill	Columbia	4		
18	-	Groovin'	Young Rascals	Atlantic	7	(1)	F L
19	3	Somethin' Stupid	Nancy & Frank Sinatra	Reprise	11	(1)	
20	19	New York Mining Disaster 1941	Bee Gees	Polydor	5	(14)	F

April 1967

This Mnth	Prev Mnth	Title	Artist	Label	Wks 20	(UK Pos)	
1	6	Happy Together	Turtles	White Whale	10	(12)	G
2	-	Somethin' Stupid	Nancy & Frank Sinatra	Reprise	10	(1)	G
3	-	This Is My Song	Petula Clark	Warner	7	(1)	
4	-	Bernadette	Four Tops	Motown	6	(8)	
5	-	Western Union	Five Americans	Abnak	6		F L
6	20	I Think We're Alone Now	Tommy James & The Shondells	Roulette	10		
7	-	A Little Bit Me, A Little Bit You	Monkees	Colgems	8	(3)	G
8	8	Dedicated To The One I Love	Mamas & The Papas	Dunhill	8	(2)	
9	-	I Never Loved A Man (The Way I Love You)	Aretha Franklin	Atlantic	7		F G
10	-	Jimmy Mack	Martha & The Vandellas	Gordy	7	(21)	
11	-	Sweet Soul Music	Arthur Conley	Atco	9 ·	(7)	F G
12	5	Penny Lane	Beatles	Capitol	6	(2)	G
13	11	There's A Kind Of Hush	Herman's Hermits	MGM	6	(7)	G
14	12	For What It's Worth (Stop, Hey What's That Sound)	Buffalo Springfield	Atco	8		F L
15	-	The Happening	Supremes	Motown	8	(6)	G
16	-	The 59th Street Bridge Song (Feelin' Groovy)	Harpers Bizarre	Warner	4	(34)	F L
17	14	Strawberry Fields Forever	Beatles	Capitol	5	(2)	G
18	-	I'm A Man	Spencer Davis Group	UA	4	(9)	L
19	-	Don't You Care	Buckinghams	Columbia	6		
20	-	At The Zoo	Simon & Garfunkel	Columbia	3		

May 1967

This Mnth	Prev Mnth	Title	Artist	Label	Wks 20	(UK Pos)	
1	15	The Happening	Supremes	Motown	8	(6)	G
2	11	Sweet Soul Music	Arthur Conley	Atco	9	(7)	F G
3	2	Somethin' Stupid	Nancy & Frank Sinatra	Reprise	10	(1)	G
4	-	Groovin'	Young Rascals	Atlantic	10	(8)	G
5	19	Don't You Care	Buckinghams	Columbia	6		
6	-	I Got Rhythm	Happenings	B.T.Puppy	7	(28)	
7	-	Respect	Aretha Franklin	Atlantic	9	(10)	G
8	-	Close Your Eyes	Peaches & Herb	Date	5		F
9	-	Release Me (And Let Me Love Again)	Engelbert Humperdinck	Parrot	8	(1)	F
10	-	You Got What It Takes	Dave Clark Five	Epic	6	(28)	L
11	-	On A Carousel	Hollies	Imperial	7	(4)	
12	7	A Little Bit Me, A Little Bit You	Monkees	Colgems	8	(3)	G
13	-	Girl, You'll Be A Woman Soon	Neil Diamond	Bang	4		
14	6	I Think We're Alone Now	Tommy James & The Shondells	Roulette	10		
15	1	Happy Together	Turtles	White Whale	10	(12)	G
16	-	Him Or Me - What's It Gonna Be	Paul Revere & The Raiders	Columbia	5		
17	-	Creeque Alley	Mamas & The Papas	Dunhill	4	(9)	
18	-	When I Was Young	Eric Burdon & The Animals	MGM	3	(45)	
19	-	Friday On My Mind	Easybeats	UA	5	(6)	F L
20	18	I'm A Man	Spencer Davis Group	UA	4	(9)	L

June 1967

This Mnth	Prev Mnth	Title	Artist	Label	Wks 20	(UK Pos)	
1	4	Groovin'	Young Rascals	Atlantic	10	(8)	G
2	7	Respect	Aretha Franklin	Atlantic	9	(10)	G
3	9	Release Me (And Let Me Love Again)	Engelbert Humperdinck	Parrot	8	(1)	F
4	-	She'd Rather Be With Me	Turtles	White Whale	6	(4)	
5	-	Somebody To Love	Jefferson Airplane	RCA	6		F
6	6	I Got Rhythm	Happenings	B.T.Puppy	7	(28)	
7	-	Little Bit O' Soul	Music Explosion	Laurie	11		F G L
8	-	Windy	Association	Warner	11		G
9	-	All I Need	Temptations	Gordy	5		
10	16	Him Or Me - What's It Gonna Be	Paul Revere & The Raiders	Columbia	5		
11	-	Mirage	Tommy James & The Shondells	Roulette	5		
12	-	Sunday Will Never Be The Same	Spanky & Our Gang	Mercury	4		F
13	17	Creeque Alley	Mamas & The Papas	Dunhill	4	(9)	
14	-	Can't Take My Eyes Off You	Frankie Valli	Philips	11		F G
15	-	Let's Live For Today	Grass Roots	Dunhill	6		F
16	-	Come On Down To My Boat	Every Mothers' Son	MGM	8		F L
17	-	San Francisco (Be Sure To Wear Flowers In Your Hair)	Scott McKenzie	Ode	8	(1)	F L
18	-	Here Comes My Baby	Tremeloes	Epic	5	(4)	F
19	-	Seven Rooms Of Gloom	Four Tops	Motown	4	(12)	
20	1	The Happening	Supremes	Motown	8	(6)	G

US
1967
APR-JUNE

◆ The price of mono albums was upped $1 to $4.98 – their first price rise since 1953, and the album chart was increased to a Top 200.

◆ Atlantic Records paid a reported $250,000 for The Bee Gees' American contract. Their UK label, Polydor, called them "The most significant talent since The Beatles".

▲ The line up at the Monterey Pop Festival included The Byrds, The Association, The Mamas & The Papas, The Who (above), Jimi Hendrix, Janis Joplin, Otis Redding, Grateful Dead, Jefferson Airplane and Buffalo Springfield.

UK 1967
JULY-SEPT

◆ The UK government banned pirate radio stations and then launched Radio 1 –their own Top 40 station.

◆ Acts at the national Jazz & Blues Festival included The Jeff Beck Group (with vocalist Rod Stewart), Donovan and newcomers Fleetwood Mac.

◆ The deaths were reported of Beatles manager Brian Epstein and Bob Dylan's inspiration folk singer/songwriter Woody Guthrie.

▲ Innovative US act The Mothers Of Invention, whose **Freak Out** album was a milestone in rock, made a successful UK debut.

July 1967

This Mnth	Prev Mnth	Title	Artist	Label	Wks 20	(US Pos)	
1	1	A Whiter Shade Of Pale	Procol Harum	Deram	11	(5)	F
2	-	Alternate Title	Monkees	RCA	8		
3	4	There Goes My Everything	Engelbert Humperdinck	Decca	13	(20)	
4	-	She'd Rather Be With Me	Turtles	London American	10	(3)	
5	-	It Must Be Him (Seul Sur Son Etoile)	Vikki Carr	Liberty	10	(3)	F L
6	-	All You Need Is Love	Beatles	Parlophone	10	(1)	
7	9	Carrie-Anne	Hollies	Parlophone	8	(9)	
8	-	See Emily Play	Pink Floyd	Columbia	7		
9	-	If I Were A Rich Man	Topol	CBS	6		F L
10	-	San Francisco (Be Sure To Wear Some Flowers In Your Hair)	Scott McKenzie	CBS	14	(4)	F L
11	18	Groovin'	Young Rascals	Atlantic	7	(1)	F L
12	15	Paper Sun	Traffic	Island	5	(94)	F
13	-	Respect	Aretha Franklin	Atlantic	5	(1)	F
14	11	Okay!	Dave Dee, Dozy, Beaky, Mick & Tich	Fontana	6		
15	-	Here Come The Nice	Small Faces	Immediate	6		
16	8	Sweet Soul Music	Arthur Conley	Atlantic	9	(2)	F L
17	-	Seven Rooms Of Gloom	Four Tops	Tamla Motown	5	(14)	
18	5	The Happening	Supremes	Tamla Motown	8	(1)	
19	-	Don't Sleep In The Subway	Petula Clark	Pye	4	(5)	
20	-	You Only Live Twice/Jackson	Nancy Sinatra	Reprise	5	(44)	

August 1967

This Mnth	Prev Mnth	Title	Artist	Label	Wks 20	(US Pos)	
1	10	San Francisco (Be Sure To Wear Some Flowers In Your Hair)	Scott McKenzie	CBS	14	(4)	F L
2	6	All You Need Is Love	Beatles	Parlophone	10	(1)	
3	-	I'll Never Fall In Love Again	Tom Jones	Decca	10	(6)	
4	-	Death Of A Clown	Dave Davies	Pye	7		F
5	-	I Was Made To Love Her	Stevie Wonder	Tamla Motown	9	(2)	
6	5	It Must Be Him (Seul Sur Son Etoile)	Vikki Carr	Liberty	10	(3)	F L
7	-	Up Up And Away	Johnny Mann Singers	Liberty	7		F L
8	-	Just Loving You	Anita Harris	CBS	15		F L
9	4	She'd Rather Be With Me	Turtles	London American	10	(3)	
10	-	Even The Bad Times Are Good	Tremeloes	CBS	9	(36)	
11	2	Alternate Title	Monkees	RCA	8		
12	-	Creeque Alley	Mamas & The Papas	RCA	6	(5)	L
13	8	See Emily Play	Pink Floyd	Columbia	7		
14	-	The House That Jack Built	Alan Price Set	Decca	7		
15	3	There Goes My Everything	Engelbert Humperdinck	Decca	13	(20)	
16	-	Let's Pretend	Lulu	Columbia	4		
17	-	Gin House Blues	Amen Corner	Deram	5		F
18	1	A Whiter Shade Of Pale	Procol Harum	Deram	11	(5)	F
19	20	You Only Live Twice/Jackson	Nancy Sinatra	Reprise	5	(44)	
20	-	Pleasant Valley Sunday	Monkees	RCA	4	(3)	

September 1967

This Mnth	Prev Mnth	Title	Artist	Label	Wks 20	(US Pos)	
1	-	The Last Waltz	Engelbert Humperdinck	Decca	20	(25)	G
2	3	I'll Never Fall In Love Again	Tom Jones	Decca	10	(6)	
3	1	San Francisco (Be Sure To Wear Some Flowers In Your Hair)	Scott McKenzie	CBS	14	(4)	
4	-	Excerpt From A Teenage Opera	Keith West	Parlophone	11		F L
5	-	Itchycoo Park	Small Faces	Immediate	11	(16)	
6	10	Even The Bad Times Are Good	Tremeloes	CBS	9	(36)	
7	-	Let's Go To San Francisco	Flowerpot Men	Deram	7		F L
8	-	We Love You/Dandelion	Rolling Stones	Decca	6	(14)	
9	8	Just Loving You	Anita Harris	CBS	15		F L
10	-	Heroes And Villains	Beach Boys	Capitol	5	(12)	
11	14	The House That Jack Built	Alan Price Set	Decca	7		
12	5	I Was Made To Love Her	Stevie Wonder	Tamla Motown	9	(2)	
13	-	Reflections	Diana Ross & The Supremes	Tamla Motown	8	(2)	
14	-	Flowers In The Rain	Move	Regal Zonophone	10		
15	-	The Day I Met Marie	Cliff Richard	Columbia	8		
16	2	All You Need Is Love	Beatles	Parlophone	10	(1)	
17	-	Hole In My Shoe	Traffic	Island	10		
18	20	Pleasant Valley Sunday	Monkees	RCA	4	(3)	
19	-	There Must Be A Way	Frankie Vaughan	Columbia	14		L
20	4	Death Of A Clown	Dave Davies	Pye	7		F

July 1967

This Mnth	Prev Mnth	Title	Artist	Label	Wks 20	(UK Pos)	
1	8	Windy	Association	Warner	11		G
2	7	Little Bit O' Soul	Music Explosion	Laurie	11		F G L
3	14	Can't Take My Eyes Off You	Frankie Valli	Philips	11		F G
4	17	San Francisco (Be Sure To Wear Flowers In Your Hair)	Scott McKenzie	Ode	8	(1)	F L
5	-	Up Up & Away	Fifth Dimension	Soul City	6		
6	-	Light My Fire	Doors	Elektra	12	(49)	F G
7	16	Come On Down To My Boat	Every Mothers' Son	MGM	8		F L
8	-	Don't Sleep In The Subway	Petula Clark	Warner	5	(12)	
9	-	A Whiter Shade Of Pale	Procol Harum	Deram	9	(1)	F
10	-	I Was Made To Love Her	Stevie Wonder	Tamla	9	(5)	G
11	-	C'mon Marianne	Four Seasons	Philips	5		
12	1	Groovin'	Young Rascals	Atlantic	10	(8)	G
13	15	Let's Live For Today	Grass Roots	Dunhill	6		F
14	-	White Rabbit	Jefferson Airplane	RCA	5		
15	-	Mercy, Mercy, Mercy	Buckinghams	Columbia	6		
16	-	The Tracks Of My Tears	Johnny Rivers	Imperial	4		
17	4	She'd Rather Be With Me	Turtles	White Whale	6	(4)	
18	2	Respect	Aretha Franklin	Atlantic	9	(10)	G
19	-	Here We Go Again	Ray Charles	ABC/TRC	4	(38)	L
20	-	Society's Child (Baby I've Been Thinking)	Janis Ian	Verve	3		F

August 1967

This Mnth	Prev Mnth	Title	Artist	Label	Wks 20	(UK Pos)	
1	6	Light My Fire	Doors	Elektra	12	(49)	F G
2	-	All You Need Is Love	Beatles	Capitol	7	(1)	G
3	10	I Was Made To Love Her	Stevie Wonder	Tamla	9	(5)	G
4	-	Pleasant Valley Sunday	Monkees	Colgems	6	(11)	G
5	9	A Whiter Shade Of Pale	Procol Harum	Deram	9	(1)	F
6	15	Mercy, Mercy, Mercy	Buckinghams	Columbia	6		
7	-	Baby I Love You	Aretha Franklin	Atlantic	7	(39)	G
8	-	A Girl Like You	Young Rascals	Atlantic	6	(37)	
9	3	Can't Take My Eyes Off You	Frankie Valli	Philips	11		F G
10	1	Windy	Association	Warner	11		G
11	-	Ode To Billie Joe	Bobbie Gentry	Capitol	10	(13)	F G L
12	-	Silence Is Golden	Tremeloes	Epic	5	(1)	L
13	-	Carrie-Ann	Hollies	Epic	6	(3)	
14	-	Cold Sweat (Part 1)	James Brown	King	6		
15	-	My Mammy	Happenings	B.T.Puppy	4	(34)	L
16	14	White Rabbit	Jefferson Airplane	RCA	5		
17	2	Little Bit O' Soul	Music Explosion	Laurie	11		F G L
18	-	Reflections	Diana Ross & The Supremes	Motown	8	(5)	G
19	-	Jackson	Nancy Sinatra & Lee Hazlewood	Reprise	4	(11)	
20	-	Heroes And Villians	Beach Boys	Brother	3	(8)	

September 1967

This Mnth	Prev Mnth	Title	Artist	Label	Wks 20	(UK Pos)	
1	11	Ode To Billie Joe	Bobbie Gentry	Capitol	10	(13)	F G L
2	18	Reflections	Diana Ross & The Supremes	Motown	8	(5)	G
3	-	Come Back When You Grow Up	Bobby Vee & The Strangers	Liberty	9		G L
4	-	The Letter	Box Tops	Mala	10	(5)	F G
5	-	Apples Peaches Pumpkin Pie	Jay & The Techniques	Smash	9		F
6	-	You're My Everything	Temptations	Gordy	6	(26)	
7	7	Baby I Love You	Aretha Franklin	Atlantic	7	(39)	G
8	2	All You Need Is Love	Beatles	Capitol	7	(1)	G
9	-	Never My Love	Association	Warner	10		G
10	-	Funky Broadway	Wilson Pickett	Atlantic	6	(43)	
11	-	(Your Love Keeps Lifting Me) Higher And Higher	Jackie Wilson	Brunswick	7	(9)	L
12	1	Light My Fire	Doors	Elektra	12	(49)	F G
13	-	Brown Eyed Girl	Van Morrison	Bang	6		F
14	-	You Know What I Mean	Turtles	White Whale	4		
15	-	I Dig Rock And Roll Music	Peter, Paul & Mary	Warner	5		
16	-	San Franciscan Nights	Eric Burdon & The Animals	MGM	3	(7)	
17	-	There Is A Mountain	Donovan	Epic	4	(8)	
18	14	Cold Sweat (Part 1)	James Brown	King	6		
19	4	Pleasant Valley Sunday	Monkees	Colgems	6	(11)	G
20	-	Words	Monkees	Colgems	4		

US 1967
JULY–SEPT

◆ Among the records forever associated with the "Summer Of Love" are: 'San Francisco (Be Sure To Wear Some Flowers In Your Hair)' by Scott McKenzie, 'Light My Fire' by The Doors and 'Whiter Shade Of Pale' by Procol Harum.

◆ Jimi Hendrix opened the show for The Monkees. Not unexpectedly, Hendrix was soon given his marching orders as his act was considered "too erotic" for young Monkee fans.

◆ James Brown hit with 'Cold Sweat', thought by many to be the first real 'funk' record. Also riding high were George Clinton's group The Parliaments, who evolved into funk supergroups Parliament and Funkadelic.

◆ A new noise reduction system for album and tape recording, developed by American technicians Ray and D.W. Dolby, was first used by Elektra Records subsidiary, Checkmate Records.

◆ The Beatles closed the year with 'Hello Goodbye' topping the transatlantic charts. However, in 1967, they were replaced as the world's most successful act by The Monkees, who, among other achievements, chalked up a (still unbeaten) record of four American chart topping albums in one calendar year.

◆ In the year that US record sales first topped the $1 billion mark and, for the first time, albums outsold singles, the gap between the American and British markets widened, with only 25% of Top 20 hits scoring in both countries. An interesting case was 'To Sir With Love' by Lulu, which topped the US chart but was treated as a B-side in Britain.

◆ Nine years after his death, Buddy Holly was still voted one of the World's Top 20 Male Singers in the important *Record Mirror* Poll.

October 1967

This Mnth	Prev Mnth	Title	Artist	Label	Wks 20	(US Pos)	
1	-	Massachusetts	Bee Gees	Polydor	10	(11)	
2	1	The Last Waltz	Engelbert Humperdinck	Decca	20	(25)	G
3	17	Hole In My Shoe	Traffic	Island	10		
4	14	Flowers In The Rain	Move	Regal Zonophone	10		
5	-	The Letter	Box Tops	Stateside	8	(1)	F
6	4	Excerpt From A Teenage Opera	Keith West	Parlophone	11		F L
7	13	Reflections	Diana Ross & The Supremes	Tamla Motown	8	(2)	
8	19	There Must Be A Way	Frankie Vaughan	Columbia	14		L
9	-	Homburg	Procol Harum	Regal Zonophone	7	(34)	
10	5	Itchycoo Park	Small Faces	Immediate	11	(16)	
11	-	From The Underworld	Herd	Fontana	8		F
12	-	When Will The Good Apples Fall	Seekers	Columbia	6		L
13	15	The Day I Met Marie	Cliff Richard	Columbia	8		
14	7	Let's Go To San Francisco	Flowerpot Men	Deram	7		F L
15	-	Baby, Now That I Found You	Foundations	Pye	9	(11)	F
16	-	Zabadak	Dave Dee, Dozy, Beaky, Mick & Tich	Fontana	8	(52)	
17	-	Ode To Billie Joe	Bobbie Gentry	Capitol	6	(1)	F
18	9	Just Loving You	Anita Harris	CBS	15		F L
19	-	Black Velvet Band	Dubliners	Major Minor	5		
20	2	I'll Never Fall In Love Again	Tom Jones	Decca	10	(6)	

November 1967

This Mnth	Prev Mnth	Title	Artist	Label	Wks 20	(US Pos)	
1	15	Baby, Now That I Found You	Foundations	Pye	9	(11)	F
2	1	Massachusetts	Bee Gees	Polydor	10	(11)	
3	16	Zabadak	Dave Dee, Dozy, Beaky, Mick & Tich	Fontana	8	(52)	
4	-	Autumn Almanac	Kinks	Pye	7		
5	2	The Last Waltz	Engelbert Humperdinck	Decca	20	(25)	G
6	-	Love Is All Around	Troggs	Page One	7	(7)	L
7	11	From The Underworld	Herd	Fontana	8		F
8	-	San Franciscan Nights	Eric Burdon & The Animals	MGM	5	(9)	
9	9	Homburg	Procol Harum	Regal Zonophone	7	(34)	
10	-	There Is A Mountain	Donovan	Pye	5	(11)	
11	8	There Must Be A Way	Frankie Vaughan	Columbia	14		L
12	-	Let The Heartaches Begin	Long John Baldry	Pye	9	(88)	F
13	3	Hole In My Shoe	Traffic	Island	10		
14	-	If The Whole World Stopped Loving	Val Doonican	Pye	13		
15	-	I Can See For Miles	Who	Track	4	(9)	
16	-	Everybody Knows	Dave Clark Five	Columbia	8	(43)	
17	4	Flowers In The Rain	Move	Regal Zonophone	10		
18	5	The Letter	Box Tops	Stateside	8	(1)	F
19	-	I Feel Love Comin' On	Felice Taylor	President	6		F L
20	12	When Will The Good Apples Fall	Seekers	Columbia	6		L

December 1967

This Mnth	Prev Mnth	Title	Artist	Label	Wks 20	(US Pos)	
1	-	Hello Goodbye	Beatles	Parlophone	10	(1)	
2	14	If The Whole World Stopped Loving	Val Doonican	Pye	13		
3	12	Let The Heartaches Begin	Long John Baldry	Pye	9	(88)	F
4	-	Something's Gotten Hold Of My Heart	Gene Pitney	Stateside	9		
5	-	I'm Comin' Home	Tom Jones	Decca	12	(57)	
6	16	Everybody Knows	Dave Clark Five	Columbia	8	(43)	
7	-	All My Love	Cliff Richard	Columbia	8		
8	-	Careless Hands	Des O'Connor	Columbia	9		F
9	-	Daydream Believer	Monkees	RCA	12	(1)	
10	-	World	Bee Gees	Polydor	10		
11	-	Thank U Very Much	Scaffold	Parlophone	8	(69)	F
12	-	Magical Mystery Tour (Double E.P.)	Beatles	Parlophone	9		
13	6	Love Is All Around	Troggs	Page One	7	(7)	L
14	-	Here We Go Round The Mulberry Bush	Traffic	Island	7		L
15	5	The Last Waltz	Engelbert Humperdinck	Decca	20	(25)	G
16	1	Baby, Now That I Found You	Foundations	Pye	9	(11)	F
17	19	I Feel Love Comin' On	Felice Taylor	President	6		F L
18	-	Kites	Simon Dupree & The Big Sound	Parlophone	8		F L
19	-	Walk Away Renee	Four Tops	Tamla Motown	8	(14)	
20	3	Zabadak	Dave Dee, Dozy, Beaky etc.	Fontana	8	(52)	

October 1967

This Mnth	Prev Mnth	Title	Artist	Label	Wks 20	(UK Pos)	
1	4	The Letter	Box Tops	Mala	10	(5)	F G
2	9	Never My Love	Association	Warner	10		G
3	-	To Sir With Love	Lulu	Epic	11		F G
4	-	How Can I Be Sure	Young Rascals	Atlantic	7		
5	-	Little Ole Man (Uptight-Everything's Alright)	Bill Cosby	Warner	6		F L
6	-	Gimme Little Sign	Brenton Wood	Double Shot	7	(8)	F L
7	-	Expressway To Your Heart	Soul Survivors	Crimson	9		F L
8	1	Ode To Billie Joe	Bobbie Gentry	Capitol	10	(13)	F G L
9	-	Soul Man	Sam & Dave	Stax	10	(24)	F G
10	3	Come Back When You Grow Up	Bobby Vee & The Strangers	Liberty	9		G L
11	11	(Your Love...) Higher And Higher	Jackie Wilson	Brunswick	7	(9)	L
12	-	Your Precious Love	Marvin Gaye & Tammi Terrell	Tamla	7		
13	-	It Must Be Him	Vikki Carr	Liberty	6	(2)	F L
14	-	Get On Up	Esquires	Bunky	6		F L
15	-	Hey Baby (They're Playing Our Song)	Buckinghams	Columbia	5		
16	5	Apples Peaches Pumpkin Pie	Jay & The Techniques	Smash	9		F
17	-	A Natural Woman (You Make Me Feel Like)	Aretha Franklin	Atlantic	6		
18	2	Reflections	Diana Ross & The Supremes	Motown	8	(5)	G
19	-	Incense And Peppermints	Strawberry Alarm Clock	Uni	12		F G L
20	15	I Dig Rock And Roll Music	Peter, Paul & Mary	Warner	5		

November 1967

This Mnth	Prev Mnth	Title	Artist	Label	Wks 20	(UK Pos)	
1	3	To Sir With Love	Lulu	Epic	11		F G
2	9	Soul Man	Sam & Dave	Stax	10	(24)	F G
3	19	Incense And Peppermints	Strawberry Alarm Clock	Uni	12		F G L
4	13	It Must Be Him	Vikki Carr	Liberty	6	(2)	F L
5	-	The Rain, The Park & Other Things	Cowsills	MGM	11		F G
6	12	Your Precious Love	Marvin Gaye & Tammi Terrell	Tamla	7		
7	-	Please Love Me Forever	Bobby Vinton	Epic	9		
8	7	Expressway To Your Heart	Soul Survivors	Crimson	9		F L
9	17	A Natural Woman (You Make Me...)	Aretha Franklin	Atlantic	6		
10	-	I Can See For Miles	Who	Decca	5	(10)	F
11	2	Never My Love	Association	Warner	10		G
12	-	I Say A Little Prayer	Dionne Warwick	Scepter	8		G
13	-	(Loneliness Made Me Realize) It's You That I Need	Temptations	Gordy	5		
14	-	Let It Out (Let It All Hang Out)	Hombres	Verve Forecast	5		F L
15	-	I'm Wondering	Stevie Wonder	Tamla	3	(22)	
16	-	Everlasting Love	Robert Knight	Rising Sons	4	(19)	F L
17	-	Daydream Believer	Monkees	Colgems	10	(5)	G
18	-	Love Is Strange	Peaches & Herb	Date	3		
19	-	Pata Pata	Miriam Makeba	Reprise	4		F L
20	4	How Can I Be Sure	Young Rascals	Atlantic	7		

December 1967

This Mnth	Prev Mnth	Title	Artist	Label	Wks 20	(UK Pos)	
1	17	Daydream Believer	Monkees	Colgems	10	(5)	G
2	-	I Heard It Through The Grapevine	Gladys Knight & The Pips	Soul	11	(47)	
3	5	The Rain, The Park & Other Things	Cowsills	MGM	11		F G
4	-	I Second That Emotion	Smokey Robinson/The Miracles	Tamla	10	(27)	G
5	3	Incense And Peppermints	Strawberry Alarm Clock	Uni	12		F G L
6	-	Hello Goodbye	Beatles	Capitol	9	(1)	G
7	12	I Say A Little Prayer	Dionne Warwick	Scepter	8		G
8	-	Boogaloo Down Broadway	Fantastic Johnny C	Phil L.A. Of Soul	9		F L
9	-	You Better Sit Down Kids	Cher	Imperial	7		
10	-	Woman, Woman	Union Gap Feat. Gary Puckett	Columbia	11	(48)	F G
11	-	In And Out Of Love	Diana Ross & The Supremes	Motown	4	(13)	
12	1	To Sir With Love	Lulu	Epic	11		F G
13	-	Judy In Disguise (With Glasses)	John Fred & His Playboy Band	Paula	11	(3)	F G L
14	-	Skinny Legs And All	Joe Tex	Dial	7		G
15	-	An Open Letter To My Teenage Son	Victor Lundberg	Liberty	3		F L
16	-	(The Lights Went Out In) Massachusetts	Bee Gees	Atco	4	(1)	
17	7	Please Love Me Forever	Bobby Vinton	Epic	9		
18	-	Bend Me, Shape Me	American Breed	Acta	10	(24)	F G L
19	-	Keep The Ball Rollin'	Jay & The Techniques	Smash	4		L
20	10	I Can See For Miles	Who	Decca	5	(10)	F

US
1967
OCT-DEC

◆ As the musical *Hair* opened off-Broadway, many of the original hippies mourned the premature death of their 'love and peace' life-style - caused by media over-exposure.

◆ *Rolling Stone* magazine was launched

◆ Unique soul stylist Otis Redding died in a plane crash. Redding composed 'Respect', a chart topper for 1967's golden girl, Aretha Franklin.

▲ The Steve Miller Band received a record $750,000 to sign with Capitol Records, and Tom Jones (above) signed a $1 million deal for live appearances. in Las Vegas.

UK 1968 JAN-MAR

◆ Music from *Magical Mystery Tour* kept the Beatles at the top, although the film itself was their first commercial and critical flop. Meanwhile, their previous project, **Sergeant Pepper**, grabbed four Grammies.

◆ US groups scoring transatlantic hits included Jon Fred & His Playboy Band ('Judy In Disguise'), The Lemon Pipers ('Green Tambourine') and The 1910 Fruitgum Co. ('Simon Says') the latter introducing bubble-gum music.

◆ Status Quo (who subsequently had more UK chart singles than The Beatles or Stones) debuted on the Top 20. Fellow superstars, Genesis, released their first single as did Elton John, described by his label as "1968's greatest new talent".

January 1968

This Mnth	Prev Mnth	Title	Artist	Label	Wks 20	(US Pos)	
1	1	Hello Goodbye	Beatles	Parlophone	10	(1)	
2	12	Magical Mystery Tour (Double E.P.)	Beatles	Parlophone	9		
3	-	Ballad Of Bonnie & Clyde	Georgie Fame	CBS	8	(7)	
4	19	Walk Away Renee	Four Tops	Tamla Motown	8	(14)	
5	9	Daydream Believer	Monkees	RCA	12	(1)	
6	5	I'm Comin' Home	Tom Jones	Decca	12	(57)	
7	11	Thank U Very Much	Scaffold	Parlophone	8	(69)	F
8	-	Everlasting Love	Love Affair	CBS	10		F
9	2	If The Whole World Stopped Loving	Val Doonican	Pye	13		
10	10	World	Bee Gees	Polydor	10		
11	18	Kites	Simon Dupree & The Big Sound	Parlophone	8		F L
12	-	Am I That Easy To Forget	Engelbert Humperdinck	Decca	9	(18)	
13	4	Something's Gotten Hold Of My Heart	Gene Pitney	Stateside	9		
14	-	Tin Soldier	Small Faces	Immediate	8	(73)	
15	14	Here We Go Round The Mulberry Bush	Traffic	Island	7		L
16	-	Judy In Disguise (With Glasses)	John Fred & His Playboy Band	Pye International	7	(1)	F L
17	8	Careless Hands	Des O'Connor	Columbia	9		F
18	-	In And Out Of Love	Diana Ross & The Supremes	Tamla Motown	7	(9)	
19	-	Everything I Am	Plastic Penny	Page One	5		F L
20	-	She Wears My Ring	Solomon King	Columbia	11		F L

February 1968

This Mnth	Prev Mnth	Title	Artist	Label	Wks 20	(US Pos)	
1	8	Everlasting Love	Love Affair	CBS	10		F
2	-	Mighty Quinn	Manfred Mann	Fontana	8	(10)	
3	12	Am I That Easy To Forget	Engelbert Humperdinck	Decca	9	(18)	
4	-	Bend Me Shape Me	Amen Corner	Deram	9		
5	16	Judy In Disguise (With Glasses)	John Fred & His Playboy Band	Pye International	7	(1)	F L
6	20	She Wears My Ring	Solomon King	Columbia	11		F L
7	-	Suddenly You Love Me	Tremeloes	CBS	8	(44)	
8	-	Gimme Little Sign	Brenton Wood	Liberty	7	(9)	F L
9	3	Ballad Of Bonnie & Clyde	Georgie Fame	CBS	8	(7)	
10	-	Pictures Of Matchstick Men	Status Quo	Pye	7	(12)	F
11	19	Everything I Am	Plastic Penny	Page One	5		F L
12	-	I Can Take Or Leave Your Lovin'	Herman's Hermits	Columbia	6	(22)	
13	-	Darlin'	Beach Boys	Capitol	9	(19)	
14	-	Fire Brigade	Move	Regal Zonophone	8		
15	-	Words	Bee Gees	Polydor	7	(15)	
16	-	Cinderella Rockafella	Esther & Abi Ofarim	Philips	9	(68)	F
17	5	Daydream Believer	Monkees	RCA	12	(1)	
18	-	Don't Stop The Carnival	Alan Price Set	Decca	4		
19	14	Tin Soldier	Small Faces	Immediate	8	(73)	
20	2	Magical Mystery Tour (Double E.P.)	Beatles	Parlophone	9		

March 1968

This Mnth	Prev Mnth	Title	Artist	Label	Wks 20	(US Pos)	
1	16	Cinderella Rockafella	Esther & Abi Ofarim	Philips	9	(68)	F
2	-	Legend Of Xanadu	Dave Dee, Dozy, Beaky, Mick & Tich	Fontana	8		
3	14	Fire Brigade	Move	Regal Zonophone	8		
4	-	Rosie	Don Partridge	Columbia	9		F
5	-	Jennifer Juniper	Donovan	Pye	6	(26)	
6	-	Delilah	Tom Jones	Decca	11	(15)	
7	2	Mighty Quinn	Manfred Mann	Fontana	8	(10)	
8	-	(Sittin' On) The Dock Of The Bay	Otis Redding	Stax	8	(1)	
9	-	Green Tambourine	Lemon Pipers	Pye International	6	(1)	F L
10	6	She Wears My Ring	Solomon King	Columbia	11		F L
11	4	Bend Me Shape Me	Amen Corner	Deram	9		
12	10	Pictures Of Matchstick Men	Status Quo	Pye	7	(12)	F
13	15	Words	Bee Gees	Polydor	7	(15)	
14	-	Me The Peaceful Heart	Lulu	Columbia	5	(53)	
15	13	Darlin'	Beach Boys	Capitol	9	(19)	
16	-	Lady Madonna	Beatles	Parlophone	6	(4)	
17	-	What A Wonderful World	Louis Armstrong	HMV	16	(32)	L
18	7	Suddenly You Love Me	Tremeloes	CBS	8	(44)	
19	-	If I Were A Carpenter	Four Tops	Tamla Motown	6	(20)	
20	8	Gimme Little Sign	Brenton Wood	Liberty	7	(9)	F L

January 1968

This Mnth	Prev Mnth	Title	Artist	Label	Wks 20	(UK Pos)	
1	13	Judy In Disguise (With Glasses)	John Fred & His Playboy Band	Paula	11	(3)	F G L
2	6	Hello Goodbye	Beatles	Capitol	9	(1)	G
3	-	Chain Of Fools	Aretha Franklin	Atlantic	9	(43)	G
4	10	Woman, Woman	Union Gap Feat. Gary Puckett	Columbia	11	(48)	F G
5	1	Daydream Believer	Monkees	Colgems	10	(5)	G
6	2	I Heard It Through The Grapevine	Gladys Knight & The Pips	Soul	11	(47)	
7	17	Bend Me, Shape Me	American Breed	Acta	10	(24)	F G L
8	-	Green Tambourine	Lemon Pipers	Buddah	9	(7)	F G L
9	4	I Second That Emotion	Smokey Robinson/The Miracles	Tamla	10	(27)	G
10	-	If I Could Build My Whole World Around You	Marvin Gaye & Tammi Terrell	Tamla	5	(41)	
11	13	Skinny Legs And All	Joe Tex	Dial	7		G
12	-	Honey Chile	Martha & The Vandellas	Gordy	6	(30)	L
13	-	Different Drum	Stone Poneys	Capitol	7		F L
14	8	Boogaloo Down Broadway	Fantastic Johnny C	Phil L.A. Of Soul	9		F L
15	-	Susan	Buckinghams	Columbia	6		L
16	-	Spooky	Classics IV	Imperial	9	(46)	F G
17	-	Nobody But Me	Human Beinz	Capitol	8		F L
18	-	Monterey	Eric Burdon & The Animals	MGM	2		
19	-	Summer Rain	Johnny Rivers	Imperial	5		
20	5	Incense And Peppermints	Strawberry Alarm Clock	Uni	12		F G L

February 1968

This Mnth	Prev Mnth	Title	Artist	Label	Wks 20	(UK Pos)	
1	-	Love Is Blue	Paul Mauriat	Philips	13	(12)	F G L
2	7	Green Tambourine	Lemon Pipers	Buddah	9	(7)	F G L
3	15	Spooky	Classics IV	Imperial	9	(46)	F G
4	20	I Wish It Would Rain	Temptations	Gordy	9	(45)	G
5	1	Judy In Disguise (With Glasses)	John Fred & His Playboy Band	Paula	11	(3)	F G L
6	-	Goin' Out Of My Head/ Can't Take My Eyes Off You	Lettermen	Capitol	6		
7	16	Nobody But Me	Human Beinz	Capitol	8		F L
8	-	(Theme From) Valley Of The Dolls	Dionne Warwick	Scepter	9	(28)	
9	3	Woman, Woman	Union Gap Feat. Gary Puckett	Columbia	11	(48)	F G
10	2	Chain Of Fools	Aretha Franklin	Atlantic	9	(43)	G
11	6	Bend Me, Shape Me	American Breed	Acta	10	(24)	F G L
12	-	Baby Now That I've Found You	Foundations	Uni	8	(1)	F G
13	-	I Wonder What She's Doing Tonight	Tommy Boyce & Bobby Hart	A&M	7		F L
14	-	(Sittin' On) The Dock Of The Bay	Otis Redding	Volt	12	(3)	F G L
15	14	Susan	Buckinghams	Columbia	6		L
16	-	Bottle Of Wine	Fireballs	Atco	6		F L
17	-	Simon Says	1910 Fruitgum Co.	Buddah	9	(2)	F G
18	-	We're A Winner	Impressions	ABC	4		
19	-	Itchycoo Park	Small Faces	Immediate	3	(3)	F L
20	2	Hello Goodbye	Beatles	Capitol	9	(1)	G

March 1968

This Mnth	Prev Mnth	Title	Artist	Label	Wks 20	(UK Pos)	
1	1	Love Is Blue	Paul Mauriat	Philips	13	(12)	F G L
2	13	(Sittin' On) The Dock Of The Bay	Otis Redding	Volt	12	(3)	F G L
3	7	(Theme From) Valley Of The Dolls	Dionne Warwick	Scepter	9	(28)	
4	16	Simon Says	1910 Fruitgum Co.	Buddah	9	(2)	F G
5	-	Just Dropped In (To See What Condition My Condition Was In)	First Edition	Reprise	6		F
6	-	La-La Means I Love You	Delfonics	Philly Groove	9	(19)	F
7	4	I Wish It Would Rain	Temptations	Gordy	9	(45)	G
8	-	Valleri	Monkees	Colgems	6	(12)	G
9	-	(Sweet Sweet Baby) Since You've Been Gone	Aretha Franklin	Atlantic	8		G
10	3	Spooky	Classics IV	Imperial	9	(46)	F G
11	-	I Thank You	Sam & Dave	Stax	5	(34)	L
12	-	Everything That Touches You	Association	Warner	5		L
13	-	The Ballad Of Bonnie And Clyde	Georgie Fame	Epic	9	(1)	F L
14	15	Bottle Of Wine	Fireballs	Atco	6		F L
15	12	I Wonder What She's Doing Tonight	Tommy Boyce & Bobby Hart	A&M	7		F L
16	-	Young Girl	Union Gap Feat. Gary Puckett	Columbia	11	(1)	G
17	-	Dance To The Music	Sly & The Family Stone	Epic	9	(7)	F
18	-	Mighty Quinn	Manfred Mann	Mercury	5	(1)	L
19	11	Baby Now That I've Found You	Foundations	Uni	8	(1)	F G
20	-	The End Of Our Road	Gladys Knight & The Pips	Soul	4		

◆ A daughter, Lisa Marie, was born to Elvis Presley, whose 26th film *Stay Away Joe* was released to little acclaim. It was also announced that Elvis was preparing a 'come-back' TV special.

◆ The first teenage rock hero, Frankie Lymon, died of a drug overdose and fellow fifties R&B teen sensation Little Willie John died in prison.

▲ Aretha Franklin earned her fourth gold single in a year (a record for female artists) with the Grammy winning 'Chain Of Fools'.

◆ Dick Clark launched a new TV show *Happening '68*, which ran for two years.

UK 1968 APR-JUNE

▲ Pink Floyd, (above) Jethro Tull and Tyrannosaurus Rex appeared at the first free concert in London's Hyde Park.

◆ American hits in Britain included: transatlantic No. 1 'Young Girl' by Gary Puckett & The Union Gap, 'Honey' by Bobby Goldsboro (which returned to the British Top 3 in 1975), 'What A Wonderful World' by 66-year-old Louis Armstrong (which debuted on the US chart in 1988!) and rock's biggest seller, 'Rock Around The Clock' by Bill Haley.

◆ The Beatles, who refused an invitation from the Queen to play at a charity show, had their 15th UK No. 1, 'Lady Madonna'.

April 1968

This Mnth	Prev Mnth	Title	Artist	Label	Wks 20	(US Pos)	
1	-	Congratulations	Cliff Richard	Columbia	9	(99)	
2	17	What A Wonderful World	Louis Armstrong	HMV	16	(32)	L
3	6	Delilah	Tom Jones	Decca	11	(15)	
4	-	If I Only Had Time	John Rowles	MCA	11		F
5	8	(Sittin' On) The Dock Of The Bay	Otis Redding	Stax	8	(1)	
6	16	Lady Madonna	Beatles	Parlophone	6	(4)	
7	-	Simon Says	1910 Fruitgum Co.	Pye International	12	(4)	F L
8	-	Step Inside Love	Cilla Black	Parlophone	5		
9	19	If I Were A Carpenter	Four Tops	Tamla Motown	6	(20)	
10	-	Jennifer Eccles	Hollies	Parlophone	6	(40)	
11	-	Can't Take My Eyes Off You	Andy Williams	CBS	9		
12	1	Cinderella Rockafella	Esther & Abi Ofarim	Philips	9	(68)	F
13	-	I Can't Let Maggie Go	Honeybus	Deram	6		F L
14	-	Captain Of Your Ship	Reperata & The Delrons	Bell	5		F L
15	-	Ain't Nothin' But A Housparty	Showstoppers	Beacon	9		F L
16	-	Valleri	Monkees	RCA	5	(3)	
17	4	Rosie	Don Partridge	Columbia	9		F
18	2	Legend Of Xanadu	Dave Dee, Dozy, Beaky, Mick & Tich	Fontana	8		
19	-	Love Is Blue (L'Amour Est Bleu)	Paul Mauriat	Philips	5	(1)	F L
20	-	Something Here In My Heart (Keeps A-Tellin' Me No)	Paper Dolls	Pye	5		F L

May 1968

This Mnth	Prev Mnth	Title	Artist	Label	Wks 20	(US Pos)	
1	2	What A Wonderful World	Louis Armstrong	HMV	16	(32)	L
2	-	Lazy Sunday	Small Faces	Immediate	7		
3	-	A Man Without Love	Engelbert Humperdinck	Decca	9	(19)	
4	7	Simon Says	1910 Fruitgum Co.	Pye International	12	(4)	F L
5	-	Young Girl	Gary Puckett & The Union Gap	CBS	12	(2)	F
6	11	Can't Take My Eyes Off You	Andy Williams	CBS	9		
7	-	I Don't Want Our Loving To Die	Herd	Fontana	8		L
8	4	If I Only Had Time	John Rowles	MCA	11		F
9	-	Honey	Bobby Goldsboro	UA	11	(1)	F
10	1	Congratulations	Cliff Richard	Columbia	9	(99)	
11	-	White Horses	Jacky	Philips	9		F L
12	10	Jennifer Eccles	Hollies	Parlophone	6	(40)	
13	-	Rainbow Valley	Love Affair	CBS	8		
14	15	Ain't Nothin' But A Housparty	Showstoppers	Beacon	9		F L
15	13	I Can't Let Maggie Go	Honeybus	Deram	6		F L
16	20	Something Here In My Heart (Keeps A-Tellin' Me No)	Paper Dolls	Pye	5		F L
17	3	Delilah	Tom Jones	Decca	11	(15)	
18	-	Sleepy Joe	Herman's Hermits	Columbia	6	(61)	
19	-	Joanna	Scott Walker	Philips	7		F
20	-	Cry Like A Baby	Box Tops	Bell	5	(2)	L

June 1968

This Mnth	Prev Mnth	Title	Artist	Label	Wks 20	(US Pos)	
1	5	Young Girl	Gary Puckett & The Union Gap	CBS	12	(2)	F
2	9	Honey	Bobby Goldsboro	UA	11	(1)	F
3	-	Jumping Jack Flash	Rolling Stones	Decca	9	(3)	
4	3	A Man Without Love	Engelbert Humperdinck	Decca	9	(19)	
5	-	This Wheel's On Fire	Julie Driscoll, Brian Auger & The Trinity	Marmalade	8		F L
6	13	Rainbow Valley	Love Affair	CBS	8		
7	-	Do You Know The Way To San José	Dionne Warwick	Pye International	8	(10)	
8	-	Blue Eyes	Don Partridge	Columbia	8		L
9	-	Hurdy Gurdy Man	Donovan	Pye	7	(5)	
10	7	I Don't Want Our Loving To Die	Herd	Fontana	8		L
11	19	Joanna	Scott Walker	Philips	7		F
12	-	Baby Come Back	Equals	President	12	(32)	F
13	1	What A Wonderful World	Louis Armstrong	HMV	16	(32)	L
14	-	I Pretend	Des O'Connor	Columbia	15		
15	2	Lazy Sunday	Small Faces	Immediate	7		
16	4	Simon Says	1910 Fruitgum Co.	Pye International	12	(4)	F L
17	18	Sleepy Joe	Herman's Hermits	Columbia	6	(61)	
18	-	Lovin' Things	Marmalade	CBS	6		F
19	-	Son Of Hickory Hollers Tramp	O.C. Smith	CBS	9	(40)	F L
20	-	Helule Helule	Tremeloes	CBS	5		

April 1968

This Mnth	Prev Mnth	Title	Artist	Label	Wks 20	(UK Pos)	
1	16	Young Girl	Union Gap Feat. Gary Puckett	Columbia	11	(1)	G
2	-	Honey	Bobby Goldsboro	UA	11	(2)	G
3	-	Cry Like A Baby	Box Tops	Mala	10	(15)	G
4	2	(Sittin' On) The Dock Of The Bay	Otis Redding	Volt	12	(3)	F G L
5	9	(Sweet Sweet Baby) Since You've Been Gone	Aretha Franklin	Atlantic	8		G
6	-	Lady Madonna	Beatles	Capitol	8	(1)	G
7	13	The Ballad Of Bonnie And Clyde	Georgie Fame	Epic	9	(1)	F L
8	6	La-La Means I Love You	Delfonics	Philly Groove	9	(19)	F
9	-	I Got The Feelin'	James Brown	King	9		
10	17	Dance To The Music	Sly & The Family Stone	Epic	9	(7)	F
11	8	Valleri	Monkees	Colgems	6	(12)	G
12	18	Mighty Quinn	Manfred Mann	Mercury	5	(1)	L
13	1	Love Is Blue	Paul Mauriat	Philips	13	(12)	F G L
14	-	If You Can Want	Smokey Robinson & The Miracles	Tamla	6	(50)	
15	-	Scarborough Fair/Canticle	Simon & Garfunkel	Columbia	5		
16	4	Simon Says	1910 Fruitgum Co.	Buddah	9	(2)	F G
17	-	Cowboys To Girls	Intruders	Gamble	9		F G L
18	-	Tighten Up	Archie Bell & The Drells	Atlantic	10		F G
19	-	Summertime Blues	Blue Cheer	Philips	6		F L
20	-	Playboy	Gene & Debbe	TRX	3		F L

May 1968

This Mnth	Prev Mnth	Title	Artist	Label	Wks 20	(UK Pos)	
1	18	Tighten Up	Archie Bell & The Drells	Atlantic	10		F G
2	2	Honey	Bobby Goldsboro	UA	11	(2)	G
3	-	The Good, The Bad & The Ugly	Hugo Montenegro & Orchestra	RCA	10	(1)	L
4	-	A Beautiful Morning	Rascals	Atlantic	9		G
5	17	Cowboys To Girls	Intruders	Gamble	9		F G L
6	1	Young Girl	Union Gap Feat. Gary Puckett	Columbia	11	(1)	G
7	-	The Unicorn	Irish Rovers	Decca	7		F L
8	-	Mrs. Robinson	Simon & Garfunkel	Columbia	10	(4)	G
9	3	Cry Like A Baby	Box Tops	Mala	10	(15)	G
10	-	Love Is All Around	Troggs	Fontana	5	(5)	L
11	6	Lady Madonna	Beatles	Capitol	8	(1)	G
12	-	Take Time To Know Her	Percy Sledge	Atlantic	5		L
13	9	I Got The Feelin'	James Brown	King	9		
14	-	Shoo-Be-Doo-Be-Doo-Da-Day	Stevie Wonder	Tamla	6	(46)	
15	-	Do You Know The Way To San José	Dionne Warwick	Scepter	4	(8)	
16	-	Ain't Nothing Like The Real Thing	Marvin Gaye & Tammi Terrell	Tamla	5	(34)	
17	19	Summertime Blues	Blue Cheer	Philips	6		F L
18	-	Funky Street	Arthur Conley	Atco	3	(46)	L
19	-	Mony Mony	Tommy James & The Shondells	Roulette	9	(1)	G
20	14	If You Can Want	Smokey Robinson & The Miracles	Tamla	6	(50)	

June 1968

This Mnth	Prev Mnth	Title	Artist	Label	Wks 20	(UK Pos)	
1	-	This Guy's In Love With You	Herb Alpert	A&M	11	(2)	G
2	8	Mrs. Robinson	Simon & Garfunkel	Columbia	10	(4)	G
3	-	Yummy Yummy Yummy	Ohio Express	Buddah	8	(5)	F G
4	1	Tighten Up	Archie Bell & The Drells	Atlantic	10		F G
5	19	Mony Mony	Tommy James & The Shondells	Roulette	9	(1)	G
6	-	MacArthur Park	Richard Harris	Dunhill	8	(4)	F G L
7	-	Think	Aretha Franklin	Atlantic	8	(26)	G
8	3	The Good, The Bad & The Ugly	Hugo Montenegro & Orchestra	RCA	10	(1)	L
9	-	The Look Of Love	Sergio Mendes & Brasil '66	A&M	8		F
10	4	A Beautiful Morning	Rascals	Atlantic	9		G
11	-	Angel Of The Morning	Merrilee Rush	Bell	8		F L
12	2	Honey	Bobby Goldsboro	UA	11	(2)	G
13	16	Ain't Nothing Like The Real Thing	Marvin Gaye & Tammi Terrell	Tamla	5	(34)	
14	-	The Horse	Cliff Nobles & Co.	Phil L.A. of Soul	9		F G L
15	-	Here Comes The Judge	Shorty Long	Soul	7	(30)	F L
16	-	Reach Out Of The Darkness	Friend And Lover	Verve	6		F L
17	5	Cowboys To Girls	Intruders	Gamble	9		F G L
18	-	I Could Never Love Another (After Loving You)	Temptations	Gordy	5	(47)	
19	-	Jumpin' Jack Flash	Rolling Stones	London	9	(1)	G
20	-	I Love You	People	Capitol	6		F L

US 1968 APR-JUNE

◆ Philadelphia soul stars who joined Detroit counterparts in the Top 10 were: The Delfonics, Archie Bell & The Drells, The Intruders and Cliff Nobles & Co.

◆ Trend-setters with debut hits included Sly & The Family Stone, and heavy metal merchants Blue Cheer and Iron Butterfly.

◆ Over half the The Beach Boys shows with Maharishi Mahesh Yogi were cancelled. Shortly afterwards, The Beatles described their association with the Maharishi as "a public mistake".

◆ Simon & Garfunkel's album **Bookends** replaced **The Graduate** at No. 1, and **Parsley, Sage, Rosemary And Thyme** gave them three in the Top 5!

UK 1968 JULY–SEPT

The Beatles launched their own label Apple and released their animated film *Yellow Submarine*. Incidentally, the group's No. 1 rivals of 1967, the Monkees, had their last US Top 20 entry with a Leiber & Stoller song, 'D.W. Washburn'.

◆ Chart topping album act Cream announced they were splitting up, as did The Yardbirds (who later evolved into Led Zeppelin). The Hollies announced they were making solo records, Janis Joplin quit Big Brother & The Holding Company and ex-Contour, Dennis Edwards, replaced lead singer David Ruffin in The Temptations, who had just scored their 13th American Top 20 single.

◆ Pete Townshend of The Who, revealed to *Rolling Stone* magazine that he was working on a rock opera entitled *Tommy*.

July 1968

This Mnth	Prev Mnth	Title	Artist	Label	Wks 20	(US Pos)	
1	12	Baby Come Back	Equals	President	12	(32)	F
2	14	I Pretend	Des O'Connor	Columbia	15		
3	19	Son Of Hickory Hollers Tramp	O.C. Smith	CBS	9	(40)	F L
4	-	Yesterday Has Gone	Cupid's Inspiration	Nems	7		F L
5	-	Yummy Yummy Yummy	Ohio Express	Pye International	9	(4)	F L
6	-	Mony Mony	Tommy James & The Shondells	Major Minor	11	(3)	F L
7	3	Jumping Jack Flash	Rolling Stones	Decca	9	(3)	
8	-	My Name Is Jack	Manfred Mann	Fontana	5		
9	-	MacArthur Park	Richard Harris	RCA	7	(2)	F L
10	8	Blue Eyes	Don Partridge	Columbia	8		L
11	18	Lovin' Things	Marmalade	CBS	6		F
12	9	Hurdy Gurdy Man	Donovan	Pye	7	(5)	
13	-	Hush Not A Word To Mary	John Rowles	MCA	5		L
14	-	Fire	Crazy World Of Arthur Brown	Track	10	(2)	F L
15	-	One More Dance	Esther & Abi Ofarim	Philips	4		L
16	1	Young Girl	Gary Puckett & The Union Gap	CBS	12	(2)	F
17	-	This Guy's In Love With You	Herb Alpert	A&M	11	(1)	
18	-	Mrs. Robinson	Simon & Garfunkel	CBS	7	(1)	
19	5	This Wheel's On Fire	Julie Driscoll, Brian Auger & The Trinity	Marmalade	8		F L
20	-	I Close My Eyes And Count To Ten	Dusty Springfield	Philips	6		

August 1968

This Mnth	Prev Mnth	Title	Artist	Label	Wks 20	(US Pos)	
1	6	Mony Mony	Tommy James & The Shondells	Major Minor	11	(3)	F L
2	14	Fire	Crazy World Of Arthur Brown	Track	10	(2)	F L
3	17	This Guy's In Love With You	Herb Alpert	A&M	11	(1)	
4	2	I Pretend	Des O'Connor	Columbia	15		
5	20	I Close My Eyes And Count To Ten	Dusty Springfield	Philips	6		
6	-	Help Yourself	Tom Jones	Decca	10	(35)	
7	18	Mrs. Robinson	Simon & Garfunkel	CBS	7	(1)	
8	-	Sunshine Girl	Herman's Hermits	Columbia	8		
9	-	Dance To The Music	Sly & The Family Stone	Direction	7	(8)	F
10	-	Do It Again	Beach Boys	Capitol	10	(20)	
11	-	Last Night In Soho	Dave Dee, Dozy, Beaky, Mick & Tich	Fontana	6		
12	-	I've Gotta Get A Message To You	Bee Gees	Polydor	11	(8)	
13	9	MacArthur Park	Richard Harris	RCA	7	(2)	F L
14	-	Keep On	Bruce Channel	Bell	6		L
15	1	Baby Come Back	Equals	President	12	(32)	F
16	-	High In The Sky	Amen Corner	Deram	9		
17	-	Days	Kinks	Pye	6		
18	5	Yummy Yummy Yummy	Ohio Express	Pye International	9	(4)	F L
19	-	I Say A Little Prayer	Aretha Franklin	Atlantic	8	(10)	
20	3	Son Of Hickory Hollers Tramp	O.C. Smith	CBS	9	(40)	F L

September 1968

This Mnth	Prev Mnth	Title	Artist	Label	Wks 20	(US Pos)	
1	12	I've Gotta Get A Message To You	Bee Gees	Polydor	11	(8)	
2	10	Do It Again	Beach Boys	Capitol	10	(20)	
3	19	I Say A Little Prayer	Aretha Franklin	Atlantic	8	(10)	
4	-	Hold Me Tight	Johnny Nash	Regal Zonophone	10	(5)	F
5	-	Hey Jude	Beatles	Apple	10	(1)	
6	-	Those Were The Days	Mary Hopkin	Apple	14	(2)	F
7	3	This Guy's In Love With You	Herb Alpert	A&M	11	(1)	
8	16	High In The Sky	Amen Corner	Deram	9		
9	6	Help Yourself	Tom Jones	Decca	10	(35)	
10	-	Jesamine	Casuals	Decca	11		F L
11	-	On The Road Again	Canned Heat	Liberty	7	(16)	F
12	-	Lady Willpower	Gary Puckett & The Union Gap	CBS	10	(2)	
13	-	Dream A Little Dream Of Me	Mama Cass	RCA	7	(12)	F
14	-	Little Arrows	Leapy Lee	MCA	13	(16)	F L
15	1	Mony Mony	Tommy James & The Shondells	Major Minor	11	(3)	F L
16	2	Fire	Crazy World Of Arthur Brown	Track	10	(2)	F L
17	-	Hard To Handle	Otis Redding	Atlantic	6	(51)	L
18	9	Dance To The Music	Sly & The Family Stone	Direction	7	(8)	F
19	-	Classical Gas	Mason Williams	Warner	8	(2)	F L
20	8	Sunshine Girl	Herman's Hermits	Columbia	8		

July 1968

This Mnth	Prev Mnth	Title	Artist	Label	Wks 20	(UK Pos)	
1	-	Grazing In The Grass	Hugh Masekela	Uni	9		F G L
2	1	This Guy's In Love With You	Herb Alpert	A&M	11	(2)	G
3	19	Jumpin' Jack Flash	Rolling Stones	London	9	(1)	G
4	-	Lady Willpower	Gary Puckett & The Union Gap	Columbia	10	(5)	G
5	14	The Horse	Cliff Nobles & Co.	Phil L.A. of Soul	9		F G L
6	-	Stoned Soul Picnic	Fifth Dimension	Soul City	9		G
7	9	The Look Of Love	Sergio Mendes & Brasil '66	A&M	8		F
8	15	Here Comes The Judge	Shorty Long	Soul	7	(30)	F L
9	11	Angel Of The Morning	Merrilee Rush	Bell	8		F L
10	16	Reach Out Of The Darkness	Friend And Lover	Verve	6		F L
11	-	Indian Lake	Cowsills	MGM	5		
12	-	Hurdy Gurdy Man	Donovan	Epic	7	(4)	
13	-	Classical Gas	Mason Williams	Warner	8	(9)	F G L
14	-	Hello, I Love You	Doors	Elektra	9	(15)	G
15	6	MacArthur Park	Richard Harris	Dunhill	8	(4)	F G L
16	3	Yummy Yummy Yummy	Ohio Express	Buddah	8	(5)	F G
17	-	Turn Around Look At Me	Vogues	Reprise	9		G
18	5	Mony Mony	Tommy James & The Shondells	Roulette	9	(1)	G
19	2	Mrs. Robinson	Simon & Garfunkel	Columbia	10	(4)	G
20	20	I Love You	People	Capitol	6		F L

August 1968

This Mnth	Prev Mnth	Title	Artist	Label	Wks 20	(UK Pos)	
1	14	Hello, I Love You	Doors	Elektra	9	(15)	G
2	-	People Got To Be Free	Rascals	Atlantic	11		G L
3	13	Classical Gas	Mason Williams	Warner	8	(9)	F G L
4	-	Born To Be Wild	Steppenwolf	Dunhill	9	(30)	F G
5	-	Sunshine Of Your Love	Cream	Atco	8	(25)	F G
6	6	Stoned Soul Picnic	Fifth Dimension	Soul City	9		G
7	17	Turn Around Look At Me	Vogues	Reprise	9		G
8	-	Light My Fire	José Feliciano	RCA	9	(6)	F G L
9	12	Hurdy Gurdy Man	Donovan	Epic	7	(4)	
10	1	Grazing In The Grass	Hugh Masekela	Uni	9		F G L
11	4	Lady Willpower	Gary Puckett & The Union Gap	Columbia	10	(5)	G
12	-	(You Keep Me) Hangin' On	Vanilla Fudge	Atco	7	(18)	F L
13	-	Stay In My Corner	Dells	Cadet	7		
14	3	Jumpin' Jack Flash	Rolling Stones	London	9	(1)	G
15	-	I Can't Stop Dancing	Archie Bell & The Drells	Atlantic	5		L
16	5	The Horse	Cliff Nobles & Co.	Phil L.A. of Soul	9		F G L
17	-	Dream A Little Dream Of Me	Mama Cass	Dunhill	4	(11)	F L
18	-	Journey To The Center Of The Mind	Amboy Dukes	Mainstream	6		F L
19	-	You're All I Need To Get By	Marvin Gaye & Tammi Terrell	Tamla	5	(19)	
20	-	Pictures Of Matchstick Men	Status Quo	Cadet Concept	4	(7)	F L

September 1968

This Mnth	Prev Mnth	Title	Artist	Label	Wks 20	(UK Pos)	
1	2	People Got To Be Free	Rascals	Atlantic	11		G L
2	-	Harper Valley P.T.A.	Jeannie C. Riley	Plantation	11	(12)	F G L
3	-	1 2 3 Red Light	1910 Fruitgum Co.	Buddah	6		G
4	4	Born To Be Wild	Steppenwolf	Dunhill	9	(30)	F G
5	8	Light My Fire	José Feliciano	RCA	9	(6)	F G L
6	-	Hush	Deep Purple	Tetragrammaton	7		F
7	-	Hey Jude	Beatles	Apple	16	(1)	G
8	-	The House That Jack Built	Aretha Franklin	Atlantic	6		
9	-	The Fool On The Hill	Sergio Mendes & Brasil '66	A&M	6		L
10	19	You're All I Need To Get By	Marvin Gaye & Tammi Terrell	Tamla	5	(19)	
11	1	Hello, I Love You	Doors	Elektra	9	(15)	G
12	-	Slip Away	Clarence Carter	Atlantic	7		F G
13	-	I've Gotta Get A Message To You	Bee Gees	Atco	7	(1)	
14	-	Fire	Crazy World Of Arthur Brown	Track	10	(1)	F G L
15	-	I Say A Little Prayer	Aretha Franklin	Atlantic	5	(4)	G
16	-	Girl Watcher	O'Kaysions	ABC	9		F G L
17	-	Time Has Come Today	Chambers Brothers	Columbia	5		F L
18	5	Sunshine Of Your Love	Cream	Atco	8	(25)	F G
19	12	(You Keep Me) Hangin' On	Vanilla Fudge	Atco	7	(18)	F L
20	-	Revolution	Beatles	Capitol	9		G

US 1968

JULY-SEPT

▲ The Newport Pop Festival was attended by 100,000 fans. Headliners included Sonny & Cher (above), The Byrds, Jefferson Airplane, Grateful Dead, Iron Butterfly, Steppenwolf, Canned Heat and token British band, Eric Burdon & The Animals.

◆ The Rascals scored their third No. 1 with 'People Got To Be Free', Tommy James & The Shondells had one of their 11 Top 20 entries with 'Mony Mony' and The Doors collected a second chart topper with 'Hello I Love You'. Although all these acts were US superstars, they all only visited the British Top 20 singles chart once.

UK 1968

OCT-DEC

◆ John Sebastian left The Lovin' Spoonful, Eric Burdon disbanded The Animals and Graham Nash left The Hollies (to form Crosby, Stills & Nash). Also Mama Cass left The Mamas & The Papas, Peter Tork quit The Monkees and Cream's farewell American tour grossed over $700,000.

◆ Double album, **The Beatles**, topped the charts, and the group's seven minute single, 'Hey Jude', quickly amassed world sales of five million. The first Beatle solo LPs were released by George and John (with Yoko), and a single on their Apple imprint, 'Those Were The Days' by Mary Hopkin became an international hit.

◆ **The Sound Of Music**, which had topped the chart for 68 weeks, passed the two million sales mark, becoming Britain's biggest selling album.

◆ For the first time more albums were sold in Britian than singles.

October 1968

This Mnth	Prev Mnth	Title	Artist	Label	Wks 20	(US Pos)	
1	6	Those Were The Days	Mary Hopkin	Apple	14	(2)	F
2	5	Hey Jude	Beatles	Apple	10	(1)	
3	10	Jesamine	Casuals	Decca	11		F L
4	14	Little Arrows	Leapy Lee	MCA	13	(16)	F L
5	12	Lady Willpower	Gary Puckett & The Union Gap	CBS	10	(2)	
6	-	My Little Lady	Tremeloes	CBS	7		
7	-	Red Balloon	Dave Clark Five	Columbia	6		
8	-	A Day Without Love	Love Affair	CBS	7		
9	4	Hold Me Tight	Johnny Nash	Regal Zonophone	10	(5)	F
10	-	Les Bicyclettes De Belsize	Engelbert Humperdinck	Decca	7	(31)	
11	19	Classical Gas	Mason Williams	Warner	8	(2)	F L
12	-	Ice In The Sun	Status Quo	Pye	6	(70)	
13	1	I've Gotta Get A Message To You	Bee Gees	Polydor	11	(8)	
14	-	Light My Fire	José Feliciano	RCA	8	(3)	F L
15	-	The Good, The Bad And The Ugly	Hugo Montenegro & Orchestra	RCA	15	(2)	F L
16	3	I Say A Little Prayer	Aretha Franklin	Atlantic	8	(10)	
17	-	Listen To Me	Hollies	Parlophone	6		
18	-	Hello, I Love You	Doors	Elektra	6	(1)	F
19	8	High In The Sky	Amen Corner	Deram	9		
20	-	Only One Woman	Marbles	Polydor	8		F L

November 1968

This Mnth	Prev Mnth	Title	Artist	Label	Wks 20	(US Pos)	
1	15	The Good, The Bad And The Ugly	Hugo Montenegro & Orchestra	RCA	15	(2)	F L
2	-	With A Little Help From My Friends	Joe Cocker	Regal Zonophone	8	(68)	F
3	-	Eloise	Barry Ryan	MGM	9	(86)	F L
4	1	Those Were The Days	Mary Hopkin	Apple	14	(2)	F
5	-	This Old Heart Of Mine	Isley Brothers	Tamla Motown	10	(12)	F
6	20	Only One Woman	Marbles	Polydor	8		F L
7	-	All Along The Watchtower	Jimi Hendrix Experience	Track	6	(20)	
8	14	Light My Fire	Jose Feliciano	RCA	8	(3)	F L
9	-	Breakin' Down The Walls Of Heartache	Johnny Johnson & The Bandwagon	Direction	11		F
10	4	Little Arrows	Leapy Lee	MCA	13	(16)	F L
11	3	Jesamine	Casuals	Decca	11		F L
12	2	Hey Jude	Beatles	Apple	10	(1)	
13	-	Elenore	Turtles	London American	5	(6)	L
14	10	Les Bicyclettes De Belsize	Engelbert Humperdinck	Decca	7	(31)	
15	-	Ain't Got No - I Got Life/ Do What You Gotta Do	Nina Simone	RCA	12	(94)	F
16	-	Lily The Pink	Scaffold	Parlophone	12		
17	17	Listen To Me	Hollies	Parlophone	6		
18	6	My Little Lady	Tremeloes	CBS	7		
19	8	A Day Without Love	Love Affair	CBS	7		
20	-	Mexico	Long John Baldry	Pye	4		L

December 1968

This Mnth	Prev Mnth	Title	Artist	Label	Wks 20	(US Pos)	
1	16	Lily The Pink	Scaffold	Parlophone	12		
2	15	Ain't Got No - I Got Life/ Do What You Gotta Do	Nina Simone	RCA	12	(94)	F
3	1	The Good, The Bad And The Ugly	Hugo Montenegro & Orchestra	RCA	15	(2)	F L
4	-	One Two Three O'Leary	Des O'Connor	Columbia	9		
5	-	Build Me Up Buttercup	Foundations	Pye	9	(3)	
6	-	I'm The Urban Spaceman	Bonzo Dog Doo-Dah Band	Liberty	10		F L
7	5	This Old Heart Of Mine	Isley Brothers	Tamla Motown	10	(12)	F
8	9	Breakin' Down The Walls Of Heartache	Johnny Johnson & The Bandwagon	Direction	11		F
9	-	Race With The Devil	Gun	CBS	7		F L
10	-	I'm A Tiger	Lulu	Columbia	10		
11	-	Sabre Dance	Love Sculpture	Parlophone	8		F L
12	3	Eloise	Barry Ryan	MGM	9	(86)	F L
13	-	May I Have The Next Dream With You	Malcolm Roberts	Major Minor	8		F
14	-	Ob-La-Di Ob-La-Da	Marmalade	CBS	10		
15	-	Harper Valley P.T.A.	Jeannie C. Riley	Polydor	5	(1)	F L
16	13	Elenore	Turtles	London American	5	(6)	L
17	-	Albatross	Fleetwood Mac	Blue Horizon	13		F
18	-	Private Number	Judy Clay & William Bell	Stax	9	(75)	F L
19	-	A Minute Of Your Time	Tom Jones	Decca	7	(48)	
20	7	All Along The Watchtower	Jimi Hendrix Experience	Track	6	(20)	

October 1968

This Mnth	Prev Mnth	Title	Artist	Label	Wks 20	(UK Pos)	
1	7	Hey Jude	Beatles	Apple	16	(1)	G
2	14	Fire	Crazy World Of Arthur Brown	Track	10	(1)	F G L
3	-	Little Green Apples	O.C. Smith	Columbia	10		F G L
4	2	Harper Valley P.T.A.	Jeannie C. Riley	Plantation	11	(12)	F G L
5	16	Girl Watcher	O'Kaysions	ABC	9		F G L
6	13	I've Gotta Get A Message To You	Bee Gees	Atco	7	(1)	
7	-	Midnight Confessions	Grass Roots	Dunhill	10		G
8	-	My Special Angel	Vogues	Reprise	6		L
9	-	Over You	Gary Puckett & The Union Gap	Columbia	7		G
10	12	Slip Away	Clarence Carter	Atlantic	7		F G
11	-	Say It Loud-I'm Black And I'm Proud	James Brown	King	6		
12	17	Time Has Come Today	Chambers Brothers	Columbia	5		F L
13	-	Those Were The Days	Mary Hopkin	Apple	11	(1)	F G
14	1	People Got To Be Free	Rascals	Atlantic	11		G L
15	20	Revolution	Beatles	Capitol	9		G
16	-	Suzie Q. (Pt. 1)	Creedence Clearwater Revival	Fantasy	6		F
17	-	Elenore	Turtles	White Whale	7	(7)	
18	15	I Say A Little Prayer	Aretha Franklin	Atlantic	5	(4)	G
19	-	Piece Of My Heart	Big Brother & The Holding Company	Columbia	5		F L
20	3	1 2 3 Red Light	1910 Fruitgum Co.	Buddah	6		G

November 1968

This Mnth	Prev Mnth	Title	Artist	Label	Wks 20	(UK Pos)	
1	1	Hey Jude	Beatles	Apple	16	(1)	G
2	13	Those Were The Days	Mary Hopkin	Apple	11	(1)	F G
3	-	Love Child	Diana Ross & The Supremes	Motown	14	(15)	G
4	-	Magic Carpet Ride	Steppenwolf	Dunhill	9		G
5	-	Hold Me Tight	Johnny Nash	Jad	9	(5)	F
6	-	White Room	Cream	Atco	7	(28)	L
7	3	Little Green Apples	O.C. Smith	Columbia	10		F G L
7	1	Elenore	Turtles	White Whale	7	(7)	
9	-	Abraham, Martin And John	Dion	Laurie	10		G L
10	7	Midnight Confessions	Grass Roots	Dunhill	10		G
11	-	Who's Making Love	Johnnie Taylor	Stax	9		F G
12	9	Over You	Gary Puckett & The Union Gap	Columbia	7		G
13	2	Fire	Crazy World Of Arthur Brown	Track	10	(1)	F G L
14	-	For Once In My Life	Stevie Wonder	Tamla	11	(3)	G
15	-	Wichita Lineman	Glen Campbell	Capitol	11	(7)	F G
16	-	Stormy	Classics IV	Imperial	9		
17	16	Suzie Q. (Pt. 1)	Creedence Clearwater Revival	Fantasy	6		F
18	19	Piece Of My Heart	Big Brother & The Holding Company	Columbia	5		F L
19	-	Sweet Blindness	Fifth Dimension	Soul City	2		
20	-	Chewy Chewy	Ohio Express	Buddah	7		G L

December 1968

This Mnth	Prev Mnth	Title	Artist	Label	Wks 20	(UK Pos)	
1	-	I Heard It Through The Grapevine	Marvin Gaye	Tamla	13	(1)	G
2	3	Love Child	Diana Ross & The Supremes	Motown	14	(15)	G
3	14	For Once In My Life	Stevie Wonder	Tamla	11	(3)	G
4	9	Abraham, Martin And John	Dion	Laurie	10		G L
5	15	Wichita Lineman	Glen Campbell	Capitol	11	(7)	F G
6	11	Who's Making Love	Johnnie Taylor	Stax	9		F G
7	16	Stormy	Classics IV	Imperial	9		
8	1	Hey Jude	Beatles	Apple	16	(1)	G
9	-	I Love How You Love Me	Bobby Vinton	Epic	10		G
10	-	Both Sides Now	Judy Collins	Elektra	6	(14)	F
11	4	Magic Carpet Ride	Steppenwolf	Dunhill	9		G
12	-	Cloud Nine	Temptations	Gordy	8	(15)	G
13	-	See Saw	Aretha Franklin	Atlantic	5		G
14	2	Those Were The Days	Mary Hopkin	Apple	11	(1)	F G
15	-	Cinnamon	Derek	Bang	7		L
16	-	I'm Gonna Make You Love Me	Diana Ross & The Supremes & The Temptations	Motown	11	(3)	G
17	20	Chewy Chewy	Ohio Express	Buddah	7		G L
18	-	Bring It On Home To Me	Eddie Floyd	Stax	5		F L
19	5	Hold Me Tight	Johnny Nash	Jad	9	(5)	F
20	-	Scarborough Fair	Sergio Mendes & Brasil '66	A&M	2		

▲ The Mamas & The Papas were sued by their label Dunhill for disbanding mid-contract, while Motown sued top producer/songwriters Holland, Dozier & Holland for $4 million, for not offering them any recordings in 1968.

◆ A bill including Marvin Gaye, Jose Feliciano, Three Dog Night, Chuck Berry, Fleetwood Mac, Joni Mitchell, The Box Tops, The Turtles, Jr. Walker and Joe Tex, attracted 100,000 to The Miami Pop Festival.

◆ Elvis Presley's long awaited TV special was widely considered a commercial and artistic triumph.

UK 1969 JAN-MAR

◆ The Beatles made their last public appearance on the roof of the Apple building singing 'Get Back'. Soon after, they had the top two US albums again; **The Beatles** and **Yellow Submarine**.

◆ Led Zeppelin debuted in the US (supported by fellow new-comers Jethro Tull). They would become one of the biggest selling and most influential acts of all time.

▲ Cream's **Goodbye Cream** album was a transatlantic Top 3 entry - although their film of the same name was panned. Meanwhile, ex-Cream members Eric Clapton (above) and Ginger Baker were planning a new group (Blind Faith) with Stevie Winwood.

January 1969

This Mnth	Prev Mnth	Title	Artist	Label	Wks 20	(US Pos)	
1	14	Ob-La-Di Ob-La-Da	Marmalade	CBS	10		
2	1	Lily The Pink	Scaffold	Parlophone	12		
3	17	Albatross	Fleetwood Mac	Blue Horizon	13		F
4	5	Build Me Up Buttercup	Foundations	Pye	9	(3)	
5	6	I'm The Urban Spaceman	Bonzo Dog Doo-Dah Band	Liberty	10		F L
6	-	For Once In My Life	Stevie Wonder	Tamla Motown	10	(2)	
7	11	Sabre Dance	Love Sculpture	Parlophone	8		F L
8	-	Something's Happening	Herman's Hermits	Columbia	8		
9	2	Ain't Got No - I Got Life/ Do What You Gotta Do	Nina Simone	RCA	12	(94)	F
10	-	Son-Of-A Preacher Man	Dusty Springfield	Philips	6	(10)	
11	18	Private Number	Judy Clay & William Bell	Stax	9	(75)	F L
12	4	One Two Three O'Leary	Des O'Connor	Columbia	9		
13	-	Blackberry Way	Move	Regal Zonophone	8		
14	10	I'm A Tiger	Lulu	Columbia	10		
15	-	Fox On The Run	Manfred Mann	Fontana	6	(97)	
16	9	Race With The Devil	Gun	CBS	7		F L
17	3	The Good, The Bad And The Ugly	Hugo Montenegro & Orchestra	RCA	15	(2)	F L
18	-	Love Child	Diana Ross & The Supremes	Tamla Motown	9	(1)	
19	-	Stop Her On Sight (SOS)/ Headline News	Edwin Starr	Polydor	5	(48)	F
20	19	A Minute Of Your Time	Tom Jones	Decca	7	(48)	

February 1969

This Mnth	Prev Mnth	Title	Artist	Label	Wks 20	(US Pos)	
1	3	Albatross	Fleetwood Mac	Blue Horizon	13		F
2	13	Blackberry Way	Move	Regal Zonophone	8		
3	6	For Once In My Life	Stevie Wonder	Tamla Motown	10	(2)	
4	-	Dancing In The Street	Martha & The Vandellas	Tamla Motown	7		F
5	-	You Got Soul	Johnny Nash	Major Minor	6	(58)	
6	-	Please Don't Go	Donald Peers	Columbia	9		F L
7	1	Ob-La-Di Ob-La-Da	Marmalade	CBS	10		
8	-	I'm Gonna Make You Love Me	Diana Ross & The Supremes & The Temptations	Tamla Motown	7	(2)	
9	-	To Love Somebody	Nina Simone	RCA	5		
10	-	(If Paradise Is) Half As Nice	Amen Corner	Immediate	7		
11	15	Fox On The Run	Manfred Mann	Fontana	6	(97)	
12	-	Where Do You Go To My Lovely	Peter Sarstedt	UA	10	(70)	F
13	8	Something's Happening	Herman's Hermits	Columbia	8		
14	-	I Guess I'll Always Love You	Isley Brothers	Tamla Motown	5	(61)	
15	11	Private Number	Judy Clay & William Bell	Stax	9	(75)	F L
16	19	Stop Her On Sight (SOS)/Headline...	Edwin Starr	Polydor	5	(48)	F
17	-	The Way It Used To Be	Engelbert Humperdinck	Decca	8	(42)	
18	-	I'll Pick A Rose For My Rose	Marv Johnson	Tamla Motown	6		L
19	2	Lily The Pink	Scaffold	Parlophone	12		
20	-	Mrs. Robinson (E.P.)	Simon & Garfunkel	CBS	1		

March 1969

This Mnth	Prev Mnth	Title	Artist	Label	Wks 20	(US Pos)	
1	12	Where Do You Go To My Lovely	Peter Sarstedt	UA	10	(70)	F
2	-	Surround Yourself With Sorrow	Cilla Black	Parlophone	9		
3	-	I Heard It Through The Grapevine	Marvin Gaye	Tamla Motown	10	(1)	
4	17	The Way It Used To Be	Engelbert Humperdinck	Decca	8	(42)	
5	6	Please Don't Go	Donald Peers	Columbia	9		F L
6	-	Gentle On My Mind	Dean Martin	Reprise	12		L
7	-	Wichita Lineman	Glen Campbell	Ember	6	(3)	F
8	-	Monsieur Dupont	Sandie Shaw	Pye	8		L
9	10	(If Paradise Is) Half As Nice	Amen Corner	Immediate	7		
10	-	First Of May	Bee Gees	Polydor	6	(37)	
11	8	I'm Gonna Make You Love Me	Diana Ross & The Supremes & The Temptations	Tamla Motown	7	(2)	
12	-	You've Lost That Lovin' Feelin'	Righteous Brothers	London American	6		
13	-	Sorry Suzanne	Hollies	Parlophone	7	(56)	
14	-	If I Can Dream	Elvis Presley	RCA	6	(12)	
15	-	Good Times (Better Times)	Cliff Richard	Columbia	7		
16	4	Dancing In The Street	Martha & The Vandellas	Tamla Motown	7		F
17	18	I'll Pick A Rose For My Rose	Marv Johnson	Tamla Motown	6		L
18	-	Games People Play	Joe South	Capitol	8	(12)	F L
19	2	Blackberry Way	Move	Regal Zonophone	8		
20	1	Albatross	Fleetwood Mac	Blue Horizon	13		F

January 1969

This Mnth	Prev Mnth	Title	Artist	Label	Wks 20	(UK Pos)	
1	1	I Heard It Through The Grapevine	Marvin Gaye	Tamla	13	(1)	G
2	16	I'm Gonna Make You Love Me	Diana Ross & The Supremes & The Temptations	Motown	11	(3)	G
3	-	Soulful Strut	Young-Holt Unlimited	Brunswick	9		F G L
4	-	Hooked On A Feeling	B.J. Thomas	Scepter	7		G
5	5	Wichita Lineman	Glen Campbell	Capitol	11	(7)	F G
6	3	For Once In My Life	Stevie Wonder	Tamla	11	(3)	G
7	-	Crimson & Clover	Tommy James & The Shondells	Roulette	13		G
8	12	Cloud Nine	Temptations	Gordy	8	(15)	G
9	-	Going Up The Country	Canned Heat	Liberty	7	(19)	L
10	-	Son-Of-A Preacher Man	Dusty Springfield	Atlantic	6	(9)	
11	15	Cinnamon	Derek	Bang	7		L
12	2	Love Child	Diana Ross & The Supremes	Motown	14	(15)	G
13	-	Touch Me	Doors	Elektra	10		G
14	-	Worst That Could Happen	Brooklyn Bridge	Buddah	7		F G L
15	9	I Love How You Love Me	Bobby Vinton	Epic	10		G
16	-	Everyday People	Sly & The Family Stone	Epic	11	(36)	G
17	-	Lo Mucho Que Te Quiero (The More I Love You)	Rene & Rene	White Whale	3		F L
18	7	Stormy	Classics IV	Imperial	9		
19	-	I Started A Joke	Bee Gees	Atco	7		
20	6	Who's Making Love	Johnnie Taylor	Stax	9		F G

February 1969

This Mnth	Prev Mnth	Title	Artist	Label	Wks 20	(UK Pos)	
1	16	Everyday People	Sly & The Family Stone	Epic	11	(36)	G
2	7	Crimson & Clover	Tommy James & The Shondells	Roulette	13		G
3	13	Touch Me	Doors	Elektra	10		G
4	14	Worst That Could Happen	Brooklyn Bridge	Buddah	7		F G L
5	-	Build Me Up Buttercup	Foundations	Uni	10	(2)	L
6	-	Can I Change My Mind	Tyrone Davis	Dakar	7		F G
7	1	I Heard It Through The Grapevine	Marvin Gaye	Tamla	13	(1)	G
8	2	I'm Gonna Make You Love Me	Diana Ross & The Supremes & The Temptations	Motown	11	(3)	G
9	19	I Started A Joke	Bee Gees	Atco	7		
10	-	Hang 'Em High	Booker T. & The M.G.'s	Stax	6		
11	-	You Showed Me	Turtles	White Whale	7		L
12	-	This Magic Moment	Jay & The Americans	UA	8		G
13	-	I'm Livin' In Shame	Diana Ross & The Supremes	Motown	4	(14)	
14	4	Hooked On A Feeling	B.J. Thomas	Scepter	7		G
15	-	If I Can Dream	Elvis Presley	RCA	6	(11)	
16	3	Soulful Strut	Young-Holt Unlimited	Brunswick	9		F G L
17	-	Baby, Baby Don't You Cry	Smokey Robinson/The Miracles	Tamla	6		
18	-	Games People Play	Joe South	Capitol	6	(6)	F
19	-	Proud Mary	Creedence Clearwater Revival	Fantasy	9	(8)	G
20	9	Going Up The Country	Canned Heat	Liberty	7	(19)	L

March 1969

This Mnth	Prev Mnth	Title	Artist	Label	Wks 20	(UK Pos)	
1	19	Proud Mary	Creedence Clearwater Revival	Fantasy	9	(8)	G
2	-	Dizzy	Tommy Roe	ABC	10	(1)	G
3	5	Build Me Up Buttercup	Foundations	Uni	10	(2)	L
4	1	Everyday People	Sly & The Family Stone	Epic	11	(36)	G
5	2	Crimson & Clover	Tommy James & The Shondells	Roulette	13		G
6	-	This Girl's In Love With You	Dionne Warwick	Scepter	7		
7	-	Traces	Classics IV	Imperial	9		G
8	-	Indian Giver	1910 Fruitgum Co.	Buddah	7		G L
9	-	Time Of The Season	Zombies	Date	8		G L
10	-	Run Away Child, Running Wild	Temptations	Gordy	8		
11	12	This Magic Moment	Jay & The Americans	UA	8		G
12	17	Baby, Baby Don't You Cry	Smokey Robinson/The Miracles	Tamla	6		
13	3	Touch Me	Doors	Elektra	10		G
14	18	Games People Play	Joe South	Capitol	6	(6)	F
15	-	My Whole World Ended (The Moment You Left Me)	David Ruffin	Motown	5		F
16	-	I've Gotta Be Me	Sammy Davis Jr.	Reprise	7		
17	-	Galveston	Glen Campbell	Capitol	9	(14)	G
18	-	Aquarius/Let The Sunshine In	Fifth Dimension	Soul City	14	(11)	G
19	11	You Showed Me	Turtles	White Whale	7		L
20	6	Can I Change My Mind	Tyrone Davis	Dakar	7		F G

◆ Elvis Presley recorded in Memphis for the first time since 1955. The session produced such hits as 'Suspicious Minds' and 'In The Ghetto'. Incidentally, Dusty Springfield's Memphis-recorded 'Son-Of-A Preacher Man' became her last transatlantic Top 10 solo entry.

◆ The Doors' leader Jim Morrison was arrested in Miami for lewd and lascivious behaviour in public and for indecent exposure and public profanity.

◆ Motown Records were riding high again. Their hits included the transatlantic toppers, 'I Heard it Through The Grapevine' by Marvin Gaye (his first British hit, which returned to the Top 10 in 1986) and **TCB,** the second joint album by The Supremes and The Temptations.

UK 1969
APR-JUNE

◆ Headliners at the first Country Music Festival in Britain included George Jones, Tammy Wynette, Conway Twitty and Loretta Lynn. Meanwhile, fellow Nashville superstar Johnny Cash appeared on a TV special with Bob Dylan, whose **Nashville Skyline** album was flying high.

◆ Several re-issued American soul singles charted. Among the acts benefiting were Motown's Isley Brothers, Jr. Walker and The Temptations. The latter, incidentally, appeared at the White House alongside The Turtles.

◆ Blind Faith's debut show in London's Hyde Park was watched by a crowd of 150,000.

◆ Meanwhile, the first successful rock opera *Tommy* by The Who simultaneously entered the UK and US album charts.

April 1969

This Mnth	Prev Mnth	Title	Artist	Label	Wks 20	(US Pos)	
1	3	I Heard It Through The Grapevine	Marvin Gaye	Tamla Motown	10	(1)	
2	-	Israelites	Desmond Dekker & The Aces	Pyramid	8	(9)	
3	6	Gentle On My Mind	Dean Martin	Reprise	12		L
4	-	Boom Bang-A-Bang	Lulu	Columbia	7		
5	-	Goodbye	Mary Hopkin	Apple	9	(13)	
6	13	Sorry Suzanne	Hollies	Parlophone	7	(56)	
7	-	In The Bad Bad Old Days	Foundations	Pye	7	(51)	L
8	-	Pinball Wizard	Who	Track	8	(19)	
9	18	Games People Play	Joe South	Capitol	8	(12)	F L
10	-	Windmills Of Your Mind	Noel Harrison	Reprise	9		F L
11	8	Monsieur Dupont	Sandie Shaw	Pye	8		L
12	-	I Can Hear Music	Beach Boys	Capitol	7	(24)	
13	2	Surround Yourself With Sorrow	Cilla Black	Parlophone	9		
14	1	Where Do You Go To My Lovely	Peter Sarstedt	UA	10	(70)	F
15	-	Get Back	Beatles with Billy Preston	Apple	10	(1)	
16	-	Come Back And Shake Me	Clodagh Rodgers	RCA	8		F
17	-	Harlem Shuffle	Bob & Earl	Island	7	(44)	F L
18	-	Cupid	Johnny Nash	Major Minor	6	(39)	
19	-	Get Ready	Temptations	Tamla Motown	5	(29)	
20	10	First Of May	Bee Gees	Polydor	6	(37)	

May 1969

This Mnth	Prev Mnth	Title	Artist	Label	Wks 20	(US Pos)	
1	15	Get Back	Beatles with Billy Preston	Apple	10	(1)	
2	-	Man Of The World	Fleetwood Mac	Immediate	9		
3	-	My Sentimental Friend	Herman's Hermits	Columbia	7		
4	5	Goodbye	Mary Hopkin	Apple	9	(13)	
5	16	Come Back And Shake Me	Clodagh Rodgers	RCA	8		F
6	-	My Way	Frank Sinatra	Reprise	9	(27)	
7	-	Behind A Painted Smile	Isley Brothers	Tamla Motown	7		
8	8	Pinball Wizard	Who	Track	8	(19)	
9	2	Israelites	Desmond Dekker & The Aces	Pyramid	8	(9)	
10	-	Dizzy	Tommy Roe	Stateside	10	(1)	L
11	-	The Boxer	Simon & Garfunkel	CBS	7	(7)	
12	-	(I'm A) Road Runner	Jr. Walker & The All Stars	Tamla Motown	6	(20)	F
13	17	Harlem Shuffle	Bob & Earl	Island	7	(44)	F L
14	18	Cupid	Johnny Nash	Major Minor	6	(39)	
15	-	Ragamuffin Man	Manfred Mann	Fontana	6		
16	3	Gentle On My Mind	Dean Martin	Reprise	12		L
17	-	Love Me Tonight	Tom Jones	Decca	6	(13)	
18	10	Windmills Of Your Mind	Noel Harrison	Reprise	9		F L
19	-	Aquarius/Let The Sunshine In (Medley)	Fifth Dimension	Liberty	4	(1)	F
20	-	I'm Living In Shame	Diana Ross & The Supremes	Tamla Motown	3	(10)	

June 1969

This Mnth	Prev Mnth	Title	Artist	Label	Wks 20	(US Pos)	
1	-	Ballad Of John And Yoko	Beatles	Apple	8	(8)	
2	10	Dizzy	Tommy Roe	Stateside	10	(1)	L
3	-	Oh Happy Day	Edwin Hawkins Singers	Buddah	8	(4)	F L
4	-	Time Is Tight	Booker T. & The M.G.'s	Stax	10	(6)	F
5	1	Get Back	Beatles with Nilly Preston	Apple	10	(1)	
6	6	My Way	Frank Sinatra	Reprise	9	(27)	
7	-	Living In The Past	Jethro Tull	Island	6	(11)	F
8	-	The Tracks Of My Tears	Smokey Robinson & The Miracles	Tamla Motown	6		F
9	2	Man Of The World	Fleetwood Mac	Immediate	9		
10	11	The Boxer	Simon & Garfunkel	CBS	7	(7)	
11	-	(Your Love Keeps Lifting Me) Higher And Higher	Jackie Wilson	MCA	6	(6)	
12	-	Big Ship	Cliff Richard	Columbia	5		
13	-	In The Ghetto	Elvis Presley	RCA	11	(3)	
14	15	Ragamuffin Man	Manfred Mann	Fontana	6		
15	17	Love Me Tonight	Tom Jones	Decca	6	(13)	
16	-	Something In The Air	Thunderclap Newman	Track	8	(37)	F L
17	3	My Sentimental Friend	Herman's Hermits	Columbia	7		
18	-	I'd Rather Go Blind	Chicken Shack	Blue Horizon	5		F L
19	-	Galveston	Glen Campbell	Ember	5	(4)	
20	7	Behind A Painted Smile	Isley Brothers	Tamla Motown	7		

US 1969 APR–JUNE

April 1969

This Mnth	Prev Mnth	Title	Artist	Label	Wks 20	(UK Pos)	
1	18	Aquarius/Let The Sunshine In	Fifth Dimension	Soul City	14	(11)	G
2	-	You've Made Me So Very Happy	Blood Sweat & Tears	Columbia	8	(35)	F G
3	2	Dizzy	Tommy Roe	ABC	10	(1)	G
4	17	Galveston	Glen Campbell	Capitol	9	(14)	G
5	-	Only The Strong Survive	Jerry Butler	Mercury	8		G
6	-	It's Your Thing	Isley Brothers	T-Neck	10	(30)	G
7	9	Time Of The Season	Zombies	Date	8		G L
8	-	Hair	Cowsills	MGM	10		G L
9	-	Twenty Five Miles	Edwin Starr	Gordy	6	(36)	F
10	10	Run Away Child, Running Wild	Temptations	Gordy	8		
11	-	Rock Me	Steppenwolf	Dunhill	6		L
12	7	Traces	Classics IV	Imperial	9		G
13	-	Sweet Cherry Wine	Tommy James & The Shondells	Roulette	6		
14	1	Proud Mary	Creedence Clearwater Revival	Fantasy	9	(8)	G
15	-	Do Your Thing	Watts 103rd Street Band	Warner	4		F
16	-	Don't Give In To Him	Gary Puckett & The Union Gap	Columbia	4		
17	8	Indian Giver	1910 Fruitgum Co.	Buddah	7		G L
18	-	Gimme Gimme Good Lovin'	Crazy Elephant	Bell	5	(12)	F L
19	-	Time Is Tight	Booker T. & The M.G.'s	Stax	6	(4)	L
20	-	Hot Smoke & Sasafrass	Bubble Puppy	International	3		F L

May 1969

This Mnth	Prev Mnth	Title	Artist	Label	Wks 20	(UK Pos)	
1	1	Aquarius/Let The Sunshine In	Fifth Dimension	Soul City	14	(11)	G
2	8	Hair	Cowsills	MGM	10		G L
3	6	It's Your Thing	Isley Brothers	T-Neck	10	(30)	G
4	-	Get Back	Beatles with Billy Preston	Apple	11	(1)	G
5	-	Love (Can Make You Happy)	Mercy	Sundi	9		F G L
6	-	The Boxer	Simon & Garfunkel	Columbia	8	(6)	
7	-	Hawaii Five-O	Ventures	Liberty	7		L
8	-	Atlantis	Donovan	Epic	8	(23)	L
9	-	These Eyes	Guess Who	RCA	9		F G
10	19	Time Is Tight	Booker T. & The M.G.'s	Stax	6	(4)	L
11	-	Oh Happy Day	Edwin Hawkins Singers	Pavilion	7	(2)	F G
12	2	You've Made Me So Very Happy	Blood Sweat & Tears	Columbia	8	(35)	F G
13	-	Gitarzan	Ray Stevens	Monument	8		G
14	13	Sweet Cherry Wine	Tommy James & The Shondells	Roulette	6		
15	5	Only The Strong Survive	Jerry Butler	Mercury	8		G
16	-	The Chokin' Kind	Joe Simon	Sound Stage 7	5		F G
17	-	Grazin' In The Grass	Friends Of Distinction	RCA	8		F G
18	18	Gimme Gimme Good Lovin'	Crazy Elephant	Bell	5	(12)	F L
19	-	Goodbye	Mary Hopkin	Apple	4	(2)	L
20	-	In The Ghetto	Elvis Presley	RCA	9	(2)	G

June 1969

This Mnth	Prev Mnth	Title	Artist	Label	Wks 20	(UK Pos)	
1	4	Get Back	Beatles with Billy Preston	Apple	11	(1)	G
2	-	Love Theme From Romeo & Juliet	Henry Mancini & His Orchestra	RCA	11		G
3	-	Bad Moon Rising	Creedence Clearwater Revival	Fantasy	10	(1)	G
4	20	In The Ghetto	Elvis Presley	RCA	9	(2)	G
5	5	Love (Can Make You Happy)	Mercy	Sundi	9		F G L
6	17	Grazin' In The Grass	Friends Of Distinction	RCA	8		F G
7	-	Too Busy Thinking About My Baby	Marvin Gaye	Tamla	9	(5)	
8	-	One	Three Dog Night	Dunhill	9		F G
9	11	Oh Happy Day	Edwin Hawkins Singers	Pavilion	7	(2)	F G
10	9	These Eyes	Guess Who	RCA	9		F G
11	1	Aquarius/Let The Sunshine In	Fifth Dimension	Soul City	14	(11)	G
12	-	Good Morning Starshine	Oliver	Jubilee	8	(6)	F
13	-	Spinning Wheel	Blood Sweat & Tears	Columbia	10		G
14	-	The Israelites	Desmond Dekker & The Aces	Uni	5	(1)	F L
15	13	Gitarzan	Ray Stevens	Monument	8		G
16	8	Atlantis	Donovan	Epic	8	(23)	L
17	-	More Today Than Yesterday	Spiral Staircase	Columbia	4		F L
18	8	Ballad Of John And Yoko	Beatles	Apple	6	(1)	G
19	-	Black Pearl	Sonny Charles & The Checkmates, Ltd.	A&M	7		F L
20	-	Love Me Tonight	Tom Jones	Parrot	6	(9)	

◆ The Beach Boys sued Capitol Records for over $2 million and announced the formation of their own Brother label.

▲ Headliners at The Newport 69 festival included Jimi Hendrix, Creedence Clearwater Revival, The Rascals, The Byrds, Joe Cocker (above), Ike & Tina Turner, Jethro Tull and Columbia's $300,000 signing Johnny Winter.

◆ The first rock musical, *Hair*, not only topped the album chart for three months, but songs from it, 'Aquarius'/'Let The Sunshine In' and 'Hair' held the top two places on the singles chart in May.

UK 1969 JULY–SEPT

▲ The Rolling Stones (above) attracted 250,000 fans to Hyde Park – during the show they paid tribute to ex-member Brian Jones who had drowned just days before. Other British shows included the Isle of Wight festival headlined by Bob Dylan, and The National Jazz & Blues Festival featuring The Who, Yes and King Crimson.

◆ The chart position of 'Ballad Of John & Yoko' by The Beatles suffered because many stations banned it for mentioning "Christ" and "Crucifixion". Other Beatle news included Paul's supposed death, and the sale of their publishing catalogue to ATV for £1 ($2.5) million.

July 1969

This Mnth	Prev Mnth	Title	Artist	Label	Wks 20	(US Pos)	
1	16	Something In The Air	Thunderclap Newman	Track	8	(37)	F L
2	13	In The Ghetto	Elvis Presley	RCA	11	(3)	
3	-	Hello Susie	Amen Corner	Immediate	6		L
4	-	Way Of Life	Family Dogg	Bell	8		F L
5	1	Ballad Of John And Yoko	Beatles	Apple	8	(8)	
6	-	Break Away	Beach Boys	Capitol	6	(63)	
7	-	Honky Tonk Women	Rolling Stones	Decca	12	(1)	
8	-	Proud Mary	Creedence Clearwater Revival	Liberty	6	(2)	F
9	7	Living In The Past	Jethro Tull	Island	6	(11)	F
10	-	Give Peace A Chance	Plastic Ono Band	Apple	7	(14)	F
11	-	It Mek	Desmond Dekker & The Aces	Pyramid	5		
12	4	Time Is Tight	Booker T. & The M.G.'s	Stax	10	(6)	F
13	-	Lights Of Cincinatti	Scott Walker	Philips	5		L
14	-	Baby Make It Soon	Marmalade	CBS	7		
15	3	Oh Happy Day	Edwin Hawkins Singers	Buddah	8	(4)	F L
16	-	Frozen Orange Juice	Peter Sarstedt	UA	4		L
17	-	Gimme Gimme Good Lovin'	Crazy Elephant	Major Minor	5	(12)	F L
18	-	Saved By The Bell	Robin Gibb	Polydor	10		F L
19	12	Big Ship	Cliff Richard	Columbia	5		
20	-	That's The Way God Planned It	Billy Preston	Apple	6	(62)	F

August 1969

This Mnth	Prev Mnth	Title	Artist	Label	Wks 20	(US Pos)	
1	7	Honky Tonk Women	Rolling Stones	Decca	12	(1)	
2	18	Saved By The Bell	Robin Gibb	Polydor	10		F L
3	-	Make Me An Island	Joe Dolan	Pye	10		F
4	10	Give Peace A Chance	Plastic Ono Band	Apple	7	(14)	F
5	-	My Cherie Amour	Stevie Wonder	Tamla Motown	9	(4)	
6	-	Goodnight Midnight	Clodagh Rodgers	RCA	8		
7	-	Conversations	Cilla Black	Parlophone	7		
8	2	In The Ghetto	Elvis Presley	RCA	11	(3)	
9	-	In The Year 2525 (Exordium & Terminus)	Zager & Evans	RCA	9	(1)	F L
10	-	Bringing On Back The Good Times	Love Affair	CBS	6		L
11	-	Early In The Morning	Vanity Fare	Page One	6	(12)	
12	-	Too Busy Thinking About My Baby	Marvin Gaye	Tamla Motown	8	(4)	
13	-	Wet Dream	Max Romeo	Unity	6		F L
14	14	Baby Make It Soon	Marmalade	CBS	7		
15	1	Something In The Air	Thunderclap Newman	Track	8	(37)	F L
16	20	That's The Way God Planned It	Billy Preston	Apple	6	(62)	F
17	11	It Mek	Desmond Dekker & The Aces	Pyramid	5		
18	-	Viva Bobbie Joe	Equals	President	8		
19	-	Goo Goo Barabajagal (Love Is Hot)	Donovan & Jeff Beck Group	Pye	4	(36)	L
20	-	Curly	Move	Regal Zonophone	7		

September 1969

This Mnth	Prev Mnth	Title	Artist	Label	Wks 20	(US Pos)	
1	-	Bad Moon Rising	Creedence Clearwater Revival	Liberty	11	(2)	
2	9	In The Year 2525 (Exordium & Terminus)	Zager & Evans	RCA	9	(1)	F L
3	-	Don't Forget To Remember	Bee Gees	Polydor	11	(73)	
4	-	Je T'Aime...Moi Non Plus	Jane Birkin & Serge Gainsbourg	Fontana/ Major Minor	13	(58)	F L
5	-	Natural Born Bugie	Humble Pie	Immediate	7		F L
6	12	Too Busy Thinking About My Baby	Marvin Gaye	Tamla Motown	8	(4)	
7	18	Viva Bobbie Joe	Equals	President	8		
8	5	My Cherie Amour	Stevie Wonder	Tamla Motown	9	(4)	
9	1	Honky Tonk Women	Rolling Stones	Decca	12	(1)	
10	-	Good Morning Starshine	Oliver	CBS	10	(3)	F L
11	-	I'll Never Fall In Love Again	Bobbie Gentry	Capitol	9		
12	2	Saved By The Bell	Robin Gibb	Polydor	10		F L
13	3	Make Me An Island	Joe Dolan	Pye	10		F
14	-	A Boy Named Sue	Johnny Cash	CBS	9	(2)	F
15	20	Curly	Move	Regal Zonophone	7		
16	11	Early In The Morning	Vanity Fare	Page One	6	(12)	
17	-	It's Getting Better	Mama Cass	Stateside	6	(30)	L
18	-	Throw Down A Line	Cliff Richard	Columbia	6		
19	-	I'm A Better Man	Engelbert Humperdinck	Decca	4	(38)	
20	-	Cloud Nine	Temptations	Tamla Motown	3	(6)	

US 1969 JULY-SEPT

July 1969

This Mnth	Prev Mnth	Title	Artist	Label	Wks 20	(UK Pos)	
1	13	Spinning Wheel	Blood Sweat & Tears	Columbia	10		G
2	-	In The Year 2525 (Exordium & Terminus)	Zager & Evans	RCA	10	(1)	F G L
3	-	Crystal Blue Persuasion	Tommy James & The Shondells	Roulette	11		G
4	8	One	Three Dog Night	Dunhill	9		F G
5	2	Love Theme From Romeo & Juliet	Henry Mancini & His Orchestra	RCA	11		G
6	12	Good Morning Starshine	Oliver	Jubilee	8	(6)	F
7	-	What Does It Take To Win Your Love	Jr. Walker & The All Stars	Soul	9	(13)	
8	18	Ballad Of John And Yoko	Beatles	Apple	6	(1)	G
9	3	Bad Moon Rising	Creedence Clearwater Revival	Fantasy	10	(1)	G
10	-	Color Him Father	Winstons	Metromedia	7		F G L
11	-	My Cherie Amour	Stevie Wonder	Tamla	8	(4)	G
12	1	Get Back	Beatles with Billy Preston	Apple	11	(1)	G
13	-	Mother Popcorn (You Got To Have A Mother For Me)	James Brown	King	8		
14	-	Baby I Love You	Andy Kim	Steed	8		F G
15	20	Love Me Tonight	Tom Jones	Parrot	6	(9)	
16	7	Too Busy Thinking About My Baby	Marvin Gaye	Tamla	9	(5)	
17	4	In The Ghetto	Elvis Presley	RCA	9	(2)	G
18	19	Black Pearl	Sonny Charles/Checkmates Ltd.	A&M	7		F L
19	-	Sweet Caroline	Neil Diamond	Uni	9	(8)	G
20	-	Ruby, Don't Take Your Love To Town	Kenny Rogers & First Edition	Reprise	6	(2)	

August 1969

This Mnth	Prev Mnth	Title	Artist	Label	Wks 20	(UK Pos)	
1	-	Honky Tonk Women	Rolling Stones	London	12	(1)	G
2	2	In The Year 2525 (Exordium &...)	Zager & Evans	RCA	10	(1)	F G L
3	3	Crystal Blue Persuasion	Tommy James & The Shondells	Roulette	11		G
4	19	Sweet Caroline	Neil Diamond	Uni	9	(8)	G
5	-	A Boy Named Sue	Johnny Cash	Columbia	10	(4)	G
6	-	Put A Little Love In Your Heart	Jackie DeShannon	Imperial	7		G L
7	20	Ruby, Don't Take Your Love...	Kenny Rogers & First Edition	Reprise	6	(2)	
8	7	What Does It Take To Win Your Love	Jr. Walker & The All Stars	Soul	9	(13)	
9	11	My Cherie Amour	Stevie Wonder	Tamla	8	(4)	G
10	14	Baby I Love You	Andy Kim	Steed	8		F G
11	-	Polk Salad Annie	Tony Joe White	Monument	6		F L
12	1	Spinning Wheel	Blood Sweat & Tears	Columbia	10		G
13	-	Get Together	Youngbloods	RCA	9		F G L
14	-	Green River	Creedence Clearwater Revival	Fantasy	10	(19)	G
15	-	Laughing	Guess Who	RCA	5		G
16	-	Lay Lady Lay	Bob Dylan	Columbia	8	(5)	
17	-	Sugar Sugar	Archies	Calendar	15	(1)	F G
18	13	Mother Popcorn (You GTo Have A...)	James Brown	King	8		
19	-	Quentin's Theme (from TV Series 'Dark Shadows')	Charles Randolph Grean Sounde	Ranwood	5		F L
20	10	Color Him Father	Winstons	Metromedia	7		F G L

September 1969

This Mnth	Prev Mnth	Title	Artist	Label	Wks 20	(UK Pos)	
1	17	Sugar Sugar	Archies	Calendar	15	(1)	F G
2	1	Honky Tonk Women	Rolling Stones	London	12	(1)	G
3	14	Green River	Creedence Clearwater Revival	Fantasy	10	(19)	G
4	5	A Boy Named Sue	Johnny Cash	Columbia	10	(4)	G
5	-	Easy To Be Hard	Three Dog Night	Dunhill	10		
6	13	Get Together	Youngbloods	RCA	9		F G L
7	-	I'll Never Fall In Love Again	Tom Jones	Parrot	11	(2)	G
8	-	I Can't Get Next To You	Temptations	Gordy	13	(13)	
9	16	Lay Lady Lay	Bob Dylan	Columbia	8	(5)	
10	-	Little Woman	Bobby Sherman	Metromedia	9		F G
11	-	Oh What A Nite	Dells	Cadet	6		L
12	-	Jean	Oliver	Crewe	9		G L
13	6	Put A Little Love In Your Heart	Jackie DeShannon	Imperial	7		G L
14	-	Hurt So Bad	Lettermen	Capitol	6		L
15	4	Sweet Caroline	Neil Diamond	Uni	9	(8)	G
16	-	This Girl Is A Woman Now	Gary Puckett & The Union Gap	Columbia	7		L
17	-	Share Your Love With Me	Aretha Franklin	Atlantic	3		
18	-	I'd Wait A Million Years	Grass Roots	Dunhill	4		
19	-	Hot Fun In The Summertime	Sly & The Family Stone	Epic	8		
20	15	Laughing	Guess Who	RCA	5		G

▲ Important pop festivals took place in Atlanta, Atlantic City, Denver, New Orleans, Newport, Seattle, Texas and Toronto. However, they were all overshadowed by the Woodstock Festival which attracted a crowd of over 400,000 to see acts like Jefferson Airplane, Jimi Hendrix (above), The Who, Creedence Clearwater Revival, Blood, Sweat and Tears and Sly & The Family Stone.

◆ Elvis netted $1 million for his first live shows since 1961 (International Hotel, Las Vegas). Also earning big bucks were album chart toppers Blind Faith, who started their sell-out stadium tour at Madison Square Garden.

UK 1969 OCT-DEC

As the year closed, Elton John first collaborated with songwriter Bernie Taupin, Rod Stewart joined The Faces, Jimi Hendrix unveiled his Band Of Gypsies and Isaac Hayes' **Hot Buttered Soul** turned gold.

◆ The Rolling Stones toured the US for the first time in three years. Their record breaking tour being marred by the death of a fan during their set at Altamont. The fateful festival was attended by 300,000 people and also starred Jefferson Airplane, Santana and Grammy winning Crosby, Stills, Nash & Young. Altamont heralded the beginning of the end of the rock festival phenomenon.

◆ The first major American rock'n'roll revival show took place in New York, and starred Bill Haley, Chuck Berry, The Platters, The Coasters and The Shirelles.

October 1969

This Mnth	Prev Mnth	Title	Artist	Label	Wks 20	(US Pos)	
1	4	Je T'Aime...Moi Non Plus	Jane Birkin & Serge Gainsbourg	Fontana/ Major Minor	13	(58)	F L
2	11	I'll Never Fall In Love Again	Bobbie Gentry	Capitol	9		
3	14	A Boy Named Sue	Johnny Cash	CBS	9	(2)	F
4	-	Lay Lady Lay	Bob Dylan	CBS	7	(7)	
5	1	Bad Moon Rising	Creedence Clearwater Revival	Liberty	11	(2)	
6	-	I'm Gonna Make You Mine	Lou Christie	Buddah	8	(10)	L
7	10	Good Morning Starshine	Oliver	CBS	10	(3)	F L
8	-	Nobody's Child	Karen Young	Major Minor	12		F L
9	3	Don't Forget To Remember	Bee Gees	Polydor	11	(73)	
10	18	Throw Down A Line	Cliff Richard	Columbia	6		
11	17	It's Getting Better	Mama Cass	Stateside	6	(30)	L
12	-	He Ain't Heavy, He's My Brother	Hollies	Parlophone	8	(7)	
13	-	Space Oddity	David Bowie	Philips	8	(15)	F
14	-	Oh Well	Fleetwood Mac	Reprise	10	(55)	
15	-	Sugar Sugar	Archies	RCA	17	(1)	F L
16	-	Hare Krishna	Radha Krishna Temple	Apple	5		F L
17	2	In The Year 2525 (Exordium & Terminus)	Zager & Evans	RCA	9	(1)	F L
18	5	Natural Born Bugie	Humble Pie	Immediate	7		F L
19	-	Do What You Gotta Do	Four Tops	Tamla Motown	1		
20	7	Viva Bobbie Joe	Equals	President	8		

November 1969

This Mnth	Prev Mnth	Title	Artist	Label	Wks 20	(US Pos)	
1	15	Sugar Sugar	Archies	RCA	17	(1)	F L
2	14	Oh Well	Fleetwood Mac	Reprise	10	(55)	
3	-	The Return Of Django	Upsetters	Upsetter	8		F L
4	-	(Call Me) Number One	Tremeloes	CBS	11		
5	12	He Ain't Heavy, He's My Brother	Hollies	Parlophone	8	(7)	
6	8	Nobody's Child	Karen Young	Major Minor	12		F L
7	-	Wonderful World Beautiful People	Jimmy Cliff	Trojan	9	(25)	F
8	6	I'm Gonna Make You Mine	Lou Christie	Buddah	8	(10)	L
9	-	Something/Come Together	Beatles	Apple	8	(1)	
10	-	Love's Been Good To Me	Frank Sinatra	Reprise	7	(75)	
11	13	Space Oddity	David Bowie	Philips	8	(15)	F
12	-	Delta Lady	Joe Cocker	Regal Zonophone	5	(69)	
13	-	Sweet Dream	Jethro Tull	Chrysalis	6		
14	-	Ruby, Don't Take Your Love To Town	Kenny Rogers & First Edition	Reprise	16	(6)	F
15	-	Yester-Me, Yester-You, Yesterday	Stevie Wonder	Tamla Motown	9	(7)	
16	-	What Does It Take To Win Your Love	Jr. Walker & The All Stars	Tamla Motown	5	(4)	
17	3	A Boy Named Sue	Johnny Cash	CBS	9	(2)	F
18	-	Cold Turkey	Plastic Ono Band	Apple	5	(30)	
19	1	Je T'Aime...Moi Non Plus	Jane Birkin & Serge Gainsbourg	Fontana/ Major Minor	13	(58)	F L
20	-	Liquidator	Harry J. & The All Stars	Trojan	13		F L

December 1969

This Mnth	Prev Mnth	Title	Artist	Label	Wks 20	(US Pos)	
1	1	Sugar Sugar	Archies	RCA	17	(1)	F L
2	14	Ruby, Don't Take Your Love To...	Kenny Rogers & First Edition	Reprise	16	(6)	F
3	-	Two Little Boys	Rolf Harris	Columbia	16		
4	15	Yester-Me, Yester-You, Yesterday	Stevie Wonder	Tamla Motown	9	(7)	
5	-	Melting Pot	Blue Mink	Philips	10		F
6	4	(Call Me) Number One	Tremeloes	CBS	11		
7	-	Suspicious Minds	Elvis Presley	RCA	11	(1)	
8	-	Winter World Of Love	Engelbert Humperdinck	Decca	9	(16)	
9	20	Liquidator	Harry J. & The All Stars	Trojan	13		F L
10	-	All I Have To Do Is Dream	Bobbie Gentry & Glen Campbell	Capitol	10	(27)	L
11	-	Onion Song	Marvin Gaye & Tammi Terrell	Tamla Motown	8	(50)	
12	9	Something/Come Together	Beatles	Apple	8	(1)	
13	7	Wonderful World Beautiful People	Jimmy Cliff	Trojan	9	(25)	F
14	-	Tracy	Cuff Links	MCA	9	(9)	F
15	-	Love Is All	Malcolm Roberts	Major Minor	6		L
16	-	Durham Town (The Leavin')	Roger Whittaker	Columbia	9		F
17	2	Oh Well	Fleetwood Mac	Reprise	10	(55)	
18	-	Without Love	Tom Jones	Decca	6	(5)	
19	13	Sweet Dream	Jethro Tull	Chrysalis	6		
20	6	Nobody's Child	Karen Young	Major Minor	12		F L

October 1969

This Mnth	Prev Mnth	Title	Artist	Label	Wks 20	(UK Pos)	
1	1	Sugar Sugar	Archies	Calendar	15	(1)	F G
2	8	I Can't Get Next To You	Temptations	Gordy	13	(13)	G
3	12	Jean	Oliver	Crewe	9		G L
4	10	Little Woman	Bobby Sherman	Metromedia	9		F G
5	19	Hot Fun In The Summertime	Sly & The Family Stone	Epic	8		
6	-	Suspicious Minds	Elvis Presley	RCA	11	(2)	G
7	5	Easy To Be Hard	Three Dog Night	Dunhill	10		
8	-	Everybody's Talkin'	Nilsson	RCA	6	(23)	F
9	-	That's The Way Love Is	Marvin Gaye	Tamla	6		
10	2	Honky Tonk Women	Rolling Stones	London	12	(1)	G
11	16	This Girl Is A Woman Now	Gary Puckett & The Union Gap	Columbia	7		L
12	-	I'm Gonna Make You Mine	Lou Christie	Buddah	5	(2)	L
13	3	Green River	Creedence Clearwater Revival	Fantasy	10	(19)	G
14	-	Wedding Bell Blues	Fifth Dimension	Soul City	10	(16)	G
15	-	Baby It's You	Smith	Dunhill	9		F L
16	-	Tracy	Cuff Links	Decca	6	(4)	F L
17	11	Oh What A Nite	Dells	Cadet	6		L
18	7	I'll Never Fall In Love Again	Tom Jones	Parrot	11	(2)	G
19	6	Get Together	Youngbloods	RCA	9		F G L
20	-	Come Together/Something	Beatles	Apple	13	(4)	G

November 1969

This Mnth	Prev Mnth	Title	Artist	Label	Wks 20	(UK Pos)	
1	14	Wedding Bell Blues	Fifth Dimension	Soul City	10	(16)	G
2	20	Come Together/Something	Beatles	Apple	13	(4)	G
3	6	Suspicious Minds	Elvis Presley	RCA	11	(2)	G
4	-	And When I Die	Blood Sweat & Tears	Columbia	10		G
5	15	Baby It's You	Smith	Dunhill	9		F L
6	2	I Can't Get Next To You	Temptations	Gordy	13	(13)	G
7	-	Smile A Little Smile For Me	Flying Machine	Janus	8		F G L
8	1	Sugar Sugar	Archies	Calendar	15	(1)	F G
9	-	Take A Letter Maria	R.B. Greaves	Atco	10		F G L
10	-	Na Na Hey Hey Kiss Him Goodbye	Steam	Fontana	11	(9)	F G L
11	5	Hot Fun In The Summertime	Sly & The Family Stone	Epic	8		
12	16	Tracy	Cuff Links	Decca	6	(4)	F L
13	-	Yester-Me, Yester-You, Yesterday	Stevie Wonder	Tamla	6	(2)	
14	-	Is That All There Is	Peggy Lee	Capitol	5		L
15	-	Down On The Corner/Fortunate Son	Creedence Clearwater Revival	Fantasy	10	(31)	G
16	-	Leaving On A Jet Plane	Peter, Paul & Mary	Warner	12	(2)	G L
17	4	Little Woman	Bobby Sherman	Metromedia	9		F G
18	-	Going In Circles	Friends Of Distinction	RCA	6		G
19	-	Baby, I'm For Real	Originals	Soul	6		F
20	3	Jean	Oliver	Crewe	9		G L

December 1969

This Mnth	Prev Mnth	Title	Artist	Label	Wks 20	(UK Pos)	
1	16	Leaving On A Jet Plane	Peter, Paul & Mary	Warner	12	(2)	G L
2	10	Na Na Hey Hey Kiss Him Goodbye	Steam	Fontana	11	(9)	F G L
3	-	Someday We'll Be Together	Diana Ross & The Supremes	Motown	13	(13)	G
4	15	Down On The Corner/Fortunate Son	Creedence Clearwater Revival	Fantasy	10	(31)	G
5	2	Come Together/Something	Beatles	Apple	13	(4)	G
6	9	Take A Letter Maria	R.B. Greaves	Atco	10		F G L
7	-	Raindrops Keep Fallin' On My Head	B.J. Thomas	Scepter	15	(38)	G
8	13	Yester-Me, Yester-You, Yesterday	Stevie Wonder	Tamla	6	(2)	
9	4	And When I Die	Blood Sweat & Tears	Columbia	10		G
10	-	Holly Holy	Neil Diamond	Uni	9		G
11	-	Eli's Coming	Three Dog Night	Dunhill	10		
12	-	Backfield In Motion	Mel & Tim	Bamboo	9		F G
13	1	Wedding Bell Blues	Fifth Dimension	Soul City	10	(16)	G
14	-	Whole Lotta Love	Led Zeppelin	Atlantic	9		F G
15	-	I Want You Back	Jackson Five	Motown	13	(2)	F G
16	-	Midnight Cowboy	Ferrante & Teicher	UA	7		L
17	7	Smile A Little Smile For Me	Flying Machine	Janus	8		F G L
18	-	Cherry Hill Park	Billy Joe Royal	Columbia	5		L
19	-	La La La (If I Had You)	Bobby Sherman	Metromedia	6		G
20	19	Baby, I'm For Real	Originals	Soul	6		F

US 1969
OCT-DEC

◆ Diana Ross' last single with The Supremes, 'Someday We'll be Together', gave the group their twelfth and final No. 1 – only Elvis Presley and The Beatles (who both added to their totals) had collected more.

◆ Tape cassettes accounted for 40% of the $1 billion spent on recorded music in 1969 – another survey showed that 75% of this amount came from the under 30s.

▲ On the album front **Led Zeppelin II** gave the group (above) the first of many transatlantic toppers, and the critically un-acclaimed heavy rockers Grand Funk Railroad debuted with **On Time**.

70s

Sly Stone

Barry Manilow

Olivia Newton-John

Left: David Bowie

Myriad musical styles thrived side-by-side in the 1970s. Sales of albums and tapes increased in leaps and bounds as rock acts spurned the single, preferring instead to concentrate on 'serious' album projects. It left the singles field wide open for the onset of the disco boom.

Rock continued to diversify, and even though the musical tastes of America and Britain were often similar, several rock superstars were little heralded beyond the shores of their homeland. For example America's Bob Seger, Three Dog Night and Grand Funk Railroad and Britain's Slade,

Barry White

147

70s

Mud and Status Quo. It was not only the era when heavy metal came of age, but also when artists like The Jackson Five, The Osmonds, David Cassidy and The Bay City Rollers caused teeny bopper pandemonium on both sides of the Atlantic.

Singer/songwriters became the norm in the 1970s. The number of cover versions which charted were minimal when compared to the first two decades of rock. Musically, it was a far more original decade than the swingin' (and stealin') sixties.

Many record producers such as Gamble and Huff, Giorgio Moroder and Mickie Most were becoming stars in their own right. This was especially true in the disco field, which ruled the singles market in impressive fashion during the late 1970s. In many cases the vocalists were faceless (and indeed interchangeable) performers who simply added their voices to already completed musical backing tracks.

As usual, black American artists played a major role in the era's music, with soul, funk and disco providing the majority of transatlantic hits. Black music had begun to diversify too, providing not only some of the most exciting and innovative sounds of the era, but also some of the best-produced MOR-oriented recordings and, on the down-side, some of the blandest disco tracks.

America and Britain were no longer the only countries supplying global hits. The multi-talented Bee Gees and Olivia Newton-John led an invasion of Australian-bred artists, while Swedish quartet Abba proved that continental Europe could also teach the pop world a thing or two.

Although its presence was not directly felt in America, punk revolutionized music. Elvis Costello may have been the only artist from the period to achieve lasting international success, but the attitude and energy of the time was to influence a legion of British pop stars in the 1980s.

The decade ended with electropop, Euro disco and synth rock making their mark. A new wave of heavy metal artists were also banging their heads on the chart door while rap, which would have a lot to say in the next two decades, was starting to enjoy its first taste of mass acceptance.

Donny and Marie Osmond

Top UK Artists in US 1970-79	
1	Elton John
2	Bee Gees
3	Paul McCartney
4	Olivia Newton-John
5	Rolling Stones
6	Ringo Starr
7	Andy Gibb
8	Rod Stewart
9	Fleetwood Mac
10	Electric Light Orchestra

Top US Artists in UK 1970-79	
1	Elvis Presley
2	Stylistics
3	Donna Summer
4	Jackson Five
5	Diana Ross
6	Donny Osmond
7	Blondie
8	Drifters
9	David Cassidy
10	Carpenters

Elvis Costello

Top Singles Artists in the UK 1970-1979

1	Abba	(Swe)	Epic
2	Rod Stewart	(UK)	Mercury/Warner/Riva
3	Slade	(UK)	Polydor
4	Elvis Presley	(US)	RCA
5	T. Rex	(UK)	Fly/EMI
6	Paul McCartney/Wings	(UK)	Apple/Capitol/Parlophone
7	Showaddywaddy	(UK)	Bell/Arista
8	Elton John	(UK)	DJM/Rocket
9	Gary Glitter	(UK)	Bell/Arista
10	Mud	(UK)	RAK
11	David Bowie	(UK)	RCA/Deram
12	Sweet	(UK)	RCA
13	Bay City Rollers	(UK)	Bell/Arista
14	Electric Light Orchestra	(UK)	Harvest/Jet
15	10cc	(UK)	UK/Mercury
16	Boney M	(WI)	Atlantic/Hansa
17	Stylistics	(US)	Avco/H&L
18	Status Quo	(UK)	Vertigo/Pye
19	Queen	(UK)	EMI
20	Hot Chocolate	(UK)	RAK

Top Singles Artists in the US 1970-1979

1	Elton John	(UK)	Uni/MCA/Rocket
2	Bee Gees	(UK)	Atco/RSO
3	Paul McCartney/Wings	(UK)	Apple/Capitol/Columbia
4	Carpenters	(US)	A&M
5	Stevie Wonder	(US)	Tamla
6	Jackson Five	(US)	Motown/Epic
7	Chicago	(US)	Columbia
8	Donna Summer	(US)	Oasis/Casablanca
9	Three Dog Night	(US)	Dunhill
10	Olivia Newton-John	(UK)	Uni/MCA/RSO
11	Eagles	(US)	Asylum
12	Barry Manilow	(US)	Bell/Arista
13	John Denver	(US)	RCA
14	Barbra Streisand	(US)	Columbia
15	Neil Diamond	(US)	Uni/MCA/Columbia
16	Tony Orlando & Dawn	(US)	Bell/Elektra
17	Helen Reddy	(Aus)	Capitol
18	Commodores	(US)	Motown
19	Diana Ross	(US)	Motown
20	Al Green	(US)	Hi

Al Green

Top UK Singles 1970-79

1	Sailing	Rod Stewart
2	You're The One That I Want	John Travolta & Olivia Newton-John
3	Mull Of Kintyre/Girls' School	Wings
4	Bohemian Rhapsody	Queen
5	Rivers Of Babylon/Brown Girl In The Ring	Boney M
6	In The Summertime	Mungo Jerry
7	The Wonder Of You	Elvis Presley
8	Summer Nights	John Travolta & Olivia Newton-John
9	Save Your Kisses For Me	Brotherhood Of Man
10	Leader Of The Pack	Shangri-Las

Top US Singles 1970-79

1	You Light Up My Life	Debby Boone
2	Night Fever	Bee Gees
3	Le Freak	Chic
4	Shadow Dancing	Andy Gibb
5	Tonight's The Night (Gonna Be Alright)	Rod Stewart
6	My Sharona	Knack
7	I Just Want To Be Your Everything	Andy Gibb
8	Joy To The World	Three Dog Night
9	The First Time Ever I Saw Your Face	Roberta Flack
10	Best Of My Love	Emotions

Abba

UK 1970 JAN-MAR

◆ American Ron Dante was the lead vocalist of transatlantic hit makers The Archies and The Cuff Links, while Englishman Tony Burrows sang in three transatlantic hit acts, Edison Lighthouse, White Plains and Brotherhood Of Man.

◆ Davy Jones quit The Monkees, British teen idol Steve Ellis left Love Affair and Joe Cocker split from the Grease Band before joining the *Mad Dogs And Englishmen* tour.

◆ Simon & Garfunkel topped the transatlantic single and album charts with the multi Grammy winning **Bridge Over Troubled Water**. The album headed the UK charts for a record 41 weeks and remained in the Top 10 for 126 weeks!

◆ The Anglo-American supergroup, Crosby, Stills, Nash & Young made their UK debut at the prestigious Royal Festival Hall.

January 1970

This Mnth	Prev Mnth	Title	Artist	Label	Wks 20	(US Pos)	
1	3	Two Little Boys	Rolf Harris	Columbia	16		
2	2	Ruby, Don't Take Your Love To Town	Kenny Rogers & First Edition	Reprise	16	(6)	F
3	10	All I Have To Do Is Dream	Bobbie Gentry & Glen Campbell	Capitol	10	(27)	L
4	7	Suspicious Minds	Elvis Presley	RCA	11	(1)	
5	14	Tracy	Cuff Links	MCA	9	(9)	F
6	1	Sugar Sugar	Archies	RCA	17	(1)	F L
7	5	Melting Pot	Blue Mink	Philips	10		F
8	-	Good Old Rock 'n' Roll	Dave Clark Five	Columbia	8		
9	-	Reflections Of My Life	Marmalade	Decca	7	(10)	
10	-	Come And Get It	Badfinger	Apple	7	(7)	F
11	4	Yester-Me, Yester-You, Yesterday	Stevie Wonder	Tamla Motown	9	(7)	
12	18	Without Love	Tom Jones	Decca	6	(5)	
13	16	Durham Town (The Leavin')	Roger Whittaker	Columbia	9		F
14	9	Liquidator	Harry J. & The All Stars	Trojan	13		F L
15	-	Love Grows (Where My Rosemary Goes)	Edison Lighthouse	Bell	10	(5)	F L
16	-	Friends	Arrival	Decca	5		F
17	8	Winter World Of Love	Engelbert Humperdinck	Decca	9	(16)	
18	11	Onion Song	Marvin Gaye & Tammi Terrell	Tamla Motown	8	(50)	
19	-	Someday We'll Be Together	Diana Ross & The Supremes	Tamla Motown	5	(1)	
20	-	Leavin' On A Jet Plane	Peter, Paul & Mary	Warner	9	(1)	L

February 1970

This Mnth	Prev Mnth	Title	Artist	Label	Wks 20	(US Pos)	
1	15	Love Grows (Where My Rosemary Goes)	Edison Lighthouse	Bell	10	(5)	F L
2	20	Leavin' On A Jet Plane	Peter, Paul & Mary	Warner	9	(1)	L
3	-	Let's Work Together	Canned Heat	Liberty	9	(26)	L
4	-	The Witch's Promise/Teacher	Jethro Tull	Chrysalis	5		
5	-	Temma Harbour	Mary Hopkin	Apple	6	(39)	
6	1	Two Little Boys	Rolf Harris	Columbia	16		
7	-	I Want You Back	Jackson Five	Tamla Motown	9	(1)	F
8	10	Come And Get It	Badfinger	Apple	7	(7)	F
9	9	Reflections Of My Life	Marmalade	Decca	7	(10)	
10	-	Wand'rin' Star	Lee Marvin	Paramount	11		F L
11	-	Venus	Shocking Blue	Penny Farthing	5	(1)	F L
12	-	I'm A Man	Chicago	CBS	6	(49)	F
13	-	Instant Karma	Lennon, Ono & The Plastic Ono Band	Apple	6	(3)	
14	2	Ruby, Don't Take Your Love To...	Kenny Rogers & First Edition	Reprise	16	(6)	F
15	-	I Can't Get Next To You	Temptations	Tamla Motown	5	(1)	
16	16	Friends	Arrival	Decca	5		F
17	-	My Baby Loves Lovin'	White Plains	Deram	5	(13)	F
18	-	Years May Come, Years May Go	Herman's Hermits	Columbia	7		
19	3	All I Have To Do Is Dream	Bobbie Gentry & Glen Campbell	Capitol	10	(27)	L
20	-	United We Stand	Brotherhood Of Man	Deram	6	(13)	F

March 1970

This Mnth	Prev Mnth	Title	Artist	Label	Wks 20	(US Pos)	
1	10	Wand'rin' Star	Lee Marvin	Paramount	11		F L
2	-	Bridge Over Troubled Water	Simon & Garfunkel	CBS	13	(1)	L
3	7	I Want You Back	Jackson Five	Tamla Motown	9	(1)	F
4	-	Let It Be	Beatles	Apple	6	(1)	
5	3	Let's Work Together	Canned Heat	Liberty	9	(26)	L
6	13	Instant Karma	Lennon/Ono/Plastic Ono Band	Apple	6	(3)	
7	-	That Same Old Feeling	Pickettywitch	Pye	8	(67)	F
8	18	Years May Come, Years May Go	Herman's Hermits	Columbia	7		
9	1	Love Grows (Where My Rosemary...)	Edison Lighthouse	Bell	10	(5)	F L
10	-	Na Na Hey Hey Kiss Him Goodbye	Steam	Fontana	6	(1)	F L
11	-	Don't Cry Daddy	Elvis Presley	RCA	7	(6)	
12	-	Can't Help Falling In Love	Andy Williams	CBS	11	(88)	
13	-	Raindrops Keep Fallin' On My Head	Sacha Distel	Warner	5		F L
14	20	United We Stand	Brotherhood Of Man	Deram	6	(13)	F
15	-	Something's Burning	Kenny Rogers & First Edition	Reprise	8	(11)	
16	-	Everybody Get Together	Dave Clark Five	Columbia	5		L
17	2	Leavin' On A Jet Plane	Peter, Paul & Mary	Warner	9	(1)	L
18	17	My Baby Loves Lovin'	White Plains	Deram	5	(13)	F
19	-	Young Gifted And Black	Bob & Marcia	Harry J.	8		F
20	-	Knock Knock Who's There	Mary Hopkin	Apple	7	(92)	

January 1970

This Mnth	Prev Mnth	Title	Artist	Label	Wks 20	(UK Pos)	
1	7	Raindrops Keep Fallin' On My Head	B.J. Thomas	Scepter	15	(38)	G
2	15	I Want You Back	Jackson Five	Motown	13	(2)	F G
3	-	Venus	Shocking Blue	Colossus	11	(8)	F G L
4	3	Someday We'll Be Together	Diana Ross & The Supremes	Motown	13	(13)	G
5	14	Whole Lotta Love	Led Zeppelin	Atlantic	9		F G
6	1	Leaving On A Jet Plane	Peter, Paul & Mary	Warner	12	(2)	G L
7	-	Don't Cry Daddy/Rubberneckin'	Elvis Presley	RCA	7	(8)	G
8	-	Jam Up Jelly Tight	Tommy Roe	ABC	7		G L
9	4	Down On The Corner/Fortunate Son	Creedence Clearwater Revival	Fantasy	10	(31)	G
10	16	Midnight Cowboy	Ferrante & Teicher	UA	7		L
11	-	Without Love (There Is Nothing)	Tom Jones	Parrot	7	(10)	G
12	19	La La La (If I Had You)	Bobby Sherman	Metromedia	6		
13	-	Jingle Jangle	Archies	Kirshner	7		G L
14	2	Na Na Hey Hey Kiss Him Goodbye	Steam	Fontana	11	(9)	F G L
15	10	Holly Holy	Neil Diamond	UNI	9		G
16	-	Early In The Morning	Vanity Fare	Page One	6	(8)	F
17	-	I'll Never Fall In Love Again	Dionne Warwick	Scepter	7		
18	-	Thank You (Falettinme Be Mice Elf Agin)/Everybody Is A Star	Sly & The Family Stone	Epic	8		G
19	11	Eli's Coming	Three Dog Night	Dunhill	10		
20	5	Come Together/Something	Beatles	Apple	13	(4)	G

February 1970

This Mnth	Prev Mnth	Title	Artist	Label	Wks 20	(UK Pos)	
1	18	Thank You (Falettinme Be Mice Elf Agin)/Everybody Is A Star	Sly & The Family Stone	Epic	8		G
2	-	Hey There Lonely Girl	Eddie Holman	ABC	8	(4)	F G L
3	2	I Want You Back	Jackson Five	Motown	13	(2)	F G
4	1	Raindrops Keep Fallin' On My Head	B.J. Thomas	Scepter	15	(38)	G
5	3	Venus	Shocking Blue	Colossus	11	(8)	F G L
6	-	No Time	Guess Who	RCA	7		
7	-	Psychedelic Shack	Temptations	Gordy	7	(33)	
8	-	Travelin' Band/Who'll Stop The Rain	Creedence Clearwater Revival	Fantasy	8	(8)	G
9	-	Bridge Over Troubled Water	Simon & Garfunkel	Columbia	12	(1)	G
10	-	Arizona	Mark Lindsay	Columbia	7		F G L
11	11	Without Love (There Is Nothing)	Tom Jones	Parrot	7	(10)	G
12	17	I'll Never Fall In Love Again	Dionne Warwick	Scepter	7		
13	-	Walk A Mile In My Shoes	Joe South	Capitol	6		L
14	-	Rainy Night In Georgia	Brook Benton	Cotillion	9		G L
15	-	Ma Belle Amie	Tee Set	Colossus	8		F L
16	5	Whole Lotta Love	Led Zeppelin	Atlantic	9		F G
17	-	The Thrill Is Gone	B.B. King	Bluesway	4		F L
18	-	The Rapper	Jaggerz	Kama Sutra	9		F G L
19	13	Jingle Jangle	Archies	Kirshner	7		G L
20	7	Don't Cry Daddy/Rubberneckin'	Elvis Presley	RCA	7	(8)	G

March 1970

This Mnth	Prev Mnth	Title	Artist	Label	Wks 20	(UK Pos)	
1	9	Bridge Over Troubled Water	Simon & Garfunkel	Columbia	12	(1)	G
2	18	The Rapper	Jaggerz	Kama Sutra	9		F G L
3	-	Give Me Just A Little More Time	Chairmen Of The Board	Invictus	9	(3)	F G
4	14	Rainy Night In Georgia	Brook Benton	Cotillion	9		G L
5	-	He Ain't Heavy, He's My Brother	Hollies	Epic	7	(3)	
6	8	Travelin' Band/Who'll Stop The Rain	Creedence Clearwater Revival	Fantasy	8	(8)	G
7	15	Ma Belle Amie	Tee Set	Colossus	8		F L
8	-	Instant Karma (We All Shine On)	John Lennon/Plastic Ono Band	Apple	10	(5)	G
9	-	Love Grows (Where My Rosemary Goes)	Edison Lighthouse	Bell	9	(1)	F G L
10	-	Let It Be	Beatles	Apple	11	(2)	G
11	-	Evil Ways	Santana	Columbia	6		F
12	1	Thank You (Falettinme Be Mice Elf Agin)/Everybody Is A Star	Sly & The Family Stone	Epic	8		G
13	-	Didn't I (Blow Your Mind This Time)	Delfonics	Philly Groove	6	(22)	G L
14	2	Hey There Lonely Girl	Eddie Holman	ABC	8	(4)	F G L
15	-	ABC	Jackson Five	Motown	11	(8)	G
16	-	Spirit In The Sky	Norman Greenbaum	Reprise	11	(1)	F G L
17	7	Psychedelic Shack	Temptations	Gordy	7	(33)	
18	4	Raindrops Keep Fallin' On My Head	B.J. Thomas	Scepter	15	(38)	G
19	-	House Of The Rising Sun	Frijid Pink	Parrot	7	(4)	F G L
20	-	Easy Come, Easy Go	Bobby Sherman	Metromedia	8		G

US 1970
JAN-MAR

◆ The last newly recorded Beatles single, 'Let It Be', entered the US Hot 100 chart at No. 6 - a record which is still unsurpassed. John Lennon's latest single 'Instant Karma', written with Phil Spector, was also an instant transatlantic hit.

◆ Shocking Blue headed a short-lived mini-invasion of the US charts by Dutch groups. They were followed up the charts by fellow countrymen Tee Set and the George Baker Selection.

◆ The R&B/soul scene mourned the deaths of singers Billy Stewart (car crash), Tammi Terrell (brain tumour), Slim Harpo (heart attack) and James Sheppard (murdered).

UK 1970 APR-JUNE

▲ Grateful Dead made their UK debut at the Hollywood Rock Music Festival, where newcomers Mungo Jerry (above, whose 'In The Summertime' would sell seven million world-wide) were the surprise hit. One of several other UK festivals was the Bath Festival Of Blues And Progressive Music, whose headliners included Led Zeppelin, The Byrds, Donovan, Santana, Steppenwolf, Pink Floyd, John Mayall and Frank Zappa.

◆ The Who performed their rock opera *Tommy* at the Metropolitan Opera House in New York. They declared it would be the last time ever they performed it in its entirety.

April 1970

This Mnth	Prev Mnth	Title	Artist	Label	Wks 20	(US Pos)	
1	2	Bridge Over Troubled Water	Simon & Garfunkel	CBS	13	(1)	L
2	12	Can't Help Falling In Love	Andy Williams	CBS	11	(88)	
3	20	Knock Knock Who's There	Mary Hopkin	Apple	7	(92)	
4	-	All Kinds Of Everything	Dana	Rex	8		F
5	19	Young Gifted And Black	Bob & Marcia	Harry J.	8		F
6	-	Spirit In The Sky	Norman Greenbaum	Reprise	11	(3)	F L
7	1	Wand'rin' Star	Lee Marvin	Paramount	11		F L
8	7	That Same Old Feeling	Pickettywitch	Pye	8	(67)	F
9	-	Gimme Dat Ding	Pipkins	Columbia	6	(9)	F L
10	-	Farewell Is A Lonely Sound	Jimmy Ruffin	Tamla Motown	7		
11	15	Something's Burning	Kenny Rogers & The First Edition	Reprise	8	(11)	
12	-	I Can't Help Myself	Four Tops	Tamla Motown	5	(1)	
13	4	Let It Be	Beatles	Apple	6	(1)	
14	-	Never Had A Dream Come True	Stevie Wonder	Tamla Motown	7	(26)	
15	-	When Julie Comes Around	Cuff Links	MCA	6	(41)	L
16	11	Don't Cry Daddy	Elvis Presley	RCA	7	(6)	
17	16	Everybody Get Together	Dave Clark Five	Columbia	5		L
18	-	Good Morning Freedom	Blue Mink	Philips	4		
19	10	Na Na Hey Hey Kiss Him Goodbye	Steam	Fontana	6	(1)	F L
20	-	You're Such A Good Looking Woman	Joe Dolan	Pye	4		L

May 1970

This Mnth	Prev Mnth	Title	Artist	Label	Wks 20	(US Pos)	
1	-	Back Home	England World Cup Squad	Pye	9		F
2	6	Spirit In The Sky	Norman Greenbaum	Reprise	11	(3)	F L
3	-	House Of The Rising Sun	Frijid Pink	Deram	8	(7)	F L
4	4	All Kinds Of Everything	Dana	Rex	8		F
5	-	Daughter Of Darkness	Tom Jones	Decca	9	(13)	
6	-	Question	Moody Blues	Threshold	9	(21)	
7	-	Yellow River	Christie	CBS	11	(23)	F
8	1	Bridge Over Troubled Water	Simon & Garfunkel	CBS	13	(1)	L
9	-	Travellin' Band	Creedence Clearwater Revival	Liberty	7	(2)	
10	2	Can't Help Falling In Love	Andy Williams	CBS	11	(88)	
11	-	I Can't Tell The Bottom From The Top	Hollies	Parlophone	5	(82)	
12	-	Brontosaurus	Move	Regal Zonophone	6		
13	14	Never Had A Dream Come True	Stevie Wonder	Tamla Motown	7	(26)	
14	-	I Don't Believe In If Anymore	Roger Whittaker	Columbia	8		
15	15	When Julie Comes Around	Cuff Links	MCA	6	(41)	L
16	9	Gimme Dat Ding	Pipkins	Columbia	6	(9)	F L
17	10	Farewell Is A Lonely Sound	Jimmy Ruffin	Tamla Motown	7		
18	-	Honey Come Back	Glen Campbell	Capitol	10	(19)	
19	18	Good Morning Freedom	Blue Mink	Philips	4		
20	-	Up The Ladder To The Roof	Supremes	Tamla Motown	6	(10)	

June 1970

This Mnth	Prev Mnth	Title	Artist	Label	Wks 20	(US Pos)	
1	7	Yellow River	Christie	CBS	11	(23)	F
2	-	In The Summertime	Mungo Jerry	Dawn	13	(3)	F
3	-	Groovin' With Mr. Bloe	Mr. Bloe	DJM	10		F L
4	18	Honey Come Back	Glen Campbell	Capitol	10	(19)	
5	1	Back Home	England World Cup Squad	Pye	9		F
6	-	Cottonfields	Beach Boys	Capitol	12		
7	-	Everything Is Beautiful	Ray Stevens	CBS	8	(1)	F
8	6	Question	Moody Blues	Threshold	9	(21)	
9	20	Up The Ladder To The Roof	Supremes	Tamla Motown	6	(10)	
10	-	Sally	Gerry Monroe	Chapter One	9		F
11	-	Abraham Martin & John	Marvin Gaye	Tamla Motown	7		
12	-	All Right Now	Free	Island	11	(4)	F
13	-	The Green Manalishi (With The Two Prong Crown)	Fleetwood Mac	Reprise	9		
14	-	ABC	Jackson Five	Tamla Motown	5	(1)	
15	14	I Don't Believe In If Anymore	Roger Whittaker	Columbia	8		
16	5	Daughter Of Darkness	Tom Jones	Decca	9	(13)	
17	-	Goodbye Sam Hello Samantha	Cliff Richard	Columbia	10		
18	2	Spirit In The Sky	Norman Greenbaum	Reprise	11	(3)	F L
19	-	It's All In The Game	Four Tops	Tamla Motown	9	(24)	
20	-	Down The Dustpipe	Status Quo	Pye	6		

April 1970

This Mnth	Prev Mnth	Title	Artist	Label	Wks 20	(UK Pos)	
1	10	Let It Be	Beatles	Apple	11	(2)	G
2	15	ABC	Jackson Five	Motown	11	(8)	G
3	8	Instant Karma (We All Shine On)	John Lennon	Apple	10	(5)	G
4	16	Spirit In The Sky	Norman Greenbaum	Reprise	11	(1)	F G L
5	1	Bridge Over Troubled Water	Simon & Garfunkel	Columbia	12	(1)	G
6	9	Love Grows (Where My Rosemary...)	Edison Lighthouse	Bell	9	(1)	F G L
7	-	Come And Get It	Badfinger	Apple	7	(4)	F
8	19	House Of The Rising Sun	Frijid Pink	Parrot	7	(4)	F G L
9	20	Easy Come, Easy Go	Bobby Sherman	Metromedia	8		G
10	-	American Woman/No Sugar Tonight	Guess Who	RCA	12	(19)	G
11	-	Up The Ladder To The Roof	Supremes	Motown	6	(6)	
12	-	Love Or Let Me Be Lonely	Friends Of Distinction	RCA	8		L
13	2	The Rapper	Jaggerz	Kama Sutra	9		F G L
14	-	The Bells	Originals	Soul	4		L
15	-	Turn Back The Hands Of Time	Tyrone Davis	Dakar	8		G L
16	-	Call Me	Aretha Franklin	Atlantic	4		
17	3	Give Me Just A Little More Time	Chairmen Of The Board	Invictus	9	(3)	F G
18	-	Something's Burning	Kenny Rogers & First Edition	Reprise	5	(8)	
19	5	He Ain't Heavy, He's My Brother	Hollies	Epic	7	(3)	
20	4	Rainy Night In Georgia	Brook Benton	Cotillion	9		G L

May 1970

This Mnth	Prev Mnth	Title	Artist	Label	Wks 20	(UK Pos)	
1	10	American Woman/No Sugar Tonight	Guess Who	RCA	12	(19)	G
2	1	Let It Be	Beatles	Apple	11	(2)	G
3	-	Vehicle	Ides Of March	Warner	7	(31)	F L
4	2	ABC	Jackson Five	Motown	11	(8)	G
5	-	Everything Is Beautiful	Ray Stevens	Barnaby	9	(6)	G
6	15	Turn Back The Hands Of Time	Tyrone Davis	Dakar	8		G L
7	4	Spirit In The Sky	Norman Greenbaum	Reprise	11	(1)	F G L
8	-	Cecilia	Simon & Garfunkel	Columbia	9		G
9	-	Up Around The Bend/ Run Through The Jungle	Creedence Clearwater Revival	Fantasy	8	(3)	G
10	-	Reflections Of My Life	Marmalade	London	8	(3)	F L
11	-	Love On A Two-Way Street	Moments	Stang	10		F G
12	12	Love Or Let Me Be Lonely	Friends Of Distinction	RCA	8		L
13	-	Woodstock	Crosby, Stills, Nash & Young	Atlantic	7		F
14	-	For The Love Of Him	Bobbi Martin	UA	7		L
15	3	Instant Karma (We All Shine On)	John Lennon/Plastic Ono Band	Apple	10	(5)	G
16	-	Which Way You Goin' Billy	Poppy Family	London	8	(7)	F G L
17	-	Get Ready	Rare Earth	Rare Earth	11		F
18	18	Something's Burning	Kenny Rogers & First Edition	Reprise	5	(8)	
19	-	The Letter	Joe Cocker	A&M	5	(39)	F
20	7	Come And Get It	Badfinger	Apple	7	(4)	F

June 1970

This Mnth	Prev Mnth	Title	Artist	Label	Wks 20	(UK Pos)	
1	-	The Long And Winding Road/ For You Blue	Beatles	Apple	8		G
2	16	Which Way You Goin' Billy	Poppy Family	London	8	(7)	F G L
3	17	Get Ready	Rare Earth	Rare Earth	11		F
4	11	Love On A Two-Way Street	Moments	Stang	10		F G
5	-	The Love You Save	Jackson Five	Motown	11	(7)	G
6	5	Everything Is Beautiful	Ray Stevens	Barnaby	9	(6)	G
7	9	Up Around The Bend/Run Through...	Creedence Clearwater Revival	Fantasy	8	(3)	G
8	-	Lay Down (Candles In The Rain)	Melanie	Buddah	10		F
9	-	Ride Captain Ride	Blues Image	Atco	9		F G L
10	-	Mama Told Me (Not To Come)	Three Dog Night	Dunhill	11	(3)	G
11	-	Ball Of Confusion (That's What The World Is Today)	Temptations	Gordy	11	(7)	G
12	8	Cecilia	Simon & Garfunkel	Columbia	9		G
13	-	Hitchin' A Ride	Vanity Fare	Page One	9	(16)	G L
14	19	The Letter	Joe Cocker	A&M	5	(39)	F
15	-	Make Me Smile	Chicago	Columbia	7		F
16	-	The Wonder Of You/ Mama Liked The Roses	Elvis Presley	RCA	7	(1)	G
17	-	My Baby Loves Lovin'	White Plains	Deram	6	(9)	F L
18	1	American Woman/No Sugar Tonight	Guess Who	RCA	12	(19)	G
19	-	Daughter Of Darkness	Tom Jones	Parrot	4	(5)	
20	-	Band Of Gold	Freda Payne	Invictus	11	(1)	F G

◆ As John, Paul, George and Ringo immersed themselves in solo projects, rumours were rife that The Beatles were to split. The group's final film *Let it Be* was released and, unsurprisingly, its soundtrack topped the charts. In America the album replaced Paul's solo effort, **McCartney,** at the top, in the same week the group's last official US single, 'The Long And Winding Road', became their 20th and last No. 1.

◆ The film *Woodstock* was premiered and its triple album soundtrack quickly turned to gold. Also selling well was 'Woodstock' by Crosby, Stills, Nash & Young which was taken from their chart topping **Deja Vu** album.

◆ Velvet-voiced soul stylist Brook Benton scored the last of his 16 Top 20 hits with a Tony Joe White song, 'Rainy Night In Georgia'.

153

UK 1970 JULY-SEPT

◆ Just weeks before his untimely death, Jimi Hendrix appeared at the Isle Of Wight Festival which also showcased The Who, The Doors, Chicago, Emerson, Lake & Palmer, The Moody Blues and Free, whose debut hit, 'All Right Now', returned to the UK Top 20 in 1973 and again in 1991.

◆ EMI increased the price of singles to 47.5p ($1.25).

◆ At a time when past superstar Bing Crosby was celebrating selling over 300 million records, future super-star Phil Collins joined Genesis, and Olivia Newton-John recorded with Toomorrow.

◆ The *Melody Maker* poll showed Janis Joplin as Top Female Singer and, after eight years, The Beatles were replaced as Top Group by Led Zeppelin. Incidentally, Zeppelin billed their sixth US tour as "The Greatest Live Event Since The Beatles".

July 1970

This Mnth	Prev Mnth	Title	Artist	Label	Wks 20	(US Pos)	
1	2	In The Summertime	Mungo Jerry	Dawn	13	(3)	F
2	12	All Right Now	Free	Island	11	(4)	F
3	-	Up Around The Bend	Creedence Clearwater Revival	Liberty	8	(4)	
4	19	It's All In The Game	Four Tops	Tamla Motown	9	(24)	
5	3	Groovin' With Mr. Bloe	Mr. Bloe	DJM	10		F L
6	6	Cottonfields	Beach Boys	Capitol	12		
7	10	Sally	Gerry Monroe	Chapter One	9		F
8	17	Goodbye Sam Hello Samantha	Cliff Richard	Columbia	10		
9	-	Love Of The Common People	Nicky Thomas	Trojan	7		F L
10	-	Lola	Kinks	Pye	10	(9)	
11	-	Something	Shirley Bassey	UA	12	(55)	
12	13	The Green Manalishi (With The Two Prong Crown)	Fleetwood Mac	Reprise	9		
13	20	Down The Dustpipe	Status Quo	Pye	6		
14	-	The Wonder Of You	Elvis Presley	RCA	16	(9)	
15	1	Yellow River	Christie	CBS	11	(23)	F
16	4	Honey Come Back	Glen Campbell	Capitol	10	(19)	
17	-	Lady D'Arbanville	Cat Stevens	Island	8		
18	11	Abraham Martin & John	Marvin Gaye	Tamla Motown	7		
19	-	Neanderthal Man	Hotlegs	Fontana	9	(22)	F L
20	-	Love Like A Man	Ten Years After	Deram	6	(98)	F L

August 1970

This Mnth	Prev Mnth	Title	Artist	Label	Wks 20	(US Pos)	
1	14	The Wonder Of You	Elvis Presley	RCA	16	(9)	
2	19	Neanderthal Man	Hotlegs	Fontana	9	(22)	F L
3	10	Lola	Kinks	Pye	10	(9)	
4	11	Something	Shirley Bassey	UA	12	(55)	
5	2	All Right Now	Free	Island	11	(4)	F
6	1	In The Summertime	Mungo Jerry	Dawn	13	(3)	F
7	-	Rainbow	Marmalade	Decca	8	(51)	
8	-	I'll Say Forever My Love	Jimmy Ruffin	Tamla Motown	8	(77)	
9	-	Natural Sinner	Fair Weather	RCA	6		F L
10	-	The Tears Of A Clown	Smokey Robinson & The Miracles	Tamla Motown	10	(1)	
11	3	Up Around The Bend	Creedence Clearwater Revival	Liberty	8	(4)	
12	17	Lady D'Arbanville	Cat Stevens	Island	8		
13	4	It's All In The Game	Four Tops	Tamla Motown	9	(24)	
14	20	Love Like A Man	Ten Years After	Deram	6	(98)	F L
15	-	Big Yellow Taxi	Joni Mitchell	Reprise	5	(67)	F L
16	-	The Love You Save	Jackson Five	Tamla Motown	4	(1)	
17	-	25 Or 6 To 4	Chicago	CBS	7	(4)	
18	-	Signed, Sealed, Delivered I'm Yours	Stevie Wonder	Tamla Motown	5	(3)	
19	9	Love Of The Common People	Nicky Thomas	Trojan	7		F L
20	-	Sweet Inspiration	Johnny Johnson & The Bandwagon	Bell	5		

September 1970

This Mnth	Prev Mnth	Title	Artist	Label	Wks 20	(US Pos)	
1	10	The Tears Of A Clown	Smokey Robinson/The Miracles	Tamla Motown	10	(1)	
2	1	The Wonder Of You	Elvis Presley	RCA	16	(9)	
3	-	Give Me Just A Little More Time	Chairmen Of The Board	Invictus	8	(3)	F
4	-	Mama Told Me Not To Come	Three Dog Night	Stateside	8	(1)	F L
5	-	Band Of Gold	Freda Payne	Invictus	11	(3)	F L
6	-	Make It With You	Bread	Elektra	7	(1)	F
7	-	Love Is Life	Hot Chocolate	RAK	8		F
8	-	Wild World	Jimmy Cliff	Island	5		L
9	17	25 Or 6 To 4	Chicago	CBS	7	(4)	
10	7	Rainbow	Marmalade	Decca	8	(51)	
11	-	You Can Get It If You Really Want	Desmond Dekker	Trojan	10		
12	-	Which Way You Goin' Billy	Poppy Family	Decca	7	(2)	F L
13	2	Neanderthal Man	Hotlegs	Fontana	9	(22)	F L
14	4	Something	Shirley Bassey	UA	12	(55)	
15	20	Sweet Inspiration	Johnny Johnson & The Bandwagon	Bell	5		
16	-	Montego Bay	Bobby Bloom	Polydor	8	(8)	F L
17	-	It's So Easy	Andy Williams	CBS	4		
18	9	Natural Sinner	Fair Weather	RCA	6		F L
19	-	Don't Play That Song	Aretha Franklin	Atlantic	5	(11)	
20	-	Black Night	Deep Purple	Harvest	10	(66)	F

US 1970 JULY-SEPT

July 1970

This Mnth	Prev Mnth	Title	Artist	Label	Wks 20	(UK Pos)	
1	10	Mama Told Me (Not To Come)	Three Dog Night	Dunhill	11	(3)	G
2	5	The Love You Save	Jackson Five	Motown	11	(7)	G
3	11	Ball Of Confusion (That's What The World Is Today)	Temptations	Gordy	11	(7)	G
4	20	Band Of Gold	Freda Payne	Invictus	11	(1)	F G
5	9	Ride Captain Ride	Blues Image	Atco	9		F G L
6	-	(They Long To Be) Close To You	Carpenters	A&M	9	(6)	F G
7	8	Lay Down (Candles In The Rain)	Melanie	Buddah	10		F
8	13	Hitchin' A Ride	Vanity Fare	Page One	9	(16)	G L
9	-	Gimme Dat Ding	Pipkins	Capitol	5	(6)	F L
10	-	O-O-O Child	Five Stairsteps	Buddah	8		F G L
11	16	The Wonder Of You/ Mama Liked The Roses	Elvis Presley	RCA	7	(1)	G
12	1	The Long And Winding Road/For...	Beatles	Apple	8		G
13	-	Make It With You	Bread	Elektra	12	(5)	F G
14	-	Tighter, Tighter	Alive & Kicking	Roulette	9		F L
15	3	Get Ready	Rare Earth	Rare Earth	11		F
16	-	A Song Of Joy	Miguel Rios	A&M	5	(16)	F L
17	-	Signed Sealed Delivered I'm Yours	Stevie Wonder	Tamla	10	(15)	G
18	-	United We Stand	Brotherhood Of Man	Deram	4	(10)	F L
19	-	Are You Ready	Pacific Gas & Electric	Columbia	5		F L
20	17	My Baby Loves Lovin'	White Plains	Deram	6	(9)	F L

August 1970

This Mnth	Prev Mnth	Title	Artist	Label	Wks 20	(UK Pos)	
1	6	(They Long To Be) Close To You	Carpenters	A&M	9	(6)	F G
2	13	Make It With You	Bread	Elektra	12	(5)	F G
3	-	Spill The Wine	Eric Burdon & War	MGM	9		F L
4	17	Signed Sealed Delivered I'm Yours	Stevie Wonder	Tamla	10	(15)	G
5	-	War	Edwin Starr	Gordy	11	(3)	G L
6	4	Band Of Gold	Freda Payne	Invictus	11	(1)	F G
7	-	In The Summertime	Mungo Jerry	Janus	8	(1)	F G L
8	14	Tighter, Tighter	Alive & Kicking	Roulette	9		F L
9	1	Mama Told Me (Not To Come)	Three Dog Night	Dunhill	11	(3)	G
10	3	Ball Of Confusion (That's What...)	Temptations	Gordy	11	(7)	G
11	-	I Just Can't Help Believing	B.J. Thomas	Scepter	7		
12	10	O-O-O Child	Five Stairsteps	Buddah	8		F G L
13	-	(If You Let Me Make Love To You Then) Why Can't I Touch You?	Ronnie Dyson	Columbia	5		F L
14	-	Patches	Clarence Carter	Atlantic	9	(2)	L
15	2	The Love You Save	Jackson Five	Motown	11	(7)	G
16	-	Lay A Little Lovin' On Me	Robin McNamara	Steed	5		F L
17	-	25 Or 6 To 4	Chicago	Columbia	8	(7)	
18	-	Ain't No Mountain High Enough	Diana Ross	Motown	11	(6)	F
19	-	Ohio	Crosby, Stills, Nash & Young	Atlantic	3		L
20	5	Ride Captain Ride	Blues Image	Atco	9		F G L

September 1970

This Mnth	Prev Mnth	Title	Artist	Label	Wks 20	(UK Pos)	
1	5	War	Edwin Starr	Gordy	11	(3)	G L
2	18	Ain't No Mountain High Enough	Diana Ross	Motown	11	(6)	F
3	-	Lookin' Out My Back Door/ Long As I Can See The Light	Creedence Clearwater Revival	Fantasy	10	(20)	G
4	14	Patches	Clarence Carter	Atlantic	9	(2)	L
5	17	25 Or 6 To 4	Chicago	Columbia	8	(7)	
6	7	In The Summertime	Mungo Jerry	Janus	8	(1)	F G L
7	-	Julie, Do Ya Love Me	Bobby Sherman	Metromedia	9		G
8	2	Make It With You	Bread	Elektra	12	(5)	F G
9	-	Candida	Dawn	Bell	11	(9)	F G
10	-	Don't Play That Song	Aretha Franklin	Atlantic	5	(13)	G
11	-	Snowbird	Anne Murray	Capitol	8	(23)	F G
12	3	Spill The Wine	Eric Burdon & War	MGM	9		F L
13	-	Cracklin' Rosie	Neil Diamond	UNI	10	(3)	G
14	-	(I Know) I'm Losing You	Rare Earth	Rare Earth	6		
15	4	Signed Sealed Delivered I'm Yours	Stevie Wonder	Tamla	10	(15)	G
16	-	I (Who Have Nothing)	Tom Jones	Parrot	5	(16)	
17	-	Hi-De-Ho	Blood Sweat & Tears	Columbia	4		L
18	-	Groovy Situation	Gene Chandler	Mercury	4		G L
19	13	(If You Let Me Make Love To You...	Ronnie Dyson	Columbia	5		F L
20	-	Rubber Duckie	Ernie	Columbia	3		F L

◆ Elton John embarked on his debut American tour as Elvis Presley (whose 'The Wonder Of You' was his first newly recorded UK chart topper for eight years) started his first for 14 years.

▲ As Motown announced that the Jackson Five (above) had sold 10 million records in just nine months, ex-Motown producers Holland, Dozier & Holland's label Invictus scored a transatlantic smash with 'Band Of Gold' by Freda Payne – the first UK No. 1 by a black American female.

UK 1970
OCT-DEC

◆ While solo albums by John Lennon and George Harrison climbed the charts, Paul McCartney filed for the dissolution of Beatles Co.

▲ Double Grammy winners, The Carpenters (above), had their first transatlantic hit , '(They Long To Be) Close To You'. Also debuting on the UK chart were Neil Diamond, Gilbert O' Sullivan and T-Rex, while the US chart welcomed Dawn, James Taylor, and the stars of the latest pop-oriented TV series, The Partridge Family, featuring teen idol David Cassidy.

◆ The price of all record papers in Britain rose to 5p (12c).

October 1970

This Mnth	Prev Mnth	Title	Artist	Label	Wks 20	(US Pos)	
1	5	Band Of Gold	Freda Payne	Invictus	11	(3)	F L
2	20	Black Night	Deep Purple	Harvest	10	(66)	F
3	11	You Can Get It If You Really Want	Desmond Dekker	Trojan	10		
4	-	Paranoid	Black Sabbath	Vertigo	8	(61)	F
5	16	Montego Bay	Bobby Bloom	Polydor	8	(8)	F L
6	-	Me And My Life	Tremeloes	CBS	9		L
7	-	Ain't No Mountain High Enough	Diana Ross	Tamla Motown	7	(1)	F
8	-	(They Long To Be) Close To You	Carpenters	A&M	8	(1)	F
9	12	Which Way You Goin' Billy	Poppy Family	Decca	7	(2)	F L
10	-	Patches	Clarence Carter	Atlantic	8	(4)	F L
11	-	Ball Of Confusion	Temptations	Tamla Motown	7	(3)	
12	-	Woodstock	Matthews Southern Comfort	Uni	8	(23)	F L
13	1	The Tears Of A Clown	Smokey Robinson & The Miracles	Tamla Motown	10	(1)	
14	3	Give Me Just A Little More Time	Chairmen Of The Board	Invictus	8	(3)	F
15	2	The Wonder Of You	Elvis Presley	RCA	16	(9)	
16	-	Strange Band	Family	Reprise	5		F
17	-	Black Pearl	Horace Faith	Trojan	4		F L
18	-	Still Water (Love)	Four Tops	Tamla Motown	6	(11)	
19	7	Love Is Life	Hot Chocolate	RAK	8		F
20	-	Gasoline Alley Bred	Hollies	Parlophone	4		

November 1970

This Mnth	Prev Mnth	Title	Artist	Label	Wks 20	(US Pos)	
1	12	Woodstock	Matthews Southern Comfort	Uni	8	(23)	F L
2	10	Patches	Clarence Carter	Atlantic	8	(4)	F L
3	-	War	Edwin Starr	Tamla Motown	8	(1)	
4	-	Indian Reservation	Don Fardon	Young Blood	11	(20)	F L
5	-	Voodoo Chile	Jimi Hendrix Experience	Track	10		L
6	-	The Witch	Rattles	Decca	5	(79)	F L
7	-	Ruby Tuesday	Melanie	Buddah	7	(52)	F
8	-	San Bernadino	Christie	CBS	6	(100)	L
9	6	Me And My Life	Tremeloes	CBS	9		L
10	2	Black Night	Deep Purple	Harvest	10	(66)	F
11	-	It's Wonderful	Jimmy Ruffin	Tamla Motown	8		
12	1	Band Of Gold	Freda Payne	Invictus	11	(3)	F L
13	11	Ball Of Confusion	Temptations	Tamla Motown	7	(3)	
14	-	Cracklin' Rosie	Neil Diamond	Uni	13	(1)	F
15	-	I Hear You Knocking	Dave Edmunds	MAM	12	(4)	F
16	-	Julie, Do Ya Love Me	White Plains	Deram	9		
17	-	Ride A White Swan	T. Rex	Fly	14	(76)	F
18	4	Paranoid	Black Sabbath	Vertigo	8	(61)	F
19	18	Still Water (Love)	Four Tops	Tamla Motown	6	(11)	
20	-	I've Lost You	Elvis Presley	RCA	8	(32)	

December 1970

This Mnth	Prev Mnth	Title	Artist	Label	Wks 20	(US Pos)	
1	15	I Hear You Knocking	Dave Edmunds	MAM	12	(4)	F
2	-	When I'm Dead And Gone	McGuinness Flint	Capitol	10	(47)	F
3	14	Cracklin' Rosie	Neil Diamond	Uni	13	(1)	F
4	-	It's Only Make Believe	Glen Campbell	Capitol	10	(10)	
5	-	You've Got Me Dangling On A String	Chairmen Of The Board	Invictus	10	(38)	
6	17	Ride A White Swan	T. Rex	Fly	14	(76)	F
7	5	Voodoo Chile	Jimi Hendrix Experience	Track	10		
8	-	I'll Be There	Jackson Five	Tamla Motown	11	(1)	
9	-	Home Lovin' Man	Andy Williams	CBS	9		
10	4	Indian Reservation	Don Fardon	Young Blood	11	(20)	F L
11	-	My Prayer	Gerry Monroe	Chapter One	7		
12	-	Grandad	Clive Dunn	Columbia	14		F L
13	-	Nothing Rhymed	Gilbert O'Sullivan	MAM	7		F
14	20	I've Lost You	Elvis Presley	RCA	8	(32)	
15	16	Julie, Do Ya Love Me	White Plains	Deram	9		
16	-	Lady Barbara	Herman's Hermits	RAK	6		L
17	-	Blame It On The Pony Express	Johnny Johnson & The Bandwagon	Bell	8		L
18	11	It's Wonderful	Jimmy Ruffin	Tamla Motown	8		
19	8	San Bernadino	Christie	CBS	6	(100)	L
20	1	Woodstock	Matthews Southern Comfort	Uni	8	(23)	F L

October 1970

This Mnth	Prev Mnth	Title	Artist	Label	Wks 20	(UK Pos)	
1	-	I'll Be There	Jackson Five	Motown	14	(4)	G
2	13	Cracklin' Rosie	Neil Diamond	Uni	10	(3)	G
3	9	Candida	Dawn	Bell	11	(9)	F G
4	-	All Right Now	Free	Island	10	(2)	F L
5	-	Green Eyed Lady	Sugarloaf	Liberty	10		F
6	2	Ain't No Mountain High Enough	Diana Ross	Motown	11	(6)	F
7	-	We've Only Just Begun	Carpenters	A&M	13	(28)	G
8	7	Julie, Do Ya Love Me	Bobby Sherman	Metromedia	9		G
9	3	Lookin' Out My Back Door/Long As...	Creedence Clearwater Revival	Fantasy	10	(20)	G
10	-	Fire And Rain	James Taylor	Warner	10	(42)	F
11	-	Lola	Kinks	Reprise	6	(2)	
12	-	Express Yourself	Charles Wright & The Watts 103rd Street Rhythm Band	Warner	5		L
13	-	Indiana Wants Me	R. Dean Taylor	Rare Earth	8	(2)	F L
14	11	Snowbird	Anne Murray	Capitol	8	(23)	F G
15	14	(I Know) I'm Losing You	Rare Earth	Rare Earth	6		
16	-	Still Water (Love)	Four Tops	Motown	7	(10)	
17	1	War	Edwin Starr	Gordy	11	(3)	G L
18	-	It's A Shame	Spinners	V.I.P.	3	(20)	F
19	-	Look What They've Done To My Song Ma	New Seekers Featuring Eve Graham	Elektra	4	(44)	F
20	-	It's Only Make Believe	Glen Campbell	Capitol	4	(4)	

November 1970

This Mnth	Prev Mnth	Title	Artist	Label	Wks 20	(UK Pos)	
1	1	I'll Be There	Jackson Five	Motown	14	(4)	G
2	7	We've Only Just Begun	Carpenters	A&M	13	(28)	G
3	-	I Think I Love You	Partridge Family	Bell	14	(18)	F G
4	10	Fire And Rain	James Taylor	Warner	10	(42)	F
5	13	Indiana Wants Me	R. Dean Taylor	Rare Earth	8	(2)	F L
6	-	The Tears Of A Clown	Smokey Robinson/The Miracles	Tamla	12	(1)	G
7	5	Green Eyed Lady	Sugarloaf	Liberty	10		F
8	-	Gypsy Woman	Brian Hyland	Uni	9	(42)	G L
9	-	Montego Bay	Bobby Bloom	L&R/MGM	6	(3)	F L
10	-	Somebody's Been Sleeping	100 Proof Aged In Soul	Hot Wax	6		F G L
11	-	It Don't Matter To Me	Bread	Elektra	5		
12	-	Cry Me A River	Joe Cocker	A&M	5		
13	4	All Right Now	Free	Island	10	(2)	F L
14	2	Cracklin' Rosie	Neil Diamond	Uni	10	(3)	G
15	-	Super Bad (Pts 1 & 2)	James Brown	King	5		
16	-	Heaven Help Us All	Stevie Wonder	Tamla	6	(29)	
17	3	Candida	Dawn	Bell	11	(9)	F G
18	11	Lola	Kinks	Reprise	6	(2)	
19	-	Engine Number 9	Wilson Pickett	Atlantic	4		
20	-	You Don't Have To Say You Love Me/Patch It Up	Elvis Presley	RCA	4	(9)	

December 1970

This Mnth	Prev Mnth	Title	Artist	Label	Wks 20	(UK Pos)	
1	6	The Tears Of A Clown	Smokey Robinson/The Miracles	Tamla	12	(1)	G
2	3	I Think I Love You	Partridge Family	Bell	14	(18)	F G
3	-	One Less Bell To Answer	Fifth Dimension	Bell	12		G
4	-	My Sweet Lord/Isn't It A Pity	George Harrison	Apple	12	(1)	F G
5	8	Gypsy Woman	Brian Hyland	Uni	9	(42)	G L
6	-	Black Magic Woman	Santana	Columbia	9		
7	-	No Matter What	Badfinger	Apple	5	(5)	
8	1	I'll Be There	Jackson Five	Motown	14	(4)	G
9	-	Does Anybody Really Know What Time It Is	Chicago	Columbia	9		
10	2	We've Only Just Begun	Carpenters	A&M	13	(28)	G
11	-	Stoned Love	Supremes	Motown	9	(3)	G
12	-	Knock Three Times	Dawn	Bell	13	(1)	G
13	-	5-10-15-20 (25-30 Years Of Love)	Presidents	Sussex	7		F L
14	-	Share The Land	Guess Who	RCA	5		
15	16	Heaven Help Us All	Stevie Wonder	Tamla	6	(29)	
16	4	Fire And Rain	James Taylor	Warner	10	(42)	F
17	20	You Don't Have To Say.../Patch...	Elvis Presley	RCA	4	(9)	
18	-	Domino	Van Morrison	Warner	4		L
19	9	Montego Bay	Bobby Bloom	L&R/MGM	6	(3)	F L
20	-	See Me, Feel Me	Who	Decca	2		

◆ Janis Joplin died of a heroin overdose three days after the funeral of Jimi Hendrix. Shortly afterwards President Nixon appealed for the screening of rock lyrics and banning of songs promoting drug use.

◆ In the USA in 1970, 8.5 million tape players were sold. Casey Kasem launched the long running radio show, *American Top 40*, and the majority of the planned 48 Rock Festivals were legally stopped.

◆ In December, Creedence Clearwater Revival received six gold albums and five gold singles – all earned since 1969.

◆ Jim Morrison played his last shows as lead singer of The Doors. Morrison was also sentenced to eight months hard labour for indecent exposure and profanity on stage in Miami. He was still appealing the sentence when he died in 1971.

157

▲ George Harrison's triple LP, **All Things Must Pass,** topped the American charts, and his single 'My Sweet Lord' was a transatlantic No. 1. Soon after, a court ruled that he had "unconsciously plagiarized" The Chiffons' (with whom The Beatles had toured in 1964) 'He's So Fine' when writing this hit.

◆ The UK album chart became a Top 50.

◆ The Rolling Stones played their last British dates before moving to France for tax reasons.

◆ Swedish quartet, The Engaged Couples, made their debut at a Gothenburg nightclub. They later changed their name to Abba and found world-wide fame.

January 1971

This Mnth	Prev Mnth	Title	Artist	Label	Wks 20	(US Pos)	
1	12	Grandad	Clive Dunn	Columbia	14		F L
2	1	I Hear You Knocking	Dave Edmunds	MAM	12	(4)	F
3	6	Ride A White Swan	T. Rex	Fly	14	(76)	F
4	8	I'll Be There	Jackson Five	Tamla Motown	11	(1)	
5	2	When I'm Dead And Gone	McGuinness Flint	Capitol	10	(47)	F
6	3	Cracklin' Rosie	Neil Diamond	Uni	13	(1)	F
7	17	Blame It On The Pony Express	Johnny Johnson & The Bandwagon	Bell	8		L
8	4	It's Only Make Believe	Glen Campbell	Capitol	10	(10)	
9	-	Ape Man	Kinks	Pye	9	(45)	
10	9	Home Lovin' Man	Andy Williams	CBS	9		
11	13	Nothing Rhymed	Gilbert O'Sullivan	MAM	7		F
12	-	My Sweet Lord	George Harrison	Apple	12	(1)	F
13	-	Black Skin Blue Eyed Boys	Equals	President	6		L
14	5	You've Got Me Dangling On A String	Chairmen Of The Board	Invictus	10	(38)	
15	-	Amazing Grace	Judy Collins	Elektra	13	(15)	
16	-	The Pushbike Song	Mixtures	Polydor	13	(44)	F L
17	-	You Don't Have To Say You Love Me	Elvis Presley	RCA	6	(11)	
18	16	Lady Barbara	Herman's Hermits	RAK	6		L
19	11	My Prayer	Gerry Monroe	Chapter One	7		
20	-	You're Ready Now	Frankie Valli	Philips	6		F

February 1971

This Mnth	Prev Mnth	Title	Artist	Label	Wks 20	(US Pos)	
1	12	My Sweet Lord	George Harrison	Apple	12	(1)	F
2	16	The Pushbike Song	Mixtures	Polydor	13	(44)	F L
3	-	Stoned Love	Supremes	Tamla Motown	8	(7)	
4	-	Resurrection Shuffle	Ashton Gardner & Dyke	Capitol	9	(40)	F L
5	15	Amazing Grace	Judy Collins	Elektra	13	(15)	
6	-	No Matter What	Badfinger	Apple	8	(8)	
7	1	Grandad	Clive Dunn	Columbia	14		F L
8	-	Your Song	Elton John	DJM	6	(8)	F
9	-	Candida	Dawn	Bell	6	(3)	F
10	9	Ape Man	Kinks	Pye	9	(45)	
11	-	It's Impossible	Perry Como	RCA	11	(10)	
12	3	Ride A White Swan	T. Rex	Fly	14	(76)	F
13	20	You're Ready Now	Frankie Valli	Philips	6		F
14	-	She's A Lady	Tom Jones	Decca	5	(2)	
15	-	Baby Jump	Mungo Jerry	Dawn	9		
16	4	I'll Be There	Jackson Five	Tamla Motown	11	(1)	
17	-	Rupert	Jackie Lee	Pye	5		F L
18	17	You Don't Have To Say You Love Me	Elvis Presley	RCA	6	(11)	
19	-	(Come 'Round Here) I'm The One You Need	Smokey Robinson & The Miracles	Tamla Motown	4		
20	-	Sweet Caroline	Neil Diamond	Uni	7	(4)	

March 1971

This Mnth	Prev Mnth	Title	Artist	Label	Wks 20	(US Pos)	
1	15	Baby Jump	Mungo Jerry	Dawn	9		
2	-	Another Day	Paul McCartney	Apple	9	(5)	F
3	1	My Sweet Lord	George Harrison	Apple	12	(1)	F
4	11	It's Impossible	Perry Como	RCA	11	(10)	
5	-	Rose Garden	Lynn Anderson	CBS	10	(3)	F L
6	-	Hot Love	T. Rex	Fly	12	(72)	
7	2	The Pushbike Song	Mixtures	Polydor	13	(44)	F L
8	20	Sweet Caroline	Neil Diamond	Uni	7	(4)	
9	5	Amazing Grace	Judy Collins	Elektra	13	(15)	
10	4	Resurrection Shuffle	Ashton Gardner & Dyke	Capitol	9	(40)	F L
11	-	Tomorrow Night	Atomic Rooster	B&C	5		F
12	3	Stoned Love	Supremes	Tamla Motown	8	(7)	
13	-	Everything's Tuesday	Chairmen Of The Board	Invictus	5	(38)	
14	-	Bridget The Midget (The Queen Of The Blues)	Ray Stevens	CBS	9	(50)	
15	-	Power To The People	John Lennon & The Plastic Ono Band	Apple	6	(11)	
16	-	Strange Kind Of Woman	Deep Purple	Harvest	5		
17	-	Forget Me Not	Martha & The Vandellas	Tamla Motown	3	(93)	L
18	-	Who Put The Lights Out	Dana	Rex	3		
19	-	Rose Garden	New World	RAK	5		F
20	-	Jack In The Box	Clodagh Rodgers	RCA	6		L

This Mnth	Prev Mnth	Title	Artist	Label	Wks 20	(UK Pos)	
1	4	My Sweet Lord/Isn't It A Pity	George Harrison	Apple	12	(1)	F G
2	12	Knock Three Times	Dawn	Bell	13	(1)	G
3	3	One Less Bell To Answer	Fifth Dimension	Bell	12		G
4	6	Black Magic Woman	Santana	Columbia	9		
5	2	I Think I Love You	Partridge Family	Bell	14	(18)	F G
6	-	Lonely Days	Bee Gees	Atco	7	(33)	G
7	11	Stoned Love	Supremes	Motown	9	(3)	G
8	-	Stoney End	Barbra Streisand	Columbia	8	(27)	
9	-	Groove Me	King Floyd	Chimneyville	10		F G L
10	1	The Tears Of A Clown	Smokey Robinson & The Miracles	Tamla	12	(1)	G
11	-	It's Impossible	Perry Como	RCA	9	(4)	L
12	-	Rose Garden	Lynn Anderson	Columbia	10	(3)	F G L
13	-	Your Song	Elton John	Uni	7	(7)	F
14	9	Does Anybody Really Know What Time It Is	Chicago	Columbia	9		
15	-	River Deep-Mountain High	Supremes & Four Tops	Motown	5	(11)	
16	-	Pay To The Piper	Chairmen Of The Board	Invictus	3	(34)	L
17	-	For The Good Times	Ray Price	Columbia	6		F L
18	-	I Hear You Knocking	Dave Edmunds	MAM	7	(1)	F L
19	18	Domino	Van Morrison	Warner	4		L
20	-	If I Were Your Woman	Gladys Knight & The Pips	Soul	5		

This Mnth	Prev Mnth	Title	Artist	Label	Wks 20	(UK Pos)	
1	-	One Bad Apple	Osmonds	MGM	10		F G
2	2	Knock Three Times	Dawn	Bell	13	(1)	G
3	12	Rose Garden	Lynn Anderson	Columbia	10	(3)	F G L
4	18	I Hear You Knocking	Dave Edmunds	MAM	7	(1)	F L
5	-	Mama's Pearl	Jackson Five	Motown	7	(25)	
6	-	If You Could Read My Mind	Gordon Lightfoot	Reprise	8	(30)	F
7	9	Groove Me	King Floyd	Chimneyville	10		F G L
8	6	Lonely Days	Bee Gees	Atco	7	(33)	G
9	1	My Sweet Lord/Isn't It A Pity	George Harrison	Apple	12	(1)	F G
10	-	Watching Scotty Grow	Bobby Goldsboro	UA	5		L
11	-	Mr. Bojangles	Nitty Gritty Dirt Band	Liberty	8		F
12	13	Your Song	Elton John	Uni	7	(7)	F
13	-	Sweet Mary	Wadsworth Mansion	Sussex	5		F L
14	20	If I Were Your Woman	Gladys Knight & The Pips	Soul	5		
15	-	Amos Moses	Jerry Reed	RCA	7		F G
16	3	One Less Bell To Answer	Fifth Dimension	Bell	12		G
17	-	Amazing Grace	Judy Collins	Elektra	5	(5)	
18	8	Stoney End	Barbra Streisand	Columbia	8	(27)	
19	-	Theme From Love Story	Henry Mancini & His Orchestra	RCA	5		L
20	-	Have You Ever Seen The Rain	Creedence Clearwater Revival	Fantasy	6	(36)	G

This Mnth	Prev Mnth	Title	Artist	Label	Wks 20	(UK Pos)	
1	-	Me And Bobby McGee	Janis Joplin	Columbia	10		F G L
2	-	Just My Imagination (Running Away With Me)	Temptations	Gordy	11	(8)	G
3	1	One Bad Apple	Osmonds	MGM	10		F G
4	-	She's A Lady	Tom Jones	Parrot	9	(13)	G
5	-	For All We Know	Carpenters	A&M	9	(18)	G
6	-	Proud Mary	Ike & Tina Turner	Liberty	7		G L
7	-	Doesn't Somebody Want To Be Wanted	Partridge Family	Bell	10		G
8	6	If You Could Read My Mind	Gordon Lightfoot	Reprise	8	(30)	F
9	5	Mama's Pearl	Jackson Five	Motown	7	(25)	
10	15	Amos Moses	Jerry Reed	RCA	7		F G
11	20	Have You Ever Seen The Rain	Creedence Clearwater Revival	Fantasy	6	(36)	G
12	-	Help Me Make It Through The Night	Sammi Smith	Mega	7		F G L
13	-	What's Going On	Marvin Gaye	Tamla	11		G
14	11	Mr. Bojangles	Nitty Gritty Dirt Band	Liberty	8		F
15	-	What Is Life	George Harrison	Apple	6		
16	13	Sweet Mary	Wadsworth Mansion	Sussex	5		F L
17	19	Theme From Love Story	Henry Mancini & His Orchestra	RCA	5		L
18	-	(Where Do I Begin) Love Story	Andy Williams	Columbia	6	(4)	L
19	-	Cried Like A Baby	Bobby Sherman	Metromedia	3		L
20	-	Temptation Eyes	Grass Roots	Dunhill	5		

US 1971 JAN-MAR

◆ As the Jackson Five celebrated their fourth successive No. 1, The Osmonds scored their first with the Jackson Five-inspired 'One Bad Apple', which the hitherto MOR-oriented act had recorded in funky Muscle Shoals.

◆ The Allman Brothers (including ex-Muscle Shoals session guitarist Duane Allman) recorded **At Fillmore East,** which put southern rock on the map.

◆ There was a resurgence of interest in country with Ray Price, Lynn Anderson, Sammi Smith, Jerry Reed and The Nitty Gritty Dirt Band charting. Nashville writer Kris Kristofferson (later a movie star) had two compositions in the Top 20, including chart topper, 'Me and Bobby McGee', and black country singer Charley Pride collected three gold albums.

UK 1971 APR-JUNE

◆ **Sticky Fingers,** the Rolling Stones first album on their own eponymous label, was a transatlantic No. 1, a feat their debut single, 'Brown Sugar', almost equalled.

◆ Dickie Valentine, Britain's last major home-grown heart-throb before the arrival of rock'n'roll, died in a car crash.

◆ The small house where Elvis Presley was born in Tupelo, Mississippi, was opened to the public.

◆ Ringo Starr had his first solo hit with his composition. 'It Don't Come Easy', which fellow ex-Beatle, George Harrison produced.

◆ Eric Clapton won a poll in *NME* for Greatest All-Time Guitarist with Jimi Hendrix and B.B. King in runner-up positions.

◆ The Beatles box office record at New York's Shea Stadium was broken by heavy rockers Grand Funk Railroad.

April 1971

This Mnth	Prev Mnth	Title	Artist	Label	Wks 20	(US Pos)	
1	6	Hot Love	T. Rex	Fly	12	(72)	
2	14	Bridget The Midget (The Queen Of The Blues)	Ray Stevens	CBS	9	(50)	
3	5	Rose Garden	Lynn Anderson	CBS	10	(3)	F L
4	20	Jack In The Box	Clodagh Rodgers	RCA	6		L
5	-	There Goes My Everything	Elvis Presley	RCA	6	(21)	
6	-	Walkin'	C.C.S.	RAK	7		
7	2	Another Day	Paul McCartney	Apple	9	(5)	F
8	-	If Not For You	Olivia Newton-John	Pye International	6	(25)	F
9	15	Power To The People	John Lennon	Apple	6	(11)	
10	-	(Where Do I Begin) Love Story	Andy Williams	CBS	8	(9)	
11	-	Double Barrel	Dave & Ansil Collins	Technique	9	(22)	F
12	1	Baby Jump	Mungo Jerry	Dawn	9		
13	4	It's Impossible	Perry Como	RCA	11	(10)	
14	-	Mozart Symphony No. 40 In G Minor	Waldo De Los Rios	A&M	10	(67)	F L
15	16	Strange Kind Of Woman	Deep Purple	Harvest	5		
16	8	Sweet Caroline	Neil Diamond	Uni	7	(4)	
17	-	Funny Funny	Sweet	RCA	6		F
18	3	My Sweet Lord	George Harrison	Apple	12	(1)	F
19	7	The Pushbike Song	Mixtures	Polydor	13	(44)	F L
20	-	Something Old, Something New	Fantastics	Bell	3		F L

May 1971

This Mnth	Prev Mnth	Title	Artist	Label	Wks 20	(US Pos)	
1	-	Knock Three Times	Dawn	Bell	13	(1)	
2	-	Brown Sugar/Bitch/Let It Rock	Rolling Stones	Rolling Stone	9	(1)	
3	11	Double Barrel	Dave & Ansil Collins	Technique	9	(22)	F
4	-	It Don't Come Easy	Ringo Starr	Apple	8	(4)	F
5	14	Mozart Symphony No. 40 In G Minor	Waldo De Los Rios	A&M	10	(67)	F L
6	-	Indiana Wants Me	R. Dean Taylor	Tamla Motown	9	(5)	
7	-	Remember Me	Diana Ross	Tamla Motown	7	(16)	
8	1	Hot Love	T. Rex	Fly	12	(72)	
9	-	Jig A Jig	East Of Eden	Deram	6		F L
10	10	(Where Do I Begin) Love Story	Andy Williams	CBS	8	(9)	
11	-	Heaven Must Have Sent You	Elgins	Tamla Motown	9	(50)	F L
12	-	Malt And Barley Blues	McGuinness Flint	Capitol	7		L
13	-	Un Banc, Un Arbre, Une Rue	Severine	Philips	4		F L
14	2	Bridget The Midget (The Queen Of The Blues)	Ray Stevens	CBS	9	(50)	
15	-	My Brother Jake	Free	Island	7		
16	-	Sugar Sugar	Sakkarin	RCA	5		F L
17	17	Funny Funny	Sweet	RCA	6		F
18	-	It's A Sin To Tell A Lie	Gerry Monroe	Chapter One	5		L
19	-	Rosetta	Fame And Price Together	CBS	5		L
20	20	Something Old, Something New	Fantastics	Bell	3		F L

June 1971

This Mnth	Prev Mnth	Title	Artist	Label	Wks 20	(US Pos)	
1	1	Knock Three Times	Dawn	Bell	13	(1)	
2	-	I Did What I Did For Maria	Tony Christie	MCA	9		F
3	11	Heaven Must Have Sent You	Elgins	Tamla Motown	9	(50)	F L
4	-	I'm Gonna Run Away From You	Tami Lynn	Mojo	8		F L
5	-	I Am ...I Said	Neil Diamond	Uni	8	(4)	
6	6	Indiana Wants Me	R. Dean Taylor	Tamla Motown	9	(5)	
7	-	Lady Rose	Mungo Jerry	Dawn	7		
8	-	Banner Man	Blue Mink	Regal Zonophone	9		
9	15	My Brother Jake	Free	Island	7		
10	-	Chirpy Chirpy Cheep Cheep	Middle Of The Road	RCA	12		F
11	-	Rags To Riches	Elvis Presley	RCA	6	(33)	
12	2	Brown Sugar/Bitch/Let It Rock	Rolling Stones	Rolling Stone	9	(1)	
13	-	He's Gonna Step On You Again	John Kongos	Fly	8	(70)	F
14	12	Malt And Barley Blues	McGuinness Flint	Capitol	7		L
15	-	Oh You Pretty Thing	Peter Noone	Rak	6		F L
16	9	Jig A Jig	East Of Eden	Deram	6		F L
17	-	I Think Of You	Perry Como	RCA	5	(53)	
18	-	Don't Let It Die	Hurricane Smith	Columbia	8		F
19	-	Co-Co	Sweet	RCA	10	(99)	
20	5	Mozart Symphony No. 40 In G Minor	Waldo De Los Rios	A&M	10	(67)	F L

160

April 1971

This Mnth	Prev Mnth	Title	Artist	Label	Wks 20	(UK Pos)	
1	13	What's Going On	Marvin Gaye	Tamla	11		G
2	2	Just My Imagination (Running Away With Me)	Temptations	Gordy	11	(8)	G
3	-	Joy To The World	Three Dog Night	Dunhill	13	(24)	G
4	1	Me And Bobby McGee	Janis Joplin	Columbia	10		F G L
5	-	Another Day/Oh Woman Oh Why Oh Why	Paul McCartney	Apple	9	(2)	F
6	5	For All We Know	Carpenters	A&M	9	(18)	G
7	4	She's A Lady	Tom Jones	Parrot	9	(13)	G
8	7	Doesn't Somebody Want To Be...	Partridge Family	Bell	10		G
9	-	Put Your Hand In The Hand	Ocean	Kama Sutra	9		F G L
10	6	Proud Mary	Ike & Tina Turner	Liberty	7		G L
11	-	One Toke Over The Line	Brewer And Shipley	Kama Sutra	6		F L
12	-	Never Can Say Goodbye	Jackson Five	Motown	10	(33)	G
13	12	Help Me Make It Through The Night	Sammi Smith	Mega	7		F G L
14	-	Wild World	Cat Stevens	A&M	5		F
15	-	I Am ...I Said	Neil Diamond	Uni	7	(4)	
16	18	(Where Do I Begin) Love Story	Andy Williams	Columbia	6	(4)	L
17	15	What Is Life	George Harrison	Apple	6		
18	-	If	Bread	Elektra	8		
19	-	Stay Awhile	Bells	Polydor	6		F G L
20	-	Oye Como Va	Santana	Columbia	3		

May 1971

This Mnth	Prev Mnth	Title	Artist	Label	Wks 20	(UK Pos)	
1	3	Joy To The World	Three Dog Night	Dunhill	13	(24)	G
2	12	Never Can Say Goodbye	Jackson Five	Motown	10	(33)	G
3	9	Put Your Hand In The Hand	Ocean	Kama Sutra	9		F G L
4	18	If	Bread	Elektra	8		
5	-	Bridge Over Troubled Water/ Brand New Me	Aretha Franklin	Atlantic	8		G
6	-	Brown Sugar	Rolling Stones	Rolling Stone	10	(2)	G
7	-	Me And You And A Dog Named Boo	Lobo	Big Tree	8	(4)	F
8	-	Chick-A-Boom	Daddy Dewdrop	Sunflower	8		F L
9	19	Stay Awhile	Bells	Polydor	6		F G L
10	15	I Am ...I Said	Neil Diamond	Uni	7	(4)	
11	-	Want Ads	Honey Cone	Hot Wax	11		F G
12	1	What's Going On	Marvin Gaye	Tamla	11		G
13	-	Love Her Madly	Doors	Elektra	6		
14	-	It Don't Come Easy	Ringo Starr	Apple	9	(4)	F G
15	-	Sweet And Innocent	Donny Osmond	MGM	9		F G
16	-	Power To The People	John Lennon/Plastic Ono Band	Apple	4	(7)	
17	5	Another Day/Oh Woman Oh Why...	Paul McCartney	Apple	9	(2)	F
18	2	Just My Imagination (Running...)	Temptations	Gordy	11	(8)	G
19	-	Here Comes The Sun	Richie Havens	Stormy Forest	4		F L
20	-	Superstar	Murray Head	Decca	5	(47)	F

June 1971

This Mnth	Prev Mnth	Title	Artist	Label	Wks 20	(UK Pos)	
1	11	Want Ads	Honey Cone	Hot Wax	11		F G
2	-	Rainy Days And Mondays	Carpenters	A&M	10		G
3	6	Brown Sugar	Rolling Stones	Rolling Stone	10	(2)	G
4	-	It's Too Late/I Feel The Earth Move	Carole King	Ode	12	(6)	F G
5	14	It Don't Come Easy	Ringo Starr	Apple	9	(4)	F G
6	1	Joy To The World	Three Dog Night	Dunhill	13	(24)	G
7	-	Treat Her Like A Lady	Cornelius Brothers/Sister Rose	UA	10		F G
8	15	Sweet And Innocent	Donny Osmond	MGM	9		F G
9	-	I'll Meet You Halfway	Partridge Family	Bell	6		
10	-	Indian Reservation (The Lament Of The Cherokee Reservation Indian)	Raiders	Columbia	12		G L
11	5	Bridge Over Troubled Water/Brand...	Aretha Franklin	Atlantic	8		G
12	-	When You're Hot, You're Hot	Jerry Reed	RCA	7		L
13	-	I Don't Know How To Love Him	Helen Reddy	Capitol	5		F
14	7	Me And You And A Dog Named Boo	Lobo	Big Tree	8	(4)	F G
15	2	Never Can Say Goodbye	Jackson Five	Motown	10	(33)	G
16	-	Don't Knock My Love (Pt. 1)	Wilson Pickett	Atlantic	5		G L
17	20	Superstar	Murray Head	Decca	5	(47)	F
18	-	Double Lovin'	Osmonds	MGM	4		
19	-	Don't Pull Your Love	Hamilton, Joe Frank & Reynolds	Dunhill	8		F G
20	-	Nathan Jones	Supremes	Motown	4	(5)	

◆ The Beach Boys, The Allman Brothers, Albert King, The J. Geils Band and Mountain appeared on the final bill at the Fillmore East venue. Days later the Fillmore West too closed – an era had ended.

◆ Singer/songwriter Carole King's double Grammy wining album, **Tapestry,** hit the top. It would stay on the chart for over 300 weeks!

▲ Ed Sullivan's last TV show aired. Among the guests were Gladys Knight & The Pips.

◆ Diana Ross was signed to play Billie Holiday in the Motown backed film, *Lady Sings The Blues.*

UK 1971

JULY-SEPT

▲ Glitter-Rock (aka Glam Rock) was off and running in Britain, thanks to hits from Sweet, T-Rex (above) and chart newcomers Slade.

◆ The Tams seven-year-old 'Hey Girl Don't Bother Me' was one of several re-issues on the British chart – others came from Tami Lynn, The Elgins and even Elvis with a coupling of 'Heartbreak Hotel' and 'Hound Dog'.

◆ Louis Armstrong, the oldest person to top either the American or British charts, died age 71. Armstrong, who first charted in 1926, paid his last visit to the US Top 40 in 1988, 62 years later!).

July 1971

This Mnth	Prev Mnth	Title	Artist	Label	Wks 20	(US Pos)	
1	10	Chirpy Chirpy Cheep Cheep	Middle Of The Road	RCA	12		F
2	19	Co-Co	Sweet	RCA	10	(99)	
3	18	Don't Let It Die	Hurricane Smith	Columbia	8		F
4	8	Banner Man	Blue Mink	Regal Zonophone	9		
5	-	Me And You And A Dog Named Boo	Lobo	Philips	9	(5)	F
6	-	Get It On	T. Rex	Fly	9	(10)	
7	-	Black And White	Greyhound	Trojan	8		F
8	13	He's Gonna Step On You Again	John Kongos	Fly	8	(70)	F
9	-	Just My Imagination (Runnin' Away With Me)	Temptations	Tamla Motown	8	(1)	
10	-	Monkey Spanner	Dave & Ansil Collins	Technique	8		L
11	4	I'm Gonna Run Away From You	Tami Lynn	Mojo	8		F L
12	-	Tom-Tom Turnaround	New World	RAK	10		
13	2	I Did What I Did For Maria	Tony Christie	MCA	9		F
14	-	Pied Piper	Bob & Marcia	Trojan	5		L
15	7	Lady Rose	Mungo Jerry	Dawn	7		
16	-	River Deep-Mountain High	Supremes & Four Tops	Tamla	6	(14)	
17	-	I Don't Blame You At All	Smokey Robinson & The Miracles	Tamla Motown	5	(18)	
18	-	When You Are A King	White Plains	Deram	5		L
19	-	Never Ending Song Of Love	New Seekers	Philips	12		F
20	-	Tonight	Move	Harvest	5		

August 1971

This Mnth	Prev Mnth	Title	Artist	Label	Wks 20	(US Pos)	
1	19	Never Ending Song Of Love	New Seekers	Philips	12		F
2	6	Get It On	T. Rex	Fly	9	(10)	
3	-	I'm Still Waiting	Diana Ross	Tamla Motown	11	(63)	
4	-	Devil's Answer	Atomic Rooster	B&C	7		L
5	-	In My Own Time	Family	Reprise	8		
6	1	Chirpy Chirpy Cheep Cheep	Middle Of The Road	RCA	12		F
7	12	Tom-Tom Turnaround	New World	RAK	10		
8	-	Won't Get Fooled Again	Who	Track	6	(15)	
9	-	What Are You Doing Sunday	Dawn	Bell	7	(39)	
10	5	Me And You And A Dog Named Boo	Lobo	Philips	9	(5)	F
11	2	Co-Co	Sweet	RCA	10	(99)	
12	-	Heartbreak Hotel/Hound Dog	Elvis Presley	RCA	5		
13	-	Leap Up And Down (Wave Your Knickers In The Air)	St. Cecilia	Polydor	7		F L
14	-	Soldier Blue	Buffy Sainte-Marie	RCA	8		F L
15	10	Monkey Spanner	Dave & Ansil Collins	Technique	8		L
16	-	Let Your Yeah Be Yeah	Pioneers	Trojan	6		F L
17	-	Bangla Desh	George Harrison	Apple	4	(23)	
18	7	Black And White	Greyhound	Trojan	8		F
19	-	Get Down And Get With It	Slade	Polydor	4		F
20	-	Hey Girl Don't Bother Me	Tams	Probe	11	(41)	F L

September 1971

This Mnth	Prev Mnth	Title	Artist	Label	Wks 20	(US Pos)	
1	20	Hey Girl Don't Bother Me	Tams	Probe	11	(41)	F L
2	3	I'm Still Waiting	Diana Ross	Tamla Motown	11	(63)	
3	1	Never Ending Song Of Love	New Seekers	Philips	12		F
4	-	Did You Ever	Nancy Sinatra & Lee Hazlewood	Reprise	9		L
5	9	What Are You Doing Sunday	Dawn	Bell	7	(39)	
6	14	Soldier Blue	Buffy Sainte-Marie	RCA	8		F L
7	-	Back Street Luv	Curved Air	Warner	6		F L
8	-	Nathan Jones	Supremes	Tamla Motown	7	(16)	
9	-	It's Too Late	Carole King	A&M	6	(1)	L
10	16	Let Your Yeah Be Yeah	Pioneers	Trojan	6		F L
11	5	In My Own Time	Family	Reprise	8		
12	-	I Believe (In Love)	Hot Chocolate	RAK	6		
13	-	Maggie May	Rod Stewart	Mercury	14	(1)	F
14	-	You've Got A Friend	James Taylor	Warner	9	(1)	F L
15	-	Tweedle Dee Tweedle Dum	Middle Of The Road	RCA	9		
16	-	Cousin Norman	Marmalade	Decca	7		
17	2	Get It On	T. Rex	Fly	9	(10)	
18	17	Bangla Desh	George Harrison	Apple	4	(23)	
19	-	Tap Turns On The Water	C.C.S.	RAK	7		L
20	-	For All We Know	Shirley Bassey	UA	10		

July 1971

This Mnth	Prev Mnth	Title	Artist	Label	Wks 20	(UK Pos)	
1	4	It's Too Late/I Feel The Earth Move	Carole King	Ode	12	(6)	F G
2	10	Indian Reservation (The Lament...)	Raiders	Columbia	12		G L
3	-	You've Got A Friend	James Taylor	Warner	10	(4)	G
4	19	Don't Pull Your Love	Hamilton, Joe Frank & Reynolds	Dunhill	8		F G
5	7	Treat Her Like A Lady	Cornelius Brothers/Sister Rose	UA	10		F G
6	-	Mr. Big Stuff	Jean Knight	Stax	11		F G L
7	2	Rainy Days And Mondays	Carpenters	A&M	10		G
8	-	Draggin' The Line	Tommy James	Roulette	8		F
9	-	How Can You Mend A Broken Heart	Bee Gees	Atco	12		G
10	-	Sooner Or Later	Grass Roots	Dunhill	5		
11	-	That's The Way I've Always Heard It Should Be	Carly Simon	Elektra	6		F
12	-	She's Not Just Another Woman	8th Day	Invictus	6		F G L
13	-	Take Me Home, Country Roads	John Denver	RCA	11		F G
14	12	When You're Hot, You're Hot	Jerry Reed	RCA	7		L
15	1	Want Ads	Honey Cone	Hot Wax	11		F G
16	3	Brown Sugar	Rolling Stones	Rolling Stone	10	(2)	G
17	5	It Don't Come Easy	Ringo Starr	Apple	9	(4)	F G
18	-	Never Ending Song Of Love	Delaney & Bonnie & Friends	Atco	6		F
19	-	Here Comes That Rainy Day Feeling Again	Fortunes	Capitol	5		L
20	-	I Don't Want To Do Wrong	Gladys Knight & The Pips	Soul	5		

August 1971

This Mnth	Prev Mnth	Title	Artist	Label	Wks 20	(UK Pos)	
1	9	How Can You Mend A Broken Heart	Bee Gees	Atco	12		G
2	6	Mr. Big Stuff	Jean Knight	Stax	11		F G L
3	13	Take Me Home, Country Roads	John Denver	RCA	11		F G
4	3	You've Got A Friend	James Taylor	Warner	10	(4)	G
5	-	Mercy Mercy Me (The Ecology)	Marvin Gaye	Tamla	8		
6	-	Beginnings/Colour My World	Chicago	Columbia	8		
7	8	Draggin' The Line	Tommy James	Roulette	8		F
8	-	Signs	Five Man Electrical Band	Lionel	8		F G L
9	2	Indian Reservation (The Lament...)	Raiders	Columbia	12		G L
10	-	Liar	Three Dog Night	Dunhill	7		
11	1	It's Too Late/I Feel The Earth Move	Carole King	Ode	12	(6)	F G
12	-	What The World Need Now Is Love/Abraham, Martin & John	Tom Clay	Mowest	5		F L
13	-	Sweet Hitch-Hiker	Creedence Clearwater Revival	Fantasy	6	(36)	L
14	-	Smiling Faces Sometime	Undisputed Truth	Gordy	9		F G L
15	-	Spanish Harlem	Aretha Franklin	Atlantic	9	(14)	G
16	18	Never Ending Song Of Love	Delaney & Bonnie & Friends	Atco	6		F
17	-	Bring The Boys Home	Freda Payne	Invictus	5		L
18	-	Hot Pants (She Got To Use What She Got To Get What She Wants)	James Brown	People	5		
19	-	Riders On The Storm	Doors	Elektra	4	(68)	L
20	-	Go Away Little Girl	Donny Osmond	MGM	10		G

September 1971

This Mnth	Prev Mnth	Title	Artist	Label	Wks 20	(UK Pos)	
1	20	Go Away Little Girl	Donny Osmond	MGM	10		G
2	15	Spanish Harlem	Aretha Franklin	Atlantic	9	(14)	G
3	-	Ain't No Sunshine	Bill Withers	Sussex	9		F G
4	-	Uncle Albert/Admiral Halsey	Paul & Linda McCartney	Apple	10		G
5	14	Smiling Faces Sometime	Undisputed Truth	Gordy	9		F G L
6	1	How Can You Mend A Broken Heart	Bee Gees	Atco	12		G
7	-	I Just Want To Celebrate	Rare Earth	Rare Earth	6		
8	-	Maggie May/Reason To Believe	Rod Stewart	Mercury	13	(1)	F G
9	-	Whatcha See Is Whatcha Get	Dramatics	Volt	7		F
10	-	Night They Drove Old Dixie Down	Joan Baez	Vanguard	11	(6)	F G L
11	3	Take Me Home, Country Roads	John Denver	RCA	11		F G
12	-	Stick-Up	Honey Cone	Hot Wax	7		G
13	8	Signs	Five Man Electrical Band	Lionel	8		F G L
14	-	Superstar	Carpenters	A&M	11	(18)	G
15	10	Liar	Three Dog Night	Dunhill	7		
16	13	Sweet Hitch-Hiker	Creedence Clearwater Revival	Fantasy	6	(36)	L
17	-	I Woke Up In Love This Morning	Partridge Family	Bell	6		
18	-	Won't Get Fooled Again	Who	Decca	4	(9)	
19	-	Do You Know What I Mean	Lee Michaels	A&M	10		F L
20	5	Mercy Mercy Me (The Ecology)	Marvin Gaye	Tamla	8		

US 1971
JULY-SEPT

▲ *The Concerts For Bangla Desh* took place at Madison Square Garden. George Harrison organized the event which also starred Eric Clapton, Ringo Starr (above), Badfinger and Bob Dylan.

◆ Jim Morrison, leader of The Doors, died of a heart attack on the day the group's 'Riders On The Storm' entered the Hot 100. It became their sixth and last Top 20 entry.

◆ Top sax session man, King Curtis (Ousley), was murdered. Aretha Franklin, Stevie Wonder, Brook Benton and Duane Allman were among those attending his funeral.

UK 1971 OCT-DEC

◆ English comedian Benny Hill topped the chart with the novelty 'Ernie (The Fastest Milkman In The West)', which was loosely based on an earlier record by American humorist Frank Gallup.

◆ Superstars Michael Jackson and Al Green had their first major solo hits with 'Got To Be There' and 'Tired Of Being Alone' respectively. Other chart newcomers included David Cassidy in America and The Bay City Rollers in the UK.

◆ Led Zeppelin's untitled fourth album, which contained the FM classic 'Stairway To Heaven', was released. It spent five years on the American chart and sold eleven million in the US alone.

◆ British rock musical *Jesus Christ Superstar* opened on Broadway, and London's new 'in' venue, the Rainbow Theatre, announced that Alice Cooper, The Who and The Faces would be among its first headliners.

October 1971

This Mnth	Prev Mnth	Title	Artist	Label	Wks 20	(US Pos)	
1	13	Maggie May	Rod Stewart	Mercury	14	(1)	F
2	15	Tweedle Dee Tweedle Dum	Middle Of The Road	RCA	9		
3	14	You've Got A Friend	James Taylor	Warner	9	(1)	F L
4	1	Hey Girl Don't Bother Me	Tams	Probe	11	(41)	F L
5	4	Did You Ever	Nancy Sinatra & Lee Hazlewood	Reprise	9		L
6	20	For All We Know	Shirley Bassey	UA	10		
7	19	Tap Turns On The Water	C.C.S.	RAK	7		L
8	-	Witch Queen Of New Orleans	Redbone	Epic	8	(21)	F L
9	-	Freedom Come Freedom Go	Fortunes	Capitol	7	(72)	
10	16	Cousin Norman	Marmalade	Decca	7		
11	-	Simple Game	Four Tops	Tamla Motown	8	(90)	
12	-	Sultana	Titanic	CBS	7		F L
13	-	Life Is A Long Song/Up The Pool	Jethro Tull	Chrysalis	5		L
14	8	Nathan Jones	Supremes	Tamla Motown	7	(16)	
15	-	Butterfly	Danyel Gerard	CBS	5	(78)	F L
16	12	I Believe (In Love)	Hot Chocolate	RAK	6		
17	-	Another Time Another Place	Engelbert Humperdinck	Decca	4	(43)	
18	-	You Don't Have To Be In The Army To Fight In The War	Mungo Jerry	Dawn	3		
19	7	Back Street Luv	Curved Air	Warner	6		F L
20	-	Keep On Dancing	Bay City Rollers	Bell	5		F

November 1971

This Mnth	Prev Mnth	Title	Artist	Label	Wks 20	(US Pos)	
1	-	Coz I Luv You	Slade	Polydor	10		
2	1	Maggie May	Rod Stewart	Mercury	14	(1)	F
3	-	Till	Tom Jones	Decca	10	(41)	
4	-	Tired Of Being Alone	Al Green	London American	6	(11)	F
5	8	Witch Queen Of New Orleans	Redbone	Epic	8	(21)	F L
6	-	Johnny Reggae	Piglets	Bell	7		F L
7	-	I Will Return	Springwater	Polydor	6		F L
8	11	Simple Game	Four Tops	Tamla Motown	8	(90)	
9	-	The Night They Drove Old Dixie Down	Joan Baez	Vanguard	7	(3)	L
10	-	Banks Of The Ohio	Olivia Newton-John	Pye International	8	(94)	
11	-	Gypsys Tramps & Thieves	Cher	MCA	9	(1)	
12	-	Look Around	Vince Hill	Columbia	6		L
13	-	Jeepster	T. Rex	Fly	10		
14	12	Sultana	Titanic	CBS	7		F L
15	-	Brandy	Scott English	Horse	5	(91)	F L
16	-	Ernie (The Fastest Milkman In The West)	Benny Hill	Columbia	10		L
17	6	For All We Know	Shirley Bassey	UA	10		
18	2	Tweedle Dee Tweedle Dum	Middle Of The Road	RCA	9		
19	-	Run, Baby Run (Back Into My Arms)	Newbeats	London American	6		L
20	-	Surrender	Diana Ross	Tamla Motown	5	(38)	

December 1971

This Mnth	Prev Mnth	Title	Artist	Label	Wks 20	(US Pos)	
1	16	Ernie (The Fastest Milkman In The...)	Benny Hill	Columbia	10		L
2	13	Jeepster	T. Rex	Fly	10		
3	1	Coz I Luv You	Slade	Polydor	10		
4	-	Tokoloshe Man	John Kongos	Fly	7		L
5	11	Gypsys Tramps & Thieves	Cher	MCA	9	(1)	
6	-	Theme From 'Shaft'	Isaac Hayes	Stax	8	(1)	F
7	-	Something Tells Me (Something Is Gonna Happen Tonight)	Cilla Black	Parlophone	8		L
8	10	Banks Of The Ohio	Olivia Newton-John	Pye International	8	(94)	
9	-	No Matter How I Try	Gilbert O'Sullivan	MAM	9		
10	3	Till	Tom Jones	Decca	10	(41)	
11	6	Johnny Reggae	Piglets	Bell	7		F L
12	19	Run, Baby Run (Back Into My Arms)	Newbeats	London American	6		L
13	-	Softly Whispering I Love You	Congregation	Columbia	8	(29)	F L
14	-	Sing A Song Of Freedom	Cliff Richard	Columbia	4		
15	7	I Will Return	Springwater	Polydor	6		F L
16	20	Surrender	Diana Ross	Tamla Motown	5	(38)	
17	-	I'd Like To Teach The World To Sing	New Seekers	Polydor	12	(7)	
18	-	Soley Soley	Middle Of The Road	RCA	8		L
19	-	It Must Be Love	Labi Siffre	Pye International	6		F
20	-	Fireball	Deep Purple	Harvest	6		L

October 1971

This Mnth	Prev Mnth	Title	Artist	Label	Wks 20	(UK Pos)	
1	8	Maggie May/Reason To Believe	Rod Stewart	Mercury	13	(1)	F G
2	14	Superstar	Carpenters	A&M	11	(18)	G
3	-	Yo-Yo	Osmonds	MGM	10		G
4	10	The Night They Drove Old Dixie Down	Joan Baez	Vanguard	11	(6)	F G L
5	19	Do You Know What I Mean	Lee Michaels	A&M	10		F L
6	1	Go Away Little Girl	Donny Osmond	MGM	10		G
7	4	Uncle Albert/Admiral Halsey	Paul & Linda McCartney	Apple	10		G
8	-	If You Really Love Me	Stevie Wonder	Tamla	8	(20)	
9	-	Sweet City Woman	Stampeders	Bell	7		F L
10	-	Gypsys Tramps & Thieves	Cher	Kapp	11	(4)	G
11	3	Ain't No Sunshine	Bill Withers	Sussex	9		F G
12	-	Tired Of Being Alone	Al Green	Hi	10	(4)	F G
13	5	Smiling Faces Sometime	Undisputed Truth	Gordy	9		F G L
14	-	I've Found Someone Of My Own	Free Movement	Decca	7		F L
15	-	Theme From 'Shaft'	Isaac Hayes	Enterprise	10	(4)	F G
16	-	So Far Away/Smackwater Jack	Carole King	Ode	5		
17	2	Spanish Harlem	Aretha Franklin	Atlantic	9	(14)	G
18	-	Trapped By A Thing Called Love	Denise La Salle	Westbound	5		F G L
19	-	Peace Train	Cat Stevens	A&M	8		
20	12	Stick-Up	Honey Cone	Hot Wax	7		G

November 1971

This Mnth	Prev Mnth	Title	Artist	Label	Wks 20	(UK Pos)	
1	10	Gypsys Tramps & Thieves	Cher	Kapp	11	(4)	G
2	15	Theme From 'Shaft'	Isaac Hayes	Enterprise	10	(4)	F G
3	-	Imagine	John Lennon & The Plastic Ono Band	Apple	8	(6)	
4	1	Maggie May/Reason To Believe	Rod Stewart	Mercury	13	(1)	F G
5	19	Peace Train	Cat Stevens	A&M	8		
6	-	Have You Seen Her	Chi-Lites	Brunswick	10	(3)	F
7	3	Yo-Yo	Osmonds	MGM	10		G
8	-	Baby I'm A Want You	Bread	Elektra	7	(14)	G
9	14	I've Found Someone Of My Own	Free Movement	Decca	7		F L
10	-	Got To Be There	Michael Jackson	Motown	11	(5)	F
11	-	Inner City Blues (Makes Me Wanna Holler)	Marvin Gaye	Tamla	4		
12	2	Superstar	Carpenters	A&M	11	(18)	G
13	-	Family Affair	Sly & The Family Stone	Epic	11	(15)	G
14	-	Desiderata	Les Crane	Warner	5	(7)	F L
15	-	Everybody's Everything	Santana	Columbia	4		
16	-	Rock Steady	Aretha Franklin	Atlantic	5		G
17	-	Never My Love	Fifth Dimension	Bell	5		
18	5	Do You Know What I Mean	Lee Michaels	A&M	10		F L
19	12	Tired Of Being Alone	Al Green	Hi	10	(4)	F G
20	-	Easy Loving	Freddie Hart	Capitol	5		F G L

December 1971

This Mnth	Prev Mnth	Title	Artist	Label	Wks 20	(UK Pos)	
1	13	Family Affair	Sly & The Family Stone	Epic	11	(15)	G
2	6	Have You Seen Her	Chi-Lites	Brunswick	10	(3)	F
3	10	Got To Be There	Michael Jackson	Motown	11	(5)	F
4	-	An Old Fashioned Love Song	Three Dog Night	Dunhill	8		G
5	2	Theme From 'Shaft'	Isaac Hayes	Enterprise	10	(4)	F G
6	-	Brand New Key	Melanie	Neighborhood	12	(4)	G L
7	8	Baby I'm A Want You	Bread	Elektra	7	(14)	G
8	-	All I Ever Need Is You	Sonny & Cher	Kapp	7	(8)	
9	-	Cherish	David Cassidy	Bell	8	(2)	F G L
10	1	Gypsys Tramps & Thieves	Cher	Kapp	11	(4)	G
11	-	Scorpio	Dennis Coffey & The Detroit Guitar Band	Sussex	11		F
12	-	American Pie (Pts 1 & 2)	Don McLean	UA	14	(2)	F G
13	-	Respect Yourself	Staple Singers	Stax	6		F
14	14	Desiderata	Les Crane	Warner	5	(7)	F L
15	16	Rock Steady	Aretha Franklin	Atlantic	5		G
16	-	Hey Girl/I Knew You When	Donny Osmond	MGM	7		G
17	3	Imagine	John Lennon/PlasticOno Band	Apple	8	(6)	
18	-	You Are Everything	Stylistics	Avco	10		F G
19	-	Stones	Neil Diamond	Uni	3		
20	-	Where Did Our Love Go	Donnie Elbert	All Platinum	3	(8)	F L

US 1971

OCT-DEC

◆ US record and tape sales increased to $1.7 billion - 60% being purchased by under 30s.

▲ The Faces concert at Madison Square Garden sold out in record time. The group's lead vocalist Rod Stewart (above) topped both the transatlantic album and single charts with his first Top 20 entries, 'Maggie May' and **Every Picture Tells A Story** respectively. John Lennon also hit No. 1 on both sides of the water with his debut solo set, **Imagine.**

◆ Legendary rocker Gene Vincent died of a bleeding ulcer, and up-and-coming superstar Duane Allman was killed in a motorcycle accident.

165

UK 1972 JAN-MAR

◆ Pink Floyd previewed their **Dark Side Of The Moon** album at London's new home of rock music, The Rainbow Theatre. The LP, which was released a year later, smashed all records for chart longevity.

◆ As Paul McCartney (& Wings) played his first dates since leaving The Beatles, John Lennon was having problems renewing his US visa. Ringo Starr, meanwhile, was making a film about Britain's latest pop sensations, T-Rex, whose live shows were "creating hysteria not seen since the early days of The Beatles".

◆ Shortly after Badfinger scored their biggest US hit with 'Day After Day', the suicidal song, 'Without You', written by group members Pete Ham and Tom Evans, gave Nilsson a Grammy winning transatlantic No. 1. Tragically, both writers later committed suicide.

January 1972

This Mnth	Prev Mnth	Title	Artist	Label	Wks 20	(US Pos)	
1	17	I'd Like To Teach The World To Sing	New Seekers	Polydor	12	(7)	
2	13	Softly Whispering I Love You	Congregation	Columbia	8	(29)	F L
3	-	Mother Of Mine	Neil Reid	Decca	14		F L
4	18	Soley Soley	Middle Of The Road	RCA	8		L
5	1	Ernie (The Fastest Milkman In The West)	Benny Hill	Columbia	10		L
6	-	I Just Can't Help Believing	Elvis Presley	RCA	8		
7	7	Something Tells Me (Something Is Gonna Happen Tonight)	Cilla Black	Parlophone	8		L
8	-	Sleepy Shores	Johnny Pearson Orchestra	Penny Farthing	7		F L
9	2	Jeepster	T. Rex	Fly	10		
10	9	No Matter How I Try	Gilbert O'Sullivan	MAM	9		
11	-	Brand New Key	Melanie	Buddah	7	(1)	L
12	-	Horse With No Name	America	Warner	7	(1)	F L
13	6	Theme From 'Shaft'	Isaac Hayes	Stax	8	(1)	F
14	-	Stay With Me	Faces	Warner	5	(17)	F
15	-	Morning Has Broken	Cat Stevens	Island	4	(6)	
16	-	Morning	Val Doonican	Philips	6		L
17	4	Tokoloshe Man	John Kongos	Fly	7		L
18	-	Telegram Sam	T. Rex	T. Rex	7	(67)	
19	-	Where Did Our Love Go	Donnie Elbert	London American	5	(15)	F
20	-	Let's Stay Together	Al Green	London American	7	(1)	

February 1972

This Mnth	Prev Mnth	Title	Artist	Label	Wks 20	(US Pos)	
1	18	Telegram Sam	T. Rex	T. Rex	7	(67)	
2	-	Son Of My Father	Chicory Tip	CBS	9		F
3	3	Mother Of Mine	Neil Reid	Decca	14		F L
4	-	Have You Seen Her	Chi-Lites	MCA	7	(3)	F
5	1	I'd Like To Teach The World To Sing	New Seekers	Polydor	12	(7)	
6	12	Horse With No Name	America	Warner	7	(1)	F L
7	-	Look Wot You Dun	Slade	Polydor	7		
8	20	Let's Stay Together	Al Green	London American	7	(1)	
9	-	American Pie	Don McLean	UA	11	(1)	F
10	11	Brand New Key	Melanie	Buddah	7	(1)	L
11	-	All I Ever Need Is You	Sonny & Cher	MCA	6	(7)	L
12	-	Storm In A Teacup	Fortunes	Capitol	6		L
13	14	Stay With Me	Faces	Warner	5	(17)	F
14	-	Moon River	Greyhound	Trojan	4		
15	19	Where Did Our Love Go	Donnie Elbert	London American	5	(15)	F
16	-	Day After Day	Badfinger	Apple	6	(4)	L
17	-	Without You	Nilsson	RCA	13	(1)	F L
18	6	I Just Can't Help Believing	Elvis Presley	RCA	8		
19	-	Baby I'm A Want You	Bread	Elektra	4	(3)	
20	-	Got To Be There	Michael Jackson	Tamla Motown	6	(4)	F

March 1972

This Mnth	Prev Mnth	Title	Artist	Label	Wks 20	(US Pos)	
1	17	Without You	Nilsson	RCA	13	(1)	F L
2	9	American Pie	Don McLean	UA	11	(1)	F
3	2	Son Of My Father	Chicory Tip	CBS	9		F
4	-	Beg Steal Or Borrow	New Seekers	Polydor	9	(81)	
5	-	Mother & Child Reunion	Paul Simon	CBS	7	(4)	F
6	20	Got To Be There	Michael Jackson	Tamla Motown	6	(4)	F
7	-	Blue Is The Colour	Chelsea F.C.	Penny Farthing	7		F L
8	-	Alone Again (Naturally)	Gilbert O'Sullivan	MAM	7	(1)	
9	7	Look Wot You Dun	Slade	Polydor	7		
10	-	Meet Me On The Corner	Lindisfarne	Charisma	6		F
11	-	Poppa Joe	Sweet	RCA	5		
12	3	Mother Of Mine	Neil Reid	Decca	14		F L
13	12	Storm In A Teacup	Fortunes	Capitol	6		L
14	-	I Can't Help Myself	Donnie Elbert	Avco	5	(22)	L
15	16	Day After Day	Badfinger	Apple	6	(4)	L
16	4	Have You Seen Her	Chi-Lites	MCA	7	(3)	F
17	-	Hold Your Head Up	Argent	Epic	7	(5)	F
18	-	Floy Joy	Supremes	Tamla Motown	6	(16)	
19	-	Say You Don't Mind	Colin Blunstone	Epic	3		F L
20	-	Desiderata	Les Crane	Warner	7	(8)	F L

January 1972

This Mnth	Prev Mnth	Title	Artist	Label	Wks 20	(UK Pos)	
1	12	American Pie (Pts 1 & 2)	Don McLean	UA	14	(2)	F G
2	6	Brand New Key	Melanie	Neighborhood	12	(4)	G L
3	-	Let's Stay Together	Al Green	Hi	12	(7)	G
4	-	Sunshine	Jonathan Edwards	Capricorn	10		F G L
5	11	Scorpio	Dennis Coffey & The Detroit Guitar Band	Sussex	11		F
6	1	Family Affair	Sly & The Family Stone	Epic	11	(15)	G
7	-	I'd Like To Teach The World To Sing	New Seekers	Elektra	7	(1)	G L
8	18	You Are Everything	Stylistics	Avco	10		F G
9	3	Got To Be There	Michael Jackson	Motown	11	(5)	F
10	-	Clean Up Woman	Betty Wright	Alston	8		F G L
11	-	Day After Day	Badfinger	Apple	9	(10)	G
12	-	Sugar Daddy	Jackson Five	Motown	5		
13	16	Hey Girl/I Knew You When	Donny Osmond	MGM	7		G
14	-	Drowning In The Sea Of Love	Joe Simon	Spring	7		G
15	-	I'd Like To Teach The World To Sing	Hillside Singers	Metromedia	5		F L
16	9	Cherish	David Cassidy	Bell	8	(2)	F G L
17	-	Never Been To Spain	Three Dog Night	Dunhill	8		
18	4	An Old Fashioned Love Song	Three Dog Night	Dunhill	8		G
19	2	Have You Seen Her	Chi-Lites	Brunswick	10	(3)	F
20	-	One Monkey Don't Stop No Show (Pt. 1)	Honey Cone	Hot Wax	4		L

February 1972

This Mnth	Prev Mnth	Title	Artist	Label	Wks 20	(UK Pos)	
1	3	Let's Stay Together	Al Green	Hi	12	(7)	G
2	-	Without You	Nilsson	RCA	11	(1)	G
3	1	American Pie (Pts 1 & 2)	Don McLean	UA	14	(2)	F G
4	-	Precious And Few	Climax	Carousel	10		F G L
5	-	Hurting Each Other	Carpenters	A&M	8		G
6	17	Never Been To Spain	Three Dog Night	Dunhill	8		
7	-	Down By The Lazy River	Osmonds	MGM	10	(40)	G
8	-	Joy	Apollo 100	Mega	8		F L
9	11	Day After Day	Badfinger	Apple	9	(10)	G
10	2	Brand New Key	Melanie	Neighborhood	12	(4)	G L
11	-	The Lion Sleeps Tonight	Robert John	Atlantic	11		F G
12	-	Sweet Seasons	Carole King	Ode	6		
13	-	Anticipation	Carly Simon	Elektra	6		
14	4	Sunshine	Jonathan Edwards	Capricorn	10		F G L
15	-	Everything I Own	Bread	Elektra	8	(32)	
16	10	Clean Up Woman	Betty Wright	Alston	8		F G L
17	-	Black Dog	Led Zeppelin	Atlantic	2		
18	5	Scorpio	Dennis Coffey & The Detroit Guitar Band	Sussex	11		F
19	-	Don't Say You Don't Remember	Beverly Bremmers	Scepter	5		F L
20	-	Stay With Me	Faces	Warner	4	(6)	F L

March 1972

This Mnth	Prev Mnth	Title	Artist	Label	Wks 20	(UK Pos)	
1	2	Without You	Nilsson	RCA	11	(1)	G
2	-	Heart Of Gold	Neil Young	Reprise	10	(10)	F G L
3	11	The Lion Sleeps Tonight	Robert John	Atlantic	11		F G
4	15	Everything I Own	Bread	Elektra	8	(32)	
5	4	Precious And Few	Climax	Carousel	10		F G L
6	7	Down By The Lazy River	Osmonds	MGM	10	(40)	G
7	-	A Horse With No Name	America	Warner	12	(3)	F G
8	-	The Way Of Love	Cher	Kapp	7		
9	-	Mother And Child Reunion	Paul Simon	Columbia	8	(5)	F
10	5	Hurting Each Other	Carpenters	A&M	8		G
11	-	Puppy Love	Donny Osmond	MGM	8	(1)	G
12	-	Bang A Gong (Get It On)	T. Rex	Fly	6	(1)	F L
13	-	Jungle Fever	Chakachas	Polydor	7	(29)	F G L
14	12	Sweet Seasons	Carole King	Ode	6		
15	-	I Gotcha	Joe Tex	Dial	13		G
16	8	Joy	Apollo 100	Mega	8		F L
17	1	Let's Stay Together	Al Green	Hi	12	(7)	G
18	3	American Pie (Pts 1 & 2)	Don McLean	UA	14	(2)	F G
19	-	In The Rain	Dramatics	Volt	8		L
20	19	Don't Say You Don't Remember	Beverly Bremmers	Scepter	5		F L

◆ Three outstanding black female vocalists died: Big Maybelle (Smith), soul stylist Linda Jones and gospel queen Mahalia Jackson (40,000 people filed past her coffin). Other deaths reported included David Seville, creator of The Chipmunks, and 1920s hit-maker Gene Austin, often called "The first superstar".

◆ The 50s nostalgia musical *Grease* opened, it ran on Broadway for a record 3,388 performances.

▲ Don McLean's (above) 'American Pie' and album of the same title topped the charts. Another singer-song-writer achieving that feat was Neil Young with 'Heart Of Gold' and **Harvest.**

UK 1972 APR-JUNE

◆ Among the record nine re-issued singles in the UK Top 50 were Procol Harum's 'A Whiter Shade of Pale' and tracks by The Chiffons and The Drifters.

◆ Clyde McPhatter, founder of The Drifters and one of the most imitated R&B singers in the 1950s, died of drink related causes.

◆ The Electric Light Orchestra and Roxy Music made their UK debuts, as Slade embarked on their first UK tour (supported by Status Quo). Other firsts included David Bowie's chart album, **The Rise And Fall Of Ziggy Stardust And The Spiders From Mars,** and Bob Marley's first hit as composer of American reggae star Johnny Nash's 'Stir It Up'.

◆ British songwriters penned the US chart - toppers 'The First Time Ever I Saw Your Face' (Ewan MacColl) and 'The Candy Man' (Anthony Newley/ Leslie Bricusse).

April 1972

This Mnth	Prev Mnth	Title	Artist	Label	Wks 20	(US Pos)	
1	1	Without You	Nilsson	RCA	13	(1)	F L
2	4	Beg Steal Or Borrow	New Seekers	Polydor	9	(81)	
3	-	Amazing Grace	Royal Scots Dragoon Guards	RCA	11	(11)	F
4	-	Sweet Talkin' Guy	Chiffons	London American	8		L
5	17	Hold Your Head Up	Argent	Epic	7	(5)	F
6	-	Back Off Boogaloo	Ringo Starr	Apple	8	(9)	
7	8	Alone Again (Naturally)	Gilbert O'Sullivan	MAM	7	(1)	
8	-	The Young New Mexican Puppeteer	Tom Jones	Decca	7	(80)	
9	20	Desiderata	Les Crane	Warner	7	(8)	F L
10	-	Heart Of Gold	Neil Young	Reprise	5	(1)	F L
11	10	Meet Me On The Corner	Lindisfarne	Charisma	6		F
12	2	American Pie	Don McLean	UA	11	(1)	F
13	18	Floy Joy	Supremes	Tamla Motown	6	(16)	
14	-	Until It's Time For You To Go	Elvis Presley	RCA	6	(40)	
15	-	Debora/One Inch Rock	Tyrannosaurus Rex	Magni Fly	6		
16	-	Run Run Run	Jo Jo Gunne	Asylum	7	(27)	F L
17	-	Crying Laughing Loving Lying	Labi Siffre	Pye International	5		
18	-	It's One Of Those Nights (Yes Love)	Partridge Family	Bell	5	(20)	
19	-	Come What May	Vicky Leandros	Philips	8		F L
20	5	Mother & Child Reunion	Paul Simon	CBS	7	(4)	F

May 1972

This Mnth	Prev Mnth	Title	Artist	Label	Wks 20	(US Pos)	
1	3	Amazing Grace	Royal Scots Dragoon Guards	RCA	11	(11)	F
2	-	Could It Be Forever/Cherish	David Cassidy	Bell	9	(37)	F
3	19	Come What May	Vicky Leandros	Philips	8		F L
4	-	A Thing Called Love	Johnny Cash	CBS	7		L
5	-	Rocket Man	Elton John	DJM	8	(6)	
6	-	Metal Guru	T. Rex	EMI	8		
7	-	Tumbling Dice	Rolling Stones	Rolling Stone	6	(7)	
8	-	Radancer	Marmalade	Decca	6		
9	16	Run Run Run	Jo Jo Gunne	Asylum	7	(27)	F L
10	6	Back Off Boogaloo	Ringo Starr	Apple	8	(9)	
11	4	Sweet Talkin' Guy	Chiffons	London American	8		L
12	-	At The Club/Saturday Night At The Movies	Drifters	Atlantic	9	(43)	
13	15	Debora/One Inch Rock	Tyrannosaurus Rex	Magni Fly	6		
14	-	Oh Babe What Would You Say?	Hurricane Smith	Columbia	7	(3)	L
15	-	Take A Look Around	Temptations	Tamla Motown	5	(30)	
16	-	Leeds United	Leeds United F.C.	Chapter One	5		F L
17	8	The Young New Mexican Puppeteer	Tom Jones	Decca	7	(80)	
18	1	Without You	Nilsson	RCA	13	(1)	F L
19	-	Stir It Up	Johnny Nash	CBS	5	(12)	
20	14	Until It's Time For You To Go	Elvis Presley	RCA	6	(40)	

June 1972

This Mnth	Prev Mnth	Title	Artist	Label	Wks 20	(US Pos)	
1	6	Metal Guru	T. Rex	EMI	8		
2	-	Vincent	Don McLean	UA	9	(12)	
3	12	At The Club/Saturday Night At The Movies	Drifters	Atlantic	9	(43)	
4	-	Lady Eleanor	Lindisfarne	Charisma	6	(82)	
5	14	Oh Babe What Would You Say?	Hurricane Smith	Columbia	7	(3)	L
6	-	California Man	Move	Harvest	8		
7	5	Rocket Man	Elton John	DJM	8	(6)	
8	-	Rockin' Robin	Michael Jackson	Tamla Motown	7	(2)	
9	-	Take Me Bak 'Ome	Slade	Polydor	9	(97)	
10	-	Sister Jane	New World	RAK	6		L
11	2	Could It Be Forever/Cherish	David Cassidy	Bell	9	(37)	F
12	-	Mary Had A Little Lamb	Wings	Apple	7	(28)	
13	1	Amazing Grace	Royal Scots Dragoon Guards	RCA	11	(11)	F
14	-	Isn't Life Strange	Moody Blues	Threshold	4	(29)	
15	-	Rock & Roll Part 2	Gary Glitter	Bell	10	(7)	F
16	3	Come What May	Vicky Leandros	Philips	8		F L
17	-	Doobedood'ndoobe Doobedood'ndoobe	Diana Ross	Tamla Motown	3		
18	-	A Whiter Shade Of Pale	Procol Harum	Magnifly	4		
19	4	A Thing Called Love	Johnny Cash	CBS	7		L
20	16	Leeds United	Leeds United F.C.	Chapter One	5		F L

April 1972

This Mnth	Prev Mnth	Title	Artist	Label	Wks 20	(UK Pos)	
1	7	A Horse With No Name	America	Warner	12	(3)	F G
2	-	The First Time Ever I Saw Your Face	Roberta Flack	Atlantic	14	(14)	F G
3	15	I Gotcha	Joe Tex	Dial	13		G
4	-	Rockin' Robin	Michael Jackson	Motown	9	(3)	G
5	2	Heart Of Gold	Neil Young	Reprise	10	(10)	F G L
6	19	In The Rain	Dramatics	Volt	8		L
7	11	Puppy Love	Donny Osmond	MGM	8	(1)	G
8	-	Betcha By Golly, Wow	Stylistics	Avco	10	(13)	G
9	-	Day Dreaming	Aretha Franklin	Atlantic	9		G
10	-	A Cowboy's Work Is Never Done	Sonny & Cher	Kapp	8		L
11	9	Mother And Child Reunion	Paul Simon	Columbia	8	(5)	F
12	3	The Lion Sleeps Tonight	Robert John	Atlantic	11		F G
13	13	Jungle Fever	Chakachas	Polydor	7	(29)	F G L
14	-	Doctor My Eyes	Jackson Browne	Asylum	6		F
15	-	Roundabout	Yes	Atlantic	5		F
16	-	Look What You Done For Me	Al Green	Hi	9	(44)	G
17	-	The Family Of Man	Three Dog Night	Dunhill	5		
18	1	Without You	Nilsson	RCA	11	(1)	G
19	-	Baby Blue	Badfinger	Apple	4		L
20	-	Vincent/Castles In The Air	Don McLean	UA	6	(1)	

May 1972

This Mnth	Prev Mnth	Title	Artist	Label	Wks 20	(UK Pos)	
1	2	The First Time Ever I Saw Your Face	Roberta Flack	Atlantic	14	(14)	F G
2	-	I'll Take You There	Staple Singers	Stax	10	(30)	G
3	3	I Gotcha	Joe Tex	Dial	13		G
4	-	Oh Girl	Chi-Lites	Brunswick	11	(14)	G L
5	16	Look What You Done For Me	Al Green	Hi	9	(44)	G
6	8	Betcha By Golly, Wow	Stylistics	Avco	10	(13)	G
7	4	Rockin' Robin	Michael Jackson	Motown	9	(3)	G
8	9	Day Dreaming	Aretha Franklin	Atlantic	9		G
9	-	Tumbling Dice	Rolling Stones	Rolling Stone	6	(5)	
10	-	Back Off Boogaloo	Ringo Starr	Apple	5	(2)	
11	-	Morning Has Broken	Cat Stevens	A&M	8	(9)	
12	-	Hot Rod Lincoln	Commander Cody & His Lost Planet Airmen	Paramount	7		F L
13	1	A Horse With No Name	America	Warner	12	(3)	F G
14	-	The Candy Man	Sammy Davis Jr.	MGM	9		G L
15	14	Doctor My Eyes	Jackson Browne	Asylum	6		F
16	20	Vincent/Castles In The Air	Don McLean	UA	6	(1)	
17	-	Sylvia's Mother	Dr. Hook	Columbia	8	(2)	F G
18	-	Little Bitty Pretty One	Jackson Five	Motown	4		
19	17	The Family Of Man	Three Dog Night	Dunhill	5		
20	-	Slippin' Into Darkness	War	UA	4		G

June 1972

This Mnth	Prev Mnth	Title	Artist	Label	Wks 20	(UK Pos)	
1	14	The Candy Man	Sammy Davis Jr.	MGM	9		G L
2	2	I'll Take You There	Staple Singers	Stax	10	(30)	G
3	4	Oh Girl	Chi-Lites	Brunswick	11	(14)	G L
4	-	Song Sung Blue	Neil Diamond	Uni	9	(14)	G
5	-	Nice To Be With You	Gallery	Sussex	7		F G L
6	17	Sylvia's Mother	Dr. Hook	Columbia	8	(2)	F G
7	-	Outa-Space	Billy Preston	A&M	8	(44)	F G
8	-	(Last Night) I Didn't Get To Sleep At All	Fifth Dimension	Bell	7		G
9	1	The First Time Ever I Saw Your Face	Roberta Flack	Atlantic	14	(14)	F G
10	11	Morning Has Broken	Cat Stevens	A&M	8	(9)	
11	-	Troglodyte (Cave Man)	Jimmy Castor Bunch	RCA	7		F G
12	9	Tumbling Dice	Rolling Stones	Rolling Stone	6	(5)	
13	-	Lean On Me	Bill Withers	Sussex	10	(18)	G
14	-	It's Going To Take Some Time	Carpenters	A&M	4		
15	-	Diary	Bread	Elektra	5		
16	-	Walkin' In The Rain With The One I Love	Love Unlimited	Uni	4	(14)	F G L
17	12	Hot Rod Lincoln	Commander Cody & His Lost Planet Airmen	Paramount	7		F L
18	5	Look What You Done For Me	Al Green	Hi	9	(44)	G
19	-	Amazing Grace	Royal Scots Dragoon Guards	RCA	4	(1)	F L
20	-	I Saw The Light	Todd Rundgren	Bearsville	3	(36)	F

◆ The Mar Y Sol (Sea And Sun) Festival in Puerto Rica was attended by 30,000. Headlining acts included The Allman Brothers, Black Sabbath, Emerson Lake & Palmer and The J. Geils Band.

◆ For the first time, the top eight singles on the US chart (May) were all by African-American artists.

◆ John Hammond, who discovered Bob Dylan, also signed his latest find, Bruce Springsteen, to Columbia Records.

◆ Elvis Presley finally made his live New York debut at Madison Square Garden.

◆ Two songs associated with 1950s hit maker Bobby Day returned to the Top 20. They were 'Rockin' Robin', which hit by Michael Jackson, and Day's composition, 'Little Bitty Pretty One', which was now successful for Michael's group, the Jackson Five.

UK 1972
JULY-SEPT

▲ Wembley Stadium hosted its first pop concert and 45,000 50s fans turned out to watch Bill Haley, Chuck Berry (above), Little Richard, Jerry Lee Lewis and Bo Diddley (filmed as *The London Rock And Roll Show*)

◆ The successful album-oriented TV show, *The Old Grey Whistle Test*, kicked off - it helped launch many less commercial acts in the 1970s.

◆ The Rolling Stones' 30 city US tour was seen by 750,000 people, who paid a record $4 million for tickets.

July 1972

This Mnth	Prev Mnth	Title	Artist	Label	Wks 20	(US Pos)	
1	-	Puppy Love	Donny Osmond	MGM	12	(3)	F
2	15	Rock & Roll Part 2	Gary Glitter	Bell	10	(7)	F
3	9	Take Me Bak 'Ome	Slade	Polydor	9	(97)	
4	-	Little Willie	Sweet	RCA	8	(3)	
5	-	Circles	New Seekers	Polydor	8	(87)	
6	-	Sylvia's Mother	Dr. Hook	CBS	8	(5)	F
7	-	I Can See Clearly Now	Johnny Nash	CBS	9	(1)	
8	-	An American Trilogy	Elvis Presley	RCA	5	(66)	
9	2	Vincent	Don McLean	UA	9	(12)	
10	8	Rockin' Robin	Michael Jackson	Tamla Motown	7	(2)	
11	-	Ooh-Wakka-Doo-Wakka-Day	Gilbert O'Sullivan	MAM	6		
12	-	Breaking Up Is Hard To Do	Partridge Family	Bell	9	(28)	
13	-	Join Together	Who	Track	6	(17)	
14	6	California Man	Move	Harvest	8		L
15	12	Mary Had A Little Lamb	Paul McCartney	Apple	7	(28)	
16	-	Seaside Shuffle	Terry Dactyl & The Dinosaurs	UK	8		F L
17	-	School's Out	Alice Cooper	Warner	9	(7)	F
18	-	Mad About You	Bruce Ruffin	Rhino	5		L
19	-	Walkin' In The Rain With The One I Love	Love Unlimited	Uni	4	(14)	F
20	-	Little Bit Of Love	Free	Island	5		

August 1972

This Mnth	Prev Mnth	Title	Artist	Label	Wks 20	(US Pos)	
1	17	School's Out	Alice Cooper	Warner	9	(7)	F
2	16	Seaside Shuffle	Terry Dactyl & The Dinosaurs	UK	8		F L
3	1	Puppy Love	Donny Osmond	MGM	12	(3)	F
4	-	Silver Machine	Hawkwind	UA	10		F L
5	12	Breaking Up Is Hard To Do	Partridge Family	Bell	9	(28)	
6	-	Popcorn	Hot Butter	Pye International	8	(9)	F L
7	6	Sylvia's Mother	Dr. Hook	CBS	8	(5)	F
8	2	Rock & Roll Part 2	Gary Glitter	Bell	10	(7)	F
9	7	I Can See Clearly Now	Johnny Nash	CBS	9	(1)	
10	-	You Wear It Well	Rod Stewart	Mercury	7	(13)	
11	-	All The Young Dudes	Mott The Hoople	CBS	6	(37)	F
12	5	Circles	New Seekers	Polydor	8	(87)	
13	-	It's Four In The Morning	Faron Young	Mercury	10	(92)	F L
14	-	10538 Overture	Electric Light Orchestra	Harvest	6		F
15	-	Run To Me	Bee Gees	Polydor	5	(16)	
16	-	Automatically Sunshine	Supremes	Tamla Motown	4	(37)	L
17	-	Layla	Derek & The Dominoes	Polydor	5	(10)	F L
18	-	Starman	David Bowie	RCA	6	(65)	
19	18	Mad About You	Bruce Ruffin	Rhino	5		L
20	-	The Loco-Motion	Little Eva	London American	5		L

September 1972

This Mnth	Prev Mnth	Title	Artist	Label	Wks 20	(US Pos)	
1	-	Mama Weer All Crazee Now	Slade	Polydor	7	(76)	
2	10	You Wear It Well	Rod Stewart	Mercury	7	(13)	
3	13	It's Four In The Morning	Faron Young	Mercury	10	(92)	F L
4	-	Sugar Me	Lynsey De Paul	MAM	6		F
5	-	Virginia Plain	Roxy Music	Island	6		F
6	-	Standing In The Road	Blackfoot Sue	Jam	6		F L
7	11	All The Young Dudes	Mott The Hoople	CBS	6	(37)	F
8	-	How Can I Be Sure	David Cassidy	Bell	8	(25)	
9	-	I Get The Sweetest Feeling	Jackie Wilson	MCA	6	(34)	
10	-	Children Of The Revolution	T. Rex	EMI	7		
11	-	Ain't No Sunshine	Michael Jackson	Tamla Motown	6		
12	4	Silver Machine	Hawkwind	UA	10		F L
13	17	Layla	Derek & The Dominoes	Polydor	5	(10)	F L
14	1	School's Out	Alice Cooper	Warner	9	(7)	F
15	-	Too Young	Donny Osmond	MGM	5	(13)	
16	-	Living In Harmony	Cliff Richard	Columbia	4		
17	20	The Loco-Motion	Little Eva	London American	5		L
18	6	Popcorn	Hot Butter	Pye International	8	(9)	F L
19	-	Come On Over To My Place	Drifters	Atlantic	6	(60)	
20	-	Wig Wam Bam	Sweet	RCA	7		

July 1972

This Mnth	Prev Mnth	Title	Artist	Label	Wks 20	(UK Pos)	
1	13	Lean On Me	Bill Withers	Sussex	10	(18)	G
2	-	Too Late To Turn Back Now	Cornelius Brothers & Sister Rose	UA	9		G L
3	-	Daddy Don't You Walk So Fast	Wayne Newton	Chelsea	10		G L
4	-	(If Loving You Is Wrong) I Don't Wanna Be Right	Luther Ingram	Koko	11		F L
5	7	Outa-Space	Billy Preston	A&M	8	(44)	F G
6	4	Song Sung Blue	Neil Diamond	Uni	9	(14)	G
7	-	Brandy (You're A Fine Girl)	Looking Glass	Epic	11		F G L
8	-	Rocket Man	Elton John	Uni	8	(2)	
9	-	Alone Again (Naturally)	Gilbert O'Sullivan	MAM	10	(3)	F G
10	-	How Do You Do?	Mouth & McNeal	Philips	8		F G L
11	-	Where Is The Love	Roberta Flack & Donny Hathaway	Atlantic	8	(29)	G
12	1	The Candy Man	Sammy Davis Jr.	MGM	9		G L
13	-	School's Out	Alice Cooper	Warner	7	(1)	F
14	-	Layla	Derek & The Dominoes	Atco	7	(4)	F L
15	11	Troglodyte (Cave Man)	Jimmy Castor Bunch	RCA	7		F G
16	-	Take It Easy	Eagles	Asylum	6		F
17	-	Too Young	Donny Osmond	MGM	5	(5)	
18	-	I Need You	America	Warner	5		
19	5	Nice To Be With You	Gallery	Sussex	7		F G L
20	-	Long Cool Woman (In A Black Dress)	Hollies	Epic	9	(32)	G

August 1972

This Mnth	Prev Mnth	Title	Artist	Label	Wks 20	(UK Pos)	
1	9	Alone Again (Naturally)	Gilbert O'Sullivan	MAM	10	(3)	F G
2	7	Brandy (You're A Fine Girl)	Looking Glass	Epic	11		F G L
3	4	(If Loving...) I Don't Wanna Be Right	Luther Ingram	Koko	11		F L
4	20	Long Cool Woman (In A Black Dress)	Hollies	Epic	9	(32)	G
5	3	Daddy Don't You Walk So Fast	Wayne Newton	Chelsea	10		G L
6	-	I'm Still In Love With You	Al Green	Hi	8	(35)	G
7	11	Where Is The Love	Roberta Flack/Donny Hathaway	Atlantic	8	(29)	G
8	-	Coconut	Nilsson	RCA	6	(42)	L
9	2	Too Late To Turn Back Now	Cornelius Brothers/Sister Rose	UA	9		G L
10	-	Goodbye To Love	Carpenters	A&M	5	(9)	
11	-	Hold You Head Up	Argent	Epic	6	(5)	F L
12	-	The Happiest Girl In The Whole U.S.A.	Donna Fargo	Dot	5		F G
13	13	School's Out	Alice Cooper	Warner	7	(1)	F
14	10	How Do You Do?	Mouth & McNeal	Philips	8		F G L
15	-	You Don't Mess Around With Jim	Jim Croce	ABC	5		F
16	14	Layla	Derek & The Dominoes	Atco	7	(4)	F L
17	1	Lean On Me	Bill Withers	Sussex	10	(18)	G
18	-	Motorcycle Mama	Sailcat	Elektra	5		F L
19	-	Baby Don't Get Hooked On Me	Mac Davis	Columbia	9	(29)	F G
20	-	Hold Her Tight	Osmonds	MGM	4		

September 1972

This Mnth	Prev Mnth	Title	Artist	Label	Wks 20	(UK Pos)	
1	19	Baby Don't Get Hooked On Me	Mac Davis	Columbia	9	(29)	F G
2	-	Black & White	Three Dog Night	Dunhill	6		G
3	-	Back Stabbers	O'Jays	Philly International	8	(14)	F G
4	-	Saturday In The Park	Chicago	Columbia	7		G
5	4	Long Cool Woman (In A Black Dress)	Hollies	Epic	9	(32)	G
6	-	Rock And Roll Part 2	Gary Glitter	Bell	5	(2)	F L
7	6	I'm Still In Love With You	Al Green	Hi	8	(35)	G
8	2	Brandy (You're A Fine Girl)	Looking Glass	Epic	11		F G L
9	-	Go All The Way	Raspberries	Capitol	8		F G
10	1	Alone Again (Naturally)	Gilbert O'Sullivan	MAM	10	(3)	F G
11	-	Ben	Michael Jackson	Motown	9	(7)	G
12	-	Honky Cat	Elton John	Uni	4	(31)	
13	-	Everybody Plays The Fool	Main Ingredient	RCA	8		F G
14	-	Power Of Love	Joe Simon	Spring	4		G
15	-	Guitar Man	Bread	Elektra	5	(16)	
16	15	You Don't Mess Around With Jim	Jim Croce	ABC	5		F
17	11	Hold You Head Up	Argent	Epic	6	(5)	F L
18	-	Use Me	Bill Withers	Sussex	8		G L
19	-	Play Me	Neil Diamond	Uni	6		
20	10	Goodbye To Love	Carpenters	A&M	5	(9)	

US 1972
JULY-SEPT

◆ Both the Pocono International Raceway Festival (Emerson, Lake & Palmer, Humble Pie, J. Geils Band, etc.), and the Bull Island Festival (Canned Heat, Black Oak Arkansas, Brownsville Station, etc.) attracted 200,000 fans. However, the first charity festival, *The Festival Of Hope*, (Jefferson Airplane, Stephen Stills, James Brown, etc.) lost money.

◆ Smokey Robinson announced he was leaving The Miracles, as Curtis Mayfield (who had earlier left fellow R&B headliners, The Impressions) moved towards the top with his solo album **Super Fly.**

◆ New names on the chart included The Eagles, Jim Croce and Alice Cooper, while Derek & The Dominoes introduced the world to 'Layla' and veteran R&B group The O'Jays gave new label Philly International their first hit.

UK 1972
OCT-DEC

◆ Compilation albums of 1950s hits held the top spot for 14 consecutive weeks, and re-issues of earlier hits continued to clog the charts, the latest coming from Americans Neil Sedaka, The Shangri-Las, Chris Montez and Roy C.

◆ With Osmond-mania at its height in the UK, nine-year-old Little Jimmy's minor US hit, 'Long Haired Lover From Liverpool', became the biggest British seller by any of the family.

◆ The Moody Blues US tour was a resounding success. The group, who had a transatlantic hit with the five-year-old, 'Nights in White Satin', topped the album chart with **Seventh Sojourn**.

◆ Filming started on *That'll Be The Day*, which starred future British pop idol David Essex, Keith Moon (The Who), Ringo Starr and the early UK rocker Billy Fury.

October 1972

This Mnth	Prev Mnth	Title	Artist	Label	Wks 20	(US Pos)	
1	-	Mouldy Old Dough	Lieutenant Pigeon	Decca	11		F
2	8	How Can I Be Sure	David Cassidy	Bell	8	(25)	
3	-	You're A Lady	Peter Skellern	Decca	7	(50)	F
4	-	I Didn't Know I Loved You (Till I Saw You Rock 'n' Roll)	Gary Glitter	Bell	7	(35)	
5	20	Wig Wam Bam	Sweet	RCA	7		
6	-	Donna	10cc	UK	9		F
7	10	Children Of The Revolution	T. Rex	EMI	7		
8	-	Burning Love	Elvis Presley	RCA	6	(2)	
9	-	In A Broken Dream	Python Lee Jackson	Youngblood	7	(56)	F L
10	15	Too Young	Donny Osmond	MGM	5	(13)	
11	-	Big Six	Judge Dread	Big Shot	8		F
12	-	Elected	Alice Cooper	Warner	7	(26)	
13	-	John I'm Only Dancing	David Bowie	RCA	5		
14	-	There Are More Questions Than Answers	Johnny Nash	CBS	6		
15	-	Clair	Gilbert O'Sullivan	MAM	8	(2)	
16	19	Come On Over To My Place	Drifters	Atlantic	6	(60)	
17	3	It's Four In The Morning	Faron Young	Mercury	10	(92)	F L
18	1	Mama Weer All Crazee Now	Slade	Polydor	7	(76)	
19	-	Suzanne Beware Of The Devil	Dandy Livingstone	Horse	5		F L
20	-	Goodbye To Love/I Won't Last A Day Without You	Carpenters	A&M	6	(7)	

November 1972

This Mnth	Prev Mnth	Title	Artist	Label	Wks 20	(US Pos)	
1	15	Clair	Gilbert O'Sullivan	MAM	8	(2)	
2	1	Mouldy Old Dough	Lieutenant Pigeon	Decca	11		F
3	-	Leader Of The Pack	Shangri-Las	Kama Sutra	6		
4	-	Loop Di Love	Shag	UK	7		F L
5	-	My Ding-A-Ling	Chuck Berry	Chess	10	(1)	
6	6	Donna	10cc	UK	9		F
7	12	Elected	Alice Cooper	Warner	7	(26)	
8	9	In A Broken Dream	Python Lee Jackson	Youngblood	7	(56)	F L
9	20	Goodbye To Love/I Won't Last A...	Carpenters	A&M	6	(7)	
10	-	Crazy Horses	Osmonds	MGM	12	(14)	F
11	-	Why	Donny Osmond	MGM	9	(13)	
12	-	Crocodile Rock	Elton John	DJM	10	(1)	
13	-	Let's Dance	Chris Montez	London American	5		L
14	-	Hallelujah Freedom	Junior Campbell	Deram	5		F
15	-	I'm Stone In Love With You	Stylistics	Avco	5	(10)	
16	-	Here I Go Again	Archie Bell & The Drells	Atlantic	3		F
17	14	There Are More Questions Than...	Johnny Nash	CBS	6		
18	-	Burlesque	Family	Reprise	5		L
19	8	Burning Love	Elvis Presley	RCA	6	(2)	
20	3	You're A Lady	Peter Skellern	Decca	7	(50)	F

December 1972

This Mnth	Prev Mnth	Title	Artist	Label	Wks 20	(US Pos)	
1	5	My Ding-A-Ling	Chuck Berry	Chess	10	(1)	
2	10	Crazy Horses	Osmonds	MGM	12	(14)	F
3	-	Gudbuy T'Jane	Slade	Polydor	9	(68)	
4	11	Why	Donny Osmond	MGM	9	(13)	
5	-	Long Haired Lover From Liverpool	Little Jimmy Osmond	MGM	14	(38)	F
6	-	Solid Gold Easy Action	T. Rex	EMI	8		
7	12	Crocodile Rock	Elton John	DJM	10	(1)	
8	-	Ben	Michael Jackson	Tamla Motown	8	(1)	
9	-	Angel/What Made Milwaukee Famous	Rod Stewart	Mercury	5	(40)	
10	-	Happy Xmas (War Is Over)	John & Yoko/Plastic Ono Band	Apple	5		
11	-	Stay With Me	Blue Mink	Regal Zonophone	5		
12	-	Shotgun Wedding	Roy 'C'	UK	7		L
13	-	Lookin' Through The Windows	Jackson Five	Tamla Motown	6	(16)	
14	-	Rock Me Baby	David Cassidy	Bell	5	(38)	
15	-	Nights In White Satin	Moody Blues	Deram	6	(2)	
16	-	Lay Down	Strawbs	A&M	4		F
17	1	Clair	Gilbert O'Sullivan	MAM	8	(2)	
18	-	Help Me Make It Through The Night	Gladys Knight & The Pips	Tamla Motown	7	(33)	
19	15	I'm Stone In Love With You	Stylistics	Avco	5	(10)	
20	-	Little Drummer Boy	Royal Scots Dragoon Guards	RCA	4		L

172

October 1972

This Mnth	Prev Mnth	Title	Artist	Label	Wks 20	(UK Pos)	
1	18	Use Me	Bill Withers	Sussex	8		G L
2	-	Burning Love	Elvis Presley	RCA	9	(7)	G
3	11	Ben	Michael Jackson	Motown	9	(7)	G
4	-	My Ding-A-Ling	Chuck Berry	Chess	9	(1)	F G
5	13	Everybody Plays The Fool	Main Ingredient	RCA	8		F G
6	-	Nights In White Satin	Moody Blues	Deram	12	(19)	G
7	9	Go All The Way	Raspberries	Capitol	8		F G
8	-	Garden Party	Rick Nelson	Decca	8	(41)	G L
9	-	Popcorn	Hot Butter	Musicor	6	(5)	F L
10	-	Tight Rope	Leon Russell	Shelter	5		F
11	3	Back Stabbers	O'Jays	Philly International	8	(14)	F G
12	19	Play Me	Neil Diamond	Uni	6		
13	1	Baby Don't Get Hooked On Me	Mac Davis	Columbia	9	(29)	F G
14	-	Freddie's Dead	Curtis Mayfield	Curtom	7		F G
15	-	Why/Lonely Boy	Donny Osmond	MGM	4	(3)	
16	-	Goodtime Charlie's Got The Blues	Danny O'Keefe	Signpost	5		F L
17	-	You Wear It Well	Rod Stewart	Mercury	3	(1)	
18	-	Speak To The Sky	Rick Springfield	Capitol	5		F
19	-	I Can See Clearly Now	Johnny Nash	Epic	10	(5)	G
20	2	Black & White	Three Dog Night	Dunhill	6		G

November 1972

This Mnth	Prev Mnth	Title	Artist	Label	Wks 20	(UK Pos)	
1	19	I Can See Clearly Now	Johnny Nash	Epic	10	(5)	G
2	-	I'd Love You To Want Me	Lobo	Big Tree	7	(5)	G
3	6	Nights In White Satin	Moody Blues	Deram	12	(19)	G
4	-	I'll Be Around	Spinners	Atlantic	7		G
5	14	Freddie's Dead	Curtis Mayfield	Curtom	7		F G
6	-	I Am Woman	Helen Reddy	Capitol	11		G
7	-	Papa Was A Rollin' Stone	Temptations	Gordy	9	(14)	G
8	4	My Ding-A-Ling	Chuck Berry	Chess	9	(1)	G L
9	8	Garden Party	Rick Nelson	Decca	8	(41)	G L
10	-	If I Could Reach You	Fifth Dimension	Bell	6		L
11	-	Convention '72	Delegates	Mainstream	3		F L
12	-	Witchy Woman	Eagles	Asylum	5		
13	-	Summer Breeze	Seals & Crofts	Warner	6		F
14	2	Burning Love	Elvis Presley	RCA	9	(7)	G
15	-	Listen To The Music	Doobie Brothers	Warner	5	(29)	F
16	-	If You Don't Know Me By Now	Harold Melvin & The Blue Notes	Philly International	8	(9)	F G
17	-	You Ought To Be With Me	Al Green	Hi	8		G
18	16	Goodtime Charlie's Got The Blues	Danny O'Keefe	Signpost	5		F L
19	3	Ben	Michael Jackson	Motown	9	(7)	G
20	-	Ventura Highway	America	Warner	6	(43)	

December 1972

This Mnth	Prev Mnth	Title	Artist	Label	Wks 20	(UK Pos)	
1	6	I Am Woman	Helen Reddy	Capitol	11		G
2	-	Me And Mrs. Jones	Billy Paul	Philly International	11	(12)	F G L
3	17	You Ought To Be With Me	Al Green	Hi	8		G
4	-	It Never Rains In Southern California	Albert Hammond	Mums	8		F G L
5	7	Papa Was A Rollin' Stone	Temptations	Gordy	9	(14)	G
6	-	Clair	Gilbert O'Sullivan	MAM	10	(1)	G
7	16	If You Don't Know Me By Now	Harold Melvin & The Blue Notes	Philly International	8	(9)	F G
8	1	I Can See Clearly Now	Johnny Nash	Epic	10	(5)	G
9	-	Funny Face	Donna Fargo	Dot	9		G L
10	-	Rockin' Pneumonia & The Boogie Woogie Flu	Johnny Rivers	UA	10		G
11	20	Ventura Highway	America	Warner	6	(43)	
12	-	Something's Wrong With Me	Austin Roberts	Chelsea	7		F
13	-	I'm Stone In Love With You	Stylistics	Avco	5	(9)	G
14	-	You're So Vain	Carly Simon	Elektra	12	(3)	G
15	13	Summer Breeze	Seals & Crofts	Warner	6		F
16	-	Superfly	Curtis Mayfield	Curtom	8		G L
17	2	I'd Love You To Want Me	Lobo	Big Tree	7	(5)	G
18	-	Keeper Of The Castle	Four Tops	Dunhill	6	(18)	
19	-	Crazy Horses	Osmonds	MGM	4	(2)	
20	-	Your Mama Don't Dance	Loggins & Messina	Columbia	8		F G

US 1972 OCT-DEC

◆ In the year that American sales of records and tapes topped $2 billion, the public demanded more escapism and less political statement in their music.

◆ Chuck Berry scored his biggest hit with the double-entendre transatlantic No. 1, 'My Ding-A-Ling'. Coincidentally, in October, 50s favourites Chuck, Rick Nelson and Elvis simultaneously had their last Top 10 entries.

▲ Don Kirshner launched the TV series *In Concert*. Initial guests included Alice Cooper (above), The Allman Brothers, Blood, Sweat & Tears and Chuck Berry.

UK 1973 JAN-MAR

▲ Local glam rock greats, Sweet, Gary Glitter, T-Rex, David Bowie and Slade vied for the affection of British teeny boppers with American super-stars The Osmonds and David Cassidy (above).

◆ Pink Floyd's album **Dark Side Of The Moon** entered the US chart, where it has remained for a record smashing 17 years (selling over 12 million copies)!

◆ Although not shown in the UK, Elvis' special *Aloha From Hawaii* attracted the biggest world-wide TV audience to date, and the soundtrack album quickly amassed over a million advance orders.

January 1973

This Mnth	Prev Mnth	Title	Artist	Label	Wks 20	(US Pos)	
1	5	Long Haired Lover From Liverpool	Little Jimmy Osmond	MGM	14	(38)	F
2	-	The Jean Genie	David Bowie	RCA	8	(71)	
3	-	Hi Hi Hi/C Moon	Wings	Apple	6	(10)	
4	6	Solid Gold Easy Action	T. Rex	EMI	8		
5	2	Crazy Horses	Osmonds	MGM	12	(14)	F
6	-	Ball Park Incident	Wizzard	Harvest	6		F
7	-	You're So Vain	Carly Simon	Elektra	8	(1)	F
8	-	Blockbuster	Sweet	RCA	10	(73)	
9	-	Big Seven	Judge Dread	Big Shot	7		
10	-	Always On My Mind	Elvis Presley	RCA	5		
11	3	Gudbuy T'Jane	Slade	Polydor	9	(68)	
12	12	Shotgun Wedding	Roy 'C'	UK	7		L
13	15	Nights In White Satin	Moody Blues	Deram	6	(2)	
14	10	Happy Xmas (War Is Over)	John & Yoko & The Plastic Ono Band	Apple	5		
15	1	My Ding-A-Ling	Chuck Berry	Chess	10	(1)	
16	18	Help Me Make It Through The Night	Gladys Knight & The Pips	Tamla Motown	7	(33)	
17	8	Ben	Michael Jackson	Tamla Motown	8	(1)	
18	-	Do You Wanna Touch Me (Oh Yeah)	Gary Glitter	Bell	7		
19	-	Wishing Well	Free	Island	5		
20	-	Can't Keep It In	Cat Stevens	Island	4		

February 1973

This Mnth	Prev Mnth	Title	Artist	Label	Wks 20	(US Pos)	
1	8	Blockbuster	Sweet	RCA	10	(73)	
2	18	Do You Wanna Touch Me (Oh Yeah)	Gary Glitter	Bell	7		
3	-	Part Of The Union	Strawbs	A&M	9		L
4	-	Daniel	Elton John	DJM	6	(2)	
5	7	You're So Vain	Carly Simon	Elektra	8	(1)	F
6	1	Long Haired Lover From Liverpool	Little Jimmy Osmond	MGM	14	(38)	F
7	-	Sylvia	Focus	Polydor	6	(89)	L
8	-	Roll Over Beethoven	Electric Light Orchestra	Harvest	5	(42)	
9	-	Paper Plane	Status Quo	Vertigo	5		
10	19	Wishing Well	Free	Island	5		
11	-	Whiskey In The Jar	Thin Lizzy	Decca	6		F
12	-	If You Don't Know Me By Now	Harold Melvin & The Blue Notes	CBS	4	(3)	F
13	2	The Jean Genie	David Bowie	RCA	8	(71)	
14	-	Superstition	Stevie Wonder	Tamla Motown	5	(1)	
15	-	Me And Mrs. Jones	Billy Paul	Epic	4	(1)	F L
16	-	Cindy Incidentally	Faces	Warner	7	(48)	
17	-	Baby I Love You	Dave Edmunds	Rockfield	6		
18	-	Lookin' Through The Eyes Of Love	Partridge Family	Bell	5	(39)	
19	6	Ball Park Incident	Wizzard	Harvest	6		F
20	20	Can't Keep It In	Cat Stevens	Island	4		

March 1973

This Mnth	Prev Mnth	Title	Artist	Label	Wks 20	(US Pos)	
1	-	Cum On Feel The Noize	Slade	Polydor	7	(98)	
2	-	Feel The Need In Me	Detroit Emeralds	Janus	7	(90)	F
3	-	20th Century Boy	T. Rex	EMI	6		
4	16	Cindy Incidentally	Faces	Warner	7	(48)	
5	-	The Twelfth Of Never	Donny Osmond	MGM	9	(8)	
6	-	Killing Me Softly With His Song	Roberta Flack	Atlantic	8	(1)	
7	-	Hello Hurray	Alice Cooper	Warner	8	(35)	
8	3	Part Of The Union	Strawbs	A&M	9		L
9	-	Power To All Our Friends	Cliff Richard	EMI	7		
10	1	Blockbuster	Sweet	RCA	10	(73)	
11	-	Gonna Make You An Offer You Can't Refuse	Jimmy Helms	Cube	5		F L
12	7	Sylvia	Focus	Polydor	6	(89)	L
13	-	Doctor My Eyes	Jackson Five	Tamla Motown	5		
14	17	Baby I Love You	Dave Edmunds	Rockfield	6		
15	-	Get Down	Gilbert O'Sullivan	MAM	8	(7)	
16	11	Whiskey In The Jar	Thin Lizzy	Decca	6		F
17	2	Do You Wanna Touch Me (Oh Yeah)	Gary Glitter	Bell	7		
18	18	Lookin' Through The Eyes Of Love	Partridge Family	Bell	5	(39)	
19	-	Never Never Never	Shirley Bassey	UA	8	(48)	L
20	-	Heart Of Stone	Kenny	RAK	6		F L

January 1973

This Mnth	Prev Mnth	Title	Artist	Label	Wks 20	(UK Pos)	
1	14	You're So Vain	Carly Simon	Elektra	12	(3)	G
2	-	Superstition	Stevie Wonder	Tamla	9	(11)	G
3	2	Me And Mrs. Jones	Billy Paul	Philly International	11	(12)	F G L
4	20	Your Mama Don't Dance	Loggins & Messina	Columbia	8		F G
5	6	Clair	Gilbert O'Sullivan	MAM	10	(1)	G
6	-	Crocodile Rock	Elton John	MCA	12	(5)	G
7	10	Rockin' Pneumonia & The Boogie...	Johnny Rivers	UA	10		G
8	16	Superfly	Curtis Mayfield	Curtom	8		G L
9	9	Funny Face	Donna Fargo	Dot	9		G L
10	-	Why Can't We Live Together	Timmy Thomas	Glades	8	(12)	F L
11	-	Oh Babe What Would You Say	Hurricane Smith	Capitol	8	(4)	F L
12	18	Keeper Of The Castle	Four Tops	Dunhill	6	(18)	
13	-	Don't Let Me Be Lonely Tonight	James Taylor	Warner	4		
14	-	Trouble Man	Marvin Gaye	Tamla	6		
15	4	It Never Rains In Southern California	Albert Hammond	Mums	8		F G L
16	-	Hi, Hi, Hi	Wings	Apple	5	(5)	
17	-	Living In The Past	Jethro Tull	Chrysalis	6	(3)	F
18	-	The World Is A Ghetto	War	UA	6		G
19	3	You Ought To Be With Me	Al Green	Hi	8		G
20	-	Do It Again	Steely Dan	ABC	7	(39)	F

February 1973

This Mnth	Prev Mnth	Title	Artist	Label	Wks 20	(UK Pos)	
1	6	Crocodile Rock	Elton John	MCA	12	(5)	G
2	1	You're So Vain	Carly Simon	Elektra	12	(3)	G
3	11	Oh Babe What Would You Say	Hurricane Smith	Capitol	8	(4)	F L
4	20	Do It Again	Steely Dan	ABC	7	(39)	F
5	10	Why Can't We Live Together	Timmy Thomas	Glades	8	(12)	F L
6	-	Dueling Banjos	Eric Weissberg & Steve Mandell	Warner	10	(17)	F G L
7	-	Could It Be I'm Falling In Love	Spinners	Atlantic	8	(11)	G
8	2	Superstition	Stevie Wonder	Tamla	9	(11)	G
9	-	Don't Expect Me To Be Your Friend	Lobo	Big Tree	7		L
10	-	Killing Me Softly With His Song	Roberta Flack	Atlantic	12	(6)	G
11	18	The World Is A Ghetto	War	UA	6		G
12	-	Rocky Mountain High	John Denver	RCA	7		
13	14	Trouble Man	Marvin Gaye	Tamla	6		
14	-	Dancing In The Moonlight	King Harvest	Perception	7		F L
15	4	Your Mama Don't Dance	Loggins & Messina	Columbia	8		F G
16	-	Last Song	Edward Bear	Capitol	9		F L
17	-	Love Train	O'Jays	Philly International	9	(9)	G
18	-	Daddy's Home	Jermaine Jackson	Motown	7		F
19	16	Hi, Hi, Hi	Wings	Apple	5	(5)	
20	3	Me And Mrs. Jones	Billy Paul	Philly International	11	(12)	F G L

March 1973

This Mnth	Prev Mnth	Title	Artist	Label	Wks 20	(UK Pos)	
1	10	Killing Me Softly With His Song	Roberta Flack	Atlantic	12	(6)	G
2	17	Love Train	O'Jays	Philly International	9	(9)	G
3	-	Also Sprach Zarathustra (2001)	Deodata	CTI	8	(7)	F L
4	16	Last Song	Edward Bear	Capitol	9		F L
5	6	Dueling Banjos	Eric Weissberg & Steve Mandell	Warner	10	(17)	F G L
6	-	The Cover Of 'Rolling Stone'	Dr. Hook	Columbia	7		G
7	7	Could It Be I'm Falling In Love	Spinners	Atlantic	8	(11)	G
8	-	Neither One Of Us (Wants To Be The First To Say Goodbye)	Gladys Knight & The Pips	Soul	9	(31)	
9	-	Danny's Song	Anne Murray	Capitol	9		
10	-	Break Up To Make Up	Stylistics	Avco	7	(34)	G
11	1	Crocodile Rock	Elton John	MCA	12	(5)	G
12	-	Ain't No Woman (Like The One I've Got)	Four Tops	Dunhill	9		G
13	18	Daddy's Home	Jermaine Jackson	Motown	7		F
14	12	Rocky Mountain High	John Denver	RCA	7		
15	-	I'm Just A Singer (In A Rock 'n' Roll Band)	Moody Blues	Threshold	4	(36)	
16	2	You're So Vain	Carly Simon	Elektra	12	(3)	G
17	-	Sing	Carpenters	A&M	9		G
18	-	Call Me (Come Back Home)	Al Green	Hi	6		G
19	9	Don't Expect Me To Be Your Friend	Lobo	Big Tree	7		L
20	-	The Night The Lights Went Out In Georgia	Vicki Lawrence	Bell	10		F G L

US 1973
JAN-MAR

◆ Columbia Records showcased Bruce Springsteen at the trendy Max's Kansas City club in New York to promote his debut LP, **Greetings From Asbury Park, N.J.**, which initially sold few copies.

◆ TV series *Midnight Special* was launched as a more MOR-slanted rival to the successful *In Concert*.

◆ Recently wed Carly Simon's transatlantic hit, 'You're So Vain', turned gold at the same time as husband James Taylor's album **One Man Dog**.

◆ Kiss, who originally owed a little to the ground-breaking New York Dolls, made their live debut. The Dolls, incidentally, also influenced several British acts and helped sow the seeds of the punk music revolution.

175

UK 1973 APR-JUNE

◆ As John Lennon denied that The Beatles would re-unite, the group's compilation album **1967-1970** was replaced at the top of the US chart by **Red Rose Speedway** from Paul McCartney & Wings. This in turn was followed by George Harrison's **Living In The Material World.** For the record, Paul, who starred in the TV special *James Paul McCartney*, was enjoying his biggest US solo hit, 'My Love'.

▲ Fleetwood Mac's re-issued instrumental 'Albatross' peaked at No. 2, narrowly failing to become the first record to top the UK chart on two separate occasions.

April 1973

This Mnth	Prev Mnth	Title	Artist	Label	Wks 20	(US Pos)	
1	-	Tie A Yellow Ribbon Round The Old Oak Tree	Dawn	Bell	17	(1)	
2	15	Get Down	Gilbert O'Sullivan	MAM	8	(7)	
3	-	I'm A Clown/Some Kind Of A Summer	David Cassidy	Bell	8		
4	5	The Twelfth Of Never	Donny Osmond	MGM	9	(8)	
5	-	Tweedle Dee	Little Jimmy Osmond	MGM	7	(59)	
6	-	Hello Hello I'm Back Again	Gary Glitter	Bell	10		
7	9	Power To All Our Friends	Cliff Richard	EMI	7		
8	19	Never Never Never	Shirley Bassey	UA	8	(48)	L
9	-	Love Train	O'Jays	CBS	6	(1)	
10	-	Pyjamarama	Roxy Music	Island	6		
11	-	All Because Of You	Geordie	EMI	6		F
12	-	Drive-In Saturday	David Bowie	RCA	7		
13	-	Crazy	Mud	RAK	5		F
14	20	Heart Of Stone	Kenny	RAK	6		F L
15	-	My Love	Paul McCartney & Wings	Apple	6	(1)	
16	-	Amanda	Stuart Gillies	Philips	5		F L
17	6	Killing Me Softly With His Song	Roberta Flack	Atlantic	8	(1)	
18	2	Feel The Need In Me	Detroit Emeralds	Janus	7	(90)	F
19	-	Why Can't We Live Together	Timmy Thomas	Mojo	4	(3)	F L
20	1	Cum On Feel The Noize	Slade	Polydor	7	(98)	

May 1973

This Mnth	Prev Mnth	Title	Artist	Label	Wks 20	(US Pos)	
1	1	Tie A Yellow Ribbon Round The Old Oak Tree	Dawn	Bell	17	(1)	
2	-	Hell Raiser	Sweet	RCA	6		
3	-	See My Baby Jive	Wizzard	Harvest	10		
4	6	Hello Hello I'm Back Again	Gary Glitter	Bell	10		
5	12	Drive-In Saturday	David Bowie	RCA	7		
6	-	Giving It All Away	Roger Daltrey	Track	6	(83)	F
7	-	Brother Louie	Hot Chocolate	RAK	6		
8	-	And I Love You So	Perry Como	RCA	12	(29)	
9	15	My Love	Paul McCartney & Wings	Apple	6	(1)	
10	-	No More Mr. Nice Guy	Alice Cooper	Warner	4	(25)	
11	11	All Because Of You	Geordie	EMI	6		F
12	-	Also Sprach Zarathustra (2001)	Deodata	CTI	5	(2)	F L
13	-	Wonderful Dream	Ann-Marie David	Epic	4		F L
14	5	Tweedle Dee	Little Jimmy Osmond	MGM	7	(59)	
15	-	One And One Is One	Medicine Head	Polydor	7		F
16	2	Get Down	Gilbert O'Sullivan	MAM	8	(7)	
17	3	I'm A Clown/Some Kind Of A...	David Cassidy	Bell	8		
18	-	Big Eight	Judge Dread	Big Shot	5		
19	-	Can The Can	Suzi Quatro	RAK	7	(56)	F
20	-	Broken Down Angel	Nazareth	Mooncrest	5		F

June 1973

This Mnth	Prev Mnth	Title	Artist	Label	Wks 20	(US Pos)	
1	19	Can The Can	Suzi Quatro	RAK	7	(56)	F
2	-	Rubber Bullets	10cc	UK	9	(73)	
3	3	See My Baby Jive	Wizzard	Harvest	10		
4	15	One And One Is One	Medicine Head	Polydor	7		F
5	-	Albatross	Fleetwood Mac	CBS	8		
6	8	And I Love You So	Perry Como	RCA	12	(29)	
7	-	The Groover	T. Rex	EMI	5		
8	-	Stuck In The Middle With You	Stealer's Wheel	A&M	6	(6)	F L
9	1	Tie A Yellow Ribbon Round The..	Dawn	Bell	17	(1)	
10	-	Walking In The Rain	Partridge Family	Bell	5		L
11	-	You Are The Sunshine Of My Life	Stevie Wonder	Tamla Motown	5	(1)	
12	-	Welcome Home	Peters & Lee	Philips	15		F
13	-	Snoopy Vs. The Red Baron	Hotshots	Mooncrest	8		F L
14	-	Give Me Love (Give Me Peace On Earth)	George Harrison	Apple	6	(1)	
15	2	Hell Raiser	Sweet	RCA	6		
16	-	Walk On The Wild Side	Lou Reed	RCA	4	(16)	F L
17	-	Live And Let Die	Wings	Apple	7	(2)	
18	20	Broken Down Angel	Nazareth	Mooncrest	5		F
19	-	Skweeze Me Pleeze Me	Slade	Polydor	6		
20	12	Also Sprach Zarathustra (2001)	Deodata	CTI	5	(2)	F L

April 1973

This Mnth	Prev Mnth	Title	Artist	Label	Wks 20	(UK Pos)	
1	20	The Night The Lights Went Out In Georgia	Vicki Lawrence	Bell	10		F G L
2	-	Tie A Yellow Ribbon Round The Old Oak Tree	Dawn	Bell	14	(1)	G
3	17	Sing	Carpenters	A&M	9		G
4	8	Neither One Of Us (Wants To Be...)	Gladys Knight & The Pips	Soul	9	(31)	
5	-	The Cisco Kid	War	UA	7		G
6	12	Ain't No Woman (Like The One...)	Four Tops	Dunhill	9		G
7	-	Masterpiece	Temptations	Gordy	6		L
8	9	Danny's Song	Anne Murray	Capitol	9		
9	-	Little Willy	Sweet	Bell	9	(4)	F G
10	1	Killing Me Softly With His Song	Roberta Flack	Atlantic	12	(6)	G
11	10	Break Up To Make Up	Stylistics	Avco	7	(34)	G
12	-	The Twelfth Of Never	Donny Osmond	MGM	6	(1)	G
13	-	Stir It Up	Johnny Nash	Epic	5	(13)	L
14	-	You Are The Sunshine Of My Life	Stevie Wonder	Tamla	10	(7)	G
15	18	Call Me (Come Back Home)	Al Green	Hi	6		G
16	-	Stuck In The Middle With You	Stealer's Wheel	A&M	9	(8)	F L
17	3	Also Sprach Zarathustra (2001)	Deodata	CTI	8	(7)	F L
18	-	Drift Away	Dobie Gray	Decca	9		G L
19	2	Love Train	O'Jays	Philly International	9	(9)	G
20	-	Peaceful	Helen Reddy	Capitol	4		

May 1973

This Mnth	Prev Mnth	Title	Artist	Label	Wks 20	(UK Pos)	
1	2	Tie A Yellow Ribbon Round The...	Dawn	Bell	14	(1)	G
2	14	You Are The Sunshine Of My Life	Stevie Wonder	Tamla	10	(7)	G
3	9	Little Willy	Sweet	Bell	9	(4)	F G
4	-	Frankenstein	Edgar Winter Group	Epic	10	(18)	F G
5	18	Drift Away	Dobie Gray	Decca	9		G L
6	-	Daniel	Elton John	MCA	9	(4)	G
7	16	Stuck In The Middle With You	Stealer's Wheel	A&M	9	(8)	F L
8	1	The Night The Lights Went Out In...	Vicki Lawrence	Bell	10		F G L
9	-	My Love	Paul McCartney & Wings	Apple	10	(9)	G
10	5	The Cisco Kid	War	UA	7		G
11	-	Wildflower	Skylark	Capitol	9		F L
12	-	Reeling In The Years	Steely Dan	ABC	6		
13	-	Pillow Talk	Sylvia	Vibration	11	(14)	F G
14	12	The Twelfth Of Never	Donny Osmond	MGM	6	(1)	G
15	-	Hocus Pocus	Focus	Sire	7	(20)	F L
16	3	Sing	Carpenters	A&M	9		G
17	-	Daisy A Day	Jud Strunk	MGM	4		F L
18	-	Funky Worm	Ohio Players	Westbound	3		F G
19	7	Masterpiece	Temptations	Gordy	6		L
20	-	I'm Gonna Love You Just A Little More Baby	Barry White	20th Century	9	(23)	F G

June 1973

This Mnth	Prev Mnth	Title	Artist	Label	Wks 20	(UK Pos)	
1	9	My Love	Paul McCartney & Wings	Apple	10	(9)	G
2	13	Pillow Talk	Sylvia	Vibration	11	(14)	F G
3	20	I'm Gonna Love You Just A Little...	Barry White	20th Century	9	(23)	F G
4	-	Playground In My Mind	Clint Holmes	Epic	10		F G L
5	6	Daniel	Elton John	MCA	9	(4)	G
6	4	Frankenstein	Edgar Winter Group	Epic	10	(18)	F G
7	-	Give Me Love (Give Me Peace On Earth)	George Harrison	Apple	9	(8)	G
8	-	Will It Go Round In Circles	Billy Preston	A&M	11		G
9	-	Right Place Wrong Time	Dr. John	Atco	8		F L
10	-	Kodachrome	Paul Simon	Columbia	8		
11	-	Long Train Running	Doobie Brothers	Warner	7		
12	1	Tie A Yellow Ribbon Round The...	Dawn	Bell	14	(1)	G
13	-	One Of A Kind (Love Affair)	Spinners	Atlantic	5		G
14	2	You Are The Sunshine Of My Life	Stevie Wonder	Tamla	10	(7)	G
15	15	Hocus Pocus	Focus	Sire	7	(20)	F L
16	-	Shambala	Three Dog Night	Dunhill	11		G
17	5	Drift Away	Dobie Gray	Decca	9		G L
18	-	Bad, Bad Leroy Brown	Jim Croce	ABC	12		G
19	11	Wildflower	Skylark	Capitol	9		F L
20	3	Little Willy	Sweet	Bell	9	(4)	F G

US 1973
APR-JUNE

◆ Led Zeppelin set off on a US tour modestly labelled, "The biggest and most profitable rock & roll tour in the history of the United States" – which, at the time, it probably was.

◆ Attracting big audiences were Paul Simon's and the Electric Light Orchestra's first tours, Bread's last and Carole King's free concert in Central Park. Also drawing the crowds was a British Re-Invasion show featuring Herman's Hermits, Gerry & The Pacemakers, The Searchers and Wayne Fontana & The Mindbenders.

◆ Guests on *American Bandstand*'s 20th anniversary show included Three Dog Night, Paul Revere and The Raiders and Little Richard, with Fabian, Conway Twitty and Annette appearing on film.

UK 1973 JULY-SEPT

◆ 'Monster Mash' by Bobby 'Boris' Pickett & The Crypt Kickers, which had topped the US chart in 1962, not only returned to the Top 10 but also hit in re-issue-mad Britain for the first time.

◆ David Bowie and Jethro Tull (who topped the US LP chart with **A Passion Play**) announced that their touring days were over. The Everly Brothers split up and Ray Davis quit The Kinks. More permanent, however, was the dissolution of The Doors and Eno's departure from Roxy Music.

◆ The first Reading Festival was held with headliners including Traffic, Eric Burdon and the transatlantically successful Dutch rockers, Focus.

◆ Much to his annoyance George Harrison had to pay £1 million in taxes on the money raised by his charity album, **The Concert For Bangla Desh.**

July 1973

This Mnth	Prev Mnth	Title	Artist	Label	Wks 20	(US Pos)	
1	12	Welcome Home	Peters & Lee	Philips	15		F
2	19	Skweeze Me Pleeze Me	Slade	Polydor	6		
3	-	Life On Mars	David Bowie	RCA	8		
4	-	Born To Be With You	Dave Edmunds	Rockfield	7		
5	13	Snoopy Vs. The Red Baron	Hotshots	Mooncrest	8		F L
6	-	Take Me To The Mardi Gras	Paul Simon	CBS	5		
7	2	Rubber Bullets	10cc	UK	9	(73)	
8	-	Saturday Night's Alright For Fighting	Elton John	DJM	5	(12)	
9	-	I'm The Leader Of The Gang (I Am)	Gary Glitter	Bell	8		
10	5	Albatross	Fleetwood Mac	CBS	8		
11	-	Going Home	Osmonds	MGM	6	(36)	
12	-	Alright Alright Alright	Mungo Jerry	Dawn	6		
13	-	Randy	Blue Mink	EMI	5		L
14	17	Live And Let Die	Wings	Apple	7	(2)	
15	-	Gaye	Clifford T. Ward	Charisma	5		F L
16	14	Give Me Love (Give Me Peace On Earth)	George Harrison	Apple	6	(1)	
17	-	Honaloochie Boogie	Mott The Hoople	CBS	3		
18	7	The Groover	T. Rex	EMI	5		
19	-	Can You Do It	Geordie	EMI	4		L
20	-	Step By Step	Joe Simon	Mojo	3	(37)	F L

August 1973

This Mnth	Prev Mnth	Title	Artist	Label	Wks 20	(US Pos)	
1	9	I'm The Leader Of The Gang (I Am)	Gary Glitter	Bell	8		
2	1	Welcome Home	Peters & Lee	Philips	15		F
3	-	Yesterday Once More	Carpenters	A&M	8	(2)	
4	-	48 Crash	Suzi Quatro	RAK	5		
5	12	Alright Alright Alright	Mungo Jerry	Dawn	6		
6	-	Spanish Eyes	Al Martino	Capitol	13		L
7	11	Going Home	Osmonds	MGM	6	(36)	
8	-	You Can Do Magic	Limmie & The Family Cookin'	Avco	7	(84)	F
9	3	Life On Mars	David Bowie	RCA	8		
10	-	Touch Me In The Morning	Diana Ross	Tamla Motown	6	(1)	
11	-	Ying Tong Song	Goons	Decca	4		L
12	-	Bad Bad Boy	Nazareth	Mooncrest	5		
13	-	(Dancing) On A Saturday Night	Barry Blue	Bell	9		F
14	-	Young Love	Donny Osmond	MGM	7	(25)	
15	-	Smarty Pants	First Choice	Bell	5	(56)	L
16	13	Randy	Blue Mink	EMI	5		L
17	15	Gaye	Clifford T. Ward	Charisma	5		F L
18	-	All Right Now	Free	Island	3		
19	-	Rising Sun	Medicine Head	Polydor	5		L
20	-	Summer (The First Time)	Bobby Goldsboro	UA	5	(21)	

September 1973

This Mnth	Prev Mnth	Title	Artist	Label	Wks 20	(US Pos)	
1	-	Angel Fingers	Wizzard	Harvest	8		
2	14	Young Love	Donny Osmond	MGM	7	(25)	
3	-	Rock On	David Essex	CBS	7	(5)	F
4	13	(Dancing) On A Saturday Night	Barry Blue	Bell	9		F
5	6	Spanish Eyes	Al Martino	Capitol	13		L
6	-	Angie	Rolling Stones	Rolling Stone	5	(1)	
7	8	You Can Do Magic	Limmie & The Family Cookin'	Avco	7	(84)	F
8	-	Oh No Not My Baby	Rod Stewart	Mercury	5	(59)	
9	-	Say, Has Anybody Seen My Sweet Gypsy Rose	Dawn	Bell	5	(3)	L
10	-	Like Sister And Brother	Drifters	Bell	6		
11	3	Yesterday Once More	Carpenters	A&M	8	(2)	
12	-	Ballroom Blitz	Sweet	RCA	6	(5)	
13	-	Pick Up The Pieces	Hudson-Ford	A&M	4		F
14	-	Monster Mash	Bobby 'Boris' Pickett & The Crypt Kickers	London American	6	(10)	F L
15	-	The Dean And I	10cc	UK	4		
16	20	Summer (The First Time)	Bobby Goldsboro	UA	5	(21)	
17	-	Eye Level	Simon Park Orchestra	Columbia	10		F G L
18	2	Welcome Home	Peters & Lee	Philips	15		F
19	-	For The Good Times	Perry Como	RCA	10		L
20	1	I'm The Leader Of The Gang (I Am)	Gary Glitter	Bell	8		

July 1973

This Mnth	Prev Mnth	Title	Artist	Label	Wks 20	(UK Pos)	
1	8	Will It Go Round In Circles	Billy Preston	A&M	11		G
2	18	Bad, Bad Leroy Brown	Jim Croce	ABC	12		G
3	10	Kodachrome	Paul Simon	Columbia	8		
4	16	Shambala	Three Dog Night	Dunhill	11		G
5	-	Yesterday Once More	Carpenters	A&M	9	(2)	G
6	7	Give Me Love (Give Me Peace On...)	George Harrison	Apple	9	(8)	G
7	-	Smoke On The Water	Deep Purple	Warner	9	(21)	G L
8	4	Playground In My Mind	Clint Holmes	Epic	10		F G L
9	-	Boogie Woogie Bugle Boy	Bette Midler	Atlantic	6		
10	-	Diamond Girl	Seals & Crofts	Warner	7		
11	-	Natural High	Bloodstone	London	6	(40)	F G L
12	9	Right Place Wrong Time	Dr. John	Atco	8		F L
13	1	My Love	Paul McCartney & Wings	Apple	10	(9)	G
14	11	Long Train Running	Doobie Brothers	Warner	7		
15	-	Money	Pink Floyd	Harvest	5		F
16	3	I'm Gonna Love You Just A Little...	Barry White	20th Century	9	(23)	F G
17	-	Monster Mash	Bobby 'Boris' Pickett & The Crypt Kickers	Parrott	7	(3)	F L
18	-	Touch Me In The Morning	Diana Ross	Motown	12	(9)	
19	-	Behind Closed Doors	Charlie Rich	Epic	4	(16)	F G
20	-	The Morning After (Song From The Poseidon Adventure)	Maureen McGovern	20th Century	9		F G

August 1973

This Mnth	Prev Mnth	Title	Artist	Label	Wks 20	(UK Pos)	
1	-	Live And Let Die	Paul McCartney & Wings	Apple	8	(9)	G
2	20	The Morning After (Song From...)	Maureen McGovern	20th Century	9		F G
3	-	Brother Louie	Stories	Kama Sutra	11		F G L
4	18	Touch Me In The Morning	Diana Ross	Motown	12	(9)	
5	2	Bad, Bad Leroy Brown	Jim Croce	ABC	12		G
6	-	Let's Get It On	Marvin Gaye	Tamla	15	(31)	G
7	-	Get Down	Gilbert O'Sullivan	MAM	8	(1)	G L
8	-	Uneasy Rider	Charlie Daniels Band	Kama Sutra	5		F
9	7	Smoke On The Water	Deep Purple	Warner	9	(21)	G L
10	-	Feelin' Stronger Every Day	Chicago	Columbia	9		
11	17	Monster Mash	Bobby 'Boris' Pickett & Crypt...	Parrott	7	(3)	F L
12	-	I Believe In You (You Believe In Me)	Johnnie Taylor	Stax	8		G
13	5	Yesterday Once More	Carpenters	A&M	9	(2)	G
14	-	Delta Dawn	Helen Reddy	Capitol	10		G
15	10	Diamond Girl	Seals & Crofts	Warner	7		
16	-	Say, Has Anybody Seen My Sweet Gypsy Rose	Dawn Featuring Tony Orlando	Bell	9	(12)	G
17	4	Shambala	Three Dog Night	Dunhill	11		G
18	-	Here I Am (Come And Take Me)	Al Green	Hi	8		G
19	-	If You Want Me To Stay	Sly & The Family Stone	Epic	8		G L
20	1	Will It Go Round In Circles	Billy Preston	A&M	11		G

September 1973

This Mnth	Prev Mnth	Title	Artist	Label	Wks 20	(UK Pos)	
1	6	Let's Get It On	Marvin Gaye	Tamla	15	(31)	G
2	14	Delta Dawn	Helen Reddy	Capitol	10		G
3	16	Say, Has Anybody Seen My Sweet...	Dawn Featuring Tony Orlando	Bell	9	(12)	G
4	3	Brother Louie	Stories	Kama Sutra	11		F G L
5	-	We're An American Band	Grand Funk	Capitol	10		F G
6	-	Loves Me Like A Rock	Paul Simon	Columbia	10	(39)	G
7	4	Touch Me In The Morning	Diana Ross	Motown	12	(9)	
8	1	Live And Let Die	Paul McCartney & Wings	Apple	8	(9)	G
9	-	Half-Breed	Cher	MCA	11		G
10	-	Higher Ground	Stevie Wonder	Tamla	9	(29)	
11	-	Gypsy Man	War	UA	6		
12	-	That Lady	Isley Brothers	T-Neck	10	(14)	G
13	18	Here I Am (Come And Take Me)	Al Green	Hi	8		G
14	-	Saturday Night's Alright For Fighting	Elton John	MCA	6	(7)	
15	-	My Maria	B.W. Stevenson	RCA	7		F L
16	2	The Morning After (Song From...)	Maureen McGovern	20th Century	8		F G
17	7	Get Down	Gilbert O'Sullivan	MAM	8	(1)	G L
18	19	If You Want Me To Stay	Sly & The Family Stone	Epic	8		G L
19	10	Feelin' Stronger Every Day	Chicago	Columbia	9		
20	-	Ramblin' Man	Allman Brothers Band	Capricorn	9		F L

US 1973 JULY-SEPT

▲ The best attended Rock Festival of the era was the Summer Jam Festival at Watkins Glen (New York), where 600,000 saw the Grateful Dead (above), The Band and The Allman Brothers.

◆ Jim Croce, whose course was set for superstardom, died in a plane crash. Ex-Byrds Clarence White and Gram Parsons also met untimely ends as did Larry Finnegan, who had a major hit in 1962 with 'Dear One'.

◆ Neil Young was the first artist to appear at the Roxy Theatre in L.A., and country singer/songwriter Willie Nelson held the first of his famous Independence Day all-star picnics.

UK 1973
OCT-DEC

◆ It was announced that David Bowie had sold over eight million units in Britain in two years, making him the biggest seller since The Beatles.

▲ Hottest producer/ songwriters in Britain in 1973 were Nicky Chinn & Mike Chapman, who were responsible for hits from Sweet, (above), American rocker Suzi Quatro and new teen idols Mud.

◆ Gary Glitter and Slade had million sellers with UK-only hits that entered the charts in pole position, 'I Love You Love Me Love' and 'Merry Xmas Everybody' respectively.

October 1973

This Mnth	Prev Mnth	Title	Artist	Label	Wks 20	(US Pos)	
1	17	Eye Level	Simon Park Orchestra	Columbia	10		F G L
2	-	My Friend Stan	Slade	Polydor	6		
3	-	Nutbush City Limits	Ike & Tina Turner	UA	7	(22)	L
4	12	Ballroom Blitz	Sweet	RCA	6	(5)	
5	14	Monster Mash	Bobby 'Boris' Pickett & The Crypt Kickers	London American	6	(10)	F L
6	-	The Laughing Gnome	David Bowie	Deram	6		
7	19	For The Good Times	Perry Como	RCA	10		L
8	-	Daydreamer/The Puppy Song	David Cassidy	Bell	8		
9	-	Caroline	Status Quo	Vertigo	8		
10	-	Goodbye Yellow Brick Road	Elton John	DJM	7	(2)	
11	1	Angel Fingers	Wizzard	Harvest	8		
12	-	Joybringer	Manfred Mann's Earth Band	Vertigo	5		L
13	-	A Hard Rain's Gonna Fall	Bryan Ferry	Island	5		F
14	-	Sorrow	David Bowie	RCA	8		
15	-	Ghetto Child	Detroit Spinners	Atlantic	6	(29)	
16	8	Oh No Not My Baby	Rod Stewart	Mercury	5	(59)	
17	5	Spanish Eyes	Al Martino	Capitol	13		L
18	-	All The Way From Memphis	Mott The Hoople	CBS	4		
19	-	Showdown	Electric Light Orchestra	Harvest	5	(53)	
20	-	That Lady (Pt. 1)	Isley Brothers	Epic	2	(6)	

November 1973

This Mnth	Prev Mnth	Title	Artist	Label	Wks 20	(US Pos)	
1	-	Let Me In	Osmonds	MGM	9	(36)	
2	14	Sorrow	David Bowie	RCA	8		
3	8	Daydreamer/The Puppy Song	David Cassidy	Bell	8		
4	-	Top Of The World	Carpenters	A&M	8	(1)	
5	-	Dyna-Mite	Mud	RAK	7		
6	1	Eye Level	Simon Park Orchestra	Columbia	10		F G L
7	-	I Love You Love Me Love	Gary Glitter	Bell	12		G
8	15	Ghetto Child	Detroit Spinners	Atlantic	6	(29)	
9	7	For The Good Times	Perry Como	RCA	10		L
10	-	Photograph	Ringo Starr	Apple	5	(1)	
11	-	This Flight Tonight	Nazareth	Mooncrest	5		
12	9	Caroline	Status Quo	Vertigo	8		
13	-	When I Fall In Love	Donny Osmond	MGM	9	(14)	
14	10	Goodbye Yellow Brick Road	Elton John	DJM	7	(2)	
15	-	Do You Wanna Dance	Barry Blue	Bell	6		
16	19	Showdown	Electric Light Orchestra	Harvest	5	(53)	
17	-	Deck Of Cards	Max Bygraves	Pye	5		L
18	-	Paper Roses	Marie Osmond	MGM	11	(5)	F L
19	2	My Friend Stan	Slade	Polydor	6		
20	-	Won't Somebody Dance With Me	Lynsey De Paul	MAM	5		

December 1973

This Mnth	Prev Mnth	Title	Artist	Label	Wks 20	(US Pos)	
1	7	I Love You Love Me Love	Gary Glitter	Bell	12		G
2	-	My Coo-Ca-Choo	Alvin Stardust	Magnet	12		F
3	-	You Won't Find Another Fool Like Me	New Seekers	Polydor	12		
4	18	Paper Roses	Marie Osmond	MGM	11	(5)	F L
5	-	Lamplight	David Essex	CBS	11	(71)	
6	-	Merry Xmas Everybody	Slade	Polydor	7		G
7	-	Why Oh Why Oh Why	Gilbert O'Sullivan	MAM	10		
8	-	Roll Away The Stone	Mott The Hoople	CBS	9		
9	-	I Wish It Could Be Christmas Everyday	Wizzard	Harvest	7		
10	-	Street Life	Roxy Music	Island	8		
11	13	When I Fall In Love	Donny Osmond	MGM	9	(14)	
12	5	Dyna-Mite	Mud	RAK	7		
13	1	Let Me In	Osmonds	MGM	9	(36)	
14	-	Truck On (Tyke)	T. Rex	EMI	7		
15	-	The Show Must Go On	Leo Sayer	Chrysalis	9		F
16	15	Do You Wanna Dance	Barry Blue	Bell	6		
17	-	Helen Wheels	Paul McCartney & Wings	Apple	4	(10)	
18	-	Forever	Roy Wood	Harvest	9		
19	-	Loving And Free/Amoureuse	Kiki Dee	Rocket	5		F
20	10	Photograph	Ringo Starr	Apple	5	(1)	

October 1973

This Mnth	Prev Mnth	Title	Artist	Label	Wks 20	(UK Pos)	
1	9	Half-Breed	Cher	MCA	11		G
2	-	Angie	Rolling Stones	Rolling Stone	10	(5)	G
3	20	Ramblin' Man	Allman Brothers Band	Capricorn	9		F L
4	1	Let's Get It On	Marvin Gaye	Tamla	15	(31)	G
5	-	Midnight Train To Georgia	Gladys Knight & The Pips	Buddah	12	(10)	G
6	10	Higher Ground	Stevie Wonder	Tamla	9	(29)	
7	12	That Lady	Isley Brothers	T-Neck	10	(14)	G
8	-	Keep On Truckin' (Pt 1)	Eddie Kendricks	Tamla	13	(18)	F G
9	6	Loves Me Like A Rock	Paul Simon	Columbia	10	(39)	G
10	5	We're An American Band	Grand Funk	Capitol	10		F G
11	-	Yes We Can Can	Pointer Sisters	Blue Thumb	7		F
12	-	Heartbeat - It's A Lovebeat	DeFranco Family	20th Century	9		F G
13	-	Paper Roses	Marie Osmond	MGM	9	(2)	F G L
14	-	All I Know	Garfunkel	Columbia	7		F
15	15	My Maria	B.W. Stevenson	RCA	7		F L
16	2	Delta Dawn	Helen Reddy	Capitol	10		G
17	-	Knockin' On Heaven's Door	Bob Dylan	Columbia	6	(14)	L
18	-	Free Ride	Edgar Winter Group	Epic	4		L
19	-	Basketball Jones Feat. Tyrone Shoelaces	Cheech & Chong	Ode	4		F
20	-	China Grove	Doobie Brothers	Warner	4		

November 1973

This Mnth	Prev Mnth	Title	Artist	Label	Wks 20	(UK Pos)	
1	8	Keep On Truckin' (Pt 1)	Eddie Kendricks	Tamla	13	(18)	F G
2	5	Midnight Train To Georgia	Gladys Knight & The Pips	Buddah	12	(10)	G
3	12	Heartbeat - It's A Lovebeat	DeFranco Family	20th Century	9		F G
4	-	Photograph	Ringo Starr	Apple	9	(8)	G
5	2	Angie	Rolling Stones	Rolling Stone	10	(5)	G
6	13	Paper Roses	Marie Osmond	MGM	9	(2)	F G L
7	-	Space Race	Billy Preston	A&M	9		G
8	-	Top Of The World	Carpenters	A&M	11	(5)	G
9	1	Half-Breed	Cher	MCA	11		G
10	-	Just You 'n' Me	Chicago	Columbia	9		G
11	14	All I Know	Garfunkel	Columbia	7		F
12	-	I Got A Name	Jim Croce	ABC	6		
13	3	Ramblin' Man	Allman Brothers Band	Capricorn	9		F L
14	-	You're A Special Part Of Me	Marvin Gaye & Diana Ross	Motown	5		
15	-	The Love I Lost (Part 1)	Harold Melvin & The Blue Notes	Philly International	7	(21)	G
16	-	Goodbye Yellow Brick Road	Elton John	MCA	9	(6)	G
17	17	Knockin' On Heaven's Door	Bob Dylan	Columbia	6	(14)	L
18	4	Let's Get It On	Marvin Gaye	Tamla	15	(31)	G
19	-	Why Me	Kris Kristofferson	Monument	3		F G L
20	-	The Most Beautiful Girl	Charlie Rich	Epic	11	(2)	G

December 1973

This Mnth	Prev Mnth	Title	Artist	Label	Wks 20	(UK Pos)	
1	16	Goodbye Yellow Brick Road	Elton John	MCA	9	(6)	G
2	20	The Most Beautiful Girl	Charlie Rich	Epic	11	(2)	G
3	8	Top Of The World	Carpenters	A&M	11	(5)	G
4	10	Just You 'n' Me	Chicago	Columbia	9		G
5	-	Hello It's Me	Todd Rundgren	Bearsville	8		L
6	-	Leave Me Alone (Ruby Red Dress)	Helen Reddy	Capitol	8		G
7	-	Time In A Bottle	Jim Croce	ABC	11		G
8	4	Photograph	Ringo Starr	Apple	9	(8)	G
9	-	The Joker	Steve Miller Band	Capitol	11		F G
10	-	If You're Ready Come Go With Me	Staple Singers	Stax	6	(34)	G
11	7	Space Race	Billy Preston	A&M	9		G
12	15	The Love I Lost (Part 1)	Harold Melvin & The Blue Notes	Philly International	7	(21)	G
13	1	Keep On Truckin' (Pt 1)	Eddie Kendricks	Tamla	13	(18)	F G
14	-	Never, Never Gonna Give Ya Up	Barry White	20th Century	11	(14)	G
15	2	Midnight Train To Georgia	Gladys Knight & The Pips	Buddah	12	(10)	G
16	-	Show And Tell	Al Wilson	Rocky Road	11		F G L
17	-	Smokin' In The Boys Room	Brownsville Station	Big Tree	8	(27)	F G L
18	3	Heartbeat - It's A Lovebeat	DeFranco Family	20th Century	9		F G
19	-	Living For The City	Stevie Wonder	Tamla	9	(15)	
20	-	Rockin' Roll Baby	Stylistics	Avco	4	(6)	

US
1973
OCT-DEC

◆ In 1973, rock continued to fragment and progressive FM radio no longer seemed to be breaking new acts. *Rolling Stone* added politics and art to the magazine's musical content and wondered if "rock had run out of new things to say".

◆ In the year when 75% of new albums failed to break even, Virgin released its successful debut LP, **Tubular Bells** by Mike Oldfield. It was a year when soul was supreme, southern rock was on the rise and female vocalists accounted for a record nine US No. 1s.

◆ Top entertainer Bobby Darin died of heart problems aged 37, and gospel great Sister Rosetta Tharpe and hit comedian Allan Sherman also passed away.

◆ CBGB's opened in New York – the club would help launch the careers of acts like Blondie, The Ramones and Talking Heads.

181

UK 1974 JAN-MAR

▲ Newcomers who were creating interest included: Queen, Leo Sayer (above), Alvin Stardust, Bad Company, The Wombles, and a new-look Bay City Rollers.

◆ The main winners in the *NME* poll were David Bowie (Top Male), Diana Ross (Top Female) and Yes (Top Group). Incidentally, Yes, who quickly sold out their Madison Square Garden shows, scored their first UK chart top-per with the LP **Tales From Topographic Oceans.**

January 1974

This Mnth	Prev Mnth	Title	Artist	Label	Wks 20	(US Pos)	
1	3	You Won't Find Another Fool Like Me	New Seekers	Polydor	12		
2	15	The Show Must Go On	Leo Sayer	Chrysalis	9		F
3	6	Merry Xmas Everybody	Slade	Polydor	7		G
4	2	My Coo-Ca-Choo	Alvin Stardust	Magnet	12		F
5	-	Dance With The Devil	Cozy Powell	RAK	10	(49)	F
6	1	I Love You Love Me Love	Gary Glitter	Bell	12		G
7	18	Forever	Roy Wood	Harvest	9		
8	4	Paper Roses	Marie Osmond	MGM	11	(5)	F L
9	-	Radar Love	Golden Earring	Track	6	(13)	F L
10	9	I Wish It Could Be Christmas Everyday	Wizzard	Harvest	7		
11	-	Pool Hall Richard/I Wish It Would Rain	Faces	Warner	7		
12	-	Love On A Mountain Top	Robert Knight	Monument	10		F
13	5	Lamplight	David Essex	CBS	11	(71)	
14	-	Teenage Rampage	Sweet	RCA	6		
15	-	Tiger Feet	Mud	RAK	8		
16	8	Roll Away The Stone	Mott The Hoople	CBS	9		
17	-	Solitaire	Andy Williams	CBS	8		L
18	10	Street Life	Roxy Music	Island	8		
19	7	Why Oh Why Oh Why	Gilbert O'Sullivan	MAM	10		
20	14	Truck On (Tyke)	T. Rex	EMI	7		

February 1974

This Mnth	Prev Mnth	Title	Artist	Label	Wks 20	(US Pos)	
1	15	Tiger Feet	Mud	RAK	8		
2	14	Teenage Rampage	Sweet	RCA	6		
3	17	Solitaire	Andy Williams	CBS	8		L
4	-	The Man Who Sold The World	Lulu	Polydor	6		
5	5	Dance With The Devil	Cozy Powell	RAK	10	(49)	F
6	-	Devil Gate Drive	Suzi Quatro	RAK	7		
7	-	Rockin' Roll Baby	Stylistics	Avco	6	(14)	
8	-	All Of My Life	Diana Ross	Tamla Motown	6		
9	2	The Show Must Go On	Leo Sayer	Chrysalis	9		F
10	-	The Wombling Song	Wombles	CBS	7		F
11	1	You Won't Find Another Fool Like Me	New Seekers	Polydor	12		
12	-	How Come	Ronnie Lane	GM	4		F L
13	9	Radar Love	Golden Earring	Track	6	(13)	F L
14	7	Forever	Roy Wood	Harvest	9		
15	12	Love On A Mountain Top	Robert Knight	Monument	10		F
16	-	Jealous Mind	Alvin Stardust	Magnet	6		
17	4	My Coo-Ca-Choo	Alvin Stardust	Magnet	12		
18	-	Teenage Lament '74	Alice Cooper	Warner	3	(48)	L
19	-	Teenage Dream	Marc Bolan & T. Rex	EMI	3		
20	-	Rebel Rebel	David Bowie	RCA	5	(64)	

March 1974

This Mnth	Prev Mnth	Title	Artist	Label	Wks 20	(US Pos)	
1	-	The Air That I Breathe	Hollies	Polydor	7	(6)	
2	-	Billy, Don't Be A Hero	Paper Lace	Bus Stop	9	(96)	F
3	16	Jealous Mind	Alvin Stardust	Magnet	6		
4	-	You're Sixteen	Ringo Starr	Apple	7	(1)	L
5	-	The Most Beautiful Girl	Charlie Rich	CBS	9	(1)	F
6	6	Devil Gate Drive	Suzi Quatro	RAK	7		
7	-	Remember (Sha-La-La)	Bay City Rollers	Bell	6		
8	-	Jet	Paul McCartney & Wings	Apple	6	(7)	
9	10	The Wombling Song	Wombles	CBS	7		F
10	-	It's You	Freddie Starr	Tiffany	6		F L
11	20	Rebel Rebel	David Bowie	RCA	5	(64)	
12	-	I Get A Little Sentimental Over You	New Seekers	Polydor	6		L
13	-	Candle In The Wind	Elton John	DJM	6		
14	-	Ma He's Making Eyes At Me	Lena Zavaroni	Philips	6	(91)	F L
15	-	Emma	Hot Chocolate	RAK	7	(8)	
16	-	School Love	Barry Blue	Bell	5		L
17	1	Tiger Feet	Mud	Rak	8		
18	-	Seasons In The Sun	Terry Jacks	Bell	9	(1)	F
19	-	Never, Never Gonna Give Ya Up	Barry White	Pye International	4	(7)	F
20	-	Love's Theme	Love Unlimited Orchestra	Pye	6	(1)	F L

January 1974

This Mnth	Prev Mnth	Title	Artist	Label	Wks 20	(UK Pos)	
1	9	The Joker	Steve Miller Band	Capitol	11		F G
2	16	Show And Tell	Al Wilson	Rocky Road	11		F G L
3	7	Time In A Bottle	Jim Croce	ABC	11		
4	17	Smokin' In The Boys Room	Brownsville Station	Big Tree	8	(27)	F G L
5	-	I've Got To Use My Imagination	Gladys Knight & The Pips	Buddah	9		G
6	-	You're Sixteen	Ringo Starr	Apple	10	(4)	G
7	-	The Way We Were	Barbra Streisand	Columbia	12	(31)	G
8	19	Living For The City	Stevie Wonder	Tamla	9	(15)	
9	14	Never, Never Gonna Give Ya Up	Barry White	20th Century	11	(14)	G
10	-	Let Me Be There	Olivia Newton-John	MCA	10		F G
11	-	Love's Theme	Love Unlimited Orchestra	20th Century	11	(10)	F G L
12	-	Helen Wheels	Paul McCartney & Wings	Apple	7	(12)	
13	2	The Most Beautiful Girl	Charlie Rich	Epic	11	(2)	G
14	6	Leave Me Alone (Ruby Red Dress)	Helen Reddy	Capitol	8		G
15	-	Until You Come Back To Me (That's What I'm Gonna Do)	Aretha Franklin	Atlantic	12	(26)	G
16	-	When I Fall In Love	Donny Osmond	MGM	4	(4)	L
17	-	Me And Baby Brother	War	UA	5	(21)	
18	1	Goodbye Yellow Brick Road	Elton John	MCA	9	(6)	G
19	-	Americans	Byron MacGregor	Westbound	6		F G L
20	3	Top Of The World	Carpenters	A&M	11	(5)	G

February 1974

This Mnth	Prev Mnth	Title	Artist	Label	Wks 20	(UK Pos)	
1	7	The Way We Were	Barbra Streisand	Columbia	12	(31)	G
2	11	Love's Theme	Love Unlimited Orchestra	20th Century	11	(10)	F G L
3	6	You're Sixteen	Ringo Starr	Apple	10	(4)	G
4	15	Until You Come Back To Me (That's What I'm Gonna Do)	Aretha Franklin	Atlantic	12	(26)	G
5	-	Spiders & Snakes	Jim Stafford	MGM	9	(14)	F
6	19	Americans	Byron MacGregor	Westbound	6		F G L
7	10	Let Me Be There	Olivia Newton-John	MCA	10		F G
8	-	Jungle Boogie	Kool & The Gang	De-Lite	11		F G
9	2	Show And Tell	Al Wilson	Rocky Road	11		F G L
10	-	Rock On	David Essex	Columbia	10	(3)	F G L
11	-	Boogie Down	Eddie Kendricks	Tamla	10	(39)	G
12	5	I've Got To Use My Imagination	Gladys Knight & The Pips	Buddah	9		G
13	-	Seasons In The Sun	Terry Jacks	Bell	10	(1)	F G L
14	-	Put Your Hands Together	O'Jays	Philly International	6		
15	1	The Joker	Steve Miller Band	Capitol	11	(1)	F G
16	4	Smokin' In The Boys Room	Brownsville Station	Big Tree	8	(27)	F G L
17	-	I Love	Tom T. Hall	Mercury	5		F L
18	-	Doo Doo Doo Doo Doo (Heartbreaker)	Rolling Stones	Rolling Stone	3		
19	8	Living For The City	Stevie Wonder	Tamla	9	(15)	
20	3	Time In A Bottle	Jim Croce	ABC	11		G

March 1974

This Mnth	Prev Mnth	Title	Artist	Label	Wks 20	(UK Pos)	
1	13	Seasons In The Sun	Terry Jacks	Bell	10	(1)	F G L
2	11	Boogie Down	Eddie Kendricks	Tamla	10	(39)	G
3	-	Dark Lady	Cher	MCA	8	(36)	G
4	-	Sunshine On My Shoulders	John Denver	RCA	10		G
5	-	Mockingbird	Carly Simon & James Taylor	Elektra	8	(34)	G
6	8	Jungle Boogie	Kool & The Gang	De-Lite	11		F G
7	1	The Way We Were	Barbra Streisand	Columbia	12	(31)	G
8	10	Rock On	David Essex	Columbia	10	(3)	F G L
9	-	Jet	Paul McCartney & Wings	Apple	7	(7)	
10	-	Eres Tu (Touch The Wind)	Mocedades	Tara	7		F L
11	5	Spiders & Snakes	Jim Stafford	MGM	9	(14)	F
12	-	Bennie And The Jets	Elton John	MCA	11	(37)	G
13	-	Hooked On A Feeling	Blue Swede	EMI	9		F G
14	-	Come And Get Your Love	Redbone	Epic	10		F G L
15	2	Love's Theme	Love Unlimited Orchestra	20th Century	11	(10)	F G L
16	4	Until You Come Back To Me (That's What I'm Gonna Do)	Aretha Franklin	Atlantic	12	(26)	G
17	-	The Lord's Prayer	Sister Janet Mead	A&M	7		F G L
18	-	Trying To Hold On To My Woman	Lamont Dozier	ABC	4		F L
19	14	Put Your Hands Together	O'Jays	Philly International	6		
20	-	A Love Song	Anne Murray	Capitol	4		

◆ Many new faces appeared as the new year started: Jefferson Starship evolved from Jefferson Airplane, debut LPs from Billy Joel and Kiss were on release, and Olivia Newton-John, Kool & The Gang and The Steve Miller Band (whose 'The Joker' was a UK chart topper in 1990), made their Top 20 debuts.

◆ Bob Dylan's long-awaited US tour was an unqualified success. Dylan, who turned down $2 million for the film rights to the tour, was topping the album chart with **Planet Waves.**

◆ Dick Clark launched the American Music Awards. Twenty years later, the AMA are still running second only to the Grammys.

◆ In January, the late Jim Croce had the top two albums and a No. 1 single, 'Time In A Bottle'. No other rock performer (Elvis included) has equalled this posthumous achievement.

183

UK 1974
APR-JUNE

◆ Rick Wakeman quit Yes and his solo album **Journey To The Centre Of The Earth** reached the transatlantic Top 3. Also stretching their wings were Bill Wyman, who became the first Rolling Stone to release a solo album and The Who's Roger Daltrey, who staged his first solo concert.

◆ *NME* writers selected **Sergeant Pepper** (The Beatles), **Blonde On Blonde** (Bob Dylan) and **Pet Sounds** (Beach Boys) as the three greatest albums ever recorded.

◆ Newcomers The Rubettes, Showaddywaddy, Cockney Rebel, The Glitter Band, and Anglo-US acts Sparks and The Arrows joined Britain's mid-70s chart regulars.

◆ As Blue Swede put Sweden on the US musical map, Abba gave Scandinavia its biggest British hit, with their Eurovision Song Contest winner, 'Waterloo'.

April 1974

This Mnth	Prev Mnth	Title	Artist	Label	Wks 20	(US Pos)	
1	18	Seasons In The Sun	Terry Jacks	Bell	9	(1)	F
2	-	Angel Face	Glitter Band	Bell	7		F
3	-	Everyday	Slade	Polydor	5		
4	-	Remember Me This Way	Gary Glitter	Bell	7		
5	-	You Are Everything	Diana Ross	Tamla Motown	7		
6	2	Billy, Don't Be A Hero	Paper Lace	Bus Stop	9	(96)	F
7	15	Emma	Hot Chocolate	RAK	7	(8)	
8	-	The Cat Crept In	Mud	RAK	6		
9	-	Doctor's Orders	Sunny	CBS	5		F L
10	-	Seven Seas Of Rhye	Queen	EMI	6		F
11	-	Remember You're A Womble	Wombles	CBS	9		
12	5	The Most Beautiful Girl	Charlie Rich	CBS	9	(1)	F
13	12	I Get A Little Sentimental Over You	New Seekers	Polydor	6		L
14	-	I'm Gonna Knock On Your Door	Little Jimmy Osmond	MGM	4		L
15	-	Waterloo	Abba	Epic	7	(6)	F
16	-	Homely Girl	Chi-Lites	Brunswick	6	(54)	
17	-	Rock Around The Clock	Bill Haley & His Comets	MCA	5		L
18	-	A Walkin' Miracle	Limmie & The Family Cookin'	Avco	5		L
19	-	Long Live Love	Olivia Newton-John	Pye International	4		
20	-	Jambalaya	Carpenters	A&M	5		

May 1974

This Mnth	Prev Mnth	Title	Artist	Label	Wks 20	(US Pos)	
1	15	Waterloo	Abba	Epic	7	(6)	F
2	-	Don't Stay Away Too Long	Peters & Lee	Philips	8		
3	-	Shang-A-Lang	Bay City Rollers	Bell	6		
4	-	Sugar Baby Love	Rubettes	Polydor	7	(37)	F
5	11	Remember You're A Womble	Wombles	CBS	9		
6	-	Rock 'n' Roll Winter	Wizzard	Warner	4		
7	16	Homely Girl	Chi-Lites	Brunswick	6	(54)	
8	-	The Night Chicago Died	Paper Lace	Bus Stop	6	(1)	
9	18	A Walkin' Miracle	Limmie & The Family Cookin'	Avco	5		L
10	-	Red Dress	Alvin Stardust	Magnet	5		
11	8	The Cat Crept In	Mud	RAK	6		
12	1	Seasons In The Sun	Terry Jacks	Bell	9	(1)	F
13	-	This Town Ain't Big Enough For Both Of Us	Sparks	Island	6		F
14	-	He's Misstra Know It All	Stevie Wonder	Tamla Motown	5		
15	-	I Can't Stop	Osmonds	MCA	5	(96)	
16	5	You Are Everything	Diana Ross	Tamla Motown	7		
17	9	Doctor's Orders	Sunny	CBS	5		F L
18	-	Long Legged Woman Dressed In Black	Mungo Jerry	Dawn	5		L
19	-	Spiders & Snakes	Jim Stafford	MGM	4	(3)	F
20	-	Break The Rules	Status Quo	Vertigo	4		

June 1974

This Mnth	Prev Mnth	Title	Artist	Label	Wks 20	(US Pos)	
1	-	Hey Rock And Roll	Showaddywaddy	Bell	8		F
2	-	There's A Ghost In My House	R. Dean Taylor	Tamla Motown	7		L
3	-	The Streak	Ray Stevens	Janus	7	(1)	
4	13	This Town Ain't Big Enough For Both Of Us	Sparks	Island	6		F
5	4	Sugar Baby Love	Rubettes	Polydor	7	(37)	F
6	-	Judy Teen	Cockney Rebel	EMI	6		F
7	-	Always Yours	Gary Glitter	Bell	6		
8	-	Jarrow Song	Alan Price	Warner	5		L
9	8	The Night Chicago Died	Paper Lace	Bus Stop	6	(1)	
10	-	A Touch Too Much	Arrows	RAK	5		F L
11	-	I See A Star	Mouth & McNeal	Decca	5		F L
12	-	Go (Before You Break My Heart)	Gigliola Cinquetti	CBS	4		L
13	-	She	Charles Aznavour	Barclay	8		F L
14	-	If I Didn't Care	David Cassidy	Bell	4		
15	2	Don't Stay Away Too Long	Peters & Lee	Philips	8		
16	-	Liverpool Lou	Scaffold	Warner	4		L
17	-	I'd Love You To Want Me	Lobo	UK	6	(2)	L
18	-	One Man Band	Leo Sayer	Chrysalis	5	(96)	
19	-	The In Crowd	Bryan Ferry	Island	4		
20	3	Shang-A-Lang	Bay City Rollers	Bell	6		

184

April 1974

This Mnth	Prev Mnth	Title	Artist	Label	Wks 20	(UK Pos)	
1	12	Bennie And The Jets	Elton John	MCA	11	(37)	G
2	13	Hooked On A Feeling	Blue Swede	EMI	9		F G
3	-	TSOP (The Sound Of Philadelphia)	MFSB Featuring The Three Degrees	Philly International	10	(22)	F G L
4	14	Come And Get Your Love	Redbone	Epic	10		F G L
5	-	Best Thing That Ever Happened To Me	Gladys Knight & The Pips	Buddah	9	(7)	G
6	4	Sunshine On My Shoulders	John Denver	RCA	10		G
7	-	Oh My My	Ringo Starr	Apple	7		
8	17	The Lord's Prayer	Sister Janet Mead	A&M	7		F G L
9	1	Seasons In The Sun	Terry Jacks	Bell	10	(1)	F G L
10	-	Lookin' For A Love	Bobby Womack	UA	6		F G L
11	-	The Loco-Motion	Grand Funk	Capitol	10		G
12	-	I'll Have To Say I Love You In A Song	Jim Croce	ABC	5		L
13	-	A Very Special Love Song	Charlie Rich	Epic	4		
14	5	Mockingbird	Carly Simon & James Taylor	Elektra	8	(34)	G
15	-	Dancing Machine	Jackson Five	Motown	13		
16	-	Just Don't Want To Be Lonely	Main Ingredient	RCA	7	(27)	G L
17	3	Dark Lady	Cher	MCA	8	(36)	G
18	9	Jet	Paul McCartney & Wings	Apple	7	(7)	
19	-	Tubular Bells	Mike Oldfield	Virgin	6	(31)	F L
20	-	The Show Must Go On	Three Dog Night	Dunhill	9		G

May 1974

This Mnth	Prev Mnth	Title	Artist	Label	Wks 20	(UK Pos)	
1	-	The Streak	Ray Stevens	Barnaby	11	(1)	G
2	15	Dancing Machine	Jackson Five	Motown	13		G
3	11	The Loco-Motion	Grand Funk	Capitol	10		G
4	-	The Entertainer	Marvin Hamlisch	MCA	9	(25)	F G L
5	20	The Show Must Go On	Three Dog Night	Dunhill	9		G
6	1	Bennie And The Jets	Elton John	MCA	11	(37)	G
7	-	(I've Been) Searchin' So Long	Chicago	Columbia	7		
8	3	TSOP (The Sound Of Philadelphia)	MFSB Feat The Three Degrees	Philly International	10	(22)	F G L
9	-	Midnight At The Oasis	Maria Muldaur	Reprise	8	(21)	F
10	-	You Make Me Feel Brand New	Stylistics	Avco	11	(2)	G
11	-	Band On The Run	Paul McCartney & Wings	Apple	10	(3)	G
12	19	Tubular Bells	Mike Oldfield	Virgin	6	(31)	F L
13	5	Best Thing That Ever Happened To Me	Gladys Knight & The Pips	Buddah	9	(7)	G
14	-	I Won't Last A Day Without You	Carpenters	A&M	6	(32)	
15	2	Hooked On A Feeling	Blue Swede	EMI	9		F G
16	-	Help Me	Joni Mitchell	Asylum	6		F L
17	16	Just Don't Want To Be Lonely	Main Ingredient	RCA	7	(27)	G L
18	-	Oh Very Young	Cat Stevens	A&M	6		
19	7	Oh My My	Ringo Starr	Apple	7		
20	4	Come And Get Your Love	Redbone	Epic	10		F G L

June 1974

This Mnth	Prev Mnth	Title	Artist	Label	Wks 20	(UK Pos)	
1	10	You Make Me Feel Brand New	Stylistics	Avco	11	(2)	G
2	-	Billy, Don't Be A Hero	Bo Donaldson & The Heywoods	ABC	9		F G L
3	-	Sundown	Gordon Lightfoot	Reprise	10	(33)	G
4	11	Band On The Run	Paul McCartney & Wings	Apple	10	(3)	G
5	1	The Streak	Ray Stevens	Barnaby	11	(1)	G
6	2	Dancing Machine	Jackson Five	Motown	13		G
7	-	Be Thankful For What You Got	William DeVaughn	Roxbury	7		F G L
8	4	The Entertainer	Marvin Hamlisch	MCA	9	(25)	F G L
9	9	Midnight At The Oasis	Maria Muldaur	Reprise	8	(21)	F
10	-	If You Love Me (Let Me Know)	Olivia Newton-John	MCA	8		G
11	-	For The Love Of Money	O'Jays	Philly International	6		G
12	-	Hollywood Swinging	Kool & The Gang	De-Lite	6		G
13	16	Help Me	Joni Mitchell	Asylum	6		F L
14	-	My Girl Bill	Jim Stafford	MGM	4	(20)	
15	-	Rock The Boat	Hues Corporation	RCA	7	(6)	F G
16	18	Oh Very Young	Cat Stevens	A&M	6		
17	3	The Loco-Motion	Grand Funk	Capitol	10		G
18	-	Rock Your Baby	George McCrae	TK	7	(1)	F G L
19	-	You Won't See Me	Anne Murray	Capitol	7		
20	5	The Show Must Go On	Three Dog Night	Dunhill	9		G

US 1974 APR-JUNE

▲ The California Jam Festival which was seen by 200,000, was also taped for TV. Among the headliners were The Eagles (above), Emerson, Lake & Palmer, Black Sabbath and Deep Purple.

◆ Grand Funk Railroad scored their biggest hit with a revival of 'The Loco-Motion' and Three Dog Night collected their last Top 10 entry with a cover of Leo Sayer's, 'The Show Must Go On'. Although both acts were enormously successful in their homeland, they had little UK success.

◆ After seeing a show in Boston, Jon Landau of *Rolling Stone* made his famous remark, "I have seen rock & roll's future, and his name is Bruce Springsteen".

UK 1974 JULY-SEPT

American oldies on the UK chart included Gary Puckett's 'Young Girl', 'Baby Love' by The Supremes and Jimmy Ruffin's 'What Becomes Of The Broken Hearted'.

The Moody Blues opened the world's first quadrophonic (a system with four separate soundtracks as compared to stereo's two) recording studio in West London. One of the first projects recorded there was **Blue Jays,** a transatlantic Top 20 album by Moody members Justin Hayward & John Lodge.

Steely Dan played their last show for three years, James Taylor toured the US with up-and-coming star Linda Ronstadt, and the re-formed Crosby, Stills, Nash & Young appeared at Wembley supported by Joni Mitchell and The Band.

July 1974

This Mnth	Prev Mnth	Title	Artist	Label	Wks 20	(US Pos)	
1	13	She	Charles Aznavour	Barclay	8		F L
2	-	Kissin' In The Back Row Of The Movies	Drifters	Bell	8		
3	-	Bangin' Man	Slade	Polydor	5		
4	-	Rock Your Baby	George McCrae	Jayboy	9	(1)	F
5	17	I'd Love You To Want Me	Lobo	UK	6	(2)	L
6	-	Young Girl	Gary Puckett & The Union Gap	CBS	6		L
7	-	Band On The Run	Paul McCartney & Wings	Apple	6	(1)	
8	7	Always Yours	Gary Glitter	Bell	6		
9	-	Banana Rock	Wombles	CBS	5		
10	-	Wall Street Shuffle	10cc	UK	5		
11	1	Hey Rock And Roll	Showaddywaddy	Bell	8		F
12	18	One Man Band	Leo Sayer	Chrysalis	5	(96)	
13	-	Born With A Smile On My Face	Stephanie De Sykes	Bradley's	6		F
14	-	The Six Teens	Sweet	RCA	5		
15	-	If You Go Away	Terry Jacks	Bell	4	(68)	L
16	3	The Streak	Ray Stevens	Janus	7	(1)	
17	-	When Will I See You Again	Three Degrees	Philly International	10	(2)	
18	-	Guilty	Pearls	Bell	4		F L
19	-	Beach Baby	First Class	UK	4	(4)	F L
20	-	Going Down The Road	Roy Wood	Harvest	3		

August 1974

This Mnth	Prev Mnth	Title	Artist	Label	Wks 20	(US Pos)	
1	17	When Will I See You Again	Three Degrees	Philly International	10	(2)	
2	-	You Make Me Feel Brand New	Stylistics	Avco	9	(2)	
3	4	Rock Your Baby	George McCrae	Jayboy	9	(1)	F
4	-	Summerlove Sensation	Bay City Rollers	Bell	7		
5	13	Born With A Smile On My Face	Stephanie De Sykes	Bradley's	6		F
6	-	Rocket	Mud	RAK	5		
7	-	Rock The Boat	Hues Corporation	RCA	5	(1)	F L
8	-	What Becomes Of The Brokenhearted	Jimmy Ruffin	Tamla Motown	8		
9	-	Amateur Hour	Sparks	Island	5		
10	7	Band On The Run	Paul McCartney & Wings	Apple	6	(1)	
11	-	I'm Leaving It (All) Up To You	Donny & Marie Osmond	MGM	8	(4)	F
12	-	I Shot The Sheriff	Eric Clapton	RSO	4	(1)	F
13	-	It's Only Rock 'n Roll (But I Like It)	Rolling Stones	Rolling Stone	4	(16)	
14	-	Tonight	Rubettes	Polydor	5		
15	2	Kissin' In The Back Row Of The...	Drifters	Bell	8		
16	-	Love Me For A Reason	Osmonds	MGM	7	(10)	
17	-	Mr. Soft	Cockney Rebel	EMI	5		
18	6	Young Girl	Gary Puckett & The Union Gap	CBS	6		L
19	-	Honey Honey	Sweet Dreams	Bradley's	6	(68)	F L
20	-	Just For You	Glitter Band	Bell	4		

September 1974

This Mnth	Prev Mnth	Title	Artist	Label	Wks 20	(US Pos)	
1	-	Kung Fu Fighting	Carl Douglas	Pye	8	(1)	F L
2	16	Love Me For A Reason	Osmonds	MGM	7	(10)	
3	-	Annie's Song	John Denver	RCA	9	(1)	F L
4	-	Y Viva Espana	Sylvia	Sonet	8		L
5	11	I'm Leaving It (All) Up To You	Donny & Marie Osmond	MGM	8	(4)	F
6	-	Hang On In There Baby	Johnny Bristol	MGM	7	(8)	F L
7	-	You You You	Alvin Stardust	Magnet	6		
8	1	When Will I See You Again	Three Degrees	Philly International	10	(2)	
9	8	What Becomes Of The Brokenhearted	Jimmy Ruffin	Tamla Motown	8		
10	-	Queen Of Clubs	KC & The Sunshine Band	Jayboy	6	(66)	F
11	-	Na Na Na	Cozy Powell	RAK	6		L
12	-	Can't Get Enough Of Your Love, Babe	Barry White	Pye International	6	(1)	
13	19	Honey Honey	Sweet Dreams	Bradley's	6	(68)	F L
14	2	You Make Me Feel Brand New	Stylistics	Avco	9	(2)	
15	17	Mr. Soft	Cockney Rebel	EMI	5		
16	-	The Black Eyed Boys	Paper Lace	Bus Stop	4	(41)	L
17	-	Baby Love	Diana Ross & The Supremes	Tamla Motown	3		L
18	-	Rock 'n' Roll Lady	Showaddywaddy	Bell	4		
19	-	Rock Me Gently	Andy Kim	Capitol	5	(1)	F L
20	-	Long Tall Glasses	Leo Sayer	Chrysalis	5	(9)	

US 1974 JULY-SEPT

July 1974

This Mnth	Prev Mnth	Title	Artist	Label	Wks 20	(UK Pos)	
1	18	Rock Your Baby	George McCrae	TK	7	(1)	F G L
2	-	Annie's Song	John Denver	RCA	8	(1)	G
3	15	Rock The Boat	Hues Corporation	RCA	7	(6)	F G
4	-	Rock And Roll Heaven	Righteous Brothers	Haven	7		
5	-	On And On	Gladys Knight & The Pips	Buddah	7		G
6	-	Don't Let The Sun Go Down On Me	Elton John	MCA	6	(16)	G
7	-	The Air That I Breathe	Hollies	Epic	7	(2)	G L
8	-	Rikki Don't Lose That Number	Steely Dan	ABC	7	(58)	
9	3	Sundown	Gordon Lightfoot	Reprise	10	(33)	G
10	2	Billy, Don't Be A Hero	Bo Donaldson & The Heywoods	ABC	9		F G L
11	19	You Won't See Me	Anne Murray	Capitol	7		
12	10	If You Love Me (Let Me Know)	Olivia Newton-John	MCA	8		G
13	-	Sideshow	Blue Magic	Atco	10		F G L
14	-	One Hell Of A Woman	Mac Davis	Columbia	6		
15	-	Feel Like Makin' Love	Roberta Flack	Atlantic	8	(34)	G
16	-	Radar Love	Golden Earring	Track	5	(7)	F
17	12	Hollywood Swinging	Kool & The Gang	De-Lite	6		G
18	1	You Make Me Feel Brand New	Stylistics	Avco	11	(2)	G
19	-	Please Come To Boston	Dave Loggins	Epic	7		F L
20	-	Waterloo	Abba	Atlantic	7	(1)	F

August 1974

This Mnth	Prev Mnth	Title	Artist	Label	Wks 20	(UK Pos)	
1	-	The Night Chicago Died	Paper Lace	Mercury	8	(3)	F G L
2	15	Feel Like Makin' Love	Roberta Flack	Atlantic	8	(34)	G
3	-	(You're) Having My Baby	Paul Anka & Odia Coates	UA	8	(6)	G
4	-	Tell Me Something Good	Rufus	ABC	7		F G
5	-	Wildwood Weed	Jim Stafford	MGM	7		L
6	19	Please Come To Boston	Dave Loggins	Epic	7		F L
7	20	Waterloo	Abba	Atlantic	7	(1)	F
8	13	Sideshow	Blue Magic	Atco	10		F G L
9	-	I Shot The Sheriff	Eric Clapton	RSO	7	(9)	G
10	-	Call On Me	Chicago	Columbia	5		
11	-	I'm Leaving It (All) Up To You	Donny & Marie Osmond	MGM	7	(2)	F G
12	2	Annie's Song	John Denver	RCA	8	(1)	G
13	6	Don't Let The Sun Go Down On Me	Elton John	MCA	6	(16)	G
14	-	Keep On Smilin'	Wet Willie	Capricorn	5		F L
15	-	Rock Me Gently	Andy Kim	Capitol	9	(2)	G L
16	-	You And Me Against The World	Helen Reddy	Capitol	6		
17	8	Rikki Don't Lose That Number	Steely Dan	ABC	7	(58)	
18	-	Takin' Care Of Business	Bachman-Turner Overdrive	Mercury	5		F
19	4	Rock And Roll Heaven	Righteous Brothers	Haven	7		
20	-	Shinin' On	Grand Funk	Capitol	4		

September 1974

This Mnth	Prev Mnth	Title	Artist	Label	Wks 20	(UK Pos)	
1	15	Rock Me Gently	Andy Kim	Capitol	9	(2)	G L
2	-	Nothing From Nothing	Billy Preston	A&M	10		G
3	9	I Shot The Sheriff	Eric Clapton	RSO	7	(9)	G
4	3	(You're) Having My Baby	Paul Anka & Odia Coates	UA	8	(6)	G
5	-	Can't Get Enough Of Your Love, Babe	Barry White	20th Century	6	(8)	G
6	-	Then Came You	Dionne Warwick	Warner	11	(29)	G
7	-	I Honestly Love You	Olivia Newton-John	MCA	8	(22)	G
8	-	Clap For The Wolfman	Guess Who	RCA	7		L
9	-	You Haven't Done Nothin	Stevie Wonder	Tamla	12	(30)	G
10	11	I'm Leaving It (All) Up To You	Donny & Marie Osmond	MGM	7	(2)	F G
11	-	Hang On In There Baby	Johnny Bristol	MGM	7	(3)	F L
12	4	Tell Me Something Good	Rufus	ABC	7		F G
13	-	Beach Baby	First Class	UK	6	(13)	F L
14	-	Another Saturday Night	Cat Stevens	A&M	5	(19)	L
15	16	You And Me Against The World	Helen Reddy	Capitol	6		
16	-	Sweet Home Alabama	Lynyrd Skynyrd	MCA	9		F
17	1	The Night Chicago Died	Paper Lace	Mercury	8	(3)	F G L
18	-	Who Do You Think You Are	Bo Donaldson & The Heywoods	ABC	3		F L
19	-	It's Only Rock 'n' Roll (But I Like It)	Rolling Stones	Rolling Stone	3	(10)	
20	-	Earache My Eye - Feat. Alice Bowie	Cheech & Chong	Ode	4		L

◆ George Harrison unveiled his Dark Horse label and Led Zeppelin's recently launched label, Swan Song, had a No. 1 with Bad Company's eponymously titled album.

◆ Dance hits from George McCrae, The Hues Corporation, Barry White, Johnny Bristol and KC & The Sunshine Band laid the foundations for the forthcoming world-wide disco craze. For the record, Bristol, also penned The Osmonds transatlantic Top 10 hit, 'Love Me For A Reason'.

▲ Surprisingly, British-born, Australian-raised Olivia Newton-John was voted No. 1 female country singer (tied with Dolly Parton) in the *Billboard* Awards.

UK 1974 OCT-DEC

◆ John Denver, one of America's top selling acts of the 1970s, had his only British hit single with 'Annie's Song', written about his wife.

◆ Mike Oldfield's 15-month-old **Tubular Bells** replaced his **Hergest Ridge** at the top of the British album chart.

▲ The Drifters, who started as a trend-setting R&B act in 1953, were now resident in Britain and scored their third successive UK-written Top 10 hit, 'Down On The Beach Tonight'. Another American R&B group who would soon follow in their footsteps were female Philadelphian trio The Three Degrees (above).

October 1974

This Mnth	Prev Mnth	Title	Artist	Label	Wks 20	(US Pos)	
1	-	Sad Sweet Dreamer	Sweet Sensation	Pye	7	(14)	F
2	3	Annie's Song	John Denver	RCA	9	(1)	F L
3	-	Gee Baby	Peter Shelley	Magnet	6	(81)	F
4	19	Rock Me Gently	Andy Kim	Capitol	5	(1)	F L
5	-	Everything I Own	Ken Boothe	Trojan	9		F
6	20	Long Tall Glasses	Leo Sayer	Chrysalis	5	(9)	
7	1	Kung Fu Fighting	Carl Douglas	Pye	8	(1)	F L
8	6	Hang On In There Baby	Johnny Bristol	MGM	7	(8)	F L
9	-	Far Far Away	Slade	Polydor	5		
10	-	I Get A Kick Out Of You	Gary Shearston	Charisma	5		F L
11	-	Farewell/Bring It On Home To Me	Rod Stewart	Mercury	4		
12	-	Reggae Tune	Andy Fairweather-Low	A&M	4		F
13	-	(You're) Having My Baby	Paul Anka & Odia Coates	UA	6	(1)	L
14	-	All Of Me Loves All Of You	Bay City Rollers	Bell	6		
15	7	You You You	Alvin Stardust	Magnet	6		
16	12	Can't Get Enough Of Your Love...	Barry White	Pye International	6	(1)	
17	-	I Can't Leave You Alone	George McCrae	Jayboy	5	(50)	
18	-	Knock On Wood	David Bowie	RCA	4		
19	10	Queen Of Clubs	KC & The Sunshine Band	Jayboy	6	(66)	F
20	-	Gonna Make You A Star	David Essex	CBS	9		

November 1974

This Mnth	Prev Mnth	Title	Artist	Label	Wks 20	(US Pos)	
1	20	Gonna Make You A Star	David Essex	CBS	9		
2	-	Killer Queen	Queen	EMI	6	(12)	
3	5	Everything I Own	Ken Boothe	Trojan	9		F
4	-	(Hey There) Lonely Girl	Eddie Holman	ABC	7		F L
5	14	All Of Me Loves All Of You	Bay City Rollers	Bell	6		
6	-	You're The First, The Last, My Everything	Barry White	20th Century	9	(2)	
7	9	Far Far Away	Slade	Polydor	5		
8	-	Down On The Beach Tonight	Drifters	Bell	5		
9	-	Let's Put It All Together	Stylistics	Avco	5	(18)	
10	-	Let's Get Together Again	Glitter Band	Bell	5		
11	-	Pepper Box	Peppers	Spark	5		F L
12	13	(You're) Having My Baby	Paul Anka & Odia Coates	UA	6	(1)	L
13	-	Juke Box Jive	Rubettes	Polydor	9		
14	17	I Can't Leave You Alone	George McCrae	Jayboy	5	(50)	
15	-	The Wild One	Suzi Quatro	RAK	5		
16	-	All I Want Is You	Roxy Music	Island	6		
17	-	Oh Yes! You're Beautiful	Gary Glitter	Bell	7		
18	-	No Honestly	Lynsey De Paul	Jet	4		
19	-	Never Turn Your Back On Mother Earth	Sparks	Island	4		
20	-	Magic	Pilot	EMI	5	(5)	F

December 1974

This Mnth	Prev Mnth	Title	Artist	Label	Wks 20	(US Pos)	
1	6	You're The First, The Last, My...	Barry White	20th Century	9	(2)	
2	-	You Ain't Seen Nothin' Yet	Bachman-Turner Overdrive	Mercury	9	(1)	F L
3	13	Juke Box Jive	Rubettes	Polydor	9		
4	17	Oh Yes! You're Beautiful	Gary Glitter	Bell	7		
5	-	Lonely This Christmas	Mud	RAK	8		
6	-	My Boy	Elvis Presley	RCA	9	(20)	
7	-	Tell Him	Hello	Bell	6		F
8	-	Get Dancing	Disco Tex & The Sex-O-Lettes	Chelsea	8	(10)	F
9	-	Streets Of London	Ralph McTell	Reprise	9		F L
10	-	Ire Feelings (Skanga)	Rupie Edwards	Cactus	6		F L
11	-	Lucy In The Sky With Diamonds	Elton John	DJM	8	(1)	
12	1	Gonna Make You A Star	David Essex	CBS	9		
13	-	Wombling Merry Christmas	Wombles	CBS	5		
14	20	Magic	Pilot	EMI	5	(5)	F
15	-	You Can Make Me Dance Sing Or Anything	Rod Stewart & The Faces	Warner	4		L
16	-	The In Betweenies/Father Christmas Do Not Touch Me	Goodies	Bradley's	6		F
17	-	Too Good To Be Forgotten	Chi-Lites	Brunswick	4		
18	4	(Hey There) Lonely Girl	Eddie Holman	ABC	7		F L
19	-	Down Down	Status Quo	Vertigo	8		
20	2	Killer Queen	Queen	EMI	6	(12)	

October 1974

This Mnth	Prev Mnth	Title	Artist	Label	Wks 20	(UK Pos)	
1	6	Then Came You	Dionne Warwick	Warner	11	(29)	G
2	9	You Haven't Done Nothin	Stevie Wonder	Tamla	12	(30)	G
3	2	Nothing From Nothing	Billy Preston	A&M	10		G
4	7	I Honestly Love You	Olivia Newton-John	MCA	8	(22)	G
5	-	Can't Get Enough	Bad Company	Swan Song	8	(15)	F
6	-	The Bitch Is Back	Elton John	MCA	7	(15)	
7	-	Steppin' Out (Gonna Boogie Tonight)	Tony Orlando & Dawn	Bell	6		
8	-	Jazzman	Carole King	Ode	8		
9	-	Stop And Smell The Roses	Mac Davis	Columbia	6		
10	-	Never My Love	Blue Swede	EMI	4		L
11	13	Beach Baby	First Class	UK	6	(13)	F L
12	16	Sweet Home Alabama	Lynyrd Skynyrd	MCA	9		F
13	14	Another Saturday Night	Cat Stevens	A&M	5	(19)	L
14	11	Hang On In There Baby	Johnny Bristol	MGM	7	(3)	F L
15	-	Love Me For A Reason	Osmonds	MGM	3	(1)	L
16	20	Earache My Eye - Feat. Alice Bowie	Cheech & Chong	Ode	4		L
17	-	You Little Trustmaker	Tymes	RCA	4	(18)	L
18	-	You Ain't Seen Nothin' Yet	Bachman-Turner Overdrive	Mercury	8	(2)	G
19	-	Do It Baby	Miracles	Tamla	5		
20	-	Skin Tight	Ohio Players	Mercury	3		G

November 1974

This Mnth	Prev Mnth	Title	Artist	Label	Wks 20	(UK Pos)	
1	-	Do It ('Til You're Satisfied)	B.T. Express	Roadshow	9	(52)	F G
2	18	You Ain't Seen Nothin' Yet	Bachman-Turner Overdrive	Mercury	8	(2)	G
3	-	Tin Man	America	Warner	7		
4	-	My Melody Of Love	Bobby Vinton	ABC	7		G L
5	-	Whatever Gets You Thru The Night	John Lennon & The Plastic Ono Nuclear Band	Apple	6	(36)	
6	-	I Can Help	Billy Swan	Monument	7	(6)	F G L
7	-	Back Home Again	John Denver	RCA	7		G
8	-	Longfellow Serenade	Neil Diamond	Columbia	5		
9	-	Everlasting Love	Carl Carlton	ABC	6		F L
10	2	You Haven't Done Nothin	Stevie Wonder	Tamla	12	(30)	G
11	8	Jazzman	Carole King	Ode	8		
12	-	Life Is A Rock (But The Radio Rolled Me)	Reunion	RCA	5	(33)	F L
13	-	When Will I See You Again	Three Degrees	Philly International	9	(1)	G L
14	6	The Bitch Is Back	Elton John	MCA	7	(15)	
15	-	Kung Fu Fighting	Carl Douglas	20th Century	9	(1)	F G L
16	-	Carefree Highway	Gordon Lightfoot	Reprise	4		
17	-	The Need To Be	Jim Weatherly	Buddah	4		F L
18	-	Cat's In The Cradle	Harry Chapin	Elektra	7		F G L
19	-	I've Got The Music In Me	Kiki Dee	Rocket	5	(19)	F L
20	5	Can't Get Enough	Bad Company	Swan Song	8	(15)	F

December 1974

This Mnth	Prev Mnth	Title	Artist	Label	Wks 20	(UK Pos)	
1	15	Kung Fu Fighting	Carl Douglas	20th Century	9	(1)	F G L
2	-	Angie Baby	Helen Reddy	Capitol	9	(5)	G
3	18	Cat's In The Cradle	Harry Chapin	Elektra	7		F G L
4	13	When Will I See You Again	Three Degrees	Philly International	9	(1)	G L
5	-	You're The First, The Last, My Everything	Barry White	20th Century	9	(1)	G
6	6	I Can Help	Billy Swan	Monument	7	(6)	F G L
7	-	Junior's Farm /Sally G	Paul McCartney & Wings	Apple	9	(16)	
8	-	Lucy In The Sky With Diamonds	Elton John	MCA	8	(10)	G
9	-	Sha-La-La (Make Me Happy)	Al Green	Hi	7	(20)	G
10	1	Do It ('Til You're Satisfied)	B.T. Express	Roadshow	9	(52)	F G
11	-	You Got The Love	Rufus Featuring Chaka Khan	ABC	6		
12	-	Laughter In The Rain	Neil Sedaka	Rocket	11	(15)	
13	-	Only You	Ringo Starr	Apple	6	(28)	
14	-	Boogie On Reggae Woman	Stevie Wonder	Tamla	9	(12)	G
15	4	My Melody Of Love	Bobby Vinton	ABC	7		G L
16	-	Please Mr. Postman	Carpenters	A&M	8	(2)	G
17	-	Wishing You Were Here	Chicago	Columbia	5		
18	-	Must Of Got Lost	J. Geils Band	Atlantic	4		F
19	-	Fairytale	Pointer Sisters	Blue Thumb	3		
20	-	Mandy	Barry Manilow	Bell	8	(11)	F G

US 1974 OCT-DEC

◆ George Harrison was the first ex-Beatle to tour America - he did so to half empty houses. John Lennon fared better; he had his first solo No. 1, 'Whatever Gets You Thru The Night', from the chart topping **Walls And Bridges** album. To celebrate, Lennon appeared on stage with Elton John at Madison Square Garden. Elton ended 1974 with his **Greatest Hits** topping the transatlantic charts.

◆ Comparative veterans scoring Top 20 hits included Bobby Vinton, Neil Sedaka, The Three Degrees, Billy Swann and The J. Geils Band.

◆ The Beach Boys' first No. 1 LP for ten years, **Endless Summer,** was replaced at the top by Olivia Newton-John's **If You Love Me, Let Me Know,** which contained her Grammy winning 'I Honestly Love You'.

UK 1975 JAN-MAR

◆ A Warner Brothers Records show featuring The Doobie Brothers, Little Feat, Tower Of Power and Graham Central Station, made a successful European tour.

◆ American acts whose current records were faring far better in Britain included: actor Telly Savalas, The Tymes, The Moments & Whatnauts, Johnny Mathis and Love Unlimited.

▲ Disco was taking over with hits by Gloria Gaynor, Disco Tex, Barry White (above), Shirley & Co., Labelle and B. T. Express. Another type of dance music selling well in the UK was northern soul – the biggest hit from obscure Canadian band Wigan's Chosen Few.

January 1975

This Mnth	Prev Mnth	Title	Artist	Label	Wks 20	(US Pos)	
1	9	Streets Of London	Ralph McTell	Reprise	9		F L
2	19	Down Down	Status Quo	Vertigo	8		
3	5	Lonely This Christmas	Mud	RAK	8		
4	-	The Bump	Kenny	RAK	6		F
5	-	Never Can Say Goodbye	Gloria Gaynor	MGM	5	(9)	F
6	-	Ms Grace	Tymes	RCA	5	(91)	L
7	8	Get Dancing	Disco Tex & The Sex-O-Lettes	Chelsea	8	(10)	F
8	-	I Can Help	Billy Swan	Monument	7	(1)	F L
9	13	Wombling Merry Christmas	Wombles	CBS	5		
10	6	My Boy	Elvis Presley	RCA	9	(20)	
11	16	The In Betweenies/Father Christmas Do Not Touch Me	Goodies	Bradley's	6		F
12	3	Juke Box Jive	Rubettes	Polydor	9		
13	-	Stardust	David Essex	CBS	4		
14	-	Are You Ready To Rock	Wizzard	Warner	5		L
15	2	You Ain't Seen Nothin' Yet	Bachman-Turner Overdrive	Mercury	9	(1)	F L
16	-	Help Me Make It Through The Night	John Holt	Trojan	6		F L
17	-	Crying Over You	Ken Boothe	Trojan	4		L
18	-	Morning Side Of The Mountain	Donny & Marie Osmond	MGM	5	(8)	
19	1	You're The First, The Last, My...	Barry White	20th Century	9	(2)	
20	11	Lucy In The Sky With Diamonds	Elton John	DJM	8	(1)	

February 1975

This Mnth	Prev Mnth	Title	Artist	Label	Wks 20	(US Pos)	
1	-	January	Pilot	EMI	6	(87)	L
2	-	Goodbye My Love	Glitter Band	Bell	6		
3	-	Sugar Candy Kisses	Mac & Katie Kissoon	Polydor	5		F
4	-	Please Mr. Postman	Carpenters	A&M	7	(1)	
5	4	The Bump	Kenny	RAK	6		F
6	18	Morning Side Of The Mountain	Donny & Marie Osmond	MGM	5	(8)	
7	-	Angie Baby	Helen Reddy	Capitol	6	(1)	F L
8	6	Ms Grace	Tymes	RCA	5	(91)	L
9	5	Never Can Say Goodbye	Gloria Gaynor	MGM	5	(9)	F
10	-	Make Me Smile (Come Up And See Me)	Steve Harley & Cockney Rebel	EMI	6	(96)	
11	-	Black Superman (Muhammad Ali)	Johnny Wakelin & The Kinshasa Band	Pye	4	(21)	F
12	-	Promised Land	Elvis Presley	RCA	5	(14)	
13	16	Help Me Make It Through The Night	John Holt	Trojan	6		F L
14	-	Footsee	Wigan's Chosen Few	Disco Demand	5		F L
15	-	Now I'm Here	Queen	EMI	5		
16	-	Shame, Shame, Shame	Shirley And Company	All Platinum	5	(12)	F L
17	-	Purely By Coincidence	Sweet Sensation	Pye	4		L
18	-	Star On A TV Show	Stylistics	Avco	4	(47)	
19	-	Boogie On Reggae Woman	Stevie Wonder	Tamla Motown	3	(3)	
20	-	The Secrets That You Keep	Mud	RAK	5		

March 1975

This Mnth	Prev Mnth	Title	Artist	Label	Wks 20	(US Pos)	
1	-	If	Telly Savalas	MCA	7		F L
2	-	Only You Can	Fox	GTO	7	(53)	F
3	-	Bye Bye Baby	Bay City Rollers	Bell	11		
4	10	Make Me Smile (Come Up And See...)	Steve Harley & Cockney Rebel	EMI	6	(96)	
5	20	The Secrets That You Keep	Mud	RAK	5		
6	-	My Eyes Adored You	Frankie Valli	Private Stock	5	(1)	
7	-	Pick Up The Pieces	Average White Band	Atlantic	5	(1)	F
8	-	There's A Whole Lot Of Loving	Guys & Dolls	Magnet	7		F
9	4	Please Mr. Postman	Carpenters	A&M	7	(1)	
10	-	What Am I Gonna Do With You	Barry White	20th Century	6	(8)	
11	16	Shame, Shame, Shame	Shirley And Company	All Platinum	5	(12)	F L
12	-	Girls	Moments And Whatnauts	All Platinum	6		F
13	-	Please Tell Him I Said Hello	Dana	GTO	6		
14	-	Fancy Pants	Kenny	RAK	6		
15	-	Mandy	Barry Manilow	Arista	4	(1)	F
16	-	I'm Stone In Love With You	Johnny Mathis	CBS	6		
17	-	I Can Do It	Rubettes	State	6		
18	-	Dreamer	Supertramp	A&M	4	(15)	F
19	14	Footsee	Wigan's Chosen Few	Disco Demand	5		F L
20	-	It May Be Winter Outside (But In My Heart It's Spring)	Love Unlimited	20th Century	4	(83)	L

January 1975

This Mnth	Prev Mnth	Title	Artist	Label	Wks 20	(UK Pos)	
1	12	Laughter In The Rain	Neil Sedaka	Rocket	11	(15)	
2	8	Lucy In The Sky With Diamonds	Elton John	MCA	8	(10)	G
3	20	Mandy	Barry Manilow	Bell	8	(11)	F G
4	16	Please Mr. Postman	Carpenters	A&M	8	(2)	G
5	5	You're The First, The Last, My Everything	Barry White	20th Century	9	(1)	G
6	14	Boogie On Reggae Woman	Stevie Wonder	Tamla	9	(12)	G
7	7	Junior's Farm/Sally G	Paul McCartney & Wings	Apple	9	(16)	
8	-	One Man Woman/One Woman Man	Paul Anka & Odia Coates	UA	7		
9	-	Morning Side Of The Mountain	Donny & Marie Osmond	MGM	7	(5)	
10	13	Only You	Ringo Starr	Apple	6	(28)	
11	-	Fire	Ohio Players	Mercury	8		G
12	-	Never Can Say Goodbye	Gloria Gaynor	MGM	7	(2)	F
13	1	Kung Fu Fighting	Carl Douglas	20th Century	9	(1)	F G L
14	2	Angie Baby	Helen Reddy	Capitol	9	(5)	G
15	-	Pick Up The Pieces	Average White Band	Atlantic	9	(6)	F G
16	-	Doctor's Orders	Carol Douglas	Midland Int.	6		F L
17	-	Bungle In The Jungle	Jethro Tull	Chrysalis	5		L
18	-	Some Kind Of Wonderful	Grand Funk	Capitol	8		
19	-	You're No Good	Linda Ronstadt	Capitol	6		F G
20	-	Get Dancin'	Disco Tex & The Sex-O-Lettes	Chelsea	5	(8)	F L

February 1975

This Mnth	Prev Mnth	Title	Artist	Label	Wks 20	(UK Pos)	
1	15	Pick Up The Pieces	Average White Band	Atlantic	9	(6)	F G
2	19	You're No Good	Linda Ronstadt	Capitol	6		F G
3	-	Best Of My Love	Eagles	Asylum	10		G
4	11	Fire	Ohio Players	Mercury	8		G
5	18	Some Kind Of Wonderful	Grand Funk	Capitol	8		
6	-	Black Water	Doobie Brothers	Warner	10		G
7	6	Boogie On Reggae Woman	Stevie Wonder	Tamla	9	(12)	G
8	-	Lonely People	America	Warner	6		
9	1	Laughter In The Rain	Neil Sedaka	Rocket	11	(15)	
10	-	My Eyes Adored You	Frankie Valli	Private Stock	9	(5)	G
11	-	#9 Dream	John Lennon	Apple	5	(23)	
12	-	Look In My Eyes Pretty Woman	Tony Orlando & Dawn	Bell	4		
13	20	Get Dancin'	Disco Tex & The Sex-O-Lettes	Chelsea	5	(8)	F L
14	16	Doctor's Orders	Carol Douglas	Midland Int.	6		F L
15	4	Please Mr. Postman	Carpenters	A&M	8	(2)	G
16	-	Sweet Surrender	John Denver	RCA	3		
17	-	Have You Never Been Mellow	Olivia Newton-John	MCA	9		G
18	3	Mandy	Barry Manilow	Bell	8	(11)	F G
19	-	Nightingale	Carole King	Ode	4		
20	9	Morning Side Of The Mountain	Donny & Marie Osmond	MGM	7	(5)	

March 1975

This Mnth	Prev Mnth	Title	Artist	Label	Wks 20	(UK Pos)	
1	10	My Eyes Adored You	Frankie Valli	Private Stock	9	(5)	G
2	-	Lady Marmalade (Voulez-Vous Coucher Avec Moi)	Labelle	Epic	9	(17)	F G L
3	17	Have You Never Been Mellow	Olivia Newton-John	MCA	9		G
4	6	Black Water	Doobie Brothers	Warner	10		G
5	-	Lovin' You	Minnie Riperton	Epic	9	(2)	F G L
6	-	Express	B.T. Express	Roadshow	9	(34)	G L
7	-	Lady	Styx	Wooden Nickel	6		F
8	-	Don't Call Us We'll Call You	Sugarloaf/Jerry Corbetta	Claridge	6		L
9	-	Poetry Man	Phoebe Snow	Shelter	7		F L
10	8	Lonely People	America	Warner	6		
11	3	Best Of My Love	Eagles	Asylum	10		G
12	-	You Are So Beautiful	Joe Cocker	A&M	6		
13	-	Can't Get It Out Of My Head	Electric Light Orchestra	UA	6		F
14	-	No No Song/Snookeroo	Ringo Starr	Apple	6		L
15	-	Philadelphia Freedom	Elton John	MCA	14	(12)	G
16	1	Pick Up The Pieces	Average White Band	Atlantic	9	(6)	F G
17	-	Shame Shame Shame	Shirley And Company	Vibration	3	(6)	F L
18	-	I'm A Woman	Maria Muldaur	Reprise	4		L
19	-	Sad Sweet Dreamer	Sweet Sensation	Pye	3	(1)	F
20	5	Some Kind Of Wonderful	Grand Funk	Capitol	8		

US 1975 JAN-MAR

◆ In just four hours Led Zeppelin sold the 60,000 seats for their Madison Square Garden appearances. All their six albums were simultaneously situated in the US chart (a record), including the group's first Swan Song LP, **Physical Graffiti,** which topped the transatlantic charts.

◆ Influential performers and forefathers of r'n'r', Louis Jordan and T-Bone Walker, both died. Early rockers, Bill Haley and Chuck Berry, both owed much to Jordan, and Walker's influence can be heard in many rock and R&B guitar stars' work.

◆ Britain successfully sent "soul to Newcastle" in the shape of Sweet Sensation and the Average White Band, the latter's debut hit topping the American chart.

UK 1975 APR-JUNE

▲ A 12 city American tour by The Beach Boys and Chicago (whose **Chicago VIII** was a chart topper) was seen by 700,000 who paid over $7 million. The Beach Boys then joined Elton John (above), Rufus and The Eagles, playing to 80,000 at London's Wembley Stadium. For the record books, Elton's **Captain Fantastic And The Brown Dirt Cowboy** became the first album to enter the US LP charts at No. 1.

◆ Oldies on the UK chart included Tammy Wynette's 1968 US hit 'Stand By Your Man', Desmond Dekker's 'Israelites' and Bobby Goldsboro's 'Honey'.

April 1975

This Mnth	Prev Mnth	Title	Artist	Label	Wks 20	(US Pos)	
1	3	Bye Bye Baby	Bay City Rollers	Bell	11		
2	-	Fox On The Run	Sweet	RCA	6	(5)	
3	-	Swing Your Daddy	Jim Gilstrap	Chelsea	7	(55)	F L
4	-	Love Me Love My Dog	Peter Shelley	Magnet	6		L
5	-	Funky Gibbon/Sick Man Blues	Goodies	Bradley's	6	(79)	
6	8	There's A Whole Lot Of Loving	Guys & Dolls	Magnet	7		F
7	12	Girls	Moments And Whatnauts	All Platinum	6		F
8	14	Fancy Pants	Kenny	RAK	6		
9	17	I Can Do It	Rubettes	State	6		
10	-	Honey	Bobby Goldsboro	UA	6		L
11	-	Play Me Like You Play Your Guitar	Duane Eddy & Rebelettes	GTO	5		
12	-	The Ugly Duckling	Mike Reid	Pye	4		F L
13	10	What Am I Gonna Do With You	Barry White	20th Century	6	(8)	
14	-	Let Me Be The One	Shadows	EMI	3		
15	-	Philadelphia Freedom	Elton John	DJM	6	(1)	
16	-	Skiing In The Snow	Wigan's Ovation	Spark	4		F L
17	-	Life Is A Minestone	10cc	Mercury	5		
18	-	Oh Boy	Mud	RAK	6		
19	-	Reach Out I'll Be There	Gloria Gaynor	MGM	4	(60)	
20	-	Loving You	Minnie Riperton	Epic	6	(1)	F L

May 1975

This Mnth	Prev Mnth	Title	Artist	Label	Wks 20	(US Pos)	
1	18	Oh Boy	Mud	RAK	6		
2	20	Loving You	Minnie Riperton	Epic	6	(1)	F L
3	-	Stand By Your Man	Tammy Wynette	Epic	8		F
4	-	Hurt So Good	Susan Cadogan	Magnet	6		F L
5	-	Let Me Try Again	Tammy Jones	Epic	6		F L
6	10	Honey	Bobby Goldsboro	UA	6		L
7	-	I Wanna Dance Wit Choo'	Disco Tex & The Sex-O-Lettes	Chelsea	5	(23)	L
8	-	The Way We Were/Try To Remember (Medley)	Gladys Knight & The Pips	Buddah	7	(11)	
9	-	Sing Baby Sing	Stylistics	Avco	7		
10	-	Only Yesterday	Carpenters	A&M	5	(4)	
11	-	The Night	Frankie Valli & Four Seasons	Mowest	5		
12	-	Whispering Grass	Windsor Davies & Don Estelle	EMI	9		F L
13	1	Bye Bye Baby	Bay City Rollers	Bell	11		
14	-	Thanks For The Memory (Wham Bam Thank You Mam)	Slade	Polydor	5		
15	-	Take Good Care Of Yourself	Three Degrees	Philly Int.	4		
16	-	A Little Love And Understanding	Gilbert Becaud	Decca	5		F L
17	-	The Tears I Cried	Glitter Band	Bell	5		
18	-	Don't Do It Baby	Mac & Katie Kissoon	State	4		
19	-	Three Steps To Heaven	Showaddywaddy	Bell	8		
20	-	Send In The Clowns	Judy Collins	Elektra	5	(19)	L

June 1975

This Mnth	Prev Mnth	Title	Artist	Label	Wks 20	(US Pos)	
1	12	Whispering Grass	Windsor Davies & Don Estelle	EMI	9		F L
2	19	Three Steps To Heaven	Showaddywaddy	Bell	8		
3	-	I'm Not In Love	10cc	Mercury	8	(2)	
4	-	The Proud One	Osmonds	MGM	6	(22)	L
5	3	Stand By Your Man	Tammy Wynette	Epic	8		F
6	9	Sing Baby Sing	Stylistics	Avco	7		
7	-	The Hustle	Van McCoy	Avco	8	(1)	F
8	8	The Way We Were/Try To Remember (Medley)	Gladys Knight & The Pips	Buddah	7	(11)	
9	-	Listen To What The Man Said	Wings	Capitol	5	(1)	
10	20	Send In The Clowns	Judy Collins	Elektra	5	(19)	L
11	-	Disco Stomp	Hamilton Bohannon	Brunswick	7		F L
12	-	Disco Queen	Hot Chocolate	RAK	4	(28)	
13	-	Autobahn	Kraftwerk	Vertigo	5	(25)	F
14	-	Tears On My Pillow	Johnny Nash	CBS	9		L
15	-	Roll Over Lay Down	Status Quo	Vertigo	5		
16	-	The Israelites	Desmond Dekker & The Aces	Cactus	5		
17	-	Oh What A Shame	Roy Wood	Jet	4		L
18	-	Doing Alright With The Boys	Gary Glitter	Bell	4		L
19	-	Baby I Love You, OK	Kenny	RAK	4		
20	14	Thanks For The Memory (Wham Bam Thank You Mam)	Slade	Polydor	5		

April 1975

This Mnth	Prev Mnth	Title	Artist	Label	Wks 20	(UK Pos)	
1	15	Philadelphia Freedom	Elton John	MCA	14	(12)	G
2	5	Lovin' You	Minnie Riperton	Epic	9	(2)	F G L
3	-	(Hey Won't You Play) Another Somebody Done Somebody Wrong Song	B.J. Thomas	ABC	10		G
4	14	No No Song/Snookeroo	Ringo Starr	Apple	6		L
5	-	Chevy Van	Sammy Johns	GRC	8		F G L
6	-	Supernatural Thing Part 1	Ben E. King	Atlantic	5		
7	-	What Am I Gonna Do With You	Barry White	20th Century	4	(5)	
8	-	Emma	Hot Chocolate	Big Tree	6	(3)	F
9	2	Lady Marmalade (Voulez-Vous Coucher Avec Moi)	Labelle	Epic	9	(17)	F G L
10	6	Express	B.T. Express	Roadshow	9	(34)	G L
11	-	Before The Next Teardrop Falls	Freddy Fender	ABC/Dot	11		F G
12	-	He Don't Love You (Like I Love You)	Tony Orlando & Dawn	Elektra	7		G
13	9	Poetry Man	Phoebe Snow	Shelter	7		F L
14	-	Walking In Rhythm	Blackbyrds	Fantasy	8	(23)	F
15	-	Once You Get Started	Rufus	ABC	5		
16	-	L-O-V-E (Love)	Al Green	Hi	5	(24)	
17	-	Shining Star	Earth, Wind & Fire	Columbia	11		F G
18	12	You Are So Beautiful	Joe Cocker	A&M	6		
19	-	Long Tall Glasses (I Can Dance)	Leo Sayer	Warner	6	(4)	F
20	-	Harry Truman	Chicago	Columbia	3		

May 1975

This Mnth	Prev Mnth	Title	Artist	Label	Wks 20	(UK Pos)	
1	11	Before The Next Teardrop Falls	Freddy Fender	ABC/Dot	11		F G
2	17	Shining Star	Earth, Wind & Fire	Columbia	11		F G
3	12	He Don't Love You (Like I Love You)	Tony Orlando & Dawn	Elektra	7		G
4	-	Only Yesterday	Carpenters	A&M	6	(7)	
5	-	Jackie Blue	Ozark Mountain Daredevils	A&M	7		F L
6	-	How Long	Ace	Anchor	8	(20)	F L
7	-	Thank God I'm A Country Boy	John Denver	RCA	8		G
8	-	I Don't Like To Sleep Alone	Paul Anka & Odia Coates	UA	7		
9	1	Philadelphia Freedom	Elton John	MCA	14	(12)	G
10	3	(Hey...) Another Somebody Done...	B.J. Thomas	ABC	10		G
11	14	Walking In Rhythm	Blackbyrds	Fantasy	8	(23)	F
12	-	Sister Golden Hair	America	Warner	8		G
13	-	Bad Time	Grand Funk	Capitol	7		L
14	-	Old Days	Chicago	Columbia	7		
15	-	Killer Queen	Queen	Elektra	5	(2)	F
16	19	Long Tall Glasses (I Can Dance)	Leo Sayer	Warner	6	(4)	F
17	-	When Will I Be Loved	Linda Ronstadt	Capitol	10		
18	-	Love Won't Let Me Wait	Major Harris	Atlantic	9	(37)	F G L
19	5	Chevy Van	Sammy Johns	GRC	8		F G L
20	-	It's A Miracle	Barry Manilow	Arista	3		

June 1975

This Mnth	Prev Mnth	Title	Artist	Label	Wks 20	(UK Pos)	
1	17	When Will I Be Loved	Linda Ronstadt	Capitol	10		
2	-	Love Will Keep Us Together	Captain & Tennille	A&M	13	(32)	F G
3	12	Sister Golden Hair	America	Warner	8		G
4	-	I'm Not Lisa	Jessi Colter	Capitol	7		F L
5	18	Love Won't Let Me Wait	Major Harris	Atlantic	9	(37)	F G L
6	-	Wildfire	Michael Murphey	Epic	7		F G
7	-	Get Down, Get Down (Get On The Floor)	Joe Simon	Spring	5		L
8	-	Cut The Cake	Average White Band	Atlantic	6	(31)	L
9	13	Bad Time	Grand Funk	Capitol	7		L
10	7	Thank God I'm A Country Boy	John Denver	RCA	8		G
11	14	Old Days	Chicago	Columbia	7		
12	-	Only Women	Alice Cooper	Atlantic	6		
13	-	The Hustle	Van McCoy	Avco	8	(3)	F G L
14	-	Take Me In Your Arms (Rock Me)	Doobie Brothers	Warner	4		
15	-	Listen To What The Man Said	Wings	Capitol	9	(6)	G
16	9	Philadelphia Freedom	Elton John	MCA	14	(12)	G
17	-	Magic	Pilot	EMI	7	(11)	F G L
18	6	How Long	Ace	Anchor	8	(20)	F L
19	1	Before The Next Teardrop Falls	Freddy Fender	ABC/Dot	11		F G
20	-	Bad Luck (Pt. 1)	Harold Melvin & The Blue Notes	Philly Int.	3		

◆ Apple Records was dissolved, Ten Years After called it a day and Sonny & Cher got divorced (Cher wed Gregg Allman four days later). Also, Ritchie Blackmore deserted Deep Purple to form Rainbow, Lemmy left Hawkwind to form Motorhead, and Alan Longmuir quit The Bay City Rollers.

◆ Highly respected record executives Clive Davis (Columbia/ Arista) and Kenny Gamble and Leon Huff (Philly International) were indicted on payola charges.

◆ Jefferson Starship attracted 60,000 to Central Park, Stevie Wonder played to 125,000 at the Washington Monument, and The Rolling Stones started their first US tour with guitarist Ron Wood, which grossed over $13 million.

UK 1975
JULY-SEPT

◆ Paul McCartney, who had yet to score a solo No. 1 single in his homeland, notched up his fourth American chart topping single, 'Listen To What The Man Said', and another transatlantic album top-per, **Venus And Mars.**

◆ Soon after David Bowie announced "rock'n'roll is dead", he had his biggest American hit with 'Fame', co-written with John Lennon.

◆ The UK album chart increased to a Top 60.

◆ The Great American Music Fair in New York state, starred Jefferson Starship (whose **Red Octopus** topped the chart) and The Doobie Brothers. Britain's Knebworth Festival was headlined by Pink Floyd, the re-formed Steve Miller Band and Captain Beefheart.

July 1975

This Mnth	Prev Mnth	Title	Artist	Label	Wks 20	(US Pos)	
1	14	Tears On My Pillow	Johnny Nash	CBS	9		L
2	-	Misty	Ray Stevens	Janus	7	(14)	L
3	7	The Hustle	Van McCoy	Avco	8	(1)	F
4	-	Have You Seen Her/Oh Girl	Chi-Lites	Brunswick	5		
5	3	I'm Not In Love	10cc	Mercury	8	(2)	
6	-	Give A Little Love	Bay City Rollers	Bell	7		
7	11	Disco Stomp	Hamilton Bohannon	Brunswick	7		F L
8	-	Eighteen With A Bullet	Pete Wingfield	Island	5	(15)	F L
9	-	Barbados	Typically Tropical	Gull	9		F L
10	1	Whispering Grass	Windsor Davies & Don Estelle	EMI	9		F L
11	18	Doing Alright With The Boys	Gary Glitter	Bell	4		L
12	-	Moonshine Sally	Mud	RAK	4		
13	-	Rollin' Stone	David Essex	CBS	4		
14	-	Je T'Aime (Moi Non Plus)	Judge Dread	Cactus	6		
15	2	Three Steps To Heaven	Showaddywaddy	Bell	8		
16	-	Jive Talkin'	Bee Gees	RSO	7	(1)	
17	-	Sealed With A Kiss	Brian Hyland	ABC	8		L
18	-	D.I.V.O.R.C.E.	Tammy Wynette	Epic	4	(63)	
19	-	My White Bicycle	Nazareth	Mooncrest	4		
20	19	Baby I Love You, OK	Kenny	RAK	4		

August 1975

This Mnth	Prev Mnth	Title	Artist	Label	Wks 20	(US Pos)	
1	9	Barbados	Typically Tropical	Gull	9		F L
2	-	Can't Give You Anything (But My Love)	Stylistics	Avco	8	(51)	
3	-	If You Think You Know How To Love Me	Smokey	RAK	7	(96)	F
4	6	Give A Little Love	Bay City Rollers	Bell	7		
5	16	Jive Talkin'	Bee Gees	RSO	7	(1)	
6	-	The Last Farewell	Roger Whittaker	EMI	9	(19)	
7	-	It's Been So Long	George McCrae	Jayboy	7		
8	17	Sealed With A Kiss	Brian Hyland	ABC	8		L
9	-	It's In His Kiss	Linda Lewis	Arista	5		L
10	-	Blanket On The Ground	Billie Jo Spears	UA	6	(78)	F
11	-	Delilah	Sensational Alex Harvey Band	Vertigo	5		F
12	-	Sailing	Rod Stewart	Warner	9	(58)	
13	1	Tears On My Pillow	Johnny Nash	CBS	9		L
14	-	Sherry	Adrian Baker	Magnet	4		F L
15	-	Dolly My Love	Moments	All Platinum	5		L
16	-	That's The Way (I Like It)	KC & The Sunshine Band	Jayboy	6	(1)	
17	14	Je T'Aime (Moi Non Plus)	Judge Dread	Cactus	6		
18	-	The Best Thing That Ever Happened	Gladys Knight & The Pips	Buddah	6	(3)	
19	2	Misty	Ray Stevens	Janus	7	(14)	L
20	-	El Bimbo	Bimbo Jet	EMI	4	(43)	F L

September 1975

This Mnth	Prev Mnth	Title	Artist	Label	Wks 20	(US Pos)	
1	12	Sailing	Rod Stewart	Warner	9	(58)	
2	6	The Last Farewell	Roger Whittaker	EMI	9	(19)	
3	-	Moonlighting	Leo Sayer	Chrysalis	6		
4	-	Summertime City	Mike Batt	Epic	5		F L
5	-	Funky Moped/Magic Roundabout	Jasper Carrott	DJM	10		F L
6	-	A Child's Prayer	Hot Chocolate	RAK	5		
7	2	Can't Give You Anything (But My Love)	Stylistics	Avco	8	(51)	
8	16	That's The Way (I Like It)	KC & The Sunshine Band	Jayboy	6	(1)	
9	-	I'm On Fire	5000 Volts	Philips	6	(26)	F
10	-	Heartbeat	Showaddywaddy	Bell	5		
11	-	Julie Ann	Kenny	RAK	5		L
12	7	It's Been So Long	George McCrae	Jayboy	7		
13	-	Hold Me Close	David Essex	CBS	8		
14	18	The Best Thing That Ever Happened	Gladys Knight & The Pips	Buddah	6	(3)	
15	10	Blanket On The Ground	Billie Jo Spears	UA	6	(78)	F
16	-	There Goes My First Love	Drifters	Bell	8		
17	-	Motor Biking	Chris Spedding	RAK	4		F L
18	-	Fattie Bum-Bum	Carl Malcolm	UK	5		F L
19	-	Love In The Sun	Glitter Band	Bell	4		
20	-	I Only Have Eyes For You	Art Garfunkel	CBS	8	(18)	F

July 1975

This Mnth	Prev Mnth	Title	Artist	Label	Wks 20	(UK Pos)	
1	13	The Hustle	Van McCoy	Avco	8	(3)	F G L
2	15	Listen To What The Man Said	Wings	Capitol	9	(6)	G
3	2	Love Will Keep Us Together	Captain & Tennille	A&M	13	(32)	F G
4	-	One Of These Nights	Eagles	Asylum	11	(23)	
5	-	Please Mr. Please	Olivia Newton-John	MCA	9		G
6	-	I'm Not In Love	10cc	Mercury	8	(1)	F
7	-	Swearin' To God	Frankie Valli	Private Stock	5	(31)	
8	17	Magic	Pilot	EMI	7	(11)	F G L
9	-	Rockin' Chair	Gwen McCrae	Cat	5		F L
10	6	Wildfire	Michael Murphey	Epic	7		F G
11	-	Midnight Blue	Melissa Manchester	Arista	8		F
12	-	The Way We Were/Try To Remember (Medley)	Gladys Knight & The Pips	Buddah	6	(4)	
13	-	Jive Talkin'	Bee Gees	RSO	9	(5)	G
14	5	Love Won't Let Me Wait	Major Harris	Atlantic	9	(37)	F G L
15	1	When Will I Be Loved	Linda Ronstadt	Capitol	10		
16	-	Dynomite	Bazuka	A&M	6		F
17	-	Someone Saved My Life Tonight	Elton John	MCA	8	(22)	G
18	-	Misty	Ray Stevens	Barnaby	4	(2)	L
19	4	I'm Not Lisa	Jessi Colter	Capitol	7		F L
20	-	Why Can't We Be Friends?	War	UA	9		G

August 1975

This Mnth	Prev Mnth	Title	Artist	Label	Wks 20	(UK Pos)	
1	4	One Of These Nights	Eagles	Asylum	11	(23)	
2	13	Jive Talkin'	Bee Gees	RSO	9	(5)	G
3	17	Someone Saved My Life Tonight	Elton John	MCA	8	(22)	G
4	-	Rhinestone Cowboy	Glen Campbell	Capitol	14	(4)	G
5	5	Please Mr. Please	Olivia Newton-John	MCA	9		G
6	20	Why Can't We Be Friends?	War	UA	9		G
7	-	Fallin' In Love	Hamilton, Joe Frank & Reynolds	Playboy	8		G L
8	-	How Sweet It Is (To Be Loved By You)	James Taylor	Warner	9		
9	11	Midnight Blue	Melissa Manchester	Arista	8		F
10	-	Get Down Tonight	KC & The Sunshine Band	TK	6	(21)	F G
11	6	I'm Not In Love	10cc	Mercury	8	(1)	F
12	-	At Seventeen	Janis Ian	Columbia	8		L
13	-	Fight The Power Pt. 1	Isley Brothers	T-Neck	8		G L
14	-	The Rockford Files	Mike Post	MGM	5		F
15	1	The Hustle	Van McCoy	Avco	8	(3)	F G L
16	2	Listen To What The Man Said	Wings	Capitol	9	(6)	G
17	3	Love Will Keep Us Together	Captain & Tennille	A&M	13	(32)	F G
18	16	Dynomite	Bazuka	A&M	6		F L
19	-	Could It Be Magic	Barry Manilow	Arista	8	(25)	
20	-	Mornin' Beautiful	Tony Orlando & Dawn	Elektra	4		L

September 1975

This Mnth	Prev Mnth	Title	Artist	Label	Wks 20	(UK Pos)	
1	4	Rhinestone Cowboy	Glen Campbell	Capitol	14	(4)	G
2	-	Fame	David Bowie	RCA	8	(17)	G
3	12	At Seventeen	Janis Ian	Columbia	8		L
4	13	Fight The Power Pt. 1	Isley Brothers	T-Neck	8		G L
5	-	I'm Sorry/Calypso	John Denver	RCA	12		G
6	19	Could It Be Magic	Barry Manilow	Arista	8	(25)	
7	7	Fallin' In Love	Hamilton, Joe Frank & Reynolds	Playboy	8		G L
8	-	Wasted Days And Wasted Nights	Freddy Fender	ABC/Dot	9		G
9	-	Run Joey Run	David Geddes	Big Tree	6		F
10	10	Get Down Tonight	KC & The Sunshine Band	TK	6	(21)	F G
11	-	Feel Like Makin' Love	Bad Company	Swan Song	6	(20)	
12	-	Ballroom Blitz	Sweet	Capitol	10	(2)	
13	-	That's The Way Of The World	Earth, Wind & Fire	Columbia	6		
14	-	Ain't No Way To Treat A Lady	Helen Reddy	Capitol	6		
15	8	How Sweet It Is (To Be Loved By You)	James Taylor	Warner	9		
16	2	Jive Talkin'	Bee Gees	RSO	9	(5)	G
17	-	Third Rate Romance	Amazing Rhythm Aces	ABC	4		F L
18	-	Dance With Me	Orleans	Asylum	7		F
19	1	One Of These Nights	Eagles	Asylum	11	(23)	
20	-	I Believe There's Nothing Stronger Than Our Love	Paul Anka & Odia Coates	UA	4		

▲ As the Grand Ole Opry celebrated its 50th birthday, country singer Glen Campbell (above) topped the pop chart with 'Rhinestone Cowboy', and the death was announced of legendary performer Lefty Frizzell.

◆ Other news included Peter Gabriel leaving Genesis, with drummer Phil Collins taking over vocals, and Stevie Wonder re-signing with Motown for a record $13 million.

◆ Soul superstar Jackie Wilson went into a coma after suffering a massive heart attack on stage. He remained in the coma until his death in early 1984.

UK 1975 OCT-DEC

▲ Queen's (above) 'Bohemian Rhapsody' topped the UK chart (returning to No. 1 in 1991) selling over a million. **Greatest Hits** LPs by Perry Como and Jim Reeves made No. 1, and hit oldies included Chubby Checker's 'Let's Twist Again', 'David Bowie's 'Space Oddity' and the 1937 recording 'The Trail Of The Lonesome Pine' by Laurel & Hardy!

◆ In the week Elton John again entered the American LP chart at No. 1 with **Rock Of The Westies**, Bob Dylan's Rolling Thunder Revue rolled across the USA and the Sex Pistols made their London debut.

October 1975

This Mnth	Prev Mnth	Title	Artist	Label	Wks 20	(US Pos)	
1	13	Hold Me Close	David Essex	CBS	8		
2	20	I Only Have Eyes For You	Art Garfunkel	CBS	8	(18)	F
3	16	There Goes My First Love	Drifters	Bell	8		
4	-	It's Time For Love	Chi-Lites	Brunswick	5	(94)	
5	-	Una Paloma Blanca	Jonathan King	UK	6		L
6	-	Who Loves You	Four Seasons	Warner	5	(3)	
7	-	S.O.S.	Abba	Epic	6	(15)	
8	-	Scotch On The Rocks	Band Of The Black Watch	Spark	7		F L
9	-	Feelings	Morris Albert	Decca	6	(6)	F L
10	5	Funky Moped/Magic Roundabout	Jasper Carrott	DJM	10		F L
11	-	Paloma Blanca	George Baker Selection	Warner	4	(26)	F L
12	18	Fattie Bum-Bum	Carl Malcolm	UK	5		F L
13	9	I'm On Fire	5000 Volts	Philips	6	(26)	F
14	1	Sailing	Rod Stewart	Warner	9	(58)	
15	-	Space Oddity	David Bowie	RCA	8	(15)	
16	-	L-L-Lucy	Mud	Private Stock	4		
17	-	Don't Play Your Rock 'n' Roll To Me	Smokey	RAK	4		
18	3	Moonlighting	Leo Sayer	Chrysalis	6		
19	10	Heartbeat	Showaddywaddy	Bell	5		
20	-	Big Ten	Judge Dread	Cactus	4		

November 1975

This Mnth	Prev Mnth	Title	Artist	Label	Wks 20	(US Pos)	
1	15	Space Oddity	David Bowie	RCA	8	(15)	
2	-	Love Is The Drug	Roxy Music	Island	6	(30)	
3	-	D.I.V.O.R.C.E.	Billy Connolly	Polydor	6		F L
4	-	Rhinestone Cowboy	Glen Campbell	Capitol	6	(1)	L
5	-	Love Hurts	Jim Capaldi	Island	6	(97)	F L
6	-	You Sexy Thing	Hot Chocolate	RAK	9	(3)	
7	2	I Only Have Eyes For You	Art Garfunkel	CBS	8	(18)	F
8	-	Imagine	John Lennon	Apple	5		G
9	-	Hold Back The Night	Trammps	Buddah	5	(35)	F
10	-	Blue Guitar	Justin Hayward & John Lodge	Threshold	5	(94)	F
11	-	What A Diff'rence A Day Makes	Esther Phillips	Kudu	5	(20)	F L
12	-	Bohemian Rhapsody	Queen	EMI	14	(9)	G
13	9	Feelings	Morris Albert	Decca	6	(6)	F L
14	-	New York Groove	Hello	Bell	4		L
15	-	Sky High	Jigsaw	Splash	5	(3)	F L
16	7	S.O.S.	Abba	Epic	6	(15)	
17	3	There Goes My First Love	Drifters	Bell	8		
18	-	This Old Heart Of Mine	Rod Stewart	Riva	5		
19	-	Right Back Where We Started From	Maxine Nightingale	UA	5	(2)	F
20	-	Money Honey	Bay City Rollers	Bell	8	(9)	

December 1975

This Mnth	Prev Mnth	Title	Artist	Label	Wks 20	(US Pos)	
1	12	Bohemian Rhapsody	Queen	EMI	14	(9)	G
2	6	You Sexy Thing	Hot Chocolate	RAK	9	(3)	
3	-	The Trail Of The Lonesome Pine	Laurel & Hardy With The Avalon Boys	UA	7		F L
4	-	Na Na Is The Saddest Word	Stylistics	Avco	7		
5	20	Money Honey	Bay City Rollers	Bell	8	(9)	
6	-	Let's Twist Again	Chubby Checker	London American	8		
7	-	All Around My Hat	Steeleye Span	Chrysalis	7		L
8	-	I Believe In Father Christmas	Greg Lake	Manticore	6	(95)	F L
9	-	Happy To Be On An Island In The Sun	Demis Roussos	Philips	7		F
10	-	Show Me You're A Woman	Mud	Private Stock	6		
11	18	This Old Heart Of Mine	Rod Stewart	Riva	5		
12	-	Golden Years	David Bowie	RCA	7	(10)	
13	5	Love Hurts	Jim Capaldi	Island	6	(97)	F L
14	8	Imagine	John Lennon	Apple	5		G
15	-	Renta Santa	Chris Hill	Philips	3		F
16	-	It's Gonna Be A Cold Cold Christmas	Dana	GTO	5		
17	15	Sky High	Jigsaw	Splash	5	(3)	F L
18	3	D.I.V.O.R.C.E.	Billy Connolly	Polydor	6		F L
19	-	In For A Penny	Slade	Polydor	3		
20	-	Wide Eyed And Legless	Andy Fairweather-Low	A&M	7		L

October 1975

This Mnth	Prev Mnth	Title	Artist	Label	Wks 20	(UK Pos)	
1	5	I'm Sorry/Calypso	John Denver	RCA	12		G
2	-	Bad Blood	Neil Sedaka	Rocket	6		G
3	12	Ballroom Blitz	Sweet	Capitol	10	(2)	
4	-	Miracles	Jefferson Starship	Grunt	7		
5	18	Dance With Me	Orleans	Asylum	7		F
6	-	Lyin' Eyes	Eagles	Asylum	8	(23)	
7	-	Feelings	Morris Albert	RCA	11	(4)	F G L
8	2	Fame	David Bowie	RCA	8	(17)	G
9	-	They Just Can't Stop It The (Games People Play)	Spinners	Atlantic	9		G
10	-	Mr. Jaws	Dickie Goodman	Cash	5		F G L
11	14	Ain't No Way To Treat A Lady	Helen Reddy	Capitol	6		
12	-	It Only Takes A Minute	Tavares	Capitol	6	(46)	F
13	-	Who Loves You	Four Seasons	Warner	9	(6)	
14	-	Rocky	Austin Roberts	Private Stock	3	(22)	L
15	-	Brazil	Ritchie Family	20th Century	5	(41)	F
16	1	Rhinestone Cowboy	Glen Campbell	Capitol	14	(4)	G
17	9	Run Joey Run	David Geddes	Big Tree	6		F
18	-	Heat Wave/Love Is A Rose	Linda Ronstadt	Asylum	8		
19	-	Island Girl	Elton John	MCA	9	(14)	G
20	-	Something Better To Do	Olivia Newton-John	MCA	6		

November 1975

This Mnth	Prev Mnth	Title	Artist	Label	Wks 20	(UK Pos)	
1	19	Island Girl	Elton John	MCA	9	(14)	G
2	13	Who Loves You	Four Seasons	Warner	9	(6)	
3	-	This Will Be	Natalie Cole	Capitol	7	(32)	F
4	6	Lyin' Eyes	Eagles	Asylum	8	(23)	
5	-	The Way I Want To Touch You	Captain & Tennille	A&M	9	(28)	G
6	7	Feelings	Morris Albert	RCA	11	(4)	F G L
7	4	Miracles	Jefferson Starship	Grunt	7		
8	-	That's The Way (I Like It)	KC & The Sunshine Band	TK	10	(4)	G
9	18	Heat Wave/Love Is A Rose	Linda Ronstadt	Asylum	8		
10	-	Low Rider	War	UA	8	(12)	
11	9	They Just Can't Stop It The (Games People Play)	Spinners	Atlantic	9		G
12	1	I'm Sorry/Calypso	John Denver	RCA	12		G
13	-	Fly Robin Fly	Silver Convention	Midland Int.	8	(28)	F G
14	-	Sky High	Jigsaw	Chelsea	10	(9)	F L
15	-	Nights On Broadway	Bee Gees	RSO	8		
16	-	Let's Do It Again	Staple Singers	Curtom	8		G L
17	-	Do It Any Way You Wanna	Peoples Choice	TSOP	5	(36)	F G L
18	20	Something Better To Do	Olivia Newton-John	MCA	6		
19	2	Bad Blood	Neil Sedaka	Rocket	6		G
20	-	My Little Town	Simon & Garfunkel	Columbia	6		L

December 1975

This Mnth	Prev Mnth	Title	Artist	Label	Wks 20	(UK Pos)	
1	16	Let's Do It Again	Staple Singers	Curtom	8		G L
2	8	That's The Way (I Like It)	KC & The Sunshine Band	TK	10	(4)	G
3	13	Fly Robin Fly	Silver Convention	Midland Int.	8	(28)	F G
4	-	Saturday Night	Bay City Rollers	Arista	9		F G
5	14	Sky High	Jigsaw	Chelsea	10	(9)	F L
6	-	Love Rollercoaster	Ohio Players	Mercury	12		G
7	-	Theme From Mahogany (Do You Know Where You're Going To)	Diana Ross	Motown	10	(5)	
8	-	I Write The Songs	Barry Manilow	Arista	13		G
9	15	Nights On Broadway	Bee Gees	RSO	8		
10	-	Fox On The Run	Sweet	Capitol	8	(2)	G
11	-	Our Day Will Come	Frankie Valli	Private Stock	5		
12	20	My Little Town	Simon & Garfunkel	Columbia	6		L
13	-	I Love Music (Pt. 1)	O'Jays	Philly Int.	10	(13)	G
14	1	Island Girl	Elton John	MCA	9	(14)	G
15	5	The Way I Want To Touch You	Captain & Tennille	A&M	9	(28)	G
16	-	Convoy	C.W. McCall	MGM	9	(2)	F G L
17	10	Low Rider	War	UA	8	(12)	
18	-	Venus And Mars Rock Show	Wings	Capitol	3		
19	-	I Want'a Do Something Freaky To You	Leon Haywood	20th Century	4		F L
20	-	Times Of Your Life	Paul Anka	UA	8		L

◆ A record 35 singles topped the US chart in 1975 and sales of records and tapes rose to $2.36 billion.

◆ Bruce Springsteen simultaneously made the front cover of *Time* and *Newsweek*, and soon after made his debut in the Top 40 with 'Born To Run'.

◆ *Saturday Night Live* bowed in on NBC. The first show included Grammy winner Janis Ian, whose **Between The Lines** topped the LP chart. Simon & Garfunkel briefly re-united the following week to plug 'My Little Town'. For the record, Simon's **Still Crazy After All These Years** headed the US album charts and Garfunkel's Flamingos-cloned 'I Only Have Eyes For You' topped the UK singles chart.

UK
1976
JAN-MAR

◆ Thirteen years after taking the US charts by storm, The Four Seasons had their only transatlantic No. 1, 'December '63 (Oh What A Night)'.

◆ In Britain, album chart toppers included 1950s star Slim Whitman and 1960s chart regular Roy Orbison, whilst 1940s favourite Glenn Miller returned to the singles chart!

◆ Despite minimal British success Fleetwood Mac (with new members Stevie Nicks and Lindsey Buckingham) headed up the US LP chart with their eponymous album - it took 58 weeks to reach No. 1!

◆ Ringo Starr became the third ex-Beatle to score two solo American chart toppers. Only John Lennon had so far failed to reach the top spot twice.

◆ Teeny bop idol Gary Glitter made the first of several "farewell" appearances.

January 1976

This Mnth	Prev Mnth	Title	Artist	Label	Wks 20	(US Pos)	
1	1	Bohemian Rhapsody	Queen	EMI	14	(9)	G
2	-	Glass Of Champagne	Sailor	Epic	8		F
3	-	Mamma Mia	Abba	Epic	8	(32)	
4	6	Let's Twist Again	Chubby Checker	London American	8		
5	20	Wide Eyed And Legless	Andy Fairweather-Low	A&M	7		L
6	3	The Trail Of The Lonesome Pine	Laurel & Hardy/Avalon Boys	UA	7		F L
7	-	In Dulce Jubilo/On Horseback	Mike Oldfield	Virgin	4		F
8	-	King Of The Cops	Billy Howard	Penny Farthing	6		F L
9	8	I Believe In Father Christmas	Greg Lake	Manticore	6	(95)	F L
10	-	Love Machine	Miracles	Tamla Motown	7	(1)	L
11	12	Golden Years	David Bowie	RCA	7	(10)	
12	16	It's Gonna Be A Cold Cold...	Dana	GTO	5		
13	-	We Do It	R & J Stone	RCA	7		F L
14	-	Forever & Ever	Slik	Bell	7		F L
15	-	Itchycoo Park	Small Faces	Immediate	5		L
16	-	Let The Music Play	Barry White	20th Century	4	(32)	
17	-	Can I Take You Home Little Girl	Drifters	Bell	7		
18	9	Happy To Be On An Island In The Sun	Demis Roussos	Philips	7		F
19	2	You Sexy Thing	Hot Chocolate	RAK	9	(3)	
20	-	If I Could	David Essex	CBS	4		

February 1976

This Mnth	Prev Mnth	Title	Artist	Label	Wks 20	(US Pos)	
1	14	Forever & Ever	Slik	Bell	7		F L
2	-	December '63 (Oh What A Night)	Four Seasons	Warner	8	(1)	
3	3	Mamma Mia	Abba	Epic	8	(32)	
4	-	Love To Love You Baby	Donna Summer	GTO	6	(2)	F
5	10	Love Machine	Miracles	Tamla Motown	7	(1)	L
6	-	Rodrigo's Guitar Concerto De Aranjuez	Manuel & His Music Of The Mountains	EMI	6		F L
7	13	We Do It	R & J Stone	RCA	7		F L
8	-	No Regrets	Walker Brothers	GTO	5		L
9	-	I Love To Love (But My Baby Loves To Dance)	Tina Charles	CBS	7		F
10	-	Convoy	C.W. McCall	MGM	7	(1)	F L
11	-	Dat	Pluto Shervington	Opal	5		F
12	-	Moonlight Serenade/Little Brown Jug/In The Mood	Glenn Miller	RCA	5		L
13	-	It Should Have Been Me	Yvonne Fair	Tamla Motown	5	(85)	F L
14	-	Low Rider	War	UA	5	(7)	F
15	1	Bohemian Rhapsody	Queen	EMI	14	(9)	G
16	-	Evil Woman	Electric Light Orchestra	Jet	4	(10)	
17	-	Squeeze Box	Who	Polydor	6	(16)	
18	-	Walk Away From Love	David Ruffin	Tamla	4	(9)	F L
19	-	Midnight Rider	Paul Davidson	Tropical	4		F L
20	-	Rain	Status Quo	Vertigo	5		

March 1976

This Mnth	Prev Mnth	Title	Artist	Label	Wks 20	(US Pos)	
1	9	I Love To Love (But My Baby...)	Tina Charles	CBS	7		F
2	10	Convoy	C.W. McCall	MGM	7	(1)	F L
3	-	Love Really Hurts Without You	Billy Ocean	GTO	8	(22)	F
4	2	December '63 (Oh What A Night)	Four Seasons	Warner	8	(1)	
5	-	You Don't Have To Say You Love Me	Guys & Dolls	Magnet	5		L
6	-	People Like You And People Like Me	Glitter Band	Bell	6		L
7	-	Save Your Kisses For Me	Brotherhood Of Man	Pye	13	(27)	G
8	13	It Should Have Been Me	Yvonne Fair	Tamla Motown	5	(85)	F L
9	6	Rodrigo's Guitar Concerto...	Manuel/Music Of The Mountains	EMI	6		F L
10	-	You See The Trouble With Me	Barry White	20th Century	7		
11	-	I Wanna Stay With You	Gallagher & Lyle	A&M	6	(49)	F
12	-	(Do The) Spanish Hustle	Fatback Band	Polydor	4		
13	20	Rain	Status Quo	Vertigo	5		
14	11	Dat	Pluto Shervington	Opal	5		F
15	-	Funky Weekend	Stylistics	Avco	4	(76)	
16	-	Falling Apart At The Seams	Marmalade	Target	6	(49)	L
17	-	Miss You Nights	Cliff Richard	EMI	4		
18	-	Yesterday	Beatles	Apple	6		
19	17	Squeeze Box	Who	Polydor	6	(16)	
20	-	I Love Music	O'Jays	Philly International	4	(5)	

US 1976 JAN-MAR

January 1976

This Mnth	Prev Mnth	Title	Artist	Label	Wks 20	(UK Pos)	
1	8	I Write The Songs	Barry Manilow	Arista	13		G
2	6	Love Rollercoaster	Ohio Players	Mercury	12		G
3	7	Theme From Mahogany (Do You Know Where You're Going To)	Diana Ross	Motown	10	(5)	
4	16	Convoy	C.W. McCall	MGM	9	(2)	F G L
5	13	I Love Music (Pt. 1)	O'Jays	Philly Int.	10	(13)	G
6	-	Love To Love You Baby	Donna Summer	Oasis	11	(4)	F G
7	20	Times Of Your Life	Paul Anka	UA	8		L
8	-	You Sexy Thing	Hot Chocolate	Big Tree	12	(2)	G
9	-	Walk Away From Love	David Ruffin	Motown	6	(10)	L
10	10	Fox On The Run	Sweet	Capitol	8	(2)	G
11	-	Sing A Song	Earth, Wind & Fire	Columbia	8		G
12	4	Saturday Night	Bay City Rollers	Arista	9		F G
13	-	Country Boy (You Got Your Feet In L.A.)	Glen Campbell	Capitol	6		
14	-	Rock And Roll All Nite (Live Version)	Kiss	Casablanca	5		F
15	-	Fly Away	John Denver	RCA	5		L
16	-	50 Ways To Leave Your Lover	Paul Simon	Columbia	10	(23)	G
17	2	That's The Way (I Like It)	KC & The Sunshine Band	TK	10	(4)	G
18	-	Evil Woman	Electric Light Orchestra	UA	8	(10)	
19	1	Let's Do It Again	Staple Singers	Curtom	8		G L
20	-	Love Machine	Miracles	Tamla	11	(3)	G L

February 1976

This Mnth	Prev Mnth	Title	Artist	Label	Wks 20	(UK Pos)	
1	16	50 Ways To Leave Your Lover	Paul Simon	Columbia	10	(23)	G
2	-	Theme From S.W.A.T.	Rhythm Heritage	ABC	8		F G
3	8	You Sexy Thing	Hot Chocolate	Big Tree	12	(2)	G
4	6	Love To Love You Baby	Donna Summer	Oasis	11	(4)	F G
5	20	Love Machine	Miracles	Tamla	11	(3)	G L
6	1	I Write The Songs	Barry Manilow	Arista	13		G
7	-	Breaking Up Is Hard To Do	Neil Sedaka	Rocket	8		
8	-	All By Myself	Eric Carmen	Arista	10	(12)	F G
9	-	Take It To The Limit	Eagles	Asylum	9	(12)	
10	-	Love Hurts	Nazareth	A&M	9		F G L
11	11	Sing A Song	Earth, Wind & Fire	Columbia	8		G
12	18	Evil Woman	Electric Light Orchestra	UA	8	(10)	
13	2	Love Rollercoaster	Ohio Players	Mercury	12		G
14	-	December '63 (Oh What A Night)	Four Seasons	Warner	12	(1)	G L
15	-	Wake Up Everybody (Pt. 1)	Harold Melvin & The Blue Notes	Philly Int.	6	(23)	L
16	4	Convoy	C.W. McCall	MGM	9	(2)	F G L
17	-	Lonely Night (Angel Face)	Captain & Tennille	A&M	10		G
18	-	Grow Some Funk Of Your Own/ I Feel Like A Bullet	Elton John	MCA	3		
19	-	Dream Weaver	Gary Wright	Warner	10		F G
20	7	Times Of Your Life	Paul Anka	UA	8		L

March 1976

This Mnth	Prev Mnth	Title	Artist	Label	Wks 20	(UK Pos)	
1	14	December '63 (Oh What A Night)	Four Seasons	Warner	12	(1)	G L
2	8	All By Myself	Eric Carmen	Arista	10	(12)	F G
3	19	Dream Weaver	Gary Wright	Warner	10		F G
4	17	Lonely Night (Angel Face)	Captain & Tennille	A&M	10		G
5	9	Take It To The Limit	Eagles	Asylum	9	(12)	
6	5	Love Machine	Miracles	Tamla	11	(3)	G L
7	-	Sweet Thing	Rufus Featuring Chaka Khan	ABC	9		G L
8	-	Disco Lady	Johnnie Taylor	Columbia	10	(25)	PL
9	-	Dream On	Aerosmith	Columbia	8		F
10	-	Junk Food Junkie	Larry Groce	Warner	5		F L
11	2	Theme From S.W.A.T.	Rhythm Heritage	ABC	8		F G
12	-	Fanny (Be Tender With My Love)	Bee Gees	RSO	6		
13	-	Money Honey	Bay City Rollers	Arista	6	(3)	
14	10	Love Hurts	Nazareth	A&M	9		F G L
15	-	Golden Years	David Bowie	RCA	8	(8)	
16	1	50 Ways To Leave Your Lover	Paul Simon	Columbia	10	(23)	G
17	-	Right Back Where We Started From	Maxine Nightingale	UA	12	(8)	F G
18	-	Let Your Love Flow	Bellamy Brothers	Warner	9	(7)	F L
19	3	You Sexy Thing	Hot Chocolate	Big Tree	12	(2)	G
20	-	Deep Purple	Donny & Marie Osmond	MGM	6	(25)	L

◆ R&B stars Howlin' Wolf, Arthur Gunter and Buster Brown died, as did previous hit makers Percy Faith, Sal Mineo, Free's Paul Kossoff and Supreme, Florence Ballard.

◆ A new award, the platinum album, was introduced for albums selling over one million copies. First recipient was **Eagles/Their Greatest Hits 1971-1974** - which went on to sell 14 million copies!

▲ German based producer/composer Giorgio Moroder's latest discovery, American disco diva Donna Summer, had the first of her numerous hits with a controversial, heavy breathing opus, 'Love To Love You Baby'.

UK 1976 APR-JUNE

▲ The Rolling Stones, whose **Black And Blue** headed the American LP listings, played six nights at Earl's Court in London as part of their eight-week European tour. Other major UK events included The Who at Charlton Athletic Football Club and David Bowie (above) at Wembley. Also gigging were The Sex Pistols, America's Patti Smith, The Stranglers, The Damned and AC/DC.

◆ All The Beatles' previous singles were re-issued, with five making the Top 40, and 'Yesterday', which was never previously released, reached the Top 10. Incidentally, the group turned down a $30 million American offer to re-unite.

April 1976

This Mnth	Prev Mnth	Title	Artist	Label	Wks 20	(US Pos)	
1	7	Save Your Kisses For Me	Brotherhood Of Man	Pye	13	(27)	G
2	-	Music	John Miles	Decca	7	(88)	
3	10	You See The Trouble With Me	Barry White	20th Century	7		
4	-	Fernando	Abba	Epic	12	(13)	
5	-	I'm Mandy Fly Me	10cc	Mercury	6	(60)	
6	-	Jungle Rock	Hank Mizell	Charly	9		F L
7	-	Pinball Wizard	Elton John	DJM	4		
8	-	Theme From Mahogany (Do You Know Where You're Going To)	Diana Ross	Tamla Motown	5	(1)	
9	3	Love Really Hurts Without You	Billy Ocean	GTO	8	(22)	F
10	18	Yesterday	Beatles	Apple	6		
11	-	Girls Girls Girls	Sailor	Epic	5		L
12	11	I Wanna Stay With You	Gallagher & Lyle	A&M	6	(49)	F
13	16	Falling Apart At The Seams	Marmalade	Target	6	(49)	L
14	-	Hello Happiness	Drifters	Bell	5		
15	-	Love Me Like I Love You	Bay City Rollers	Bell	5		
16	-	Don't Stop It Now	Hot Chocolate	RAK	5	(42)	
17	-	Hey Jude	Beatles	Apple	4		
18	6	People Like You And People Like Me	Glitter Band	Bell	6		L
19	1	I Love To Love (But My Baby Loves To Dance)	Tina Charles	CBS	7		F
20	-	S-S-S-Single Bed	Fox	GTO	7		L

May 1976

This Mnth	Prev Mnth	Title	Artist	Label	Wks 20	(US Pos)	
1	4	Fernando	Abba	Epic	12	(13)	
2	1	Save Your Kisses For Me	Brotherhood Of Man	Pye	13	(27)	G
3	6	Jungle Rock	Hank Mizell	Charly	9		F L
4	20	S-S-S-Single Bed	Fox	GTO	7		L
5	-	Silver Star	Four Seasons	Warner	5	(38)	L
6	-	More, More, More	Andrea True Connection	Buddah	7	(4)	F L
7	-	Arms Of Mary	Sutherland Brothers And Quiver	CBS	5	(81)	F L
8	-	Get Up And Boogie (That's Right)	Silver Convention	Magnet	6	(2)	F L
9	-	No Charge	J.J. Barrie	Power Exchange	7		F L
10	-	Convoy GB	Laurie Lingo & The Dipsticks	State	5		F L
11	-	Can't Help Falling In Love	Stylistics	Avco	6		
12	-	Fool To Cry	Rolling Stones	Rolling Stone	6	(10)	
13	-	Life Is Too Short Girl	Sheer Elegance	Pye International	6		L
14	8	Theme From Mahogany (Do You Know Where You're Going To)	Diana Ross	Tamla Motown	5	(1)	
15	-	My Resistance Is Low	Robin Sarstedt	Decca	5		F L
16	-	Combine Harvester (Brand New Key)	Wurzels	EMI	7		F
17	-	Love Hangover	Diana Ross	Tamla Motown	6	(1)	
18	-	Disco Connection	Isaac Hayes	ABC	5		L
19	11	Girls Girls Girls	Sailor	Epic	5		L
20	15	Love Me Like I Love You	Bay City Rollers	Bell	5		

June 1976

This Mnth	Prev Mnth	Title	Artist	Label	Wks 20	(US Pos)	
1	16	Combine Harvester (Brand New Key)	Wurzels	EMI	7		F
2	-	Silly Love Songs	Wings	Parlophone	8	(1)	
3	9	No Charge	J.J. Barrie	Power Exchange	7		F L
4	-	You To Me Are Everything	Real Thing	Pye International	8	(64)	F
5	15	My Resistance Is Low	Robin Sarstedt	Decca	5		F L
6	-	You Just Might See Me Cry	Our Kid	Polydor	7		F L
7	-	Let Your Love Flow	Bellamy Brothers	Warner	8	(1)	F
8	12	Fool To Cry	Rolling Stones	Rolling Stone	6	(10)	
9	1	Fernando	Abba	Epic	12	(13)	
10	-	Tonight's The Night (Gonna Be Alright)	Rod Stewart	Riva	7	(1)	
11	-	Jolene	Dolly Parton	RCA	6	(60)	F
12	-	Heart On My Sleeve	Gallagher & Lyle	A&M	7	(67)	L
13	-	Show Me The Way	Peter Frampton	A&M	5	(6)	F L
14	-	Devil Woman	Cliff Richard	EMI	4	(6)	
15	-	Midnight Train To Georgia	Gladys Knight & The Pips	Buddah	4	(1)	
16	-	This Is It	Melba Moore	Buddah	4	(91)	F
17	-	Young Hearts Run Free	Candi Staton	Warner	9	(20)	F
18	17	Love Hangover	Diana Ross	Tamla Motown	6	(1)	
19	-	Shake It Down	Mud	Private Stock	2		
20	-	Let's Stick Together	Bryan Ferry	Island	7		

US 1976 APR-JUNE

April 1976

This Mnth	Prev Mnth	Title	Artist	Label	Wks 20	(UK Pos)	
1	8	Disco Lady	Johnnie Taylor	Columbia	10	(25)	P L
2	18	Let Your Love Flow	Bellamy Brothers	Warner	9	(7)	F L
3	17	Right Back Where We Started From	Maxine Nightingale	UA	12	(8)	F G
4	4	Lonely Night (Angel Face)	Captain & Tennille	A&M	10		G
5	3	Dream Weaver	Gary Wright	Warner	10		F G
6	-	Only Sixteen	Dr. Hook	Capitol	7		G
7	-	Boogie Fever	Sylvers	Capitol	11		F G
8	-	Sweet Love	Commodores	Motown	6	(32)	
9	-	Show Me The Way	Peter Frampton	A&M	10	(10)	F
10	9	Dream On	Aerosmith	Columbia	8		F
11	-	Bohemian Rhapsody	Queen	Elektra	9	(1)	G
12	7	Sweet Thing	Rufus Featuring Chaka Khan	ABC	9		G L
13	1	December '63 (Oh What A Night)	Four Seasons	Warner	12	(1)	G L
14	-	There's A Kind Of Hush (All Over The World)	Carpenters	A&M	4	(22)	
15	15	Golden Years	David Bowie	RCA	8	(8)	
16	-	Welcome Back	John Sebastian	Reprise	10		F G L
17	-	Fooled Around And Fell In Love	Elvin Bishop	Capricorn	9	(34)	F G L
18	13	Money Honey	Bay City Rollers	Arista	6	(3)	
19	20	Deep Purple	Donny & Marie Osmond	MGM	6	(25)	L
20	-	I Do, I Do, I Do, I Do, I Do	Abba	Atlantic	3	(38)	

May 1976

This Mnth	Prev Mnth	Title	Artist	Label	Wks 20	(UK Pos)	
1	16	Welcome Back	John Sebastian	Reprise	10		F G L
2	17	Fooled Around And Fell In Love	Elvin Bishop	Capricorn	9	(34)	F G L
3	-	Silly Love Songs	Wings	Capitol	12	(2)	G
4	7	Boogie Fever	Sylvers	Capitol	11		F G
5	-	Love Hangover	Diana Ross	Motown	10	(10)	
6	-	Get Up And Boogie	Silver Convention	Midland Int.	11	(7)	G L
7	3	Right Back Where We Started From	Maxine Nightingale	UA	12	(8)	F G
8	-	Shannon	Henry Gross	Lifesong	9		F G L
9	9	Show Me The Way	Peter Frampton	A&M	10	(10)	F
10	-	Tryin' To Get The Feeling Again	Barry Manilow	Arista	7		
11	-	Happy Days	Pratt & McClain	Reprise	7	(31)	F L
12	-	Sara Smile	Daryl Hall & John Oates	RCA	11		F G
13	-	Misty Blue	Dorothy Moore	Malaco	11	(5)	F L
14	2	Let Your Love Flow	Bellamy Brothers	Warner	9	(7)	F L
15	1	Disco Lady	Johnnie Taylor	Columbia	10	(25)	P L
16	-	Fool To Cry	Rolling Stones	Rolling Stone	6	(6)	
17	-	Rhiannon (Will You Ever Win)	Fleetwood Mac	Reprise	6	(46)	
18	11	Bohemian Rhapsody	Queen	Elektra	9	(1)	G
19	-	Strange Magic	Electric Light Orchestra	UA	5	(38)	
20	8	Sweet Love	Commodores	Motown	6	(32)	

June 1976

This Mnth	Prev Mnth	Title	Artist	Label	Wks 20	(UK Pos)	
1	3	Silly Love Songs	Wings	Capitol	12	(2)	G
2	6	Get Up And Boogie	Silver Convention	Midland Int.	11	(7)	G L
3	13	Misty Blue	Dorothy Moore	Malaco	11	(5)	F L
4	5	Love Hangover	Diana Ross	Motown	10	(10)	
5	12	Sara Smile	Daryl Hall & John Oates	RCA	11		F G
6	-	Shop Around	Captain & Tennille	A&M	10		G
7	-	More, More, More (Pt. 1)	Andrea True Connection	Buddah	10	(5)	F G L
8	8	Shannon	Henry Gross	Lifesong	9		F G L
9	11	Happy Days	Pratt & McClain	Reprise	7	(31)	F L
10	-	I'll Be Good To You	Brothers Johnson	A&M	8		F G
11	-	Love Is Alive	Gary Wright	Warner	14		
12	-	Afternoon Delight	Starland Vocal Band	Windsong	10	(18)	F G L
13	1	Welcome Back	John Sebastian	Reprise	10		F G L
14	16	Fool To Cry	Rolling Stones	Rolling Stone	6	(6)	
15	-	Kiss And Say Goodbye	Manhattans	Columbia	11	(4)	F G
16	17	Rhiannon (Will You Ever Win)	Fleetwood Mac	Reprise	6	(46)	
17	-	Takin' It To The Streets	Doobie Brothers	Warner	3		
18	-	Movin'	Brass Construction	UA	4	(23)	F L
19	-	Never Gonna Fall In Love Again	Eric Carmen	Arista	6		
20	-	I Want You	Marvin Gaye	Tamla	4		

◆ Paul McCartney & Wings played to a record indoor crowd of 67,000 in Seattle, during their debut US tour. They topped the charts with 'Silly Love Songs' and their LP, **Wings At The Speed of Sound** (which stopped The Beatles' **Rock'n'Roll Music** hitting No. 1).

◆ Johnnie Taylor's US-only hit, 'Disco Lady', became the first certified platinum single (two million sales). Meanwhile, disco ladies Diana Ross, Silver Convention and The Andrea True Connection were scoring transatlantic Top 20 hits.

◆ The biggest selling live LP, **Frampton Comes Alive**, by ex-UK teen idol Peter Frampton topped the US chart. The double album has sold over six million copies.

◆ Eddy Arnold's 'Cowboy' made him the first artist to have had 100 singles on the country charts.

UK 1976

JULY-SEPT

◆ A UK visit by The Ramones helped heightened interest in punk. The Sex Pistols appeared on TV, and The Clash, The Buzzcocks and Siouxsie & The Banshees made their live debuts. Stiff Records was launched and the first issue of fanzine *Sniffin' Glue* hit the streets.

◆ The Rolling Stones, Lynyrd Skynyrd, and 10cc attracted 200,000 to the Knebworth Festival, while 60,000 attended Queen's Hyde Park concert and Grateful Dead and Santana packed the crowds into Wembley.

◆ Britain's top solo artist, Cliff Richard, finally cracked the US Top 10 with 'Devil Woman'. His 20 date Russian tour was also a great success.

◆ Elton John, who topped the UK chart for the first time with 'Don't Go Breaking My Heart', played a record-breaking seven nights at Madison Square Garden.

July 1976

This Mnth	Prev Mnth	Title	Artist	Label	Wks 20	(US Pos)	
1	17	Young Hearts Run Free	Candi Staton	Warner	9	(20)	F
2	-	The Roussos Phenomenon E.P.	Demis Roussos	Philips	9		
3	-	A Little Bit More	Dr. Hook	Capitol	11	(11)	
4	-	Kiss And Say Goodbye	Manhattans	CBS	8	(1)	F
5	4	You To Me Are Everything	Real Thing	Pye International	8	(64)	F
6	-	Don't Go Breaking My Heart	Elton John & Kiki Dee	Rocket	11	(1)	
7	20	Let's Stick Together	Bryan Ferry	Island	7		
8	6	You Just Might See Me Cry	Our Kid	Polydor	7		F L
9	-	Misty Blue	Dorothy Moore	Contempo	9	(3)	F
10	-	You're My Best Friend	Queen	EMI	5	(16)	
11	10	Tonight's The Night (Gonna Be Alright)	Rod Stewart	Riva	7	(1)	
12	-	Leader Of The Pack	Shangri-Las	Charly/Contempo	5		L
13	-	It Only Takes A Minute	One Hundred Ton & A Feather	UK	5		F L
14	-	The Boys Are Back In Town	Thin Lizzy	Vertigo	5	(12)	
15	-	You Are My Love	Liverpool Express	Warner	6		F
16	-	Heaven Must Be Missing An Angel	Tavares	Capitol	7	(15)	F
17	12	Heart On My Sleeve	Gallagher & Lyle	A&M	7	(67)	L
18	2	Silly Love Songs	Wings	Parlophone	8	(1)	
19	-	I Love To Boogie	T. Rex	EMI	5		
20	-	Man To Man	Hot Chocolate	RAK	4		

August 1976

This Mnth	Prev Mnth	Title	Artist	Label	Wks 20	(US Pos)	
1	6	Don't Go Breaking My Heart	Elton John & Kiki Dee	Rocket	11	(1)	
2	3	A Little Bit More	Dr. Hook	Capitol	11	(11)	
3	-	Jeans On	David Dundas	Air	6	(17)	F L
4	16	Heaven Must Be Missing An Angel	Tavares	Capitol	7	(15)	F
5	-	In Zaire	Johnny Wakelin	Pye	6		L
6	-	Now Is The Time	Jimmy James & The Vagabonds	Pye	6		F L
7	-	Dr Kiss Kiss	5000 Volts	Philips	6		L
8	-	Let 'Em In	Wings	Parlophone	8	(3)	
9	9	Misty Blue	Dorothy Moore	Contempo	9	(3)	F
10	-	You Should Be Dancing	Bee Gees	RSO	7	(1)	
11	2	The Roussos Phenomenon E.P.	Demis Roussos	Philips	9		
12	-	Mystery Song	Status Quo	Vertigo	5		
13	-	Harvest For The World	Isley Brothers	Epic	4	(63)	
14	4	Kiss And Say Goodbye	Manhattans	CBS	8	(1)	F
15	-	Here Comes The Sun	Steve Harley	EMI	4		
16	-	You Don't Have To Go	Chi-Lites	Brunswick	7		L
17	-	Extended Play (E.P.)	Bryan Ferry	Island	6		
18	-	What I've Got In Mind	Billie Jo Spears	UA	5		L
19	1	Young Hearts Run Free	Candi Staton	Warner	9	(20)	F
20	-	You'll Never Find Another Love Like Mine	Lou Rawls	Philly International	4	(2)	F L

September 1976

This Mnth	Prev Mnth	Title	Artist	Label	Wks 20	(US Pos)	
1	-	Dancing Queen	Abba	Epic	12	(1)	
2	8	Let 'Em In	Wings	Parlophone	8	(3)	
3	-	The Killing Of Georgie	Rod Stewart	Riva	7	(30)	
4	16	You Don't Have To Go	Chi-Lites	Brunswick	7		L
5	-	(Light Of Experience) Doina De Jale	Georghe Zamfir	Epic	6		F L
6	-	Can't Get By Without You	Real Thing	Pye	8		
7	-	16 Bars	Stylistics	H & L	7		L
8	1	Don't Go Breaking My Heart	Elton John & Kiki Dee	Rocket	11	(1)	
9	18	What I've Got In Mind	Billie Jo Spears	UA	5		L
10	-	Aria	Acker Bilk	Pye	6		L
11	-	Blinded By The Light	Manfred Mann's Earth Band	Bronze	6	(1)	F
12	-	I Am A Cider Drinker (Paloma Blanca)	Wurzels	EMI	5		L
13	-	I Only Wanna Be With You	Bay City Rollers	Bell	6	(12)	
14	17	Extended Play (E.P.)	Bryan Ferry	Island	6		
15	10	You Should Be Dancing	Bee Gees	RSO	7	(1)	
16	-	Mississippi	Pussycat	Sonet	13		F L
17	2	A Little Bit More	Dr. Hook	Capitol	11	(11)	
18	-	Dance Little Lady Dance	Tina Charles	CBS	6		
19	20	You'll Never Find Another Love Like Mine	Lou Rawls	Philly International	4	(2)	F L
20	5	In Zaire	Johnny Wakelin	Pye	6		L

July 1976

This Mnth	Prev Mnth	Title	Artist	Label	Wks 20	(UK Pos)	
1	12	Afternoon Delight	Starland Vocal Band	Windsong	10	(18)	F G L
2	15	Kiss And Say Goodbye	Manhattans	Columbia	11	(4)	F G
3	10	I'll Be Good To You	Brothers Johnson	A&M	8		F G
4	11	Love Is Alive	Gary Wright	Warner	14		
5	-	Moonlight Feels Right	Starbuck	Private Stock	9		F L
6	-	Got To Get You Into My Life	Beatles	Capitol	8		
7	6	Shop Around	Captain & Tennille	A&M	10		G
8	7	More, More, More (Pt. 1)	Andrea True Connection	Buddah	10	(5)	F G L
9	1	Silly Love Songs	Wings	Capitol	12	(2)	G
10	-	Rock And Roll Music	Beach Boys	Brother	10	(36)	
11	-	Let Her In	John Travolta	Midland Int.	5		F
12	-	Get Closer	Seals & Crofts	Warner	6		
13	3	Misty Blue	Dorothy Moore	Malaco	11	(5)	F L
14	-	Take The Money And Run	Steve Miller Band	Capitol	6		
15	-	If You Know What I Mean	Neil Diamond	Columbia	6	(35)	
16	5	Sara Smile	Daryl Hall & John Oates	RCA	11		F G
17	-	Don't Go Breaking My Heart	Elton John & Kiki Dee	Rocket	9	(1)	G
18	-	The Boys Are Back In Town	Thin Lizzy	Mercury	5	(8)	F L
19	19	Never Gonna Fall In Love Again	Eric Carmen	Arista	6		
20	2	Get Up And Boogie	Silver Convention	Midland Int.	11	(7)	G L

August 1976

This Mnth	Prev Mnth	Title	Artist	Label	Wks 20	(UK Pos)	
1	17	Don't Go Breaking My Heart	Elton John & Kiki Dee	Rocket	9	(1)	G
2	-	You Should Be Dancing	Bee Gees	RSO	10	(5)	G
3	-	Let 'Em In	Wings	Capitol	8	(2)	G
4	-	You'll Never Find Another Love Like Mine	Lou Rawls	Philly Int.	9	(10)	G L
5	4	Love Is Alive	Gary Wright	Warner	14		
6	-	I'd Really Love To See You Tonight	England Dan & John Ford Coley	Big Tree	11		F G
7	10	Rock And Roll Music	Beach Boys	Brother	10	(36)	
8	2	Kiss And Say Goodbye	Manhattans	Columbia	11	(4)	F G
9	-	(Shake, Shake, Shake) Shake Your Booty	KC & The Sunshine Band	TK	12	(22)	G
10	-	This Masquerade	George Benson	Warner	7		F
11	-	Turn The Beat Around	Vicki Sue Robinson	RCA	6		F L
12	-	Play That Funky Music	Wild Cherry	Epic	13	(7)	F G L
13	-	A Fifth Of Beethoven	Walter Murphy/Big Apple Band	Private Stock	14	(28)	F G L
14	-	Baby, I Love Your Way	Peter Frampton	A&M	5	(43)	
15	1	Afternoon Delight	Starland Vocal Band	Windsong	10	(18)	F G L
16	5	Moonlight Feels Right	Starbuck	Private Stock	9		F L
17	6	Got To Get You Into My Life	Beatles	Capitol	8		
18	-	Say You Love Me	Fleetwood Mac	Reprise	9	(40)	
19	-	I'm Easy	Keith Carradine	ABC	4		F L
20	15	If You Know What I Mean	Neil Diamond	Columbia	6	(35)	

September 1976

This Mnth	Prev Mnth	Title	Artist	Label	Wks 20	(UK Pos)	
1	12	Play That Funky Music	Wild Cherry	Epic	13	(7)	F G L
2	9	(Shake, Shake, Shake) Shake Your Booty	KC & The Sunshine Band	TK	12	(22)	G
3	6	I'd Really Love To See You Tonight	England Dan & John Ford Coley	Big Tree	11		F G
4	4	You'll Never Find Another Love Like Mine	Lou Rawls	Philly Int.	9	(10)	G L
5	13	A Fifth Of Beethoven	Walter Murphy/Big Apple Band	Private Stock	14	(28)	F G L
6	-	Lowdown	Boz Scaggs	Columbia	9	(28)	F G
7	-	Summer	War	UA	6		G L
8	2	You Should Be Dancing	Bee Gees	RSO	10	(5)	G
9	-	Devil Woman	Cliff Richard	Rocket	9	(9)	F G
10	-	If You Leave Me Now	Chicago	Columbia	12	(1)	G
11	18	Say You Love Me	Fleetwood Mac	Reprise	9	(40)	
12	1	Don't Go Breaking My Heart	Elton John & Kiki Dee	Rocket	9	(1)	G
13	3	Let 'Em In	Paul McCartney	Capitol	8	(2)	G
14	-	With Your Love	Jefferson Starship	Grunt	6		
15	-	Disco Duck	Rick Dees & His Cast Of Idiots	RSO	12	(6)	F G L
16	-	A Little Bit More	Dr. Hook	Capitol	7	(2)	
17	-	Still The One	Orleans	Asylum	8		
18	10	This Masquerade	George Benson	Warner	7		F
19	-	Getaway	Earth, Wind & Fire	Columbia	6		G
20	-	Heaven Must Be Missing An Angel	Tavares	Capitol	4	(4)	G L

US
1976
JULY-SEPT

◆ NBC filmed a Beach Boys concert at Anaheim Stadium, California. It was the first time Brian Wilson had participated in 12 years. The result was seen in their 15th Anniversary TV special, *The Beach Boys: It's OK.* Incidentally, their **20 Golden Greats** led the UK listings for 10 weeks.

▲ Joining the droves of disco artists in the charts were soulful singers: Lou Rawls, The Isley Brothers, The Manhattans, Dorothy Moore (above) and Candi Staton.

◆ Deep Purple and The Allman Brothers disbanded, and Loggins and Messina split up.

UK 1976
OCT-DEC

▲ 'New Rose' by The Damned, widely accepted as the first British punk single, was released. The Sex Pistols (above) debut disc 'Anarchy In The UK' charted, but EMI offended by their "disgraceful... aggressive behaviour", withdrew the record, paid them off with £40,000 ($100,000) and dropped them!

◆ Chicago, had their only transatlantic topper with the Grammy winning AOR classic 'If You Leave Me Now'.

◆ London based LBC became Britain's first commercial radio station.

October 1976

This Mnth	Prev Mnth	Title	Artist	Label	Wks 20	(US Pos)	
1	16	Mississippi	Pussycat	Sonet	13		F L
2	1	Dancing Queen	Abba	Epic	12	(1)	
3	-	Sailing	Rod Stewart	Warner	8	(58)	
4	6	Can't Get By Without You	Real Thing	Pye	8		
5	-	When Forever Has Gone	Demis Roussos	Philips	7		L
6	-	Disco Duck	Rick Dees & His Cast Of Idiots	RSO	6	(1)	F L
7	-	Howzat	Sherbet	Epic	7	(61)	F L
8	-	Girl Of My Best Friend	Elvis Presley	RCA	6		
9	18	Dance Little Lady Dance	Tina Charles	CBS	6		
10	13	I Only Wanna Be With You	Bay City Rollers	Bell	6	(12)	
11	-	Hurt	Manhattans	CBS	8	(97)	L
12	-	If You Leave Me Now	Chicago	CBS	12	(1)	
13	-	The Best Disco In Town	Ritchie Family	Polydor	5	(17)	F L
14	12	I Am A Cider Drinker (Paloma Blanca)	Wurzels	EMI	5		L
15	-	Summer Of My Life	Simon May	Pye	6		F L
16	-	Don't Take Away The Music	Tavares	Capitol	7	(34)	
17	10	Aria	Acker Bilk	Pye	6		L
18	11	Blinded By The Light	Manfred Mann's Earth Band	Bronze	6	(1)	F
19	-	I'll Meet You At Midnight	Smokie	RAK	5		
20	-	Loving And Free/Amoureuse	Kiki Dee	Rocket	5		

November 1976

This Mnth	Prev Mnth	Title	Artist	Label	Wks 20	(US Pos)	
1	12	If You Leave Me Now	Chicago	CBS	12	(1)	
2	1	Mississippi	Pussycat	Sonet	13		F L
3	-	You Make Me Feel Like Dancing	Leo Sayer	Chrysalis	7	(1)	
4	16	Don't Take Away The Music	Tavares	Capitol	7	(34)	
5	-	Play That Funky Music	Wild Cherry	Epic	7	(1)	F L
6	11	Hurt	Manhattans	CBS	8	(97)	L
7	5	When Forever Has Gone	Demis Roussos	Philips	7		L
8	-	If Not You	Dr. Hook	Capitol	6	(55)	
9	-	Under The Moon Of Love	Showaddywaddy	Bell	12		
10	-	Couldn't Get It Right	Climax Blues Band	BTM	6	(3)	F L
11	7	Howzat	Sherbet	Epic	7	(61)	F L
12	15	Summer Of My Life	Simon May	Pye	6		F L
13	-	Dancing With The Captain	Paul Nicholas	RSO	5		
14	-	Substitute	Who	Polydor	5		
15	-	Love And Affection	Joan Armatrading	A&M	5		F
16	-	Beautiful Noise	Neil Diamond	CBS	4		
17	-	Lost In France	Bonnie Tyler	RCA	5		F
18	-	Somebody To Love	Queen	EMI	8	(13)	
19	-	Jaws	Lalo Schifrin	CTI	4		F L
20	3	Sailing	Rod Stewart	Warner	8	(58)	

December 1976

This Mnth	Prev Mnth	Title	Artist	Label	Wks 20	(US Pos)	
1	9	Under The Moon Of Love	Showaddywaddy	Bell	12		
2	18	Somebody To Love	Queen	EMI	8	(13)	
3	-	Money Money Money	Abba	Epic	10	(56)	
4	-	Livin' Thing	Electric Light Orchestra	Jet	8	(13)	
5	-	When A Child Is Born (Soleado)	Johnny Mathis	CBS	8		
6	-	Love Me	Yvonne Elliman	RSO	8	(14)	F
7	1	If You Leave Me Now	Chicago	CBS	12	(1)	
8	3	You Make Me Feel Like Dancing	Leo Sayer	Chrysalis	7	(1)	
9	-	Lean On Me	Mud	Private Stock	7		L
10	-	Portsmouth	Mike Oldfield	Virgin	9		
11	-	Get Back	Rod Stewart	Riva	6		
12	17	Lost In France	Bonnie Tyler	RCA	5		F
13	8	If Not You	Dr. Hook	Capitol	6	(55)	
14	-	Sorry Seems To Be The Hardest Word	Elton John	Rocket	3	(6)	
15	-	Living Next Door To Alice	Smokie	RAK	7	(25)	
16	-	Bionic Santa	Chris Hill	Philips	5		L
17	-	Little Does She Know	Kursaal Flyers	CBS	6		F L
18	-	Dr. Love	Tina Charles	CBS	8		L
19	-	Stop Me (If You've Heard It All Before)	Billy Ocean	GTO	4		
20	-	Rock'n Me	Steve Miller Band	Mercury	4	(1)	F

October 1976

This Mnth	Prev Mnth	Title	Artist	Label	Wks 20	(UK Pos)	
1	15	Disco Duck	Rick Dees & His Cast Of Idiots	RSO	12	(6)	F G L
2	5	A Fifth Of Beethoven	Walter Murphy/Big Apple Band	Private Stock	14	(28)	F G L
3	10	If You Leave Me Now	Chicago	Columbia	12	(1)	G
4	1	Play That Funky Music	Wild Cherry	Epic	13	(7)	F G L
5	6	Lowdown	Boz Scaggs	Columbia	9	(28)	F G
6	2	(Shake, Shake...) Shake Your Booty	KC & The Sunshine Band	TK	12	(22)	G
7	17	Still The One	Orleans	Asylum	8		
8	-	She's Gone	Daryl Hall & John Oates	Atlantic	9	(42)	
9	9	Devil Woman	Cliff Richard	Rocket	9	(9)	F G
10	-	Rock'n Me	Steve Miller Band	Capitol	9	(11)	
11	3	I'd Really Love To See You Tonight	England Dan & John Ford Coley	Big Tree	11		F G
12	-	That'll Be The Day	Linda Ronstadt	Asylum	6		
13	-	Love So Right	Bee Gees	RSO	9	(41)	G
14	-	Magic Man	Heart	Mushroom	7		F
15	-	I Only Want To Be With You	Bay City Rollers	Arista	5	(4)	
16	-	Wreck Of The Edmund Fitzgerald	Gordon Lightfoot	Reprise	9	(40)	L
17	16	A Little Bit More	Dr. Hook	Capitol	7	(2)	
18	19	Getaway	Earth, Wind & Fire	Columbia	6		G
19	-	(Don't Fear) The Reaper	Blue Oyster Cult	Columbia	7	(16)	F L
20	11	Say You Love Me	Fleetwood Mac	Reprise	9	(40)	

November 1976

This Mnth	Prev Mnth	Title	Artist	Label	Wks 20	(UK Pos)	
1	16	Wreck Of The Edmund Fitzgerald	Gordon Lightfoot	Reprise	9	(40)	L
2	-	Tonight's The Night (Gonna Be Alright)	Rod Stewart	Warner	12	(5)	G
3	1	Disco Duck	Rick Dees & His Cast Of Idiots	RSO	12	(6)	F G L
4	13	Love So Right	Bee Gees	RSO	9	(41)	G
5	-	Muskrat Love	Captain & Tennille	A&M	11		G
6	10	Rock'n Me	Steve Miller Band	Capitol	9	(11)	
7	-	Just To Be Close To You	Commodores	Motown	6		
8	-	The Rubberband Man	Spinners	Atlantic	11	(16)	G
9	-	Beth	Kiss	Casablanca	10		G
10	-	Do You Feel Like We Do	Peter Frampton	A&M	4	(39)	
11	3	If You Leave Me Now	Chicago	Columbia	12	(1)	G
12	-	Nadia's Theme (The Young & The Restless)	Barry DeVorzon & Perry Botkin	A&M	11		F G L
13	-	More Than A Feeling	Boston	Epic	11	(22)	F
14	-	You Are The Woman	Firefall	Atlantic	8		F
15	19	(Don't Fear) The Reaper	Blue Oyster Cult	Columbia	7	(16)	F L
16	-	Fernando	Abba	Atlantic	5	(1)	
17	8	She's Gone	Daryl Hall & John Oates	Atlantic	9	(42)	
18	-	Nights Are Forever Without You	England Dan & John Ford Coley	Big Tree	8		
19	14	Magic Man	Heart	Mushroom	7		F
20	-	I Never Cry	Alice Cooper	Warner	8		G

December 1976

This Mnth	Prev Mnth	Title	Artist	Label	Wks 20	(UK Pos)	
1	2	Tonight's The Night (Gonna Be...)	Rod Stewart	Warner	12	(5)	G
2	8	The Rubberband Man	Spinners	Atlantic	11	(16)	G
3	-	You Don't Have To Be A Star (To Be In My Show)	Marilyn McCoo & Billy Davis Jr	ABC	11	(7)	F G
4	13	More Than A Feeling	Boston	Epic	11	(22)	F
5	-	You Make Me Feel Like Dancing	Leo Sayer	Warner	13	(2)	G
6	5	Muskrat Love	Captain & Tennille	A&M	11		G
7	-	Sorry Seems To Be The Hardest Word	Elton John	MCA/Rocket	8	(11)	G
8	12	Nadia's Theme (Young & Restless)	Barry DeVorzon & Perry Botkin	A&M	11		F G L
9	4	Love So Right	Bee Gees	RSO	9	(41)	G
10	14	You Are The Woman	Firefall	Atlantic	8		F
11	18	Nights Are Forever Without You	England Dan & John Ford Coley	Big Tree	8		
12	-	After The Lovin'	Engelbert Humperdinck	Epic	9		G L
13	20	I Never Cry	Alice Cooper	Warner	8		G
14	-	Dazz	Brick	Bang	11	(36)	F
15	-	Stand Tall	Burton Cummings	Portrait	8		F G L
16	9	Beth	Kiss	Casablanca	10		G
17	1	Wreck Of The Edmund Fitzgerald	Gordon Lightfoot	Reprise	9	(40)	L
18	-	Hot Line	Sylvers	Capitol	10		G
19	-	Love Me	Yvonne Elliman	RSO	7	(6)	F
20	-	I Wish	Stevie Wonder	Tamla	12	(5)	G

◆ Record and tape sales for the year went up to $2.74 billion, thanks partly to disco, whose rhythms were also being heard in rock and jazz.

◆ The Band's final performance was filmed as *The Last Waltz*. Appearing with them were Bob Dylan, Van Morrison, Neil Diamond, Muddy Waters, Joni Mitchell, Neil Young, Eric Clapton and Ringo Starr.

◆ Noteworthy rock acts enjoying their first Top 20 singles included: Heart, England Dan & John Ford Coley, Firefall, Blue Oyster Cult and Boston, whose eponymous album became the fastest-selling debut LP.

◆ Stevie Wonder's long-awaited album, **Songs In The Key Of Life,** headed the US charts for 14 weeks and earned Stevie a couple of Grammies.

UK 1977

JAN-MAR

◆ American actor David Soul's version of the British-written 'Don't Give Up On Us', topped the transatlantic charts and sold a million copies in the UK alone. Interestingly, teen-heartthrob Soul had previously recorded unsuccessfully in 1966 as The Covered Man (advertisements showed him with a bag on his head)!

◆ A&M signed The Sex Pistols (including new member Sid Vicious) and just nine days later, after pressure from the label's head office in Los Angeles, paid them off with £75,000 ($185,000).

◆ Two American acts faring better in Britain were Manhattan Transfer with the chart-topping single, 'Chanson D'Amour', and 53-year-old country singer Slim Whitman who had a No. 1 album, **Red River Valley** – neither record charted Stateside.

January 1977

This Mnth	Prev Mnth	Title	Artist	Label	Wks 20	(US Pos)	
1	-	Don't Give Up On Us	David Soul	Private Stock	12	(1)	F G
2	1	Under The Moon Of Love	Showaddywaddy	Bell	12		
3	3	Money Money Money	Abba	Epic	10	(56)	
4	5	When A Child Is Born (Soleado)	Johnny Mathis	CBS	8		
5	18	Dr. Love	Tina Charles	CBS	8		L
6	10	Portsmouth	Mike Oldfield	Virgin	9		
7	15	Living Next Door To Alice	Smokie	RAK	7	(25)	
8	-	Things We Do For Love	10cc	Mercury	8	(5)	
9	-	Side Show	Barry Biggs	Dynamic	9		F L
10	-	Don't Cry For Me Argentina	Julie Covington	MCA	10		F
11	-	Wild Side Of Life	Status Quo	Vertigo	9		
12	-	I Wish	Stevie Wonder	Tamla Motown	6	(1)	
13	2	Somebody To Love	Queen	EMI	8	(13)	
14	-	Grandma's Party	Paul Nicholas	RSO	8		L
15	-	You're More Than A Number In My Little Red Book	Drifters	Arista	6		L
16	9	Lean On Me	Mud	Private Stock	7		L
17	-	Isn't She Lovely	David Parton	Pye	7		F L
18	4	Livin' Thing	Electric Light Orchestra	Jet	8	(13)	
19	-	Fairytale	Dana	GTO	6		L
20	16	Bionic Santa	Chris Hill	Philips	5		L

February 1977

This Mnth	Prev Mnth	Title	Artist	Label	Wks 20	(US Pos)	
1	10	Don't Cry For Me Argentina	Julie Covington	MCA	10		F
2	1	Don't Give Up On Us	David Soul	Private Stock	12	(1)	F G
3	-	When I Need You	Leo Sayer	Chrysalis	9	(1)	
4	9	Side Show	Barry Biggs	Dynamic	9		F L
5	17	Isn't She Lovely	David Parton	Pye	7		F L
6	-	Don't Leave Me This Way	Harold Melvin & The Blue Notes	Philly Int.	7		L
7	-	Daddy Cool	Boney M	Atlantic	6	(65)	F
8	-	Jack In The Box	Moments	All Platinum	6		L
9	-	Boogie Nights	Heatwave	GTO	10	(2)	F
10	-	Car Wash	Rose Royce	MCA	6	(1)	F
11	-	Suspicion	Elvis Presley	RCA	6		
12	15	You're More Than A Number In My Little Red Book	Drifters	Arista	6		L
13	-	Chanson D'Amour	Manhattan Transfer	Atlantic	11		F
14	-	Sing Me	Brothers	Bus Stop	6		F L
15	-	Don't Believe A Word	Thin Lizzy	Vertigo	4		
16	8	Things We Do For Love	10cc	Mercury	8	(5)	
17	11	Wild Side Of Life	Status Quo	Vertigo	9		
18	-	This Is Tomorrow	Bryan Ferry	Polydor	6		
19	-	Romeo	Mr. Big	EMI	7	(87)	F L
20	12	I Wish	Stevie Wonder	Tamla Motown	6	(1)	

March 1977

This Mnth	Prev Mnth	Title	Artist	Label	Wks 20	(US Pos)	
1	13	Chanson D'Amour	Manhattan Transfer	Atlantic	11		F
2	9	Boogie Nights	Heatwave	GTO	10	(2)	F
3	3	When I Need You	Leo Sayer	Chrysalis	9	(1)	
4	19	Romeo	Mr. Big	EMI	7	(87)	F L
5	-	Knowing Me Knowing You	Abba	Epic	11	(14)	
6	-	Sound And Vision	David Bowie	RCA	9	(69)	
7	-	Torn Between Two Lovers	Mary MacGregor	Ariola America	8	(1)	F L
8	1	Don't Cry For Me Argentina	Julie Covington	MCA	10		F
9	-	When	Showaddywaddy	Arista	8		
10	18	This Is Tomorrow	Bryan Ferry	Polydor	6		
11	-	Baby I Know	Rubettes	State	7		L
12	-	Rockaria	Electric Light Orchestra	Jet	5		
13	-	What Can I Say	Boz Scaggs	CBS	5	(42)	F
14	6	Don't Leave Me This Way	Harold Melvin & The Blue Notes	Philly Int.	7		L
15	14	Sing Me	Brothers	Bus Stop	6		F L
16	2	Don't Give Up On Us	David Soul	Private Stock	12	(1)	F G
17	-	Moody Blue	Elvis Presley	RCA	5	(31)	
18	-	Don't Leave Me This Way	Thelma Houston	Motown	4	(1)	F L
19	8	Jack In The Box	Moments	All Platinum	6		L
20	-	Going In With My Eyes Open	David Soul	Private Stock	6	(54)	

January 1977

This Mnth	Prev Mnth	Title	Artist	Label	Wks 20	(UK Pos)	
1	5	**You Make Me Feel Like Dancing**	Leo Sayer	Warner	13	(2)	G
2	20	**I Wish**	Stevie Wonder	Tamla	12	(5)	G
3	-	**Car Wash**	Rose Royce	MCA	12	(9)	F G
4	14	**Dazz**	Brick	Bang	11	(36)	F
5	3	**You Don't Have To Be A Star (To Be In My Show)**	Marilyn McCoo & Billy Davis Jr	ABC	11	(7)	F G
6	1	**Tonight's The Night (Gonna Be Alright)**	Rod Stewart	Warner	12	(5)	G
7	18	**Hot Line**	Sylvers	Capitol	10		G
8	12	**After The Lovin'**	Engelbert Humperdinck	Epic	9		G L
9	-	**New Kid In Town**	Eagles	Asylum	12	(20)	G
10	7	**Sorry Seems To Be The Hardest Word**	Elton John	MCA/Rocket	8	(11)	G
11	2	**The Rubberband Man**	Spinners	Atlantic	11	(16)	G
12	15	**Stand Tall**	Burton Cummings	Portrait	8		F G L
13	-	**Walk This Way**	Aerosmith	Columbia	6		
14	-	**Somebody To Love**	Queen	Elektra	7	(2)	
15	-	**Blinded By The Light**	Manfred Mann's Earth Band	Warner	10	(6)	F G L
16	-	**Torn Between Two Lovers**	Mary MacGregor	Ariola America	12	(4)	F G L
17	-	**Livin' Thing**	Electric Light Orchestra	UA	6	(4)	
18	-	**Lost Without You Love**	Bread	Elektra	8	(27)	L
19	4	**More Than A Feeling**	Boston	Epic	11	(22)	F
20	-	**Enjoy Yourself**	Jacksons	Epic	9	(42)	G

February 1977

This Mnth	Prev Mnth	Title	Artist	Label	Wks 20	(UK Pos)	
1	9	**New Kid In Town**	Eagles	Asylum	12	(20)	G
2	16	**Torn Between Two Lovers**	Mary MacGregor	Ariola America	12	(4)	F G L
3	15	**Blinded By The Light**	Manfred Mann's Earth Band	Warner	10	(6)	F G L
4	-	**Evergreen (Love Theme From 'A Star Is Born')**	Barbra Streisand	Columbia	15	(3)	G
5	3	**Car Wash**	Rose Royce	MCA	12	(9)	F G
6	20	**Enjoy Yourself**	Jacksons	Epic	9	(42)	G
7	-	**I Like Dreamin'**	Kenny Nolan	20th Century	12		F G
8	-	**Fly Like An Eagle**	Steve Miller Band	Capitol	12		G
9	2	**I Wish**	Stevie Wonder	Tamla	12	(5)	G
10	4	**Dazz**	Brick	Bang	11	(36)	F
11	-	**Weekend In New England**	Barry Manilow	Arista	7		
12	18	**Lost Without You Love**	Bread	Elektra	8	(27)	L
13	-	**Night Moves**	Bob Seger & Silver Bullet Band	Capitol	8		
14	-	**Dancing Queen**	Abba	Atlantic	12	(1)	G
15	7	**Hot Line**	Sylvers	Capitol	10		G
16	-	**Year Of The Cat**	Al Stewart	Janus	6	(31)	F
17	-	**Hard Luck Woman**	Kiss	Casablanca	5		
18	13	**Walk This Way**	Aerosmith	Columbia	6		
19	-	**Go Your Own Way**	Fleetwood Mac	Warner	5	(38)	
20	1	**You Make Me Feel Like Dancing**	Leo Sayer	Warner	13	(2)	G

March 1977

This Mnth	Prev Mnth	Title	Artist	Label	Wks 20	(UK Pos)	
1	4	**Evergreen (From 'A Star Is Born')**	Barbra Streisand	Columbia	15	(3)	G
2	8	**Fly Like An Eagle**	Steve Miller Band	Capitol	12		G
3	14	**Dancing Queen**	Abba	Atlantic	12	(1)	G
4	13	**Night Moves**	Bob Seger & Silver Bullet Band	Capitol	8		
5	7	**I Like Dreamin'**	Kenny Nolan	20th Century	12		F G
6	-	**Rich Girl**	Daryl Hall & John Oates	RCA	10		G
7	2	**Torn Between Two Lovers**	Mary MacGregor	Ariola America	12	(4)	F G L
8	-	**Don't Leave Me This Way**	Thelma Houston	Tamla	12	(13)	F G L
9	-	**Things We Do For Love**	10cc	Mercury	10	(6)	G L
10	3	**Blinded By The Light**	Manfred Mann's Earth Band	Warner	10	(6)	F G L
11	-	**Don't Give Up On Us**	David Soul	Private Stock	9	(1)	F G L
12	1	**New Kid In Town**	Eagles	Asylum	12	(20)	G
13	16	**Year Of The Cat**	Al Stewart	Janus	6	(31)	F
14	-	**Boogie Child**	Bee Gees	RSO	6		
15	-	**Maybe I'm Amazed**	Wings	Capitol	7	(28)	
16	-	**Carry On Wayward Son**	Kansas	Kirshner	7	(51)	F
17	19	**Go Your Own Way**	Fleetwood Mac	Warner	5	(38)	
18	-	**I've Got Love On My Mind**	Natalie Cole	Capitol	10		G
19	11	**Weekend In New England**	Barry Manilow	Arista	7		
20	-	**So In To You**	Atlanta Rhythm Section	Polydor	10		F

US 1977
JAN-MAR

▲ *American Bandstand* celebrated its 25th Birthday. Chuck Berry, Johnny Rivers, Seals & Crofts, Jr. Walker and The Pointer Sisters (above) joined the party.

◆ **Night Moves** gave veteran rocker Bob Seger the first of many American Top 20 albums, and the title track returned him to the Top 20 after an eight-year absence.

◆ Progressive rockers Kansas, who sold millions of LPs in the 1970s, made their Top 20 single debut with 'Carry on Wayward Son'.

UK 1977

APR-JUNE

◆ Despite a radio ban (due to its "treasonous sentiments"), The Sex Pistols' 'God Save The Queen' topped some British charts at the height of the Queen's Silver Jubilee celebrations.

◆ US cult heroes Blondie, Television, Talking Heads and The Ramones toured the UK, and The Damned became the first UK punk act to perform at CBGB's in New York.

▲ Debuting in the UK Top 20 were Genesis (above) with 'Spot The Pigeon' and their former lead singer, Peter Gabriel, with 'Solsbury Hill'.

April 1977

This Mnth	Prev Mnth	Title	Artist	Label	Wks 20	(US Pos)	
1	5	Knowing Me Knowing You	Abba	Epic	11	(14)	
2	20	Going In With My Eyes Open	David Soul	Private Stock	6	(54)	
3	-	I Don't Want To Put A Hold On You	Berni Flint	EMI	8		F L
4	-	Red Light Spells Danger	Billy Ocean	GTO	9		
5	9	When	Showaddywaddy	Arista	8		
6	-	Sunny	Boney M	Atlantic	6		
7	6	Sound And Vision	David Bowie	RCA	9	(69)	
8	-	Oh Boy	Brotherhood Of Man	Pye	7		
9	1	Chanson D'Amour	Manhattan Transfer	Atlantic	11		F
10	-	You Don't Have To Be A Star (To Be In My Show)	Marilyn McCoo & Billy Davis Jr	ABC	5	(1)	F L
11	17	Moody Blue	Elvis Presley	RCA	5	(31)	
12	-	Free	Deniece Williams	CBS	9	(25)	F
13	-	Have I The Right?	Dead End Kids	CBS	7		F L
14	-	Sir Duke	Stevie Wonder	Motown	7	(1)	
15	-	Lay Back In The Arms Of Someone	Smokie	RAK	6		
16	-	Love Hit Me	Maxine Nightingale	UA	3		L
17	-	Gimme Some	Brendon	Magnet	5		F L
18	7	Torn Between Two Lovers	Mary MacGregor	Ariola America	8	(1)	F L
19	-	Pearl's A Singer	Elkie Brooks	A&M	6		F
20	2	Boogie Nights	Heatwave	GTO	10	(2)	F

May 1977

This Mnth	Prev Mnth	Title	Artist	Label	Wks 20	(US Pos)	
1	-	I Don't Want To Talk About It/First Cut Is The Deepest	Rod Stewart	Riva	10	(46)	
2	12	Free	Deniece Williams	CBS	9	(25)	F
3	-	Ain't Gonna Bump No More (With No Big Fat Woman)	Joe Tex	Epic	8	(12)	F L
4	14	Sir Duke	Stevie Wonder	Motown	7	(1)	
5	-	The Shuffle	Van McCoy	H & L	8		L
6	-	Whodunit	Tavares	Capitol	7	(22)	
7	-	Evergreen (From 'A Star Is Born')	Barbra Streisand	CBS	12	(1)	
8	-	Hotel California	Eagles	Asylum	5	(1)	L
9	-	Good Morning Judge	10cc	Mercury	7	(69)	
10	-	Lucille	Kenny Rogers	UA	10	(5)	
11	13	Have I The Right?	Dead End Kids	CBS	7		F L
12	4	Red Light Spells Danger	Billy Ocean	GTO	9		
13	-	Mah Na Mah Na	Piero Umiliani	EMI International	5	(55)	F L
14	19	Pearl's A Singer	Elkie Brooks	A&M	6		F
15	-	Solsbury Hill	Peter Gabriel	Charisma	5	(68)	F
16	1	Knowing Me Knowing You	Abba	Epic	11	(14)	
17	-	Got To Give It Up	Marvin Gaye	Motown	6	(1)	
18	-	How Much Love	Leo Sayer	Chrysalis	5	(17)	
19	-	Lonely Boy	Andrew Gold	Asylum	5	(7)	F
20	3	I Don't Want To Put A Hold On You	Berni Flint	EMI	8		F L

June 1977

This Mnth	Prev Mnth	Title	Artist	Label	Wks 20	(US Pos)	
1	10	Lucille	Kenny Rogers	UA	10	(5)	
2	1	I Don't Want To Talk About It/First...	Rod Stewart	Riva	10	(46)	
3	7	Evergreen (From 'A Star Is Born')	Barbra Streisand	CBS	12	(1)	
4	-	God Save The Queen	Sex Pistols	Virgin	6		F
5	3	Ain't Gonna Bump No More (With...)	Joe Tex	Epic	8	(12)	F L
6	-	Show You The Way To Go	Jacksons	Epic	7	(28)	
7	-	You're Moving Out Today	Carole Bayer Sager	Elektra	7	(69)	F L
8	-	Halfway Down The Stairs	Muppets	Pye	6		F
9	5	The Shuffle	Van McCoy	H & L	8		L
10	17	Got To Give It Up	Marvin Gaye	Motown	6	(1)	
11	9	Good Morning Judge	10cc	Mercury	7	(69)	
12	-	Telephone Line	Electric Light Orchestra	Jet	7	(7)	
13	-	Lido Shuffle	Boz Scaggs	CBS	7	(11)	L
14	-	O.K.	Rock Follies	Polydor	4		F L
15	-	Baby Don't Change Your Mind	Gladys Knight & The Pips	Buddah	7	(52)	
16	-	So You Win Again	Hot Chocolate	RAK	10	(31)	
17	-	Too Hot To Handle/Slip Your Disc To This	Heatwave	GTO	7		
18	-	Fanfare For The Common Man	Emerson, Lake & Palmer	Atlantic	10		F L
19	13	Mah Na Mah Na	Piero Umiliani	EMI International	5	(55)	F L
20	-	Spot The Pigeon (E.P.)	Genesis	Charisma	2		F

April 1977

This Mnth	Prev Mnth	Title	Artist	Label	Wks 20	(UK Pos)	
1	8	Don't Leave Me This Way	Thelma Houston	Tamla	12	(13)	F G L
2	11	Don't Give Up On Us	David Soul	Private Stock	9	(1)	F G L
3	-	Southern Nights	Glen Campbell	Capitol	11	(28)	G L
4	-	Hotel California	Eagles	Asylum	13	(8)	G
5	18	I've Got Love On My Mind	Natalie Cole	Capitol	10		G
6	9	Things We Do For Love	10cc	Mercury	10	(6)	G L
7	6	Rich Girl	Daryl Hall & John Oates	RCA	10		G
8	1	Evergreen (Love Theme From 'A Star Is Born')	Barbra Streisand	Columbia	15	(3)	G
9	20	So In To You	Atlanta Rhythm Section	Polydor	10		F
10	3	Dancing Queen	Abba	Atlantic	12	(1)	G
11	-	Right Time Of The Night	Jennifer Warnes	Arista	9		F
12	-	When I Need You	Leo Sayer	Warner	10	(1)	G
13	-	Tryin' To Love Two	William Bell	Mercury	5		F G L
14	-	I Wanna Get Next To You	Rose Royce	MCA	6	(14)	L
15	16	Carry On Wayward Son	Kansas	Kirshner	7	(51)	F
16	15	Maybe I'm Amazed	Wings	Capitol	7	(28)	
17	-	Couldn't Get It Right	Climax Blues Band	Sire	9	(10)	F
18	-	Lido Shuffle	Boz Scaggs	Columbia	7	(13)	
19	2	Fly Like An Eagle	Steve Miller Band	Capitol	12		G
20	-	Sir Duke	Stevie Wonder	Tamla	5	(2)	G

May 1977

This Mnth	Prev Mnth	Title	Artist	Label	Wks 20	(UK Pos)	
1	12	When I Need You	Leo Sayer	Warner	10	(1)	G
2	4	Hotel California	Eagles	Asylum	13	(8)	G
3	17	Couldn't Get It Right	Climax Blues Band	Sire	9	(10)	F
4	-	I'm Your Boogie Man	KC & The Sunshine Band	TK	11	(41)	
5	20	Sir Duke	Stevie Wonder	Tamla	5	(2)	G
6	3	Southern Nights	Glen Campbell	Capitol	11	(28)	G L
7	-	Got To Give It Up (Pt.1)	Marvin Gaye	Tamla	12	(7)	G
8	11	Right Time Of The Night	Jennifer Warnes	Arista	9		F
9	-	Dreams	Fleetwood Mac	Warner	9	(24)	G
10	-	Lucille	Kenny Rogers	UA	9	(1)	G
11	9	So In To You	Atlanta Rhythm Section	Polydor	10		F
12	18	Lido Shuffle	Boz Scaggs	Columbia	7	(13)	
13	-	Gonna Fly Now (Theme From 'Rocky')	Bill Conti	UA	10		F G L
14	-	Lonely Boy	Andrew Gold	Asylum	9	(11)	F L
15	14	I Wanna Get Next To You	Rose Royce	MCA	6	(14)	L
16	-	Feels Like The First Time	Foreigner	Atlantic	8	(39)	F
17	-	Hello Stranger	Yvonne Elliman	RSO	5	(26)	
18	1	Don't Leave Me This Way	Thelma Houston	Tamla	12	(13)	F G L
19	5	I've Got Love On My Mind	Natalie Cole	Capitol	10		G
20	-	Can't Stop Dancin'	Captain & Tennille	A&M	5		

June 1977

This Mnth	Prev Mnth	Title	Artist	Label	Wks 20	(UK Pos)	
1	7	Got To Give It Up (Pt.1)	Marvin Gaye	Tamla	12	(7)	G
2	9	Dreams	Fleetwood Mac	Warner	9	(24)	G
3	13	Gonna Fly Now (Theme From 'Rocky')	Bill Conti	UA	10		F G L
4	16	Feels Like The First Time	Foreigner	Atlantic	8	(39)	F
5	10	Lucille	Kenny Rogers	UA	9	(1)	G
6	-	Undercover Angel	Alan O'Day	Pacific	13	(43)	F G L
7	14	Lonely Boy	Andrew Gold	Asylum	9	(11)	F L
8	4	I'm Your Boogie Man	KC & The Sunshine Band	TK	11	(41)	
9	-	Angel In Your Arms	Hot	Big Tree	12		F G L
10	-	Jet Airliner	Steve Miller Band	Capitol	9		
11	3	Couldn't Get It Right	Climax Blues Band	Sire	9	(10)	F
12	-	Life In The Fast Lane	Eagles	Asylum	5		
13	-	Ain't Gonna Bump No More (With No Big Fat Woman)	Joe Tex	Epic	5	(2)	G L
14	-	Heard It In A Love Song	Marshall Tucker Band	Capricorn	5		F L
15	-	Da Doo Ron Ron	Shaun Cassidy	Warner	10		F G
16	-	Looks Like We Made It	Barry Manilow	Arista	11		G
17	1	When I Need You	Leo Sayer	Warner	10	(1)	G
18	-	Margaritaville	Jimmy Buffett	ABC	9		F L
19	2	Hotel California	Eagles	Asylum	13	(8)	G
20	-	My Heart Belongs To Me	Barbra Streisand	Columbia	9		

US 1977

APR-JUNE

◆ Making their New York debuts were Dolly Parton at the Bottom Line, Olivia Newton-John at the Metropolitan Opera House and Club 54, which would become the world's best known disco.

◆ Led Zeppelin broke the attendance record for a single act show when 76,000 saw them perform at the Silverdrome in Pontiac, Michigan.

◆ Elvis Presley made his last appearance at the Market Square Arena, Indianapolis.

◆ Fleetwood Mac's **Rumours** (which went on to sell 14 million copies!) topped the album chart for 31 weeks. It stopped The Beatles scoring their last No. 1 with **The Beatles At The Hollywood Bowl.**

UK 1977
JULY-SEPT

◆ Connie Francis' **20 All Time Greats** became the first album ever by a female soloist to top the UK chart. For the record, it was quickly dethroned by Elvis' **40 Greatest Hits.**

▲ The Bay City Rollers (above), whose star had already waned in the UK, scored their last American Top 20 entry as new teen idols, Shaun Cassidy (David's brother) and Andy Gibb (Brother of the Bee Gees), debuted on the chart.

◆ Marc Bolan, front man of the highly successful glam rock duo T-Rex, died in a car crash. He was a major figure in British rock music.

July 1977

This Mnth	Prev Mnth	Title	Artist	Label	Wks 20	(US Pos)	
1	16	So You Win Again	Hot Chocolate	RAK	10	(31)	
2	18	Fanfare For The Common Man	Emerson, Lake & Palmer	Atlantic	10		F L
3	15	Baby Don't Change Your Mind	Gladys Knight & The Pips	Buddah	7	(52)	
4	-	Ma Baker	Boney M	Atlantic	10	(96)	
5	-	I Feel Love	Donna Summer	GTO	9	(6)	
6	6	Show You The Way To Go	Jacksons	Epic	7	(28)	
7	-	Sam	Olivia Newton-John	EMI	7	(20)	
8	-	Peaches/Go Buddy Go	Stranglers	UA	7		F
9	-	Angelo	Brotherhood Of Man	Pye	11		
10	-	Pretty Vacant	Sex Pistols	Virgin	5		
11	-	Oh Lori	Alessi	A&M	8		F L
12	7	You're Moving Out Today	Carole Bayer Sager	Elektra	7	(69)	F L
13	1	Lucille	Kenny Rogers	UA	10	(5)	
14	3	Evergreen (Love Theme From 'A Star Is Born')	Barbra Streisand	CBS	12	(1)	
15	-	Slow Down	John Miles	Decca	6	(34)	L
16	-	You're Gonna Get Next To Me	Bo Kirkland & Ruth Davis	EMI International	5		F L
17	-	Feel The Need In Me	Detroit Emeralds	Atlantic	8	(90)	L
18	-	Do What You Wanna Do	T-Connection	TK	3	(46)	F
19	12	Telephone Line	Electric Light Orchestra	Jet	7	(7)	
20	8	Halfway Down The Stairs	Muppets	Pye	6		F

August 1977

This Mnth	Prev Mnth	Title	Artist	Label	Wks 20	(US Pos)	
1	9	Angelo	Brotherhood Of Man	Pye	11		
2	5	I Feel Love	Donna Summer	GTO	9	(6)	
3	-	You Got What It Takes	Showaddywaddy	Arista	8		
4	-	Float On	Floaters	ABC	9	(2)	F L
5	4	Ma Baker	Boney M	Atlantic	10	(96)	
6	-	We're All Alone	Rita Coolidge	A&M	8	(7)	F L
7	-	The Crunch	Rah Band	Good Earth	8		F
8	-	It's Your Life	Smokie	RAK	6		
9	-	Easy	Commodores	Motown	6	(4)	
10	-	Something Better Change/ Straighten Out	Stranglers	UA	5		
11	2	Fanfare For The Common Man	Emerson, Lake & Palmer	Atlantic	10		F L
12	1	So You Win Again	Hot Chocolate	RAK	10	(31)	
13	-	That's What Friends Are For	Deniece Williams	CBS	7		
14	-	Roadrunner	Jonathan Richman & The Modern Lovers	Berserkley	3		F
15	10	Pretty Vacant	Sex Pistols	Virgin	5		
16	-	Nights On Broadway	Candi Staton	Warner	8		
17	11	Oh Lori	Alessi	A&M	8		F L
18	-	Nobody Does It Better	Carly Simon	Elektra	8	(2)	
19	-	Way Down	Elvis Presley	RCA	10	(18)	
20	17	Feel The Need In Me	Detroit Emeralds	Atlantic	8	(90)	L

September 1977

This Mnth	Prev Mnth	Title	Artist	Label	Wks 20	(US Pos)	
1	19	Way Down	Elvis Presley	RCA	10	(18)	
2	-	Magic Fly	Space	Pye International	8		F L
3	-	Silver Lady	David Soul	Private Stock	11	(52)	
4	-	Oxygene Part IV	Jean-Michel Jarre	Polydor	7		F L
5	4	Float On	Floaters	ABC	9	(2)	F L
6	-	Deep Down Inside	Donna Summer	Casablanca	7		
7	16	Nights On Broadway	Candi Staton	Warner	8		
8	18	Nobody Does It Better	Carly Simon	Elektra	8	(2)	
9	1	Angelo	Brotherhood Of Man	Pye	11		
10	13	That's What Friends Are For	Deniece Williams	CBS	7		
11	3	You Got What It Takes	Showaddywaddy	Arista	8		
12	-	Telephone Man	Meri Wilson	Pye International	7	(18)	F L
13	7	The Crunch	Rah Band	Good Earth	8		F
14	-	Do Anything You Wanna Do	Rods	Island	7		F L
15	-	Tulane	Steve Gibbons Band	Polydor	4		F L
16	-	Dancin' In The Moonlight (It's Caught Me In The Spotlight)	Thin Lizzy	Vertigo	4		
17	-	Looking After Number One	Boomtown Rats	Ensign	5		F
18	-	Best Of My Love	Emotions	CBS	7	(1)	F
19	2	I Feel Love	Donna Summer	GTO	9	(6)	
20	-	Wonderous Stories	Yes	Atlantic	7		F L

July 1977

This Mnth	Prev Mnth	Title	Artist	Label	Wks 20	(UK Pos)	
1	16	Looks Like We Made It	Barry Manilow	Arista	11		G
2	15	Da Doo Ron Ron	Shaun Cassidy	Warner	10		F G
3	-	I Just Want To Be Your Everything	Andy Gibb	RSO	18	(26)	F G
4	6	Undercover Angel	Alan O'Day	Pacific	13	(43)	F G L
5	-	I'm In You	Peter Frampton	A&M	10	(41)	
6	20	My Heart Belongs To Me	Barbra Streisand	Columbia	9		
7	9	Angel In Your Arms	Hot	Big Tree	12		F G L
8	18	Margaritaville	Jimmy Buffett	ABC	9		F L
9	-	Do You Wanna Make Love	Peter McCann	20th Century	10		F G L
10	3	Gonna Fly Now (Theme From 'Rocky')	Bill Conti	UA	10		F G L
11	10	Jet Airliner	Steve Miller Band	Capitol	9		
12	-	Best Of My Love	Emotions	Columbia	15	(4)	F G
13	-	(Your Love Has Lifted Me) Higher And Higher	Rita Coolidge	A&M	13	(48)	F G
14	1	Got To Give It Up (Pt.1)	Marvin Gaye	Tamla	12	(7)	G
15	-	Whatcha Gonna Do	Pablo Cruise	A&M	10		F
16	-	You And Me	Alice Cooper	Warner	7		
17	2	Dreams	Fleetwood Mac	Warner	9	(24)	G
18	-	Knowing Me Knowing You	Abba	Atlantic	5	(1)	
19	-	You Made Me Believe In Magic	Bay City Rollers	Arista	6	(34)	L
20	-	Easy	Commodores	Motown	9	(9)	G

August 1977

This Mnth	Prev Mnth	Title	Artist	Label	Wks 20	(UK Pos)	
1	3	I Just Want To Be Your Everything	Andy Gibb	RSO	18	(26)	F G
2	12	Best Of My Love	Emotions	Columbia	15	(4)	F G
3	13	(Your Love Has Lifted Me) Higher And Higher	Rita Coolidge	A&M	13	(48)	F G
4	5	I'm In You	Peter Frampton	A&M	10	(41)	
5	20	Easy	Commodores	Motown	9	(9)	G
6	15	Whatcha Gonna Do	Pablo Cruise	A&M	10		F
7	9	Do You Wanna Make Love	Peter McCann	20th Century	10		F G L
8	-	Just A Song Before I Go	Crosby, Stills & Nash	Atlantic	7		
9	-	Handy Man	James Taylor	Columbia	9		
10	-	Don't Stop	Fleetwood Mac	Warner	10	(32)	
11	16	You And Me	Alice Cooper	Warner	7		
12	6	My Heart Belongs To Me	Barbra Streisand	Columbia	9		
13	19	You Made Me Believe In Magic	Bay City Rollers	Arista	6	(34)	L
14	2	Da Doo Ron Ron	Shaun Cassidy	Warner	10		F G
15	-	Barracuda	Heart	Portrait	7		
16	-	Float On	Floaters	ABC	7	(1)	F G L
17	1	Looks Like We Made It	Barry Manilow	Arista	11		G
18	-	Smoke From A Distant Fire	Sanford/Townsend Band	Warner	6		F L
19	-	Telephone Line	Electric Light Orchestra	UA	10	(8)	G
20	-	Strawberry Letter 23	Brothers Johnson	A&M	7	(35)	G

September 1977

This Mnth	Prev Mnth	Title	Artist	Label	Wks 20	(UK Pos)	
1	2	Best Of My Love	Emotions	Columbia	15	(4)	F G
2	1	I Just Want To Be Your Everything	Andy Gibb	RSO	18	(26)	F G
3	16	Float On	Floaters	ABC	7	(1)	F G L
4	10	Don't Stop	Fleetwood Mac	Warner	10	(32)	
5	9	Handy Man	James Taylor	Columbia	9		
6	20	Strawberry Letter 23	Brothers Johnson	A&M	7	(35)	G
7	19	Telephone Line	Electric Light Orchestra	UA	10	(8)	G
8	3	(Your Love Has Lifted Me) Higher And Higher	Rita Coolidge	A&M	13	(48)	F G
9	-	Keep It Comin' Love	KC & The Sunshine Band	TK	9	(31)	
10	5	Easy	Commodores	Motown	9	(9)	G
11	18	Smoke From A Distant Fire	Sanford/Townsend Band	Warner	6		F L
12	-	Cold As Ice	Foreigner	Atlantic	11	(24)	
13	-	Star Wars (Main Title)	London Symphony Orchestra	20th Century	4		F
14	-	Star Wars Theme/Cantina Band	Meco	Millenium	10	(7)	F G
15	8	Just A Song Before I Go	Crosby, Stills & Nash	Atlantic	7		
16	-	That's Rock 'n' Roll	Shaun Cassidy	Warner	11		G
17	-	On And On	Stephen Bishop	ABC	7		F L
18	15	Barracuda	Heart	Portrait	7		
19	-	Swayin' To The Music (Slow Dancin')	Johnny Rivers	Big Tree	9		G L
20	-	Nobody Does It Better	Carly Simon	Elektra	11	(7)	G

US 1977

JULY-SEPT

◆ Elvis Presley, the most important and influential artist of the rock era, died and was mourned world-wide. In America, the demand for Presley product far out-stripped the quantities that RCA (at full stretch) could produce. In Britain he had nine singles simultaneously in the UK chart and a staggering 27 albums in the Top 100! Some estimates say that 20 million Elvis records were sold world-wide the day after his death!

◆ Grateful Dead attracted over 100,000 to the Old Bridge Concert in New Jersey. Kool & The Gang were seen by a similar sized crowd at Maryland's Brute Music Festival, and The Doobie Brothers and Thin Lizzy helped make Britain's Reading Festival successful.

◆ The Commodores (who included singer/ songwriter Lionel Richie) started a 70-city American tour which grossed over $6 million.

UK 1977

OCT-DEC

◆ Bing Crosby died. The well-loved singer, who had amassed 299 American Top 20 hits, found himself back in the British Top 10 with the evergreen, 'White Christmas'.

◆ Donna Summer's transatlantic disco hit 'I Feel Love', with its hypnotic synth-sequencer riffs, laid the foundation stone for Euro disco and techno-pop.

▲ Understandably, British punk had few initial takers Stateside. However the Sex Pistols chart topping UK debut LP **Never Mind the Bollocks** and Elvis Costello's (above) **My Aim Is True** (which included musical contributions from Huey Lewis) were minor US successes.

October 1977

This Mnth	Prev Mnth	Title	Artist	Label	Wks 20	(US Pos)	
1	3	Silver Lady	David Soul	Private Stock	11	(52)	
2	-	Black Is Black	La Belle Epoque	Harvest	9		F L
3	18	Best Of My Love	Emotions	CBS	7	(1)	F
4	-	I Remember Elvis Presley (The King Is Dead)	Danny Mirror	Sonet	6		F L
5	1	Way Down	Elvis Presley	RCA	10	(18)	
6	-	Yes Sir I Can Boogie	Baccara	RCA	9		F
7	-	You're In My Heart	Rod Stewart	Riva	8	(4)	
8	-	From New York To L.A.	Patsy Gallant	EMI	5		F L
9	2	Magic Fly	Space	Pye International	8		F L
10	-	Black Betty	Ram Jam	Epic	8	(18)	F
11	-	No More Heroes	Stranglers	UA	6		
12	12	Telephone Man	Meri Wilson	Pye International	7	(18)	F L
13	20	Wonderous Stories	Yes	Atlantic	7		F L
14	6	Deep Down Inside	Donna Summer	Casablanca	7		
15	-	Star Wars Theme - Cantina Band	Meco	RCA	5	(1)	F L
16	4	Oxygene Part IV	Jean-Michel Jarre	Polydor	7		F L
17	-	Rockin' All Over The World	Status Quo	Vertigo	10		
18	-	Sunshine After The Rain	Elkie Brooks	A&M	4		
19	-	I Remember Yesterday	Donna Summer	GTO	5		
20	-	Holidays In The Sun	Sex Pistols	Virgin	5		

November 1977

This Mnth	Prev Mnth	Title	Artist	Label	Wks 20	(US Pos)	
1	-	The Name Of The Game	Abba	Epic	9	(12)	
2	17	Rockin' All Over The World	Status Quo	Vertigo	10		
3	-	We Are The Champions	Queen	EMI	8	(4)	
4	6	Yes Sir I Can Boogie	Baccara	RCA	9		F
5	7	You're In My Heart	Rod Stewart	Riva	8	(4)	
6	-	2-4-6-8 Motorway	Tom Robinson Band	EMI	6		F
7	2	Black Is Black	La Belle Epoque	Harvest	9		F L
8	-	Calling Occupants Of Interplanetary Craft	Carpenters	A&M	6	(32)	L
9	-	How Deep Is Your Love	Bee Gees	RSO	11	(1)	
10	-	Needles And Pins	Smokie	RAK	6	(68)	
11	-	Dancin' Party	Showaddywaddy	Arista	9		
12	-	Live In Trouble	Barron Knights	Epic	5		
13	-	Virginia Plain	Roxy Music	Polydor	5		
14	10	Black Betty	Ram Jam	Epic	8	(18)	F
15	20	Holidays In The Sun	Sex Pistols	Virgin	5		
16	-	Daddy Cool/The Girl Can't Help It	Darts	Magnet	10		F
17	1	Silver Lady	David Soul	Private Stock	11	(52)	
18	-	She's Not There	Santana	CBS	5	(27)	F L
19	-	Mull Of Kintyre/Girls' School	Wings	Capitol	13	(33)	P
20	-	Hot Track E.P.	Nazareth	Mountain	4		L

December 1977

This Mnth	Prev Mnth	Title	Artist	Label	Wks 20	(US Pos)	
1	19	Mull Of Kintyre/Girls' School	Wings	Capitol	13	(33)	P
2	-	The Floral Dance	Brighouse & Rastrick Brass Band	Transatlantic	10		F L
3	9	How Deep Is Your Love	Bee Gees	RSO	11	(1)	
4	-	I Will	Ruby Winters	Creole	9		F
5	16	Daddy Cool/The Girl Can't Help It	Darts	Magnet	10		F
6	11	Dancin' Party	Showaddywaddy	Arista	9		
7	-	Egyptian Reggae	Jonathan Richman & The Modern Lovers	Berserkley	6		L
8	-	Belfast	Boney M	Atlantic	7		
9	3	We Are The Champions	Queen	EMI	8	(4)	
10	-	Love's Unkind	Donna Summer	GTO	10		
11	2	Rockin' All Over The World	Status Quo	Vertigo	10		
12	-	White Christmas	Bing Crosby	MCA	4		G
13	-	It's A Heartache	Bonnie Tyler	RCA	9	(3)	
14	-	Love Of My Life	Dooleys	GTO	5		
15	-	Put Your Love In Me	Hot Chocolate	RAK	6		
16	1	The Name Of The Game	Abba	Epic	9	(12)	
17	-	Mary Of The Fourth Form	Boomtown Rats	Ensign	5		
18	-	Watching The Detectives	Elvis Costello	Stiff	5		F
19	-	My Way	Elvis Presley	RCA	6	(22)	
20	12	Live In Trouble	Barron Knights	Epic	5		

October 1977

This Mnth	Prev Mnth	Title	Artist	Label	Wks 20	(UK Pos)	
1	9	Keep It Comin' Love	KC & The Sunshine Band	TK	9	(31)	
2	20	Nobody Does It Better	Carly Simon	Elektra	11	(7)	G
3	-	You Light Up My Life	Debby Boone	Warner	16	(48)	F P L
4	16	That's Rock 'n' Roll	Shaun Cassidy	Warner	11		G
5	14	Star Wars Theme/Cantina Band	Meco	Millenium	10	(7)	F G
6	-	Boogie Nights	Heatwave	Epic	13	(2)	F P
7	12	Cold As Ice	Foreigner	Atlantic	11	(24)	
8	-	Brick House	Commodores	Motown	9	(32)	
9	-	I Feel Love	Donna Summer	Casablanca	10	(1)	G
10	19	Swayin' To The Music (Slow Dancin')	Johnny Rivers	Big Tree	9		G L
11	2	I Just Want To Be Your Everything	Andy Gibb	RSO	18	(26)	F G
12	1	Best Of My Love	Emotions	Columbia	15	(4)	F G
13	-	It's Ecstasy When You Lay Down Next To Me	Barry White	20th Century	9	(40)	G L
14	-	Don't It Make My Brown Eyes Blue	Crystal Gayle	UA	14	(5)	F G
15	17	On And On	Stephen Bishop	ABC	7		F L
16	-	The King Is Gone	Ronnie McDowell	Scorpion	5		F G L
17	4	Don't Stop	Fleetwood Mac	Warner	10	(32)	
18	7	Telephone Line	Electric Light Orchestra	UA	10	(8)	G
19	6	Strawberry Letter 23	Brothers Johnson	A&M	7	(35)	G
20	-	Heaven On The 7th Floor	Paul Nicholas	RSO	9	(40)	F G L

November 1977

This Mnth	Prev Mnth	Title	Artist	Label	Wks 20	(UK Pos)	
1	3	You Light Up My Life	Debby Boone	Warner	16	(48)	F P L
2	6	Boogie Nights	Heatwave	Epic	13	(2)	F P
3	14	Don't It Make My Brown Eyes Blue	Crystal Gayle	UA	14	(5)	F G
4	13	It's Ecstasy When You Lay Down Next To Me	Barry White	20th Century	9	(40)	G L
5	-	Baby What A Big Surprise	Chicago	Columbia	9	(41)	
6	-	How Deep Is Your Love	Bee Gees	RSO	21	(3)	G
7	2	Nobody Does It Better	Carly Simon	Elektra	11	(7)	G
8	20	Heaven On The 7th Floor	Paul Nicholas	RSO	9	(40)	F G L
9	-	We're All Alone	Rita Coolidge	A&M	10	(6)	
10	9	I Feel Love	Donna Summer	Casablanca	10	(1)	G
11	-	Blue Bayou	Linda Ronstadt	Asylum	11	(35)	G
12	4	That's Rock 'n' Roll	Shaun Cassidy	Warner	11		G
13	-	Just Remember I Love You	Firefall	Atlantic	5		
14	8	Brick House	Commodores	Motown	9	(32)	
15	-	Help Is On Its Way	Little River Band	Harvest	4		F
16	-	You Make Lovin' Fun	Fleetwood Mac	Warner	6	(45)	
17	-	It's So Easy	Linda Ronstadt	Asylum	8		
18	5	Star Wars Theme/Cantina Band	Meco	Millenium	10	(7)	F G
19	-	We Just Disagree	Dave Mason	Columbia	4		F L
20	-	Back In Love Again	L.T.D.	A&M	10		G L

December 1977

This Mnth	Prev Mnth	Title	Artist	Label	Wks 20	(UK Pos)	
1	1	You Light Up My Life	Debby Boone	Warner	16	(48)	F P L
2	6	How Deep Is Your Love	Bee Gees	RSO	21	(3)	G
3	11	Blue Bayou	Linda Ronstadt	Asylum	11	(35)	G
4	3	Don't It Make My Brown Eyes Blue	Crystal Gayle	UA	14	(5)	F G
5	17	It's So Easy	Linda Ronstadt	Asylum	8		
6	20	Back In Love Again	L.T.D.	A&M	10		G L
7	-	Baby Come Back	Player	RSO	14	(32)	F G
8	9	We're All Alone	Rita Coolidge	A&M	10	(6)	
9	-	Here You Come Again	Dolly Parton	RCA	9	(75)	F G
10	-	Sentimental Lady	Bob Welch	Capitol	8		F
11	-	Isn't It Time	Babys	Chrysalis	6	(45)	F
12	-	Slip Slidin' Away	Paul Simon	Columbia	10	(36)	
13	5	Baby What A Big Surprise	Chicago	Columbia	9	(41)	
14	16	You Make Lovin' Fun	Fleetwood Mac	Warner	6	(45)	
15	8	Heaven On The 7th Floor	Paul Nicholas	RSO	9	(40)	F G L
16	-	You Can't Turn Me Off (In The Middle Of Turning Me On)	High Inergy	Gordy	7		F L
17	-	You're In My Heart	Rod Stewart	Warner	12	(3)	G
18	-	Come Sail Away	Styx	A&M	9		
19	2	Boogie Nights	Heatwave	Epic	13	(2)	F P
20	-	Hey Deanie	Shaun Cassidy	Warner	9		G L

◆ American sales of records (including the new twelve inch disco singles) and tapes zoomed to $3.5 billion, with the latter accounting for a quarter of business. Disco still ruled the singles charts with hits coming not only from America and the UK but also from Scandinavia, The Netherlands, France and Spain.

▲ In America, Pat Boone's daughter, Debbie topped the chart for a record 10 weeks with the Grammy and Academy Award winning, 'You Light Up My Life'. In Britain, Paul McCartney & Wings' (above) 'Mull Of Kintyre' sold over two million copies to become Britain's biggest-selling single.

UK 1978

JAN-MAR

◆ British acts working the USA included Genesis, David Bowie, The Stranglers, The Jam and The Sex Pistols, whose leader, Johnny Rotten, announced at the end of their short and controversial tour, that they were disbanding. Fellow punk pioneers, The Damned, also called it a day (re-uniting later) and *Sniffin' Glue* ceased publication. Punk had peaked and its more widely acceptable, close relative "new wave" was now "in".

◆ Pink Floyd's Dave Gilmour helped Kate Bush get a record deal with EMI. The multi-talented teenager's first single 'Wuthering Heights' shot her to instant stardom in Britain. Meanwhile, in Ireland, U2 won a record audition in a major local talent competition.

◆ Nineteen years after his death Buddy Holly & The Crickets' **20 Golden Greats** topped the UK album chart.

January 1978

This Mnth	Prev Mnth	Title	Artist	Label	Wks 20	(US Pos)	
1	1	Mull Of Kintyre/Girls' School	Wings	Capitol	13	(33)	P
2	10	Love's Unkind	Donna Summer	GTO	10		
3	13	It's A Heartache	Bonnie Tyler	RCA	9	(3)	
4	2	The Floral Dance	Brighouse & Rastrick Brass Band	Transatlantic	10		F L
5	-	Don't It Make My Brown Eyes Blue	Crystal Gayle	UA	8	(2)	F
6	-	Dance Dance Dance (Yowsah Yowsah Yowsah)	Chic	Atlantic	8	(6)	F
7	-	Uptown Top Ranking	Althia And Donna	Lightning	8		F L
8	3	How Deep Is Your Love	Bee Gees	RSO	11	(1)	
9	-	Let's Have A Quiet Night In	David Soul	Private Stock	7		
10	4	I Will	Ruby Winters	Creole	9		F
11	-	Native New Yorker	Odyssey	RCA	7	(21)	F
12	-	Who Pays The Ferryman	Yannis Markopoulos	BBC	4		F L
13	5	Daddy Cool/The Girl Can't Help It	Darts	Magnet	10		F
14	-	Figaro	Brotherhood Of Man	Pye	9		
15	-	Jamming/Punky Reggae Party	Bob Marley & The Wailers	Island	5		
16	-	Only Women Bleed	Julie Covington	Virgin	4		L
17	-	I Love You	Donna Summer	Casablanca	3	(37)	
18	19	My Way	Elvis Presley	RCA	6	(22)	
19	-	Lovely Day	Bill Withers	CBS	6	(30)	
20	-	If I Had Words	Scott Fitzgerald & Yvonne Keeley	Pepper	7		F L

February 1978

This Mnth	Prev Mnth	Title	Artist	Label	Wks 20	(US Pos)	
1	14	Figaro	Brotherhood Of Man	Pye	9		
2	-	Take A Chance On Me	Abba	Epic	10	(3)	
3	20	If I Had Words	Scott Fitzgerald/Yvonne Keeley	Pepper	7		F L
4	7	Uptown Top Ranking	Althia And Donna	Lightning	8		F L
5	-	Come Back My Love	Darts	Magnet	10		
6	-	Sorry I'm A Lady	Baccara	RCA	5		L
7	1	Mull Of Kintyre/Girls' School	Wings	Capitol	13	(33)	P
8	11	Native New Yorker	Odyssey	RCA	7	(21)	F
9	19	Lovely Day	Bill Withers	CBS	6	(30)	
10	-	Wishing On A Star	Rose Royce	Warner	8		
11	-	Hotlegs/I Was Only Joking	Rod Stewart	Riva	6	(28)	
12	-	Mr. Blue Sky	Electric Light Orchestra	Jet	8	(35)	
13	2	Love's Unkind	Donna Summer	GTO	10		
14	-	Love Is Like Oxygen	Sweet	Polydor	5	(8)	L
15	-	The Groove Line	Heatwave	GTO	5	(7)	
16	15	Jamming/Punky Reggae Party	Bob Marley & TheWailers	Island	5		
17	-	Drummer Man	Tonight	Target	3		F L
18	-	Just One More Night	Yellow Dog	Virgin	5		F L
19	3	It's A Heartache	Bonnie Tyler	RCA	9	(3)	
20	6	Dance Dance Dance (Yowsah...)	Chic	Atlantic	8	(6)	F

March 1978

This Mnth	Prev Mnth	Title	Artist	Label	Wks 20	(US Pos)	
1	-	Wuthering Heights	Kate Bush	EMI	9		F
2	2	Take A Chance On Me	Abba	Epic	10	(3)	
3	5	Come Back My Love	Darts	Magnet	10		
4	10	Wishing On A Star	Rose Royce	Warner	8		
5	-	Denis	Blondie	Chrysalis	9		F
6	-	Stayin' Alive	Bee Gees	RSO	7	(1)	
7	-	Baker Street	Gerry Rafferty	UA	10	(2)	F
8	-	I Can't Stand The Rain	Eruption	Atlantic	8	(18)	F
9	12	Mr. Blue Sky	Electric Light Orchestra	Jet	8	(35)	
10	-	Matchstalk Men And Matchstalk Cats And Dogs	Brian & Michael	Pye	11		F L
11	-	Is This Love	Bob Marley & The Wailers	Island	6		
12	18	Just One More Night	Yellow Dog	Virgin	5		F L
13	-	Emotions	Samantha Sang	Private Stock	8	(3)	F L
14	1	Figaro	Brotherhood Of Man	Pye	9		
15	-	Free (E.P.)	Free	Island	4		L
16	-	Fantasy	Earth, Wind & Fire	CBS	4	(32)	
17	14	Love Is Like Oxygen	Sweet	Polydor	5	(8)	L
18	3	If I Had Words	Scott Fitzgerald/Yvonne Keeley	Pepper	7		F L
19	-	Ally's Tartan Army	Andy Cameron	Klub	5		F L
20	-	I Love The Sound Of Breaking Glass	Nick Lowe & His Cowboy Outfit	Radar	4		F

January 1978

This Mnth	Prev Mnth	Title	Artist	Label	Wks 20	(UK Pos)	
1	7	Baby Come Back	Player	RSO	14	(32)	F G
2	2	How Deep Is Your Love	Bee Gees	RSO	21	(3)	G
3	17	You're In My Heart	Rod Stewart	Warner	12	(3)	G
4	9	Here You Come Again	Dolly Parton	RCA	9	(75)	F G
5	12	Slip Slidin' Away	Paul Simon	Columbia	10	(36)	
6	20	Hey Deanie	Shaun Cassidy	Warner	9		G L
7	-	We Are The Champions	Queen	Elektra	11	(2)	G
8	18	Come Sail Away	Styx	A&M	9		
9	-	Short People	Randy Newman	Warner	11		F G L
10	6	Back In Love Again	L.T.D.	A&M	10		G L
11	-	Stayin' Alive	Bee Gees	RSO	16	(4)	P
12	-	Just The Way You Are	Billy Joel	Columbia	13	(19)	F G
13	10	Sentimental Lady	Bob Welch	Capitol	8		F
14	3	Blue Bayou	Linda Ronstadt	Asylum	11	(35)	G
15	1	You Light Up My Life	Debby Boone	Warner	16	(48)	F P L
16	-	Runaround Sue	Leif Garrett	Atlantic	5		
17	-	(Love Is) Thicker Than Water	Andy Gibb	RSO	14		G
18	16	You Can't Turn Me Off (In The Middle Of Turning Me On)	High Inergy	Gordy	7		F L
19	-	Sometimes When We Touch	Dan Hill	20th Century	10	(13)	F G
20	-	Turn To Stone	Electric Light Orchestra	Jet	5	(18)	

February 1978

This Mnth	Prev Mnth	Title	Artist	Label	Wks 20	(UK Pos)	
1	11	Stayin' Alive	Bee Gees	RSO	16	(4)	P
2	17	(Love Is) Thicker Than Water	Andy Gibb	RSO	14		G
3	12	Just The Way You Are	Billy Joel	Columbia	13	(19)	F G
4	7	We Are The Champions	Queen	Elektra	11	(2)	G
5	19	Sometimes When We Touch	Dan Hill	20th Century	10	(13)	F G
6	9	Short People	Randy Newman	Warner	11		F G L
7	-	Emotion	Samantha Sang	Private Stock	12	(11)	F P L
8	-	Dance, Dance, Dance (Yowsah, Yowsah, Yowsah)	Chic	Atlantic	10	(6)	F G
9	1	Baby Come Back	Player	RSO	14	(32)	F G
10	2	How Deep Is Your Love	Bee Gees	RSO	21	(3)	G
11	-	I Go Crazy	Paul Davis	Bang	11		F
12	3	You're In My Heart	Rod Stewart	Warner	12	(3)	G
13	-	Lay Down Sally	Eric Clapton	RSO	14	(39)	G
14	-	Peg	Steely Dan	ABC	6		
15	6	Hey Deanie	Shaun Cassidy	Warner	9		G L
16	-	Night Fever	Bee Gees	RSO	15	(1)	P
17	-	Theme From 'Close Encounters Of The Third Kind'	John Williams	Arista	4		L
18	-	Serpentine Fire	Earth, Wind & Fire	Columbia	6		
19	-	Don't Let Me Be Misunderstood	Santa Esmeralda	Casablanca	3	(41)	F L
20	-	Desiree	Neil Diamond	Columbia	3	(39)	

March 1978

This Mnth	Prev Mnth	Title	Artist	Label	Wks 20	(UK Pos)	
1	16	Night Fever	Bee Gees	RSO	15	(1)	P
2	1	Stayin' Alive	Bee Gees	RSO	16	(4)	P
3	2	(Love Is) Thicker Than Water	Andy Gibb	RSO	14		G
4	7	Emotion	Samantha Sang	Private Stock	12	(11)	F P L
5	13	Lay Down Sally	Eric Clapton	RSO	14	(39)	G
6	5	Sometimes When We Touch	Dan Hill	20th Century	10	(13)	F G
7	11	I Go Crazy	Paul Davis	Bang	11		F
8	8	Dance, Dance, Dance (Yowsah...)	Chic	Atlantic	10	(6)	F G
9	-	Can't Smile Without You	Barry Manilow	Arista	12	(43)	G
10	3	Just The Way You Are	Billy Joel	Columbia	13	(19)	F G
11	-	Thunder Island	Jay Ferguson	Asylum	8		F L
12	-	The Name Of The Game	Abba	Atlantic	4	(1)	
13	-	What's Your Name	Lynyrd Skynyrd	MCA	6		L
14	-	If I Can't Have You	Yvonne Elliman	RSO	12	(4)	G L
15	14	Peg	Steely Dan	ABC	6		
16	10	How Deep Is Your Love	Bee Gees	RSO	21	(3)	G
17	-	Falling	Leblanc & Carr	Big Tree	4		F L
18	-	Happy Anniversary	Little River Band	Harvest	4		
19	-	Wonderful World	Art Garfunkel, James Taylor & Paul Simon	Columbia	4		L
20	4	We Are The Champions	Queen	Elektra	11	(2)	G

▲ Not only did The Bee Gees have the top two singles in March, they also composed and produced the top four – an unprecedented achievement.

◆ The film *Saturday Night Fever* took disco to even greater heights - the soundtrack (heavily featuring The Bee Gees) topped the charts for six months, and sold 11 million in America, 25 million worldwide.

◆ Another film doing the rounds was the chronologically confusing *American Hot Wax* - loosely based on r'n'r DJ Alan Freed's life.

◆ Santana, Foreigner, Heart, Ted Nugent and Aerosmith were among the acts attracting 250,000 people to California Jam II.

UK 1978
APR-JUNE

◆ As The Bee Gees scored their only transatlantic topper of the 1970s with the Grammy winning, 'Night Fever', its parent album, **Saturday Night Fever,** started an 18 week run (a record for the decade) at the top in Britain.

▲ Boney M's double-sided chart topper, 'Rivers Of Babylon'/ 'Brown Girl In The Ring', which sold over two million in Britain, was the only American Top 40 entry for these regular European hit makers.

◆ All 90,000 tickets for Bob Dylan's Wembley concert were sold in less than eight hours.

April 1978

This Mnth	Prev Mnth	Title	Artist	Label	Wks 20	(US Pos)	
1	10	Matchstalk Men And Matchstalk...	Brian & Michael	Pye	11		F L
2	-	I Wonder Why	Showaddywaddy	Arista	7		
3	7	Baker Street	Gerry Rafferty	UA	10	(2)	F
4	-	If You Can't Give Me Love	Suzi Quatro	RAK	8	(45)	
5	5	Denis	Blondie	Chrysalis	9		F
6	1	Wuthering Heights	Kate Bush	EMI	9		F
7	-	Follow You Follow Me	Genesis	Charisma	7	(23)	
8	-	Never Let Her Slip Away	Andrew Gold	Asylum	8	(67)	
9	-	With A Little Luck	Wings	Parlophone	5	(1)	
10	-	Night Fever	Bee Gees	RSO	12	(1)	
11	8	I Can't Stand The Rain	Eruption	Atlantic	8	(18)	F
12	-	Too Much, Too Little, Too Late	Johnny Mathis/Deniece Williams	CBS	9	(1)	
13	20	I Love The Sound Of Breaking Glass	Nick Lowe & His Cowboy Outfit	Radar	4		F
14	19	Ally's Tartan Army	Andy Cameron	Klub	5		F L
15	-	Walk In Love	Manhattan Transfer	Atlantic	5		
16	-	Every 1's A Winner	Hot Chocolate	RAK	6	(6)	
17	-	Singin' In The Rain (Pt. 1)	Sheila B. Devotion	Carrere	4		F
18	-	Sometimes When We Touch	Dan Hill	20th Century	5	(3)	F L
19	11	Is This Love	Bob Marley & The Wailers	Island	6		
20	-	More Like The Movies	Dr. Hook	Capitol	5		

May 1978

This Mnth	Prev Mnth	Title	Artist	Label	Wks 20	(US Pos)	
1	-	Rivers Of Babylon/Brown Girl In The Ring	Boney M	Atlantic/Hansa	22	(30)	P
2	10	Night Fever	Bee Gees	RSO	12	(1)	
3	12	Too Much, Too Little, Too Late	Johnny Mathis/Deniece Williams	CBS	9	(1)	
4	-	Automatic Lover	Dee D. Jackson	Mercury	5		F L
5	8	Never Let Her Slip Away	Andrew Gold	Asylum	8	(67)	
6	-	Boy From New York City	Darts	Magnet	8		
7	-	Because The Night	Patti Smith Group	Arista	6	(13)	F L
8	-	Let's All Chant	Michael Zager Band	Private Stock	6	(36)	F L
9	1	Matchstalk Men And Matchstalk...	Brian & Michael	Pye	11		F L
10	-	Jack And Jill	Raydio	Arista	5	(8)	F
11	-	If I Can't Have You	Yvonne Elliman	RSO	7	(1)	L
12	-	Love Is In The Air	John Paul Young	Ariola	6	(7)	F L
13	-	She's So Modern	Boomtown Rats	Ensign	6		
14	-	Do It Again	Raffaella Carra	Epic	5		F L
15	4	If You Can't Give Me Love	Suzi Quatro	RAK	8	(45)	
16	-	More Than A Woman	Tavares	Capitol	6	(32)	
17	-	Everybody Dance	Chic	Atlantic	5	(38)	
18	2	I Wonder Why	Showaddywaddy	Arista	7		
19	-	Bad Old Days	Co-Co	Ariola/Hansa	3		F L
20	-	(I'm Always Touched By Your) Presence Dear	Blondie	Chrysalis	5		

June 1978

This Mnth	Prev Mnth	Title	Artist	Label	Wks 20	(US Pos)	
1	1	Rivers Of Babylon/Brown Girl In...	Boney M	Atlantic/Hansa	22	(30)	P
2	-	You're The One That I Want	John Travolta & Olivia Newton-John	RSO	17	(1)	F P
3	6	Boy From New York City	Darts	Magnet	8		
4	11	If I Can't Have You	Yvonne Elliman	RSO	7	(1)	L
5	2	Night Fever	Bee Gees	RSO	12	(1)	
6	-	Ca Plane Pour Moi	Plastic Bertrand	Sire	7		F L
7	-	Oh Carol	Smokie	RAK	6		
8	12	Love Is In The Air	John Paul Young	Ariola	6	(7)	F L
9	-	Davy's On The Road Again	Manfred Mann's Earth Band	Bronze	5		L
10	-	Annie's Song	James Galway	RCA Red Seal	8		F L
11	16	More Than A Woman	Tavares	Capitol	6	(32)	
12	-	Miss You	Rolling Stones	Rolling Stone	6	(1)	
13	7	Because The Night	Patti Smith Group	Arista	6	(13)	F L
14	-	The Smurf Song	Father Abraham & The Smurfs	Decca	11		F
15	-	Ole Ola (Muhler Brasileira)	Rod Stewart	Riva	3		
16	-	What A Waste	Ian Dury & The Blockheads	Stiff	4		F
17	-	Making Up Again	Goldie	Bronze	5		F L
18	-	Hi Tension	Hi Tension	Island	3		F
19	-	It Sure Brings Out The Love In Your Eyes	David Soul	Private Stock	4		L
20	-	Come To Me	Ruby Winters	Creole	4		L

April 1978

This Mnth	Prev Mnth	Title	Artist	Label	Wks 20	(UK Pos)	
1	1	Night Fever	Bee Gees	RSO	15	(1)	P
2	9	Can't Smile Without You	Barry Manilow	Arista	12	(43)	G
3	5	Lay Down Sally	Eric Clapton	RSO	14	(39)	G
4	14	If I Can't Have You	Yvonne Elliman	RSO	12	(4)	G L
5	2	Stayin' Alive	Bee Gees	RSO	16	(4)	P
6	-	Dust In The Wind	Kansas	Kirshner	8		G
7	-	The Closer I Get To You	Roberta Flack/Donny Hathaway	Atlantic	11	(42)	G
8	-	Jack And Jill	Raydio	Arista	8	(11)	F G
9	-	Our Love	Natalie Cole	Capitol	8		G
10	-	With A Little Luck	Wings	Capitol	11	(5)	
11	4	Emotion	Samantha Sang	Private Stock	12	(11)	F P L
12	-	We'll Never Have To Say Goodbye Again	England Dan/John Ford Coley	Big Tree	5		
13	-	Runnin' On Empty	Jackson Browne	Asylum	6		
14	3	(Love Is) Thicker Than Water	Andy Gibb	RSO	14		G
15	-	You're The One That I Want	John Travolta & Olivia Newton-John	RSO	13	(1)	P
16	11	Thunder Island	Jay Ferguson	Asylum	8		F L
17	-	Count On Me	Jefferson Starship	Grunt	8		
18	-	Ebony Eyes	Bob Welch	Capitol	4		
19	-	Goodbye Girl	David Gates	Elektra	4		F L
20	7	I Go Crazy	Paul Davis	Bang	11		F

May 1978

This Mnth	Prev Mnth	Title	Artist	Label	Wks 20	(UK Pos)	
1	10	With A Little Luck	Wings	Capitol	11	(5)	
2	7	The Closer I Get To You	Roberta Flack/Donny Hathaway	Atlantic	11	(42)	G
3	4	If I Can't Have You	Yvonne Elliman	RSO	12	(4)	G L
4	-	Too Much, Too Little, Too Late	Johnny Mathis/Deniece Williams	Columbia	11	(3)	G L
5	15	You're The One That I Want	John Travolta & Olivia Newton-John	RSO	13	(1)	P
6	1	Night Fever	Bee Gees	RSO	15	(1)	P
7	-	Shadow Dancing	Andy Gibb	RSO	15	(42)	G
8	17	Count On Me	Jefferson Starship	Grunt	8		
9	-	Feels So Good	Chuck Mangione	A&M	10		F
10	-	Imaginary Lover	Atlanta Rhythm Section	Polydor	7		
11	2	Can't Smile Without You	Barry Manilow	Arista	12	(43)	G
12	-	Disco Inferno	Trammps	Atlantic	6	(16)	F L
13	-	This Time I'm In It For Love	Player	RSO	7		L
14	-	On Broadway	George Benson	Warner	7		
15	6	Dust In The Wind	Kansas	Kirshner	8		G
16	3	Lay Down Sally	Eric Clapton	RSO	14	(39)	G
17	-	Baby Hold On	Eddie Money	Columbia	5		F
18	-	Love Is Like Oxygen	Sweet	Capitol	9	(9)	L
19	-	Take A Chance On Me	Abba	Atlantic	11	(1)	G
20	8	Jack And Jill	Raydio	Arista	8	(11)	F G

June 1978

This Mnth	Prev Mnth	Title	Artist	Label	Wks 20	(UK Pos)	
1	7	Shadow Dancing	Andy Gibb	RSO	15	(42)	G
2	5	You're The One That I Want	John Travolta & Olivia Newton-John	RSO	13	(1)	P
3	4	Too Much, Too Little, Too Late	Johnny Mathis/Deniece Williams	Columbia	11	(3)	G L
4	-	Baker Street	Gerry Rafferty	UA	12	(3)	F G
5	-	It's A Heartache	Bonnie Tyler	RCA	11	(4)	F G
6	19	Take A Chance On Me	Abba	Atlantic	11	(1)	G
7	9	Feels So Good	Chuck Mangione	A&M	10		F
8	18	Love Is Like Oxygen	Sweet	Capitol	9	(9)	L
9	14	On Broadway	George Benson	Warner	7		
10	-	You Belong To Me	Carly Simon	Elektra	7		
11	-	Dance With Me	Peter Brown	Drive	9	(57)	L
12	1	With A Little Luck	Wings	Capitol	11	(5)	
13	-	Use Ta Be My Girl	O'Jays	Philly Int.	9	(12)	G L
14	-	The Groove Line	Heatwave	Epic	9	(12)	G L
15	2	The Closer I Get To You	Roberta Flack/Donny Hathaway	Atlantic	11	(42)	G
16	13	This Time I'm In It For Love	Player	RSO	7		L
17	-	Two Out Of Three Ain't Bad	Meat Loaf	Epic	7	(69)	F G
18	17	Baby Hold On	Eddie Money	Columbia	5		F
19	-	Still The Same	Bob Seger & Silver Bullet Band	Capitol	8		
20	-	Because The Night	Patti Smith Group	Arista	5	(5)	F L

US
1978
APR-JUNE

◆ The record breaking Bee Gees wrote four successive No. 1 singles and produced three of them. A few weeks later, their younger brother, Andy Gibb, scored his third successive chart topper with his third release, 'Shadow Dancing'.

◆ Films opening Stateside included *FM* featuring Tom Petty, Linda Ronstadt and REO Speedwagon and *Thank God It's Friday* starring Donna Summer and The Commodores. Also premiering were *Grease* with John Travolta and Olivia Newton-John and *The Buddy Holly Story*.

◆ Meat Loaf made his Top 20 debut with 'Two Out Of Three Ain't Bad', as his album **Bat Out Of Hell** climbed the transatlantic charts. The LP went on to sell over 25 million world-wide.

UK 1978
JULY-SEPT

▲ The soundtrack album to John Travolta's latest box office smash *Grease* topped the American album chart for three months and it repeated that feat in Britain. It contained the transatlantic smash duets, 'You're The One That I Want' and 'Summer Nights' by Travolta and Olivia Newton-John (both selling over a million in the UK alone), as well as the chart topping title song by Frankie Valli.

◆ Headliners at the Reading Festival included Foreigner, The Jam, Ultravox, Status Quo and Patti Smith.

July 1978

This Mnth	Prev Mnth	Title	Artist	Label	Wks 20	(US Pos)	
1	2	You're The One That I Want	John Travolta & Olivia Newton-John	RSO	17	(1)	F P
2	14	The Smurf Song	Father Abraham & The Smurfs	Decca	11		F
3	-	Dancing In The City	Marshall Hain	Harvest	9	(43)	F L
4	-	Airport	Motors	Virgin	7		F
5	10	Annie's Song	James Galway	RCA Red Seal	8		F L
6	-	Like Clockwork	Boomtown Rats	Ensign	7		
7	-	Man With The Child In His Eyes	Kate Bush	EMI	6	(85)	
8	-	A Little Bit Of Soap	Showaddywaddy	Arista	6		
9	12	Miss You	Rolling Stones	Rolling Stone	6	(1)	
10	-	Substitute	Clout	Carrere	9	(67)	F L
11	-	Boogie Oogie Oogie	Taste Of Honey	Capitol	8	(1)	F L
12	-	No One Is Innocent/My Way	Sex Pistols	Virgin	5		
13	1	Rivers Of Babylon/Brown Girl In...	Boney M	Atlantic/Hansa	22	(30)	P
14	-	Mind Blowing Decisions	Heatwave	GTO	4		
15	-	Used Ta Be My Girl	O'Jays	Philly International	5	(4)	L
16	-	Wild West Hero	Electric Light Orchestra	Jet	6		
17	-	Run For Home	Lindisfarne	Mercury	5	(33)	
18	17	Making Up Again	Goldie	Bronze	5		F L
19	9	Davy's On The Road Again	Manfred Mann's Earth Band	Bronze	5		L
20	-	Argentine Melody (Cancion De Argentina)	San Jose	MCA	3		F L

August 1978

This Mnth	Prev Mnth	Title	Artist	Label	Wks 20	(US Pos)	
1	1	You're The One That I Want	John Travolta & Olivia Newton-John	RSO	17	(1)	F P
2	10	Substitute	Clout	Carrere	9	(67)	F L
3	11	Boogie Oogie Oogie	Taste Of Honey	Capitol	8	(1)	F L
4	13	Rivers Of Babylon/Brown Girl In...	Boney M	Atlantic/Hansa	22	(30)	P
5	-	Three Times A Lady	Commodores	Motown	10	(1)	
6	-	Forever Autumn	Justin Hayward	CBS	6	(47)	L
7	2	The Smurf Song	Father Abraham & The Smurfs	Decca	11		F
8	-	5-7-0-5	City Boy	Vertigo	5	(27)	F L
9	-	If The Kids Are United	Sham 69	Polydor	5		
10	-	It's Raining	Darts	Magnet	8		
11	3	Dancing In The City	Marshall Hain	Harvest	9	(43)	F L
12	-	Northern Lights	Renaissance	Warner	5		F L
13	16	Wild West Hero	Electric Light Orchestra	Jet	6		
14	-	Supernature	Cerrone	Atlantic	5	(70)	F L
15	8	A Little Bit Of Soap	Showaddywaddy	Arista	6		
16	6	Like Clockwork	Boomtown Rats	Ensign	7		
17	-	Dreadlock Holiday	10cc	Mercury	9	(44)	L
18	-	Come Back And Finish What You Started	Gladys Knight & The Pips	Buddah	5		
19	-	Stay	Jackson Browne	Asylum	4	(20)	F L
20	-	Baby Stop Crying	Bob Dylan	CBS	5		L

September 1978

This Mnth	Prev Mnth	Title	Artist	Label	Wks 20	(US Pos)	
1	5	Three Times A Lady	Commodores	Motown	10	(1)	
2	17	Dreadlock Holiday	10cc	Mercury	9	(44)	L
3	4	Rivers Of Babylon/Brown Girl In...	Boney M	Atlantic/Hansa	22	(30)	P
4	-	Oh What A Circus	David Essex	Mercury	8		
5	-	Jilted John	Jilted John	EMI International	7		F L
6	10	It's Raining	Darts	Magnet	8		
7	1	You're The One That I Want	John Travolta/O. Newton-John	RSO	17	(1)	F P
8	-	Kiss You All Over	Exile	RAK	6	(1)	F L
9	-	British Hustle/Peace On Earth	Hi Tension	Island	5		L
10	-	Hong Kong Garden	Siouxsie & The Banshees	Polydor	5		F
11	14	Supernature	Cerrone	Atlantic	5	(70)	F L
12	-	Grease	Frankie Valli	RSO	6	(1)	L
13	-	Picture This	Blondie	Chrysalis	6		
14	-	Summer Nights	John Travolta/O. Newton-John	RSO	11	(5)	G
15	-	An Everlasting Love	Andy Gibb	RSO	5	(5)	F L
16	-	Summer Night City	Abba	Epic	5		
17	-	It's Only Make Believe	Child	Ariola Hansa	5		F L
18	-	Forget About You	Motors	Virgin	4		L
19	-	Again And Again	Status Quo	Vertigo	4		
20	-	Love Don't Live Here Anymore	Rose Royce	Whitfield	7	(32)	

July 1978

This Mnth	Prev Mnth	Title	Artist	Label	Wks 20	(UK Pos)	
1	1	Shadow Dancing	Andy Gibb	RSO	15	(42)	G
2	4	Baker Street	Gerry Rafferty	UA	12	(3)	F G
3	19	Still The Same	Bob Seger & The Silver Bullet Band	Capitol	8		
4	13	Use Ta Be My Girl	O'Jays	Philly Int.	9	(12)	G L
5	-	Miss You	Rolling Stones	Rolling Stone	12	(3)	G
6	6	Take A Chance On Me	Abba	Atlantic	11	(1)	G
7	14	The Groove Line	Heatwave	Epic	9	(12)	G L
8	5	It's A Heartache	Bonnie Tyler	RCA	11	(4)	F G
9	-	Last Dance	Donna Summer	Casablanca	11	(51)	G
10	-	Grease	Frankie Valli	RSO	11	(3)	P L
11	11	Dance With Me	Peter Brown	Drive	9	(57)	L
12	-	Love Will Find A Way	Pablo Cruise	A&M	8		
13	17	Two Out Of Three Ain't Bad	Meat Loaf	Epic	7	(69)	F G
14	-	Three Times A Lady	Commodores	Motown	12	(1)	G
15	10	You Belong To Me	Carly Simon	Elektra	7		
16	-	Bluer Than Blue	Michael Johnson	EMI America	6		F
17	-	Runaway	Jefferson Starship	Grunt	4		
18	8	Love Is Like Oxygen	Sweet	Capitol	9	(9)	L
19	-	Hot Blooded	Foreigner	Atlantic	12	(42)	G
20	-	Copacabana (At The Copa)	Barry Manilow	Arista	7	(42)	G

August 1978

This Mnth	Prev Mnth	Title	Artist	Label	Wks 20	(UK Pos)	
1	14	Three Times A Lady	Commodores	Motown	12	(1)	G
2	10	Grease	Frankie Valli	RSO	11	(3)	P L
3	5	Miss You	Rolling Stones	Rolling Stone	12	(3)	G
4	9	Last Dance	Donna Summer	Casablanca	11	(51)	G
5	19	Hot Blooded	Foreigner	Atlantic	12	(42)	G
6	12	Love Will Find A Way	Pablo Cruise	A&M	8		
7	-	Boogie Oogie Oogie	Taste Of Honey	Capitol	14	(3)	F P
8	-	Magnet And Steel	Walter Egan	Columbia	8		F G L
9	20	Copacabana (At The Copa)	Barry Manilow	Arista	7	(42)	G
10	-	An Everlasting Love	Andy Gibb	RSO	10	(10)	G
11	-	Hopelessly Devoted To You	Olivia Newton-John	RSO	12	(2)	G
12	-	Life's Been Good	Joe Walsh	Asylum	7	(14)	F
13	-	My Angel Baby	Toby Beau	RCA	7		F L
14	1	Shadow Dancing	Andy Gibb	RSO	15	(42)	G
15	2	Baker Street	Gerry Rafferty	UA	12	(3)	F G
16	-	I'm Not Gonna Let It Bother Me Tonight	Atlanta Rhythm Section	Polydor	4		
17	-	Kiss You All Over	Exile	Warner	15	(6)	F G L
18	-	Shame	Evelyn 'Champagne' King	RCA	7	(39)	F G
19	4	Use Ta Be My Girl	O'Jays	Philly Int.	9	(12)	G L
20	3	Still The Same	Bob Seger & Silver Bullet Band	Capitol	8		

September 1978

This Mnth	Prev Mnth	Title	Artist	Label	Wks 20	(UK Pos)	
1	7	Boogie Oogie Oogie	Taste Of Honey	Capitol	14	(3)	F P
2	1	Three Times A Lady	Commodores	Motown	12	(1)	G
3	11	Hopelessly Devoted To You	Olivia Newton-John	RSO	12	(2)	G
4	17	Kiss You All Over	Exile	Warner	15	(6)	F G L
5	5	Hot Blooded	Foreigner	Atlantic	12	(42)	G
6	10	An Everlasting Love	Andy Gibb	RSO	10	(10)	G
7	-	Summer Nights	John Travolta & Olivia Newton-John	RSO	9	(1)	G L
8	-	Hot Child In The City	Nick Gilder	Chrysalis	14		F P L
9	-	Don't Look Back	Boston	Epic	9	(43)	
10	-	Love Is In The Air	John Paul Young	Scotti Bros	11	(5)	F L
11	2	Grease	Frankie Valli	RSO	11	(3)	P L
12	-	Got To Get You Into My Life	Earth, Wind & Fire	Columbia	6	(33)	G
13	-	Fool (If You Think It's Over)	Chris Rea	UA	7	(30)	F L
14	18	Shame	Evelyn 'Champagne' King	RCA	7	(39)	F G
15	-	Reminiscing	Little River Band	Harvest	10		
16	-	You And I	Rick James	Gordy	6	(46)	F
17	-	You Needed Me	Anne Murray	Capitol	13	(22)	G
18	3	Miss You	Rolling Stones	Rolling Stone	12	(3)	G
19	-	Hollywood Nights	Bob Seger & The Silver Bullet Band	Capitol	6	(42)	
20	-	Whenever I Call You 'Friend'	Kenny Loggins	Columbia	10		F

US
1978
JULY-SEPT

◆ The Rolling Stones, whose 'Miss You' and **Some Girls** headed the singles and album charts respectively, broke the indoor attendance record when more than 80,000 people paid over $1 million to see them at the New Orleans Superdome.

◆ Despite the involvement of The Bee Gees, the film *Sergeant Pepper's Lonely Hearts Club Band* was a resounding miss.

◆ Steve Miller and The Eagles drew 65,000 to a gig in Bloomington, and both Bob Dylan's and Fleetwood Mac's US tours were sell-outs. Other successful live events included Canada Jam, with headliners The Doobie Brothers, Kansas and The Commodores, and Grateful Dead's performance at the Egyptian pyramids.

UK 1978 OCT-DEC

◆ *Smash Hits* was launched. It became the most successful teen magazine in Britain.

◆ The film *Grease* continued to spawn hits, with three songs, 'Summer Nights', 'Sandy' and 'Hopelessly Devoted To You', taking slots in the British Top 4 in November.

▲ The Cars, who were voted Best New Band in *Rolling Stone*, started a European tour. Their debut hit, 'My Best Friend's Girl', was the first picture disc to be successfully marketed in Britain.

◆ Sex Pistol Sid Vicious was charged in New York with the murder of his girlfriend

October 1978

This Mnth	Prev Mnth	Title	Artist	Label	Wks 20	(US Pos)	
1	14	Summer Nights	John Travolta & Olivia Newton-John	RSO	11	(5)	G
2	-	Rasputin	Boney M	Atlantic/Hansa	7		
3	20	Love Don't Live Here Anymore	Rose Royce	Whitfield	7	(32)	
4	-	Lucky Stars	Dean Friedman	Lifesong	6		F L
5	-	I Can't Stop Lovin' You (Though I Try)	Leo Sayer	Chrysalis	6		
6	-	Sandy	John Travolta	Polydor	7		
7	-	Sweet Talkin' Woman	Electric Light Orchestra	Jet	7	(17)	
8	12	Grease	Frankie Valli	RSO	6	(1)	L
9	-	You Make Me Feel (Mighty Real)	Sylvester	Fantasy	5	(36)	F L
10	-	Now That We've Found Love	Third World	Island	4	(47)	F
11	-	Talking In Your Sleep	Crystal Gayle	UA	5	(18)	L
12	-	Blame It On The Boogie	Jacksons	Epic	7	(54)	
13	16	Summer Night City	Abba	Epic	5		
14	-	Rat Trap	Boomtown Rats	Ensign	9		
15	-	Macarthur Park	Donna Summer	Casablanca	6	(1)	
16	2	Dreadlock Holiday	10cc	Mercury	9	(44)	L
17	-	A Rose Has To Die	Dooleys	GTO	4		
18	8	Kiss You All Over	Exile	RAK	6	(1)	F L
19	1	Three Times A Lady	Commodores	Motown	10	(1)	
20	4	Oh What A Circus	David Essex	Mercury	8		

November 1978

This Mnth	Prev Mnth	Title	Artist	Label	Wks 20	(US Pos)	
1	14	Rat Trap	Boomtown Rats	Ensign	9		
2	1	Summer Nights	John Travolta/O. Newton-John	RSO	11	(5)	G
3	6	Sandy	John Travolta	Polydor	7		
4	-	Hopelessly Devoted To You	Olivia Newton-John	RSO	5	(3)	
5	-	Darlin'	Frankie Miller	Chrysalis	7		F L
6	15	Macarthur Park	Donna Summer	Casablanca	6	(1)	
7	-	My Best Friend's Girl	Cars	Elektra	5	(35)	F
8	12	Blame It On The Boogie	Jacksons	Epic	7	(54)	
9	2	Rasputin	Boney M	Atlantic/Hansa	7		
10	-	Pretty Little Angel Eyes	Showaddywaddy	Arista	6		
11	7	Sweet Talkin' Woman	Electric Light Orchestra	Jet	7	(17)	
12	-	Instant Replay	Dan Hartman	Sky	6	(29)	F
13	-	Givin' Up Givin' In	Three Degrees	Ariola	5		
14	-	Public Image	Public Image Ltd.	Virgin	4		F
15	-	Bicycle Race/Fat Bottomed Girls	Queen	EMI	4	(24)	
16	-	Da Ya Think I'm Sexy	Rod Stewart	Riva	9	(1)	
17	4	Lucky Stars	Dean Friedman	Lifesong	6		F L
18	-	Dippety Day	Father Abraham & The Smurfs	Decca	5		
19	-	Hurry Up Harry	Sham 69	Polydor	5		
20	-	Hanging On The Telephone	Blondie	Chrysalis	7		

December 1978

This Mnth	Prev Mnth	Title	Artist	Label	Wks 20	(US Pos)	
1	-	Mary's Boy Child-Oh My Lord	Boney M	Atlantic/Hansa	7	(85)	G
2	16	Da Ya Think I'm Sexy	Rod Stewart	Riva	9	(1)	
3	-	Too Much Heaven	Bee Gees	RSO	9	(1)	
4	-	A Taste Of Aggro	Barron Knights	Epic	8		
5	-	I Lost My Heart To A Starship Trooper	Sarah Brightman & Hot Gossip	Ariola	8		F
6	-	Y.M.C.A.	Village People	Mercury	10	(2)	F G
7	-	Le Freak	Chic	Atlantic	10	(1)	
8	-	Always And Forever/Mind Blowing Decisions	Heatwave	GTO	9	(18)	
9	20	Hanging On The Telephone	Blondie	Chrysalis	7		
10	-	You Don't Bring Me Flowers	Barbra & Neil	Columbia	6	(1)	
11	1	Rat Trap	Boomtown Rats	Ensign	9		
12	-	Lay Your Love On Me	Racey	RAK	9		F
13	-	Don't Cry Out Loud	Elkie Brooks	A&M	5		
14	4	Hopelessly Devoted To You	Olivia Newton-John	RSO	5	(3)	
15	10	Pretty Little Angel Eyes	Showaddywaddy	Arista	6		
16	7	My Best Friend's Girl	Cars	Elektra	5	(35)	F
17	-	Greased Lightning	John Travolta	Polydor	5	(47)	
18	-	Song For Guy	Elton John	Rocket	6		
19	12	Instant Replay	Dan Hartman	Sky	6	(29)	F
20	-	In The Bush	Musique	CBS	5	(58)	F L

October 1978

This Mnth	Prev Mnth	Title	Artist	Label	Wks 20	(UK Pos)	
1	8	Hot Child In The City	Nick Gilder	Chrysalis	14		F P L
2	4	Kiss You All Over	Exile	Warner	15	(6)	F G L
3	1	Boogie Oogie Oogie	Taste Of Honey	Capitol	14	(3)	F P
4	15	Reminiscing	Little River Band	Harvest	10		
5	17	You Needed Me	Anne Murray	Capitol	13	(22)	G
6	20	Whenever I Call You 'Friend'	Kenny Loggins	Columbia	10		F
7	10	Love Is In The Air	John Paul Young	Scotti Bros	11	(5)	F L
8	7	Summer Nights	John Travolta & Olivia Newton-John	RSO	9	(1)	G L
9	9	Don't Look Back	Boston	Epic	9	(43)	
10	-	MacArthur Park	Donna Summer	Casablanca	12	(5)	G
11	-	How Much I Feel	Ambrosia	Warner	11		
12	-	Right Down The Line	Gerry Rafferty	UA	6		
13	3	Hopelessly Devoted To You	Olivia Newton-John	RSO	12	(2)	G
14	-	Get Off	Foxy	Dash	7		F L
15	-	Double Vision	Foreigner	Atlantic	9		G
16	19	Hollywood Nights	Bob Seger & The Silver Bullet Band	Capitol	6	(42)	
17	-	You Never Done It Like That	Captain & Tennille	A&M	8	(63)	
18	-	Back In The U.S.A.	Linda Ronstadt	Asylum	4		
19	2	Three Times A Lady	Commodores	Motown	12	(1)	G
20	-	Beast Of Burden	Rolling Stones	Rolling Stone	4		

November 1978

This Mnth	Prev Mnth	Title	Artist	Label	Wks 20	(UK Pos)	
1	10	MacArthur Park	Donna Summer	Casablanca	12	(5)	G
2	15	Double Vision	Foreigner	Atlantic	9		G
3	5	You Needed Me	Anne Murray	Capitol	13	(22)	G
4	11	How Much I Feel	Ambrosia	Warner	11		
5	1	Hot Child In The City	Nick Gilder	Chrysalis	14		F P L
6	2	Kiss You All Over	Exile	Warner	15	(6)	F G L
7	-	I Just Wanna Stop	Gino Vannelli	A&M	9		F
8	6	Whenever I Call You 'Friend'	Kenny Loggins	Columbia	10		F
9	17	You Never Done It Like That	Captain & Tennille	A&M	8	(63)	
10	-	You Don't Bring Me Flowers	Barbra & Neil	Columbia	12	(5)	G
11	-	Ready To Take A Chance Again	Barry Manilow	Arista	5		
12	-	I Love The Night Life (Disco 'Round)	Alicia Bridges	Polydor	12	(32)	F G L
13	20	Beast Of Burden	Rolling Stones	Rolling Stone	4		
14	4	Reminiscing	Little River Band	Harvest	10		
15	-	Time Passages	Al Stewart	Arista	9		L
16	14	Get Off	Foxy	Dash	7		F L
17	-	(Our Love) Don't Throw It All Away	Andy Gibb	RSO	10	(32)	G
18	-	Sharing The Night Together	Dr. Hook	Capitol	10	(43)	G
19	-	Le Freak	Chic	Atlantic	17	(7)	P
20	-	Who Are You	Who	Decca	5	(18)	

December 1978

This Mnth	Prev Mnth	Title	Artist	Label	Wks 20	(UK Pos)	
1	19	Le Freak	Chic	Atlantic	17	(7)	P
2	10	You Don't Bring Me Flowers	Barbra & Neil	Columbia	12	(5)	G
3	7	I Just Wanna Stop	Gino Vannelli	A&M	9		F
4	12	I Love The Night Life (Disco 'Round)	Alicia Bridges	Polydor	12	(32)	F G L
5	-	My Life	Billy Joel	Columbia	12	(12)	G
6	-	Too Much Heaven	Bee Gees	RSO	11	(3)	P
7	18	Sharing The Night Together	Dr. Hook	Capitol	10	(43)	G
8	1	MacArthur Park	Donna Summer	Casablanca	12	(5)	G
9	17	(Our Love) Don't Throw It All Away	Andy Gibb	RSO	10	(32)	G
10	15	Time Passages	Al Stewart	Arista	9		L
11	-	Y.M.C.A.	Village People	Casablanca	17	(1)	F P
12	4	How Much I Feel	Ambrosia	Warner	11		
13	-	Hold The Line	Toto	Columbia	10	(14)	F G
14	-	Strange Way	Firefall	Atlantic	7		L
15	-	How You Gonna See Me Now	Alice Cooper	Warner	6	(61)	
16	-	Ooh Baby Baby	Linda Ronstadt	Asylum	7		
17	2	Double Vision	Foreigner	Atlantic	9		G
18	-	Promises	Eric Clapton	RSO	6	(37)	
19	-	Alive Again	Chicago	Columbia	6		
20	-	Straight On	Heart	Portrait	4		

US 1978
OCT-DEC

◆ American record and tape sales topped $4 billion for the first time in 1978. Disco remained supreme, pop prospered, funk fared well, new wave caused more than a ripple of interest and rock ruled on the album chart - there was room for many styles to be simultaneously successful.

◆ Solo albums by the four members of Kiss (who were now also stars of a regular cartoon series) all shipped gold.

◆ CBS Records became the first label to hike their album prices up a dollar to $8.98.

◆ Both Bruce Springsteen and Queen headlined at Madison Square Garden, while on the other coast, the last acts to play San Francisco's famous Winterland Theater were Grateful Dead (their 48th show there) and The Blues Brothers.

UK 1979 JAN-MAR

◆ British single sales continued to amaze, with hits from the Village People ('Y.M.C.A.') and Blondie ('Heart Of Glass') selling over a million and Ian Dury's new wave disco track, 'Hit Me With Your Rhythm Stick', only narrowly missing.

▲ British success for local groups Dire Straits and Police (above), only came after their respective singles 'Sultans Of Swing' and 'Roxanne' charted in America.

◆ *Rolling Stone* reported that it now cost between $350,000-500,000 to produce, promote and support a new album release in America.

January 1979

This Mnth	Prev Mnth	Title	Artist	Label	Wks 20	(US Pos)	
1	6	Y.M.C.A.	Village People	Mercury	10	(2)	F G
2	-	Hit Me With Your Rhythm Stick	Ian Dury & The Blockheads	Stiff	10		
3	12	Lay Your Love On Me	Racey	RAK	9		F
4	-	September	Earth, Wind & Fire	CBS	7	(8)	
5	18	Song For Guy	Elton John	Rocket	6		
6	7	Le Freak	Chic	Atlantic	10	(1)	
7	-	A Little More Love	Olivia Newton-John	EMI	6	(3)	
8	4	A Taste Of Aggro	Barron Knights	Epic	8		
9	-	Hello This Is Joannie (Telephone Answering Machine Song)	Paul Evans	Spring	5		F L
10	10	You Don't Bring Me Flowers	Barbra & Neil	Columbia	6	(1)	
11	1	Mary's Boy Child-Oh My Lord	Boney M	Atlantic/Hansa	7	(85)	G
12	3	Too Much Heaven	Bee Gees	RSO	9	(1)	
13	-	I'm Every Woman	Chaka Khan	Warner	7	(21)	F
14	5	I Lost My Heart To A Starship Trooper	Sarah Brightman & Hot Gossip	Ariola	8		F
15	-	One Nation Under A Groove (Pt. 1)	Funkadelic	Warner	4	(28)	F L
16	-	Car 67	Driver 67	Logo	5		F L
17	-	I'll Put You Together Again	Hot Chocolate	RAK	4		
18	-	Women In Love	Three Degrees	Ariola	8		
19	-	Heart Of Glass	Blondie	Chrysalis	8	(1)	G
20	8	Always And Forever/Mind Blowing Decisions	Heatwave	GTO	9	(18)	

February 1979

This Mnth	Prev Mnth	Title	Artist	Label	Wks 20	(US Pos)	
1	19	Heart Of Glass	Blondie	Chrysalis	8	(1)	G
2	18	Women In Love	Three Degrees	Ariola	8		
3	-	Chiquitita	Abba	Epic	7	(29)	
4	-	Don't Cry For Me Argentina	Shadows	EMI	6		
5	2	Hit Me With Your Rhythm Stick	Ian Dury & The Blockheads	Stiff	10		
6	-	I Was Made For Dancin'	Leif Garrett	Scotti Bros	5	(10)	F L
7	-	Contact	Edwin Starr	20th Century	6	(65)	
8	16	Car 67	Driver 67	Logo	5		F L
9	4	September	Earth, Wind & Fire	CBS	7	(8)	
10	-	Milk And Alcohol	Dr. Feelgood	UA	5		F L
11	-	Tragedy	Bee Gees	RSO	7	(1)	
12	1	Y.M.C.A.	Village People	Mercury	10	(2)	F G
13	7	A Little More Love	Olivia Newton-John	EMI	6	(3)	
14	-	My Life	Billy Joel	CBS	4	(3)	
15	-	Oliver's Army	Elvis Costello	Radar	9		
16	-	King Rocker	Generation X	Chrysalis	4		F L
17	-	Just The Way You Are	Barry White	20th Century	5		
18	9	Hello This Is Joannie (Telephone...)	Paul Evans	Spring	5		F L
19	-	I Will Survive	Gloria Gaynor	Polydor	9	(1)	
20	3	Lay Your Love On Me	Racey	RAK	9		F

March 1979

This Mnth	Prev Mnth	Title	Artist	Label	Wks 20	(US Pos)	
1	19	I Will Survive	Gloria Gaynor	Polydor	9	(1)	
2	15	Oliver's Army	Elvis Costello	Radar	9		
3	11	Tragedy	Bee Gees	RSO	7	(1)	
4	-	Lucky Number	Lene Lovich	Stiff	7		F
5	-	Can You Feel The Force	Real Thing	Pye	7		
6	-	Something Else/Friggin' In The Riggin'	Sex Pistols	Virgin	7		
7	-	I Want Your Love	Chic	Atlantic	7	(7)	
8	1	Heart Of Glass	Blondie	Chrysalis	8	(1)	G
9	-	Keep On Dancin'	Gary's Gang	CBS	5	(41)	F L
10	7	Contact	Edwin Starr	20th Century	6	(65)	
11	-	Get Down	Gene Chandler	20th Century	5	(53)	F L
12	-	Into The Valley	Skids	Virgin	6		F
13	3	Chiquitita	Abba	Epic	7	(29)	
14	-	Painter Man	Boney M	Atlantic/Hansa	3		
15	-	Get It	Darts	Magnet	4		
16	-	Waiting For An Alibi	Thin Lizzy	Vertigo	4		
17	-	In The Navy	Village People	Mercury	6	(3)	
18	-	Don't Stop Me Now	Queen	EMI	4	(86)	
19	-	Sound Of The Suburbs	Members	Virgin	4		F L
20	6	I Was Made For Dancin'	Leif Garrett	Scotti Bros	5	(10)	F L

January 1979

This Mnth	Prev Mnth	Title	Artist	Label	Wks 20	(UK Pos)	
1	1	Le Freak	Chic	Atlantic	17	(7)	P
2	6	Too Much Heaven	Bee Gees	RSO	11	(3)	P
3	5	My Life	Billy Joel	Columbia	12	(12)	G
4	11	Y.M.C.A.	Village People	Casablanca	17	(1)	F P
5	2	You Don't Bring Me Flowers	Barbra & Neil	Columbia	12	(5)	G
6	13	Hold The Line	Toto	Columbia	10	(14)	F G
7	16	Ooh Baby Baby	Linda Ronstadt	Asylum	7		
8	-	A Little More Love	Olivia Newton-John	MCA	15	(4)	G
9	-	Every 1's A Winner	Hot Chocolate	Infinity	7	(12)	G L
10	18	Promises	Eric Clapton	RSO	6	(37)	
11	-	September	Earth, Wind & Fire	Arc	9	(3)	G
12	7	Sharing The Night Together	Dr. Hook	Capitol	10	(43)	G
13	-	Da Ya Think I'm Sexy	Rod Stewart	Warner	13	(1)	G
14	9	(Our Love) Don't Throw It All Away	Andy Gibb	RSO	10	(32)	G
15	-	Lotta Love	Nicolette Larson	Warner	10		F L
16	-	We've Got Tonite	Bob Seger & The Silver Bullet Band	Capitol	5	(41)	
17	-	Fire	Pointer Sisters	Planet	13	(34)	G
18	15	How You Gonna See Me Now	Alice Cooper	Warner	6	(61)	
19	-	New York Groove	Ace Frehley	Casablanca	6		F L
20	4	I Love The Night Life (Disco 'Round)	Alicia Bridges	Polydor	12	(32)	F G L

February 1979

This Mnth	Prev Mnth	Title	Artist	Label	Wks 20	(UK Pos)	
1	13	Da Ya Think I'm Sexy	Rod Stewart	Warner	13	(1)	G
2	4	Y.M.C.A.	Village People	Casablanca	17	(1)	F P
3	8	A Little More Love	Olivia Newton-John	MCA	15	(4)	G
4	1	Le Freak	Chic	Atlantic	17	(7)	P
5	17	Fire	Pointer Sisters	Planet	13	(34)	G
6	-	I Will Survive	Gloria Gaynor	Polydor	15	(1)	G L
7	15	Lotta Love	Nicolette Larson	Warner	10		F L
8	9	Every 1's A Winner	Hot Chocolate	Infinity	7	(12)	G L
9	-	Somewhere In The Night	Barry Manilow	Arista	6	(42)	
10	-	I Was Made For Dancin'	Leif Garrett	Scotti Bros	7	(4)	L
11	11	September	Earth, Wind & Fire	Arc	9	(3)	G
12	-	Got To Be Real	Cheryl Lynn	Columbia	7		F G L
13	2	Too Much Heaven	Bee Gees	RSO	11	(3)	P
14	-	Shake It	Ian Matthews	Mushroom	6		F L
15	-	Heaven Knows	Donna Summer	Casablanca	10	(34)	G
16	-	Soul Man	Blues Brothers	Atlantic	5		F
17	-	Tragedy	Bee Gees	RSO	11	(1)	P
18	19	New York Groove	Ace Frehley	Casablanca	6		F L
19	-	No Tell Lover	Chicago	Columbia	5		
20	3	My Life	Billy Joel	Columbia	12	(12)	G

March 1979

This Mnth	Prev Mnth	Title	Artist	Label	Wks 20	(UK Pos)	
1	6	I Will Survive	Gloria Gaynor	Polydor	15	(1)	G L
2	17	Tragedy	Bee Gees	RSO	11	(1)	P
3	1	Da Ya Think I'm Sexy	Rod Stewart	Warner	13	(1)	G
4	15	Heaven Knows	Donna Summer	Casablanca	10	(34)	G
5	-	What A Fool Believes	Doobie Brothers	Warner	10	(31)	G
6	-	Shake Your Groove Thing	Peaches & Herb	Polydor	8	(26)	G
7	5	Fire	Pointer Sisters	Planet	13	(34)	G
8	-	Sultans Of Swing	Dire Straits	Warner	9	(8)	F
9	3	A Little More Love	Olivia Newton-John	MCA	15	(4)	G
10	-	What You Won't Do For Love	Bobby Caldwell	Clouds	6		F L
11	-	Don't Cry Out Loud	Melissa Manchester	Arista	7		
12	2	Y.M.C.A.	Village People	Casablanca	17	(1)	F P
13	4	Le Freak	Chic	Atlantic	17	(7)	P
14	-	Lady	Little River Band	Harvest	7		
15	-	Knock On Wood	Amii Stewart	Ariola	10	(6)	F G L
16	-	Every Time I Think Of You	Babys	Chrysalis	4		L
17	7	Lotta Love	Nicolette Larson	Warner	10		F L
18	-	Big Shot	Billy Joel	Columbia	3		
19	12	Got To Be Real	Cheryl Lynn	Columbia	7		F G L
20	-	I Just Fall In Love Again	Anne Murray	Capitol	7	(58)	

US 1979
JAN-MAR

◆ A UNICEF benefit concert in New York starred The Bee Gees, Olivia Newton-John, Abba, Linda Ronstadt, Rod Stewart, Donna Summer, John Denver and Earth Wind & Fire.

◆ Sid Vicious died of a heroin overdose before his murder trial. Soul star Donny Hathaway leapt to his death, and 1966 No. 1 chart – topper SSgt. Barry Sadler was arrested for killing a songwriter.

◆ The rockumentary *The Heroes Of Rock & Roll* was aired. It included clips of Chuck Berry, Buddy Holly, Bob Dylan, The Beatles, The Rolling Stones, Bruce Springsteen and the two Elvis', Presley and Costello.

◆ Stephen Stills became the first rock artist to record digitally. Digital recording was the biggest advance since stereo. Instead of recording on tape, sounds are sampled 40-50,000 a second, and the information stored in binary numbers.

UK 1979 APR-JUNE

The film *Quadrophenia*, based on The Who album, and featuring Sting and Toyah, premiered in London on the night of The Who's first gig with new drummer Kenny Jones (Keith Moon having died in September 1978). Soon afterwards, The Who's movie *The Kids Are Alright* premiered in New York.

Ex-Beatles Paul McCartney, George Harrison and Ringo Starr played together at Eric Clapton's wedding to Harrison's ex-wife Patti – the subject of Clapton's composition 'Layla'.

Art Garfunkel's 'Bright Eyes', from the animated film *Watership Down*, topped the UK chart selling over a million copies. Surprisingly it failed to chart in his homeland.

For the first time in 16 years The Shadows had two successive Top 10 hits, 'Don't Cry For Me Argentina' and 'Theme From The Deer Hunter'.

April 1979

This Mnth	Prev Mnth	Title	Artist	Label	Wks 20	(US Pos)	
1	-	Bright Eyes	Art Garfunkel	CBS	11		G L
2	-	Cool For Cats	Squeeze	A&M	7		
3	-	Some Girls	Racey	RAK	7		
4	17	In The Navy	Village People	Mercury	6	(3)	
5	1	I Will Survive	Gloria Gaynor	Polydor	9	(1)	
6	-	Shake Your Body (Down To The Ground)	Jacksons	Epic	6	(7)	
7	-	Sultans Of Swing	Dire Straits	Vertigo	5	(4)	F
8	-	He's The Greatest Dancer	Sister Sledge	Atlantic/Cotillion	5	(9)	
9	-	Silly Thing/Who Killed Bambi	Sex Pistols	Virgin	4		
10	-	The Runner	Three Degrees	Ariola	4		
11	7	I Want Your Love	Chic	Atlantic	7	(7)	
12	-	Hallelujah	Milk & Honey	Polydor	4		F L
13	6	Something Else/Friggin' In The Riggin'	Sex Pistols	Virgin	7		
14	-	Pop Muzik	M	MCA	9	(1)	F
15	-	Wow	Kate Bush	EMI	4		
16	-	Turn The Music Up	Players Association	Vanguard	4		F L
17	-	I Don't Wanna Lose You	Kandidate	RAK	5		F L
18	4	Lucky Number	Lene Lovich	Stiff	7		F
19	2	Oliver's Army	Elvis Costello	Radar	9		
20	-	The Logical Song	Supertramp	A&M	5	(6)	

May 1979

This Mnth	Prev Mnth	Title	Artist	Label	Wks 20	(US Pos)	
1	1	Bright Eyes	Art Garfunkel	CBS	11		G L
2	14	Pop Muzik	M	MCA	9	(1)	F
3	-	Hooray Hooray It's A Holi-Holiday	Boney M	Atlantic/Hansa	6		
4	-	Does Your Mother Know	Abba	Epic	6	(19)	
5	-	Knock On Wood	Amii Stewart	Atlantic/Hansa	6	(1)	F
6	-	Reunited	Peaches & Herb	CBS	7	(1)	F L
7	3	Some Girls	Racey	RAK	7		
8	-	Goodnight Tonight	Wings	Parlophone	5	(5)	
9	20	The Logical Song	Supertramp	A&M	5	(6)	
10	-	Dance Away	Roxy Music	Polydor	10	(44)	
11	-	One Way Ticket	Eruption	Atlantic/Hansa	6		L
12	-	Sunday Girl	Blondie	Chrysalis	8		
13	-	Banana Splits (Tra La La Song)	Dickies	A&M	3		F L
14	6	Shake Your Body (Down To The...)	Jacksons	Epic	6	(7)	
15	-	Parisienne Walkways	Gary Moore	MCA	5		F
16	12	Hallelujah	Milk & Honey	Polydor	4		F L
17	-	Love You Inside Out	Bee Gees	RSO	3	(1)	
18	-	Boys Keep Swingin'	David Bowie	RCA	6		
19	-	Roxanne	Police	A&M	5	(32)	F
20	2	Cool For Cats	Squeeze	A&M	7		

June 1979

This Mnth	Prev Mnth	Title	Artist	Label	Wks 20	(US Pos)	
1	10	Dance Away	Roxy Music	Polydor	10	(44)	
2	12	Sunday Girl	Blondie	Chrysalis	8		
3	-	Boogie Wonderland	Earth, Wind & Fire With The Emotions	CBS	7	(6)	
4	-	Ring My Bell	Anita Ward	TK	7	(1)	F L
5	-	Ain't No Stoppin' Us Now	McFadden & Whitehead	Philly Int.	6	(13)	F L
6	-	Theme From The Deer Hunter (Cavatina)	Shadows	EMI	6		
7	-	Are 'Friends' Electric	Tubeway Army	Beggars Banquet	10		F L
8	-	Shine A Little Love	Electric Light Orchestra	Jet	6	(8)	
9	6	Reunited	Peaches & Herb	CBS	7	(1)	F L
10	-	Up The Junction	Squeeze	A&M	6		
11	-	We Are Family	Sister Sledge	Atlantic	4	(2)	
12	2	Pop Muzik	M	MCA	9	(1)	F
13	-	The Lone Ranger	Quantum Jump	Electric	5		F L
14	-	Hot Stuff	Donna Summer	Casablanca	4	(1)	
15	18	Boys Keep Swingin'	David Bowie	RCA	6		
16	-	H.A.P.P.Y. Radio	Edwin Starr	RCA	5	(79)	L
17	4	Does Your Mother Know	Abba	Epic	6	(19)	
18	-	Masquerade	Skids	Virgin	4		
19	15	Parisienne Walkways	Gary Moore	MCA	5		F
20	-	Night Owl	Gerry Rafferty	UA	5		L

April 1979

This Mnth	Prev Mnth	Title	Artist	Label	Wks 20	(UK Pos)	
1	1	I Will Survive	Gloria Gaynor	Polydor	15	(1)	G L
2	15	Knock On Wood	Amii Stewart	Ariola	10	(6)	F G L
3	5	What A Fool Believes	Doobie Brothers	Warner	10	(31)	G
4	-	Music Box Dancer	Frank Mills	Polydor	8		F G L
5	-	Heart Of Glass	Blondie	Chrysalis	10	(1)	F G
6	-	Reunited	Peaches & Herb	Polydor	13	(4)	P
7	2	Tragedy	Bee Gees	RSO	11	(1)	P
8	8	Sultans Of Swing	Dire Straits	Warner	9	(8)	F
9	-	Stumblin' In	Suzi Quatro & Chris Norman	RSO	10	(41)	F G L
10	-	I Want Your Love	Chic	Atlantic	8	(4)	G
11	-	Goodnight Tonight	Wings	Columbia	11	(5)	G
12	-	In The Navy	Village People	Casablanca	9	(2)	G L
13	14	Lady	Little River Band	Harvest	7		
14	-	He's The Greatest Dancer	Sister Sledge	Cotillion	8	(6)	F
15	-	Take Me Home	Cher	Casablanca	7		G
16	20	I Just Fall In Love Again	Anne Murray	Capitol	7	(58)	
17	6	Shake Your Groove Thing	Peaches & Herb	Polydor	8	(26)	G
18	3	Da Ya Think I'm Sexy	Rod Stewart	Warner	13	(1)	G
19	-	Livin' It Up (Friday Night)	Bell & James	A&M	3	(59)	F G L
20	-	Shake Your Body (Down To The Ground)	Jacksons	Epic	11	(4)	G

May 1979

This Mnth	Prev Mnth	Title	Artist	Label	Wks 20	(UK Pos)	
1	6	Reunited	Peaches & Herb	Polydor	13	(4)	P
2	12	In The Navy	Village People	Casablanca	9	(2)	G L
3	9	Stumblin' In	Suzi Quatro & Chris Norman	RSO	10	(41)	F G L
4	11	Goodnight Tonight	Wings	Columbia	11	(5)	G
5	-	Hot Stuff	Donna Summer	Casablanca	16	(11)	G
6	5	Heart Of Glass	Blondie	Chrysalis	10	(1)	F G
7	20	Shake Your Body (Down To The Ground)	Jacksons	Epic	11	(4)	G
8	-	Love You Inside Out	Bee Gees	RSO	10	(13)	G
9	2	Knock On Wood	Amii Stewart	Ariola	10	(6)	F G L
10	14	He's The Greatest Dancer	Sister Sledge	Cotillion	8	(6)	F
11	15	Take Me Home	Cher	Casablanca	7		G
12	-	Love Is The Answer	England Dan/John Ford Coley	Big Tree	7		L
13	10	I Want Your Love	Chic	Atlantic	8	(4)	G
14	-	Love Takes Time	Orleans	Infinity	5		L
15	4	Music Box Dancer	Frank Mills	Polydor	8		F G L
16	-	We Are Family	Sister Sledge	Cotillion	9	(8)	G L
17	-	Just When I Needed You Most	Randy Vanwarmer	Bearsville	9	(8)	F G L
18	-	The Logical Song	Supertramp	A&M	10	(7)	
19	-	Disco Nights (Rock Freak)	G.Q.	Arista	6	(42)	F G
20	3	What A Fool Believes	Doobie Brothers	Warner	10	(31)	G

June 1979

This Mnth	Prev Mnth	Title	Artist	Label	Wks 20	(UK Pos)	
1	5	Hot Stuff	Donna Summer	Casablanca	16	(11)	G
2	16	We Are Family	Sister Sledge	Cotillion	9	(8)	G L
3	17	Just When I Needed You Most	Randy Vanwarmer	Bearsville	9	(8)	F G L
4	8	Love You Inside Out	Bee Gees	RSO	10	(13)	G
5	-	Ring My Bell	Anita Ward	Juana	13	(1)	F G L
6	18	The Logical Song	Supertramp	A&M	10	(7)	
7	-	Chuck E.'s In Love	Rickie Lee Jones	Warner	9	(18)	F L
8	1	Reunited	Peaches & Herb	Polydor	13	(4)	P
9	-	She Believes In Me	Kenny Rogers	UA	9	(42)	G
10	-	Bad Girls	Donna Summer	Casablanca	12	(14)	G
11	-	You Take My Breath Away	Rex Smith	Columbia	7		F G L
12	-	Boogie Wonderland	Earth, Wind & Fire With The Emotions	Arc	9	(4)	
13	7	Shake Your Body (Down To The Ground)	Jacksons	Epic	11	(4)	G
14	4	Goodnight Tonight	Wings	Columbia	11	(5)	G
15	-	Rock 'n' Roll Fantasy	Bad Company	Swan Song	6		
16	19	Disco Nights (Rock Freak)	G.Q.	Arista	6	(42)	F G
17	-	Minute By Minute	Doobie Brothers	Warner	5	(47)	
18	-	Deeper Than The Night	Olivia Newton-John	MCA	4	(64)	
19	-	Makin' It	David Naughton	RSO	11		F G L
20	2	In The Navy	Village People	Casablanca	9	(2)	G L

▲ African-Americans with top transatlantic hits included: Earth Wind & Fire (above) with The Emotions, Peaches & Herb, Anita Ward, McFadden & Whitehead, Donna Summer, Amii Stewart and The Jacksons.

◆ The California Music Festival starred top US rockers Van Halen (prior to their ten month world tour), Cheap Trick, Aerosmith, Ted Nugent and Ireland's Boomtown Rats (with Bob Geldof).

◆ Lowell George, the well-respected leader of recently disbanded rock group Little Feat, died of drug related causes.

UK 1979 JULY-SEPT

▲ West Indian sounds continued to gain popularity thanks in part to ska-based 2-Tone music, whose foremost purveyors, The Specials and Madness (above), debuted on the British chart.

◆ *Rolling Stone* called videotapes "The newest selling tool in rock", citing David Bowie's 'Boys Keep Swinging' and Queen's 'Bohemian Rhapsody' as good examples.

◆ Electro-pop pioneer Gary Numan quickly duplicated his group, Tubeway Army's, No. 1 single and album successes with the solo releases 'Cars' and **The Pleasure Principle.**

July 1979

This Mnth	Prev Mnth	Title	Artist	Label	Wks 20	(US Pos)	
1	7	**Are 'Friends' Electric**	Tubeway Army	Beggars Banquet	10		F L
2	-	**Silly Games**	Janet Kay	Scope	6		F L
3	-	**C'mon Everybody**	Sex Pistols	Virgin	5		L
4	-	**Light My Fire/137 Disco Heaven (Medley)**	Amii Stewart	Atlantic	5	(69)	
5	10	**Up The Junction**	Squeeze	A&M	6		
6	20	**Night Owl**	Gerry Rafferty	UA	5		L
7	-	**Lady Lynda**	Beach Boys	Caribou	4		
8	-	**Good Times**	Chic	Atlantic	5	(1)	
9	-	**Wanted**	Dooleys	GTO	7		
10	-	**Girls Talk**	Dave Edmunds	Swansong	5	(65)	
11	4	**Ring My Bell**	Anita Ward	TK	7	(1)	F L
12	-	**Babylon's Burning**	Ruts	Virgin	4		F L
13	-	**I Don't Like Mondays**	Boomtown Rats	Ensign	9	(73)	
14	13	**The Lone Ranger**	Quantum Jump	Electric	5		F L
15	1	**Dance Away**	Roxy Music	Polydor	10	(44)	
16	-	**Living On The Front Line**	Eddy Grant	Ensign	4		F
17	-	**Breakfast In America**	Supertramp	A&M	4	(62)	L
18	-	**Maybe**	Thom Pace	RSO	4		F L
19	-	**Born To Be Alive**	Patrick Hernandez	Gem	5	(16)	F L
20	-	**My Sharona**	Knack	Capitol	3	(1)	F L

August 1979

This Mnth	Prev Mnth	Title	Artist	Label	Wks 20	(US Pos)	
1	13	**I Don't Like Mondays**	Boomtown Rats	Ensign	9	(73)	
2	-	**We Don't Talk Anymore**	Cliff Richard	EMI	10	(7)	
3	-	**Angel Eyes/Voulez Vous**	Abba	Epic	6	(64)	
4	-	**Can't Stand Losing You**	Police	A&M	6		
5	9	**Wanted**	Dooleys	GTO	7		
6	-	**Reasons To Be Cheerful (Pt 3)**	Ian Dury & The Blockheads	Stiff	5		L
7	-	**Hersham Boys**	Sham 69	Polydor	4		L
8	-	**After The Love Has Gone**	Earth, Wind & Fire	CBS	6	(2)	
9	-	**The Diary Of Horace Wimp**	Electric Light Orchestra	Jet	5		
10	-	**Beat The Clock**	Sparks	Virgin	4		L
11	10	**Girls Talk**	Dave Edmunds	Swansong	5	(65)	
12	-	**Duke Of Earl**	Darts	Magnet	6		
13	-	**Bang Bang**	B.A. Robertson	Asylum	7		F
14	19	**Born To Be Alive**	Patrick Hernandez	Gem	5	(16)	F L
15	20	**My Sharona**	Knack	Capitol	3	(1)	F L
16	-	**Gangsters**	Specials	2 Tone	6		F
17	17	**Breakfast In America**	Supertramp	A&M	4	(62)	L
18	-	**Angel Eyes**	Roxy Music	Polydor	7		
19	2	**Silly Games**	Janet Kay	Scope	6		F L
20	1	**Are 'Friends' Electric**	Tubeway Army	Beggars Banquet	10		F L

September 1979

This Mnth	Prev Mnth	Title	Artist	Label	Wks 20	(US Pos)	
1	2	**We Don't Talk Anymore**	Cliff Richard	EMI	10	(7)	
2	-	**Cars**	Gary Numan	Beggars Banquet	8	(9)	F
3	13	**Bang Bang**	B.A. Robertson	Asylum	7		F
4	-	**Street Life**	Crusaders	MCA	6	(36)	F L
5	-	**Don't Bring Me Down**	Electric Light Orchestra	Jet	6	(4)	
6	18	**Angel Eyes**	Roxy Music	Polydor	7		
7	-	**If I Said You Had A Beautiful Body, Would You Hold It Against Me**	Bellamy Brothers	Warner	7	(39)	L
8	-	**Just When I Needed You Most**	Randy Vanwarmer	Bearsville	5	(4)	F L
9	-	**Love's Gotta Hold On Me**	Dollar	Carrere	6		
10	-	**Money**	Flying Lizards	Virgin	5	(50)	F L
11	16	**Gangsters**	Specials	2 Tone	6		F
12	1	**I Don't Like Mondays**	Boomtown Rats	Ensign	9	(73)	
13	-	**Message In A Bottle**	Police	A&M	7	(74)	
14	8	**After The Love Has Gone**	Earth, Wind & Fire	CBS	6	(2)	
15	-	**Gotta Go Home/El Lute**	Boney M	Atlantic/Hansa	4		L
16	-	**Ooh! What A Life**	Gibson Brothers	Island	5		F
17	-	**Strut Your Funky Stuff**	Frantique	Philly Int.	4		F L
18	-	**Sail On**	Commodores	Motown	4	(4)	
19	12	**Duke Of Earl**	Darts	Magnet	6		
20	-	**Reggae For It Now**	Bill Lovelady	Charisma	4		F L

July 1979

This Mnth	Prev Mnth	Title	Artist	Label	Wks 20	(UK Pos)	
1	10	Bad Girls	Donna Summer	Casablanca	12	(14)	G
2	5	Ring My Bell	Anita Ward	Juana	13	(1)	F G L
3	1	Hot Stuff	Donna Summer	Casablanca	16	(11)	G
4	19	Makin' It	David Naughton	RSO	11		F G L
5	12	Boogie Wonderland	Earth, Wind & Fire With The Emotions	Arc	9	(4)	
6	-	I Want You To Want Me	Cheap Trick	Epic	9	(29)	F G
7	-	Gold	John Stewart	RSO	9	(43)	F L
8	9	She Believes In Me	Kenny Rogers	UA	9	(42)	G
9	-	Shine A Little Love	Electric Light Orchestra	Jet	9	(6)	
10	-	Good Times	Chic	Atlantic	11	(5)	G L
11	7	Chuck E.'s In Love	Rickie Lee Jones	Warner	9	(18)	F L
12	-	When You're In Love With A Beautiful Woman	Dr. Hook	Capitol	10	(1)	G
13	6	The Logical Song	Supertramp	A&M	10	(7)	
14	-	Ain't No Stoppin' Us Now	McFadden & Whitehead	Philly Int.	7	(5)	F P L
15	2	We Are Family	Sister Sledge	Cotillion	9	(8)	G L
16	-	I Can't Stand It No More	Peter Frampton	A&M	4		L
17	-	You Can't Change That	Raydio	Arista	7		
18	-	The Main Event/Fight	Barbra Streisand	Columbia	9		G
19	-	Dance The Night Away	Van Halen	Warner	4		F
20	4	Love You Inside Out	Bee Gees	RSO	10	(13)	G

August 1979

This Mnth	Prev Mnth	Title	Artist	Label	Wks 20	(UK Pos)	
1	10	Good Times	Chic	Atlantic	11	(5)	G L
2	1	Bad Girls	Donna Summer	Casablanca	12	(14)	G
3	-	My Sharona	Knack	Capitol	14	(6)	F G
4	18	The Main Event/Fight	Barbra Streisand	Columbia	9		G
5	2	Ring My Bell	Anita Ward	Juana	13	(1)	F G L
6	12	When You're In Love With A Beautiful Woman	Dr. Hook	Capitol	10	(1)	G
7	-	Mama Can't Buy You Love	Elton John	MCA	8		G
8	17	You Can't Change That	Raydio	Arista	7		
9	-	After The Love Has Gone	Earth, Wind & Fire	Arc	10	(4)	G
10	7	Gold	John Stewart	RSO	9	(43)	F L
11	4	Makin' It	David Naughton	RSO	11		F G L
12	-	Sad Eyes	Robert John	EMI America	13	(31)	G L
13	-	I Was Made For Lovin' You	Kiss	Casablanca	6	(50)	G
14	-	Lead Me On	Maxine Nightingale	Windsong	9		G L
15	-	The Devil Went Down To Georgia	Charlie Daniels Band	Epic	8	(14)	G
16	3	Hot Stuff	Donna Summer	Casablanca	16	(11)	G
17	-	Don't Bring Me Down	Electric Light Orchestra	Jet	10	(3)	G
18	6	I Want You To Want Me	Cheap Trick	Epic	9	(29)	F G
19	-	I'll Never Love This Way Again	Dionne Warwick	Arista	14		G
20	14	Ain't No Stoppin' Us Now	McFadden & Whitehead	Philly Int.	7	(5)	F P L

September 1979

This Mnth	Prev Mnth	Title	Artist	Label	Wks 20	(UK Pos)	
1	3	My Sharona	Knack	Capitol	14	(6)	F G
2	9	After The Love Has Gone	Earth, Wind & Fire	Arc	10	(4)	G
3	15	The Devil Went Down To Georgia	Charlie Daniels Band	Epic	8	(14)	G
4	12	Sad Eyes	Robert John	EMI America	13	(31)	G L
5	17	Don't Bring Me Down	Electric Light Orchestra	Jet	10	(3)	G
6	14	Lead Me On	Maxine Nightingale	Windsong	9		G L
7	-	Lonesome Loser	Little River Band	Capitol	9		
8	19	I'll Never Love This Way Again	Dionne Warwick	Arista	14		G
9	1	Good Times	Chic	Atlantic	11	(5)	G L
10	-	Sail On	Commodores	Motown	10	(8)	
11	-	Rise	Herb Alpert	A&M	13	(13)	G
12	7	Mama Can't Buy You Love	Elton John	MCA	8		G
13	-	Don't Stop Till You Get Enough	Michael Jackson	Epic	9	(3)	G
14	4	The Main Event/Fight	Barbra Streisand	Columbia	9		G
15	-	Heaven Must Have Sent You	Bonnie Pointer	Motown	8		F L
16	-	Let's Go	Cars	Elektra	4	(51)	F
17	-	Bad Case Of Loving You (Doctor, Doctor)	Robert Palmer	Island	5	(61)	
18	-	Cruel To Be Kind	Nick Lowe	Columbia	4	(12)	F L
19	-	Goodbye Stranger	Supertramp	A&M	5	(57)	
20	-	Pop Muzik	M	Sire	13	(2)	F G L

US 1979 JULY-SEPT

◆ Chic, the disco group featuring Bernard Edwards and Nile Rodgers (producer/ writers of Sister Sledge's hits), scored their fourth transatlantic Top 10 hit, 'Good Times'.

◆ Recent hit makers Van McCoy ('The Hustle') and Minnie Ripperton ('Loving You') died, as did Norrie Paramor, arguably Britain's most successful record producer.

◆ The *No Nukes* shows at Madison Square Garden featured such headliners as Bruce Springsteen, James Taylor, The Doobie Brothers and Crosby, Stills & Nash. Other successful live shows included The Cars in Central Park, The Who (plus AC/DC and The Stranglers) at Wembley, and Led Zeppelin's first UK date for four years at Knebworth. Zeppelin, incidentally, scored their eighth and last successive UK No. 1 LP with **In Through The Out Door.**

UK 1979
OCT-DEC

◆ Almost overnight The Police became teen idols. They had two consecutive chart toppers, 'Message in A Bottle' and 'Walking on The Moon', and the first of five successive No. 1 LPs, **Regatta De Blanc.**

▲ Among the year's top record deals were Paul McCartney signing to Columbia for $20 million, and Paul Simon's (above) seven album deal with Warner, which was reportedly worth $14 million.

◆ As the decade closed, The Sugarhill Gang's 'Rapper's Delight' introduced the world to rap music. Initially rap was considered a novelty that could not possibly have a future!

October 1979

This Mnth	Prev Mnth	Title	Artist	Label	Wks 20	(US Pos)	
1	-	Video Killed The Radio Star	Buggles	Island	6	(40)	F
2	13	Message In A Bottle	Police	A&M	7	(74)	
3	-	Don't Stop Till You Get Enough	Michael Jackson	Epic	7	(1)	
4	-	Dreaming	Blondie	Chrysalis	6	(27)	
5	-	Whatever You Want	Status Quo	Vertigo	6		
6	-	Since You've Been Gone	Rainbow	Polydor	6	(57)	F
7	-	One Day At A Time	Lena Martell	Pye	8		F L
8	-	Every Day Hurts	Sad Café	RCA	6		F
9	2	Cars	Gary Numan	Beggars Banquet	8	(9)	F
10	7	If I Said You Had A Beautiful Body...	Bellamy Brothers	Warner	7	(39)	L
11	-	When You're In Love With A Beautiful Woman	Dr. Hook	Capitol	9	(6)	
12	-	The Chosen Few	Dooleys	GTO	5		L
13	-	Kate Bush On Stage E.P.	Kate Bush	EMI	3		
14	9	Love's Gotta Hold On Me	Dollar	Carrere	6		
15	-	Queen Of Hearts	Dave Edmunds	Swansong	5		L
16	-	O.K. Fred	Erroll Dunkley	Scope	5		F L
17	-	Cruel To Be Kind	Nick Lowe	Radar	5	(12)	L
18	18	Sail On	Commodores	Motown	4	(4)	
19	-	Gimme Gimme Gimme (A Man After Midnight)	Abba	Epic	6		
20	-	Tusk	Fleetwood Mac	Warner	5	(8)	

November 1979

This Mnth	Prev Mnth	Title	Artist	Label	Wks 20	(US Pos)	
1	11	When You're In Love With A...	Dr. Hook	Capitol	9	(6)	
2	7	One Day At A Time	Lena Martell	Pye	8		F L
3	-	Crazy Little Thing Called Love	Queen	EMI	7	(1)	
4	19	Gimme Gimme Gimme (A Man...)	Abba	Epic	6		
5	-	The Eton Rifles	Jam	Polydor	5		
6	8	Every Day Hurts	Sad Café	RCA	6		F
7	-	Still	Commodores	Motown	6	(1)	
8	20	Tusk	Fleetwood Mac	Warner	5	(8)	
9	-	Gonna Get Along Without You Now	Viola Wills	Ariola/Hansa	5		F L
10	-	On My Radio	Selecter	2 Tone	3		F
11	-	She's In Love With You	Suzi Quatro	RAK	4	(41)	L
12	1	Video Killed The Radio Star	Buggles	Island	6	(40)	F
13	-	The Sparrow	Ramblers	Decca	5		F L
14	-	No More Tears (Enough Is Enough)	Barbra Streisand & Donna Summer	Casablanca/CBS	8	(1)	
15	-	A Message To You Rudy/Nite Klub	Specials	2 Tone	4		
16	12	The Chosen Few	Dooleys	GTO	5		L
17	3	Don't Stop Till You Get Enough	Michael Jackson	Epic	7	(1)	
18	16	O.K. Fred	Erroll Dunkley	Scope	5		F L
19	-	Knocked It Off	B.A. Robertson	Asylum	4		
20	-	Ladies Night	Kool & The Gang	Mercury	4	(8)	F

December 1979

This Mnth	Prev Mnth	Title	Artist	Label	Wks 20	(US Pos)	
1	-	Walking On The Moon	Police	A&M	7		
2	-	Another Brick In The Wall (Pt. 2)	Pink Floyd	Harvest	8	(1)	G L
3	14	No More Tears (Enough Is Enough)	Barbra Streisand & D. Summer	Casablanca/CBS	8	(1)	
4	-	Que Sera Mi Vida (If You Should Go)	Gibson Brothers	Island	8		
5	-	I Only Want To Be With You	Tourists	Logo	7	(83)	F
6	-	Rapper's Delight	Sugarhill Gang	Sugarhill	7	(36)	F L
7	1	When You're In Love With A...	Dr. Hook	Capitol	9	(6)	
8	-	Confusion/Last Train To London	Electric Light Orchestra	Jet	6	(37)	
9	3	Crazy Little Thing Called Love	Queen	EMI	7	(1)	
10	-	One Step Beyond	Madness	Stiff	6		
11	-	I Have A Dream	Abba	Epic	6		
12	-	My Simple Heart	Three Degrees	Ariola	6		L
13	-	Day Trip To Bangor (Didn't We Have A Lovely Time)	Fiddler's Dram	Dingles	5		F L
14	-	Complex	Gary Numan	Beggars Banquet	4		
15	-	Off The Wall	Michael Jackson	Epic	4	(10)	
16	7	Still	Commodores	Motown	6	(1)	
17	-	Wonderful Christmastime	Paul McCartney	Parlophone	5		
18	-	Union City Blue	Blondie	Chrysalis	5		
19	-	Brass In Pocket	Pretenders	Real	9	(14)	F
20	5	The Eton Rifles	Jam	Polydor	5		

US 1979 OCT-DEC

October 1979

This Mnth	Prev Mnth	Title	Artist	Label	Wks 20	(UK Pos)	
1	11	Rise	Herb Alpert	A&M	13	(13)	G
2	13	Don't Stop Till You Get Enough	Michael Jackson	Epic	9	(3)	G
3	10	Sail On	Commodores	Motown	10	(8)	
4	20	Pop Muzik	M	Sire	13	(2)	F G L
5	4	Sad Eyes	Robert John	EMI America	13	(31)	G L
6	8	I'll Never Love This Way Again	Dionne Warwick	Arista	14		G
7	-	Dim All The Lights	Donna Summer	Casablanca	11	(29)	
8	1	My Sharona	Knack	Capitol	14	(6)	F G
9	7	Lonesome Loser	Little River Band	Capitol	9		
10	-	Heartache Tonight	Eagles	Asylum	12	(40)	G
11	15	Heaven Must Have Sent You	Bonnie Pointer	Motown	8		F L
12	-	You Decorated My Life	Kenny Rogers	UA	8		
13	-	Still	Commodores	Motown	13	(4)	G
14	2	After The Love Has Gone	Earth, Wind & Fire	Arc	10	(4)	G
15	-	Dirty White Boy	Foreigner	Atlantic	5		
16	-	Tusk	Fleetwood Mac	Warner	7	(6)	
17	5	Don't Bring Me Down	Electric Light Orchestra	Jet	10	(3)	G
18	18	Cruel To Be Kind	Nick Lowe	Columbia	4	(12)	F L
19	-	Please Don't Go	KC & The Sunshine Band	TK	15	(3)	
20	-	Born To Be Alive	Patrick Hernandez	Columbia	5	(10)	F G L

November 1979

This Mnth	Prev Mnth	Title	Artist	Label	Wks 20	(UK Pos)	
1	7	Dim All The Lights	Donna Summer	Casablanca	11	(29)	G
2	13	Still	Commodores	Motown	13	(4)	G
3	10	Heartache Tonight	Eagles	Asylum	12	(40)	G
4	-	Babe	Styx	A&M	12	(6)	G
5	-	No More Tears (Enough Is Enough)	Barbra Streisand & Donna Summer	Casablanca/CBS	9	(3)	G
6	4	Pop Muzik	M	Sire	13	(2)	F G L
7	1	Rise	Herb Alpert	A&M	13	(13)	G
8	12	You Decorated My Life	Kenny Rogers	UA	8		
9	16	Tusk	Fleetwood Mac	Warner	7	(6)	
10	19	Please Don't Go	KC & The Sunshine Band	TK	15	(3)	
11	-	Ships	Barry Manilow	Arista	8		
12	2	Don't Stop Till You Get Enough	Michael Jackson	Epic	9	(3)	G
13	-	Good Girls Don't	Knack	Capitol	5	(66)	L
14	-	Send One Your Love	Stevie Wonder	Tamla	12	(52)	
15	15	Dirty White Boy	Foreigner	Atlantic	5		
16	6	I'll Never Love This Way Again	Dionne Warwick	Arista	14		G
17	-	Broken Hearted Me	Anne Murray	Capitol	5		
18	-	Come To Me	France Joli	Prelude	4		F L
19	-	You're Only Lonely	J.D. Souther	Columbia	8		F
20	-	Take The Long Way Home	Supertramp	A&M	7		

December 1979

This Mnth	Prev Mnth	Title	Artist	Label	Wks 20	(UK Pos)	
1	4	Babe	Styx	A&M	12	(6)	G
2	10	Please Don't Go	KC & The Sunshine Band	TK	15	(3)	
3	-	Escape (The Pina Colada Song)	Rupert Holmes	Infinity	12	(23)	F G
4	2	Still	Commodores	Motown	13	(4)	G
5	5	No More Tears (Enough Is Enough)	Barbra Streisand & Donna Summer	Casablanca/CBS	9	(3)	G
6	14	Send One Your Love	Stevie Wonder	Tamla	12	(52)	
7	19	You're Only Lonely	J.D. Souther	Columbia	8		F
8	-	Do That To Me One More Time	Captain & Tennille	Casablanca	17	(7)	G L
9	20	Take The Long Way Home	Supertramp	A&M	7		
10	-	Ladies Night	Kool & The Gang	De-Lite	10	(9)	G
11	3	Heartache Tonight	Eagles	Asylum	12	(40)	G
12	-	Cool Change	Little River Band	Capitol	9		
13	-	Rock With You	Michael Jackson	Epic	13	(7)	G
14	11	Ships	Barry Manilow	Arista	8		
15	-	We Don't Talk Anymore	Cliff Richard	EMI America	10	(1)	
16	-	Head Games	Foreigner	Atlantic	6		
17	6	Pop Muzik	M	Sire	13	(2)	F G L
18	17	Broken Hearted Me	Anne Murray	Capitol	5		
19	1	Dim All The Lights	Donna Summer	Casablanca	11	(29)	G
20	-	Better Love Next Time	Dr. Hook	Capitol	8	(8)	

◆ In 1979, the value of record sales in the USA dropped 11% to $3.7 billion (albums accounting for 90% of the total), and platinum and gold record awards plummeted by almost 50%. The decrease in disco sales and increase in home taping were thought to be the main causes.

◆ A survey showed that 50% of the highest rated American radio stations were broadcasting on FM.

◆ Eleven fans were crushed to death in the rush for good seats at a Who concert in Cincinatti.

◆ The Eagles' Grammy winning fifth and last chart topper, 'Heartache Tonight', came from their fourth successive No. 1 album, **The Long Run.**

80s

Chrissie Hynde

Blondie

Michael Hutchence of INXS

Left: Prince

The 1980s was a decade when rock music continued to diversify. The ever expanding fields of heavy metal and rap added excitement to the scene, and dance music recovered from the death of disco to flourish in the latter part of the ten-year period. It was also a time when female vocalists, led by Madonna Louise Ciccone, smashed down invisible barriers, more recording artists than ever before became millionaires, and British performers staged a second major invasion of the USA.

Top US Artists in UK 1980-89	
1	Madonna
2	Michael Jackson
3	Stevie Wonder
4	Prince
5	Whitney Houston
6	Kool & The Gang
7	Lionel Richie
8	Diana Ross
9	Blondie
10	Gloria Estefan

80s

Rock, which reached thirty-something during the decade, gained a respectability it had previously never enjoyed. Veteran acts like Paul McCartney, The Rolling Stones and The Who packed stadiums world-wide, alongside contemporary superstars such as Dire Straits, Michael Jackson, Bruce Springsteen and U2. Another of the era's great success stories, Prince, showed that white rock added to black music was a winning combination, while artists such as New Kids On The Block, Rick Astley, Lisa Stansfield and Paul Young again proved that sounding black was no hindrance to a white act's career.

Top UK Artists in US 1980-89	
1	Phil Collins
2	George Michael
3	Duran Duran
4	Paul McCartney
5	Billy Ocean
6	Elton John
7	Olivia Newton-John
8	Culture Club
9	Rod Stewart
10	Sheena Easton

The 1980s also saw the rise in importance of female vocalists like Madonna, Whitney Houston, Janet Jackson and Kylie Minogue in Britain, who dominated the charts and shattered many records previously held by the their male counterparts.

On the technical front, it was the decade when CDs came, conquered and virtually made vinyl extinct. Encouraged by the superior quality of sound made possible by CD, consumer spending on recorded music spiralled as worn-out vinyl recordings were replaced by CD versions. New sales records were set: an estimated 40 million people purchased Michael Jackson's *Thriller,* making it the best-selling album of all time. In Britain, fuelled by CD sales, Dire Straits' *Brothers In Arms* became the first album to top the three million sales mark.

Cher

With the advent of MTV, the video also grew in importance and became the essential marketing tool for a single. This meant that an artist's image became as important as their sound, which no doubt helped the careers of photogenic performers such as Culture Club, Duran Duran and New Kids On The Block. Videos became more sophisticated and the production of a video was almost as important as the song itself.

Above all though, the 1980s will be best remembered as the decade of the charity record. Many previous recording projects and live shows had donated their proceeds to good causes, but it took Bob Geldof's Band Aid/Live Aid venture in 1984/1985 to capture the public's imagination and really start the charity bandwagon rolling. By the time the decade faded into history, vast fortunes had been raised to help the needy, with Band Aid alone amassing $140 (£90) million.

Milli Vanilli

Frankie Goes to Hollywood   *Bon Jovi*

Pet Shop Boys

Top Singles Artists in the UK 1980-89

1	Madonna	(US)	Sire/Geffen
2	Shakin' Stevens	(UK)	Epic
3	Michael Jackson	(US)	Epic/Motown
4	Cliff Richard	(UK)	EMI
5	Madness	(UK)	Stiff
6	David Bowie	(UK)	RCA/EMI America/Virgin
7	UB40	(UK)	Graduate/Dep International
8	Phil Collins	(UK)	Virgin
9	Duran Duran	(UK)	EMI/Parlophone
10	Wham!	(UK)	Innervision/Epic
11	Adam & The Ants	(UK)	CBS/Decca/Ego
12	Queen	(UK)	EMI/Parlophone
13	Pet Shop Boys	(UK)	Parlophone
14	Paul McCartney	(UK)	Parlophone
15	Spandau Ballet	(UK)	Reformation/Chrysalis
16	Status Quo	(UK)	Vertigo
17	Bananarama	(UK)	Deram/London
18	Kylie Minogue	(Aus)	PWL
19	Stevie Wonder	(US)	Motown
20	Police	(UK/US)	A&M

Sting

Top Singles Artists in the US 1980-89

1	Michael Jackson	(US)	Epic
2	Madonna	(US)	Sire/Geffen
3	Daryl Hall & John Oates	(US)	RCA/Arista
4	Prince	(US)	Warner/Paisley Park
5	Lionel Richie	(US)	Motown
6	Phil Collins	(UK)	Atlantic
7	Whitney Houston	(US)	Arista
8	Huey Lewis & The News	(US)	Chrysalis
9	George Michael	(UK)	Columbia
10	Duran Duran	(UK)	Harvest/Capitol
11	Billy Joel	(US)	Columbia
12	John Cougar Mellencamp	(US)	Riva/Mercury
13	Kenny Rogers	(US)	UA/Liberty /RCA
14	Bruce Springsteen	(US)	Columbia
15	Kool & The Gang	(US)	De-Lite/Mercury
16	Air Supply	(Aus)	Arista
17	Bon Jovi	(US)	Mercury
18	Cyndi Lauper	(US)	Portrait/Epic
19	Stevie Wonder	(US)	Tamla /Motown
20	Chicago	(US)	Full Moon/Warner/Reprise

Top US Singles 1980-89

1	Physical	Olivia Newton-John
2	Bette Davis Eyes	Kim Carnes
3	Endless Love	Diana Ross & Lionel Richie
4	Every Breath You Take	Police
5	Eye Of The Tiger	Survivor
6	Flashdance....What A Feeling	Irene Cara
7	I Love Rock 'n' Roll	Joan Jett & The Blackhearts
8	Say Say Say	Paul McCartney & Michael Jackson
9	Call Me	Blondie
10	Ebony And Ivory	Paul McCartney & Stevie Wonder

Top UK Singles 1980-89

1	Relax	Frankie Goes To Hollywood
2	Do They Know It's Christmas?	Band Aid
3	Blue Monday	New Order
4	In The Air Tonight	Phil Collins
5	Two Tribes	Frankie Goes To Hollywood
6	Last Christmas	Wham!
7	Drive	Cars
8	Holiday	Madonna
9	Ride On Time	Black Box
10	I Just Called To Say I Love You	Stevie Wonder

UK 1980
JAN-MAR

◆ American records faring better in Britain included chart toppers 'Together We Are Beautiful' by Fern Kinney and 'Atomic' by Blondie.

◆ Among the past hit makers who died as the decade dawned were Mantovani (the most successful British act in the US before The Beatles), R&B legends Amos Milburn and Professor Longhair, early rocker Larry Williams and million selling 1950s British balladeer David Whitfield.

▲ The first indie LP chart in the UK showed **Dirk Wears White Socks** by Adam & The Ants at No. 1.

January 1980

This Mnth	Prev Mnth	Title	Artist	Label	Wks 20	(US Pos)	
1	19	Brass In Pocket	Pretenders	Real	9	(14)	F
2	2	Another Brick In The Wall (Pt. 2)	Pink Floyd	Harvest	8	(1)	G L
3	11	I Have A Dream	Abba	Epic	6		
4	-	Please Don't Go	KC & The Sunshine Band	TK	6	(1)	
5	-	With You I'm Born Again	Billy Preston & Syreeta	Motown	5	(4)	L
6	13	Day Trip To Bangor (Didn't We Have A Lovely Time)	Fiddler's Dram	Dingles	5		F L
7	5	I Only Want To Be With You	Tourists	Logo	7	(83)	F
8	-	My Girl	Madness	Stiff	6		
9	-	Tears Of A Clown/Ranking Full Stop	Beat	2 Tone	7		F
10	-	I'm In The Mood For Dancing	Nolans	Epic	8		F
11	6	Rapper's Delight	Sugarhill Gang	Sugarhill	7	(36)	F L
12	12	My Simple Heart	Three Degrees	Ariola	6		L
13	1	Walking On The Moon	Police	A&M	7		
14	-	Is It Love You're After	Rose Royce	Whitfield	6		
15	-	Green Onions	Booker T. & The M.G.'s	Atlantic	4		L
16	-	London Calling	Clash	CBS	3		
17	-	John I'm Only Danncing (Again)	David Bowie	RCA	5		
18	-	Better Love Next Time	Dr. Hook	Capitol	4	(12)	
19	-	Babe	Styx	A&M	6	(1)	F L
20	17	Wonderful Christmastime	Paul McCartney	Parlophone	5		

February 1980

1	-	Too Much Too Young E.P. (Special AKA Live!)	Specials	2 Tone	6		
2	-	Coward Of The County	Kenny Rogers	UA	8	(3)	
3	10	I'm In The Mood For Dancing	Nolans	Epic	8		F
4	-	Someone's Looking At You	Boomtown Rats	Ensign	5		
5	-	It's Different For Girls	Joe Jackson	A&M	5		
6	8	My Girl	Madness	Stiff	6		
7	19	Babe	Styx	A&M	6	(1)	F L
8	-	Captain Beaky/Wilfred The Weasel	Keith Michel	Polydor	5		F L
9	-	And The Beat Goes On	Whispers	Solar	7	(19)	F
10	-	I Hear You Now	Jon & Vangelis	Polydor	6	(58)	F
11	1	Brass In Pocket	Pretenders	Real	9	(14)	F
12	-	7 Teen	Regents	Rialto	4		F L
13	5	With You I'm Born Again	Billy Preston & Syreeta	Motown	5	(4)	L
14	-	Carrie	Cliff Richard	EMI	6	(34)	
15	15	Green Onions	Booker T. & The M.G.'s	Atlantic	4		L
16	4	Please Don't Go	KC & The Sunshine Band	TK	6	(1)	
17	-	Atomic	Blondie	Chrysalis	6	(39)	
18	-	Rock With You	Michael Jackson	Epic	5	(1)	
19	-	I Can't Stand Up For Falling Down	Elvis Costello	F. Beat	5		
20	-	Living By Numbers	New Muzik	GTO	3		F L

March 1980

1	-	Together We Are Beautiful	Fern Kinney	WEA	7		F L
2	-	Take That Look Off Your Face	Marti Webb	Polydor	6		F
3	17	Atomic	Blondie	Chrysalis	6	(39)	
4	-	Games Without Frontiers	Peter Gabriel	Charisma	5	(48)	
5	-	All Night Long	Rainbow	Polydor	6		
6	-	Turning Japanese	Vapors	UA	7	(36)	F L
7	9	And The Beat Goes On	Whispers	Solar	7	(19)	F
8	2	Coward Of The County	Kenny Rogers	UA	8	(3)	
9	14	Carrie	Cliff Richard	EMI	6	(34)	
10	19	I Can't Stand Up For Falling Down	Elvis Costello	F. Beat	5		
11	-	So Lonely	Police	A&M	5		
12	-	Going Underground/Dreams Of Children	Jam	Polydor	6		
13	-	Dance Yourself Dizzy	Liquid Gold	Polo	8		F
14	-	Do That To Me One More Time	Captain & Tennille	Casablanca	4	(1)	F L
15	18	Rock With You	Michael Jackson	Epic	5	(1)	
16	-	Hands Off-She's Mine	Beat	Go Feet	4		
17	-	Working My Way Back To You-Forgive Me, Girl (Medley)	Detroit Spinners	Atlantic	9	(2)	
18	-	So Good To Be Back Home Again	Tourists	Logo	5		L
19	-	Riders In The Sky	Shadows	EMI	4		L
20	-	Cuba/Better Do It Salsa	Gibson Brothers	Island	3	(81)	

January 1980

This Mnth	Prev Mnth	Title	Artist	Label	Wks 20	(UK Pos)	
1	13	Rock With You	Michael Jackson	Epic	13	(7)	G
2	3	Escape (The Pina Colada Song)	Rupert Holmes	Infinity	12	(23)	F G
3	8	Do That To Me One More Time	Captain & Tennille	Casablanca	17	(7)	G L
4	6	Send One Your Love	Stevie Wonder	Tamla	12	(52)	
5	-	Coward Of The County	Kenny Rogers	UA	8	(1)	G
6	15	We Don't Talk Anymore	Cliff Richard	EMI America	10	(1)	
7	2	Please Don't Go	KC & The Sunshine Band	TK	15	(3)	
8	-	Cruisin'	Smokey Robinson	Tamla	12		F
9	10	Ladies Night	Kool & The Gang	De-Lite	10	(9)	G
10	-	The Long Run	Eagles	Asylum	10	(66)	
11	12	Cool Change	Little River Band	Capitol	9		
12	20	Better Love Next Time	Dr. Hook	Capitol	8	(8)	
13	4	Still	Commodores	Motown	13	(4)	G
14	-	I Wanna Be Your Lover	Prince	Warner	6	(41)	F G
15	1	Babe	Styx	A&M	12	(6)	G
16	-	Sara	Fleetwood Mac	Warner	7	(37)	
17	-	Jane	Jefferson Starship	Grunt	6	(21)	L
18	-	This Is It	Kenny Loggins	Columbia	8		
19	-	Crazy Little Thing Called Love	Queen	Elektra	14	(2)	
20	-	Don't Do Me Like That	Tom Petty & The Heartbreakers	Backstreet	6		F

February 1980

This Mnth	Prev Mnth	Title	Artist	Label	Wks 20	(UK Pos)	
1	3	Do That To Me One More Time	Captain & Tennille	Casablanca	17	(7)	G L
2	1	Rock With You	Michael Jackson	Epic	13	(7)	G
3	19	Crazy Little Thing Called Love	Queen	Elektra	14	(2)	
4	8	Cruisin'	Smokey Robinson	Tamla	12		F
5	5	Coward Of The County	Kenny Rogers	UA	8	(1)	G
6	-	Yes, I'm Ready	Teri DeSario With K.C.	Casablanca	9		F G L
7	16	Sara	Fleetwood Mac	Warner	7	(37)	
8	-	Longer	Dan Fogelberg	Full Moon	9	(59)	F
9	-	On The Radio	Donna Summer	Casablanca	9	(32)	G
10	18	This Is It	Kenny Loggins	Columbia	8		
11	-	Desire	Andy Gibb	RSO	10		
12	10	The Long Run	Eagles	Asylum	10	(66)	
13	20	Don't Do Me Like That	Tom Petty & The Heartbreakers	Backstreet	6		F
14	2	Escape (The Pina Colada Song)	Rupert Holmes	Infinity	12	(23)	F G
15	-	Romeo's Tune	Steve Forbert	Nemperor	5		F L
16	-	Daydream Believer	Anne Murray	Capitol	7	(61)	L
17	-	An American Dream	Nitty Gritty Dirt Band	UA	5		L
18	-	Working My Way Back To You/ Forgive Me, Girl	Spinners	Atlantic	12	(1)	G
19	-	Deja Vu	Dionne Warwick	Arista	3		
20	14	I Wanna Be Your Lover	Prince	Warner	6	(41)	F G

March 1980

This Mnth	Prev Mnth	Title	Artist	Label	Wks 20	(UK Pos)	
1	3	Crazy Little Thing Called Love	Queen	Elektra	14	(2)	
2	-	Another Brick In The Wall	Pink Floyd	Columbia	15	(1)	G L
3	11	Desire	Andy Gibb	RSO	10		
4	8	Longer	Dan Fogelberg	Full Moon	9	(59)	F
5	18	Working My Way Back To You/ Forgive Me, Girl	Spinners	Atlantic	12	(1)	G
6	9	On The Radio	Donna Summer	Casablanca	9	(32)	G
7	6	Yes I'm Ready	Teri DeSario With K.C.	Casablanca	9		F G L
8	-	Him	Rupert Holmes	MCA	7	(31)	L
9	-	The Second Time Around	Shalamar	Solar	9	(45)	F
10	-	Too Hot	Kool & The Gang	De-Lite	10	(23)	
11	1	Do That To Me One More Time	Captain & Tennille	Casablanca	17	(7)	G L
12	-	How Do I Make You	Linda Ronstadt	Asylum	9		
13	-	Call Me	Blondie	Chrysalis	16	(1)	G
14	-	Special Lady	Ray, Goodman & Brown	Polydor	9		F G L
15	-	Ride Like The Wind	Christopher Cross	Warner	11	(69)	F
16	16	Daydream Believer	Anne Murray	Capitol	7	(61)	L
17	4	Cruisin'	Smokey Robinson	Tamla	12		F
18	2	Rock With You	Michael Jackson	Epic	13	(7)	G
19	-	Refugee	Tom Petty & The Heartbreakers	Backstreet	4		
20	-	I Can't Tell You Why	Eagles	Asylum	9		L

◆ Pink Floyd, who were touring America, headed the LP chart for 15 weeks with **The Wall,** and their single 'Another Brick In The Wall' was a transatlantic million seller. Also Floyd's **Dark Side Of The Moon** broke the longevity record on the album chart, which previously stood at 302 weeks.

◆ 'Rock With You' gave Michael Jackson his second successive No. 1, and his first solo album for six years. **Off The Wall** hit the Transatlantic Top 5 and went platinum.

◆ AC/DC's lead singer Bon Scott died of drink related causes, as the Australian act earned their first platinum album, **Highway To Hell.**

◆ Making their first forays into the American chart were Prince, Tom Petty, Air Supply and Christopher Cross, whilst in Britain, local acts, UB40, Shakin' Stevens, Def Leppard, OMD and Iron Maiden debuted.

UK 1980 APR-JUNE

◆ 'Mirror In The Bathroom' by 2-Tone act The Beat, was the UK's first digitally recorded hit. Another first was The Police's 'Six Pack' – six separate singles sold as a package – which reached the Top 20.

◆ American records creating much more interest in Britain included dance tracks from Crown Heights Affair and Teena Marie, a soulful duet by Roberta Flack & the late Donny Hathaway, and the chart topping ten-year-old theme to the TV series *M*A*S*H*.

◆ Peter Gabriel's third (of four!) eponymous albums gave him his first chart topper. It came soon after his previous group, Genesis, had their first No. 1 with **Duke.**

◆ The Jam's 'Going Underground' became the first record to enter the chart at No. 1 since 1973. The trio were also voted Top Group in the *NME* Poll.

April 1980

This Mnth	Prev Mnth	Title	Artist	Label	Wks 20	(US Pos)	
1	17	Working My Way Back To You...	Detroit Spinners	Atlantic	9	(2)	
2	13	Dance Yourself Dizzy	Liquid Gold	Polo	8		F
3	-	King/Food For Thought	UB40	Graduate	7		F
4	-	Sexy Eyes	Dr. Hook	Capitol	6	(5)	L
5	12	Going Underground/Dreams Of...	Jam	Polydor	6		
6	-	Work Rest & Play (E.P.)	Madness	Stiff	5		
7	-	Poison Ivy	Lambrettas	Rocket	5		F
8	-	Call Me	Blondie	Chrysalis	5	(1)	
9	-	Turn It On Again	Genesis	Charisma	4	(58)	
10	-	January February	Barbara Dickson	Epic	6		
11	6	Turning Japanese	Vapors	UA	7	(36)	F L
12	-	Stomp!	Brothers Johnson	A&M	5	(7)	F L
13	-	Talk Of The Town	Pretenders	Real	4		
14	-	Silver Dream Machine (Pt. 1)	David Essex	Mercury	7		
15	-	Geno	Dexy's Midnight Runners	Late Night Feelings	8		F
16	1	Together We Are Beautiful	Fern Kinney	WEA	7		F L
17	-	Living After Midnight	Judas Priest	CBS	4		
18	-	Don't Push It, Don't Force It	Leon Haywood	20th Century	6	(49)	F L
19	-	Echo Beach	Martha & The Muffins	Dindisc	4		F L
20	-	Coming Up	Paul McCartney	Parlophone	5	(1)	

May 1980

This Mnth	Prev Mnth	Title	Artist	Label	Wks 20	(US Pos)	
1	15	Geno	Dexy's Midnight Runners	Late Night...	8		F
2	-	What's Another Year	Johnny Logan	Epic	6		F
3	-	No Doubt About It	Hot Chocolate	RAK	8		
4	20	Coming Up	Paul McCartney	Parlophone	5	(1)	
5	-	Mirror In The Bathroom	Beat	Go Feet	5		
6	-	She's Out Of My Life	Michael Jackson	Epic	5	(10)	
7	14	Silver Dream Machine (Pt. 1)	David Essex	Mercury	7		
8	-	Hold On To My Love	Jimmy Ruffin	RSO	5	(10)	L
9	8	Call Me	Blondie	Chrysalis	5	(1)	
10	-	I Shoulda Loved Ya	Narada Michael Walden	Atlantic	5	(66)	F
11	-	The Groove	Rodney Franklin	CBS	4		F L
12	-	Toccata	Sky	Ariola	4		F L
13	-	Theme From M*A*S*H (Suicide Is Painless)	Mash	CBS	7		F L
14	-	My Perfect Cousin	Undertones	Sire	3		
15	-	Over You	Roxy Music	Polydor	7	(80)	
16	-	Don't Make Waves	Nolans	Epic	4		
17	-	We Are Glass	Gary Numan	Beggars Banquet	5		
18	-	Check Out The Groove	Bobby Thurston	Epic	3		F L
19	3	King/Food For Thought	UB40	Graduate	7		F
20	-	The Golden Years (E.P.)	Motorhead	Bronze	3		F

June 1980

This Mnth	Prev Mnth	Title	Artist	Label	Wks 20	(US Pos)	
1	-	Crying	Don McLean	EMI	9	(5)	
2	13	Theme From M*A*S*H (Suicide...)	Mash	CBS	7		F L
3	-	Funkytown	Lipps Inc.	Casablanca	8	(1)	F L
4	3	No Doubt About It	Hot Chocolate	Rak	8		
5	-	Back Together Again	Roberta Flack/Donny Hathaway	Atlantic	7	(56)	
6	-	Rat Race/Rude Buoys Outa Jail	Specials	2 Tone	6		
7	-	Let's Get Serious	Jermaine Jackson	Motown	5	(9)	F
8	15	Over You	Roxy Music	Polydor	7	(80)	
9	-	You Gave Me Love	Crown Heights Affair	De-Lite	6		F L
10	-	Everybody's Got To Learn Sometime	Korgis	Rialto	6	(18)	L
11	-	Behind The Groove	Teena Marie	Motown	5		F L
12	17	We Are Glass	Gary Numan	Beggars Banquet	5		
13	6	She's Out Of My Life	Michael Jackson	Epic	5	(10)	
14	-	Messages	Orchestral Manoeuvres In The Dark	Dindisc	4		F
15	-	Midnite Dynamos	Matchbox	Magnet	5		
16	-	Substitute	Liquid Gold	Polo	4		L
17	-	Let's Go Round Again Pt. 1	Average White Band	RCA	5	(53)	L
18	-	Breaking The Law	Judas Priest	CBS	3		L
19	-	D-a-a-ance	Lambrettas	Rocket	3		L
20	-	Simon Templar/Two Pints Of Lager And A Packet Of Crisps Please	Splodgenessabounds	Deram	4		F L

April 1980

This Mnth	Prev Mnth	Title	Artist	Label	Wks 20	(UK Pos)	
1	13	Call Me	Blondie	Chrysalis	16	(1)	G
2	2	Another Brick In The Wall	Pink Floyd	Columbia	15	(1)	G L
3	15	Ride Like The Wind	Christopher Cross	Warner	11	(69)	F
4	14	Special Lady	Ray, Goodman & Brown	Polydor	9		F G L
5	5	Working My Way Back To You/ Forgive Me, Girl	Spinners	Atlantic	12	(1)	G
6	-	With You I'm Born Again	Billy Preston & Syreeta	Motown	8	(2)	L
7	10	Too Hot	Kool & The Gang	De-Lite	10	(23)	
8	20	I Can't Tell You Why	Eagles	Asylum	9		L
9	-	Fire Lake	Bob Seger & The Silver Bullet Band	Capitol	8		
10	-	Lost In Love	Air Supply	Arista	12		F
11	1	Crazy Little Thing Called Love	Queen	Elektra	14	(2)	
12	-	Off The Wall	Michael Jackson	Epic	7	(7)	G
13	-	You May Be Right	Billy Joel	Columbia	7		
14	-	Sexy Eyes	Dr. Hook	Capitol	11	(4)	G L
15	8	Him	Rupert Holmes	MCA	7	(31)	L
16	-	Hold On To My Love	Jimmy Ruffin	RSO	6	(7)	L
17	12	How Do I Make You	Linda Ronstadt	Asylum	9		
18	3	Desire	Andy Gibb	RSO	10		
19	-	Don't Fall In Love With A Dreamer	Kenny Rogers & Kim Carnes	UA	11		
20	9	The Second Time Around	Shalamar	Solar	9	(45)	F

May 1980

This Mnth	Prev Mnth	Title	Artist	Label	Wks 20	(UK Pos)	
1	1	Call Me	Blondie	Chrysalis	16	(1)	G
2	10	Lost In Love	Air Supply	Arista	12		F
3	14	Sexy Eyes	Dr. Hook	Capitol	11	(4)	G L
4	3	Ride Like The Wind	Christopher Cross	Warner	11	(69)	F
5	19	Don't Fall In Love With A Dreamer	Kenny Rogers & Kim Carnes	UA	11		
6	-	Funkytown	Lipps Inc.	Casablanca	11	(2)	F P L
7	-	Biggest Part Of Me	Ambrosia	Warner	12		
8	-	Hurt So Bad	Linda Ronstadt	Asylum	9		
9	6	With You I'm Born Again	Billy Preston & Syreeta	Motown	8	(2)	L
10	2	Another Brick In The Wall	Pink Floyd	Columbia	15	(1)	G L
11	13	You May Be Right	Billy Joel	Columbia	7		
12	-	Cars	Gary Numan	Atco	10	(1)	F L
13	-	I Can't Help It	Andy Gibb & Olivia Newton-John	RSO	5		
14	-	Stomp!	Brothers Johnson	A&M	7	(6)	L
15	9	Fire Lake	Bob Seger & Silver Bullet Band	Capitol	8		
16	-	Coming Up (Live At Glasgow)	Paul McCartney	Columbia	14	(2)	G
17	-	Against The Wind	Bob Seger & Silver Bullet Band	Capitol	9		
18	-	Breakdown Dead Ahead	Boz Scaggs	Columbia	5		
19	-	Pilot Of The Airwaves	Charlie Dore	Island	5	(66)	F L
20	16	Hold On To My Love	Jimmy Ruffin	RSO	6	(7)	L

June 1980

This Mnth	Prev Mnth	Title	Artist	Label	Wks 20	(UK Pos)	
1	6	Funkytown	Lipps Inc.	Casablanca	11	(2)	F P L
2	16	Coming Up (Live At Glasgow)	Paul McCartney	Columbia	14	(2)	G
3	-	The Rose	Bette Midler	Atlantic	12		G
4	7	Biggest Part Of Me	Ambrosia	Warner	12		
5	17	Against The Wind	Bob Seger & Silver Bullet Band	Capitol	9		
6	-	It's Still Rock And Roll To Me	Billy Joel	Columbia	14	(14)	G
7	-	Little Jeannie	Elton John	MCA	13	(33)	G
8	1	Call Me	Blondie	Chrysalis	16	(1)	G
9	-	Steal Away	Robbie Dupree	Elektra	11		F
10	12	Cars	Gary Numan	Atco	10	(1)	F L
11	-	She's Out Of My Life	Michael Jackson	Epic	7	(3)	G
12	-	Cupid/I've Loved You For A Long Time	Spinners	Atlantic	12	(4)	L
13	5	Don't Fall In Love With A Dreamer	Kenny Rogers & Kim Carnes	UA	11		
14	-	Let's Get Serious	Jermaine Jackson	Motown	8	(8)	
15	8	Hurt So Bad	Linda Ronstadt	Asylum	9		
16	-	Let Me Love You Tonight	Pure Prairie League	Casablanca	8		F L
17	-	Brass In Pocket	Pretenders	Sire	7	(1)	F
18	-	Shining Star	Manhattans	Columbia	10	(45)	G L
19	14	Stomp!	Brothers Johnson	A&M	7	(6)	L
20	3	Sexy Eyes	Dr. Hook	Capitol	11	(4)	G L

◆ The live version of Paul McCartney's 'Coming Up' was an American No. 1, while the studio version of the same song became a major UK success.

▲ The combination of top German disco producer Giorgio Moroder and Blondie resulted in the group's second successive transatlantic topper, 'Call Me'. It happened in the month that top disco, Club 54, closed its doors.

◆ Movies going on release included John Travolta's *Urban Cowboy*, *The Blues Brothers* (featuring Aretha Franklin, James Brown and Ray Charles) and *Roadie*, which starred Meat Loaf.

UK 1980 JULY-SEPT

◆ Critically acclaimed Manchester group Joy Division's 'Love Will Tear Us Apart' reached the Top 20 shortly after the group's leader Ian Curtis had committed suicide.

▲ Scottish singer Sheena Easton found herself with two singles in the Top 10 after being the subject of the TV series *The Big Time*. She went on to win the Grammy for Best New Artist of 1981.

◆ The first cassette only single, 'C30, C60, C90 Go' by Bow Wow Wow (which encouraged home-taping) was a minor British hit.

◆ Stars of the Reading Festival included metal merchants Iron Maiden, Def Leppard, UFO and Whitesnake.

July 1980

This Mnth	Prev Mnth	Title	Artist	Label	Wks 20	(US Pos)	
1	-	Xanadu	Olivia Newton-John/ Electric Light Orchestra	Jet	8	(8)	
2	-	Jump To The Beat	Stacy Lattisaw	Atlantic	7		F L
3	-	Use It Up And Wear It Out	Odyssey	RCA	8		
4	1	Crying	Don McLean	EMI	9	(5)	
5	-	Cupid-I've Loved You For A Long Time (Medley)	Detroit Spinners	Atlantic	6	(4)	L
6	-	My Way Of Thinking/I Think It's Going To Rain	UB40	Graduate	6		
7	-	Could You Be Loved	Bob Marley & The Wailers	Island	6		
8	3	Funkytown	Lipps Inc.	Casablanca	8	(1)	F L
9	-	Waterfalls	Paul McCartney	Parlophone	5		
10	10	Everybody's Got To Learn Sometime	Korgis	Rialto	6	(18)	L
11	-	Babooshka	Kate Bush	EMI	6		
12	20	Simon Templar/Two Pints Of Lager...	Splodgenessabounds	Deram	4		F L
13	-	To Be Or Not To Be	B.A. Robertson	Asylum	3		
14	-	More Than I Can Say	Leo Sayer	Chrysalis	6	(2)	
15	5	Back Together Again	Roberta Flack/Donny Hathaway	Atlantic	7	(56)	
16	-	747 (Strangers In The Night)	Saxon	Carrere	4		
17	11	Behind The Groove	Teena Marie	Motown	5		F L
18	-	Emotional Rescue	Rolling Stones	Rolling Stone	5	(3)	
19	-	Let's Hang On	Darts	Magnet	4		L
20	-	Love Will Tear Us Apart	Joy Division	Factory	4		F

August 1980

This Mnth	Prev Mnth	Title	Artist	Label	Wks 20	(US Pos)	
1	-	The Winner Takes It All	Abba	Epic	7	(8)	
2	-	Upside Down	Diana Ross	Motown	7	(1)	
3	-	9 to 5 (a.k.a. Morning Train)	Sheena Easton	EMI	9	(1)	F
4	-	Oops Upside Your Head	Gap Band	Mercury	8		F
5	-	Ashes To Ashes	David Bowie	RCA	7		
6	14	More Than I Can Say	Leo Sayer	Chrysalis	6	(2)	
7	3	Use It Up And Wear It Out	Odyssey	RCA	8		
8	-	Oh Yeah (On The Radio)	Roxy Music	Polydor	5		
9	-	Give Me The Night	George Benson	Warner	5	(4)	F
10	11	Babooshka	Kate Bush	EMI	6		
11	-	Start	Jam	Polydor	6		
12	7	Could You Be Loved	Bob Marley & The Wailers	Island	6		
13	-	Tom Hark	Piranhas	Sire	6		F
14	-	Feels Like I'm In Love	Kelly Marie	Calibre	9		F L
15	-	Funkin' For Jamaica (N.Y.)	Tom Browne	Arista	4		F L
16	1	Xanadu	Olivia Newton-John/E.L.O.	Jet	8	(8)	
17	-	There There My Dear	Dexy's Midnight Runners	Late Night Feelings	5		
18	-	Mariana	Gibson Brothers	Island	3		L
19	-	Lip Up Fatty	Bad Manners	Magnet	4		F
20	-	Sunshine Of Your Smile	Mike Berry	Polydor	6		L

September 1980

This Mnth	Prev Mnth	Title	Artist	Label	Wks 20	(US Pos)	
1	14	Feels Like I'm In Love	Kelly Marie	Calibre	9		F L
2	11	Start	Jam	Polydor	6		
3	-	Eighth Day	Hazel O'Connor	A&M	6		F
4	5	Ashes To Ashes	David Bowie	RCA	7		
5	-	One Day I'll Fly Away	Randy Crawford	Warner	6		F
6	-	It's Only Love/Beyond The Reef	Elvis Presley	RCA	6	(51)	L
7	3	9 to 5	Sheena Easton	EMI	9	(1)	F
8	-	Dreaming	Cliff Richard	EMI	6	(10)	
9	-	Modern Girl	Sheena Easton	EMI	6	(18)	
10	-	Master Blaster (Jammin')	Stevie Wonder	Motown	6	(5)	
11	20	Sunshine Of Your Smile	Mike Berry	Polydor	6		L
12	13	Tom Hark	Piranhas	Sire	6		F
13	-	Another One Bites The Dust	Queen	EMI	5	(1)	
14	-	I Die: You Die	Gary Numan	Beggars Banquet	4		
15	-	Can't Stop The Music	Village People	Mercury	4		L
16	-	Bank Robber	Clash	CBS	4		
17	-	Don't Stand So Close To Me	Police	A&M	7	(10)	
18	-	It's Still Rock And Roll To Me	Billy Joel	CBS	6	(1)	
19	1	The Winner Takes It All	Abba	Epic	7	(8)	
20	-	Baggy Trousers	Madness	Stiff	7		

July 1980

This Mnth	Prev Mnth	Title	Artist	Label	Wks 20	(UK Pos)	
1	6	It's Still Rock And Roll To Me	Billy Joel	Columbia	14	(14)	G
2	2	Coming Up (Live At Glasgow)	Paul McCartney	Columbia	14	(2)	G
3	7	Little Jeannie	Elton John	MCA	13	(33)	G
4	12	Cupid/I've Loved You For A Long Time	Spinners	Atlantic	12	(4)	L
5	3	The Rose	Bette Midler	Atlantic	12		G
6	9	Steal Away	Robbie Dupree	Elektra	11		F
7	-	Magic	Olivia Newton-John	MCA	12	(32)	G
8	18	Shining Star	Manhattans	Columbia	10	(45)	G L
9	16	Let Me Love You Tonight	Pure Prairie League	Casablanca	8		F L
10	-	Tired Of Toein' The Line	Rocky Burnette	EMI America	8	(58)	F L
11	14	Let's Get Serious	Jermaine Jackson	Motown	8	(8)	
12	1	Funkytown	Lipps Inc.	Casablanca	11	(2)	F P L
13	-	One Fine Day	Carole King	Capitol	7		L
14	5	Against The Wind	Bob Seger & The Silver Bullet Band	Capitol	9		
15	-	Take Your Time (Do It Right) (Pt. 1)	S.O.S. Band	Tabu	9	(51)	F G L
16	-	In America	Charlie Daniels Band	Epic	5		L
17	-	More Love	Kim Carnes	EMI America	9		
18	4	Biggest Part Of Me	Ambrosia	Warner	12		
19	-	Emotional Rescue	Rolling Stones	Rolling Stone	10	(9)	
20	-	I'm Alive	Electric Light Orchestra	MCA	3	(20)	G

August 1980

This Mnth	Prev Mnth	Title	Artist	Label	Wks 20	(UK Pos)	
1	7	Magic	Olivia Newton-John	MCA	12	(32)	G
2	-	Sailing	Christopher Cross	Warner	9	(48)	
3	15	Take Your Time (Do It Right) (Pt. 1)	S.O.S. Band	Tabu	9	(51)	F G L
4	19	Emotional Rescue	Rolling Stones	Rolling Stone	10	(9)	
5	1	It's Still Rock And Roll To Me	Billy Joel	Columbia	14	(14)	G
6	-	Upside Down	Diana Ross	Motown	14	(2)	G
7	8	Shining Star	Manhattans	Columbia	10	(45)	G L
8	17	More Love	Kim Carnes	EMI America	9		
9	3	Little Jeannie	Elton John	MCA	13	(33)	G
10	-	Fame	Irene Cara	RSO	10	(1)	F
11	4	Cupid/I've Loved You For A Long Time	Spinners	Atlantic	12	(4)	L
12	-	Let My Love Open The Door	Pete Townshend	Atco	5	(46)	F L
13	2	Coming Up (Live At Glasgow)	Paul McCartney	Columbia	14	(2)	G
14	-	Give Me The Night	George Benson	Warner	10	(7)	
15	-	All Out Of Love	Air Supply	Arista	12	(11)	G
16	-	Misunderstanding	Genesis	Atlantic	4	(42)	F
17	10	Tired Of Toein' The Line	Rocky Burnette	EMI America	8	(58)	F L
18	-	Into The Night	Benny Mardones	Polydor	6		F
19	-	Late In The Evening	Paul Simon	Warner	10	(58)	L
20	-	Take A Little Rhythm	Ali Thomson	A&M	3		F L

September 1980

This Mnth	Prev Mnth	Title	Artist	Label	Wks 20	(UK Pos)	
1	6	Upside Down	Diana Ross	Motown	14	(2)	G
2	15	All Out Of Love	Air Supply	Arista	12	(11)	G
3	10	Fame	Irene Cara	RSO	10	(1)	F
4	14	Give Me The Night	George Benson	Warner	10	(7)	
5	-	Lookin' For Love	Johnny Lee	Full Moon	8		F G L
6	19	Late In The Evening	Paul Simon	Warner	10	(58)	L
7	-	Another One Bites The Dust	Queen	Elektra	18	(7)	G
8	4	Emotional Rescue	Rolling Stones	Rolling Stone	10	(9)	
9	-	Drivin' My Life Away	Eddie Rabbitt	Elektra	10		G
10	2	Sailing	Christopher Cross	Warner	9	(48)	
11	-	One In A Million You	Larry Graham	Warner	4		F G L
12	-	I'm Alright	Kenny Loggins	Columbia	8		
13	-	You're The Only Woman (You & I)	Ambrosia	Warner	6		L
14	1	Magic	Olivia Newton-John	MCA	12	(32)	G
15	-	Xanadu	Olivia Newton-John/ Electric Light Orchestra	MCA	7	(1)	
16	-	You'll Accomp'ny Me	Bob Seger & Silver Bullet Band	Capitol	5		
17	18	Into The Night	Benny Mardones	Polydor	6		F
18	-	All Over The World	Electric Light Orchestra	MCA	5	(11)	
19	3	Take Your Time (Do It Right) (Pt. 1)	S.O.S. Band	Tabu	9	(51)	F G L
20	-	Woman In Love	Barbra Streisand	Columbia	13	(1)	G

US 1980 JULY-SEPT

◆ A crowd of 400,000 flocked to Central Park to see Elton John, and half a million thronged to a Beach Boys concert in Washington.

◆ John Bonham, the drummer of Led Zeppelin, died after a heavy drinking bout. The platinum selling group cancelled their planned US tour and disbanded.

◆ In America, British acts Elton John, Genesis, Pete Townshend, Ali Thomson and Olivia Newton-John hit with records that had missed the UK Top 40. In Britain, American artists Stacy Lattisaw, Odyssey, Tom Browne, The Village People and Randy Crawford charted with US pop flops.

◆ Debut hits by Americans Benny Mardones ('Into The Night' in America) and The Gap Band ('Oops Upside Your Head' in Britain) both returned to the Top 20 later in the decade.

UK 1980 OCT-DEC

◆ The Police had the year's top UK single and album with the Grammy winning 'Don't Stand So Close To Me' and **Zenyatta Mondatta**, both of which entered at No. 1.

◆ Abba's 'Super Trooper' gave them their ninth and last chart topper, as the album of the same name chalked up over a million British advance orders.

◆ Cliff Richard, who had recently received the MBE from the Queen, scored his third and last US Top 10 entry with his 76th British solo hit, 'Dreaming'.

◆ Paul McCartney received a rhodium plated record from *The Guinness Book Of Records* for being the most successful songwriter of all time.

October 1980

This Mnth	Prev Mnth	Title	Artist	Label	Wks 20	(US Pos)	
1	17	Don't Stand So Close To Me	Police	A&M	7	(10)	
2	-	D.I.S.C.O.	Ottawan	Carrere	7		F
3	20	Baggy Trousers	Madness	Stiff	7		
4	10	Master Blaster (Jammin')	Stevie Wonder	Motown	6	(5)	
5	-	My Old Piano	Diana Ross	Motown	5		
6	-	If You're Lookin' For A Way Out	Odyssey	RCA	8		
7	-	Et Les Oiseaux Chantaient (And The Birds Were Singing)	Sweet People	Polydor	4		F L
8	-	Amigo	Black Slate	Ensign	4		F L
9	-	What You're Proposing	Status Quo	Vertigo	4		
10	-	Woman In Love	Barbra Streisand	CBS	8	(1)	
11	-	When You Ask About Love	Matchbox	Magnet	7		
12	5	One Day I'll Fly Away	Randy Crawford	Warner	6		F
13	-	Killer On The Loose	Thin Lizzy	Vertigo	4		
14	1	Feels Like I'm In Love	Kelly Marie	Calibre	9		F L
15	-	Searching	Change	WEA	3		
16	-	Gotta Pull Myself Together	Nolans	Epic	5		
17	13	Another One Bites The Dust	Queen	EMI	5	(1)	
18	-	Casanova	Coffee	De-Lite	4		F L
19	-	Stereotype/International Jet Set	Specials	2 Tone	1		
20	6	It's Only Love/Beyond The Reef	Elvis Presley	RCA	6	(51)	L

November 1980

This Mnth	Prev Mnth	Title	Artist	Label	Wks 20	(US Pos)	
1	10	Woman In Love	Barbra Streisand	CBS	8	(1)	
2	-	The Tide Is High	Blondie	Chrysalis	9	(1)	
3	-	Special Brew	Bad Manners	Magnet	6		
4	-	Fashion	David Bowie	RCA	6	(70)	
5	-	Enola Gay	Orchestral Manoeuvres In The Dark	Dindisc	7		
6	-	I Could Be So Good For You	Dennis Waterman	EMI	6		F L
7	-	Dog Eat Dog	Adam & The Ants	CBS	6		F
8	-	Super Trouper	Abba	Epic	9	(45)	
9	-	Never Knew Love Like This Before	Stephanie Mills	20th Century	7	(6)	F L
10	11	When You Ask About Love	Matchbox	Magnet	7		
11	6	If You're Lookin' For A Way Out	Odyssey	RCA	8		
12	9	What You're Proposing	Status Quo	Vertigo	4		
13	2	D.I.S.C.O.	Ottawan	Carrere	7		F
14	-	The Earth Dies Screaming/Dream A Lie	UB40	Graduate	5		
15	16	Gotta Pull Myself Together	Nolans	Epic	5		
16	-	Celebration	Kool & The Gang	De-Lite	5	(1)	
17	3	Baggy Trousers	Madness	Stiff	7		
18	-	(Just Like) Starting Over	John Lennon	Geffen	10	(1)	
19	-	All Out Of Love	Air Supply	Arista	4	(2)	F L
20	-	The Same Old Scene	Roxy Music	Polydor	3		

December 1980

This Mnth	Prev Mnth	Title	Artist	Label	Wks 20	(US Pos)	
1	8	Super Trouper	Abba	Epic	9	(45)	
2	-	There's No One Quite Like Grandma	St. Winifred's School Choir	MFP	6		F L
3	-	Embarrassment	Madness	Stiff	8		
4	-	Stop The Cavalry	Jona Lewie	Stiff	8		L
5	-	Banana Republic	Boomtown Rats	Ensign	7		L
6	18	(Just Like) Starting Over	John Lennon	Geffen	10	(1)	
7	-	To Cut A Long Story Short	Spandau Ballet	Reformation	8		F
8	-	De Do Do Do, De Da Da Da	Police	A&M	6	(10)	
9	2	The Tide Is High	Blondie	Chrysalis	9	(1)	
10	-	Do You Feel My Love	Eddy Grant	Ensign	4		
11	-	Runaway Boys	Stray Cats	Arista	6		F
12	-	Antmusic	Adam & The Ants	CBS	12		
13	16	Celebration	Kool & The Gang	De-Lite	5	(1)	
14	-	Lady	Kenny Rogers	UA	5	(1)	
15	9	Never Knew Love Like This Before	Stephanie Mills	20th Century	7	(6)	F L
16	6	I Could Be So Good For You	Dennis Waterman	EMI	6		F L
17	-	Lies/Don't Drive My Car	Status Quo	Vertigo	6		
18	-	Happy Xmas (War Is Over)	John & Yoko & The Plastic Ono Band	Apple	5		
19	-	Flash	Queen	EMI	8	(42)	
20	-	Rock 'n' Roll Ain't Noise Pollution	AC/DC	Atlantic	3		F

October 1980

This Mnth	Prev Mnth	Title	Artist	Label	Wks 20	(UK Pos)	
1	7	Another One Bites The Dust	Queen	Elektra	18	(7)	G
2	20	Woman In Love	Barbra Streisand	Columbia	13	(1)	G
3	1	Upside Down	Diana Ross	Motown	14	(2)	G
4	2	All Out Of Love	Air Supply	Arista	12	(11)	G
5	-	Real Love	Doobie Brothers	Warner	8		
6	12	I'm Alright	Kenny Loggins	Columbia	8		
7	9	Drivin' My Life Away	Eddie Rabbitt	Elektra	10		G
8	-	He's So Shy	Pointer Sisters	Planet	11		G
9	6	Late In The Evening	Paul Simon	Warner	10	(58)	L
10	15	Xanadu	Olivia Newton-John/ Electric Light Orchestra	MCA	7	(1)	
11	4	Give Me The Night	George Benson	Warner	10	(7)	
12	-	Never Knew Love Like This Before	Stephanie Mills	20th Century	10	(4)	F G L
13	-	The Wanderer	Donna Summer	Geffen	9	(48)	G
14	-	Jesse	Carly Simon	Warner	6		G
15	5	Lookin' For Love	Johnny Lee	Full Moon	8		F G L
16	-	Lady	Kenny Rogers	Liberty	16	(12)	
17	-	Look What You've Done To Me	Boz Scaggs	Columbia	5		
18	-	Hot Rod Hearts	Robbie Dupree	Elektra	6		L
19	18	All Over The World	Electric Light Orchestra	MCA	5	(11)	
20	-	I'm Comin' Out	Diana Ross	Motown	9	(13)	

November 1980

This Mnth	Prev Mnth	Title	Artist	Label	Wks 20	(UK Pos)	
1	2	Woman In Love	Barbra Streisand	Columbia	13	(1)	G
2	16	Lady	Kenny Rogers	Liberty	16	(12)	
3	1	Another One Bites The Dust	Queen	Elektra	18	(7)	G
4	13	The Wanderer	Donna Summer	Geffen	9	(48)	G
5	20	I'm Comin' Out	Diana Ross	Motown	9	(13)	
6	-	Master Blaster (Jammin')	Stevie Wonder	Tamla	13	(2)	
7	12	Never Knew Love Like This Before	Stephanie Mills	20th Century	10	(4)	F G L
8	8	He's So Shy	Pointer Sisters	Planet	11		G
9	-	Dreaming	Cliff Richard	EMI America	8	(8)	
10	-	More Than I Can Say	Leo Sayer	Warner	12	(2)	G L
11	-	(Just Like) Starting Over	John Lennon	Geffen	16	(1)	G
12	-	Lovely One	Jacksons	Epic	5	(29)	
13	5	Real Love	Doobie Brothers	Warner	8		
14	-	You've Lost That Lovin' Feeling	Daryl Hall & John Oates	RCA	7	(55)	
15	-	Love On The Rocks	Neil Diamond	Columbia	13	(17)	
16	3	Upside Down	Diana Ross	Motown	14	(2)	G
17	-	Whip It	Devo	Warner	7	(51)	F G L
18	-	Hit Me With Your Best Shot	Pat Benatar	Chrysalis	11		F G
19	14	Jesse	Carly Simon	Warner	6		G
20	-	Dreamer	Supertramp	A&M	4	(13)	

December 1980

This Mnth	Prev Mnth	Title	Artist	Label	Wks 20	(UK Pos)	
1	2	Lady	Kenny Rogers	Liberty	16	(12)	
2	10	More Than I Can Say	Leo Sayer	Warner	12	(2)	G L
3	11	(Just Like) Starting Over	John Lennon	Geffen	16	(1)	G
4	15	Love On The Rocks	Neil Diamond	Columbia	13	(17)	
5	-	Hungry Heart	Bruce Springsteen	Columbia	10	(44)	F
6	3	Another One Bites The Dust	Queen	Elektra	18	(7)	G
7	6	Master Blaster (Jammin')	Stevie Wonder	Tamla	13	(2)	
8	-	Guilty	Barbra Streisand & Barry Gibb	Columbia	11	(34)	G
9	18	Hit Me With Your Best Shot	Pat Benatar	Chrysalis	11		F G
10	-	Every Woman In The World	Air Supply	Arista	13		
11	1	Woman In Love	Barbra Streisand	Columbia	13	(1)	G
12	-	Tell It Like It Is	Heart	Epic	8		
13	-	The Tide Is High	Blondie	Chrysalis	14	(1)	G
14	14	You've Lost That Lovin' Feeling	Daryl Hall & John Oates	RCA	7	(55)	
15	-	De Do Do Do, De Da Da Da	Police	A&M	8	(5)	F
16	5	I'm Comin' Out	Diana Ross	Motown	9	(13)	
17	-	Passion	Rod Stewart	Warner	12	(17)	
18	-	It's My Turn	Diana Ross	RCA	10	(16)	
19	-	Never Be The Same	Christopher Cross	Warner	5		
20	9	Dreaming	Cliff Richard	EMI America	8	(8)	

▲ John Lennon's murder shook the world, as Elvis Presley's death had in 1977. Lennon's comeback album, **Double Fantasy,** and its debut single, '(Just Like) Starting Over', shot to the top, as sales of all his (and The Beatles') earlier records increased dramatically.

◆ In the year that video discs were introduced, the sale of pre-recorded audio tapes now accounted for 39% of all album sales. However, the total sales of record and tapes continued to drop, with 34 million fewer units being sold than in 1979.

◆ Kenny Rogers' biggest hit, 'Lady', was written and produced by fellow star Lionel Richie.

UK 1981 JAN-MAR

◆ In January, the late John Lennon held three of the Top 4 places in the UK chart. His recordings of 'Woman' and the re-released 'Imagine' hit the top as did Roxy Music's interpretation of his composition 'Jealous Guy'.

◆ Erstwhile punks Adam & The Ants had five singles and two albums in the charts in February, with the Brit Award winning **Kings Of The Wild Frontier** heading the LP chart for 12 weeks.

▲ Major new artists on the UK charts included Phil Collins (whose first solo album **Face Value** entered at No. 1), 'new romantics' Spandau Ballet and Duran Duran (above), Kim Wilde and influential bands New Order and Ultravox.

January 1981

This Mnth	Prev Mnth	Title	Artist	Label	Wks 20	(US Pos)	
1	-	Imagine	John Lennon	Apple	9		
2	12	Antmusic	Adam & The Ants	CBS	12		
3	18	Happy Xmas (War Is Over)	John & Yoko & The Plastic Ono Band	Apple	5		
4	6	(Just Like) Starting Over	John Lennon	Geffen	10	(1)	
5	4	Stop The Cavalry	Jona Lewie	Stiff	8		L
6	-	Do Nothing/Maggie's Farm	Specials	2 Tone	5		
7	19	Flash	Queen	EMI	8	(42)	
8	8	De Do Do Do, De Da Da Da	Police	A&M	6	(10)	
9	-	Woman	John Lennon	Geffen	7	(2)	
10	-	Too Nice To Talk To	Beat	Go Feet	4		
11	2	There's No One Quite Like Grandma	St. Winifred's School Choir	MFP	6		F L
12	-	In The Air Tonight	Phil Collins	Virgin	6	(19)	F
13	-	I Am The Beat	Look	MCA	5		F L
14	-	Rabbit	Chas & Dave	Rockney	6		
15	3	Embarrassment	Madness	Stiff	8		
16	1	Super Trouper	Abba	Epic	9	(45)	
17	-	Don't Stop The Music	Yarbrough & Peoples	Mercury	6	(19)	F L
18	17	Lies/Don't Drive My Car	Status Quo	Vertigo	6		
19	11	Runaway Boys	Stray Cats	Arista	6		F
20	-	I Ain't Gonna Stand For It	Stevie Wonder	Motown	4	(11)	

February 1981

This Mnth	Prev Mnth	Title	Artist	Label	Wks 20	(US Pos)	
1	9	Woman	John Lennon	Geffen	7	(2)	
2	-	Vienna	Ultravox	Chrysalis	10		F
3	12	In The Air Tonight	Phil Collins	Virgin	6	(19)	F
4	-	I Surrender	Rainbow	Polydor	6		
5	-	Shaddup You Face	Joe Dolce Music Theatre	Epic	6	(53)	F L
6	-	Return Of The Los Palmas 7	Madness	Stiff	7		
7	-	Oldest Swinger In Town	Fred Wedlock	Rocket	5		F L
8	-	Romeo And Juliet	Dire Straits	Vertigo	6		
9	-	Rapture	Blondie	Chrysalis	5	(1)	
10	1	Imagine	John Lennon	Apple	9		
11	-	Fade To Grey	Visage	Polydor	5		F
12	2	Antmusic	Adam & The Ants	CBS	12		
13	-	Rock This Town	Stray Cats	Arista	5	(9)	
14	17	Don't Stop The Music	Yarbrough & Peoples	Mercury	6	(19)	F L
15	-	We'll Bring The House Down	Slade	Cheapskate	4		
16	-	St. Valentine's Day Massacre E.P.	Motorhead & Girlschool	Bronze	5		
17	-	(Do) The Hucklebuck	Coast To Coast	Polydor	8		F L
18	-	Young Parisians	Adam & The Ants	Decca	4		
19	-	Message Of Love	Pretenders	Real	3		
20	-	Jealous Guy	Roxy Music	EG	7		

March 1981

This Mnth	Prev Mnth	Title	Artist	Label	Wks 20	(US Pos)	
1	20	Jealous Guy	Roxy Music	EG	7		
2	-	Kings Of The Wild Frontier	Adam & The Ants	CBS	6		
3	17	(Do) The Hucklebuck	Coast To Coast	Polydor	8		F L
4	2	Vienna	Ultravox	Chrysalis	10		F
5	-	Kids In America	Kim Wilde	RAK	8	(25)	F
6	-	This Ole House	Shakin' Stevens	Epic	9		
7	5	Shaddup You Face	Joe Dolce Music Theatre	Epic	6	(53)	F L
8	-	Four From Toyah E.P.	Toyah	Safari	7		F
9	-	Reward	Teardrop Explodes	Vertigo	4		F
10	-	Southern Freeez	Freeez	Beggars Banquet	4		F
11	16	St. Valentine's Day Massacre E.P.	Motorhead & Girlschool	Bronze	5		
12	-	Something 'Bout You Baby I Like	Status Quo	Vertigo	4		
13	-	You Better You Bet	Who	Polydor	4	(18)	L
14	4	I Surrender	Rainbow	Polydor	6		
15	-	Once In A Lifetime	Talking Heads	Sire	3	(91)	F
16	-	Lately	Stevie Wonder	Motown	7	(64)	
17	-	Star	Kiki Dee	Ariola	4		L
18	6	Return Of The Los Palmas 7	Madness	Stiff	7		
19	-	(Somebody) Help Me Out	Beggar & Co	Ensign	3		F L
20	-	I Missed Again	Phil Collins	Virgin	3	(19)	

January 1981

This Mnth	Prev Mnth	Title	Artist	Label	Wks 20	(UK Pos)	
1	3	(Just Like) Starting Over	John Lennon	Geffen	16	(1)	G
2	4	Love On The Rocks	Neil Diamond	Columbia	13	(17)	
3	13	The Tide Is High	Blondie	Chrysalis	14	(1)	G
4	10	Every Woman In The World	Air Supply	Arista	13		
5	8	Guilty	Barbra Streisand & Barry Gibb	Columbia	11	(34)	G
6	17	Passion	Rod Stewart	Warner	12	(17)	
7	5	Hungry Heart	Bruce Springsteen	Columbia	10	(44)	F
8	18	It's My Turn	Diana Ross	RCA	10	(16)	
9	-	I Love A Rainy Night	Eddie Rabbitt	Elektra	14	(53)	G
10	12	Tell It Like It Is	Heart	Epic	8		
11	-	Celebration	Kool & The Gang	De-Lite	16	(7)	P
12	1	Lady	Kenny Rogers	Liberty	16	(12)	
13	-	I Made It Through The Rain	Barry Manilow	Arista	6	(37)	
14	15	De Do Do Do, De Da Da Da	Police	A&M	8	(5)	F
15	2	More Than I Can Say	Leo Sayer	Warner	12	(2)	G L
16	-	Hey Nineteen	Steely Dan	MCA	10		L
17	9	Hit Me With Your Best Shot	Pat Benatar	Chrysalis	11		F G
18	-	Giving It Up For Your Love	Delbert McClinton	Capitol	9		F L
19	-	Time Is Time	Andy Gibb	RSO	4		L
20	-	9 To 5	Dolly Parton	RCA	12	(47)	G

February 1981

This Mnth	Prev Mnth	Title	Artist	Label	Wks 20	(UK Pos)	
1	9	I Love A Rainy Night	Eddie Rabbitt	Elektra	14	(53)	G
2	20	9 To 5	Dolly Parton	RCA	12	(47)	G
3	11	Celebration	Kool & The Gang	De-Lite	16	(7)	P
4	3	The Tide Is High	Blondie	Chrysalis	14	(1)	G
5	-	Woman	John Lennon	Geffen	13	(1)	G
6	-	Keep On Loving You	REO Speedwagon	Epic	13	(7)	F P
7	6	Passion	Rod Stewart	Warner	12	(17)	
8	18	Giving It Up For Your Love	Delbert McClinton	Capitol	9		F L
9	-	Same Old Lang Syne	Dan Fogelberg	Full Moon	7		
10	1	(Just Like) Starting Over	John Lennon	Geffen	16	(1)	G
11	-	The Best Of Times	Styx	A&M	12	(42)	
12	16	Hey Nineteen	Steely Dan	MCA	10		L
13	-	The Winner Takes It All	Abba	Atlantic	11	(1)	L
14	4	Every Woman In The World	Air Supply	Arista	13		
15	-	I Ain't Gonna Stand For It	Stevie Wonder	Tamla	7	(10)	
16	-	Crying	Don McLean	Millenium	12	(1)	L
17	8	It's My Turn	Diana Ross	RCA	10	(16)	
18	-	Miss Sun	Boz Scaggs	Columbia	5		L
19	-	Hello Again	Neil Diamond	Capitol	10	(51)	
20	-	Together	Tierra	Boardwalk	5		F L

March 1981

This Mnth	Prev Mnth	Title	Artist	Label	Wks 20	(UK Pos)	
1	5	Woman	John Lennon	Geffen	13	(1)	G
2	6	Keep On Loving You	REO Speedwagon	Epic	13	(7)	F P
3	2	9 To 5	Dolly Parton	RCA	12	(47)	G
4	11	The Best Of Times	Styx	A&M	12	(42)	
5	16	Crying	Don McLean	Millenium	12	(1)	L
6	-	Rapture	Blondie	Chrysalis	12	(5)	G L
7	1	I Love A Rainy Night	Eddie Rabbitt	Elektra	14	(53)	G
8	19	Hello Again	Neil Diamond	Capitol	10	(51)	
9	13	The Winner Takes It All	Abba	Atlantic	11	(1)	L
10	3	Celebration	Kool & The Gang	De-Lite	16	(7)	P
11	-	What Kind Of Fool	Barbra Streisand & Barry Gibb	Columbia	7		
12	-	Kiss On My List	Daryl Hall & John Oates	RCA	12	(33)	G
13	15	I Ain't Gonna Stand For It	Stevie Wonder	Tamla	7	(10)	
14	8	Giving It Up For Your Love	Delbert McClinton	Capitol	9		F L
15	-	While You See A Chance	Steve Winwood	Island	8	(45)	F
16	4	The Tide Is High	Blondie	Chrysalis	14	(1)	G
17	-	Don't Stand So Close To Me	Police	A&M	7	(1)	
18	-	Just The Two Of Us	Grover Washington Jr.	Elektra	12	(34)	F L
19	-	Games People Play	Alan Parsons Project	Arista	3		F
20	-	A Little In Love	Cliff Richard	EMI America	5	(15)	L

◆ Bill Haley died. The performer, widely acknowledged as the first rock'n'roll star, had sold over 25 million copies of 'Rock Around The Clock' – the biggest selling single in the rock era.

◆ AOR rock pioneers, REO Speedwagon, whose 'Keep On Loving You' introduced them to the Top 20, replaced John Lennon at the peak of the LP chart with **Hi Infidelity**. The album was on top 15 weeks, selling over seven million copies.

◆ Blondie's transatlantic hit 'Rapture', one of the first rap releases by a white artist, brought rap back to the forefront of pop music.

UK 1981

APR-JUNE

◆ The first demonstration of the compact disc took place in Europe. The revolutionary digital playback system for music, which utilised laser beam technology, eventually replaced vinyl as the most popular system of carrying recorded sound.

◆ Among the UK chart toppers were Michael Jackson's first No. 1, 'One Day In Your Life' (which missed the American Top 40), and 'Stand And Deliver' by Adam & The Ants, which entered in pole position.

◆ Toni Basil's **Word of Mouth** (which included the future No. 1 'Mickey') claimed to be the first album to be simultaneously released on record and video.

◆ Thanks to the success of the film *Urban Cowboy*, country music was thriving in the USA. In Britain the biggest country hit was 'Teddy Bear' a five-year-old American single by the late Red Sovine.

April 1981

This Mnth	Prev Mnth	Title	Artist	Label	Wks 20	(US Pos)	
1	6	This Ole House	Shakin' Stevens	Epic	9		
2	-	Making Your Mind Up	Bucks Fizz	RCA	8		F
3	16	Lately	Stevie Wonder	Motown	7	(64)	
4	-	Einstein A Go-Go	Landscape	RCA	7		F L
5	5	Kids In America	Kim Wilde	RAK	8	(25)	F
6	-	Intuition	Linx	Chrysalis	6		
7	-	It's A Love Thing	Whispers	Solar	7	(28)	L
8	-	Chi Mai (Theme From 'The Life And Times Of David Lloyd George')	Ennio Morricone	BBC	8		F L
9	-	Good Thing Going (We've Got A Good Thing Going)	Sugar Minott	RCA	6		F L
10	-	Capstick Comes Home/ The Sheffield Grinder	Tony Capstick	Dingles	4		F L
11	-	Night Games	Graham Bonnett	Vertigo	5		F L
12	-	Can You Feel It	Jacksons	Epic	6	(77)	
13	-	D-Days	Hazel O'Connor	Albion	5		
14	8	Four From Toyah E.P.	Toyah	Safari	7		F
15	-	Attention To Me	Nolans	Epic	7		
16	1	Jealous Guy	Roxy Music	EG	7		
17	3	(Do) The Hucklebuck	Coast To Coast	Polydor	8		F L
18	-	Just A Feeling	Bad Manners	Magnet	5		
19	-	Mind Of A Toy	Visage	Polydor	3		
20	-	And The Bands Played On	Saxon	Carrere	4		

May 1981

This Mnth	Prev Mnth	Title	Artist	Label	Wks 20	(US Pos)	
1	-	Stars On 45	Starsound	CBS	8	(1)	F
2	-	Stand And Deliver	Adam & The Ants	CBS	8		
3	-	You Drive Me Crazy	Shakin' Stevens	Epic	8		
4	-	Grey Day	Madness	Stiff	6		
5	8	Chi Mai (Theme From...)	Ennio Morricone	BBC	8		F L
6	2	Making Your Mind Up	Bucks Fizz	RCA	8		F
7	-	Chequered Love	Kim Wilde	Rak	5		
8	-	Ossie's Dream (Spurs Are On Their Way To Wembley)	Tottenham Hotspur F.A. Cup Final Squad	Rockney	4		F
9	-	Swords Of A Thousand Men	Ten Pole Tudor	Stiff	6		F
10	-	Keep On Loving You	REO Speedwagon	Epic	5	(1)	F
11	9	Good Thing Going (We've Got A...)	Sugar Minott	RCA	6		F L
12	12	Can You Feel It	Jacksons	Epic	6	(77)	
13	15	Attention To Me	Nolans	Epic	7		
14	-	Musclebound/Glow	Spandau Ballet	Reformation	5		
15	-	Stray Cat Strut	Stray Cats	Arista	4	(3)	L
16	-	Only Crying	Keith Marshall	Arrival	4		F L
17	11	Night Games	Graham Bonnett	Vertigo	5		F L
18	-	Bette Davis Eyes	Kim Carnes	EMI America	5	(1)	F L
19	-	I Want To Be Free	Toyah	Safari	6		
20	7	It's A Love Thing	Whispers	Solar	7	(28)	L

June 1981

This Mnth	Prev Mnth	Title	Artist	Label	Wks 20	(US Pos)	
1	-	Being With You	Smokey Robinson	Motown	7	(2)	F L
2	-	One Day In Your Life	Michael Jackson	Motown	8	(55)	
3	-	More Than In Love	Kate Robbins & Beyond	RCA	6		F L
4	-	How 'Bout Us	Champaign	CBS	7	(12)	F L
5	2	Stand And Deliver	Adam & The Ants	CBS	8		
6	3	You Drive Me Crazy	Shakin' Stevens	Epic	8		
7	-	Will You	Hazel O'Connor	A&M	5		L
8	-	Going Back To My Roots	Odyssey	RCA	7		
9	-	Funeral Pyre	Jam	Polydor	3		
10	19	I Want To Be Free	Toyah	Safari	6		
11	-	Teddy Bear	Red Sovine	Starday	4	(40)	F L
12	-	All Stood Still	Ultravox	Chrysalis	5		
13	-	Ain't No Stoppin'	Enigma	Creole	5		F
14	1	Stars On 45	Starsound	CBS	8	(1)	F
15	9	Swords Of A Thousand Men	Ten Pole Tudor	Stiff	6		F
16	7	Chequered Love	Kim Wilde	RAK	5		
17	-	Memory	Elaine Paige	Polydor	6		F
18	-	Chariots Of Fire - Titles	Vangelis	Polydor	3	(1)	F L
19	18	Bette Davis Eyes	Kim Carnes	EMI America	5	(1)	F L
20	-	Ghost Town	Specials	2 Tone	8		

April 1981

This Mnth	Prev Mnth	Title	Artist	Label	Wks 20	(UK Pos)	
1	12	Kiss On My List	Daryl Hall & John Oates	RCA	12	(33)	G
2	6	Rapture	Blondie	Chrysalis	12	(5)	G L
3	18	Just The Two Of Us	Grover Washington Jr.	Elektra	12	(34)	F L
4	-	Morning Train (9 To 5)	Sheena Easton	EMI America	9	(3)	F G
5	4	The Best Of Times	Styx	A&M	12	(42)	
6	15	While You See A Chance	Steve Winwood	Island	8	(45)	F
7	1	Woman	John Lennon	Geffen	13	(1)	G
8	-	Angel Of The Morning	Juice Newton	Capitol	11	(43)	F G
9	5	Crying	Don McLean	Millenium	12	(1)	L
10	17	Don't Stand So Close To Me	Police	A&M	7	(1)	
11	2	Keep On Loving You	REO Speedwagon	Epic	13	(7)	F P
12	-	Being With You	Smokey Robinson	Tamla	13	(1)	G
13	-	I Can't Stand It	Eric Clapton	RSO	8		
14	8	Hello Again	Neil Diamond	Capitol	10	(51)	
15	-	Her Town Too	James Taylor & J. D. Souther	Columbia	6		L
16	-	Somebody's Knockin'	Terri Gibbs	MCA	5		F L
17	11	What Kind Of Fool	Barbra Streisand & Barry Gibb	Columbia	7		
18	3	9 To 5	Dolly Parton	RCA	12	(47)	G
19	9	The Winner Takes It All	Abba	Atlantic	11	(1)	L
20	-	Living Inside Myself	Gino Vannelli	Arista	11		L

May 1981

This Mnth	Prev Mnth	Title	Artist	Label	Wks 20	(UK Pos)	
1	12	Being With You	Smokey Robinson	Tamla	13	(1)	G
2	-	Bette Davis Eyes	Kim Carnes	EMI America	16	(10)	G
3	3	Just The Two Of Us	Grover Washington Jr.	Elektra	12	(34)	F L
4	8	Angel Of The Morning	Juice Newton	Capitol	11	(43)	F G
5	-	Take It On The Run	REO Speedwagon	Epic	11	(19)	G
6	20	Living Inside Myself	Gino Vannelli	Arista	11		L
7	4	Morning Train (9 To 5)	Sheena Easton	EMI America	9	(3)	F G
8	-	Sukiyaki	Taste Of Honey	Capitol	11		G L
9	-	Too Much Time On My Hands	Styx	A&M	8		
10	1	Kiss On My List	Daryl Hall & John Oates	RCA	12	(33)	G
11	-	Watching The Wheels	John Lennon	Geffen	6	(30)	
12	-	Stars On 45 (Medley)	Stars On 45	Radio	11	(2)	F G L
13	-	Sweetheart	Franke & The Knockouts	Millennium	8		F L
14	13	I Can't Stand It	Eric Clapton	RSO	8		
15	-	A Woman Needs Love (Just Like You Do)	Ray Parker Jr. & Raydio	Arista	12		
16	2	Rapture	Blondie	Chrysalis	12	(5)	G L
17	-	How 'Bout Us	Champaign	Columbia	6	(5)	F L
18	15	Her Town Too	James Taylor & J. D. Souther	Columbia	6		L
19	6	While You See A Chance	Steve Winwood	Island	8	(45)	F
20	-	America	Neil Diamond	Capitol	10		

June 1981

This Mnth	Prev Mnth	Title	Artist	Label	Wks 20	(UK Pos)	
1	2	Bette Davis Eyes	Kim Carnes	EMI America	16	(10)	G
2	12	Stars On 45 (Medley)	Stars On 45	Radio	11	(2)	F G L
3	8	Sukiyaki	Taste Of Honey	Capitol	11		G L
4	15	A Woman Needs Love (Just Like You Do)	Ray Parker Jr. & Raydio	Arista	12		
5	-	All Those Years Ago	George Harrison	Dark Horse	9	(13)	
6	1	Being With You	Smokey Robinson	Tamla	13	(1)	G
7	20	America	Neil Diamond	Capitol	10		
8	6	Living Inside Myself	Gino Vannelli	Arista	11		L
9	5	Take It On The Run	REO Speedwagon	Epic	11	(19)	G
10	-	The One That You Love	Air Supply	Arista	11		G
11	-	This Little Girl	Gary U.S. Bonds	EMI America	8	(43)	L
12	-	You Make My Dreams	Daryl Hall & John Oates	RCA	10		
13	13	Sweetheart	Franke & The Knockouts	Millennium	8		F L
14	-	I Love You	Climax Blues Band	Warner	6		L
15	-	Jessie's Girl	Rick Springfield	RCA	16	(43)	G
16	-	What Are We Doin' In Love	Dottie West & Kenny Rogers	Liberty	6		F L
17	3	Just The Two Of Us	Grover Washington Jr.	Elektra	12	(34)	F L
18	17	How 'Bout Us	Champaign	Columbia	6	(5)	F L
19	-	Elvira	Oak Ridge Boys	MCA	10		F G
20	-	Theme From 'Greatest American Hero' (Believe It Or Not)	Joey Scarbury	Elektra	14		F G L

◆ A Dutch session group called Starsound in Britain, and known as both as Stars On 45 and Stars On Long Play in America, started a world-wide medley craze with their smash, 'Stars On 45'.

◆ Bob Marley, the world's best known and most successful reggae artist, died of cancer. He was given a statesmen's funeral in Jamaica.

▲ Daryl Hall & John Oates, who became the most successful duo in the rock era, scored the first of their five No. 1 singles with 'Kiss On My List'.

◆ Wings, Steely Dan and Yes announced that they were to disband.

UK 1981

JULY-SEPT

◆ A recording of the month's most watched event, the wedding of Prince Charles and Princess Diana, was on sale just two days later and quickly topped the album chart.

◆ When Soft Cell's revival of the northern soul favourite, 'Tainted Love' was re-issued it became Britain's Top Single of 1981. It also went on to spend a record 43 weeks in the US Hot 100.

◆ Meat Loaf's long-awaited album, **Dead Ringer,** was the first LP by an American artist to enter the British chart at No. 1.

◆ The most successful purveyors of 2-Tone music, The Specials, topped the chart with their last single, 'Ghost Train'. It was their seventh Top 10 entry in two years.

◆ British-born Olivia Newton-John received her own plaque on the prestigious Hollywood Walk Of Fame.

July 1981

This Mnth	Prev Mnth	Title	Artist	Label	Wks 20	(US Pos)	
1	20	Ghost Town	Specials	2 Tone	8		
2	-	Can Can	Bad Manners	Magnet	8		
3	2	One Day In Your Life	Michael Jackson	Motown	8	(55)	
4	-	Body Talk	Imagination	R&B	9		F
5	-	Stars On 45 (Vol 2)	Starsound	CBS	6		
6	8	Going Back To My Roots	Odyssey	RCA	7		
7	-	Wordy Rappinghood	Tom Tom Club	Island	5		F L
8	-	No Woman No Cry	Bob Marley & The Wailers	Island	6		
9	17	Memory	Elaine Paige	Polydor	6		F
10	-	Motorhead Live	Motorhead	Bronze	4		L
11	-	You Might Need Somebody	Randy Crawford	Warner	5		
12	1	Being With You	Smokey Robinson	Motown	7	(2)	F L
13	-	Dancing On The Floor (Hooked On Love)	Third World	CBS	6		L
14	-	Razzamatazz	Quincy Jones	A&M	3		L
15	-	Chant No. 1 (I Don't Need This Pressure On)	Spandau Ballet	Reformation	7		
16	-	Piece Of The Action	Bucks Fizz	RCA	5		
17	-	Lay All Your Love On Me	Abba	Epic	4		
18	3	More Than In Love	Kate Robbins & Beyond	RCA	6		F L
19	-	Sat In Your Lap	Kate Bush	EMI	4		
20	11	Teddy Bear	Red Sovine	Starday	4	(40)	F L

August 1981

This Mnth	Prev Mnth	Title	Artist	Label	Wks 20	(US Pos)	
1	-	Green Door	Shakin' Stevens	Epic	6		
2	-	Hooked On Classics	Royal Philharmonic Orchestra	RCA	7	(10)	F L
3	-	Happy Birthday	Stevie Wonder	Motown	7		
4	15	Chant No. 1 (I Don't Need This Pressure On)	Spandau Ballet	Reformation	7		
5	-	Back To The Sixties	Tight Fit	Jive	6	(89)	F
6	-	Girls On Film	Duran Duran	EMI	6		
7	-	Love Action (I Believe In Love)	Human League	Virgin	7		
8	-	Hold On Tight	Electric Light Orchestra	Jet	9	(10)	
9	1	Ghost Town	Specials	2 Tone	8		
10	-	For Your Eyes Only	Sheena Easton	EMI	5	(4)	
11	-	Japanese Boy	Aneka	Hansa	7		F L
12	-	Walk Right Now	Jacksons	Epic	5	(73)	
13	2	Can Can	Bad Manners	Magnet	8		
14	-	Tainted Love	Soft Cell	Some Bizzare	9	(8)	F
15	-	Caribbean Disco	Lobo	Polydor	5		F L
16	-	Water On Glass/Boys	Kim Wilde	RAK	4		
17	5	Stars On 45 (Vol 2)	Starsound	CBS	6		
18	-	New Life	Depeche Mode	Mute	6		F
19	-	Beach Boy Gold	Gidea Park	Sonet	4		F L
20	13	Dancing On The Floor (Hooked...)	Third World	CBS	6		L

September 1981

This Mnth	Prev Mnth	Title	Artist	Label	Wks 20	(US Pos)	
1	14	Tainted Love	Soft Cell	Some Bizzare	9	(8)	F
2	11	Japanese Boy	Aneka	Hansa	7		F L
3	-	Prince Charming	Adam & The Ants	CBS	7		
4	-	Wired For Sound	Cliff Richard	EMI	6	(71)	
5	8	Hold On Tight	Electric Light Orchestra	Jet	9	(10)	
6	7	Love Action (I Believe In Love)	Human League	Virgin	7		
7	-	Souvenir	Orchestral Manoeuvres In The Dark	Dindisc	6		
8	-	Hands Up (Give Me Your Heart)	Ottawan	Carrere	8		L
9	-	Start Me Up	Rolling Stones	Rolling Stone	4	(2)	
10	-	One In Ten	UB40	Dep International	5		
11	-	She's Got Claws	Gary Numan	Beggars Banquet	4		
12	-	Pretend	Alvin Stardust	Stiff	6		
13	-	Slow Hand	Pointer Sisters	Planet	5	(2)	F
14	-	Abacab	Genesis	Charisma	4	(26)	
15	2	Hooked On Classics	Royal Philharmonic Orchestra	RCA	7	(10)	F L
16	-	Endless Love	Diana Ross & Lionel Richie	Motown	6	(1)	
17	-	Everybody Salsa	Modern Romance	WEA	3		F
18	-	The Thin Wall	Ultravox	Chrysalis	4		
19	15	Caribbean Disco	Lobo	Polydor	5		F L
20	1	Green Door	Shakin' Stevens	Epic	6		

July 1981

This Mnth	Prev Mnth	Title	Artist	Label	Wks 20	(UK Pos)	
1	1	Bette Davis Eyes	Kim Carnes	EMI America	16	(10)	G
2	10	The One That You Love	Air Supply	Arista	11		G
3	15	Jessie's Girl	Rick Springfield	RCA	16	(43)	G
4	5	All Those Years Ago	George Harrison	Dark Horse	9	(13)	
5	19	Elvira	Oak Ridge Boys	MCA	10		F G
6	12	You Make My Dreams	Daryl Hall & John Oates	RCA	10		
7	20	Theme From 'Greatest American Hero' (Believe It Or Not)	Joey Scarbury	Elektra	14		F G L
8	-	I Don't Need You	Kenny Rogers	Liberty	11		
9	2	Stars On 45 (Medley)	Stars On 45	Radio	11	(2)	F G L
10	-	Slow Hand	Pointer Sisters	Planet	13	(10)	G
11	4	A Woman Needs Love (Just Like...)	Ray Parker Jr. & Raydio	Arista	12		
12	-	Hearts	Marty Balin	EMI America	11		F L
13	-	The Boy From New York City	Manhattan Transfer	Atlantic	10		F L
14	-	Gemini Dream	Moody Blues	Threshold	6		
15	11	This Little Girl	Gary U.S. Bonds	EMI America	8	(43)	L
16	7	America	Neil Diamond	Capitol	10		
17	3	Sukiyaki	Taste Of Honey	Capitol	11		G L
18	-	Queen Of Hearts	Juice Newton	Capitol	13		G
19	-	Winning	Santana	Columbia	3		
20	-	Modern Girl	Sheena Easton	EMI America	3	(8)	

August 1981

This Mnth	Prev Mnth	Title	Artist	Label	Wks 20	(UK Pos)	
1	7	Theme From 'Greatest American...'	Joey Scarbury	Elektra	14		F G L
2	3	Jessie's Girl	Rick Springfield	RCA	16	(43)	G
3	-	Endless Love	Diana Ross & Lionel Richie	Motown	15	(7)	G
4	10	Slow Hand	Pointer Sisters	Planet	13	(10)	G
5	8	I Don't Need You	Kenny Rogers	Liberty	11		
6	13	The Boy From New York City	Manhattan Transfer	Atlantic	10		F L
7	5	Elvira	Oak Ridge Boys	MCA	10		F G
8	18	Queen Of Hearts	Juice Newton	Capitol	13		G
9	-	(There's) No Gettin' Over Me	Ronnie Milsap	RCA	11		
10	12	Hearts	Marty Balin	EMI America	11		F L
11	-	Lady You Bring Me Up	Commodores	Motown	10	(56)	
12	2	The One That You Love	Air Supply	Arista	11		G
13	-	Stop Draggin' My Heart Around	Stevie Nicks With Tom Petty & The Heartbreakers	Modern	10	(50)	F
14	-	Who's Crying Now	Journey	Columbia	11	(46)	
15	1	Bette Davis Eyes	Kim Carnes	EMI America	16	(10)	G
16	-	Urgent	Foreigner	Atlantic	11	(54)	
17	-	It's Now Or Never	John Schneider	Scotti Bros	5		F L
18	-	Touch Me When We're Dancing	Carpenters	A&M	5		L
19	6	You Make My Dreams	Daryl Hall & John Oates	RCA	10		
20	-	Time	Alan Parsons Project	Arista	6		

September 1981

This Mnth	Prev Mnth	Title	Artist	Label	Wks 20	(UK Pos)	
1	3	Endless Love	Diana Ross & Lionel Richie	Motown	15	(7)	G
2	13	Stop Draggin' My Heart Around	S. Nicks/T. Petty/Heartbreakers	Modern	10	(50)	F
3	8	Queen Of Hearts	Juice Newton	Capitol	13		G
4	16	Urgent	Foreigner	Atlantic	11	(54)	
5	9	(There's) No Gettin' Over Me	Ronnie Milsap	RCA	11		
6	4	Slow Hand	Pointer Sisters	Planet	13	(10)	G
7	14	Who's Crying Now	Journey	Columbia	11	(46)	
8	11	Lady You Bring Me Up	Commodores	Motown	10	(56)	
9	-	Step By Step	Eddie Rabbitt	Elektra	10		
10	-	Arthur's Theme (Best That You Can Do)	Christopher Cross	Warner	13	(7)	G
11	2	Jessie's Girl	Rick Springfield	RCA	16	(43)	G
12	-	Hold On Tight	Electric Light Orchestra	Jet	7	(4)	
13	1	Theme From 'Greatest American...'	Joey Scarbury	Elektra	14		F G L
14	-	Start Me Up	Rolling Stones	Rolling Stone	13	(7)	
15	-	Cool Love	Pablo Cruise	A&M	6		L
16	-	The Beach Boys Medley	Beach Boys	Capitol	5	(47)	
17	-	The Breakup Song (They Don't Write 'Em)	Greg Kihn Band	Beserkley	5		F
18	5	I Don't Need You	Kenny Rogers	Liberty	11		
19	-	Really Wanna Know You	Gary Wright	Warner	3		L
20	-	For Your Eyes Only	Sheena Easton	Liberty	9	(8)	

◆ For the first time three female soloists had No. 1 albums within a three month period: Kim Carnes with **Mistaken Identity,** Pat Benatar with **Precious Time** and **Bella Donna** by Stevie Nicks.

▲ Lionel Richie was the first person to produce the top pop, R&B and country records in the same week. Also his duet with Diana Ross (above), 'Endless Love', a nine week chart topper, became Motown's biggest ever seller.

◆ Newsworthy shows included Simon & Garfunkel's re-union in front of 500,000 in Central Park and a 36-city tour by The Jacksons, which grossed $5.5 million.

UK 1981 OCT-DEC

◆ The Rolling Stones American tour grossed a record $35 million, with each Stone supposedly pocketing $4 million.

▲ The Human League's 'Don't You Want Me' sold almost 1.5 million in the UK alone. Six months later it topped the American chart and opened the doors there to other British synth bands. Incidentally, the group's **Dare** album also reached No. 1 in Britain.

◆ Queen's **Greatest Hits** album topped the chart. It became one of the most successful albums of all time in the UK, spending over 300 weeks on the chart and selling over three million copies in the UK alone.

October 1981

This Mnth	Prev Mnth	Title	Artist	Label	Wks 20	(US Pos)	
1	-	The Birdie Song (Birdie Dance)	Tweets	PRT	8		F L
2	-	It's My Party	Dave Stewart & Barbara Gaskin	Broken	8	(72)	L
3	-	Under Your Thumb	Godley & Creme	Polydor	6		F
4	3	Prince Charming	Adam & The Ants	CBS	7		
5	8	Hands Up (Give Me Your Heart)	Ottawan	Carrere	8		L
6	-	Thunder In Mountains	Toyah	Safari	5		
7	-	Invisible Sun	Police	A&M	4		
8	-	Just Can't Get Enough	Depeche Mode	Mute	5		
9	-	Shut Up	Madness	Stiff	5		
10	-	Happy Birthday	Altered Images	Epic	7		F
11	-	O Superman	Laurie Anderson	Warner	4		F L
12	-	Open Your Heart	Human League	Virgin	5		
13	12	Pretend	Alvin Stardust	Stiff	6		
14	16	Endless Love	Diana Ross & Lionel Richie	Motown	6	(1)	
15	-	A Good Year For The Roses	Elvis Costello	F. Beat	6		L
16	-	It's Raining	Shakin' Stevens	Epic	5		
17	-	Absolute Beginners	Jam	Polydor	4		
18	7	Souvenir	Orchestral Manoeuvres In The Dark	Dindisc	6		
19	-	Walkin' In The Sunshine	Bad Manners	Magnet	5		
20	1	Tainted Love	Soft Cell	Some Bizzare	9	(8)	F

November 1981

This Mnth	Prev Mnth	Title	Artist	Label	Wks 20	(US Pos)	
1	-	Every Little Thing She Does Is Magic	Police	A&M	6	(3)	
2	-	Joan Of Arc	Orchestral Manoeuvres In The Dark	Dindisc	5		
3	-	When She Was My Girl	Four Tops	Casablanca	5	(11)	
4	-	Under Pressure	Queen & David Bowie	EMI	6	(29)	
5	10	Happy Birthday	Altered Images	Epic	7		F
6	-	Begin The Beguine (Volver A Empezar)	Julio Iglesias	CBS	8		F
7	-	Labelled With Love	Squeeze	A&M	6		
8	-	Favourite Shirts (Boy Meets Girl)	Haircut 100	Arista	5		F
9	-	Tonight I'm Yours (Don't Hurt Me)	Rod Stewart	Riva	6	(20)	
10	2	It's My Party	Dave Stewart & Barbara Gaskin	Broken	8	(72)	L
11	-	Physical	Olivia Newton-John	EMI	6	(1)	
12	-	Let's Groove	Earth, Wind & Fire	CBS	6	(3)	L
13	15	A Good Year For The Roses	Elvis Costello	F. Beat	6		L
14	-	Bed Sitter	Soft Cell	Some Bizzare	7		
15	-	I Go To Sleep	Pretenders	Real	5		
16	-	Hold Me	B.A. Robertson & Maggie Bell	Swansong	5		L
17	-	When You Were Sweet Sixteen	Fureys & Davey Arthur	Ritz	4		F L
18	1	The Birdie Song (Birdie Dance)	Tweets	PRT	8		F L
19	12	Open Your Heart	Human League	Virgin	5		
20	-	Why Do Fools Fall In Love	Diana Ross	Capitol	8	(7)	

December 1981

This Mnth	Prev Mnth	Title	Artist	Label	Wks 20	(US Pos)	
1	-	Don't You Want Me	Human League	Virgin	9	(1)	G
2	-	Daddy's Home	Cliff Richard	EMI	8	(23)	
3	6	Begin The Beguine (Volver A...)	Julio Iglesias	CBS	8		F
4	20	Why Do Fools Fall In Love	Diana Ross	Capitol	8	(7)	
5	14	Bed Sitter	Soft Cell	Some Bizzare	7		
6	-	One Of Us	Abba	Epic	7		L
7	-	Ant Rap	Adam & The Ants	CBS	7		
8	-	It Must Be Love	Madness	Stiff	7	(33)	
9	12	Let's Groove	Earth, Wind & Fire	CBS	6	(3)	L
10	-	Wedding Bells	Godley & Creme	Polydor	6		
11	4	Under Pressure	Queen & David Bowie	EMI	6	(29)	
12	-	Land Of Make Believe	Bucks Fizz	RCA	10		
13	15	I Go To Sleep	Pretenders	Real	5		
14	-	Rock 'n' Roll	Status Quo	Vertigo	6		
15	-	Cambodia	Kim Wilde	RAK	6		
16	-	Ay Ay Ay Ay Moosey	Modern Romance	WEA	4		
17	-	Spirits In The Material World	Police	A&M	5	(11)	
18	-	Mirror Mirror (Mon Amour)	Dollar	WEA	8		
19	-	Four More From Toyah E.P.	Toyah	Safari	2		L
20	8	Favourite Shirts (Boy Meets Girl)	Haircut 100	Arista	5		F

248

October 1981

This Mnth	Prev Mnth	Title	Artist	Label	Wks 20	(UK Pos)	
1	10	Arthur's Theme (Best That You Can Do)	Christopher Cross	Warner	13	(7)	G
2	1	Endless Love	Diana Ross & Lionel Richie	Motown	15	(7)	G
3	14	Start Me Up	Rolling Stones	Rolling Stone	13	(7)	
4	20	For Your Eyes Only	Sheena Easton	Liberty	9	(8)	
5	9	Step By Step	Eddie Rabbitt	Elektra	10		
6	-	Private Eyes	Daryl Hall & John Oates	RCA	12	(32)	G
7	2	Stop Draggin' My Heart Around	Stevie Nicks With Tom Petty & The Heartbreakers	Modern	10	(50)	F
8	7	Who's Crying Now	Journey	Columbia	11	(46)	
9	-	The Night Owls	Little River Band	Capitol	11		
10	-	Hard To Say	Dan Fogelberg	Full Moon	7		
11	-	I've Done Everything For You	Rick Springfield	RCA	7		
12	4	Urgent	Foreigner	Atlantic	11	(54)	
13	-	Tryin' To Live My Life Without You	Bob Seger & Silver Bullet Band	Capitol	7		
14	12	Hold On Tight	Electric Light Orchestra	Jet	7	(4)	
15	-	Share Your Love	Kenny Rogers	Liberty	6		
16	3	Queen Of Hearts	Juice Newton	Capitol	13		G
17	-	When She Was My Girl	Four Tops	Casablanca	6	(3)	L
18	5	(There's) No Gettin' Over Me	Ronnie Milsap	RCA	11		
19	-	Here I Am (Just When You Thought I Was Over You)	Air Supply	Arista	9		
20	-	Super Freak (Pt. 1)	Rick James	Gordy	4		L

November 1981

This Mnth	Prev Mnth	Title	Artist	Label	Wks 20	(UK Pos)	
1	6	Private Eyes	Daryl Hall & John Oates	RCA	12	(32)	G
2	3	Start Me Up	Rolling Stones	Rolling Stone	13	(7)	
3	-	Physical	Olivia Newton-John	MCA	17	(7)	P
4	-	Waiting For A Girl Like You	Foreigner	Atlantic	16	(8)	G
5	13	Tryin' To Live My Life Without You	Bob Seger & Silver Bullet Band	Capitol	7		
6	19	Here I Am (Just When You...)	Air Supply	Arista	9		
7	1	Arthur's Theme (Best That You...)	Christopher Cross	Warner	13	(7)	G
8	9	The Night Owls	Little River Band	Capitol	11		
9	-	Every Little Thing She Does Is Magic	Police	A&M	9	(1)	
10	-	Oh No	Commodores	Motown	10	(44)	
11	-	The Theme From Hill Street Blues	Mike Post Feat. Larry Carlton	Elektra	6	(25)	L
12	11	I've Done Everything For You	Rick Springfield	RCA	7		
13	-	Why Do Fools Fall In Love	Diana Ross	RCA	9	(4)	
14	17	When She Was My Girl	Four Tops	Casablanca	6	(3)	L
15	4	For Your Eyes Only	Sheena Easton	Liberty	9	(8)	
16	-	Young Turks	Rod Stewart	Warner	10	(11)	
17	10	Hard To Say	Dan Fogelberg	Full Moon	7		
18	-	The Old Songs	Barry Manilow	Arista	5	(48)	
19	-	Let's Groove	Earth, Wind & Fire	Arc	12	(3)	G
20	-	We're In This Love Together	Al Jarreau	Warner	7	(55)	F L

December 1981

This Mnth	Prev Mnth	Title	Artist	Label	Wks 20	(UK Pos)	
1	3	Physical	Olivia Newton-John	MCA	17	(7)	G
2	4	Waiting For A Girl Like You	Foreigner	Atlantic	16	(8)	G
3	19	Let's Groove	Earth, Wind & Fire	Arc	12	(3)	G
4	16	Young Turks	Rod Stewart	Warner	10	(11)	
5	10	Oh No	Commodores	Motown	10	(44)	
6	13	Why Do Fools Fall In Love	Diana Ross	RCA	9	(4)	
7	-	Harden My Heart	Quarterflash	Geffen	15	(49)	F
8	9	Every Little Thing She Does Is Magic	Police	A&M	9	(1)	
9	-	Don't Stop Believing	Journey	Columbia	7	(62)	
10	-	I Can't Go For That (No Can Do)	Daryl Hall & John Oates	RCA	15	(8)	G
11	-	Leather And Lace	Stevie Nicks	Modern	12		
12	-	Trouble	Lindsey Buckingham	Asylum	10	(31)	F L
13	6	Here I Am (Just When You...)	Air Supply	Arista	9		
14	-	Yesterday's Songs	Neil Diamond	Columbia	7		
15	-	Comin' In And Out Of Your Life	Barbra Streisand	Columbia	10	(66)	L
16	1	Private Eyes	Daryl Hall & John Oates	RCA	12	(32)	G
17	-	Turn Your Love Around	George Benson	Warner	11	(29)	L
18	-	The Sweetest Thing (I've Ever Known)	Juice Newton	Capitol	13		
19	2	Start Me Up	Rolling Stones	Rolling Stone	13	(7)	
20	-	Centerfold	J. Geils Band	EMI America	15	(3)	G

US 1981
OCT-DEC

◆ In 1981, the CD was first demonstrated, home video games took off and home taping increased. Also, MTV first appeared on the screen, Top 40 radio audiences decreased, and Sony sold 1.5 million of their new portable Walkman cassette players.

◆ Several major record labels upped the price of singles to $1.99 (30 months earlier they had been just $1.29).

◆ Trend setting punk-funk artist Rick James returned to the Top 20 with 'Super Freak'. The song was later utilized by MC Hammer in his million selling 'U Can't Touch This'.

◆ In November a record three Australian acts were in the Top 10: Little River Band, Air Supply and Rick Springfield as Australian raised Olivia Newton-John headed for a 10-week residency at the top with 'Physical'.

UK 1982 JAN-MAR

◆ Retro rock'n'roller Shakin' Stevens scored his third No. 1 with 'Oh Julie' (covered in America by Barry Manilow) and The Jam had their third chart topping single with 'Town Called Malice' and their only No. 1 LP, **The Gift.**

▲ UB40's new record deal with Dep International was described as "The best since Paul McCartney signed with Columbia".

◆ After years of hassles, George Harrison was able to present a cheque for $8.8 million to UNICEF, earned from his *Concert For Bangla Desh* project.

January 1982

This Mnth	Prev Mnth	Title	Artist	Label	Wks 20	(US Pos)	
1	12	Land Of Make Believe	Bucks Fizz	RCA	10		
2	1	Don't You Want Me	Human League	Virgin	9	(1)	G
3	-	Get Down On It	Kool & The Gang	De-Lite	7	(10)	
4	18	Mirror Mirror (Mon Amour)	Dollar	WEA	8		
5	-	I'll Find My Way Home	Jon & Vangelis	Polydor	8	(51)	L
6	7	Ant Rap	Adam & The Ants	CBS	7		
7	6	One Of Us	Abba	Epic	7		L
8	8	It Must Be Love	Madness	Stiff	7	(33)	
9	-	The Model/Computer Love	Kraftwerk	EMI	7		
10	-	Oh Julie	Shakin' Stevens	Epic	7		
11	-	I Could Be Happy	Altered Images	Epic	7		
12	-	Waiting For A Girl Like You	Foreigner	Atlantic	8	(2)	F
13	2	Daddy's Home	Cliff Richard	EMI	8	(23)	
14	-	Being Boiled	Human League	Virgin	5		
15	10	Wedding Bells	Godley & Creme	Polydor	6		
16	14	Rock 'n' Roll	Status Quo	Vertigo	6		
17	-	Dead Ringer For Love	Meat Loaf	Epic	6		
18	-	Young Turks	Rod Stewart	Riva	4	(5)	
19	-	Golden Brown	Stranglers	Liberty	7		
20	17	Spirits In The Material World	Police	A&M	5	(11)	

February 1982

This Mnth	Prev Mnth	Title	Artist	Label	Wks 20	(US Pos)	
1	19	Golden Brown	Stranglers	Liberty	7		
2	9	The Model/Computer Love	Kraftwerk	EMI	7		
3	-	Maid Of Orleans (The Waltz Joan Of Arc)	Orchestral Manoeuvres In The Dark	Dindisc	7		
4	-	Town Called Malice/Precious	Jam	Polydor	6		
5	10	Oh Julie	Shakin' Stevens	Epic	7		
6	17	Dead Ringer For Love	Meat Loaf	Epic	6		
7	-	Arthur's Theme (Best That You Can Do)	Christopher Cross	Warner	6	(1)	F L
8	-	The Lion Sleeps Tonight	Tight Fit	Jive	9		
9	-	Say Hello Wave Goodbye	Soft Cell	Some Bizzare	6		
10	-	Love Plus One	Haircut 100	Arista	7	(37)	
11	-	I Can't Go For That (No Can Do)	Daryl Hall & John Oates	RCA	5	(1)	F
12	1	Land Of Make Believe	Bucks Fizz	RCA	10		
13	-	Drowning In Berlin	Mobiles	Rialto	5		F L
14	-	Senses Working Overtime	XTC	Virgin	5		L
15	-	Easier Said Than Done	Shakatak	Polydor	4		F
16	-	Centrefold	J. Geils Band	EMI America	6	(1)	F L
17	3	Get Down On It	Kool & The Gang	De-Lite	7	(10)	
18	14	Bein' Boiled	Human League	Virgin	5		
19	-	Let's Get It Up	AC/DC	Atlantic	2	(44)	
20	12	Waiting For A Girl Like You	Foreigner	Atlantic	8	(2)	F

March 1982

This Mnth	Prev Mnth	Title	Artist	Label	Wks 20	(US Pos)	
1	8	The Lion Sleeps Tonight	Tight Fit	Jive	9		
2	-	Mickey	Toni Basil	Radialchoice	6	(1)	F L
3	10	Love Plus One	Haircut 100	Arista	7	(37)	
4	-	It Ain't What You Do It's The Way That You Do It	Fun Boy Three & Bananarama	Chrysalis	5		
5	-	Seven Tears	Goombay Dance Band	Epic	7		F L
6	16	Centrefold	J. Geils Band	EMI America	6	(1)	F L
7	-	Poison Arrow	ABC	Neutron	6	(25)	
8	-	See You	Depeche Mode	Mute	5		
9	-	Go Wild In The Country	Bow Wow Wow	RCA	5		F
10	-	Run To The Hills	Iron Maiden	EMI	5		F
11	-	Classic	Adrian Gurvitz	RAK	5		F L
12	-	Just An Illusion	Imagination	R&B	7		
13	4	Town Called Malice/Precious	Jam	Polydor	6		
14	-	Quiereme Mucho (Yours)	Julio Iglesias	CBS	4		
15	-	Cardiac Arrest	Madness	Stiff	4		
16	-	Layla	Derek & The Dominoes	RSO	5		F L
17	9	Say Hello Wave Goodbye	Soft Cell	Some Bizzare	6		
18	-	Party Fears Two	Associates	Associates	3		F
19	-	Deutscher Girls	Adam & The Ants	Ego	4		
20	3	Maid Of Orleans (The Waltz Joan Of Arc)	Orchestral Manoeuvres In The Dark	Dindisc	7		

January 1982

This Mnth	Prev Mnth	Title	Artist	Label	Wks 20	(UK Pos)	
1	1	Physical	Olivia Newton-John	MCA	17	(7)	P
2	2	Waiting For A Girl Like You	Foreigner	Atlantic	16	(8)	G
3	10	I Can't Go For That (No Can Do)	Daryl Hall & John Oates	RCA	15	(8)	G
4	3	Let's Groove	Earth, Wind & Fire	Arc	12	(3)	G
5	7	Harden My Heart	Quarterflash	Geffen	15	(49)	F
6	20	Centerfold	J. Geils Band	EMI America	15	(3)	G
7	11	Leather And Lace	Stevie Nicks	Modern	12		
8	17	Turn Your Love Around	George Benson	Warner	11	(29)	L
9	18	The Sweetest Thing (I've Ever Known)	Juice Newton	Capitol	13		
10	12	Trouble	Lindsey Buckingham	Asylum	10	(31)	F L
11	15	Comin' In And Out Of Your Life	Barbra Streisand	Columbia	10	(66)	L
12	-	Hooked On Classics	Royal Philharmonic Orchestra	RCA	8	(2)	F L
13	4	Young Turks	Rod Stewart	Warner	10	(11)	
14	-	Cool Night	Paul Davis	Arista	9		
15	6	Why Do Fools Fall In Love	Diana Ross	RCA	9	(4)	
16	14	Yesterday's Songs	Neil Diamond	Columbia	7		
17	-	Someone Could Lose A Heart Tonight	Eddie Rabbitt	Elektra	4		
18	-	Shake It Up	Cars	Elektra	11		
19	-	Waiting On A Friend	Rolling Stones	Rolling Stone	7	(50)	
20	9	Don't Stop Believing	Journey	Columbia	7	(62)	

February 1982

This Mnth	Prev Mnth	Title	Artist	Label	Wks 20	(UK Pos)	
1	6	Centerfold	J. Geils Band	EMI America	15	(3)	G
2	3	I Can't Go For That (No Can Do)	Daryl Hall & John Oates	RCA	15	(8)	G
3	5	Harden My Heart	Quarterflash	Geffen	15	(49)	F
4	18	Shake It Up	Cars	Elektra	11		
5	-	Open Arms	Journey	Columbia	11		
6	9	The Sweetest Thing (I've Ever Known)	Juice Newton	Capitol	13		
7	-	Sweet Dreams	Air Supply	Arista	11		
8	1	Physical	Olivia Newton-John	MCA	17	(7)	P
9	8	Turn Your Love Around	George Benson	Warner	11	(29)	L
10	-	Leader Of The Band	Dan Fogelberg	Full Moon	10		
11	-	That Girl	Stevie Wonder	Tamla	9	(39)	
12	-	Take It Easy On Me	Little River Band	Capitol	9		
13	2	Waiting For A Girl Like You	Foreigner	Atlantic	16	(8)	G
14	19	Waiting On A Friend	Rolling Stones	Rolling Stone	7	(50)	
15	7	Leather And Lace	Stevie Nicks	Modern	12		
16	14	Cool Night	Paul Davis	Arista	9		
17	-	Mirror Mirror	Diana Ross	RCA	6	(36)	
18	-	You Could Have Been With Me	Sheena Easton	EMI America	5	(54)	
19	12	Hooked On Classics	Royal Philharmonic Orchestra	RCA	8	(2)	F L
20	-	I Love Rock 'n' Roll	Joan Jett & The Blackhearts	Boardwalk	14	(4)	F G

March 1982

This Mnth	Prev Mnth	Title	Artist	Label	Wks 20	(UK Pos)	
1	20	I Love Rock 'n' Roll	Joan Jett & The Blackhearts	Boardwalk	14	(4)	F G
2	5	Open Arms	Journey	Columbia	11		
3	1	Centerfold	J. Geils Band	EMI America	15	(3)	G
4	11	That Girl	Stevie Wonder	Tamla	9	(39)	
5	7	Sweet Dreams	Air Supply	Arista	11		
6	-	We Got The Beat	Go-Go's	IRS	12		G
7	4	Shake It Up	Cars	Elektra	11		
8	17	Mirror Mirror	Diana Ross	RCA	6	(36)	
9	-	Pac-Man Fever	Buckner & Garcia	Columbia	7		F G L
10	-	Make A Move On Me	Olivia Newton-John	MCA	8	(43)	
11	10	Leader Of The Band	Dan Fogelberg	Full Moon	10		
12	-	Bobbie Sue	Oak Ridge Boys	MCA	4		L
13	-	Spirits In The Material World	Police	A&M	5	(12)	
14	12	Take It Easy On Me	Little River Band	Capitol	9		
15	-	Key Largo	Bertie Higgins	Kat Family	10		F L
16	-	Chariots Of Fire - Titles	Vangelis	Polydor	12	(12)	F L
17	-	Through The Years	Kenny Rogers	Liberty	5		
18	2	I Can't Go For That (No Can Do)	Daryl Hall & John Oates	RCA	15	(8)	G
19	-	Freeze-Frame	J. Geils Band	EMI America	10	(27)	G L
20	-	Should I Do It	Pointer Sisters	Planet	5	(50)	

US 1982

JAN-MAR

◆ Anglo-American rockers Foreigner scored their first British Top 10 hit with, 'Waiting For A Girl Like You'. This single, their 10th major US hit, spent a record 10 weeks at No. 2 in the USA. It came from the album 4, which spent 10 weeks at No. 1.

◆ Oddly, two top transatlantic hits had been originally recorded unsuccessfully on producer Mickie Most's RAK label; America's No. 1 'I Love Rock 'n' Roll' by Joan Jett (first released by The Arrows) and 'Mickey' by Toni Basil (previously by Racey).

◆ After 32 weeks climbing the chart, **Beauty & The Beat** by The Go-Go's' became the first rock album by a female group to reach the top.

UK 1982
APR-JUNE

▲ In their homeland, British supergroup Asia's eponymous album, which headed the US chart for nine weeks, failed to make the Top 10.

◆ Adam & The Ants split and Adam's first solo effort, 'Goody Two Shoes', topped the UK listings and became his first US Top 20 entry.

◆ The Rolling Stones made their first British appearance in six years. Their two shows at Wembley attracted 140,000 fans.

◆ After nine consecutive Top 10 hits, Madness finally made the UK top spot with 'House Of Fun'.

April 1982

This Mnth	Prev Mnth	Title	Artist	Label	Wks 20	(US Pos)	
1	-	My Camera Never Lies	Bucks Fizz	RCA	5		
2	-	Ain't No Pleasing You	Chas & Dave	Rockney	6		
3	5	Seven Tears	Goombay Dance Band	Epic	7		F L
4	12	Just An Illusion	Imagination	R&B	7		
5	-	Give Me Back My Heart	Dollar	WEA	6		
6	-	Ghosts	Japan	Virgin	5		
7	-	More Than This	Roxy Music	EG	5		
8	-	Ebony And Ivory	Paul McCartney & Stevie Wonder	Parlophone	7	(1)	
9	16	Layla	Derek & The Dominoes	RSO	5		F L
10	14	Quiereme Mucho (Yours)	Julio Iglesias	CBS	4		
11	-	Papa's Got A Brand New Pigbag	Pigbag	Y	5		F L
12	-	Have You Ever Been In Love	Leo Sayer	Chrysalis	3		
13	-	Dear John	Status Quo	Vertigo	4		
14	-	Is It A Dream	Classix Nouveaux	Liberty	3		F L
15	-	Night Birds	Shakatak	Polydor	4		
16	-	One Step Further	Bardo	Epic	4		F L
17	-	See Those Eyes	Altered Images	Epic	4		
18	7	Poison Arrow	ABC	Neutron	6	(25)	
19	-	Damned Don't Cry	Visage	Polydor	3		
20	-	Blue Eyes	Elton John	Rocket	4	(12)	

May 1982

This Mnth	Prev Mnth	Title	Artist	Label	Wks 20	(US Pos)	
1	-	I Won't Let You Down	PhD	WEA	7		F L
2	8	Ebony And Ivory	Paul McCartney & Stevie Wonder	Parlophone	7	(1)	
3	-	A Little Peace	Nicole	CBS	6		F L
4	-	I Love Rock 'n' Roll	Joan Jett & The Blackhearts	Epic	6	(1)	F L
5	-	Only You	Yazoo	Mute	7	(67)	F
6	-	Really Saying Something	Bananarama With Funboy Three	Deram	5		
7	-	This Time (We'll Get It Right)/ England We'll Fly The Flag	England World Cup Squad	England	5		
8	-	We Have A Dream	Scotland World Cup Squad	WEA	5		L
9	-	Girl Crazy	Hot Chocolate	RAK	6		
10	11	Papa's Got A Brand New Pigbag	Pigbag	Y	5		F L
11	-	Goody Two Shoes	Adam Ant	CBS	7	(12)	
12	16	One Step Further	Bardo	Epic	4		F L
13	-	Forget Me Nots	Patrice Rushen	Elektra	5	(23)	F L
14	-	House Of Fun	Madness	Stiff	6		
15	-	Fantasy Island	Tight Fit	Jive	7		
16	-	I Can Make You Feel Good	Shalamar	Solar	5		
17	-	Fantastic Day	Haircut 100	Arista	5		
18	-	Shirley	Shakin' Stevens	Epic	2		
19	-	The Look Of Love (Part 1)	ABC	Neutron	7	(18)	
20	-	Instinction	Spandau Ballet	Chrysalis	4		

June 1982

This Mnth	Prev Mnth	Title	Artist	Label	Wks 20	(US Pos)	
1	11	Goody Two Shoes	Adam Ant	CBS	7	(12)	
2	-	Torch	Soft Cell	Some Bizzare	6		
3	19	The Look Of Love (Part 1)	ABC	Neutron	7	(18)	
4	14	House Of Fun	Madness	Stiff	6		
5	-	Hungry Like The Wolf	Duran Duran	EMI	8	(3)	
6	-	I've Never Been To Me	Charlene	Motown	6	(3)	F L
7	15	Fantasy Island	Tight Fit	Jive	7		L
8	-	Mama Used To Say	Junior	Mercury	7	(30)	F
9	5	Only You	Yazoo	Mute	7	(67)	F
10	-	I'm A Wonderful Thing (Baby)	Kid Creole & The Coconuts	Ze	5		F
11	-	I Want Candy	Bow Wow Wow	RCA	4	(62)	L
12	-	Work That Body	Diana Ross	Capitol	5	(44)	
13	-	3 X 3 (E.P.)	Genesis	Charisma	4	(32)	
14	-	We Take Mystery (To Bed)	Gary Numan	Beggars Banquet	2		
15	-	Island Of Lost Souls	Blondie	Chrysalis	4	(37)	L
16	-	Club Country	Associates	Associates	4		L
17	13	Forget Me Nots	Patrice Rushen	Elektra	5	(23)	F L
18	1	I Won't Let You Down	PhD	WEA	7		F L
19	-	Inside Out	Odyssey	RCA	7		L
20	-	Do I Do	Stevie Wonder	Motown	3	(13)	

April 1982

This Mnth	Prev Mnth	Title	Artist	Label	Wks 20	(UK Pos)	
1	1	I Love Rock 'n' Roll	Joan Jett & The Blackhearts	Boardwalk	14	(4)	F G
2	6	We Got The Beat	Go-Go's	IRS	12		G
3	16	Chariots Of Fire - Titles	Vangelis	Polydor	12	(12)	F L
4	19	Freeze-Frame	J. Geils Band	EMI America	10	(27)	G L
5	-	Don't Talk To Strangers	Rick Springfield	RCA	14		
6	10	Make A Move On Me	Olivia Newton-John	MCA	8	(43)	
7	15	Key Largo	Bertie Higgins	Kat Family	10		F L
8	-	Do You Believe In Love	Huey Lewis & The News	Chrysalis	7	(9)	F
9	2	Open Arms	Journey	Columbia	11		
10	4	That Girl	Stevie Wonder	Tamla	9	(39)	
11	-	Edge Of Seventeen (Just Like The White Winged Dove)	Stevie Nicks	Modern	6		
12	-	(Oh) Pretty Woman	Van Halen	Warner	6		
13	-	'65 Love Affair	Paul Davis	Arista	11		L
14	9	Pac-Man Fever	Buckner & Garcia	Columbia	7		F G L
15	-	867-5309/Jenny	Tommy Tutone	Columbia	10		F L
16	-	One Hundred Ways	Quincy Jones/James Ingram	A&M	3		L
17	20	Should I Do It	Pointer Sisters	Planet	5	(50)	
18	-	Ebony And Ivory	Paul McCartney & Stevie Wonder	Columbia	12	(1)	G
19	5	Sweet Dreams	Air Supply	Arista	11		
20	-	Find Another Fool	Quarterflash	Geffen	4		

May 1982

This Mnth	Prev Mnth	Title	Artist	Label	Wks 20	(UK Pos)	
1	18	Ebony And Ivory	Paul McCartney & Stevie Wonder	Columbia	12	(1)	G
2	5	Don't Talk To Strangers	Rick Springfield	RCA	14		
3	15	867-5309/Jenny	Tommy Tutone	Columbia	10		F L
4	-	I've Never Been To Me	Charlene	Motown	9	(1)	F G L
5	3	Chariots Of Fire	Vangelis	Polydor	12	(12)	F L
6	13	'65 Love Affair	Paul Davis	Arista	11		L
7	1	I Love Rock 'n' Roll	Joan Jett & The Blackhearts	Boardwalk	14	(4)	F G
8	-	The Other Woman	Ray Parker Jr.	Arista	10		
9	-	Did It In A Minute	Daryl Hall & John Oates	RCA	8		
10	4	Freeze-Frame	J. Geils Band	EMI America	10	(27)	G L
11	-	Get Down On It	Kool & The Gang	De-Lite	7	(3)	
12	-	Always On My Mind	Willie Nelson	Columbia	11	(49)	G
13	2	We Got The Beat	Go-Go's	IRS	12		G
14	-	Don't You Want Me	Human League	A&M	15	(1)	F G
15	-	The Beatles Movie Medley	Beatles	Capitol	6	(10)	L
16	-	Heat Of The Moment	Asia	Geffen	11	(46)	F
17	-	Empty Garden (Hey Hey Johnny)	Elton John	Geffen	6	(51)	
18	8	Do You Believe In Love	Huey Lewis & The News	Chrysalis	7	(9)	F
19	-	Man On Your Mind	Little River Band	Capitol	6		
20	-	Goin' Down	Greg Guidry	Columbia	5		F L

June 1982

This Mnth	Prev Mnth	Title	Artist	Label	Wks 20	(UK Pos)	
1	1	Ebony And Ivory	Paul McCartney & Stevie Wonder	Columbia	12	(1)	G
2	14	Don't You Want Me	Human League	A&M	15	(1)	F G
3	12	Always On My Mind	Willie Nelson	Columbia	11	(49)	G
4	-	Rosanna	Toto	Columbia	15	(12)	
5	8	The Other Woman	Ray Parker Jr.	Arista	10		
6	16	Heat Of The Moment	Asia	Geffen	11	(46)	F
7	-	Crimson And Clover	Joan Jett & The Blackhearts	Boardwalk	6	(60)	
8	2	Don't Talk To Strangers	Rick Springfield	RCA	14		
9	-	It's Gonna Take A Miracle	Deniece Williams	Arc/Columbia	6		
10	3	867-5309/Jenny	Tommy Tutone	Columbia	10		F L
11	-	Let It Whip	Dazz Band	Motown	11		F L
12	-	Body Language	Queen	Elektra	4	(25)	
13	-	Hurts So Good	John Cougar	Riva	19		G
14	4	I've Never Been To Me	Charlene	Motown	9	(1)	F G L
15	-	Love's Been A Little Bit Hard On Me	Juice Newton	Capitol	10		
16	-	Making Love	Roberta Flack	Atlantic	5		
17	19	Man On Your Mind	Little River Band	Capitol	6		
18	6	'65 Love Affair	Paul Davis	Arista	11		L
19	-	Caught Up In You	38 Special	A&M	8		F
20	-	Tainted Love	Soft Cell	Sire	9	(1)	F L

US
1982
APR-JUNE

◆ **Tug of War,** Paul McCartney's last transatlantic No. 1 album, contained the duet 'Ebony And Ivory', which gave vocal partner Stevie Wonder his first British No. 1. McCartney, also became the first song-writer with two compositions simultaneously on both the American soul and country charts.

◆ The Hot Soul Singles chart was re-named the Black Singles chart.

◆ Charlene's minor 1977 hit, 'I've Never Been To Me', climbed into the transatlantic Top 3. It was Motown's biggest hit by a white artist.

◆ Peace Sunday at California's Rose Bowl attracted 85,000 to watch the likes of Bob Dylan, Stevie Wonder, Linda Ronstadt, Tom Petty and Stevie Nicks, while over a million attended the New York Peace Rally starring James Taylor, Jackson Browne (with Bruce Springsteen) and Gary 'U.S.' Bonds.

UK 1982 JULY-SEPT

◆ 'Come On Eileen' by Dexy's Midnight Runners which sold over a million in the UK, was Britain's top single of 1982 and went on to top the American charts too.

◆ Thanks to the TV series *Fame* (based on the 1980 film), Irene Cara's 'Fame' headed the British listings (two years after reaching the US Top 5). The film's soundtrack album also hit No. 1, being replaced by the million selling **Kids From Fame** from the TV series.

◆ Prince Charles' first Prince's Trust Rock Gala featured a super-group which included Phil Collins, Pete Townshend, Robert Plant, Midge Ure and Kate Bush.

◆ Survivor become the first US rock group to top the British charts in six years with their American No. 1, 'Eye of The Tiger'.

July 1982

This Mnth	Prev Mnth	Title	Artist	Label	Wks 20	(US Pos)	
1	-	Abracadabra	Steve Miller Band	Mercury	7	(1)	
2	-	Fame	Irene Cara	RSO	10	(4)	F
3	19	Inside Out	Odyssey	RCA	7		L
4	-	Happy Talk	Captain Sensible	A&M	4		F
5	-	A Night To Remember	Shalamar	Solar	6	(44)	
6	-	Music And Lights	Imagination	R&B	5		L
7	-	Da Da Da	Trio	Mobile Suit	5		F L
8	-	Shy Boy	Bananarama	London	7	(83)	
9	-	Now Those Days Are Gone	Bucks Fizz	RCA	5		
10	-	It Started With A Kiss	Hot Chocolate	RAK	8		
11	-	Don't Go	Yazoo	Mute	6		
12	-	No Regrets	Midge Ure	Chrysalis	5		F
13	6	I've Never Been To Me	Charlene	Motown	6	(3)	F L
14	-	Iko Iko	Natasha	Towerbell	5		F L
15	-	Driving In My Car	Madness	Stiff	6		
16	-	Come On Eileen	Dexy's Midnight Runners	Mercury	11	(1)	G
17	12	Work That Body	Diana Ross	Capitol	5	(44)	
18	-	Just Who Is The Five O'Clock Hero	Jam	Polydor	3		
19	-	Beatles Movie Medley	Beatles	Parlophone	4	(12)	
20	-	Night Train	Visage	Polydor	4		L

August 1982

This Mnth	Prev Mnth	Title	Artist	Label	Wks 20	(US Pos)	
1	16	Come On Eileen	Dexy's Midnight Runners	Mercury	11	(1)	G
2	2	Fame	Irene Cara	RSO	10	(4)	F
3	11	Don't Go	Yazoo	Mute	6		
4	10	It Started With A Kiss	Hot Chocolate	RAK	8		
5	-	Eye Of The Tiger	Survivor	Scotti Brothers	10	(1)	F
6	15	Driving My Car	Madness	Stiff	6		
7	-	Strange Little Girl	Stranglers	Liberty	5		
8	-	Stool Pigeon	Kid Creole & The Coconuts	Ze	5		
9	-	Can't Take My Eyes Off You	Boystown Gang	ERC	6		F L
10	-	My Girl Lollipop (My Boy Lollipop)	Bad Manners	Magnet	3		L
11	8	Shy Boy	Bananarama	London	7	(83)	
12	-	What	Soft Cell	Some Bizzare	5		
13	-	The Clapping Song	Belle Stars	Stiff	4		F
14	7	Da Da Da	Trio	Mobile Suit	5		F L
15	-	I Second That Emotion	Japan	Hansa	6		L
16	-	I Eat Cannibals Pt. 1	Toto Coelo	Radialchoice	5	(66)	F L
17	-	The Only Way Out	Cliff Richard	EMI	4	(64)	
18	-	Save A Prayer	Duran Duran	EMI	6	(16)	
19	-	Arthur Daley ('E's Alright)	Firm	Bark	3		F
20	-	John Wayne Is Big Leggy	Haysi Fantayzee	Regard	4		F

September 1982

This Mnth	Prev Mnth	Title	Artist	Label	Wks 20	(US Pos)	
1	5	Eye Of The Tiger	Survivor	Scotti Brothers	10	(1)	F
2	18	Save A Prayer	Duran Duran	EMI	6	(16)	
3	-	Walking On Sunshine	Rocker's Revenge	London	8		F L
4	-	Private Investigations	Dire Straits	Vertigo	6		
5	1	Come On Eileen	Dexy's Midnight Runners	Mercury	11	(1)	G
6	-	Hi-Fidelity	Kids From 'Fame' (Featuring Valerie Landsberg)	RCA	6		F
7	-	All Of My Heart	ABC	Neutron	5		
8	-	Give Me Your Heart Tonight	Shakin' Stevens	Epic	4		
9	12	What	Soft Cell	Some Bizzare	5		
10	-	The Message	Grandmaster Flash, Melle Mel & The Furious Five	Sugar Hill	4	(62)	F
11	-	The Bitterest Pill (I Ever Had To Swallow)	Jam	Polydor	5		
12	16	I Eat Cannibals Pt. 1	Toto Coelo	Radialchoice	5	(66)	F L
13	-	There It Is	Shalamar	Solar	7		
14	9	Can't Take My Eyes Off You	Boystown Gang	ERC	6		F L
15	-	Nobody's Fool	Haircut 100	Arista	4		L
16	-	Today	Talk Talk	EMI	4		F
17	-	Saddle Up	David Christie	KR	5		F L
18	20	John Wayne Is Big Leggy	Haysi Fantayzee	Regard	4		F
19	-	Why	Carly Simon	WEA	5	(74)	
20	2	Fame	Irene Cara	RSO	10	(4)	F

July 1982

This Mnth	Prev Mnth	Title	Artist	Label	Wks 20	(UK Pos)	
1	4	Rosanna	Toto	Columbia	15	(12)	
2	2	Don't You Want Me	Human League	A&M	15	(1)	F G
3	13	Hurts So Good	John Cougar	Riva	19		G
4	-	Eye Of The Tiger	Survivor	Scotti Brothers	18	(1)	F G
5	11	Let It Whip	Dazz Band	Motown	11		F L
6	-	Hold Me	Fleetwood Mac	Warner	11		
7	15	Love's Been A Little Bit Hard On Me	Juice Newton	Capitol	10		
8	20	Tainted Love	Soft Cell	Sire	9	(1)	F L
9	-	Only The Lonely	Motels	Capitol	12		F
10	-	Abracadabra	Steve Miller Band	Capitol	17	(2)	G L
11	19	Caught Up In You	38 Special	A&M	8		F
12	-	Keep The Fire Burnin'	REO Speedwagon	Epic	10		
13	6	Heat Of The Moment	Asia	Geffen	11	(46)	F
14	-	Do I Do	Stevie Wonder	Tamla	6	(10)	
15	1	Ebony And Ivory	Paul McCartney & Stevie Wonder	Columbia	12	(1)	G
16	-	Hard To Say I'm Sorry	Chicago	Full Moon	15	(4)	G
17	-	Even The Nights Are Better	Air Supply	Arista	10	(44)	
18	-	Any Day Now	Ronnie Milsap	RCA	5		L
19	3	Always On My Mind	Willie Nelson	Columbia	11	(49)	G
20	-	Wasted On The Way	Crosby, Stills & Nash	Atlantic	10		

August 1982

This Mnth	Prev Mnth	Title	Artist	Label	Wks 20	(UK Pos)	
1	4	Eye Of The Tiger	Survivor	Scotti Brothers	18	(1)	F G
2	3	Hurts So Good	John Cougar	Riva	19		G
3	10	Abracadabra	Steve Miller Band	Capitol	17	(2)	G L
4	6	Hold Me	Fleetwood Mac	Warner	11		
5	16	Hard To Say I'm Sorry	Chicago	Full Moon	15	(4)	G
6	17	Even The Nights Are Better	Air Supply	Arista	10	(44)	
7	12	Keep The Fire Burnin'	REO Speedwagon	Epic	10		
8	-	Vacation	Go-Go's	IRS	7		
9	20	Wasted On The Way	Crosby, Stills & Nash	Atlantic	10		
10	-	Take It Away	Paul McCartney	Columbia	9	(15)	
11	1	Rosanna	Toto	Columbia	15	(12)	
12	-	You Should Hear How She Talks About You	Melissa Manchester	Arista	10		L
13	9	Only The Lonely	Motels	Capitol	12		F
14	-	Love Is In Control (Finger On The Trigger)	Donna Summer	Warner	8	(18)	
15	-	Love Will Turn You Around	Kenny Rogers	Liberty	7		
16	2	Don't You Want Me	Human League	A&M	15	(1)	F G
17	5	Let It Whip	Dazz Band	Motown	11		F L
18	-	Jack & Diane	John Cougar	Riva	14	(25)	G
19	-	Eye In The Sky	Alan Parsons Project	Arista	13		
20	-	American Music	Pointer Sisters	Planet	5		

September 1982

This Mnth	Prev Mnth	Title	Artist	Label	Wks 20	(UK Pos)	
1	3	Abracadabra	Steve Miller Band	Capitol	17	(2)	G L
2	5	Hard To Say I'm Sorry	Chicago	Full Moon	15	(4)	G
3	1	Eye Of The Tiger	Survivor	Scotti Brothers	18	(1)	F G
4	18	Jack & Diane	John Cougar	Riva	14	(25)	G
5	12	You Should Hear How She Talks About You	Melissa Manchester	Arista	10		L
6	2	Hurts So Good	John Cougar	Riva	19		G
7	6	Even The Nights Are Better	Air Supply	Arista	10	(44)	
8	4	Hold Me	Fleetwood Mac	Warner	11		
9	10	Take It Away	Paul McCartney	Columbia	9	(15)	
10	19	Eye In The Sky	Alan Parsons Project	Arista	13		
11	14	Love Is In Control (Finger On The...)	Donna Summer	Warner	8	(18)	
12	-	Who Can It Be Now?	Men At Work	Columbia	14	(45)	F
13	15	Love Will Turn You Around	Kenny Rogers	Liberty	7		
14	9	Wasted On The Way	Crosby, Stills & Nash	Atlantic	10		
15	8	Vacation	Go-Go's	IRS	7		
16	-	You Can Do Magic	America	Capitol	11	(59)	L
17	-	Think I'm In Love	Eddie Money	Columbia	7		
18	-	Somebody's Baby	Jackson Browne	Asylum	9		
19	-	Blue Eyes	Elton John	Geffen	5	(8)	
20	20	American Music	Pointer Sisters	Planet	5		

US
1982
JULY-SEPT

▲ 'The Message' by Grandmaster Flash (above) was the first successful rap record with to address social problems in America, and showed what could be achieved through that medium. Another equally important black music recording was 'Planet Rock' by Afrika Bambaataa, which helped lay the foundations of hip-hop.

◆ The Us Festival drew 400,000 to California. Headliners included Fleetwood Mac, Tom Petty, Police, Pat Benatar, The Cars, The Kinks and Eddie Money.

255

UK 1982 OCT-DEC

▲ Big American hits from the first British invasion, 'Love Me Do' by The Beatles and 'House Of The Rising Sun' by The Animals returned to the UK chart. Debuting on that chart were Culture Club, Wham! (above) and Tears for Fears – artists who would help lead the second UK invasion.

◆ Whilst The Who made their (first) farewell tour of the US, Britain's top singles group, The Jam, quit while they were still at the top. Their last release, 'Beat Surrender', entered the chart at No. 1.

◆ The 1980s most influential British pop TV show, *The Tube*, was launched.

October 1982

This Mnth	Prev Mnth	Title	Artist	Label	Wks 20	(US Pos)	
1	-	Pass The Dutchie	Musical Youth	MCA	6	(10)	F
2	-	Zoom	Fat Larry's Band	Virgin	7		F L
3	-	Do You Really Want To Hurt Me	Culture Club	Virgin	9	(2)	F
4	-	Hard To Say I'm Sorry	Chicago	Full Moon	6	(1)	
5	-	Starmaker	Kids From 'Fame'	RCA	7		
6	-	Love Come Down	Evelyn King	EMI	7	(17)	F L
7	-	Jackie Wilson Said	Dexy's Midnight Runners	Mercury	4		
8	13	There It Is	Shalamar	Solar	7		
9	-	Love Me Do	Beatles	Parlophone	5		L
10	-	Just What I Always Wanted	Mari Wilson	Compact	5		F L
11	-	Lifeline	Spandau Ballet	Chrysalis	5		
12	-	Annie I'm Not Your Daddy	Kid Creole & The Coconuts	Ze	5		L
13	11	The Bitterest Pill (I Ever Had To Swallow)	Jam	Polydor	5		
14	-	Friend Or Foe	Adam Ant	CBS	4		
15	1	Eye Of The Tiger	Survivor	Scotti Brothers	10	(1)	F
16	3	Walking On Sunshine	Rocker's Revenge	London	8		F L
17	19	Why	Carly Simon	WEA	5	(74)	
18	-	House Of The Rising Sun	Animals	RAK	4		L
19	-	Danger Games	Pinkees	Creole	2		F L
20	-	Mad World	Tears For Fears	Mercury	7		F

November 1982

This Mnth	Prev Mnth	Title	Artist	Label	Wks 20	(US Pos)	
1	-	I Don't Wanna Dance	Eddy Grant	Ice	7	(53)	
2	-	Heartbreaker	Dionne Warwick	Arista	6	(10)	
3	20	Mad World	Tears For Fears	Mercury	7		F
4	3	Do You Really Want To Hurt Me	Culture Club	Virgin	9	(2)	F
5	-	(Sexual) Healing	Marvin Gaye	CBS	6	(3)	
6	-	Theme From Harry's Game	Clannad	RCA	4		F
7	-	Maneater	Daryl Hall & John Oates	RCA	4	(1)	
8	-	Ooh La La La (Let's Go Dancing)	Kool & The Gang	De-Lite	4	(30)	
9	-	The Girl Is Mine	Michael Jackson & Paul McCartney	Epic	3	(2)	
10	5	Starmaker	Kids From 'Fame'	RCA	7		
11	-	Mirror Man	Human League	Virgin	8	(30)	
12	-	I Wanna Do It With You	Barry Manilow	Arista	5		
13	-	Young Guns (Go For It)	Wham!	Innervision	9		F
14	-	Living On The Ceiling	Blancmange	London	6		F
15	12	Annie I'm Not Your Daddy	Kid Creole & The Coconuts	Ze	5		L
16	9	Love Me Do	Beatles	Parlophone	5		L
17	-	I'll Be Satisfied	Shakin' Stevens	Epic	4		
18	-	Caroline (Live At The N.E.C.)	Status Quo	Vertigo	3		
19	-	Rio	Duran Duran	EMI	5	(14)	
20	11	Lifeline	Spandau Ballet	Chrysalis	5		

December 1982

This Mnth	Prev Mnth	Title	Artist	Label	Wks 20	(US Pos)	
1	-	Save Your Love	Renee And Renato	Hollywood	10		F L
2	-	Beat Surrender	Jam	Polydor	6		L
3	-	Time (Clock Of The Heart)	Culture Club	Virgin	8	(2)	
4	11	Mirror Man	Human League	Virgin	8	(30)	
5	-	Truly	Lionel Richie	Motown	7	(1)	
6	13	Young Guns (Go For It)	Wham!	Innervision	9		F
7	-	Our House	Madness	Stiff	8	(7)	
8	14	Living On The Ceiling	Blancmange	London	6		F
9	-	Best Years Of Our Lives	Modern Romance	WEA	8		
10	-	The Shakin' Stevens E.P.	Shakin' Stevens	Epic	4		
11	1	I Don't Wanna Dance	Eddy Grant	Ice	7	(53)	
12	19	Rio	Duran Duran	EMI	5	(14)	
13	-	Peace On Earth/Little Drummer Boy	David Bowie & Bing Crosby	RCA	4		
14	-	Wishing (If I Had A Photograph Of You)	Flock Of Seagulls	Jive	4	(26)	F L
15	-	Hymn	Ultravox	Chrysalis	8		
16	-	The Other Side Of Love	Yazoo	Mute	4		
17	-	You Can't Hurry Love	Phil Collins	Virgin	10	(10)	
18	2	Heartbreaker	Dionne Warwick	Arista	6	(10)	
19	-	Friends	Shalamar	Solar	6		
20	-	A Winter's Tale	David Essex	Mercury	6		

US 1982 OCT-DEC

October 1982

This Mnth	Prev Mnth	Title	Artist	Label	Wks 20	(UK Pos)	
1	4	Jack & Diane	John Cougar	Riva	14	(25)	G
2	12	Who Can It Be Now?	Men At Work	Columbia	14	(45)	F
3	10	Eye In The Sky	Alan Parsons Project	Arista	13		
4	-	I Keep Forgettin' (Everytime You're Near)	Michael McDonald	Warner	8	(43)	F
5	18	Somebody's Baby	Jackson Browne	Asylum	9		
6	1	Abracadabra	Steve Miller Band	Capitol	17	(2)	G L
7	16	You Can Do Magic	America	Capitol	11	(59)	L
8	-	Heart Attack	Olivia Newton-John	MCA	11	(46)	
9	2	Hard To Say I'm Sorry	Chicago	Full Moon	15	(4)	G
10	-	I Ran (So Far Away)	Flock Of Seagulls	Jive/Arista	6	(43)	F L
11	-	Up Where We Belong	Joe Cocker & Jennifer Warnes	Island	11	(7)	G
12	3	Eye Of The Tiger	Survivor	Scotti Brothers	18	(1)	F G
13	-	Break It To Me Gently	Juice Newton	Capitol	6		L
14	19	Blue Eyes	Elton John	Geffen	5	(8)	
15	-	Gypsy	Fleetwood Mac	Warner	4	(46)	
16	-	Hold On	Santana	Columbia	6		L
17	5	You Should Hear How She Talks About You	Melissa Manchester	Arista	10		L
18	-	Heartlight	Neil Diamond	Columbia	9	(47)	L
19	-	Gloria	Laura Branigan	Atlantic	16	(6)	F G
20	6	Hurts So Good	John Cougar	Riva	19		G

November 1982

This Mnth	Prev Mnth	Title	Artist	Label	Wks 20	(UK Pos)	
1	11	Up Where We Belong	Joe Cocker & Jennifer Warnes	Island	11	(7)	G
2	8	Heart Attack	Olivia Newton-John	MCA	11	(46)	
3	-	Truly	Lionel Richie	Motown	11	(6)	G
4	19	Gloria	Laura Branigan	Atlantic	16	(6)	F G
5	18	Heartlight	Neil Diamond	Columbia	9	(47)	L
6	2	Who Can It Be Now?	Men At Work	Columbia	14	(45)	F
7	1	Jack & Diane	John Cougar	Riva	14	(25)	G
8	-	Muscles	Diana Ross	RCA	8	(15)	
9	-	Mickey	Toni Basil	Chrysalis	12	(2)	F G L
10	-	Maneater	Daryl Hall & John Oates	RCA	14	(6)	G
11	-	Steppin' Out	Joe Jackson	A&M	10	(6)	F
12	4	I Keep Forgettin' (Everytime...)	Michael McDonald	Warner	8	(43)	F
13	7	You Can Do Magic	America	Capitol	11	(59)	L
14	3	Eye In The Sky	Alan Parsons Project	Arista	13		
15	-	The Girl Is Mine	Paul McCartney & Michael Jackson	Epic	12	(8)	G
16	-	Dirty Laundry	Don Henley	Asylum	12	(59)	F G
17	-	Rock This Town	Stray Cats	EMI America	8	(9)	F
18	-	Nobody	Sylvia	RCA	4		G L
19	-	You Don't Want Me Anymore	Steel Breeze	RCA	3		F L
20	-	The One You Love	Glenn Frey	Asylum	4		F

December 1982

This Mnth	Prev Mnth	Title	Artist	Label	Wks 20	(UK Pos)	
1	9	Mickey	Toni Basil	Chrysalis	12	(2)	F G L
2	10	Maneater	Daryl Hall & John Oates	RCA	14	(6)	G
3	4	Gloria	Laura Branigan	Atlantic	16	(6)	F G
4	3	Truly	Lionel Richie	Motown	11	(6)	G
5	15	The Girl Is Mine	Paul McCartney & Michael Jackson	Epic	12	(8)	G
6	11	Steppin' Out	Joe Jackson	A&M	10	(6)	F
7	16	Dirty Laundry	Don Henley	Asylum	12	(59)	F G
8	-	Sexual Healing	Marvin Gaye	Columbia	13	(4)	G L
9	17	Rock This Town	Stray Cats	EMI America	8	(9)	F
10	-	It's Raining Again	Supertramp	A&M	7	(26)	L
11	8	Muscles	Diana Ross	RCA	8	(15)	
12	-	Down Under	Men At Work	Columbia	15	(1)	G
13	-	Shadows Of The Night	Pat Benatar	Chrysalis	6	(50)	
14	1	Up Where We Belong	Joe Cocker & Jennifer Warnes	Island	11	(7)	G
15	-	Heartbreaker	Dionne Warwick	Arista	9	(2)	
16	5	Heartlight	Neil Diamond	Columbia	9	(47)	L
17	-	Africa	Toto	Columbia	12	(3)	
18	-	Rock The Casbah	Clash	Epic	10	(15)	F L
19	2	Heart Attack	Olivia Newton-John	MCA	11	(46)	
20	-	You And I	Eddie Rabbitt	Elektra	12		L

◆ Rock videos came of age in 1982, as MTV gained importance and many clubs added video screens. It was a year when AOR rockers ruled the American album charts, rap showed it had teeth and synth-rock started to thrive. Nonetheless, record and tape sales dropped (by 3%) for the fourth consecutive year to $3.59 billion.

◆ Thanks partly to MTV, Australian group Men At Work topped the singles chart with 'Who Can It be Now?', and the album lists for 15 weeks with **Business As Usual.**

▲ Stars at the Jamaican World Music Festival included Rick James, Gladys Knight, Aretha Franklin, and Joe Jackson (above).

UK 1983 JAN-MAR

▲ Noteworthy new-comers on the UK chart included future transat-lantic stars U2 (above, whose album **War** entered at No. 1), The Eurythmics and the Thompson Twins.

◆ Shortly after disbanding, The Jam had a record 15 singles in the UK Top 100, and lead singer Paul Weller, signed a £250,000 deal for his new act Style Council.

◆ As the first of the revolutionary CD discs (which stores sounds digitally, thus eliminating most distortion) went on sale, Human League released the (supposed) first video single containing three of their hits.

January 1983

This Mnth	Prev Mnth	Title	Artist	Label	Wks 20	(US Pos)	
1	17	You Can't Hurry Love	Phil Collins	Virgin	10	(10)	
2	20	A Winter's Tale	David Essex	Mercury	6		
3	1	Save Your Love	Renee And Renato	Hollywood	10		F L
4	-	Orville's Song	Keith Harris & Orville	BBC	5		F L
5	-	Down Under	Men At Work	Epic	7	(1)	F L
6	9	Best Years Of Our Lives	Modern Romance	WEA	8		
7	7	Our House	Madness	Stiff	8	(7)	
8	-	The Story Of The Blues	Wah!	Eternal	6		F
9	3	Time (Clock Of The Heart)	Culture Club	Virgin	8	(2)	
10	-	Buffalo Gals	Malcolm McLaren & The World's Famous Supreme Team	Charisma	7		F
11	15	Hymn	Ultravox	Chrysalis	8		
12	-	Electric Avenue	Eddy Grant	Ice	5	(2)	
13	-	Heartache Avenue	Maisonettes	Ready Steady Go!	4		F L
14	10	The Shakin' Stevens E.P.	Shakin' Stevens	Epic	4		
15	-	All The Love In The World	Dionne Warwick	Arista	5		
16	13	Peace On Earth/Little Drummer Boy	David Bowie & Bing Crosby	RCA	4		
17	-	Steppin' Out	Joe Jackson	A&M	5	(6)	L
18	-	Cacharpaya (Andes Pumpsa Daesi)	Incantation	Beggars Banquet	4		F L
19	-	European Female	Stranglers	Epic	3		
20	-	If You Can't Stand The Heat	Bucks Fizz	RCA	6		

February 1983

This Mnth	Prev Mnth	Title	Artist	Label	Wks 20	(US Pos)	
1	-	Too Shy	Kajagoogoo	EMI	8	(5)	F
2	5	Down Under	Men At Work	Epic	7	(1)	F L
3	-	Sign Of The Times	Belle Stars	Stiff	7	(75)	L
4	-	Change	Tears For Fears	Mercury	6	(73)	
5	-	Up Where We Belong	Joe Cocker & Jennifer Warnes	Island	6	(1)	
6	12	Electric Avenue	Eddy Grant	Ice	5	(2)	
7	-	Wham Rap	Wham!	Innervision	5		
8	-	Gloria	Laura Branigan	Atlantic	6	(2)	F
9	-	Billie Jean	Michael Jackson	Epic	10	(1)	
10	-	Oh Diane	Fleetwood Mac	Warner	5		
11	1	You Can't Hurry Love	Phil Collins	Virgin	10	(10)	
12	-	Africa	Toto	CBS	6	(1)	
13	-	The Cutter	Echo & The Bunnymen	Korova	4		
14	8	The Story Of The Blues	Wah!	Eternal	6		F
15	-	Last Night A D.J. Saved My Life	Indeep	Sound Of New York	4		F L
16	-	New Year's Day	U2	Island	3	(53)	F
17	-	Never Gonna Give You Up	Musical Youth	MCA	5		L
18	-	Christian	China Crisis	Virgin	3		F
19	17	Steppin' Out	Joe Jackson	A&M	5	(6)	L
20	-	The Tunnel Of Love	Fun Boy Three	Chrysalis	5		

March 1983

This Mnth	Prev Mnth	Title	Artist	Label	Wks 20	(US Pos)	
1	-	Total Eclipse Of The Heart	Bonnie Tyler	CBS	8	(1)	
2	-	Sweet Dreams (Are Made Of This)	Eurythmics	RCA	7	(1)	F
3	9	Billie Jean	Michael Jackson	Epic	10	(1)	
4	-	Rock The Boat	Forrest	CBS	6		F
5	12	Africa	Toto	CBS	6	(1)	
6	-	Na Na Hey Hey Kiss Him Goodbye	Bananarama	London	5		
7	1	Too Shy	Kajagoogoo	EMI	8	(5)	F
8	-	Love On Your Side	Thompson Twins	Arista	5	(45)	F
9	-	Speak Like A Child	Style Council	Polydor	5		F
10	-	Tomorrow's (Just Another Day)/ Madness (Is All In The Mind)	Madness	Stiff	4		
11	17	Never Gonna Give You Up	Musical Youth	MCA	5		L
12	-	High Life	Modern Romance	WEA	3		
13	-	She Means Nothing To Me	Phil Everly & Cliff Richard	Capitol	4		F L
14	-	Baby, Come To Me	Patti Austin & James Ingram	Qwest	5	(1)	F L
15	-	Communication	Spandau Ballet	Reformation	4	(59)	
16	-	Rip It Up	Orange Juice	Polydor	5		F L
17	20	The Tunnel Of Love	Fun Boy Three	Chrysalis	5		
18	-	Is There Something I Should Know	Duran Duran	EMI	5	(4)	
19	4	Change	Tears For Fears	Mercury	6	(73)	
20	-	Let's Dance	David Bowie	EMI America	8	(1)	

258

January 1983

This Mnth	Prev Mnth	Title	Artist	Label	Wks 20	(UK Pos)	
1	5	The Girl Is Mine	Paul McCartney & Michael Jackson	Epic	12	(8)	G
2	12	Down Under	Men At Work	Columbia	15	(1)	G
3	7	Dirty Laundry	Don Henley	Asylum	12	(59)	F G
4	2	Maneater	Daryl Hall & John Oates	RCA	14	(6)	G
5	8	Sexual Healing	Marvin Gaye	Columbia	13	(4)	G L
6	1	Mickey	Toni Basil	Chrysalis	12	(2)	F P L
7	17	Africa	Toto	Columbia	12	(3)	
8	-	Baby Come To Me	Patti Austin With James Ingram	Qwest	13	(11)	F G L
9	18	Rock The Casbah	Clash	Epic	10	(15)	F L
10	3	Gloria	Laura Branigan	Atlantic	16	(6)	F G
11	20	You And I	Eddie Rabbitt	Elektra	12		L
12	15	Heartbreaker	Dionne Warwick	Arista	9	(2)	
13	6	Steppin' Out	Joe Jackson	A&M	10	(6)	F
14	-	The Other Guy	Little River Band	Capitol	9		L
15	-	You Can't Hurry Love	Phil Collins	Atlantic	9	(1)	
16	-	Shame On The Moon	Bob Seger & The Silver Bullet Band	Capitol	13		
17	9	Rock This Town	Stray Cats	EMI America	8	(9)	F
18	4	Truly	Lionel Richie	Motown	11	(6)	G
19	-	Heart To Heart	Kenny Loggins	Columbia	8		
20	-	Goody Two Shoes	Adam Ant	Epic	7	(1)	F L

February 1983

This Mnth	Prev Mnth	Title	Artist	Label	Wks 20	(UK Pos)	
1	8	Baby Come To Me	Patti Austin With James Ingram	Qwest	13	(11)	F G L
2	2	Down Under	Men At Work	Columbia	15	(1)	G
3	16	Shame On The Moon	Bob Seger & The Silver Bullet Band	Capitol	13		
4	-	Stray Cat Strut	Stray Cats	EMI America	8	(11)	
5	7	Africa	Toto	Columbia	12	(3)	
6	11	You And I	Eddie Rabbitt	Elektra	12		L
7	5	Sexual Healing	Marvin Gaye	Columbia	13	(4)	G L
8	20	Goody Two Shoes	Adam Ant	Epic	7	(1)	F L
9	-	Pass The Dutchie	Musical Youth	MCA	6	(1)	F L
10	15	You Can't Hurry Love	Phil Collins	Atlantic	9	(1)	
11	-	Billie Jean	Michael Jackson	Epic	12	(1)	G
12	-	Do You Really Want To Hurt Me	Culture Club	Epic	12	(1)	F
13	4	Maneater	Daryl Hall & John Oates	RCA	14	(6)	G
14	14	The Other Guy	Little River Band	Capitol	9		L
15	-	Hungry Like The Wolf	Duran Duran	Harvest	12	(5)	F
16	9	Rock The Casbah	Clash	Epic	10	(15)	F L
17	-	Your Love Is Driving Me Crazy	Sammy Hagar	Geffen	5		F L
18	19	Heart To Heart	Kenny Loggins	Columbia	8		
19	-	All Right	Christopher Cross	Warner	9	(51)	
20	-	Allentown	Billy Joel	Columbia	8		

March 1983

This Mnth	Prev Mnth	Title	Artist	Label	Wks 20	(UK Pos)	
1	11	Billie Jean	Michael Jackson	Epic	12	(1)	G
2	12	Do You Really Want To Hurt Me	Culture Club	Epic	12	(1)	F
3	15	Hungry Like The Wolf	Duran Duran	Harvest	12	(5)	F
4	3	Shame On The Moon	Bob Seger & The Silver Bullet Band	Capitol	13		
5	-	Back On The Chain Gang	Pretenders	Sire	9	(17)	
6	-	You Are	Lionel Richie	Motown	11	(43)	
7	-	We've Got Tonight	Kenny Rogers/Sheena Easton	Liberty	9	(28)	
8	4	Stray Cat Strut	Stray Cats	EMI America	8	(11)	
9	-	Separate Ways (Worlds Apart)	Journey	Columbia	10		
10	-	One On One	Daryl Hall & John Oates	RCA	9	(63)	
11	-	Mr. Roboto	Styx	A&M	11		G
12	-	Twilight Zone	Golden Earring	21	8		L
13	19	All Right	Christopher Cross	Warner	9	(51)	
14	1	Baby Come To Me	Patti Austin/James Ingram	Qwest	13	(11)	F G L
15	-	I Know There's Something Going On	Frida	Atlantic	7	(43)	F L
16	-	Come On Eileen	Dexy's Midnight Runners	Mercury	11	(1)	F L
17	6	You And I	Eddie Rabbitt	Elektra	12		L
18	2	Down Under	Men At Work	Columbia	15	(1)	G
19	-	Jeopardy	Greg Kihn Band	Beserkley	11	(63)	L
20	9	Pass The Dutchie	Musical Youth	MCA	6	(1)	F L

US 1983 JAN-MAR

◆ Michael Jackson's Grammy winning **Thriller** album (which eventually sold a record 40 million copies worldwide) started a stunning 37 weeks run at the top. Incidentally, 'Billie Jean' the first single spawned from it became a No. 1 on both sides of the Atlantic as did 'Down Under' by Australia's Men At Work and 'Total Eclipse Of The Heart' by Welsh songstress Bonnie Tyler.

◆ The new British invasion started, and by March one third of the Hot 100 records were by British born acts.

◆ Toto, who were scoring their biggest hit with 'Africa', collected a record five Grammy Awards.

◆ Karen Carpenter, the voice that sold fifty million albums by The Carpenters, died of heartbeat irregularities brought about by anorexia nevosa.

◆ Led Zeppelin earned their tenth successive gold award for **Coda.**

259

UK 1983
APR-JUNE

◆ Police scored the last of their five UK No. 1 singles and albums with 'Every Breath You Take' and **Synchronicity**. Both records also topped the US chart, with the latter holding sway for 17 weeks.

◆ David Bowie signed a $10 million deal with EMI, and the first release 'Let's Dance' (co-produced with Nile Rodgers) became his biggest transatlantic hit. He also launched his *Serious Moonlight* tour, which would be seen by over 2.5 million people around the world.

◆ Teenage American group New Edition (featuring 14-year-old Bobby Brown) topped the British chart with 'Candy Girl', but missed the US Top 40.

◆ 'Blue Monday', the 12-inch only release from New Order, was released. It became the UK's biggest selling single on that particular format and spent nearly a year on the chart.

April 1983

This Mnth	Prev Mnth	Title	Artist	Label	Wks 20	(US Pos)	
1	20	Let's Dance	David Bowie	EMI America	8	(1)	
2	18	Is There Something I Should Know	Duran Duran	EMI	5	(4)	
3	-	Church Of The Poison Mind	Culture Club	Virgin	6	(10)	
4	-	Boxer Beat	Joboxers	RCA	5		F
5	-	Breakaway	Tracey Ullman	Stiff	6	(70)	F
6	-	Beat It	Michael Jackson	Epic	6	(1)	
7	-	Words	F.R. David	Carrere	7	(62)	F L
8	-	Ooh To Be Ah	Kajagoogoo	EMI	5		
9	9	Speak Like A Child	Style Council	Polydor	5		F
10	2	Sweet Dreams (Are Made Of This)	Eurythmics	RCA	7	(1)	F
11	1	Total Eclipse Of The Heart	Bonnie Tyler	CBS	8	(1)	
12	-	Blue Monday	New Order	Factory	8		F
13	-	Fields Of Fire (400 Miles)	Big Country	Mercury	4	(52)	F
14	-	True	Spandau Ballet	Reformation	8	(4)	
15	-	Snot Rap	Kenny Everett	RCA	3		F L
16	-	Love Is A Stranger	Eurythmics	RCA	4	(23)	
17	-	Don't Talk To Me About Love	Altered Images	Epic	4		L
18	-	The House That Jack Built	Tracie	Respond	3		F L
19	16	Rip It Up	Orange Juice	Polydor	5		F L
20	-	Whistle Down The Wind	Nick Heyward	Arista	4		F

May 1983

This Mnth	Prev Mnth	Title	Artist	Label	Wks 20	(US Pos)	
1	14	True	Spandau Ballet	Reformation	8	(4)	
2	-	Temptation	Heaven 17	Virgin	7		F
3	-	Dancing Tight	Galaxy Featuring Phil Fearon	Ensign	6		F
4	-	(Keep Feeling) Fascination	Human League	Virgin	6	(8)	
5	-	Candy Girl	New Edition	London	6	(46)	F
6	7	Words	F.R. David	Carrere	7	(62)	F L
7	-	Pale Shelter	Tears For Fears	Mercury	4		
8	-	Can't Get Used To Losing You	Beat	Go Feet	5		L
9	-	Our Lips Are Sealed	Fun Boy Three	Chrysalis	5		L
10	-	We Are Detective	Thompson Twins	Arista	4		
11	6	Beat It	Michael Jackson	Epic	6	(1)	
12	-	Blind Vision	Blancmange	London	4		
13	-	Bad Boys	Wham!	Innervision	8	(60)	
14	1	Let's Dance	David Bowie	EMI America	8	(1)	
15	-	What Kinda Boy You Looking For (Girl)	Hot Chocolate	RAK	4		
16	-	True Love Ways	Cliff Richard	EMI	4		
17	-	Friday Night (Live Version)	Kids From 'Fame'	RCA	4		L
18	3	Church Of The Poison Mind	Culture Club	Virgin	6	(10)	
19	-	Every Breath You Take	Police	A&M	8	(1)	
20	-	Nobody's Diary	Yazoo	Mute	7		

June 1983

This Mnth	Prev Mnth	Title	Artist	Label	Wks 20	(US Pos)	
1	19	Every Breath You Take	Police	A&M	8	(1)	
2	13	Bad Boys	Wham!	Innervision	8	(60)	
3	20	Nobody's Diary	Yazoo	Mute	7		
4	-	Buffalo Soldier	Bob Marley & The Wailers	Island	6		
5	-	China Girl	David Bowie	EMI America	5	(10)	
6	-	Love Town	Booker Newberry III	Polydor	5		F L
7	-	Flashdance....What A Feeling	Irene Cara	Casablanca	9	(1)	L
8	5	Candy Girl	New Edition	London	4	(46)	L
9	-	Just Got Lucky	Joboxers	RCA	4	(36)	L
10	-	Baby Jane	Rod Stewart	Warner	9	(14)	
11	-	Lady Love Me (One More Time)	George Benson	Warner	5	(30)	
12	-	Waiting For A Train	Flash And The Pan	Ensign	5		F L
13	-	I Guess That's Why They Call It The Blues	Elton John	Rocket	6	(4)	
14	8	Can't Get Used To Losing You	Beat	Go Feet	5		L
15	-	Wanna Be Startin' Something	Michael Jackson	Epic	3	(5)	
16	2	Temptation	Heaven 17	Virgin	7		F
17	-	Money Go Round (Pt.1)	Style Council	Polydor	3		
18	-	Hang On Now	Kajagoogoo	EMI	3	(78)	
19	1	True	Spandau Ballet	Reformation	8	(4)	
20	-	Dark Is The Night	Shakatak	Polydor	2		

April 1983

This Mnth	Prev Mnth	Title	Artist	Label	Wks 20	(UK Pos)	
1	1	Billie Jean	Michael Jackson	Epic	12	(1)	G
2	16	Come On Eileen	Dexy's Midnight Runners	Mercury	11	(1)	F L
3	11	Mr. Roboto	Styx	A&M	11		G
4	-	Beat It	Michael Jackson	Epic	15	(3)	G
5	19	Jeopardy	Greg Kihn Band	Beserkley	11	(63)	L
6	3	Hungry Like The Wolf	Duran Duran	Harvest	12	(5)	F
7	9	Separate Ways (Worlds Apart)	Journey	Columbia	10		
8	10	One On One	Daryl Hall & John Oates	RCA	9	(63)	
9	2	Do You Really Want To Hurt Me	Culture Club	Epic	12	(1)	F
10	-	Der Kommissar	After The Fire	Epic	11	(47)	F L
11	7	We've Got Tonight	Kenny Rogers/Sheena Easton	Liberty	9	(28)	
12	6	You Are	Lionel Richie	Motown	11	(43)	
13	-	She Blinded Me With Science	Thomas Dolby	Capitol	11	(49)	F L
14	-	Let's Dance	David Bowie	EMI America	12	(1)	G
15	5	Back On The Chain Gang	Pretenders	Sire	9	(17)	
16	-	Little Red Corvette	Prince & The Revolution	Warner	10	(2)	
17	15	I Know There's Something Going On	Frida	Atlantic	7	(43)	F L
18	-	Even Now	Bob Seger & The Silver Bullet Band	Capitol	5	(73)	
19	-	Overkill	Men At Work	Columbia	11	(21)	
20	12	Twilight Zone	Golden Earring	21	8		L

May 1983

This Mnth	Prev Mnth	Title	Artist	Label	Wks 20	(UK Pos)	
1	4	Beat It	Michael Jackson	Epic	15	(3)	G
2	14	Let's Dance	David Bowie	EMI America	12	(1)	G
3	19	Overkill	Men At Work	Columbia	11	(21)	
4	13	She Blinded Me With Science	Thomas Dolby	Capitol	11	(49)	F L
5	-	Flashdance....What A Feeling	Irene Cara	Casablanca	16	(2)	G
6	5	Jeopardy	Greg Kihn Band	Beserkley	11	(63)	L
7	16	Little Red Corvette	Prince & The Revolution	Warner	10	(2)	
8	-	Solitaire	Laura Branigan	Atlantic	8		
9	10	Der Kommissar	After The Fire	Epic	11	(47)	F L
10	-	My Love	Lionel Richie	Motown	8	(70)	
11	2	Come On Eileen	Dexy's Midnight Runners	Mercury	11	(1)	F L
12	-	Time (Clock Of The Heart)	Culture Club	Epic	11	(3)	
13	-	I Won't Hold You Back	Toto	Columbia	7	(37)	
14	-	Straight From The Heart	Bryan Adams	A&M	5	(51)	F
15	-	Photograph	Def Leppard	Mercury	6	(66)	F
16	-	Rio	Duran Duran	Capitol	4	(9)	
17	3	Mr. Roboto	Styx	A&M	11		G
18	-	Affair Of The Night	Rick Springfield	RCA	9		
19	-	There's Always Something There To Remind Me	Naked Eyes	EMI America	7	(59)	F
20	18	Even Now	Bob Seger & The Silver Bullet Band	Capitol	5	(73)	

June 1983

This Mnth	Prev Mnth	Title	Artist	Label	Wks 20	(UK Pos)	
1	5	Flashdance....What A Feeling	Irene Cara	Casablanca	16	(2)	G
2	12	Time (Clock Of The Heart)	Culture Club	Epic	11	(3)	
3	2	Let's Dance	David Bowie	EMI America	12	(1)	G
4	3	Overkill	Men At Work	Columbia	11	(21)	
5	-	Electric Avenue	Eddy Grant	Portrait	12	(2)	F G L
6	1	Beat It	Michael Jackson	Epic	15	(3)	G
7	-	Don't Let It End	Styx	A&M	9	(56)	
8	10	My Love	Lionel Richie	Motown	8	(70)	
9	18	Affair Of The Night	Rick Springfield	RCA	9		
10	19	There's Always Something There To Remind Me	Naked Eyes	EMI America	7	(59)	F
11	-	Family Man	Daryl Hall & John Oates	RCA	7	(15)	
12	-	Faithfully	Journey	Columbia	7		
13	4	She Blinded Me With Science	Thomas Dolby	Capitol	11	(49)	F L
14	-	Never Gonna Let You Go	Sergio Mendes	A&M	12	(45)	L
15	-	Every Breath You Take	Police	A&M	16	(1)	G
16	-	Too Shy	Kajagoogoo	EMI America	8	(1)	F L
17	7	Little Red Corvette	Prince & The Revolution	Warner	10	(2)	
18	-	She's A Beauty	Tubes	Capitol	7		F L
19	8	Solitaire	Laura Branigan	Atlantic	8		
20	-	Wanna Be Startin' Something	Michael Jackson	Epic	10	(8)	

US 1983

APR-JUNE

◆ For the first time ever, over 60% of the Hot 100 were recorded by non-American artists – the majority being British!

▲ Michael Jackson's 'Beat It' video, with its 150 extras, cost a then record $70,000. The Grammy winning single soon joined its predecessor, 'Billie Jean', in the Top 5.

◆ The Us '83 Festival which attracted half the estimated 600,000 crowd, lost $10 million. Headliners David Bowie and Van Halen received $1 million each. Other performers included Men At Work, U2, The Pretenders and The Stray Cats.

UK
1983
JULY–SEPT

◆ David Bowie had ten albums in the British Top 100 (a feat bettered only by Elvis Presley), including the transatlantic Top 5 hit, **Let's Dance.**

▲ Stars of the Castle Donnington Rock Festival included ZZ Top (above), Meat Loaf, Twisted Sister and Whitesnake. Other successful live shows included Barry Manilow at Blenheim Palace, and The Prince's Trust Gala which included Duran Duran and Dire Straits.

◆ For the first time 90% of UK hits were available on twelve inch singles.

July 1983

This Mnth	Prev Mnth	Title	Artist	Label	Wks 20	(US Pos)	
1	10	Baby Jane	Rod Stewart	Warner	9	(14)	
2	-	Wherever I Lay My Hat (That's My Home)	Paul Young	CBS	9	(70)	F
3	-	I.O.U.	Freeez	Beggars Banquet	9		L
4	-	Moonlight Shadow	Mike Oldfield	Virgin	9		
5	7	Flashdance....What A Feeling	Irene Cara	Casablanca	9	(1)	L
6	-	Come Live With Me	Heaven 17	Virgin	7		
7	-	War Baby	Tom Robinson	Panic	5		L
8	-	Who's That Girl	Eurythmics	RCA	6	(21)	
9	-	Double Dutch	Malcolm McLaren	Charisma	9		
10	-	It's Over	Funk Masters	Master Funk	4		F L
11	-	Dead Giveaway	Shalamar	Solar	5	(22)	
12	13	I Guess That's Why They Call It The Blues	Elton John	Rocket	6	(4)	
13	1	Every Breath You Take	Police	A&M	8	(1)	
14	-	Rock 'n' Roll Is King	Electric Light Orchestra	Jet	4	(19)	L
15	-	Take That Situation	Nick Heyward	Arista	3		
16	-	Cruel Summer	Bananarama	London	5	(9)	
17	-	Wrapped Around Your Finger	Police	A&M	4	(8)	
18	-	The Trooper	Iron Maiden	EMI	3		
19	5	China Girl	David Bowie	EMI America	5	(10)	
20	-	When We Were Young	Bucks Fizz	RCA	3		

August 1983

This Mnth	Prev Mnth	Title	Artist	Label	Wks 20	(US Pos)	
1	-	Give It Up	KC & The Sunshine Band	Epic	9	(18)	L
2	-	Club Tropicana	Wham!	Innervision	7		
3	9	Double Dutch	Malcolm McLaren	Charisma	9		
4	3	I.O.U.	Freeez	Beggars Banquet	9		L
5	2	Wherever I Lay My Hat (That's My Home)	Paul Young	CBS	9	(70)	F
6	-	Long Hot Summer	Style Council	Polydor	5		
7	-	Gold	Spandau Ballet	Reformation	6	(29)	
8	-	I'm Still Standing	Elton John	Rocket	6	(12)	
9	-	Everything Counts	Depeche Mode	Mute	5		
10	-	The Crown	Gary Byrd & The GB Experience	Motown	5		F L
11	8	Who's That Girl	Eurythmics	RCA	6	(21)	
12	-	Rockit	Herbie Hancock	CBS	5	(71)	L
13	-	Big Log	Robert Plant	WEA	4	(20)	F L
14	16	Cruel Summer	Bananarama	London	5	(9)	
15	-	Wings Of A Dove	Madness	Stiff	6		
16	17	Wrapped Around Your Finger	Police	A&M	4	(8)	
17	-	It's Late	Shakin' Stevens	Epic	3		
18	4	Moonlight Shadow	Mike Oldfield	Virgin	9		
19	-	Watching You Watching Me	David Grant	Chrysalis	5		
20	6	Come Live With Me	Heaven 17	Virgin	7		

September 1983

This Mnth	Prev Mnth	Title	Artist	Label	Wks 20	(US Pos)	
1	-	Red Red Wine	UB40	Dep International	10	(34)	
2	15	Wings Of A Dove	Madness	Stiff	6		
3	-	Tonight I Celebrate My Love	Peabo Bryson & Roberta Flack	Capitol	7	(16)	F
4	-	What Am I Gonna Do	Rod Stewart	Warner	7	(35)	
5	-	Mama	Genesis	Virgin/Charisma	7	(73)	
6	-	Walking In The Rain	Modern Romance	WEA	6		L
7	1	Give It Up	KC & The Sunshine Band	Epic	9	(18)	L
8	-	The Sun Goes Down (Living It Up)	Level 42	Polydor	5		F
9	-	Karma Chameleon	Culture Club	Virgin	11	(1)	G
10	7	Gold	Spandau Ballet	Reformation	6	(29)	
11	8	I'm Still Standing	Elton John	Rocket	6	(12)	
12	-	Come Back And Stay	Paul Young	CBS	5	(22)	
13	-	Dolce Vita	Ryan Paris	Carrere	5		F L
14	2	Club Tropicana	Wham!	Innervision	7		
15	-	Chance	Big Country	Mercury	5		
16	6	Long Hot Summer	Style Council	Polydor	5		
17	-	Ol' Rag Blues	Status Quo	Vertigo	4		
18	19	Watching You Watching Me	David Grant	Chrysalis	5		
19	-	Confusion	New Order	Factory	3		
20	-	Modern Love	David Bowie	EMI America	6	(14)	

July 1983

This Mnth	Prev Mnth	Title	Artist	Label	Wks 20	(UK Pos)	
1	15	**Every Breath You Take**	Police	A&M	16	(1)	G
2	5	**Electric Avenue**	Eddy Grant	Portrait	12	(2)	F G L
3	1	**Flashdance....What A Feeling**	Irene Cara	Casablanca	16	(2)	G
4	14	**Never Gonna Let You Go**	Sergio Mendes	A&M	12	(45)	L
5	20	**Wanna Be Startin' Something**	Michael Jackson	Epic	10	(8)	
6	-	**Come Dancing**	Kinks	Arista	8	(12)	L
7	-	**Our House**	Madness	Geffen	7	(5)	F L
8	-	**Is There Something I Should Know**	Duran Duran	Capitol	9	(1)	
9	16	**Too Shy**	Kajagoogoo	EMI America	8	(1)	F L
10	-	**Stand Back**	Stevie Nicks	Modern	10		
11	2	**Time (Clock Of The Heart)**	Culture Club	Epic	11	(3)	
12	-	**She Works Hard For The Money**	Donna Summer	Mercury	11	(25)	
13	-	**Sweet Dreams (Are Made Of This)**	Eurythmics	RCA	13	(2)	F G
14	-	**1999**	Prince & The Revolution	Warner	6	(2)	
15	7	**Don't Let It End**	Styx	A&M	9	(56)	
16	-	**I'm Still Standing**	Elton John	Geffen	6	(4)	
17	11	**Family Man**	Daryl Hall & John Oates	RCA	7	(15)	
18	-	**Baby Jane**	Rod Stewart	Warner	4	(1)	
19	-	**Maniac**	Michael Sembello	Casablanca	13	(43)	F L
20	18	**She's A Beauty**	Tubes	Capitol	7		F L

August 1983

This Mnth	Prev Mnth	Title	Artist	Label	Wks 20	(UK Pos)	
1	1	**Every Breath You Take**	Police	A&M	16	(1)	G
2	13	**Sweet Dreams (Are Made Of This)**	Eurythmics	RCA	13	(2)	F G
3	12	**She Works Hard For The Money**	Donna Summer	Mercury	11	(25)	
4	19	**Maniac**	Michael Sembello	Casablanca	13	(43)	F L
5	10	**Stand Back**	Stevie Nicks	Modern	10		
6	8	**Is There Something I Should Know**	Duran Duran	Capitol	9	(1)	
7	-	**It's A Mistake**	Men At Work	Columbia	8	(33)	L
8	-	**(Keep Feeling) Fascination**	Human League	A&M	9	(2)	
9	3	**Flashdance....What A Feeling**	Irene Cara	Casablanca	16	(2)	G
10	-	**Puttin' On The Ritz**	Taco	RCA	9		F G L
11	4	**Never Gonna Let You Go**	Sergio Mendes	A&M	12	(45)	L
12	-	**I'll Tumble 4 Ya**	Culture Club	Epic	8		
13	-	**China Girl**	David Bowie	EMI America	6	(2)	
14	-	**Hot Girls In Love**	Loverboy	Columbia	6		F
15	2	**Electric Avenue**	Eddy Grant	Portrait	12	(2)	F G L
16	5	**Wanna Be Startin' Something**	Michael Jackson	Epic	10	(8)	
17	-	**Human Nature**	Michael Jackson	Epic	7		
18	-	**The Safety Dance**	Men Without Hats	Backstreet	11	(6)	F
19	-	**Take Me To Heart**	Quarterflash	Geffen	4		
20	-	**Lawyers In Love**	Jackson Browne	Asylum	6		

September 1983

This Mnth	Prev Mnth	Title	Artist	Label	Wks 20	(UK Pos)	
1	4	**Maniac**	Michael Sembello	Casablanca	13	(43)	F L
2	2	**Sweet Dreams (Are Made Of This)**	Eurythmics	RCA	13	(2)	F G
3	-	**Tell Her About It**	Billy Joel	Columbia	9	(4)	
4	18	**The Safety Dance**	Men Without Hats	Backstreet	11	(6)	F
5	10	**Puttin' On The Ritz**	Taco	RCA	9		F G L
6	-	**Total Eclipse Of The Heart**	Bonnie Tyler	Columbia	14	(1)	G L
7	1	**Every Breath You Take**	Police	A&M	16	(1)	G
8	17	**Human Nature**	Michael Jackson	Epic	7		
9	-	**Don't Cry**	Asia	Geffen	7	(33)	L
10	-	**Making Love Out Of Nothing At All**	Air Supply	Arista	13		G
11	-	**(She's) Sexy + 17**	Stray Cats	EMI America	8	(29)	L
12	3	**She Works Hard For The Money**	Donna Summer	Mercury	11	(25)	
13	12	**I'll Tumble 4 Ya**	Culture Club	Epic	8		
14	20	**Lawyers In Love**	Jackson Browne	Asylum	6		
15	8	**(Keep Feeling) Fascination**	Human League	A&M	9	(2)	
16	-	**Far From Over**	Frank Stallone	RSO	6	(68)	F L
17	7	**It's A Mistake**	Men At Work	Columbia	8	(33)	L
18	-	**King Of Pain**	Police	A&M	9	(17)	
19	-	**Promises, Promises**	Naked Eyes	EMI America	6		L
20	-	**True**	Spandau Ballet	Chrysalis	9	(1)	F L

US 1983
JULY-SEPT

◆ In April half the American Top 30 singles were by British artists, and in June, British acts had their best ever showing on the US Hot 100. Included among the hit makers were veterans of the first British Invasion, The Kinks and The Hollies.

◆ In Britain, UB40 had their first No. 1, with a revival of Neil Diamond's 'Red Red Wine', while in America, Canadian quintet Sheriff had a minor hit with 'When I'm With You'. Both records returned to top the US charts in the late 1980s.

◆ The Police performed in front of 70,000 at Shea Stadium and Run DMC and L.L. Cool J. headlined a controversial rap tour. Also Simon & Garfunkel started a reunion tour and Diana Ross staged a free show in Central Park.

UK 1983 OCT-DEC

▲ Culture Club's only transatlantic chart topper, 'Karma Chameleon', was Britain's top single in 1983, selling nearly 1.5 million.

◆ In 1983, Michael Jackson not only had the biggest album, **Thriller,** he also earned the first platinum music video for *The Making Of Thriller*, and amassed seven US Top 10 singles –. the best yearly performance since The Beatles in 1964!

◆ British group Pink Floyd's **Dark Side of The Moon** logged its 491st chart week in America, beating the existing record set Johnny Mathis' **Greatest Hits** album.

October 1983

This Mnth	Prev Mnth	Title	Artist	Label	Wks 20	(US Pos)	
1	9	Karma Chameleon	Culture Club	Virgin	11	(1)	G
2	20	Modern Love	David Bowie	EMI America	6	(14)	
3	-	They Don't Know	Tracey Ullman	Stiff	6	(8)	
4	-	Dear Prudence	Siouxsie & The Banshees	Wonderland	6		
5	-	New Song	Howard Jones	WEA	6	(27)	F
6	1	Red Red Wine	UB40	Dep International	10	(34)	
7	-	This Is Not A Love Song	Public Image Ltd.	Virgin	5		
8	-	Blue Monday	New Order	Factory	7		
9	-	In Your Eyes	George Benson	Warner	6		
10	-	All Night Long (All Night)	Lionel Richie	Motown	8	(1)	
11	-	(Hey You) The Rocksteady Crew	Rocksteady Crew	Virgin	6		F L
12	12	Come Back And Stay	Paul Young	CBS	5	(22)	
13	3	Tonight I Celebrate My Love	Peabo Bryson & Roberta Flack	Capitol	7	(16)	F
14	-	Superman (Gioca Jouer)	Black Lace	Flair	5		F
15	-	Tahiti (From Mutiny On The Bounty)	David Essex	Mercury	5		L
16	5	Mama	Genesis	Virgin/Charisma	7	(73)	
17	-	Big Apple	Kajagoogoo	EMI	4		L
18	-	The Safety Dance	Men Without Hats	Statik	6	(3)	F L
19	13	Dolce Vita	Ryan Paris	Carrere	5		F L
20	15	Chance	Big Country	Mercury	5		

November 1983

1	-	Uptown Girl	Billy Joel	CBS	12	(3)	
2	10	All Night Long (All Night)	Lionel Richie	Motown	8	(1)	
3	-	Say Say Say	Paul McCartney & Michael Jackson	Parlophone	9	(1)	
4	-	Cry Just A Little Bit	Shakin' Stevens	Epic	7	(67)	
5	-	Puss 'n Boots	Adam Ant	CBS	4		
6	-	The Love Cats	Cure	Fiction	5		
7	1	Karma Chameleon	Culture Club	Virgin	11	(1)	G
8	18	The Safety Dance	Men Without Hats	Statik	6	(3)	F L
9	-	The Sun And The Rain	Madness	Stiff	4	(72)	
10	-	Union Of The Snake	Duran Duran	EMI	4	(3)	
11	-	Never Never	Assembly	Mute	4		F L
12	-	Please Don't Make Me Cry	UB40	Dep International	5		
13	11	(Hey You) The Rocksteady Crew	Rocksteady Crew	Virgin	6		F L
14	3	They Don't Know	Tracey Ullman	Stiff	6	(8)	
15	5	New Song	Howard Jones	WEA	6	(27)	F
16	-	Love Of The Common People	Paul Young	CBS	10	(45)	
17	-	Solid Bond In Your Heart	Style Council	Polydor	3		
18	-	Undercover Of The Night	Rolling Stones	Rolling Stone	3	(9)	
19	-	Calling Your Name	Marilyn	Mercury	4		F L
20	-	Unconditional Love	Donna Summer	Mercury	2	(43)	

December 1983

1	-	Only You	Flying Pickets	10	7		F
2	16	Love Of The Common People	Paul Young	CBS	10	(45)	
3	-	Hold Me Now	Thompson Twins	Arista	9	(3)	
4	-	My Oh My	Slade	RCA	7	(37)	
5	-	Let's Stay Together	Tina Turner	Capitol	8	(26)	F
6	1	Uptown Girl	Billy Joel	CBS	12	(3)	
7	-	Victims	Culture Club	Virgin	6		
8	-	Please Don't Fall In Love	Cliff Richard	EMI	6		
9	-	Move Over Darling	Tracey Ullman	Stiff	5		
10	-	Islands In The Stream	Kenny Rogers & Dolly Parton	RCA	7	(1)	L
11	-	Tell Her About It	Billy Joel	CBS	7	(1)	
12	-	Thriller	Michael Jackson	Epic	9	(4)	
13	19	Calling Your Name	Marilyn	Mercury	4		F L
14	-	Marguerita Time	Status Quo	Vertigo	6		
15	3	Say Say Say	Paul McCartney & Michael Jackson	Parlophone	9	(1)	
16	-	What Is Love	Howard Jones	WEA	8	(33)	
17	11	Never Never	Assembly	Mute	4		F L
18	4	Cry Just A Little Bit	Shakin' Stevens	Epic	7	(67)	
19	-	Right By Your Side	Eurythmics	RCA	4	(29)	
20	-	That's All!	Genesis	Charisma/virgin	4	(6)	

October 1983

This Mnth	Prev Mnth	Title	Artist	Label	Wks 20	(UK Pos)	
1	6	Total Eclipse Of The Heart	Bonnie Tyler	Columbia	14	(1)	G L
2	10	Making Love Out Of Nothing At All	Air Supply	Arista	13		G
3	20	True	Spandau Ballet	Chrysalis	9	(1)	F L
4	-	Islands In The Stream	Kenny Rogers & Dolly Parton	RCA	15	(7)	G
5	18	King Of Pain	Police	A&M	9	(17)	
6	-	One Thing Leads To Another	Fixx	MCA	9		
7	4	The Safety Dance	Men Without Hats	Backstreet	11	(6)	F
8	-	All Night Long (All Night)	Lionel Richie	Motown	15	(2)	G
9	3	Tell Her About It	Billy Joel	Columbia	9	(4)	
10	11	(She's) Sexy + 17	Stray Cats	EMI America	8	(29)	L
11	-	Telefone (Long Distance Love Affair)	Sheena Easton	EMI America	9		
12	-	Delirious	Prince & The Revolution	Warner	8		
13	-	Burning Down The House	Talking Heads	Sire	5		F L
14	16	Far From Over	Frank Stallone	RSO	6	(68)	F L
15	19	Promises, Promises	Naked Eyes	EMI America	6		L
16	-	Suddenly Last Summer	Motels	Capitol	8		
17	-	How Am I Supposed To Live Without You	Laura Branigan	Atlantic	6		
18	1	Maniac	Michael Sembello	Casablanca	13	(43)	F L
19	-	Uptown Girl	Billy Joel	Columbia	13	(1)	G
20	-	If Anyone Falls	Stevie Nicks	Modern	4		

November 1983

This Mnth	Prev Mnth	Title	Artist	Label	Wks 20	(UK Pos)	
1	8	All Night Long (All Night)	Lionel Richie	Motown	15	(2)	G
2	4	Islands In The Stream	Kenny Rogers & Dolly Parton	RCA	15	(7)	G
3	-	Say Say Say	Paul McCartney & Michael Jackson	Columbia	16	(2)	G
4	19	Uptown Girl	Billy Joel	Columbia	13	(1)	G
5	1	Total Eclipse Of The Heart	Bonnie Tyler	Columbia	14	(1)	G L
6	-	Cum On Feel The Noize	Quiet Riot	Pasha	11	(45)	F G L
7	6	One Thing Leads To Another	Fixx	MCA	9		
8	-	Love Is A Battlefield	Pat Benatar	Chrysalis	12	(17)	
9	16	Suddenly Last Summer	Motels	Capitol	8		L
10	12	Delirious	Prince & The Revolution	Warner	8		
11	2	Making Love Out Of Nothing At All	Air Supply	Arista	13		G
12	11	Telefone (Long Distance Love Affair)	Sheena Easton	EMI America	9		
13	-	Say It Isn't So	Daryl Hall & John Oates	RCA	13	(69)	
14	-	Heart And Soul	Huey Lewis & The News	Chrysalis	7		
15	-	P.Y.T. (Pretty Young Thing)	Michael Jackson	Epic	6	(11)	L
16	-	Crumblin' Down	John Cougar Mellencamp	Riva	6		
17	3	True	Spandau Ballet	Chrysalis	9	(1)	F L
18	-	Modern Love	David Bowie	EMI America	5	(2)	
19	-	Tonight I Celebrate My Love	Peabo Bryson & Roberta Flack	Capitol	8	(2)	F
20	-	Church Of The Poison Mind	Culture Club	Epic	8	(2)	

December 1983

This Mnth	Prev Mnth	Title	Artist	Label	Wks 20	(UK Pos)	
1	3	Say Say Say	Paul McCartney & Michael Jackson	Columbia	16	(2)	G
2	13	Say It Isn't So	Daryl Hall & John Oates	RCA	13	(69)	
3	1	All Night Long (All Night)	Lionel Richie	Motown	15	(2)	G
4	4	Uptown Girl	Billy Joel	Columbia	13	(1)	G
5	-	Union Of The Snake	Duran Duran	Capitol	10	(3)	
6	8	Love Is A Battlefield	Pat Benatar	Chrysalis	12	(17)	
7	-	Owner Of A Lonely Heart	Yes	Atco	13	(28)	L
8	-	Twist Of Fate	Olivia Newton-John	MCA	10	(57)	
9	2	Islands In The Stream	Kenny Rogers & Dolly Parton	RCA	15	(7)	G
10	20	Church Of The Poison Mind	Culture Club	Epic	8	(2)	
11	6	Cum On Feel The Noize	Quiet Riot	Pasha	11	(45)	F G L
12	-	Undercover Of The Night	Rolling Stones	Rolling Stone	8	(11)	
13	16	Crumblin' Down	John Cougar Mellencamp	Riva	6		
14	-	Why Me?	Irene Cara	Geffen/Network	7		
15	-	Break My Stride	Matthew Wilder	Private I	11	(4)	F L
16	-	Major Tom (Coming Home)	Peter Schilling	Elektra	7	(42)	F L
17	-	I Guess That's Why They Call It The Blues	Elton John	Geffen	10	(5)	
18	-	Synchronicity II	Police	A&M	6	(17)	
19	14	Heart And Soul	Huey Lewis & The News	Chrysalis	7		
20	-	Talking In Your Sleep	Romantics	Nemperor	12		F L

US 1983

OCT-DEC

◆ Total record and tape sales in 1983 went up 3% to $3.7 billion, with tapes outselling records for the first time.

◆ The success of MTV, and videos in general, meant an act's image was now almost as important as their sound. This situation not only benefited the British invaders, it boosted heavy metal sales and helped Michael Jackson and Prince crossover to the pop market (they were among the very few black artists seen on MTV).

◆ Jim Steinman (known for his work with Meat Loaf) produced October's top two by Bonnie Tyler (the first Welsh artist to reach No. 1) and Air Supply.

◆ Winners of the first *Billboard* Video Awards included Michael Jackson, ZZ Top, Duran Duran and Eurythmics.

UK 1984 JAN-MAR

◆ As 'Nobody Told Me' gave John Lennon his last transatlantic Top 20 hit, Paul McCartney scored his only British No. 1 of the 1980s, 'Pipes Of Peace', which, oddly, failed to chart Stateside.

◆ Despite being banned by the BBC, 'Relax' by Frankie Goes To Hollywood became one of Britain's biggest ever sellers.

◆ The *NME* Poll showed New Order as Best Group, their 'Blue Monday' as Top Record, and fellow Mancunians The Smiths as Best New Group. Incidentally, in January, The Smiths' first three releases held the top three rungs on the Independent chart.

◆ Culture Club, fronted by gender bender Boy George, were mobbed at the airport by over 2,500 fans when they arrived in North America for a two-month tour.

January 1984

This Mnth	Prev Mnth	Title	Artist	Label	Wks 20	(US Pos)	
1	-	Pipes Of Peace	Paul McCartney	Parlophone	6		
2	16	What Is Love	Howard Jones	WEA	8	(33)	
3	-	Relax	Frankie Goes To Hollywood	ZTT	25	(10)	F G
4	14	Marguerita Time	Status Quo	Vertigo	6		
5	11	Tell Her About It	Billy Joel	CBS	7	(1)	
6	2	Love Of The Common People	Paul Young	CBS	10	(45)	
7	-	A Rockin' Good Way	Shaky & Bonnie	CBS	5		
8	-	That's Living (Alright)	Joe Fagin	Towerbell	7		F L
9	10	Islands In The Stream	Kenny Rogers & Dolly Parton	RCA	7	(1)	L
10	3	Hold Me Now	Thompson Twins	Arista	9	(3)	
11	1	Only You	Flying Pickets	10	7		F
12	7	Victims	Culture Club	Virgin	6		
13	-	Bird Of Paradise	Snowy White	Towerbell	4		F L
14	4	My Oh My	Slade	RCA	7	(37)	
15	-	Nobody Told Me	John Lennon	Ono/Polydor	3	(5)	L
16	12	Thriller	Michael Jackson	Epic	9	(4)	
17	-	Wonderland	Big Country	Mercury	4	(86)	
18	-	Running With The Night	Lionel Richie	Motown	2	(7)	
19	-	Wishful Thinking	China Crisis	Virgin	4		
20	5	Let's Stay Together	Tina Turner	Capitol	8	(26)	F

February 1984

This Mnth	Prev Mnth	Title	Artist	Label	Wks 20	(US Pos)	
1	3	Relax	Frankie Goes To Hollywood	ZTT	25	(10)	F G
2	-	Radio Ga Ga	Queen	EMI	6	(16)	
3	-	Girls Just Want To Have Fun	Cyndi Lauper	Portrait	7	(2)	F
4	-	Break My Stride	Matthew Wilder	Epic	7	(5)	F L
5	-	Doctor Doctor	Thompson Twins	Arista	7	(11)	
6	8	That's Living (Alright)	Joe Fagin	Towerbell	7		F L
7	-	Holiday	Madonna	Sire	5	(16)	F
8	-	New Moon On Monday	Duran Duran	EMI	4	(10)	
9	-	(Feels Like) Heaven	Fiction Factory	CBS	4		F L
10	-	99 Red Balloons	Nena	Epic	8	(2)	F L
11	-	My Ever Changing Moods	Style Council	Polydor	4		
12	-	Here Comes The Rain Again	Eurythmics	RCA	5	(4)	
13	-	The Killing Moon	Echo & The Bunnymen	Korova	3		
14	-	What Difference Does It Make	Smiths	Rough Trade	4		F
15	-	Somebody's Watching Me	Rockwell	Motown	6	(2)	F L
16	-	Love Theme From 'The Thorn Birds'	Juan Martin	WEA	2		F L
17	-	Wouldn't It Be Good	Nik Kershaw	MCA	7	(46)	F
18	17	Wonderland	Big Country	Mercury	4	(86)	
19	-	Michael Caine	Madness	Stiff	3		
20	1	Pipes Of Peace	Paul McCartney	Parlophone	6		

March 1984

This Mnth	Prev Mnth	Title	Artist	Label	Wks 20	(US Pos)	
1	10	99 Red Balloons	Nena	Epic	8	(2)	F L
2	-	Joanna/Tonight	Kool & The Gang	De-Lite	7	(2)	
3	-	Street Dance	Break Machine	Record Shack	8		F
4	17	Wouldn't It Be Good	Nik Kershaw	MCA	7	(46)	F
5	1	Relax	Frankie Goes To Hollywood	ZTT	25	(10)	F G
6	-	Hello	Lionel Richie	Motown	10	(1)	
7	-	An Innocent Man	Billy Joel	CBS	7	(10)	
8	15	Somebody's Watching Me	Rockwell	Motown	6	(2)	F L
9	-	It's Raining Men	Weather Girls	CBS	6	(46)	F L
10	-	Jump	Van Halen	Warner	5	(1)	F
11	-	What Do I Do	Phil Fearon & Galaxy	Ensign	5		
12	-	The Music Of Torvill & Dean EP	Richard Hartley/ Michael Reed Orchestra	Safari	5		F L
13	-	Run Runaway	Slade	RCA	5	(20)	
14	-	Robert De Niro's Waiting	Bananarama	London	5	(95)	
15	5	Doctor Doctor	Thompson Twins	Arista	7	(11)	
16	-	Your Love Is King	Sade	Epic	5	(54)	F
17	-	Hide And Seek	Howard Jones	WEA	5		
18	-	It's A Miracle	Culture Club	Virgin	5	(13)	
19	2	Radio Ga Ga	Queen	EMI	6	(16)	
20	11	My Ever Changing Moods	Style Council	Polydor	4		

January 1984

This Mnth	Prev Mnth	Title	Artist	Label	Wks 20	(UK Pos)	
1	7	Owner Of A Lonely Heart	Yes	Atco	13	(28)	L
2	1	Say Say Say	Paul McCartney & Michael Jackson	Columbia	16	(2)	G
3	20	Talking In Your Sleep	Romantics	Nemperor	12		F L
4	15	Break My Stride	Matthew Wilder	Private I	11	(4)	F L
5	17	I Guess That's Why They Call It The Blues	Elton John	Geffen	10	(5)	
6	8	Twist Of Fate	Olivia Newton-John	MCA	10	(57)	
7	-	Karma Chameleon	Culture Club	Virgin	13	(1)	G
8	2	Say It Isn't So	Daryl Hall & John Oates	RCA	13	(69)	
9	5	Union Of The Snake	Duran Duran	Capitol	10	(3)	
10	-	Running With The Night	Lionel Richie	Motown	8	(9)	
11	-	Joanna	Kool & The Gang	De-Lite	10	(2)	
12	-	That's All!	Genesis	Atlantic	8	(16)	
13	12	Undercover Of The Night	Rolling Stones	Rolling Stone	8	(11)	
14	3	All Night Long (All Night)	Lionel Richie	Motown	15	(2)	G
15	4	Uptown Girl	Billy Joel	Columbia	13	(1)	G
16	-	Think Of Laura	Christopher Cross	Warner	6		L
17	-	Pink Houses	John Cougar Mellencamp	Riva	5		
18	6	Love Is A Battlefield	Pat Benatar	Chrysalis	12	(17)	
19	-	The Curly Shuffle	Jump 'N The Saddle	Atlantic	3		F L
20	-	I Still Can't Get Over You	Ray Parker Jr.	Arista	5		

February 1984

This Mnth	Prev Mnth	Title	Artist	Label	Wks 20	(UK Pos)	
1	7	Karma Chameleon	Culture Club	Virgin	13	(1)	G
2	11	Joanna	Kool & The Gang	De-Lite	10	(2)	
3	-	Jump	Van Halen	Warner	13	(7)	G
4	3	Talking In Your Sleep	Romantics	Nemperor	12		F L
5	12	That's All!	Genesis	Atlantic	8	(16)	
6	1	Owner Of A Lonely Heart	Yes	Atco	13	(28)	L
7	-	99 Luftballons	Nena	Epic	10	(1)	F G L
8	10	Running With The Night	Lionel Richie	Motown	8	(9)	
9	-	Let The Music Play	Shannon	Mirage	8	(14)	F G L
10	-	Girls Just Want To Have Fun	Cyndi Lauper	Portrait	10	(2)	F G
11	16	Think Of Laura	Christopher Cross	Warner	6		L
12	-	An Innocent Man	Billy Joel	Columbia	7	(8)	
13	-	Thriller	Michael Jackson	Epic	8	(10)	G
14	4	Break My Stride	Matthew Wilder	Private I	11	(4)	F L
15	5	I Guess That's Why They Call It The Blues	Elton John	Geffen	10	(5)	
16	17	Pink Houses	John Cougar Mellencamp	Riva	5		
17	-	Nobody Told Me	John Lennon	Polydor	7	(6)	L
18	-	Wrapped Around Your Finger	Police	A&M	7	(7)	L
19	20	I Still Can't Get Over You	Ray Parker Jr.	Arista	5		
20	-	Somebody's Watching Me	Rockwell	Motown	10	(6)	F G L

March 1984

This Mnth	Prev Mnth	Title	Artist	Label	Wks 20	(UK Pos)	
1	3	Jump	Van Halen	Warner	13	(7)	G
2	20	Somebody's Watching Me	Rockwell	Motown	10	(6)	F G L
3	10	Girls Just Want To Have Fun	Cyndi Lauper	Portrait	10	(2)	F G
4	7	99 Luftballons	Nena	Epic	10	(1)	F G L
5	-	Footloose	Kenny Loggins	Columbia	12	(6)	G
6	-	Here Comes The Rain Again	Eurythmics	RCA	10	(8)	
7	-	I Want A New Drug	Huey Lewis & The News	Chrysalis	8		
8	13	Thriller	Michael Jackson	Epic	8	(10)	G
9	17	Nobody Told Me	John Lennon	Polydor	7	(6)	L
10	-	Automatic	Pointer Sisters	Planet	8	(2)	
11	-	Got A Hold On Me	Christine McVie	Warner	6		F L
12	-	Adult Education	Daryl Hall & John Oates	RCA	8	(63)	
13	-	New Moon On Monday	Duran Duran	Capitol	6	(9)	
14	1	Karma Chameleon	Culture Club	Virgin	13	(1)	G
15	18	Wrapped Around Your Finger	Police	A&M	7	(7)	L
16	-	The Language Of Love	Dan Fogelberg	Full Moon	5		L
17	-	Against All Odds (Take A Look At Me Now)	Phil Collins	Atlantic	10	(2)	G
18	9	Let The Music Play	Shannon	Mirage	8	(14)	F G L
19	-	Miss Me Blind	Culture Club	Virgin	8		
20	-	Hold Me Now	Thompson Twins	Arista	11	(4)	F

US
1984
JAN-MAR

◆ Michael Jackson's **Thriller,** with world sales of 30 million, became the biggest selling record ever. Jackson, also received a record eight Grammy Awards and seven American Music Awards.

◆ Nena's German recording '99 Luftballons' was an international hit, albeit in an English lyric version in Britain.

▲ Two new American women creating a stir were Cyndi Lauper (above), who won Best New Act in the Grammy Awards and Madonna.

◆ Jackie Wilson, one of the all-time greats of soul music, died after spending over eight years in a coma.

UK 1984
APR-JUNE

◆ The Beatles, who had recently had streets named after them in Liverpool, were made Freemen of that city – it's highest honour. Also in Liverpool, the Beatles City Exhibition Centre opened and the Cavern Club was re-launched.

◆ Frankie Goes To Hollywood's second single, 'Two Tribes', entered at No. 1 and spent nine weeks at the summit. Soon afterwards 'Relax' moved back up to No. 2. Both singles sold over a million in the UK.

▲ Elton John (above), Kool & The Gang and Brits winner Paul Young (whose No Parlez album sold over a million) performed in front of 72,000 at Wembley Stadium.

April 1984

This Mnth	Prev Mnth	Title	Artist	Label	Wks 20	(US Pos)	
1	6	Hello	Lionel Richie	Motown	10	(1)	
2	-	You Take Me Up	Thompson Twins	Arista	6	(44)	
3	-	A Love Worth Waiting For	Shakin' Stevens	Epic	6		
4	-	People Are People	Depeche Mode	Mute	6	(13)	
5	-	Glad It's All Over/Damned On 45	Captain Sensible	A&M	5		L
6	-	Against All Odds (Take A Look At Me Now)	Phil Collins	Virgin	8	(1)	
7	14	Robert De Niro's Waiting	Bananarama	London	5	(95)	
8	-	I Want To Break Free	Queen	EMI	9	(45)	
9	-	Nelson Mandela	Special AKA	2 Tone	4		L
10	18	It's A Miracle	Culture Club	Virgin	5	(13)	
11	-	Ain't Nobody	Rufus & Chaka Khan	Warner	6	(22)	F
12	9	It's Raining Men	Weather Girls	CBS	6	(46)	F L
13	-	(When You Say You Love Somebody) In The Heart	Kool & The Gang	De-Lite	4		
14	11	What Do I Do	Phil Fearon & Galaxy	Ensign	5		
15	-	Wood Beez (Pray Like Aretha Franklin)	Scritti Politti	Virgin	3	(91)	F
16	-	P.Y.T. (Pretty Young Thing)	Michael Jackson	Epic	3	(10)	
17	16	Your Love Is King	Sade	Epic	5	(54)	F
18	-	The Reflex	Duran Duran	EMI	8	(1)	
19	-	Don't Tell Me	Blancmange	London	6		L
20	-	Cherry Oh Baby	UB40	Dep International	3		

May 1984

This Mnth	Prev Mnth	Title	Artist	Label	Wks 20	(US Pos)	
1	18	The Reflex	Duran Duran	EMI	8	(1)	
2	-	Automatic	Pointer Sisters	Planet	7	(5)	
3	6	Against All Odds (Take A Look At...)	Phil Collins	Virgin	8	(1)	
4	8	I Want To Break Free	Queen	EMI	9	(45)	
5	-	One Love/People Get Ready	Bob Marley & The Wailers	Island	5		L
6	-	Locomotion	O.M.D.	Virgin	7		
7	-	When You're Young And In Love	Flying Pickets	10	5		L
8	19	Don't Tell Me	Blancmange	London	6		L
9	-	Footloose	Kenny Loggins	CBS	4	(1)	F L
10	-	Let's Hear It For The Boy	Deniece Williams	CBS	7	(1)	L
11	1	Hello	Lionel Richie	Motown	10	(1)	
12	-	Dancing Girls	Nik Kershaw	MCA	3		
13	-	The Lebanon	Human League	Virgin	3	(64)	
14	-	I'm Falling	Bluebells	London	4		F
15	-	Love Games	Belle & The Devotions	CBS	2		F L
16	-	Wake Me Up Before You Go Go	Wham!	Epic	8	(1)	
17	-	Break Dance Party	Break Machine	Record Shack	4		L
18	13	(When You Say You...) In The Heart	Kool & The Gang	De-Lite	4		
19	-	Somebody Else's Guy	Jocelyn Brown	4th & Broadway	3	(75)	F
20	2	You Take Me Up	Thompson Twins	Arista	6	(44)	

June 1984

This Mnth	Prev Mnth	Title	Artist	Label	Wks 20	(US Pos)	
1	16	Wake Me Up Before You Go Go	Wham!	Epic	8	(1)	
2	-	Two Tribes	Frankie Goes To Hollywood	ZTT	14	(43)	G
3	-	Smalltown Boy	Bronski Beat	Forbidden Fruit	7	(48)	F
4	-	High Energy	Evelyn Thomas	Record Shack	5	(85)	F L
5	10	Let's Hear It For The Boy	Deniece Williams	CBS	7	(1)	L
6	-	Dancing With Tears In My Eyes	Ultravox	Chrysalis	5		
7	-	Only When You Leave	Spandau Ballet	Reformation	4	(34)	
8	-	Relax	Frankie Goes To Hollywood	ZTT	25	(10)	F G
9	-	Sad Songs (Say So Much)	Elton John	Rocket	5	(5)	
10	-	Pearl In The Shell	Howard Jones	WEA	4		
11	-	Searchin' (I Gotta Find A Man)	Hazell Dean	Proto	5		F
12	-	Groovin' (You're The Best Thing)/Big Boss Groove	Style Council	Polydor	5		
13	-	I Won't Let The Sun Go Down On Me	Nik Kershaw	MCA	8		
14	1	The Reflex	Duran Duran	EMI	8	(1)	
15	-	Farewell My Summer Love	Michael Jackson	Motown	5	(38)	
16	-	Heaven Knows I'm Miserable Now	Smiths	Rough Trade	5		
17	-	I Feel Like Buddy Holly	Alvin Stardust	Stiff	5		
18	-	Thinking Of You	Sister Sledge	Cotillion/Atlantic	6		
19	2	Automatic	Pointer Sisters	Planet	7	(5)	
20	4	I Want To Break Free	Queen	EMI	9	(45)	

April 1984

This Mnth	Prev Mnth	Title	Artist	Label	Wks 20	(UK Pos)	
1	5	Footloose	Kenny Loggins	Columbia	12	(6)	G
2	17	Against All Odds (Take A Look At Me Now)	Phil Collins	Atlantic	10	(2)	G
3	-	Hello	Lionel Richie	Motown	14	(1)	G
4	2	Somebody's Watching Me	Rockwell	Motown	10	(6)	F G L
5	19	Miss Me Blind	Culture Club	Virgin	8		
6	10	Automatic	Pointer Sisters	Planet	9	(2)	
7	20	Hold Me Now	Thompson Twins	Arista	11	(4)	F
8	6	Here Comes The Rain Again	Eurythmics	RCA	10	(8)	
9	12	Adult Education	Daryl Hall & John Oates	RCA	8	(63)	
10	-	Love Somebody	Rick Springfield	RCA	8		
11	-	They Don't Know	Tracey Ullman	MCA	7	(2)	F L
12	1	Jump	Van Halen	Warner	13	(7)	G
13	-	You Might Think	Cars	Elektra	8		
14	-	Eat It	Weird Al Yankovic	Rock 'n' Roll	5	(36)	F L
15	-	To All The Girls I've Loved Before	Julio Iglesias & Willie Nelson	Columbia	9	(17)	F G
16	3	Girls Just Want To Have Fun	Cyndi Lauper	Portrait	10	(2)	F G
17	7	I Want A New Drug	Huey Lewis & The News	Chrysalis	8		
18	-	Girls	Dwight Twilley	EMI America	4		L
19	-	Tonight	Kool & The Gang	De-Lite	6	(2)	
20	-	Let's Hear It For The Boy	Deniece Williams	Columbia	11	(2)	G L

May 1984

This Mnth	Prev Mnth	Title	Artist	Label	Wks 20	(UK Pos)	
1	3	Hello	Lionel Richie	Motown	14	(1)	G
2	20	Let's Hear It For The Boy	Deniece Williams	Columbia	11	(2)	G L
3	7	Hold Me Now	Thompson Twins	Arista	11	(4)	F
4	15	To All The Girls I've Loved Before	Julio Iglesias & Willie Nelson	Columbia	9	(17)	F G
5	2	Against All Odds (Take A Look At Me Now)	Phil Collins	Atlantic	10	(2)	G
6	10	Love Somebody	Rick Springfield	RCA	8		
7	-	Time After Time	Cyndi Lauper	Portrait	11	(3)	
8	-	Oh, Sherrie	Steve Perry	Columbia	11		
9	13	You Might Think	Cars	Elektra	8		
10	1	Footloose	Kenny Loggins	Columbia	12	(6)	G
11	-	Head Over Heels	Go-Go's	IRS	7		L
12	-	Breakdance	Irene Cara	Geffen	8		L
13	11	They Don't Know	Tracey Ullman	MCA	7	(2)	F L
14	-	The Reflex	Duran Duran	Capitol	11	(1)	
15	-	The Longest Time	Billy Joel	Columbia	5	(25)	
16	-	Sister Christian	Night Ranger	MCA	8		F
17	19	Tonight	Kool & The Gang	De-Lite	6	(2)	
18	-	Authority Song	John Cougar Mellencamp	Riva	4		
19	5	Miss Me Blind	Culture Club	Virgin	8		
20	-	The Heart Of Rock 'n' Roll	Huey Lewis & The News	Chrysalis	9		

June 1984

This Mnth	Prev Mnth	Title	Artist	Label	Wks 20	(UK Pos)	
1	7	Time After Time	Cyndi Lauper	Portrait	11	(3)	
2	14	The Reflex	Duran Duran	Capitol	11	(1)	
3	2	Let's Hear It For The Boy	Deniece Williams	Columbia	11	(2)	G L
4	8	Oh, Sherrie	Steve Perry	Columbia	11		
5	20	The Heart Of Rock 'n' Roll	Huey Lewis & The News	Chrysalis	9		
6	-	Self Control	Laura Branigan	Atlantic	10	(5)	
7	-	Jump (For My Love)	Pointer Sisters	Planet	11	(6)	
8	-	Dancing In The Dark	Bruce Springsteen	Columbia	13	(4)	G
9	16	Sister Christian	Night Ranger	MCA	8		F
10	-	Borderline	Madonna	Sire	8	(2)	
11	1	Hello	Lionel Richie	Motown	14	(1)	G
12	12	Breakdance	Irene Cara	Geffen	8		L
13	-	Eyes Without A Face	Billy Idol	Chrysalis	10	(18)	F
14	-	When Doves Cry	Prince	Warner	14	(4)	P
15	-	It's A Miracle	Culture Club	Virgin	6	(4)	
16	-	Almost Paradise...Love Theme From Footloose	Mike Reno & Ann Wilson	Columbia	9		F L
17	-	I'll Wait	Van Halen	Warner	5		
18	4	To All The Girls I've Loved Before	Julio Iglesias & Willie Nelson	Columbia	9	(17)	F G
19	-	You Can't Get What You Want (Till You Know What You Want)	Joe Jackson	A&M	4		L
20	-	Stay The Night	Chicago	Full Moon	3		

◆ British artists held a record forty places on the Hot 100.

◆ Transatlantic toppers included: 'Wake Me Up Before You Go Go' by Wham!, 'The Reflex' by Duran Duran (remixed by Nile Rodgers) and Lionel Richie's 'Hello'. Richie was on a 50-date American tour with Tina Turner.

◆ Among the hit makers who died were: soul superstar Marvin Gaye, Ral Donner, and R&B great Z.Z. Hill and top tunesmiths Meredith Wilson and Jimmy Kennedy.

◆ The soundtrack to the film *Footloose* was on top for 10 weeks. It included the transatlantic hits 'Let's Hear It For The Boy' (Deniece Williams) and 'Footloose' (Kenny Loggins).

UK 1984 JULY-SEPT

◆ Stevie Wonder's 36th British hit 'I Just Called To Say I Love You' was not only his first solo No. 1, but also Motown's first UK million seller. It was the third British million seller in a row to head the chart (following 'Two Tribes' and 'Careless Whisper') – a record unlikely to be broken.

▲ Americans in Britain included Van Halen and Motley Crue, who appeared at the Castle Donnington Festival, Bob Dylan, who was joined on stage by local notables Bono, Van Morrison and Eric Clapton, and Billy Joel (above), who, after his Wembley show was screened on TV, found himself with six albums in the British chart.

July 1984

This Mnth	Prev Mnth	Title	Artist	Label	Wks 20	(US Pos)	
1	2	Two Tribes	Frankie Goes To Hollywood	ZTT	14	(43)	G
2	-	Relax	Frankie Goes To Hollywood	ZTT	25	(10)	F G
3	-	Time After Time	Cyndi Lauper	Portrait	7	(1)	
4	13	I Won't Let The Sun Go Down On Me	Nik Kershaw	MCA	8		
5	-	Hole In My Shoe	neil	WEA	6		F L
6	-	Jump (For My Love)	Pointer Sisters	Planet	5	(3)	
7	-	White Lines (Don't Don't Do It)	Grandmaster Flash, Melle Mel & The Furious Five	Sugar Hill	12		L
8	-	When Doves Cry	Prince	Warner	8	(1)	F
9	-	Breakin'...There's No Stopping Us	Ollie & Jerry	Polydor	5	(9)	F L
10	-	What's Love Got To Do With It	Tina Turner	Capitol	10	(1)	
11	-	Love Resurrection	Alison Moyet	CBS	5	(82)	F
12	-	Young At Heart	Bluebells	London	6		
13	-	Sister Of Mercy	Thompson Twins	Arista	3		
14	3	Smalltown Boy	Bronski Beat	Forbidden	7	(48)	F
15	-	Talking Loud And Clear	Orchestral Manoeuvres In The Dark	Virgin	4		
16	15	Farewell My Summer Love	Michael Jackson	Motown	6	(38)	
17	-	Stuck On You	Lionel Richie	Motown	4	(3)	
18	1	Wake Me Up Before You Go Go	Wham!	Epic	8	(1)	
19	-	Everybody's Laughing	Phil Fearon & Galaxy	Ensign	5		
20	18	Thinking Of You	Sister Sledge	Cotillion/Atlantic	6		

August 1984

This Mnth	Prev Mnth	Title	Artist	Label	Wks 20	(US Pos)	
1	1	Two Tribes	Frankie Goes To Hollywood	ZTT	14	(43)	G
2	-	Careless Whisper	George Michael	Epic	12	(1)	F G
3	10	What's Love Got To Do With It	Tina Turner	Capitol	10	(1)	
4	-	Agadoo	Black Lace	Flair	10		
5	-	Relax	Frankie Goes To Hollywood	ZTT	25	(10)	F G
6	8	When Doves Cry	Prince	Warner	8	(1)	F
7	-	Whatever I Do (Wherever I Go)	Hazell Dean	Proto	7		
8	5	Hole In My Shoe	neil	WEA	6		F L
9	-	It's A Hard Life	Queen	EMI	4	(72)	
10	-	Self Control	Laura Branigan	Atlantic	7	(4)	L
11	7	White Lines (Don't Don't Do It)	Grandmaster Flash, Melle Mel & The Furious Five	Sugar Hill	12		L
12	-	Like To Get To Know You Well	Howard Jones	WEA	7	(49)	
13	19	Everybody's Laughing	Phil Fearon & Galaxy	Ensign	5		
14	-	On The Wings Of Love	Jeffrey Osborne	A&M	5	(29)	L
15	-	Down On The Street	Shakatak	Polydor	4		L
16	-	Closest Thing To Heaven	Kane Gang	Kitchenware	5		F L
17	-	I Just Called To Say I Love You	Stevie Wonder	Motown	13	(1)	G
18	3	Time After Time	Cyndi Lauper	Portrait	7	(1)	
19	-	Stuck On You	Trevor Walters	Sanity	4		F L
20	12	Young At Heart	Bluebells	London	6		

September 1984

This Mnth	Prev Mnth	Title	Artist	Label	Wks 20	(US Pos)	
1	16	I Just Called To Say I Love You	Stevie Wonder	Motown	13	(1)	G
2	2	Careless Whisper	George Michael	Epic	12	(1)	F G
3	4	Agadoo	Black Lace	Flair	10		
4	-	Ghostbusters	Ray Parker Jr.	Arista	17	(1)	
5	-	Dr. Beat	Miami Sound Machine	Epic	7		F
6	11	Like To Get To Know You Well	Howard Jones	WEA	7	(49)	
7	-	Passengers	Elton John	Rocket	5		
8	-	Pride (In The Name Of Love)	U2	Island	7	(33)	
9	9	Self Control	Laura Branigan	Atlantic	7	(4)	L
10	-	Big In Japan	Alphaville	WEA International	5	(66)	F L
11	-	Lost In Music	Sister Sledge	Cotillion/Atlantic	6		
12	-	Master And Servant	Depeche Mode	Mute	4	(87)	
13	-	I'll Fly For You	Spandau Ballet	Reformation	4		
14	6	Whatever I Do (Wherever I Go)	Hazell Dean	Proto	7		
15	-	Madame Butterfly	Malcolm McLaren	Charisma	4		L
16	1	Two Tribes	Frankie Goes To Hollywood	ZTT	14	(43)	G
17	10	White Lines (Don't Don't Do It)	Grandmaster Flash, Melle Mel & The Furious Five	Sugar Hill	12		L
18	-	A Letter To You	Shakin' Stevens	Epic	4		
19	-	Blue Jean	David Bowie	EMI America	4	(8)	
20	18	Stuck On You	Trevor Walters	Sanity	4		F L

July 1984

This Mnth	Prev Mnth	Title	Artist	Label	Wks 20	(UK Pos)	
1	14	When Doves Cry	Prince	Warner	14	(4)	P
2	8	Dancing In The Dark	Bruce Springsteen	Columbia	13	(4)	G
3	13	Eyes Without A Face	Billy Idol	Chrysalis	10	(18)	F
4	7	Jump (For My Love)	Pointer Sisters	Planet	11	(6)	
5	-	Ghostbusters	Ray Parker Jr.	Arista	13	(2)	G
6	16	Almost Paradise...Love Theme From Footloose	Mike Reno & Ann Wilson	Columbia	9		F L
7	-	Legs	ZZ Top	Warner	8	(16)	
8	-	Infatuation	Rod Stewart	Warner	8	(27)	
9	6	Self Control	Laura Branigan	Atlantic	10	(5)	
10	2	The Reflex	Duran Duran	Capitol	11	(1)	
11	-	State Of Shock	Jacksons	Epic	8	(14)	G
12	-	Sad Songs (Say So Much)	Elton John	Geffen	9	(7)	
13	-	Doctor! Doctor!	Thompson Twins	Arista	6	(3)	
14	-	Magic	Cars	Elektra	7		
15	5	The Heart Of Rock 'n' Roll	Huey Lewis & The News	Chrysalis	9		
16	-	Breakin'...There's No Stopping Us	Ollie & Jerry	Polydor	6	(5)	F L
17	1	Time After Time	Cyndi Lauper	Portrait	11	(3)	
18	-	What's Love Got To Do With It	Tina Turner	Capitol	13	(3)	F G
19	-	I Can Dream About You	Dan Hartman	MCA	8	(12)	F L
20	3	Let's Hear It For The Boy	Deniece Williams	Columbia	11	(2)	G L

August 1984

This Mnth	Prev Mnth	Title	Artist	Label	Wks 20	(UK Pos)	
1	5	Ghostbusters	Ray Parker Jr.	Arista	13	(2)	G
2	1	When Doves Cry	Prince	Warner	14	(4)	P
3	18	What's Love Got To Do With It	Tina Turner	Capitol	13	(3)	F G
4	11	State Of Shock	Jacksons	Epic	8	(14)	G
5	-	Stuck On You	Lionel Richie	Motown	11	(12)	
6	19	I Can Dream About You	Dan Hartman	MCA	8	(12)	F L
7	12	Sad Songs (Say So Much)	Elton John	Geffen	9	(7)	
8	2	Dancing In The Dark	Bruce Springsteen	Columbia	13	(4)	G
9	-	Sunglasses At Night	Corey Hart	EMI America	9		F
10	-	Missing You	John Waite	EMI America	11	(9)	F L
11	8	Infatuation	Rod Stewart	Warner	8	(27)	
12	-	If Ever You're In My Arms Again	Peabo Bryson	Elektra	7		
13	16	Breakin'...There's No Stopping Us	Ollie & Jerry	Polydor	6	(5)	F L
14	-	Round And Round	Ratt	Atlantic	6		F L
15	-	She Bop	Cyndi Lauper	Portrait	11	(46)	
16	-	Panama	Van Halen	Warner	4	(61)	
17	-	If This Is It	Huey Lewis & The News	Chrysalis	10	(39)	
18	7	Legs	ZZ Top	Warner	8	(16)	
19	3	Eyes Without A Face	Billy Idol	Chrysalis	10	(18)	F
20	-	The Warrior	Scandal Featuring Patty Smyth	Columbia	9		F L

September 1984

This Mnth	Prev Mnth	Title	Artist	Label	Wks 20	(UK Pos)	
1	10	Missing You	John Waite	EMI America	11	(9)	F L
2	3	What's Love Got To Do With It	Tina Turner	Capitol	13	(3)	F G
3	15	She Bop	Cyndi Lauper	Portrait	11	(46)	
4	-	Let's Go Crazy	Prince & The Revolution	Warner	11	(7)	G
5	-	Drive	Cars	Elektra	10	(5)	
6	17	If This Is It	Huey Lewis & The News	Chrysalis	10	(39)	
7	20	The Warrior	Scandal Featuring Patty Smyth	Columbia	9		F L
8	5	Stuck On You	Lionel Richie	Motown	11	(12)	
9	1	Ghostbusters	Ray Parker Jr.	Arista	13	(2)	G
10	-	The Glamorous Life	Sheila E	Warner	8		F
11	9	Sunglasses At Night	Corey Hart	EMI America	9		F
12	-	Cruel Summer	Bananarama	London	6	(8)	F
13	-	Cover Me	Bruce Springsteen	Columbia	8	(16)	
14	-	I Just Called To Say I Love You	Stevie Wonder	Motown	12	(1)	G
15	2	When Doves Cry	Prince & The Revolution	Warner	14	(4)	P
16	-	Lights Out	Peter Wolf	EMI America	6		F
17	-	Dynamite	Jermaine Jackson	Arista	5		
18	12	If Ever You're In My Arms Again	Peabo Bryson	Elektra	7		
19	-	Hard Habit To Break	Chicago	Full Moon	11	(8)	
20	-	Rock Me Tonite	Billy Squier	Capitol	5		L

US 1984 JULY-SEPT

◆ The Jackson's *Victory* tour was the year's top road show. Their three days at New Jersey's Giant's Stadium alone grossed $4.5 million. Michael Jackson reportedly gave the $5 million he made from the tour to charity.

▲ The soundtrack to Prince's film *Purple Rain* sold a million in its first week. It led the lists for 24 weeks. The first two singles from it, 'When Doves Cry' and 'Let's Go Crazy', also hit the top.

◆ Lionel Richie was seen singing 'All Night Long' by 2.6 billion people around the globe at the opening of the Olympic Games in Los Angeles.

UK 1984
OCT-DEC

◆ Bob Geldof and Midge Ure organized an all-star group, Band Aid, whose 'Do They Know It's Christmas' not only raised a fortune for the starving in Ethiopia but also became Britain's biggest ever seller (over 3.5 million).

▲ The year's most successful act in the UK, Frankie Goes To Hollywood, amassed record British advance orders of over a million for their debut album, **Welcome To the Pleasuredome.** In addition, 'The Power Of Love', became their third consecutive No. 1 single, thus equalling a record established by fellow Liverpudlians Gerry & The Pacemakers in 1963.

October 1984

This Mnth	Prev Mnth	Title	Artist	Label	Wks 20	(US Pos)	
1	1	I Just Called To Say I Love You	Stevie Wonder	Motown	13	(1)	G
2	-	The War Song	Culture Club	Virgin	5	(17)	
3	-	Freedom	Wham!	Epic	8	(3)	
4	4	Ghostbusters	Ray Parker Jr.	Arista	17	(1)	
5	-	No More Lonely Nights (Ballad)	Paul McCartney	Parlophone	6	(6)	
6	-	Drive	Cars	Elektra	6	(3)	
7	-	Together In Electric Dreams	Giorgio Moroder & Phil Oakey	Virgin	6		L
8	-	Why?	Bronski Beat	Forbidden Fruit	5		
9	8	Pride (In The Name Of Love)	U2	Island	7	(33)	
10	-	Shout To The Top	Style Council	Polydor	4		
11	-	Purple Rain	Prince & The Revolution	Warner	4	(2)	
12	11	Lost In Music	Sister Sledge	Cotillion/Atlantic	6		
13	-	Missing You	John Waite	EMI	6	(1)	F L
14	-	If It Happens Again	UB40	Dep International	4		
15	-	I'm Gonna Tear Your Playhouse Down	Paul Young	CBS	3	(13)	
16	-	All Cried Out	Alison Moyet	CBS	6		
17	-	Love Kills	Freddie Mercury	CBS	4	(69)	F
18	19	Blue Jean	David Bowie	Emi America	4	(8)	
19	-	I Feel For You	Chaka Khan	Warner	8	(3)	
20	2	Careless Whisper	George Michael	Epic	12	(1)	F G

November 1984

This Mnth	Prev Mnth	Title	Artist	Label	Wks 20	(US Pos)	
1	19	I Feel For You	Chaka Khan	Warner	8	(3)	
2	-	The Wild Boys	Duran Duran	Parlophone	6	(2)	
3	3	Freedom	Wham!	Epic	8	(3)	
4	-	The Wanderer	Status Quo	Vertigo	5		
5	-	Caribbean Queen (No More Love On The Run)	Billy Ocean	Jive	6	(1)	
6	16	All Cried Out	Alison Moyet	CBS	6		
7	-	I Should Have Known Better	Jim Diamond	A&M	8		F
8	-	Never Ending Story	Limahl	EMI	7	(17)	L
9	-	Too Late For Goodbyes	Julian Lennon	Charisma	5	(5)	F
10	5	No More Lonely Nights (Ballad)	Paul McCartney	Parlophone	6	(6)	
11	7	Together In Electric Dreams	Giorgio Moroder & Phil Oakey	Virgin	6		L
12	-	Gimme All Your Lovin'	ZZ Top	Warner	4	(37)	F
13	-	Love's Great Adventure	Ultravox	Chrysalis	5		
14	-	Hard Habit To Break	Chicago	Full Moon	4	(3)	
15	-	I'm So Excited	Pointer Sisters	Planet	4	(9)	
16	1	I Just Called To Say I Love You	Stevie Wonder	Motown	13	(1)	G
17	-	The Riddle	Nik Kershaw	MCA	9		
18	13	Missing You	John Waite	EMI	6	(1)	F L
19	-	Sexcrime (Nineteen Eighty Four)	Eurythmics	Virgin	7	(81)	
20	6	Drive	Cars	Elektra	6	(3)	

December 1984

This Mnth	Prev Mnth	Title	Artist	Label	Wks 20	(US Pos)	
1	-	The Power Of Love	Frankie Goes To Hollywood	ZTT	8		
2	18	The Riddle	Nik Kershaw	MCA	9		
3	-	We All Stand Together	Paul McCartney	Parlophone	7		
4	-	Like A Virgin	Madonna	Sire	10	(1)	
5	-	Do They Know It's Christmas	Band Aid	Mercury	8	(13)	F P
6	-	Teardrops	Shakin' Stevens	Epic	6		
7	7	I Should Have Known Better	Jim Diamond	A&M	8		F
8	-	Last Christmas/Everything She Wants	Wham!	Epic	8	(1)	G
9	20	Sexcrime (Nineteen Eighty Four)	Eurythmics	Virgin	7	(81)	
10	-	I Won't Run Away	Alvin Stardust	Chrysalis	6		L
11	1	I Feel For You	Chaka Khan	Warner	8	(3)	
12	-	Fresh	Kool & The Gang	De-Lite	7	(9)	
13	-	Nellie The Elephant	Toy Dolls	Volume	6		F L
14	-	Do The Conga	Black Lace	Flair	6		L
15	-	One Night In Bangkok	Murray Head	RCA	7	(3)	F L
16	8	Never Ending Story	Limahl	EMI	7	(17)	L
17	-	Everything Must Change	Paul Young	CBS	7	(56)	
18	-	Another Rock And Roll Christmas	Gary Glitter	Arista	3		L
19	15	Hard Habit To Break	Chicago	Full Moon	4	(3)	
20	-	Shout	Tears For Fears	Mercury	9	(1)	

US 1984 OCT-DEC

October 1984

This Mnth	Prev Mnth	Title	Artist	Label	Wks 20	(UK Pos)	
1	14	I Just Called To Say I Love You	Stevie Wonder	Motown	12	(1)	G
2	4	Let's Go Crazy	Prince & The Revolution	Warner	11	(7)	G
3	19	Hard Habit To Break	Chicago	Full Moon	11	(8)	
4	-	Caribbean Queen (No More Love On The Run)	Billy Ocean	Jive	11	(6)	F G
5	-	Lucky Star	Madonna	Sire	8	(14)	
6	5	Drive	Cars	Elektra	10	(5)	
7	13	Cover Me	Bruce Springsteen	Columbia	8	(16)	
8	-	On The Dark Side	John Cafferty & The Beaver Brown Band	Scotti Brothers	6		F
9	1	Missing You	John Waite	EMI America	11	(9)	F L
10	-	I'm So Excited	Pointer Sisters	Planet	6	(11)	
11	10	The Glamorous Life	Sheila E	Warner	8		F
12	-	Purple Rain	Prince & The Revolution	Warner	9	(8)	G
13	3	She Bop	Cyndi Lauper	Portrait	11	(46)	
14	-	Wake Me Up Before You Go-Go	Wham!	Columbia	11	(1)	F G
15	7	The Warrior	Scandal Featuring Patty Smyth	Columbia	9		F L
16	-	Some Guys Have All The Luck	Rod Stewart	Warner	5	(15)	
17	12	Cruel Summer	Bananarama	London	6	(8)	F
18	-	Blue Jean	David Bowie	EMI America	7	(6)	
19	2	What's Love Got To Do With It	Tina Turner	Capitol	13	(3)	F G
20	-	Are We Ourselves?	Fixx	MCA	3		

November 1984

This Mnth	Prev Mnth	Title	Artist	Label	Wks 20	(UK Pos)	
1	12	Purple Rain	Prince & The Revolution	Warner	9	(8)	G
2	14	Wake Me Up Before You Go-Go	Wham!	Columbia	11	(1)	F G
3	4	Caribbean Queen (No More Love On The Run)	Billy Ocean	Jive	11	(6)	F G
4	1	I Just Called To Say I Love You	Stevie Wonder	Motown	12	(1)	G
5	-	Out Of Touch	Daryl Hall & John Oates	RCA	12	(48)	
6	-	Better Be Good To Me	Tina Turner	Capitol	8	(45)	
7	-	I Feel For You	Chaka Khan	Warner	11	(1)	F G L
8	-	Strut	Sheena Easton	EMI America	8		
9	18	Blue Jean	David Bowie	EMI America	7	(6)	
10	3	Hard Habit To Break	Chicago	Full Moon	11	(8)	
11	-	Desert Moon	Dennis Deyoung	A&M	7		F L
12	-	All Through The Night	Cyndi Lauper	Portrait	9	(64)	
13	-	Penny Lover	Lionel Richie	Motown	9	(18)	
14	8	On The Dark Side	John Cafferty & The Beaver Brown Band	Scotti Brothers	6		F
15	5	Lucky Star	Madonna	Sire	8	(14)	
16	-	No More Lonely Nights	Paul McCartney	Columbia	9	(2)	
17	10	I'm So Excited	Pointer Sisters	Planet	6	(11)	
18	-	Cool It Now	New Edition	MCA	11		F G
19	16	Some Guys Have All The Luck	Rod Stewart	Warner	5	(15)	
20	-	The Wild Boys	Duran Duran	Capitol	11	(2)	

December 1984

This Mnth	Prev Mnth	Title	Artist	Label	Wks 20	(UK Pos)	
1	5	Out Of Touch	Daryl Hall & John Oates	RCA	12	(48)	
2	20	The Wild Boys	Duran Duran	Capitol	11	(2)	
3	7	I Feel For You	Chaka Khan	Warner	11	(1)	F G L
4	-	Sea Of Love	Honeydrippers	Es Paranza	10	(56)	F L
5	2	Wake Me Up Before You Go-Go	Wham!	Columbia	11	(1)	F G
6	-	Like A Virgin	Madonna	Sire	11	(3)	G
7	16	No More Lonely Nights	Paul McCartney	Columbia	9	(2)	
8	18	Cool It Now	New Edition	MCA	11		F G
9	-	We Belong	Pat Benatar	Chrysalis	10	(22)	
10	12	All Through The Night	Cyndi Lauper	Portrait	9	(64)	
11	13	Penny Lover	Lionel Richie	Motown	9	(18)	
12	-	Valotte	Julian Lennon	Atlantic	8	(55)	F
13	-	All I Need	Jack Wagner	Qwest	9		F L
14	-	I Can't Hold Back	Survivor	Scotti Brothers	7		
15	6	Better Be Good To Me	Tina Turner	Capitol	8	(45)	
16	1	Purple Rain	Prince & The Revolution	Warner	9	(8)	G
17	8	Strut	Sheena Easton	EMI America	8		
18	-	Run To You	Bryan Adams	A&M	8	(11)	
19	-	Born In The U.S.A.	Bruce Springsteen	Columbia	7	(5)	
20	-	You're The Inspiration	Chicago	Full Moon	10	(14)	

◆ American record and tape sales in 1984 shot up 17% to $4.46 billion, 8% higher than the industry's best year (1978). In the year that cassette singles were introduced, pre-recorded cassette sales rocketed by 100%, and the fledgling CD accounted for $4.2 million, with the industry predicting that they would replace vinyl by 1992.

◆ It was the year the British invaded the singles chart and Prince was king of the albums. Also enjoying a good year were Hall & Oates, who scored their sixth and last No. 1 with 'Out of Touch', and Bruce Springsteen, whose 11-country *Born In The USA* tour was seen by 4.7 million in 61 cities.

◆ Video Award winners included Herbie Hancock's 'Rockit' (five MTV awards), 'Two Tribes' (Best British video) and 'You Might Think' by The Cars (Best Video at the First International Video Awards).

273

UK 1985 JAN-MAR

◆ Bruce Springsteen's 12 million selling **Born In The USA** topped the transatlantic charts as 'Dancing In The Dark' gave him his first major British hit. Also debuting in the Top 20 were the production team of Stock, Aitken & Waterman with 'You Spin Me Round' by Dead Or Alive, which took a record 15 weeks on the chart to reach the top.

◆ *Record Mirror* Poll winners included George Michael (Top Male), Sade (Top Female) and Frankie Goes To Hollywood (Top Group).

◆ Queen, Rod Stewart, Yes, Iron Maiden, AC/DC, Whitesnake, The Scorpions and Ozzy Osbourne were among the headliners at the massive *Rock In Rio* festival.

January 1985

This Mnth	Prev Mnth	Title	Artist	Label	Wks 20	(US Pos)	
1	5	Do They Know It's Christmas	Band Aid	Mercury	8	(13)	F P
2	8	Last Christmas/Everything She Wants	Wham!	Epic	8	(1)	G
3	-	I Want To Know What Love Is	Foreigner	Atlantic	9	(1)	L
4	4	Like A Virgin	Madonna	Sire	10	(1)	
5	4	Ghostbusters	Ray Parker Jr.	Arista	17	(1)	
6	20	Shout	Tears For Fears	Mercury	9	(1)	
7	3	We All Stand Together	Paul McCartney	Parlophone	7		
8	18	Everything Must Change	Paul Young	CBS	7	(56)	
9	13	Nellie The Elephant	Toy Dolls	Volume	6		F L
10	-	I Know Him So Well	Elaine Paige & Barbara Dickson	RCA	10		L
11	-	Step Off (Pt. 1)	Grandmaster Melle Mel & The Furious Five	Sugar Hill	4		F L
12	-	1999/Little Red Corvette	Prince & The Revolution	Warner	7	(12)	
13	-	Since Yesterday	Strawberry Switchblade	Korova	5		F L
14	1	The Power Of Love	Frankie Goes To Hollywood	ZTT	8		
15	-	Police Officer	Smiley Culture	Fashion	3		F L
16	2	The Riddle	Nik Kershaw	MCA	9		
17	12	Fresh	Kool & The Gang	De-Lite	7	(9)	
18	-	Love & Pride	King	CBS	8	(55)	F
19	-	Atmosphere	Russ Abbot	Spirit	7		F
20	-	Friends	Amii Stewart	RCA	4		

February 1985

This Mnth	Prev Mnth	Title	Artist	Label	Wks 20	(US Pos)	
1	9	I Know Him So Well	Elaine Paige & Barbara Dickson	RCA	10		L
2	17	Love & Pride	King	CBS	8	(55)	F
3	-	Solid	Ashford & Simpson	Capitol	8	(12)	F L
4	3	I Want To Know What Love Is	Foreigner	Atlantic	9	(1)	L
5	11	1999/Little Red Corvette	Prince & The Revolution	Warner	7	(12)	
6	-	Dancing In The Dark	Bruce Springsteen	CBS	9	(2)	F
7	18	Atmosphere	Russ Abbot	Spirit	7		F
8	-	Close (To The Edit)	Art Of Noise	ZTT	4		F
9	5	Shout	Tears For Fears	Mercury	9	(1)	
10	-	A New England	Kirsty MacColl	Stiff	5		
11	-	Run To You	Bryan Adams	A&M	6	(6)	F
12	-	Things Can Only Get Better	Howard Jones	WEA	6	(5)	
13	12	Since Yesterday	Strawberry Switchblade	Korova	5		F L
14	-	Sussudio	Phil Collins	Virgin	4	(1)	
15	-	Loverboy	Billy Ocean	Jive	5	(2)	
16	-	Thinking Of You	Colour Field	Chrysalis	4		F L
17	-	You Spin Me Round (Like A Record)	Dead Or Alive	Epic	8	(11)	F
18	-	Nightshift	Commodores	Motown	8	(3)	
19	4	Like A Virgin	Madonna	Sire	10	(1)	
20	-	Yah Mo B There	James Ingram & Michael McDonald	A&M	2	(19)	

March 1985

This Mnth	Prev Mnth	Title	Artist	Label	Wks 20	(US Pos)	
1	17	You Spin Me Round (Like A Record)	Dead Or Alive	Epic	8	(11)	F
2	-	Material Girl	Madonna	Sire	6	(2)	
3	1	I Know Him So Well	Elaine Paige & Barbara Dickson	RCA	10		L
4	18	Nightshift	Commodores	Motown	8	(3)	
5	-	Kiss Me	Stephen 'Tin Tin' Duffy	10	6		F
6	-	Easy Lover	Philip Bailey & Phil Collins	CBS	9	(2)	F L
7	-	That Ole Devil Called Love	Alison Moyet	CBS	6		
8	-	The Last Kiss	David Cassidy	Arista	5		L
9	-	Everytime You Go Away	Paul Young	CBS	6	(1)	
10	-	Do What You Do	Jermaine Jackson	Arista	6	(13)	L
11	6	Dancing In The Dark	Bruce Springsteen	CBS	9	(2)	F
12	-	Let's Go Crazy/Take Me With You	Prince & The Revolution	Warner	4	(1)	
13	3	Solid	Ashford & Simpson	Capitol	8	(12)	F L
14	2	Love & Pride	King	CBS	8	(55)	F
15	-	We Close Our Eyes	Go West	Chrysalis	8	(41)	F
16	12	Things Can Only Get Better	Howard Jones	WEA	6	(5)	
17	-	Wide Boy	Nik Kershaw	MCA	6		
18	-	Pie Jesu	Sarah Brightman & Paul Miles-Kingston	HMV	5		
19	10	A New England	Kirsty MacColl	Stiff	5		
20	-	The Boys Of Summer	Don Henley	Geffen	3	(5)	F L

January 1985

This Mnth	Prev Mnth	Title	Artist	Label	Wks 20	(UK Pos)	
1	6	Like A Virgin	Madonna	Sire	11	(3)	G
2	13	All I Need	Jack Wagner	Qwest	9		F L
3	20	You're The Inspiration	Chicago	Full Moon	10	(14)	
4	2	The Wild Boys	Duran Duran	Capitol	11	(2)	
5	18	Run To You	Bryan Adams	A&M	8	(11)	
6	-	I Want To Know What Love Is	Foreigner	Atlantic	11	(1)	G
7	9	We Belong	Pat Benatar	Chrysalis	10	(22)	
8	-	Easy Lover	Philip Bailey & Phil Collins	Columbia	10	(1)	F G L
9	4	Sea Of Love	Honeydrippers	Es Paranza	10	(56)	F L
10	19	Born In The U.S.A.	Bruce Springsteen	Columbia	7	(5)	
11	8	Cool It Now	New Edition	MCA	11		F G
12	-	The Boys Of Summer	Don Henley	Geffen	8	(12)	
13	-	Careless Whisper	Wham! Feat. George Michael	Columbia	12	(1)	F G
14	12	Valotte	Julian Lennon	Atlantic	8	(55)	F
15	1	Out Of Touch	Daryl Hall & John Oates	RCA	12	(48)	
16	-	I Would Die 4 U	Prince & The Revolution	Warner	6	(58)	
17	-	Do What You Do	Jermaine Jackson	Arista	7	(6)	
18	-	Do They Know It's Christmas	Band Aid	Columbia	4	(1)	F G L
19	-	Loverboy	Billy Ocean	Jive	9	(15)	
20	-	Jamie	Ray Parker Jr.	Arista	5		L

February 1985

1	13	Careless Whisper	Wham! Feat.George Michael	Columbia	12	(1)	F G
2	6	I Want To Know What Love Is	Foreigner	Atlantic	11	(1)	G
3	8	Easy Lover	Philip Bailey & Phil Collins	Columbia	10	(1)	F G L
4	19	Loverboy	Billy Ocean	Jive	9	(15)	
5	-	Method Of Modern Love	Daryl Hall & John Oates	RCA	7	(21)	
6	-	Neutron Dance	Pointer Sisters	Planet	9	(31)	
7	12	The Boys Of Summer	Don Henley	Geffen	8	(12)	
8	-	The Heat Is On	Glenn Frey	MCA	10	(12)	
9	3	You're The Inspiration	Chicago	Full Moon	10	(14)	
10	-	Can't Fight This Feeling	REO Speedwagon	Epic	10	(16)	G
11	-	California Girls	David Lee Roth	Warner	7	(68)	F
12	-	Solid	Ashford & Simpson	Capitol	5	(3)	F L
13	1	Like A Virgin	Madonna	Sire	11	(3)	G
14	-	Sugar Walls	Sheena Easton	EMI America	7		
15	16	I Would Die 4 U	Prince & The Revolution	Warner	6	(58)	
16	-	The Old Man Down The Road	John Fogerty	Warner	6		F
17	-	Mr. Telephone Man	New Edition	MCA	4	(19)	
18	-	Misled	Kool & The Gang	De-Lite	6	(28)	
19	-	Call To The Heart	Giuffria	MCA	2		F L
20	2	All I Need	Jack Wagner	Qwest	9		F L

March 1985

1	10	Can't Fight This Feeling	REO Speedwagon	Epic	10	(16)	G
2	8	The Heat Is On	Glenn Frey	MCA	10	(12)	
3	-	Material Girl	Madonna	Sire	8	(3)	
4	-	Too Late For Goodbyes	Julian Lennon	Atlantic	8	(6)	L
5	1	Careless Whisper	Wham! Feat. George Michael	Columbia	12	(1)	F G
6	11	California Girls	David Lee Roth	Warner	7	(68)	F
7	-	One More Night	Phil Collins	Atlantic	9	(4)	
8	-	Lovergirl	Teena Marie	Epic	9		F L
9	-	Private Dancer	Tina Turner	Capitol	7	(26)	
10	6	Neutron Dance	Pointer Sisters	Planet	9	(31)	
11	2	I Want To Know What Love Is	Foreigner	Atlantic	11	(1)	G
12	-	High On You	Survivor	Scotti Brothers	5		
13	-	Only The Young	Journey	Geffen	5		
14	-	Relax	Frankie Goes To Hollywood	Island	5	(1)	F L
15	14	Sugar Walls	Sheena Easton	EMI America	7		
16	4	Loverboy	Billy Ocean	Jive	9	(15)	
17	18	Misled	Kool & The Gang	De-Lite	6	(28)	
18	16	The Old Man Down The Road	John Fogerty	Warner	6		F
19	-	Just Another Night	Mick Jagger	Columbia	5	(32)	F
20	3	Easy Lover	Philip Bailey & Phil Collins	Columbia	10	(1)	F G L

US 1985
JAN-MAR

▲ Madonna's 'Like A Virgin', produced by Nile Rodgers, topped the US single and album charts. The first female singer to simultaneously head both charts.

◆ Tina Turner picked up four Grammy Awards, Prince received a record 10 American Music Award nominations, and Brits winners included Prince, Paul Young, Alison Moyet and Wham!

◆ Anglo-American rock group Foreigner had their only transatlantic No. 1 with 'I Want To Know What Love Is', taken from **Agent Provocateur,** their sixth successive US Top 10 album.

275

▲ Few Chinese noticed as Wham! became the first western pop group to play in China and to have records released there. In contrast, few Britons could have been unaware of Bruce Springsteen's (above) UK tour. He was an unqualified success, and all his seven albums returned to the chart.

◆ Two records by black American female acts topped the British chart despite having caused little interest in their homeland. They were 'Move Closer' by Phyllis Nelson and 'Frankie' by Sister Sledge.

April 1985

This Mnth	Prev Mnth	Title	Artist	Label	Wks 20	(US Pos)	
1	-	Everybody Wants To Rule The World	Tears For Fears	Mercury	9	(1)	
2	6	Easy Lover	Philip Bailey & Phil Collins	CBS	9	(2)	F L
3	-	Welcome To The Pleasure Dome	Frankie Goes To Hollywood	ZTT	5	(48)	
4	15	We Close Our Eyes	Go West	Chrysalis	8	(41)	F
5	-	Move Closer	Phyllis Nelson	Carrere	11		F L
6	-	We Are The World	USA For Africa	CBS	6	(1)	F L
7	-	Could It Be I'm Falling In Love	David Grant & Jaki Graham	Chrysalis	6		
8	18	Pie Jesu	Sarah Brightman & Paul Miles-Kingston	HMV	5		
9	7	That Ole Devil Called Love	Alison Moyet	CBS	6		
10	9	Everytime You Go Away	Paul Young	CBS	6	(1)	
11	-	One More Night	Phil Collins	Virgin	5	(1)	
12	-	Clouds Across The Moon	Rah Band	RCA	5		L
13	-	Spend The Night	Coolnotes	Abstract Dance	4		F
14	17	Wide Boy	Nik Kershaw	MCA	6		
15	-	The Heat Is On	Glenn Frey	MCA	4	(2)	F L
16	10	Do What You Do	Jermaine Jackson	Arista	6	(13)	L
17	5	Kiss Me	Stephen 'Tin Tin' Duffy	10	6		F
18	2	Material Girl	Madonna	Sire	6	(2)	
19	-	I Feel Love	Bronski Beat & Marc Almond	Forbidden Fruit	7		
20	-	Don't You (Forget About Me)	Simple Minds	Virgin	5	(1)	

May 1985

This Mnth	Prev Mnth	Title	Artist	Label	Wks 20	(US Pos)	
1	-	19	Paul Hardcastle	Chrysalis	9	(15)	F
2	5	Move Closer	Phyllis Nelson	Carrere	11		F L
3	19	I Feel Love	Bronski Beat & Marc Almond	Forbidden Fruit	7		
4	1	Everybody Wants To Rule The World	Tears For Fears	Mercury	9	(1)	
5	-	Feel So Real	Steve Arrington	Atlantic	7		F L
6	-	Rhythm Of The Night	DeBarge	Gordy	6	(3)	F L
7	20	Don't You (Forget About Me)	Simple Minds	Virgin	5	(1)	
8	6	We Are The World	USA For Africa	CBS	6	(1)	F L
9	-	The Unforgettable Fire	U2	Island	3		
10	-	I Was Born To Love You	Freddie Mercury	CBS	5	(76)	
11	-	Walls Come Tumbling Down!	Style Council	Polydor	4		
12	-	A View To Kill	Duran Duran	Parlophone	7	(1)	
13	-	Love Don't Live Here Anymore	Jimmy Nail	Virgin	6		F
14	11	One More Night	Phil Collins	Virgin	5	(1)	
15	12	Clouds Across The Moon	Rah Band	RCA	5		L
16	-	Kayleigh	Marillion	EMI	9		
17	7	Could It Be I'm Falling In Love	David Grant & Jaki Graham	Chrysalis	6		
18	-	Slave To Love	Bryan Ferry	EG	6		
19	-	Lover Come Back To Me	Dead Or Alive	Epic	3	(75)	
20	-	I Want Your Lovin' (Just A Little Bit)	Curtis Hairston	London	2		F L

June 1985

This Mnth	Prev Mnth	Title	Artist	Label	Wks 20	(US Pos)	
1	16	Kayleigh	Marillion	EMI	9		
2	-	You'll Never Walk Alone	The Crowd	Spartan	6		F L
3	1	19	Paul Hardcastle	Chrysalis	9	(15)	F
4	12	A View To Kill	Duran Duran	Parlophone	7	(1)	
5	-	Suddenly	Billy Ocean	Jive	8	(4)	
6	-	Obsession	Animotion	Mercury	6	(6)	F L
7	-	The Word Girl	Scritti Politti Feat. Ranking Ann	Virgin	6		
8	-	Frankie	Sister Sledge	Atlantic	10	(75)	
9	-	Crazy For You	Madonna	Geffen	10	(1)	
10	-	Out In The Fields	Gary Moore & Phil Lynott	10	6		
11	-	History	Mai Tai	Virgin	7		F
12	-	Cherish	Kool & The Gang	De-Lite	12	(2)	L
13	-	Walking On Sunshine	Katrina & The Waves	Capitol	5	(9)	F L
14	13	Love Don't Live Here Anymore	Jimmy Nail	Virgin	6		F
15	-	Axel F	Harold Faltermeyer	MCA	9	(3)	F L
16	6	Rhythm Of The Night	DeBarge	Gordy	6	(3)	F L
17	-	Ben	Marti Webb	Starblend	6		
18	-	Call Me	Go West	Chrysalis	3	(54)	
19	3	I Feel Love	Bronski Beat & Marc Almond	Forbidden Fruit	7		
20	-	Johnny Come Home	Fine Young Cannibals	London	7	(76)	F

April 1985

This Mnth	Prev Mnth	Title	Artist	Label	Wks 20	(UK Pos)	
1	-	We Are The World	USA For Africa	Columbia	9	(1)	F P L
2	-	Crazy For You	Madonna	Geffen	11	(2)	G
3	7	One More Night	Phil Collins	Atlantic	9	(4)	
4	-	Nightshift	Commodores	Motown	8	(3)	L
5	-	Rhythm Of The Night	DeBarge	Gordy	9	(4)	
6	-	I'm On Fire	Bruce Springsteen	Columbia	7	(5)	
7	-	Obsession	Animotion	Mercury	8	(5)	F
8	3	Material Girl	Madonna	Sire	8	(3)	
9	-	Don't You (Forget About Me)	Simple Minds	A&M	11	(7)	F
10	-	One Night In Bangkok	Murray Head	RCA	9	(12)	L
11	-	Missing You	Diana Ross	RCA	6		L
12	8	Lovergirl	Teena Marie	Epic	9		F L
13	-	All She Wants To Do Is Dance	Don Henley	Geffen	7		
14	-	Some Like It Hot	Power Station	Capitol	8	(14)	F
15	1	Can't Fight This Feeling	REO Speedwagon	Epic	10	(16)	G
16	-	Somebody	Bryan Adams	A&M	5	(35)	
17	-	Along Comes A Woman	Chicago	Full Moon	3		
18	-	Smooth Operator	Sade	Portrait	8	(19)	F
19	19	Just Another Night	Mick Jagger	Columbia	5	(32)	F
20	4	Too Late For Goodbyes	Julian Lennon	Atlantic	8	(6)	L

May 1985

This Mnth	Prev Mnth	Title	Artist	Label	Wks 20	(UK Pos)	
1	9	Don't You (Forget About Me)	Simple Minds	A&M	11	(7)	F
2	2	Crazy For You	Madonna	Geffen	11	(2)	G
3	10	One Night In Bangkok	Murray Head	RCA	9	(12)	L
4	-	Everything She Wants	Wham!	Columbia	10	(2)	
5	1	We Are The World	USA For Africa	Columbia	9	(1)	F P L
6	18	Smooth Operator	Sade	Portrait	8	(19)	F
7	14	Some Like It Hot	Power Station	Capitol	8	(14)	F
8	5	Rhythm Of The Night	DeBarge	Gordy	9	(4)	
9	-	Everybody Wants To Rule The World	Tears For Fears	Mercury	11	(2)	F
10	-	Axel F	Harold Faltermeyer	MCA	8	(2)	F L
11	7	Obsession	Animotion	Mercury	8	(5)	F
12	-	Suddenly	Billy Ocean	Jive	9	(4)	
13	13	All She Wants To Do Is Dance	Don Henley	Geffen	7		
14	-	Don't Come Around Here No More	Tom Petty & The Heartbreakers	MCA	6	(50)	
15	4	Nightshift	Commodores	Motown	8	(3)	L
16	-	Things Can Only Get Better	Howard Jones	Elektra	9	(6)	F
17	-	Fresh	Kool & The Gang	De-Lite	7	(11)	
18	-	That Was Yesterday	Foreigner	Atlantic	4	(28)	
19	-	In My House	Mary Jane Girls	Gordy	9		F L
20	-	Heaven	Bryan Adams	A&M	10	(38)	

June 1985

This Mnth	Prev Mnth	Title	Artist	Label	Wks 20	(UK Pos)	
1	9	Everybody Wants To Rule The World	Tears For Fears	Mercury	11	(2)	F
2	20	Heaven	Bryan Adams	A&M	10	(38)	
3	16	Things Can Only Get Better	Howard Jones	Elektra	9	(6)	F
4	-	Sussudio	Phil Collins	Atlantic	9	(12)	
5	19	In My House	Mary Jane Girls	Gordy	9		F L
6	12	Suddenly	Billy Ocean	Jive	9	(4)	
7	4	Everything She Wants	Wham!	Columbia	10	(2)	
8	10	Axel F	Harold Faltermeyer	MCA	8	(2)	F L
9	-	Angel	Madonna	Sire	8	(5)	G
10	-	Walking On Sunshine	Katrina & The Waves	Capitol	7	(8)	F
11	-	A View To Kill	Duran Duran	Capitol	10	(2)	
12	-	Raspberry Beret	Prince & The Revolution	Paisley Park	9	(25)	
13	-	The Search Is Over	Survivor	Scotti Brothers	8		
14	1	Don't You (Forget About Me)	Simple Minds	A&M	11	(7)	F
15	17	Fresh	Kool & The Gang	De-Lite	7	(11)	
16	-	Smuggler's Blues	Glenn Frey	MCA	6	(22)	
17	-	Would I Lie To You?	Eurythmics	RCA	8	(17)	
18	6	Smooth Operator	Sade	Portrait	8	(19)	F
19	-	Voices Carry	Til Tuesday	Epic	7		F L
20	-	You Give Good Love	Whitney Houston	Arista	10		F

◆ A galaxy of top American artists recorded Michael Jackson & Lionel Richie's song 'We Are The World' under the name USA For Africa. The Grammy winning single inspired by Britain's Band Aid hit No. 1 in just four weeks and sold over four million copies – making it the fastest mover and biggest seller of the decade. The **We Are The World** album hit the summit in two weeks and went triple platinum.

◆ Two tribute records to Marvin Gaye were simultaneous hits: 'Nightshift' (also about Jackie Wilson) by The Commodores and 'Missing You' by Diana Ross. Oddly, neither act has yet returned to the US Top 20.

◆ At the end of May, Madonna was the only all-American act in the US Top 10 – seven of the others being British and one, The Power Station, being Anglo-American.

UK 1985 JULY-SEPT

◆ 'Dancing In The Street' by David Bowie & Mick Jagger, entered the UK chart at No. 1. Proceeds from the hit helped the starving in Ethiopia.

◆ In September, a record nine re-issued singles were simultaneously in the UK Top 40, including re-mixes of Amii Stewart's 1979 'Knock On Wood' and 'Light My Fire' – the earliest of dozens of dance re-mixes to chart in Britain.

◆ Dire Straits scored simultaneous US chart-toppers with **Brothers In Arms** (which eventually sold six million in America, nearly four million in the UK and topped the chart in 22 countries!), and the Grammy winning 'Money For Nothing' on which co-writer Sting apeared.

July 1985

This Mnth	Prev Mnth	Title	Artist	Label	Wks 20	(US Pos)	
1	8	**Frankie**	Sister Sledge	Atlantic	10	(75)	
2	15	**Axel F**	Harold Faltermeyer	MCA	9	(3)	F L
3	9	**Crazy For You**	Madonna	Geffen	10	(1)	
4	12	**Cherish**	Kool & The Gang	De-Lite	12	(2)	L
5	-	**I'm On Fire/Born In The U.S.A.**	Bruce Springsteen	CBS	7	(6)	
6	-	**There Must Be An Angel (Playing With My Heart)**	Eurythmics	RCA	8	(22)	
7	-	**My Toot Toot**	Denise La Salle	Epic	6		F L
8	17	**Ben**	Marti Webb	Starblend	6		
9	20	**Johnny Come Home**	Fine Young Cannibals	London	7	(76)	F
10	-	**Live Is Life**	Opus	Polydor	7	(32)	F L
11	11	**History**	Mai Tai	Virgin	7		F
12	5	**Suddenly**	Billy Ocean	Jive	8	(4)	
13	-	**Head Over Heels**	Tears For Fears	Mercury	4	(3)	
14	-	**Round And Round**	Jaki Graham	EMI	4		
15	1	**Kayleigh**	Marillion	EMI	9		
16	-	**Into The Groove**	Madonna	Sire	10		
17	2	**You'll Never Walk Alone**	The Crowd	Spartan	6		F L
18	-	**Turn It Up**	Conway Brothers	10	3		F L
19	-	**Money's Too Tight (To Mention)**	Simply Red	Elektra	3	(28)	F
20	-	**Living On Video**	Trans-X	Boiling Point	5	(61)	F L

August 1985

This Mnth	Prev Mnth	Title	Artist	Label	Wks 20	(US Pos)	
1	16	**Into The Groove**	Madonna	Sire	10		
2	-	**We Don't Need Another Hero (Thunderdome)**	Tina Turner	Capitol	7	(2)	
3	-	**Money For Nothing**	Dire Straits	Vertigo	8	(1)	
4	6	**There Must Be An Angel (Playing With My Heart)**	Eurythmics	RCA	8	(22)	
5	-	**I Got You Babe**	UB40 Feat Chrissie Hynde	Dep International	8	(28)	
6	-	**Holiday**	Madonna	Sire	5		
7	-	**White Wedding**	Billy Idol	Chrysalis	8	(36)	
8	-	**Running Up That Hill**	Kate Bush	EMI	6	(30)	
9	-	**Drive**	Cars	Elektra	7		L
10	10	**Live Is Life**	Opus	Polydor	7	(32)	F L
11	4	**Cherish**	Kool & The Gang	De-Lite	12	(2)	L
12	-	**Say I'm Your No. 1**	Princess	Supreme	6		F
13	1	**Frankie**	Sister Sledge	Atlantic	10	(75)	
14	2	**Axel F**	Harold Faltermeyer	MCA	9	(3)	F L
15	-	**Don Quixote**	Nik Kershaw	MCA	3		L
16	-	**Tarzan Boy**	Baltimora	Columbia	7	(13)	F L
17	-	**Excitable**	Amazulu	Island	3		F
18	20	**Living On Video**	Trans-X	Boiling Point	5	(61)	F L
19	-	**Alone Without You**	King	CBS	5		
20	14	**Round And Round**	Jaki Graham	EMI	4		

September 1985

This Mnth	Prev Mnth	Title	Artist	Label	Wks 20	(US Pos)	
1	-	**Dancing In The Street**	David Bowie & Mick Jagger	EMI America	7	(7)	
2	-	**Holding Out For A Hero**	Bonnie Tyler	CBS	8	(34)	L
3	16	**Tarzan Boy**	Baltimora	Columbia	7	(13)	F L
4	5	**I Got You Babe**	UB40 Feat. Chrissie Hynde	Dep International	8	(28)	
5	-	**Part Time Lover**	Stevie Wonder	Motown	5	(1)	
6	-	**Body And Soul**	Mai Tai	Virgin	6		L
7	1	**Into The Groove**	Madonna	Sire	10		
8	-	**Knock On Wood/Light My Fire**	Amii Stewart	Sedition	5		L
9	9	**Drive**	Cars	Elektra	7		L
10	-	**Lavender**	Marillion	EMI	5		
11	8	**Running Up That Hill**	Kate Bush	EMI	6	(30)	
12	12	**Say I'm Your No. 1**	Princess	Supreme	6		F
13	-	**If I Was**	Midge Ure	Chrysalis	7		
14	-	**Angel**	Madonna	Sire	5	(5)	
15	19	**Alone Without You**	King	CBS	5		
16	-	**The Power Of Love**	Huey Lewis & The News	Chrysalis	5	(1)	F
17	3	**Money For Nothing**	Dire Straits	Vertigo	8	(1)	
18	-	**Lean On Me (Ah-Li-Ayo)**	Red Box	Sire	8		F
19	-	**Body Rock**	Maria Vidal	EMI America	5	(48)	F L
20	-	**I Can Dream About You**	Dan Hartman	MCA	3	(6)	L

July 1985

This Mnth	Prev Mnth	Title	Artist	Label	Wks 20	(UK Pos)	
1	11	A View To Kill	Duran Duran	Capitol	10	(2)	
2	12	Raspberry Beret	Prince & The Revolution	Paisley Park	9	(25)	
3	-	Everytime You Go Away	Paul Young	Columbia	11	(4)	F
4	4	Sussudio	Phil Collins	Atlantic	9	(12)	
5	20	You Give Good Love	Whitney Houston	Arista	10		F
6	13	The Search Is Over	Survivor	Scotti Brothers	8		
7	-	Glory Days	Bruce Springsteen	Columbia	8	(17)	
8	-	If You Love Somebody Set Them Free	Sting	A&M	10	(26)	F
9	17	Would I Lie To You?	Eurythmics	RCA	8	(17)	
10	19	Voices Carry	Til Tuesday	Epic	7		F L
11	-	Shout	Tears For Fears	Mercury	9	(4)	
12	-	Sentimental Street	Night Ranger	MCA/Camel	7		
13	2	Heaven	Bryan Adams	A&M	10	(38)	
14	-	The Goonies 'R' Good Enough	Cyndi Lauper	Portrait	5		
15	-	Never Surrender	Corey Hart	EMI America	9		
16	-	Get It On (Bang A Gong)	Power Station	Capitol	6	(22)	L
17	-	19	Paul Hardcastle	Chrysalis	4	(1)	F L
18	9	Angel	Madonna	Sire	8	(5)	G
19	-	Who's Holding Donna Now	DeBarge	Gordy	6		L
20	-	Crazy In The Night (Barking At Airplanes)	Kim Carnes	EMI America	2		L

August 1985

This Mnth	Prev Mnth	Title	Artist	Label	Wks 20	(UK Pos)	
1	11	Shout	Tears For Fears	Mercury	9	(4)	
2	-	The Power Of Love	Huey Lewis & The News	Chrysalis	10	(9)	
3	15	Never Surrender	Corey Hart	EMI America	9		
4	-	Freeway Of Love	Aretha Franklin	Arista	9	(68)	
5	8	If You Love Somebody Set Them...	Sting	A&M	10	(26)	F
6	3	Everytime You Go Away	Paul Young	Columbia	11	(4)	F
7	-	St. Elmo's Fire (Man In Motion)	John Parr	Atlantic	10	(6)	F L
8	-	Summer Of '69	Bryan Adams	A&M	7	(42)	
9	-	We Don't Need Another Hero (Thunderdome)	Tina Turner	Capitol	9	(3)	
10	19	Who's Holding Donna Now	DeBarge	Gordy	6		L
11	7	Glory Days	Bruce Springsteen	Columbia	8	(17)	
12	-	What About Love?	Heart	Capitol	6	(14)	
13	16	Get It On (Bang A Gong)	Power Station	Capitol	6	(22)	L
14	5	You Give Good Love	Whitney Houston	Arista	10		F
15	-	Cherish	Kool & The Gang	De-Lite	10	(4)	
16	-	You Spin Me Round (Like A Record)	Dead Or Alive	Epic	5	(1)	F
17	-	You're Only Human (Second Wind)	Billy Joel	Columbia	7		
18	-	People Are People	Depeche Mode	Sire	5	(4)	F
19	-	Don't Lose My Number	Phil Collins	Atlantic	9		
20	-	Invincible (Theme From The Legend Of Billie Jean)	Pat Benatar	Chrysalis	6	(53)	

September 1985

This Mnth	Prev Mnth	Title	Artist	Label	Wks 20	(UK Pos)	
1	-	Money For Nothing	Dire Straits	Warner	10	(4)	
2	7	St. Elmo's Fire (Man In Motion)	John Parr	Atlantic	10	(6)	F L
3	15	Cherish	Kool & The Gang	De-Lite	10	(4)	
4	9	We Don't Need Another Hero (...)	Tina Turner	Capitol	9	(3)	
5	19	Don't Lose My Number	Phil Collins	Atlantic	9		
6	-	Freedom	Wham!	Columbia	8	(1)	
7	2	The Power Of Love	Huey Lewis & The News	Chrysalis	10	(9)	
8	-	Pop Life	Prince & The Revolution	Paisley Park	6	(60)	
9	-	Oh Sheila	Ready For The World	MCA	10	(50)	F
10	-	Dress You Up	Madonna	Sire	8	(5)	
11	4	Freeway Of Love	Aretha Franklin	Arista	9	(68)	
12	-	Dare Me	Pointer Sisters	RCA	7	(17)	L
13	20	Invincible (From The Legend Of...)	Pat Benatar	Chrysalis	6	(53)	
14	8	Summer Of '69	Bryan Adams	A&M	7	(42)	
15	-	Take On Me	A-Ha	Warner	10	(2)	F
16	17	You're Only Human (Second Wind)	Billy Joel	Columbia	7		
17	-	Saving All My Love For You	Whitney Houston	Arista	10	(1)	
18	-	Lonely Ol' Night	John Cougar Mellencamp	Riva	8		
19	-	Dancing In The Street	Mick Jagger & David Bowie	EMI America	6	(1)	L
20	-	Smokin' In The Boys Room	Motley Crue	Elektra	4	(71)	F

US
1985
JULY-SEPT

◆ Rock music's greatest live show, *Live Aid* (which included over two dozen top rock acts), was staged in both London and Philadelphia. A TV audience of approximately 1.6 billion people in 170 countries watched the show which raised $80 million (£50 million) for famine relief in Africa.

▲ A record eight consecutive US chart-toppers were by non-American acts. Among the seven UK No. 1s were two by Tears For Fears whose **Songs From The Big Chair** headed the LP chart.

◆ Michael Jackson purchased The Beatles' publishing company, ATV, for $34 million.

279

UK 1985

OCT-DEC

▲ It was claimed that Dire Straits 'Brothers In Arms' was the first commercially succssseful CD single.

◆ American Jennifer Rush topped the chart with 'The Power Of Love'. It became the first UK million seller by a female artist. In her homeland it failed to reach the Top 40. The song, however, became an American No. 1 by French-Canadian Celine Dion in 1994.

◆ Whitney Houston scored a transatlantic No. 1 with her Grammy winning 'Saving All My Love For You'. It came from her 14 million sell-ing eponymous debut album - the biggest selling album ever by a female artist.

October 1985

This Mnth	Prev Mnth	Title	Artist	Label	Wks 20	(US Pos)	
1	-	The Power Of Love	Jennifer Rush	CBS	11	(57)	F G
2	13	If I Was	Midge Ure	Chrysalis	7		
3	-	Trapped	Colonel Abrams	MCA	10		F L
4	18	Lean On Me (Ah-Li-Ayo)	Red Box	Sire	8		F
5	-	Rebel Yell	Billy Idol	Chrysalis	6	(46)	
6	-	Take On Me	A-Ha	Warner	8	(1)	F
7	-	St. Elmo's Fire (Man In Motion)	John Parr	London	6	(1)	F L
8	1	Dancing In The Street	David Bowie & Mick Jagger	EMI America	7	(7)	
9	2	Holding Out For A Hero	Bonnie Tyler	CBS	8	(34)	L
10	-	Alive And Kicking	Simple Minds	Virgin	6	(3)	
11	14	Angel	Madonna	Sire	5	(5)	
12	-	Gambler	Madonna	Geffen	6		
13	-	Miami Vice Theme	Jan Hammer	MCA	4	(1)	F
14	10	Lavender	Marillion	EMI	5		
15	19	Body Rock	Maria Vidal	EMI America	5	(48)	F L
16	16	The Power Of Love	Huey Lewis & The News	Chrysalis	5	(1)	F
17	-	Slave To The Rhythm	Grace Jones	ZTT	4		
18	-	Nikita	Elton John	Rocket	7	(7)	
19	-	Single Life	Cameo	Club	3		F
20	-	The Lodgers	Style Council	Polydor	3		

November 1985

This Mnth	Prev Mnth	Title	Artist	Label	Wks 20	(US Pos)	
1	1	The Power Of Love	Jennifer Rush	CBS	11	(57)	F G
2	-	A Good Heart	Feargal Sharkey	Virgin	10	(67)	F
3	6	Take On Me	A-Ha	Warner	8	(1)	F
4	18	Nikita	Elton John	Rocket	7	(7)	
5	-	Don't Break My Heart	UB40	Dep International	8		
6	-	Something About You	Level 42	Polydor	6	(7)	
7	3	Trapped	Colonel Abrams	MCA	10		F L
8	-	I'm Your Man	Wham!	Epic	8	(3)	
9	-	Road To Nowhere	Talking Heads	EMI	6		
10	-	One Vision	Queen	EMI	4	(61)	
11	12	Gambler	Madonna	Geffen	6		
12	-	Sisters Are Doin' It For Themselves	Eurythmics & Aretha Franklin	RCA	5	(18)	
13	-	Stairway To Heaven	Far Corporation	Arista	4	(89)	F L
14	7	St. Elmo's Fire (Man In Motion)	John Parr	London	6	(1)	F L
15	-	The Show	Doug E. Fresh & The Get Fresh Crew	Cooltempo	6		F L
16	-	The Taste Of Your Tears	King	CBS	5		L
17	-	Election Day	Arcadia	Odeon	4	(6)	F L
18	10	Alive And Kicking	Simple Minds	Virgin	6	(3)	
19	-	See The Day	Dee C. Lee	CBS	8		F L
20	13	Miami Vice Theme	Jan Hammer	MCA	4	(1)	F

December 1985

This Mnth	Prev Mnth	Title	Artist	Label	Wks 20	(US Pos)	
1	-	Saving All My Love For You	Whitney Houston	Arista	9	(1)	F
2	8	I'm Your Man	Wham!	Epic	8	(3)	
3	19	See The Day	Dee C. Lee	CBS	8		F L
4	-	Separate Lives	Phil Collins & Marilyn Martin	Virgin	8	(1)	
5	-	Do They Know It's Christmas	Band Aid	Mercury	5		P L
6	-	Merry Christmas Everyone	Shakin' Stevens	Epic	6		
7	-	Dress You Up	Madonna	Sire	6	(5)	
8	-	West End Girls	Pet Shop Boys	Parlophone	8	(1)	F
9	2	A Good Heart	Feargal Sharkey	Virgin	10	(67)	F
10	-	Say You, Say Me	Lionel Richie	Motown	7	(1)	
11	15	The Show	Doug E. Fresh & The Get Fresh Crew	Cooltempo	6		F L
12	-	We Built This City	Starship	RCA	6	(1)	F
13	-	Last Christmas	Wham!	Epic	4		
14	-	Santa Claus Is Comin' To Town/ My Home Town	Bruce Springsteen	Epic	4		
15	5	Don't Break My Heart	UB40	Dep International	8		
16	-	Don't Look Down-The Sequel	Go West	Chrysalis	6	(39)	
17	-	Walking In The Air	Aled Jones	HMV	5		F L
18	9	Road To Nowhere	Talking Heads	EMI	6		
19	-	Spies Like Us	Paul McCartney	Parlophone	6	(7)	
20	-	Hit That Perfect Beat	Bronski Beat	Forbidden Fruit	7		

October 1985

This Mnth	Prev Mnth	Title	Artist	Label	Wks 20	(UK Pos)	
1	15	Take On Me	A-Ha	Warner	10	(2)	F
2	17	Saving All My Love For You	Whitney Houston	Arista	10	(1)	
3	9	Oh Sheila	Ready For The World	MCA	10	(50)	F
4	-	Part Time Lover	Stevie Wonder	Tamla	10	(3)	
5	1	Money For Nothing	Dire Straits	Warner	10	(4)	
6	18	Lonely Ol' Night	John Cougar Mellencamp	Riva	8		
7	-	Miami Vice Theme	Jan Hammer	MCA	9	(5)	F L
8	19	Dancing In The Street	Mick Jagger & David Bowie	EMI America	6	(1)	L
9	-	Fortress Around Your Heart	Sting	A&M	7	(49)	
10	3	Cherish	Kool & The Gang	De-Lite	10	(4)	
11	-	I'm Goin' Down	Bruce Springsteen	Columbia	6		
12	-	Head Over Heels	Tears For Fears	Mercury	9	(12)	
13	10	Dress You Up	Madonna	Sire	7	(5)	
14	-	Lovin' Every Minute Of It	Loverboy	Columbia	7		
15	6	Freedom	Wham!	Columbia	8	(1)	
16	-	You Belong To The City	Glenn Frey	MCA	9		
17	5	Don't Lose My Number	Phil Collins	Atlantic	9		
18	-	I'm Gonna Tear Your Playhouse Down	Paul Young	Columbia	5	(9)	
19	-	We Built This City	Starship	Grunt	10	(12)	F
20	-	Cry	Godley & Creme	Polydor	5	(19)	F L

November 1985

This Mnth	Prev Mnth	Title	Artist	Label	Wks 20	(UK Pos)	
1	19	We Built This City	Starship	Grunt	10	(12)	F
2	16	You Belong To The City	Glenn Frey	MCA	9		
3	7	Miami Vice Theme	Jan Hammer	MCA	9	(5)	F L
4	-	Separate Lives	Phil Collins & Marilyn Martin	Atlantic	13	(4)	
5	12	Head Over Heels	Tears For Fears	Mercury	9	(12)	
6	4	Part Time Lover	Stevie Wonder	Tamla	10	(3)	
7	-	Broken Wings	Mr. Mister	RCA	11	(4)	F
8	-	Never	Heart	Capitol	8	(8)	
9	-	Lay Your Hands On Me	Thompson Twins	Arista	8	(13)	
10	-	Be Near Me	ABC	Mercury	7	(26)	
11	-	Who's Zoomin' Who	Aretha Franklin	Arista	7	(11)	
12	2	Saving All My Love For You	Whitney Houston	Arista	10	(1)	
13	1	Take On Me	A-Ha	Warner	10	(2)	F
14	-	You Are My Lady	Freddie Jackson	Capitol	6	(49)	L
15	-	Election Day	Arcadia	Capitol	10	(7)	F L
16	-	Sleeping Bag	ZZ Top	Warner	8	(27)	L
17	-	One Night Love Affair	Bryan Adams	A&M	5		
18	14	Lovin' Every Minute Of It	Loverboy	Columbia	7		
19	9	Fortress Around Your Heart	Sting	A&M	7	(49)	
20	-	Party All The Time	Eddie Murphy	Columbia	11		F G L

December 1985

This Mnth	Prev Mnth	Title	Artist	Label	Wks 20	(UK Pos)	
1	-	Say You, Say Me	Lionel Richie	Motown	12	(8)	G
2	7	Broken Wings	Mr. Mister	RCA	11	(4)	F
3	4	Separate Lives	Phil Collins & Marilyn Martin	Atlantic	13	(4)	
4	20	Party All The Time	Eddie Murphy	Columbia	11		F G L
5	-	Alive & Kicking	Simple Minds	A&M	10	(7)	
6	15	Election Day	Arcadia	Capitol	10	(7)	F L
7	-	I Miss You	Klymaxx	MCA/Constell.	11		F
8	16	Sleeping Bag	ZZ Top	Warner	8	(27)	L
9	-	Small Town	John Cougar Mellencamp	Riva	8	(53)	
10	-	That's What Friends Are For	Dionne Warwick & Friends	Arista	13	(16)	G
11	8	Never	Heart	Capitol	8	(8)	
12	1	We Built This City	Starship	Grunt	10	(12)	F
13	-	Perfect Way	Scritti Politti	Warner	6	(48)	F L
14	-	Tonight She Comes	Cars	Elektra	8		
15	11	Who's Zoomin' Who	Aretha Franklin	Arista	7	(11)	
16	-	Walk Of Life	Dire Straits	Warner	10	(2)	
17	2	You Belong To The City	Glenn Frey	MCA	9		
18	-	Talk To Me	Stevie Nicks	Modern	10	(68)	
19	9	Lay Your Hands On Me	Thompson Twins	Arista	8	(13)	
20	-	Burning Heart	Survivor	Scotti Brothers	11	(5)	

US
1985
OCT-DEC

◆ 1985 was the year many stars actively became involved in charity work, helping to raise much money for deserving causes. Apart from helping bring the famine in Africa to the public's attention, recording artists alerted many to such serious issues as AIDS and environmental damage.

◆ Total record and tape sales held steady in the USA, where compact discs now accounted for 21 million of the 643 million units sold (a rise of 250%!). In Britain cassette albums outsold records for the first time in 1985.

◆ Previous hit makers who died this year included 1950's idol Ricky Nelson, the grandfather of rock'n'roll, Joe Turner, orchestra leader Nelson Riddle and Ian Stewart (an original Rolling Stone).

UK 1986 JAN-MAR

An *NME* survey showed that Madonna was the UK's Top Singles Artist in 1985 and that Bruce Springsteen was Top Album Artist.

◆ 'The Sun Always Shines On T.V.' by teeny bop idols A-Ha became the first record by a Norwegian act to top the UK chart. Their previous single, 'Take On Me', had headed the American chart, thanks partly to an outstanding video.

◆ After a Dire Straits concert was shown on TV, all the group's previous five albums joined the record-breaking **Brothers In Arms** in the chart.

◆ Among the American re-releases hitting the heights were 'Borderline' by Madonna, 'The Power of Love' by Huey Lewis & The News and, perhaps most surprisingly, 'Theme From New York New York' by Frank Sinatra.

January 1986

This Mnth	Prev Mnth	Title	Artist	Label	Wks 20	(US Pos)	
1	8	West End Girls	Pet Shop Boys	Parlophone	8	(1)	F
2	20	Hit That Perfect Beat	Bronski Beat	Forbidden Fruit	7		
3	-	The Sun Always Shines On T.V.	A-Ha	Warner	7	(20)	
4	1	Saving All My Love For You	Whitney Houston	Arista	9	(1)	F
5	-	Saturday Love	Cherelle & Alexander O'Neal	Tabu	5	(26)	F L
6	-	Girlie Girlie	Sophia George	Winner	5		F L
7	6	Merry Christmas Everyone	Shakin' Stevens	Epic	6		
8	-	Walk Of Life	Dire Straits	Vertigo	6	(7)	L
9	17	Walking In The Air	Aled Jones	HMV	5		F L
10	-	You Little Thief	Feargal Sharkey	Virgin	4		
11	-	Broken Wings	Mr Mister	RCA	4	(1)	F
12	7	Dress You Up	Madonna	Sire	6	(5)	
13	5	Do They Know It's Christmas	Band Aid	Mercury	5		P L
14	2	I'm Your Man	Wham!	Epic	8	(3)	
15	4	Separate Lives	Phil Collins & Marilyn Martin	Virgin	8	(1)	
16	-	Alice I Want You Just For Me	Full Force	CBS	3		F L
17	13	Last Christmas	Wham!	Epic	4		
18	-	Who's Zoomin' Who	Aretha Franklin	Arista	3	(7)	
19	-	Russians	Sting	A&M	3	(16)	
20	-	It's Alright (Baby's Coming Back)	Eurythmics	RCA	4	(78)	

February 1986

This Mnth	Prev Mnth	Title	Artist	Label	Wks 20	(US Pos)	
1	-	When The Going Gets Tough, The Tough Get Going	Billy Ocean	Jive	8	(2)	
2	-	Borderline	Madonna	Sire	6	(10)	
3	3	The Sun Always Shines On T.V.	A-Ha	Warner	7	(20)	
4	-	Only Love	Nana Mouskouri	Philips	6		F L
5	-	System Addict	Five Star	Tent	6		
6	8	Walk Of Life	Dire Straits	Vertigo	6	(7)	L
7	-	Living In America	James Brown	Scotti Bros	6	(4)	
8	-	Eloise	Damned	MCA	6		L
9	-	The Phantom Of The Opera	Sarah Brightman/Steve Harley	Polydor	4		
10	-	Starting Together	Su Pollard	Rainbow	5		F L
11	-	The Captain Of Her Heart	Double	Polydor	4	(16)	F L
12	-	How Will I Know	Whitney Houston	Arista	6	(1)	
13	-	Suspicious Minds	Fine Young Cannibals	London	5		
14	11	Broken Wings	Mr Mister	RCA	4	(1)	F
15	-	Chain Reaction	Diana Ross	Capitol	10	(66)	
16	5	Saturday Love	Cherrelle & Alexander O'Neal	Tabu	5	(26)	F L
17	-	Rise	Public Image Ltd.	Virgin	5		L
18	-	Pull Up To The Bumper/La Vie En Rose	Grace Jones	Island	4		L
19	-	Burning Heart	Survivor	Scotti Brothers	5	(2)	L
20	-	Sanctify Yourself	Simple Minds	Virgin	3	(14)	

March 1986

This Mnth	Prev Mnth	Title	Artist	Label	Wks 20	(US Pos)	
1	15	Chain Reaction	Diana Ross	Capitol	10	(66)	
2	-	Manic Monday	Bangles	CBS	6	(2)	F
3	1	When The Going Gets Tough, The Tough Get Going	Billy Ocean	Jive	8	(2)	
4	-	Love Missile F1-11	Sigue Sigue Sputnik	Parlophone	4		F
5	-	Absolute Beginners	David Bowie	Virgin	5	(53)	
6	-	Hi Ho Silver	Jim Diamond	A&M	7		L
7	10	Starting Together	Su Pollard	Rainbow	5		F L
8	19	Burning Heart	Survivor	Scotti Brothers	5	(2)	L
9	-	Theme From New York New York	Frank Sinatra	Reprise	3	(32)	L
10	-	(Nothin' Serious) Just Buggin'	Whistle	Champion	4		F L
11	12	How Will I Know	Whitney Houston	Arista	6	(1)	
12	-	Living Doll	Cliff Richard & The Young Ones	WEA	7		
13	-	Kiss	Prince & The Revolution	Paisley Park	4	(1)	
14	-	The Power Of Love/Do You Believe In Love	Huey Lewis & The News	Chrysalis	4		
15	8	Eloise	Damned	MCA	6		L
16	-	Don't Waste My Time	Paul Hardcastle	Chrysalis	4		
17	-	Move Away	Culture Club	Virgin	4	(12)	L
18	-	Kyrie	Mr. Mister	RCA	5	(1)	L
19	-	Digging Your Scene	Blow Monkeys	RCA	4	(14)	F
20	-	Touch Me (I Want Your Body)	Samantha Fox	Jive	6	(4)	F

January 1986

This Mnth	Prev Mnth	Title	Artist	Label	Wks 20	(UK Pos)	
1	1	Say You, Say Me	Lionel Richie	Motown	12	(8)	G
2	10	That's What Friends Are For	Dionne Warwick & Friends	Arista	13	(16)	G
3	4	Party All The Time	Eddie Murphy	Columbia	11		F G L
4	5	Alive & Kicking	Simple Minds	A&M	10	(7)	
5	7	I Miss You	Klymaxx	MCA/Constell.	11		F
6	18	Talk To Me	Stevie Nicks	Modern	10	(68)	
7	9	Small Town	John Cougar Mellencamp	Riva	8	(53)	
8	20	Burning Heart	Survivor	Scotti Brothers	11	(5)	
9	16	Walk Of Life	Dire Straits	Warner	10	(2)	
10	14	Tonight She Comes	Cars	Elektra	8		
11	-	My Hometown	Bruce Springsteen	Columbia	7	(9)	
12	-	I'm Your Man	Wham!	Columbia	8	(1)	
13	6	Election Day	Arcadia	Capitol	10	(7)	F L
14	2	Broken Wings	Mr. Mister	RCA	11	(4)	F
15	3	Separate Lives	Phil Collins & Marilyn Martin	Atlantic	13	(4)	
16	-	Spies Like Us	Paul McCartney	Columbia	6	(16)	L
17	-	Go Home	Stevie Wonder	Tamla	6	(67)	
18	-	It's Only Love	Bryan Adams & Tina Turner	A&M	5	(29)	
19	-	When The Going Gets Tough, The Tough Get Going	Billy Ocean	Jive	8	(1)	
20	-	Conga	Miami Sound Machine	Epic	8		F

February 1986

This Mnth	Prev Mnth	Title	Artist	Label	Wks 20	(UK Pos)	
1	8	Burning Heart	Survivor	Scotti Brothers	11	(5)	
2	19	When The Going Gets Tough, The Tough Get Going	Billy Ocean	Jive	8	(1)	
3	2	That's What Friends Are For	Dionne Warwick & Friends	Arista	13	(16)	G
4	-	How Will I Know	Whitney Houston	Arista	10	(5)	
5	-	Kyrie	Mr. Mister	RCA	9	(11)	
6	-	Living In America	James Brown	Scotti Bros	7	(5)	L
7	-	The Sweetest Taboo	Sade	Portrait	7	(31)	
8	12	I'm Your Man	Wham!	Columbia	8	(1)	
9	20	Conga	Miami Sound Machine	Epic	8		F
10	-	Sara	Starship	Grunt	9	(66)	
11	16	Spies Like Us	Paul McCartney	Columbia	6	(16)	L
12	6	Talk To Me	Stevie Nicks	Modern	10	(68)	
13	-	Life In A Northern Town	Dream Academy	Warner	7	(15)	F L
14	17	Go Home	Stevie Wonder	Tamla	6	(67)	
15	-	Silent Running (On Dangerous Ground)	Mike + The Mechanics	Atlantic	7	(21)	F
16	1	Say You, Say Me	Lionel Richie	Motown	12	(8)	G
17	11	My Hometown	Bruce Springsteen	Columbia	7	(9)	
18	-	A Love Bizarre	Sheila E	Paisley Park	4		L
19	9	Walk Of Life	Dire Straits	Warner	10	(2)	
20	-	Secret Lovers	Atlantic Starr	A&M	10	(10)	F

March 1986

This Mnth	Prev Mnth	Title	Artist	Label	Wks 20	(UK Pos)	
1	10	Sara	Starship	Grunt	9	(66)	
2	-	These Dreams	Heart	Capitol	9	(8)	
3	20	Secret Lovers	Atlantic Starr	A&M	10	(10)	F
4	5	Kyrie	Mr. Mister	RCA	9	(11)	
5	4	How Will I Know	Whitney Houston	Arista	10	(5)	
6	-	R.O.C.K In The U.S.A. (A Salute To '60s Rock)	John Cougar Mellencamp	Riva	8	(67)	
7	-	Rock Me Amadeus	Falco	A&M	9	(1)	F
8	-	King For A Day	Thompson Twins	Arista	7	(22)	L
9	-	Nikita	Elton John	Geffen	5	(3)	
10	15	Silent Running (On Dangerous...)	Mike + The Mechanics	Atlantic	7	(21)	F
11	-	What You Need	INXS	Atlantic	9	(51)	F
12	7	The Sweetest Taboo	Sade	Portrait	7	(31)	
13	6	Living In America	James Brown	Scotti Bros	7	(5)	L
14	-	Kiss	Prince & The Revolution	Paisley Park	10	(6)	G
15	-	This Could Be The Night	Loverboy	Columbia	5		
16	13	Life In A Northern Town	Dream Academy	Warner	7	(15)	F L
17	-	Let's Go All The Way	Sly Fox	Capitol	8	(3)	F L
18	2	When The Going Gets Tough, The...	Billy Ocean	Jive	8	(1)	
19	-	Sanctify Yourself	Simple Minds	A&M	4	(10)	L
20	-	Manic Monday	Bangles	Columbia	9	(2)	F

◆ Stevie Wonder and Bob Dylan were among the many acts staging shows to celebrate Martin Luther King Jr.'s birthday becoming a national holiday.

◆ Exactly thirty years after cutting his debut record, James Brown had his biggest and last major transatlantic hit, 'Living In America'.

▲ In March a record four of the Top 5, and 13 of the Top 40 albums featured female singers, one of whom, Sade, won the Grammy for Best New Act.

◆ Lionel Richie's 'Say You, Say Me' gave him a record nine successful years when (at least) one of his compositions had reached No. 1.

◆ Bob Geldof received an honorary knighthood from the Queen for his charity work. Among the current charity hits were 'Everybody Wants To Run the World' (the theme to Sports Aid's *Race Against Time*) by Tears For Fears and an update of 'Living Doll' by Cliff Richard & The Young Ones (for Comic Relief).

◆ Sam Cooke's 'Wonderful World' (from 1960) and Marvin Gaye's 'I Heard it Through The Grapevine' (from 1968), were the first of many oldies that hit after being heard in Levis' jeans advertisements.

◆ Shortly before his last gig with Wham!, George Michael's 'A Different Corner' became the first British No. 1, sung, written, produced, arranged and played (all instruments!) by the same person.

April 1986

This Mnth	Prev Mnth	Title	Artist	Label	Wks 20	(US Pos)	
1	12	**Living Doll**	Cliff Richard & The Young Ones	WEA	7		
2	-	**A Different Corner**	George Michael	Epic	7	(7)	
3	-	**Rock Me Amadeus**	Falco	A&M	9	(1)	F
4	20	**Touch Me (I Want Your Body)**	Samantha Fox	Jive	6	(4)	F
5	-	**A Kind Of Magic**	Queen	EMI	8	(42)	
6	-	**Wonderful World**	Sam Cooke	RCA	6		L
7	-	**You To Me Are Everything**	Real Thing	PRT	7		
8	-	**Peter Gunn**	Art Of Noise & Duane Eddy	China	4	(50)	
9	-	**Secret Lovers**	Atlantic Starr	A&M	6	(3)	F
10	-	**Train Of Thought**	A-Ha	Warner	3		
11	-	**Look Away**	Big Country	Mercury	5		
12	-	**All The Things She Said**	Simple Minds	Virgin	5	(28)	
13	1	**Chain Reaction**	Diana Ross	Capitol	10	(66)	
14	5	**Absolute Beginners**	David Bowie	Virgin	5	(53)	
15	-	**E=MC^2**	Big Audio Dynamite	CBS	4		F L
16	-	**What Have You Done For Me Lately**	Janet Jackson	A&M	6	(4)	F
17	-	**Can't Wait Another Minute**	Five Star	Tent	7	(41)	
18	-	**Just Say No**	Grange Hill Cast	BBC	3		F L
19	6	**Hi Ho Silver**	Jim Diamond	A&M	7		L
20	18	**Kyrie**	Mr. Mister	RCA	5	(1)	L

May 1986

This	Prev	Title	Artist	Label	Wks	(US)	
1	-	**Lessons In Love**	Level 42	Polydor	7	(12)	
2	3	**Rock Me Amadeus**	Falco	A&M	9	(1)	F
3	-	**On My Own**	Patti Labelle/Michael McDonald	MCA	8	(1)	F L
4	-	**The Chicken Song**	Spitting Image	Virgin	6		F L
5	-	**Live To Tell**	Madonna	Sire	6	(1)	
6	16	**What Have You Done For Me Lately**	Janet Jackson	A&M	6	(4)	F
7	-	**Sledgehammer**	Peter Gabriel	Virgin	8	(1)	
8	17	**Can't Wait Another Minute**	Five Star	Tent	7	(41)	
9	-	**Greatest Love Of All**	Whitney Houston	Arista	5	(1)	
10	2	**A Different Corner**	George Michael	Epic	7	(7)	
11	-	**Snooker Loopy**	Matchroom Mob With Chas & Dave	Rockney	4		F L
12	-	**Spirit In The Sky**	Doctor & The Medics	IRS	9	(69)	F L
13	-	**I Heard It Through The Grapevine**	Marvin Gaye	Tamla Motown	4		L
14	-	**Why Can't This Be Love**	Van Halen	Warner	4	(3)	L
15	5	**A Kind Of Magic**	Queen	EMI	8	(42)	
16	18	**Just Say No**	Grange Hill Cast	BBC	3		F L
17	-	**There'll Be Sad Songs (To Make You Cry)**	Billy Ocean	Jive	4	(1)	
18	-	**Rolling Home**	Status Quo	Vertigo	3		
19	11	**Look Away**	Big Country	Mercury	5		
20	-	**You And Me Tonight**	Aurra	10	4		F L

June 1986

This	Prev	Title	Artist	Label	Wks	(US)	
1	12	**Spirit In The Sky**	Doctor & The Medics	IRS	9	(69)	F L
2	-	**Holding Back The Years**	Simply Red	WEA	8	(1)	
3	-	**I Can't Wait**	Nu Shooz	Atlantic	7	(3)	F L
4	-	**Addicted To Love**	Robert Palmer	Island	7	(1)	
5	7	**Sledgehammer**	Peter Gabriel	Virgin	8	(1)	
6	-	**Can't Get By Without You**	Real Thing	PRT	6		L
7	-	**The Edge Of Heaven/Where Did Your Heart Go**	Wham!	Epic	6	(10)	L
8	-	**Hunting High And Low**	A-Ha	Warner	5		
9	-	**Set Me Free**	Jaki Graham	EMI	5		
10	-	**Everybody Wants To Run The World**	Tears For Fears	Mercury	3		
11	-	**Too Good To Be Forgotten**	Amazulu	Island	6		
12	-	**Vienna Calling**	Falco	A&M	4	(18)	L
13	4	**The Chicken Song**	Spitting Image	Virgin	6		F L
14	-	**Happy Hour**	Housemartins	Go! Discs	7		F
15	3	**On My Own**	Patti Labelle/Michael McDonald	MCA	8	(1)	F L
16	-	**New Beginning (Mamba Seyra)**	Bucks Fizz	Polydor	5		L
17	1	**Lessons In Love**	Level 42	Polydor	7	(12)	
18	-	**My Favourite Waste Of Time**	Owen Paul	Epic	7		F L
19	-	**Opportunities (Let's Make Lots Of Money)**	Pet Shop Boys	Parlophone	4	(10)	
20	-	**Amityville (The House On The Hill)**	Lovebug Starski	Epic	4		F L

April 1986

This Mnth	Prev Mnth	Title	Artist	Label	Wks 20	(UK Pos)	
1	14	Kiss	Prince & The Revolution	Paisley Park	10	(6)	G
2	7	Rock Me Amadeus	Falco	A&M	9	(1)	F
3	20	Manic Monday	Bangles	Columbia	9	(2)	F
4	-	Addicted To Love	Robert Palmer	Island	10	(5)	
5	-	West End Girls	Pet Shop Boys	EMI America	11	(1)	
6	11	What You Need	INXS	Atlantic	9	(51)	F
7	-	Harlem Shuffle	Rolling Stones	Rolling Stone	8	(13)	
8	17	Let's Go All The Way	Sly Fox	Capitol	8	(3)	F L
9	6	R.O.C.K In The U.S.A. (A Salute To '60s Rock)	John Cougar Mellencamp	Riva	8	(67)	
10	-	Why Can't This Be Love	Van Halen	Warner	8	(8)	
11	-	Tender Love	Force M.D's	Warner	6	(23)	F L
12	3	Secret Lovers	Atlantic Starr	A&M	10	(10)	F
13	-	What Have You Done For Me Lately	Janet Jackson	A&M	9	(3)	F
14	-	Your Love	Outfield	Columbia	8		F
15	2	These Dreams	Heart	Capitol	9	(8)	
16	-	Take Me Home	Phil Collins	Atlantic	8	(19)	
17	-	American Storm	Bob Seger & Silver Bullet Band	Capitol	5		
18	-	I Can't Wait	Stevie Nicks	Modern	3	(54)	
19	-	I Think It's Love	Jermaine Jackson	Arista	3		L
20	-	Bad Boy	Miami Sound Machine	Epic	7	(16)	

May 1986

This Mnth	Prev Mnth	Title	Artist	Label	Wks 20	(UK Pos)	
1	-	Greatest Love Of All	Whitney Houston	Arista	9	(8)	
2	5	West End Girls	Pet Shop Boys	EMI America	11	(1)	F
3	13	What Have You Done For Me Lately	Janet Jackson	A&M	9	(3)	F
4	-	Live To Tell	Madonna	Sire	10	(2)	
5	-	If You Leave	Orchestral Manoeuvres In The Dark	A&M	9	(48)	F
6	10	Why Can't This Be Love	Van Halen	Warner	8	(8)	
7	-	On My Own	Patti Labelle/Michael McDonald	MCA	11	(2)	G L
8	16	Take Me Home	Phil Collins	Atlantic	8	(19)	
9	4	Addicted To Love	Robert Palmer	Island	10	(5)	
10	20	Bad Boy	Miami Sound Machine	Epic	7	(16)	
11	14	Your Love	Outfield	Columbia	8		F
12	-	I Can't Wait	Nu Shooz	Atlantic	9	(2)	F L
13	-	Something About You	Level 42	Polydor	9	(6)	F
14	-	All I Need Is A Miracle	Mike + The Mechanics	Atlantic	7	(53)	
15	1	Kiss	Prince & The Revolution	Paisley Park	10	(6)	G
16	7	Harlem Shuffle	Rolling Stones	Rolling Stone	8	(13)	
17	-	Is It Love	Mr. Mister	RCA	6		L
18	-	Be Good To Yourself	Journey	Columbia	6		
19	-	Move Away	Culture Club	Virgin	5	(7)	L
20	3	Manic Monday	Bangles	Columbia	9	(2)	F

June 1986

This Mnth	Prev Mnth	Title	Artist	Label	Wks 20	(UK Pos)	
1	7	On My Own	Patti Labelle/Michael McDonald	MCA	11	(2)	G L
2	-	There'll Be Sad Songs (To Make You Cry)	Billy Ocean	Jive	10	(12)	
3	4	Live To Tell	Madonna	Sire	10	(2)	
4	-	Crush On You	Jets	MCA	8	(5)	F
5	12	I Can't Wait	Nu Shooz	Atlantic	9	(2)	F L
6	-	A Different Corner	George Michael	Columbia	6	(1)	
7	-	No One Is To Blame	Howard Jones	Elektra	8	(16)	
8	-	Holding Back The Years	Simply Red	Elektra	8	(2)	F
9	1	Greatest Love Of All	Whitney Houston	Arista	9	(8)	
10	-	Who's Johnny	El DeBarge	Gordy	8		F L
11	13	Something About You	Level 42	Polydor	9	(6)	F
12	-	Nothin' At All	Heart	Capitol	6	(38)	
13	14	All I Need Is A Miracle	Mike + The Mechanics	Atlantic	7	(53)	
14	-	I Wanna Be A Cowboy	Boys Don't Cry	Profile	5		F L
15	5	If You Leave	Orchestral Manoeuvres In The Dark	A&M	9	(48)	F
16	-	Nasty	Janet Jackson	A&M	8	(19)	
17	-	Invisible Touch	Genesis	Atlantic	8	(15)	
18	-	Sledgehammer	Peter Gabriel	Geffen	10	(4)	F
19	18	Be Good To Yourself	Journey	Columbia	6		
20	17	Is It Love	Mr. Mister	RCA	6		L

◆ Interestingly, Patti Labelle and Michael McDonald only met _after_ they had recorded and made the video for their aptly named chart topper, 'On My Own'. The record gave both artists long-awaited British Top 10 debuts.

▲ In June, Whitney Houston, Patti Labelle and Janet Jackson (above) held the Top 3 positions on the album chart. It was the first time that either females or black artists had achieved this feat. Whitney also became the first female to score three successive No. 1 singles.

◆ A record 20 British artists were simultaneously resident in the Top 40 in June.

UK 1986 JULY-SEPT

◆ Madonna's self-penned and produced, 'Papa Don't Preach' was a transatlantic topper, as was her album **True Blue,** the first LP by an American female to enter the UK chart at the summit.

◆ Chicago club DJ, Farley 'Jackmaster' Funk's 'Love Can't Turn You Around' is generally regarded as the earliest "house music" hit.

◆ Frankie Goes To Hollywood announced they were to disband, septet Madness shrunk to a quartet and Stiff Records closed – it was the end of another era in British pop.

◆ Peter Gabriel's 'Sledgehammer' replaced 'Invisible Touch' by his old band Genesis at the top of the American chart.

July 1986

This Mnth	Prev Mnth	Title	Artist	Label	Wks 20	(US Pos)	
1	-	Papa Don't Preach	Madonna	Sire	9	(1)	
2	18	My Favourite Waste Of Time	Owen Paul	Epic	7		F L
3	7	The Edge Of Heaven/Where Did Your Heart Go	Wham!	Epic	6	(10)	L
4	14	Happy Hour	Housemartins	Go! Discs	7		F
5	-	Let's Go All The Way	Sly Fox	Capitol	6	(7)	F L
6	-	Venus	Bananarama	London	5	(1)	
7	11	Too Good To Be Forgotten	Amazulu	Island	6		
8	-	Every Beat Of My Heart	Rod Stewart	Warner	6	(83)	
9	3	I Can't Wait	Nu Shooz	Atlantic	7	(3)	F L
10	-	Sing Our Own Song	UB40	Dep International	4		
11	-	The Lady In Red	Chris De Burgh	A&M	9	(3)	F
12	16	New Beginning (Mamba Seyra)	Bucks Fizz	Polydor	5		L
13	-	Bang Zoom (Let's Go Go)	Real Roxanne With Hitman Howie Tee	Cooltempo	4		F L
14	-	Do Ya Do Ya (Wanna Please Me)	Samantha Fox	Jive	3	(87)	
15	8	Hunting High And Low	A-Ha	Warner	5		
16	-	Paranoimia	Art Of Noise	China	3	(34)	
17	-	Camouflage	Stan Ridgway	IRS	6		F L
18	1	Spirit In The Sky	Doctor & The Medics	IRS	9	(69)	F L
19	-	It's 'Orrible Being In Love (When You're 8½)	Claire & Friends	BBC	3		F L
20	-	Higher Love	Steve Winwood	Island	3	(1)	F

August 1986

This Mnth	Prev Mnth	Title	Artist	Label	Wks 20	(US Pos)	
1	11	The Lady In Red	Chris De Burgh	A&M	9	(3)	F
2	-	So Macho/Cruising	Sinitta	Fanfare	9		F
3	-	I Want To Wake Up With You	Boris Gardiner	Revue	9		
4	17	Camouflage	Stan Ridgway	IRS	6		F L
5	-	Ain't Nothing Goin' On But The Rent	Gwen Guthrie	Boiling Point	7	(42)	F L
6	1	Papa Don't Preach	Madonna	Sire	9	(1)	
7	-	Anyone Can Fall In Love	Anita Dobson	BBC	4		F L
8	5	Let's Go All The Way	Sly Fox	Capitol	6	(7)	F L
9	-	Find The Time	Five Star	Tent	4		
10	-	Calling All The Heroes	It Bites	Virgin	5		F L
11	8	Every Beat Of My Heart	Rod Stewart	Warner	6	(83)	
12	-	What's The Colour Of Money?	Hollywood Beyond	WEA	5		F L
13	-	Shout	Lulu	Jive/Decca	4		
14	-	Panic	Smiths	Rough Trade	4		
15	-	I Didn't Mean To Turn You On	Robert Palmer	Island	4	(2)	
16	-	Dancing On The Ceiling	Lionel Richie	Motown	4	(2)	
17	-	Brother Louie	Modern Talking	RCA	6		F L
18	-	I Can Prove It	Phil Fearon	Ensign	4		L
19	-	We Don't Have To ...	Jermaine Stewart	10	9	(5)	F
20	10	Sing Our Own Song	UB40	Dep International	4		

September 1986

This Mnth	Prev Mnth	Title	Artist	Label	Wks 20	(US Pos)	
1	-	Don't Leave Me This Way	Communards	London	9	(40)	F
2	19	We Don't Have To ...	Jermaine Stewart	10	9	(5)	F
3	3	I Want To Wake Up With You	Boris Gardiner	Revue	9		
4	-	Glory Of Love	Peter Cetera	Full Moon	7	(1)	F L
5	-	(I Just) Died In Your Arms	Cutting Crew	Siren	6	(1)	F L
6	-	Rage Hard	Frankie Goes To Hollywood	ZTT	4		
7	17	Brother Louie	Modern Talking	RCA	6		F L
8	-	Word Up	Cameo	Club	7	(6)	
9	-	Holiday Rap	M.C. Miker 'G' & Deejay Sven	Debut	3		F L
10	-	Love Can't Turn Around	Farley 'Jackmaster' Funk	D.J. International	6		F L
11	2	So Macho/Cruising	Sinitta	Fanfare	9		F
12	-	Walk This Way	Run D.M.C.	London	6	(4)	F
13	-	Thorn In My Side	Eurythmics	RCA	7	(68)	
14	-	Human	Human League	Virgin	5	(1)	L
15	-	Rain Or Shine	Five Star	Tent	7		
16	-	When I Think Of You	Janet Jackson	A&M	4	(1)	
17	1	The Lady In Red	Chris De Burgh	A&M	9	(3)	F
18	-	You Give Love A Bad Name	Bon Jovi	Vertigo	3	(1)	F
19	-	Sweet Freedom	Michael McDonald	MCA	3	(7)	L
20	5	Ain't Nothing Goin' On But The Rent	Gwen Guthrie	Boiling Point	7	(42)	F L

July 1986

This Mnth	Prev Mnth	Title	Artist	Label	Wks 20	(UK Pos)	
1	17	Invisible Touch	Genesis	Atlantic	8	(15)	
2	16	Nasty	Janet Jackson	A&M	8	(19)	
3	8	Holding Back The Years	Simply Red	Elektra	8	(2)	F
4	18	Sledgehammer	Peter Gabriel	Geffen	10	(4)	F
5	-	Danger Zone	Kenny Loggins	Columbia	8	(45)	
6	2	There'll Be Sad Songs (To Make You Cry)	Billy Ocean	Jive	10	(12)	
7	10	Who's Johnny	El DeBarge	Gordy	8		F L
8	-	Glory Of Love	Peter Cetera	Full Moon	10	(3)	F
9	-	Your Wildest Dreams	Moody Blues	Threshold	6		L
10	7	No One Is To Blame	Howard Jones	Elektra	8	(16)	
11	-	Love Touch	Rod Stewart	Warner	7	(27)	
12	-	Mad About You	Belinda Carlisle	IRS	9	(67)	F
13	-	Opportunities (Let's Make Lots Of Money)	Pet Shop Boys	EMI America	6	(11)	
14	-	Papa Don't Preach	Madonna	Sire	9	(1)	
15	-	When The Heart Rules The Mind	GTR	Arista	4		F L
16	-	Tuff Enuff	Fabulous Thunderbirds	CBS Associated	6		F L
17	-	Like A Rock	Bob Seger & Silver Bullet Band	Capitol	5		
18	1	On My Own	Patti Labelle/Michael McDonald	MCA	11	(2)	G L
19	4	Crush On You	Jets	MCA	8	(5)	F
20	-	Modern Woman	Billy Joel	Epic	5		

August 1986

This Mnth	Prev Mnth	Title	Artist	Label	Wks 20	(UK Pos)	
1	14	Papa Don't Preach	Madonna	Sire	9	(1)	
2	8	Glory Of Love	Peter Cetera	Full Moon	10	(3)	F
3	12	Mad About You	Belinda Carlisle	IRS	9	(67)	F
4	-	Higher Love	Steve Winwood	Island	9	(13)	
5	-	Venus	Bananarama	London	9	(8)	
6	-	We Don't Have To Take Our Clothes Off	Jermaine Stewart	Arista	7	(2)	F L
7	-	Rumors	Timex Social Club	Jay	8	(13)	F L
8	-	Dancing On The Ceiling	Lionel Richie	Motown	11	(7)	
9	4	Sledgehammer	Peter Gabriel	Geffen	10	(4)	F
10	-	Take My Breath Away	Berlin	Columbia	9	(1)	F L
11	11	Love Touch	Rod Stewart	Warner	7	(27)	
12	-	Sweet Freedom	Michael McDonald	MCA	8	(12)	L
13	-	The Edge Of Heaven	Wham!	Columbia	5	(1)	L
14	5	Danger Zone	Kenny Loggins	Columbia	8	(45)	
15	-	Friends And Lovers	Gloria Loring & Carl Anderson	USA Carrere	10		F L
16	1	Invisible Touch	Genesis	Atlantic	8	(15)	
17	-	You Should Be Mine (The Woo Woo Song)	Jeffrey Osborne	A&M	4		F
18	2	Nasty	Janet Jackson	A&M	8	(19)	
19	-	Stuck With You	Huey Lewis & The News	Chrysalis	9	(12)	
20	-	Baby Love	Regina	Atlantic	7	(50)	F L

September 1986

This Mnth	Prev Mnth	Title	Artist	Label	Wks 20	(UK Pos)	
1	19	Stuck With You	Huey Lewis & The News	Chrysalis	9	(12)	
2	8	Dancing On The Ceiling	Lionel Richie	Motown	11	(7)	
3	15	Friends And Lovers	Gloria Loring & Carl Anderson	USA Carrere	10		F L
4	10	Take My Breath Away	Berlin	Columbia	9	(1)	F L
5	-	Walk This Way	Run D.M.C.	Profile	8	(8)	F L
6	5	Venus	Bananarama	London	9	(8)	
7	-	Words Get In The Way	Miami Sound Machine	Epic	8		
8	-	Don't Forget Me (When I'm Gone)	Glass Tiger	Manhattan	9	(29)	F
9	-	Dreamtime	Daryl Hall	RCA	7	(28)	F L
10	4	Higher Love	Steve Winwood	Island	9	(13)	
11	20	Baby Love	Regina	Atlantic	7	(50)	F L
12	12	Sweet Freedom	Michael McDonald	MCA	8	(12)	L
13	-	Love Zone	Billy Ocean	Jive	6	(49)	
14	-	When I Think Of You	Janet Jackson	A&M	9	(10)	
15	-	Two Of Hearts	Stacey Q	Atlantic	7		F L
16	1	Papa Don't Preach	Madonna	Sire	9	(1)	
17	-	The Captain Of Her Heart	Double	A&M	4	(8)	F L
18	-	Throwing It All Away	Genesis	Atlantic	8	(22)	
19	7	Rumors	Timex Social Club	Jay	8	(13)	F L
20	-	Man Size Love	Klymaxx	MCA	3		

US 1986

JULY-SEPT

▲ Run DMC's *Raising Hell* tour (including fellow rappers L.L. Cool J, Whodini and The Beastie Boys) sparked off mini-riots at several venues. Run DMC's **Raising Hell** LP was the first platinum rap album, and 'Walk This Way' (featuring Aerosmith's Steve Tyler) (above) was the earliest hit to combine the rap and rock genres.

◆ Janet Jackson became the youngest singer to top the album charts since Little Stevie Wonder in 1963.

◆ The Monkees, with six of their albums back on the charts, had a successful US tour with another reformed 1960's band, Herman's Hermits.

287

UK 1986

OCT-DEC

African Americans collecting their debut transatlantic hits included Cameo, Gregory Abbott, Oran 'Juice' Jones and Anita Baker.

◆ 'Take My Breath Away' (from the five million selling **Top Gun** soundtrack) gave Berlin a transatlantic chart-topper. It also returned to the British Top 3 in 1990.

▲ In October, for the first time the top three US singles were by different solo female singers, Janet Jackson, Tina Turner (above) and Cyndi Lauper. A month later female vocalists held a record Top 5 slots on the UK chart.

October 1986

This Mnth	Prev Mnth	Title	Artist	Label	Wks 20	(US Pos)	
1	-	**True Blue**	Madonna	Sire	7	(3)	
2	15	**Rain Or Shine**	Five Star	Tent	7		
3	1	**Don't Leave Me This Way**	Communards	London	9	(40)	F
4	-	**You Can Call Me Al**	Paul Simon	Warner	6	(23)	
5	-	**Every Loser Wins**	Nick Berry	BBC	6		F
6	-	**In The Army Now**	Status Quo	Vertigo	7		
7	8	**Word Up**	Cameo	Club	7	(6)	
8	13	**Thorn In My Side**	Eurythmics	RCA	7	(68)	
9	-	**Suburbia**	Pet Shop Boys	Parlophone	5	(70)	
10	-	**I've Been Losing You**	A-Ha	Warner	4		
11	-	**All I Ask Of You**	Cliff Richard & Sarah Brightman	Polydor	8		
12	-	**Walk Like An Egyptian**	Bangles	CBS	8	(1)	
13	2	**We Don't Have To ...**	Jermaine Stewart	10	9	(5)	F
14	-	**(Forever) Live And Die**	Orchestral Manoeuvres In The Dark	Virgin	5	(19)	
15	-	**Always There**	Marti Webb	BBC	5		L
16	12	**Walk This Way**	Run D.M.C.	London	6	(4)	F
17	5	**(I Just) Died In Your Arms**	Cutting Crew	Siren	6	(1)	F L
18	-	**True Colors**	Cyndi Lauper	Portrait	5	(1)	
19	-	**Stuck With You**	Huey Lewis & The News	Chrysalis	4	(1)	L
20	-	**Montego Bay**	Amazulu	Island	3	(90)	L

November 1986

This Mnth	Prev Mnth	Title	Artist	Label	Wks 20	(US Pos)	
1	-	**Take My Breath Away**	Berlin	CBS	11	(1)	F
2	-	**You Keep Me Hangin' On**	Kim Wilde	MCA	7	(1)	
3	12	**Walk Like An Egyptian**	Bangles	CBS	8	(1)	
4	-	**Showing Out (Get Fresh At The Weekend)**	Mel & Kim	Supreme	6	(78)	F
5	6	**In The Army Now**	Status Quo	Vertigo	7		
6	5	**Every Loser Wins**	Nick Berry	BBC	6		F
7	-	**Breakout**	Swing Out Sister	Mercury	7	(6)	F
8	11	**All I Ask Of You**	Cliff Richard & Sarah Brightman	Polydor	8		
9	-	**Livin' On A Prayer**	Bon Jovi	Vertigo	10	(1)	
10	-	**The Final Countdown**	Europe	Epic	10	(8)	F
11	-	**Through The Barricades**	Spandau Ballet	Reformation	5		L
12	-	**Don't Give Up**	Peter Gabriel & Kate Bush	Virgin	4	(72)	
13	-	**Notorious**	Duran Duran	EMI	4	(2)	
14	-	**For America**	Red Box	Sire	5		L
15	-	**Midas Touch**	Midnight Star	Solar	4	(42)	L
16	1	**True Blue**	Madonna	Sire	7	(3)	
17	-	**Don't Get Me Wrong**	Pretenders	Real	4	(10)	
18	4	**You Can Call Me Al**	Paul Simon	Warner	6	(23)	
19	-	**Each Time You Break My Heart**	Nick Kamen	WEA	5		F
20	-	**French Kissin' In The USA**	Debbie Harry	Chrysalis	7	(57)	F L

December 1986

This Mnth	Prev Mnth	Title	Artist	Label	Wks 20	(US Pos)	
1	10	**The Final Countdown**	Europe	Epic	10	(8)	F
2	-	**Sometimes**	Erasure	Mute	10		F
3	-	**Caravan Of Love**	Housemartins	Go! Discs	6		
4	-	**The Rain**	Oran 'Juice' Jones	Def Jam	8	(9)	F L
5	9	**Livin' On A Prayer**	Bon Jovi	Vertigo	10	(1)	
6	1	**Take My Breath Away**	Berlin	CBS	11	(1)	F
7	-	**Open Your Heart**	Madonna	Sire	6	(1)	
8	-	**Shake You Down**	Gregory Abbott	CBS	7	(1)	F L
9	-	**Reet Petite**	Jackie Wilson	SMP	9		
10	-	**So Cold The Night**	Communards	London	6		
11	19	**Each Time You Break My Heart**	Nick Kamen	WEA	5		F
12	20	**French Kissin' In The USA**	Debbie Harry	Chrysalis	7	(57)	F L
13	-	**Cry Wolf**	A-Ha	Warner	6	(50)	
14	7	**Breakout**	Swing Out Sister	Mercury	7	(6)	F
15	-	**The Skye Boat Song**	Roger Whittaker & Des O'Connor	Tembo	5		L
16	-	**Is This Love**	Alison Moyet	CBS	9		
17	2	**You Keep Me Hangin' On**	Kim Wilde	MCA	7	(1)	
18	4	**Showing Out (Get Fesh At The Weekend)**	Mel & Kim	Supreme	6	(78)	F
19	-	**Big Fun**	Gap Band	Total Experience	8		
20	-	**Land Of Confusion**	Genesis	Virgin	7	(4)	

October 1986

This Mnth	Prev Mnth	Title	Artist	Label	Wks 20	(UK Pos)	
1	14	When I Think Of You	Janet Jackson	A&M	9	(10)	
2	-	Typical Male	Tina Turner	Capitol	9	(33)	
3	18	Throwing It All Away	Genesis	Atlantic	8	(22)	
4	15	Two Of Hearts	Stacey Q	Atlantic	7		F L
5	-	True Colors	Cyndi Lauper	Portrait	8	(12)	
6	8	Don't Forget Me (When I'm Gone)	Glass Tiger	Manhattan	9	(29)	F
7	-	Heartbeat	Don Johnson	Epic	7	(46)	F L
8	1	Stuck With You	Huey Lewis & The News	Chrysalis	9	(12)	
9	-	All Cried Out	Lisa Lisa & Cult Jam With Full Force	Columbia	7		F
10	-	I Didn't Mean To Turn You On	Robert Palmer	Island	8	(9)	
11	3	Friends And Lovers	Gloria Loring & Carl Anderson	USA Carrere	10		F L
12	9	Dreamtime	Daryl Hall	RCA	7	(28)	F L
13	-	A Matter Of Trust	Billy Joel	Columbia	5	(52)	
14	-	Sweet Love	Anita Baker	Elektra	6	(13)	F
15	-	Heaven In Your Eyes	Loverboy	Columbia	5		L
16	-	Amanda	Boston	MCA	8		
17	-	Human	Human League	A&M	10	(8)	L
18	5	Walk This Way	Run D.M.C.	Profile	8	(8)	F L
19	-	Missionary Man	Eurythmics	RCA	5	(31)	L
20	13	Love Zone	Billy Ocean	Jive	6	(49)	

November 1986

This Mnth	Prev Mnth	Title	Artist	Label	Wks 20	(UK Pos)	
1	17	Human	Human League	A&M	10	(8)	L
2	16	Amanda	Boston	MCA	8		
3	-	True Blue	Madonna	Sire	8	(1)	
4	-	You Give Love A Bad Name	Bon Jovi	Mercury	9	(14)	F
5	-	Take Me Home Tonight	Eddie Money	Columbia	8		
6	-	Word Up	Cameo	Atlanta Artists	8	(3)	F L
7	10	I Didn't Mean To Turn You On	Robert Palmer	Island	8	(9)	
8	-	The Next Time I Fall	Peter Cetera & Amy Grant	Full Moon	8		
9	5	True Colors	Cyndi Lauper	Portrait	8	(12)	
10	-	Hip To Be Square	Huey Lewis & The News	Chrysalis	9	(41)	
11	-	The Rain	Oran 'Juice' Jones	Def Jam	6	(4)	F L
12	-	Love Will Conquer All	Lionel Richie	Motown	7	(45)	
13	-	I'll Be Over You	Toto	Columbia	5		L
14	-	The Way It Is	Bruce Hornsby & The Range	RCA	11	(15)	F
15	2	Typical Male	Tina Turner	Capitol	9	(33)	
16	14	Sweet Love	Anita Baker	Elektra	6	(13)	F
17	-	Everybody Have Fun Tonight	Wang Chung	Geffen	10		
18	-	To Be A Lover	Billy Idol	Chrysalis	9	(22)	
19	1	When I Think Of You	Janet Jackson	A&M	9	(10)	
20	-	Walk Like An Egyptian	Bangles	Columbia	11	(3)	G

December 1986

This Mnth	Prev Mnth	Title	Artist	Label	Wks 20	(UK Pos)	
1	20	Walk Like An Egyptian	Bangles	Columbia	11	(3)	G
2	14	The Way It Is	Bruce Hornsby & The Range	RCA	11	(15)	F
3	17	Everybody Have Fun Tonight	Wang Chung	Geffen	10		
4	-	Notorious	Duran Duran	Capitol	10	(7)	
5	10	Hip To Be Square	Huey Lewis & The News	Chrysalis	9	(41)	
6	-	Shake You Down	Gregory Abbott	Columbia	11	(6)	F G L
7	18	To Be A Lover	Billy Idol	Chrysalis	9	(22)	
8	8	The Next Time I Fall	Peter Cetera & Amy Grant	Full Moon	8		
9	-	Stand By Me	Ben E. King	Atlantic	9	(1)	L
10	4	You Give Love A Bad Name	Bon Jovi	Mercury	9	(14)	F
11	-	C'Est La Vie	Robbie Nevil	Manhattan/EMI	10	(3)	F
12	-	Don't Get Me Wrong	Pretenders	Sire	7	(10)	L
13	-	War	Bruce Springsteen	Columbia	7	(18)	
14	-	Control	Janet Jackson	A&M	9	(42)	
15	6	Word Up	Cameo	Atlanta Artists	8	(3)	F L
16	12	Love Will Conquer All	Lionel Richie	Motown	7	(45)	
17	1	Human	Human League	A&M	10	(8)	L
18	-	Is This Love	Survivor	Scotti Brothers	8		L
19	-	Land Of Confusion	Genesis	Atlantic	10	(14)	
20	-	Victory	Kool & The Gang	Mercury	7	(30)	

US 1986 OCT-DEC

◆ American record and tape shipments rose 6% to $4.65 billion, with CD sales up 139% to $930 million. Singles sales however were down 22%.

◆ The five album box set **Bruce Springsteen & The E Street Band Live/1975-85** entered at No. 1. Springsteen was only the third artist to accomplish this feat – Elton John and Stevie Wonder had previously done so but with single albums.

◆ In 1986, the *Rock And Roll Hall Of Fame* chose Cleveland as its home. The initial artists inducted being: Chuck Berry, James Brown, Sam Cooke, Fats Domino, The Everly Brothers, Alan Freed, Buddy Holly, Jerry Lee Lewis, Little Richard, Sun Records owner Sam Phillips and Elvis Presley.

UK 1987 JAN-MAR

◆ Ben E. King's 25-year-old 'Stand By Me' was a transatlantic Top 10 hit, while in Britain, Percy Sledge's 1966 smash, 'When A Man Loves A Woman', scored again. Jackie Wilson's 29-year-old 'Reet Petite' hit the top and half the Top 10 in March were re-issues.

▲ *Record Mirror's* readers poll showed Prince as Top Male, Madonna as Top Female and The Smiths (above) as Top Group.

◆ The Beatles' initial four albums were released on compact disc and instantly took the Top 4 places on the CD chart.

January 1987

This Mnth	Prev Mnth	Title	Artist	Label	Wks 20	(US Pos)	
1	9	Reet Petite	Jackie Wilson	SMP	9		
2	16	Is This Love	Alison Moyet	CBS	9		
3	19	Big Fun	Gap Band	Total Experience	8		
4	-	Jack Your Body	Steve 'Silk' Hurley	DJ International	7		F L
5	-	No More The Fool	Elkie Brooks	Legend	8		L
6	3	Caravan Of Love	Housemartins	Go! Discs	6		
7	-	C'est La Vie	Robbie Nevil	Manhattan	5	(2)	F L
8	2	Sometimes	Erasure	Mute	10		F
9	1	The Final Countdown	Europe	Epic	10	(8)	F
10	7	Open Your Heart	Madonna	Sire	6	(1)	
11	4	The Rain	Oran 'Juice' Jones	Def Jam	8	(9)	F L
12	13	Cry Wolf	A-Ha	Warner	6	(50)	
13	-	Surrender	Swing Out Sister	Mercury	4		L
14	-	Hymn To Her	Pretenders	Real	5		L
15	8	Shake You Down	Gregory Abbott	CBS	7	(1)	F L
16	-	It Didn't Matter	Style Council	Polydor	3		
17	-	I Knew You Were Waiting (For Me)	Aretha Franklin & George Michael	Epic	6	(1)	L
18	-	Down To Earth	Curiosity Killed The Cat	Mercury	8		F
19	5	Livin' On A Prayer	Bon Jovi	Vertigo	10	(1)	
20	10	So Cold The Night	Communards	London	6		

February 1987

This Mnth	Prev Mnth	Title	Artist	Label	Wks 20	(US Pos)	
1	17	I Knew You Were Waiting (For Me)	Aretha Franklin & George Michael	Epic	6	(1)	L
2	-	Heartache	Pepsi & Shirlie	Polydor	6	(78)	F
3	18	Down To Earth	Curiosity Killed The Cat	Mercury	8		F
4	-	Almaz	Randy Crawford	Warner	5		L
5	-	It Doesn't Have To Be That Way	Blow Monkeys	RCA	4		L
6	-	Male Stripper	Man 2 Man Meet Man Parrish	Bolts	7		F L
7	-	Stand By Me	Ben E. King	Atlantic	7	(9)	F L
8	-	I Love My Radio	Taffy	Transglobal	4		F L
9	-	When A Man Loves A Woman	Percy Sledge	Atlantic	6		L
10	4	Jack Your Body	Steve 'Silk' Hurley	Dj International	7		
11	-	Stay Out Of My Life	Five Star	Tent	4		
12	-	The Music Of The Night/Wishing You Were Somehow Here Again	Michael Crawford/ Sarah Brightman	Polydor	4		F L
13	-	Running In The Family	Level 42	Polydor	6	(83)	
14	-	You Sexy Thing	Hot Chocolate	EMI	4		L
15	5	No More The Fool	Elkie Brooks	Legend	8		L
16	7	C'est La Vie	Robbie Nevil	Manhattan	5	(2)	F L
17	-	Coming Around Again	Carly Simon	Arista	5	(18)	L
18	-	Shoplifters Of The World Unite	Smiths	Rough Trade	2		
19	2	Is This Love	Alison Moyet	CBS	9		
20	-	Once Bitten Twice Shy	Vesta Williams	A&M	3		F L

March 1987

This Mnth	Prev Mnth	Title	Artist	Label	Wks 20	(US Pos)	
1	-	Everything I Own	Boy George	Virgin	6		F
2	-	I Get The Sweetest Feeling	Jackie Wilson	SMP	6		
3	-	Live It Up	Mental As Anything	Epic	7		F L
4	-	The Great Pretender	Freddie Mercury	Parlophone	6		
5	7	Stand By Me	Ben E. King	Atlantic	7	(9)	F L
6	-	Respectable	Mel & Kim	Supreme	9		
7	9	When A Man Loves A Woman	Percy Sledge	Atlantic	6		L
8	-	Crush On You	Jets	MCA	6	(3)	F L
9	6	Male Stripper	Man 2 Man Meet Man Parrish	Bolts	7		F L
10	13	Running In The Family	Level 42	Polydor	6	(83)	
11	-	Weak In The Presence Of Beauty	Alison Moyet	CBS	6		
12	-	Moonlighting ('Theme')	Al Jarreau	WEA	4	(23)	F L
13	-	Respect Yourself	Bruce Willis	Motown	4	(5)	F
14	-	The Right Thing	Simply Red	WEA	4	(27)	
15	-	It Doesn't Have To Be	Erasure	Mute	5		
16	3	Down To Earth	Curiosity Killed The Cat	Mercury	8		F
17	17	Coming Around Again	Carly Simon	Arista	5	(18)	L
18	-	With Or Without You	U2	Island	6	(1)	
19	-	Sign 'O' The Times	Prince	Paisley Park	5	(3)	
20	-	(You Gotta) Fight For Your Right (To Party)	Beastie Boys	Def Jam	3	(7)	F

US 1987 JAN-MAR

January 1987

This Mnth	Prev Mnth	Title	Artist	Label	Wks 20	(UK Pos)	
1	11	**C'Est La Vie**	Robbie Nevil	Manhattan/EMI	10	(3)	F
2	6	**Shake You Down**	Gregory Abbott	Columbia	11	(6)	F G L
3	4	**Notorious**	Duran Duran	Capitol	10	(7)	
4	14	**Control**	Janet Jackson	A&M	9	(42)	
5	-	**At This Moment**	Billy Vera & The Beaters	Rhino	9		F G L
6	1	**Walk Like An Egyptian**	Bangles	Columbia	11	(3)	G
7	19	**Land Of Confusion**	Genesis	Atlantic	10	(14)	
8	-	**Open Your Heart**	Madonna	Sire	8	(4)	
9	18	**Is This Love**	Survivor	Scotti Brothers	8		L
10	3	**Everybody Have Fun Tonight**	Wang Chung	Geffen	10		
11	-	**Someday**	Glass Tiger	Manhattan	8	(66)	L
12	20	**Victory**	Kool & The Gang	Mercury	7	(30)	
13	-	**Change Of Heart**	Cyndi Lauper	Portrait	6	(67)	
14	2	**The Way It Is**	Bruce Hornsby & The Range	RCA	11	(15)	F
15	13	**War**	Bruce Springsteen	Columbia	7	(18)	
16	-	**Touch Me (I Want Your Body)**	Samantha Fox	Jive	7	(3)	F
17	9	**Stand By Me**	Ben E. King	Atlantic	9	(1)	L
18	-	**Livin' On A Prayer**	Bon Jovi	Mercury	10	(4)	
19	12	**Don't Get Me Wrong**	Pretenders	Sire	7	(10)	L
20	-	**Keep Your Hands To Yourself**	Georgia Satellites	Elektra	9	(69)	F L

February 1987

This Mnth	Prev Mnth	Title	Artist	Label	Wks 20	(UK Pos)	
1	18	**Livin' On A Prayer**	Bon Jovi	Mercury	10	(4)	
2	20	**Keep Your Hands To Yourself**	Georgia Satellites	Elektra	9	(69)	F L
3	-	**Will You Still Love Me**	Chicago	Warner	8		
4	16	**Touch Me (I Want Your Body)**	Samantha Fox	Jive	7	(3)	F
5	-	**Jacob's Ladder**	Huey Lewis & The News	Chrysalis	8		
6	8	**Open Your Heart**	Madonna	Sire	8	(4)	
7	13	**Change Of Heart**	Cyndi Lauper	Portrait	6	(67)	
8	-	**You Got It All**	Jets	MCA	8		
9	-	**Ballerina Girl**	Lionel Richie	Motown	7	(17)	
10	5	**At This Moment**	Billy Vera & The Beaters	Rhino	9		F G L
11	-	**Love You Down**	Ready For The World	MCA	6	(60)	L
12	-	**Somewhere Out There**	Linda Ronstadt/James Ingram	MCA	8	(8)	
13	-	**Respect Yourself**	Bruce Willis	Motown	7	(7)	F L
14	-	**Big Time**	Peter Gabriel	Geffen	7	(13)	L
15	-	**(You Gotta) Fight For Your Right (To Party)**	Beastie Boys	Def Jam	6	(11)	F L
16	-	**We're Ready**	Boston	Epic	5		
17	-	**Nobody's Fool**	Cinderella	Mercury	4		F
18	7	**Land Of Confusion**	Genesis	Atlantic	10	(14)	
19	11	**Someday**	Glass Tiger	Manhattan	8	(66)	L
20	-	**Stop To Love**	Luther Vandross	Epic	4	(24)	F

March 1987

This Mnth	Prev Mnth	Title	Artist	Label	Wks 20	(UK Pos)	
1	12	**Somewhere Out There**	Linda Ronstadt/James Ingram	MCA	8	(8)	
2	-	**Let's Wait Awhile**	Janet Jackson	A&M	7	(3)	
3	-	**Lean On Me**	Club Nouveau	Warner	8	(3)	F G L
4	5	**Jacob's Ladder**	Huey Lewis & The News	Chrysalis	8		
5	-	**Mandolin Rain**	Bruce Hornsby & The Range	RCA	8	(70)	
6	-	**Nothing's Gonna Stop Us Now**	Starship	Grunt	10	(1)	
7	1	**Livin' On A Prayer**	Bon Jovi	Mercury	10	(4)	
8	-	**Tonight Tonight Tonight**	Genesis	Atlantic	7	(18)	
9	13	**Respect Yourself**	Bruce Willis	Motown	7	(7)	F L
10	14	**Big Time**	Peter Gabriel	Geffen	7	(13)	L
11	8	**You Got It All**	Jets	MCA	8		
12	-	**Come Go With Me**	Expose	Arista	8		F
13	15	**(You Gotta) Fight For Your Right (To Party)**	Beastie Boys	Def Jam	6	(11)	F L
14	-	**The Final Countdown**	Europe	Epic	6	(1)	F
15	2	**Keep Your Hands To Yourself**	Georgia Satellites	Elektra	9	(69)	F L
16	-	**Don't Dream It's Over**	Crowded House	Capitol	10	(27)	F
17	-	**I Knew You Were Waiting (For Me)**	Aretha Franklin & George Michael	Arista	8	(1)	
18	-	**Let's Go**	Wang Chung	Geffen	5		L
19	-	**I Wanna Go Back**	Eddie Money	Columbia	4		
20	-	**Brand New Lover**	Dead Or Alive	Epic	4	(31)	L

◆ It was announced that DAT (digital audio tapes) and CDV (compact disc videos) machines would soon be on the market.

◆ The Beastie Boys' **Licensed To Ill** became the first rap album to top the chart. The white trio's first single '(You Gotta) Fight For Your Right (To Party)' was also a transatlantic hit.

▲ Huey Lewis & The News scored their third and last American No. 1 with 'Jacob's Ladder'. It was one of five Top 10 hits from their chart-topping **Fore** album.

◆ Paul Simon picked up a Grammy for Album Of The Year for **Graceland** and the Brit Award for Best International Solo Artist.

291

UK 1987
APR-JUNE

◆ Wembley hosted one of many shows raising money for AIDS research. Its stars included George Michael, Elton John, Boy George, Kim Wilde, and US soul duo Womack and Womack. Also having sell out Wembley appearances were Lionel Ritchie, U2, Duran Duran, David Bowie, Luther Vandross, Tina Turner and The Pretenders.

◆ Headliners at Switzerland's Montreux Rock Festival included Whitney Houston, Cameo, Duran Duran, Spandau Ballet, Run DMC and The Beastie Boys. The latter two then toured Britain where The Beasties received a hammering from the British press for their alleged anti-social behaviour.

◆ Britain's most popular new teeny bop stars were Curiosity Killed the Cat, Wet Wet Wet and the shortlived, but transatlantically successful, Johnny Hates Jazz.

April 1987

This Mnth	Prev Mnth	Title	Artist	Label	Wks 20	(US Pos)	
1	-	Let It Be	Ferry Aid	The Sun	5		F L
2	-	La Isla Bonita	Madonna	Sire	8	(4)	
3	6	Respectable	Mel & Kim	Supreme	9		
4	-	Lean On Me	Club Nouveau	King Jay	7	(1)	F L
5	-	Let's Wait Awhile	Janet Jackson	Breakout	6	(2)	
6	18	With Or Without You	U2	Island	6	(1)	
7	-	If You Let Me Stay	Terence Trent D'Arby	CBS	7	(68)	F
8	-	Can't Be With You Tonight	Judy Boucher	Orbitone	9		F
9	-	Ever Fallen In Love	Fine Young Cannibals	London	6		
10	11	Weak In The Presence Of Beauty	Alison Moyet	CBS	6		
11	-	Living In A Box	Living In A Box	Chrysalis	8	(17)	F
12	-	The Irish Rover	Pogues & The Dubliners	Stiff	3		
13	1	Everything I Own	Boy George	Virgin	6		F
14	2	I Get The Sweetest Feeling	Jackie Wilson	SMP	6		
15	-	Ordinary Day	Curiosity Killed The Cat	Mercury	3		
16	-	The Slightest Touch	Five Star	Tent	6		
17	-	Wanted Dead Or Alive	Bon Jovi	Vertigo	4	(7)	
18	19	Sign 'O' The Times	Prince	Paisley Park	5	(3)	
19	13	Respect Yourself	Bruce Willis	Motown	4	(5)	F
20	-	Big Time	Peter Gabriel	Charisma	3	(8)	

May 1987

This Mnth	Prev Mnth	Title	Artist	Label	Wks 20	(US Pos)	
1	-	Nothing's Gonna Stop Us Now	Starship	RCA	11	(1)	L
2	8	Can't Be With You Tonight	Judy Boucher	Orbitone	9		F
3	-	A Boy From Nowhere	Tom Jones	Epic	8		
4	11	Living In A Box	Living In A Box	Chrysalis	8	(17)	F
5	-	(Something Inside) So Strong	Labi Siffre	China	7		L
6	2	La Isla Bonita	Madonna	Sire	8	(4)	
7	-	Another Step (Closer To You)	Kim Wilde & Junior	MCA	7		
8	16	The Slightest Touch	Five Star	Tent	6		
9	-	Big Love	Fleetwood Mac	Warner	5	(5)	
10	-	Shattered Dreams	Johnny Hates Jazz	Virgin	6	(2)	F
11	-	Back And Forth	Cameo	Club	5	(50)	L
12	-	I Wanna Dance With Somebody (Who Loves Me)	Whitney Houston	Arista	10	(1)	
13	4	Lean On Me	Club Nouveau	King Jay	7	(1)	F L
14	-	Incommunicado	Marillion	EMI	3		
15	-	April Skies	Jesus And Mary Chain	Blanco	3		
16	-	To Be With You Again	Level 42	Polydor	3		
17	7	If You Let Me Stay	Terence Trent D'Arby	CBS	7	(68)	F
18	-	Lil' Devil	Cult	Beggars Banquet	4		
19	-	Boops (Here To Go)	Sly And Robbie	4th & Broadway	3		F L
20	-	Hold Me Now	Johnny Logan	Epic	7		L

June 1987

This Mnth	Prev Mnth	Title	Artist	Label	Wks 20	(US Pos)	
1	12	I Wanna Dance With Somebody (Who Loves Me)	Whitney Houston	Arista	10	(1)	
2	20	Hold Me Now	Johnny Logan	Epic	7		L
3	1	Nothing's Gonna Stop Us Now	Starship	RCA	11	(1)	L
4	-	I Want Your Sex	George Michael	Epic	5	(2)	
5	-	Star Trekkin'	Firm	Bark	7		L
6	-	I Still Haven't Found What I'm Looking For	U2	Island	4	(1)	
7	-	Jack Mix II	Mirage	Debut	5		F
8	-	Victim Of Love	Erasure	Mute	4		
9	-	Nothing's Gonna Stop Me Now	Samantha Fox	Jive	5	(80)	
10	-	Under The Boardwalk	Bruce Willis	Motown	10	(59)	L
11	-	Goodbye Stranger	Pepsi & Shirlie	Polydor	4		L
12	10	Shattered Dreams	Johnny Hates Jazz	Virgin	6	(2)	F
13	-	Wishing I Was Lucky	Wet Wet Wet	Precious	5	(58)	F
14	-	You're The Voice	John Farnham	Wheatley	6	(82)	F L
15	-	Serious	Donna Allen	Portrait	3	(21)	F
16	-	It's A Sin	Pet Shop Boys	Parlophone	8	(9)	
17	-	When Smokey Sings	ABC	Neutron	4	(5)	L
18	-	Looking For A New Love	Jody Watley	MCA	3	(2)	F L
19	-	Is This Love	Whitesnake	EMI	5	(2)	
20	-	No Sleep Till Brooklyn	Beastie Boys	Def Jam	3		

292

April 1987

This Mnth	Prev Mnth	Title	Artist	Label	Wks 20	(UK Pos)	
1	6	Nothing's Gonna Stop Us Now	Starship	Grunt	10	(1)	
2	17	I Knew You Were Waiting (For Me)	Aretha Franklin/George Michael	Arista	8	(1)	
3	16	Don't Dream It's Over	Crowded House	Capitol	10	(27)	F
4	3	Lean On Me	Club Nouveau	Warner	8	(3)	F G L
5	-	Sign 'O' The Times	Prince	Paisley Park	8	(10)	
6	-	Midnight Blue	Lou Gramm	Atlantic	7		F
7	12	Come Go With Me	Expose	Arista	8		F
8	-	Looking For A New Love	Jody Watley	MCA	10	(13)	F
9	-	The Finer Things	Steve Winwood	Island	8		
10	8	Tonight Tonight Tonight	Genesis	Atlantic	7	(18)	
11	-	(I Just) Died In Your Arms	Cutting Crew	Virgin	8	(4)	F
12	-	Walking Down Your Street	Bangles	Columbia	5	(16)	
13	18	Let's Go	Wang Chung	Geffen	5		L
14	-	La Isla Bonita	Madonna	Sire	8	(1)	
15	2	Let's Wait Awhile	Janet Jackson	A&M	7	(3)	
16	14	The Final Countdown	Europe	Epic	6	(1)	F
17	-	With Or Without You	U2	Island	10	(4)	F
18	-	Stone Love	Kool & The Gang	Mercury	6	(45)	L
19	5	Mandolin Rain	Bruce Hornsby & The Range	RCA	8	(70)	
20	-	What You Get Is What You See	Tina Turner	Capitol	3	(30)	

May 1987

This Mnth	Prev Mnth	Title	Artist	Label	Wks 20	(UK Pos)	
1	17	With Or Without You	U2	Island	10	(4)	F
2	8	Looking For A New Love	Jody Watley	MCA	10	(13)	F
3	11	(I Just) Died In Your Arms	Cutting Crew	Virgin	8	(4)	F
4	-	Lady In Red	Chris De Burgh	A&M	9	(1)	F L
5	14	La Isla Bonita	Madonna	Sire	8	(1)	
6	-	Heat Of The Night	Bryan Adams	A&M	7	(50)	
7	-	Big Love	Fleetwood Mac	Warner	7	(9)	
8	-	You Keep Me Hangin' On	Kim Wilde	MCA	8	(2)	F L
9	-	Always	Atlantic Starr	Warner	10	(3)	
10	-	Right On Track	Breakfast Club	MCA	7	(54)	F L
11	3	Don't Dream It's Over	Crowded House	Capitol	10	(27)	F
12	5	Sign 'O' The Times	Prince	Paisley Park	8	(10)	
13	-	Talk Dirty To Me	Poison	Enigma	4	(67)	F
14	-	I Know What I Like	Huey Lewis & The News	Chrysalis	5		
15	-	Nothing's Gonna Change My Love For You	Glenn Medeiros	Amherst	6	(1)	F
16	2	I Knew You Were Waiting (For Me)	Aretha Franklin/George Michael	Arista	8	(1)	
17	-	Wanted Dead Or Alive	Bon Jovi	Mercury	8	(13)	
18	9	The Finer Things	Steve Winwood	Island	8		
19	-	Head To Toe	Lisa Lisa & Cult Jam	Columbia	10		
20	-	What's Going On	Cyndi Lauper	Portrait	5	(57)	

June 1987

This Mnth	Prev Mnth	Title	Artist	Label	Wks 20	(UK Pos)	
1	19	Head To Toe	Lisa Lisa & Cult Jam	Columbia	10		
2	9	Always	Atlantic Starr	Warner	10	(3)	
3	-	In Too Deep	Genesis	Atlantic	8	(19)	
4	-	I Wanna Dance With Somebody (Who Loves Me)	Whitney Houston	Arista	11	(1)	G
5	8	You Keep Me Hangin' On	Kim Wilde	MCA	8	(2)	F L
6	-	Diamonds	Herb Alpert	A&M	7	(27)	L
7	17	Wanted Dead Or Alive	Bon Jovi	Mercury	8	(13)	
8	-	Alone	Heart	Capitol	11	(3)	
9	-	Just To See Her	Smokey Robinson	Tamla	7	(52)	
10	-	Songbird	Kenny G	Arista	8	(22)	F
11	4	Lady In Red	Chris De Burgh	A&M	9	(1)	F L
12	-	Meet Me Half Way	Kenny Loggins	Columbia	6		
13	1	With Or Without You	U2	Island	10	(4)	F
14	-	Shakedown	Bob Seger & The Silver Bullet Band	MCA	10		L
15	-	Lessons In Love	Level 42	Polydor	4	(3)	L
16	-	Don't Disturb The Groove	System	Atlantic	7		F L
17	7	Big Love	Fleetwood Mac	Warner	7	(9)	
18	15	Nothing's Gonna Change My Love For You	Glenn Medeiros	Amherst	6	(1)	F
19	10	Right On Track	Breakfast Club	MCA	7	(54)	F L
20	-	Point Of No Return	Expose	Arista	7		

◆ U2's transatlantic No. 1 album **The Joshua Tree,** which had sold 250,000 in its first week in the UK, shipped over two million in America in just six weeks.

◆ Madonna scored her 11th consecutive Top 5 hit with 'La Isla Bonita' – a feat bettered only by Elvis and The Beatles. In Britain, it was her 14th Top 10 entry and her fourth No. 1 – both records for a female artist.

◆ **Whitney,** became the first album to enter both the US and UK charts at No. 1. For the record, Miss Houston's Grammy winning 'I Wanna Dance With Somebody' was produced by Narada Michael Walden, who was also responsible for another transatlantic topper, 'Nothing's Gonna Stop Us Now' by Starship.

UK 1987
JULY-SEPT

◆ The video for Peter Gabriel's 'Sledgehammer' won a record 10 MTV awards.

◆ Cliff Richard scored his 50th British Top 10 hit, 'My Pretty One', and Bananarama collected their 13th chart entry – a record for a British female group.

▲ Rick Astley had Britain's biggest selling single of 1987, 'Never Gonna Give You Up'.

◆ Debuting in the US Top 20 were future chart regulars Debbie Gibson and Richard Marx, while the UK list welcomed relative veterans Linda Ronstadt (with her 12th US Top 20 entry, 'Somewhere Out There') and Def Leppard.

July 1987

This Mnth	Prev Mnth	Title	Artist	Label	Wks 20	(US Pos)	
1	16	It's A Sin	Pet Shop Boys	Parlophone	8	(9)	
2	10	Under The Boardwalk	Bruce Willis	Motown	10	(59)	L
3	-	Wishing Well	Terence Trent D'Arby	CBS	6	(1)	
4	5	Star Trekkin'	Firm	Bark	7		L
5	-	Always	Atlantic Starr	Warner	8	(1)	L
6	-	The Living Daylights	A-Ha	Warner	5		
7	1	I Wanna Dance With Somebody (Who Loves Me)	Whitney Houston	Arista	10	(1)	
8	-	My Pretty One	Cliff Richard	EMI	4		
9	-	Who's That Girl	Madonna	Sire	7	(1)	
10	-	Sweetest Smile	Black	A&M	4		F
11	-	Alone	Heart	Capitol	7	(1)	F
12	-	F.L.M.	Mel & Kim	Supreme	5		
13	14	You're The Voice	John Farnham	Wheatley	6	(82)	F L
14	-	Misfit	Curiosity Killed The Cat	Mercury	4	(42)	
15	19	Is This Love	Whitesnake	EMI	5	(2)	
16	-	Higher And Higher	Jackie Wilson	SMP	2		L
17	-	Jive Talkin'	Boogie Box High	Hardback	5		F L
18	-	Let's Dance	Chris Rea	Magnet	4	(81)	F
19	17	When Smokey Sings	ABC	Neutron	4	(5)	L
20	-	La Bamba	Los Lobos	Slash	6	(1)	F

August 1987

This Mnth	Prev Mnth	Title	Artist	Label	Wks 20	(US Pos)	
1	20	La Bamba	Los Lobos	Slash	6	(1)	F
2	-	I Just Can't Stop Loving You	Michael Jackso	Epic	6	(1)	
3	-	Call Me	Spagna	CBS	6		F L
4	-	True Faith	New Order	Factory	6		
5	9	Who's That Girl	Madonna	Sire	7	(1)	
6	11	Alone	Heart	Capitol	7	(1)	F
7	5	Always	Atlantic Starr	Warner	8	(1)	L
8	-	Labour Of Love	Hue & Cry	Circa	6		F
9	-	Never Gonna Give You Up	Rick Astley	RCA	10	(1)	F
10	-	Toy Boy	Sinitta	Fanfare	8		
11	-	Animal	Def Leppard	Bludgeon Riffola	5	(19)	F
12	-	Sweet Little Mystery	Wet Wet Wet	Precious	6		
13	-	Somewhere Out There	Linda Ronstadt/James Ingram	MCA	4	(2)	F
14	-	What Have I Done To Deserve This	Pet Shop Boys & Dusty Springfield	Parlophone	6	(2)	
15	17	Jive Talkin'	Boogie Box High	Hardback	5		F L
16	1	It's A Sin	Pet Shop Boys	Parlophone	8	(9)	
17	-	Just Don't Want To Be Lonely	Freddie McGregor	Germain	4		F L
18	-	She's On It	Beastie Boys	Def Jam	4		L
19	2	Under The Boardwalk	Bruce Willis	Motown	10	(59)	L
20	-	Funky Town	Pseudo Echo	RCA	4	(6)	F L

September 1987

This Mnth	Prev Mnth	Title	Artist	Label	Wks 20	(US Pos)	
1	9	Never Gonna Give You Up	Rick Astley	RCA	10	(1)	F
2	-	Wipeout	Fat Boys & Beach Boys	Urban	7	(12)	F
3	-	Heart And Soul	T'Pau	Siren	6	(4)	F
4	14	What Have I Done To Deserve This	Pet Shop Boys & Dusty Springfield	Parlophone	6	(2)	
5	-	Some People	Cliff Richard	EMI	7		
6	10	Toy Boy	Sinitta	Fanfare	8		
7	-	Pump Up The Volume	M/A/R/R/S	4AD	8	(13)	F L
8	-	Where The Streets Have No Name	U2	Island	3	(13)	
9	-	Wonderful Life	Black	A&M	5		L
10	12	Sweet Little Mystery	Wet Wet Wet	Precious	6		
11	-	Casanova	Levert	Atlantic	5	(5)	F L
12	-	Causing A Commotion	Madonna	Sire	5	(2)	
13	-	Bridge To Your Heart	Wax	RCA	5		F L
14	3	Call Me	Spagna	CBS	6		F L
15	-	House Nation	House Master Boyz & The Rude Boy Of House	Magnetic Dance	4		F L
16	-	It's Over	Level 42	Polydor	4		
17	2	I Just Can't Stop Loving You	Michael Jackson	Epic	6	(1)	
18	-	I Don't Want To Be A Hero	Johnny Hates Jazz	Virgin	5	(31)	
19	-	U Got The Look	Prince	Paisley Park	4	(2)	
20	-	Bad	Michael Jackson	Epic	5	(1)	

294

US 1987
JULY-SEPT

July 1987

This Mnth	Prev Mnth	Title	Artist	Label	Wks 20	(UK Pos)	
1	8	Alone	Heart	Capitol	11	(3)	
2	4	I Wanna Dance With Somebody (...)	Whitney Houston	Arista	11	(1)	G
3	14	Shakedown	Bob Seger & Silver Bullet Band	MCA	10		L
4	16	Don't Disturb The Groove	System	Atlantic	7		F L
5	20	Point Of No Return	Expose	Arista	7		
6	-	Funky Town	Pseudo Echo	RCA	6	(8)	F L
7	-	Something So Strong	Crowded House	Capitol	7		L
8	-	I Still Haven't Found What I'm Looking For	U2	Island	9	(6)	
9	10	Songbird	Kenny G	Arista	8	(22)	F
10	-	I Want Your Sex	George Michael	Columbia	9	(3)	G
11	-	Rhythm Is Gonna Get You	Gloria Estefan & The Miami Sound Machine	Epic	7	(16)	
12	1	Head To Toe	Lisa Lisa & Cult Jam	Columbia	10		
13	-	Heart And Soul	T'Pau	Virgin	9	(4)	F L
14	-	Girls Girls Girls	Motley Crue	Elektra	6	(26)	
15	3	In Too Deep	Genesis	Atlantic	8	(19)	
16	9	Just To See Her	Smokey Robinson	Tamla	7	(52)	
17	-	Kiss Him Goodbye	Nylons	Open Air	5		F L
18	-	Every Little Kiss	Bruce Hornsby & The Range	RCA	4		
19	-	Cross My Broken Heart	Jets	MCA	6		
20	2	Always	Atlantic Starr	Warner	10	(3)	

August 1987

This Mnth	Prev Mnth	Title	Artist	Label	Wks 20	(UK Pos)	
1	8	I Still Haven't Found What I'm...	U2	Island	9	(6)	
2	-	Who's That Girl	Madonna	Sire	8	(1)	
3	-	Luka	Suzanne Vega	A&M	7	(23)	F L
4	10	I Want Your Sex	George Michael	Columbia	9	(3)	G
5	-	La Bamba	Los Lobos	Slash	9	(1)	F L
6	-	Don't Mean Nothing	Richard Marx	Manhattan	7		F
7	13	Heart And Soul	T'Pau	Virgin	9	(4)	F L
8	-	Only In My Dreams	Debbie Gibson	Atlantic	8	(11)	F
9	-	Rock Steady	Whispers	Solar	7	(38)	L
10	3	Shakedown	Bob Seger & Silver Bullet Band	MCA	10		L
11	19	Cross My Broken Heart	Jets	MCA	6		
12	11	Rhythm Is Gonna Get You	Gloria Estefan/Miami Sound...	Epic	7	(16)	
13	1	Alone	Heart	Capitol	11	(3)	
14	-	I Just Can't Stop Loving You	Michael Jackson	Epic	8	(1)	G
15	-	It's Not Over ('Til It's Over)	Starship	Grunt	5		
16	-	Wot's It To Ya	Robbie Nevil	Manhattan	4	(43)	L
17	-	Love Power	Dionne Warwick & Jeffrey Osborne	Arista	5	(63)	L
18	-	Can't We Try	Dan Hill (with Vonda Shepard)	Columbia	7		L
19	-	Back In The High Life Again	Steve Winwood	Island	3	(53)	
20	-	Didn't We Almost Have It All	Whitney Houston	Arista	9	(14)	

September 1987

This Mnth	Prev Mnth	Title	Artist	Label	Wks 20	(UK Pos)	
1	14	I Just Can't Stop Loving You	Michael Jackson	Epic	8	(1)	G
2	20	Didn't We Almost Have It All	Whitney Houston	Arista	9	(14)	
3	5	La Bamba	Los Lobos	Slash	9	(1)	F L
4	-	Here I Go Again	Whitesnake	Geffen	11	(9)	F
5	-	When Smokey Sings	ABC	Mercury	8	(11)	L
6	-	Doing It All For My Baby	Huey Lewis & The News	Chrysalis	6		
7	18	Can't We Try	Dan Hill (with Vonda Shepard)	Columbia	7		L
8	-	I Heard A Rumour	Bananarama	London	7	(14)	L
9	8	Only In My Dreams	Debbie Gibson	Atlantic	8	(11)	F
10	-	Touch Of Grey	Grateful Dead	Arista	6		F L
11	-	Lost In Emotion	Lisa Lisa & Cult Jam	Columbia	8	(58)	L
12	2	Who's That Girl	Madonna	Sire	8	(1)	
13	-	Wipeout	Fat Boys & Beach Boys	Tin Pan Apple	6	(2)	F
14	-	Carrie	Europe	Epic	8	(22)	L
15	6	Don't Mean Nothing	Richard Marx	Manhattan	7		F
16	-	I Need Love	L.L. Cool J	Def Jam	4	(8)	F
17	-	U Got The Look	Prince	Paisley Park	9	(11)	
18	9	Rock Steady	Whispers	Solar	7	(38)	L
19	17	Love Power	Dionne Warwick & Jeffrey Osborne	Arista	5	(63)	L
20	-	Who Will You Run To	Heart	Capitol	6	(30)	

◆ 'Whose That Girl' (Madonna), 'La Bamba' (Los Lobos) and 'I Just Can't Stop Loving You' (Michael Jackson) followed each other in the No. 1 spot in both the USA and Britain. Siedah Garrett who sang with Jackson on his 11th No. 1, also sang on Madonna's chart-topper.

◆ Michael Jackson's first album since 1982, **Bad,** shipped a record 2.25 million copies in America, and sold a record 380,000 in its first week in the UK.

◆ The reformed Doobie Brothers, James Taylor, Santana and Bonnie Raitt played at a disarmament festival in Russia, while fellow Americans Bon Jovi, Metallica and Cinderella headlined Britain's Castle Donnington festival.

UK 1987
OCT-DEC

◆ Half the songs on December's UK chart were oldies. Among them were re-issues of 'When I Fall In Love' by Nat 'King' Cole (1957) and 'My Baby Just Cares For Me' by Nina Simone (1959).

◆ 1987 was the year when "sampling" surfaced, three inch CDs were unsuccessfully launched, Japanese company Sony bought CBS Records and MTV debuted in Europe.

◆ Performers inducted in the *Rock And Roll Hall Of Fame* in 1987 were The Coasters, Eddie Cochran, Bo Diddley, Aretha Franklin, Marvin Gaye, Bill Haley, B.B. King, Clyde McPhatter, Rick Nelson, Roy Orbison, Carl Perkins, Smokey Robinson, Joe Turner, Muddy Waters and Jackie Wilson.

October 1987

This Mnth	Prev Mnth	Title	Artist	Label	Wks 20	(US Pos)	
1	-	Crockett's Theme	Jan Hammer	MCA	8		L
2	-	Full Metal Jacket (I Wanna Be Your Drill Instructor)	Abigail Mead & Nigel Goulding	Warner	6		F L
3	7	Pump Up The Volume	M/A/R/R/S	4AD	8	(13)	F L
4	-	You Win Again	Bee Gees	Warner	8	(75)	
5	-	Crazy Crazy Nights	Kiss	Vertigo	5	(65)	F
6	20	Bad	Michael Jackson	Epic	5	(1)	
7	1	Never Gonna Give You Up	Rick Astley	RCA	10	(1)	F
8	-	I Need Love	L.L. Cool J	CBS	5	(14)	F L
9	-	The Circus	Erasure	Mute	5		
10	5	Some People	Cliff Richard	EMI	7		
11	-	I Found Lovin'	Fatback Band	Master Mix	4		L
12	-	Love In The First Degree/Mr. Sleaze	Bananarama/S.A.W.	London	6	(48)	
13	12	Causing A Commotion	Madonna	Sire	5	(2)	
14	-	This Corrosion	Sisters Of Mercy	Merciful Release	3		F
15	-	Mony Mony	Billy Idol	Chrysalis	6	(1)	
16	-	Faith	George Michael	Epic	5	(1)	
17	-	Little Lies	Fleetwood Mac	Warner	5	(4)	
18	-	The Real Thing	Jellybean Feat.\ Steven Dante	Chrysalis	4	(82)	F
19	15	House Nation	House Master Boyz/Rude Boy...	Magnetic Dance	4		F L
20	-	Walk The Dinosaur	Was (Not Was)	Fontana	5	(7)	F

November 1987

This Mnth	Prev Mnth	Title	Artist	Label	Wks 20	(US Pos)	
1	-	China In Your Hand	T'Pau	Siren	11		
2	-	Got My Mind Set On You	George Harrison	Dark Horse	9	(1)	L
3	-	Whenever You Need Somebody	Rick Astley	RCA	6		
4	4	You Win Again	Bee Gees	Warner	8	(75)	
5	-	Never Can Say Goodbye	Communards	London	7	(51)	
6	16	Faith	George Michael	Epic	5	(1)	
7	12	Love In The First Degree/Mr. Sleaze	Bananarama/S.A.W.	London	6	(48)	
8	-	(I've Had) The Time Of My Life	Bill Medley & Jennifer Warnes	RCA	4	(1)	F
9	-	My Baby Just Cares For Me	Nina Simone	Charly	4		L
10	-	Barcelona	Freddie Mercury/M. Caballé	Polydor	4		
11	-	Here I Go Again	Whitesnake	EMI	5	(1)	
12	17	Little Lies	Fleetwood Mac	Warner	5	(4)	
13	-	Jack Mix IV	Mirage	Debut	4		L
14	-	So Emotional	Whitney Houston	Arista	6	(1)	
15	15	Mony Mony	Billy Idol	Chrysalis	6	(1)	
16	-	Criticize	Alexander O'Neal	Tabu	8	(70)	
17	1	Crockett's Theme	Jan Hammer	MCA	8		L
18	20	Walk The Dinosaur	Was (Not Was)	Fontana	5	(7)	F
19	-	I Don't Think That Man Should Sleep Alone	Ray Parker Jr.	Geffen	3	(68)	L
20	9	The Circus	Erasure	Mute	5		

December 1987

This Mnth	Prev Mnth	Title	Artist	Label	Wks 20	(US Pos)	
1	1	China In Your Hand	T'Pau	Siren	11		
2	-	Always On My Mind	Pet Shop Boys	Parlophone	8	(4)	
3	-	The Way You Make Me Feel	Michael Jackson	Epic	7	(1)	
4	-	When I Fall In Love/My Arms Keep Missing You	Rick Astley	RCA	6		
5	-	What Do You Want To Make Those Eyes At Me For	Shakin' Stevens	Epic	5		
6	-	Letter From America	Proclaimers	Chrysalis	6		F
7	-	Love Letters	Alison Moyet	CBS	6		L
8	2	Got My Mind Set On You	George Harrison	Dark Horse	9	(1)	L
9	16	Criticize	Alexander O'Neal	Tabu	8	(70)	
10	-	Rockin' Around The Christmas Tree	Mel & Kim (Smith & Wilde)	Supreme	5		
11	-	Fairytale Of New York	Pogues Feat. Kirsty MacColl	Pogue Mahone	6		F
12	-	Who Found Who	Jellybean Featuring Elisa Fiorillo	Chrysalis	6	(16)	
13	14	So Emotional	Whitney Houston	Arista	6	(1)	
14	5	Never Can Say Goodbye	Communards	London	7	(51)	
15	-	The Look Of Love	Madonna	Sire	5		
16	-	Once Upon A Long Ago	Paul McCartney	Parlophone	3		
17	-	When I Fall In Love	Nat 'King' Cole	Capitol	4		L
18	-	Heaven Is A Place On Earth	Belinda Carlisle	Virgin	10	(1)	F
19	-	Ev'ry Time We Say Goodbye	Simply Red	Elektra	3		
20	-	Some Guys Have All The Luck	Maxi Priest	10		4	F

October 1987

This Mnth	Prev Mnth	Title	Artist	Label	Wks 20	(UK Pos)	
1	11	Lost In Emotion	Lisa Lisa & Cult Jam	Columbia	8	(58)	L
2	17	U Got The Look	Prince	Paisley Park	9	(11)	
3	-	Bad	Michael Jackson	Epic	7	(3)	
4	-	Causing A Commotion	Madonna	Sire	8	(4)	
5	4	Here I Go Again	Whitesnake	Geffen	11	(9)	F
6	-	Casanova	Levert	Atlantic	7	(9)	F L
7	14	Carrie	Europe	Epic	8	(22)	L
8	-	Let Me Be The One	Expose	Arista	7		
9	20	Who Will You Run To	Heart	Capitol	6	(30)	
10	-	I Think We're Alone Now	Tiffany	MCA	9	(1)	F
11	8	I Heard A Rumour	Bananarama	London	7	(14)	L
12	-	Paper In Fire	John Cougar Mellencamp	Mercury	6		
13	-	Mony Mony	Billy Idol	Chrysalis	9	(7)	
14	-	Little Lies	Fleetwood Mac	Warner	8	(5)	
15	2	Didn't We Almost Have It All	Whitney Houston	Arista	9	(14)	
16	-	Breakout	Swing Out Sister	Mercury	8	(4)	F L
17	-	Jump Start	Natalie Cole	EMI Manhattan	4	(36)	
18	-	One Heartbeat	Smokey Robinson	Tamla	4		L
19	-	It's A Sin	Pet Shop Boys	EMI Manhattan	6	(1)	
20	-	Brilliant Disguise	Bruce Springsteen	Columbia	7	(20)	

November 1987

This Mnth	Prev Mnth	Title	Artist	Label	Wks 20	(UK Pos)	
1	13	Mony Mony	Billy Idol	Chrysalis	9	(7)	
2	-	(I've Had) The Time Of My Life	Bill Medley & Jennifer Warnes	RCA	9	(6)	F L
3	10	I Think We're Alone Now	Tiffany	MCA	9	(1)	F
4	-	Heaven Is A Place On Earth	Belinda Carlisle	MCA	11	(1)	
5	20	Brilliant Disguise	Bruce Springsteen	Columbia	7	(20)	
6	16	Breakout	Swing Out Sister	Mercury	8	(4)	F L
7	-	Should've Known Better	Richard Marx	EMI Manhattan	8	(50)	
8	14	Little Lies	Fleetwood Mac	Warner	8	(5)	
9	-	I've Been In Love Before	Cutting Crew	Virgin	5	(24)	L
10	4	Causing A Commotion	Madonna	Sire	8	(4)	
11	-	Faith	George Michael	Columbia	10	(2)	
12	19	It's A Sin	Pet Shop Boys	EMI Manhattan	6	(1)	
13	-	We'll Be Together	Sting	A&M	7	(41)	
14	-	The One I Love	R.E.M.	IRS	6	(16)	F
15	3	Bad	Michael Jackson	Epic	7	(3)	
16	-	I Won't Forget You	Poison	Enigma	4		
17	-	Shake Your Love	Debbie Gibson	Atlantic	10	(7)	
18	8	Let Me Be The One	Expose	Arista	7		
19	-	Where The Streets Have No Name	U2	Island	4	(4)	
20	-	Is This Love	Whitesnake	Geffen	10	(9)	L

December 1987

This Mnth	Prev Mnth	Title	Artist	Label	Wks 20	(UK Pos)	
1	11	Faith	George Michael	Columbia	10	(2)	
2	20	Is This Love	Whitesnake	Geffen	10	(9)	L
3	-	So Emotional	Whitney Houston	Arista	11	(5)	
4	17	Shake Your Love	Debbie Gibson	Atlantic	10	(7)	
5	4	Heaven Is A Place On Earth	Belinda Carlisle	MCA	11	(1)	
6	-	Got My Mind Set On You	George Harrison	Dark Horse	11	(2)	L
7	-	Don't You Want Me	Jody Watley	MCA	9	(55)	
8	-	Catch Me I'm Falling	Pretty Poison	Virgin	8		F L
9	7	Should've Known Better	Richard Marx	EMI Manhattan	8	(50)	
10	2	(I've Had) The Time Of My Life	Bill Medley & Jennifer Warnes	RCA	9	(6)	F L
11	13	We'll Be Together	Sting	A&M	7	(41)	
12	-	Valerie	Steve Winwood	Island	7	(19)	
13	-	The Way You Make Me Feel	Michael Jackson	Epic	9	(3)	
14	-	Cherry Bomb	John Cougar Mellencamp	Mercury	7		
15	-	Dude (Looks Like A Lady)	Aerosmith	Geffen	6	(20)	
16	14	The One I Love	R.E.M.	IRS	6	(16)	F
17	-	Tell It To My Heart	Taylor Dayne	Arista	9	(3)	F
18	-	Need You Tonight	INXS	Atlantic	11	(2)	
19	-	Candle In The Wind (Live)	Elton John	MCA	7	(5)	
20	1	Mony Mony	Billy Idol	Chrysalis	9	(7)	

US 1987

OCT–DEC

◆ American record and tape shipments were up 19.7% to $5.56 billion, with CD sales up 93% to 100 million.

◆ Paul Simon organized a charity show at Madison Square Garden for New York's homeless children. Among the stars appearing were Billy Joel, Bruce Springsteen, Dion and Chaka Khan.

▲ Revivals of two hits by Tommy James & The Shondells followed each other at the top: 'I Think We're Alone Now' by Tiffany and 'Mony Mony' by Billy Idol (above).

◆ The *Dirty Dancing* soundtrack topped the US album chart for 18 weeks.

UK 1988
JAN-MAR

▲ Female artists scored a record three successive No. 1s when Australian soap star Kylie Minogue followed transatlantic toppers, Belinda Carlisle (above) and Tiffany to the top spot.

♦ House and acid house music were huge in Britain. However, they did not travel well and the vast majority of UK hits in this vein failed to reach the US Hot 100.

♦ Expose became the first group to have four American Top 10 singles on their debut LP. Surprisingly, the female trio, whose next three singles also graced the Top 10, never had a major UK hit.

January 1988

This Mnth	Prev Mnth	Title	Artist	Label	Wks 20	(US Pos)	
1	18	Heaven Is A Place On Earth	Belinda Carlisle	Virgin	10	(1)	F
2	2	Always On My Mind	Pet Shop Boys	Parlophone	8	(4)	
3	-	House Arrest	Krush	Club	7		F L
4	-	Stutter Rap (No Sleep 'Til Bedtime)	Morris Minor & The Majors	10/Virgin	5		F L
5	-	Angel Eyes (Home And Away)	Wet Wet Wet	Precious	6		
6	-	I Found Someone	Cher	Geffen	4	(10)	
7	-	Sign Your Name	Terence Trent D'Arby	CBS	6	(4)	
8	-	I Think We're Alone Now	Tiffany	MCA	9	(1)	F
9	-	Come Into My Life	Joyce Sims	London	5		L
10	11	Fairytale Of New York	Pogues Feat. Kirsty MacColl	Pogue Mahone	6		F
11	-	All Day And All Of The Night	Stranglers	Epic	4		
12	3	The Way You Make Me Feel	Michael Jackson	Epic	7	(1)	
13	7	Love Letters	Alison Moyet	CBS	6		L
14	-	Rise To The Occasion	Climie Fisher	EMI	4		F
15	4	When I Fall In Love/My Arms Keep Missing You	Rick Astley	RCA	6		
16	10	Rockin' Around The Christmas Tree	Mel & Kim (Smith & Wilde)	10	5		
17	17	When I Fall In Love	Nat 'King' Cole	Capitol	4		
18	-	Heatseeker	AC/DC	Atlantic	3		
19	-	When Will I Be Famous	Bros	CBS	6	(83)	F
20	-	Rok Da House	Beatmasters Feat. Cookie Crew	Rhythm King	5		F

February 1988

This Mnth	Prev Mnth	Title	Artist	Label	Wks 20	(US Pos)	
1	8	I Think We're Alone Now	Tiffany	MCA	9	(1)	F
2	-	Tell It To My Heart	Taylor Dayne	Arista	6	(7)	F
3	-	I Should Be So Lucky	Kylie Minogue	PWL	10	(28)	F
4	19	When Will I Be Famous	Bros	CBS	6	(83)	F
5	-	Get Outta My Dreams Get Into My Car	Billy Ocean	Jive	6	(1)	L
6	-	Candle In The Wind (Live)	Elton John	Rocket	5	(6)	
7	-	Shake Your Love	Debbie Gibson	Atlantic	5	(4)	F
8	-	Say It Again	Jermaine Stewart	10	5	(27)	
9	-	The Jack That House Built	Jack 'n' Chill	Oval	5		F L
10	-	Beat Dis	Bomb The Bass	Mister-Ron	5		F
11	20	Rok Da House	Beatmasters Feat. Cookie Crew	Rhythm King	5		F
12	7	Sign Your Name	Terence Trent D'Arby	CBS	6	(4)	
13	1	Heaven Is A Place On Earth	Belinda Carlisle	Virgin	10	(1)	F
14	-	O L'Amour	Dollar	London	5		L
15	-	Valentine	T'Pau	Siren	4		
16	-	Gimme Hope Jo'anna	Eddy Grant	Ice	5		L
17	3	House Arrest	Krush	Club	7		F L
18	-	Hot In The City	Billy Idol	Chrysalis	4	(23)	L
19	-	Tower Of Strength	Mission	Mercury	4		
20	-	Suedehead	Morrissey	HMV	3		F

March 1988

This Mnth	Prev Mnth	Title	Artist	Label	Wks 20	(US Pos)	
1	3	I Should Be So Lucky	Kylie Minogue	PWL	10	(28)	F
2	-	Together Forever	Rick Astley	RCA	5	(1)	
3	-	Joe Le Taxi	Vanessa Paradis	FA Prods	6		F
4	10	Beat Dis	Bomb The Bass	Mister-Ron	5		F
5	-	Crash	Primitives	Lazy	5		F L
6	5	Get Outta My Dreams Get Into My Car	Billy Ocean	Jive	6	(1)	L
7	-	Doctorin' The House	Coldcut Featuring Yazz & The Plastic Population	Ahead Of Our Time	5		F
8	-	Don't Turn Around	Aswad	Mango	5		F
9	-	Ship Of Fools	Erasure	Mute	5		
10	16	Gimme Hope Jo'anna	Eddy Grant	Ice	5		L
11	-	I Get Weak	Belinda Carlisle	Virgin	5	(2)	
12	20	Suedehead	Morrissey	HMV	3		F
13	-	Love Is Contagious	Taja Sevelle	Paisley	3		F L
14	-	Drop The Boy	Bros	CBS	7		
15	-	Never/These Dreams	Heart	Capitol	5	(4)	
16	2	Tell It To My Heart	Taylor Dayne	Arista	6	(7)	F
17	-	That's The Way It Is	Mel & Kim	Supreme	3		L
18	-	Hazy Shade Of Winter	Bangles	Def Jam	3	(2)	
19	-	Can I Play With Madness	Iron Maiden	EMI	4		
20	-	Could've Been	Tiffany	MCA	5	(1)	

US 1988 JAN-MAR

January 1988

This Mnth	Prev Mnth	Title	Artist	Label	Wks 20	(UK Pos)	
1	6	Got My Mind Set On You	George Harrison	Dark Horse	11	(2)	L
2	13	The Way You Make Me Feel	Michael Jackson	Epic	9	(3)	
3	18	Need You Tonight	INXS	Atlantic	11	(2)	
4	3	So Emotional	Whitney Houston	Arista	11	(5)	
5	-	Could've Been	Tiffany	MCA	10	(4)	
6	-	Hazy Shade Of Winter	Bangles	Def Jam	10	(11)	
7	19	Candle In The Wind (Live)	Elton John	MCA	7	(5)	
8	17	Tell It To My Heart	Taylor Dayne	Arista	9	(3)	F
9	2	Is This Love	Whitesnake	Geffen	10	(9)	L
10	-	Seasons Change	Expose	Arista	11		
11	4	Shake Your Love	Debbie Gibson	Atlantic	10	(7)	
12	1	Faith	George Michael	Columbia	10	(2)	
13	14	Cherry Bomb	John Cougar Mellencamp	Mercury	7		
14	-	I Want To Be Your Man	Roger	Reprise	7	(61)	F L
15	7	Don't You Want Me	Jody Watley	MCA	9	(55)	
16	-	Hungry Eyes	Eric Carmen	RCA	9		
17	-	There's The Girl	Heart	Capitol	6	(34)	
18	-	I Could Never Take The Place Of Your Man	Prince	Paisley Park	5	(29)	
19	8	Catch Me I'm Falling	Pretty Poison	Virgin	8		F L
20	12	Valerie	Steve Winwood	Island	7	(19)	

February 1988

This Mnth	Prev Mnth	Title	Artist	Label	Wks 20	(UK Pos)	
1	10	Seasons Change	Expose	Arista	11		
2	5	Could've Been	Tiffany	MCA	10	(4)	
3	-	What Have I Done To Deserve This	Pet Shop Boys/Dusty Springfield	EMI Manhattan	8	(2)	
4	16	Hungry Eyes	Eric Carmen	RCA	9		
5	-	Say You Will	Foreigner	Atlantic	7	(71)	
6	14	I Want To Be Your Man	Roger	Reprise	7	(61)	F L
7	-	She's Like The Wind	Patrick Swayze (With Wendy Fraser)	RCA	8	(17)	F L
8	-	Father Figure	George Michael	Columbia	9	(11)	
9	-	Don't Shed A Tear	Paul Carrack	Chrysalis	6	(60)	F L
10	-	Never Gonna Give You Up	Rick Astley	RCA	10	(1)	F
11	3	Need You Tonight	INXS	Atlantic	11	(2)	
12	6	Hazy Shade Of Winter	Bangles	Def Jam	10	(11)	
13	-	Can't Stay Away From You	Gloria Estefan & The Miami Sound Machine	Epic	5	(7)	
14	-	I Get Weak	Belinda Carlisle	MCA	8	(10)	
15	-	Pump Up The Volume	M/A/R/R/S	4th & Broadway	5	(1)	F G L
16	-	Tunnel Of Love	Bruce Springsteen	Columbia	4	(45)	
17	-	Everywhere	Fleetwood Mac	Warner	4	(4)	L
18	-	I Live For Your Love	Natalie Cole	EMI Manhattan	4	(23)	
19	-	I Found Someone	Cher	Geffen	6	(5)	
20	-	Just Like Paradise	David Lee Roth	Warner	6	(27)	L

March 1988

This Mnth	Prev Mnth	Title	Artist	Label	Wks 20	(UK Pos)	
1	10	Never Gonna Give You Up	Rick Astley	RCA	10	(1)	F
2	8	Father Figure	George Michael	Columbia	9	(11)	
3	14	I Get Weak	Belinda Carlisle	MCA	8	(10)	
4	-	Endless Summer Nights	Richard Marx	EMI Manhattan	9	(50)	
5	-	Man In The Mirror	Michael Jackson	Epic	10	(21)	
6	7	She's Like The Wind	Patrick Swayz/Wendy Fraser	RCA	8	(17)	F L
7	-	Out Of The Blue	Debbie Gibson	Atlantic	9	(19)	
8	20	Just Like Paradise	David Lee Roth	Warner	6	(27)	L
9	-	I Want Her	Keith Sweat	Vintertainment	8	(26)	F
10	-	Get Outta My Dreams Get Into My Car	Billy Ocean	Jive	10	(3)	
11	-	Hysteria	Def Leppard	Mercury	5	(26)	
12	13	Can't Stay Away From You	Gloria Estefan/Miami Sound...	Epic	5	(7)	
13	-	Rocket 2 U	Jets	MCA	7	(69)	
14	19	I Found Someone	Cher	Geffen	6	(5)	
15	-	(Sittin' On) The Dock Of The Bay	Michael Bolton	Columbia	5		
16	3	What Have I Done To Deserve This	Pet Shop Boys/Dusty Springfield	EMI Manhattan	8	(2)	
17	-	Girlfriend	Pebbles	MCA	9	(8)	F
18	-	Devil Inside	INXS	Atlantic	8	(47)	
19	-	Be Still My Beating Heart	Sting	A&M	3		
20	-	Love Overboard	Gladys Knight & The Pips	MCA	3	(42)	L

◆ Whitney Houston became the first artist to sell five million of her two debut albums, and her chart topping 'So Emotional' gave producer Narada Michael Walden his fourth No. 1 in nine months.

◆ Gripes at the Grammies included the fact that there were no awards for rap, hard rock or heavy metal and that the Best Female Rock award had been dropped. The year's winners included U2, Sting, Paul Simon and Jody Watley.

◆ George Michael's first solo album, **Faith,** headed the US chart for 12 weeks (a record for a British male singer) and 'Father Figure' gave him his sixth No. 1 single.

◆ Andy Gibb died aged 30. He was the only singer to place his first three singles in the top slot in the USA.

UK 1988

APR–JUNE

◆ Nelson Mandela's 70th birthday show was the most star-studded event since 'Live Aid'. Appearing were such notables as Bryan Adams, The Bee Gees, Natalie Cole, Phil Collins, Dire Straits, Eurythmics, Al Green, Whitney Houston, George Michael, Salt-N-Pepa, Sting and Stevie Wonder. The suprise hit of the show was Grammy winning American newcomer Tracy Chapman.

◆ Bros, whose UK tour incited mass hysteria among Britain's teeny-boppers, topped the chart with a re-issue of their first single 'I Owe You Nothing'.

◆ Rick Astley, The Bee Gees, Phil Collins, The Four Tops, Mark Knopfler, T'Pau and Wet Wet Wet appeared at the Prince's Trust Rock Gala at Wembley. Also scoring at that venue this quarter were Def Leppard, Fleetwood Mac, INXS, Rush, Simply Red and Bruce Springsteen.

April 1988

This Mnth	Prev Mnth	Title	Artist	Label	Wks 20	(US Pos)	
1	-	Heart	Pet Shop Boys	Parlophone	7		
2	-	Love Changes (Everything)	Climie Fisher	EMI	6	(23)	L
3	14	Drop The Boy	Bros	CBS	7		
4	20	Could've Been	Tiffany	MCA	5	(1)	
5	-	Everywhere	Fleetwood Mac	Warner	5	(14)	L
6	8	Don't Turn Around	Aswad	Mango	5		F
7	-	Cross My Broken Heart	Sinitta	Fanfare	5		
8	-	Who's Leaving Who	Hazell Dean	EMI	7		
9	-	Pink Cadillac	Natalie Cole	Manhattan	6	(5)	F
10	-	I'm Not Scared	Eighth Wonder	CBS	6		F
11	-	Theme From S'Express	S'Express	Rhythm King	7	(91)	F
12	19	Can I Play With Madness	Iron Maiden	EMI	4		
13	-	I Want You Back	Bananarama	London	6		
14	-	Stay On These Roads	A-Ha	Warner	4		
15	-	Prove Your Love	Taylor Dayne	Arista	4	(7)	L
16	-	Girlfriend	Pebbles	MCA	3	(5)	F L
17	-	Mary's Prayer	Danny Wilson	Virgin	6	(23)	F L
18	1	I Should Be So Lucky	Kylie Minogue	PWL	10	(28)	F
19	-	I Want You Back '88	Michael Jackson With The Jackson Five	Epic	5	(1)	
20	-	Only In My Dreams	Debbie Gibson	Atlantic	3	(4)	

May 1988

This Mnth	Prev Mnth	Title	Artist	Label	Wks 20	(US Pos)	
1	-	Perfect	Fairground Attraction	RCA	8	(80)	F
2	11	Theme From S'express	S'express	Rhythm King	7	(91)	F
3	-	Blue Monday 1988	New Order	Factory	6	(68)	
4	-	With A Little Help From My Friends/ She's Leaving Home	Wet Wet Wet/ Billy Bragg & Cara Tivey	Childline	7		
5	-	Loadsamoney (Doin' Up The House)	Harry Enfield	Mercury	4		F L
6	17	Mary's Prayer	Danny Wilson	Virgin	6	(23)	F L
7	-	Anfield Rap (Red Machine In Full Effect)	Liverpool F.C.	Virgin	4		L
8	13	I Want You Back	Bananarama	London	6		
9	-	Got To Be Certain	Kylie Minogue	PWL	8		
10	8	Who's Leaving Who	Hazell Dean	EMI	7		
11	9	Pink Cadillac	Natalie Cole	Manhattan	6	(5)	F
12	-	Divine Emotions	Narada	Reprise	4		L
13	19	I Want You Back '88	Michael Jackson/Jackson Five	Epic	5	(1)	
14	-	Alphabet Street	Prince	Paisley Park	3	(8)	
15	-	Circle In The Sand	Belinda Carlisle	Virgin	5	(7)	
16	-	The King Of Rock 'n' Roll	Prefab Sprout	Kitchenware	4		F L
17	1	Heart	Pet Shop Boys	Parlophone	7		
18	-	Somewhere In My Heart	Aztec Camera	WEA	6		
19	-	Let's All Chant	Mick And Pat	PWL	4		F L
20	-	Pump Up The Bitter	Star Turn On 45 Pints	Pacific	2		F L

June 1988

This Mnth	Prev Mnth	Title	Artist	Label	Wks 20	(US Pos)	
1	4	With A Little Help From My Friends/ She's Leaving Home	Wet Wet Wet/ Billy Bragg & Cara Tivey	Childline	7		
2	9	Got To Be Certain	Kylie Minogue	PWL	8		
3	-	Doctorin' The Tardis	Timelords	KLF Comms.	5	(66)	F L
4	18	Somewhere In My Heart	Aztec Camera	WEA	6		
5	-	Voyage Voyage	Desireless	CBS	6		F L
6	15	Circle In The Sand	Belinda Carlisle	Virgin	5	(7)	
7	-	I Owe You Nothing	Bros	CBS	7		
8	-	My One Temptation	Mica Paris	4th & Broadway	5	(97)	F
9	-	Wild World	Maxi Priest	10	6	(25)	
10	-	Boys (Summertime Love)	Sabrina	CBS	6		F L
11	1	Perfect	Fairground Attraction	RCA	8	(80)	F
12	-	Check This Out	L.A. Mix	Breakout	4		F L
13	-	I Saw Him Standing There	Tiffany	MCA	3	(7)	
14	-	Everyday Is Like Sunday	Morrissey	HMV	3		
15	16	The King Of Rock 'n' Roll	Prefab Sprout	Kitchenware	4		F L
16	-	Chains Of Love	Erasure	Mute	4	(12)	
17	-	Tribute (Right On)	Pasadenas	CBS	7	(52)	F
18	-	Give A Little Love	Aswad	Mango	3		L
19	-	The Twist (Yo, Twist)	Fat Boys/Chubby Checker	Urban	7	(16)	L
20	-	Love Will Save The Day	Whitney Houston	Arista	2	(9)	

US 1988 APR-JUNE

April 1988

This Mnth	Prev Mnth	Title	Artist	Label	Wks 20	(UK Pos)	
1	10	Get Outta My Dreams Get Into My Car	Billy Ocean	Jive	10	(3)	
2	18	Devil Inside	INXS	Atlantic	8	(47)	
3	-	Where Do Broken Hearts Go	Whitney Houston	Arista	10	(14)	
4	-	Wishing Well	Terence Trent D'Arby	Columbia	10	(4)	F
5	5	Man In The Mirror	Michael Jackson	Epic	10	(21)	
6	17	Girlfriend	Pebbles	MCA	9	(8)	F
7	-	Angel	Aerosmith	Geffen	9	(69)	
8	-	I Saw Him Standing There	Tiffany	MCA	6	(8)	
9	13	Rocket 2 U	Jets	MCA	7	(69)	
10	7	Out Of The Blue	Debbie Gibson	Atlantic	9	(19)	
11	-	Pink Cadillac	Natalie Cole	EMI Manhattan	7	(5)	
12	4	Endless Summer Nights	Richard Marx	EMI Manhattan	9	(50)	
13	-	Prove Your Love	Taylor Dayne	Arista	7	(8)	
14	-	Anything For You	Gloria Estefan & The Miami Sound Machine	Epic	10	(10)	
15	-	Some Kind Of Lover	Jody Watley	MCA	6		
16	9	I Want Her	Keith Sweat	Vintertainment	8	(26)	F
17	-	One Step Up	Bruce Springsteen	Columbia	5		
18	-	Electric Blue	Icehouse	Chrysalis	7	(53)	L
19	15	(Sittin' On) The Dock Of The Bay	Michael Bolton	Columbia	5		
20	1	Never Gonna Give You Up	Rick Astley	RCA	10	(1)	F

May 1988

This Mnth	Prev Mnth	Title	Artist	Label	Wks 20	(UK Pos)	
1	14	Anything For You	Gloria Estefan & The Miami Sound Machine	Epic	10	(10)	
2	-	Shattered Dreams	Johnny Hates Jazz	Virgin	9	(5)	F L
3	-	One More Try	George Michael	Columbia	9	(8)	
4	-	Always On My Mind	Pet Shop Boys	EMI Manhattan	7	(1)	
5	-	Naughty Girls (Need Love Too)	Samantha Fox	Jive	9	(31)	
6	-	I Don't Want To Live Without You	Foreigner	Atlantic	7		L
7	4	Wishing Well	Terence Trent D'Arby	Columbia	10	(4)	F
8	18	Electric Blue	Icehouse	Chrysalis	7	(53)	L
9	-	Wait	White Lion	Atlantic	6		F
10	11	Pink Cadillac	Natalie Cole	EMI Manhattan	7	(5)	
11	7	Angel	Aerosmith	Geffen	9	(69)	
12	-	Two Occasions	Deele	Solar	5		F L
13	-	Everything Your Heart Desires	Daryl Hall & John Oates	Arista	7		
14	-	Piano In The Dark	Brenda Russell & Joe Esposito	A&M	6	(23)	F L
15	3	Where Do Broken Hearts Go	Whitney Houston	Arista	10	(14)	
16	-	Together Forever	Rick Astley	RCA	9	(2)	
17	13	Prove Your Love	Taylor Dayne	Arista	7	(8)	
18	-	Dreaming	Orchestral Manoeuvres In The Dark	A&M	3	(50)	L
19	-	Make It Real	Jets	MCA	9		L
20	-	Circle In The Sand	Belinda Carlisle	MCA	6	(4)	

June 1988

This Mnth	Prev Mnth	Title	Artist	Label	Wks 20	(UK Pos)	
1	3	One More Try	George Michael	Columbia	9	(8)	
2	16	Together Forever	Rick Astley	RCA	9	(2)	
3	-	Foolish Beat	Debbie Gibson	Atlantic	8	(9)	
4	19	Make It Real	Jets	MCA	9		L
5	-	Dirty Diana	Michael Jackson	Epic	8	(4)	
6	13	Everything Your Heart Desires	Daryl Hall & John Oates	Arista	7		
7	-	The Valley Road	Bruce Hornsby & The Range	RCA	8	(44)	
8	20	Circle In The Sand	Belinda Carlisle	MCA	6	(4)	
9	2	Shattered Dreams	Johnny Hates Jazz	Virgin	9	(5)	F L
10	-	Alphabet Street	Prince	Paisley Park	6	(9)	
11	-	The Flame	Cheap Trick	Epic	9		
12	5	Naughty Girls (Need Love Too)	Samantha Fox	Jive	9	(31)	
13	14	Piano In The Dark	Brenda Russell & Joe Esposito	A&M	6	(23)	F L
14	-	Kiss Me Deadly	Lita Ford	RCA	6	(75)	F
15	-	Mercedes Boy	Pebbles	MCA	8	(42)	
16	-	I Still Believe	Brenda K. Starr	MCA	7		F L
17	-	Nothin' But A Good Time	Poison	Enigma	6	(48)	
18	-	We All Sleep Alone	Cher	Geffen	4	(47)	
19	-	Pour Some Sugar On Me	Def Leppard	Mercury	9	(18)	
20	6	I Don't Want To Live Without You	Foreigner	Atlantic	7		L

▲ Whitney Houston became the first artist in history to score seven successive No. 1 singles, and with 'Foolish Beat', 17-year-old Debbie Gibson (above) became the first teenager to write, produce and sing on a US No. 1.

◆ Velvet voiced early 1960s hitmaker Brook Benton died, as did Dave Prater of Sam & Dave and fellow soul singer Carolyn Franklin.

◆ The American *Monsters Of Rock* tour starring Van Halen, Metallica, The Scorpions and Dokken was expected to attract 2 million fans. In actuality, some of the stadiums where the heavy metal acts played were less than half full.

UK 1988
JULY-SEPT

◆ Two fans died at the *Monsters Of Rock* festival at Castle Donnington. Headlining were Iron Maiden, Kiss, Guns N' Roses, Megadeth and David Lee Roth. Britain's biggest crowd for years, 125,000, watched Michael Jackson in Liverpool. Jackson, who had six albums charting, also attracted 500,000 to his seven Wembley dates.

◆ The Hollies' 19-year-old 'He Ain't Heavy, He's My Brother' hit the top. Other oldies returning included 'Lovely Day' by Bill Withers, 'Easy' by The Commodores and 'Reach Out I'll Be There' by The Four Tops. In America the 1962 hit 'Do You Love Me' by The Contours re-charted.

◆ Tracy Chapman became the first female singer to top the transatlantic LP charts with a debut album, and Kylie Minogue became the youngest to hit the top. Minogue's LP sold two million in the UK – a record for a female artist.

July 1988

This Mnth	Prev Mnth	Title	Artist	Label	Wks 20	(US Pos)	
1	-	Nothing's Gonna Change My Love For You	Glenn Medeiros	London	8	(12)	F
2	-	Push It/Tramp	Salt 'n' Pepa	Champion/ffrr	8	(19)	F
3	19	The Twist (Yo, Twist)	Fat Boys/Chubby Checker	Urban	7	(16)	L
4	7	I Owe You Nothing	Bros	CBS	7		
5	-	Fast Car	Tracy Chapman	Elektra	6	(6)	F L
6	-	Breakfast In Bed	UB40 Featuring Chrissie Hynde	Dep International	6		
7	10	Boys (Summertime Love)	Sabrina	CBS	6		F L
8	-	I Don't Want To Talk About It	Everything But The Girl	Blanco Y Negro	6		F
9	-	In The Air Tonight	Phil Collins	Virgin	5		
10	-	Roses Are Red	Mac Band Featuring The McCampbell Brothers	MCA	7		F L
11	17	Tribute (Right On)	Pasadenas	CBS	7	(52)	F
12	-	Dirty Diana	Michael Jackson	Epic	5	(1)	
13	-	I Want Your Love	Transvision Vamp	MCA	6		F
14	-	Don't Blame It On That Girl/ Wap Bam Boogie	Matt Bianco	WEA	6		L
15	9	Wild World	Maxi Priest	10	6	(25)	
16	-	Foolish Beat	Debbie Gibson	Atlantic	5	(1)	
17	3	Doctorin' The Tardis	Timelords	KLF	5	(66)	F L
18	-	You Came	Kim Wilde	MCA	7	(41)	
19	-	Love Bites	Def Leppard	Bludgeon Riffola	4	(1)	
20	-	Tougher Than The Rest	Bruce Springsteen	CBS	3		

August 1988

This Mnth	Prev Mnth	Title	Artist	Label	Wks 20	(US Pos)	
1	-	The Only Way Is Up	Yazz & The Plastic Population	Big Life	9	(96)	
2	-	The Loco-Motion	Kylie Minogue	PWL	7	(3)	
3	18	You Came	Kim Wilde	MCA	7	(41)	
4	-	I Need You	B.V.S.M.P.	Debut	6		F L
5	-	Superfly Guy	S'Express	Rhythm King	6		
6	-	Find My Love	Fairground Attraction	RCA	6		L
7	-	The Evil That Men Do	Iron Maiden	EMI	3		
8	1	Nothing's Gonna Change My Love...	Glenn Medeiros	London	8	(12)	F
9	-	Reach Out I'll Be There	Four Tops	Motown	5		
10	-	Hands To Heaven	Breathe	Siren	6	(2)	F L
11	2	Push It/Tramp	Salt 'n' Pepa	Champion/ffrr	8	(19)	F
12	-	The Harder I Try	Brother Beyond	Parlophone	6		F
13	13	I Want Your Love	Transvision Vamp	MCA	6		F
14	-	Martha's Harbour	All About Eve	Mercury	3		F L
15	8	I Don't Want To Talk About It	Everything But The Girl	Blanco Y Negro	6		F
16	-	Hustle! (To The Music...)	Funky Worm	Fon	4		F L
17	10	Roses Are Red	Mac Band/McCampbell Brothers	MCA	7		F L
18	-	My Love	Julio Iglesias (featuring Stevie Wonder)	CBS	5	(80)	L
19	-	Good Tradition	Tanita Tikaram	WEA	4		F L
20	12	Dirty Diana	Michael Jackson	Epic	5	(1)	

September 1988

This Mnth	Prev Mnth	Title	Artist	Label	Wks 20	(US Pos)	
1	-	Groovy Kind Of Love	Phil Collins	Virgin	10	(1)	
2	-	Teardrops	Womack & Womack	4th & Broadway	11		
3	12	The Harder I Try	Brother Beyond	Parlophone	6		F
4	1	The Only Way Is Up	Yazz & The Plastic Population	Big Life	9	(96)	
5	-	He Ain't Heavy, He's My Brother	Hollies	EMI	7		L
6	-	Megablast/Don't Make Me Wait	Bomb The Bass	Mister-Ron	5		
7	-	The Race	Yello	Mercury	6		F L
8	18	My Love	Julio Iglesias/Stevie Wonder	CBS	5	(80)	L
9	2	The Loco-Motion	Kylie Minogue	PWL	7	(3)	
10	10	Hands To Heaven	Breathe	Siren	6	(2)	F L
11	-	Lovely Day	Bill Withers	CBS	5		L
12	-	I Quit	Bros	CBS	3		
13	-	Anything For You	Gloria Estefan/Miami Sound...	Epic	6	(1)	
14	-	Rush Hour	Jane Wiedlin	Manhattan	4	(9)	F L
15	-	Nothing Can Divide Us	Jason Donovan	PWL	7		F
16	-	Touchy!	A-Ha	Warner	3		
17	4	I Need You	B.V.S.M.P.	Debut	6		F L
18	-	I'm Gonna Be	Proclaimers	Chrysalis	5		
19	-	Big Fun	Inner City	10	7		F
20	6	Find My Love	Fairground Attraction	RCA	6		L

July 1988

This Mnth	Prev Mnth	Title	Artist	Label	Wks 20	(UK Pos)	
1	19	Pour Some Sugar On Me	Def Leppard	Mercury	9	(18)	
2	11	The Flame	Cheap Trick	Epic	9		
3	-	New Sensation	INXS	Atlantic	7	(25)	
4	-	Hold On To The Nights	Richard Marx	EMI Manhattan	9	(60)	
5	15	Mercedes Boy	Pebbles	MCA	8	(42)	
6	-	Roll With It	Steve Winwood	Virgin	9	(53)	
7	-	Hands To Heaven	Breathe	A&M	10	(4)	F
8	-	Make Me Lose Control	Eric Carmen	Arista	8		L
9	-	Nite And Day	Al B. Sure!	Warner	7	(44)	F L
10	5	Dirty Diana	Michael Jackson	Epic	8	(4)	
11	3	Foolish Beat	Debbie Gibson	Atlantic	8	(9)	
12	-	Rush Hour	Jane Wiedlin	EMI Manhattan	6	(12)	F L
13	17	Nothin' But A Good Time	Poison	Enigma	6	(48)	
14	-	Sign Your Name	Terence Trent D'Arby	Columbia	8	(2)	L
15	7	The Valley Road	Bruce Hornsby & The Range	RCA	8	(44)	
16	4	Make It Real	Jets	MCA	9		L
17	-	1-2-3	Gloria Estefan & The Miami Sound Machine	Epic	8	(9)	
18	-	Lost In You	Rod Stewart	Warner	5	(21)	
19	-	Parents Just Don't Understand	D.J. Jazzy Jeff & Fresh Prince	Jive	5		F
20	16	I Still Believe	Brenda K. Starr	MCA	7		F L

August 1988

This Mnth	Prev Mnth	Title	Artist	Label	Wks 20	(UK Pos)	
1	6	Roll With It	Steve Winwood	Virgin	9	(53)	
2	-	I Don't Wanna Go On With You Like That	Elton John	MCA	8	(30)	
3	-	Monkey	George Michael	Columbia	8	(13)	
4	7	Hands To Heaven	Breathe	A&M	10	(4)	F
5	8	Make Me Lose Control	Eric Carmen	Arista	8		L
6	-	I Don't Wanna Live Without Your Love	Chicago	Reprise	8		
7	17	1-2-3	Gloria Estefan & The Miami Sound Machine	Epic	8	(9)	
8	14	Sign Your Name	Terence Trent D'Arby	Columbia	8	(2)	L
9	-	Fast Car	Tracy Chapman	Elektra	8	(5)	F L
10	-	Sweet Child O' Mine	Guns N' Roses	Geffen	10	(6)	F
11	-	Love Will Save The Day	Whitney Houston	Arista	5	(10)	
12	4	Hold On To The Nights	Richard Marx	EMI Manhattan	9	(60)	
13	-	Simply Irresistible	Robert Palmer	EMI Manhattan	9	(44)	
14	-	Just Got Paid	Johnny Kemp	Columbia	5	(68)	F L
15	-	Perfect World	Huey Lewis & The News	Chrysalis	7	(48)	
16	-	Do You Love Me	Contours	Motown	4		L
17	1	Pour Some Sugar On Me	Def Leppard	Mercury	9	(18)	
18	-	When It's Love	Van Halen	Warner	6	(28)	
19	-	The Twist (Yo, Twist)	Fat Boys With Chubby Checker	Tin Pan Apple	3	(2)	L
20	19	Parents Just Don't Understand	D.J. Jazzy Jeff & Fresh Prince	Jive	5		F

September 1988

This Mnth	Prev Mnth	Title	Artist	Label	Wks 20	(UK Pos)	
1	10	Sweet Child O' Mine	Guns N' Roses	Geffen	10	(6)	F
2	13	Simply Irresistible	Robert Palmer	EMI Manhattan	9	(44)	
3	15	Perfect World	Huey Lewis & The News	Chrysalis	7	(48)	
4	-	I'll Always Love You	Taylor Dayne	Arista	10	(41)	
5	-	Don't Worry Be Happy	Bobby McFerrin	EMI Manhattan	9	(2)	F L
6	-	If It Isn't Love	New Edition	MCA	8		L
7	18	When It's Love	Van Halen	Warner	6	(28)	
8	3	Monkey	George Michael	Columbia	8	(13)	
9	-	Nobody's Fool	Kenny Loggins	Columbia	6		L
10	-	Another Part Of Me	Michael Jackson	Epic	6	(15)	
11	-	It Would Take A Strong Strong Man	Rick Astley	RCA	6		
12	-	One Good Woman	Peter Cetera	Full Moon	7		
13	9	Fast Car	Tracy Chapman	Elektra	8	(5)	F L
14	-	Love Bites	Def Leppard	Mercury	8	(11)	
15	2	I Don't Wanna Go On With You...	Elton John	MCA	8	(30)	
16	6	I Don't Wanna Live Without Your...	Chicago	Reprise	8		
17	-	Don't Be Cruel	Cheap Trick	Epic	8		
18	-	I Hate Myself For Loving You	Joan Jett & The Blackhearts	Blackheart	6	(46)	
19	-	A Nightmare On My Street	D.J. Jazzy Jeff & Fresh Prince	Jive	4		
20	11	Love Will Save The Day	Whitney Houston	Arista	5	(10)	

US 1988
JULY-SEPT

◆ Grateful Dead's nine days at Madison Square Gardens broke the box office record set by Neil Diamond.

▲ For the first time three heavy metal albums held the top rungs. The acts concerned were Van Halen, Def Leppard and Guns N' Roses (above). Def Leppard's multi-platinum **Hysteria** was also the first heavy metal album to spawn four Top 10 hit singles.

◆ Motown Records was bought by MCA for $61 million.

◆ MTV Award winners included Guns N' Roses, Cher, Suzanne Vega and Australian rockers INXS, who collected five.

UK 1988 OCT-DEC

◆ U2's film *Rattle And Hum* premiered, and the double album soundtrack sold a record one million copies in its first week in America and 300,000 in Britain.

▲ Britain's fastest selling single of 1988 was 'Mistletoe And Wine', which gave Cliff Richard his 100th chart record and his 55th Top 10 hit (equalling Elvis Presley's record).

◆ Roy Orbison died. The 60s star was currently charting with the supergroup The Traveling Wilburys.

◆ Stock, Aitken & Waterman wrote and produced a record six singles in the Top 30 in October.

October 1988

This Mnth	Prev Mnth	Title	Artist	Label	Wks 20	(US Pos)	
1	-	One Moment In Time	Whitney Houston	Arista	8	(5)	
2	2	Teardrops	Womack & Womack	4th & Broadway	11		
3	5	He Ain't Heavy, He's My Brother	Hollies	EMI	7		L
4	-	Don't Worry Be Happy	Bobby McFerrin	Manhattan	5	(1)	F L
5	-	Desire	U2	Island	4	(3)	
6	-	She Wants To Dance With Me	Rick Astley	RCA	7	(6)	
7	1	Groovy Kind Of Love	Phil Collins	Virgin	10	(1)	
8	-	A Little Respect	Erasure	Mute	8	(14)	
9	15	Nothing Can Divide Us	Jason Donovan	PWL	7		F
10	-	Wee Rule	Wee Papa Girl Rappers	Jive	6		F L
11	19	Big Fun	Inner City	10	7		F
12	-	Orinoco Flow	Enya	WEA	6	(24)	F
13	-	We Call It Acieed	D. Mob Feat. Gary Haisman	ffrr	6		F
14	11	Lovely Day	Bill Withers	CBS	5		L
15	-	Domino Dancing	Pet Shop Boys	Parlophone	4	(18)	
16	-	Never Trust A Stranger	Kim Wilde	MCA	5		
17	-	Je Ne Sais Pas Pourquoi	Kylie Minogue	PWL	6		
18	-	Riding On A Train	Pasadenas	CBS	5		
19	-	Harvest For The World	Christians	Island	4		
20	-	Burn It Up	Beatmasters With P.P. Arnold	Rhythm King	4		

November 1988

This Mnth	Prev Mnth	Title	Artist	Label	Wks 20	(US Pos)	
1	-	Stand Up For Your Love Rights	Yazz	Big Life	6		
2	17	Je Ne Sais Pas Pourquoi	Kylie Minogue	PWL	6		
3	12	Orinoco Flow	Enya	WEA	6	(24)	F
4	-	The First Time	Robin Beck	Mercury	9		F L
5	-	Girl You Know It's True	Milli Vanilli	Cooltempo	6	(2)	F
6	-	She Makes My Day	Robert Palmer	EMI	5		
7	-	Real Gone Kid	Deacon Blue	CBS	5		F
8	-	He Ain't No Competition	Brother Beyond	Parlophone	4		
9	-	Need You Tonight	INXS	Mercury	5	(1)	F
10	-	Missing You	Chris De Burgh	A&M	6		L
11	-	Kiss	Art Of Noise & Tom Jones	China	4	(31)	L
12	-	1-2-3	Gloria Estefan & The Miami Sound Machine	Epic	3	(3)	
13	13	We Call It Acieed	D. Mob Feat. Gary Haisman	ffrr	6		F
14	-	Twist And Shout	Salt 'n' Pepa	ffrr	4		
15	1	One Moment In Time	Whitney Houston	Arista	8	(5)	
16	-	The Clairvoyant	Iron Maiden	EMI	3		
17	8	A Little Respect	Erasure	Mute	8	(14)	
18	-	Let's Stick Together	Bryan Ferry	EG	2		
19	19	Harvest For The World	Christians	Island	4		
20	-	Left To My Own Devices	Pet Shop Boys	Parlophone	4	(84)	

December 1988

This Mnth	Prev Mnth	Title	Artist	Label	Wks 20	(US Pos)	
1	-	Mistletoe And Wine	Cliff Richard	EMI	7		
2	-	Cat Among The Pigeons/Silent Night	Bros	CBS	6		
3	-	Especially For You	Kylie Minogue/Jason Donovan	PWL	10		
4	-	Suddenly	Angry Anderson	Food For Thought	8		F L
5	-	Two Hearts	Phil Collins	Virgin	8	(1)	
6	-	Crackers International (E.P.)	Erasure	Mute	10		
7	4	The First Time	Robin Beck	Mercury	9		F L
8	-	Smooth Criminal	Michael Jackson	Epic	8	(7)	
9	-	Take Me To Your Heart	Rick Astley	RCA	7		
10	-	Good Life	Inner City	10	8	(73)	
11	-	Burning Bridges (On And Off And On Again)	Status Quo	Vertigo	6		
12	10	Missing You	Chris De Burgh	A&M	6		L
13	-	Angel Of Harlem	U2	Island	4	(14)	
14	-	Say A Little Prayer	Bomb The Bass	Rhythm King	5		
15	20	Left To My Own Devices	Pet Shop Boys	Parlophone	4	(84)	
16	-	Downtown '88	Petula Clark	PRT	4		L
17	9	Need You Tonight	INXS	Mercury	5	(1)	F
18	-	Buffalo Stance	Neneh Cherry	Circa	7	(3)	F
19	-	Fine Time	New Order	Factory	4		
20	-	Loco In Acapulco	Four Tops	Arista	5		L

October 1988

This Mnth	Prev Mnth	Title	Artist	Label	Wks 20	(UK Pos)	
1	-	Red Red Wine	UB40	A&M	9		F
2	14	Love Bites	Def Leppard	Mercury	8	(11)	
3	-	Groovy Kind Of Love	Phil Collins	Atlantic	8	(1)	
4	5	Don't Worry Be Happy	Bobby McFerrin	EMI Manhattan	9	(2)	F L
5	-	What's On Your Mind (Pure Energy)	Information Society	Tommy Boy	8		F
6	17	Don't Be Cruel	Cheap Trick	Epic	8		
7	-	Don't You Know What The Night Can Do	Steve Winwood	Virgin	7		
8	-	Don't Be Cruel	Bobby Brown	MCA	8	(13)	FG
9	-	Wild Wild West	Escape Club	Atlantic	10		F
10	12	One Good Woman	Peter Cetera	Full Moon	7		
11	4	I'll Always Love You	Taylor Dayne	Arista	10	(41)	
12	-	Kokomo	Beach Boys	Elektra	8	(25)	G L
13	18	I Hate Myself For Loving You	Joan Jett & The Blackhearts	Blackheart	6	(46)	
14	-	Never Tear Us Apart	INXS	Atlantic	6	(24)	
15	-	The Loco-Motion	Kylie Minogue	Geffen	9	(2)	F L
16	-	Forever Young	Rod Stewart	Warner	4	(57)	
17	-	True Love	Glenn Frey	MCA	5		L
18	-	One Moment In Time	Whitney Houston	Arista	7	(1)	
19	-	Please Don't Go Girl	New Kids On The Block	Columbia	5		F
20	1	Sweet Child O' Mine	Guns N' Roses	Geffen	10	(6)	F

November 1988

This Mnth	Prev Mnth	Title	Artist	Label	Wks 20	(UK Pos)	
1	-	Bad Medicine	Bon Jovi	Mercury	8	(17)	
2	9	Wild Wild West	Escape Club	Atlantic	10		F
3	12	Kokomo	Beach Boys	Elektra	8	(25)	G L
4	15	The Loco-Motion	Kylie Minogue	Geffen	9	(2)	F L
5	-	Desire	U2	Island	8	(1)	
6	-	Baby I Love Your Way/Freebird Medley	Will To Power	Epic	9	(6)	F
7	-	How Can I Fall	Breathe	A&M	10	(48)	
8	-	Kissing A Fool	George Michael	Columbia	6	(18)	
9	18	One Moment In Time	Whitney Houston	Arista	7	(1)	
10	-	Look Away	Chicago	Reprise	11		
11	3	Groovy Kind Of Love	Phil Collins	Atlantic	8	(1)	
12	-	I Don't Want Your Love	Duran Duran	Capitol	9	(14)	
13	-	Don't Know What You Got (Till It's Gone)	Cinderella	Mercury	5	(54)	
14	14	Never Tear Us Apart	INXS	Atlantic	6	(24)	
15	-	Giving You The Best That I Got	Anita Baker	Elektra	10	(55)	
16	-	Another Lover	Giant Steps	A&M	6		F L
17	-	Waiting For A Star To Fall	Boy Meets Girl	RCA	10	(9)	F L
18	5	What's On Your Mind (Pure Energy)	Information Society	Tommy Boy	8		F
19	1	Red Red Wine	UB40	A&M	9	(1)	F
20	7	Don't You Know What The Night...	Steve Winwood	Virgin	7		

December 1988

This Mnth	Prev Mnth	Title	Artist	Label	Wks 20	(UK Pos)	
1	10	Look Away	Chicago	Reprise	11		
2	-	Every Rose Has Its Thorn	Poison	Enigma	10	(13)	
3	15	Giving You The Best That I Got	Anita Baker	Elektra	10	(55)	
4	-	My Prerogative	Bobby Brown	MCA	10	(6)	
5	17	Waiting For A Star To Fall	Boy Meets Girl	RCA	10	(9)	F L
6	6	Baby I Love Your Way/Freebird Medley	Will To Power	Epic	9	(6)	F
7	-	Welcome To The Jungle	Guns N' Roses	Geffen	8	(24)	
8	12	I Don't Want Your Love	Duran Duran	Capitol	9	(14)	
9	7	How Can I Fall	Breathe	A&M	10	(48)	
10	-	Walk On Water	Eddie Money	Columbia	8		
11	-	Two Hearts	Phil Collins	Atlantic	9	(6)	
12	-	In Your Room	Bangles	Columbia	8	(35)	
13	-	The Promise	When In Rome	Virgin	7	(58)	F L
14	-	Don't Rush Me	Taylor Dayne	Arista	9		
15	5	Desire	U2	Island	8	(1)	
16	-	Finish What Ya Started	Van Halen	Warner	5		L
17	1	Bad Medicine	Bon Jovi	Mercury	8	(17)	
18	-	Armageddon It	Def Leppard	Mercury	8	(20)	
19	-	I Remember Holding You	Boys Club	MCA	6		F L
20	8	Kissing A Fool	George Michael	Columbia	6	(18)	

US 1988

OCT-DEC

◆ American record and tape shipments reached a new high of $6.25 billion, with CD business increasing 47%. It was also a record year in Britain, with sales of over $1 billion, and CDs showing a 60% increase.

▲ Among the acts enjoying their first Top 20 entries were future superstars Bobby Brown (above), Guns N' Roses and New Kids On The Block.

◆ John Lennon & Paul McCartney's composition 'Yesterday' clocked up a record five millionth play on American radio.

◆ Bruce Springsteen, Sting, Peter Gabriel and Tracy Chapman toured under the banner *Human Rights Now*.

UK 1989 JAN-MAR

◆ A new album chart was introduced which contained only multi-artist albums, leaving the main chart for solo artist sets.

◆ American producers L.A. & Babyface had five singles simultaneously in the US Top 40. In Britain, Stock, Aitken & Waterman scored their 80th UK Top 75 hit in less than five years, and in March produced three of the Top 4 singles.

◆ The quasi-religious video for Madonna's transatlantic topper, 'Like A Prayer', caused a major controversy, resulting in Pepsi dropping an $8 million advertising campaign.

◆ Michael Jackson's **Moonwalker** replaced **Thriller** as the top selling all time music video and other top sellers included U2's **Rattle And Hum** and Bruce Springsteen's **Anthology 1978-1988.**

January 1989

This Mnth	Prev Mnth	Title	Artist	Label	Wks 20	(US Pos)	
1	3	Especially For You	Kylie Minogue/Jason Donovan	PWL	10		
2	6	Crackers International (E.P.)	Erasure	Mute	10		
3	18	Buffalo Stance	Neneh Cherry	Circa	7	(3)	F
4	10	Good Life	Inner City	10	8	(73)	
5	-	She Drives Me Crazy	Fine Young Cannibals	London	6	(1)	
6	-	The Living Years	Mike + The Mechanics	WEA	7	(1)	F
7	4	Suddenly	Angry Anderson	Food For Thought	8		F L
8	-	Four Letter Word	Kim Wilde	MCA	6		
9	-	Baby I Love Your Way/Freebird	Will To Power	Epic	5	(1)	F L
10	20	Loco In Acapulco	Four Tops	Arista	5		L
11	-	Something's Gotten Hold Of My Heart	Marc Almond Featuring Gene Pitney	Parlophone	9		
12	-	You Got It	Roy Orbison	Virgin	6	(9)	
13	-	Waiting For A Star To Fall	Boy Meets Girl	RCA	4	(5)	F L
14	-	Cuddly Toy	Roachford	CBS	5		F L
15	11	Burning Bridges (On And Off...)	Status Quo	Vertigo	6		
16	-	All She Wants Is	Duran Duran	EMI	2	(22)	
17	1	Mistletoe And Wine	Cliff Richard	EMI	7		
18	-	Keeping The Dream Alive	Freiheit	CBS	4		F L
19	5	Two Hearts	Phil Collins	Virgin	8	(1)	
20	-	You Are The One	A-Ha	Warner	5		

February 1989

This Mnth	Prev Mnth	Title	Artist	Label	Wks 20	(US Pos)	
1	11	Something's Gotten Hold Of My...	Marc Almond Feat. Gene Pitney	Parlophone	9		
2	6	The Living Years	Mike + The Mechanics	WEA	7	(1)	F
3	-	Love Train	Holly Johnson	MCA	6	(65)	F
4	12	You Got It	Roy Orbison	Virgin	6	(9)	
5	-	Love Changes Everything	Michael Ball	Really Useful	8		F L
6	-	My Prerogative	Bobby Brown	MCA	6	(1)	F
7	14	Cuddly Toy	Roachford	CBS	5		F L
8	-	Wait	Robert Howard & Kym Mazelle	RCA	5		F L
9	-	Belfast Child	Simple Minds	Virgin	5		
10	-	That's The Way Love Is	Ten City	Atlantic	5		F L
11	-	Fine Time	Yazz	Big Life	4		
12	5	She Drives Me Crazy	Fine Young Cannibals	London	6	(1)	
13	-	Last Of The Famous International Playboys	Morrissey	HMV	2		
14	-	Hold Me In Your Arms	Rick Astley	RCA	4		
15	-	Stop	Sam Brown	A&M	7	(65)	F
16	1	Especially For You	Kylie Minogue/Jason Donovan	PWL	10		
17	-	Leave Me Alone	Michael Jackson	Epic	6		
18	2	Crackers International (E.P.)	Erasure	Mute	10		
19	-	It's Only Love	Simply Red	Elektra	2	(57)	
20	-	Big Area	Then Jerico	London	2		L

March 1989

This Mnth	Prev Mnth	Title	Artist	Label	Wks 20	(US Pos)	
1	-	Too Many Broken Hearts	Jason Donovan	PWL	9		
2	-	Help	Bananarama/La Na Nee Nee Noo Nioo	London	6		
3	15	Stop	Sam Brown	A&M	7	(65)	F
4	5	Love Changes Everything	Michael Ball	Really Useful	8		F L
5	-	Can't Stay Away From You	Gloria Estefan & The Miami Sound Machine	Epic	6	(6)	
6	17	Leave Me Alone	Michael Jackson	Epic	6		
7	-	Hey Music Lover	S'Express	Rhythm King	5		L
8	-	This Time I Know It's For Real	Donna Summer	Warner	8	(7)	
9	9	Belfast Child	Simple Minds	Virgin	5		
10	-	Like A Prayer	Madonna	Sire	7	(1)	
11	-	Straight Up	Paula Abdul	Siren	9	(1)	F
12	-	I Don't Want A Lover	Texas	Mercury	5	(77)	F
13	-	Blow The House Down	Living In A Box	Chrysalis	4		
14	-	I'd Rather Jack	Reynolds Girls	PWL	6		F L
15	-	Keep On Movin'	Soul II Soul Feat. Caron Wheeler	10	6	(11)	F
16	6	My Prerogative	Bobby Brown	MCA	6	(1)	F
17	-	Turn Up The Bass	Tyree Feat. Kool Rock Steady	ffrr	3		F L
18	-	Every Rose Has Its Thorn	Poison	Enigma	4	(1)	F
19	-	Paradise City	Guns N' Roses	Geffen	5	(5)	F
20	14	Hold Me In Your Arms	Rick Astley	RCA	4		

US 1989 JAN-MAR

January 1989

This Mnth	Prev Mnth	Title	Artist	Label	Wks 20	(UK Pos)	
1	11	Two Hearts	Phil Collins	Atlantic	9	(6)	
2	14	Don't Rush Me	Taylor Dayne	Arista	9		
3	4	My Prerogative	Bobby Brown	MCA	10	(6)	
4	18	Armageddon It	Def Leppard	Mercury	8	(20)	
5	2	Every Rose Has Its Thorn	Poison	Enigma	10	(13)	
6	-	When I'm With You	Sheriff	Capitol	8		F L
7	-	Smooth Criminal	Michael Jackson	Epic	7	(8)	
8	-	The Way You Love Me	Karyn White	Warner	6	(42)	F
9	-	When The Children Cry	White Lion	Atlantic	7		L
10	-	Born To Be My Baby	Bon Jovi	Mercury	9	(22)	
11	-	Put A Little Love In Your Heart	Annie Lennox & Al Green	A&M	6	(28)	F
12	12	In Your Room	Bangles	Columbia	8	(35)	
13	19	I Remember Holding You	Boys Club	MCA	6		F L
14	-	All This Time	Tiffany	MCA	7	(47)	L
15	5	Waiting For A Star To Fall	Boy Meets Girl	RCA	10	(9)	F L
16	-	Straight Up	Paula Abdul	Virgin	9	(3)	F G
17	3	Giving You The Best That I Got	Anita Baker	Elektra	10	(55)	
18	-	Wild Thing	Tone Loc	Delicious Vinyl	8	(21)	F P
19	-	Holding On	Steve Winwood	Virgin	4		
20	1	Look Away	Chicago	Reprise	11		

February 1989

This Mnth	Prev Mnth	Title	Artist	Label	Wks 20	(UK Pos)	
1	16	Straight Up	Paula Abdul	Virgin	9	(3)	F G
2	18	Wild Thing	Tone Loc	Delicious Vinyl	8	(21)	F P
3	10	Born To Be My Baby	Bon Jovi	Mercury	9	(22)	
4	6	When I'm With You	Sheriff	Capitol	8		F L
5	-	The Lover In Me	Sheena Easton	MCA	8	(15)	
6	-	She Wants To Dance With Me	Rick Astley	RCA	6	(6)	
7	-	Lost In Your Eyes	Debbie Gibson	Atlantic	9	(34)	
8	9	When The Children Cry	White Lion	Atlantic	7		L
9	-	What I Am	Edie Brickell & New Bohemians	Geffen	7	(31)	F L
10	-	Walking Away	Information Society	Tommy Boy	5		L
11	-	You Got It (The Right Stuff)	New Kids On The Block	Columbia	8	(1)	
12	-	I Wanna Have Some Fun	Samantha Fox	Jive	6	(63)	L
13	14	All This Time	Tiffany	MCA	7	(47)	L
14	-	Surrender To Me	Ann Wilson & Robin Zander	Capitol	7		L
15	8	The Way You Love Me	Karyn White	Warner	6	(42)	F
16	-	Dial My Heart	Boys	Motown	5	(61)	F L
17	4	Armageddon It	Def Leppard	Mercury	8	(20)	
18	-	Angel Of Harlem	U2	Island	3	(9)	
19	-	The Living Years	Mike + The Mechanics	Atlantic	8	(2)	L
20	2	Don't Rush Me	Taylor Dayne	Arista	9		

March 1989

This Mnth	Prev Mnth	Title	Artist	Label	Wks 20	(UK Pos)	
1	7	Lost In Your Eyes	Debbie Gibson	Atlantic	9	(34)	
2	19	The Living Years	Mike + The Mechanics	Atlantic	8	(2)	L
3	-	Roni	Bobby Brown	MCA	6	(21)	
4	-	Girl You Know It's True	Milli Vanilli	Arista	9	(3)	F G
5	-	Paradise City	Guns N' Roses	Geffen	6	(6)	
6	-	My Heart Can't Tell You No	Rod Stewart	Warner	8	(49)	
7	11	You Got It (The Right Stuff)	New Kids On The Block	Columbia	8	(1)	
8	-	Eternal Flame	Bangles	Columbia	8	(1)	L
9	-	The Look	Roxette	EMI	8	(7)	F
10	1	Straight Up	Paula Abdul	Virgin	9	(3)	F G
11	-	Don't Tell Me Lies	Breathe	A&M	5	(45)	L
12	5	The Lover In Me	Sheena Easton	MCA	8	(15)	
13	14	Surrender To Me	Ann Wilson & Robin Zander	Capitol	7		L
14	-	You're Not Alone	Chicago	Reprise	4		
15	-	Walk The Dinosaur	Was (Not Was)	Chrysalis	5	(10)	L
16	-	She Drives Me Crazy	Fine Young Cannibals	IRS	9	(5)	F
17	9	What I Am	Edie Brickell & New Bohemians	Geffen	7	(31)	F L
18	-	Dreamin'	Vanessa Williams	Wing	7	(74)	F
19	2	Wild Thing	Tone Loc	Delicious Vinyl	8	(21)	F P
20	-	I Beg Your Pardon	Kon Kan	Atlantic	4	(5)	F L

◆ Due to the drop in singles sales the qualification for an American gold record was halved to 500,000, and a platinum to 1 million, while in Britain sales of 600,000 earned a platinum record and 400,000 a gold.

◆ *Rock And Roll Hall Of Fame* inductees for 1988/89 were The Beach Boys, The Beatles, Dion, The Drifters, Bob Dylan, Otis Redding, Rolling Stones, The Supremes, The Temptations and Stevie Wonder.

◆ The first CDs to sell a million were U2's **The Joshua Tree,** the **Dirty Dancing** soundtrack, Def Leppard's **Hysteria** and George Michael's **Faith.**

◆ Many disagreed with the choice of progressive rock band Jethro Tull as the first Hard Rock & Heavy Metal Grammy winner, and with white pop star George Michael winning the American Music Awards for Top R&B Male and Top R&B Album.

UK 1989 APR-JUNE

◆ Wembley crowd-pullers included The Bee Gees, Bobby Brown, Bob Dylan, Elton John, R.E.M., Diana Ross and Stevie Wonder.

▲ Stock, Aitken & Waterman scored a record three successive No. 1s with singles by Kylie Minogue (above), Jason Donovan and an all star group featuring Gerry (& The Pacemakers) Marsden, whose re-recording of 'Ferry Cross The Mersey' was the eighth charity chart topper in five years, and the fourth to enter at No. 1.

◆ 'Eternal Flame' by The Bangles was the only record by a female group to top the transatlantic charts in the 1980s.

April 1989

This Mnth	Prev Mnth	Title	Artist	Label	Wks 20	(US Pos)	
1	-	Eternal Flame	Bangles	CBS	9	(1)	L
2	10	Like A Prayer	Madonna	Sire	7	(1)	
3	11	Straight Up	Paula Abdul	Siren	9	(1)	F
4	-	I Beg Your Pardon	Kon Kan	Atlantic	7	(15)	F L
5	1	Too Many Broken Hearts	Jason Donovan	PWL	9		
6	8	This Time I Know It's For Real	Donna Summer	Warner	8	(7)	
7	-	If You Don't Know Me By Now	Simply Red	Elektra	7	(1)	
8	-	Baby I Don't Care	Transvision Vamp	MCA	8		
9	-	Americanos	Holly Johnson	MCA	7		
10	15	Keep On Movin'	Soul II Soul Feat. Caron Wheeler	10	6	(11)	F
11	19	Paradise City	Guns N' Roses	Geffen	5	(5)	F
12	-	When Love Comes To Town	U2 With B.B. King	Island	3	(68)	
13	-	People Hold On	Coldcut Feat. Lisa Stansfield	Ahead Of Our Time	4		L
14	-	Good Thing	Fine Young Cannibals	London	5	(1)	
15	14	I'd Rather Jack	Reynolds Girls	PWL	6		F L
16	-	Lullaby	Cure	Fiction	3	(74)	
17	-	I Haven't Stopped Dancing Yet	Pat & Mick	PWL	3		F L
18	-	International Rescue	Fuzzbox	WEA	4		F
19	-	Don't Be Cruel	Bobby Brown	MCA	3	(8)	
20	5	Can't Stay Away From You	Gloria Estefan/Miami Sound...	Epic	6	(6)	

May 1989

This Mnth	Prev Mnth	Title	Artist	Label	Wks 20	(US Pos)	
1	-	Hand On Your Heart	Kylie Minogue	PWL	7		
2	-	Requiem	London Boys	WEA	7		F
3	-	Miss You Like Crazy	Natalie Cole	EMI	8	(7)	
4	1	Eternal Flame	Bangles	CBS	9	(1)	L
5	-	I Want It All	Queen	Parlophone	4	(50)	
6	-	Bring Me Edelweiss	Edelweiss	WEA	5		F L
7	-	Beds Are Burning	Midnight Oil	CBS/Sprint	5	(17)	F L
8	-	Ferry 'Cross The Mersey	Christians/Holly Johnson/Paul McCartney/Gerry Marsden & Stock Aitken Waterman	PWL	5		F L
9	8	Baby I Don't Care	Transvision Vamp	MCA	8		
10	-	I'm Every Woman	Chaka Khan	Warner	4		L
11	9	Americanos	Holly Johnson	MCA	7		
12	7	If You Don't Know Me By Now	Simply Red	Elektra	7	(1)	
13	-	The Look	Roxette	EMI	4	(1)	F
14	-	Who's In The House	Beatmasters	Rhythm King	4		
15	-	Electric Youth	Debbie Gibson	Atlantic	3	(11)	
16	-	Every Little Step	Bobby Brown	MCA	4	(3)	
17	-	Your Mama Don't Dance	Poison	Capitol	3	(10)	
18	14	Good Thing	Fine Young Cannibals	London	5	(1)	
19	-	Manchild	Neneh Cherry	Circa	5		
20	-	Where Has All The Love Gone	Yazz	Big Life	3		

June 1989

This Mnth	Prev Mnth	Title	Artist	Label	Wks 20	(US Pos)	
1	-	Sealed With A Kiss	Jason Donovan	PWL	5		
2	3	Miss You Like Crazy	Natalie Cole	EMI	8	(7)	
3	-	Express Yourself	Madonna	Sire	5	(2)	
4	-	The Best Of Me	Cliff Richard	EMI	4		
5	-	Right Back Where We Started From	Sinitta	Fanfare	7	(84)	
6	-	Back To Life (However Do You Want Me)	Soul II Soul Featuring Caron Wheeler	10	10	(4)	
7	-	Sweet Child O' Mine	Guns N' Roses	Geffen	6	(1)	
8	8	Ferry 'Cross The Mersey	Christians, Holly Johnson etc.	PWL	5		F L
9	19	Manchild	Neneh Cherry	Circa	5		
10	-	I Don't Wanna Get Hurt	Donna Summer	Warner	5		
11	-	On The Inside (Theme 'Prisoner-Cell Block H')	Lynne Hamilton	A1	4		F L
12	-	I Drove All Night	Cyndi Lauper	Epic	6	(6)	
13	1	Hand On Your Heart	Kylie Minogue	PWL	7		
14	2	Requiem	London Boys	WEA	7		F
15	-	Song For Whoever	Beautiful South	Go! Discs	7		F
16	-	It Is Time To Get Funky	D. Mob Featuring LRS	London	5		
17	6	Bring Me Edelweiss	Edelweiss	WEA	5		F L
18	16	Every Little Step	Bobby Brown	MCA	4	(3)	
19	-	Batdance	Prince	Warner	5	(1)	
20	-	Just Keep Rockin'	Double Trouble & Rebel M.C.	Desire	7		F

April 1989

This Mnth	Prev Mnth	Title	Artist	Label	Wks 20	(UK Pos)	
1	9	The Look	Roxette	EMI	8	(7)	F
2	16	She Drives Me Crazy	Fine Young Cannibals	IRS	9	(5)	F
3	-	Like A Prayer	Madonna	Sire	9	(1)	G
4	8	Eternal Flame	Bangles	Columbia	8	(1)	L
5	4	Girl You Know It's True	Milli Vanilli	Arista	9	(3)	F G
6	-	Funky Cold Medina	Tone Loc	Delicious	7	(13)	G L
7	-	Stand	R.E.M.	Warner	6	(48)	
8	-	I'll Be There For You	Bon Jovi	Mercury	10	(18)	
9	-	Heaven Help Me	Deon Estus	Mika/Polydor	6	(41)	F L
10	6	My Heart Can't Tell You No	Rod Stewart	Warner	8	(49)	
11	-	Second Chance	Thirty Eight Special	A&M	8		L
12	-	Your Mama Don't Dance	Poison	Enigma	5	(13)	
13	18	Dreamin'	Vanessa Williams	Wing	7	(74)	F
14	-	Superwoman	Karyn White	Warner	5	(11)	
15	-	You Got It	Roy Orbison	Virgin	6	(3)	L
16	15	Walk The Dinosaur	Was (Not Was)	Chrysalis	5	(10)	L
17	-	Room To Move	Animotion	Polydor	5		L
18	-	Rocket	Def Leppard	Mercury	4	(15)	
19	2	The Living Years	Mike + The Mechanics	Atlantic	8	(2)	L
20	-	Real Love	Jody Watley	MCA	8	(31)	

May 1989

This Mnth	Prev Mnth	Title	Artist	Label	Wks 20	(UK Pos)	
1	20	Real Love	Jody Watley	MCA	8	(31)	
2	-	Forever Your Girl	Paula Abdul	Virgin	9	(24)	
3	8	I'll Be There For You	Bon Jovi	Mercury	10	(18)	
4	-	Soldier Of Love	Donny Osmond	Capitol	8	(29)	
5	-	Rock On	Michael Damian	Cypress	8		F L
6	3	Like A Prayer	Madonna	Sire	9	(1)	G
7	-	Patience	Guns N' Roses	Geffen	7	(10)	
8	-	After All	Cher & Peter Cetera	Geffen	7		
9	-	Wind Beneath My Wings	Bette Midler	Atlantic	10	(5)	G
10	11	Second Chance	Thirty Eight Special	A&M	8		L
11	-	Electric Youth	Debbie Gibson	Atlantic	5	(14)	
12	-	Every Little Step	Bobby Brown	MCA	9	(6)	
13	-	I'll Be Loving You (Forever)	New Kids On The Block	Columbia	8	(5)	
14	6	Funky Cold Medina	Tone Loc	Delicious	7	(13)	G L
15	-	Thinking Of You	Sa-Fire	Polydor/Cutting	6		F L
16	-	Cult Of Personality	Living Colour	Epic	4	(67)	F L
17	-	Close My Eyes Forever	Lita Ford (& Ozzy Osbourne)	RCA	7	(47)	L
18	-	Everlasting Love	Howard Jones	Elektra	5	(62)	L
19	-	Iko Iko	Belle Stars	Capitol	4	(35)	F L
20	2	She Drives Me Crazy	Fine Young Cannibals	IRS	9	(5)	F

June 1989

This Mnth	Prev Mnth	Title	Artist	Label	Wks 20	(UK Pos)	
1	13	I'll Be Loving You (Forever)	New Kids On The Block	Columbia	8	(5)	
2	9	Wind Beneath My Wings	Bette Midler	Atlantic	10	(5)	G
3	12	Every Little Step	Bobby Brown	MCA	9	(6)	
4	-	Buffalo Stance	Neneh Cherry	Virgin	9	(3)	F
5	-	Satisfied	Richard Marx	EMI	8	(52)	
6	5	Rock On	Michael Damian	Cypress	8		F L
7	-	Baby Don't Forget My Number	Milli Vanilli	Arista	9	(16)	
8	7	Patience	Guns N' Roses	Geffen	7	(10)	
9	17	Close My Eyes Forever	Lita Ford (& Ozzy Osbourne)	RCA	7	(47)	L
10	-	Good Thing	Fine Young Cannibals	I.R.S.	9	(7)	
11	-	This Time I Know It's For Real	Donna Summer	Atlantic	6	(3)	L
12	-	Cry	Waterfront	Polydor	6	(17)	F L
13	4	Soldier Of Love	Donny Osmond	Capitol	8	(29)	
14	2	Forever Your Girl	Paula Abdul	Virgin	9	(24)	
15	-	Miss You Like Crazy	Natalie Cole	EMI	8	(2)	
16	-	Where Are You Now	Jimmy Harnen With Synch	WTG	5		F L
17	-	I Drove All Night	Cyndi Lauper	Epic	6	(7)	L
18	1	Real Love	Jody Watley	MCA	8	(31)	
19	-	If You Don't Know Me By Now	Simply Red	Elektra	9	(2)	L
20	18	Everlasting Love	Howard Jones	Elektra	5	(62)	L

US 1989
APR-JUNE

◆ For the first time over half the Top 10 black albums were by rap artists. *Billboard* introduced an all-rap chart, and MTV banned NWA's 'Straight Outta Compton' video for being too "pro-gang".

◆ The first non-vinyl Hot 100 hits were 'Me Myself And I' by De La Soul and 'Right Next To Me' by Whistle.

◆ As veteran rockers The Who (they earned $30 million from their shows) and Beach Boys started successful US tours. Old singles by The Belle Stars, Jimmy Harnen & Synch, Benny Mardones and Real Life climbed the Hot 100.

◆ The second World Music Video Awards (seen by satellite in 46 countries) selected Michael Jackson's 'Dirty Diana' as the Top Promotional Video.

UK 1989 JULY-SEPT

In America, Madonna scored a record 16th successive Top 5 single with 'Cherish', and in the UK Kylie Minogue's sixth release 'Wouldn't Change A Thing' became her sixth Top 2 single - no artist had ever achieved a better chart start.

◆ Soul II Soul's second transatlantic hit, 'Back To Life', was one of the most influential records of the decade. The group were the year's top selling twelve inch act in America.

◆ In September, Italian records held the top three places in the UK dance chart with the chart topping 'Ride On Time' by Black Box outselling all other singles in 1989.

◆ Phonogram bought Island Records for $480 (£300) million with shareholders U2 making $48 (£30) million from the deal.

July 1989

This Mnth	Prev Mnth	Title	Artist	Label	Wks 20	(US Pos)	
1	6	Back To Life (However Do You Want Me)	Soul II Soul Featuring Caron Wheeler	10	10	(4)	
2	-	London Nights	London Boys	Teldec/WEA	7		
3	15	Song For Whoever	Beautiful South	Go! Discs	7		F
4	-	You'll Never Stop Me From Loving You	Sonia	Chrysalis	8		F
5	-	Licence To Kill	Gladys Knight	MCA	7		L
6	-	It's Alright	Pet Shop Boys	Parlophone	4		
7	19	Batdance	Prince	Warner	5	(1)	
8	-	Ain't Nobody	Rufus & Chaka Khan	Warner	7	(22)	L
9	-	On Our Own	Bobby Brown	MCA	6	(2)	
10	-	Wind Beneath My Wings	Bette Midler	Atlantic	6	(1)	F L
11	12	I Drove All Night	Cyndi Lauper	Epic	6	(6)	
12	-	All I Want Is You	U2	Island	3	(83)	
13	-	Breakthru'	Queen	Parlophone	3		
14	-	Superwoman	Karyn White	Warner	4	(8)	F L
15	-	Don't Wanna Lose You	Gloria Estefan	Epic	6	(1)	
16	20	Just Keep Rockin'	Double Trouble & Rebel M.C.	Desire	7		F
17	5	Right Back Where We Started From	Sinitta	Fanfare	7	(84)	
18	-	Voodoo Ray (EP)	A Guy Called Gerald	Rham!	4		F L
19	1	Sealed With A Kiss	Jason Donovan	PWL	5		
20	-	Patience	Guns N' Roses	Geffen	3	(4)	

August 1989

This Mnth	Prev Mnth	Title	Artist	Label	Wks 20	(US Pos)	
1	-	Swing The Mood	Jive Bunny & The Mastermixers	Music Factory	10	(11)	F
2	-	Wouldn't Change A Thing	Kylie Minogue	PWL	6		
3	-	French Kiss	Lil Louis	ffrr	7	(50)	F
4	-	Poison	Alice Cooper	Epic	7	(7)	L
5	4	You'll Never Stop Me From Loving...	Sonia	Chrysalis	8		F
6	15	Don't Wanna Lose You	Gloria Estefan	Epic	6	(1)	
7	-	Toy Soldiers	Martika	CBS	6	(1)	F
8	-	Too Much	Bros	CBS	4		
9	9	On Our Own	Bobby Brown	MCA	6	(2)	
10	-	You're History	Shakespear's Sister	ffrr	4		F
11	-	Losing My Mind	Liza Minnelli	Epic	3		F L
12	-	Ride On Time	Black Box	De Construction	14		F
13	-	Blame It On The Boogie	Big Fun	Jive	6		F
14	8	Ain't Nobody	Rufus & Chaka Khan	Warner	7	(22)	L
15	10	Wind Beneath My Wings	Bette Midler	Atlantic	6	(1)	F L
16	2	London Nights	London Boys	Teldec/WEA	7		
17	-	Hey D.J. I Can't Dance To That Music You're Playing/Ska Train	Beatmasters Featuring Betty Boo	Rhythm King	6		L
18	-	Days	Kirsty MacColl	Virgin	4		L
19	-	Do The Right Thing	Redhead Kingpin & The FBI	10	3		F L
20	1	Back To Life (However Do You ...)	Soul II Soul Feat. Caron Wheeler	10	10	(4)	

September 1989

This Mnth	Prev Mnth	Title	Artist	Label	Wks 20	(US Pos)	
1	12	Ride On Time	Black Box	De Construction	14		F
2	1	Swing The Mood	Jive Bunny & The Mastermixers	Music Factory	10	(11)	F
3	-	Sowing The Seeds Of Love	Tears For Fears	Fontana	5	(2)	
4	-	Right Here Waiting	Richard Marx	EMI	7	(1)	F
5	13	Blame It On The Boogie	Big Fun	Jive	6		F
6	-	Every Day (I Love You More)	Jason Donovan	PWL	4		
7	-	I Need Your Lovin'	Alyson Williams	Def Jam	7		L
8	-	The Time Warp	Damian	Jive	5		F L
9	-	The Best	Tina Turner	Capitol	7	(15)	
10	-	I Just Don't Have The Heart	Cliff Richard	EMI	5		
11	-	Numero Uno	Starlight	City Beat	6		F L
12	17	Hey D.J. I Can't Dance To That Music You're Playing/Ska Train	Beatmasters Featuring Betty Boo	Rhythm King	6		L
13	-	Pump Up The Jam	Technotronic Featuring Felly	Swanyard	9	(2)	F
14	-	Cherish	Madonna	Sire	5	(2)	
15	4	Poison	Alice Cooper	Epic	7	(7)	L
16	-	If Only I Could	Sydney Youngblood	Circa	9		F
17	7	Toy Soldiers	Martika	CBS	6	(1)	F
18	3	French Kiss	Lil Louis	ffrr	7	(50)	F
19	2	Wouldn't Change A Thing	Kylie Minogue	PWL	6		
20	-	Personal Jesus	Depeche Mode	Mute	3	(28)	

July 1989

This Mnth	Prev Mnth	Title	Artist	Label	Wks 20	(UK Pos)	
1	-	Express Yourself	Madonna	Sire	7	(5)	
2	19	If You Don't Know Me By Now	Simply Red	Elektra	9	(2)	L
3	-	Toy Soldiers	Martika	Columbia	9	(5)	
4	10	Good Thing	Fine Young Cannibals	I.R.S.	9	(7)	
5	7	Baby Don't Forget My Number	Milli Vanilli	Arista	9	(16)	
6	15	Miss You Like Crazy	Natalie Cole	EMI	8	(2)	
7	-	Batdance	Prince	Warner	8	(2)	G
8	-	What You Don't Know	Expose	Arista	6		
9	-	So Alive	Love And Rockets	RCA	8		F L
10	-	On Our Own	Bobby Brown	MCA	10	(4)	G
11	-	Lay Your Hands On Me	Bon Jovi	Mercury	7	(18)	
12	5	Satisfied	Richard Marx	EMI	8	(52)	
13	17	I Drove All Night	Cyndi Lauper	Epic	6	(7)	L
14	-	The Doctor	Doobie Brothers	Capitol	5	(73)	L
15	4	Buffalo Stance	Neneh Cherry	Virgin	9	(3)	F
16	-	Once Bitten Twice Shy	Great White	Capitol	9		F L
17	-	Crazy About Her	Rod Stewart	Warner	5		
18	-	I Like It	Dino	4th & Broadway	8		F
19	11	This Time I Know It's For Real	Donna Summer	Atlantic	6	(3)	L
20	-	I Won't Back Down	Tom Petty	MCA	5	(28)	

August 1989

This Mnth	Prev Mnth	Title	Artist	Label	Wks 20	(UK Pos)	
1	-	Right Here Waiting	Richard Marx	EMI	10	(2)	G
2	10	On Our Own	Bobby Brown	MCA	10	(4)	G
3	-	Cold Hearted	Paula Abdul	Virgin	11	(46)	
4	16	Once Bitten Twice Shy	Great White	Capitol	9		F L
5	7	Batdance	Prince	Warner	8	(2)	G
6	-	Don't Wanna Lose You	Gloria Estefan	Epic	9	(6)	
7	18	I Like It	Dino	4th & Broadway	8		F
8	-	Hangin' Tough	New Kids On The Block	Columbia	8	(1)	G
9	9	So Alive	Love And Rockets	RCA	8		F L
10	-	Secret Rendezvous	Karyn White	Warner	8	(22)	
11	3	Toy Soldiers	Martika	Columbia	9	(5)	
12	-	Friends	Jody Watley With Eric B & Rakim	MCA	6	(21)	L
13	11	Lay Your Hands On Me	Bon Jovi	Mercury	7	(18)	
14	-	The End Of The Innocence	Don Henley	Geffen	5	(48)	L
15	-	Angel Eyes	Jeff Healey Band	Arista	7		F L
16	2	If You Don't Know Me By Now	Simply Red	Elektra	9	(2)	L
17	-	Sacred Emotion	Donny Osmond	Capitol	4		L
18	-	Shower Me With Your Love	Surface	Columbia	7		
19	-	Keep On Movin'	Soul Ii Soul	Virgin	6	(5)	F G
20	-	I'm That Type Of Guy	L.L. Cool J	Def Jam	3	(43)	

September 1989

This Mnth	Prev Mnth	Title	Artist	Label	Wks 20	(UK Pos)	
1	-	Heaven	Warrant	Columbia	9		F
2	-	Girl I'm Gonna Miss You	Milli Vanilli	Arista	9	(2)	
3	6	Don't Wanna Lose You	Gloria Estefan	Epic	9	(6)	
4	-	If I Could Turn Back Time	Cher	Geffen	9	(6)	
5	3	Cold Hearted	Paula Abdul	Virgin	11	(46)	
6	8	Hangin' Tough	New Kids On The Block	Columbia	8	(1)	G
7	-	18 And Life	Skid Row	Atlantic	9	(12)	F
8	18	Shower Me With Your Love	Surface	Columbia	7		
9	-	Cherish	Madonna	Sire	8	(3)	
10	1	Right Here Waiting	Richard Marx	EMI	10	(2)	G
11	15	Angel Eyes	Jeff Healey Band	Arista	7		F L
12	-	One	Bee Gees	Warner	5	(71)	L
13	-	Miss You Much	Janet Jackson	A&M	10	(22)	G
14	19	Keep On Movin'	Soul II Soul	Virgin	6	(5)	FG
15	-	Kisses On The Wind	Neneh Cherry	Virgin	4	(20)	L
16	10	Secret Rendezvous	Karyn White	Warner	8	(22)	
17	14	The End Of The Innocence	Don Henley	Geffen	5	(48)	L
18	12	Friends	Jody Watley With Eric B & Rakim	MCA	6	(21)	L
19	-	Love Song	Cure	Elektra	6	(18)	F
20	-	Don't Look Back	Fine Young Cannibals	IRS	5	(34)	L

US 1989
JULY-SEPT

◆ New Kids On The Block, America's hottest new act, simultaneously headed the single and album chart with 'Hangin' Tough'. Other successful new artists included hard rockers, Warrant, Skid Row and Great White.

◆ Producer/songwriters L.A. & Babyface scored their twelfth No. 1 black hit in two years with Babyface's own single 'It's No Crime'.

▲ The Moscow Peace Festival starred Bon Jovi (above), Motley Crue, Ozzy Osbourne, The Scorpions, Skid Row and Cinderella.

◆ WEA announced they were phasing out production of seven inch vinyl records in 1990.

UK 1989 OCT-DEC

▲ Jive Bunny & The Mastermixers scored their third successive No. 1 in five months with 'Let's Party', while in the US 'Angelia' gave Richard Marx (above) his seventh successive Top 10 hit.

◆ In October, songwriter Diane Warren became the first female to pen the Top 2 and had five of her songs simultaneously climbing the Top 100. In Britain, Stock, Aitken & Waterman were equally popular, producing 11 of the year's Top 40 British singles.

October 1989

This Mnth	Prev Mnth	Title	Artist	Label	Wks 20	(US Pos)	
1	1	Ride On Time	Black Box	De Construction	14		F
2	13	Pump Up The Jam	Technotronic Featuring Felly	Swanyard	9	(2)	F
3	16	If Only I Could	Sydney Youngblood	Circa	9		F
4	-	Street Tuff	Rebel MC/Double Trouble	Desire	8		L
5	-	That's What I Like	Jive Bunny & The Mastermixers	Music Factory	8	(69)	
6	-	We Didn't Start The Fire	Billy Joel	CBS	6	(1)	
7	-	Girl I'm Gonna Miss You	Milli Vanilli	Cooltempo	8	(1)	L
8	-	Sweet Surrender	Wet Wet Wet	Precious	5		
9	-	Drama!	Erasure	Mute	4		
10	-	If I Could Turn Back Time	Cher	Geffen	7	(3)	
11	-	Leave A Light On	Belinda Carlisle	Virgin	6	(11)	
12	-	You Keep It All In	Beautiful South	Go! Discs	5		
13	4	Right Here Waiting	Richard Marx	EMI	7	(1)	F
14	-	Room In Your Heart	Living In A Box	Chrysalis	7		L
15	9	The Best	Tina Turner	Capitol	7	(15)	
16	-	Wishing On A Star	Fresh 4 Featuring Lizz E	10	3		F L
17	-	Chocolate Box	Bros	CBS	2		
18	-	Name And Number	Curiosity Killed The Cat	Mercury	3		
19	-	The Road To Hell (Pt. 2)	Chris Rea	WEA	5		
20	14	Cherish	Madonna	Sire	5	(2)	

November 1989

This Mnth	Prev Mnth	Title	Artist	Label	Wks 20	(US Pos)	
1	-	All Around The World	Lisa Stansfield	Arista	7	(3)	
2	7	Girl I'm Gonna Miss You	Milli Vanilli	Cooltempo	8	(1)	L
3	5	That's What I Like	Jive Bunny & The Mastermixers	Music Factory	8	(69)	L
4	-	Never Too Late	Kylie Minogue	PWL	5		
5	-	Another Day In Paradise	Phil Collins	Virgin	5	(1)	
6	4	Street Tuff	Rebel MC/Double Trouble	Desire	8		L
7	-	I Feel The Earth Move	Martika	CBS	6	(25)	
8	14	Room In Your Heart	Living In A Box	Chrysalis	7		L
9	-	You Got It (The Right Stuff)	New Kids On The Block	CBS	8	(3)	F
10	11	Leave A Light On	Belinda Carlisle	Virgin	6	(11)	
11	-	Don't Know Much	Linda Ronstadt (featuring Aaron Neville)	Elektra	7	(2)	L
12	-	Grand Piano	Mixmaster	BCM	4		F L
13	10	If I Could Turn Back Time	Cher	Geffen	7	(3)	
14	19	The Road To Hell (Pt. 2)	Chris Rea	WEA	5		
15	-	Infinite Dreams	Iron Maiden	EMI	2		
16	1	Ride On Time	Black Box	De Construction	14		F
17	-	I Want That Man	Deborah Harry	Chrysalis	4		L
18	-	Never Too Much (89 Remix)	Luther Vandross	Epic	3	(33)	
19	-	C'mon And Get My Love	D. Mob Featuring Cathy Dennis	Ffrr	4	(10)	
20	3	If Only I Could	Sydney Youngblood	Circa	9		F

December 1989

This Mnth	Prev Mnth	Title	Artist	Label	Wks 20	(US Pos)	
1	11	Don't Know Much	Linda Ronstadt (featuring Aaron Neville)	Elektra	7	(2)	L
2	9	You Got It (The Right Stuff)	New Kids On The Block	CBS	8	(3)	F
3	-	Lambada	Kaoma	CBS	9	(46)	F L
4	-	When You Come Back To Me	Jason Donovan	PWL	8		
5	-	Get A Life	Soul II Soul	10	8	(54)	
6	-	Eve Of The War	Jeff Wayne	CBS	6		F L
7	-	Let's Party	Jive Bunny & The Mastermixers	Music Factory	5		
8	-	I Don't Wanna Lose You	Tina Turner	Capitol	5	(9)	
9	-	Donald Where's Your Troosers	Andy Stewart	Stone	5	(77)	F L
10	-	Dear Jessie	Madonna	Sire	6		
11	-	Do They Know It's Christmas?	Band Aid II	PWL/Polydor	4		F L
12	-	Homely Girl	UB40	Dep International	4		
13	-	Can't Shake The Feeling	Big Fun	Jive	5		
14	-	Got To Get	Rob 'n' Raz Featuring Leila K	Arista	9		F L
15	1	All Around The World	Lisa Stansfield	Arista	7	(3)	
16	-	Fool's Gold/What The World Is Waiting For	Stone Roses	Silvertone	4		F
17	5	Another Day In Paradise	Phil Collins	Virgin	5	(1)	
18	-	In Private	Dusty Springfield	Parlophone	4		L
19	-	Sister	Bros	CBS	3		
20	-	Pacific	808 State	ZTT	4		F

US 1989 OCT-DEC

October 1989

This Mnth	Prev Mnth	Title	Artist	Label	Wks 20	(UK Pos)	
1	13	Miss You Much	Janet Jackson	A&M	10	(22)	G
2	-	Sowing The Seeds Of Love	Tears For Fears	Fontana	8	(5)	L
3	19	Love Song	Cure	Elektra	6	(18)	F
4	-	Listen To Your Heart	Roxette	EMI	8	(6)	
5	-	Bust A Move	Young M.C.	Delicious Vinyl	11	(73)	F G L
6	-	Mixed Emotions	Rolling Stones	Columbia	6	(36)	L
7	-	It's No Crime	Babyface	Solar	6		F
8	9	Cherish	Madonna	Sire	8	(3)	
9	-	Love In An Elevator	Aerosmith	Geffen	6	(13)	
10	2	Girl I'm Gonna Miss You	Milli Vanilli	Arista	9	(2)	
11	-	Cover Girl	New Kids On The Block	Columbia	7	(4)	
12	-	Dr. Feelgood	Motley Crue	Elektra	6	(50)	
13	1	Heaven	Warrant	Columbia	9		F
14	-	When I Looked At Him	Expose	Arista	5		
15	4	If I Could Turn Back Time	Cher	Geffen	9	(6)	
16	-	Rock Wit'cha	Bobby Brown	MCA	7	(33)	
17	-	When I See You Smile	Bad English	Epic	8	(61)	F
18	-	Healing Hands	Elton John	MCA	4	(1)	
19	7	18 And Life	Skid Row	Atlantic	9	(12)	F
20	-	It's Not Enough	Starship	RCA	5		L

November 1989

This Mnth	Prev Mnth	Title	Artist	Label	Wks 20	(UK Pos)	
1	17	When I See You Smile	Bad English	Epic	8	(61)	F
2	-	Blame It On The Rain	Milli Vanilli	Arista	10	(53)	G
3	4	Listen To Your Heart	Roxette	EMI	8	(6)	
4	-	Love Shack	B-52's	Reprise	8	(2)	F
5	-	(It's Just) The Way You Love Me	Paula Abdul	Virgin	8	(74)	
6	11	Cover Girl	New Kids On The Block	Columbia	7	(4)	
7	-	Angelia	Richard Marx	EMI	7	(45)	
8	1	Miss You Much	Janet Jackson	A&M	10	(22)	G
9	-	We Didn't Start The Fire	Billy Joel	Columbia	10	(7)	
10	-	Poison	Alice Cooper	Epic	6	(2)	L
11	2	Sowing The Seeds Of Love	Tears For Fears	Fontana	8	(5)	L
12	-	Didn't I (Blow Your Mind)	New Kids On The Block	Columbia	6	(8)	
13	-	Back To Life	Soul II Soul Feat. Caron Wheeler	Virgin	11	(1)	G L
14	16	Rock Wit'cha	Bobby Brown	MCA	7	(33)	
15	5	Bust A Move	Young M.C.	Delicious Vinyl	11	(73)	F G L
16	9	Love In An Elevator	Aerosmith	Geffen	6	(13)	
17	-	Don't Know Much	Linda Ronstadt (featuring Aaron Neville)	Elektra	11	(2)	
18	-	Get On Your Feet	Gloria Estefan	Epic	4	(23)	
19	-	Don't Close You Eyes	Kix	Atlantic	6		F L
20	12	Dr. Feelgood	Motley Crue	Elektra	6	(50)	

December 1989

This Mnth	Prev Mnth	Title	Artist	Label	Wks 20	(UK Pos)	
1	9	We Didn't Start The Fire	Billy Joel	Columbia	10	(7)	
2	-	Another Day In Paradise	Phil Collins	Atlantic	10	(2)	
3	17	Don't Know Much	Linda Ronstadt (feat uring Aaron Neville)	Elektra	11	(2)	
4	13	Back To Life	Soul II Soul Feat. Caron Wheeler	Virgin	11	(1)	G L
5	-	With Every Beat Of My Heart	Taylor Dayne	Arista	9	(53)	
6	2	Blame It On The Rain	Milli Vanilli	Arista	10	(53)	G
7	-	Rhythm Nation	Janet Jackson	A&M	9	(23)	
8	-	Pump Up The Jam	Technotronic Featuring Felly	SBK	12	(2)	F G
9	-	Living In Sin	Bon Jovi	Mercury	7	(35)	
10	5	(It's Just) The Way You Love Me	Paula Abdul	Virgin	8	(74)	
11	-	Just Like Jesse James	Cher	Geffen	8	(11)	
12	7	Angelia	Richard Marx	EMI	7	(45)	
13	4	Love Shack	B-52's	Reprise	8	(2)	F
14	-	This One's For The Children	New Kids On The Block	Columbia	6	(9)	
15	19	Don't Close You Eyes	Kix	Atlantic	6		F L
16	-	Everything	Jody Watley	MCA	10	(74)	
17	-	How Am I Supposed To Live Without You	Michael Bolton	Columbia	10	(3)	
18	-	Leave A Light On	Belinda Carlisle	MCA	5	(4)	L
19	1	When I See You Smile	Bad English	Epic	8	(61)	F
20	10	Poison	Alice Cooper	Epic	6	(2)	L

◆ The year's singles sales decreased 35% and vinyl LPs dropped 59%. However, CD sales rose 24%, cassette singles increased by 240%, and total sales increased to $6.46 billion. In Britain, CDs now outsold vinyl.

◆ In the last year of the decade: Dick Clark left *American Bandstand*, relatively few British artists scored Stateside, Michael Jackson's *Bad* tour (seen by 4.4 million in 15 countries) grossed $125 million, and The Rolling Stones and The Who were America's top live attractions. The decade ended with an updating of 'Do They Know It's Christmas' by Band Aid II (current UK stars) at No. 1 in Britain.

◆ Janet Jackson and her ex-choreographer, Paula Abdul, topped the album chart. Jackson with **Rhythm Nation 1814,** crammed full of future Top 5 hits, and Abdul's **Forever Your Girl** which became the first debut LP to include four No. 1s.

90s

Above: *PM Dawn*

Jade

Snow

The first four years of the 1990s have surely laid the foundations for another interesting and certainly unpredictable musical decade. There can be little doubt that it will be the most revolutionary yet, at least as far as musical technology is concerned.

Many music industry people are convinced that, given time, the MiniDisc, the Digital Compact Cassette, CD-I, CD-Rom and CD Video will become top selling carriers of recorded music and record-related information. Equally exciting is the thought that interactive cable networks and digital music channels are just around the corner. These will make high quality digital music of all kinds available to everyone at the push of a button.

Hammer

Who, back in the days of the breakable ten inch 78 rpm single, could have foreseen these changes?

Over the last four decades, sales figures for records have spiralled upwards. In the mid-1950s, an album that sold 250,000 copies was considered very successful, whereas in 1993, world-wide sales of 10 million are not unusual. To launch a new artist in the 1950s was relatively inexpensive. Today, costs are so prohibitive that only major companies can regularly play the game; however, the rewards can more than compensate for the risk.

Rock music itself has, of course, changed drastically since the early days, its evolution taking it in many varied directions, with each of these sub-genres either evolving in their own right or simply evaporating as interest in them waned. The musical children of rock'n'roll do not all bear a striking resemblance to their revolutionary parent. The term rock music now covers a multitude of styles, appealing to an audience wider than ever.

It is interesting to note that not all the stars of the 1950s are well and truly off the scene. In 1993, Tony Bennett, Rosemary Clooney, Little Richard, Etta James and Chet Atkins were all nominated for Grammy Awards and Frank Sinatra narrowly missed the top of the transatlantic album chart. In Britain, that same year also saw the late Buddy Holly top the album chart and Cliff Richard continue his unprecedented string of hits.

REM

Sinead O'Connor

Top Singles Artists In The US 1990-93		
1 **Mariah Carey**	(US)	Columbia
2 **Janet Jackson**	(US)	Virgin
3 **Madonna**	(US)	Sire/Maverick
4 **Whitney Houston**	(US)	Arista
5 **Michael Bolton**	(US)	Columbia
6 **Boyz II Men**	(US)	Motown
7 **Paula Abdul**	(US)	Virgin/Captive
8 **Wilson Phillips**	(US)	SBK
9 **Bryan Adams**	(Can)	A&M
10 **Color Me Badd**	(US)	Giant
11 **Michael Jackson**	(US)	Epic
12 **Roxette**	(Swe)	EMI
13 **Rod Stewart**	(UK)	Warner
14 **Hammer**	(US)	Capitol
15 **En Vogue**	(US)	Atco East West
16 **Amy Grant**	(US)	A&M
17 **Prince**	(US)	Paisley Park
18 **George Michael**	(UK)	Columbia
19 **Bobby Brown**	(US)	MCA
20 **SWV**	(US)	RCA

Top Singles Artists In The UK 1990-93		
1 **Madonna**	(US)	Sire/Maverick
2 **Kylie Minogue**	(Aus)	PWL
3 **Take That**	(UK)	RCA
4 **New Kids On The Block**	(US)	CBS
5 **Snap**	(US/Ger)	Arista
6 **2 Unlimited**	(Neth)	PWL Continental
7 **Michael Jackson**	(US)	Epic
8 **Erasure**	(UK)	Mute
9 **Guns N' Roses**	(US)	Geffen
10 **Whitney Houston**	(US)	Arista
11 **KLF**	(UK)	KLF Communications
12 **Shamen**	(UK)	One Little Indian
13 **Roxette**	(Swe)	EMI
14 **Rod Stewart**	(UK)	Warner
15 **Pet Shop Boys**	(UK)	Parlophone
16 **Queen**	(UK)	Parlophone
17 **Prince**	(US)	Paisley Park
18 **Bryan Adams**	(Can)	A&M
19 **Cliff Richard**	(UK)	EMI
20 **Hammer**	(US)	Capitol

UK 1990

JAN-MAR

◆ Ruby Turner became the first female British singer to top the US black music chart. A month later Lisa Stansfield followed in her footsteps.

◆ Veteran rock acts on successful world tours included Paul McCart-ney and David Bowie, whose **Changesbowie** was a UK No. 1.

▲ Phil Collins' **...But Seriously** sold a million in Britain in a record five weeks, topping the charts for 15 weeks. Oddly, for a week in February, Collins' 'I Wish It Would Rain Down' was the only male vocal record in the UK Top 10!

January 1990

This Mnth	Prev Mnth	Title	Artist	Label	Wks 20	(US Pos)	
1	-	Hangin' Tough	New Kids On The Block	CBS	6	(1)	
2	5	Get A Life	Soul II Soul	10	8	(54)	
3	4	When You Come Back To Me	Jason Donovan	PWL	8		
4	-	Touch Me	49ers	4th & Broadway	7		F
5	14	Got To Get	Rob 'n' Raz Featuring Leila K	Arista	9		F L
6	-	Got To Have Your Love	Mantronix Featuring Wondress	Capitol	7	(82)	F
7	-	Tears On My Pillow	Kylie Minogue	PWL	6		
8	-	The Magic Number/Buddy	De La Soul	Big Life	5		
9	11	Do They Know It's Christmas?	Band Aid II	PWL/Polydor	4		F L
10	10	Dear Jessie	Madonna	Sire	6		
11	3	Lambada	Kaoma	CBS	9	(46)	F L
12	-	Put Your Hands Together	D. Mob Featuring Nuff Juice	London	4		L
13	-	You Make Me Feel (Mighty Real)	Jimmy Somerville	London	4	(87)	
14	-	Going Back To My Roots/Rich In Paradise	FPI Project	Rumour	4		F L
15	-	Deep Heat '89	Latino Rave	Deep Heat	6		F L
16	-	Could Have Told You So	Halo James	Epic	5		F L
17	7	Let's Party	Jive Bunny & The Mastermixers	Music Factory	5		
18	-	Listen To Your Heart	Sonia	Chrysalis	3		
19	-	Nothing Compares 2 U	Sinead O'Connor	Ensign	10	(1)	F L
20	9	Donald Where's Your Troosers	Andy Stewart	Stone	5	(77)	F L

February 1990

This Mnth	Prev Mnth	Title	Artist	Label	Wks 20	(US Pos)	
1	19	Nothing Compares 2 U	Sinead O'Connor	Ensign	10	(1)	F L
2	-	Get Up (Before The Night Is Over)	Technotronic Feat. Ya Kid K	Swanyard	7	(7)	
3	-	Happenin' All Over Again	Lonnie Gordon	Supreme	6		F L
4	7	Tears On My Pillow	Kylie Minogue	PWL	6		
5	6	Got To Have Your Love	Mantronix Featuring Wondress	Capitol	7	(82)	F
6	-	I Wish It Would Rain Down	Phil Collins	Virgin	5	(3)	
7	-	Dub Be Good To Me	Beats International Featuring Lindy Layton	Go Beat	10	(76)	F
8	4	Touch Me	49ers	4th & Broadway	7		F
9	-	Walk On By	Sybil	PWL	5	(74)	
10	-	Instant Replay	Yell!	Fanfare	4		F L
11	-	I Don't Know Anybody Else	Black Box	Deconstruction	5	(23)	
12	16	Could Have Told You So	Halo James	Epic	5		F L
13	-	Live Together	Lisa Stansfield	Arista	3		
14	-	Nothing Ever Happens	Del Amitri	A&M	4		F
15	1	Hangin' Tough	New Kids On The Block	CBS	6	(1)	
16	-	Enjoy The Silence	Depeche Mode	Mute	6	(8)	
17	-	Just Like Jesse James	Cher	Geffen	4	(8)	
18	13	You Make Me Feel (Mighty Real)	Jimmy Somerville	London	4	(87)	
19	-	18 And Life	Skid Row	Atlantic	2	(4)	F
20	-	How Am I Supposed To Live Without You	Michael Bolton	CBS	6	(1)	F

March 1990

This Mnth	Prev Mnth	Title	Artist	Label	Wks 20	(US Pos)	
1	7	Dub Be Good To Me	Beats International/Lindy Layton	Go Beat	10	(76)	F
2	20	How Am I Supposed To Live...	Michael Bolton	CBS	6	(1)	F
3	-	The Brits 1990	Various Artists	RCA	5		F L
4	-	Infinity	Guru Josh	Deconstruction	5		F L
5	-	Love Shack	B-52's	Reprise	8	(3)	
6	1	Nothing Compares 2 U	Sinead O'Connor	Ensign	10	(1)	F L
7	-	Blue Savannah	Erasure	Mute	7		
8	-	That Sounds Good To Me	Jive Bunny & The Mastermixers	Music Factory	3		
9	-	Moments In Soul	Jt And The Big Family	Champion	4		F L
10	-	Lily Was Here	David A. Stewart Featuring Candy Dulfer	Anxious	7	(11)	F L
11	-	I'll Be Loving You (Forever)	New Kids On The Block	CBS	4	(1)	
12	16	Enjoy The Silence	Depeche Mode	Mute	6	(8)	
13	11	I Don't Know Anybody Else	Black Box	Deconstruction	5	(23)	
14	-	Strawberry Fields Forever	Candy Flip	Debut	7		F L
15	2	Get Up (Before The Night Is Over)	Technotronic Feat. Ya Kid K	Swanyard	7	(7)	
16	-	The Power	Snap	Arista	10	(2)	F
17	-	Elephant Stone	Stone Roses	Silvertone	2		
18	-	Downtown Train	Rod Stewart	Warner	4	(3)	
19	-	Black Betty	Ram Jam	Epic	3		L
20	-	Birdhouse In Your Soul	They Might Be Giants	Elektra	6		F L

January 1990

This Mnth	Prev Mnth	Title	Artist	Label	Wks 20	(UK Pos)	
1	8	Pump Up The Jam	Technotronic Featuring Felly	SBK	12	(2)	F G
2	17	How Am I Supposed To Live Without You	Michael Bolton	Columbia	10	(3)	
3	2	Another Day In Paradise	Phil Collins	Atlantic	10	(2)	
4	16	Everything	Jody Watley	MCA	10	(74)	
5	7	Rhythm Nation	Janet Jackson	A&M	9	(23)	
6	-	Downtown Train	Rod Stewart	Warner	10	(10)	
7	-	Just Between You And Me	Lou Gramm	Atlantic	7		L
8	-	Free Fallin'	Tom Petty	MCA	8	(64)	L
9	3	Don't Know Much	Linda Ronstadt (Featuring Aaron Neville)	Elektra	11	(2)	
10	-	Two To Make It Right	Seduction	Vendetta	11		F
11	-	Love Song	Tesla	Geffen	9		F
12	14	This One's For The Children	New Kids On The Block	Columbia	6	(9)	
13	5	With Every Beat Of My Heart	Taylor Dayne	Arista	9	(53)	
14	11	Just Like Jesse James	Cher	Geffen	8	(11)	
15	-	Swing The Mood	Jive Bunny & The Mastermixers	Atco	6	(1)	F L
16	-	When The Night Comes	Joe Cocker	Capitol	6	(65)	L
17	-	I Remember You	Skid Row	Atlantic	6	(36)	L
18	-	Opposites Attract	Paula Abdul (duet with The Wild Pair)	Virgin	9	(2)	
19	-	Janie's Got A Gun	Aerosmith	Geffen	7		
20	1	We Didn't Start The Fire	Billy Joel	Columbia	10	(7)	

February 1990

This Mnth	Prev Mnth	Title	Artist	Label	Wks 20	(UK Pos)	
1	18	Opposites Attract	Paula Abdul (with The Wild Pair)	Virgin	9	(2)	
2	10	Two To Make It Right	Seduction	Vendetta	11		F
3	-	Dangerous	Roxette	EMI	8	(6)	
4	19	Janie's Got A Gun	Aerosmith	Geffen	7		
5	-	What Kind Of Man Would I Be?	Chicago	Reprise	6		L
6	-	Escapade	Janet Jackson	A&M	10	(17)	
7	6	Downtown Train	Rod Stewart	Warner	10	(10)	
8	-	All Or Nothing	Milli Vanilli	Arista	6	(74)	L
9	2	How Am I Supposed To Live Without You	Michael Bolton	Columbia	10	(3)	
10	-	We Can't Go Wrong	Cover Girls	Capitol	6		F
11	17	I Remember You	Skid Row	Atlantic	6	(36)	L
12	-	Here We Are	Gloria Estefan	Epic	6	(23)	
13	-	Roam	B-52's	Reprise	9	(17)	L
14	-	Tell Me Why	Expose	Arista	5		
15	-	Price Of Love	Bad English	Epic	7		L
16	8	Free Fallin'	Tom Petty	MCA	8	(64)	L
17	-	Peace In Our Time	Eddie Money	Columbia	4		L
18	-	No More Lies	Michel'le	Ruthless	7		F L
19	1	Pump Up The Jam	Technotronic Featuring Felly	SBK	12	(2)	F G
20	4	Everything	Jody Watley	MCA	10	(74)	

March 1990

This Mnth	Prev Mnth	Title	Artist	Label	Wks 20	(UK Pos)	
1	6	Escapade	Janet Jackson	A&M	10	(17)	
2	-	Black Velvet	Alannah Myles	Atlantic	10	(2)	F L
3	13	Roam	B-52's	Reprise	9	(17)	L
4	-	Love Will Lead You Back	Taylor Dayne	Arista	9	(69)	
5	-	I Wish It Would Rain Down	Phil Collins	Atlantic	8	(7)	
6	-	I Go To Extremes	Billy Joel	Columbia	7	(70)	L
7	3	Dangerous	Roxette	EMI	8	(6)	
8	15	Price Of Love	Bad English	Epic	7		L
9	18	No More Lies	Michel'le	Ruthless	7		F L
10	-	All Around The World	Lisa Stansfield	Arista	10	(1)	F G
11	-	C'mon And Get My Love	D. Mob	Ffrr	7	(15)	F L
12	-	I'll Be Your Everything	Tommy Page	Sire	7	(53)	F L
13	1	Opposites Attract	Paula Abdul (with The Wild Pair)	Virgin	9	(2)	
14	-	Keep It Together	Madonna	Sire	5		
15	-	Just A Friend	Biz Markie	Cold Chillin'	5	(55)	F G L
16	-	Get Up! (Before The Night Is Over)	Technotronic	SBK	7	(2)	
17	12	Here We Are	Gloria Estefan	Epic	6	(23)	
18	-	Too Late To Say Goodbye	Richard Marx	EMI	5	(38)	
19	-	Don't Wanna Fall In Love	Jane Child	Warner	9	(22)	F L
20	-	No Myth	Michael Penn	RCA	5		F L

◆ New Kids On The Block's **Hangin' Tough** became the first music video to sell a million copies. The title song also gave them a Transatlantic No. 1. NKOTB, whose merchandise was flooding the States, were also winners at the American Music Awards alongside Paula Abdul (who also grabbed a handful of *Rolling Stone* awards) and Bobby Brown.

◆ Michael Jackson received an award for selling over 110 million records in the 1980s, and Gloria Estefan was presented with a Golden Globe for sales of over five million albums outside the United States.

◆ For the first time three girl groups were simultaneously situated in the Top 10, The Cover Girls, Seduction and Expose. The latter, also equalled a 23-year-old record set by The Supremes by scoring their seventh Top 10 single in two years.

◆ Top Americans appearing successfully in Britain included Anita Baker, Bobby Brown, Heart, Billy Joel, Metallica, New Kids On The Block and Prince.

◆ Stars at a Wembley show, celebrating the release from a South African prison of Nelson Mandela, included Tracy Chapman, Peter Gabriel, Patti Labelle, Simple Minds and Neil Young. An all-star John Lennon tribute show in Liverpool featured Natalie Cole, Terence Trent D'Arby, Roberta Flack, Hall & Oates, Cyndi Lauper, Kylie Minogue and Wet Wet Wet. Headliners at a huge charity show at Knebworth included Phil Collins, Paul McCartney, Pink Floyd and Status Quo.

◆ Between February and April, Iron Maiden had 10 different twin pack twelve inch records enter the album Top 20. They were re-issues of their earlier singles and were ineligible for the singles chart.

April 1990

This Mnth	Prev Mnth	Title	Artist	Label	Wks 20	(US Pos)	
1	-	Vogue	Madonna	Sire	10	(1)	
2	16	The Power	Snap	Arista	10	(2)	F
3	-	Black Velvet	Alannah Myles	Atlantic	8	(1)	F L
4	-	Kingston Town	UB40	Dep International	8		
5	-	Don't Miss The Partyline	Bizz Nizz	Cooltempo	5		F L
6	5	Love Shack	B-52's	Reprise	8	(3)	
7	-	Step On	Happy Mondays	Factory	7	(57)	
8	-	Hang On To Your Love	Jason Donovan	PWL	4		
9	-	All I Wanna Do Is Make Love To You	Heart	Capitol	8	(2)	L
10	14	Strawberry Fields Forever	Candy Flip	Debut	7		F L
11	20	Birdhouse In Your Soul	They Might Be Giants	Elektra	6		F L
12	-	Opposites Attract	Paula Abdul (with The Wild Pair)	Siren	9	(1)	
13	-	Ghetto Heaven	Family Stand	Atlantic	8		F L
14	10	Lily Was Here	David A. Stewart/Candy Dulfer	Anxious	7	(11)	F L
15	7	Blue Savannah	Erasure	Mute	7		
16	-	This Beat Is Technotronic	Technotronic Feat. MC Eric	Swanyard	3		
17	-	Killer	Adamski	MCA	13		
18	-	Mamma Gave Birth To The Soul Children	Queen Latifah & De La Soul	Tommy Boy	4		F L
19	1	Dub Be Good To Me	Beats International/Lindy Layton	Go Beat	10	(76)	F
20	-	Everybody Needs Somebody To Love	Blues Brothers	Atlantic	3		F L

May 1990

This Mnth	Prev Mnth	Title	Artist	Label	Wks 20	(US Pos)	
1	17	Killer	Adamski	MCA	13		
2	-	Dirty Cash	Adventures Of Stevie V	Mercury	9	(25)	F L
3	12	Opposites Attract	Paula Abdul (with The Wild Pair)	Siren	9	(1)	
4	1	Vogue	Madonna	Sire	10	(1)	
5	-	Better The Devil You Know	Kylie Minogue	PWL	6		
6	3	Black Velvet	Alannah Myles	Atlantic	8	(1)	F L
7	-	Cover Girl	New Kids On The Block	CBS	5	(2)	
8	-	A Dream's A Dream	Soul II Soul	Virgin	4	(85)	
9	4	Kingston Town	UB40	Dep International	8		
10	-	Hold On	En Vogue	Atlantic	6	(2)	F L
11	2	The Power	Snap	Arista	10	(2)	F
12	9	All I Wanna Do Is Make Love To You	Heart	Capitol	8	(2)	L
13	-	Won't Talk About It	Beats International	Go Beat	5	(76)	L
14	13	Ghetto Heaven	Family Stand	Atlantic	8		F L
15	-	Take Your Time	Mantronix Featuring Wondress	Capitol	4		L
16	7	Step On	Happy Mondays	Factory	7	(57)	
17	-	I Still Haven't Found What I'm Looking For	Chimes	CBS	5		F L
18	-	How Can We Be Lovers	Michael Bolton	CBS	4	(3)	
19	-	November Spawned A Monster	Morrissey	HMV	2		
20	-	Something Happened On The Way To Heaven	Phil Collins	Virgin	3	(4)	L

June 1990

This Mnth	Prev Mnth	Title	Artist	Label	Wks 20	(US Pos)	
1	-	World In Motion	Englandneworder	Factory	9		L
2	1	Killer	Adamski	MCA	13		
3	-	Hear The Drummer (Get Wicked)	Chad Jackson	Big Wave	6		F L
4	-	Doin' The Doo	Betty Boo	Rhythm King	7		F
5	-	Sacrifice/Healing Hands	Elton John	Rocket	10	(18)	
6	-	Venus	Don Pablo's Animals	Rumour	6		F L
7	-	It Must Have Been Love	Roxette	EMI	9	(1)	
8	2	Dirty Cash	Adventures Of Stevie V	Mercury	9	(25)	F L
9	-	Step By Step	New Kids On The Block	CBS	3	(1)	
10	-	The Only One I Know	Charlatans	Situation Two	5		F
11	5	Better The Devil You Know	Kylie Minogue	PWL	6		
12	-	Oops Up	Snap	Arista	8	(35)	
13	-	Hold On	Wilson Phillips	SBK	7	(1)	F
14	-	Nessun Dorma	Luciano Pavarotti	Decca	6		F
15	10	Hold On	En Vogue	Atlantic	6	(2)	F L
16	17	I Still Haven't Found What I'm...	Chimes	CBS	5		F L
17	-	Star	Erasure	Mute	4		
18	-	The Only Rhyme That Bites	MC Tunes Versus 808 State	ZTT	6		F
19	-	Papa Was A Rolling Stone	Was (Not Was)	Fontana	3		
20	7	Cover Girl	New Kids On The Block	CBS	5	(2)	

April 1990

This Mnth	Prev Mnth	Title	Artist	Label	Wks 20	(UK Pos)	
1	19	Don't Wanna Fall In Love	Jane Child	Warner	9	(22)	F L
2	10	All Around The World	Lisa Stansfield	Arista	10	(1)	F G
3	-	Nothing Compares 2 U	Sinead O'Connor	Chrysalis	12	(1)	F G L
4	12	I'll Be Your Everything	Tommy Page	Sire	7	(53)	F L
5	-	I Wanna Be Rich	Calloway	Solar	10		F L
6	-	Here And Now	Luther Vandross	Epic	7	(43)	
7	4	Love Will Lead You Back	Taylor Dayne	Arista	9	(69)	
8	-	How Can We Be Lovers	Michael Bolton	Columbia	8	(10)	
9	-	Whole Wide World	A'me Lorain	RCA	6		F L
10	-	Forever	Kiss	Mercury	6	(65)	L
11	-	Without You	Motley Crue	Elektra	6	(39)	
12	2	Black Velvet	Alannah Myles	Atlantic	10	(2)	F L
13	-	Whip Appeal	Babyface	Solar	6		L
14	16	Get Up! (Before The Night Is Over)	Technotronic	SBK	7	(2)	
15	5	I Wish It Would Rain Down	Phil Collins	Atlantic	8	(7)	
16	-	What It Takes	Aerosmith	Geffen	7		
17	-	Heartbeat	Seduction	Vendetta	5	(75)	
18	-	All I Wanna Do Is Make Love To You	Heart	Capitol	10	(8)	
19	-	All My Life	Linda Ronstadt (Featuring Aaron Neville)	Elektra	4		L
20	-	Sending All My Love	Linear	Atlantic	11		F L

May 1990

This Mnth	Prev Mnth	Title	Artist	Label	Wks 20	(UK Pos)	
1	3	Nothing Compares 2 U	Sinead O'Connor	Chrysalis	12	(1)	F G L
2	-	Vogue	Madonna	Sire	11	(1)	G
3	18	All I Wanna Do Is Make Love To You	Heart	Capitol	10	(8)	
4	5	I Wanna Be Rich	Calloway	Solar	10		F L
5	-	Hold On	Wilson Phillips	SBK	13	(6)	F
6	-	Alright	Janet Jackson	A&M	9	(20)	
7	20	Sending All My Love	Linear	Atlantic	11		F L
8	8	How Can We Be Lovers	Michael Bolton	Columbia	8	(10)	
9	-	Poison	Bell Biv Devoe	MCA	12	(19)	F G
10	16	What It Takes	Aerosmith	Geffen	7		
11	-	This Old Heart Of Mine	Rod Stewart With Ronald Isley	Warner	6	(51)	
12	-	It Must Have Been Love	Roxette	EMI	12	(3)	
13	-	Love Child	Sweet Sensation	Atco	5		
14	1	Don't Wanna Fall In Love	Jane Child	Warner	9	(22)	F L
15	13	Whip Appeal	Babyface	Solar	6		L
16	2	All Around The World	Lisa Stansfield	Arista	10	(1)	F G
17	-	U Can't Touch This	M.C. Hammer	Capitol	9	(3)	F
18	-	The Humpty Dance	Digital Underground	Tommy Boy	8		F G L
19	-	Ooh La La (I Can't Get Over You)	Perfect Gentlemen	Columbia	4		F L
20	-	Room At The Top	Adam Ant	MCA	3	(13)	F L

June 1990

This Mnth	Prev Mnth	Title	Artist	Label	Wks 20	(UK Pos)	
1	12	It Must Have Been Love	Roxette	EMI	12	(3)	
2	5	Hold On	Wilson Phillips	SBK	13	(6)	F
3	9	Poison	Bell Biv Devoe	MCA	12	(19)	F G
4	2	Vogue	Madonna	Sire	11	(1)	G
5	-	Step By Step	New Kids On The Block	Columbia	9	(2)	G
6	3	All I Wanna Do Is Make Love To You	Heart	Capitol	10	(8)	
7	-	Ready Or Not	After 7	Virgin	9		F
8	17	U Can't Touch This	M.C. Hammer	Capitol	9	(3)	F
9	-	Do You Remember?	Phil Collins	Atlantic	7	(57)	
10	-	Hold On	En Vogue	Atlantic	12	(5)	F G
11	6	Alright	Janet Jackson	A&M	9	(20)	
12	7	Sending All My Love	Linear	Atlantic	11		F L
13	18	The Humpty Dance	Digital Underground	Tommy Boy	8		F G L
14	-	I'll Be Your Shelter	Taylor Dayne	Arista	7	(43)	
15	1	Nothing Compares 2 U	Sinead O'Connor	Chrysalis	12	(1)	F G L
16	-	She Ain't Worth It	Glenn Medeiros (Featuring Bobby Brown)	MCA	10	(12)	L
17	-	Children Of The Night	Richard Marx	EMI	4	(54)	
18	19	Ooh La La (I Can't Get Over You)	Perfect Gentlemen	Columbia	4		F L
19	-	Rub You The Right Way	Johnny Gill	Motown	10		F
20	-	Baby, It's Tonight	Jude Cole	Reprise	5		F L

US 1990

APR-JUNE

◆ Two different songs with the same title, 'Hold On', introduced the world to two of the early 1990's top acts, En Vogue and Wilson Phillips.

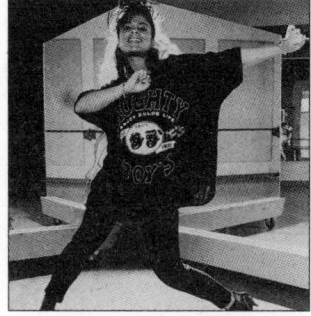

▲ Paula Abdul (above) broke Connie Francis' 28-year-old record when she clocked up 68 consecutive weeks in the US Top 40.

◆ Grammy and Brits winner Sinead O'Connor's 'Nothing Compares 2 U' and I **Do Not Want What I Haven't Got** topped the transatlantic single and album charts respectively – she was the first Irish female to reach the US No. 1 spot.

UK 1990

JULY-SEPT

▲ Pink Floyd's *The Wall* show in Berlin drew 200,000 people and an estimated one billion saw it on TV. Among those appearing were Bryan Adams, The Band, Van Morrison, Sinead O'Connor (above) and The Scorpions.

◆ Elton John's 'Sacrifice' not only helped him equal Elvis Presley's American record of (at least) one Top 40 hit a year for 21 years, it also gave him his first British solo chart topper, 'Sacrifice'/'Healing Hands'. Elton also scored his first No. 1 British album for 16 years with **Sleeping With The Past.**

July 1990

This Mnth	Prev Mnth	Title	Artist	Label	Wks 20	(US Pos)	
1	5	Sacrifice/Healing Hands	Elton John	Rocket	10	(18)	
2	-	Mona	Craig McLachlan & Check 1-2	Epic	8		F
3	7	It Must Have Been Love	Roxette	EMI	9	(1)	
4	14	Nessun Dorma	Luciano Pavarotti	Decca	6		F
5	-	U Can't Touch This	M.C. Hammer	Capitol	11	(8)	F
6	-	Thunderbirds Are Go	FAB Featuring MC Parker	Brothers Org.	5		F L
7	12	Oops Up	Snap	Arista	8	(35)	
8	1	World In Motion	Englandneworder	Factory	9		L
9	-	Close To You	Maxi Priest	10	6	(1)	
10	-	Turtle Power	Partners In Kryme	SBK	8	(13)	F L
11	-	One Love	Stone Roses	Silvertone	4		
12	13	Hold On	Wilson Phillips	SBK	7	(1)	F
13	-	She Ain't Worth It	Glenn Medeiros Featuring Bobby Brown	London	4	(1)	L
14	-	Hanky Panky	Madonna	Sire	6	(10)	
15	18	The Only Rhyme That Bites	MC Tunes Versus 808 State	ZTT	6		F
16	-	I'm Free	Soup Dragons	Raw TV/Big Life	8	(79)	F L
17	-	Rockin' Over The Beat	Technotronic Featuring Ya Kid K	Swanyard	5	(95)	
18	-	Naked In The Rain	Blue Pearl	W.A.U.!Mr.Modo	9		F
19	-	Thinking Of You	Maureen	Urban	4		F L
20	4	Doin' The Doo	Betty Boo	Rhythm King	7		F

August 1990

This Mnth	Prev Mnth	Title	Artist	Label	Wks 20	(US Pos)	
1	10	Turtle Power	Partners In Kryme	SBK	8	(13)	F L
2	-	Tom's Diner	DNA Featuring Suzanne Vega	A&M	7	(5)	F
3	18	Naked In The Rain	Blue Pearl	W.A.U.!Mr.Modo	9		F
4	5	U Can't Touch This	M.C. Hammer	Capitol	11	(8)	F
5	16	I'm Free	Soup Dragons	Raw TV/Big Life	8	(79)	F L
6	14	Hanky Panky	Madonna	Sire	6	(10)	
7	-	Tonight	New Kids On The Block	CBS	8	(7)	
8	-	Itsy Bitsy Teeny Weeny Yellow Polka Dot Bikini	Bombalurina	Carpet	8		F
9	1	Sacrifice/Healing Hands	Elton John	Rocket	10	(18)	
10	-	Thieves In The Temple	Prince	Paisley Park	3	(6)	
11	17	Rockin' Over The Beat	Technotronic Feat. Ya Kid K	Swanyard	5	(95)	
12	-	Listen To Your Heart/Dangerous	Roxette	EMI	5	(1)	
13	2	Mona	Craig McLachlan & Check 1-2	Epic	8		F
14	-	Hardcore Uproar	Together	Ffrr	4		F L
15	-	LFO	LFO	Warp	3		F L
16	-	Where Are You Baby?	Betty Boo	Rhythm King	6		
17	-	California Dreamin'/Carry The Blame	River City People	EMI	5		F L
18	-	Blaze Of Glory	Jon Bon Jovi	Vertigo	3	(1)	F L
19	3	It Must Have Been Love	Roxette	EMI	9	(1)	
20	-	Tricky Disco	Tricky Disco	Warp	3		F L

September 1990

This Mnth	Prev Mnth	Title	Artist	Label	Wks 20	(US Pos)	
1	-	The Joker	Steve Miller Band	Capitol	7		L
2	-	Groove Is In The Heart	Deee-Lite	Elektra	8	(4)	F L
3	-	Four Bacharach & David Songs (EP)	Deacon Blue	CBS	6		
4	8	Itsy Bitsy Teeny Weeny Yellow Polka Dot Bikini	Bombalurina	Carpet	8		F
5	-	What Time Is Love	KLF/Children Of The Revolution	KLF Comms.	7	(57)	F
6	16	Where Are You Baby?	Betty Boo	Rhythm King	6		
7	7	Tonight	New Kids On The Block	CBS	8	(7)	
8	-	Vision Of Love	Mariah Carey	CBS	5	(1)	F
9	-	The Space Jungle	Adamski	MCA	4		L
10	-	Show Me Heaven	Maria McKee	Epic	9		F L
11	-	Groovy Train	Farm	Produce	5	(41)	F
12	-	Praying For Time	George Michael	Epic	4	(1)	
13	-	Holy Smoke	Iron Maiden	EMI	2		
14	3	Naked In The Rain	Blue Pearl	W.A.U.!Mr.Modo	9		F
15	-	I've Been Thinking About You	Londonbeat	Anxious	7	(1)	L
16	12	Listen To Your Heart/Dangerous	Roxette	EMI	5	(1)	
17	-	Can Can You Party	Jive Bunny & The Mastermixers	Music Factory	3		
18	-	Rhythm Of The Rain	Jason Donovan	PWL	2		
19	2	Tom's Diner	DNA Featuring Suzanne Vega	A&M	7	(5)	F
20	-	Silhouettes	Cliff Richard	EMI	4		

July 1990

This Mnth	Prev Mnth	Title	Artist	Label	Wks 20	(UK Pos)	
1	16	She Ain't Worth It	Glenn Medeiros Featuring Bobby Brown	MCA	10	(12)	L
2	10	Hold On	En Vogue	Atlantic	12	(5)	F G
3	-	Cradle Of Love	Billy Idol	Chrysalis	11	(34)	L
4	5	Step By Step	New Kids On The Block	Columbia	9	(2)	G
5	19	Rub You The Right Way	Johnny Gill	Motown	10		F
6	-	The Power	Snap	Arista	10	(1)	F G
7	1	It Must Have Been Love	Roxette	EMI	12	(3)	
8	-	Enjoy The Silence	Depeche Mode	Sire	7	(6)	
9	-	Vision Of Love	Mariah Carey	Columbia	12	(9)	F
10	-	Girls Nite Out	Tyler Collins	RCA	7		F L
11	14	I'll Be Your Shelter	Taylor Dayne	Arista	7	(43)	
12	-	When I'm Back On My Feet Again	Michael Bolton	Columbia	6	(44)	
13	3	Poison	Bell Biv Devoe	MCA	12	(19)	F G
14	9	Do You Remember?	Phil Collins	Atlantic	7	(57)	
15	2	Hold On	Wilson Phillips	SBK	13	(6)	F
16	-	King Of Wishful Thinking	Go West	EMI	7	(18)	F
17	-	Mentirosa	Mellow Man Ace	Capitol	4		F L
18	-	You Can't Deny It	Lisa Stansfield	Arista	3		L
19	-	Hanky Panky	Madonna	Sire	3	(2)	
20	-	If Wishes Came True	Sweet Sensation	Atco	10		L

August 1990

This Mnth	Prev Mnth	Title	Artist	Label	Wks 20	(UK Pos)	
1	9	Vision Of Love	Mariah Carey	Columbia	12	(9)	F
2	20	If Wishes Came True	Sweet Sensation	Atco	10		L
3	-	Come Back To Me	Janet Jackson	A&M	8	(20)	
4	6	The Power	Snap	Arista	10	(1)	F G
5	-	Unskinny Bop	Poison	Enigma	10	(15)	
6	3	Cradle Of Love	Billy Idol	Chrysalis	11	(34)	L
7	-	Do Me	Bell Biv Devoe	MCA	11	(56)	L
8	5	Rub You The Right Way	Johnny Gill	Motown	10		F
9	-	Blaze Of Glory	Jon Bon Jovi	Mercury	10	(13)	F G
10	-	Have You Seen Her	M.C. Hammer	Capitol	9	(8)	
11	16	King Of Wishful Thinking	Go West	EMI	7	(18)	F
12	-	Jerk Out	Time	Paisley Park	6		L
13	1	She Ain't Worth It	Glenn Medeiros Featuring Bobby Brown	MCA	10	(12)	L
14	-	Epic	Faith No More	Slash	7	(25)	F L
15	-	Release Me	Wilson Phillips	SBK	10	(36)	
16	-	Could This Be Love	Seduction	A&M	5		L
17	-	Make You Sweat	Keith Sweat	Vintertainment	8		
18	10	Girls Nite Out	Tyler Collins	RCA	7		F L
19	12	When I'm Back On My Feet Again	Michael Bolton	Columbia	6	(44)	
20	2	Hold On	En Vogue	Atlantic	12	(5)	F G

September 1990

This Mnth	Prev Mnth	Title	Artist	Label	Wks 20	(UK Pos)	
1	15	Release Me	Wilson Phillips	SBK	10	(36)	
2	9	Blaze Of Glory	Jon Bon Jovi	Mercury	10	(13)	F G
3	7	Do Me	Bell Biv Devoe	MCA	11	(56)	L
4	-	(Can't Live Without Your) Love And Affection	Nelson	DGC	10	(54)	F
5	5	Unskinny Bop	Poison	Enigma	10	(15)	
6	10	Have You Seen Her	M.C. Hammer	Capitol	9	(8)	
7	-	Thieves In The Temple	Prince	Paisley Park	6	(7)	
8	-	Close To You	Maxi Priest	Charisma	11	(7)	F
9	2	If Wishes Came True	Sweet Sensation	Atco	10		L
10	-	Something Happened On The Way To Heaven	Phil Collins	Atlantic	7	(15)	L
11	-	Tonight	New Kids On The Block	Columbia	5	(3)	
12	3	Come Back To Me	Janet Jackson	A&M	8	(20)	
13	-	Praying For Time	George Michael	Columbia	8	(6)	
14	1	Vision Of Love	Mariah Carey	Columbia	12	(9)	F
15	-	Oh Girl	Paul Young	Columbia	6	(25)	L
16	14	Epic	Faith No More	Slash	7	(25)	F L
17	-	My, My, My	Johnny Gill	Motown	6		L
18	-	Can't Stop Falling Into Love	Cheap Trick	Epic	3		L
19	12	Jerk Out	Time	Paisley Park	6		L
20	-	Heart Of Stone	Taylor Dayne	Arista	4		

◆ M.C. Hammer's **Please Hammer Don't Hurt 'Em** topped the album chart for 21 weeks (spending a record 32 consecutive weeks in the Top 2), selling over 10 million copies.

◆ New Kids On The Block, who had three of the Top 4 US music videos, signed a $10 million sponsorship deal with McDonalds. Incidentally, in July, Maurice Starr, the group's producer/manager, had discovered three of the top four singles artists, the others being Bell Biv Devoe and Bobby Brown.

◆ Madonna chalked up her 20th US Top 10 single in six years – only Elvis and The Beatles could beat that.

◆ Guitar hero Stevie Ray Vaughan died in a helicopter crash and soul giant Curtis Mayfield was paralysed after a lighting rack fell on him during a show.

UK 1990 OCT-DEC

◆ Bobby Vinton's 1963 US chart topper, 'Blue Velvet', hit in Britain as Berlin's 'Take My Breath Away' returned. The Righteous Brothers' 'You've Lost That Lovin' Feeling' spent a record third time in the Top 10, and the duo's 25-year-old 'Unchained Melody' became the year's top seller.

◆ In October, for the first time since March 1986, there were no Stock Aitken & Waterman records in the Top 40. They had produced over 100 Top 75 entries.

◆ In the USA, New Kids On The Block had five albums charting simultaneously. In Britain their seven Top 10 singles in 1990 equalled Bill Haley & The Comets' 1956 record. NKOTB reportedly earned $115 million in 1990.

October 1990

This Mnth	Prev Mnth	Title	Artist	Label	Wks 20	(US Pos)	
1	10	Show Me Heaven	Maria McKee	Epic	9		F L
2	-	Blue Velvet	Bobby Vinton	Epic	8		L
3	-	The Anniversary Waltz - Part 1	Status Quo	Vertigo	6		
4	15	I've Been Thinking About You	Londonbeat	Anxious	7	(1)	L
5	-	I Can't Stand It	Twenty 4 Seven Featuring Captain Hollywood	BCM	6		F
6	-	Megamix	Technotronic	Swanyard	5		L
7	-	A Little Time	Beautiful South	Go! Discs	8		
8	-	So Hard	Pet Shop Boys	Parlophone	3	(62)	
9	-	Have You Seen Her	M.C. Hammer	Capitol	4	(4)	
10	-	Fascinating Rhythm	Bass-O-Matic	Virgin	5		F L
11	2	Groove Is In The Heart	Deee-Lite	Elektra	8	(4)	F L
12	1	The Joker	Steve Miller Band	Capitol	7		L
13	-	It's A Shame (My Sister)	Monie Love Feat. True Image	Cooltempo	4	(26)	
14	-	Let's Try Again/Didn't I Blow Your Mind	New Kids On The Block	CBS	3	(53)	
15	-	I'm Your Baby Tonight	Whitney Houston	Arista	6	(1)	
16	11	Groovy Train	Farm	Produce	5	(41)	F
17	-	Unchained Melody	Righteous Brothers	Verve	11	(13)	
18	-	Kinky Afro	Happy Mondays	Factory	4		
19	-	From A Distance	Cliff Richard	EMI	3		
20	-	Cult Of Snap	Snap	Arista	3		

November 1990

This Mnth	Prev Mnth	Title	Artist	Label	Wks 20	(US Pos)	
1	17	Unchained Melody	Righteous Brothers	Verve	11	(13)	
2	7	A Little Time	Beautiful South	Go! Discs	8		
3	-	Don't Worry	Kim Appleby	Parlophone	8		F
4	-	Take My Breath Away	Berlin	CBS	6		L
5	-	Step Back In Time	Kylie Minogue	PWL	4		
6	-	(We Want) The Same Thing	Belinda Carlisle	MCA	5		
7	-	Fog On The Tyne (Revisited)	Gazza And Lindisfarne	Best	4		F L
8	-	Fantasy	Black Box	De Construction	6		
9	15	I'm Your Baby Tonight	Whitney Houston	Arista	6	(1)	
10	-	I'll Be Your Baby Tonight	Robert Palmer And UB40	EMI	6		
11	1	Show Me Heaven	Maria McKee	Epic	9		F L
12	-	Unbelievable	EMF	Parlophone	8	(1)	F
13	-	To Love Somebody	Jimmy Somerville	London	4		L
14	-	Working Man	Rita McNeil	Polydor	4		F L
15	18	Kinky Afro	Happy Mondays	Factory	4		
16	-	Cubik/Olympic	808 State	ZTT	3		
17	-	Ice Ice Baby	Vanilla Ice	SBK	10	(1)	F
18	3	The Anniversary Waltz - Part 1	Status Quo	Vertigo	6		
19	-	Close To Me	Cure	Elektra	3	(97)	
20	2	Blue Velvet	Bobby Vinton	Epic	8		L

December 1990

This Mnth	Prev Mnth	Title	Artist	Label	Wks 20	(US Pos)	
1	17	Ice Ice Baby	Vanilla Ice	SBK	10	(1)	F
2	12	Unbelievable	EMF	Parlophone	8	(1)	F
3	1	Unchained Melody	Righteous Brothers	Verve	11	(13)	
4	-	Saviour's Day	Cliff Richard	EMI	6		
5	-	Justify My Love	Madonna	Sire	6	(1)	
6	-	All Together Now	Farm	Produce	8		
7	3	Don't Worry	Kim Appleby	Parlophone	8		F
8	-	You've Lost That Lovin' Feeling/Ebb Tide	Righteous Brothers	Verve	6		L
9	-	Kinky Boots	Patrick MacNee & Honor Blackman	Deram	4		F L
10	-	Wicked Game	Chris Isaak	London	5	(6)	F
11	-	Mary Had A Little Boy	Snap	Arista	6		
12	-	Pray	M.C. Hammer	Capitol	7	(2)	
13	-	Sadness Part 1	Enigma	Virgin Int.	9	(5)	L
14	-	It Takes Two	Rod Stewart & Tina Turner	Warner	4		
15	-	Falling	Julee Cruise	Warner	4		F L
16	-	This One's For The Children	New Kids On The Block	CBS	4	(7)	
17	8	Fantasy	Black Box	De Construction	6		
18	-	The Grease Megamix	John Travolta/O. Newton-John	Polydor	6		L
19	-	Just This Side Of Love	Malandra Burrows	YTV	4		F L
20	-	King Of The Road (EP)	Proclaimers	Chrysalis	3		L

October 1990

This Mnth	Prev Mnth	Title	Artist	Label	Wks 20	(UK Pos)	
1	-	I Don't Have The Heart	James Ingram	Warner	10		L
2	13	Praying For Time	George Michael	Columbia	8	(6)	
3	8	Close To You	Maxi Priest	Charisma	11	(7)	F
4	-	Ice Ice Baby	Vanilla Ice	SBK	11	(1)	F G
5	-	Black Cat	Janet Jackson	A&M	7	(15)	
6	4	(Can't Live Without Your) Love And Affection	Nelson	DGC	10	(54)	F
7	-	Romeo	Dino	Island	6		L
8	-	Giving You The Benefit	Pebbles	MCA	7	(73)	
9	-	Can't Stop	After 7	Virgin	8	(54)	
10	-	Everybody Everybody	Black Box	RCA	7	(16)	F
11	10	Something Happened On The Way To Heaven	Phil Collins	Atlantic	7	(15)	L
12	-	Suicide Blonde	INXS	Atlantic	5	(11)	
13	-	Love Takes Time	Mariah Carey	Columbia	14	(37)	
14	15	Oh Girl	Paul Young	Columbia	6	(25)	L
15	-	Unchained Melody	Righteous Brothers	Verve	6	(1)	G
16	2	Blaze Of Glory	Jon Bon Jovi	Mercury	10	(13)	F G
17	3	Do Me	Bell Biv Devoe	MCA	11	(56)	L
18	17	My, My, My	Johnny Gill	Motown	6		L
19	-	Pray	M.C. Hammer	Capitol	7	(8)	
20	1	Release Me	Wilson Phillips	SBK	10	(36)	

November 1990

This Mnth	Prev Mnth	Title	Artist	Label	Wks 20	(UK Pos)	
1	13	Love Takes Time	Mariah Carey	Columbia	14	(37)	
2	19	Pray	M.C. Hammer	Capitol	7	(8)	
3	-	More Than Words Can Say	Alias	EMI	8		F
4	4	Ice Ice Baby	Vanilla Ice	SBK	11	(1)	F G
5	-	Groove Is In The Heart	Deee-Lite	Elektra	10	(2)	F L
6	1	I Don't Have The Heart	James Ingram	Warner	10		L
7	-	I'm Your Baby Tonight	Whitney Houston	Arista	12	(5)	
8	-	Something To Believe In	Poison	Enigma	11	(35)	L
9	-	Knockin' Boots	Candyman	Epic	5		F G L
10	8	Giving You The Benefit	Pebbles	MCA	7	(73)	
11	5	Black Cat	Janet Jackson	A&M	7	(15)	
12	-	Feels Good	Tony! Toni! Tone!	Wing	9		F
13	-	Because I Love You (The Postman Song)	Stevie B	LMR	12	(6)	L
14	-	From A Distance	Bette Midler	Atlantic	12	(45)	G L
15	-	Cherry Pie	Warrant	Columbia	5	(35)	
16	9	Can't Stop	After 7	Virgin	8	(54)	
17	-	So Close	Daryl Hall John Oates	Arista	5	(69)	L
18	-	Hippychick	Soho	Atco	4	(8)	F L
19	12	Suicide Blonde	INXS	Atlantic	5	(11)	
20	3	Close To You	Maxi Priest	Charisma	11	(7)	F

December 1990

This Mnth	Prev Mnth	Title	Artist	Label	Wks 20	(UK Pos)	
1	13	Because I Love You (The Postman Song)	Stevie B	LMR	12	(6)	L
2	14	From A Distance	Bette Midler	Atlantic	12	(45)	G L
3	7	I'm Your Baby Tonight	Whitney Houston	Arista	12	(5)	
4	-	Impulsive	Wilson Phillips	SBK	10	(42)	
5	-	Tom's Diner	DNA Featuring Suzanne Vega	A&M	10	(2)	F L
6	-	Justify My Love	Madonna	Sire	10	(2)	G
7	-	The Way You Do The Things You Do	UB40	Virgin	10	(49)	
8	8	Something To Believe In	Poison	Enigma	11	(35)	L
9	1	Love Takes Time	Mariah Carey	Columbia	14	(37)	
10	-	High Enough	Damn Yankees	Warner	13		F
11	5	Groove Is In The Heart	Deee-Lite	Elektra	10	(2)	F L
12	-	Freedom	George Michael	Columbia	8	(28)	
13	-	Miracle	Jon Bon Jovi	Mercury	6	(29)	L
14	-	Sensitivity	Ralph Tresvant	MCA	11	(18)	F L
15	-	Love Will Never Do (Without You)	Janet Jackson	A&M	11	(34)	
16	12	Feels Good	Tony! Toni! Tone!	Wing	9		F
17	3	More Than Words Can Say	Alias	EMI	8		F
18	-	Stranded	Heart	Capitol	5	(60)	L
19	17	So Close	Daryl Hall John Oates	Arista	5	(69)	L
20	-	Wiggle It	2 In A Room	Cutting	5	(3)	F L

US
1990
OCT-DEC

◆ Record and tape sales in 1990 increased 14% with total shipments of $7.5 billion. Vinyl albums were down 60% and CD sales up 33%.

▲ The year ended with Vanilla Ice's (above) 'Ice Ice Baby' becoming rap's first No. 1, Taylor Dayne's run of seven successive Top 10 hits ending, and with Milli Vanilli, returning their Grammy Award after it was discovered that they had not sung on their hits.

◆ Matsushita bought MCA Records for $3 billion and CBS Records changed their name to Sony.

◆ *Billboard's* Hot Black Singles chart was renamed Hot R&B Singles.

323

UK 1991 JAN-MAR

◆ Another spate of re-entries hit the UK Top 20 including records by Bill Medley & Jennifer Warnes, The Clash, Madonna, John Travolta & Olivia Newton-John, Free, while Patsy Cline's 1961 American hit, 'Crazy' made its UK debut.

◆ Eric Clapton played a record 24 nights at London's prestigious Royal Albert Hall.

◆ Michael Jackson, whose **Bad** album had now passed the 25 million sales mark globally, signed the world's biggest record deal (reportedly worth somewhere between $50 million and a billion!) with Sony.

◆ George Michael and Andrew Ridgeley of Wham! briefly reunited on stage at *Rock In Rio II*. Among the other acts appearing at the big Brazilian festival were Prince, Guns N' Roses and Top UK band Happy Mondays.

January 1991

This Mnth	Prev Mnth	Title	Artist	Label	Wks 20	(US Pos)	
1	13	Sadness Part 1	Enigma	Virgin Int.	9	(5)	L
2	-	Crazy	Seal	ZTT	9	(8)	F
3	18	The Grease Megamix	John Travolta/O. Newton-John	Polydor	6		L
4	1	Ice Ice Baby	Vanilla Ice	SBK	10	(1)	F
5	-	Bring Your Daughter...To The Slaughter	Iron Maiden	EMI	3		
6	6	All Together Now	Farm	Produce	8		
7	-	Gonna Make You Sweat	C&C Music Factory/F. Williams	CBS	6	(1)	F
8	-	3 A.M. Eternal	KLF/Children Of The Revolution	KLF Comms.	8	(5)	
9	-	(I've Had) The Time Of My Life	Bill Medley & Jennifer Warnes	RCA	4		L
10	8	You've Lost That Lovin' Feeling	Righteous Brothers	Verve	6		L
11	12	Pray	M.C. Hammer	Capitol	7	(2)	
12	11	Mary Had A Little Boy	Snap	Arista	6		
13	-	International Bright Young Thing	Jesus Jones	Food	3		F L
14	-	I Can't Take The Power	Off-Shore	CBS	4		F L
15	5	Justify My Love	Madonna	Sire	6	(1)	L
16	-	Mercy Mercy Me - I Want You	Robert Palmer	EMI	4	(16)	L
17	-	Innuendo	Queen	Parlophone	3		
18	4	Saviour's Day	Cliff Richard	EMI	6		
19	-	The Total Mix	Black Box	De Construction	4		
20	-	All The Man That I Need	Whitney Houston	Arista	3	(1)	

February 1991

This Mnth	Prev Mnth	Title	Artist	Label	Wks 20	(US Pos)	
1	-	Do The Bartman	Simpsons	Geffen	10		F
2	8	3 A.M. Eternal	KLF/Children Of The Revolution	KLF Comms.	8	(5)	
3	-	Wiggle It	2 In A Room	Big Life	6	(15)	F L
4	-	(I Wanna Give You) Devotion	Nomad/MC Mikee Freedom	Rumour	8		F
5	-	What Do I Have To Do	Kylie Minogue	PWL	5		
6	-	Only You	Praise	Epic	5		F L
7	-	I Believe	EMF	Parlophone	4		
8	-	Hippychick	Soho	S&M/Savage	5	(14)	F L
9	-	Get Here	Oleta Adams	Fontana	7	(5)	F L
10	-	Cry For Help	Rick Astley	RCA	5	(7)	L
11	2	Crazy	Seal	ZTT	9	(8)	F
12	-	Play That Funky Music	Vanilla Ice	SBK	4	(4)	L
13	17	Innuendo	Queen	Parlophone	3		
14	1	Sadness Part 1	Enigma	Virgin Int.	9	(5)	L
15	-	You Got The Love	Source Featuring Candi Staton	Truelove	7		F L
16	-	G.L.A.D.	Kim Appleby	Parlophone	3		
17	7	Gonna Make You Sweat	C&C Music Factory/F. Williams	CBS	6	(1)	
18	-	In Yer Face	808 State	ZTT	4		
19	-	All Right Now	Free	Island	5		L
20	16	Mercy Mercy Me - I Want You	Robert Palmer	EMI	4	(16)	L

March 1991

This Mnth	Prev Mnth	Title	Artist	Label	Wks 20	(US Pos)	
1	-	Should I Stay Or Should I Go	Clash	CBS	6		
2	15	You Got The Love	Source Featuring Candi Staton	Truelove	7		F L
3	1	Do The Bartman	Simpsons	Geffen	10		F
4	-	The Stonk	Hale & Pace & The Stonkers	London	5		F L
5	-	Crazy For You	Madonna	Sire	4		
6	-	Because I Love You (Postman Song)	Stevie B	LMR	6	(1)	F L
7	-	Move Your Body (Elevation)	Xpansions	Optimism	5		F L
8	-	Joyride	Roxette	EMI	7	(1)	
9	4	(I Wanna Give You) Devotion	Nomad/MC Mikee Freedom	Rumour	8		F
10	-	The One And Only	Chesney Hawkes	Chrysalis	6	(10)	F L
11	-	It's Too Late	Quartz Introducing Dina Carroll	Mercury	6		F L
12	-	Rhythm Of My Heart	Rod Stewart	Warner	8		
13	19	All Right Now	Free	Island	5		L
14	9	Get Here	Oleta Adams	Fontana	7	(5)	F L
15	-	Where The Streets Have No Name-Can't Take My Eyes Off You/How Can You Expect To Be Taken Seriously	Pet Shop Boys	EMI	4	(72)	
16	-	Love Rears It's Ugly Head	Living Colour	Epic	5		F L
17	2	3 A.M. Eternal	KLF/Children Of The Revolution	KLF Comms.	8	(5)	
18	-	Let There Be Love	Simple Minds	Virgin	4		
19	18	In Yer Face	808 State	ZTT	4		
20	-	Secret Love	Bee Gees	Warner	5		

January 1991

This Mnth	Prev Mnth	Title	Artist	Label	Wks 20	(UK Pos)	
1	6	Justify My Love	Madonna	Sire	10	(2)	G
2	15	Love Will Never Do (Without You)	Janet Jackson	A&M	11	(34)	
3	10	High Enough	Damn Yankees	Warner	13		F
4	-	The First Time	Surface	Columbia	12	(60)	
5	14	Sensitivity	Ralph Tresvant	MCA	11	(18)	F L
6	1	Because I Love You (The Postman Song)	Stevie B	LMR	12	(6)	L
7	-	Gonna Make You Sweat	C&C Music Factory Featuring Freedom Williams	Columbia	11	(3)	F G
8	2	From A Distance	Bette Midler	Atlantic	12	(45)	G L
9	5	Tom's Diner	DNA Featuring Suzanne Vega	A&M	10	(2)	F L
10	-	Play That Funky Music	Vanilla Ice	SBK	8	(10)	L
11	-	After The Rain	Nelson	DGC	9		
12	4	Impulsive	Wilson Phillips	SBK	10	(42)	
13	-	I'm Not In Love	Will To Power	Epic	6	(29)	L
14	-	Miles Away	Winger	Atlantic	7	(56)	L
15	3	I'm Your Baby Tonight	Whitney Houston	Arista	12	(5)	
16	-	Just Another Dream	Cathy Dennis	Polydor	5	(13)	F
17	7	The Way You Do The Things You Do	UB40	Virgin	10	(49)	
18	-	I'll Give All My Love To You	Keith Sweat	Vintertainment	6		
19	12	Freedom	George Michael	Columbia	8	(28)	
20	-	All The Man That I Need	Whitney Houston	Arista	10	(13)	

February 1991

This Mnth	Prev Mnth	Title	Artist	Label	Wks 20	(UK Pos)	
1	7	Gonna Make You Sweat	C&C Music Factory Featuring Freedom Williams	Columbia	11	(3)	F G
2	4	The First Time	Surface	Columbia	12	(60)	
3	20	All The Man That I Need	Whitney Houston	Arista	10	(13)	
4	-	One More Try	Timmy T	Quality	12		F G L
5	-	Where Does My Heart Beat Now	Celine Dion	Epic	9	(73)	F
6	10	Play That Funky Music	Vanilla Ice	SBK	8	(10)	L
7	18	I'll Give All My Love To You	Keith Sweat	Vintertainment	6		
8	2	Love Will Never Do (Without You)	Janet Jackson	A&M	11	(34)	
9	-	Someday	Mariah Carey	Columbia	10	(38)	
10	-	Disappear	INXS	Atlantic	6	(21)	L
11	5	Sensitivity	Ralph Tresvant	MCA	11	(18)	F L
12	11	After The Rain	Nelson	DGC	9		
13	-	I Saw Red	Warrant	Columbia	6		L
14	-	Wicked Game	Chris Isaak	Reprise	6	(10)	F L
15	13	I'm Not In Love	Will To Power	Epic	6	(29)	L
16	1	Justify My Love	Madonna	Sire	10	(2)	G
17	-	Love Makes Things Happen	Pebbles	MCA	4		L
18	16	Just Another Dream	Cathy Dennis	Polydor	5	(13)	F
19	-	Around The Way Girl	L.L. Cool J	Def Jam	8	(36)	
20	3	High Enough	Damn Yankees	Warner	13		F

March 1991

This Mnth	Prev Mnth	Title	Artist	Label	Wks 20	(UK Pos)	
1	4	One More Try	Timmy T	Quality	12		F G L
2	9	Someday	Mariah Carey	Columbia	10	(38)	
3	-	Coming Out Of The Dark	Gloria Estefan	Epic	9	(25)	L
4	-	This House	Tracie Spencer	Capitol	8	(65)	F L
5	-	Get Here	Oleta Adams	Fontana	7	(4)	F L
6	3	All The Man That I Need	Whitney Houston	Arista	10	(13)	
7	-	Show Me The Way	Styx	A&M	6		L
8	-	Hold You Tight	Tara Kemp	Giant	10	(69)	F
9	-	All This Time	Sting	A&M	6	(22)	
10	5	Where Does My Heart Beat Now	Celine Dion	Epic	9	(73)	F
11	-	Rescue Me	Madonna	Sire	5	(3)	
12	-	I've Been Thinking About You	Londonbeat	Radioactive	10	(2)	F
13	-	You're In Love	Wilson Phillips	SBK	10	(29)	
14	1	Gonna Make You Sweat	C&C Music Factory Featuring Freedom Williams	Columbia	11	(3)	F G
15	-	Signs	Tesla	Geffen	8	(70)	L
16	19	Around The Way Girl	L.L. Cool J	Def Jam	8	(36)	
17	-	Iesha	Another Bad Creation	Motown	9		F
18	14	Wicked Game	Chris Isaak	Reprise	6	(10)	F L
19	-	Sadeness Part 1	Enigma	Charisma	8	(1)	F L
20	-	Waiting For Love	Alias	EMI	3		L

US
1991
JAN-MAR

◆ A record seven of March's Top 10 were by female singers. Among them were Grammy winning Mariah Carey, whose 'Someday' was her third successive No. 1, with all three hits coming from her chart topping eponymous album.

▲ As Whitney Houston (above) equalled Madonna's (female) record of nine No. 1s, it was reported that the latter had sold 54 million albums and 26 million singles worldwide.

◆ Vanilla Ice's **To The Extreme** sold five million in 12 weeks. It was the first No. 1 not available on vinyl.

◆ Janet Jackson became the first artist to score seven Top 5 singles from one album.

325

UK 1991 APR-JUNE

▲ New Kids On The Block ended their European tour at Wembley. They had played 31 dates and grossed $8.8 million.

◆ As sister Dannii scored her second successive hit, Kylie Minogue became the first artist to see her first 13 hit singles all go into the Top 10.

◆ Small Faces' singer Steve Marriott died in a fire, and David Ruffin died of drug-related causes. Michael Jackson paid for Ruffin's star-studded funeral at which Aretha Franklin and Stevie Wonder paid tributes to the ex-Temptation.

April 1991

This Mnth	Prev Mnth	Title	Artist	Label	Wks 20	(US Pos)	
1	-	Sit Down	James	Fontana	8		F
2	-	The Whole Of The Moon	Waterboys	Ensign	6		F L
3	10	The One And Only	Chesney Hawkes	Chrysalis	6	(10)	F L
4	12	Rhythm Of My Heart	Rod Stewart	Warner	8		
5	-	Rescue Me	Madonna	Sire	5	(9)	
6	-	The Size Of A Cow	Wonder Stuff	Polydor	5		
7	8	Joyride	Roxette	EMI	7	(1)	
8	-	Deep, Deep Trouble	Simpsons Feat. Bart & Homer	Geffen	5	(69)	L
9	-	Love & Kisses	Dannii Minogue	MCA	5		F
10	-	Human Nature	Gary Clail On-U Sound System	Perfecto	5		F L
11	-	Anthem	N-Joi	Deconstruction	5		F
12	20	Secret Love	Bee Gees	Warner	5		
13	-	I've Got News For You	Feargal Sharkey	Virgin	4		L
14	11	It's Too Late	Quartz Introducing Dina Carroll	Mercury	6		F L
15	18	Let There Be Love	Simple Minds	Virgin	4		
16	-	The Shoop Shoop Song (It's In His Kiss)	Cher	Geffen	11	(33)	
17	15	Where The Streets Have No Name...	Pet Shop Boys	EMI	4	(72)	
18	-	Snap Mega Mix	Snap	Arista	3		
19	-	Sailing On The Seven Seas	OMD	Virgin	8		
20	4	The Stonk	Hale & Pace & The Stonkers	London	5		F L

May 1991

This Mnth	Prev Mnth	Title	Artist	Label	Wks 20	(US Pos)	
1	16	The Shoop Shoop Song (It's In His...)	Cher	Geffen	11	(33)	
2	-	Last Train To Trancentral	KLF	KLF Comms.	7		
3	19	Sailing On The Seven Seas	OMD	Virgin	8		
4	-	Senza Una Donna (Without A Woman)	Zucchero & Paul Young	London	6		F
5	-	Touch Me (All Night Long)	Cathy Dennis	Polydor	6	(2)	
6	-	Promise Me	Beverley Craven	Epic	8		F L
7	-	There's No Other Way	Blur	Food	5	(82)	F L
8	-	Gypsy Woman (La Da Dee)	Crystal Waters	A&M	6	(8)	F
9	-	Get The Message	Electronic	Factory	4		
10	-	Born Free	Vic Reeves & The Roman Numerals	Sense	4		F
11	1	Sit Down	James	Fontana	8		F
12	-	Tainted Love	Soft Cell/Marc Almond	Mercury	5		L
13	-	Ring Ring Ring (Ha Ha Hey)	De La Soul	Big Life	4		L
14	2	The Whole Of The Moon	Waterboys	Ensign	6		F L
15	-	Future Love (EP)	Seal	ZTT	3		
16	-	Fading Like A Flower (Every Time You Leave)	Roxette	EMI	3	(2)	
17	-	I Wanna Sex You Up	Color Me Badd	Giant	9	(2)	F
18	-	Quadrophonia	Quadrophonia	ARS	2		F L
19	-	Anasthasia	T99	Citybeat	2		F L
20	-	Baby Baby	Amy Grant	A&M	7	(1)	F L

June 1991

This Mnth	Prev Mnth	Title	Artist	Label	Wks 20	(US Pos)	
1	17	I Wanna Sex You Up	Color Me Badd	Giant	9	(2)	F
2	1	The Shoop Shoop Song (It's In His...)	Cher	Geffen	11	(33)	
3	20	Baby Baby	Amy Grant	A&M	7	(1)	F L
4	6	Promise Me	Beverley Craven	Epic	8		F L
5	-	Shiny Happy People	R.E.M.	Warner	6	(10)	
6	8	Gypsy Woman (La Da Dee)	Crystal Waters	A&M	6	(8)	F
7	-	Thinking About Your Love	Kenny Thomas	Cooltempo	8		
8	-	Shocked	Kylie Minogue	PWL	4		
9	-	Any Dream Will Do	Jason Donovan	Really Useful	9		
10	-	Do You Want Me	Salt-N-Pepa	ffrr	6	(21)	
11	12	Tainted Love	Soft Cell/Marc Almond	Mercury	5		L
12	-	Light My Fire	Doors	Elektra	3		L
13	-	Only Fools (Never Fall In Love)	Sonia	IQ	5		
14	-	Holiday	Madonna	Sire	3		
15	2	Last Train To Trancentral	KLF	KLF Comms.	7		
16	5	Touch Me (All Night Long)	Cathy Dennis	Polydor	6	(2)	
17	-	Move That Body	Technotronic Featuring Reggie	ARS	3		
18	-	The Motown Song	Rod Stewart	Warner	4	(10)	
19	-	Success	Dannii Minogue	MCA	3		
20	-	Chorus	Erasure	Mute	6		

April 1991

This Mnth	Prev Mnth	Title	Artist	Label	Wks 20	(UK Pos)	
1	13	You're In Love	Wilson Phillips	SBK	10	(29)	
2	12	I've Been Thinking About You	Londonbeat	Radioactive	10	(2)	F
3	-	Baby Baby	Amy Grant	A&M	11	(2)	
4	8	Hold You Tight	Tara Kemp	Giant	10	(69)	F
5	-	Joyride	Roxette	EMI	9	(4)	
6	19	Sadeness Part 1	Enigma	Charisma	8	(1)	F L
7	-	Rico Suave	Gerardo	Interscope	6		L
8	-	Cry For Help	Rick Astley	RCA	7	(7)	L
9	-	I Like The Way (The Kissing Game)	Hi-Five	Jive	12	(43)	F
10	3	Coming Out Of The Dark	Gloria Estefan	Epic	9	(25)	L
11	17	Iesha	Another Bad Creation	Motown	9		F
12	-	Here We Go	C&C Music Factory Featuring Freedom Williams & Zelma Davis	Columbia	9	(20)	
13	-	Touch Me (All Night Long)	Cathy Dennis	Polydor	10	(5)	
14	15	Signs	Tesla	Geffen	8	(70)	L
15	-	I Touch Myself	Divinyls	Virgin	8	(10)	F L
16	1	One More Try	Timmy T	Quality	12		F G L
17	-	Voices That Care	Voices That Care	Giant	6		F L
18	-	Round And Round	Tevin Campbell	Qwest	5		F
19	-	Rhythm Of My Heart	Rod Stewart	Warner	8		
20	4	This House	Tracie Spencer	Capitol	8	(65)	F L

May 1991

This Mnth	Prev Mnth	Title	Artist	Label	Wks 20	(UK Pos)	
1	9	I Like The Way (The Kissing Game)	Hi-Five	Jive	12	(43)	F
2	13	Touch Me (All Night Long)	Cathy Dennis	Polydor	10	(5)	
3	12	Here We Go	C&C Music Factory/Freedom Williams/Zelma Davis	Columbia	9	(20)	
4	3	Baby Baby	Amy Grant	A&M	11	(2)	
5	15	I Touch Myself	Divinyls	Virgin	8	(10)	F L
6	5	Joyride	Roxette	EMI	9	(4)	
7	19	Rhythm Of My Heart	Rod Stewart	Warner	8		
8	-	I Don't Wanna Cry	Mariah Carey	Columbia	10		
9	-	More Than Words	Extreme	A&M	11	(2)	F
10	-	Silent Lucidity	Queensryche	EMI	7	(18)	F L
11	-	I Wanna Sex You Up	Color Me Badd	Giant	13	(1)	F P
12	8	Cry For Help	Rick Astley	RCA	7	(7)	L
13	-	Love Is A Wonderful Thing	Michael Bolton	Columbia	8	(23)	
14	-	Losing My Religion	R.E.M.	Warner	9	(19)	
15	17	Voices That Care	Voices That Care	Giant	6		F L
16	-	You Don't Have To Go Home Tonight	Triplets	Mercury	4		F L
17	-	More Than Ever	Nelson	DGC	4		L
18	1	You're In Love	Wilson Phillips	SBK	10	(29)	
19	-	Save Some Love	Keedy	Arista	4		F L
20	2	I've Been Thinking About You	Londonbeat	Radioactive	10	(2)	F

June 1991

This Mnth	Prev Mnth	Title	Artist	Label	Wks 20	(UK Pos)	
1	-	Rush Rush	Paula Abdul	Virgin	11	(6)	
2	11	I Wanna Sex You Up	Color Me Badd	Giant	13	(1)	F P
3	9	More Than Words	Extreme	A&M	11	(2)	F
4	13	Love Is A Wonderful Thing	Michael Bolton	Columbia	8	(23)	
5	14	Losing My Religion	R.E.M.	Warner	9	(19)	
6	8	I Don't Wanna Cry	Mariah Carey	Columbia	10		
7	-	Unbelievable	EMF	EMI	12	(3)	F
8	-	Power Of Love-Love Power	Luther Vandross	Epic	8	(46)	
9	-	Strike It Up	Black Box	RCA	5	(16)	L
10	1	I Like The Way (The Kissing Game)	Hi-Five	Jive	12	(43)	F
11	-	Playground	Another Bad Creation	Motown	5		L
12	-	Right Here, Right Now	Jesus Jones	SBK	10	(31)	F
13	-	Miracle	Whitney Houston	Arista	5		
14	-	Couple Days Off	Huey Lewis & The News	EMI	4		L
15	-	Here I Am (Come And Take Me)	UB40	Virgin	7	(46)	
16	2	Touch Me (All Night Long)	Cathy Dennis	Polydor	10	(5)	
17	10	Silent Lucidity	Queensryche	EMI	7	(18)	F L
18	-	How Can I Ease The Pain	Lisa Fischer	Elektra	5		F L
19	7	Rhythm Of My Heart	Rod Stewart	Warner	8		
20	-	Gypsy Woman (She's Homeless)	Crystal Waters	Mercury	6	(2)	F L

US 1991

APR-JUNE

◆ When *Billboard* changed their method of calculating album charts, country and rap records fared much better. Also, records entering at No. 1 were no longer rare.

◆ NWA's album **Efil4zaggin** was the first No. 1 LP since Led Zeppelin's **Presence** in 1976, which did not contain a hit single.

◆ Session singer Yvette Marine claimed she had sung lead on some Paula Abdul tracks. This did not seem to affect Abdul's sales as 'Rush Rush' and **Spellbound** hit the top.

◆ 'I Touch Myself' by The Divinyls was songwriters Billy Steinberg & Tom Kelly sixth major hit by different female vocalists. The others, 'Like A Virgin' (Madonna), 'True Colors' (Cyndi Lauper), 'Alone' (Heart), 'Eternal Flame' (Bangles), 'So Emotional' (Whitney Houston), were all chart topping singles.

UK 1991 JULY-SEPT

▲ Bryan Adams' recording of '(Everything I Do) I Do It For You' was the world's top selling single in 1991. It sold over three million in America, and became the first million seller for six years in Britain, where it spent a record 16 successive weeks at the top.

◆ It was expected that seven million people in 25 countries would pay approximately £70 ($100) million to see Dire Straits on tour.

◆ Opera singer Luciano Pavarotti topped the album chart with **Essential Pavarotti II,** and at times he had three entries in the music video Top 10.

July 1991

This Mnth	Prev Mnth	Title	Artist	Label	Wks 20	(US Pos)	
1	-	(Everything I Do) I Do It For You	Bryan Adams	A&M	22	(1)	G
2	9	Any Dream Will Do	Jason Donovan	Really Useful	9		
3	20	Chorus	Erasure	Mute	6		
4	-	Rush Rush	Paula Abdul	Virgin	7	(1)	
5	7	Thinking About Your Love	Kenny Thomas	Cooltempo	8		
6	-	You Could Be Mine	Guns N' Roses	Geffen	7	(29)	
7	-	Now That We've Found Love	Heavy D. & The Boyz	MCA	8	(11)	F L
8	-	Always There	Incognito Featuring Jocelyn Brown	Talkin Loud	5		F
9	1	I Wanna Sex You Up	Color Me Badd	Giant	9	(2)	F
10	10	Do You Want Me	Salt-N-Pepa	ffrr	6	(21)	
11	-	Things That Make You Go Hmmmm....	C&C Music Factory Featuring Freedom Williams	Columbia	7	(4)	L
12	-	7 Ways To Love	Cola Boy	Arista	4		F L
13	-	Pandora's Box	OMD	Virgin	5		L
14	-	Are You Mine?	Bros	Columbia	3		L
15	-	It Ain't Over 'Til It's Over	Lenny Kravitz	Virgin America	4	(2)	F
16	-	Love And Understanding	Cher	Geffen	5	(17)	L
17	-	I Touch Myself	Divinyls	Virgin America	5	(4)	F L
18	-	More Than Words	Extreme	A&M	8	(1)	
19	18	The Motown Song	Rod Stewart	Warner	4	(10)	
20	-	Move Any Mountain	Shamen	One Little Indian	7	(38)	F

August 1991

This Mnth	Prev Mnth	Title	Artist	Label	Wks 20	(US Pos)	
1	1	(Everything I Do) I Do It For You	Bryan Adams	A&M	22	(1)	G
2	18	More Than Words	Extreme	A&M	8	(1)	
3	-	I'm Too Sexy	Right Said Fred	Tug	11	(1)	F
4	20	Move Any Mountain	Shamen	One Little Indian	7	(38)	F
5	7	Now That We've Found Love	Heavy D. & The Boyz	MCA	8	(11)	F L
6	-	All For Love	Color Me Badd	Giant	6	(1)	L
7	-	Winter In July	Bomb The Bass	Rhythm King	5		L
8	-	Set Adrift On Memory Bliss	P.M. Dawn	Gee Street	5	(1)	F
9	11	Things That Make You Go Hmmmm....	C&C Music Factory Featuring Freedom Williams	Columbia	7	(4)	L
10	-	Summertime	D.J. Jazzy Jeff & Fresh Prince	Jive	5	(4)	F
11	-	Twist & Shout	Deacon Blue	Columbia	4		
12	13	Pandora's Box	OMD	Virgin	5		L
13	2	Any Dream Will Do	Jason Donovan	Really Useful	9		
14	-	Charly	Prodigy	XL	7		F
15	-	Enter Sandman	Metallica	Vertigo	2	(16)	
16	6	You Could Be Mine	Guns N' Roses	Geffen	7	(29)	
17	-	Sunshine On A Rainy Day	Zoe	M&G	9		F L
18	-	Jump To The Beat	Dannii Minogue	MCA	3		
19	-	Happy Together	Jason Donovan	PWL	4		
20	16	Love And Understanding	Cher	Geffen	5	(17)	L

September 1991

This Mnth	Prev Mnth	Title	Artist	Label	Wks 20	(US Pos)	
1	1	(Everything I Do) I Do It For You	Bryan Adams	A&M	22	(1)	G
2	3	I'm Too Sexy	Right Said Fred	Tug	11	(1)	F
3	-	Insanity	Oceanic	Dead Dead Good	11		F
4	14	Charly	Prodigy	XL	7		F
5	17	Sunshine On A Rainy Day	Zoe	M&G	9		F L
6	-	Let's Talk About Sex	Salt-N-Pepa	ffrr	9	(13)	
7	-	Gett Off	Prince/New Power Generation	Paisley Park	5	(21)	
8	-	What Can You Do For Me	Utah Saints	ffrr	7		F
9	-	I'll Be Back	Arnee & The Terminaters	Epic	4		F L
10	-	Love...Thy Will Be Done	Martika	Columbia	5	(10)	
11	-	Love To Hate You	Erasure	Mute	6		
12	-	Peace	Sabrina Johnson	East West	6		F L
13	8	Set Adrift On Memory Bliss	P.M. Dawn	Gee Street	5	(1)	F
14	-	Everybody's Free (To Feel Good)	Rozalla	Pulse 8	6	(37)	F
15	6	All For Love	Color Me Badd	Giant	6	(1)	L
16	-	20th Century Boy	Marc Bolan & T. Rex	Marc On Wax	4		L
17	-	Don't Cry	Guns N' Roses	Geffen	2	(10)	
18	2	More Than Words	Extreme	A&M	8	(1)	
19	-	Good Vibrations	Marky Mark & The Funky Bunch Featuring Loleatta Holloway	Interscope	3	(1)	F L
20	-	Something Got Me Started	Simply Red	East West	4	(23)	

July 1991

This Month	Prev Mnth	Title	Artist	Label	Wks 20	(UK Pos)	
1	7	Unbelievable	EMF	EMI	12	(3)	F
2	1	Rush Rush	Paula Abdul	Virgin	11	(6)	
3	12	Right Here, Right Now	Jesus Jones	SBK	10	(31)	F
4	2	I Wanna Sex You Up	Color Me Badd	Giant	13	(1)	F P
5	-	Place In This World	Michael W. Smith	Reunion	7		F L
6	-	P.A.S.S.I.O.N.	Rythm Syndicate	Impact	9	(58)	F
7	-	Piece Of My Heart	Tara Kemp	Giant	6		L
8	-	(Everything I Do) I Do It For You	Bryan Adams	A&M	13	(1)	P
9	15	Here I Am (Come And Take Me)	UB40	Virgin	7	(46)	
10	-	Summertime	D.J. Jazzy Jeff & Fresh Prince	Jive	9	(8)	G
11	8	Power Of Love/Love Power	Luther Vandross	Epic	8	(46)	
12	-	Lily Was Here	David A. Stewart Introducing Candy Dulfer	Anxious	5	(6)	F L
13	20	Gypsy Woman (She's Homeless)	Crystal Waters	Mercury	6	(2)	F L
14	-	Every Heartbeat	Amy Grant	A&M	10	(25)	
15	-	It Ain't Over 'Til It's Over	Lenny Kravitz	Virgin America	9	(11)	F L
16	3	More Than Words	Extreme	A&M	11	(2)	F
17	-	The Dream Is Still Alive	Wilson Phillips	SBK	5		
18	-	Temptation	Corina	Cutting	7		F L
19	-	Walking In Memphis	Marc Cohn	Atlantic	5	(22)	F L
20	-	Fading Like A Flower (Every Time You Leave)	Roxette	EMI	8	(12)	L

August 1991

This Month	Prev Mnth	Title	Artist	Label	Wks 20	(UK Pos)	
1	8	(Everything I Do) I Do It For You	Bryan Adams	A&M	13	(1)	P
2	14	Every Heartbeat	Amy Grant	A&M	10	(25)	
3	15	It Ain't Over 'Til It's Over	Lenny Kravitz	Virgin America	9	(11)	F L
4	20	Fading Like A Flower (Every Time...)	Roxette	EMI	8	(12)	L
5	10	Summertime	D.J. Jazzy Jeff & Fresh Prince	Jive	9	(8)	G
6	-	Wind Of Change	Scorpions	Mercury	10	(2)	F L
7	18	Temptation	Corina	Cutting	7		F L
8	6	P.A.S.S.I.O.N.	Rythm Syndicate	Impact	9	(58)	F
9	-	3 A.M. Eternal	KLF	Arista	7	(1)	F
10	-	I Can't Wait Another Minute	Hi-Five	Jive	10		
11	-	The Promise Of A New Day	Paula Abdul	Captive/Virgin	9	(52)	
12	-	Motownphilly	Boyz II Men	Motown	12	(23)	F G
13	3	Right Here, Right Now	Jesus Jones	SBK	10	(31)	F
14	-	Crazy	Seal	Sire	7	(2)	F L
15	-	I'll Be There	Escape Club	Atlantic	5		L
16	-	Things That Make You Go Hmmmm....	C&C Music Factory Featuring Freedom Williams	Columbia	9	(4)	L
17	1	Unbelievable	EMF	EMI	12	(3)	F
18	-	Unforgettable	Natalie Cole	Elektra	6	(19)	L
19	-	Time, Love And Tenderness	Michael Bolton	Columbia	8	(28)	
20	-	Too Many Walls	Cathy Dennis	Polydor	9	(17)	L

September 1991

This Month	Prev Mnth	Title	Artist	Label	Wks 20	(UK Pos)	
1	-	I Adore Mi Amor	Color Me Badd	Giant	10	(44)	
2	12	Motownphilly	Boyz II Men	Motown	12	(23)	F G
3	16	Things That Make You Go	C&C Music Factory/F. Williams	Columbia	9	(4)	L
4	-	Good Vibrations	Marky Mark & The Funky Bunch Loleatta Holloway	Interscope	9	(14)	F
5	1	(Everything I Do) I Do It For You	Bryan Adams	A&M	13	(1)	P
6	11	The Promise Of A New Day	Paula Abdul	Captive/Virgin	9	(52)	
7	19	Time, Love And Tenderness	Michael Bolton	Columbia	8	(28)	
8	20	Too Many Walls	Cathy Dennis	Polydor	9	(17)	L
9	-	Love Of A Lifetime	Firehouse	Epic	7		
10	-	Emotions	Mariah Carey	Columbia	11	(17)	
11	-	The Motown Song	Rod Stewart	Warner	6	(10)	
12	-	Now That We Found Love	Heavy D. & The Boyz	Uptown	7	(2)	F L
13	9	3 A.M. Eternal	KLF	Arista	7	(1)	F
14	10	I Can't Wait Another Minute	Hi-Five	Jive	10		
15	-	Shiny Happy People	R.E.M.	Warner	5	(6)	L
16	-	Something To Talk About	Bonnie Raitt	Capitol	8		F
17	6	Wind Of Change	Scorpions	Mercury	10	(2)	F L
18	-	Do Anything	Natural Selection	East West	12	(69)	F L
19	14	Crazy	Seal	Sire	7	(2)	F L
20	2	Every Heartbeat	Amy Grant	A&M	10	(25)	

◆ **Ropin' the Wind** by Garth Brooks, which shipped 2.6 million in its first week, was the first country album ever to enter in pole position. It remained at the top for 18 weeks, and has sold over nine million copies.

◆ Metallica's self titled album entered the transatlantic charts at No. 1 – a first for a heavy metal act.

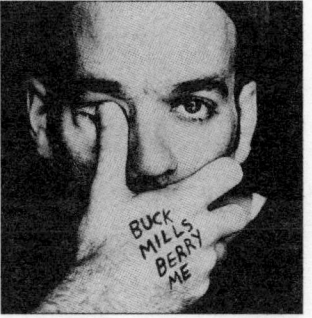

▲ R.E.M. snared a record six MTV awards including Best Video for 'Losing My Religion'.

◆ AMA award winners Aerosmith signed a $40 million deal with Columbia, and Motley Crue re-signed to Elektra for a similar amount.

UK 1991
OCT-DEC

In 1991, more singles charted than ever, records tended to enter higher and have shorter chart life spans. It was a year when dance music thrived, twelve inch singles outsold seven inches, more European artists charted, and only a handful of British hit acts repeated their success Stateside.

The Rolling Stones signed to Virgin for $40 million, while Madonna's new deal guaranteed her at least $5 million per album.

▲ Freddie Mercury died. His group Queen ended the year as Britain's top album act and top singles group, and their **Greatest Hits** album was certified as a three million seller.

October 1991

This Mnth	Prev Mnth	Title	Artist	Label	Wks 20	(US Pos)	
1	1	(Everything I Do) I Do It For You	Bryan Adams	A&M	22	(1)	G
2	-	Wind Of Change	Scorpions	Mercury	7	(4)	F L
3	3	Insanity	Oceanic	Dead Dead Good	11		F
4	6	Let's Talk About Sex	Salt-N-Pepa	ffrr	9	(13)	
5	-	Saltwater	Julian Lennon	Virgin	6		L
6	11	Love To Hate You	Erasure	Mute	6		
7	14	Everybody's Free (To Feel Good)	Rozalla	Pulse 8	6	(37)	F
8	-	Always Look On The Bright Side Of Life	Monty Python	Virgin	5		F L
9	-	World In Union	Kiri Te Kanawa	Columbia	7		F L
10	-	Get Ready For This	2 Unlimited	PWL Continental	8	(76)	F
11	12	Peace	Sabrina Johnson	East West	6		F L
12	5	Sunshine On A Rainy Day	Zoe	M&G	9		F L
13	2	I'm Too Sexy	Right Said Fred	Tug	11	(1)	F
14	-	Best Of You	Kenny Thomas	Cooltempo	3		
15	-	Such A Feeling	Bizarre Inc	Vinyl Solution	5		F
16	-	Change	Lisa Stansfield	Arista	4	(30)	
17	-	Live Your Life Be Free	Belinda Carlisle	Virgin	3		
18	-	Dizzy	Vic Reeves & The Wonder Stuff	Sense	8		L
19	20	Something Got Me Started	Simply Red	East West	4	(23)	
20	-	Baby Love	Dannii Minogue	MCA	2		

November 1991

This Mnth	Prev Mnth	Title	Artist	Label	Wks 20	(US Pos)	
1	18	Dizzy	Vic Reeves & The Wonder Stuff	Sense	8		L
2	10	Get Ready For This	2 Unlimited	PWL Continental	8	(76)	F
3	1	(Everything I Do) I Do It For You	Bryan Adams	A&M	22	(1)	G
4	-	Rhythm Is A Mystery	K-Klass	De Construction	4		F L
5	-	The Fly	U2	Island	3	(58)	
6	-	If You Were Here With Me Now	Kylie Minogue/Keith Washington	PWL	5		
7	9	World In Union	Kiri Te Kanawa	Columbia	7		F L
8	-	Activ 8 (Come With Me)	Altern 8	Network	5		F
9	-	Is There Anybody Out There?	Bassheads	De Construction	4		F
10	-	Black Or White	Michael Jackson	Epic	9	(1)	
11	-	No Son Of Mine	Genesis	Virgin	3	(12)	
12	-	Playing With Knives	Bizarre Inc	Vinyl Solution	3		
13	2	Wind Of Change	Scorpions	Mercury	7	(4)	F L
14	8	Always Look On The Bright Side Of Life	Monty Python	Virgin	5		F L
15	-	American Pie	Don McLean	Liberty	4		L
16	-	Killer (EP)	Seal	ZTT	3	(100)	L
17	-	When A Man Loves A Woman	Michael Bolton	Columbia	3	(1)	
18	-	Go	Moby	Outer-Rhythm	4		F L
19	3	Insanity	Oceanic	Dead Dead Good	11		F
20	-	DJs Take Control/Way In My Brain	SL2	XL	2		F

December 1991

This Mnth	Prev Mnth	Title	Artist	Label	Wks 20	(US Pos)	
1	-	Don't Let The Sun Go Down On Me	George Michael & Elton John	Epic	6	(1)	
2	-	When You Tell Me That You Love Me	Diana Ross	EMI	9		
3	-	Justified And Ancient	KLF Feat. Tammy Wynette	KLF Comms.	9	(11)	
4	10	Black Or White	Michael Jackson	Epic	9	(1)	
5	-	Driven By You	Brian May	Parlophone	6		F
6	-	Ride Like The Wind	East Side Beat	ffrr	6		F L
7	-	Too Blind To See It	Kym Sims	Atco	8	(38)	
8	-	Stars	Simply Red	East West	6	(44)	
9	-	Bohemian Rhapsody/These Are The Days Of Our Lives	Queen	Parlophone	10	(2)	P
10	-	Don't Talk Just Kiss	Right Said Fred/Jocelyn Brown	Tug	7	(76)	
11	-	Live And Let Die	Guns N' Roses	Geffen	4	(33)	
12	8	Activ 8 (Come With Me)	Altern 8	Network	5		F
13	-	Smells Like Teen Spirit	Nirvana	DGC	3	(6)	F
14	-	We Should Be Together	Cliff Richard	EMI	3		
15	-	Rocket Man (I Think It's Going To Be A Long Long Time)	Kate Bush	Mercury	4		
16	1	Dizzy	Vic Reeves & The Wonder Stuff	Sense	8		L
17	-	If You Go Away	New Kids On The Block	Columbia	2		L
18	-	Addams Groove	Hammer	Capitol	7	(7)	
19	-	Sound	James	Fontana	3		
20	-	The Bare Necessities Megamix	UK Mixmasters	Connect	4		F L

US 1991 OCT-DEC

October 1991

This Mnth	Prev Mnth	Title	Artist	Label	Wks 20	(UK Pos)	
1	10	Emotions	Mariah Carey	Columbia	11	(17)	
2	18	Do Anything	Natural Selection	East West	12	(69)	F L
3	-	Romantic	Karyn White	Warner	11	(23)	
4	4	Good Vibrations	Marky Mark & The Funky Bunch Featuring Loleatta Holloway	Interscope	9	(14)	F
5	-	Hole Hearted	Extreme	A&M	9	(12)	L
6	1	I Adore Mi Amor	Color Me Badd	Giant	10	(44)	
7	16	Something To Talk About	Bonnie Raitt	Capitol	8		F
8	-	Can't Stop This Thing We Started	Bryan Adams	A&M	11	(12)	
9	-	Everybody Plays The Fool	Aaron Neville	A&M	5		L
10	9	Love Of A Lifetime	Firehouse	Epic	7		
11	-	Real Real Real	Jesus Jones	SBK	6	(19)	L
12	-	Love...Thy Will Be Done	Martika	Columbia	5	(9)	L
13	2	Motownphilly	Boyz II Men	Motown	12	(23)	F G
14	-	Cream	Prince & The New Power Generation.	Paisley Park	12	(15)	
15	-	Don't Want To Be A Fool	Luther Vandross	Epic	5		
16	15	Shiny Happy People	R.E.M.	Warner	5	(6)	L
17	-	O.P.P.	Naughty By Nature	Tommy Boy	14	(35)	F P
18	12	Now That We Found Love	Heavy D. & The Boyz	Uptown	7	(2)	F L
19	-	Enter Sandman	Metallica	Elektra	3	(5)	F L
20	5	(Everything I Do) I Do It For You	Bryan Adams	A&M	13	(1)	P

November 1991

This Mnth	Prev Mnth	Title	Artist	Label	Wks 20	(UK Pos)	
1	14	Cream	Prince/New Power Generation	Paisley Park	12	(15)	
2	8	Can't Stop This Thing We Started	Bryan Adams	A&M	11	(12)	
3	-	When A Man Loves A Woman	Michael Bolton	Columbia	12	(8)	
4	-	It's So Hard To Say Goodbye To Yesterday	Boyz II Men	Motown	14		
5	17	O.P.P.	Naughty By Nature	Tommy Boy	14	(35)	F P
6	3	Romantic	Karyn White	Warner	11	(23)	
7	-	Set Adrift On Memory Bliss	P.M. Dawn	Gee Street/Island	13	(3)	F
8	-	Set The Night To Music	Roberta Flack With Maxi Priest	Atlantic	8		L
9	2	Do Anything	Natural Selection	East West	12	(69)	F L
10	-	Don't Cry	Guns N' Roses	Geffen	12	(8)	
11	1	Emotions	Mariah Carey	Columbia	11	(17)	
12	-	That's What Love Is For	Amy Grant	A&M	11	(60)	
13	-	The One And Only	Chesney Hawkes	Chrysalis	7	(1)	F L
14	-	Blowing Kisses In The Wind	Paula Abdul	Captive	10		
15	11	Real Real Real	Jesus Jones	SBK	6	(19)	L
16	-	I Wonder Why	Curtis Stigers	Arista	4	(5)	F L
17	5	Hole Hearted	Extreme	A&M	9	(12)	L
18	-	Let's Talk About Sex	Salt-N-Pepa	Next Plateau	8	(2)	L
19	-	Black Or White	Michael Jackson	Epic	12	(1)	G
20	15	Don't Want To Be A Fool	Luther Vandross	Epic	5		

December 1991

This Mnth	Prev Mnth	Title	Artist	Label	Wks 20	(UK Pos)	
1	19	Black Or White	Michael Jackson	Epic	12	(1)	G
2	4	It's So Hard To Say Goodbye To Yesterday	Boyz II Men	Motown	14		
3	7	Set Adrift On Memory Bliss	P.M. Dawn	Gee Street/Island	13	(3)	F
4	3	When A Man Loves A Woman	Michael Bolton	Columbia	12	(8)	
5	-	All 4 Love	Color Me Badd	Giant	15	(5)	
6	14	Blowing Kisses In The Wind	Paula Abdul	Captive	10		
7	-	Can't Let Go	Mariah Carey	Columbia	14	(20)	
8	-	Finally	Ce Ce Peniston	A&M	14	(2)	F L
9	12	That's What Love Is For	Amy Grant	A&M	11	(60)	
10	-	Wildside	Marky Mark & The Funky Bunch	Intercope	8	(42)	L
11	-	2 Legit 2 Quit	Hammer	Capitol	13	(60)	G L
12	1	Cream	Prince/New Power Generation	Paisley Park	12	(15)	
13	-	Keep Coming Back	Richard Marx	Capitol	7	(55)	
14	5	O.P.P.	Naughty By Nature	Tommy Boy	14	(35)	F P
15	18	Let's Talk About Sex	Salt-N-Pepa	Next Plateau	8	(2)	L
16	-	No Son Of Mine	Genesis	Atlantic	9	(6)	
17	10	Don't Cry	Guns N' Roses	Geffen	12	(8)	
18	2	Can't Stop This Thing We Started	Bryan Adams	A&M	11	(12)	
19	8	Set The Night To Music	Roberta Flack With Maxi Priest	Atlantic	8		L
20	-	Smells Like Teen Spirit	Nirvana	Geffen	13	(7)	F G L

◆ Thanks to CDs, the value of America's music sales in 1991 went up 3.8% to $7.8 billion.

◆ Michael Jackson's album **Dangerous** entered the transatlantic charts at No. 1. It shipped four million in America, and sold a record 200,000 in three days in the UK. Its lead-off single, 'Black Or White', was the first American record to enter the UK chart at No. 1 since 1960.

◆ Guns N' Roses' albums **Use Your Illusion I** and **II** entered the American and UK charts in the top two rungs (bettering a record set by The Beatles).

◆ Mariah Carey became the first artist to have her first five hits reach No. 1 and the youngest act to score five No. 1s – records previously held by Elvis.

UK 1992 JAN-MAR

◆ Following Freddie Mercury's death, Queen had the top 4 music videos and 'Bohemian Rhapsody' became the first record ever to top the charts twice (selling over a million on both occasions). It's double A-side, 'These Are The Days Of Our Lives', was voted Record of The Year at the Brit Awards.

◆ Inducted into the *Rock And Roll Hall Of Fame* between 1989-92 were Eric Clapton, The Four Tops, Jimi Hendrix, The Impressions, The Kinks, John Lee Hooker, Jimmy Page, Simon & Garfunkel, Ike & Tina Tuner and The Who.

◆ A survey showed that Phonogram was the most successful record company. The Dutch conglomerate was responsible for 18.5% of world-sales.

January 1992

This Mnth	Prev Mnth	Title	Artist	Label	Wks 20	(US Pos)	
1	9	Bohemian Rhapsody/These Are The Days Of Our Lives	Queen	Parlophone	10	(2)	P
2	3	Justified And Ancient	KLF Feat. Tammy Wynette	KLF Comms.	9	(11)	
3	7	Too Blind To See It	Kym Sims	Atco	8	(38)	F
4	18	Addams Groove	Hammer	Capitol	7	(7)	
5	10	Don't Talk Just Kiss	Right Said Fred/Jocelyn Brown	Tug	7	(76)	
6	-	Goodnight Girl	Wet Wet Wet	Precious	9		
7	-	Everybody In The Place (EP)	Prodigy	XL	5		
8	2	When You Tell Me That You Love Me	Diana Ross	EMI	9		
9	-	We Got A Love Thang	Ce Ce Peniston	A&M	5	(20)	F
10	1	Don't Let The Sun Go Down On Me	George Michael & Elton John	Epic	6	(1)	
11	-	God Gave Rock & Roll To You Ii	Kiss	Interscope	5		L
12	11	Live And Let Die	Guns N' Roses	Geffen	4	(33)	
13	-	I Can't Dance	Genesis	Virgin	5	(7)	
14	5	Driven By You	Brian May	Parlophone	6		F
15	4	Black Or White	Michael Jackson	Epic	9	(1)	
16	-	Give Me Just A Little More Time	Kylie Minogue	PWL	5		
17	-	Different Strokes	Isotonik	Ffrreedom	2		F L
18	-	Feel So High	Des'ree	Dusted Sound	4		F L
19	-	(Can You) Feel The Passion	Blue Pearl	Big Life	3		L
20	-	Twilight Zone	2 Unlimited	PWL Continental	7	(49)	

February 1992

This Mnth	Prev Mnth	Title	Artist	Label	Wks 20	(US Pos)	
1	6	Goodnight Girl	Wet Wet Wet	Precious	9		
2	-	Stay	Shakespears Sister	London	14	(4)	
3	20	Twilight Zone	2 Unlimited	PWL Continental	7	(49)	
4	-	I'm Doing Fine Now	Pasadenas	Columbia	7		
5	-	I Wonder Why	Curtis Stigers	Arista	6	(9)	F
6	16	Give Me Just A Little More Time	Kylie Minogue	PWL	5		
7	-	Remember The Time/Come Together	Michael Jackson	Epic	4	(3)	
8	-	My Girl	Temptations	Epic	8		L
9	1	Bohemian Rhapsody/These Are The Days Of Our Lives	Queen	Parlophone	10	(2)	P
10	-	The Bouncer	Kicks Like A Mule	Tribal Bass	4		F L
11	-	For Your Babies	Simply Red	East West	5		
12	11	God Gave Rock & Roll To You Ii	Kiss	Interscope	5		L
13	-	I Love Your Smile	Shanice	Motown	7	(2)	F L
14	13	I Can't Dance	Genesis	Virgin	5	(7)	
15	-	It's A Fine Day	Opus III	PWL Int.	5		F L
16	7	Everybody In The Place (EP)	Prodigy	XL	5		
17	-	Thought I'd Died And Gone To Heaven	Bryan Adams	A&M	4	(13)	L
18	-	Welcome To The Cheap Seats (EP)	Wonder Stuff	Polydor	3		
19	-	Dixie-Narco (EP)	Primal Scream	Creation	2		L
20	-	It Must Be Love	Madness	Virgin	5		L

March 1992

This Mnth	Prev Mnth	Title	Artist	Label	Wks 20	(US Pos)	
1	2	Stay	Shakespears Sister	London	14	(4)	
2	13	I Love Your Smile	Shanice	Motown	7	(2)	F L
3	8	My Girl	Temptations	Epic	8		L
4	-	America: What Time Is Love?	KLF	KLF Comms.	4	(57)	L
5	-	Weather With You	Crowded House	Capitol	5		
6	15	It's A Fine Day	Opus III	PWL Int.	5		F L
7	-	November Rain	Guns N' Roses	Geffen	3	(3)	
8	-	Tears In Heaven	Eric Clapton	Reprise	5	(2)	L
9	-	Finally	Ce Ce Peniston	A&M	6	(5)	
10	-	To Be With You	Mr. Big	Atlantic	7	(1)	F L
11	20	It Must Be Love	Madness	Virgin	5		L
12	4	I'm Doing Fine Now	Pasadenas	Columbia	7		
13	-	Deeply Dippy	Right Said Fred	Tug	10		
14	-	Come As You Are	Nirvana	DGC	2	(32)	
15	-	Human Touch	Bruce Springsteen	Columbia	2	(16)	L
16	-	I Know	New Atlantic	3 Beat	4		F L
17	17	Thought I'd Died And Gone To Heaven	Bryan Adams	A&M	4	(13)	L
18	-	Let's Get Rocked	Def Leppard	Bludgeon Riffola	4	(15)	
19	-	Dragging Me Down	Inspiral Carpets	Cow	3		L
20	-	Rave Generator	Toxic Two	PWL Int.	3		F L

January 1992

This Mnth	Prev Mnth	Title	Artist	Label	Wks 20	(UK Pos)	
1	1	Black Or White	Michael Jackson	Epic	12	(1)	G
2	5	All 4 Love	Color Me Badd	Giant	15	(5)	
3	7	Can't Let Go	Mariah Carey	Columbia	14	(20)	
4	8	Finally	Ce Ce Peniston	A&M	14	(2)	F L
5	-	Don't Let The Sun Go Down On Me	George Michael & Elton John	Columbia	13	(1)	
6	2	It's So Hard To Say Goodbye To Yesterday	Boyz II Men	Motown	14		L
7	11	2 Legit 2 Quit	Hammer	Capitol	13	(60)	G L
8	20	Smells Like Teen Spirit	Nirvana	Geffen	13	(7)	F G L
9	-	I Love Your Smile	Shanice	Motown	14	(2)	F
10	-	Diamonds And Pearls	Prince & The New Power Generation	Paisley Park	12	(25)	
11	-	Addams Groove	Hammer	Capitol	8	(4)	
12	3	Set Adrift On Memory Bliss	P.M. Dawn	Gee Street/Island	13	(3)	F
13	10	Wildside	Marky Mark & The Funky Bunch	Intercope	8	(42)	L
14	16	No Son Of Mine	Genesis	Atlantic	9	(6)	
15	4	When A Man Loves A Woman	Michael Bolton	Columbia	12	(8)	
16	6	Blowing Kisses In The Wind	Paula Abdul	Captive	10		
17	-	Mysterious Ways	U2	Island	8	(13)	
18	-	Tell Me What You Want Me To Do	Tevin Campbell	Qwest	12	(63)	L
19	-	I'm Too Sexy	Right Said Fred	Charisma	13	(2)	F G L
20	-	The Way I Feel About You	Karyn White	Warner	7	(65)	L

February 1992

This Mnth	Prev Mnth	Title	Artist	Label	Wks 20	(UK Pos)	
1	19	I'm Too Sexy	Right Said Fred	Charisma	13	(2)	F G L
2	9	I Love Your Smile	Shanice	Motown	14	(2)	F
3	10	Diamonds And Pearls	Prince/New Power Generation	Paisley Park	12	(25)	
4	5	Don't Let The Sun Go Down On Me	George Michael & Elton John	Columbia	13	(1)	
5	-	To Be With You	Mr. Big	Atlantic	13	(3)	F
6	2	All 4 Love	Color Me Badd	Giant	15	(5)	
7	8	Smells Like Teen Spirit	Nirvana	Geffen	13	(7)	F G L
8	18	Tell Me What You Want Me To Do	Tevin Campbell	Qwest	12	(63)	L
9	-	Remember The Time	Michael Jackson	Epic	13	(3)	
10	4	Finally	Ce Ce Peniston	A&M	14	(2)	F L
11	3	Can't Let Go	Mariah Carey	Columbia	14	(20)	
12	20	The Way I Feel About You	Karyn White	Warner	7	(65)	L
13	17	Mysterious Ways	U2	Island	8	(13)	
14	-	Good For Me	Amy Grant	A&M	10	(60)	
15	7	2 Legit 2 Quit	Hammer	Capitol	13	(60)	G L
16	-	Masterpiece	Atlantic Starr	Warner	14		
17	1	Black Or White	Michael Jackson	Epic	12	(1)	G
18	-	Vibeology	Paula Abdul	Captive	5	(19)	
19	-	Save The Best For Last	Vanessa Williams	Wing	17	(3)	
20	-	Tears In Heaven	Eric Clapton	Duck	16	(5)	G

March 1992

This Mnth	Prev Mnth	Title	Artist	Label	Wks 20	(UK Pos)	
1	5	To Be With You	Mr. Big	Atlantic	13	(3)	F
2	19	Save The Best For Last	Vanessa Williams	Wing	17	(3)	
3	9	Remember The Time	Michael Jackson	Epic	13	(3)	
4	1	I'm Too Sexy	Right Said Fred	Charisma	13	(2)	F G L
5	20	Tears In Heaven	Eric Clapton	Duck	16	(5)	G
6	2	I Love Your Smile	Shanice	Motown	14	(2)	F
7	16	Masterpiece	Atlantic Starr	Warner	14		L
8	14	Good For Me	Amy Grant	A&M	10	(60)	
9	-	I Can't Dance	Genesis	Virgin	9	(7)	
10	8	Tell Me What You Want Me To Do	Tevin Campbell	Qwest	12	(63)	L
11	-	Breakin' My Heart (Pretty Brown Eyes)	Mint Condition	Perspective	9		F L
12	-	Missing You Now	Michael Bolton	Columbia	7	(28)	
13	3	Diamonds And Pearls	Prince/New Power Geneartion	Paisley Park	12	(25)	
14	-	Justified And Ancient	KLF Feat. Tammy Wynette	Arista	5	(2)	L
15	-	Make It Happen	Mariah Carey	Columbia	11	(17)	
16	-	Beauty And The Beast	Celine Dion & Peabo Bryson	Epic	9	(9)	
17	-	If You Go Away	NKOTB (New Kids On The Block)	Columbia	3		L
18	4	Don't Let The Sun Go Down On Me	George Michael & Elton John	Columbia	13	(1)	
19	-	Uhh Ahh	Boyz II Men	Motown	6		
20	7	Smells Like Teen Spirit	Nirvana	Geffen	13	(7)	F G L

US 1992
JAN-MAR

◆ Garth Brooks became the first artist since Herb Alpert in 1966 to have two albums in the Top 3 simultaneously. He also had a further LP in the Top 20 and his total sales were approaching 16 million.

▲ The royalties earned by George Michael (above) and Elton John's transatlantic topper, 'Don't Let The Sun Go Down On Me', went to a variety of AIDS charities.

◆ Paula Abdul's 'Vibeology' ended a run of eight successive Top 10 entries. Like Abdul, New Kids On The Block were now accused of not singing all the lead vocals on their records.

333

UK 1992

APR-JUNE

◆ Bruce Springsteen's albums **Human Touch** and **Lucky Town** entered the UK chart in positions 1 and 2 (Nos. 2 and 3 in the USA) - the feat is more remarkable considering only three days sales were taken into account as the albums were released on a Thursday rather than Monday as is usual in the UK.

◆ Stars appearing in a successful tribute show for Freddie Mercury at Wembley included David Bowie, Def Leppard, Guns N' Roses, Elton John, Metallica, George Michael, Liza Minnelli, Robert Plant, Queen, Lisa Stansfield and U2.

◆ U2, who at times had seven albums on the UK chart, signed a £10 ($15) million publishing deal with Phonogram.

◆ Def Leppard's **Adrenalize** entered the transatlantic charts at No. 1, shipping two million copies in its first week in the USA.

April 1992

This Mnth	Prev Mnth	Title	Artist	Label	Wks 20	(US Pos)	
1	13	Deeply Dippy	Right Said Fred	Tug	10		
2	1	Stay	Shakespears Sister	London	14	(4)	
3	10	To Be With You	Mr. Big	Atlantic	7	(1)	F L
4	-	Save The Best For Last	Vanessa Williams	Polydor	7	(1)	F L
5	-	Joy	Soul II Soul	Ten	4		L
6	9	Finally	Ce Ce Peniston	A&M	6	(5)	
7	-	Why	Annie Lennox	RCA	5	(34)	F
8	18	Let's Get Rocked	Def Leppard	Bludgeon Riffola	4	(15)	
9	-	Evapor 8	Altern 8	Network	3		
10	-	On A Ragga Tip	SL2	XL	9		L
11	-	You're All That Matters To Me	Curtis Stigers	Arista	7	(98)	L
12	-	Breath Of Life	Erasure	Mute	4		
13	-	Viva Las Vegas	ZZ Top	Warner	4		L
14	8	Tears In Heaven	Eric Clapton	Reprise	5	(2)	L
15	-	You	Ten Sharp	Columbia	7		F L
16	-	Be Quick Or Be Dead	Iron Maiden	EMI	2		
17	-	(I Want To Be) Elected	Mr. Bean & Smear Campaign	London	3		F L
18	-	Take My Advice	Kym Sims	Atco	2	(86)	L
19	-	Time To Make You Mine	Lisa Stansfield	Arista	4		
20	-	The Only Living Boy In New Cross	Carter-Unstoppable Sex Machine	Big Cat	3		

May 1992

This Mnth	Prev Mnth	Title	Artist	Label	Wks 20	(US Pos)	
1	-	Please Don't Go	KWS	Network	12	(6)	F
2	10	On A Ragga Tip	SL2	XL	9		L
3	-	Hang On In There Baby	Curiosity	RCA	6		L
4	1	Deeply Dippy	Right Said Fred	Tug	10		
5	-	The Days Of Pearly Spencer	Marc Almond	Some Bizzare	4		L
6	-	Workaholic	2 Unlimited	PWL Continental	4		
7	-	My Lovin'	En Vogue	East West America	5	(2)	
8	11	You're All That Matters To Me	Curtis Stigers	Arista	7	(98)	L
9	-	Everything About You	Ugly Kid Joe	Mercury	7	(9)	F
10	-	Nothing Else Matters	Metallica	Vertigo	3	(35)	
11	-	Knockin' On Heaven's Door	Guns N' Roses	Geffen	6		
12	-	Temple Of Love (1992)	Sisters Of Mercy	Merciful Release	3		
13	15	You	Ten Sharp	Columbia	7		F L
14	-	I Don't Care	Shakespears Sister	London	4	(55)	
15	-	In The Closet	Michael Jackson	Epic	3	(6)	
16	4	Save The Best For Last	Vanessa Williams	Polydor	7	(1)	F L
17	-	Beauty And The Beast	Celine Dion & Peabo Bryson	Epic	3	(9)	F L
18	-	Keep On Walkin'	Ce Ce Peniston	A&M	3	(15)	L
19	-	Song For Love	Extreme	A&M	3		
20	20	The Only Living Boy In New Cross	Carter-Unstoppable Sex Machine	Big Cat	3		

June 1992

This Mnth	Prev Mnth	Title	Artist	Label	Wks 20	(US Pos)	
1	1	Please Don't Go	KWS	Network	12	(6)	F
2	-	Hazard	Richard Marx	Capitol	10	(9)	F
3	-	Jump	Kris Kross	Ruffhouse	6	(1)	F
4	-	Abba-Esque (EP)	Erasure	Mute	8		
5	-	Something Good	Utah Saints	ffrr	7	(98)	
6	-	Heartbeat	Nick Berry	Columbia	5		L
7	-	Toofunky	George Michael	Epic	5	(10)	
8	9	Everything About You	Ugly Kid Joe	Mercury	7	(9)	F
9	-	It Only Takes A Minute	Take That	RCA	6		F
10	11	Knockin' On Heaven's Door	Guns N' Roses	Geffen	6		
11	-	The One	Elton John	Rocket	5	(9)	L
12	-	Friday, I'm In Love	Cure	Fiction	4	(18)	L
13	-	Blue Room	Orb	Big Life	3		F
14	2	On A Ragga Tip	SL2	XL	9		L
15	7	My Lovin'	En Vogue	East West America	5	(2)	
16	-	Midlife Crisis	Faith No More	Slash	2		F
17	-	Even Better Than The Real Thing	U2	Island	6	(32)	
18	-	Ain't 2 Proud 2 Beg	TLC	Arista	3	(6)	F L
19	-	I'll Be There	Mariah Carey	Columbia	6	(1)	
20	14	I Don't Care	Shakespears Sister	London	4	(55)	

April 1992

This Mnth	Prev Mnth	Title	Artist	Label	Wks 20	(UK Pos)	
1	2	Save The Best For Last	Vanessa Williams	Wing	17	(3)	
2	5	Tears In Heaven	Eric Clapton	Duck	16	(5)	G
3	7	Masterpiece	Atlantic Starr	Warner	14		L
4	15	Make It Happen	Mariah Carey	Columbia	11	(17)	
5	3	Remember The Time	Michael Jackson	Epic	13	(3)	
6	11	Breakin' My Heart (Pretty Brown Eyes)	Mint Condition	Perspective	9		F L
7	-	Ain't Too Proud 2 Beg	TLC	Laface	12	(13)	F G
8	-	Jump	Kris Kross	Ruffhouse	15	(2)	F P
9	-	Bohemian Rhapsody	Queen	Hollywood	9	(1)	L
10	16	Beauty And The Beast	Celine Dion & Peabo Bryson	Epic	9	(9)	
11	9	I Can't Dance	Genesis	Virgin	9	(7)	
12	-	My Lovin' (You're Never Gonna Get It)	En Vogue	Atlantic	16	(4)	
13	-	Hazard	Richard Marx	Capitol	9	(3)	
14	4	I'm Too Sexy	Right Said Fred	Charisma	13	(2)	F G L
15	1	To Be With You	Mr. Big	Atlantic	13	(3)	F
16	-	Live And Learn	Joe Public	Columbia	13	(43)	F L
17	-	Everything Changes	Kathy Troccoli	Reunion	6		F L
18	-	Human Touch/Better Days	Bruce Springsteen	Columbia	7	(11)	L
19	8	Good For Me	Amy Grant	A&M	10	(60)	
20	14	Justified And Ancient	KLF Feat. Tammy Wynette	Arista	5	(2)	L

May 1992

This Mnth	Prev Mnth	Title	Artist	Label	Wks 20	(UK Pos)	
1	8	Jump	Kris Kross	Ruffhouse	15	(2)	F P
2	12	My Lovin' (You're Never Gonna Get It)	En Vogue	Atlantic	16	(4)	
3	9	Bohemian Rhapsody	Queen	Hollywood	9	(1)	L
4	1	Save The Best For Last	Vanessa Williams	Wing	17	(3)	
5	16	Live And Learn	Joe Public	Columbia	13	(43)	F L
6	2	Tears In Heaven	Eric Clapton	Duck	16	(5)	G
7	-	Under The Bridge	Red Hot Chili Peppers	Warner	15	(26)	F L
8	7	Ain't Too Proud 2 Beg	TLC	Laface	12	(13)	F G
9	-	Everything About You	Ugly Kid Joe	Star Dog	7	(3)	F
10	-	One	U2	Island	8		L
11	-	In The Closet	Michael Jackson	Epic	8	(8)	
12	4	Make It Happen	Mariah Carey	Columbia	11	(17)	
13	13	Hazard	Richard Marx	Capitol	9	(3)	
14	-	Thought I'd Died And Gone To Heaven	Bryan Adams	A&M	7	(8)	
15	-	Baby Got Back	Sir Mix-A-Lot	Def American	20	(56)	F P
16	-	Damn I Wish I Was Your Lover	Sophie B. Hawkins	Columbia	11	(14)	F L
17	-	Let's Get Rocked	Def Leppard	Mercury	5	(2)	
18	3	Masterpiece	Atlantic Starr	Warner	14		L
19	-	If You Asked Me To	Celine Dion	Epic	12	(60)	L
20	10	Beauty And The Beast	Celine Dion & Peabo Bryson	Epic	9	(9)	

June 1992

This Mnth	Prev Mnth	Title	Artist	Label	Wks 20	(UK Pos)	
1	-	I'll Be There	Mariah Carey	Columbia	11	(2)	
2	1	Jump	Kris Kross	Ruffhouse	15	(2)	F P
3	7	Under The Bridge	Red Hot Chili Peppers	Warner	15	(26)	F L
4	15	Baby Got Back	Sir Mix-A-Lot	Def American	20	(56)	F P
5	2	My Lovin' (You're Never Gonna...)	En Vogue	Atlantic	16	(4)	
6	16	Damn I Wish I Was Your Lover	Sophie B. Hawkins	Columbia	11	(14)	F L
7	19	If You Asked Me To	Celine Dion	Epic	12	(60)	L
8	5	Live And Learn	Joe Public	Columbia	13	(43)	F L
9	-	Achy Breaky Heart	Billy Ray Cyrus	Mercury	16	(3)	F G L
10	-	Tennessee	Arrested Development	Chrysalis	11	(18)	F
11	11	In The Closet	Michael Jackson	Epic	8	(8)	
12	-	The Best Things In Life Are Free	Luther Vandross/Janet Jackson	Perspective	12	(2)	L
13	-	Hold On My Heart	Genesis	Atlantic	8	(16)	L
14	8	Ain't Too Proud 2 Beg	TLC	Laface	12	(13)	F G
15	-	Wishing On A Star	Cover Girls	Epic	10	(38)	L
16	-	Just Another Day	Jon Secada	SBK	18	(5)	F
17	6	Tears In Heaven	Eric Clapton	Duck	16	(5)	G
18	4	Save The Best For Last	Vanessa Williams	Wing	17	(3)	
19	-	Come & Talk To Me	Jodeci	Uptown/MCA	13		F
20	-	Just Take My Heart	Mr. Big	Atlantic	2	(26)	L

US 1992
APR-JUNE

▲ Schoolboy rap duo Kris Kross (above) topped both the single and album charts with their debut releases, 'Jump' and **Totally Krossed Out.** Other noteworthy chart new-comers included Arrested Development, TLC, Red Hot Chili Peppers, Jodeci and Jon Secada.

◆ The soundtrack to *Wayne's World* hit the top, launching Queen's 'Bohemian Rhapsody' back into the Top 10. Queen also had America's top music video and four albums climbing the chart.

◆ Mariah Carey's sixth chart topper, 'I'll Be There', entered the Hot 100 at No. 13 – the highest first week placing since 'Let It Be' by The Beatles in 1970.

UK 1992 JULY-SEPT

▲ Elton John overtook The Beatles when he collected his 50th US Top 40 entry with 'The One'. Madonna's (above) 'This Used To Be My Playground', not only gave her a (female) record 10th American No. 1, but also meant she had more UK Top 10 hits than The Beatles. Morrissey (ex-lead singer of The Smiths) sold out the Hollywood Bowl in 23 minutes breaking another record set by The Beatles.

◆ Prince signed a world-wide record and publishing deal with Warner estimated to be worth $100 million.

July 1992

This Mnth	Prev Mnth	Title	Artist	Label	Wks 20	(US Pos)	
1	4	Abba-Esque (EP)	Erasure	Mute	8		
2	19	I'll Be There	Mariah Carey	Columbia	6	(1)	
3	-	Rhythm Is A Dancer	Snap	Arista	16	(5)	
4	-	Ain't No Doubt	Jimmy Nail	East West	9		L
5	-	Sesame's Treet	Smart E's	Suburban Base	6	(60)	F L
6	2	Hazard	Richard Marx	Capitol	10	(9)	
7	-	A Trip To Trumpton	Urban Hype	Faze	5		F L
8	5	Something Good	Utah Saints	ffrr	7	(98)	
9	17	Even Better Than The Real Thing	U2	Island	6	(32)	
10	-	One Shining Moment	Diana Ross	EMI	6		
11	-	Sexy MF/Strollin'	Prince/New Power Generation	Paisley Park	4	(66)	
12	6	Heartbeat	Nick Berry	Columbia	5		L
13	-	I Drove All Night	Roy Orbison	MCA	6		
14	-	Disappointed	Electronic	Parlophone	2		L
15	-	L.S.I.	Shamen	One Little Indian	6		
16	1	Please Don't Go	KWS	Network	12	(6)	F L
17	7	Toofunky	George Michael	Epic	5	(10)	
18	-	Shake Your Head	Was (Not Was)	Fontana	8		L
19	-	This Used To Be My Playground	Madonna	Sire	6	(1)	
20	9	It Only Takes A Minute	Take That	RCA	6		F

August 1992

This Mnth	Prev Mnth	Title	Artist	Label	Wks 20	(US Pos)	
1	3	Rhythm Is A Dancer	Snap	Arista	16	(5)	
2	4	Ain't No Doubt	Jimmy Nail	East West	9		L
3	-	Achy Breaky Heart	Billy Ray Cyrus	Mercury	8	(4)	F L
4	-	Barcelona	Freddie Mercury & Montserrat Caballe	Polydor	5		
5	19	This Used To Be My Playground	Madonna	Sire	6	(1)	
6	18	Shake Your Head	Was (Not Was)	Fontana	8		L
7	-	Just Another Day	Jon Secada	SBK	10	(5)	F L
8	-	The Best Things In Life Are Free	Luther Vandross/Janet Jackson	Epic	10	(10)	L
9	-	Don't You Want Me	Felix	Deconstruction	8		F
10	15	L.S.I.	Shamen	One Little Indian	6		
11	5	Sesame's Treet	Smart E's	Suburban Base	6	(60)	F L
12	13	I Drove All Night	Roy Orbison	MCA	6		
13	-	Baker Street	Undercover	PWL Int.	11		F
14	-	This Charming Man	Smiths	WEA	2		
15	-	Book Of Days	Enya	WEA	3		L
16	-	Who Is It	Michael Jackson	Epic	4	(14)	
17	-	Rock Your Baby	KWS	Network	4		L
18	-	How Do You Do!	Roxette	EMI	4	(58)	
19	-	Magic Friend	2 Unlimited	PWL Continental	4		
20	7	A Trip To Trumpton	Urban Hype	Faze	5		F L

September 1992

This Mnth	Prev Mnth	Title	Artist	Label	Wks 20	(US Pos)	
1	1	Rhythm Is A Dancer	Snap	Arista	16	(5)	
2	-	Ebeneezer Goode	Shamen	One Little Indian	8		
3	13	Baker Street	Undercover	PWL Int.	11		F
4	8	The Best Things In Life Are Free	Luther Vandross/Janet Jackson	Epic	10	(10)	L
5	-	Too Much Love Will Kill You	Brian May	Parlophone	6		
6	7	Just Another Day	Jon Secada	SBK	10	(5)	F L
7	-	It's My Life	Dr. Alban	Arista	9	(88)	F
8	-	My Destiny	Lionel Richie	Motown	9		L
9	3	Achy Breaky Heart	Billy Ray Cyrus	Mercury	8	(4)	F L
10	-	Walking On Broken Glass	Annie Lennox	RCA	5	(14)	
11	9	Don't You Want Me	Felix	Deconstruction	8		F
12	-	House Of Love	East 17	London	4		F
13	-	Theme From M*A*S*H (Suicide Is Painless)/(Everything I Do) I Do It For You	Manic Street Preachers/ Fatima Mansions	Columbia	4		
14	-	Iron Lion Zion	Bob Marley & The Wailers	Tuff Gong	5		L
15	17	Rock Your Baby	KWS	Network	4		L
16	-	Jam	Michael Jackson	Epic	2	(26)	
17	-	Take This Heart	Richard Marx	Capitol	2	(20)	L
18	4	Barcelona	Freddie Mercury & Montserrat Caballe	Polydor	5		
19	-	Fire/Jericho	Prodigy	XL	2		
20	-	Rest In Peace	Extreme	A&M	2	(96)	

July 1992

This Mnth	Prev Mnth	Title	Artist	Label	Wks 20	(UK Pos)	
1	4	Baby Got Back	Sir Mix-A-Lot	Def American	20	(56)	F P
2	1	I'll Be There	Mariah Carey	Columbia	11	(2)	L
3	3	Under The Bridge	Red Hot Chili Peppers	Warner	15	(26)	F L
4	9	Achy Breaky Heart	Billy Ray Cyrus	Mercury	16	(3)	F G L
5	7	If You Asked Me To	Celine Dion	Epic	12	(60)	L
6	10	Tennessee	Arrested Development	Chrysalis	11	(18)	F
7	15	Wishing On A Star	Cover Girls	Epic	10	(38)	L
8	-	Baby-Baby-Baby	TLC	Laface	18	(55)	G L
9	6	Damn I Wish I Was Your Lover	Sophie B. Hawkins	Columbia	11	(14)	F L
10	16	Just Another Day	Jon Secada	SBK	18	(5)	F
11	-	Life Is A Highway	Tom Cochrane	Capitol	15	(62)	F L
12	-	This Used To Be My Playground	Madonna	Sire	11	(3)	
13	2	Jump	Kris Kross	Ruffhouse	15	(2)	F P
14	-	Toofunky	George Michael	Columbia	9	(4)	L
15	12	The Best Things In Life Are Free	Luther Vandross & Janet Jackson	Perspective	12	(2)	L
16	5	My Lovin' (You're Never Gonna Get It)	En Vogue	Atlantic	16	(4)	
17	-	November Rain	Guns N' Roses	Geffen	14	(4)	L
18	19	Come & Talk To Me	Jodeci	Uptown/MCA	13		F
19	-	Warm It Up	Kris Kross	Columbia	7	(16)	
20	13	Hold On My Heart	Genesis	Atlantic	8	(16)	L

August 1992

This Mnth	Prev Mnth	Title	Artist	Label	Wks 20	(UK Pos)	
1	8	Baby-Baby-Baby	TLC	Laface	18	(55)	G L
2	12	This Used To Be My Playground	Madonna	Sire	11	(3)	
3	-	End Of The Road	Boyz II Men	Motown	21	(1)	G
4	1	Baby Got Back	Sir Mix-A-Lot	Def American	20	(56)	F P
5	17	November Rain	Guns N' Roses	Geffen	14	(4)	L
6	10	Just Another Day	Jon Secada	SBK	18	(5)	F
7	11	Life Is A Highway	Tom Cochrane	Capitol	15	(62)	F L
8	4	Achy Breaky Heart	Billy Ray Cyrus	Mercury	16	(3)	F G L
9	-	Giving Him Something He Can Feel	En Vogue	Atco	11	(44)	
10	18	Come & Talk To Me	Jodeci	Uptown/MCA	13		F
11	-	Move This	Technotronic Featuring Ya Kid K	SBK	8		L
12	-	Humpin' Around	Bobby Brown	MCA	11	(19)	
13	-	Stay	Shakespears Sister	London	9	(1)	F L
14	19	Warm It Up	Kris Kross	Columbia	7	(16)	
15	14	Toofunky	George Michael	Columbia	9	(4)	L
16	-	The One	Elton John	MCA	10	(10)	L
17	7	Wishing On A Star	Cover Girls	Epic	10	(38)	L
18	-	Keep On Walkin'	Ce Ce Peniston	A&M	4	(10)	L
19	2	I'll Be There	Mariah Carey	Columbia	11	(2)	L
20	5	If You Asked Me To	Celine Dion	Epic	12	(60)	L

September 1992

This Mnth	Prev Mnth	Title	Artist	Label	Wks 20	(UK Pos)	
1	3	End Of The Road	Boyz II Men	Motown	21	(1)	G
2	1	Baby-Baby-Baby	TLC	Laface	18	(55)	G L
3	12	Humpin' Around	Bobby Brown	MCA	11	(19)	
4	5	November Rain	Guns N' Roses	Geffen	14	(4)	L
5	13	Stay	Shakespears Sister	London	9	(1)	F L
6	-	Sometimes Love Just Ain't Enough	Patty Smyth With Don Henley	MCA	16	(22)	F L
7	-	Jump Around	House Of Pain	Tommy Boy	16	(8)	F G L
8	6	Just Another Day	Jon Secada	SBK	18	(5)	F
9	9	Giving Him Something He Can Feel	En Vogue	Atco	11	(44)	
10	11	Move This	Technotronic Featuring Ya Kid K	SBK	8		L
11	16	The One	Elton John	MCA	10	(10)	L
12	2	This Used To Be My Playground	Madonna	Sire	11	(3)	
13	4	Baby Got Back	Sir Mix-A-Lot	Def American	20	(56)	F P
14	-	She's Playing Hard To Get	Hi-Five	Jive	12	(55)	L
15	-	Please Don't Go	KWS	Next Plateau	9	(1)	F L
16	7	Life Is A Highway	Tom Cochrane	Capitol	15	(62)	F L
17	-	All I Want	Toad The Wet Sprocket	Columbia	7		F
18	-	Do I Have To Say The Words?	Bryan Adams	A&M	7	(30)	
19	-	People Everyday	Arrested Development	Chrysalis	10	(2)	
20	10	Come & Talk To Me	Jodeci	Uptown/MCA	13		F

◆ **Some Gave All** by Billy Ray Cyrus became the first debut album to top the chart in two weeks and the first to hold the top spot for 17 weeks. Cyrus' transatlantic hit, 'Achy Breaky Heart', was the first million selling country single since 'Islands In The Stream' by Kenny Rogers and Dolly Parton in 1983.

◆ In September, LA & Babyface became the first producers to hold the Top 3 chart placings with records by different acts (Boyz II Men, TLC and Bobby Brown).

◆ Richard Marx scored his twelfth successive Top 20 entry with 'Take This Heart', and Michael Jackson missed the Top 20 for the first time since 1979 with 'Jam'. For the record, Jackson's **Dangerous** album had now sold over 15 million globally in just 10 months.

337

UK 1992
OCT-DEC

◆ American shows by Elton John, George Michael, Lionel Richie, Madonna and Billy Idol raised over $7 million for AIDS research. At the same time, Elton, signed his publishing to Warner for a world record $26 million.

▲ U2 (above) grossed $64 million from their 1992 US tour. Barbra Streisand's new record contract with Columbia was slated to earn her a similar figure.

◆ The Wedding Present equalled a record set in 1957 by Elvis Presley by scoring twelve chart records in a year. Like many of their 1992 British contemporaries, however, the group made little impact in America.

October 1992

This Mnth	Prev Mnth	Title	Artist	Label	Wks 20	(US Pos)	
1	-	Sleeping Satellite	Tasmin Archer	EMI	9	(32)	F
2	-	End Of The Road	Boyz II Men	Motown	12	(1)	F L
3	7	It's My Life	Dr. Alban	Arista	9	(88)	F
4	2	Ebeneezer Goode	Shamen	One Little Indian	8		
5	-	I'm Gonna Get You	Bizarre Inc. Feat. Angie Brown	Vinyl Solution	8	(47)	
6	-	Erotica	Madonna	Maverick	5	(3)	
7	3	Baker Street	Undercover	PWL Int.	11		F
8	-	A Million Love Songs (EP)	Take That	RCA	5		
9	-	Tetris	Doctor Spin	Carpet	5		F L
10	14	Iron Lion Zion	Bob Marley & The Wailers	Tuff Gong	5		L
11	8	My Destiny	Lionel Richie	Motown	9		L
12	-	Love Song/Alive And Kicking	Simple Minds	Virgin	3		L
13	-	Keep The Faith	Bon Jovi	Jambco	4	(29)	
14	-	My Name Is Prince	Prince/New Power Generation	Paisley Park	3	(36)	L
15	-	People Everyday	Arrested Development	Cooltempo	8	(8)	F
16	-	Sentinel	Mike Oldfield	WEA	3		L
17	1	Rhythm Is A Dancer	Snap	Arista	16	(5)	
18	4	The Best Things In Life Are Free	Luther Vandross/Janet Jackson	Epic	10	(10)	L
19	5	Too Much Love Will Kill You	Brian May	Parlophone	6		
20	13	Theme From M*A*S*H.../(...) I Do It...	Manic St. Preachers/Fatima...	Columbia	4		

November 1992

This Mnth	Prev Mnth	Title	Artist	Label	Wks 20	(US Pos)	
1	2	End Of The Road	Boyz II Men	Motown	12	(1)	F L
2	15	People Everyday	Arrested Development	Cooltempo	8	(8)	F
3	-	Would I Lie To You?	Charles & Eddie	Capitol	12	(13)	F L
4	-	Boss Drum	Shamen	One Little Indian	5		
5	-	Never Let Her Slip Away	Undercover	PWL Int.	5		L
6	-	Run To You	Rage	Pulse 8	5		F L
7	-	I Will Always Love You	Whitney Houston	Arista	17	(1)	G
8	-	Be My Baby	Vanessa Paradis	Remark	6		L
9	-	Supermarioland	Ambassadors Of Funk/MC Mario	Living Beat	5		F L
10	5	I'm Gonna Get You	Bizarre Inc Feat Angie Brown	Vinyl Solution	8	(47)	
11	-	Temptation	Heaven 17	Virgin	8		L
12	1	Sleeping Satellite	Tasmin Archer	EMI	9	(32)	F
13	-	Invisible Touch (Live)	Genesis	Virgin	2		L
14	-	Who Needs Love (Like That)	Erasure	Mute	3		L
15	-	Out Of Space/Ruff In The Jungle Bizness	Prodigy	XL	9		
16	-	Yesterdays/November Rain	Guns N' Roses	Geffen	3	(3)	
17	-	Montreux EP	Simply Red	East West	7		L
18	13	Keep The Faith	Bon Jovi	Jambco	4	(29)	
19	-	Hello (Turn Your Radio On)	Shakespears Sister	London	2		L
20	-	Free Your Mind/Giving Him Something He Can Feel	En Vogue	East West America	3	(8)	L

December 1992

This Mnth	Prev Mnth	Title	Artist	Label	Wks 20	(US Pos)	
1	6	I Will Always Love You	Whitney Houston	Arista	17	(1)	G
2	-	Heal The World	Michael Jackson	Epic	8	(27)	L
3	3	Would I Lie To You?	Charles & Eddie	Capitol	12	(13)	F L
4	-	Tom Traubert's Blues (Waltzing Matilda)	Rod Stewart	Warner	5		
5	-	Slam Jam	WWF Superstars	Arista	5		F
6	14	Out Of Space/Ruff In The Jungle...	Prodigy	XI	9		
7	-	Could It Be Magic	Take That	RCA	9		
8	10	Temptation	Heaven 17	Virgin	8		L
9	-	I Still Believe In You	Cliff Richard	EMI	4		
10	-	Deeper And Deeper	Madonna	Maverick	5	(7)	
11	-	Boney M Megamix	Boney M	Arista	5		L
12	-	In My Defence	Freddie Mercury	Parlophone	4		L
13	-	Phorever People	Shamen	One Little Indian	7		
14	16	Montreux EP	Simply Red	East West	7		L
15	-	Step It Up	Stereo MCs	4th & Broadway	7		
16	-	If We Hold On Together	Diana Ross	EMI	6		L
17	1	End Of The Road	Boyz II Men	Motown	12	(1)	F L
18	-	Miami Hit Mix/Christmas Through Your Eyes	Gloria Estefan	Epic	5		
19	2	People Everyday	Arrested Development	Cooltempo	8	(8)	F
20	5	Never Let Her Slip Away	Undercover	PWL Int.	5		L

October 1992

This Mnth	Prev Mnth	Title	Artist	Label	Wks 20	(UK Pos)	
1	1	End Of The Road	Boyz II Men	Motown	21	(1)	G
2	6	Sometimes Love Just Ain't Enough	Patty Smyth With Don Henley	MCA	16	(22)	F L
3	7	Jump Around	House Of Pain	Tommy Boy	16	(8)	F G L
4	14	She's Playing Hard To Get	Hi-Five	Jive	12	(55)	L
5	-	I'd Die Without You	P.M. Dawn	Laface	19	(30)	
6	15	Please Don't Go	KWS	Next Plateau	9	(1)	F L
7	19	People Everyday	Arrested Development	Chrysalis	10	(2)	
8	-	When I Look Into Your Eyes	Firehouse	Epic	8	(65)	L
9	2	Baby-Baby-Baby	TLC	Laface	18	(55)	G L
10	3	Humpin' Around	Bobby Brown	MCA	11	(19)	
11	-	Erotica	Madonna	Maverick	7	(3)	
12	-	How Do You Talk To An Angel	Heights	Capitol	13		F L
13	-	Free Your Mind	En Vogue	Atco	8	(16)	
14	-	Have You Ever Needed Someone So Bad	Def Leppard	Mercury	9	(16)	L
15	-	Rhythm Is A Dancer	Snap	Arista	20	(1)	L
16	4	November Rain	Guns N' Roses	Geffen	14	(4)	L
17	18	Do I Have To Say The Words?	Bryan Adams	A&M	7	(30)	
18	-	Real Love	Mary J. Blige	Uptown	16	(26)	F L
19	-	Forever Love	Color Me Badd	Giant	4		L
20	5	Stay	Shakespears Sister	London	9	(1)	F L

November 1992

This Mnth	Prev Mnth	Title	Artist	Label	Wks 20	(UK Pos)	
1	12	How Do You Talk To An Angel	Heights	Capitol	13		F L
2	1	End Of The Road	Boyz II Men	Motown	21	(1)	G
3	5	I'd Die Without You	P.M. Dawn	Laface	19	(30)	
4	-	If I Ever Fall In Love	Shai	Gasoline Alley	18	(36)	F G
5	-	Rump Shaker	Wreckx-N-Effect	MCA	17	(24)	F P L
6	15	Rhythm Is A Dancer	Snap	Arista	20	(1)	L
7	2	Sometimes Love Just Ain't Enough	Patty Smyth With Don Henley	MCA	16	(22)	F L
8	-	What About Your Friends	TLC	Laface	16	(59)	L
9	18	Real Love	Mary J. Blige	Uptown	16	(26)	F L
10	3	Jump Around	House Of Pain	Tommy Boy	16	(8)	F G L
11	11	Erotica	Madonna	Maverick/Sire	7	(3)	
12	-	Good Enough	Bobby Brown	MCA	15	(41)	
13	-	I Will Always Love You	Whitney Houston	Arista	19	(1)	P
14	13	Free Your Mind	En Vogue	Atco East West	8	(16)	
15	-	Layla	Eric Clapton	Duck	8	(45)	L
16	-	Walking On Broken Glass	Annie Lennox	Arista	8	(8)	L
17	14	Have You Ever Needed Someone So Bad	Def Leppard	Mercury	9	(16)	L
18	-	Would I Lie To You?	Charles & Eddie	Capitol	7	(1)	F L
19	-	Love Is On The Way	Saigon Kick	Third Stone	10		F L
20	7	People Everyday	Arrested Development	Chrysalis	10	(2)	

December 1992

This Mnth	Prev Mnth	Title	Artist	Label	Wks 20	(UK Pos)	
1	13	I Will Always Love You	Whitney Houston	Arista	19	(1)	P
2	4	If I Ever Fall In Love	Shai	Gasoline Alley	18	(36)	F G
3	5	Rump Shaker	Wreckx-N-Effect	MCA	17	(24)	F P L
4	3	I'd Die Without You	P.M. Dawn	Laface	19	(30)	
5	-	In The Still Of The Night (I'll Remember)	Boyz II Men	Motown	14	(27)	G L
6	1	How Do You Talk To An Angel	Heights	Capitol	13		F L
7	6	Rhythm Is A Dancer	Snap	Arista	20	(1)	L
8	12	Good Enough	Bobby Brown	MCA	15	(41)	
9	9	Real Love	Mary J. Blige	Uptown	16	(26)	F L
10	8	What About Your Friends	TLC	Laface	16	(59)	L
11	-	To Love Somebody	Michael Bolton	Columbia	9	(16)	
12	-	Saving Forever For You	Shanice	Motown	14	(42)	L
13	19	Love Is On The Way	Saigon Kick	Third Stone	10		F L
14	15	Layla	Eric Clapton	Duck	8	(45)	L
15	-	Do You Believe In Us	Jon Secada	SBK	9	(30)	
16	2	End Of The Road	Boyz II Men	Motown	21	(1)	G
17	-	Deeper And Deeper	Madonna	Maverick	9	(6)	
18	16	Walking On Broken Glass	Annie Lennox	Arista	8	(8)	L
19	7	Sometimes Love Just Ain't Enough	Patty Smyth With Don Henley	MCA	16	(22)	F L
20	-	Little Miss Can't Be Wrong	Spin Doctors	Epic	5	(23)	F

◆ With CDs now out-selling cassettes, shipments of recorded music in America jumped 15.2% to over $9 billion.

◆ In October, Garth Brooks had four albums in the Top 20, and his LP **The Chase** was the first album to be certified quintuple platinum in its first month. By November, a record-shattering 40% of the Top 25 albums were by country artists!

◆ Boyz II Men's transatlantic topper, 'End Of The Road', spent an unprecedented 13 weeks at No. 1. They were one of a record nine black vocalists in the Top 10 of December.

◆ Bob Dylan celebrated his 30th anniversary with an all-star Madison Square Garden show. The Beatles celebrated their 30th anniversary by having a record 11 albums in the Catalog Top 50 (including **Sgt. Pepper** at No. 1).

339

UK 1993 JAN-MAR

◆ R.E.M. were voted Top Group of 1992 in the *NME* Poll and their **Automatic For The People** (which narrowly missed becoming a transatlantic No. 1) collected the trophy for Top Album.

◆ Thirty-four years after his death, Buddy Holly's album **Words of Love** topped the UK chart.

▲ At the end of March, for the first time, reggae records held the top three places on the UK chart. They were 'Oh Carolina' by Shaggy, 'Informer' by Snow (above) and 'Mr. Loverman' by Shabba Ranks.

January 1993

This Mnth	Prev Mnth	Title	Artist	Label	Wks 20	(US Pos)	
1	1	I Will Always Love You	Whitney Houston	Arista	17	(1)	G
2	7	Could It Be Magic	Take That	RCA	9		
3	-	Exterminate!	Snap Featuring Niki Haris	Arista	8		
4	2	Heal The World	Michael Jackson	Epic	8	(27)	L
5	13	Phorever People	Shamen	One Little Indian	7		
6	-	Mr. Wendal/Revolution	Arrested Development	Cooltempo	5	(6)	
7	3	Would I Lie To You?	Charles & Eddie	Capitol	12	(13)	F L
8	-	I'm Easy/Be Aggressive	Faith No More	Slash	5	(58)	L
9	-	The Love I Lost	West End Featuring Sybil	PWL Sanctuary	9		F L
10	5	Slam Jam	WWF Superstars	Arista	5		F
11	-	We Are Family	Sister Sledge	Atlantic	4		
12	-	Open Your Mind	Usura	Deconstruction	5		F L
13	18	Miami Hit Mix/Christmas Through Your Eyes	Gloria Estefan	Epic	5		
14	-	Sweet Harmony	Beloved	East West	5		L
15	-	After All	Frank And Walters	Setanta	3		F L
16	11	Boney M Megamix	Boney M	Arista	5		L
17	6	Out Of Space/Ruff In The Jungle Bizness	Prodigy	XL	9		
18	-	Someday (I'm Coming Back)	Lisa Stansfield	Arista	5		
19	-	Steam	Peter Gabriel	Realworld	3	(32)	L
20	-	No Limit	2 Unlimited	PWL Continental	13		

February 1993

This Mnth	Prev Mnth	Title	Artist	Label	Wks 20	(US Pos)	
1	20	No Limit	2 Unlimited	PWL Continental	13		
2	1	I Will Always Love You	Whitney Houston	Arista	17	(1)	G
3	-	Deep	East 17	London	8		
4	9	The Love I Lost	West End Featuring Sybil	PWL Sanctuary	9		F L
5	-	Little Bird/Love Song For A Vampire	Annie Lennox	RCA	8	(49)	L
6	-	Ordinary World	Duran Duran	Parlophone	6	(3)	
7	3	Exterminate!	Snap Featuring Niki Haris	Arista	8		
8	-	How Can I Love You More?	M People	Deconstruction	4		F
9	-	Why Can't I Wake Up With You?	Take That	RCA	4		
10	-	I'm Every Woman	Whitney Houston	Arista	6	(4)	
11	-	Stairway To Heaven	Rolf Harris	Vertigo	3		L
12	14	Sweet Harmony	Beloved	East West	5		L
13	12	Open Your Mind	Usura	Deconstruction	5		F L
14	-	Are You Gonna Go My Way	Lenny Kravitz	Virgin America	7		
15	11	We Are Family	Sister Sledge	Atlantic	4		
16	-	Independence	Lulu	Dome	3		
17	-	Give In To Me	Michael Jackson	Epic	6		
18	-	You're In A Bad Way	Saint Etienne	Heavenly	2		F L
19	-	Ruby Tuesday	Rod Stewart	Warner	3		
20	-	I Feel You	Depeche Mode	Mute	2	(37)	

March 1993

This Mnth	Prev Mnth	Title	Artist	Label	Wks 20	(US Pos)	
1	1	No Limit	2 Unlimited	PWL Continental	13		
2	-	Oh Carolina	Shaggy	Greensleeves	12	(59)	F L
3	17	Give In To Me	Michael Jackson	Epic	6		
4	5	Little Bird/Love Song For A Vampire	Annie Lennox	RCA	8	(49)	L
5	14	Are You Gonna Go My Way	Lenny Kravitz	Virgin America	7		
6	-	Mr. Loverman	Shabba Ranks	Epic	8	(40)	
7	-	Stick It Out	Right Said Fred & Friends	Tug	5		L
8	10	I'm Every Woman	Whitney Houston	Arista	6	(4)	
9	-	Animal Nitrate	Suede	Nude	3		L
10	-	Informer	Snow	East West America	11	(1)	F L
11	3	Deep	East 17	London	8		
12	-	Too Young To Die	Jamiroquai	Sony S²	3		F
13	-	Cat's In The Cradle	Ugly Kid Joe	Mercury	6	(6)	L
14	-	Shortsharpshock (EP)	Therapy?	A&M	2		F
15	-	Bad Girl	Madonna	Maverick	3	(36)	
16	9	Why Can't I Wake Up With You?	Take That	RCA	4		
17	-	Looking Through Patient Eyes	P.M. Dawn	Gee Street	4	(6)	L
18	-	Young At Heart	Bluebells	London	8		
19	-	Fear Of The Dark (Live)	Iron Maiden	EMI	2		
20	-	Peace In Our Time	Cliff Richard	EMI	2		L

January 1993

This Mnth	Prev Mnth	Title	Artist	Label	Wks 20	(UK Pos)	
1	1	I Will Always Love You	Whitney Houston	Arista	19	(1)	P
2	2	If I Ever Fall In Love	Shai	Gasoline Alley	18	(36)	F G
3	3	Rump Shaker	Wreckx-N-Effect	MCA	17	(24)	F P L
4	5	In The Still Of The Night (I'll Remember)	Boyz II Men	Motown	14	(27)	G L
5	12	Saving Forever For You	Shanice	Motown	14	(42)	L
6	7	Rhythm Is A Dancer	Snap	Arista	20	(1)	L
7	8	Good Enough	Bobby Brown	MCA	15	(41)	
8	4	I'd Die Without You	P.M. Dawn	Laface	19	(30)	
9	17	Deeper And Deeper	Madonna	Maverick	9	(6)	
10	9	Real Love	Mary J. Blige	Uptown	16	(26)	F L
11	10	What About Your Friends	TLC	Laface	16	(59)	L
12	-	A Whole New World (Aladdin's Theme)	Peabo Bryson & Regina Belle	Columbia	15	(12)	L
13	-	When She Cries	Restless Heart	RCA	8		F L
14	11	To Love Somebody	Michael Bolton	Columbia	9	(16)	
15	-	7	Prince/New Power Generation	Paisley Park	11	(27)	L
16	-	Faithful	Go West	EMI	6	(13)	L
17	13	Love Is On The Way	Saigon Kick	Third Stone	10		F L
18	-	Mr. Wendal	Arrested Development	Chrysalis	15	(4)	L
19	6	How Do You Talk To An Angel	Heights	Capitol	13		F L
20	-	Flex	Mad Cobra	Columbia	2		F L

February 1993

This Mnth	Prev Mnth	Title	Artist	Label	Wks 20	(UK Pos)	
1	1	I Will Always Love You	Whitney Houston	Arista	19	(1)	P
2	12	A Whole New World (Aladdin's Theme)	Peabo Bryson & Regina Belle	Columbia	15	(12)	L
3	-	Ordinary World	Duran Duran	Capitol	12	(6)	
4	5	Saving Forever For You	Shanice	Motown	14	(42)	L
5	2	If I Ever Fall In Love	Shai	Gasoline Alley	18	(36)	F G
6	18	Mr. Wendal	Arrested Development	Chrysalis	15	(4)	L
7	15	7	Prince/New Power Generation	Paisley Park	11	(27)	L
8	-	I'm Every Woman	Whitney Houston	Arista	11	(4)	
9	4	In The Still Of The Night (I'll Remember)	Boyz II Men	Motown	14	(27)	G L
10	-	Here We Go Again!	Portrait	Capitol	9	(37)	F L
11	3	Rump Shaker	Wreckx-N-Effect	MCA	17	(24)	F P L
12	-	Nuthin' But A "G" Thang	Dr. Dre	Death Row	19		F G
13	-	Hip Hop Hurray	Naughty By Nature	Tommy Boy	14	(20)	G L
14	6	Rhythm Is A Dancer	Snap	Arista	20	(1)	L
15	-	Don't Walk Away	Jade	Giant	19	(7)	L
16	9	Deeper And Deeper	Madonna	Maverick	9	(6)	
17	-	Informer	Snow	Atco	15	(2)	F
18	13	When She Cries	Restless Heart	RCA	8		F L
19	-	Get Away	Bobby Brown	MCA	5		L
20	7	Good Enough	Bobby Brown	MCA	15	(41)	

March 1993

This Mnth	Prev Mnth	Title	Artist	Label	Wks 20	(UK Pos)	
1	17	Informer	Snow	Atco	15	(2)	F
2	12	Nuthin' But A "G" Thang	Dr. Dre	Death Row	19		F G
3	2	A Whole New World (Aladdin's...)	Peabo Bryson & Regina Belle	Columbia	15	(12)	L
4	3	Ordinary World	Duran Duran	Capitol	12	(6)	
5	8	I'm Every Woman	Whitney Houston	Arista	11	(4)	
6	15	Don't Walk Away	Jade	Giant	19	(7)	L
7	-	Freak Me	Silk	Keia	18	(46)	F G L
8	6	Mr. Wendal	Arrested Development	Chrysalis	15	(4)	L
9	1	I Will Always Love You	Whitney Houston	Arista	19	(1)	P
10	-	Bed Of Roses	Bon Jovi	Jambco	10	(13)	L
11	13	Hip Hop Hurray	Naughty By Nature	Tommy Boy	14	(20)	G L
12	-	I Have Nothing	Whitney Houston	Arista	13	(3)	L
13	-	Comforter	Shai	Gasoline Alley	13		
14	-	Two Princes	Spin Doctors	Epic	14	(3)	L
15	7	7	Prince/New Power Generation	Paisley Park	11	(27)	L
16	-	I Got A Man	Positive K	Island	8	(43)	F L
17	10	Here We Go Again!	Portrait	Capitol	9	(37)	F L
18	-	The Right Kind Of Love	Jeremy Jordan	Giant	5		F L
19	-	Cat's In The Cradle	Ugly Kid Joe	Stardog	8	(7)	L
20	19	Get Away	Bobby Brown	MCA	5		L

◆ Whitney Houston's soundtrack album **The Bodyguard** sold a record six million copies in just eight weeks. Her transatlantic topper, 'I Will Always Love You', became the top selling single ever by a female vocalist in Britain. It also headed the US chart for a record 14 weeks selling over three million in two months.

◆ Madonna's string of 27 consecutive Top 20 hits ended when 'Bad Girl' missed the mark.

◆ Eric Clapton picked up six Grammy Awards including Best Male Vocalist and Best Record and Song of The Year for 'Tears In Heaven', while **Unplugged,** voted Album Of The Year, moved to the top.

◆ Stars at President Clinton's inaugural Gala at the Capital Centre included Chuck Berry, Fleetwood Mac (re-united for the show), Aretha Franklin, Elton John and Barbra Streisand.

UK 1993

APR-JUNE

▲ Depeche Mode, whose 'Walking in My Shoes' was their 21st Top 20 entry, entered the transatlantic charts at No. 1 with their album **Songs Of Faith & Devotion.**

◆ In April, nine of the British Top 10 were dance records, and at times only five of the Top 20 records were by British artists - two more firsts.

◆ U2 signed a six album record deal worth over £130 ($200) million with Island.

April 1993

This Mnth	Prev Mnth	Title	Artist	Label	Wks 20	(US Pos)	
1	18	Young At Heart	Bluebells	London	8		L
2	10	Informer	Snow	East West America	11	(1)	F L
3	2	Oh Carolina	Shaggy	Greensleeves	12	(59)	F L
4	-	When I'm Good And Ready	Sybil	PWL Int.	8		L
5	6	Mr. Loverman	Shabba Ranks	Epic	8	(40)	
6	-	Show Me Love	Robin S.	Champion	6	(5)	F
7	-	Don't Walk Away	Jade	Giant	6	(4)	F
8	-	Ain't No Love (Ain't No Use)	Sub Sub Featuring Melanie Williams	Rob's	8		F L
9	1	No Limit	2 Unlimited	PWL Continental	13		
10	-	U Got 2 Know	Cappella	Internal	7		
11	13	Cat's In The Cradle	Ugly Kid Joe	Mercury	6	(6)	L
12	-	Fever	Madonna	Maverick	3		
13	-	Regret	New Order	London	3	(28)	
14	-	Go Away	Gloria Estefan	Epic	4		L
15	-	Wind It Up (Rewound)	Prodigy	XL	3		
16	-	Come Undone	Duran Duran	Parlophone	4	(7)	L
17	-	Wrestlemania	WWF Superstars	Arista	3		L
18	-	Slow It Down	East 17	London	3		
19	-	I Have Nothing	Whitney Houston	Arista	6	(4)	
20	-	Jump They Say	David Bowie	Arista	2		L

May 1993

This Mnth	Prev Mnth	Title	Artist	Label	Wks 20	(US Pos)	
1	-	Five Live (EP)	George Michael & Queen	Parlophone	7		L
2	-	All That She Wants	Ace Of Base	London	12	(2)	F
3	-	Sweat (A La La La La Long)	Inner Circle	Magnet	8	(16)	F
4	-	That's The Way Love Goes	Janet Jackson	Virgin	6	(1)	
5	-	Tribal Dance	2 Unlimited	PWL Continental	7		
6	19	I Have Nothing	Whitney Houston	Arista	6	(4)	
7	-	Everybody Hurts	REM	Warner	8	(29)	L
8	8	Ain't No Love (Ain't No Use)	Sub Sub Feat. Melanie Williams	Rob's	8		F L
9	2	Informer	Snow	East West	11	(1)	F L
10	1	Young At Heart	Bluebells	London	8		L
11	-	Housecall	Shabba Ranks Feat. Maxi Priest	Epic	5	(37)	L
12	-	(I Can't Help) Falling In Love With You	UB40	Dep International	12	(1)	
13	10	U Got 2 Know	Cappella	Internal	7		
14	-	Believe In Me	Utah Saints	ffrr	3		L
15	4	When I'm Good And Ready	Sybil	PWL Int.	8		L
16	-	In These Arms	Bon Jovi	Jambco	3	(28)	
17	-	I Don't Wanna Fight	Tina Turner	Parlophone	5	(9)	
18	-	Jump Around	House Of Pain	Ruffness	4	(3)	F L
19	6	Show Me Love	Robin S.	Champion	6	(5)	F
20	-	Express	Dina Carroll	A&M	3		

June 1993

This Mnth	Prev Mnth	Title	Artist	Label	Wks 20	(US Pos)	
1	12	(I Can't Help) Falling In Love With You	UB40	Dep International	12	(1)	
2	2	All That She Wants	Ace Of Base	London	12	(2)	F
3	-	Two Princes	Spin Doctors	Epic	10	(7)	F L
4	-	What Is Love	Haddaway	Arista	12	(11)	F
5	-	Three Little Pigs	Green Jelly	Zoo	5	(17)	F L
6	3	Sweat (A La La La La Long)	Inner Circle	Magnet	8	(16)	F
7	-	In All The Right Places	Lisa Stansfield	Arista	7		
8	-	Dreams	Gabrielle	Go.Beat	11	(32)	F
9	-	Shout	Louchie Lou & Michie One	ffrr	5		F L
10	-	Tease Me	Chaka Demus & Pliers	Mango	13		F
11	-	Can You Forgive Her?	Pet Shop Boys	Parlophone	3		
12	-	Do You See The Light (Looking For)	Snap Featuring Niki Haris	Arista	4		L
13	5	Tribal Dance	2 Unlimited	PWL Continental	7		
14	-	Blow Your Mind	Jamiroquai	Sony S²	3		L
15	17	I Don't Wanna Fight	Tina Turner	Parlophone	5	(9)	
16	1	Five Live (EP)	George Michael & Queen	Parlophone	7		L
17	18	Jump Around	House Of Pain	Ruffness	4	(3)	F L
18	4	That's The Way Love Goes	Janet Jackson	Virgin	6	(1)	
19	-	Have I Told You Lately	Rod Stewart	Warner	5	(5)	L
20	-	One Night In Heaven	M People	Deconstruction	8		

US 1993 APR-JUNE

April 1993

This Mnth	Prev Mnth	Title	Artist	Label	Wks 20	(UK Pos)	
1	1	Informer	Snow	Atco	15	(2)	F
2	7	Freak Me	Silk	Keia	18	(46)	F G L
3	2	Nuthin' But A "G" Thang	Dr. Dre	Death Row	19		F G
4	12	I Have Nothing	Whitney Houston	Arista	13	(3)	L
5	6	Don't Walk Away	Jade	Giant	19	(7)	L
6	19	Cat's In The Cradle	Ugly Kid Joe	Stardog	8	(7)	L
7	14	Two Princes	Spin Doctors	Epic	14	(3)	L
8	-	Love Is	Vanessa Williams & Brian McKnight	Giant	14		L
9	13	Comforter	Shai	Gasoline Alley	13		
10	10	Bed Of Roses	Bon Jovi	Jambco	10	(13)	L
11	-	I'm So Into You	SWV	RCA	15	(17)	F L
12	4	Ordinary World	Duran Duran	Capitol	12	(6)	
13	8	Mr. Wendal	Arrested Development	Chrysalis	15	(4)	L
14	11	Hip Hop Hurray	Naughty By Nature	Tommy Boy	14	(20)	G L
15	-	Ditty	Paperboy	Next Plateau	12		F G L
16	5	I'm Every Woman	Whitney Houston	Arista	11	(4)	
17	-	Looking Through Patient Eyes	P.M. Dawn	Gee Street	14	(11)	L
18	16	I Got A Man	Positive K	Island	8	(43)	F L
19	3	A Whole New World (Aladdin's Theme)	Peabo Bryson & Regina Belle	Columbia	15	(12)	L
20	-	It Was A Good Day	Ice Cube	Priority	5	(27)	F

May 1993

This Mnth	Prev Mnth	Title	Artist	Label	Wks 20	(UK Pos)	
1	2	Freak Me	Silk	Keia	18	(46)	F G L
2	-	That's The Way Love Goes	Janet Jackson	Virgin	16	(2)	G
3	8	Love Is	Vanessa Williams/B. McKnight	Giant	14		L
4	3	Nuthin' But A "G" Thang	Dr. Dre	Death Row	19		F G
5	4	I Have Nothing	Whitney Houston	Arista	13	(3)	L
6	1	Informer	Snow	Atco	15	(2)	F
7	11	I'm So Into You	SWV	RCA	15	(17)	F L
8	17	Looking Through Patient Eyes	P.M. Dawn	Gee Street	14	(11)	L
9	5	Don't Walk Away	Jade	Giant	19	(7)	L
10	-	Knockin' Da Boots	H-Town	Luke	15		F G L
11	15	Ditty	Paperboy	Next Plateau	12		F G L
12	7	Two Princes	Spin Doctors	Epic	14	(3)	L
13	-	Weak	SWV	RCA	17	(33)	G
14	-	Who Is It	Michael Jackson	Epic	5	(10)	
15	9	Comforter	Shai	Gasoline Alley	13		
16	14	Hip Hop Hurray	Naughty By Nature	Tommy Boy	14	(20)	G L
17	20	It Was A Good Day	Ice Cube	Priority	5	(27)	F
18	-	Have I Told You Lately	Rod Stewart	Warner	13	(5)	
19	-	The Crying Game	Boy George	SBK	4	(22)	F L
20	6	Cat's In The Cradle	Ugly Kid Joe	Stardog	8	(7)	L

June 1993

This Mnth	Prev Mnth	Title	Artist	Label	Wks 20	(UK Pos)	
1	2	That's The Way Love Goes	Janet Jackson	Virgin	16	(2)	G
2	1	Freak Me	Silk	Keia	18	(46)	F G L
3	13	Weak	SWV	RCA	17	(33)	G
4	10	Knockin' Da Boots	H-Town	Luke	15		F G L
5	-	Show Me Love	Robin S.	Big Beat	13	(6)	F L
6	18	Have I Told You Lately	Rod Stewart	Warner	13	(5)	
7	8	Looking Through Patient Eyes	P.M. Dawn	Gee Street	14	(11)	L
8	-	Come Undone	Duran Duran	Capitol	11	(13)	L
9	-	Bad Boys	Inner Circle	Big Beat	8	(52)	F
10	7	I'm So Into You	SWV	RCA	15	(17)	F L
11	3	Love Is	Vanessa Williams/B. McKnight	Giant	14		L
12	-	Dre Day	Dr. Dre	Death Row	10		L
13	-	I'll Never Get Over You (Getting Over Me)	Expose	Arista	12	(75)	L
14	4	Nuthin' But A "G" Thang	Dr. Dre	Death Row	19		F G
15	-	Whoomp! (There It Is)	Tag Team	Life/Bellmark	28		F P L
16	9	Don't Walk Away	Jade	Giant	19	(7)	L
17	11	Ditty	Paperboy	Next Plateau	12		F G L
18	-	(I Can't Help) Falling In Love With You	UB40	Virgin	19	(1)	G L
19	-	Dazzey Duks	Duice	TMR/Bellmark	11		F G L
20	-	More And More	Captain Hollywood Project	Imago	6	(23)	F L

◆ Janet Jackson's album, **Janet,** entered the transatlantic charts at No. 1. Jam & Lewis were apparently paid $3 million to produce the album which sold 6 million in 1993.

◆ As rap lifestyles and lyrics made the headlines, rappers charting included Dr Dre, Arrested Development, Paperboy, Naughty By Nature, Positive K and Ice Cube. Also hitting were the Tag Team (whose 'Whoomp! (There It Is)' spent a record 24 weeks in the Top 10) and Duice (whose 'Dazzey Duks' was on the sales chart for over a year).

◆ Soul stars Arthur Alexander and Marv Johnson died, as did Conway Twitty, who had amassed a record 40 country No. 1 hits.

◆ Barbra Streisand's **Back To Broadway** had a million advance orders and Billy Ray Cyrus' sophomore album, **It Won't Be The Last,** collected 1.5 million orders.

UK 1993 JULY-SEPT

◆ **Black Sunday** by controversial rappers Cyprus Hill entered the American album chart in pole position, as did Billy Joel's only album for four years, **River Of Dreams, In Pieces** by Garth Brooks and U2's **Zooropa**, the latter repeating the feat in Britain.

◆ European music conglomerate Polygram bought Motown Records' 30,000 masters for $325 million, as the label re-signed Boyz II Men in a deal that could earn the act $30 million.

◆ British acts Cream, Elton John, The Animals, John Lennon, Van Morrison and Rod Stewart joined other 1993 *Rock And Roll Hall Of Fame* inductees: The Band, Ruth Brown, Creedence Clearwater Revival, The Doors, Duane Eddy, Grateful Dead, Etta James, Frankie Lymon & The Teenagers, Bob Marley and Sly & The Family Stone.

July 1993

This Mnth	Prev Mnth	Title	Artist	Label	Wks 20	(US Pos)	
1	8	Dreams	Gabrielle	Go.Beat	11	(32)	F
2	4	What Is Love	Haddaway	Arista	12	(11)	F
3	10	Tease Me	Chaka Demus & Pliers	Mango	13		F
4	20	One Night In Heaven	M People	Deconstruction	8		
5	-	What's Up	4 Non Blondes	Interscope	11	(16)	F L
6	1	(I Can't Help) Falling In Love With You	UB40	Dep International	12	(1)	
7	-	I Will Survive	Gloria Gaynor	Polydor	6		L
8	-	Pray	Take That	RCA	7		
9	19	Have I Told You Lately	Rod Stewart	Warner	5	(5)	L
10	3	Two Princes	Spin Doctors	Epic	10	(7)	F L
11	-	Will You Be There	Michael Jackson	Epic	4	(7)	L
12	2	All That She Wants	Ace Of Base	London	12	(2)	F
13	-	If I Can't Have You	Kim Wilde	MCA	4		L
14	-	Almost Unreal	Roxette	EMI	5	(94)	
15	-	This Is It	Dannii Minogue	MCA	5		L
16	7	In All The Right Places	Lisa Stansfield	Arista	7		
17	-	Living On My Own	Freddie Mercury	Parlophone	9		L
18	-	Nothin' My Love Can't Fix	Joey Lawrence	EMI	3	(19)	F L
19	-	I Wanna Love You	Jade	Giant	3	(16)	L
20	-	Can't Get Enough Of Your Love	Taylor Dayne	Arista	3	(20)	L

August 1993

This Mnth	Prev Mnth	Title	Artist	Label	Wks 20	(US Pos)	
1	17	Living On My Own	Freddie Mercury	Parlophone	9		L
2	-	The Key The Secret	Urban Cookie Collective	Pulse 8	10		F
3	5	What's Up	4 Non Blondes	Interscope	11	(16)	F L
4	-	The River Of Dreams	Billy Joel	Columbia	9	(3)	L
5	8	Pray	Take That	RCA	7		
6	-	It Keeps Rainin' (Tears From My Eyes)	Bitty McLean	Brilliant	9		F L
7	3	Tease Me	Chaka Demus & Pliers	Mango	13		F
8	-	Mr. Vain	Culture Beat	Epic	11	(20)	F
9	-	Nuff Vibes (EP)	Apache Indian	Island	6		L
10	1	Dreams	Gabrielle	Go.Beat	11	(32)	F
11	-	Rain	Madonna	Maverick	4	(14)	L
12	-	Looking Up	Michelle Gayle	RCA	4		F L
13	14	Almost Unreal	Roxette	EMI	5	(94)	
14	-	Higher Ground	UB40	Dep International	5	(46)	L
15	-	Luv 4 Luv	Robin S.	Champion	4		L
16	-	I Will Always Love You	Sarah Washington	Almighty	4		F L
17	2	What Is Love	Haddaway	Arista	12	(11)	F
18	-	Dreamlover	Mariah Carey	Columbia	6	(1)	
19	15	This Is It	Dannii Minogue	MCA	5		L
20	-	Right Here	SWV	RCA	8	(2)	L

September 1993

This Mnth	Prev Mnth	Title	Artist	Label	Wks 20	(US Pos)	
1	8	Mr. Vain	Culture Beat	Epic	11	(20)	F
2	6	It Keeps Rainin' (Tears From My Eyes)	Bitty McLean	Brilliant	9		F L
3	20	Right Here	SWV	RCA	8	(2)	L
4	4	The River Of Dreams	Billy Joel	Columbia	9	(3)	L
5	-	Boom! Shake The Room	Jazzy Jeff & Fresh Prince	Jive	10	(13)	F L
6	1	Living On My Own	Freddie Mercury	Parlophone	9		L
7	-	Faces	2 Unlimited	PWL Continental	4		
8	18	Dreamlover	Mariah Carey	Columbia	6	(1)	
9	-	Go West	Pet Shop Boys	Parlophone	6		
10	2	The Key The Secret	Urban Cookie Collective	Pulse 8	10		F
11	9	Nuff Vibes (EP)	Apache Indian	Island	6		L
12	14	Higher Ground	UB40	Dep International	5	(46)	L
13	-	Heart-Shaped Box	Nirvana	Geffen	2		L
14	-	Creep	Radiohead	Parlophone	3	(34)	F L
15	-	Slave To The Vibe	Aftershock	Virgin	5		F L
16	-	She Don't Let Nobody	Chaka Demus & Pliers	Mango	7		
17	-	Moving On Up	M People	Deconstruction	7		
18	-	Rubberband Girl	Kate Bush	EMI	2	(88)	L
19	-	Disco Inferno	Tina Turner	Parlophone	3		
20	-	It Must Have Been Love	Roxette	EMI	4		L

344

US 1993 JULY-SEPT

July 1993

This Mnth	Prev Mnth	Title	Artist	Label	Wks 20	(UK Pos)	
1	3	Weak	SWV	RCA	17	(33)	G
2	18	(I Can't Help) Falling In Love With You	UB40	Virgin	19	(1)	G L
3	15	Whoomp! (There It Is)	Tag Team	Life/Bellmark	28		F P L
4	1	That's The Way Love Goes	Janet Jackson	Virgin	16	(2)	L
5	4	Knockin' Da Boots	H-Town	Luke	15		F G L
6	5	Show Me Love	Robin S.	Big Beat	13	(6)	F L
7	6	Have I Told You Lately	Rod Stewart	Warner	13	(5)	
8	13	I'll Never Get Over You (Getting Over Me)	Expose	Arista	12	(75)	L
9	-	Lately	Jodeci	Uptown/MCA	15		L
10	12	Dre Day	Dr. Dre	Death Row	10		L
11	-	Slam	Onyx	Ral/Chaos	10	(31)	F G L
12	-	I'm Gonna Be (500 Miles)	Proclaimers	Chrysalis	12		F L
13	19	Dazzey Duks	Duice	TMR/Bellmark	11		F G L
14	8	Come Undone	Duran Duran	Capitol	11	(13)	L
15	-	Whoot, There It Is	95 South	Wrap	10		F G L
16	-	What's Up	4 Non Blondes	Interscope	9	(2)	F L
17	-	I Don't Wanna Fight	Tina Turner	Virgin	11	(7)	L
18	-	If I Had No Loot	Tony! Toni! Tone!	Wing	11	(44)	
19	9	Bad Boys	Inner Circle	Big Beat	8	(52)	F
20	2	Freak Me	Silk	Keia	18	(46)	F G L

August 1993

This Mnth	Prev Mnth	Title	Artist	Label	Wks 20	(UK Pos)	
1	2	(I Can't Help) Falling In Love With You	UB40	Virgin	19	(1)	G L
2	3	Whoomp! (There It Is)	Tag Team	Life/Bellmark	28		F P L
3	12	I'm Gonna Be (500 Miles)	Proclaimers	Chrysalis	12		F L
4	9	Lately	Jodeci	Uptown/MCA	15		L
5	11	Slam	Onyx	Ral/Chaos	10	(31)	F G L
6	18	If I Had No Loot	Tony! Toni! Tone!	Wing	11	(44)	
7	1	Weak	SWV	RCA	17	(33)	G
8	-	Runaway Train	Soul Asylum	Columbia	12	(7)	F L
9	-	If	Janet Jackson	Virgin	16	(14)	
10	17	I Don't Wanna Fight	Tina Turner	Virgin	11	(7)	L
11	-	Dreamlover	Mariah Carey	Columbia	19	(9)	G
12	15	Whoot, There It Is	95 South	Wrap	10		F G L
13	6	Show Me Love	Robin S.	Big Beat	13	(6)	F L
14	-	Right Here (Human Nature)	SWV	RCA	14	(3)	L
15	4	That's The Way Love Goes	Janet Jackson	Virgin	16	(2)	L
16	8	I'll Never Get Over You (Getting Over Me)	Expose	Arista	12	(75)	L
17	-	Will You Be There	Michael Jackson	Epic	9	(9)	L
18	13	Dazzey Duks	Duice	TMR/Bellmark	11		F G L
19	16	What's Up	4 Non Blondes	Interscope	9	(2)	F L
20	5	Knockin' Da Boots	H-Town	Luke	15		F G L

September 1993

This Mnth	Prev Mnth	Title	Artist	Label	Wks 20	(UK Pos)	
1	11	Dreamlover	Mariah Carey	Columbia	19	(9)	G
2	1	(I Can't Help) Falling In Love With...	UB40	Virgin	19	(1)	G L
3	2	Whoomp! (There It Is)	Tag Team	Life/Bellmark	28		F P L
4	9	If	Janet Jackson	Virgin	16	(14)	
5	14	Right Here (Human Nature)	SWV	RCA	14	(3)	L
6	8	Runaway Train	Soul Asylum	Columbia	12	(7)	F L
7	4	Lately	Jodeci	Uptown/MCA	15		L
8	17	Will You Be There	Michael Jackson	Epic	9	(9)	L
9	-	The River Of Dreams	Billy Joel	Columbia	14	(3)	L
10	-	Baby I'm Yours	Shai	Gasoline Alley	9		L
11	6	If I Had No Loot	Tony! Toni! Tone!	Wing	11	(44)	
12	3	I'm Gonna Be (500 Miles)	Proclaimers	Chrysalis	12		F L
13	-	One Last Cry	Brian McKnight	Giant	7		L
14	-	I Get Around	2Pac	Interscope	8		F L
15	-	Rain	Madonna	Maverick	6	(7)	L
16	-	Another Sad Love Song	Toni Braxton	Laface	11	(51)	F
17	5	Slam	Onyx	Ral/Chaos	10	(31)	F G L
18	10	I Don't Wanna Fight	Tina Turner	Virgin	11	(7)	L
19	-	Boom! Shake The Room	Jazzy Jeff & Fresh Prince	Jive	4	(1)	L
20	-	Cryin'	Aerosmith	Geffen	9	(17)	L

▲ Rapper Snoop Doggy Dogg gave himself up on a murder charge (immediately after presenting En Vogue with an MTV award). He was released on a $1 million bail.

◆ Among the acts playing gigs to help Mid-West flood victims were Bon Jovi, John Mellencamp, Van Halen and country superstars Clint Black and Wynonna.

◆ Garth Brooks, who had a record four albums in the country Top 5, sold out 200,000 tickets for three shows at the Texas Stadium in a record-crushing 305 minutes!

UK 1993 OCT-DEC

In America, only 10 different singles made No. 1 in 1993 (a record low), and records, in general, stayed on the charts longer. In contrast, in Britain, more records than ever charted and a hit's life-span was shorter than ever. 1993 was the year of the American rock act, and the worst year for British artists in the US charts since the British Invasion in 1964.

♦ British teen idols Take That became the first act to have three successive singles enter at No. 1. They also had three of the country's Top 4 videos.

♦ Meat Loaf's **Bat Out Of Hell II** was Britain's top album of 1993, and his single 'I'd Do Anything For Love (But I Won't Do That)' also topped the transatlantic charts.

October 1993

This Mnth	Prev Mnth	Title	Artist	Label	Wks 20	(US Pos)	
1	5	Boom! Shake The Room	Jazzy Jeff & Fresh Prince	Jive	10	(13)	F L
2	17	Moving On Up	M People	Deconstruction	7		
3	16	She Don't Let Nobody	Chaka Demus & Pliers	Mango	7		
4	-	I'd Do Anything For Love (But I Won't Do That)	Meat Loaf	Virgin	12	(1)	
5	-	Relight My Fire	Take That Featuring Lulu	RCA	5		
6	-	Stay	Eternal	EMI	6		F L
7	-	Relax	Frankie Goes To Hollywood	ZTT	5		
8	-	Life	Haddaway	Logic	5	(83)	L
9	9	Go West	Pet Shop Boys	Parlophone	6		L
10	1	Mr. Vain	Culture Beat	Epic	11	(20)	F
11	-	U Got 2 Let The Music	Cappella	Internal	6		L
12	-	One Love	Prodigy	XL	4		L
13	-	Going Nowhere	Gabrielle	Go.Beat	4		L
14	-	Don't Be A Stranger	Dina Carroll	A&M	11		L
15	3	Right Here	SWV	RCA	8	(2)	L
16	-	Here We Go	Stakka Bo	Polydor	4		F L
17	-	Please Forgive Me	Bryan Adams	A&M	9	(7)	L
18	-	Play Dead	Bjork & David Arnold	Island	4		F
19	20	It Must Have Been Love	Roxette	EMI	4		L
20	-	Both Sides Of The Story	Phil Collins	Virgin	2	(25)	L

November 1993

This Mnth	Prev Mnth	Title	Artist	Label	Wks 20	(US Pos)	
1	4	I'd Do Anything For Love (But I Won't Do That)	Meat Loaf	Virgin	12	(1)	
2	17	Please Forgive Me	Bryan Adams	A&M	9	(7)	L
3	14	Don't Be A Stranger	Dina Carroll	A&M	11		
4	-	Got To Get It	Culture Beat	Epic	5		L
5	11	U Got 2 Let The Music	Cappella	Internal	6		L
6	-	Hero	Mariah Carey	Columbia	8	(1)	L
7	-	Feels Like Heaven	Urban Cookie Collective	Pulse 8	4		L
8	-	Runaway Train	Soul Asylum	Columbia	5	(5)	F L
9	-	True Love	Elton John & Kiki Dee	Rocket	6	(56)	L
10	-	Real Love '93	Time Frequency	Internal Affairs	3		L
11	-	Again	Janet Jackson	Virgin	6	(1)	L
12	-	Feel Like Making Love	Pauline Henry	Sony S²	4		F L
13	-	Ain't It Fun	Guns N' Roses	Geffen	2		L
14	-	Little Fluffy Clouds	Orb	Big Life	2		L
15	1	Boom! Shake The Room	Jazzy Jeff & Fresh Prince	Jive	10	(13)	F L
16	6	Stay	Eternal	EMI	6		F L
17	-	Queen Of The Night	Whitney Houston	Arista	2		L
18	-	Long Train Runnin'	Doobie Brothers	Warner	4		F L
19	20	Both Sides Of The Story	Phil Collins	Virgin	2	(25)	L
20	-	Said I Love You....But I Lied	Michael Bolton	Columbia	2	(10)	L

December 1993

This Mnth	Prev Mnth	Title	Artist	Label	Wks 20	(US Pos)	
1	-	Mr. Blobby	Mr. Blobby	Destiny Music	4		F L
2	9	True Love	Elton John & Kiki Dee	Rocket	6	(56)	L
3	-	For Whom The Bell Tolls	Bee Gees	Polydor	4		L
4	2	Please Forgive Me	Bryan Adams	A&M	9	(7)	L
5	-	It's Alright	East 17	London	4		L
6	-	Babe	Take That	RCA	2		L
7	-	Stay (Faraway, So Close)	U2	Island	3	(66)	L
8	-	Don't Look Any Further	M People	Deconstruction	4		L
9	-	Twist And Shout	Chaka Demus & Pliers Featuring Jack Radics & Taxi Gang	Mango	2		L
10	11	Again	Janet Jackson	Virgin	6	(1)	L
11	-	The Perfect Year	Dina Carroll	A&M	3		L
12	3	Don't Be A Stranger	Dina Carroll	A&M	11		
13	18	Long Train Runnin'	Doobie Brothers	Warner	4		F L
14	-	Bat Out Of Hell	Meat Loaf	Epic	2		L
15	1	I'd Do Anything For Love (But I...)	Meat Loaf	Virgin	12	(1)	
16	-	Controversy	Prince	Paisley Park	2		L
17	-	The Power Of Love	Frankie Goes To Hollywood	ZTT	2		L
18	-	Y.M.C.A.	Village People	Bell	2		L
19	6	Hero	Mariah Carey	Columbia	8	(1)	L
20	-	I Wouldn't Normally Do This Kind Of Thing	Pet Shop Boys	Parlophone	3		L

346

October 1993

This Mnth	Prev Mnth	Title	Artist	Label	Wks 20	(UK Pos)	
1	1	**Dreamlover**	Mariah Carey	Columbia	19	(9)	G
2	5	**Right Here (Human Nature)**	SWV	RCA	14	(3)	L
3	9	**The River Of Dreams**	Billy Joel	Columbia	14	(3)	L
4	3	**Whoomp! (There It Is)**	Tag Team	Life/Bellmark	28		F P L
5	4	**If**	Janet Jackson	Virgin	16	(14)	
6	-	**I'd Do Anything For Love (But I Won't Do That)**	Meat Loaf	MCA	12	(1)	G L
7	-	**Just Kickin' It**	Xscape	Columbia	12	(49)	F G L
8	16	**Another Sad Love Song**	Toni Braxton	Laface	11	(51)	F
9	-	**Hey Mr. D.J.**	Zhane	Flavor Unit	13	(26)	F L
10	-	**All That She Wants**	Ace Of Base	Arista	11	(1)	F G L
11	2	**(I Can't Help) Falling In Love With...**	UB40	Virgin	19	(1)	G L
12	14	**I Get Around**	2Pac	Interscope	8		F L
13	20	**Cryin'**	Aerosmith	Geffen	9	(17)	L
14	-	**Two Steps Behind**	Def Leppard	Mercury	7	(32)	L
15	8	**Will You Be There**	Michael Jackson	Epic	9	(9)	L
16	-	**Anniversary**	Tony! Toni! Tone!	Wing	9		L
17	6	**Runaway Train**	Soul Asylum	Columbia	12	(7)	F L
18	-	**Sweat (A La La La La Long)**	Inner Circle	Big Beat	7	(3)	L
19	-	**What Is Love**	Haddaway	Arista	10	(2)	F L
20	-	**Again**	Janet Jackson	Virgin	8	(6)	G L

November 1993

This Mnth	Prev Mnth	Title	Artist	Label	Wks 20	(UK Pos)	
1	6	**I'd Do Anything For Love (But I Won't Do That)**	Meat Loaf	MCA	12	(1)	G L
2	10	**All That She Wants**	Ace Of Base	Arista	11	(1)	F G L
3	20	**Again**	Janet Jackson	Virgin	8	(6)	G L
4	7	**Just Kickin' It**	Xscape	Columbia	12	(49)	F G L
5	-	**Gangsta Lean**	DRS	Capitol	8		F G L
6	-	**Shoop**	Salt-N-Pepa	Next Plateau	9	(29)	L
7	9	**Hey Mr. D.J.**	Zhane	Flavor Unit	13	(26)	F L
8	4	**Whomp! (There It Is)**	Tag Team	Life/Bellmark	28		F P L
9	1	**Dreamlover**	Mariah Carey	Columbia	19	(9)	G
10	-	**Hero**	Mariah Carey	Columbia	7	(7)	G L
11	16	**Anniversary**	Tony! Toni! Tone!	Wing	9		L
12	-	**Breathe Again**	Toni Braxton	Laface	8		L
13	19	**What Is Love**	Haddaway	Arista	10	(2)	F L
14	3	**The River Of Dreams**	Billy Joel	Columbia	14	(3)	L
15	-	**Please Forgive Me**	Bryan Adams	A&M	6	(2)	
16	-	**Can We Talk**	Tevin Campbell	Qwest	8		L
17	8	**Another Sad Love Song**	Toni Braxton	Laface	11	(51)	F
18	2	**Right Here (Human Nature)**	SWV	RCA	14	(3)	L
19	-	**Keep Ya Head Up**	2Pac	Interscope	6		L
20	-	**Said I Love You....But I Lied**	Michael Bolton	Columbia	6	(15)	L

December 1993

This Mnth	Prev Mnth	Title	Artist	Label	Wks 20	(UK Pos)	
1	3	**Again**	Janet Jackson	Virgin	8	(6)	G L
2	1	**I'd Do Anything For Love (But I Won't Do That)**	Meat Loaf	MCA	12	(1)	G L
3	2	**All That She Wants**	Ace Of Base	Arista	11	(1)	F G L
4	10	**Hero**	Mariah Carey	Columbia	7	(7)	G L
5	6	**Shoop**	Salt-N-Pepa	Next Plateau	9	(29)	L
6	5	**Gangsta Lean**	DRS	Capitol	8		F G L
7	12	**Breathe Again**	Toni Braxton	Laface	8		L
8	15	**Please Forgive Me**	Bryan Adams	A&M	6	(2)	
9	-	**All For Love**	Bryan Adams/Rod Stewart/Sting	A&M	4		L
10	4	**Just Kickin' It**	Xscape	Columbia	12	(49)	F G L
11	20	**Said I Love You....But I Lied**	Michael Bolton	Columbia	6	(15)	L
12	16	**Can We Talk**	Tevin Campbell	Qwest	8		L
13	8	**Whoomp! (There It Is)**	Tag Team	Life/Bellmark	28		F P L
14	19	**Keep Ya Head Up**	2Pac	Interscope	6		L
15	7	**Hey Mr. D.J.**	Zhane	Flavor Unit	13	(26)	F L
16	9	**Dreamlover**	Mariah Carey	Columbia	19	(9)	G
17	-	**What's My Name?**	Snoop Doggy Dogg	Death Row/ Interscope	2	(20)	F L
18	13	**What Is Love**	Haddaway	Arista	10	(2)	F L
19	-	**Linger**	Cranberries	Island	3	(74)	F L
20	-	**Come Baby Come**	K7	Tommy Boy	3	(13)	F L

US
1993
OCT-DEC

◆ CDs now clearly outsold cassettes and vinyl on both sides of the Atlantic, with total sales in recession-hit Britain up by 13.5%. The MiniDisc and the Digital Compact Cassette enjoyed their first full year on the market though few noticed.

◆ Neil Diamond collected his 28th gold album, **Up On The Roof.** The only artist with more, the late Elvis Presley, chalked up his 45th, **From Nashville To Memphis.**

▲ Mariah Carey became the only artist in history to reach the Top 5 with her first 10 singles (nine of them made the Top 2!).

347

LISTINGS BY ARTIST

	US Top 20 Ent	UK Top 20 Ent
ABBA (S/N)		
Angel Eyes/Voulez Vous		8/79
Chiquitita		2/79
Dancing Queen	2/77	9/76
Does Your Mother Know		5/79
Fernando	11/76	4/76
Gimme Gimme Gimme (A Man After Midnight)		10/79
I Do, I Do, I Do, I Do, I Do	4/76	
I Have A Dream		12/79
Knowing Me Knowing You	7/77	3/77
Lay All Your Love On Me		7/81
Mamma Mia		1/76
Money Money Money		12/76
The Name Of The Game	3/78	11/77
One Of Us		12/81
S.O.S.		10/75
Summer Night City		9/78
Super Trouper		11/80
Take A Chance On Me	5/78	2/78
Waterloo	7/74	4/74
The Winner Takes It All	2/81	8/80
Russ ABBOT (UK)		
Atmosphere		1/85
Gregory ABBOTT (US)		
Shake You Down	12/86	12/86
ABC (UK)		
All Of My Heart		9/82
Be Near Me	11/85	
The Look Of Love (Part 1)		5/82
Poison Arrow		3/82
When Smokey Sings	9/87	6/87
Paula ABDUL (US)		
Blowing Kisses In The Wind	11/91	
Cold Hearted	8/89	
Forever Your Girl	5/89	
(It's Just) The Way You Love Me	11/89	
The Promise Of A New Day	8/91	
Rush Rush	6/91	7/91
Straight Up	1/89	3/89
Vibeology	2/92	
Paula ABDUL (duet with The Wild Pair) (US)		
Opposites Attract	1/90	4/90
Colonel ABRAMS (US)		
Trapped		10/85
AC/DC (Aus/UK)		
Heatseeker		1/88
Let's Get It Up		2/82
Rock 'n' Roll Ain't Noise Pollution		12/80
ACE OF BASE (S)		
All That She Wants	10/93	5/93
ACE (UK)		
How Long	5/75	
Johnny ACE (US)		
Pledging My Love	3/55	
AD LIBS (US)		
The Boy From New York City	2/65	
ADAM & THE ANTS (UK)		
Ant Rap		12/81
Antmusic		12/80
Deutscher Girls		3/82
Dog Eat Dog		11/80
Kings Of The Wild Frontier		3/81
Prince Charming		9/81
Stand And Deliver		5/81
Young Parisians		2/81
ADAM ANT (UK)		
Friend Or Foe		10/82
Goody Two Shoes	1/83	5/82
Puss 'n Boots		11/83
Room At The Top	5/90	
Bryan ADAMS (C)		
Can't Stop This Thing We Started	10/91	
Do I Have To Say The Words?	9/92	
(Everything I Do) I Do It For You	7/91	7/91
Heat Of The Night	5/87	
Heaven	5/85	
One Night Love Affair	11/85	
Please Forgive Me	11/93	10/93
Run To You	12/84	2/85
Somebody	4/85	
Straight From The Heart	5/83	
Summer Of '69	8/85	
Thought I'd Died And Gone To Heaven	5/92	2/92
Bryan ADAMS & Tina Turner (C/US)		
It's Only Love	1/86	
Bryan ADAMS/Rod Stewart/Sting (C/UK)		
All For Love	12/93	
Oleta ADAMS (US)		
Get Here	3/91	2/91
ADAMSKI (UK)		
Killer		4/90
The Space Jungle		9/90
Cannonball ADDERLEY (US)		
Mercy, Mercy, Mercy	2/67	
ADVENTURES OF STEVIE V (UK)		
Dirty Cash		5/90
AEROSMITH (US)		
Angel	4/88	
Cryin'	9/93	
Dream On	3/76	
Dude (Looks Like A Lady)	12/87	
Janie's Got A Gun	1/90	
Love In An Elevator	10/89	
Walk This Way	1/77	
What It Takes	4/90	
AFTER 7 (US)		
Can't Stop	10/90	
Ready Or Not	6/90	
AFTER THE FIRE (UK)		
Der Kommissar	4/83	
AFTERSHOCK (US)		
Slave To The Vibe		9/93
A-HA (N)		
Cry Wolf		12/86
Hunting High And Low		6/86
I've Been Losing You		10/86
The Living Daylights		7/87
Stay On These Roads		4/88
The Sun Always Shines On T.V.		1/86
Take On Me	9/85	10/85
Touchy!		9/88
Train Of Thought		4/86
You Are The One		1/89
AIR SUPPLY (Aus/UK)		
All Out Of Love	8/80	11/80
Even The Nights Are Better	7/82	
Every Woman In The World	12/80	
Here I Am (Just When You Thought I Was Over You)	10/81	
Lost In Love	4/80	
Making Love Out Of Nothing At All	9/83	
The One That You Love	6/81	
Sweet Dreams	2/82	
Jewel AKENS (US)		
The Birds And The Bees	3/65	
Morris ALBERT (Bra)		
Feelings	10/75	10/75
ALESSI (US)		
Oh Lori		7/77
ALIAS (US)		
More Than Words Can Say	11/90	
Waiting For Love	3/91	
ALIVE & KICKING (US)		
Tighter, Tighter	7/70	
ALL ABOUT EVE (UK)		
Martha's Harbour		8/88
Donna ALLEN (US)		
Serious		6/87
ALLISONS (UK)		
Are You Sure		3/61
ALLMAN BROTHERS BAND (US)		
Ramblin' Man	9/73	
Marc ALMOND (UK)		
The Days Of Pearly Spencer		5/92
❖ with *Bronski Beat* I Feel Love		4/85
Marc ALMOND featuring Gene Pitney (UK/US)		
Something's Gotten Hold Of My Heart		1/89
Herb ALPERT (US)		
Diamonds	6/87	
The Lonely Bull	11/62	
Rise	9/79	
Spanish Flea		1/66
A Taste Of Honey	11/65	
This Guy's In Love With You	6/68	7/68
Zorba The Greek	2/66	
ALPHAVILLE (G)		
Big In Japan		9/84
ALTERED IMAGES (UK)		
Don't Talk To Me About Love		4/83

Code to Nationalities

A Austria		**Jap** Japan	
Aus Australia		**Ken** Kenya	
B Belgium		**N** Norway	
Bra Brazil		**NZ** New Zealand	
C Canada		**R** Romania	
CZ Czechoslovakia		**S** Sweden	
D Denmark		**SA** South Africa	
F France		**Spa** Spain	
G Germany		**Swi** Switzerland	
Gre Greece		**UK** United Kingdom	
H Holland		**US** United States	
I Ireland		**WI** West Indies	
Ice Iceland		**Y** Yugoslavia	
Isr Israel		❖ Shared hit	
Ita Italy		★ Reissue	
J Jamaica			

	US Top 20 Ent	UK Top 20 Ent
Happy Birthday		10/81
I Could Be Happy		1/82
See Those Eyes		4/82
ALTERN 8 (UK)		
Activ 8 (Come With Me)		11/91
Evapor 8		4/92
ALTHIA AND DONNA (J)		
Uptown Top Ranking		1/78
AMAZING RHYTHM ACES (US)		
Third Rate Romance	9/75	
AMAZULU (UK)		
Excitable		8/85
Montego Bay		10/86
Too Good To Be Forgotten		6/86
AMBASSADORS OF FUNK featuring MC Mario (US)		
Supermarioland		11/92
AMBOY DUKES (US)		
Journey To The Center Of The Mind	8/68	
AMBROSIA (US)		
Biggest Part Of Me	5/80	
How Much I Feel	10/78	
You're The Only Woman (You & I)	9/80	
AMEN CORNER (UK)		
Bend Me Shape Me		2/68
Gin House Blues		8/67
Hello Susie		7/69
High In The Sky		8/68
(If Paradise Is) Half As Nice		2/69
AMERICA (US)		
A Horse With No Name	3/72	1/72
I Need You	7/72	
Lonely People	2/75	
Sister Golden Hair	5/75	
Tin Man	11/74	
Ventura Highway	11/72	
You Can Do Magic	9/82	
AMERICAN BREED (US)		
Bend Me, Shape Me	12/67	
AMES BROTHERS (US)		
It Only Hurts For A Little While	7/56	
The Man With The Banjo	4/54	
Melodie D'Amour	11/57	
My Bonnie Lassie	10/55	
The Naughty Lady Of Shady Lane	12/54	2/55
You You You	1/54	
Ed AMES (US)		
My Cup Runneth Over	3/67	
Angry ANDERSON (Aus)		
Suddenly		12/88
Bill ANDERSON (US)		
Still	6/63	
Carl ANDERSON (US)		
❖ with Gloria Loring Friends And Lovers	8/86	
Laurie ANDERSON (US)		
O Superman		10/81
Lynn ANDERSON (US)		
Rose Garden	1/71	3/71
Chris ANDREWS (UK)		
To Whom It Concerns		1/66
Yesterday Man		10/65
ANEKA (UK)		
Japanese Boy		8/81
ANGELS (US)		
My Boyfriend's Back	8/63	
ANIMALS (UK)		
Bring It On Home To Me		5/65
Don't Bring Me Down	7/66	6/66
Don't Let Me Be Misunderstood		2/65
House Of The Rising Sun	8/64	7/64
★ House Of The Rising Sun		10/82
I'm Crying		10/64
Inside-Looking Out		3/66
It's My Life		11/65
We Gotta Get Out Of This Place		7/65
Eric Burdon & The ANIMALS (UK)		
Help Me Girl		11/66
Monterey	1/68	
San Franciscan Nights	9/67	11/67
See See Rider	10/66	
When I Was Young	5/67	
ANIMOTION (US)		
Obsession	4/85	6/85
Room To Move	4/89	
Paul ANKA (C)		
(All Of A Sudden) My Heart Sings	2/59	2/59

	US Top 20 Ent	UK Top 20 Ent
Dance On Little Girl	7/61	
Diana	8/57	8/57
I Love You Baby		11/57
It's Time To Cry	12/59	
Lonely Boy	6/59	8/59
Love Me Warm And Tender	4/62	
My Home Town	6/60	
Puppy Love	3/60	
Put Your Head On My Shoulder	9/59	11/59
Times Of Your Life	12/75	
You Are My Destiny	2/58	2/58
Paul ANKA with Odia Coates (C/US)		
I Believe There's Nothing Stronger Than Our Love	9/75	
I Don't Like To Sleep Alone	5/75	
One Man Woman/One Woman Man	1/75	
(You're) Having My Baby	8/74	10/74
ANNETTE (US)		
O Dio Mio	3/60	
Pineapple Princess	9/60	
Tall Paul	2/59	
ANOTHER BAD CREATION (US)		
Iesha	3/91	
Playground	6/91	
Billie ANTHONY (UK)		
This Ole House		10/54
Ray ANTHONY (US)		
Dragnet		1/54
Peter Gunn	2/59	
APACHE INDIAN (UK)		
Nuff Vibes (EP)		8/93
APOLLO 100 (UK)		
Joy	2/72	
KIM APPLEBY (UK)		
Don't Worry		11/90
G.L.A.D.		2/91
APPLEJACKS (US)		
Mexican Hat Rock	11/58	
APPLEJACKS (UK)		
Tell Me When		4/64
ARCADIA (UK)		
Election Day	11/85	11/85
Tasmin ARCHER (UK)		
Sleeping Satellite		10/92
ARCHIES (US)		
Jingle Jangle	1/70	
Sugar Sugar	8/69	10/69
ARGENT (UK)		
Hold Your Head Up	8/72	3/72
Joan ARMATRADING (UK)		
Love And Affection		11/76
Louis ARMSTRONG (US)		
Hello, Dolly!	3/64	6/64
Theme From The Threepenny Opera		4/56
What A Wonderful World		3/68
ARNEE & The Terminaters (UK)		
I'll Be Back		9/91
Eddy ARNOLD (US)		
Make The World Go Away	12/65	3/66
P.P. ARNOLD (US) See Beatmasters with P.P. Arnold		
ARRESTED DEVELOPMENT (US)		
Mr. Wendal	1/93	1/93
People Everyday	9/92	10/92
Tennessee	6/92	
Steve ARRINGTON (US)		
Feel So Real		5/85
ARRIVAL (UK)		
Friends		1/70
ARROWS (US/UK)		
A Touch Too Much		6/74
ART OF NOISE (UK)		
Close (To The Edit)		2/85
ART OF NOISE featuring Duane Eddy (UK/US)		
Peter Gunn		4/86
ART OF NOISE featuring Max Headroom (UK/C)		
Paranoimia		7/86
ART OF NOISE featuring Tom Jones (UK)		
Kiss		11/88
ASHFORD & SIMPSON (US)		
Solid	2/85	2/85
ASHTON GARDNER & DYKE (UK)		
Resurrection Shuffle		2/71
ASIA (UK)		
Don't Cry	9/83	
Heat Of The Moment	5/82	

	US Top 20 Ent	UK Top 20 Ent
ASSEMBLY (UK)		
Never Never		11/83
ASSOCIATES (UK)		
Club Country		6/82
Party Fears Two		3/82
ASSOCIATION (US)		
Along Comes Mary	7/66	
Cherish	9/66	
Everything That Touches You	3/68	
Never My Love	9/67	
Windy	6/67	
Rick ASTLEY (UK)		
Cry For Help	4/91	2/91
Hold Me In Your Arms		2/89
It Would Take A Strong Strong Man	9/88	
Never Gonna Give You Up	2/88	8/87
She Wants To Dance With Me	2/89	10/88
Take Me To Your Heart		12/88
Together Forever	5/88	3/88
When I Fall In Love/My Arms Keep Missing You		12/87
Whenever You Need Somebody		11/87
ASWAD (UK)		
Don't Turn Around		3/88
Give A Little Love		6/88
ATLANTA RHYTHM SECTION (US)		
I'm Not Gonna Let It Bother Me Tonight	8/78	
Imaginary Lover	5/78	
So In To You	3/77	
ATLANTIC STARR (US)		
Always	5/87	7/87
Masterpiece	2/92	
Secret Lovers	2/86	4/86
ATOMIC ROOSTER (UK)		
Devil's Answer		8/71
Tomorrow Night		3/71
Winifred ATWELL (UK)		
Charleston		7/54
Dixieland		9/54
Left Bank		8/56
Let's Have A Ball		12/57
Let's Have A Ding Dong		11/55
Let's Have A Party		1/54
★ Let's Have A Party		12/54
Let's Have Another Party		11/54
Make It A Party		11/56
Piano Party		12/59
Poor People Of Paris		3/56
The Story Of Three Loves		7/54
AURRA (US)		
You And Me Tonight		5/86
Patti AUSTIN (duet with James Ingram) (US)		
Baby Come To Me	1/83	3/83
Frankie AVALON (US)		
Bobby Sox To Stockings	6/59	
A Boy Without A Girl	7/59	
Dede Dinah	2/58	
Ginger Bread	8/58	
Just Ask Your Heart	9/59	
Venus	3/59	
Why	12/59	
AVERAGE WHITE BAND (UK)		
Cut The Cake	6/75	
Let's Go Round Again Pt. 1		6/80
Pick Up The Pieces	1/75	3/75
AVONS (UK)		
Seven Little Girls Sitting In The Back Seat		12/59
Charles AZNAVOUR (F)		
She		6/74
AZTEC CAMERA (UK)		
Somewhere In My Heart		5/88
Eric B & Rakim (US) See Jody Watley with Eric B. & Rakim		
Stevie B (US)		
Because I Love You (The Postman Song)	11/90	3/91
B.V.S.M.P. (US)		
I Need You		8/88
BABYFACE (US)		
It's No Crime	10/89	
Whip Appeal	4/90	
BABYS (UK)		
Every Time I Think Of You	3/79	
Isn't It Time	12/77	
BACCARA (Spa)		

	US Top 20 Ent	UK Top 20 Ent
Sorry I'm A Lady		2/78
Yes Sir I Can Boogie		10/77
Burt BACHARACH (US)		
Trains And Boats And Planes		6/65
BACHELORS (I)		
Charmaine		3/63
Diane	6/64	2/64
I Believe		4/64
I Wouldn't Trade You For The World		9/64
Marie		6/65
No Arms Could Ever Hold You		12/64
Ramona		6/64
The Sound Of Silence		4/66
BACHMAN-TURNER OVERDRIVE (C)		
Takin' Care Of Business	8/74	
You Ain't Seen Nothin' Yet	10/74	12/74
BAD COMPANY (UK)		
Can't Get Enough	10/74	
Feel Like Makin' Love	9/75	
Rock 'n' Roll Fantasy	6/79	
BAD ENGLISH (UK/US)		
Price Of Love	2/90	
When I See You Smile	10/89	
BAD MANNERS (UK)		
Can Can		7/81
Just A Feeling		4/81
Lip Up Fatty		8/80
My Girl Lollipop (My Boy Lollipop)		8/82
Special Brew		11/80
Walkin' In The Sunshine		10/81
BADFINGER (UK)		
Baby Blue	4/72	
Come And Get It	4/70	1/70
Day After Day	1/72	2/72
No Matter What	12/70	2/71
Joan BAEZ (US)		
The Night They Drove Old Dixie Down	9/71	11/71
There But For Fortune		7/65
Philip BAILEY with Phil Collins (US/UK)		
Easy Lover	1/85	3/85
Adrian BAKER (UK)		
Sherry		8/75
Anita BAKER (US)		
Giving You The Best That I Got	11/88	
Sweet Love	10/86	
George BAKER SELECTION (H)		
Paloma Blanca		10/75
Lavern BAKER (US)		
I Cried A Tear	2/59	
Long John BALDRY (UK)		
Let The Heartaches Begin		11/67
Mexico		11/68
Marty BALIN (US)		
Hearts	7/81	
Kenny BALL (UK)		
The Green Leaves Of Summer		6/62
March Of The Siamese Children		2/62
Midnight In Moscow	3/62	11/61
Samantha		3/61
So Do I		8/62
Sukiyaki		2/63
Michael BALL (UK)		
Love Changes Everything		2/89
Hank BALLARD & The Midnighters (UK)		
Finger Poppin' Time	8/60	
Let's Go, Let's Go, Let's Go	11/60	
BALTIMORA (I)		
Tarzan Boy		8/85
BANANARAMA (UK)		
Cruel Summer	9/84	7/83
I Heard A Rumour	9/87	
I Want You Back		4/88
❖ with *Fun Boy Three* It Ain't What You Do		
It's The Way That You Do It		3/82
Love In The First Degree		10/87
Na Na Hey Hey Kiss Him Goodbye		3/83
Robert De Niro's Waiting		3/84
Shy Boy		7/82
Venus	8/86	7/86
BANANARAMA/La Na Nee Nee Noo Noo (UK)		
Help		3/89
BANANARAMA with The Fun Boy Three (UK)		
Really Saying Something		5/82
BAND AID (UK/I)		
Do They Know It's Christmas	1/85	12/84

	US Top 20 Ent	UK Top 20 Ent
★ Do They Know It's Christmas		12/85
BAND AID II (UK/Aus)		
Do They Know It's Christmas?		12/89
BANGLES (US)		
Eternal Flame	3/89	4/89
Hazy Shade Of Winter	1/88	3/88
In Your Room	12/88	
Manic Monday	3/86	3/86
Walk Like An Egyptian	11/86	10/86
Walking Down Your Street	4/87	
Chris BARBER JAZZ BAND (UK)		
Petite Fleur (Little Flower)	2/59	2/59
BARDO (UK)		
One Step Further		4/82
Bobby BARE (US)		
All American Boy	1/59	
500 Miles Away From Home	11/63	
J.J. BARRIE (C)		
No Charge		5/76
BARRON KNIGHTS (UK)		
Call Up The Groups		7/64
Live In Trouble		11/77
Merrie Gentle Pops		1/66
Pop Go The Workers		4/65
A Taste Of Aggro		12/78
John BARRY SEVEN (UK)		
Walk Don't Run		9/60
Len BARRY (US)		
Like A Baby		2/66
1-2-3	11/65	11/65
TONI BASIL (US)		
Mickey	11/82	3/82
Fontella BASS (US)		
Rescue Me	11/65	12/65
BASS-O-MATIC (UK)		
Fascinating Rhythm		10/90
Shirley BASSEY (UK)		
As I Love You		1/59
As Long As He Needs Me		8/60
Banana Boat Song		3/57
Climb Ev'ry Mountain		8/61
For All We Know		9/71
Goldfinger	3/65	
I (Who Have Nothing)		10/63
I'll Get By		12/61
Kiss Me Honey Honey Kiss Me		1/59
Never Never Never		3/73
Reach For The Stars		8/61
Something		7/70
What Now My Love		10/62
You'll Never Know		5/61
BASSHEADS (UK)		
Is There Anybody Out There?		11/91
Mike BATT (UK)		
Summertime City		9/75
Les BAXTER (US)		
The High And The Mighty	8/54	
The Poor People Of Paris	2/56	
Unchained Melody	4/55	5/55
Wake The Town And Tell The People	8/55	
BAY CITY ROLLERS (UK)		
All Of Me Loves All Of You		10/74
Bye Bye Baby		3/75
Give A Little Love		7/75
I Only Want To Be With You	10/76	9/76
Keep On Dancing		10/71
Love Me Like I Love You		4/76
Money Honey	3/76	11/75
Remember (Sha-La-La)		3/74
Saturday Night	12/75	
Shang-A-Lang		5/74
Summerlove Sensation		8/74
You Made Me Believe In Magic	7/77	
BAZUKA (US)		
Dynomite	7/75	
BEACH BOYS (US)		
Barbara Ann	1/66	3/66
Be True To Your School	12/63	
The Beach Boys Medley	9/81	
Break Away		7/69
California Girls	8/65	
Cottonfields		6/70
Dance, Dance, Dance	12/64	
Darlin'		2/68
Do It Again		8/68

	US Top 20 Ent	UK Top 20 Ent
Do You Wanna Dance?	4/65	
Fun, Fun, Fun	3/64	
God Only Knows		8/66
Good Vibrations	11/66	11/66
Help Me, Rhonda	5/65	
Heroes And Villains	8/67	9/67
I Can Hear Music		4/69
I Get Around	6/64	8/64
Kokomo	10/88	
Lady Lynda		7/79
Rock And Roll Music	7/76	
Sloop John B	4/66	5/66
Surfer Girl	9/63	
Surfin' Safari	10/62	
Surfin' U.S.A.	4/63	
Then I Kissed Her		5/67
When I Grow Up (To Be A Man)	10/64	
❖ with *The Fat Boys* Wipeout	9/87	9/87
Wouldn't It Be Nice	9/66	
BEASTIE BOYS (US)		
No Sleep Till Brooklyn		6/87
She's On It		8/87
(You Gotta) Fight For Your Right (To Party)	2/87	3/87
BEAT (UK)		
Can't Get Used To Losing You		5/83
Hands Off-She's Mine		3/80
Mirror In The Bathroom		5/80
Tears Of A Clown/Ranking Full Stop		1/80
Too Nice To Talk To		1/81
BEATLES (UK)		
All You Need Is Love	8/67	7/67
And I Love Her	9/64	
Ballad Of John And Yoko	6/69	6/69
Beatles Hits E.P.		12/63
The Beatles Movie Medley	5/82	7/82
Can't Buy Me Love	4/64	3/64
Come Together/Something	10/69	11/69
Day Tripper	1/66	12/65
Do You Want To Know A Secret	4/64	
Eight Days A Week	3/65	
Eleanor Rigby	9/66	8/66
From Me To You		4/63
Got To Get You Into My Life	7/76	
A Hard Day's Night	7/64	7/64
Hello Goodbye	12/67	12/67
Help!	8/65	8/65
Hey Jude	9/68	9/68
★ Hey Jude		4/76
I Feel Fine	12/64	12/64
I Want To Hold Your Hand	1/64	12/63
Lady Madonna	4/68	3/68
Let It Be	3/70	3/70
The Long And Winding Road/For You Blue	6/70	
Love Me Do	5/64	10/82
Magical Mystery Tour (Double E.P.)		12/67
Nowhere Man	3/66	
P.S. I Love You	6/64	
Paperback Writer	6/66	6/66
Penny Lane	3/67	2/67
Please Please Me	2/64	2/63
Revolution	9/68	
She Loves You	8/64	8/63
She's A Woman	12/64	
Strawberry Fields Forever	3/67	2/67
Ticket To Ride	5/65	4/65
Twist And Shout	3/64	7/63
We Can Work It Out	12/65	12/65
With The Beatles L.P.		12/63
Yellow Submarine	9/66	8/66
Yesterday	10/65	3/76
BEATLES with Billy Preston (UK/US)		
Get Back	5/69	4/69
BEATMASTERS featuring Betty Boo (UK)		
Hey D.J. I Can't Dance To That Music You're Playing/Ska Train		8/89
BEATMASTERS featuring The Cookie Crew (UK)		
Rok Da House		1/88
BEATMASTERS featuring Merlin (UK)		
Who's In The House		5/89
BEATMASTERS with P.P. Arnold (UK/US)		
Burn It Up		10/88
BEATS INTERNATIONAL (UK)		
Won't Talk About It		5/90
BEATS INTERNATIONAL featuring Lindy Layton (UK)		

	US Top 20 Ent	UK Top 20 Ent
Dub Be Good To Me		2/90
BEAU BRUMMELS (US)		
Just A Little	6/65	
Laugh, Laugh	2/65	
BEAUTIFUL SOUTH (UK)		
A Little Time		10/90
Song For Whoever		6/89
You Keep It All In		10/89
Gilbert BECAUD (F)		
A Little Love And Understanding		5/75
Jeff BECK (UK)		
❖ with Donovan Goo Goo Barabajagal (Love Is Hot)		8/69
Hi-Ho Silver Lining		5/67
Robin BECK (US)		
The First Time		11/88
BEE GEES (UK)		
Boogie Child	3/77	
Don't Forget To Remember		9/69
Fanny (Be Tender With My Love)	3/76	
First Of May		3/69
For Whom The Bell Tolls		12/93
How Can You Mend A Broken Heart	7/71	
How Deep Is Your Love	11/77	11/77
I Started A Joke	1/69	
I've Gotta Get A Message To You	9/68	8/68
Jive Talkin'	7/75	7/75
(The Lights Went Out In) Massachusetts	12/67	10/67
Lonely Days	1/71	
Love So Right	10/76	
Love You Inside Out	5/79	5/79
New York Mining Disaster 1941		5/67
Night Fever	2/78	4/78
Nights On Broadway	11/75	
One	9/89	
Run To Me		8/72
Secret Love		3/91
Stayin' Alive	1/78	3/78
Too Much Heaven	12/78	12/78
Tragedy	2/79	2/79
Words		2/68
World		12/67
You Should Be Dancing	8/76	8/76
You Win Again		10/87
BEGGAR & CO (UK)		
(Somebody) Help Me Out		3/81
Harry BELAFONTE (US)		
Banana Boat (Day-O)	1/57	3/57
Island In The Sun		6/57
Jamaica Farewell	1/57	
Mama Look At Bubu	4/57	
Mary's Boy Child		11/57
★ Mary's Boy Child		12/58
BELL & JAMES (US)		
Livin' It Up (Friday Night)	4/79	
BELL BIV DEVOE (US)		
Do Me	8/90	
Poison	5/90	
BELL NOTES (US)		
I've Had It	3/59	
Archie BELL & The Drells (US)		
Here I Go Again		11/72
I Can't Stop Dancing	8/68	
Tighten Up	4/68	
Freddie BELL & THE BELLBOYS (US)		
Giddy-Up-A-Ding-Dong		10/56
Maggie BELL (UK) See B.A. Robertson & Maggie Bell		
William BELL (US)		
❖ with Judy Clay Private Number		12/68
Tryin' To Love Two	4/77	
BELLAMY BROTHERS (US)		
If I Said You Had A Beautiful Body Would You Hold It Against Me		9/79
Let Your Love Flow	3/76	6/76
BELLE & The Devotions (UK)		
Love Games		5/84
BELLE STARS (UK)		
The Clapping Song		8/82
Iko Iko	5/89	
Sign Of The Times		2/83
Regina BELLE (US) See Peabo Bryson & Regina Belle		
BELLS (C)		
Stay Awhile	4/71	
BELOVED (UK)		
Sweet Harmony		1/93
Pat BENATAR (US)		
Hit Me With Your Best Shot	11/80	
Invincible (Theme From The Legend Of Billie Jean)	8/85	
Love Is A Battlefield	11/83	
Shadows Of The Night	12/82	
We Belong	12/84	
Boyd BENNETT & His Rockets (US)		
Seventeen	8/55	
Cliff BENNETT & The Rebel Rousers (UK)		
Got To Get You Into My Life		9/66
One Way Love		10/64
Tony BENNETT (US)		
In The Middle Of An Island/I Am	9/57	
Rags To Riches	1/54	
Stranger In Paradise	1/54	4/55
There'll Be No Teardrops Tonight	4/54	
George BENSON (US)		
Give Me The Night	8/80	8/80
In Your Eyes		10/83
Lady Love Me (One More Time)		6/83
On Broadway	5/78	
This Masquerade	8/76	
Turn Your Love Around	12/81	
Brook BENTON (US)		
❖ with Dinah Washington Baby (You Got What It Takes)	2/60	
The Boll Weevil Song	6/61	
Endlessly	6/59	
Hotel Happiness	12/62	
It's Just A Matter Of Time	3/59	
Kiddio	9/60	
Rainy Night In Georgia	2/70	
❖ with Dinah Washington A Rockin' Good Way	6/60	
So Many Ways	11/59	
Think Twice	3/61	
BERLIN (US)		
Take My Breath Away	8/86	11/86
★ Take My Breath Away		11/90
Elmer BERNSTEIN (US)		
Main Title From 'The Man With The Golden Arm'	4/56	
Staccato's Theme		12/59
Chuck BERRY (US)		
Johnny B. Goode	5/58	
Maybellene	8/55	
Memphis Tennessee		10/63
My Ding-A-Ling	10/72	11/72
No Particular Place To Go	7/64	6/64
Rock & Roll Music	11/57	
School Day	4/57	
Sweet Little Sixteen	3/58	
Dave BERRY (UK)		
The Crying Game		9/64
Little Things		4/65
Mama		8/66
Mike BERRY (UK)		
Don't You Think It's Time		1/63
Sunshine Of Your Smile		8/80
Nick BERRY (UK)		
Every Loser Wins		10/86
Heartbeat		6/92
BEVERLEY SISTERS (UK)		
I Saw Mommy Kissing Santa Claus		1/54
Little Donkey		12/59
The Little Drummer Boy		2/59
B-52'S (US)		
Love Shack	11/89	3/90
Roam	2/90	
BIG AUDIO DYNAMITE (UK)		
E=MC²		4/86
BIG BEN BANJO BAND (UK)		
Let's Get Together No. 1		12/54
BIG BOPPER (US)		
Chantilly Lace	10/58	1/59
BIG BROTHER & The Holding Company (US)		
Piece Of My Heart	10/68	
BIG COUNTRY (UK)		
Chance		9/83
Fields Of Fire (400 Miles)		4/83
Look Away		4/86
Wonderland		1/84
BIG FUN (UK)		
Blame It On The Boogie		8/89
Can't Shake The Feeling		12/89
Barry BIGGS (J)		
Side Show		1/77
Acker BILK (UK)		
Aria		9/76
Buona Sera		1/61
Lonely		10/62
Stranger On The Shore	4/62	8/62
Summer Set		2/60
That's My Home		8/61
BILLY & LILLIE (US)		
La Dee Dah	1/58	
BILLY JOE & The Checkmates (US)		
Percolator (Twist)	3/62	
BIMBO JET (F)		
El Bimbo		8/75
Jane BIRKIN & Serge Gainsbourg (UK/F)		
Je T'Aime...Moi Non Plus		9/69
Elvin BISHOP (US)		
Fooled Around And Fell In Love	4/76	
Stephen BISHOP (US)		
On And On	9/77	
BIZ MARKIE (US)		
Just A Friend	3/90	
BIZARRE INC (UK)		
Playing With Knives		11/91
Such A Feeling		10/91
BIZARRE INC featuring Angie Brown (UK)		
I'm Gonna Get You		10/92
BIZZ NIZZ (US/B)		
Don't Miss The Partyline		4/90
BJORK & David Arnold (Ice/UK)		
Play Dead		10/93
BLACK (UK)		
Sweetest Smile		7/87
Wonderful Life		9/87
Bill BLACK('S) COMBO (US)		
Don't Be Cruel	10/60	
Smokie-Part 2	1/60	
White Silver Sands	4/60	
Cilla BLACK (UK)		
Alfie		4/66
Anyone Who Had A Heart		2/64
Conversations		8/69
Don't Answer Me		6/66
A Fool Am I		11/66
It's For You		8/64
Love's Just A Broken Heart		2/66
Something Tells Me (Something Is Gonna Happen Tonight)		12/71
Step Inside Love		4/68
Surround Yourself With Sorrow		3/69
You're My World		5/64
You've Lost That Lovin' Feelin'		1/65
Jeanne BLACK (US)		
He'll Have To Stay	5/60	
BLACK BOX (Ita)		
Everybody Everybody	10/90	
Fantasy		11/90
I Don't Know Anybody Else		2/90
Ride On Time		8/89
Strike It Up	6/91	
The Total Mix		1/91
BLACKBYRDS (US)		
Walking In Rhythm	4/75	
BLACKFOOT SUE (UK)		
Standing In The Road		9/72
BLACK LACE (UK)		
Agadoo		8/84
Do The Conga		12/84
Superman (Gioca Jouer)		10/83
BLACK SABBATH (UK)		
Paranoid		10/70
BLACK SLATE (UK/J)		
Amigo		10/80
Band Of The BLACK WATCH (UK)		
Scotch On The Rocks		10/75
BLANCMANGE (UK)		
Blind Vision		5/83
Don't Tell Me		4/84
Living On The Ceiling		11/82
Billy BLAND (US)		
Let The Little Girl Dance	5/60	5/60
Marcie BLANE (US)		
Bobby's Girl	11/62	

	US Top 20 Ent	UK Top 20 Ent
Archie BLEYER (US)		
Hernando's Hideaway	6/54	
Mary J. BLIGE (US)		
Real Love	10/92	
BLONDIE (US)		
Atomic		2/80
Call Me	3/80	4/80
Denis		3/78
Dreaming		10/79
Hanging On The Telephone		11/78
Heart Of Glass	4/79	1/79
(I'm Always Touched By Your) Presence Dear		5/78
Island Of Lost Souls		6/82
Picture This		9/78
Rapture	3/81	2/81
Sunday Girl		5/79
The Tide Is High	12/80	11/80
Union City Blue		12/79
BLOOD SWEAT & TEARS (US)		
And When I Die	11/69	
Hi-De-Ho	9/70	
Spinning Wheel	6/69	
You've Made Me So Very Happy	4/69	
BLOODSTONE (US)		
Natural High	7/73	
Bobby BLOOM (US)		
Montego Bay	11/70	9/70
BLOW MONKEYS (UK)		
Digging Your Scene		3/86
It Doesn't Have To Be This Way		2/87
BLUE PEARL (UK/US)		
(Can You) Feel The Passion		1/92
Naked In The Rain		7/90
Barry BLUE (UK)		
(Dancing) On A Saturday Night		8/73
Do You Wanna Dance		11/73
School Love		3/74
BLUEBELLS (UK)		
I'm Falling		5/84
Young At Heart		7/84
★ Young At Heart		3/93
BLUE CHEER (US)		
Summertime Blues	4/68	
BLUE MAGIC (US)		
Sideshow	7/74	
BLUE MINK (UK/US)		
Banner Man		6/71
Good Morning Freedom		4/70
Melting Pot		12/69
Randy		7/73
Stay With Me		12/72
BLUE OYSTER CULT (US)		
(Don't Fear) The Reaper	10/76	
BLUES BROTHERS (US)		
Everybody Needs Somebody To Love		4/90
Soul Man	2/79	
BLUES IMAGE (US)		
Ride Captain Ride	6/70	
BLUES MAGOOS (US)		
(We Ain't Got) Nothin' Yet	1/67	
BLUE SWEDE (S)		
Hooked On A Feeling	3/74	
Never My Love	10/74	
Colin BLUNSTONE (UK)		
Say You Don't Mind		3/72
BLUR (UK)		
There's No Other Way		5/91
BOB & EARL (US)		
Harlem Shuffle		4/69
BOB & MARCIA (J)		
Pied Piper		7/71
Young Gifted And Black		3/70
BOBBETTES (US)		
Mr. Lee	9/57	
Hamilton BOHANNON (US)		
Disco Stomp		6/75
Marc BOLAN (UK) see T-Rex		
Michael BOLTON (US)		
How Am I Supposed To Live Without You	12/89	2/90
How Can We Be Lovers	4/90	5/90
Love Is A Wonderful Thing	5/91	
Missing You Now	3/92	
Said I Love You...But I Lied	11/93	11/93
(Sittin' On) The Dock Of The Bay	3/88	
Time, Love And Tenderness	8/91	
To Love Somebody	12/92	
When A Man Loves A Woman	11/91	11/91
When I'm Back On My Feet Again	7/90	
BOMB THE BASS (UK)		
Beat Dis		2/88
Megablast/Don't Make Me Wait		9/88
Say A Little Prayer		12/88
Winter In July		8/91
BOMBALURINA (UK)		
Itsy Bitsy Teeny Weeny Yellow Polka Dot Bikini		8/90
BON JOVI (US)		
Bad Medicine	11/88	
Bed Of Roses	3/93	
Born To Be My Baby	1/89	
I'll Be There For You	4/89	
In These Arms		5/93
Keep The Faith		10/92
Lay Your Hands On Me	7/89	
Livin' On A Prayer	1/87	11/86
Living In Sin	12/89	
Wanted Dead Or Alive	5/87	4/87
You Give Love A Bad Name	11/86	9/86
Jon BON JOVI (US)		
Blaze Of Glory	8/90	8/90
Miracle	12/90	
Gary U.S. BONDS (US)		
Dear Lady Twist	2/62	
New Orleans	11/60	
Quarter To Three	6/61	8/61
School Is Out	8/61	
This Little Girl	6/81	
Twist, Twist Senora	4/62	
BONEY M (WI)		
Belfast		12/77
Boney M Megamix		12/92
Daddy Cool		2/77
Gotta Go Home/El Lute		9/79
Hooray Hooray It's A Holi-Holiday		5/79
Ma Baker		7/77
Mary's Boy Child-Oh My Lord		12/78
Painter Man		3/79
Rasputin		10/78
Rivers Of Babylon/Brown Girl In The Ring		5/78
Sunny		4/77
Graham BONNETT (UK)		
Night Games		4/81
BONZO DOG DOO-DAH BAND (UK)		
I'm The Urban Spaceman		12/68
Betty BOO (UK)		
Doin' The Doo		6/90
❖ with Beatmasters Hey DJ I Can't Dance To That Music You're Playing		8/89
Where Are You Baby?		8/90
BOOGIE BOX HIGH (UK)		
Jive Talkin'		7/87
BOOKER T. & The M.G.'s (US)		
Green Onions	9/62	1/80
Hang 'Em High	2/69	
Time Is Tight	4/69	6/69
BOOMTOWN RATS (I)		
Banana Republic		12/80
I Don't Like Mondays		7/79
Like Clockwork		7/78
Looking After Number One		9/77
Mary Of The Fourth Form		12/77
Rat Trap		10/78
She's So Modern		5/78
Someone's Looking At You		2/80
Debby BOONE (US)		
You Light Up My Life	10/77	
Pat BOONE (US)		
Ain't That A Shame	7/55	11/55
April Love/When The Swallows Come Back To Capistrano	11/57	12/57
At My Front Door (Crazy Little Mama)	11/55	
Don't Forbid Me	1/57	2/57
Friendly Persuasion/Chains Of Love	10/56	1/57
I Almost Lost My Mind	6/56	8/56
I'll Be Home	2/56	5/56
If Dreams Came True	8/58	
It's Too Soon To Know	2/58	4/58
Johnny Will		12/61
Love Letters In The Sand	5/57	7/57
The Main Attraction		12/62
Moody River	6/61	7/61
Remember You're Mine/There's A Gold Mine In The Sky	8/57	10/57
Speedy Gonzales	7/62	7/62
Sugar Moon/Cherie I Love You	5/58	7/58
Two Hearts	5/55	
Why Baby Why	3/57	
A Wonderful Time Up There/It's Too Soon To Know	2/58	4/58
Ken BOOTHE (J)		
Crying Over You		1/75
Everything I Own		10/74
BOSTON (US)		
Amanda	10/86	
Don't Look Back	9/78	
More Than A Feeling	11/76	
We're Ready	2/87	
Eve BOSWELL (Hun)		
Pickin' A Chicken		1/56
Judy BOUCHER (UK)		
Can't Be With You Tonight		4/87
BOW WOW WOW (UK)		
Go Wild In The Country		3/82
I Want Candy		6/82
Jimmy BOWEN (US)		
I'm Stickin' With You	4/57	
David BOWIE (UK)		
Absolute Beginners		3/86
Ashes To Ashes		8/80
Blue Jean	10/84	9/84
Boys Keep Swingin'		5/79
China Girl	8/83	6/83
Drive-In Saturday		4/73
Fame	9/75	
Fashion		11/80
Golden Years	3/76	12/75
The Jean Genie		1/73
John I'm Only Dancing		10/72
John I'm Only Dancing (Again)		1/80
Jump They Say		4/93
Knock On Wood		10/74
The Laughing Gnome		10/73
Let's Dance	4/83	3/83
Life On Mars		7/73
Modern Love	11/83	9/83
Rebel Rebel		2/74
Sorrow		10/73
Sound And Vision		3/77
Space Oddity		10/69
★ Space Oddity		10/75
Starman		8/72
❖ with Queen Under Pressure		11/81
David BOWIE & Bing Crosby (UK/US)		
Peace On Earth-Little Drummer Boy		12/82
David BOWIE & Mick Jagger (UK)		
Dancing In The Street	9/85	9/85
BOX TOPS (US)		
Cry Like A Baby	4/68	5/68
The Letter	9/67	10/67
BOY GEORGE (UK)		
The Crying Game	5/93	
Everything I Own		3/87
BOY MEETS GIRL (US)		
Waiting For A Star To Fall	11/88	1/89
Tommy BOYCE & Bobby Hart (US)		
I Wonder What She's Doing Tonight	2/68	
Jimmy BOYD (US)		
I Saw Mommy Kissing Santa Claus		1/54
BOYS CLUB (US)		
I Remember Holding You	12/88	
BOYS DON'T CRY (UK)		
I Wanna Be A Cowboy	6/86	
BOYS (US)		
Dial My Heart	2/89	
BOYSTOWN GANG (US)		
Can't Take My Eyes Off You		8/82
BOYZ II MEN (US)		
End Of The Road	8/92	10/92
In The Still Of The Night (I'll Remember)	12/92	
It's So Hard To Say Goodbye To Yesterday	11/91	
Motownphilly	8/91	
Uhh Ahh	3/92	
Jan BRADLEY (US)		
Mama Didn't Lie	3/63	

	US Top 20 Ent	UK Top 20 Ent
Billy BRAGG with Cara Tivey (UK)		
She's Leaving Home		5/88
Johnny BRANDON (UK)		
Tomorrow		3/55
Laura BRANIGAN (US)		
Gloria	10/82	2/83
How Am I Supposed To Live Without You	10/83	
Self Control	6/84	8/84
Solitaire	5/83	
BRASS CONSTRUCTION (US)		
Movin'	6/76	
Los BRAVOS (Spa/G)		
Black Is Black	9/66	7/66
Toni BRAXTON (US)		
Another Sad Love Song	9/93	
Breathe Again	11/93	
BREAD (US)		
Baby I'm A Want You	11/71	2/72
Diary	6/72	
Everything I Own	2/72	
Guitar Man	9/72	
If	4/71	
It Don't Matter To Me	11/70	
Lost Without Your Love	1/77	
Make It With You	7/70	9/70
BREAK MACHINE (US)		
Break Dance Party		5/84
Street Dance		3/84
BREAKFAST CLUB (US)		
Right On Track	5/87	
BREATHE (UK)		
Don't Tell Me Lies	3/89	
Hands To Heaven	7/88	8/88
How Can I Fall	11/88	
Beverly BREMMERS (US)		
Don't Say You Don't Remember	2/72	
BRENDON (UK)		
Gimme Some		4/77
Walter BRENNAN (US)		
Old Rivers	5/62	
Tony BRENT (UK)		
Cindy Oh Cindy		12/56
Girl Of My Dreams		9/58
Three Coins In The Fountain		8/54
Bernard BRESSLAW (UK)		
Mad Passionate Love		9/58
BREWER AND SHIPLEY (US)		
One Toke Over The Line	4/71	
Teresa BREWER (US)		
Jilted	5/54	
Let Me Go, Lover!	12/54	2/55
Ricochet	1/54	
A Sweet Old Fashioned Girl	7/56	8/56
A Tear Fell	3/56	4/56
BRIAN & MICHAEL (UK)		
Matchstalk Men And Matchstalk Cats And Dogs		3/78
BRICK (US)		
Dazz	12/76	
Edie BRICKELL & The New Bohemians (US)		
What I Am	2/89	
Alicia BRIDGES (US)		
I Love The Night Life (Disco 'Round)	11/78	
BRIGHOUSE AND RASTRICK BRASS BAND (UK)		
The Floral Dance		12/77
Sarah BRIGHTMAN (UK)		
✤ with Cliff Richard All I Ask Of You		10/86
Wishing You Were Somehow Here Again		2/87
Sarah BRIGHTMAN & Hot Gossip (UK)		
I Lost My Heart To A Starship Trooper		12/78
Sarah BRIGHTMAN & Paul Miles-Kingston (UK)		
Pie Jesu		3/85
Sarah BRIGHTMAN & Steve Harley (UK)		
The Phantom Of The Opera		2/86
Johnny BRISTOL (US)		
Hang On In There Baby	9/74	9/74
BRONSKI BEAT (UK)		
Hit That Perfect Beat		12/85
Smalltown Boy		6/84
Why?		10/84
BRONSKI BEAT & Marc Almond (UK)		
I Feel Love		4/85
BROOK BROTHERS (UK)		
Warpaint		4/61
BROOKLYN BRIDGE (US)		

	US Top 20 Ent	UK Top 20 Ent
Worst That Could Happen	1/69	
Donnie BROOKS (US)		
Mission Bell	8/60	
Elkie BROOKS (UK)		
Don't Cry Out Loud		12/78
No More The Fool		1/87
Pearl's A Singer		4/77
Sunshine After The Rain		10/77
BROS (UK)		
Are You Mine?		7/91
Cat Among The Pigeons/Silent Night		12/88
Chocolate Box		10/89
Drop The Boy		3/88
I Owe You Nothing		6/88
I Quit		9/88
Sister		12/89
Too Much		8/89
When Will I Be Famous		1/88
BROTHER BEYOND (UK)		
The Harder I Try		8/88
He Ain't No Competition		11/88
BROTHERHOOD OF MAN (UK)		
Angelo		7/77
Figaro		1/78
Oh Boy		4/77
Save Your Kisses For Me		3/76
United We Stand	7/70	2/70
BROTHERS FOUR (US)		
Greenfields	4/60	
BROTHERS JOHNSON (US)		
I'll Be Good To You	6/76	
Stomp!	5/80	4/80
Strawberry Letter 23	8/77	
BROTHERS (UK)		
Sing Me		2/77
Crazy World Of Arthur BROWN (UK)		
Fire	9/68	7/68
Bobby BROWN (US)		
Don't Be Cruel	10/88	4/89
Every Little Step	5/89	5/89
Get Away	2/93	
Good Enough	11/92	
Humpin' Around	8/92	
My Prerogative	12/88	2/89
On Our Own	7/89	7/89
Rock Wit'cha	10/89	
Roni	3/89	
✤ with Glenn Medeiros She Ain't Worth It	6/90	7/90
James BROWN (US)		
Cold Sweat (Part 1)	8/67	
Hot Pants (She Got To Use What She Got To Get What She Wants)	8/71	
I Got The Feelin'	4/68	
I Got You (I Feel Good)	11/65	
It's A Man's Man's Man's World	6/66	
Living In America	2/86	2/86
Mother Popcorn (You Got To Have A Mother For Me)	7/69	
Papa's Got A Brand New Bag	8/65	
Say It Loud-I'm Black And I'm Proud	10/68	
Super Bad (Pts 1 & 2)	11/70	
Jocelyn BROWN (US)		
✤ with Incognito Always There		7/91
✤ with Right Said Fred Don't Talk Just Kiss		12/91
Somebody Else's Guy		5/84
Joe BROWN & The Bruvvers (UK)		
It Only Took A Minute		12/62
A Picture Of You		6/62
That's What Love Will Do		2/63
Peter BROWN (US)		
Dance With Me	6/78	
Sam BROWN (UK)		
Stop		2/89
Jackson BROWNE (US)		
Doctor My Eyes	4/72	
Lawyers In Love	8/83	
Runnin' On Empty	4/78	
Somebody's Baby	9/82	
Stay		8/78
Tom BROWNE (US)		
Funkin' For Jamaica (N.Y.)		8/80
BROWNS (US)		
The Old Lamplighter	4/60	
Scarlet Ribbons	12/59	
The Three Bells	8/59	9/59

	US Top 20 Ent	UK Top 20 Ent
BROWNSVILLE STATION (US)		
Smokin' In The Boys Room	12/73	
Dave BRUBECK QUARTET (US)		
Take Five		11/61
Tommy BRUCE & The Bruisers (UK)		
Ain't Misbehavin'		6/60
Dora BRYAN (UK)		
All I Want For Christmas Is A Beatle		12/63
Anita BRYANT (US)		
In My Little Corner Of The World	8/60	
Paper Roses	5/60	
Peabo BRYSON (US)		
✤ with Celine Dion Beauty And The Beast	3/92	5/92
If Ever You're In My Arms Again	8/84	
Peabo BRYSON & Regina Belle (US)		
A Whole New World (Aladdin's Theme)	1/93	
Peabo BRYSON & Roberta Flack (US)		
Tonight I Celebrate My Love	11/83	9/83
B.T. EXPRESS (US)		
Do It ('Til You're Satisfied)	11/74	
Express	3/75	
BUBBLE PUPPY (US)		
Hot Smoke & Sasafrass	4/69	
BUCHANAN & GOODMAN (US)		
The Flying Saucer (Parts 1 & 2)	8/56	
Lindsey BUCKINGHAM (US)		
Trouble	12/81	
BUCKINGHAMS (US)		
Don't You Care	4/67	
Hey Baby (They're Playing Our Song)	10/67	
Kind Of A Drag	1/67	
Mercy, Mercy, Mercy	7/67	
Susan	1/68	
BUCKNER & GARCIA (US)		
Pac-Man Fever	3/82	
BUCKS FIZZ (UK)		
If You Can't Stand The Heat		1/83
Land Of Make Believe		12/81
Making Your Mind Up		4/81
My Camera Never Lies		4/82
New Beginning (Mamba Seyra)		6/86
Now Those Days Are Gone		7/82
Piece Of The Action		7/81
When We Were Young		7/83
BUFFALO SPRINGFIELD (US)		
For What It's Worth (Stop, Hey What's That Sound)	3/67	
Jimmy BUFFETT (US)		
Margaritaville	6/77	
BUGGLES (UK)		
Video Killed The Radio Star		10/79
B. BUMBLE & The Stingers (US)		
Nut Rocker		4/62
Eric BURDON & War (UK/US)		
Spill The Wine	8/70	
Johnny BURNETTE (US)		
Dreamin'	8/60	10/60
Little Boy Sad	3/61	
You're Sixteen	12/60	1/61
Rocky BURNETTE (US)		
Tired Of Toein' The Line	7/80	
Ray BURNS (UK)		
Mobile		2/55
That's How A Love Song Was Born		9/55
Malandra BURROWS (UK)		
Just This Side Of Love		12/90
Lou BUSCH (US)		
Zambesi		2/56
Kate BUSH (UK)		
Babooshka		7/80
✤ with Peter Gabriel Don't Give Up		11/86
Kate Bush On Stage E.P.		10/79
Man With The Child In His Eyes		7/78
Rocket Man (I Think It's Going To Be A Long Long Time)		12/91
Rubberband Girl		9/93
Running Up That Hill		8/85
Sat In Your Lap		7/81
Wow		4/79
Wuthering Heights		3/78
Jerry BUTLER (US)		
He Will Break Your Heart	11/60	
Moon River	12/61	
Only The Strong Survive	4/69	
Jerry BUTLER & Betty Everett (US)		

353

	US Top 20 Ent	UK Top 20 Ent
Let It Be Me	10/64	
Jerry BUTLER & The Impressions (US)		
For Your Precious Love	7/58	
Max BYGRAVES (UK)		
Deck Of Cards		11/73
Fings Ain't What They Used T'Be		3/60
Gilly Gilly Ossenfeffer Katzenellen		
Bogen By The Sea		9/54
Heart		4/57
Heart Of My Heart		5/54
Jingle Bell Rock		12/59
Meet Me On The Corner		11/55
You Need Hands/Tulips From Amsterdam		5/58
Max BYGRAVES & The Tanner Sisters (UK)		
Friends And Neighbours		6/54
Charlie BYRD (US) See Stan Getz & Charlie Byrd		
Gary BYRD & The GB Experience (UK)		
The Crown		8/83
BYRDS (US)		
All I Really Want To Do		8/65
Eight Miles High	5/66	
Mr. Tambourine Man	6/65	7/65
Turn! Turn! Turn!	11/65	
Edward BYRNES & Connie Stevens (US)		
Kookie, Kookie (Lend Me Your Comb)	5/59	
C&C MUSIC FACTORY featuring Freedom Williams (US)		
Gonna Make You Sweat	1/91	1/91
Things That Make You Go Hmmmm...	8/91	7/91
C&C MUSIC FACTORY featuring Freedom Williams & Zelma Davis (US)		
Here We Go	4/91	
Fantastic Johnny C (US)		
Boogaloo Down Broadway	12/67	
C.C.S. (UK)		
Tap Turns On The Water		9/71
Walkin'		4/71
CADETS (US)		
Stranded In The Jungle	7/56	
Susan CADOGAN (UK)		
Hurt So Good		5/75
John CAFFERTY & The Beaver Brown Band (US)		
On The Dark Side	10/84	
Bobby CALDWELL (US)		
What You Won't Do For Love	3/79	
CALLOWAY (US)		
I Wanna Be Rich	4/90	
Eddie CALVERT (UK)		
Cherry Pink And Apple Blossom White		4/55
John And Julie		8/55
Mandy		2/58
Midnight		8/54
Oh, Mein Papa	1/54	1/54
Stranger In Paradise		5/55
Zambesi		3/56
CAMEO (US)		
Back And Forth	5/87	
Single Life		10/85
Word Up	11/86	9/86
Andy CAMERON (UK)		
Ally's Tartan Army		3/78
Glen CAMPBELL (US)		
✤ with Bobbie Gentry All I Have To Do Is Dream		12/69
Country Boy (You Got Your Feet In L.A.)	1/76	
Galveston	3/69	6/69
Honey Come Back		5/70
It's Only Make Believe	10/70	12/70
Rhinestone Cowboy	8/75	11/75
Southern Nights	4/77	
Wichita Lineman	11/68	3/69
Junior CAMPBELL (UK)		
Hallelujah Freedom		11/72
Tevin CAMPBELL (US)		
Can We Talk	11/93	
Round And Round	4/91	
Tell Me What You Want Me To Do	1/92	
CANDY FLIP (UK)		
Strawberry Fields Forever		3/90
CANDYMAN (US)		
Knockin' Boots	11/90	
CANNED HEAT (US)		
Going Up The Country	1/69	
Let's Work Together		2/70
On The Road Again		9/68

	US Top 20 Ent	UK Top 20 Ent
Freddy CANNON (US)		
Action	9/65	
Palisades Park	6/62	
Tallahassee Lassie	6/59	
Way Down Yonder In New Orleans	12/59	1/60
Jim CAPALDI (UK)		
Love Hurts		11/75
CAPITOLS (US)		
Cool Jerk	6/66	
CAPPELLA (Ita/UK)		
U Got 2 Know		4/93
U Got 2 Let The Music		10/93
CAPRIS (US)		
There's A Moon Out Tonight	2/61	
Tony CAPSTICK (UK)		
Capstick Comes Home/Sheffield Grinder		4/81
CAPTAIN & TENNILLE (US)		
Can't Stop Dancin'	5/77	
Do That To Me One More Time	12/79	3/80
Lonely Night (Angel Face)	2/76	
Love Will Keep Us Together	6/75	
Muskrat Love	11/76	
Shop Around	6/76	
The Way I Want To Touch You	11/75	
You Never Done It Like That	10/78	
CAPTAIN HOLLYWOOD PROJECT (US/G)		
More And More	6/93	
✤ with Twenty 4 Seven I Can't Stand It		10/90
CAPTAIN SENSIBLE (UK)		
Glad It's All Over/Damned On 45		4/84
Happy Talk		7/82
Irene CARA (US)		
Breakdance	5/84	
Fame	8/80	7/82
Flashdance...What A Feeling	5/83	6/83
Why Me?	12/83	
CARAVELLES (UK)		
You Don't Have To Be A Baby To Cry	12/63	8/63
Mariah CAREY (US)		
Can't Let Go	12/91	
Dreamlover	8/93	8/93
Emotions	9/91	
Hero	11/93	11/93
I Don't Wanna Cry	5/91	
I'll Be There	6/92	6/92
Love Takes Time	10/90	
Make It Happen	3/92	
Someday	2/91	
Vision Of Love	7/90	9/90
Belinda CARLISLE (US)		
Circle In The Sand	5/88	5/88
Heaven Is A Place On Earth	11/87	12/87
I Get Weak	2/88	3/88
Leave A Light On	12/89	10/89
Live Your Life Be Free		10/91
Mad About You	7/86	
(We Want) The Same Thing		11/90
Carl CARLTON (US)		
Everlasting Love	11/74	
Eric CARMEN (US)		
All By Myself	2/76	
Hungry Eyes	1/88	
Make Me Lose Control	7/88	
Never Gonna Fall In Love Again	6/76	
Kim CARNES (US)		
Bette Davis Eyes	5/81	5/81
Crazy In The Night (Barking At Airplanes)	7/85	
✤ with Kenny Rogers Don't Fall In Love With A Dreamer	4/80	
More Love	7/80	
CARPENTERS (US)		
Calling Occupants Of Interplanetary Craft		11/77
For All We Know	3/71	
Goodbye To Love	8/72	10/72
Hurting Each Other	2/72	
I Won't Last A Day Without You	5/74	10/72
It's Going To Take Some Time	6/72	
Jambalaya		4/74
Only Yesterday	5/75	5/75
Please Mr. Postman	12/74	2/75
Rainy Days And Mondays	6/71	
Sing	3/73	
Superstar	9/71	
There's A Kind Of Hush (All Over The World)	4/76	

	US Top 20 Ent	UK Top 20 Ent
(They Long To Be) Close To You	7/70	10/70
Top Of The World	11/73	11/73
Touch Me When We're Dancing	8/81	
We've Only Just Begun	10/70	
Yesterday Once More	7/73	8/73
Cathy CARR (US)		
Ivory Tower	4/56	
Pearl CARR & Teddy Johnson (UK)		
Sing Little Birdie		4/59
Vikki CARR (US)		
It Must Be Him	10/67	7/67
Raffaella CARRA (ITA)		
Do It Again		5/78
Paul CARRACK (UK)		
Don't Shed A Tear	2/88	
Keith CARRADINE (US)		
I'm Easy	8/76	
David CARROLL (US)		
Melody Of Love	2/55	
Dina CARROLL (UK)		
Don't Be A Stranger		10/93
Express		5/93
✤ with Quartz It's Too Late		3/91
The Perfect Year		12/93
Ronnie CARROLL (UK)		
Roses Are Red		8/62
Say Wonderful Things		3/63
Walk Hand In Hand		8/56
Jasper CARROTT (UK)		
Funky Moped/Magic Roundabout		9/75
CARS (US)		
Drive	9/84	10/84
★ Drive		8/85
Let's Go	9/79	
Magic	7/84	
My Best Friend's Girl		11/78
Shake It Up	1/82	
Tonight She Comes	12/85	
You Might Think	4/84	
CARTER-THE UNSTOPPABLE SEX MACHINE (UK)		
The Only Living Boy In New Cross		4/92
Clarence CARTER (US)		
Patches	8/70	10/70
Slip Away	9/68	
Mel CARTER (US)		
Hold Me Thrill Me Kiss Me	8/65	
CASCADES (US)		
Rhythm Of The Rain	2/63	3/63
Alvin CASH & The Crawlers (US)		
Twine Time	2/65	
Johnny CASH (US)		
A Boy Named Sue	8/69	9/69
Guess Things Happen That Way/Come In Stranger	7/58	
I Walk The Line	11/56	
A Thing Called Love		5/72
CASINOS (US)		
Then You Can Tell Me Goodbye	2/67	
Mama CASS (US)		
It's Getting Better		9/69
David CASSIDY (US)		
Cherish	12/71	5/12
Could It Be Forever/Cherish		5/72
Daydreamer/The Puppy Song		10/73
How Can I Be Sure		9/72
I'm A Clown/Some Kind Of A Summer		4/73
If I Didn't Care		6/74
The Last Kiss		3/85
Rock Me Baby		12/72
Shaun CASSIDY (US)		
Da Doo Ron Ron	6/77	
Hey Deanie	12/77	
That's Rock 'n' Roll	9/77	
CASTAWAYS (US)		
Liar, Liar	10/65	
Jimmy CASTOR BUNCH (US)		
Troglodyte (Cave Man)	6/72	
CASUALS (UK)		
Jesamine		9/68
George CATES (US)		
Moonglow And Theme From 'Picnic'	5/56	
CATHY JEAN & The Roommates (US)		
Please Love Me Forever	4/61	
CERRONE (F)		
Supernature		8/78

354

	US Top 20 Ent	UK Top 20 Ent
Peter CETERA (US)		
✤ with Cher After All	5/89	
Glory Of Love	7/86	9/86
One Good Woman	9/88	
Peter CETERA & Amy Grant (US)		
The Next Time I Fall	11/86	
Frank CHACKSFIELD (UK)		
Ebb Tide	1/54	2/54
In Old Lisbon		3/56
CHAD & JEREMY (UK)		
A Summer Song	10/64	
Willow Weep For Me	1/65	
CHAIRMEN OF THE BOARD (US)		
Everything's Tuesday		3/71
Give Me Just A Little More Time	3/70	9/70
Pay To The Piper	1/71	
You've Got Me Dangling On A String		12/70
CHAKACHAS (B)		
Jungle Fever	3/72	
Richard CHAMBERLAIN (US)		
Theme From Doctor Kildare (Three Stars Will Shine Tonight)	7/62	6/62
CHAMBERS BROTHERS (US)		
Time Has Come Today	9/68	
CHAMPAIGN (US)		
How 'Bout Us	5/81	6/81
CHAMPS (US)		
Tequila	3/58	4/58
Gene CHANDLER (US)		
Duke Of Earl	2/62	
Get Down		3/79
Groovy Situation	9/70	
CHANGE (US)		
Searching		10/80
Bruce CHANNEL (US)		
Hey! Baby	2/62	3/62
Keep On		8/68
CHANTAYS (US)		
Pipeline	4/63	
CHANTELS (US)		
Look In My Eyes	10/61	
Maybe	2/58	
Harry CHAPIN (US)		
Cat's In The Cradle	11/74	
Tracy CHAPMAN (US)		
Fast Car	8/88	7/88
CHARLATANS (UK)		
The Only One I Know		6/90
CHARLENE (US)		
I've Never Been To Me	5/82	6/82
CHARLES & EDDIE (US)		
Would I Lie To You?	11/92	11/92
Jimmy CHARLES (US)		
A Million To One	9/60	
Ray CHARLES (US)		
Busted	10/63	
Crying Time	2/66	
Georgia On My Mind	10/60	
Here We Go Again	7/67	
Hit The Road Jack	10/61	10/61
I Can't Stop Loving You	5/62	6/62
One Mint Julep	4/61	
Take These Chains From My Heart	5/63	5/63
Unchain My Heart	1/62	
What'd I Say (Pt. 1)	8/59	
You Are My Sunshine	12/62	
You Don't Know Me	8/62	9/62
Your Cheatin' Heart		12/62
Ray CHARLES SINGERS (US)		
Love Me With All Your Heart	5/64	
Sonny CHARLES & The Checkmates, Ltd. (US)		
Black Pearl	6/69	
Tina CHARLES (UK)		
Dance Little Lady Dance		9/76
Dr. Love		12/76
I Love To Love (But My Baby Loves To Dance)		2/76
CHARMS (US)		
Hearts Of Stone	12/54	
Ivory Tower	5/56	
CHAS & DAVE (UK)		
Ain't No Pleasing You		4/82
Rabbit		1/81
✤ with The Matchroom Mob Snooker Loopy		5/86
CHEAP TRICK (US)		
Can't Stop Falling Into Love	9/90	
Don't Be Cruel	9/88	
The Flame	6/88	
I Want You To Want Me	7/79	
Chubby CHECKER (US)		
Birdland	6/63	
Dancin' Party	7/62	
The Fly	10/61	
The Hucklebuck	11/60	
Let's Twist Again	7/61	1/62
★ Let's Twist Again		12/75
Limbo Rock	11/62	
Loddy Lo	12/63	
Pony Time	2/61	
Popeye (The Hitchhiker)	10/62	
Slow Twistin'	3/62	
The Twist	8/60	
★ The Twist	12/61	1/62
✤ with The Fat Boys The Twist (Yo, Twist)	8/88	6/88
CHEECH & CHONG (US)		
Basketball Jones Feat Tyrone Shoelaces	10/73	
Earache My Eye - Feat. Alice Bowie	9/74	
CHEERS (US)		
(Bazoom) I Need Your Lovin'	11/54	
Black Denim Trousers	10/55	
CHELSEA F.C. (UK)		
Blue Is The Colour		3/72
CHER (US)		
All I Really Want To Do	8/65	9/65
Bang Bang (My Baby Shot Me Down)	4/66	4/66
Dark Lady	3/74	
Gypsys Tramps & Thieves	10/71	11/71
Half-Breed	9/73	
I Found Someone	2/88	1/88
If I Could Turn Back Time	9/89	10/89
Just Like Jesse James	12/89	2/90
Love And Understanding		7/91
The Shoop Shoop Song (It's In His Kiss)		4/91
Take Me Home	4/79	
The Way Of Love	3/72	
We All Sleep Alone	6/88	
You Better Sit Down Kids	12/67	
CHER & Peter Cetera (US)		
After All	5/89	
CHERELLE & Alexander O'Neal (US)		
Saturday Love		1/86
Don CHERRY (US)		
Band Of Gold	12/55	2/56
Neneh CHERRY (US)		
Buffalo Stance	6/89	12/88
Kisses On The Wind	9/89	
Manchild		5/89
CHIC (US)		
Dance, Dance, Dance (Yowsah, Yowsah, Yowsah)	2/78	1/78
Everybody Dance		5/78
Good Times	7/79	7/79
I Want Your Love	4/79	3/79
Le Freak	11/78	12/78
CHICAGO (US)		
Alive Again	12/78	
Along Comes A Woman	4/85	
Baby What A Big Surprise	11/77	
Beginnings/Colour My World	8/71	
Call On Me	8/74	
Does Anybody Really Know What Time It Is	12/70	
Feelin' Stronger Every Day	8/73	
Hard Habit To Break	9/84	11/84
Hard To Say I'm Sorry	7/82	10/82
Harry Truman	4/75	
I Don't Wanna Live Without Your Love	8/88	
I'm A Man		2/70
(I've Been) Searchin' So Long	5/74	
If You Leave Me Now	9/76	10/76
Just You 'n' Me	11/73	
Look Away	11/88	
Make Me Smile	6/70	
No Tell Lover	2/79	
Old Days	5/75	
Saturday In The Park	9/72	
Stay The Night	6/84	
25 Or 6 To 4	8/70	8/70
What Kind Of Man Would I Be?	2/90	
Will You Still Love Me	2/87	
Wishing You Were Here	12/74	
You're Not Alone	3/89	
You're The Inspiration	12/84	
CHICKEN SHACK (UK)		
I'd Rather Go Blind		6/69
CHICORY TIP (UK)		
Son Of My Father		2/72
CHIFFONS (US)		
He's So Fine	3/63	5/63
One Fine Day	6/63	
Sweet Talkin' Guy	6/66	4/72
CHILD (UK)		
It's Only Make Believe		9/78
Jane CHILD (US)		
Don't Wanna Fall In Love	3/90	
CHI-LITES (US)		
Have You Seen Her	11/71	2/72
★ Have You Seen Her/Oh Girl		7/75
Homely Girl		4/74
It's Time For Love		10/75
Oh Girl	5/72	
Too Good To Be Forgotten		12/74
You Don't Have To Go		8/76
CHIMES (UK)		
I Still Haven't Found What I'm Looking For		5/90
CHIMES (US)		
Once In A While	1/61	
CHINA CRISIS (UK)		
Christian		2/83
Wishful Thinking		1/84
CHIPMUNKS (US)		
Alvin's Harmonica	3/59	
The Chipmunk Song	12/58	
Ragtime Cowboy Joe		8/59
CHORDETTES (US)		
Born To Be With You	7/56	9/56
Lollipop	3/58	4/58
Mr. Sandman	11/54	1/55
Never On Sunday	8/61	
CHORDS (US)		
Sh-Boom	7/54	
CHRISTIANS (UK)		
Harvest For The World		10/88
CHRISTIANS, Holly Johnson, Paul McCartney, Gerry Marsden & Stock Aitken Waterman (UK)		
Ferry 'Cross The Mersey		5/89
CHRISTIE (UK)		
San Bernadino		11/70
Yellow River		5/70
David CHRISTIE (F)		
Saddle Up		9/82
Lou CHRISTIE (US)		
I'm Gonna Make You Mine	10/69	10/69
Lightnin' Strikes	2/66	3/66
Two Faces Have I	5/63	
Tony CHRISTIE (UK)		
I Did What I Did For Maria		6/71
CINDERELLA (US)		
Don't Know What You Got (Till It's Gone)	11/88	
Nobody's Fool	2/87	
Gigliola CINQUETTI (Ita)		
Go (Before You Break My Heart)		6/74
Non Ho L'Eta Per Amarti		6/64
CITY BOY (UK)		
5-7-0-5		8/78
Gary CLAIL ON-U SOUND SYSTEM (UK)		
Human Nature		4/91
CLAIRE & FRIENDS (UK)		
It's 'Orrible Being In Love (When You're 8½)		7/86
CLANNAD (I)		
Theme From Harry's Game		11/82
Jimmy CLANTON (US)		
Go Jimmy Go	1/60	
Just A Dream	8/58	
Venus In Blue Jeans	10/62	
Eric CLAPTON (UK)		
I Can't Stand It	4/81	
I Shot The Sheriff	8/74	8/74
Lay Down Sally	2/78	
Layla	11/92	
Promises	12/78	
Tears In Heaven	2/92	3/92
Claudine CLARK (US)		
Party Lights	8/62	
Dave CLARK FIVE (UK)		

	US Top 20 Ent	UK Top 20 Ent
Any Way You Want It	1/65	
Because	8/64	
Bits And Pieces	4/64	2/64
Can't You See That She's Mine	7/64	6/64
Catch Us If You Can	9/65	8/65
Come Home	3/65	
Do You Love Me	6/64	
Everybody Get Together		3/70
Everybody Knows		11/67
Glad All Over	3/64	12/63
Good Old Rock 'n' Roll		1/70
I Like It Like That	7/65	
Over And Over	12/65	
Red Balloon		10/68
You Got What It Takes	5/67	
Dee CLARK (US)		
Raindrops	6/61	
Petula CLARK (UK)		
Alone		11/57
Baby Lover		3/58
Don't Sleep In The Subway	7/67	7/67
Downtown	1/65	12/64
★ Downtown '88		12/88
I Couldn't Live Without Your Love	8/66	7/66
I Know A Place	4/65	
The Little Shoemaker		6/54
Majorca		2/55
My Friend The Sea		12/61
My Love	2/66	2/66
Romeo		7/61
Sailor		1/61
A Sign Of The Times	4/66	
Suddenly There's A Valley		12/55
This Is My Song	4/67	2/67
With All My Heart		8/57
Ya Ya Twist		7/62
Sanford CLARK (US)		
The Fool	8/56	
CLASH (UK)		
Bank Robber		9/80
London Calling		1/80
Rock The Casbah	12/82	
★ Should I Stay Or Should I Go		3/91
CLASSICS IV (US)		
Spooky	1/68	
Stormy	11/68	
Traces	3/69	
CLASSIX NOUVEAUX (UK)		
Is It A Dream		4/82
Judy CLAY & William Bell (US)		
Private Number		12/68
Tom CLAY (US)		
What The World Needs Now Is Love/ Abraham, Martin & John	8/71	
Jimmy CLIFF (J)		
Wild World		9/70
Wonderful World Beautiful People		11/69
Buzz CLIFFORD (US)		
Baby Sittin' Boogie	2/61	4/61
Mike CLIFFORD (US)		
Close To Cathy	11/62	
CLIMAX (US)		
Precious And Few	2/72	
CLIMAX BLUES BAND (UK)		
Couldn't Get It Right	4/77	11/76
I Love You	6/81	
CLIMIE FISHER (UK)		
Love Changes (Everything)		4/88
Rise To The Occasion		1/88
Patsy CLINE (US)		
Crazy	11/61	
I Fall To Pieces	8/61	
Rosemary CLOONEY (US)		
Hey There	7/54	10/55
Mambo Italiano	11/54	1/55
Man		2/54
This Ole House	8/54	12/54
Where Will The Baby's Dimple Be		5/55
CLOUT (SA)		
Substitute		7/78
CLUB NOUVEAU (US)		
Lean On Me	3/87	4/87
COAST TO COAST (UK)		
(Do) The Hucklebuck		2/81
COASTERS (US)		

	US Top 20 Ent	UK Top 20 Ent
Along Came Jones	6/59	
Charlie Brown	2/59	4/59
Poison Ivy	9/59	
Searchin'/Young Blood	6/57	
Yakety Yak	6/58	9/58
Odia COATES (US) see Paul Anka with Odia Coates		
Eddie COCHRAN (US)		
C'mon Everybody		3/59
Summertime Blues	9/58	
Three Steps To Heaven		5/60
Weekend		7/61
Tom COCHRANE (C)		
Life Is A Highway	7/92	
Joe COCKER (UK)		
Cry Me A River	11/70	
Delta Lady		11/69
The Letter	5/70	
When The Night Comes	1/90	
With A Little Help From My Friends		11/68
You Are So Beautiful	3/75	
Joe COCKER & Jennifer Warnes (UK/US)		
Up Where We Belong	10/82	2/83
COCKNEY REBEL (UK) see Steve Harley		
CO-CO (UK)		
Bad Old Days		5/78
COMMANDER CODY & His Lost Planet Airmen (US)		
Hot Rod Lincoln	5/72	
COFFEE (US)		
Casanova		10/80
Dennis COFFEY & The Detroit Guitar Band (US)		
Scorpio	12/71	
Alma COGAN (UK)		
Bell Bottom Blues		3/54
Dreamboat		6/55
Go On By		10/55
I Can't Tell A Waltz From A Tango		12/54
Little Things Mean A Lot		8/54
Never Do A Tango With An Eskimo		12/55
Willie Can		4/56
Marc COHN (US)		
Walking In Memphis	7/91	
COLA BOY (UK)		
7 Ways To Love		7/91
COLDCUT featuring Yazz & The Plastic Population (UK)		
Doctorin' The House		3/88
COLDCUT featuring Lisa Stansfield (UK)		
People Hold On		4/89
Cozy COLE (US)		
Topsy II	10/58	
Jude COLE (US)		
Baby, It's Tonight	6/90	
Nat 'King' COLE (US)		
Answer Me, My Love	3/54	
A Blossom Fell/If I May	5/55	3/55
Darling Je Vous Aime Beaucoup	3/55	
Dear Lonely Hearts	12/62	
Dreams Can Tell A Lie		2/56
Forgive My Heart	11/55	
Hajji Baba	11/54	
Let There Be Love		8/62
Looking Back/Do I Like It	5/58	
Love Me As If There Were No Tomorrow		11/56
Make Her Mine		10/54
Ramblin' Rose	9/62	10/62
Send For Me/My Personal Possession	7/57	
Smile	10/54	9/54
Tenderly		4/54
That Sunday, That Summer	10/63	
Those Lazy-Hazy-Crazy Days Of Summer	6/63	
Too Young To Go Steady		6/56
When I Fall In Love	4/57	
★ When I Fall In Love		12/87
Natalie COLE (US)		
I Live For Your Love	2/88	
I've Got Love On My Mind	3/77	
Jump Start	10/87	
Miss You Like Crazy	6/89	5/89
Our Love	4/78	
Pink Cadillac	4/88	4/88
This Will Be	11/75	
Unforgettable	8/91	
Dave & Ansil COLLINS (J)		
Double Barrel		4/71
Monkey Spanner		7/71
Judy COLLINS (US)		

	US Top 20 Ent	UK Top 20 Ent
Amazing Grace	2/71	1/71
Both Sides Now	12/68	
Send In The Clowns		5/75
Phil COLLINS (UK)		
Against All Odds (Take A Look At Me Now)	3/84	4/84
Another Day In Paradise	12/89	11/89
Both Sides Of The Story		10/93
Do You Remember?	6/90	
Don't Lose My Number	8/85	
✦ with Philip Bailey Easy Lover	1/85	3/85
Groovy Kind Of Love	10/88	9/88
I Missed Again		3/81
I Wish It Would Rain Down	3/90	2/90
In The Air Tonight		1/81
★ In The Air Tonight		7/88
One More Night	3/85	4/85
Something Happened On The Way To Heaven	9/90	5/90
Sussudio	6/85	2/85
Take Me Home	4/86	
Two Hearts	12/88	12/88
You Can't Hurry Love	1/83	12/82
Phil COLLINS & Marilyn Martin (UK/US)		
Separate Lives	11/85	12/85
Tyler COLLINS (US)		
Girls Nite Out	7/90	
COLOR ME BADD (US)		
All 4 Love	12/91	8/91
Forever Love	10/92	
I Adore Mi Amor	9/91	
I Wanna Sex You Up	5/91	5/91
COLOUR FIELD (UK)		
Thinking Of You		2/85
Jessi COLTER (US)		
I'm Not Lisa	6/75	
COMMODORES (US)		
Brick House	10/77	
Easy	7/77	8/77
Just To Be Close To You	11/76	
Lady You Bring Me Up	8/81	
Nightshift	4/85	2/85
Oh No	11/81	
Sail On	9/79	9/79
Still	10/79	11/79
Sweet Love	4/76	
Three Times A Lady	7/78	8/78
COMMUNARDS (UK)		
Don't Leave Me This Way		9/86
Never Can Say Goodbye		11/87
So Cold The Night		12/86
Perry COMO (US)		
And I Love You So		5/73
Catch A Falling Star/Magic Moments	2/58	3/58
Delaware		3/60
For The Good Times		9/73
Hot Diggity (Dog Ziggity Boom)	3/56	6/56
I Know		7/59
I May Never Pass This Way Again		6/58
I Think Of You		6/71
Idle Gossip		6/54
It's Impossible	1/71	2/71
Just Born/Ivy Rose	11/57	
Kewpie Doll	5/58	5/58
Ko Ko Mo (I Love You So)	2/55	
Love Makes The World Go Round		11/58
Magic Moments	2/58	2/58
Mandolins In The Moonlight		12/58
More	6/56	10/56
Papa Loves Mambo	10/54	
Round And Round	3/57	
Tina Marie	9/55	
Tomboy		3/59
Wanted	3/54	6/54
You Alone	1/54	
CONGREGATION (UK)		
Softly Whispering I Love You		12/71
Arthur CONLEY (US)		
Funky Street	5/68	
Sweet Soul Music	4/67	6/67
Ray CONNIFF & The Singers (US)		
Somewhere, My Love	7/66	
Billy CONNOLLY (UK)		
D.I.V.O.R.C.E.		11/75
Bill CONTI (US)		
Gonna Fly Now (Theme From 'Rocky')	5/77	

	US Top 20 Ent	UK Top 20 Ent
CONTOURS (US)		
Do You Love Me	10/62	
★ Do You Love Me	8/88	
CONWAY BROTHERS (US)		
Turn It Up		7/85
Russ CONWAY (UK)		
China Tea		8/59
Lucky Five		6/60
More And More Party Pops		12/59
More Party Pops		12/58
Roulette		5/59
Royal Event		3/60
Side Saddle		3/59
Snow Coach		11/59
Toy Balloons		1/62
Sam COOKE (US)		
Another Saturday Night	5/63	
Chain Gang	9/60	10/60
Cupid		8/61
Frankie And Johnny	9/63	
Good News	3/64	
Good Times	7/64	
Little Red Rooster	11/63	
Nothing Can Change This Love	11/62	
Send Me Some Lovin'	3/63	
Shake	2/65	
Twistin' The Night Away	3/62	3/62
Wonderful World	6/60	4/86
You Send Me	10/57	
COOKIE CREW (UK) See Beatmasters featuring The Cookie Crew		
COOKIES (US)		
Don't Say Nothin'(Bad About My Baby)	4/63	
Rita COOLIDGE (US)		
We're All Alone	11/77	8/77
(Your Love Has Lifted Me) Higher And Higher	7/77	
COOLNOTES (UK)		
Spend The Night		4/85
Alice COOPER (US)		
Elected		10/72
Hello Hurray		3/73
How You Gonna See Me Now	12/78	
I Never Cry	11/76	
No More Mr. Nice Guy		5/73
Only Women	6/75	
Poison	11/89	8/89
School's Out	7/72	7/72
Teenage Lament '74		2/74
You And Me	7/77	
Jill COREY (US)		
Love Me To Pieces	8/57	
CORINA (US)		
Temptation	7/91	
CORNELIUS BROTHERS & Sister Rose (US)		
Too Late To Turn Back Now	7/72	
Treat Her Like A Lady	6/71	
Don CORNELL (US)		
The Bible Tells Me So	9/55	
Hold My Hand	9/54	9/54
Dave 'Baby' CORTEZ (US)		
The Happy Organ	4/59	
Rinky Dink	9/62	
Bill COSBY (US)		
Little Ole Man (Uptight-Everything's Alright)	10/67	
Elvis COSTELLO (US)		
A Good Year For The Roses		10/81
I Can't Stand Up For Falling Down		2/80
Oliver's Army		2/79
Watchin' The Detectives		12/77
Billy COTTON & His Band (UK)		
Friends And Neighbours		4/54
John COUGAR (US) See John (Cougar) Mellencamp		
COUNT FIVE (US)		
Psychotic Reaction	10/66	
COVER GIRLS (US)		
We Can't Go Wrong	2/90	
Wishing On A Star	6/92	
Julie COVINGTON (UK)		
Don't Cry For Me Argentina		1/77
Only Women Bleed		1/78
COWBOY CHURCH SUNDAY SCHOOL (US)		
Open Up Your Heart (And Let The Sunshine In)	2/55	
COWSILLS (US)		

	US Top 20 Ent	UK Top 20 Ent
Hair	4/69	
Indian Lake	7/68	
The Rain, The Park & Other Things	11/67	
Michael COX (UK)		
Angela Jones		7/60
Floyd CRAMER (US)		
Last Date	11/60	
On The Rebound	3/61	5/61
San Antonio Rose	7/61	
CRANBERRIES (I)		
Linger	12/93	
Les CRANE (US)		
Desiderata	11/71	3/72
Beverley CRAVEN (UK)		
Promise Me		5/91
Johnny CRAWFORD (US)		
Cindy's Birthday	6/62	
Rumors	12/62	
Michael CRAWFORD (UK)		
The Music Of The Night		2/87
Randy CRAWFORD (US)		
Almaz		2/87
One Day I'll Fly Away		9/80
You Might Need Somebody		7/81
CRAZY ELEPHANT (US)		
Gimme Gimme Good Lovin'	4/69	7/69
CRAZY WORLD OF ARTHUR BROWN (UK) See Arthur Brown		
CREAM (UK)		
I Feel Free		1/67
Sunshine Of Your Love	8/68	
White Room	11/68	
CREEDENCE CLEARWATER REVIVAL (US)		
Bad Moon Rising	6/69	9/69
Down On The Corner/Fortunate Son	11/69	
Green River	8/69	
Have You Ever Seen The Rain	2/71	
Lookin' Out My Back Door/Long As I Can See The Light	9/70	
Proud Mary	2/69	7/69
Suzie Q. (Pt. 1)	10/68	
Sweet Hitch-Hiker	8/71	
Travelin' Band/Who'll Stop The Rain	2/70	5/70
Up Around The Bend/Run Through The Jungle	5/70	7/70
KID CREOLE & The Coconuts (US)		
Annie I'm Not Your Daddy		10/82
I'm A Wonderful Thing (Baby)		6/82
Stool Pigeon		8/82
CRESCENDOS (US)		
Oh Julie	2/58	
CRESTS (US)		
16 Candles	1/59	
Step By Step	4/60	
CREW-CUTS (C)		
Angels In The Sky	1/56	
Crazy 'Bout You, Baby	6/54	
Don't Be Angry	5/55	
Earth Angel	2/55	4/55
Gum Drop	9/55	
Ko Ko Mo (I Love You So)	2/55	
Oop-Shoop	10/54	
Sh-Boom	7/54	10/54
A Story Untold	7/55	
Bernard CRIBBINS (UK)		
Hole In The Ground		3/62
Right Said Fred		7/62
CRICKETS (US)		
Don't Ever Change		7/62
Maybe Baby		3/58
Oh, Boy!	1/58	1/58
That'll Be The Day	8/57	10/57
Think It Over		8/58
Jim CROCE (US)		
Bad, Bad Leroy Brown	6/73	
I Got A Name	11/73	
I'll Have To Say I Love You In A Song	4/74	
Time In A Bottle	12/73	
You Don't Mess Around With Jim	8/72	
Bing CROSBY (US)		
Around The World	6/57	
Changing Partners	3/54	
Count Your Blessings	1/55	
✤ with David Bowie Peace On Earth-Little Drummer Boy		12/82

	US Top 20 Ent	UK Top 20 Ent
✤ with Grace Kelly True Love	10/56	12/56
White Christmas		12/77
CROSBY, STILLS & NASH (US/UK)		
Just A Song Before I Go	8/77	
Wasted On The Way	7/82	
CROSBY, STILLS, NASH & YOUNG (US/UK/C)		
Ohio	8/70	
Woodstock	5/70	
Christopher CROSS (US)		
All Right	2/83	
Arthur's Theme (Best That You Can Do)	9/81	2/82
Never Be The Same	12/80	
Ride Like The Wind	3/80	
Sailing	8/80	
Think Of Laura	1/84	
The CROWD (UK)		
You'll Never Walk Alone		6/85
CROWDED HOUSE (Aus/NZ)		
Don't Dream It's Over	3/87	
Something So Strong	7/87	
Weather With You		3/92
CROWN HEIGHTS AFFAIR (US)		
You Gave Me Love		6/80
Julee CRUISE (US)		
Falling		12/90
CRUSADERS (US)		
Street Life		9/79
CRYSTALS (US)		
Da Doo Ron Ron	6/63	6/63
He's A Rebel	10/62	
He's Sure The Boy I Love	2/63	
Then He Kissed Me	9/63	9/63
Uptown	5/62	
CUFF LINKS (US)		
Tracy	10/69	12/69
When Julie Comes Around		4/70
CULT (UK)		
Lil' Devil		5/87
CULTURE BEAT (G/UK/US)		
Got To Get It		11/93
Mr. Vain		8/93
CULTURE CLUB (UK)		
Church Of The Poison Mind	11/83	4/83
Do You Really Want To Hurt Me	2/83	10/82
I'll Tumble 4 Ya	8/83	
It's A Miracle	6/84	3/84
Karma Chameleon	1/84	9/83
Miss Me Blind	3/84	
Move Away	5/86	3/86
Time (Clock Of The Heart)	5/83	12/82
Victims		12/83
The War Song		10/84
Smiley CULTURE (UK)		
Police Officer		1/85
Burton CUMMINGS (C)		
Stand Tall	12/76	
CUPID'S INSPIRATION (UK)		
Yesterday Has Gone		7/68
CURE (UK)		
Close To Me		11/90
Friday, I'm In Love		6/92
The Love Cats		11/83
Love Song	9/89	
Lullaby		4/89
CURIOSITY KILLED THE CAT (aka Curiosity) (UK)		
Down To Earth		1/87
Hang On In There Baby		5/92
Misfit		7/87
Name And Number		10/89
Ordinary Day		4/87
CURVED AIR (UK)		
Back Street Luv		9/71
CUTTING CREW (UK)		
(I Just) Died In Your Arms	4/87	9/86
I've Been In Love Before	11/87	
CYRKLE (US)		
Red Rubber Ball	6/66	
Billy Ray CYRUS (US)		
Achy Breaky Heart	6/92	8/92
D. MOB featuring Cathy Dennis (UK)		
C'mon And Get My Love	3/90	11/89
D. MOB featuring Gary Haisman (UK)		
We Call It Acieed		10/88
D. MOB featuring LRS (UK)		

357

	US Top 20 Ent	UK Top 20 Ent
It Is Time To Get Funky		6/89
D. MOB featuring Nuff Juice (UK)		
Put Your Hands Together		1/90
D.J. JAZZY JEFF & The Fresh Prince (US)		
Boom! Shake The Room	9/93	9/93
A Nightmare On My Street	9/88	
Parents Just Don't Understand	7/88	
Summertime	7/91	8/91
Terry DACTYL & The Dinosaurs (UK)		
Seaside Shuffle		7/72
DADDY DEWDROP (US)		
Chick-A-Boom	5/71	
DALE & GRACE (US)		
I'm Leaving It Up To You	11/63	
Stop And Think It Over	2/64	
Alan DALE (US)		
Sweet And Gentle	7/55	
Jim DALE (UK)		
Be My Girl		11/57
Roger DALTREY (UK)		
Giving It All Away		5/73
DAMIAN (UK)		
The Time Warp		9/89
Michael DAMIAN (US)		
Rock On	5/89	
DAMITA JO (US)		
I'll Be There	8/61	
DAMN YANKEES (US)		
High Enough	12/90	
DAMNED (UK)		
Eloise		2/86
Vic DAMONE (US)		
On The Street Where You Live	6/56	5/58
DANA (UK)		
All Kinds Of Everything		4/70
Fairytale		1/77
It's Gonna Be A Cold Cold Christmas		12/75
Please Tell Him I Said Hello		3/75
Who Put The Lights Out		3/71
Vic DANA (US)		
Red Roses For A Blue Lady	4/65	
CHARLIE DANIELS BAND (US)		
The Devil Went Down To Georgia	8/79	
In America	7/80	
Uneasy Rider	8/73	
Johnny DANKWORTH (UK)		
African Waltz		4/61
Experiments With Mice		7/56
DANNY & The Juniors (US)		
At The Hop	12/57	1/58
DANNY WILSON (UK)		
Mary's Prayer		4/88
DANTE & The Evergreens (US)		
Alley-Oop	7/60	
Steven DANTE (UK) See Jellybean featuring Steven Dante		
Terence Trent D'ARBY (US)		
If You Let Me Stay		4/87
Sign Your Name	7/88	1/88
Wishing Well	4/88	7/87
Bobby DARIN (US)		
Beyond The Sea	2/60	2/60
Clementine		4/60
Dream Lover	5/59	6/59
18 Yellow Roses	6/63	
If I Were A Carpenter	10/66	11/66
Irresistible You	2/62	
Lazy River		3/61
Mack The Knife	9/59	10/59
Multiplication		1/62
Queen Of The Hop	11/58	
Splish Splash	7/58	
Things	8/62	8/62
You Must Have Been A Beautiful Baby	10/61	10/61
You're The Reason I'm Living	2/63	
James DARREN (US)		
Conscience	5/62	
Goodbye Cruel World	11/61	
Her Royal Majesty	3/62	
DARTELLS (US)		
Hot Pastrami	5/63	
DARTS (UK)		
Boy From New York City		5/78
Come Back My Love		2/78
Daddy Cool/The Girl Can't Help It		11/77

	US Top 20 Ent	UK Top 20 Ent
Duke Of Earl		8/79
Get It		3/79
It's Raining		8/78
Let's Hang On		7/80
DAVID & JONATHAN (UK)		
Lovers Of The World Unite		8/66
Michelle		2/66
Ann-Marie DAVID (F)		
Wonderful Dream		5/73
F.R. DAVID (F)		
Words		4/83
Paul DAVIDSON (J)		
Midnight Rider		2/76
Dave DAVIES (UK)		
Death Of A Clown		8/67
Windsor DAVIES & Don Estelle (UK)		
Whispering Grass		5/75
Billie DAVIS (UK)		
Tell Him		3/63
❖ with Mike Sarne Will I What		9/62
Mac DAVIS (US)		
Baby Don't Get Hooked On Me	8/72	
One Hell Of A Woman	7/74	
Stop And Smell The Roses	10/74	
Paul DAVIS (US)		
Cool Night	1/82	
I Go Crazy	2/78	
'65 Love Affair	4/82	
Sammy DAVIS JR. (US)		
The Candy Man	5/72	
Hey There	9/54	
I've Gotta Be Me	3/69	
Love Me Or Leave Me	6/55	9/55
Something's Gotta Give	6/55	9/55
Skeeter DAVIS (US)		
The End Of The World	3/63	
I Can't Stay Mad At You	10/63	
SPENCER DAVIS GROUP (UK)		
Gimme Some Lovin'	2/67	11/66
I'm A Man	4/67	2/67
Keep On Runnin'		1/66
Somebody Help Me		4/66
When I Come Home		9/66
Tyrone DAVIS (US)		
Can I Change My Mind	2/69	
Turn Back The Hands Of Time	4/70	
DAWN (US)		
Candida	9/70	2/71
Knock Three Times	12/70	5/71
Tie A Yellow Ribbon Round The Old Oak Tree	4/73	4/73
What Are You Doing Sunday		8/71
DAWN featuring Tony Orlando (US)		
Say, Has Anybody Seen My Sweet Gypsy Rose	8/73	9/73
Tony Orlando & DAWN (US)		
He Don't Love You (Like I Love You)	4/75	
Look In My Eyes Pretty Woman	2/75	
Mornin' Beautiful	8/75	
Steppin' Out (Gonna Boogie Tonight)	10/74	
Bobby DAY (US)		
Rock-In' Robin/Over And Over	9/58	
Doris DAY (US)		
Black Hills Of Dakota		8/54
Deadwood Stage		5/54
Everybody Loves A Lover	8/58	
I'll Never Stop Loving You	8/55	
If I Give My Heart To You	9/54	10/54
Move Over Darling		4/64
Ready Willing And Able		4/55
Secret Love	1/54	4/54
Whatever Will Be Will Be (Que Sera Sera)	7/56	7/56
Taylor DAYNE (US)		
Can't Get Enough Of Your Love		7/93
Don't Rush Me	12/88	
Heart Of Stone	9/90	
I'll Always Love You	9/88	
I'll Be Your Shelter	6/90	
Love Will Lead You Back	3/90	
Prove Your Love	4/88	4/88
Tell It To My Heart	12/87	2/88
With Every Beat Of My Heart	12/89	
DAZZ BAND (US)		
Let It Whip	6/82	
DE CASTRO SISTERS (US)		

	US Top 20 Ent	UK Top 20 Ent
Teach Me Tonight	10/54	
DEJOHN SISTERS (US)		
(My Baby Don't Love Me) No More	1/55	
DE LA SOUL (US)		
The Magic Number/Buddy		1/90
❖ with Queen Latifah Mamma Gave Birth To The Soul Children		4/90
Ring Ring Ring (Ha Ha Hey)		5/91
DEACON BLUE (UK)		
Four Bacharach & David Songs (EP)		9/90
Real Gone Kid		11/88
Twist & Shout		8/91
DEAD END KIDS (UK)		
Have I The Right?		4/77
DEAD OR ALIVE (UK)		
Brand New Lover	3/87	
Lover Come Back To Me		5/85
You Spin Me Round (Like A Record)	8/85	2/85
Hazell DEAN (UK)		
Searchin' I Gotta Find A Man)		6/84
Whatever I Do (Wherever I Go)		8/84
Who's Leaving Who		4/88
Jimmy DEAN (US)		
Big Bad John	10/61	11/61
P.T. 109	5/62	
DeBARGE (US)		
Rhythm Of The Night	4/85	5/85
Who's Holding Donna Now	7/85	
El DeBARGE (US)		
Who's Johnny	6/86	
Chris De BURGH (I)		
Lady In Red	5/87	7/86
Missing You		11/88
Diana DECKER (UK)		
Poppa Piccolino		1/54
DAVE DEE, Dozy, Beaky, Mick & Tich (UK)		
Bend It		10/66
Hideaway		7/66
Hold Tight		4/66
Last Night In Soho		8/68
Legend Of Xanadu		3/68
Okay!		6/67
Save Me		12/66
Touch Me Touch Me		4/67
Zabadak		10/67
Joey DEE & The Starliters (US)		
Peppermint Twist (Pt. 1)	12/61	2/62
Shout (Pt. 1)	4/62	
Kiki DEE (UK)		
❖ with Elton John Don't Go Breaking My Heart	7/76	7/76
I've Got The Music In Me	11/74	
Loving And Free/Amoureuse		12/73
★ Loving And Free/Amoureuse		10/76
Star		3/81
❖ with Elton John True Love		11/93
Tommy DEE (US)		
Three Stars	5/59	
DEEE-LITE (US)		
Groove Is In The Heart	11/90	9/90
DEELE (US)		
Two Occasions	5/88	
DEEP PURPLE (UK)		
Black Night		9/70
Fireball		12/71
Hush	9/68	
Smoke On The Water	7/73	
Strange Kind Of Woman		3/71
Rick DEES & His Cast Of Idiots (US)		
Disco Duck	9/76	10/76
DEF LEPPARD (UK)		
Animal		8/87
Armageddon It	12/88	
Have You Ever Needed Someone So Bad	10/92	
Hysteria	3/88	
Let's Get Rocked	5/92	3/92
Love Bites	9/88	7/88
Photograph	5/83	
Pour Some Sugar On Me	6/88	
Rocket	4/89	
Two Steps Behind	10/93	
DEFRANCO FAMILY (C)		
Heartbeat - It's A Lovebeat	10/73	
DESMOND DEKKER & The Aces (J)		
The Israelites	6/69	4/69

	US Top 20 Ent	UK Top 20 Ent
★ The Israelites		6/75
It Mek		7/69
You Can Get It If You Really Want		9/70
DEL AMITRI (UK)		
Nothing Ever Happens		2/90
DELANEY & BONNIE & Friends (US)		
Never Ending Song Of Love	7/71	
DELEGATES (US)		
Convention '72	11/72	
DELFONICS (US)		
Didn't I (Blow Your Mind This Time)	3/70	
La-La Means I Love You	3/68	
DELL-VIKINGS (US)		
Come Go With Me	3/57	
Whispering Bells	8/57	
DELLS (US)		
Oh What A Nite	9/69	
Stay In My Corner	8/68	
Chaka DEMUS & Pliers (J)		
She Don't Let Nobody		9/93
Tease Me		6/93
Chaka DEMUS & Pliers with Jack Radics & Taxi Gang (J)		
Twist And Shout		12/93
Cathy DENNIS (UK)		
✦ with D.Mob C'mon And Get My Love	3/90	11/89
Just Another Dream	1/91	
Too Many Walls	8/91	
Touch Me (All Night Long)	4/91	5/91
Jackie DENNIS (UK)		
La Dee Dah		3/58
Martin DENNY (US)		
Quiet Village	5/59	
John DENVER (US)		
Annie's Song	7/74	9/74
Back Home Again	11/74	
Fly Away	1/76	
I'm Sorry/Calypso	9/75	
Rocky Mountain High	2/73	
Sunshine On My Shoulders	3/74	
Sweet Surrender	2/75	
Take Me Home, Country Roads	7/71	
Thank God I'm A Country Boy	5/75	
Karl DENVER (UK)		
A Little Love, A Little Kiss		6/62
Marcheta		8/61
Mexicali Rose		10/61
Never Goodbye		4/62
Still		9/63
Wimoweh		2/62
DEODATA (US)		
Also Sprach Zarathustra (2001)	3/73	5/73
Lynsey DE PAUL (UK)		
No Honestly		11/74
Sugar Me		9/72
Won't Somebody Dance With Me		11/73
DEPECHE MODE (UK)		
Enjoy The Silence	7/90	2/90
Everything Counts		8/83
I Feel You		2/93
Just Can't Get Enough		10/81
Master And Servant		9/84
New Life		8/81
People Are People	8/85	4/84
Personal Jesus	9/89	
See You		3/82
DEREK (US)		
Cinnamon	12/68	
DEREK & The Dominoes (UK/US)		
Layla	7/72	8/72
★ Layla		3/82
DES'REE (UK)		
Feel So High		1/92
Teri DESARIO with K.C. (US)		
Yes, I'm Ready	2/80	
Jackie DESHANNON (US)		
Put A Little Love In Your Heart	8/69	
What The World Needs Now Is Love	7/65	
DESIRELESS (F)		
Voyage Voyage		6/88
Johnny DESMOND (US)		
Play Me Hearts And Flowers (I Wanna Cry)	4/55	
The Yellow Rose Of Texas	8/55	
Stephanie DE SYKES (UK)		
Born With A Smile On My Face		7/74
DETROIT EMERALDS (US)		

	US Top 20 Ent	UK Top 20 Ent
Feel The Need In Me		3/73
Feel The Need In Me		7/77
DETROIT SPINNERS (US) See Spinners		
William DEVAUGHN (US)		
Be Thankful For What You Got	6/74	
DEVO (US)		
Whip It	11/80	
Barry DEVORZON & Perry Botkin (US)		
Nadia's Theme (The Young & The Restless)	11/76	
DEXY'S MIDNIGHT RUNNERS (UK)		
Come On Eileen	3/83	7/82
Geno		4/80
Jackie Wilson Said		10/82
There There My Dear		8/80
Dennis DEYOUNG (US)		
Desert Moon	11/84	
Jim DIAMOND (UK)		
Hi Ho Silver		3/86
I Should Have Known Better		11/84
Neil DIAMOND (US)		
America	5/81	
Beautiful Noise		11/76
Cherry Cherry	10/66	
Cracklin' Rosie	9/70	11/70
Desiree	2/78	
Girl, You'll Be A Woman Soon	5/67	
Heartlight	10/82	
Hello Again	2/81	
Holly Holy	12/69	
I Am ...I Said	4/71	6/71
If You Know What I Mean	7/76	
Longfellow Serenade	11/74	
Love On The Rocks	11/80	
Play Me	9/72	
Song Sung Blue	6/72	
Stones	12/71	
Sweet Caroline	7/69	2/71
Yesterday's Songs	12/81	
✦ with Barbra Streisand You Don't Bring Me Flowers	11/78	12/78
DIAMONDS (C)		
The Church Bells May Ring	6/56	
Little Darlin'	3/57	6/57
The Stroll	1/58	
DICK & DEEDEE (US)		
The Mountain's High	9/61	
Thou Shalt Not Steal	1/65	
DICKIES (US)		
Banana Splits (Tra La La Song)		5/79
Barbara DICKSON (UK)		
✦ with Elaine Paige I Know Him So Well		1/85
January February		4/80
DIGITAL UNDERGROUND (US)		
The Humpty Dance	5/90	
Mark DINNING (US)		
Teen Angel	1/60	
DINO (US)		
I Like It	7/89	
Romeo	10/90	
DION & The Belmonts (US)		
A Teenager In Love	5/59	
Where Or When	1/60	
DION (US)		
Abraham, Martin And John	11/68	
Donna The Prima Donna	10/63	
Drip Drop	12/63	
Little Diane	8/62	
Lonely Teenager	12/60	
Love Came To Me	12/62	
Lovers Who Wander	5/62	
Ruby Baby	2/63	
Runaround Sue	10/61	11/61
The Wanderer	1/62	3/62
Celine DION (C)		
If You Asked Me To	5/92	
Where Does My Heart Beat Now	2/91	
Celine DION & Peabo Bryson (C/US)		
Beauty And The Beast	3/92	5/92
DIRE STRAITS (UK)		
Money For Nothing	9/85	8/85
Private Investigations		9/82
Romeo And Juliet		2/81
Sultans Of Swing	3/79	4/79
Walk Of Life	12/85	1/86
DISCO TEX & The Sex-O-Lettes (US)		

	US Top 20 Ent	UK Top 20 Ent
Get Dancin'	1/75	12/74
I Wanna Dance Wit Choo'		5/75
Sacha DISTEL (F)		
Raindrops Keep Fallin' On My Head		3/70
DIVINYLS (Aus)		
I Touch Myself	4/91	7/91
DIXIEBELLES (US)		
(Down At) Papa Joe's	11/63	
DIXIE CUPS (US)		
Chapel Of Love	5/64	
People Say	8/64	
DNA featuring Suzanne Vega (UK/US)		
Tom's Diner	12/90	8/90
Carl DOBKINS JR. (US)		
My Heart Is An Open Book	7/59	
Anita DOBSON (UK)		
Anyone Can Fall In Love		8/86
DOCTOR & The Medics (UK)		
Spirit In The Sky		5/86
DR. ALBAN (S)		
It's My Life		9/92
DR. DRE (US)		
Dre Day	6/93	
Nuthin' But A "G" Thang	2/93	
DR. FEELGOOD (UK)		
Milk And Alcohol		2/79
DR. HOOK (US)		
Better Love Next Time	12/79	1/80
The Cover of 'Rolling Stone'	3/73	
If Not You		11/76
A Little Bit More	9/76	7/76
More Like The Movies		4/78
Only Sixteen	4/76	
Sexy Eyes	4/80	4/80
Sharing The Night Together	11/78	
Sylvia's Mother	5/72	7/72
When You're In Love With A Beautiful Woman	7/79	10/79
DR. JOHN (US)		
Right Place Wrong Time	6/73	
DOCTOR SPIN (UK)		
Tetris		10/92
Ken DODD (UK)		
Let Me Cry On Your Shoulder		2/67
Love Is Like A Violin		9/60
Promises		5/66
The River		12/65
Tears		9/65
Bill DOGGETT (US)		
Honky Tonk (Parts 1 & 2)	9/56	
Joe DOLAN (US)		
Make Me An Island		8/69
You're Such A Good Looking Woman		4/70
Thomas DOLBY (UK)		
She Blinded Me With Science	4/83	
Joe DOLCE MUSIC THEATRE (US)		
Shaddup You Face		2/81
DOLLAR (UK)		
Give Me Back My Heart		4/82
Love's Gotta Hold On Me		9/79
Mirror Mirror (Mon Amour)		12/81
O L'Amour		2/88
Fats DOMINO (US)		
Be My Guest	11/59	1/60
Blue Monday	1/57	
Blueberry Hill	10/56	1/57
I Want To Walk You Home	8/59	
I'm In Love Again	5/56	9/56
I'm Ready	6/59	
I'm Walkin'	3/57	
Let The Four Winds Blow	8/61	
My Girl Josephine	12/60	
Three Nights A Week	10/60	
Valley Of Tears/It's You I Love	6/57	
Walkin' To New Orleans	7/60	
Whole Lotta Loving	12/58	
DON & JUAN (US)		
What's Your Name	3/62	
DON PABLO'S ANIMALS (US)		
Venus		6/90
Bo DONALDSON & THE HEYWOODS (US)		
Billy, Don't Be A Hero	6/74	
Who Do You Think You Are	9/74	
Lonnie DONEGAN (US)		
Battle Of New Orleans		6/59

	US Top 20 Ent	UK Top 20 Ent
Bring A Little Water Sylvie/Dead Or Alive		9/56
The Comancheros		2/62
Cumberland Gap		4/57
Does Your Chewing Gum Lose It's Flavour	9/61	2/59
Don't You Rock Me Daddy-O		1/57
Fort Worth Jail		5/59
Gamblin' Man/Putting On The Style		6/57
Grand Coolie Dam		5/58
Have A Drink On Me		6/61
I Wanna Go Home		6/60
Jack O' Diamonds		1/58
Lively		12/60
Lost John/Stewball		5/56
Michael Row The Boat		9/61
My Dixie Darling		10/57
My Old Man's A Dustman		3/60
The Party's Over		5/62
Pick A Bale Of Cotton		9/62
Rock Island Line	4/56	1/56
Sal's Got A Sugar Lip		9/59
Sally Don't You Grieve/Betty, Betty, Betty		7/58
Tom Dooley		11/58
Ral DONNER (US)		
You Don't Know What You Got (Until You Lose It)	8/61	
DONOVAN (UK)		
Atlantis	5/69	
Catch The Wind		4/65
Colours		6/65
Hurdy Gurdy Man	7/68	6/68
Jennifer Juniper		3/68
Mellow Yellow	12/66	2/67
Sunshine Superman	8/66	12/66
There Is A Mountain	9/67	11/67
DONOVAN & The Jeff Beck Group (UK)		
Goo Goo Barabajagal (Love Is Hot)		8/69
Jason DONOVAN (Aus)		
Any Dream Will Do		6/91
❖ with *Kylie Minogue* Especially For You		12/88
Every Day (I Love You More)		9/89
Hang On To Your Love		4/90
Happy Together		8/91
Nothing Can Divide Us		9/88
Rhythm Of The Rain		9/90
Sealed With A Kiss		6/89
Too Many Broken Hearts		3/89
When You Come Back To Me		12/89
DOOBIE BROTHERS (US)		
Black Water	2/75	
China Grove	10/73	
The Doctor	7/89	
Listen To The Music	11/72	
Long Train Running	6/73	11/93
Minute By Minute	6/79	
Real Love	10/80	
Take Me In Your Arms (Rock Me)	6/75	
Takin' It To The Streets	6/76	
What A Fool Believes	3/79	
DOOLEYS (UK)		
The Chosen Few		10/79
Love Of My Life		12/77
A Rose Has To Die		10/78
Wanted		7/79
Val DOONICAN (I)		
Elusive Butterfly		4/66
If The Whole World Stopped Loving		11/67
Memories Are Made Of This		3/67
Morning		1/72
The Special Years		2/65
Walk Tall		12/64
What Would I Be		11/66
DOORS (US)		
Hello, I Love You	7/68	10/68
Light My Fire	7/67	6/91
Love Her Madly	5/71	
Riders On The Storm	8/71	
Touch Me	1/69	
Charlie DORE (UK)		
Pilot Of The Airwaves	5/80	
Jimmy DORSEY (US)		
So Rare	4/57	
Lee DORSEY (US)		
Holy Cow		11/66
Working In The Coal Mine	9/66	9/66
Ya Ya	10/61	

	US Top 20 Ent	UK Top 20 Ent
Tommy DORSEY ORCHESTRA (US)		
Tea For Two Cha Cha	10/58	11/58
DOUBLE TROUBLE (UK)		
❖ with *The Rebel MC.*Street Tuff		10/89
DOUBLE TROUBLE & Rebel MC (UK)		
Just Keep Rockin'		6/89
DOUBLE (Swi)		
The Captain Of Her Heart	9/86	2/86
Carl DOUGLAS (UK)		
Kung Fu Fighting	11/74	9/74
Carol DOUGLAS (US)		
Doctor's Orders	1/75	
Craig DOUGLAS (UK)		
Heart Of A Teenage Girl		5/60
A Hundred Pounds Of Clay		4/61
Oh Lonesome Me		11/62
Only Sixteen		8/59
Our Favourite Melodies		7/62
Pretty Blue Eyes		2/60
A Teenager In Love		6/59
Time		7/61
When My Little Girl Is Smiling		4/62
Mike DOUGLAS (US)		
The Men In My Little Girl's Life	1/66	
Ronnie DOVE (US)		
One Kiss For Old Time's Sake	5/65	
DOVELLS (US)		
Bristol Stomp	10/61	
You Can't Sit Down	6/63	
Joe DOWELL (US)		
Wooden Heart	8/61	
Lamont DOZIER (US)		
Trying To Hold On To My Woman	3/74	
Charlie DRAKE (UK)		
Mr. Custer		11/60
My Boomerang Won't Come Back		10/61
Splish Splash		8/58
DRAMATICS (US)		
In The Rain	3/72	
Whatcha See Is Whatcha Get	9/71	
Rusty DRAPER (US)		
Are You Satisfied?	1/56	
The Shifting, Whispering Sands	10/55	
DREAM ACADEMY (UK)		
Life In A Northern Town	2/86	
DREAM WEAVERS (US)		
It's Almost Tomorrow	11/55	2/56
DREAMLOVERS (US)		
When We Get Married	9/61	
DRIFTERS (US)		
At The Club/Saturday Night At The Movies		5/72
Can I Take You Home Little Girl		1/76
Come On Over To My Place		9/72
Down On The Beach Tonight		11/74
Hello Happiness		4/76
Kissin' In The Back Row Of The Movies		7/74
Like Sister And Brother		9/73
On Broadway	4/63	
Please Stay	7/61	
Save The Last Dance For Me	9/60	11/60
There Goes My Baby	7/59	
There Goes My First Love		9/75
Under The Boardwalk	8/64	
Up On The Roof	1/63	
You're More Than A Number In My Little Red Book		1/77
Julie DRISCOLL, Brian Auger & The Trinity (UK)		
This Wheel's On Fire		6/68
DRIVER 67 (UK)		
Car 67		1/79
DRS (US)		
Gangsta Lean	11/93	
DUBLINERS (I)		
Black Velvet Band		10/67
❖ with *The Pogues* The Irish Rover		4/87
Seven Drunken Nights		5/67
Stephen 'Tin Tin' DUFFY (UK)		
Kiss Me		3/85
DUICE (US)		
Dazzey Duks	6/93	
Patty DUKE (US)		
Don't Just Stand There	8/65	
Candy DULFER (H) See David A. Stewart introducing Candy Dulfer		
Johnny DUNCAN & The Blue Grass Boys (US)		

	US Top 20 Ent	UK Top 20 Ent
Last Train To San Fernando		8/57
David DUNDAS (UK)		
Jeans On		8/76
Erroll DUNKLEY (J)		
O.K. Fred		10/79
Clive DUNN (UK)		
Grandad		12/70
Robbie DUPREE (US)		
Hot Rod Hearts	10/80	
Steal Away	6/80	
Simon DUPREE & The Big Sound (UK)		
Kites		12/67
DUPREES (US)		
You Belong To Me	9/62	
DURAN DURAN (UK)		
All She Wants Is		1/89
Come Undone	6/93	4/93
Girls On Film		8/81
Hungry Like The Wolf	2/83	6/82
I Don't Want Your Love	11/88	
Is There Something I Should Know	7/83	3/83
New Moon On Monday	3/84	2/84
Notorious	12/86	11/86
Ordinary World	2/93	2/93
The Reflex	5/84	4/84
Rio	5/83	11/82
Save A Prayer		8/82
Union Of The Snake	12/83	11/83
A View To Kill	6/85	5/85
The Wild Boys	11/84	11/84
Ian DURY & The Blockheads (UK)		
Hit Me With Your Rhythm Stick		1/79
Reasons To Be Cheerful (Pt 3)		8/79
What A Waste		6/78
Slim DUSTY (Aus)		
A Pub With No Beer		2/59
Bob DYLAN (US)		
Baby Stop Crying		8/78
I Want You		8/66
Knockin' On Heaven's Door	10/73	
Lay Lady Lay	8/69	10/69
Like A Rolling Stone	8/65	9/65
Positively 4th Street	10/65	11/65
Rainy Day Women #12 & 35	5/66	5/66
Subterranean Homesick Blues		5/65
Times They Are A-Changin'		4/65
Ronnie DYSON (US)		
(If You Let Me Make Love To You Then) Why Can't I Touch You	8/70	
Sheila E (US)		
The Glamorous Life	9/84	
A Love Bizarre	2/86	
EAGLES (US)		
Best Of My Love	2/75	
Heartache Tonight	10/79	
Hotel California	4/77	5/77
I Can't Tell You Why	3/80	
Life In The Fast Lane	6/77	
The Long Run	1/80	
Lyin' Eyes	10/75	
New Kid In Town	1/77	
One Of These Nights	7/75	
Take It Easy	7/72	
Take It To The Limit	2/76	
Witchy Woman	11/72	
Robert EARL (UK)		
I May Never Pass This Way Again		5/58
Wonderful Secret Of Love		3/59
EARTH, WIND & FIRE (US)		
After The Love Has Gone	8/79	8/79
Fantasy		3/78
Getaway	9/76	
Got To Get You Into My Life	9/78	
Let's Groove	11/81	11/81
September	1/79	1/79
Serpentine Fire	2/78	
Shining Star	4/75	
Sing A Song	1/76	
That's The Way Of The World	9/75	
EARTH, WIND & FIRE With The Emotions (US)		
Boogie Wonderland	6/79	6/79
EAST OF EDEN (UK)		
Jig A Jig		5/71
EAST 17 (UK)		

	US Top 20 Ent	UK Top 20 Ent
Deep		2/93
House Of Love		9/92
It's Alright		12/93
Slow It Down		4/93
EAST SIDE BEAT (ITA/UK)		
Ride Like The Wind		12/91
Sheena EASTON (UK)		
For Your Eyes Only	9/81	8/81
The Lover In Me	2/89	
Modern Girl	7/81	9/80
9 To 5 (Morning Train)	4/81	8/80
Strut	11/84	
Sugar Walls	2/85	
Telefone (Long Distance Love Affair)	10/83	
❖ with Kenny Rogers We've Got Tonight	3/83	
You Could Have Been With Me	2/82	
EASYBEATS (Aus)		
Friday On My Mind	5/67	12/66
ECHO & THE BUNNYMEN (UK)		
The Cutter		2/83
The Killing Moon		2/84
ECHOES (US)		
Baby Blue	4/61	
Billy ECKSTINE (US)		
Gigi		2/59
No One But You		11/54
EDDIE & The Hot Rods (UK) see The Rods		
Duane EDDY (US)		
Ballad Of Paladin		9/62
Because They're Young	6/60	8/60
Bonnie Came Back		3/60
(Dance With The) Guitar Man	12/62	11/62
Forty Miles Of Bad Road	7/59	9/59
Kommotion		11/60
Pepe		1/61
❖ with The Art Of Noise Peter Gunn		4/86
Peter Gunn Theme		6/59
Rebel-'Rouser	7/58	
Shazam		5/60
Some Kind-A Earthquake		1/60
Theme From Dixie		5/61
Duane EDDY & The Rebelettes (US)		
Play Me Like You Play Your Guitar		4/75
EDELWEISS (Swi)		
Bring Me Edelweiss		5/89
EDISON LIGHTHOUSE (UK)		
Love Grows (Where My Rosemary Goes)	3/70	1/70
Dave EDMUNDS (UK)		
Baby I Love You		2/73
Born To Be With You		7/73
Girls Talk		7/79
I Hear You Knocking	1/71	11/70
Queen Of Hearts		10/79
EDWARD BEAR (C)		
Last Song	2/73	
Bobby EDWARDS (US)		
You're The Reason	11/61	
Jonathan EDWARDS (US)		
Sunshine	1/72	
Rupie EDWARDS (J)		
Ire Feelings (Skanga)		12/74
Tommy EDWARDS (US)		
It's All In The Game	9/58	10/58
Love Is All We Need	12/58	
Please Mr. Sun	3/59	
Walter EGAN (US)		
Magnet And Steel	8/78	
808 STATE (UK)		
Cubik/Olympic		11/90
In Yer Face		2/91
❖ with MC Tunes The Only Rhyme		
That Bites		6/90
Pacific		12/89
8TH DAY (US)		
She's Not Just Another Woman	7/71	
EIGHTH WONDER (UK)		
I'm Not Scared		4/88
Donnie ELBERT (US)		
I Can't Help Myself		3/72
Where Did Our Love Go	12/71	1/72
ELECTRIC LIGHT ORCHESTRA (UK)		
All Over The World	9/80	
Can't Get It Out Of My Head	3/75	
Confusion/Last Train To London		12/79
The Diary Of Horace Wimp		8/79
Don't Bring Me Down	8/79	9/79
Evil Woman	1/76	2/76
Hold On Tight	9/81	8/81
I'm Alive	7/80	
Livin' Thing	1/77	12/76
Mr. Blue Sky		2/78
10538 Overture		8/72
Rock 'n' Roll Is King		7/83
Rockaria		3/77
Roll Over Beethoven		2/73
Shine A Little Love	7/79	6/79
Showdown		10/73
Strange Magic	5/76	
Sweet Talkin' Woman		10/78
Telephone Line	8/77	6/77
Turn To Stone	1/78	
Wild West Hero		7/78
❖ with Olivia Newton-John Xanadu	9/80	7/80
ELECTRIC PRUNES (US)		
I Had Too Much To Dream (Last Night)	2/67	
ELECTRONIC (UK)		
Disappointed		7/92
Get The Message		5/91
ELEGANTS (US)		
Little Star	8/58	
ELGINS (US)		
Heaven Must Have Sent You		5/71
ELIAS & His Zigzag Jive Flutes (SA)		
Tom Hark		5/58
Yvonne ELLIMAN (US)		
Hello Stranger	5/77	
If I Can't Have You	3/78	5/78
Love Me	12/76	12/76
Duke ELLINGTON (US)		
Skin Deep		3/54
Shirley ELLIS (US)		
The Clapping Song	4/65	5/65
The Name Game	1/65	
The Nitty Gritty	1/64	
EMERSON, Lake & Palmer (UK)		
Fanfare For The Common Man		6/77
EMF (UK)		
I Believe		2/91
Unbelievable	6/91	11/90
EMOTIONS (US)		
Best Of My Love	7/77	9/77
❖ with Earth, Wind & Fire Boogie		
Wonderland	6/79	6/79
EN VOGUE (US)		
Free Your Mind	10/92	11/92
Giving Him Something He Can Feel	8/92	11/92
Hold On	6/90	5/90
My Lovin' (You're Never Gonna Get It)	4/92	5/92
Harry ENFIELD (UK)		
Loadsamoney (Doin' Up The House)		5/88
ENGLAND DAN & John Ford Coley (US)		
I'd Really Love To See You Tonight	8/76	
Love Is The Answer	5/79	
Nights Are Forever Without You	11/76	
We'll Never Have To Say Goodbye Again	4/78	
ENGLAND WORLD CUP SQUAD (UK)		
Back Home		5/70
This Time (We'll Get It Right)/		
England We'll Fly The Flag		5/82
ENGLAND NEW ORDER (UK)		
World In Motion...		6/90
Scott ENGLISH (US)		
Brandy		11/71
ENIGMA (UK)		
Ain't No Stoppin'		6/81
ENIGMA (R/G)		
Sadeness Part 1	3/91	12/90
ENYA (I)		
Book Of Days		8/92
Orinoco Flow		10/88
EQUALS (UK/GUY)		
Baby Come Back		6/68
Black Skin Blue Eyed Boys		1/71
Viva Bobbie Joe		8/69
ERASURE (UK)		
Abba-Esque (E.P.)		6/92
Blue Savannah		3/90
Breath Of Life		4/92
Chains Of Love		6/88
Chorus		6/91
The Circus		10/87
Crackers International (E.P.)		12/88
Drama!		10/89
It Doesn't Have To Be		3/87
A Little Respect		10/88
Love To Hate You		9/91
Ship Of Fools		3/88
Sometimes		12/86
Star		6/90
Victim Of Love		6/87
Who Needs Love (Like That)		11/92
ERNIE (US)		
Rubber Duckie	9/70	
ERUPTION (US)		
I Can't Stand The Rain		3/78
One Way Ticket		5/79
ESCAPE CLUB (UK)		
I'll Be There	8/91	
Wild Wild West	10/88	
ESQUIRES (US)		
Get On Up	10/67	
ESSEX (US)		
Easier Said Than Done	6/63	
A Walkin' Miracle	9/63	
David ESSEX (UK)		
Gonna Make You A Star		10/74
Hold Me Close		9/75
If I Could		1/76
Lamplight		12/73
Oh What A Circus		9/78
Rock On	2/74	9/73
Rollin' Stone		7/75
Silver Dream Machine (Pt. 1)		4/80
Stardust		1/75
Tahiti (From Mutiny On The Bounty)		10/83
A Winter's Tale		12/82
Gloria ESTEFAN (US)		
Coming Out Of The Dark	3/91	
Don't Wanna Lose You	8/89	7/89
Get On Your Feet	11/89	
Go Away		4/93
Here We Are	2/90	
Miami Hit Mix/Christmas Through		
Your Eyes		12/92
Gloria ESTEFAN & The Miami Sound Machine (US)		
Anything For You	4/88	9/88
Bad Boy	4/86	
Can't Stay Away From You	2/88	3/89
Conga	1/86	
Dr. Beat		9/84
1-2-3	7/88	11/88
Rhythm Is Gonna Get You	7/87	
Words Get In The Way	9/86	
Deon ESTUS (US)		
Heaven Help Me	4/89	
ETERNAL (UK)		
Stay		10/93
EUROPE (S)		
Carrie	9/87	
The Final Countdown	3/87	11/86
EURYTHMICS (UK)		
Here Comes The Rain Again	3/84	2/84
It's Alright (Baby's Coming Back)		1/86
Love Is A Stranger		4/83
Missionary Man	10/86	
Right By Your Side		12/83
Sexcrime (Nineteen Eighty Four)		11/84
Sweet Dreams (Are Made Of This)	7/83	3/83
There Must Be An Angel (Playing With		
My Heart)		7/85
Thorn In My Side		9/86
Who's That Girl		7/83
Would I Lie To You?	6/85	
EURYTHMICS & Aretha Franklin (UK/US)		
Sisters Are Doin' It For Themselves		11/85
Maureen EVANS (UK)		
Like I Do		1/63
Paul EVANS (US)		
Happy-Go-Lucky-Me	6/60	
Hello This Is Joannie (The Telephone		
Answering Machine Song)		1/79
Midnite Special	3/60	
Paul EVANS & The Curls (US)		
Seven Little Girls Sitting In The Back Seat	11/59	
Betty EVERETT (US)		

	US Top 20 Ent	UK Top 20 Ent
❖ with *Jerry Butler* Let It Be Me	10/64	
Shoop Shoop Song (It's In His Kiss)	4/64	
Kenny EVERETT (UK)		
Snot Rap		4/83
EVERLY BROTHERS (US)		
All I Have To Do Is Dream	5/58	6/58
Bird Dog	8/58	9/58
Bye Bye Love	6/57	7/57
Cathy's Clown	5/60	4/60
Cryin' In The Rain	2/62	1/62
Devoted To You	9/58	
Ebony Eyes	2/61	
Let It Be Me	2/60	
Love Is Strange		11/65
No One Can Make My Sunshine Smile		11/62
Poor Jenny		7/59
The Price Of Love		6/65
Problems	12/58	1/59
So Sad (To Watch Good Love Go Bad)	9/60	10/60
Take A Message To Mary	5/59	
Temptation		6/61
That's Old Fashioned (That's The Way Love Should Be)	6/62	
('Til) I Kissed You	9/59	9/59
Wake Up Little Susie	10/57	11/57
Walk Right Back	3/61	2/61
When Will I Be Loved	7/60	7/60
Phil EVERLY & Cliff Richard (US/UK)		
She Means Nothing To Me		3/83
EVERY MOTHERS' SON (US)		
Come On Down To My Boat	6/67	
EVERYTHING BUT THE GIRL (UK)		
I Don't Want To Talk About It		7/88
EXCITERS (US)		
Tell Him	1/63	
EXILE (US)		
Kiss You All Over	8/78	9/78
EXPOSE (US)		
Come Go With Me	3/87	
I'll Never Get Over You (Getting Over Me)	6/93	
Let Me Be The One	10/87	
Point Of No Return	6/87	
Seasons Change	1/88	
Tell Me Why	2/90	
What You Don't Know	7/89	
When I Looked At Him	10/89	
EXTREME (US)		
Hole Hearted	10/91	
More Than Words	5/91	7/91
Rest In Peace		9/92
Song For Love		5/92
FAB featuring MC Parker (UK)		
Thunderbirds Are Go		7/90
Shelley FABARES (US)		
Johnny Angel	3/62	
FABIAN (US)		
Hound Dog Man	12/59	
Tiger	7/59	
Turn Me Loose	4/59	
Bent FABRIC (N)		
Alley Cat	9/62	
FABULOUS THUNDERBIRDS (US)		
Tuff Enuff	7/86	
FACES (UK)		
Cindy Incidentally		2/73
Pool Hall Richard/I Wish It Would Rain		1/74
Stay With Me	2/72	1/72
Rod STEWART & The Faces (UK)		
You Can Make Me Dance Sing Or Anything		12/74
Joe FAGIN (UK)		
That's Living (Alright)		1/84
Yvonne FAIR (US)		
It Should Have Been Me		2/76
FAIRGROUND ATTRACTION (UK)		
Find My Love		8/88
Perfect		5/88
FAIR WEATHER (UK)		
Natural Sinner		8/70
Andy FAIRWEATHER-LOW (UK)		
Reggae Tune		10/74
Wide Eyed And Legless		12/75
FAITH NO MORE (US)		
Epic	8/90	

	US Top 20 Ent	UK Top 20 Ent
I'm Easy/Be Aggressive		1/93
Midlife Crisis		6/92
Adam FAITH (UK)		
As You Like It		5/62
Don't That Beat All		9/62
Don't You Know It		7/61
Easy Going Me		5/61
The First Time		10/63
How About That		9/60
Lonely Pup (In A Christmas Shop)		12/60
Lonesome		2/62
Made You		7/60
Message To Martha (Kentucky Bluebird)		12/64
Poor Me		2/60
Someone Else's Baby		4/60
The Time Has Come		11/61
We Are In Love		1/64
What Do You Want		11/59
When Johnny Comes Marching Home		7/60
Who Am I/This Is It		2/61
Horace FAITH (J)		
Black Pearl		10/70
Percy FAITH (US)		
Theme From 'A Summer Place'	2/60	3/60
Marianne FAITHFULL (UK)		
As Tears Go By		9/64
Come And Stay With Me		3/65
Summer Nights		8/65
This Little Bird		5/65
FALCO (A)		
Rock Me Amadeus	3/86	4/86
Vienna Calling		6/86
Harold FALTERMEYER (G)		
Axel F	5/85	6/85
FAME AND PRICE TOGETHER (UK)		
Rosetta		5/71
Georgie FAME (UK)		
The Ballad Of Bonnie And Clyde	3/68	1/68
Get Away		7/66
Sittin' In The Park		1/67
Sunny		10/66
Yeh Yeh		1/65
FAMILY STAND (US)		
Ghetto Heaven		4/90
FAMILY (UK)		
Burlesque		11/72
In My Own Time		8/71
Strange Band		10/70
FAMILY DOGG (UK)		
Way Of Life		7/69
FANTASTICS (US)		
Something Old, Something New		4/71
FAR CORPORATION (UK/US/G/Swi)		
Stairway To Heaven		11/85
Don FARDON (UK)		
Indian Reservation		11/70
Donna FARGO (US)		
Funny Face	12/72	
The Happiest Girl In The Whole U.S.A.	8/72	
Chris FARLOWE (UK)		
Out Of Time		7/66
FARM (UK)		
All Together Now		12/90
Groovy Train		9/90
John FARNHAM (Aus)		
You're The Voice		6/87
FAT BOYS & The Beach Boys (US)		
Wipeout	9/87	9/87
FAT BOYS & Chubby Checker (US)		
The Twist (Yo, Twist)	8/88	6/88
FAT LARRY'S BAND (US)		
Zoom		10/82
FATBACK BAND (US)		
(Do The) Spanish Hustle		3/76
I Found Lovin'		10/87
FATIMA MANSION (I)		
(Everything I Do) I Do It For You		9/92
Phil FEARON & Galaxy (UK)		
Dancing Tight		5/83
Everybody's Laughing		7/84
I Can Prove It		8/86
What Do I Do		3/84
Jose FELICIANO (US)		
Light My Fire	8/68	10/68
FELIX (UK)		

	US Top 20 Ent	UK Top 20 Ent
Don't You Want Me		8/92
Freddy FENDER (US)		
Before The Next Teardrop Falls	4/75	
Wasted Days And Wasted Nights	9/75	
FENDERMEN (US)		
Mule Skinner Blues	7/60	
Jay FERGUSON (US)		
Thunder Island	3/78	
FERRANTE & TEICHER (US)		
Exodus	12/60	3/61
Midnight Cowboy	12/69	
Theme From The Appartment	9/60	
Tonight	11/61	
José FERRER (US)		
Woman (Uh-Huh)	2/54	2/54
FERRY AID (UK)		
Let It Be		4/87
Bryan FERRY (UK)		
Extended Play (E.P.)		8/76
A Hard Rain's Gonna Fall		10/73
The In Crowd		6/74
Let's Stick Together		6/76
★ Let's Stick Together		11/88
Slave To Love		5/85
This Is Tomorrow		2/77
FICTION FACTORY (UK)		
(Feels Like) Heaven		2/84
FIDDLER'S DRAM (UK)		
Day Trip To Bangor (Didn't We Have A Lovely Time)		12/79
Ernie FIELDS (US)		
In The Mood	11/59	1/60
Gracie FIELDS (UK)		
Around The World		6/57
FIESTAS (US)		
So Fine	6/59	
FIFTH DIMENSION (US)		
Aquarius/Let The Sunshine In	3/69	5/69
If I Could Reach You	11/72	
(Last Night) I Didn't Get To Sleep At All	6/72	
Never My Love	11/71	
One Less Bell To Answer	12/70	
Stoned Soul Picnic	7/68	
Sweet Blindness	11/68	
Up Up & Away	7/67	
Wedding Bell Blues	10/69	
FINE YOUNG CANNIBALS (UK)		
Don't Look Back	9/89	
Ever Fallen In Love		4/87
Good Thing	6/89	4/89
Johnny Come Home		6/85
She Drives Me Crazy	3/89	1/89
Suspicious Minds		2/86
Larry FINNEGAN (US)		
Dear One	4/62	
Elisa FIORILLO (US) See Jellybean featuring Elisa Fiorillo		
FIREBALLS (US)		
Bottle Of Wine	2/68	
FIREFALL (US)		
Just Remember I Love You	11/77	
Strange Way	12/78	
You Are The Woman	11/76	
FIREHOUSE (US)		
Love Of A Lifetime	9/91	
When I Look Into Your Eyes	10/92	
FIRM (UK)		
Arthur Daley ('E's Alright)		8/82
Star Trekkin'		6/87
FIRST CHOICE (US)		
Smarty Pants		8/73
FIRST CLASS (UK)		
Beach Baby	9/74	7/74
FIRST EDITION (US) see Kenny Rogers		
Lisa FISCHER (US)		
How Can I Ease The Pain	6/91	
Eddie FISHER (US)		
Anema E Core	4/54	
Cindy, Oh Cindy	11/56	11/56
Count Your Blessings	11/54	
Dungaree Doll	1/56	
A Girl, A Girl	4/54	
Heart	6/55	
I Need You Now	9/54	11/54
Oh! My Pa-Pa	1/54	1/54

	US Top 20 Ent	UK Top 20 Ent
Song Of The Dreamer	9/55	
Wedding Bells		3/55
Miss Toni FISHER (US)		
The Big Hurt	12/59	
Scott FITZGERALD & Yvonne Keeley (UK/H)		
If I Had Words		1/78
FIVE AMERICANS (US)		
Western Union	4/67	
FIVE MAN ELECTRICAL BAND (US)		
Signs	8/71	
FIVE STAIRSTEPS (US)		
O-O-O Child	7/70	
FIVE STAR (UK)		
Can't Wait Another Minute		4/86
Find The Time		8/86
Rain Or Shine		9/86
The Slightest Touch		4/87
Stay Out Of My Life		2/87
System Addict		2/86
5000 VOLTS (UK)		
Dr Kiss Kiss		8/76
I'm On Fire		9/75
FIXX (UK)		
Are We Ourselves?	10/84	
One Thing Leads To Another	10/83	
Roberta FLACK (US)		
Feel Like Makin' Love	7/74	
The First Time Ever I Saw Your Face	4/72	
Killing Me Softly With His Song	2/73	3/73
Making Love	6/82	
✤ with Peabo Bryson Tonight I Celebrate My Love	11/83	9/83
Roberta FLACK & Donny Hathaway (US)		
Back Together Again		6/80
The Closer I Get To You	4/78	
Where Is The Love	7/72	
Roberta FLACK with Maxi Priest (US/UK)		
Set The Night To Music	11/91	
FLAMINGOS (US)		
I Only Have Eyes For You	7/59	
FLASH AND THE PAN (Aus)		
Waiting For A Train		6/83
FLEETWOOD MAC (UK/US)		
Albatross		12/68
★ Albatross		6/73
Big Love	5/87	5/87
Don't Stop	8/77	
Dreams	5/77	
Everywhere	2/88	4/88
Go Your Own Way	2/77	
The Green Manalishi (With The Two-Prong Crown)		6/70
Gypsy	10/82	
Hold Me	7/82	
Little Lies	10/87	10/87
Man Of The World		5/69
Oh Diane		2/83
Oh Well		10/69
Rhiannon (Will You Ever Win)	5/76	
Sara	1/80	
Say You Love Me	8/76	
Tusk	10/79	10/79
You Make Lovin' Fun	11/77	
FLEETWOODS (US)		
Come Softly To Me	3/59	5/59
Mr. Blue	9/59	
Tragedy	5/61	
Berni FLINT (UK)		
I Don't Want To Put A Hold On You		4/77
FLOATERS (US)		
Float On	8/77	8/77
A FLOCK OF SEAGULLS (UK)		
I Ran (So Far Away)	10/82	
Wishing (If I Had A Photograph Of You)		12/82
FLOWERPOT MEN (UK)		
Let's Go To San Francisco		9/67
Eddie FLOYD (US)		
Bring It On Home To Me	12/68	
FLYING LIZARDS (UK)		
Money		9/79
FLYING MACHINE (UK)		
Smile A Little Smile For Me	11/69	
FLYING PICKETS (UK)		
Only You		12/83
When You're Young And In Love		5/84

	US Top 20 Ent	UK Top 20 Ent
FOCUS (H)		
Hocus Pocus	5/73	
Sylvia		2/73
Dan FOGELBERG (US)		
Hard To Say	10/81	
The Language Of Love	3/84	
Leader Of The Band	2/82	
Longer	2/80	
Same Old Lang Syne	2/81	
John FOGERTY (US)		
The Old Man Down The Road	2/85	
Wayne FONTANA (UK)		
Pamela Pamela		1/67
Wayne FONTANA & The Mindbenders (UK)		
Game Of Love	4/65	2/65
Um Um Um Um Um Um		11/64
FONTANE SISTERS (US)		
Daddy-O	12/55	
Eddie My Love	4/56	
Hearts Of Stone	12/54	
Seventeen	9/55	
Steve FORBERT (US)		
Romeo's Tune	2/80	
FORCE M.D'S (US)		
Tender Love	4/86	
Emile FORD & The Checkmates (UK)		
Counting Teardrops		12/60
On A Slow Boat To China		2/60
What Do You Want To Make Those Eyes At Me For		11/59
Frankie FORD (US)		
Sea Cruise	4/59	
Lita FORD (US)		
Kiss Me Deadly	6/88	
Lita FORD (& Ozzy Osbourne) (US/UK)		
Close My Eyes Forever	5/89	
Tennessee Ernie FORD (US)		
Ballad Of Davy Crockett	3/55	1/56
Give Me Your Word		1/55
Sixteen Tons	11/55	1/56
FOREIGNER (UK/US)		
Cold As Ice	9/77	
Dirty White Boy	10/79	
Double Vision	10/78	
Feels Like The First Time	5/77	
Head Games	12/79	
Hot Blooded	7/78	
I Don't Want To Live Without You	5/88	
I Want To Know What Love Is	1/85	1/85
Say You Will	2/88	
That Was Yesterday	5/85	
Urgent	8/81	
Waiting For A Girl Like You	11/81	1/82
FORREST (US)		
Rock The Boat		3/83
Lance FORTUNE (UK)		
Be Mine		3/60
FORTUNES (UK)		
Freedom Come Freedom Go		10/71
Here Comes That Rainy Day Feeling Again	7/71	
Here It Comes Again		10/65
Storm In A Teacup		2/72
This Golden Ring		3/66
You've Got Your Troubles	9/65	7/65
49ERS (Ita)		
Touch Me		1/90
FOUNDATIONS (UK)		
Baby Now That I've Found You	2/68	10/67
Build Me Up Buttercup	2/69	12/68
In The Bad Bad Old Days		4/69
FOUR ACES (US)		
The Gang That Sang 'Heart Of My Heart'	1/54	
Love Is A Many-Splendored Thing	9/55	11/55
Melody Of Love	2/55	
Mr. Sandman	11/54	1/55
Stranger In Paradise	1/54	5/55
Three Coins In The Fountain	5/54	7/54
FOUR KNIGHTS (US)		
I Get So Lonely	2/54	6/54
FOUR LADS (US)		
Moments To Remember	9/55	
No, Not Much!	2/56	
Skokiaan	9/54	
Standing On The Corner	5/56	
4 NON BLONDES (US)		

	US Top 20 Ent	UK Top 20 Ent
What's Up	7/93	7/93
FOUR PENNIES (UK)		
I Found Out The Hard Way		8/64
Juliet		5/64
FOUR PREPS (US)		
Big Man	5/58	6/58
Down By The Station	2/60	
26 Miles	3/58	
FOUR SEASONS (US)		
Big Girls Don't Cry	11/62	2/63
Bye, Bye, Baby (Baby Goodbye)	2/65	
C'mon Marianne	7/67	
Candy Girl	8/63	
Dawn (Go Away)	2/64	
December '63 (Oh What A Night)	2/76	2/76
Don't Think Twice (as Wonder Who)	12/65	
I've Got You Under My Skin	10/66	11/66
Let's Hang On!	11/65	12/65
Opus 17 (Don't You Worry 'Bout Me)	6/66	
Rag Doll	7/64	9/64
Ronnie	5/64	
Save It For Me	9/64	
Sherry	9/62	10/62
Silver Star		5/76
Tell It To The Rain	1/67	
Walk Like A Man	2/63	4/63
Who Loves You	10/75	10/75
Working My Way Back To You	2/66	
Frankie VALLI & FOUR SEASONS (US)		
The Night		5/75
FOUR TOPS (US)		
Ain't No Woman (Like The One I've Got)	3/73	
Baby I Need Your Loving	10/64	
Bernadette	4/67	4/67
Do What You Gotta Do		10/69
I Can't Help Myself	6/65	4/70
If I Were A Carpenter		3/68
It's All In The Game		6/70
It's The Same Old Song	8/65	
Keeper Of The Castle	12/72	
Loco In Acapulco		12/88
Reach Out I'll Be There	10/66	10/66
★ Reach Out I'll Be There		8/88
✤ with The Supremes River Deep-Mountain High	1/71	7/71
Seven Rooms Of Gloom	6/67	7/67
Simple Game		10/71
Standing In The Shadows Of Love	1/67	1/67
Still Water (Love)	10/70	10/70
Walk Away Renee		12/67
When She Was My Girl	10/81	11/81
FOUR TUNES (US)		
I Understand Just How You Feel	6/54	
FOURMOST (UK)		
Hello Little Girl		10/63
A Little Loving		5/64
FOX (UK)		
Only You Can		3/75
S-S-S-Single Bed		4/76
Samantha FOX (UK)		
Do Ya Do Ya (Wanna Please Me)		7/86
I Wanna Have Some Fun	2/89	
Naughty Girls (Need Love Too)	5/88	
Nothing's Gonna Stop Me Now		6/87
Touch Me (I Want Your Body)	1/87	3/86
Inez FOXX (US)		
Mockingbird	8/63	
FOXY (US)		
Get Off	10/78	
FPI PROJECT (Ita)		
Going Back To My Roots/Rich In Paradise		1/90
Peter FRAMPTON (UK)		
Baby, I Love Your Way	8/76	
Do You Feel Like We Do	11/76	
I Can't Stand It No More	7/79	
I'm In You	7/77	
Show Me The Way	4/76	6/76
Connie FRANCIS (US)		
Among My Souvenirs	12/59	12/59
Breakin' In A Brand New Broken Heart	5/61	7/61
Carolina Moon/Stupid Cupid		8/58
Don't Break The Heart That Loves You	3/62	
Everybody's Somebody's Fool	6/60	8/60
Frankie	6/59	
I'm Sorry I Made You Cry		7/58

	US Top 20 Ent	UK Top 20 Ent
Lipstick On Your Collar	6/59	7/59
Mama	3/60	5/60
Many Tears Ago	12/60	2/61
My Happiness	12/58	2/59
My Heart Has A Mind Of Its Own	9/60	11/60
Robot Man		6/60
Second Hand Love	6/62	
Together	7/61	9/61
Vacation	8/62	8/62
When The Boy In Your Arms (Is The Boy In Your Heart)	1/62	
Where The Boys Are	2/61	4/61
Who's Sorry Now	3/58	4/58
You Always Hurt The One You Love		1/59
FRANK AND WALTERS (I)		
After All		1/93
FRANKE & The Knockouts (US)		
Sweetheart	5/81	
FRANKIE GOES TO HOLLYWOOD (UK)		
The Power Of Love		12/84
★ The Power Of Love		12/93
Rage Hard		9/86
Relax	3/85	1/84
★ Relax		10/93
Two Tribes		6/84
Welcome To The Pleasure Dome		4/85
Aretha FRANKLIN (US)		
Baby I Love You	8/67	
Bridge Over Troubled Water/Brand New Me	5/71	
Call Me	4/70	
Chain Of Fools	1/68	
Day Dreaming	4/72	
Don't Play That Song	9/70	9/70
Freeway Of Love	8/85	
The House That Jack Built	9/68	
I Never Loved A Man (The Way I Love You)	4/67	
I Say A Little Prayer	9/68	8/68
A Natural Woman (You Make Me Feel Like)	10/67	
Respect	5/67	7/67
Rock Steady	11/71	
See Saw	12/68	
Share Your Love With Me	9/69	
✧ with Eurythmics Sisters Are Doin' It For Themselves		11/85
Spanish Harlem	8/71	
(Sweet Sweet Baby) Since You've Been Gone	3/68	
Think	6/68	
Until You Come Back To Me (That's What I'm Gonna Do)	1/74	
Who's Zoomin' Who	11/85	1/86
Aretha FRANKLIN & George Michael (US/UK)		
I Knew You Were Waiting (For Me)	3/87	1/87
Rodney FRANKLIN (US)		
The Groove		5/80
FRANTIQUE (US)		
Strut Your Funky Stuff		9/79
Stan FREBERG (US)		
Sh-Boom		11/54
John FRED & His Playboy Band (US)		
Judy In Disguise (With Glasses)	12/67	1/68
FREDDIE & The Dreamers (UK)		
I Understand		12/64
I'm Telling You Now	4/65	8/63
If You Gotta Make A Fool Of Somebody		6/63
Over You		3/64
You Were Made For Me		11/63
FREE (UK)		
All Right Now	10/70	6/70
★ All Right Now		8/73
★ All Right Now		2/91
Free (E.P.)		3/78
Little Bit Of Love		7/70
My Brother Jake		5/71
Wishing Well		1/73
FREEEZ (UK)		
I.O.U.		7/83
Southern Freeez		3/81
Bobby FREEMAN (US)		
C'mon And Swim	8/64	
Do You Want To Dance	6/58	
Ernie FREEMAN (US)		
Raunchy	11/57	
FREE MOVEMENT (US)		
I've Found Someone Of My Own	10/71	

	US Top 20 Ent	UK Top 20 Ent
Ace FREHLEY (US)		
New York Groove	1/79	
FREIHEIT (G)		
Keeping The Dream Alive		1/89
FRESH 4 featuring Lizz E (UK)		
Wishing On A Star		10/89
Doug E. FRESH & The Get Fresh Crew (US)		
The Show		11/85
Glenn FREY (US)		
The Heat Is On	2/85	4/85
The One You Love	11/82	
Smuggler's Blues	6/85	
True Love	10/88	
You Belong To The City	10/85	
FRIDA (N)		
I Know There's Something Going On	3/83	
Dean FRIEDMAN (US)		
Lucky Stars		10/78
FRIEND AND LOVER (US)		
Reach Out Of The Darkness	6/68	
FRIENDS OF DISTINCTION (US)		
Going In Circles	11/69	
Grazin' In The Grass	5/69	
Love Or Let Me Be Lonely	4/70	
FRIJID PINK (US)		
House Of The Rising Sun	3/70	5/70
FULL FORCE (US)		
Alice I Want You Just For Me		1/86
Bobby FULLER FOUR (US)		
I Fought The Law	3/66	
FUN BOY THREE (UK)		
Our Lips Are Sealed		5/83
✧ with Bananarama Really Saying Something		5/82
The Tunnel Of Love		2/83
FUN BOY THREE & Bananarama (UK)		
It Ain't What You Do It's The Way That You Do It		3/82
FARLEY 'JACKMASTER' FUNK (US)		
Love Can't Turn Around		9/86
FUNKADELIC (US)		
One Nation Under A Groove (Pt. 1)		1/79
FUNK MASTERS (UK)		
It's Over		7/83
FUNKY WORM (UK)		
Hustle! (To The Music...)		8/88
FUREYS & Davey Arthur (UK)		
When You Were Sweet Sixteen		11/81
Billy FURY (UK)		
Halfway To Paradise		6/61
I Will		5/64
I'd Never Find Another You		12/61
In Summer		8/63
In Thoughts Of You		8/65
It's Only Make Believe		8/64
Jealousy		9/61
Last Night Was Made For Love		5/62
Like I've Never Been Gone		3/63
Once Upon A Dream		8/62
When Will You Say I Love You		5/63
FUZZBOX (UK)		
International Rescue		4/89
Kenny G (US)		
Songbird	6/87	
Peter GABRIEL (UK)		
Big Time	2/87	4/87
Games Without Frontiers		3/80
Sledgehammer	6/86	5/86
Solsbury Hill		5/77
Steam		1/93
Peter GABRIEL & Kate Bush (UK)		
Don't Give Up		11/86
GABRIELLE (UK)		
Dreams		6/93
Going Nowhere		10/93
GALAXY (UK) See Phil Fearon & Galaxy		5/83
GALLAGHER & LYLE (UK)		
Heart On My Sleeve		6/76
I Wanna Stay With You		3/76
Patsy GALLANT (C)		
From New York To L.A.		10/77
GALLERY (US)		
Nice To Be With You	6/72	
James GALWAY (UK)		

	US Top 20 Ent	UK Top 20 Ent
Annie's Song		6/78
GAP BAND (US)		
Big Fun		12/86
Oops Upside Your Head		8/80
Boris GARDINER (J)		
I Want To Wake Up With You		8/86
Art GARFUNKEL (US)		
All I Know	10/73	
Bright Eyes		4/79
I Only Have Eyes For You		9/75
Art GARFUNKEL, James Taylor & Paul Simon (US)		
Wonderful World	3/78	
Gale GARNETT (US)		
We'll Sing In The Sunshine	10/64	
Leif GARRETT (US)		
I Was Made For Dancin'	2/79	2/79
Runaround Sue	1/78	
GARY'S GANG (US)		
Keep On Dancin'		3/79
David GATES (US)		
Goodbye Girl	4/78	
Marvin GAYE (US)		
Abraham Martin & John		6/70
Ain't That Peculiar	11/65	
Got To Give It Up (Pt.1)	5/77	5/77
How Sweet It Is To Be Loved By You	1/65	
I Heard It Through The Grapevine	12/68	3/69
★ I Heard It Through The Grapevine		5/86
I Want You	6/76	
I'll Be Doggone	5/65	
Inner City Blues (Makes Me Wanna Holler)	11/71	
Let's Get It On	8/73	
Mercy Mercy Me (The Ecology)	8/71	
Pride And Joy	7/63	
Sexual Healing	12/82	11/82
That's The Way Love Is	10/69	
Too Busy Thinking About My Baby	6/69	8/69
Trouble Man	1/73	
Try It Baby	7/64	
What's Going On	3/71	
✧ with Diana Ross You Are Everything		4/74
You're A Wonderful One	4/64	
Marvin GAYE & Diana Ross (US)		
You're A Special Part Of Me	11/73	
Marvin GAYE & Tammi Terrell (US)		
Ain't Nothing Like The Real Thing	5/68	
If I Could Build My Whole World Around You	1/68	
Onion Song		12/69
You're All I Need To Get By	8/68	
Your Precious Love	10/67	
Crystal GAYLE (US)		
Don't It Make My Brown Eyes Blue	10/77	1/78
Talking In Your Sleep		10/78
Michelle GAYLE (UK)		
Looking Up		8/93
Ronnie GAYLORD (US)		
Cuddle Me	3/54	
GAYLORDS (US)		
From The Vine Came The Grape	2/54	
Isle Of Capri	6/54	
The Little Shoemaker	7/54	
Gloria GAYNOR (US)		
I Will Survive	2/79	2/79
★ I Will Survive		7/93
Never Can Say Goodbye	1/75	1/75
Reach Out I'll Be There		4/75
GAZZA And Lindisfarne (UK)		
Fog On The Tyne (Revisited)		11/90
G-CLEFS (US)		
I Understand (Just How You Feel)	11/61	
David GEDDES (US)		
Run Joey Run	9/75	
J. GEILS BAND (US)		
Centerfold	12/81	2/82
Freeze-Frame	3/82	
Must Of Got Lost	12/74	
GENE & DEBBE (US)		
Playboy	4/68	
GENERATION X (UK)		
King Rocker		2/79
GENESIS (UK)		
Abacab		9/81
Follow You Follow Me		4/78
Hold On My Heart	6/92	
I Can't Dance	3/92	1/92

	US Top 20 Ent	UK Top 20 Ent
In Too Deep	6/87	
Invisible Touch	6/86	
Invisible Touch (Live)		11/92
Land Of Confusion	12/86	12/86
Mama		9/83
Misunderstanding	8/80	
No Son Of Mine	12/91	11/91
Spot The Pigeon (E.P.)		6/77
That's All!	1/84	12/83
3 X 3 (E.P.)		6/82
Throwing It All Away	9/86	
Tonight Tonight Tonight	3/87	
Turn It On Again		4/80

Bobbie GENTRY (US)

	US Top 20 Ent	UK Top 20 Ent
I'll Never Fall In Love Again		9/69
Ode To Billie Joe	8/67	10/67

Bobbie GENTRY & Glen Campbell (US)

	US Top 20 Ent	UK Top 20 Ent
All I Have To Do Is Dream		12/69

GENTRYS (US)

	US Top 20 Ent	UK Top 20 Ent
Keep On Dancing	10/65	

GEORDIE (UK)

	US Top 20 Ent	UK Top 20 Ent
All Because Of You		4/73
Can You Do It		7/73

Barbara GEORGE (US)

	US Top 20 Ent	UK Top 20 Ent
I Know (You Don't Love Me No More)	1/62	

Sophia GEORGE (J)

	US Top 20 Ent	UK Top 20 Ent
Girlie Girlie		1/86

GEORGIA SATELLITES (US)

	US Top 20 Ent	UK Top 20 Ent
Keep Your Hands To Yourself	1/87	

GERARDO (US)

	US Top 20 Ent	UK Top 20 Ent
Rico Suave	4/91	

Danyel GERARD (F)

	US Top 20 Ent	UK Top 20 Ent
Butterfly		10/71

GERRY & The Pacemakers (UK)

	US Top 20 Ent	UK Top 20 Ent
Don't Let The Sun Catch You Crying	6/64	5/64
Ferry Across The Mersey	3/65	1/65
How Do You Do It?	8/64	3/63
I Like It		6/63
I'll Be There		4/65
I'm The One		1/64
You'll Never Walk Alone		10/63

Stan GETZ & Charlie Byrd (US)

	US Top 20 Ent	UK Top 20 Ent
Desafinado		1/63

Stan GETZ & Astrud Gilberto (US)

	US Top 20 Ent	UK Top 20 Ent
The Girl From Ipanema	7/64	

GIANT STEPS (US)

	US Top 20 Ent	UK Top 20 Ent
Another Lover	11/88	

Andy GIBB (UK)

	US Top 20 Ent	UK Top 20 Ent
Desire	2/80	
An Everlasting Love	8/78	9/78
I Just Want To Be Your Everything	7/77	
(Love Is) Thicker Than Water	1/78	
(Our Love) Don't Throw It All Away	11/78	
Shadow Dancing	5/78	
Time Is Time	1/81	

Andy GIBB & Olivia Newton-John (UK)

	US Top 20 Ent	UK Top 20 Ent
I Can't Help It	5/80	

Robin GIBB (UK)

	US Top 20 Ent	UK Top 20 Ent
Saved By The Bell		7/69

Steve GIBBONS BAND (US)

	US Top 20 Ent	UK Top 20 Ent
Tulane		9/77

Georgia GIBBS (US)

	US Top 20 Ent	UK Top 20 Ent
Dance With Me Henry (Wallflower)	4/55	
Tweedle Dee	2/55	

Terri GIBBS (US)

	US Top 20 Ent	UK Top 20 Ent
Somebody's Knockin'	4/81	

Debbie GIBSON (US)

	US Top 20 Ent	UK Top 20 Ent
Electric Youth	5/89	5/89
Foolish Beat	6/88	7/88
Lost In Your Eyes	2/89	
Only In My Dreams	8/87	4/88
Out Of The Blue	3/88	
Shake Your Love	11/87	2/88

Don GIBSON (US)

	US Top 20 Ent	UK Top 20 Ent
Oh Lonesome Me/I Can't Stop Lovin' You	4/58	

GIBSON BROTHERS (F)

	US Top 20 Ent	UK Top 20 Ent
Cuba/Better Do It Salsa		3/80
Mariana		8/80
Ooh! What A Life		9/79
Que Sera Mi Vida (If You Should Go)		12/79

GIDEA PARK (UK)

	US Top 20 Ent	UK Top 20 Ent
Beach Boy Gold		8/81

Nick GILDER (UK)

	US Top 20 Ent	UK Top 20 Ent
Hot Child In The City	9/78	

Terry GILKYSON & The Easy Riders (US)

	US Top 20 Ent	UK Top 20 Ent
Marianne	2/57	

Johnny GILL (US)

	US Top 20 Ent	UK Top 20 Ent
My, My, My	9/90	
Rub You The Right Way	6/90	

Stuart GILLIES (UK)

	US Top 20 Ent	UK Top 20 Ent
Amanda		4/73

Jimmy GILMER & The Fireballs (US)

	US Top 20 Ent	UK Top 20 Ent
Sugar Shack	10/63	

Jim GILSTRAP (US)

	US Top 20 Ent	UK Top 20 Ent
Swing Your Daddy		4/75

GIRLSCHOOL (UK) See Motorhead & Girlschool

GIUFFRIA (US)

	US Top 20 Ent	UK Top 20 Ent
Call To The Heart	2/85	

Will GLAHE (A)

	US Top 20 Ent	UK Top 20 Ent
Liechtensteiner Polka	12/57	

GLASS TIGER (C)

	US Top 20 Ent	UK Top 20 Ent
Don't Forget Me (When I'm Gone)	9/86	
Someday	1/87	

Tom GLAZER & The Do-Re-Mi Children's Chorus (US)

	US Top 20 Ent	UK Top 20 Ent
On Top Of Spaghetti	7/63	

Gary GLITTER (UK)

	US Top 20 Ent	UK Top 20 Ent
Always Yours		6/74
Another Rock And Roll Christmas		12/84
Do You Wanna Touch Me (Oh Yeah)		1/73
Doing Alright With The Boys		6/75
Hello Hello I'm Back Again		4/73
I Didn't Know I Loved You (Till I Saw You Rock'n'Roll)		10/72
I Love You Love Me Love		11/73
I'm The Leader Of The Gang (I Am)		7/73
Oh Yes! You're Beautiful		11/74
Remember Me This Way		4/74
Rock And Roll Part 2	9/72	6/72

GLITTER BAND (UK)

	US Top 20 Ent	UK Top 20 Ent
Angel Face		4/74
Goodbye My Love		2/75
Just For You		8/74
Let's Get Together Again		11/74
Love In The Sun		9/75
People Like You And People Like Me		3/76
The Tears I Cried		5/75

GO WEST (UK)

	US Top 20 Ent	UK Top 20 Ent
Call Me		6/85
Don't Look Down-The Sequel		12/85
Faithful	1/93	
King Of Wishful Thinking	7/90	
We Close Our Eyes		3/85

GO-GO'S (US)

	US Top 20 Ent	UK Top 20 Ent
Head Over Heels	5/84	
Vacation	8/82	
We Got The Beat	3/82	

GODLEY & CREME (UK)

	US Top 20 Ent	UK Top 20 Ent
Cry	10/85	
Under Your Thumb		10/81
Wedding Bells		12/81

Andrew GOLD (US)

	US Top 20 Ent	UK Top 20 Ent
Lonely Boy	5/77	5/77
Never Let Her Slip Away		4/78

GOLDEN EARRING (H)

	US Top 20 Ent	UK Top 20 Ent
Radar Love	7/74	1/74
Twilight Zone	3/83	

GOLDIE (UK)

	US Top 20 Ent	UK Top 20 Ent
Making Up Again		6/78

Bobby GOLDSBORO (US)

	US Top 20 Ent	UK Top 20 Ent
Honey	4/68	5/68
★ Honey		4/75
Little Things	3/65	
See The Funny Little Clown	2/64	
Summer (The First Time)		8/73
Watching Scotty Grow	2/71	

GOODIES (UK)

	US Top 20 Ent	UK Top 20 Ent
Funky Gibbon/Sick Man Blues		4/75
The In Betweenies/Father Christmas Do Not Touch Me		12/74

Dickie GOODMAN (US)

	US Top 20 Ent	UK Top 20 Ent
Mr. Jaws	10/75	

GOOMBAY DANCE BAND (G/UK)

	US Top 20 Ent	UK Top 20 Ent
Seven Tears		3/82

GOONS (UK)

	US Top 20 Ent	UK Top 20 Ent
Bloodnok's Rock 'n' Roll Call/Ying Tong Song		9/56
I'm Walking Backwards For Christmas/Bluebottle Blues		7/56
★ Ying Tong Song		8/73

Barry GORDON (US)

	US Top 20 Ent	UK Top 20 Ent
Nuttin' For Christmas	12/55	

Lonnie GORDON (US)

	US Top 20 Ent	UK Top 20 Ent
Happenin' All Over Again		2/90

Lesley GORE (US)

	US Top 20 Ent	UK Top 20 Ent
It's My Party	6/63	6/63
Judy's Turn To Cry	8/63	
She's A Fool	11/63	
That's The Way Boys Are	4/64	
You Don't Own Me	2/64	

Eydie GORME (US)

	US Top 20 Ent	UK Top 20 Ent
Blame It On The Bossa Nova	2/63	
✤ with Steve Lawrence I Want To Stay Here	9/63	
Yes My Darling Daughter	7/62	

G.Q. (US)

	US Top 20 Ent	UK Top 20 Ent
Disco Nights (Rock Freak)	5/79	

Charlie GRACIE (US)

	US Top 20 Ent	UK Top 20 Ent
Butterfly	3/57	5/57
Fabulous		6/57
Wanderin' Eyes/I Love You So Much It Hurts		9/57

Jaki GRAHAM (UK)

	US Top 20 Ent	UK Top 20 Ent
✤ with David Grant Could It Be I'm Falling In Love		4/85
Round And Round		7/85
Set Me Free		6/86

Larry GRAHAM (US)

	US Top 20 Ent	UK Top 20 Ent
One In A Million You	9/80	

Lou GRAMM (US)

	US Top 20 Ent	UK Top 20 Ent
Just Between You And Me	1/90	
Midnight Blue	4/87	

Billy GRAMMER (US)

	US Top 20 Ent	UK Top 20 Ent
Gotta Travel On	12/58	

GRAND FUNK (US)

	US Top 20 Ent	UK Top 20 Ent
Bad Time	5/75	
The Loco-Motion	4/74	
Shinin' On	8/74	
Some Kind Of Wonderful	1/75	
We're An American Band	9/73	

GRANDMASTER FLASH, Melle Mel & The Furious Five (US)

	US Top 20 Ent	UK Top 20 Ent
The Message		9/82
White Lines (Don't Don't Do It)		7/84

GRANDMASTER MELLE MEL & The Furious Five (US)

	US Top 20 Ent	UK Top 20 Ent
Step Off (Pt. 1)		1/85

GRANGE HILL CAST (UK)

	US Top 20 Ent	UK Top 20 Ent
Just Say No		4/86

Amy GRANT (US)

	US Top 20 Ent	UK Top 20 Ent
Baby Baby	4/91	5/91
Every Heartbeat	7/91	
Good For Me	2/92	
✤ with Peter Cetera The Next Time I Fall	11/86	
That's What Love Is For	11/91	

David GRANT (UK)

	US Top 20 Ent	UK Top 20 Ent
Watching You Watching Me		8/83

David GRANT & Jaki Graham (UK)

	US Top 20 Ent	UK Top 20 Ent
Could It Be I'm Falling In Love		4/85

Earl GRANT (US)

	US Top 20 Ent	UK Top 20 Ent
The End	10/58	

Eddy GRANT (Guy)

	US Top 20 Ent	UK Top 20 Ent
Do You Feel My Love		12/80
Electric Avenue	6/83	1/83
Gimme Hope Jo'anna		2/88
I Don't Wanna Dance		11/82
Living On The Front Line		7/79

Gogi GRANT (US)

	US Top 20 Ent	UK Top 20 Ent
Suddenly There's A Valley	10/55	
The Wayward Wind	5/56	7/56

GRASS ROOTS (US)

	US Top 20 Ent	UK Top 20 Ent
I'd Wait A Million Years	9/69	
Let's Live For Today	6/67	
Midnight Confessions	10/68	
Sooner Or Later	7/71	
Temptation Eyes	3/71	

GRATEFUL DEAD (US)

	US Top 20 Ent	UK Top 20 Ent
Touch Of Grey	9/87	

Dobie GRAY (US)

	US Top 20 Ent	UK Top 20 Ent
Drift Away	4/73	
The "In" Crowd	2/65	

Charles Randolph GREAN SOUNDE (US)

	US Top 20 Ent	UK Top 20 Ent
Quentin's Theme (from TV Series 'Dark Shadows')	8/69	

GREAT WHITE (US)

	US Top 20 Ent	UK Top 20 Ent
Once Bitten Twice Shy	7/89	

R.B. GREAVES (US)

	US Top 20 Ent	UK Top 20 Ent
Take A Letter Maria	11/69	
GREEN JELLY (US)		
Three Little Pigs		6/93
Al GREEN (US)		
Call Me (Come Back Home)	3/73	
Here I Am (Come And Take Me)	8/73	
I'm Still In Love With You	8/72	
L-O-V-E (Love)	4/75	
Let's Stay Together	1/72	1/72
Look What You Done For Me	4/72	
✤ *with Annie Lennox* Put A Little Love In		
Your Heart	1/89	
Sha-La-La (Make Me Happy)	12/74	
Tired Of Being Alone	10/71	11/71
You Ought To Be With Me	11/72	
Norman GREENBAUM (US)		
Spirit In The Sky	3/70	4/70
Lorne GREENE (US)		
Ringo	11/64	
GREYHOUND (UK)		
Black And White		7/71
Moon River		2/72
Andy GRIFFITH (US)		
What It Was, Was Football	1/54	
Larry GROCE (US)		
Junk Food Junkie	3/76	
Henry GROSS (US)		
Shannon	5/76	
GTR (UK)		
When The Heart Rules The Mind	7/86	
GUESS WHO (C)		
American Woman/No Sugar Tonight	4/70	
Clap For The Wolfman	9/74	
Laughing	8/69	
No Time	2/70	
Share The Land	12/70	
These Eyes	5/69	
Greg GUIDRY (US)		
Goin' Down	5/82	
Bonnie GUITAR (US)		
Dark Moon	5/57	
GUN (UK)		
Race With The Devil		12/68
GUNS N' ROSES (US)		
Ain't It Fun		11/93
Don't Cry	11/91	9/91
Knockin' On Heaven's Door		5/92
Live And Let Die		12/91
November Rain	7/92	3/92
Paradise City	3/89	3/89
Patience	5/89	7/89
Sweet Child O' Mine	8/88	6/89
Welcome To The Jungle	12/88	
Yesterdays/November Rain		11/92
You Could Be Mine		7/91
GURU JOSH (UK)		
Infinity		3/90
Adrian GURVITZ (UK)		
Classic		3/82
Gwen GUTHRIE (US)		
Ain't Nothing Goin' On But The Rent		8/86
A GUY CALLED GERALD (UK)		
Voodoo Ray E.P.		7/89
GUYS & DOLLS (UK)		
There's A Whole Lot Of Loving		3/75
You Don't Have To Say You Love Me		3/76
H-TOWN (US)		
Knockin' Da Boots	5/93	
HADDAWAY (WI)		
Life		10/93
What Is Love	10/93	6/93
Sammy HAGAR (US)		
Your Love Is Driving Me Crazy	2/83	
HAIRCUT 100 (UK)		
Fantastic Day		5/82
Favourite Shirts (Boy Meets Girl)		11/81
Love Plus One		2/82
Nobody's Fool		9/82
Curtis HAIRSTON (US)		
I Want Your Lovin' (Just A Little Bit)		5/85
HALE & PACE & The Stonkers (UK)		
The Stonk		3/91
Bill HALEY & His Comets (US)		
Dim, Dim The Lights (I Want Some		
Atmosphere)		12/54
Don't Knock The Rock		2/57
Razzle Dazzle		10/56
Rip It Up		11/56
★ Rock Around The Clock	5/55	10/55
★ Rock Around The Clock		9/56
★ Rock Around The Clock		4/74
Rock-A-Beatin' Boogie		1/56
Rockin' Through The Rye		8/56
The Saints Rock 'n Roll		6/56
See You Later, Alligator	1/56	3/56
★ See You Later, Alligator		10/56
Shake, Rattle And Roll	9/54	12/54
Daryl HALL & John Oates (US)		
Adult Education	3/84	
Did It In A Minute	5/82	
Everything Your Heart Desires	5/88	
Family Man	6/83	
I Can't Go For That (No Can Do)	12/81	2/82
Kiss On My List	3/81	
Maneater	11/82	11/82
Method Of Modern Love	2/85	
One On One	3/83	
Out Of Touch	11/84	
Private Eyes	10/81	
Rich Girl	3/77	
Sara Smile	5/76	
Say It Isn't So	11/83	
She's Gone	10/76	
So Close	11/90	
You Make My Dreams	6/81	
You've Lost That Lovin' Feeling	11/80	
Daryl HALL (US)		
Dreamtime	9/86	
Larry HALL (US)		
Sandy	1/60	
Tom T. HALL (US)		
I Love	2/74	
Halo JAMES (UK)		
Could Have Told You So		1/90
George HAMILTON IV (US)		
A Rose And A Baby Ruth	11/56	
HAMILTON, Joe Frank & Reynolds (US)		
Don't Pull Your Love	6/71	
Fallin' In Love	8/75	
Lynne HAMILTON (AUS)		
On The Inside (Theme 'Prisoner-Cell		
Block H')		6/89
Roy HAMILTON (US)		
Don't Let Go	2/58	
Unchained Melody	5/55	
You Can Have Her	3/61	
Russ HAMILTON (UK)		
Rainbow	8/57	
We Will Make Love		6/57
Marvin HAMLISCH (US)		
The Entertainer	5/74	
HAMMER (US) also see MC Hammer		
Addams Groove	1/92	12/91
2 Legit 2 Quit	12/91	
MC HAMMER (US)		
Have You Seen Her	8/90	10/90
Pray	10/90	12/90
U Can't Touch This	5/90	7/90
Jan HAMMER (Cz)		
Crockett's Theme		10/87
Miami Vice Theme	10/85	10/85
Albert HAMMOND (UK)		
It Never Rains In Southern California	12/72	
Herbie HANCOCK (US)		
Rockit		8/83
HAPPENINGS (US)		
I Got Rhythm	5/67	
My Mammy	8/67	
See You In September	8/66	
HAPPY MONDAYS (UK)		
Kinky Afro		10/90
Step On		4/90
Paul HARDCASTLE (UK)		
Don't Waste My Time		3/86
19	7/85	5/85
Steve HARLEY (UK)		
Here Comes The Sun		8/76
✤ *with Sarah Brightman* The Phantom		
Of The Opera		2/86
Steve HARLEY & Cockney Rebel (UK)		
Judy Teen		6/74
Make Me Smile (Come Up And See Me)		2/75
Mr. Soft		8/74
Jimmy HARNEN With Sync (US)		
Where Are You Now	6/89	
HARPERS BIZARRE (US)		
The 59th Street Bridge Song		
(Feelin' Groovy)	4/67	
Anita HARRIS (UK)		
Just Loving You		8/67
Jet HARRIS (UK)		
Main Title Theme From 'Man With		
The Golden Arm'		9/62
Jet HARRIS & Tony Meehan (UK)		
Applejack		9/63
Diamonds		1/63
Scarlett O'Hara		5/63
Keith HARRIS & Orville (UK)		
Orville's Song		1/83
Major HARRIS (US)		
Love Won't Let Me Wait	5/75	
Max HARRIS (UK)		
Gurney Slade		12/60
Richard HARRIS (UK)		
MacArthur Park	6/68	7/68
Rolf HARRIS (Aus)		
Stairway To Heaven		2/93
Sun Arise		11/62
Tie Me Kangaroo Down, Sport	7/63	8/60
Two Little Boys		12/69
Ronnie HARRIS (UK)		
Story Of Tina		9/54
Thurston HARRIS (US)		
Little Bitty Pretty One	11/57	
George HARRISON (UK)		
All Those Years Ago	6/81	
Bangla Desh		8/71
Give Me Love (Give Me Peace On Earth)	6/73	6/73
Got My Mind Set On You	12/87	11/87
My Sweet Lord/Isn't It A Pity	12/70	1/71
What Is Life	3/71	
Noel HARRISON (UK)		
Windmills Of Your Mind		4/69
Wilbert HARRISON (US)		
Kansas City	5/59	
HARRY J. ALL STARS (J)		
Liquidator		11/69
Deborah HARRY (US)		
French Kissin' In The USA		11/86
I Want That Man		11/89
Corey HART (C)		
Never Surrender	7/85	
Sunglasses At Night	8/84	
Freddie HART (US)		
Easy Loving	11/71	
Richard HARTLEY/Michael Reed Orchestra (UK)		
The Music Of Torvill & Dean EP		3/84
Dan HARTMAN (US)		
I Can Dream About You	7/84	9/85
Instant Replay		11/78
Sensational Alex HARVEY BAND (UK)		
Delilah		8/75
Richie HAVENS (US)		
Here Comes The Sun	5/71	
Chesney HAWKES (UK)		
The One And Only	11/91	3/91
Edwin HAWKINS SINGERS (US)		
Oh Happy Day	5/69	6/69
Sophie B. HAWKINS (US)		
Damn I Wish I Was Your Lover	5/92	
HAWKWIND (UK)		
Silver Machine		8/72
Bill HAYES (US)		
The Ballad Of Davy Crockett	3/55	1/56
Isaac HAYES (US)		
Disco Connection		5/76
Theme From 'Shaft'	10/71	12/71
Richard HAYMAN & Jan August (US)		
A Theme From 'The Three Penny		
Opera' (Moritat)	3/56	
HAYSI FANTAYZEE (UK)		
John Wayne Is Big Leggy		8/82
Justin HAYWARD (UK)		
Forever Autumn		8/78

	US Top 20 Ent	UK Top 20 Ent
Justin HAYWARD & John Lodge (UK)		
Blue Guitar		11/75
Leon HAYWOOD (US)		
Don't Push It, Don't Force It		4/80
I Want'a Do Something Freaky To You	12/75	
Murray HEAD (UK)		
One Night In Bangkok	4/85	12/84
Superstar	5/71	
Roy HEAD (US)		
Treat Her Right	10/65	
Jeff HEALEY BAND (C)		
Angel Eyes	8/89	
HEART (US)		
All I Wanna Do Is Make Love To You	4/90	4/90
Alone	6/87	7/87
Barracuda	8/77	
Magic Man	10/76	
Never	11/85	3/88
Nothin' At All	6/86	
Straight On	12/78	
Stranded	12/90	
Tell It Like It Is	12/80	
There's The Girl	1/88	
These Dreams	3/86	3/88
What About Love?	8/85	
Who Will You Run To	9/87	
Ted HEATH (UK)		
Skin Deep		2/54
Swingin' Shepherd Blues		4/58
HEATWAVE (UK/US)		
Always And Forever/		
Mind Blowing Decisions		12/78
Boogie Nights	10/77	2/77
The Groove Line	6/78	2/78
Mind Blowing Decisions		7/78
Too Hot To Handle/Slip Your Disc To This		6/77
HEAVEN 17 (UK)		
Come Live With Me		7/83
Temptation		5/83
★ Temptation		11/92
HEAVY D. & The Boyz (US)		
Now That We Found Love	9/91	7/91
Bobby HEBB (US)		
Sunny	8/66	10/66
HEDGEHOPPERS ANONYMOUS (UK)		
It's Good News Week		10/65
HEIGHTS (US)		
How Do You Talk To An Angel	10/92	
HEINZ (UK)		
Just Like Eddie		9/63
HELLO (UK)		
New York Groove		11/75
Tell Him		12/74
Bobby HELMS (US)		
Jingle Bell Rock	1/58	
My Special Angel	11/57	
Jimmy HELMS (US)		
Gonna Make You An Offer You		
Can't Refuse		3/73
Joe HENDERSON (US)		
Snap Your Fingers	6/62	
Joe 'Mr. Piano' HENDERSON (UK)		
Sing It With Joe		6/55
Trudie		9/58
Jimi HENDRIX EXPERIENCE (US/UK)		
All Along The Watchtower		11/68
Hey Joe		1/67
Purple Haze		4/67
Voodoo Chile		11/70
The Wind Cries Mary		5/67
Don HENLEY (US)		
All She Wants To Do Is Dance	4/85	
The Boys Of Summer	1/85	3/85
Dirty Laundry	11/82	
The End Of The Innocence	8/89	
✣ with Patty Smyth Sometimes Love Just		
Ain't Enough	9/92	
Clarence 'Frogman' HENRY (US)		
But I Do	4/61	5/61
You Always Hurt The One You Love	6/61	7/61
Pauline HENRY (UK)		
Feel Like Making Love		11/93
HERD (UK)		
From The Underworld		10/67
I Don't Want Our Loving To Die		5/68

	US Top 20 Ent	UK Top 20 Ent
HERMAN'S HERMITS (UK)		
Can't You Hear My Heartbeat	3/65	
Dandy	10/66	
I Can Take Or Leave Your Lovin'		2/68
I'm Henry VIII I Am	7/65	
I'm Into Something Good	12/64	9/64
Just A Little Bit Better	10/65	9/65
Lady Barbara		12/70
Leaning On The Lamp Post	4/66	
Listen People	3/66	
Mrs. Brown You've Got A Lovely Daughter	4/65	
A Must To Avoid	1/66	1/66
My Sentimental Friend		5/69
No Milk Today		10/66
Silhouettes	5/65	3/65
Sleepy Joe		5/68
Something's Happening		1/69
Sunshine Girl		8/68
There's A Kind Of Hush	3/67	3/67
This Door Swings Both Ways	8/66	
Wonderful World	6/65	5/65
Years May Come, Years May Go		2/70
Patrick HERNANDEZ (F)		
Born To Be Alive	10/79	7/79
Nick HEYWARD (UK)		
Take That Situation		7/83
Whistle Down The Wind		4/83
Eddie HEYWOOD (US)		
✣ with Hugo Winterhalter Canadian		
Sunset	8/56	
Soft Summer Breeze	9/56	
HI TENSION (UK)		
British Hustle/Peace On Earth		9/78
Hi Tension		6/78
HI-FIVE (US)		
I Can't Wait Another Minute	8/91	
I Like The Way (The Kissing Game)	4/91	
She's Playing Hard To Get	9/92	
Al HIBBLER (US)		
He	10/55	
Unchained Melody	4/55	5/55
Bertie HIGGINS (US)		
Key Largo	3/82	
HIGH INERGY (US)		
You Can't Turn Me Off (In The Middle		
Of Turning Me On)	12/77	
HIGHWAYMEN (US)		
Cotton Fields	1/62	
Michael	8/61	9/61
Benny HILL (UK)		
Ernie (The Fastest Milkman In The West)		11/71
Chris HILL (UK)		
Bionic Santa		12/76
Renta Santa		12/75
Dan HILL (C)		
Sometimes When We Touch	1/78	4/78
Dan HILL (duet with Vonda Shepard) (C)		
Can't We Try	8/87	
Vince HILL (UK)		
Edelweiss		3/67
Look Around		11/71
Roses Of Picardy		6/67
HILLSIDE SINGERS (US)		
I'd Like To Teach The World To Sing	1/72	
HILLTOPPERS (US)		
From The Vine Came The Grape	2/54	
Marianne	3/57	
Only You (And You Alone)	12/55	2/56
Poor Butterfly	5/54	
Till Then	2/54	
Ronnie HILTON (UK)		
Around The World		6/57
A Blossom Fell		4/55
I Still Believe		12/54
No Other Love		4/56
Stars Shine In Your Eyes		9/55
Two Different Worlds		12/56
Veni Vidi Vici		12/54
Who Are We		7/56
Yellow Rose Of Texas		11/55
Joe HINTON (US)		
Funny	10/64	
Al HIRT (US)		
Java	2/64	
Edmund HOCKRIDGE (UK)		

	US Top 20 Ent	UK Top 20 Ent
Young And Foolish		2/56
Eddie HODGES (US)		
I'm Gonna Knock On Your Door	8/61	
Ron HOLDEN (US)		
Love You So	5/60	
Michael HOLLIDAY (UK)		
Gal With The Yaller Shoes		6/56
Hot Diggity		6/56
Stairway Of Love		6/58
Starry Eyed		1/60
The Story Of My Life		1/58
HOLLIES (UK)		
The Air That I Breathe	7/74	3/74
Bus Stop	9/66	7/66
Carrie-Anne	8/67	6/67
Gasoline Alley Bred		10/70
He Ain't Heavy, He's My Brother	3/70	10/69
★ He Ain't Heavy, He's My Brother		9/88
Here I Go Again		6/64
I Can't Let Go		3/66
I Can't Tell The Bottom From The Top		5/70
I'm Alive		6/65
Jennifer Eccles		4/68
Just One Look		3/64
Listen To Me		10/68
Long Cool Woman (In A Black Dress)	7/72	
Look Through Any Window		9/65
On A Carousel	5/67	3/67
Searchin'		10/63
Sorry Suzanne		3/69
Stay		1/64
Stop Stop Stop	12/66	10/66
We're Through		10/64
Yes I Will		2/65
Brenda HOLLOWAY (US)		
Every Little Bit Hurts	6/64	
Buddy HOLLY (US)		
Baby I Don't Care		8/61
Bo Diddley		6/63
Brown Eyed Handsome Man		3/63
It Doesn't Matter Anymore		3/59
Peggy Sue	12/57	1/58
Peggy Sue Got Married		10/59
Rave On		7/58
Wishing		9/63
HOLLYWOOD ARGYLES (US)		
Alley-Oop	6/60	
HOLLYWOOD BEYOND (UK)		
What's The Colour Of Money ?		8/86
HOLLYWOOD FLAMES (US)		
Buzz-Buzz-Buzz	1/58	
Eddie HOLMAN (US)		
Hey There Lonely Girl	2/70	11/74
Clint HOLMES (US)		
Playground In My Mind	6/73	
Leroy HOLMES (US)		
The High And The Mighty	8/54	
Rupert HOLMES (US)		
Escape (The Pina Colada Song)	12/79	
Him	3/80	
John HOLT (J)		
Help Me Make It Through The Night		1/75
HOMBRES (US)		
Let It Out (Let It All Hang Out)	11/67	
HOMER & JETHRO (US)		
The Battle Of Kookamonga	10/59	
HONDELLS (US)		
Little Honda	10/64	
HONEYBUS (UK)		
I Can't Let Maggie Go		4/68
HONEYCOMBS (UK)		
Have I The Right?	10/64	8/64
That's The Way		9/65
HONEY CONE (US)		
One Monkey Don't Stop No Show (Pt. 1)	1/72	
Stick-Up	9/71	
Want Ads	5/71	
HONEYDRIPPERS (UK/US)		
Sea Of Love	12/84	
Mary HOPKIN (UK)		
Goodbye	5/69	4/69
Knock Knock Who's There		3/70
Temma Harbour		2/70
Those Were The Days	10/68	9/68
Bruce HORNSBY & The Range (US)		

367

	US Top 20 Ent	UK Top 20 Ent
Every Little Kiss	7/87	
Mandolin Rain	3/87	
The Valley Road	6/88	
The Way It Is	11/86	
Johnny HORTON (US)		
The Battle Of New Orleans	5/59	
North To Alaska	11/60	
Sink The Bismarck	4/60	
HOT BUTTER (US)		
Popcorn	10/72	8/72
HOT CHOCOLATE (UK)		
Brother Louie		5/73
A Child's Prayer		9/75
Disco Queen		6/75
Don't Stop It Now		4/76
Emma	4/75	3/74
Every 1's A Winner	1/79	4/78
Girl Crazy		5/82
I Believe (In Love)		9/71
I'll Put You Together Again		1/79
It Started With A Kiss		7/82
Love Is Life		9/70
Man To Man		7/76
No Doubt About It		5/80
Put Your Love In Me		12/77
So You Win Again		6/77
What Kinda Boy You Looking For (Girl)		5/83
You Sexy Thing	1/76	11/75
★ You Sexy Thing		2/87
HOT (US)		
Angel In Your Arms	6/77	
HOTLEGS (UK)		
Neanderthal Man		7/70
HOTSHOTS (UK)		
Snoopy Vs. The Red Baron		6/73
HOUSE OF PAIN (US)		
Jump Around	9/92	5/93
HOUSEMARTINS (UK)		
Caravan Of Love		12/86
Happy Hour		6/86
HOUSE MASTER BOYZ & The Rude Boy Of House (US)		
House Nation		9/87
Thelma HOUSTON (US)		
Don't Leave Me This Way	3/77	3/77
Whitney HOUSTON (US)		
All The Man That I Need	1/91	1/91
Didn't We Almost Have It All	8/87	
Greatest Love Of All	5/86	5/86
How Will I Know	2/86	2/86
I Have Nothing	3/93	4/93
I Wanna Dance With Somebody (Who Loves Me)	6/87	5/87
I Will Always Love You	11/92	11/92
I'm Every Woman	2/93	2/93
I'm Your Baby Tonight	11/90	10/90
Love Will Save The Day	8/88	6/88
Miracle	6/91	
One Moment In Time	10/88	10/88
Queen Of The Night		11/93
Saving All My Love For You	9/85	12/85
So Emotional	12/87	11/87
Where Do Broken Hearts Go	4/88	
You Give Good Love	6/85	
Billy HOWARD (UK)		
King Of The Cops		1/76
Robert HOWARD & Kym Mazelle (UK/US)		
Wait		2/89
HUDSON-FORD (UK)		
Pick Up The Pieces		9/73
HUE & CRY (UK)		
Labour Of Love		8/87
HUES CORPORATION (US)		
Rock The Boat	6/74	8/74
HUMAN BEINZ (US)		
Nobody But Me	1/68	
HUMAN LEAGUE (UK)		
Being Boiled		1/82
Don't You Want Me	5/82	12/81
Human	10/86	9/86
(Keep Feeling) Fascination	8/83	5/83
The Lebanon		5/84
Love Action (I Believe In Love)		8/81
Mirror Man		11/82
Open Your Heart		10/81
HUMBLE PIE (UK)		
Natural Born Bugie		9/69
Engelbert HUMPERDINCK (UK)		
After The Lovin'	12/76	
Am I That Easy To Forget		1/68
Another Time Another Place		10/71
I'm A Better Man		9/69
The Last Waltz		9/67
Les Bicyclettes De Belsize		10/68
A Man Without Love		5/68
Release Me (And Let Me Love Again)	5/67	2/67
There Goes My Everything		6/67
The Way It Used To Be		2/69
Winter World Of Love		12/69
Ivory Joe HUNTER (US)		
Since I Met You Baby	12/56	
Tab HUNTER (US)		
Ninety-Nine Ways	4/57	4/57
Young Love	1/57	2/57
Steve 'Silk' HURLEY (US)		
Jack Your Body		1/87
Ferlin HUSKY (US)		
Gone	4/57	
Wings Of A Dove	2/61	
Brian HYLAND (US)		
Ginny Come Lately		6/62
Gypsy Woman	11/70	
Itsy Bitsy Teenie Weenie Yellow Polka Dot Bikini	7/60	7/60
Sealed With A Kiss	7/62	8/62
★ Sealed With A Kiss		7/75
Dick HYMAN (US)		
Moritat (A Theme From 'The Three Penny Opera')	2/56	3/56
Janis IAN (US)		
At Seventeen	8/75	
Society's Child (Baby I've Been Thinking)	7/67	
ICE CUBE (US)		
It Was A Good Day	4/93	
ICEHOUSE (NZ)		
Electric Blue	4/88	
IDES OF MARCH (US)		
Vehicle	5/70	
Billy IDOL (UK)		
Cradle Of Love	7/90	
Eyes Without A Face	6/84	
Hot In The City		2/88
Mony Mony	10/87	10/87
Rebel Yell		10/85
To Be A Lover	11/86	
White Wedding		8/85
Frank IFIELD (UK)		
Confessin'		6/63
Don't Blame Me		4/63
I Remember You	10/62	7/62
Lovesick Blues		10/62
Nobody's Darlin' But Mine		4/63
Wayward Wind		2/63
Julio IGLESIAS (Spa)		
Begin The Beguine (Volver A Empezar)		11/81
Quiereme Mucho (Yours)		3/82
Julio IGLESIAS & Willie Nelson (Spa/US)		
To All The Girls I've Loved Before	4/84	
Julio IGLESIAS (featuring Stevie Wonder) (SPa/US)		
My Love		8/88
IMAGINATION (UK)		
Body Talk		7/81
Just An Illusion		3/82
Music And Lights		7/82
IMPALAS (US)		
Sorry (I Ran All The Way Home)	4/59	
IMPRESSIONS (US)		
Amen	1/65	
❖ with Jerry Butler For Your Precious Love	7/58	
It's All Right	11/63	
Keep On Pushing	7/64	
People Get Ready	3/65	
Talking About My Baby	2/64	
We're A Winner	2/68	
INCANTATION (UK)		
Cacharpaya (Andes Pumpsa Daesi)		1/83
INCOGNITO featuring Jocelyn Brown (F/UK/US)		
Always There		7/91
INDEEP (US)		
Last Night A D.J. Saved My Life		2/83
Los INDIOS TABAJARAS (Bra)		
Maria Elena	11/63	11/63
INFORMATION SOCIETY (US)		
Walking Away	2/89	
What's On Your Mind (Pure Energy)	10/88	
Jorgen INGMANN (D)		
Apache	3/61	
James INGRAM (US)		
❖ with Patti Austin Baby Come To Me	1/83	3/83
I Don't Have The Heart	10/90	
❖ with Quincy Jones One Hundred Ways	4/82	
❖ with Linda Ronstadt Somewhere Out There	2/87	8/87
JAMES INGRAM & Michael McDonald (US)		
Yah Mo B There		2/85
Luther INGRAM (US)		
(If Loving You Is Wrong)I Don't Wanna Be Right	7/72	
INK SPOTS (US)		
Melody Of Love		5/55
INNER CIRCLE (J)		
Bad Boys	6/93	
Sweat (A La La La La Long)	10/93	5/93
INNER CITY (US)		
Big Fun		9/88
Good Life		12/88
INSPIRAL CARPETS (UK)		
Dragging Me Down		3/92
INTRUDERS (US)		
Cowboys To Girls	4/68	
INXS (Aus)		
Devil Inside	3/88	
Disappear	2/91	
Need You Tonight	12/87	11/88
Never Tear Us Apart	10/88	
New Sensation	7/88	
Suicide Blonde	10/90	
What You Need	3/86	
IRISH ROVERS (C)		
The Unicorn	5/68	
IRON MAIDEN (UK)		
Be Quick Or Be Dead		4/92
Bring Your Daughter To The Slaughter		1/91
Can I Play With Madness		3/88
The Clairvoyant		11/88
The Evil That Men Do		8/88
Fear Of The Dark (Live)		3/93
Holy Smoke		9/90
Infinite Dreams		11/89
Run To The Hills		3/82
The Trooper		7/83
Big Dee IRWIN (US)		
Swinging On A Star		12/63
Chris ISAAK (US)		
Wicked Game	2/91	12/90
ISLANDERS (US)		
The Enchanted Sea	11/59	
ISLEY BROTHERS (US)		
Behind A Painted Smile		5/69
Fight The Power Pt. 1	8/75	
Harvest For The World		8/76
I Guess I'll Always Love You		2/69
It's Your Thing	4/69	
That Lady	9/73	10/73
This Old Heart Of Mine	4/66	11/68
ISOTONIK (UK)		
Different Strokes		1/92
IT BITES (UK)		
Calling All The Heroes		8/86
Burl IVES (US)		
Funny Way Of Laughin'	5/62	
A Little Bitty Tear	1/62	2/62
IVY LEAGUE (UK)		
Funny How Love Can Be		2/65
Tossing And Turning		7/65
IVY THREE (US)		
Yogi	9/60	
JACK 'N' CHILL (UK)		
The Jack That House Built		2/88
Terry JACKS (US)		
If You Go Away		7/74
Seasons In The Sun	2/74	3/74
Chad JACKSON (UK)		

Title	US Top 20 Ent	UK Top 20 Ent
Blue Eyes	9/82	4/82
Candle In The Wind		3/74
Candle In The Wind (Live)	12/87	2/88
Crocodile Rock	1/73	11/72
Daniel	5/73	2/73
Don't Let The Sun Go Down On Me	7/74	
❖ with George Michael Don't Let The Sun Go Down On Me	1/92	12/91
Empty Garden (Hey Hey Johnny)	5/82	
Goodbye Yellow Brick Road	11/73	10/73
Grow Some Funk Of Your Own/I Feel Like A Bullet	2/76	
Healing Hands	10/89	6/90
Honky Cat	9/72	
I Don't Wanna Go On With You Like That	8/88	
I Guess That's Why They Call It The Blues	12/83	6/83
I'm Still Standing	7/83	8/83
Island Girl	10/75	
Little Jeannie	6/80	
Lucy In The Sky With Diamonds	12/74	12/74
Mama Can't Buy You Love	8/79	
Nikita	3/86	10/85
The One	8/92	6/92
Passengers		9/84
Philadelphia Freedom	3/75	4/75
Pinball Wizard		4/76
Rocket Man	7/72	5/72
Sacrifice/Healing Hands		6/90
Sad Songs (Say So Much)	7/84	6/84
Saturday Night's Alright For Fighting	9/73	7/73
Someone Saved My Life Tonight	7/75	
Song For Guy		12/78
Sorry Seems To Be The Hardest Word	12/76	12/76
Your Song	1/71	2/71
Elton JOHN & Kiki Dee (UK)		
Don't Go Breaking My Heart	7/76	7/76
True Love		11/93
Little Willie JOHN (US)		
Sleep	11/60	
Robert JOHN (US)		
The Lion Sleeps Tonight	2/72	
Sad Eyes	8/79	
JOHNNIE & JOE (US)		
Over The Mountain; Across The Sea	7/57	
JOHNNY & The Hurricanes (US)		
Beatnik Fly	3/60	3/60
Down Yonder		6/60
Ja-Da		3/61
Red River Rock	9/59	10/59
Reveille Rock		1/60
Rocking Goose		10/60
JOHNNY HATES JAZZ (UK)		
I Don't Want To Be A Hero		9/87
Shattered Dreams	5/88	5/87
Sammy JOHNS (US)		
Chevy Van	4/75	
Don JOHNSON (US)		
Heartbeat	10/86	
Holly JOHNSON (UK)		
Americanos		4/89
❖ with The Christians, Paul McCartney, Gerry Marsden & Stock Aitken Waterman Ferry 'Cross The Mersey		5/89
Love Train		2/89
Johnny JOHNSON & The Bandwagon (US)		
Blame It On The Pony Express		12/70
Breakin' Down The Walls Of Heartache		11/68
Sweet Inspiration		8/70
Laurie JOHNSON (UK)		
Sucu-Sucu		10/61
Marv JOHNSON (US)		
I Love The Way You Love	4/60	
I'll Pick A Rose For My Rose		2/69
You Got What It Takes	1/60	2/60
Michael JOHNSON (US)		
Bluer Than Blue	7/78	
Sabrina JOHNSON (US)		
Peace		9/91
JOHNSTON BROTHERS (UK)		
Hernando's Hideaway		10/55
JO JO GUNNE (US)		
Run Run Run		4/72
France JOLI (C)		
Come To Me	11/79	
JON & VANGELIS (UK/Gre)		

Title	US Top 20 Ent	UK Top 20 Ent
I Hear You Now		2/80
I'll Find My Way Home		1/82
Aled JONES (UK)		
Walking In The Air		12/85
Grace JONES (US)		
Pull Up To The Bumper/La Vie En Rose		2/86
Slave To The Rhythm		10/85
Howard JONES (UK)		
Everlasting Love	5/89	
Hide And Seek		3/84
Like To Get To Know You Well		8/84
New Song		10/83
No One Is To Blame	6/86	
Pearl In The Shell		6/84
Things Can Only Get Better	5/85	2/85
What Is Love		12/83
Jack JONES (US)		
The Race Is On	4/65	
Wives And Lovers	1/64	
Jimmy JONES (US)		
Good Timin'	5/60	6/60
Handy Man	2/60	4/60
Joe JONES (US)		
You Talk Too Much	10/60	
Oran 'Juice' JONES (US)		
The Rain	11/86	12/86
Paul JONES (UK)		
High Time		11/66
I've Been A Bad Bad Boy		2/67
Quincy JONES (US)		
Razzamatazz		7/81
Quincy JONES featuring James Ingram (US)		
One Hundred Ways	4/82	
Rickie Lee JONES (US)		
Chuck E.'s In Love	6/79	
Tammy JONES (UK)		
Let Me Try Again		5/75
Tom JONES (UK)		
A Boy From Nowhere		5/87
Daughter Of Darkness	6/70	5/70
Delilah		3/68
Detroit City		3/67
Funny Familiar Forgotten Feelings		5/67
Green Green Grass Of Home	2/67	11/66
Help Yourself		8/68
I (Who Have Nothing)	9/70	
I'll Never Fall In Love Again	9/69	8/67
I'm Comin' Home		12/67
It's Not Unusual	5/65	3/65
❖ with The Art Of Noise Kiss		11/88
Love Me Tonight	6/69	5/69
A Minute Of Your Time		12/68
She's A Lady	3/71	2/71
Till		11/71
What's New Pussycat?	7/65	9/65
With These Hands		8/65
Without Love (There Is Nothing)	1/70	12/69
The Young New Mexican Puppeteer		4/72
Janis JOPLIN (US)		
Me And Bobby Mcgee	3/71	
Jeremy JORDAN (US)		
The Right Kind Of Love	3/93	
JOURNEY (US)		
Be Good To Yourself	5/86	
Don't Stop Believing	12/81	
Faithfully	6/83	
Only The Young	3/85	
Open Arms	2/82	
Separate Ways (Worlds Apart)	3/83	
Who's Crying Now	8/81	
JOY DIVISION (UK)		
Love Will Tear Us Apart		7/80
JT & The Big Family (Ita)		
Moments In Soul		3/90
JUDAS PRIEST (UK)		
Breaking The Law		6/80
Living After Midnight		4/80
JUDGE DREAD (UK)		
Big Eight		5/73
Big Seven		1/73
Big Six		10/72
Big Ten		10/75
Je T'Aime (Moi Non Plus)		7/75
JUMP 'N THE SADDLE (US)		
The Curly Shuffle	1/84	

Title	US Top 20 Ent	UK Top 20 Ent
Rosemary JUNE (US)		
Apple Blossom Time		2/59
JUNIOR (UK)		
❖ with Kim Wilde Another Step (Closer To You)		5/87
Mama Used To Say		6/82
Jimmy JUSTICE (UK)		
Ain't That Funny		6/62
When My Little Girl Is Smiling		4/62
Bill JUSTIS (US)		
Raunchy	11/57	2/58
K-KLASS (UK)		
Rhythm Is A Mystery		11/91
K7 (US)		
Come Baby Come	12/93	
Bert KAEMPFERT (G)		
Red Roses For A Blue Lady	3/65	
Wonderland By Night	12/60	
KAJAGOOGOO (UK)		
Big Apple		10/83
Hang On Now		6/83
Ooh To Be Ah		4/83
Too Shy	6/83	2/83
KALIN TWINS (US)		
Forget Me Not	11/58	
When	7/58	8/58
Kitty KALLEN (US)		
In The Chapel In The Moonlight	7/54	
Little Things Mean A Lot	4/54	7/54
Nick KAMEN (US)		
Each Time You Break My Heart		11/86
Kiri Te KANAWA (NZ)		
World In Union		10/91
KANDIDATE (UK)		
I Don't Wanna Lose You		4/79
Eden KANE (UK)		
Boys Cry		3/64
Forget Me Not		1/62
Get Lost		9/61
I Don't Know Why		5/62
Well I Ask You		6/61
KANE GANG (UK)		
Closest Thing To Heaven		8/84
KANSAS (US)		
Carry On Wayward Son	3/77	
Dust In The Wind	4/78	
KAOMA (F)		
Lambada		12/89
KATRINA & The Waves (US/UK)		
Walking On Sunshine	6/85	6/85
Janet KAY (UK)		
Silly Games		7/79
KAYE SISTERS (UK)		
❖ with Frankie Vaughan Come Softly To Me		5/59
❖ with Frankie Vaughan Gotta Have Something In The Bank Frank		11/57
Paper Roses		8/60
KC & THE SUNSHINE BAND (US)		
Get Down Tonight	8/75	
Give It Up		8/83
I'm Your Boogie Man	5/77	
Keep It Comin' Love	9/77	
Please Don't Go	10/79	1/80
Queen Of Clubs		9/74
(Shake, Shake, Shake) Shake Your Booty	8/76	
That's The Way (I Like It)	11/75	8/75
❖ with Teri DeSario Yes, I'm Ready	2/80	
Ernie K-DOE (US)		
Mother-In-Law	4/61	
KEEDY (US)		
Save Some Love	5/91	
KEITH (US)		
98.6	1/67	
Jerry KELLER (US)		
Here Comes Summer		9/59
Johnny KEMP (US)		
Just Got Paid	8/88	
Tara KEMP (US)		
Hold You Tight	3/91	
Piece Of My Heart	7/91	
Eddie KENDRICKS (US)		
Boogie Down	2/74	
Keep On Truckin'(Pt 1)	10/73	

	US Top 20 Ent	UK Top 20 Ent
Chris KENNER (US)		
I Like It Like That (Pt.1)	7/61	
KENNY (UK)		
Baby I Love You, OK		6/75
The Bump		1/75
Fancy Pants		3/75
Heart Of Stone		3/73
Julie Ann		9/75
Nik KERSHAW (UK)		
Dancing Girls		5/84
Don Quixote		8/85
I Won't Let The Sun Go Down On Me		6/84
The Riddle		11/84
Wide Boy		3/85
Wouldn't It Be Good		2/84
Chaka KHAN (US) also see Rufus & Chaka Khan		
I Feel For You	11/84	10/84
I'm Every Woman		1/79
★ I'm Every Woman		5/89
KICKS LIKE A MULE (UK)		
The Bouncer		2/92
Johnny KIDD & The Pirates (UK)		
I'll Never Get Over You		8/63
Shakin' All Over		7/60
KIDS FROM 'FAME' (US)		
Friday Night (Live Version)		5/83
Hi-Fidelity		9/82
Starmaker		10/82
Greg KIHN BAND (US)		
The Breakup Song (They Don't Write 'Em)	9/81	
Jeopardy	3/83	
Andy KIM (US)		
Baby I Love You	7/69	
Rock Me Gently	8/74	9/74
KING FLOYD (US)		
Groove Me	1/71	
KING HARVEST (US)		
Dancing In The Moonlight	2/73	
KING (UK)		
Alone Without You		8/85
Love & Pride		1/85
The Taste Of Your Tears		11/85
B.B. KING (US)		
The Thrill Is Gone	2/70	
✤ with U2 When Love Comes To Town		4/89
Ben E. KING (US)		
Don't Play That Song (You Lied)	6/62	
Spanish Harlem	3/61	
Stand By Me	6/61	
★ Stand By Me	12/86	2/87
Supernatural Thing Part 1	4/75	
Carole KING (US)		
It Might As Well Rain Until September		9/62
It's Too Late/I Feel The Earth Move	6/71	9/71
Jazzman	10/74	
Nightingale	2/75	
One Fine Day	7/80	
So Far Away/Smackwater Jack	10/71	
Sweet Seasons	2/72	
Claude KING (US)		
Wolverton Mountain	7/62	
Dave KING (UK)		
Memories Are Made Of This		2/56
You Can't Be True To Two		4/56
Evelyn 'Champagne' KING (US)		
Love Come Down		10/82
Shame	8/78	
Jonathan KING (UK)		
Everyone's Gone To The Moon		8/65
Una Paloma Blanca		10/75
Solomon KING (US)		
She Wears My Ring		1/68
KING BROTHERS (UK)		
Mais Oui		8/60
Standing On The Corner		4/60
A White Sport Coat		6/57
KINGSMEN (US)		
The Jolly Green Giant	2/65	
Louie Louie	12/63	
KINGSTON TRIO (US)		
M.T.A.	7/59	
Reverend Mr. Black	5/63	
Tijuana Jail	4/59	
Tom Dooley	10/58	12/58
KINKS (UK)		

	US Top 20 Ent	UK Top 20 Ent
All Day And All Of The Night	2/65	11/64
Ape Man		1/71
Autumn Almanac		11/67
Come Dancing	7/83	
Days		8/68
Dead End Street		12/66
Dedicated Follower Of Fashion		3/66
Everybody's Gonna Be Happy		4/65
Lola	10/70	7/70
See My Friend		9/65
Set Me Free		6/65
Sunny Afternoon	9/66	6/66
Till The End Of The Day		1/66
Tired Of Waiting For You	4/65	2/65
Waterloo Sunset		5/67
A Well Respected Man	2/66	
You Really Got Me	11/64	8/64
Fern KINNEY (US)		
Together We Are Beautiful		3/80
Kathy KIRBY (UK)		
Dance On		9/63
Let Me Go, Lover		3/64
Secret Love		11/63
Bo KIRKLAND & Ruth Davis (US)		
You're Gonna Get Next To Me		7/77
KISS (US)		
Beth	11/76	
Crazy Crazy Nights		10/87
Forever	4/90	
God Gave Rock & Roll To You II		1/92
Hard Luck Woman	2/77	
I Was Made For Lovin' You	8/79	
Rock And Roll All Nite (Live Version)	1/76	
Mac & Katie KISSOON (UK)		
Don't Do It Baby		5/75
Sugar Candy Kisses		2/75
Eartha KITT (US)		
Santa Baby	1/54	
Somebody Bad Stole De Wedding Bell	3/54	
Under The Bridges Of Paris		4/55
KIX (US)		
Don't Close Your Eyes	11/89	
KLF (UK)		
America: What Time Is Love?		3/92
KLF featuring The Children Of The Revolution (UK)		
Last Train To Trancentral		5/91
3 A.M. Eternal	8/91	1/91
What Time Is Love		9/90
KLF featuring Tammy Wynette (UK/US)		
Justified And Ancient	3/92	12/91
KLF (AKA THE TIMELORDS) (UK)		
Doctorin' The Tardis		6/88
KLYMAXX (US)		
I Miss You	12/85	
Man Size Love	9/86	
KNACK (US)		
Good Girls Don't	11/79	
My Sharona	8/79	7/79
Gladys KNIGHT (US)		
Licence To Kill		7/89
Gladys KNIGHT & The Pips (US)		
Baby Don't Change Your Mind		6/77
Best Thing That Ever Happened To Me	4/74	8/75
Come Back And Finish What You Started		8/78
The End Of Our Road	3/68	
Every Beat Of My Heart	6/61	
Help Me Make It Through The Night		12/72
I Don't Want To Do Wrong	7/71	
I Heard It Through The Grapevine	12/67	
I've Got To Use My Imagination	1/74	
If I Were Your Woman	1/71	
Love Overboard	3/88	
Midnight Train To Georgia	10/73	6/76
Neither One Of Us (Wants To Be The First To Say Goodbye)	3/73	
On And On	7/74	
The Way We Were/Try To Remember (Medley)	7/75	5/75
Jean KNIGHT (US)		
Mr. Big Stuff	7/71	
Robert KNIGHT (US)		
Everlasting Love	11/67	
Love On A Mountain Top		1/74
Buddy KNOX (US)		
Hula Love	10/57	

	US Top 20 Ent	UK Top 20 Ent
Party Doll	3/57	
KOKOMO (US)		
Asia Minor	4/61	
KON KAN (C)		
I Beg Your Pardon	3/89	4/89
John KONGOS (SA)		
He's Gonna Step On You Again		6/71
Tokoloshe Man		12/71
KOOL & THE GANG (US)		
Celebration	1/81	11/80
Cherish	8/85	6/85
Fresh	5/85	12/84
Get Down On It	5/82	1/82
Hollywood Swinging	6/74	
Joanna	1/84	3/84
Jungle Boogie	2/74	
Ladies Night	12/79	11/79
Misled	2/85	
Ooh La La La (Let's Go Dancing)		11/82
Stone Love	4/87	
Tonight	4/84	3/84
Too Hot	3/80	
Victory	12/86	
(When You Say You Love Somebody) In The Heart		4/84
KORGIS (UK)		
Everybody's Got To Learn Sometime		6/80
KRAFTWERK (G)		
Autobahn		6/75
The Model/Computer Love		1/82
Billy J. KRAMER & The Dakotas (UK)		
Bad To Me	6/64	8/63
Do You Want To Know A Secret		5/63
From A Window		8/64
I'll Keep You Satisfied		11/63
Little Children	5/64	3/64
Trains And Boats And Planes		6/65
Lenny KRAVITZ (US)		
Are You Gonna Go My Way		2/93
It Ain't Over 'Til It's Over	7/91	7/91
KRIS KROSS (US)		
Jump	4/92	6/92
Warm It Up	7/92	
Kris KRISTOFFERSON (US)		
Why Me	11/73	
KRUSH (UK)		
House Arrest		1/88
Bob KUBAN & The In-Men (US)		
The Cheater	3/66	
KURSAAL FLYERS (UK)		
Little Does She Know		12/76
KWS (UK)		
Please Don't Go	9/92	5/92
Rock Your Baby		8/92
L.A. MIX (UK)		
Check This Out		6/88
L.L. COOL J (US)		
Around The Way Girl	2/91	
I Need Love	9/87	10/87
I'm That Type Of Guy	8/89	
L.T.D. (US)		
Back In Love Again	11/77	
LA BELLE EPOQUE (F)		
Black Is Black		10/77
Julius LA ROSA (US)		
Domani (Tomorrow)	8/55	
Eh Cumpari	1/54	
LABELLE (US)		
Lady Marmalade (Voulez-Vous Coucher Avec Moi)	3/75	
Patti LABELLE & Michael McDonald (US)		
On My Own	5/86	5/86
Cleo LAINE (UK)		
You'll Answer To Me		9/61
Frankie LAINE (US)		
Answer Me		1/54
Blowing Wild		1/54
Cool Water		6/55
Granada		3/54
Hawkeye		12/55
The Kid's Last Fight		4/54
Moonlight Gambler	1/57	12/56
My Friend		8/54
Rain Rain Rain		10/54

	US Top 20 Ent	UK Top 20 Ent
Rawhide		12/59
Sixteen Tons		1/56
Some Day	9/54	
Strange Lady In Town	7/55	
There Must Be A Reason	10/54	
A Woman In Love		9/56
Greg LAKE (UK)		
I Believe In Father Christmas		12/75
LAMBRETTAS (UK)		
D-a-a-ance		6/80
Poison Ivy		4/80
Major LANCE (US)		
Hey Little Girl	11/63	
The Monkey Time	9/63	
Um, Um, Um, Um, Um, Um	1/64	
LANDSCAPE (UK)		
Einstein A Go-Go		4/81
Ronnie LANE (UK)		
How Come		2/74
Don LANG (UK)		
Witch Doctor		6/58
Mario LANZA (US)		
Drinking Song		2/55
LARKS (US)		
The Jerk	12/64	
Nicolette LARSON (US)		
Lotta Love	1/79	
Denise LA SALLE (US)		
My Toot Toot		7/85
Trapped By A Thing Called Love	10/71	
LATINO RAVE (Various)		
Deep Heat '89		1/90
Stacy LATTISAW (US)		
Jump To The Beat		7/80
Cyndi LAUPER (US)		
All Through The Night	11/84	
Change Of Heart	1/87	
Girls Just Want To Have Fun	2/84	2/84
The Goonies 'R' Good Enough	7/85	
I Drove All Night	6/89	6/89
She Bop	8/84	
Time After Time	5/84	7/84
True Colors	10/86	10/86
What's Going On	5/87	
LAUREL & HARDY with The Avalon Boys (US)		
The Trail Of The Lonesome Pine		12/75
Joey LAWRENCE (US)		
Nothin' My Love Can't Fix		7/93
Lee LAWRENCE (UK)		
Crying In The Chapel		1/54
Suddenly There's A Valley		12/55
Steve LAWRENCE (US)		
Footsteps	4/60	4/60
Go Away Little Girl	12/62	
Party Doll	4/57	
Portrait Of My Love	5/61	
Pretty Blue Eyes	12/59	
Steve LAWRENCE & Eydie Gorme (US)		
I Want To Stay Here		9/63
Vicki LAWRENCE (US)		
The Night The Lights Went Out In Georgia	3/73	
Lindy LAYTON (UK) See Beats International featuring Lindy Layton		
Vicky LEANDROS (Gre)		
Come What May		4/72
LEBLANC & CARR (US)		
Falling	3/78	
LED ZEPPELIN (UK)		
Black Dog	2/72	
Whole Lotta Love	12/69	
Brenda LEE (US)		
All Alone Am I	10/62	2/63
As Usual	1/64	1/64
Break It To Me Gently	2/62	
Coming On Strong	11/66	
Dum Dum	7/61	
Emotions	1/61	
Everybody Loves Me But You	5/62	
Fool #1	11/61	
Here Comes That Feeling		6/62
I Want To Be Wanted	10/60	
I'm Sorry	6/60	8/60
It Started All Over Again		10/62
Let's Jump The Broomstick		3/61
Losing You	5/63	5/63

	US Top 20 Ent	UK Top 20 Ent
Rockin' Around The Christmas Tree		12/62
Speak To Me Pretty		4/62
Sweet Nothin's	3/60	4/60
That's All You Gotta Do	7/60	
Too Many Rivers	7/65	
You Can Depend On Me	4/61	
Curtis LEE (US)		
Pretty Little Angel Eyes	8/61	
Dee C. LEE (US)		
See The Day		11/85
Dickey LEE (US)		
I Saw Linda Yesterday	1/63	
Laurie (Strange Things Happen)	7/65	
Patches	9/62	
Jackie LEE (US)		
The Duck	1/66	
Rupert		2/71
Johnny LEE (US)		
Lookin' For Love	9/80	
Leapy LEE (UK)		
Little Arrows		9/68
Peggy LEE (US)		
Fever	8/58	8/58
Is That All There Is	11/69	
Mr. Wonderful		5/57
LEEDS UNITED F.C. (UK)		
Leeds United		5/72
LEFT BANKE (US)		
Walk Away Renee	10/66	
LEMON PIPERS (US)		
Green Tambourine	1/68	3/68
John LENNON/Yoko Ono/Plastic Ono Band (UK/Jap)		
Cold Turkey		11/69
Give Peace A Chance		7/69
Happy Xmas (War Is Over)		12/72
★ Happy Xmas (War Is Over)		12/80
Imagine	11/71	11/75
★ Imagine		1/81
Instant Karma (We All Shine On)	3/70	2/70
(Just Like) Starting Over	11/80	11/80
No. 9 Dream	2/75	
Nobody Told Me	2/84	1/84
Power To The People	5/71	3/71
Watching The Wheels	5/81	
Whatever Gets You Thru The Night	11/74	
Woman	2/81	1/81
Julian LENNON (UK)		
Saltwater		10/91
Too Late For Goodbyes	3/85	11/84
Valotte	12/84	
Annie LENNOX (UK)		
Little Bird/Love Song For A Vampire		2/93
Walking On Broken Glass	11/92	9/92
Why		4/92
Annie LENNOX & Al Green (UK/US)		
Put A Little Love In Your Heart	1/89	
Ketty LESTER (US)		
Love Letters	4/62	4/62
LETTERMEN (US)		
Goin' Out Of My Head/Can't Take My Eyes Off You	2/68	
Hurt So Bad	9/69	
The Way You Look Tonight	10/61	
When I Fall In Love	12/61	
LEVEL 42 (UK)		
It's Over		9/87
Lessons In Love	6/87	5/86
Running In The Family		2/87
Something About You	5/86	11/85
The Sun Goes Down (Living It Up)		9/83
To Be With You Again		5/87
LEVERT (US)		
Casanova	10/87	9/87
Jona LEWIE (UK)		
Stop The Cavalry		12/80
Barbara LEWIS (US)		
Baby, I'm Yours	8/65	
Hello Stranger	6/63	
Make Me Your Baby	11/65	
Bobby LEWIS (US)		
One Track Mind	9/61	
Tossin' And Turnin'	6/61	
Gary LEWIS & The Playboys (US)		
Count Me In	5/65	
Everybody Loves A Clown	10/65	

	US Top 20 Ent	UK Top 20 Ent
Green Grass	6/66	
My Heart's Symphony	8/66	
Save Your Heart For Me	7/65	
She's Just My Style	1/66	
Sure Gonna Miss Her	4/66	
This Diamond Ring	2/65	
Huey LEWIS & The News (US)		
Couple Days Off	6/91	
Do You Believe In Love	4/82	3/86
Doing It All For My Baby	9/87	
Heart And Soul	11/83	
The Heart Of Rock 'n' Roll	5/84	
Hip To Be Square	11/86	
I Know What I Like	5/87	
I Want A New Drug	3/84	
If This Is It	8/84	
Jacob's Ladder	2/87	
Perfect World	8/88	
The Power Of Love	8/85	9/85
★ The Power Of Love/Do You Believe In Love		3/86
Stuck With You	8/86	10/86
Jerry LEWIS (US)		
Rock-A-Bye Your Baby With A Dixie Melody	12/56	2/57
Jerry Lee LEWIS (US)		
Breathless	3/58	4/58
Great Balls Of Fire	12/57	12/57
High School Confidential		2/59
What'd I Say		5/61
Whole Lot Of Shakin' Going On	8/57	10/57
Linda LEWIS (UK)		
It's In His Kiss		8/75
Ramsey LEWIS TRIO (US)		
Hang On Sloopy	12/65	
The "In" Crowd	9/65	
John LEYTON (UK)		
Johnny Remember Me		8/61
Wild Wind		10/61
LFO (UK)		
LFO		8/90
LIEUTENANT PIGEON (UK)		
Mouldy Old Dough		10/72
Gordon LIGHTFOOT (C)		
Carefree Highway	11/74	
If You Could Read My Mind	2/71	
Sundown	6/74	
The Wreck Of The Edmund Fitzgerald	10/76	
Lil LOUIS (US)		
French Kiss		8/89
LIMAHL (UK)		
Never Ending Story		11/84
LIMMIE & THE FAMILY COOKIN' (US)		
A Walkin' Miracle		4/74
You Can Do Magic		8/73
Bob LIND (US)		
Elusive Butterfly	3/66	3/66
Kathy LINDEN (US)		
Goodbye Jimmy, Goodbye	6/59	
LINDISFARNE (UK)		
✤ with Gazza Fog On The Tyne (Revisited)		11/90
Lady Eleanor		6/72
Meet Me On The Corner		3/72
Run For Home		7/78
Mark LINDSAY (US)		
Arizona	2/70	
LINEAR (US)		
Sending All My Love	4/90	
Laurie LINGO & The Dipsticks (UK)		
Convoy GB		5/76
LINX (UK)		
Intuition		4/81
LIPPS INC. (US)		
Funkytown	5/80	6/80
LIQUID GOLD (UK)		
Dance Yourself Dizzy		3/80
Substitute		6/80
LISA LISA & Cult Jam (US)		
Head To Toe	5/87	
Lost In Emotion	9/87	
LISA LISA & CULT JAM With Full Force (US)		
All Cried Out	10/86	
LITTLE ANTHONY & The Imperials (US)		
Goin' Out Of My Head	12/64	
Hurt So Bad	3/65	

	US Top 20 Ent	UK Top 20 Ent
Tears On My Pillow	9/58	
LITTLE CAESAR & The Romans (US)		
Those Oldies But Goodies (Remind Me Of You)	6/61	
LITTLE DIPPERS (US)		
Forever	3/60	
LITTLE EVA (US)		
Keep Your Hands Off My Baby	12/62	
Let's Turkey Trot		4/63
The Loco-Motion	8/62	9/62
★ The Loco-Motion		8/72
LITTLE RICHARD (US)		
Baby Face		1/59
By The Light Of The Silvery Moon		4/59
The Girl Can't Help It		3/57
Good Golly, Miss Molly	3/58	3/58
Jenny, Jenny/Miss Ann	7/57	9/57
Keep A Knockin'	10/57	
Long Tall Sally	4/56	3/57
Lucille		7/57
LITTLE RIVER BAND (AUS)		
Cool Change	12/79	
Happy Anniversary	3/78	
Help Is On Its Way	11/77	
Lady	3/79	
Lonesome Loser	9/79	
Man On Your Mind	5/82	
The Night Owls	10/81	
The Other Guy	1/83	
Reminiscing	9/78	
Take It Easy On Me	2/82	
LIVERPOOL EXPRESS (UK)		
You Are My Love		7/76
LIVERPOOL F.C. (UK)		
Anfield Rap (Red Machine In Full Effect)		5/88
LIVING COLOUR (US)		
Cult Of Personality	5/89	
Love Rears It's Ugly Head		3/91
LIVING IN A BOX (UK)		
Blow The House Down		3/89
Living In A Box		4/87
Room In Your Heart		10/89
Dandy LIVINGSTONE (O)		
Suzanne Beware Of The Devil		10/72
LOBO (H)		
Caribbean Disco Show		8/81
LOBO (US)		
Don't Expect Me To Be Your Friend	2/73	
I'd Love You To Want Me	11/72	6/74
Me And You And A Dog Named Boo	5/71	7/71
Los LOBOS (US)		
La Bamba	8/87	7/87
Hank LOCKLIN (US)		
Please Help Me, I'm Falling	7/60	10/60
Johnny LOGAN (I)		
Hold Me Now		5/87
What's Another Year		5/80
LOGGINS & MESSINA (US)		
Your Mama Don't Dance	12/72	
Dave LOGGINS (US)		
Please Come To Boston	7/74	
Kenny LOGGINS (US)		
Danger Zone	7/86	
Footloose	3/84	5/84
Heart To Heart	1/83	
I'm Alright	9/80	
Meet Me Half Way	6/87	
Nobody's Fool	9/88	
This Is It	1/80	
Whenever I Call You 'Friend'	9/78	
LOLITA (A)		
Sailor (Your Home Is The Sea)	12/60	
LONDON BOYS (UK)		
London Nights		7/89
Requiem		5/89
LAURIE LONDON (UK)		
He's Got The Whole World (In His Hands)	4/58	12/57
LONDONBEAT (UK/US)		
I've Been Thinking About You	3/91	9/90
Shorty LONG (US)		
Here Comes The Judge	6/68	
LOOK (UK)		
I Am The Beat		1/81
LOOKING GLASS (US)		
Brandy (You're A Fine Girl)	7/72	

	US Top 20 Ent	UK Top 20 Ent
Trini LOPEZ (US)		
If I Had A Hammer	8/63	9/63
Denise LOR (US)		
If I Give My Heart To You	10/54	
A'me LORAIN (US)		
Whole Wide World	4/90	
Jerry LORDAN (UK)		
Who Could Be Bluer		3/60
Gloria LORING & Carl Anderson (US)		
Friends And Lovers	8/86	
Bonnie LOU (US)		
Tennessee Wig Walk		2/54
LOUCHIE LOU & Michie One (UK)		
Shout		6/93
John D. LOUDERMILK (US)		
Language Of Love		1/62
LOVE AFFAIR (UK)		
Bringing On Back The Good Times		8/69
A Day Without Love		10/68
Everlasting Love		1/68
Rainbow Valley		5/68
LOVE AND ROCKETS (UK)		
So Alive	7/89	
LOVE SCULPTURE (UK)		
Sabre Dance		12/68
LOVE UNLIMITED (US)		
It May Be Winter Outside (But In My Heart It's Spring)		3/75
Walkin' In The Rain With The One I Love	6/72	7/72
LOVE UNLIMITED ORCHESTRA (US)		
Love's Theme	1/74	3/74
Monie LOVE featuring True Image (UK)		
It's A Shame (My Sister)		10/90
LOVEBUG STARSKI (US)		
Amityville (The House On The Hill)		6/86
Bill LOVELADY (UK)		
Reggae For It Now		9/79
LOVERBOY (US)		
Heaven In Your Eyes	10/86	
Hot Girls In Love	8/83	
Lovin' Every Minute Of It	10/85	
This Could Be The Night	3/86	
Lene LOVICH (US)		
Lucky Number		3/79
LOVIN' SPOONFUL (US)		
Daydream	3/66	5/66
Did You Ever Have To Make Up Your Mind	5/66	
Do You Believe In Magic	10/65	
Nashville Cats	1/67	
Rain On The Roof	11/66	
Summer In The City	8/66	8/66
You Didn't Have To Be So Nice	1/66	
Jim LOWE (US)		
The Green Door	10/56	11/56
Nick LOWE (UK)		
Cruel To Be Kind	9/79	10/79
I Love The Sound Of Breaking Glass		3/78
Robin LUKE (US)		
Susie Darlin'	9/58	
LULU (UK)		
The Boat That I Row		5/67
Boom Bang-A-Bang		4/69
I'm A Tiger		12/68
Independence		2/93
Leave A Little Love		7/65
Let's Pretend		8/67
The Man Who Sold The World		2/74
Me The Peaceful Heart		3/68
❖ with Take That Relight My Fire		10/93
Shout		6/64
★ Shout		8/86
To Sir With Love	10/67	
Bob LUMAN (US)		
Let's Think About Living	10/60	10/60
Victor LUNDBERG (US)		
An Open Letter To My Teenage Son	12/67	
Arthur LYMAN (US)		
Yellow Bird	6/61	
Frankie LYMON & The Teenagers (US)		
Baby Baby		4/57
I Want You To Be My Girl	5/56	
I'm Not A Juvenile Delinquent		4/57
Why Do Fools Fall In Love	2/56	7/56
Kenny LYNCH (US)		
Up On The Roof		12/62

	US Top 20 Ent	UK Top 20 Ent
You Can Never Stop Me Loving You		7/63
Barbara LYNN (US)		
You'll Lose A Good Thing	8/62	
Cheryl LYNN (US)		
Got To Be Real	2/79	
Tami LYNN (US)		
I'm Gonna Run Away From You		6/71
Vera LYNN (US)		
A House With Love In It		12/56
My Son My Son		10/54
Phil LYNOTT (I) See Gary Moore		
LYNYRD SKYNYRD (US)		
Sweet Home Alabama	9/74	
What's Your Name	3/78	
Barbara LYON (UK)		
Stowaway		6/55
M PEOPLE (UK)		
Don't Look Any Further		12/93
How Can I Love You More?		2/93
Moving On Up		9/93
One Night In Heaven		6/93
M (UK)		
Pop Muzik	9/79	4/79
M/A/R/R/S (UK)		
Pump Up The Volume	2/88	9/87
MAC BAND featuring The McCampbell Brothers (US)		
Roses Are Red		7/88
Kirsty MacCOLL (UK)		
Days		8/89
❖ with The Pogues Fairytale Of New York		12/87
A New England		2/85
Byron MacGREGOR (US)		
Americans	1/74	
Mary MacGREGOR (US)		
Torn Between Two Lovers	1/77	3/77
Lonnie MACK (US)		
Memphis	7/63	
Giselle MacKENZIE (C)		
Hard To Get	7/55	
Ken MACKINTOSH (UK)		
The Creep		1/54
Patrick MacNEE & Honor Blackman (UK)		
Kinky Boots		12/90
MAD COBRA (J)		
Flex	1/93	
Johnny MADDOX (US)		
The Crazy Otto (Medley)	2/55	
MADNESS (UK)		
Baggy Trousers		9/80
Cardiac Arrest		3/82
Driving In My Car		7/82
Embarrassment		12/80
Grey Day		5/81
House Of Fun		5/82
It Must Be Love		12/81
★ It Must Be Love		2/92
Michael Caine		2/84
My Girl		1/80
One Step Beyond		12/79
Our House	7/83	12/82
Return Of The Los Palmas 7		2/81
Shut Up		10/81
The Sun And The Rain		11/83
Tomorrow's (Just Another Day)/Madness (Is All In The Mind)		3/83
Wings Of A Dove		8/83
Work Rest & Play (E.P.)		4/80
MADONNA (US)		
Angel	6/85	9/85
Bad Girl		3/93
Borderline	6/84	2/86
Causing A Commotion	10/87	9/87
Cherish	9/89	9/89
Crazy For You	4/85	6/85
★ Crazy For You		3/91
Dear Jessie		12/89
Deeper And Deeper	12/92	12/92
Dress You Up	9/85	12/85
Erotica	10/92	10/92
Express Yourself	7/89	4/93
Fever		4/93
Gambler		10/85
Hanky Panky	7/90	7/90
Holiday		2/84

	US Top 20 Ent	UK Top 20 Ent
★ Holiday		8/85
★ Holiday		6/91
Into The Groove		7/85
Justify My Love	12/90	12/90
Keep It Together	3/90	
La Isla Bonita	4/87	4/87
Like A Prayer	4/89	3/89
Like A Virgin	12/84	12/84
Live To Tell	5/86	5/86
The Look Of Love		12/87
Lucky Star	10/84	
Material Girl	3/85	3/85
Open Your Heart	1/87	12/86
Papa Don't Preach	7/86	7/86
Rain	9/93	8/93
Rescue Me	3/91	4/91
This Used To Be My Playground	7/92	7/92
True Blue	11/86	10/86
Vogue	5/90	4/90
Who's That Girl	8/87	7/87
MAI TAI (H)		
Body And Soul		9/85
History		6/85
MAIN INGREDIENT (US)		
Everybody Plays The Fool	9/72	
Just Don't Want To Be Lonely	4/74	
MAISONETTES (UK)		
Heartache Avenue		1/83
Miriam MAKEBA (SA)		
Pata Pata	11/67	
Carl MALCOLM (J)		
Fattie Bum-Bum		9/75
Richard MALTBY (US)		
Themes From 'The Man With The Golden Arm'	4/56	
MAMA CASS (US)		
Dream A Little Dream Of Me	8/68	9/68
MAMAS & The Papas (US)		
California Dreamin'	2/66	
Creeque Alley	5/67	8/67
Dedicated To The One I Love	3/67	5/67
I Saw Her Again	7/66	8/66
Monday Monday	4/66	5/66
Words Of Love	1/67	
MAN 2 MAN meet Man Parrish (US)		
Male Stripper		2/87
Melissa MANCHESTER (US)		
Don't Cry Out Loud	3/79	
Midnight Blue	7/75	
You Should Hear How She Talks About You	8/82	
Henry MANCINI & His Orchestra (US)		
How Soon		10/64
Love Theme From Romeo & Juliet	6/69	
Moon River	12/61	
Theme From Love Story	2/71	
MANFRED MANN (UK/SA)		
Come Tomorrow		1/65
Do Wah Diddy Diddy	9/64	7/64
5-4-3-2-1		2/64
Fox On The Run		1/69
Ha Ha Said The Clown		4/67
Hubble Bubble Toil And Trouble		5/64
If You Gotta Go Go Now		10/65
Just Like A Woman		9/66
Mighty Quinn	3/68	2/68
My Name Is Jack		7/68
Oh No Not My Baby		5/65
Pretty Flamingo		4/66
Ragamuffin Man		5/69
Semi-Detached Surburban Mr.James		11/66
Sha La La	12/64	11/64
MANFRED MANN'S EARTH BAND (UK/SA)		
Blinded By The Light	1/77	9/76
Davy's On The Road Again		6/78
Joybringer		10/73
Chuck MANGIONE (US)		
Feels So Good	5/78	
MANHATTAN TRANSFER (US)		
The Boy From New York City	7/81	
Chanson D'Amour		2/77
Walk In Love		4/78
MANHATTANS (US)		
Hurt		10/76
Kiss And Say Goodbye	6/76	7/76
Shining Star	6/80	

	US Top 20 Ent	UK Top 20 Ent
MANIC STREET PREACHERS (UK)		
Theme From M*A*S*H (Suicide Is Painless)		9/92
Barry MANILOW (US)		
Can't Smile Without You	3/78	
Copacabana (At The Copa)	7/78	
Could It Be Magic	8/75	
I Made It Through The Rain	1/81	
I Wanna Do It With You		11/82
I Write The Songs	12/75	
It's A Miracle	5/75	
Looks Like We Made It	6/77	
Mandy	12/74	3/75
The Old Songs	11/81	
Ready To Take A Chance Again	11/78	
Ships	11/79	
Somewhere In The Night	2/79	
Tryin' To Get The Feeling Again	5/76	
Weekend In New England	2/77	
Barry MANN (US)		
Who Put The Bomp (In The Bomp, Bomp, Bomp)	9/61	
Johnny MANN SINGERS (US)		
Up Up And Away		8/67
MANTOVANI (UK)		
Shadow Waltz		5/54
Swedish Rhapsody		1/54
MANTRONIX featuring Wondress (US/J)		
Got To Have Your Love		1/90
Take Your Time		5/90
MANUEL & His Music Of The Mountains (UK)		
Rodrigo's Guitar Concerto De Aranjuez		2/76
MARBLES (UK)		
Only One Woman		10/68
MARCELS (US)		
Blue Moon	3/61	4/61
Heartaches	11/61	
Little Peggy MARCH (US)		
I Will Follow Him	4/63	
Benny MARDONES (US)		
Into The Night	8/80	
Ernie MARESCA (US)		
Shout! Shout! (Knock Yourself Out)	5/62	
Kelly MARIE (UK)		
Feels Like I'm In Love		8/80
Teena MARIE (US)		
Behind The Groove		6/80
Lovergirl	3/85	
MARILLION (UK)		
Incommunicado		5/87
Kayleigh		5/85
Lavender		9/85
MARILYN (UK)		
Calling Your Name		11/83
Marino MARINI (Ita)		
Come Prima		10/58
Volare		10/58
MARKY MARK & The Funky Bunch featuring Loleatta Holloway (US)		
Good Vibrations	9/91	9/91
Wildside	12/91	
MARKETTS (US)		
Out Of Limits	1/64	
MAR-KEYS (US)		
Last Night	7/61	
Yannis MARKOPOULOS (Gre)		
Who Pays The Ferryman		1/78
Bob MARLEY & The Wailers (J)		
Buffalo Soldier		6/83
Could You Be Loved		7/80
Iron Lion Zion		9/92
Is This Love		1/78
Jamming/Funky Reggae Party		1/78
No Woman No Cry		7/81
One Love/People Get Ready		5/84
MARMALADE (UK)		
Baby Make It Soon		7/69
Cousin Norman		9/71
Falling Apart At The Seams		3/76
Lovin' Things		6/68
Ob-La-Di Ob-La-Da		12/68
Radancer		5/72
Rainbow		8/70
Reflections Of My Life	5/70	1/70
MARSHALL HAIN (UK)		
Dancing In The City		7/78

	US Top 20 Ent	UK Top 20 Ent
MARSHALL TUCKER BAND (US)		
Heard It In A Love Song	6/77	
Keith MARSHALL (UK)		
Only Crying		5/81
Lena MARTELL (UK)		
One Day At A Time		10/79
Ralph MARTERIE (US)		
Skokiaan	9/54	
MARTHA & THE MUFFINS (C)		
Echo Beach		4/80
MARTHA (REEVES) & The Vandellas (US)		
Dancing In The Street	9/64	2/69
Forget Me Not		3/71
Heat Wave	9/63	
Honey Chile		1/68
I'm Ready For Love		12/66
Jimmy Mack		4/67
Nowhere To Run		4/65
Quicksand		12/63
MARTIKA (US)		
I Feel The Earth Move		11/89
Love...Thy Will Be Done	10/91	9/91
Toy Soldiers	7/89	8/89
Bobbi MARTIN (US)		
For The Love Of Him	5/70	
Dean MARTIN (US)		
The Door Is Still Open To My Heart	10/64	
Everybody Loves Somebody	7/64	9/64
Gentle On My Mind		3/69
I Will	12/65	
Let Me Go, Lover		3/55
Mambo Italiano		2/55
Memories Are Made Of This	12/55	2/56
Naughty Lady Of Shady Lane		2/55
Return To Me	5/58	6/58
Sway	8/54	10/54
That's Amore	1/54	1/54
Under The Bridges Of Paris		4/55
Volare		9/58
Juan MARTIN (Spa)		
Love Theme From 'The Thorn Birds'		2/84
Ray MARTIN (UK)		
Swedish Rhapsody		1/54
Tony MARTIN (US)		
Here	4/54	
Stranger In Paradise	1/54	4/55
Walk Hand In Hand		7/56
Vince MARTIN With The Tarriers (US)		
Cindy, Oh Cindy	10/56	
Wink MARTINDALE (US)		
Deck Of Cards	10/59	5/63
Al MARTINO (US)		
I Love You Because	5/63	
I Love You More And More Every Day	3/64	
Spanish Eyes		8/73
The Story Of Tina		10/54
Wanted		6/54
MARVELETTES (US)		
Don't Mess With Bill	2/66	
The Hunter Gets Captured By The Game	3/67	
Playboy	6/62	
Please Mr. Postman	11/61	
Lee MARVIN (US)		
Wand'rin' Star		2/70
Richard MARX (US)		
Angelia	11/89	
Children Of The Night	6/90	
Don't Mean Nothing	8/87	
Endless Summer Nights	3/88	
Hazard	4/92	6/92
Hold On To The Nights	7/88	
Keep Coming Back	12/91	
Right Here Waiting	8/89	9/89
Satisfied	6/89	
Should've Known Better	11/87	
Take This Heart		9/92
Too Late To Say Goodbye	3/90	
MARY JANE GIRLS (US)		
In My House		5/85
Hugh MASEKELA (SA)		
Grazing In The Grass	7/68	
MASH (US)		
Theme From M*A*S*H (Suicide Is Painless)		5/80
Barbara MASON (US)		

	US Top 20 Ent	UK Top 20 Ent
Yes, I'm Ready	7/65	
Dave MASON (UK)		
We Just Disagree	11/77	
MATCHBOX (UK)		
Midnite Dynamos		6/80
When You Ask About Love		10/80
MATCHROOM MOB with Chas & Dave (UK)		
Snooker Loopy		5/86
Johnny MATHIS (US)		
A Certain Smile		10/58
Chances Are/The Twelfth Of Never	9/57	
Gina	10/62	
I'm Stone In Love With You		3/75
It's Not For Me To Say	6/57	
Misty	11/59	2/60
My Love For You		10/60
Someone		8/59
What Will My Mary Say	3/63	
When A Child Is Born (Soleado)		12/76
Johnny MATHIS & Deniece Williams (US)		
Too Much, Too Little, Too Late	5/78	4/78
Matt BIANCO (UK)		
Don't Blame It On That Girl/Wap Bam Boogie		7/88
Ian MATTHEWS (UK)		
Shake It	2/79	
MATTHEWS SOUTHERN COMFORT (UK)		
Woodstock		10/70
Susan MAUGHAN (UK)		
Bobby's Girl		11/62
MAUREEN (UK)		
Thinking Of You		7/90
Paul MAURIAT (F)		
Love Is Blue	2/68	4/68
Robert MAXWELL, His Harp & His Orchestra (US)		
Shangri-La	5/64	
Billy MAY (US)		
Main Title Theme From The Man With The Golden Arm		5/56
Brian MAY (UK)		
Driven By You		12/91
Too Much Love Will Kill You		9/92
Simon MAY (UK)		
Summer Of My Life		10/76
Curtis MAYFIELD (US)		
Freddie's Dead	10/72	
Superfly	12/72	
Kym MAZELLE (US) See Robert Howard & Kym Mazelle		
MC HAMMER (US) See Hammer		
MC MIKER 'G' & Deejay Sven (H)		
Holiday Rap		9/86
MC TUNES Versus 808 State (UK)		
The Only Rhyme That Bites		6/90
C.W. McCALL (US)		
Convoy	12/75	2/76
Peter McCANN (US)		
Do You Wanna Make Love	7/77	
Paul McCARTNEY/Wings (UK)		
Another Day/Oh Woman Oh Why Oh Why	4/71	3/71
Band On The Run	5/74	7/74
Coming Up (Live At Glasgow)	5/80	4/80
✤ with The Christians, Holly Johnson, Gerry Marsden & Stock Aitken Waterman Ferry 'Cross The Mersey		5/89
✤ with Michael Jackson The Girl Is Mine	11/82	11/82
Goodnight Tonight	4/79	5/79
Helen Wheels	1/74	12/73
Hi, Hi, Hi/C Moon	1/73	1/73
Jet	3/74	3/74
Junior's Farm/Sally G	12/74	
Let 'Em In	8/76	8/76
Listen To What The Man Said	6/75	6/75
Live And Let Die	8/73	6/73
Mary Had A Little Lamb		6/72
Maybe I'm Amazed	3/77	
Mull Of Kintyre/Girls School		11/77
My Love	5/73	4/73
No More Lonely Nights (Ballad)	11/84	10/84
Once Upon A Long Ago		12/87
Pipes Of Peace		1/84
Silly Love Songs	5/76	6/76
Spies Like Us	1/86	12/85
Take It Away	8/82	
Uncle Albert/Admiral Halsey	9/71	
Venus And Mars Rock Show	12/75	

	US Top 20 Ent	UK Top 20 Ent
Waterfalls		7/80
With A Little Luck	4/78	4/78
Wonderful Christmastime		12/79
Paul McCARTNEY & The Frog Chorus (UK)		
We All Stand Together		12/84
PAUL McCARTNEY & MICHAEL JACKSON (UK/US)		
Say Say Say	11/83	11/83
Paul McCARTNEY & Stevie Wonder (UK/US)		
Ebony And Ivory	4/82	4/82
Delbert McCLINTON (US)		
Giving It Up For Your Love	1/81	
Marilyn McCOO & Billy Davis Jr (US)		
You Don't Have To Be A Star (To Be In My Show)	12/76	4/77
Van McCOY (US)		
The Hustle	6/75	6/75
The Shuffle		5/77
McCOYS (US)		
Fever	12/65	
Hang On Sloopy	9/65	10/65
Jimmy McCRACKLIN (US)		
The Walk	3/58	
George McCRAE (US)		
I Can't Leave You Alone		10/74
It's Been So Long		8/75
Rock Your Baby	6/74	7/74
Gwen McCRAE (US)		
Rockin' Chair	7/75	
Gene McDANIELS (US)		
Chip Chip	2/62	
A Hundred Pounds Of Clay	4/61	
Tower Of Strength	10/61	
Chas McDEVITT SKIFFLE GROUP (UK)		
Freight Train		4/57
Michael McDONALD (US)		
I Keep Forgettin'(Everytime You're Near)	10/82	
✤ with Patti Labelle On My Own	5/86	5/86
Sweet Freedom	8/86	9/86
✤ with James Ingram Yah Mo B There	2/85	
Ronnie McDOWELL (US)		
The King Is Gone	10/77	
McFADDEN & WHITEHEAD (US)		
Ain't No Stoppin' Us Now	7/79	6/79
Bobby McFERRIN (US)		
Don't Worry Be Happy	9/88	10/88
Maureen McGOVERN (US)		
The Morning After (Song From The Poseidon Adventure)	7/73	
Freddie McGREGOR (J)		
Just Don't Want To Be Lonely		8/87
McGUINNESS FLINT (UK)		
Malt And Barley Blues		5/71
When I'm Dead And Gone		12/70
McGUIRE SISTERS (US)		
Goodnight, Sweetheart, Goodnight	7/54	
He	11/55	
May You Always		5/59
Muskrat Ramble	11/54	
Picnic	6/56	
Sincerely	1/55	7/55
Something's Gotta Give	6/55	
Sugartime	1/58	2/58
Barry McGUIRE (US)		
Eve Of Destruction	9/65	9/65
Maria McKEE (US)		
Show Me Heaven		9/90
Scott McKENZIE (US)		
San Francisco (Be Sure To Wear Some Flowers In Your Hair)	6/67	7/67
Brian McKNIGHT (US)		
✤ with Vanessa Williams Love Is	4/93	
One Last Cry	9/93	
Craig McLACHLAN & Check 1-2 (Aus)		
Mona		7/90
Tommy McLAIN (US)		
Sweet Dreams	8/66	
Malcolm McLAREN (UK)		
Double Dutch		7/83
Madame Butterfly		9/84
Malcolm McLAREN & The World's Famous Supreme Team (UK/US)		
Buffalo Gals		1/83
Bitty McLEAN (UK)		
It Keeps Rainin' (Tears From My Eyes)		8/93
Don McLEAN (US)		

	US Top 20 Ent	UK Top 20 Ent
American Pie (Pts 1 & 2)	12/71	2/72
★ American Pie		11/91
Crying	2/81	6/80
Vincent/Castles In The Air	4/72	6/72
Robin McNAMARA (US)		
Lay A Little Lovin' On Me	8/70	
Rita McNEIL (C)		
Working Man		11/90
Clyde McPHATTER (US)		
Lover Please	4/62	
A Lover's Question	12/58	
Ralph McTELL (UK)		
Streets Of London		12/74
Christine McVIE (UK)		
Got A Hold On Me	3/84	
Abigail MEAD & Nigel Goulding (US)		
Full Metal Jacket (I Wanna Be Your Drill Instructor)		10/87
Sister Janet MEAD (C)		
The Lord's Prayer	3/74	
MEAT LOAF		
★ Bat Out Of Hell		12/93
Dead Ringer For Love		1/82
I'd Do Anything For Love (But I Won't Do That)	10/93	10/93
Two Out Of Three Ain't Bad	6/78	
MECO		
Star Wars Theme/Cantina Band	9/77	10/77
Glenn MEDEIROS (US)		
Nothing's Gonna Change My Love For You	5/87	7/88
Glenn MEDEIROS featuring Bobby Brown (US)		
She Ain't Worth It	6/90	7/90
MEDICINE HEAD (UK)		
One And One Is One		5/73
Rising Sun		8/73
Bill MEDLEY & Jennifer Warnes (US)		
(I've Had) The Time Of My Life	11/87	11/87
★ (I've Had) The Time Of My Life		1/91
MEL & KIM (UK)		
F.L.M.		7/87
Respectable		3/87
Showing Out (Get Gresh At The Weekend)		11/86
That's The Way It Is		3/88
MEL & KIM (MEL SMITH & KIM WILDE) (UK) See Kim Wilde		
MEL & TIM (US)		
Backfield In Motion	12/69	
MELANIE		
Brand New Key	12/71	1/72
Lay Down (Candles In The Rain)	6/70	
Ruby Tuesday		11/70
John Cougar MELLENCAMP (US)		
Authority Song	5/84	
Cherry Bomb	12/87	
Crumblin' Down	11/83	
Hurts So Good	6/82	
Jack & Diane	8/82	
Lonely Ol' Night	9/85	
Paper In Fire	10/87	
Pink Houses	1/84	
R.O.C.K In The U.S.A.(A Salute To 60's Rock)	3/86	
Small Town	12/85	
MELLOW MAN ACE (US)		
Mentirosa	7/90	
Harold MELVIN & The Blue Notes (US)		
Bad Luck (Pt. 1)	6/75	
Don't Leave Me This Way		2/77
If You Don't Know Me By Now	11/72	2/73
The Love I Lost (Part 1)	11/73	
Wake Up Everybody (Pt. 1)	2/76	
MEMBERS (UK)		
Sound Of The Suburbs		3/79
MEN AT WORK (Aus)		
Down Under	12/82	1/83
It's A Mistake	8/83	
Overkill	4/83	
Who Can It Be Now?	9/82	
MEN WITHOUT HATS (C)		
The Safety Dance	8/83	10/83
Sergio MENDES (Bra)		
Never Gonna Let You Go	6/83	
Sergio MENDES & Brasil '66 (Bra)		
The Fool On The Hill	9/68	
The Look Of Love	6/68	

	US Top 20 Ent	UK Top 20 Ent
Scarborough Fair	12/68	
MENTAL AS ANYTHING (Aus)		
Live It Up		3/87
Freddie MERCURY (UK)		
The Great Pretender		3/87
I Was Born To Love You		5/85
In My Defence		12/92
Living On My Own		7/93
Love Kills		10/84
Freddie MERCURY & Montserrat Caballe (UK/Spa)		
Barcelona		11/87
★ Barcelona		8/92
MERCY (US)		
Love (Can Make You Happy)	5/69	
MERSEYBEATS (UK)		
Don't Turn Around		5/64
I Think Of You		2/64
Wishin' And Hopin'		8/64
MERSEYS (UK)		
Sorrow		5/66
METALLICA (US/D)		
Enter Sandman	10/91	8/91
Nothing Else Matters		5/92
MFSB featuring The Three Degrees (US)		
TSOP (The Sound Of Philadelphia)	4/74	
George MICHAEL (UK)		
Careless Whisper	1/85	8/84
A Different Corner	6/86	4/86
Faith	11/87	10/87
Father Figure	2/88	
Freedom	12/90	
❖ with Aretha Franklin I Knew You Were		
Waiting (For Me)	3/87	1/87
I Want Your Sex	7/87	6/87
Kissing A Fool	11/88	
Monkey	8/88	
One More Try	5/88	
Praying For Time	9/90	9/90
Toofunky	7/92	6/92
George MICHAEL & Queen (UK)		
Five Live (EP)		5/93
George MICHAEL & Elton John (UK)		
Don't Let The Sun Go Down On Me	1/92	12/91
Lee MICHAELS (US)		
Do You Know What I Mean	9/71	
MICHEL'LE (US)		
No More Lies	2/90	
Keith MICHEL (Aus)		
Captain Beaky/Wilfred The Weasel		2/80
MICK & PAT (UK) see Pat & Mick		
MICKEY & SYLVIA (US)		
Love Is Strange	2/57	
MIDDLE OF THE ROAD (UK)		
Chirpy Chirpy Cheep Cheep		6/71
Soley Soley		12/71
Tweedle Dee Tweedle Dum		9/71
Bette MIDLER (US)		
Boogie Woogie Bugle Boy	7/73	
From A Distance	11/90	
The Rose	6/80	
Wind Beneath My Wings	5/89	7/89
MIDNIGHT OIL (Aus)		
Beds Are Burning		5/89
MIDNIGHT STAR (US)		
Midas Touch		11/86
MIGIL FIVE (UK)		
Mockingbird Hill		4/64
MIKE + THE MECHANICS (UK)		
All I Need Is A Miracle	5/86	
The Living Years	2/89	1/89
Silent Running (On Dangerous Ground)	2/86	
John MILES (UK)		
Music		4/76
Slow Down		7/77
MILK & HONEY (Isr)		
Hallelujah		4/79
Chuck MILLER (US)		
The House Of Blue Lights	7/55	
Frankie MILLER (UK)		
Darlin'		11/78
Gary MILLER (UK)		
Garden Of Eden		1/57
Robin Hood		2/56
Story Of My Life		1/58
Yellow Rose Of Texas		11/55

	US Top 20 Ent	UK Top 20 Ent
Glenn MILLER (US)		
Moonlight Serenade		3/54
Moonlight Serenade/Little Brown Jug/In The Mood		2/76
Mitch MILLER (US)		
The Children's Marching Song	2/59	
Theme Song From 'Song For A Summer Night'	8/56	
The Yellow Rose Of Texas	8/55	10/55
Ned MILLER (US)		
From A Jack To A King	2/63	3/63
Roger MILLER (US)		
Chug-A-Lug	10/64	
Dang Me	7/64	
Engine Engine #9	6/65	
England Swings	12/65	
King Of The Road	2/65	5/65
Steve MILLER BAND (US)		
Abracadabra	7/82	7/82
Fly Like An Eagle	2/77	
Jet Airliner	6/77	
The Joker	12/73	9/90
Rock'n Me	10/76	12/76
Take The Money And Run	7/76	
MILLI VANILLI (F/G)		
All Or Nothing	2/90	
Baby Don't Forget My Number	6/89	
Blame It On The Rain	11/89	
Girl I'm Gonna Miss You	9/89	10/89
Girl You Know It's True	3/89	11/88
MILLIE (J) see Millie Small		
Frank MILLS (US)		
Music Box Dancer	4/79	
Garry MILLS (UK)		
Look For A Star		7/60
Hayley MILLS (UK)		
Let's Get Together	10/61	11/61
Stephanie MILLS (US)		
Never Knew Love Like This Before	10/80	11/80
Ronnie MILSAP (US)		
Any Day Now	7/82	
(There's) No Gettin' Over Me	8/81	
Garnet MIMMS & The Enchanters (US)		
Cry Baby	9/63	
MINDBENDERS (UK)		
A Groovy Kind Of Love	5/66	2/66
Sal MINEO (US)		
Start Movin' (In My Direction)	6/57	8/57
Marcello MINERBI (Ita)		
Zorba's Dance		8/65
Liza MINNELLI (US)		
Losing My Mind		8/89
Dannii MINOGUE (Aus)		
Baby Love		10/91
Jump To The Beat		8/91
Love & Kisses		4/91
Success		6/91
This Is It		7/93
Kylie MINOGUE (Aus)		
Better The Devil You Know		5/90
Give Me Just A Little More Time		1/92
Got To Be Certain		5/88
Hand On Your Heart		5/89
I Should Be So Lucky		2/88
Je Ne Sais Pas Pourquoi		10/88
The Loco-Motion	10/88	8/88
Never Too Late		11/89
Shocked		6/91
Step Back In Time		11/90
Tears On My Pillow		1/90
What Do I Have To Do		2/91
Wouldn't Change A Thing		8/89
Kylie MINOGUE & Jason Donovan (Aus)		
Especially For You		12/88
Kylie MINOGUE & Keith Washington (Aus/US)		
If You Were Here With Me Now		11/91
Sugar MINOTT (UK)		
Good Thing Going (We've Got A Good Thing Going)		4/81
MINT CONDITION (US)		
Breakin' My Heart (Pretty Brown Eyes)	3/92	
MIRACLES (US)		
Do It Baby	10/74	
Going To A Go-Go	2/66	
Love Machine	1/76	1/76

	US Top 20 Ent	UK Top 20 Ent
Mickey's Monkey	9/63	
Shop Around	1/61	
You've Really Got A Hold On Me	2/63	
Smokey Robinson & The MIRACLES (US)		
Baby, Baby Don't You Cry	2/69	
(Come 'Round Here) I'm The One You Need		2/71
I Don't Blame You At All		7/71
I Second That Emotion	12/67	
If You Can Want	4/68	
The Tears Of A Clown	11/70	8/70
The Tracks Of My Tears		6/69
MIRAGE (UK)		
Jack Mix II		6/87
Jack Mix IV		11/87
Danny MIRROR (H)		
I Remember Elvis Presley (The King Is Dead)		10/77
MISSION (UK)		
Tower Of Strength		2/88
MR. BEAN & Smear Campaign (UK)		
(I Want To Be) Elected		4/92
MR. BIG (US)		
Just Take My Heart	6/92	
To Be With You	2/92	3/92
MR. BIG (UK)		
Romeo		2/77
MR. BLOBBY (UK)		
Mr. Blobby		12/93
MR. BLOE (UK)		
Groovin' With Mr. Bloe		6/70
MR. MISTER (US)		
Broken Wings	11/85	1/86
Is It Love	5/86	
Kyrie	2/86	3/86
Guy MITCHELL (US)		
Call Rosie On The Phone		10/57
Chika Boom		1/54
Cloud Lucky Seven		1/54
Cuff Of My Shirt		2/54
Dime And A Dollar		4/54
Heartaches By The Number	11/59	1/60
Knee Deep In The Blues		3/57
Rock-A-Billy	5/57	5/57
Singing The Blues	11/56	12/56
Sippin' Soda		2/54
Joni MITCHELL (C)		
Big Yellow Taxi		8/70
Help Me	5/74	
MIXMASTER (Ita)		
Grand Piano		11/89
MIXTURES (Aus)		
The Pushbike Song		1/71
Hank MIZELL (US)		
Jungle Rock		4/76
MOBILES (UK)		
Drowning In Berlin		2/82
MOBY (US)		
Go		11/91
MOCEDADES (Spa)		
Eres Tu (Touch The Wind)	3/74	
MODERN ROMANCE (UK)		
Ay Ay Ay Ay Moosey		12/81
Best Years Of Our Lives		12/82
Everybody Salsa		9/81
High Life		3/83
Walking In The Rain		9/83
MODERN TALKING (G)		
Brother Louie		8/86
Domenico MODUGNO (Ita)		
Nel Blu Dipinto Di Blu (Volare)	8/58	9/58
MOJOS (UK)		
Everything's Alright		4/64
MOMENTS (US)		
Dolly My Love		8/75
Jack In The Box		2/77
Love On A Two-Way Street	5/70	
MOMENTS AND WHATNAUTS (US)		
Girls		3/75
Eddie MONEY (US)		
Baby Hold On	5/78	
I Wanna Go Back	3/87	
Peace In Our Time	2/90	
Take Me Home Tonight	11/86	
Think I'm In Love	9/82	

	US Top 20 Ent	UK Top 20 Ent
Never Be Anyone Else But You	3/59	
Poor Little Fool	7/58	8/58
Someday		11/58
Stood Up/Waitin' In School	1/58	
Sweeter Than You	8/59	
A Teenagers Romance/I'm Walkin'	5/57	
Teenage Idol	9/62	
Travelin' Man	5/61	6/61
A Wonder Like You	11/61	
Young Emotions	6/60	
Sandy NELSON (US)		
Let There Be Drums	12/61	12/61
Teen Beat	9/59	11/59
Willie NELSON (US)		
Always On My Mind	5/82	
✤ with Julio Iglesias To All The Girls I've Loved Before	4/84	
NENA (G)		
99 Luftballons (99 Red Balloons)	2/84	2/84
NERVOUS NORVUS (US)		
Transfusion	6/56	
Robbie NEVIL (US)		
C'est La Vie	12/86	1/87
Wot's It To Ya	8/87	
Aaron NEVILLE (US)		
✤ with Linda Ronstadt All My Life	4/90	
✤ with Linda Ronstadt Don't Know Much	11/89	11/89
Everybody Plays The Fool	10/91	
Tell It Like It Is	12/66	
NEW ATLANTIC (UK)		
I Know		3/92
NEW EDITION (US)		
Candy Girl		5/83
Cool It Now	11/84	
If It Isn't Love	9/88	
Mr. Telephone Man	2/85	
NEW KIDS ON THE BLOCK (US)		
Cover Girl	10/89	5/90
Didn't I (Blow Your Mind)	11/89	
Hangin' Tough	8/89	1/90
If You Go Away	3/92	12/91
I'll Be Loving You (Forever)	5/89	3/90
Let's Try Again/Didn't I Blow Your Mind		10/90
Please Don't Go Girl	10/88	
Step By Step	6/90	6/90
This One's For The Children	12/89	12/90
Tonight	9/90	8/90
You Got It (The Right Stuff)	2/89	11/89
NEW MUZIK (UK)		
Living By Numbers		2/80
NEW ORDER (UK)		
Blue Monday		4/83
★ Blue Monday		10/83
★ Blue Monday 1988		5/88
Confusion		9/83
Fine Time		12/88
Regret		4/93
True Faith		8/87
✤ with England World In Motion...		
NEW SEEKERS (UK)		
Beg Steal Or Borrow		3/72
Circles		7/72
I Get A Little Sentimental Over You		3/74
I'd Like To Teach The World To Sing	1/72	12/71
Never Ending Song Of Love		7/71
You Won't Find Another Fool Like Me		12/73
NEW SEEKERS featuring Eve Graham (UK)		
Look What They've Done To My Song Ma	10/70	
NEW VAUDEVILLE BAND (UK)		
Finchley Central		6/67
Peek-A-Boo		2/67
Winchester Cathedral	11/66	10/66
NEW WORLD (Aus)		
Rose Garden		3/71
Sister Jane		6/72
Tom-Tom Turnaround		7/71
NEWBEATS (US)		
Bread And Butter	9/64	
Run, Baby Run (Back Into My Arms)	11/65	11/71
Booker NEWBERRY III (US)		
Love Town		6/83
Anthony NEWLEY (UK)		
And The Heavens Cried		3/61
Do You Mind		4/60
I've Waited So Long		5/59

	US Top 20 Ent	UK Top 20 Ent
Idle On Parade (EP)		5/59
If She Should Come To You		7/60
Personality		7/59
Pop Goes The Weasel		6/61
Strawberry Fair		12/60
Why		1/60
Randy NEWMAN (US)		
Short People	1/78	
Juice NEWTON (US)		
Angel Of The Morning	4/81	
Break It To Me Gently	10/82	
Love's Been A Little Bit Hard On Me	6/82	
Queen Of Hearts	7/81	
The Sweetest Thing (I've Ever Known)	12/81	
Wayne NEWTON (US)		
Daddy Don't You Walk So Fast	7/72	
Danke Schoen	8/63	
Olivia NEWTON-JOHN (UK)		
Banks Of The Ohio		11/71
Deeper Than The Night	6/79	
✤ with John Travolta The Grease Megamix		12/90
Have You Never Been Mellow	2/75	
Heart Attack	10/82	
Hopelessly Devoted To You	8/78	11/78
✤ with Andy Gibb I Can't Help It	5/80	
I Honestly Love You	9/74	
If Not For You		4/71
If You Love Me (Let Me Know)	6/74	
Let Me Be There	1/74	
A Little More Love	1/79	1/79
Long Live Love		4/74
Magic	7/80	
Make A Move On Me	3/82	
Physical	11/81	11/81
Please Mr. Please	7/75	
Sam		7/77
Something Better To Do	10/75	
✤ with John Travolta Summer Nights	9/78	9/78
Twist Of Fate	12/83	
✤ with John Travolta You're The One That I Want	4/78	6/78
Olivia NEWTON-JOHN & Electric Light Orchestra (UK)		
Xanadu	9/80	7/80
Paul NICHOLAS (UK)		
Dancing With The Captain		11/76
Grandma's Party		1/77
Heaven On The 7th Floor	10/77	
Stevie NICKS (US)		
Edge Of Seventeen (Just Like The White Winged Dove)	4/82	
I Can't Wait	4/86	
If Anyone Falls	10/83	
Leather And Lace	12/81	
Stand Back	7/83	
Talk To Me	12/85	
Stevie NICKS with Tom Petty & The Heartbreakers (US)		
Stop Draggin' My Heart Around	8/81	
NICOLE (D)		
A Little Peace		5/82
Maxine NIGHTINGALE (UK)		
Lead Me On	8/79	
Love Hit Me		4/77
Right Back Where We Started From	3/76	11/75
NIGHT RANGER (US)		
Sentimental Street	7/85	
Sister Christian	5/84	
NILSSON (US)		
Coconut	8/72	
Everybody's Talkin'	10/69	
Without You	2/72	2/72
NINA & FREDERICK (D)		
Little Donkey		12/60
1910 FRUITGUM CO. (US)		
Indian Giver	3/69	
1 2 3 Red Light	9/68	
Simon Says	2/68	4/68
95 SOUTH (US)		
Whoot, There It Is	7/93	
NIRVANA (US)		
Come As You Are		3/92
Heart-Shaped Box		9/93
Smells Like Teen Spirit	12/91	12/91
NITTY GRITTY DIRT BAND (US)		
An American Dream	2/80	
Mr. Bojangles	2/71	

	US Top 20 Ent	UK Top 20 Ent
NKOTB (US) See New Kids On The Block		
Cliff NOBLES & CO. (US)		
The Horse	6/68	
Kenny NOLAN (US)		
I Like Dreamin'	2/77	
NOLANS (UK)		
Attention To Me		4/81
Don't Make Waves		5/80
Gotta Pull Myself Together		10/80
I'm In The Mood For Dancing		1/80
NOMAD featuring MC Mikee Freedom (UK)		
(I Wanna Give You) Devotion		2/91
Peter NOONE (UK)		
Oh You Pretty Thing		6/71
NU SHOOZ (US)		
I Can't Wait	5/86	6/86
Gary NUMAN (UK)		
Cars	5/80	9/79
Complex		12/79
I Die:You Die		9/80
She's Got Claws		9/81
We Are Glass		5/80
We Take Mystery (To Bed)		6/82
Gary NUMAN (TUBEWAY ARMY)		
Are 'Friends' Electric		6/79
NUTTY SQUIRRELS (US)		
Uh! Oh! Part 2	12/59	
NYLONS (C)		
Kiss Him Goodbye		7/87
OAK RIDGE BOYS (US)		
Bobbie Sue	3/82	
Elvira	6/81	
OBERNKIRCHEN CHILDREN'S CHOIR (G)		
Happy Wanderer		1/54
OCEAN (C)		
Put Your Hand In The Hand	4/71	
Billy OCEAN (UK)		
Caribbean Queen (No More Love On The Run)	10/84	11/84
Get Outta My Dreams Get Into My Car	3/88	2/88
Love Really Hurts Without You		3/76
Love Zone	9/86	
Loverboy	1/85	2/85
Red Light Spells Danger		4/77
Stop Me (If You've Heard It All Before)		12/76
Suddenly	5/85	6/85
There'll Be Sad Songs (To Make You Cry)	6/86	5/86
When The Going Gets Tough, The Tough Get Going	1/86	2/86
OCEANIC (UK)		
Insanity		9/91
Des O'CONNOR (UK)		
Careless Hands		12/67
I Pretend		6/68
One Two Three O'Leary		12/68
✤ with Roger Whittaker The Skye Boat Song		12/86
Hazel O'CONNOR (UK)		
D-Days		4/81
Eighth Day		9/80
Will You		6/81
Sinead O'CONNOR (I)		
Nothing Compares 2 U	4/90	1/90
Alan O'DAY (US)		
Undercover Angel	6/77	
ODYSSEY (US)		
Going Back To My Roots		6/81
If You're Lookin' For A Way Out		10/80
Inside Out		6/82
Native New Yorker		1/78
Use It Up And Wear It Out		7/80
ESTHER & ABI OFARIM (Isr)		
Cinderella Rockafella		2/68
One More Dance		7/68
OFF-SHORE (G)		
I Can't Take The Power		1/91
OHIO EXPRESS (US)		
Chewy Chewy	11/68	
Yummy Yummy Yummy	6/68	7/68
OHIO PLAYERS (US)		
Fire	1/75	
Funky Worm	5/73	
Love Rollercoaster	12/75	
Skin Tight	10/74	

	US Top 20 Ent	UK Top 20 Ent
O'JAYS (US)		
Back Stabbers	9/72	
For The Love Of Money	6/74	
I Love Music (Pt. 1)	12/75	3/76
Love Train	2/73	4/73
Put Your Hands Together	2/74	
Use Ta Be My Girl	6/78	7/78
O'KAYSIONS (US)		
Girl Watcher	9/68	
Danny O'KEEFE (US)		
Goodtime Charlie's Got The Blues	10/72	
Mike OLDFIELD (UK)		
In Dulce Jubilo/On Horseback		1/76
Moonlight Shadow		7/83
Portsmouth		12/76
Sentinel		10/92
Tubular Bells		4/74
OLIVER (US)		
Good Morning Starshine	6/69	9/69
Jean	9/69	
OLLIE & JERRY (US)		
Breakin'...There's No Stopping Us	7/84	7/84
OLYMPICS (US)		
Western Movies	8/58	10/58
OMD (UK) See Orchestral Manoeuvres In The Dark		
100 PROOF AGED IN SOUL (US)		
Somebody's Been Sleeping	11/70	
ONE HUNDRED TON & A FEATHER (UK)		
It Only Takes A Minute		7/76
Alexander O'NEAL (US)		
Criticize		11/87
✛ with Cherelle Saturday Love		1/86
ONYX (US)		
Slam	7/93	
OPUS III (UK)		
It's A Fine Day		2/92
OPUS (A)		
Live Is Life		7/85
ORANGE JUICE (UK)		
Rip It Up		3/83
ORB (UK)		
Blue Room		6/92
Little Fluffy Clouds		11/93
Roy ORBISON (US)		
Blue Angel	11/60	12/60
Blue Bayou		10/63
Cryin'	9/61	
Dream Baby	3/62	3/62
Falling		6/63
Goodnight		3/65
I Drove All Night		7/92
In Dreams	3/63	4/63
It's Over	5/64	5/64
Lana		7/66
Mean Woman Blues	10/63	
Oh Pretty Woman	9/64	9/64
Only The Lonely	7/60	9/60
Pretty Paper		12/64
Running Scared	5/61	6/61
There Won't Be Many Coming Home		12/66
Too Soon To Know		9/66
You Got It	4/89	1/89
ORCHESTRAL MANOEUVRES IN THE DARK (UK)		
Dreaming	5/88	
Enola Gay		11/80
(Forever) Live And Die		10/86
If You Leave	5/86	
Joan Of Arc		11/81
Locomotion		5/84
Maid Of Orleans (The Waltz Joan Of Arc)		2/82
Messages		6/80
Pandora's Box		7/91
Sailing On The Seven Seas		4/91
Souvenir		9/81
Talking Loud And Clear		7/84
ORIGINALS (US)		
Baby, I'm For Real	11/69	
The Bells	4/70	
Tony ORLANDO (US) also see Dawn		
Bless You		10/61
ORLEANS (US)		
Dance With Me	9/75	
Love Takes Time	5/79	
Still The One	9/76	
ORLONS (US)		

	US Top 20 Ent	UK Top 20 Ent
Don't Hang Up	11/62	
Not Me	7/63	
South Street	3/63	
The Wah-Watusi	7/62	
Jeffrey OSBORNE (US)		
✛ with Dionne Warwick Love Power	8/87	
On The Wings Of Love		8/84
You Should Be Mine (The Woo Woo Song)	8/86	
Ozzy OSBOURNE (UK) See Lita Ford (& Ozzy Osbourne)		
Donny OSMOND (US)		
Are You Lonesome Tonight/When I Fall In Love	1/74	11/73
Go Away Little Girl	8/71	
Hey Girl/I Knew You When	12/71	
Puppy Love	3/72	7/72
Sacred Emotion	8/89	
Soldier Of Love	5/89	
Sweet And Innocent	5/71	
Too Young	7/72	9/72
The Twelfth Of Never	4/73	3/73
Why/Lonely Boy	10/72	11/72
Young Love		8/73
Donny & Marie OSMOND (US)		
Deep Purple	3/76	
I'm Leaving It (All) Up To You	8/74	8/74
Morning Side Of The Mountain	1/75	1/75
Little Jimmy OSMOND (US)		
I'm Gonna Knock On Your Door		4/74
Long Haired Lover From Liverpool		12/72
Tweedle Dee		4/73
Marie OSMOND (US)		
Paper Roses	10/73	11/73
OSMONDS (US)		
Crazy Horses	12/72	11/72
Double Lovin'	6/71	
Down By The Lazy River	2/72	
Going Home		7/73
Hold Her Tight	8/72	
I Can't Stop		5/74
Let Me In		11/73
Love Me For A Reason	10/74	8/74
One Bad Apple	2/71	
The Proud One		6/75
Yo-Yo	10/71	
Gilbert O'SULLIVAN (I)		
Alone Again (Naturally)	7/72	3/72
Clair	12/72	10/72
Get Down	8/73	3/73
No Matter How I Try		12/71
Nothing Rhymed		12/70
Ooh-Wakka-Doo-Wakka-Day		7/72
Why Oh Why Oh Why		12/73
Johnny OTIS SHOW (US)		
Ma He's Making Eyes At Me		11/57
Willie And The Hand Jive	7/58	
OTTAWAN (F)		
D.I.S.C.O.		10/80
Hands Up (Give Me Your Heart)		9/81
OUR KID (UK)		
You Just Might See Me Cry		6/76
OUTFIELD (UK)		
Your Love	4/86	
OUTSIDERS (US)		
Time Won't Let Me	4/66	
OVERLANDERS (UK)		
Michelle		1/66
Reg OWEN (UK)		
Manhattan Spiritual	1/59	
OZARK MOUNTAIN DAREDEVILS (US)		
Jackie Blue	5/75	
P.M. DAWN (US)		
I'd Die Without You	10/92	
Looking Through Patient Eyes	4/93	3/93
Set Adrift On Memory Bliss	11/91	8/91
PABLO CRUISE (US)		
Cool Love	9/81	
Love Will Find A Way	7/78	
Whatcha Gonna Do	7/77	
Thom PACE (US)		
Maybe		7/79
PACIFIC GAS & ELECTRIC (US)		
Are You Ready	7/70	
Patti PAGE (US)		
Allegheny Moon	7/56	

	US Top 20 Ent	UK Top 20 Ent
Changing Partners	1/54	
Cross Over The Bridge	3/54	5/54
Go On With The Wedding	2/56	
Hush, Hush Sweet Charlotte	6/65	
Left Right Out Of Your Heart	8/58	
Mama From The Train	12/56	
Old Cape Cod	6/57	
Steam Heat	6/54	
Tommy PAGE (US)		
I'll Be Your Everything	3/90	
Elaine PAIGE (UK)		
Memory		6/81
Elaine PAIGE & Barbara Dickson (UK)		
I Know Him So Well		1/85
Robert PALMER (UK)		
Addicted To Love	4/86	6/86
Bad Case Of Loving You (Doctor, Doctor)	9/79	
I Didn't Mean To Turn You On	10/86	8/86
Mercy Mercy Me - I Want You		1/91
She Makes My Day		11/88
Simply Irresistible	8/88	
Robert PALMER & UB40 (UK)		
I'll Be Your Baby Tonight		11/90
PAPER DOLLS (UK)		
Something Here In My Heart (Keeps A-Tellin' Me No)		4/68
PAPER LACE (UK)		
Billy, Don't Be A Hero		3/74
The Black Eyed Boys		9/74
The Night Chicago Died	8/74	5/74
PAPERBOY (US)		
Ditty	4/93	
Vanessa PARADIS (F)		
Be My Baby		11/92
Joe Le Taxi		3/88
PARIS SISTERS (US)		
I Love How You Love Me	10/61	
Mica PARIS (UK)		
My One Temptation		6/88
Ryan PARIS (F)		
Dolce Vita		9/83
Simon PARK ORCHESTRA (UK)		
Eye Level		9/73
Fess PARKER (US)		
Ballad Of Davy Crockett	3/55	
Wringle Wrangle	2/57	
Ray PARKER JR. (US)		
Ghostbusters	7/84	9/84
I Don't Think That Man Should Sleep Alone		11/87
I Still Can't Get Over You	1/84	
Jamie	1/85	
The Other Woman	5/82	
Ray PARKER JR. & Raydio (US)		
Jack And Jill	4/78	5/78
A Woman Needs Love (Just Like You Do)	5/81	
You Can't Change That	7/79	
Robert PARKER (US)		
Barefootin'	6/66	
Jimmy PARKINSON (AUS)		
The Great Pretender		3/56
John PARR (UK)		
St. Elmo's Fire (Man In Motion)	8/85	10/85
Alan PARSONS PROJECT (UK)		
Eye In The Sky	8/82	
Games People Play	3/81	
Time	8/81	
Bill PARSONS (US) See Bobby Bare		
PARTNERS IN KRYME (US)		
Turtle Power		7/90
David PARTON (UK)		
Isn't She Lovely		1/77
Dolly PARTON (US)		
Here You Come Again	12/77	
✛ with Kenny Rogers Islands In The Stream	10/83	12/83
Jolene		6/76
9 To 5	1/81	
PARTRIDGE FAMILY (US)		
Breaking Up Is Hard To Do		7/72
Doesn't Somebody Want To Be Wanted	3/71	
I Think I Love You	11/70	
I Woke Up In Love This Morning	9/71	
I'll Meet You Halfway	6/71	
It's One Of Those Nights (Yes Love)		4/72
Lookin' Through The Eyes Of Love		2/73

379

	US Top 20 Ent	UK Top 20 Ent
Walking In The Rain		6/73
Don PARTRIDGE (UK)		
Blue Eyes		6/68
Rosie		3/68
PASADENAS (UK)		
I'm Doing Fine Now		2/92
Riding On A Train		10/88
Tribute (Right On)		6/88
PAT & MICK (UK)		
I Haven't Stopped Dancing Yet		4/89
Let's All Chant		5/88
PATIENCE & PRUDENCE (US)		
Gonna Get Along Without Ya Now	12/56	
Tonight You Belong To Me	9/56	
PAUL & PAULA (US)		
Hey Paula	1/63	3/63
Young Lovers	4/63	5/63
Billy PAUL (US)		
Me And Mrs. Jones	12/72	2/73
Les PAUL & Mary Ford (US)		
Hummingbird	7/55	
I'm A Fool To Care	8/54	
Vaya Con Dios	1/54	
Whither Thou Goest	10/54	
Owen PAUL (UK)		
My Favourite Waste Of Time		6/86
Luciano PAVAROTTI (Ita)		
Nessun Dorma		6/90
Freda PAYNE (US)		
Band Of Gold	6/70	9/70
Bring The Boys Home	8/71	
PEACHES & HERB (US)		
Close Your Eyes	5/67	
Love Is Strange	11/67	
Reunited	4/79	5/79
Shake Your Groove Thing	3/79	
PEARLS (UK)		
Guilty		7/74
Johnny PEARSON ORCHESTRA (UK)		
Sleepy Shores		1/72
PEBBLES (US)		
Girlfriend	3/88	4/88
Giving You The Benefit	10/90	
Love Makes Things Happen	2/91	
Mercedes Boy	6/88	
Donald PEERS (UK)		
Please Don't Go		2/69
PENGUINS (US)		
Earth Angel (Will You Be Mine)	1/55	
Ce Ce PENISTON (US)		
Finally	12/91	3/92
Keep On Walkin'	8/92	5/92
We Got A Love Thang		1/92
Michael PENN (US)		
No Myth	3/90	
PEOPLE (US)		
I Love You	6/68	
PEOPLES CHOICE (US)		
Do It Any Way You Wanna	11/75	
PEPPERS (F)		
Pepper Box		11/74
PEPSI & SHIRLIE (UK)		
Goodbye Stranger		6/87
Heartache		2/87
PERFECT GENTLEMEN (US)		
Ooh La La (I Can't Get Over You)	5/90	
Emilio PERICOLI (Ita)		
Al Di La	6/62	
Carl PERKINS (US)		
Blue Suede Shoes	3/56	5/56
Steve PERRY (US)		
Oh, Sherrie	5/84	
PET SHOP BOYS (UK)		
Always On My Mind	5/88	12/87
Can You Forgive Her?		6/93
Domino Dancing		10/88
Go West		9/93
Heart		4/88
I Wouldn't Normally Do This Kind Of Thing		12/93
It's A Sin	10/87	6/87
It's Alright		7/89
Left To My Own Devices		11/88
Opportunities (Let's Make Lots Of Money)	7/86	6/86
So Hard		10/90
Suburbia		10/86

	US Top 20 Ent	UK Top 20 Ent
West End Girls	4/86	12/85
Where The Streets Have No Name-Can't Take My Eyes Off You/How Can You Expect To Be Taken Seriously		3/91
PET SHOP BOYS & Dusty Springfield (UK)		
What Have I Done To Deserve This	2/88	8/87
PETER & GORDON (UK)		
I Go To Pieces	2/65	
Lady Godiva	11/66	
Nobody I Know	8/64	6/64
To Know You Is To Love You		7/65
True Love Ways		5/65
A World Without Love	5/64	4/64
PETER, PAUL & MARY (US)		
Blowin' In The Wind	7/63	11/63
Don't Think Twice It's All Right	10/63	
I Dig Rock And Roll Music	9/67	
If I Had A Hammer	10/62	
Leaving On A Jet Plane	11/69	1/70
Puff The Magic Dragon	4/63	
PETERS & LEE (UK)		
Don't Stay Away Too Long		5/74
Welcome Home		6/73
Paul PETERSON (US)		
My Dad	1/63	
Ray PETERSON (US)		
Corinna, Corinna	12/60	
Tell Laura I Love Her	7/60	
Tom PETTY (US)		
Free Fallin'	1/90	
I Won't Back Down	7/89	
Tom PETTY & The Heartbreakers (US)		
Don't Come Around Here No More	5/85	
Don't Do Me Like That	1/80	
Refugee	3/80	
✤ with Stevie Nicks Stop Draggin' My Heart Around	8/81	
PhD (UK)		
I Won't Let You Down		5/82
Esther PHILLIPS (US)		
What A Diff'rence A Day Makes		11/75
Little Esther PHILLIPS (US)		
Release Me	12/62	
Phil PHILLIPS With The Twilights (US)		
Sea Of Love	8/59	
Bobby 'Boris' PICKETT & The Crypt Kickers (US)		
Monster Mash	9/62	
★ Monster Mash	7/73	9/73
Wilson PICKETT (US)		
Don't Knock My Love (Pt. 1)	6/71	
Engine Number 9	11/70	
Funky Broadway	9/67	
In The Midnight Hour		10/65
Land Of 1,000 Dances	9/66	
634-5789	3/66	
PICKETTYWITCH (UK)		
That Same Old Feeling		3/70
PIGBAG (UK)		
Papa's Got A Brand New Pigbag		4/82
PIGLETS (UK)		
Johnny Reggae		11/71
P.I.L. (UK) See Public Image Ltd.		
PILOT (UK)		
January		2/75
Magic	6/75	11/74
PILTDOWN MEN (US)		
MacDonald's Cave		10/60
PINK FLOYD (UK)		
Another Brick In The Wall	3/80	12/79
Money	7/73	
See Emily Play		7/67
PINKEES (UK)		
Danger Games		10/82
PINKERTON'S ASSORTED COLOURS (UK)		
Mirror Mirror		2/66
PIONEERS (J)		
Let Your Yeah Be Yeah		8/71
PIPKINS (UK)		
Gimme Dat Ding	7/70	4/70
PIRANHAS (UK)		
Tom Hark		8/80
Gene PITNEY (US)		
Backstage		3/66
Half Heaven-Half Heartache	2/63	
I Must Be Seeing Things		3/65

	US Top 20 Ent	UK Top 20 Ent
I'm Gonna Be Strong	11/64	11/64
It Hurts To Be In Love	9/64	
Just One Smile		12/66
Last Chance To Turn Around	6/65	
Looking Through The Eyes Of Love		6/65
(The Man Who Shot) Liberty Valence	6/62	
Mecca	4/63	
Nobody Needs Your Love		6/66
Only Love Can Break A Heart	10/62	
Princess In Rags		11/65
Something's Gotten Hold Of My Heart		12/67
✤ with Marc Almond Something's Gotten Hold Of My Heart		1/89
That Girl Belongs To Yesterday		3/64
Town Without Pity	1/62	
Twenty Four Hours From Tulsa		12/63
Robert PLANT (UK)		
Big Log		8/83
PLASTIC BERTRAND (B)		
Ca Plane Pour Moi		6/78
PLASTIC ONO BAND (UK) See John Lennon		
PLASTIC PENNY (UK)		
Everything I Am		1/68
PLATTERS (US)		
Enchanted	5/59	
The Great Pretender	12/55	9/56
Harbor Lights	3/60	2/60
I'm Sorry/He's Mine	4/57	
My Prayer	7/56	11/56
Only You	10/55	9/56
Smoke Gets In Your Eyes	12/58	1/59
Twilight Time	4/58	6/58
You'll Never Ever Know/It Isn't Right	10/56	
(You've Got) The Magic Touch	4/56	
PLAYER (US)		
Baby Come Back	12/77	
This Time I'm In It For Love	5/78	
PLAYERS ASSOCIATION (US)		
Turn The Music Up		4/79
PLAYMATES (US)		
Beep Beep	11/58	
POGUES & The Dubliners (I/UK)		
The Irish Rover		4/87
POGUES featuring Kirsty MacColl (I/UK)		
Fairytale Of New York		12/87
POINTER SISTERS (US)		
American Music	8/82	
Automatic	3/84	5/84
Dare Me	9/85	
Fairytale	12/74	
Fire	1/79	
He's So Shy	10/80	
I'm So Excited	10/84	11/84
Jump (For My Love)	6/84	7/84
Neutron Dance	2/85	
Should I Do It	3/82	
Slow Hand	7/81	9/81
Yes We Can Can	10/73	
Bonnie POINTER (US)		
Heaven Must Have Sent You	9/79	
POISON (US)		
Every Rose Has Its Thorn	12/88	3/89
I Won't Forget You	11/87	
Nothin' But A Good Time	6/88	
Something To Believe In	11/90	
Talk Dirty To Me	5/87	
Unskinny Bop	8/90	
Your Mama Don't Dance	4/89	5/89
POLICE (UK/US)		
Can't Stand Losing You		8/79
De Do Do Do, De Da Da Da	12/80	12/80
Don't Stand So Close To Me	3/81	9/80
Every Breath You Take	6/83	5/83
Every Little Thing She Does Is Magic	11/81	11/81
Invisible Sun		10/81
King Of Pain	9/83	
Message In A Bottle		9/79
Roxanne		5/79
So Lonely		3/80
Spirits In The Material World	3/82	12/81
Synchronicity II	12/83	
Walking On The Moon		12/79
Wrapped Around Your Finger	2/84	7/83
SU POLLARD (UK)		
Starting Together		2/86

380

	US Top 20 Ent	UK Top 20 Ent
PONI-TAILS (US)		
Born Too Late	8/58	9/58
Brian POOLE & The Tremeloes (UK)		
Candy Man		2/64
Do You Love Me		9/63
Someone Someone		6/64
Twist And Shout		7/63
POPPY FAMILY (C)		
Which Way You Goin' Billy	5/70	9/70
PORTRAIT (US)		
Here We Go Again!	2/93	
Sandy POSEY (US)		
Born A Woman	9/66	
Single Girl	1/67	
POSITIVE K (US)		
I Got A Man	3/93	
Mike POST (US)		
The Rockford Files	8/75	
Mike POST featuring Larry Carlton (US)		
The Theme From Hill Street Blues	11/81	
Frank POURCEL'S FRENCH FIDDLES (F)		
Only You	5/59	
Cozy POWELL (UK)		
Dance With The Devil		1/74
Na Na Na		9/74
Jane POWELL (US)		
True Love	10/56	
POWER STATION (UK/US)		
Get It On (Bang A Gong)	7/85	
Some Like It Hot	4/85	
Joey POWERS (US)		
Midnight Mary	1/64	
Perez PRADO (US)		
Cherry Pink And Apple Blossom White	3/55	4/55
Patricia	6/58	8/58
PRAISE (UK)		
Only You		2/91
PRATT & McCLAIN (US)		
Happy Days	5/76	
PREFAB SPROUT (UK)		
The King Of Rock 'n' Roll		5/88
PRESIDENTS (US)		
5-10-15-20 (25-30 Years Of Love)	12/70	
Elvis PRESLEY (US)		
All Shook Up	4/57	6/57
Always On My Mind		1/73
An American Trilogy		7/72
Are You Lonesome Tonight ?	11/60	1/61
Ask Me	11/64	
Big Hunk O' Love	7/59	7/59
Blue Christmas		12/64
Blue Moon		11/56
Blue Suede Shoes		6/56
Bossa Nova Baby	11/63	
Burning Love	10/72	10/72
Can't Help Falling In Love	12/61	2/62
Crying In The Chapel	5/65	6/65
Don't Cry Daddy/Rubberneckin'	1/70	3/70
Don't/I Beg Of You	2/58	3/58
Follow That Dream E.P.		6/62
A Fool Such As I	4/59	4/59
Girl Of My Best Friend		8/60
★ Girl Of My Best Friend		10/76
Good Luck Charm	3/62	5/62
Hard Headed Woman	7/58	7/58
Heartbreak Hotel	3/56	5/56
★ Heartbreak Hotel		8/71
Hound Dog/Don't Be Cruel	8/56	9/56
I Feel So Bad	5/61	
I Got Stung	11/58	1/59
I Just Can't Help Believing		1/72
I Need Your Love Tonight	4/59	4/59
I Want You, I Need You, I Love You	6/56	9/56
I'm Yours	10/65	
I've Lost You		11/70
If Every Day Was Like Christmas		12/66
If I Can Dream	2/69	3/69
In The Ghetto	5/69	6/69
It's Now Or Never	8/60	11/60
It's Only Love/Beyond The Reef		9/80
Jailhouse Rock	10/57	1/58
Kid Galahad E.P.		11/62
King Creole		10/58
Kiss Me Quick		1/64
Kissin' Cousins	3/64	7/64
Little Sister	9/61	
Love Letters		7/66
Love Me	12/56	
Love Me Tender	10/56	12/56
(Marie's The Name) His Latest Flame	9/61	11/61
A Mess Of Blues		8/60
Moody Blue		3/77
My Boy		12/74
My Way		12/77
My Wish Came True	8/59	
One Broken Heart For Sale	3/63	3/63
One Night	11/58	1/59
Paralysed		9/57
Party		10/57
Promised Land		2/75
Rags To Riches		6/71
Return To Sender	11/62	11/62
Rock-A-Hula-Baby		2/62
Santa Bring My Baby Back To Me		11/57
She's Not You	8/62	9/62
Stuck On You	4/60	4/60
(Such An) Easy Question	7/65	
Such A Night		9/64
Surrender	2/61	5/61
Suspicion		2/77
Suspicious Minds	10/69	12/69
Teddy Bear	7/57	7/57
Tell Me Why		12/65
There Goes My Everything		4/71
Too Much	2/57	5/57
Until It's Time For You To Go		4/72
Viva Las Vegas		4/64
Way Down		8/77
Wear My Ring Around Your Neck	4/58	5/58
Wild In The Country		9/61
The Wonder Of You/Mama Liked The Roses	6/70	7/70
Wooden Heart		3/61
You Don't Have To Say You Love Me/Patch It Up	11/70	1/71
(You're The) Devil In Disguise	7/63	7/63
Billy PRESTON (US)		
✤ with The Beatles Get Back	5/69	4/69
Nothing From Nothing	9/74	
Outa-Space	6/72	
Space Race	11/73	
That's The Way God Planned It		7/69
Will It Go Round In Circles	6/73	
Billy PRESTON & Syreeta (US)		
With You I'm Born Again	4/80	1/80
Johnny PRESTON (US)		
Cradle Of Love	4/60	5/60
Feel So Fine	8/60	
Running Bear	1/60	2/60
Mike PRESTON (UK)		
Mr. Blue		11/59
PRETENDERS (C)		
Back On The Chain Gang	3/83	
Brass In Pocket	6/80	12/79
Don't Get Me Wrong	12/86	11/86
Hymn To Her		1/87
I Go To Sleep		11/81
Message Of Love		2/81
Talk Of The Town		4/80
PRETTY POISON (US)		
Catch Me I'm Falling	12/87	
PRETTY THINGS (UK)		
Don't Bring Me Down		11/64
Honey I Need		3/65
Alan PRICE (UK)		
Jarrow Song		6/74
✤ with Georgie Fame Rosetta		5/71
Alan PRICE SET (UK)		
Don't Stop The Carnival		2/68
Hi-Lili-Hi-Lo		8/66
The House That Jack Built		8/67
I Put A Spell On You		4/66
Simon Smith & His Amazing Dancing Bear		3/67
Lloyd PRICE (US)		
I'm Gonna Get Married	8/59	
Lady Luck	3/60	
Personality	6/59	7/59
Stagger Lee	1/59	3/59
Ray PRICE (US)		
For The Good Times	1/71	
Maxi PRIEST (UK)		
Close To You	9/90	7/90
✤ with Shabba Ranks Housecall		5/93
✤ with Roberta Flack Set The Night To Music	11/91	
Some Guys Have All The Luck		12/87
Wild World		6/88
Louis PRIMA (US)		
Wonderland By Night	1/61	
PRIMAL SCREAM (UK)		
Dixie-Narco (EP)		2/92
PRIMITIVES (UK)		
Crash		3/88
PRINCE (US)		
Alphabet Street	6/88	5/88
Batdance	7/89	6/89
Controversy		12/93
Cream	10/91	
Delirious	10/83	
Diamonds And Pearls	1/92	
Gett Off		9/91
I Could Never Take The Place Of Your Man	1/88	
I Wanna Be Your Lover	1/80	
I Would Die 4 U	1/85	
Kiss	3/86	3/86
Let's Go Crazy	9/84	3/85
Little Red Corvette	4/83	1/85
My Name Is Prince		10/92
1999	7/83	1/85
Pop Life	9/85	
Purple Rain	10/84	10/84
Raspberry Beret	6/85	
7	1/93	
Sexy MF/Strollin'		7/92
Sign 'O' The Times	4/87	3/87
Thieves In The Temple	9/90	8/90
U Got The Look	9/87	9/87
When Doves Cry	6/84	7/84
PRINCESS (UK)		
Say I'm Your No. 1		8/85
P.J. PROBY (US)		
Hold Me		7/64
I Apologise		3/65
Maria		12/65
Somewhere		12/64
Together		10/64
PROCLAIMERS (UK)		
I'm Gonna Be (500 Miles)	7/93	9/88
King Of The Road (E.P.)		12/90
Letter From America		12/87
PROCOL HARUM (UK)		
Homburg		10/67
A Whiter Shade Of Pale	7/67	6/67
★ A Whiter Shade Of Pale		6/72
PRODIGY (UK)		
Charly		8/91
Everybody In The Place (EP)		1/92
Fire/Jericho		9/92
One Love		10/93
Out Of Space/Ruff In The Jungle Bizness		11/92
Wind It Up (Rewound)		4/93
Dorothy PROVINE (US)		
Don't Bring Lulu		12/61
PSEUDO ECHO (AUS)		
Funky Town	7/87	8/87
PUBLIC IMAGE LTD. (UK)		
Public Image		11/78
Rise		2/86
This Is Not A Love Song		10/83
Gary PUCKETT & The Union Gap (US)		
Don't Give In To Him	4/69	
Lady Willpower	7/68	9/68
Over You	10/68	
This Girl Is A Woman Now	9/69	
Woman, Woman	12/67	
Young Girl	3/68	5/68
★ Young Girl		7/74
PURE PRAIRIE LEAGUE (US)		
Let Me Love You Tonight	6/80	
James & Bobby PURIFY (US)		
I'm Your Puppet	11/66	
BILL PURSELL (US)		
Our Winter Love	3/63	
PUSSYCAT (H)		
Mississippi		9/76

	US Top 20 Ent	UK Top 20 Ent
RESTLESS HEART (US)		
When She Cries	1/93	
REUNION (US)		
Life Is A Rock (But The Radio Rolled Me)	11/74	
Paul REVERE & The Raiders (US)		
Good Thing	1/67	
Him Or Me - What's It Gonna Be	5/67	
Hungry	7/66	
Indian Reservation (The Lament Of The Cherokee Reservation Indian)	6/71	
Just Like Me	1/66	
Kicks	4/66	
REYNOLDS GIRLS (UK)		
I'd Rather Jack		3/89
Debbie REYNOLDS (US)		
Tammy	8/57	9/57
Jody REYNOLDS (US)		
Endless Sleep	6/58	
RHYTHM HERITAGE (US)		
Theme From S.W.A.T.	2/76	
Charlie RICH (US)		
Behind Closed Doors	7/73	
The Most Beautiful Girl	11/73	3/74
A Very Special Love Song	4/74	
Cliff RICHARD (UK)		
All My Love		12/67
Bachelor Boy		12/62
The Best Of Me		6/89
Big Ship		6/69
Carrie		2/80
Congratulations		4/68
Constantly		5/64
Daddy's Home		12/81
The Day I Met Marie		9/67
Devil Woman	9/76	6/76
Do You Wanna Dance		6/62
Don't Talk To Him		11/63
Dreaming	11/80	9/80
Fall In Love With You		4/60
From A Distance		10/90
Gee Whiz It's You		4/61
A Girl Like You		6/61
Good Times (Better Times)		3/69
Goodbye Sam Hello Samantha		6/70
High Class Baby		12/58
I Could Easily Fall		12/64
I Just Don't Have The Heart		9/89
I Love You		12/60
I Still Believe In You		12/92
I'm Looking Out The Window		5/62
I'm The Lonely One		2/64
In The Country		1/67
It'll Be Me		9/62
It's All In The Game		8/63
It's All Over		4/67
A Little In Love	3/81	
Living Doll		7/59
Living In Harmony		9/72
Lucky Lips		5/63
Mean Streak		5/59
The Minute You're Gone		3/65
Miss You Nights		3/76
Mistletoe And Wine		12/88
Move It		10/58
My Pretty One		7/87
The Next Time		12/62
Nine Times Out Of Ten		9/60
On My Word		7/65
On The Beach		7/64
The Only Way Out		8/82
Peace In Our Time		3/93
Please Don't Fall In Love		12/83
Please Don't Tease		7/60
Power To All Our Friends		3/73
Saviour's Day		12/90
✤ with Phil Everly She Means Nothing To Me		3/83
Silhouettes		9/90
Sing A Song Of Freedom		12/71
Some People		9/87
Summer Holiday		2/63
Theme For A Dream		3/61
Throw Down A Line		9/69
Time Drags By		11/66
Travellin' Light		10/59
True Love Ways		5/83
The Twelfth Of Never		10/64
Visions		8/66
Voice In The Wilderness		1/60
We Don't Talk Anymore	12/79	8/79
We Should Be Together		12/91
When The Girl In Your Arms Is The Girl In Your Heart		10/61
Wind Me Up (Let Me Go)		11/65
Wired For Sound		9/81
The Young Ones		1/62
Cliff RICHARD & Sarah Brightman (UK)		
All I Ask Of You		10/86
Cliff RICHARD & The Young Ones (UK)		
Living Doll		3/86
Lionel RICHIE (US)		
All Night Long (All Night)	10/93	10/83
Ballerina Girl	2/87	
Dancing On The Ceiling	8/86	8/86
✤ with Diana Ross Endless Love	8/81	9/81
Hello	4/84	3/84
Love Will Conquer All	11/86	
My Destiny		9/92
My Love	5/83	
Penny Lover	11/84	
Running With The Night	1/84	1/84
Say You, Say Me	12/85	12/85
Stuck On You	8/84	7/84
Truly	11/82	12/82
You Are	3/83	
Jonathan RICHMAN & The Modern Lovers (US)		
Egyptian Reggae		12/77
Roadrunner		8/77
Nelson RIDDLE (US)		
Lisbon Antigua	1/56	
Stan RIDGWAY (US)		
Camouflage		7/86
RIGHT SAID FRED (UK)		
Deeply Dippy		3/92
I'm Too Sexy	1/92	8/91
RIGHT SAID FRED & Friends (UK)		
Stick It Out		3/93
RIGHT SAID FRED featuring Jocelyn Brown (UK/US)		
Don't Talk Just Kiss		12/91
RIGHTEOUS BROTHERS (US)		
Ebb Tide	12/65	
Just Once In My Life	5/65	
Rock And Roll Heaven	7/74	
Unchained Melody	8/65	9/65
★ Unchained Melody	10/90	10/90
(You're My) Soul And Inspiration	3/66	
You've Lost That Lovin' Feelin'	1/65	1/65
★ You've Lost That Lovin' Feelin'		3/69
★ You've Lost That Lovin' Feelin'/Ebb Tide		12/90
Jeannie C. RILEY (US)		
Harper Valley P.T.A.	9/68	12/68
Miguel RIOS (Spa)		
A Song Of Joy	7/70	
Waldo De Los RIOS (Bra)		
Mozart Symphony No. 40 In G Minor		4/71
RIP CHORDS (US)		
Hey Little Cobra	1/64	
Minnie RIPERTON (US)		
Lovin' You	3/75	4/75
RITCHIE FAMILY (US)		
The Best Disco In Town		10/76
Brazil	10/75	
Tex RITTER (US)		
Wayward Wind		7/56
RIVER CITY PEOPLE (UK)		
California Dreamin'/Carry The Blame		8/90
Johnny RIVERS (US)		
Baby I Need Your Lovin'	2/67	
Maybelline	9/64	
Memphis	6/64	
Mountain Of Love	11/64	
Poor Side Of Town	10/66	
Rockin' Pneumonia & The Boogie Woogie Flu	12/72	
Secret Agent Man	4/66	
Seventh Son	6/65	
Summer Rain	1/68	
Swayin' To The Music (Slow Dancin')	9/77	
The Tracks Of My Tears	7/67	
RIVIERAS (US)		
California Sun	2/64	
ROACHFORD (UK)		
Cuddly Toy		1/89
ROB 'N' RAZ featuring Leila K (S)		
Got To Get		12/89
Kate ROBBINS & Beyond (UK)		
More Than In Love		6/81
Marty ROBBINS (US)		
Devil Woman		11/62
Don't Worry	2/61	
El Paso	12/59	
A White Sport Coat (And A Pink Carnation)	5/57	
Austin ROBERTS (US)		
Rocky	10/75	
Something's Wrong With Me	12/72	
Malcolm ROBERTS (UK)		
Love Is All		12/69
May I Have The Next Dream With You		12/68
B.A. ROBERTSON (UK)		
Bang Bang		8/79
Knocked It Off		11/79
To Be Or Not To Be		7/80
B.A. ROBERTSON & Maggie Bell (UK)		
Hold Me		11/81
Don ROBERTSON (US)		
The Happy Whistler	5/56	5/56
Ivo ROBIC (Y)		
Morgen		9/59
Floyd ROBINSON (US)		
Makin' Love		10/59
Smokey ROBINSON (US) also see The Miracles		
Being With You	4/81	6/81
Cruisin'	1/80	
Just To See Her	6/87	
One Heartbeat	10/87	
Tom ROBINSON BAND (UK)		
2-4-6-8 Motorway		11/77
War Baby		7/83
Vicki Sue ROBINSON (US)		
Turn The Beat Around	8/76	
ROCK FOLLIES (UK)		
O.K.		6/77
ROCKER'S REVENGE (US)		
Walking On Sunshine		9/82
ROCKIN' BERRIES (UK)		
He's In Town		11/64
Poor Man's Son		5/65
Lord ROCKINGHAM'S XI (UK)		
Hoots Mon		10/58
ROCKSTEADY CREW (US)		
(Hey) The Rocksteady Crew		10/83
ROCKWELL (US)		
Somebody's Watching Me	2/84	2/84
Clodagh RODGERS (I)		
Come Back And Shake Me		4/69
Goodnight Midnight		8/69
Jack In The Box		3/71
Jimmie RODGERS (US)		
Are You Really Mine	9/58	
Bimbombey	12/58	
English Country Garden		7/62
Honeycomb	9/57	
Kisses Sweeter Than Wine	12/57	1/58
Secretly	5/58	
RODS (UK)		
Do Anything You Wanna Do		9/77
Tommy ROE (US)		
Dizzy	3/69	5/69
Everybody	11/63	10/63
The Folk Singer		4/63
Hooray For Hazel	10/66	
Jam Up Jelly Tight	1/70	
Sheila	8/62	9/62
Sweet Pea	7/66	
ROGER (US)		
I Want To Be Your Man	1/88	
Julie ROGERS (UK)		
The Wedding	12/64	9/64
Kenny ROGERS/First Edition (US)		
Coward Of The County	1/80	2/80
I Don't Need You	7/81	
Just Dropped In (To See What Condition My Condition Was In)	3/68	
Lady	10/80	12/80
Love Will Turn You Around	8/82	

	US Top 20 Ent	UK Top 20 Ent
Lucille	5/77	5/77
Ruby, Don't Take Your Love To Town	7/69	11/69
Share Your Love	10/81	
She Believes In Me	6/79	
Something's Burning	4/70	3/70
Through The Years	3/82	
❖ with Dottie West What Are We Doin' In Love	6/81	
You Decorated My Life	10/79	
Kenny ROGERS & Dolly Parton (US)		
Islands In The Stream	10/83	12/83
Kenny ROGERS & Kim Carnes (US)		
Don't Fall In Love With A Dreamer	4/80	
Kenny ROGERS & Sheena Easton (US/UK)		
We've Got Tonight	3/83	
ROLLING STONES (UK)		
Angie	10/73	9/73
As Tears Go By	1/66	
Beast Of Burden	10/78	
Brown Sugar	5/71	5/71
Doo Doo Doo Doo Doo (Heartbreaker)	2/74	
Emotional Rescue	7/80	7/80
Fool To Cry	5/76	5/76
Get Off Of My Cloud	10/65	11/65
Harlem Shuffle	4/86	
Have You Seen Your Mother Baby Standing In The Shadow?	10/66	10/66
Honky Tonk Women	8/69	7/69
(I Can't Get No) Satisfaction	6/65	9/65
I Wanna Be Your Man		12/63
It's All Over Now		7/64
It's Only Rock 'n Roll (But I Like It)	9/74	8/74
Jumpin' Jack Flash	6/68	6/68
The Last Time	4/65	3/65
Let's Spend The Night Together/Ruby Tuesday		2/67
Little Red Rooster		11/64
Miss You	7/78	6/78
Mixed Emotions	10/89	
Mothers Little Helper	8/66	
19th Nervous Breakdown	3/66	2/66
Not Fade Away		3/64
Paint It, Black	5/66	5/66
Ruby Tuesday	2/67	
Start Me Up	9/81	9/81
Time Is On My Side	11/64	
Tumbling Dice	5/72	5/72
Undercover Of The Night	12/83	11/83
Waiting On A Friend	1/82	
We Love You/Dandelion		9/67
ROMANTICS (UK)		
Talking In Your Sleep	12/83	
Max ROMEO (J)		
Wet Dream		8/69
Don RONDO (US)		
White Silver Sands	8/57	
RONETTES (US)		
Baby I Love You		2/64
Be My Baby	9/63	10/63
RONNY & THE DAYTONAS (US)		
G.T.O.	9/64	
Linda RONSTADT (US)		
Back In The U.S.A.	10/78	
Blue Bayou	11/77	
Heat Wave/Love Is A Rose	10/75	
How Do I Make You	3/80	
Hurt So Bad	5/80	
It's So Easy	11/77	
Ooh Baby Baby	12/78	
That'll Be The Day	10/76	
When Will I Be Loved	5/75	
You're No Good	1/75	
Linda RONSTADT & James Ingram (US)		
Somewhere Out There	2/87	8/87
Linda RONSTADT (featuring Aaron Neville) (US)		
All My Life	4/90	
Don't Know Much	11/89	11/89
ROOFTOP SINGERS (US)		
Walk Right In	1/63	2/63
ROSE ROYCE (US)		
Car Wash	1/77	2/77
I Wanna Get Next To You	4/77	
Is It Love You're After		1/80
Love Don't Live Here Anymore		9/78
Wishing On A Star		2/78

	US Top 20 Ent	UK Top 20 Ent
David ROSE & His Orchestra (US)		
The Stripper	6/62	
ROSIE & The Originals (US)		
Angel Baby	1/61	
Diana ROSS (US) also see the Supremes		
Ain't No Mountain High Enough	8/70	10/70
All Of My Life		2/74
Chain Reaction		2/86
Doobedood'ndoobe Doobedood'ndoobe		6/72
I'm Comin' Out	10/80	
I'm Still Waiting		8/71
If We Hold On Together		12/92
It's My Turn	12/80	
Love Hangover	5/76	5/76
Mirror Mirror	2/82	
Missing You	4/85	
Muscles	11/82	
My Old Piano		10/80
One Shining Moment		7/92
Remember Me		5/71
Surrender		11/71
Theme From Mahogany (Do You Know Where You're Going To)	12/75	4/76
Touch Me In The Morning	7/73	8/73
Upside Down	8/80	8/80
When You Tell Me That You Love Me		12/91
Why Do Fools Fall In Love	11/81	11/81
Work That Body		6/82
❖ with Marvin Gaye You're A Special Part Of Me	11/73	
Diana ROSS & Lionel Richie (US)		
Endless Love	8/81	9/81
Diana ROSS & Marvin Gaye (US)		
You Are Everything		4/74
Jackie ROSS (US)		
Selfish One	9/64	
Nini ROSSO (ITA)		
Il Silenzio		9/65
David Lee ROTH (US)		
California Girls	2/85	
Just Like Paradise	2/88	
Demis ROUSSOS (Gre)		
Happy To Be On An Island In The Sun		12/75
The Roussos Phenomenon E.P.		7/76
When Forever Has Gone		10/76
John ROWLES (UK)		
Hush Not A Word To Mary		7/68
If I Only Had Time		4/68
ROXETTE (S)		
Almost Unreal		7/93
Dangerous	2/90	8/90
Fading Like A Flower (Every Time You Leave)	7/91	5/91
How Do You Do!		8/92
It Must Have Been Love	5/90	6/90
★ It Must Have Been Love		9/93
Joyride	4/91	3/91
Listen To Your Heart	10/89	8/90
The Look	3/89	5/89
ROXY MUSIC (UK)		
All I Want Is You		11/74
Angel Eyes		8/79
Dance Away		5/79
Jealous Guy		2/81
Love Is The Drug		11/75
More Than This		4/82
Oh Yeah (On The Radio)		8/80
Over You		5/80
Pyjamarama		4/73
The Same Old Scene		11/80
Street Life		12/73
Virginia Plain		9/72
★ Virginia Plain		11/77
ROY 'C' (US)		
Shotgun Wedding		5/66
★ Shotgun Wedding		12/72
ROYAL GUARDSMEN (US)		
Snoopy Vs. The Red Baron	12/66	2/67
ROYAL PHILHARMONIC ORCHESTRA (UK)		
Hooked On Classics	1/82	8/81
ROYAL SCOTS DRAGOON GUARDS (UK)		
Amazing Grace	6/72	4/72
Little Drummer Boy		12/72
ROYAL TEENS (US)		
Short Shorts	2/58	

	US Top 20 Ent	UK Top 20 Ent
Billy Joe ROYAL (US)		
Cherry Hill Park	12/69	
Down In The Boondocks	8/65	
I Knew You When	11/65	
ROZALLA (Zim)		
Everybody's Free (To Feel Good)		9/91
RUBETTES (UK)		
Baby I Know		3/77
I Can Do It		3/75
Juke Box Jive		11/74
Sugar Baby Love		5/74
Tonight		8/74
RUBY & The Romantics (US)		
Our Day Will Come	3/63	
Bruce RUFFIN (J)		
Mad About You		7/72
David RUFFIN (US)		
My Whole World Ended (The Moment You Left Me)	3/69	
Walk Away From Love	1/76	2/76
Jimmy RUFFIN (US)		
Farewell Is A Lonely Sound		4/70
Hold On To My Love	4/80	5/80
I'll Say Forever My Love		8/70
It's Wonderful		11/70
What Becomes Of The Brokenhearted	10/66	12/66
★ What Becomes Of The Brokenhearted		8/74
RUFUS (US)		
Once You Get Started	4/75	
Tell Me Something Good	8/74	
RUFUS & Chaka Khan (US)		
Ain't Nobody		4/84
★ Ain't Nobody		7/89
Sweet Thing	3/76	
You Got The Love	12/74	
RUN D.M.C. (US)		
Walk This Way	9/86	9/86
Todd RUNDGREN (US)		
Hello It's Me	12/73	
I Saw The Light	6/72	
Jennifer RUSH (US)		
The Power Of Love		10/85
Merrilee RUSH (US)		
Angel Of The Morning	6/68	
Patrice RUSHEN (US)		
Forget Me Nots		5/82
Brenda RUSSELL & Joe Esposito (US)		
Piano In The Dark	5/88	
Leon RUSSELL (US)		
Tight Rope	10/72	
RUTS (UK)		
Babylon's Burning		7/79
Barry RYAN (UK)		
Eloise		11/68
Marion RYAN (UK)		
Love Me Forever		2/58
Paul & Barry RYAN (UK)		
Don't Bring Me Your Heartaches		12/65
Bobby RYDELL (US)		
The Cha Cha Cha	11/62	
Forget Him	12/63	6/63
Good Time Baby	3/61	
I'll Never Dance Again	7/62	
Kissin' Time	9/59	
Sway	12/60	1/61
Swingin' School	6/60	
Volare	8/60	
We Got Love	11/59	
Wild One	2/60	4/60
Mitch RYDER & The Detroit Wheels (US)		
Devil With A Blue Dress On & Good Golly Miss Molly	11/66	
Jenny Take A Ride!	2/66	
Sock It To Me-Baby!	3/67	
RYTHM SYNDICATE (US)		
P.A.S.S.I.O.N.	7/91	
Robin S. (US)		
Luv 4 Luv		8/93
Show Me Love	6/93	4/93
S'EXPRESS (UK)		
Hey Music Lover		3/89
Superfly Guy		8/88
Theme From S'Express		4/88
SABRINA (Ita)		

	US Top 20 Ent	UK Top 20 Ent
Boys (Summertime Love)		6/88
SAD CAFE (UK)		
Every Day Hurts		10/79
SADE (UK)		
Smooth Operator	4/85	
The Sweetest Taboo	2/86	
Your Love Is King		3/84
SSgt. Barry SADLER (US)		
The Ballad Of The Green Berets	2/66	
SAFARIS (US)		
Image Of A Girl	7/60	
SA-FIRE (US)		
Thinking Of You	5/89	
Carole Bayer SAGER (US)		
You're Moving Out Today		6/77
SAIGON KICK (US)		
Love Is On The Way	11/92	
SAILCAT (US)		
Motorcycle Mama	8/72	
SAILOR (UK)		
Girls Girls Girls		4/76
Glass Of Champagne		1/76
ST. CECILIA (UK)		
Leap Up And Down (Wave Your Knickers In The Air)		8/71
SAINT ETIENNE (UK)		
You're In A Bad Way		2/93
ST. LOUIS UNION (UK)		
Girl		2/66
Crispian ST. PETERS (UK)		
The Pied Piper	7/66	4/66
You Were On My Mind		2/66
ST. WINIFRED'S SCHOOL CHOIR (UK)		
There's No One Quite Like Grandma		12/80
Buffy SAINTE-MARIE (C)		
Soldier Blue		8/71
Kyu SAKAMOTO (Jap)		
Sukiyaki	6/63	7/63
SAKKARIN (UK)		
Sugar Sugar		5/71
SALT-N-PEPA (US)		
Do You Want Me		6/91
Let's Talk About Sex	11/91	9/91
Push It/Tramp		7/88
Shoop	11/93	
Twist And Shout		11/88
SAM & DAVE (US)		
I Thank You	3/68	
Soul Man	10/67	
SAM THE SHAM & The Pharaohs (US)		
Lil' Red Riding Hood	7/66	
Wooly Bully	5/65	7/65
SAN JOSE (UK)		
Argentine Melody (Cancion De Argentina)		7/78
SANDPIPERS (US)		
Guantanamera	9/66	10/66
Jodie SANDS (US)		
Someday		11/58
Tommy SANDS (US)		
Teen-Age Crush	3/57	
SANFORD/TOWNSEND BAND (US)		
Smoke From A Distant Fire	8/77	
Samantha SANG (Aus)		
Emotion	2/78	3/78
SANTA ESMERALDA (US/F)		
Don't Let Me Be Misunderstood	2/78	
Mongo SANTAMARIA (US)		
Watermelon Man	4/63	
SANTANA (US)		
Black Magic Woman	12/70	
Everybody's Everything	11/71	
Evil Ways	3/70	
Hold On	10/82	
Oye Como Va	4/71	
She's Not There		11/77
Winning	7/81	
SANTO & JOHNNY (US)		
Sleep Walk	8/59	
Mike SARNE with Billie Davis (UK)		
Will I What		9/62
Mike SARNE with Wendy Richard (UK)		
Come Outside		5/62
Peter SARSTEDT (UK)		
Frozen Orange Juice		7/69
Where Do You Go To My Lovely		2/69

	US Top 20 Ent	UK Top 20 Ent
Robin SARSTEDT (UK)		
My Resistance Is Low		5/76
Telly SAVALAS (US)		
If		3/75
SAXON (UK)		
And The Bands Played On		4/81
747 (Strangers In The Night)		7/80
Leo SAYER (UK)		
Have You Ever Been In Love		4/82
How Much Love		5/77
I Can't Stop Lovin' You (Though I Try)		10/78
Long Tall Glasses (I Can Dance)	4/75	9/74
Moonlighting		9/75
More Than I Can Say	11/80	7/80
One Man Band		6/74
The Show Must Go On		12/73
When I Need You	4/77	2/77
You Make Me Feel Like Dancing	12/76	11/76
SCAFFOLD (UK)		
Lily The Pink		11/68
Liverpool Lou		6/74
Thank U Very Much		12/67
Boz SCAGGS (UK)		
Breakdown Dead Ahead	5/80	
Lido Shuffle	4/77	6/77
Look What You've Done To Me	10/80	
Lowdown	9/76	
Miss Sun	2/81	
What Can I Say		3/77
SCANDAL featuring Patty Smyth (US)		
The Warrior	8/84	
Joey SCARBURY (US)		
Theme From 'Greatest American Hero' (Believe It Or Not)	6/81	
Lalo SCHIFRIN (US)		
Jaws		11/76
Peter SCHILLING (G)		
Major Tom (Coming Home)	12/83	
John SCHNEIDER (US)		
It's Now Or Never	8/81	
SCORPIONS (G)		
Wind Of Change	8/91	10/91
SCOTLAND WORLD CUP SQUAD (UK)		
We Have A Dream		5/82
Freddie SCOTT (US)		
Hey, Girl	9/63	
Jack SCOTT (US)		
Burning Bridges	5/60	
Goodbye Baby	1/59	
My True Love/Leroy	7/58	11/58
What In The World's Come Over You	2/60	3/60
Linda SCOTT (US)		
Don't Bet Money Honey	8/61	
I've Told Every Little Star	4/61	6/61
SCRITTI POLITTI (UK)		
Perfect Way	12/85	
Wood Beez (Pray Like Aretha Franklin)		4/84
SCRITTI POLITTI featuring Ranking Ann (UK)		
The Word Girl		6/85
SEAL (UK)		
Crazy	8/91	1/91
Future Love (EP)		5/91
Killer (EP)		11/91
SEALS & CROFTS (US)		
Diamond Girl	7/73	
Get Closer	7/76	
Summer Breeze	11/72	
SEARCHERS (UK)		
Ain't Gonna Kiss Ya (E.P.)		10/63
Don't Throw Your Love Away		4/64
Goodbye My Love		3/65
He's Got No Love		8/65
Love Potion Number Nine	12/64	
Needles And Pins	4/64	1/64
Someday We're Gonna Love Again		8/64
Sugar And Spice		11/63
Sweets For My Sweet		7/63
What Have They Done To The Rain		1/65
When You Walk In The Room		10/64
John SEBASTIAN (US)		
Welcome Back	4/76	
Jon SECADA (US)		
Do You Believe In Us	12/92	
Just Another Day	6/92	8/92
Harry SECOMBE (UK)		

	US Top 20 Ent	UK Top 20 Ent
On With The Motley		12/55
This Is My Song		3/67
Neil SEDAKA (US)		
Bad Blood	10/75	
Breaking Up Is Hard To Do	2/76	
Breaking Up Is Hard To Do	7/62	8/62
Calendar Girl	1/61	2/61
Happy Birthday, Sweet Sixteen	12/61	12/61
I Go Ape		5/59
Laughter In The Rain	12/74	
Little Devil	5/61	6/61
Next Door To An Angel	11/62	
Oh! Carol	11/59	11/59
Stairway To Heaven	5/60	5/60
SEDUCTION (US)		
Could This Be Love	8/90	
Heartbeat	4/90	
Two To Make It Right	1/90	
SEEKERS (AUS)		
The Carnival Is Over		11/65
Georgy Girl	1/67	3/67
I'll Never Find Another You	4/65	2/65
Morningtown Ride		12/66
Someday One Day		4/66
Walk With Me		10/66
When Will The Good Apples Fall		10/67
A World Of Our Own		5/65
Bob SEGER & The Silver Bullet Band (US)		
Against The Wind	5/80	
American Storm	4/86	
Even Now	4/83	
Fire Lake	4/80	
Hollywood Nights	9/78	
Like A Rock	7/86	
Night Moves	2/77	
Shakedown	6/87	
Shame On The Moon	1/83	
Still The Same	6/78	
Tryin' To Live My Life Without You	10/81	
We've Got Tonite	1/79	
You'll Accomp'ny Me	9/80	
SELECTER (UK)		
On My Radio		11/79
Peter SELLERS (UK)		
A Hard Day's Night		1/66
Peter SELLERS & Sophia Loren (UK/Ita)		
Goodness Gracious Me		11/60
Michael SEMBELLO (US)		
Maniac	7/83	
SENSATIONS (US)		
Let Me In	3/62	
Serendipity Singers (US)		
Don't Let The Rain Come Down (Crooked Little Man)	4/64	
Taja SEVELLE (US)		
Love Is Contagious		3/88
SEVERINE (F)		
Un Banc, Un Abre, Une Rue		5/71
David SEVILLE (US)		
Witch Doctor	4/58	6/58
SEX PISTOLS (UK)		
C'mon Everybody		7/79
God Save The Queen		6/77
Holidays In The Sun		10/77
No One Is Innocent/My Way		7/78
Pretty Vacant		7/77
Silly Thing/Who Killed Bambi		4/79
Something Else/Friggin' In The Riggin'		3/79
SHADES OF BLUE (US)		
Oh How Happy	6/66	
SHADOWS OF KNIGHT (US)		
Gloria	5/66	
SHADOWS (UK)		
Apache		8/60
Atlantis		6/63
Dance On		12/62
Don't Cry For Me Argentina		2/79
Don't Make My Baby Blue		8/65
F.B.I.		2/61
Foot Tapper		3/63
Frightened City		5/61
Geronimo		12/63
Guitar Tango		8/62
Kon-Tiki		9/61
Let Me Be The One		4/75

385

	US Top 20 Ent	UK Top 20 Ent
Man Of Mystery		11/60
Riders In The Sky		3/80
The Rise & Fall Of Flingel Bunt		5/64
The Savage		11/61
Shindig		9/63
The Stranger		11/60
Theme For Young Lovers		3/64
Theme From The Deer Hunter (Cavatina)		6/79
Wonderful Land		3/62
SHAG (UK)		
Loop Di Love		11/72
SHAGGY (J)		
Oh Carolina		3/93
SHAI (US)		
Baby I'm Yours	9/93	
Comforter	3/93	
If I Ever Fall In Love	11/92	
SHAKATAK (UK)		
Dark Is The Night		6/83
Down On The Street		8/84
Easier Said Than Done		2/82
Night Birds		4/82
SHAKESPEAR'S SISTER (UK/US)		
Hello (Turn Your Radio On)		11/92
I Don't Care		5/92
Stay	8/92	2/92
You're History		8/89
SHALAMAR (US)		
Dead Giveaway		7/83
Friends		12/82
I Can Make You Feel Good		5/82
A Night To Remember		7/82
The Second Time Around	3/80	
There It Is		9/82
SHAM 69 (UK)		
Hersham Boys		8/79
Hurry Up Harry		11/78
If The Kids Are United		8/78
SHAMEN (UK)		
Boss Drum		11/92
Ebeneezer Goode		9/92
L.S.I.		7/92
Move Any Mountain		7/91
Phorever People		12/92
SHANGRI-LAS (US)		
I Can Never Go Home Anymore	12/65	
Leader Of The Pack	11/64	2/65
★ Leader Of The Pack		11/72
★ Leader Of The Pack		7/76
Remember (Walkin' In The Sand)	9/64	11/64
SHANICE (US)		
I Love Your Smile	1/92	2/92
Saving Forever For You	12/92	
SHANNON (US)		
Let The Music Play	2/84	
Del SHANNON (US)		
Hats Off To Larry	7/61	9/61
Hey Little Girl		3/62
Keep Searchin' (We'll Follow The Sun)	1/65	2/65
Little Town Flirt	2/63	1/63
Runaway	4/61	5/61
So Long Baby	12/61	
Swiss Maid		10/62
Two Kinds Of Teardrops		5/63
Helen SHAPIRO (UK)		
Don't Treat Me Like A Child		4/61
Let's Talk About Love		5/62
Little Miss Lonely		8/62
Tell Me What He Said		3/62
Walkin' Back To Happiness		10/61
You Don't Know		7/61
Feargal SHARKEY (UK)		
A Good Heart		11/85
I've Got News For You		4/91
You Little Thief		1/86
Dee Dee SHARP (US)		
Do The Bird	4/63	
Gravy (For My Mashed Potatoes)	7/62	
Mashed Potato Time	4/62	
Ride	11/62	
Georgie SHAW (US)		
Till We Two Are One	1/54	
Sandie SHAW (UK)		
Girl Don't Come		1/65
I'll Stop At Nothing		3/65

	US Top 20 Ent	UK Top 20 Ent
Long Live Love		5/65
Message Understood		10/65
Monsieur Dupont		3/69
Nothing Comes Easy		6/66
Puppet On A String		4/67
(There's) Always Something There To Remind Me		10/64
Tomorrow		2/66
Gary SHEARSTON (UK)		
I Get A Kick Out Of You		10/74
SHEER ELEGANCE (UK)		
Life Is Too Short Girl		5/76
SHEILA B. DEVOTION (F)		
Singin' In The Rain (Pt. 1)		4/78
Peter SHELLEY (UK)		
Gee Baby		10/74
Love Me Love My Dog		4/75
Anne SHELTON (UK)		
Lay Down Your Arms		9/56
Sailor		2/61
SHEP & THE LIMELITES (US)		
Daddy's Home	5/61	
SHERBET (Aus)		
Howzat		10/76
SHERIFF (US)		
When I'm With You	1/89	
Allan SHERMAN (US)		
Hello Mudduh, Hello Fadduh	8/63	
Bobby SHERMAN (US)		
Cried Like A Baby	3/71	
Easy Come, Easy Go	3/70	
Julie, Do Ya Love Me	9/70	
La La La (If I Had You)	12/69	
Little Woman	9/69	
Pluto SHERVINGTON (J)		
Dat		2/76
SHIELDS (US)		
You Cheated	10/58	
SHIRELLES (US)		
Baby It's You	1/62	
Dedicated To The One I Love	2/61	
Foolish Little Girl	5/63	
Mama Said	5/61	
Soldier Boy	4/62	
Will You Love Me Tomorrow	1/61	2/61
SHIRLEY & COMPANY (US)		
Shame Shame Shame	3/75	2/75
SHOCKING BLUE (H)		
Venus	1/70	2/70
Troy SHONDELL (US)		
This Time	10/61	
SHOWADDYWADDY (UK)		
Dancin' Party		11/77
Heartbeat		9/75
Hey Rock And Roll		6/74
I Wonder Why		4/78
A Little Bit Of Soap		7/78
Pretty Little Angel Eyes		11/78
Rock 'n' Roll Lady		9/74
Three Steps To Heaven		5/75
Under The Moon Of Love		11/76
When		3/77
You Got What It Takes		8/77
SHOWSTOPPERS (US)		
Ain't Nothin' But A Housparty		4/68
Labi SIFFRE (UK)		
Crying Laughing Loving Lying		4/72
It Must Be Love		12/71
(Something Inside) So Strong		5/87
SIGUE SIGUE SPUTNIK (UK)		
Love Missile F1-11		3/86
SILHOUETTES (US)		
Get A Job	1/58	
SILK (US)		
Freak Me	3/93	
SILKIE (UK)		
You've Got To Hide Your Love Away		11/65
SILVER CONVENTION (G/US)		
Fly Robin Fly	11/75	
Get Up And Boogie	5/76	5/76
Harry SIMEONE CHORALE (US)		
Little Drummer Boy		2/59
Gene SIMMONS (US)		
Haunted House	9/64	
SIMON & GARFUNKEL (US)		

	US Top 20 Ent	UK Top 20 Ent
At The Zoo	4/67	
The Boxer	5/69	5/69
Bridge Over Troubled Water	2/70	3/70
Cecilia	5/70	
A Hazy Shade Of Winter	12/66	
Homeward Bound	3/66	5/66
I Am A Rock	5/66	
Mrs. Robinson	5/68	7/68
Mrs. Robinson (E.P.)		2/69
My Little Town	11/75	
Scarborough Fair/Canticle	4/68	
The Sounds Of Silence	12/65	
Carly SIMON (US)		
Anticipation	2/72	
Coming Around Again		2/87
Jesse	10/80	
Nobody Does It Better	9/77	8/77
That's The Way I've Always Heard It Should Be	7/71	
Why		9/82
You Belong To Me	6/78	
You're So Vain	12/72	1/73
Carly SIMON & James Taylor (US)		
Mockingbird	3/74	
Joe SIMON (US)		
The Chokin' Kind	5/69	
Drowning In The Sea Of Love	1/72	
Get Down, Get Down (Get On The Floor)	6/75	
Power Of Love	9/72	
Step By Step		7/73
Paul SIMON (US)		
50 Ways To Leave Your Lover	1/76	
Kodachrome	6/73	
Late In The Evening	8/80	
Loves Me Like A Rock	9/73	
Mother And Child Reunion	3/72	3/72
Slip Slidin' Away	12/77	
Take Me To The Mardi Gras		7/73
✦ with James Taylor & Art Garfunkel		
Wonderful World	3/78	
You Can Call Me Al		10/86
Nina SIMONE (US)		
Ain't Got No - I Got Life/Do What You Gotta Do		11/68
My Baby Just Cares For Me		11/87
To Love Somebody		2/69
SIMPLE MINDS (UK)		
Alive & Kicking	12/85	10/85
All The Things She Said		4/86
Belfast Child		2/89
Don't You (Forget About Me)	4/85	4/85
Let There Be Love		3/91
★ Love Song/Alive And Kicking		10/92
Sanctify Yourself	3/86	2/86
SIMPLY RED (UK)		
Ev'ry Time We Say Goodbye		12/87
For Your Babies		2/92
Holding Back The Years	6/86	6/86
If You Don't Know Me By Now	6/89	4/89
It's Only Love		2/89
Money's Too Tight (To Mention)		7/85
Montreux EP		11/92
The Right Thing		3/87
Something Got Me Started		9/91
Stars		12/91
SIMPSONS (US)		
Do The Bartman		2/91
SIMPSONS featuring Bart & Homer (US)		
Deep, Deep Trouble		4/91
Joyce SIMS (US)		
Come Into My Life		1/88
Kym SIMS (US)		
Take My Advice		4/92
Too Blind To See It		12/91
Frank SINATRA (US)		
All The Way/Chicago	12/57	12/57
Ev'rybody's Twistin'		4/62
From Here To Eternity		3/54
Granada		10/61
Hey! Jealous Lover	11/56	
High Hopes		9/59
Learnin' The Blues	6/55	8/55
Love And Marriage	11/55	1/56
Love's Been Good To Me		11/69
My Way		5/69

	US Top 20 Ent	UK Top 20 Ent
Ol' Macdonald		12/60
❖ with Nancy Sinatra Somethin' Stupid	4/67	4/67
Songs For Swinging Lovers (L.P.)		6/56
Strangers In The Night	6/66	5/66
The Tender Trap		1/56
That's Life	12/66	
Theme From New York New York		3/86
Three Coins In The Fountain	6/54	7/54
Witchcraft		2/58
You My Love		6/55
Young-At-Heart	2/54	7/54
Nancy & Frank SINATRA (US)		
Somethin' Stupid	4/67	4/67
Nancy SINATRA (US)		
How Does That Grab You Darlin'	5/66	
Sugar Town	12/66	2/67
These Boots Are Made For Walkin'	2/66	2/66
You Only Live Twice/Jackson		7/67
Nancy SINATRA & Lee Hazlewood (US)		
Did You Ever		9/71
Jackson	8/67	
SINGING DOGS (D/US)		
The Singing Dogs (Medley)		12/55
SINGING NUN (SOEUR SOURIRE) (B)		
Dominique	11/63	12/63
SINITTA (US)		
Cross My Broken Heart		4/88
Right Back Where We Started From		6/89
So Macho/Cruising		8/86
Toy Boy		8/87
SIOUXSIE & The Banshees (UK)		
Dear Prudence		10/83
Hong Kong Garden		9/78
SIR DOUGLAS QUINTET (US)		
She's About A Mover	6/65	
SIR MIX-A-LOT (US)		
Baby Got Back	5/92	
SISTER SLEDGE (US)		
Frankie		6/85
He's The Greatest Dancer	4/79	4/79
★ Lost In Music		9/84
Thinking Of You		6/84
We Are Family	5/79	6/79
★ We Are Family		1/93
SISTERS OF MERCY (UK)		
Temple Of Love (1992)		5/92
This Corrosion		10/87
Peter SKELLERN (UK)		
You're A Lady		10/72
SKID ROW (US)		
18 And Life	9/89	2/90
I Remember You	1/90	
SKIDS (UK)		
Into The Valley		3/79
Masquerade		6/79
SKIP & FLIP (US)		
Cherry Pie	5/60	
It Was I	8/59	
SKY (UK)		
Toccata		5/80
SKYLARK (US)		
Wildflower	5/73	
SKYLINERS (US)		
Since I Don't Have You	4/59	
SL2 (UK)		
DJs Take Control/Way In My Brain		11/91
On A Ragga Tip		4/92
SLADE (UK)		
Bangin' Man		7/74
Coz I Luv You		11/71
Cum On Feel The Noize		3/73
Everyday		4/74
Far Far Away		10/74
Get Down And Get With It		8/71
Gudbuy T'Jane		12/72
In For A Penny		12/75
Look Wot You Dun		2/72
Mama Weer All Crazee Now		9/72
Merry Xmas Everybody		12/73
My Friend Stan		10/73
My Oh My		12/83
Run Runaway		3/84
Skweeze Me Pleeze Me		6/73
Take Me Bak 'Ome		6/72
Thanks For The Memory (Wham Bam		

	US Top 20 Ent	UK Top 20 Ent
Thank You Mam)		5/75
We'll Bring The House Down		2/81
Percy SLEDGE (US)		
Take Time To Know Her	5/68	
When A Man Loves A Woman	5/66	6/66
★ When A Man Loves A Woman		2/87
SLIK (UK)		
Forever & Ever		1/76
SLY & The Family Stone (US)		
Dance To The Music	3/68	8/68
Everyday People	1/69	
Family Affair	11/71	
Hot Fun In The Summertime	9/69	
If You Want Me To Stay	8/73	
Thank You (Falettinme Be Mice Elf Agin)/		
Everybody Is A Star	1/70	
SLY AND ROBBIE (J)		
Boops (Here To Go)		5/87
SLY FOX (US)		
Let's Go All The Way	3/86	7/86
SMALL FACES (UK)		
All Or Nothing		8/66
Here Come The Nice		7/67
Hey Girl		5/66
Itchycoo Park	2/68	9/67
★ Itchycoo Park		1/76
Lazy Sunday		5/68
My Mind's Eye		12/66
Sha La La La Lee		2/66
Tin Soldier		1/68
What Cha Gonna Do About It		10/65
Millie SMALL (J)		
My Boy Lollipop	6/64	4/64
SMART E'S (UK)		
Sesame's Treet		7/92
SMITH (US)		
Baby It's You	10/69	
Huey (Piano) SMITH & The Clowns (US)		
Don't You Just Know It	4/58	
Hurricane SMITH (UK)		
Don't Let It Die		6/71
Oh Babe What Would You Say	1/73	5/72
Keely SMITH (US)		
You're Breakin' My Heart		4/65
Mel SMITH (UK) See Kim Wilde		
Michael W. SMITH (US)		
Place In This World	7/91	
O.C. SMITH (US)		
Little Green Apples	10/68	
Son Of Hickory Hollers Tramp		6/68
Patti SMITH GROUP (US)		
Because The Night	6/78	5/78
Rex SMITH (US)		
You Take My Breath Away	6/79	
Sammi SMITH (US)		
Help Me Make It Through The Night	3/71	
Somethin' SMITH & The Redheads (US)		
It's A Sin To Tell A Lie	6/55	
Whistling Jack SMITH (UK)		
I Was Kaiser Bill's Batman		3/67
SMITHS (UK)		
Heaven Knows I'm Miserable Now		6/84
Panic		8/86
Shoplifters Of The World Unite		2/87
This Charming Man		8/92
What Difference Does It Make		2/84
SMOKIE/SMOKEY (UK)		
Don't Play Your Rock 'n' Roll To Me		10/75
I'll Meet You At Midnight		10/76
If You Think You Know How To Love Me		8/75
It's Your Life		8/77
Lay Back In The Arms Of Someone		4/77
Living Next Door To Alice	12/76	
Needles And Pins		11/77
Oh Carol		6/78
Father Abraham & The SMURFS (H)		
Dippety Day		11/78
The Smurf Song		6/78
Patty SMYTH with Don Henley (US) also see Scandal featuring Patty Smyth		
Sometimes Love Just Ain't Enough	9/92	
SNAP (G/US)		
Cult Of Snap		10/90
Mary Had A Little Boy		12/90
Oops Up		6/90

	US Top 20 Ent	UK Top 20 Ent
The Power	7/90	3/90
Rhythm Is A Dancer	10/92	7/92
Snap Mega Mix		4/91
SNAP featuring Niki Haris (G/US)		
Do You See The Light (Looking For)		6/93
Exterminate!		1/93
SNOOP DOGGY DOGG (US)		
What's My Name?	12/93	
SNOW (C)		
Informer	2/93	3/93
Phoebe SNOW (US)		
Poetry Man	3/75	
SOFT CELL (UK)		
Bed Sitter		11/81
Say Hello Wave Goodbye		2/82
Tainted Love	6/82	8/81
★ Tainted Love		5/91
Torch		6/82
What		8/82
SOHO (UK)		
Hippychick	11/90	2/91
Jimmy SOMERVILLE (UK)		
To Love Somebody		11/90
You Make Me Feel (Mighty Real)		1/90
Joanie SOMMERS (US)		
Johnny Get Angry	7/62	
SONIA (UK)		
Listen To Your Heart		1/90
Only Fools (Never Fall In Love)		6/91
You'll Never Stop Me From Loving You		7/89
SONNY & CHER (US) also see Cher		
All I Ever Need Is You	12/71	2/72
Baby Don't Go	10/65	10/65
The Beat Goes On	2/67	
But You're Mine	11/65	
A Cowboys Work Is Never Done	4/72	
I Got You Babe	8/65	8/65
Little Man		9/66
What Now My Love		3/66
SONNY (US)		
Laugh At Me	9/65	9/65
S.O.S. BAND (US)		
Take Your Time (Do It Right) (Pt. 1)	7/80	
SOUL ASYLUM (US)		
Runaway Train	8/93	11/93
SOUL II SOUL (UK)		
A Dream's A Dream		5/90
Get A Life		12/89
Joy		4/92
SOUL II SOUL featuring Caron Wheeler (UK)		
Back To Life (However Do You Want Me)	11/89	6/89
Keep On Movin'	8/89	3/89
SOUL SURVIVORS (US)		
Expressway To Your Heart	10/67	
David SOUL (US)		
Don't Give Up On Us	3/77	1/77
Going In With My Eyes Open		3/77
It Sure Brings Out The Love In Your Eyes		6/78
Let's Have A Quiet Night In		1/78
Silver Lady		9/77
Jimmy SOUL (US)		
If You Wanna Be Happy	5/63	
SOUNDS ORCHESTRAL (UK)		
Cast Your Fate To The Wind	5/65	1/65
SOUP DRAGONS (UK)		
I'm Free		7/90
SOURCE featuring Candi Staton (UK/US)		
You Got The Love		2/91
Joe SOUTH (US)		
Games People Play	2/69	3/69
Walk A Mile In My Shoes	2/70	
J. D. SOUTHER (US)		
❖ with James Taylor Her Town Too	4/81	
You're Only Lonely	11/79	
Red SOVINE (US)		
Teddy Bear		6/81
Bob B. SOXX & THE BLUE JEANS (US)		
Zip-A-Dee Doo-Dah	12/62	
SPACE (F)		
Magic Fly		9/77
SPAGNA (Ita)		
Call Me		8/87
SPANDAU BALLET (UK)		
Chant No.1 (I Don't Need This Pressure On)		7/81
Communication		3/83

	US Top 20 Ent	UK Top 20 Ent
Gold		8/83
I'll Fly For You		9/84
Instinction		5/82
Lifeline		10/82
Musclebound/Glow		5/81
Only When You Leave		6/84
Through The Barricades		11/86
To Cut A Long Story Short		12/80
True	9/83	4/83
SPANKY & OUR GANG (US)		
Sunday Will Never Be The Same	6/67	
SPARKS (US)		
Amateur Hour		8/74
Beat The Clock		8/79
Never Turn Your Back On Mother Earth		11/74
This Town Ain't Big Enough For Both Of Us		5/74
Billie Jo SPEARS (US)		
Blanket On The Ground		8/75
What I've Got In Mind		8/76
SPECIAL AKA (UK)		
Nelson Mandela		4/84
SPECIALS (UK)		
Do Nothing/Maggie's Farm		1/81
Gangsters		8/79
Ghost Town		6/81
A Message To You Rudy/Nite Klub		11/79
Rat Race/Rude Boys Outa Jail		6/80
Stereotype/International Jet Set		10/80
Too Much Too Young E.P.		2/80
Chris SPEDDING (UK)		
Motor Biking		9/75
Johnny SPENCE (UK)		
Dr. Kildare Theme		4/62
Tracie SPENCER (US)		
This House	3/91	
SPIN DOCTORS (US)		
Little Miss Can't Be Wrong	12/92	
Two Princes	3/93	6/93
(Detroit) SPINNERS (US)		
Could It Be I'm Falling In Love	2/73	
Cupid-I've Loved You For A Long Time (Medley)	6/80	7/80
Ghetto Child		10/73
I'll Be Around	11/72	
It's A Shame	10/70	
One Of A Kind (Love Affair)	6/73	
The Rubberband Man	11/76	
They Just Can't Stop It The (Games People Play)	10/75	
Working My Way Back To You-Forgive Me, Girl	2/80	3/80
SPIRAL STAIRCASE (US)		
More Today Than Yesterday	6/69	
SPITTING IMAGE (UK)		
The Chicken Song		5/86
SPLODGENESSABOUNDS (UK)		
Simon Templar/Two Pints Of Lager And A Packet Of Crisps Please		6/80
Dusty SPRINGFIELD (UK)		
All I See Is You		10/66
Goin' Back		7/66
I Close My Eyes And Count To Ten		7/68
I Just Don't Know What To Do With Myself		7/64
I Only Want To Be With You	3/64	11/63
In Private		12/89
In The Middle Of Nowhere		7/65
Losing You		12/64
Some Of Your Lovin'		10/65
Son-Of-A Preacher Man	1/69	1/69
Stay Awhile		3/64
❖ with Pet Shop Boys What Have I Done To Deserve This	2/88	8/87
Wishin' And Hopin'	7/64	
You Don't Have To Say You Love Me	6/66	4/66
Rick SPRINGFIELD (Aus)		
Affair Of The Night	5/83	
Don't Talk To Strangers	4/82	
I've Done Everything For You	10/81	
Jessie's Girl	6/81	
Love Somebody	4/84	
Speak To The Sky	10/72	
SPRINGFIELDS (UK)		
Island Of Dreams		2/63
Say I Won't Be There		4/63
Bruce SPRINGSTEEN (US)		
Born In The U.S.A.	12/84	7/85
Brilliant Disguise	10/87	
Cover Me	9/84	
Dancing In The Dark	6/84	2/85
Glory Days	7/85	
Human Touch/Better Days	4/92	3/92
Hungry Heart	12/80	
I'm Goin' Down	10/85	
I'm On Fire	4/85	7/85
My Hometown	1/86	12/85
One Step Up	4/88	
Santa Claus Is Comin' To Town/My Hometown		12/85
Tougher Than The Rest		7/88
Tunnel Of Love	2/88	
War	12/86	
SPRINGWATER (UK)		
I Will Return		11/71
SQUEEZE (UK)		
Cool For Cats		4/79
Labelled With Love		11/81
Up The Junction		6/79
Billy SQUIER (US)		
Rock Me Tonite	9/84	
Jim STAFFORD (US)		
My Girl Bill	6/74	
Spiders & Snakes	2/74	5/74
Wildwood Weed	8/74	
Jo STAFFORD (US)		
Make Love To Me!	2/54	5/54
Suddenly There's A Valley		12/55
Terry STAFFORD (US)		
Suspicion	3/64	
STAKKA BO (S)		
Here We Go		10/93
Frank STALLONE (US)		
Far From Over	9/83	
STAMPEDERS (C)		
Sweet City Woman	10/71	
STANDELLS (US)		
Dirty Water	7/66	
Lisa STANSFIELD (UK)		
All Around The World	3/90	11/89
Change		10/91
In All The Right Places		6/93
Live Together		2/90
❖ with Coldcut People Hold On		4/89
Someday (I'm Coming Back)		1/93
Time To Make You Mine		4/92
You Can't Deny It	7/90	
STAPLE SINGERS (US)		
I'll Take You There	5/72	
If You're Ready Come Go With Me	12/73	
Let's Do It Again	11/75	
Respect Yourself	12/71	
Cyril STAPLETON (UK)		
Blue Star		9/55
The Children's Marching Song	2/59	
STARBUCK (US)		
Moonlight Feels Right	7/76	
Alvin STARDUST (UK)		
I Feel Like Buddy Holly		6/84
I Won't Run Away		12/84
Jealous Mind		2/74
My Coo-Ca-Choo		12/73
Pretend		9/81
Red Dress		5/74
You You You		9/74
STARGAZERS (UK)		
Close The Door		9/55
Crazy Otto Rag		6/55
Happy Wanderer		4/54
I See The Moon		2/54
Twenty Tiny Fingers		11/55
STARLAND VOCAL BAND (US)		
Afternoon Delight	6/76	
STARLIGHT (Ita)		
Numero Uno		9/89
Brenda K. STARR (US)		
I Still Believe	6/88	
Edwin STARR (US)		
Contact		2/79
H.A.P.P.Y. Radio		6/79
Stop Her On Sight (SOS)/Headline News		1/69
Twenty Five Miles	4/69	
War	8/70	11/70
Freddie STARR (UK)		
It's You		3/74
Kay STARR (US)		
Changing Partners	1/54	3/54
If You Love Me (Really Love Me)	5/54	
Man Upstairs	4/54	
Rock And Roll Waltz	1/56	2/56
Ringo STARR (US)		
Back Off Boogaloo	5/72	4/72
It Don't Come Easy	5/71	5/71
No No Song/Snookeroo	3/75	
Oh My My	4/74	
Only You	12/74	
Photograph	11/73	11/73
You're Sixteen	1/74	3/74
STARS ON 45 (H) See Starsound		
STARSHIP (US)		
It's Not Enough	10/89	
It's Not Over ('Til It's Over)	8/87	
Nothing's Gonna Stop Us Now	3/87	5/87
Sara	2/86	
We Built This City	10/85	12/85
STARSOUND (H)		
Stars On 45 (Medley)	5/81	5/81
Stars On 45 (Vol 2)		7/81
STAR TURN ON 45 PINTS (UK)		
Pump Up The Bitter		5/88
STATLER BROTHERS (US)		
Flowers On The Wall	1/66	
Candi STATON (US)		
Nights On Broadway		8/77
❖ with The Source You Got The Love		2/91
Young Hearts Run Free		6/76
STATUS QUO (UK)		
Again And Again		9/78
The Anniversary Waltz - Part 1		10/90
Break The Rules		5/74
Burning Bridges (On And Off And On Again)		12/88
Caroline		10/73
Caroline (Live At The N.E.C.)		11/82
Dear John		4/82
Down Down		12/74
Down The Dustpipe		6/70
Ice In The Sun		10/68
In The Army Now		10/86
Lies/Don't Drive My Car		12/80
Marguerita Time		12/83
Mystery Song		8/76
Ol' Rag Blues		9/83
Paper Plane		2/73
Pictures Of Matchstick Men	8/68	2/68
Rain		2/76
Rock 'n' Roll		12/81
Rockin' All Over The World		10/77
Roll Over Lay Down		6/75
Rolling Home		5/86
Something 'Bout You Baby I Like		3/81
The Wanderer		11/84
What You're Proposing		10/80
Whatever You Want		10/79
Wild Side Of Life		1/77
STEALER'S WHEEL (UK)		
Stuck In The Middle With You	4/73	6/73
STEAM (US)		
Na Na Hey Hey Kiss Him Goodbye	11/69	3/70
STEEL BREEZE (US)		
You Don't Want Me Anymore	11/82	
Anthony STEEL & The Radio Revellers (UK)		
West Of Zanzibar		9/54
Tommy STEELE (UK)		
Butterfingers		5/57
Come On Let's Go		11/58
Little White Bull		12/59
Nairobi		3/58
Shiralee		9/57
Singing The Blues		1/57
Tallahassee Lassie		8/59
Water Water/Handful Of Songs		9/57
What A Mouth		7/60
STEELEYE SPAN (UK)		
All Around My Hat		12/75
STEELY DAN (US)		
Do It Again	1/73	
Hey Nineteen	1/81	

	US Top 20 Ent	UK Top 20 Ent
Peg	2/78	
Reeling In The Years	5/73	
Rikki Don't Lose That Number	7/74	
STEPPENWOLF (US)		
Born To Be Wild	8/68	
Magic Carpet Ride	11/68	
Rock Me	4/69	
STEREO MCs (UK)		
Step It Up		12/92
CAT STEVENS (UK)		
Another Saturday Night	9/74	
Can't Keep It In		1/73
I'm Gonna Get Me A Gun		4/67
Lady D'Arbanville		7/70
Matthew And Son		1/67
Morning Has Broken	5/72	1/72
Oh Very Young	5/74	
Peace Train	10/71	
Wild World	4/71	
Connie STEVENS (US)		
❖ with Edward Byrnes Kookie, Kookie (Lend Me Your Comb)	5/59	
Sixteen Reasons	4/60	6/60
Dodie STEVENS (US)		
Pink Shoe Laces	3/59	
Ray STEVENS (US)		
Ahab, The Arab	7/62	
Bridget The Midget (The Queen Of The Blues)		3/71
Everything Is Beautiful	5/70	6/70
Gitarzan	5/69	
Misty	7/75	7/75
The Streak	5/74	6/74
Ricky STEVENS (UK)		
I Cried For You		12/61
Shakin' STEVENS (UK)		
Cry Just A Little Bit		11/83
Give Me Your Heart Tonight		9/82
Green Door		8/81
I'll Be Satisfied		11/82
It's Late		8/83
It's Raining		10/81
A Letter To You		9/84
A Love Worth Waiting For		4/84
Merry Christmas Everyone		12/85
Oh Julie		1/82
The Shakin' Stevens E.P.		12/82
Shirley		5/82
Teardrops		12/84
This Ole House		3/81
What Do You Want To Make Those Eyes At Me For		12/87
You Drive Me Crazy		5/81
SHAKY & BONNIE (Shakin' STEVENS & Bonnie TYLER) (UK)		
A Rockin' Good Way		1/84
B.W. STEVENSON (US)		
My Maria	9/73	
Al STEWART (UK)		
Time Passages	11/78	
Year Of The Cat	2/77	
Amii STEWART (US)		
Friends		1/85
Knock On Wood	3/79	5/79
★ Knock On Wood/Light My Fire		9/85
Light My Fire/137 Disco Heaven (Medley)		7/79
Andy STEWART (UK)		
Donald Where's Your Troosers		12/89
Billy STEWART (US)		
Summertime	8/66	
Dave STEWART & Barbara Gaskin (UK)		
It's My Party		10/81
David A. STEWART introducing Candy Dulfer (UK/H)		
Lily Was Here	7/91	3/90
Jermaine STEWART (US)		
Say It Again		2/88
We Don't Have To Take Out Clothes Off	8/86	8/86
John STEWART (US)		
Gold	7/79	
Rod STEWART (UK)		
❖ with Bryan Adams & Rod Stewart All For Love	12/93	
Angel/What Made Milwaukee Famous		12/72
Baby Jane	7/83	6/83
Crazy About Her	7/89	

	US Top 20 Ent	UK Top 20 Ent
Da Ya Think I'm Sexy	1/79	11/78
Downtown Train	1/90	3/90
Every Beat Of My Heart		7/86
Farewell/Bring It On Home To Me		10/74
Forever Young	10/88	
Get Back		12/76
Have I Told You Lately	5/93	6/93
Hotlegs/I Was Only Joking		2/78
I Don't Want To Talk About It/First Cut Is The Deepest		5/77
Infatuation	7/84	
The Killing Of Georgie		9/76
Lost In You	7/88	
Love Touch	7/86	
Maggie May/Reason To Believe	9/71	9/71
The Motown Song	9/91	6/91
My Heart Can't Tell You No	3/89	
Oh No Not My Baby		9/73
Ole Ola (Muhler Brasileira)		6/78
Passion	12/80	
Rhythm Of My Heart	4/91	3/91
Ruby Tuesday		2/93
Sailing		8/75
★ Sailing		10/76
Some Guys Have All The Luck	10/84	
This Old Heart Of Mine		11/75
Tom Traubert's Blues (Waltzing Matilda)		12/92
Tonight I'm Yours (Don't Hurt Me)		11/81
Tonight's The Night (Gonna Be Alright)	11/76	6/76
What Am I Gonna Do		9/83
You Wear It Well	10/72	8/72
You're In My Heart	12/77	10/77
Young Turks	11/81	1/82
Rod STEWART & Tina Turner (UK/US)		
It Takes Two		12/90
Rod STEWART with Ronald Isley (UK/US)		
This Old Heart Of Mine	5/90	
Curtis STIGERS (US)		
I Wonder Why	11/91	2/92
You're All That Matters To Me		4/92
STING (UK)		
❖ with Bryan Adams & Rod Stewart All For Love	12/93	
All This Time	3/91	
Be Still My Beating Heart	3/88	
Fortress Around Your Heart	10/85	
If You Love Somebody Set Them Free	7/85	
Russians		1/86
We'll Be Together	11/87	
STOCK AITKEN WATERMAN (UK)		
❖ with Christians, Holly Johnson, Paul McCartney, Gerry Marsden Ferry 'Cross The Mersey		5/89
Mr Sleaze		10/87
Morris STOLOFF (US)		
Moonglow And Theme From 'Picnic'	4/56	6/56
Stone PONEYS (US)		
Different Drum	1/68	
STONE ROSES (UK)		
Elephant Stone		3/90
Fool's Gold/What The World Is Waiting For		12/89
One Love		7/90
R & J STONE (UK)		
We Do It		1/76
STORIES (US)		
Brother Louie	8/73	
Gale STORM (US)		
Dark Moon	5/57	
I Hear You Knocking	11/55	
Teenage Prayer	1/56	
Why Do Fools Fall In Love	3/56	
STRANGELOVES (US)		
I Want Candy	8/65	
STRANGLERS (UK)		
All Day And All Of The Night		1/88
European Female		1/83
Golden Brown		1/82
No More Heroes		10/77
Peaches/Go Buddy Go		7/77
Something Better Change/Straighten Out		8/77
Strange Little Girl		8/82
STRAWBERRY ALARM CLOCK (US)		
Incense And Peppermints	10/67	
STRAWBERRY SWITCHBLADE (UK)		
Since Yesterday		1/85

	US Top 20 Ent	UK Top 20 Ent
STRAWBS (UK)		
Lay Down		12/72
Part Of The Union		2/73
STRAY CATS (US)		
Rock This Town	11/82	2/81
Runaway Boys		12/80
(She's) Sexy + 17	9/83	
Stray Cat Strut	2/83	5/81
Barbra STREISAND (US)		
Comin' In And Out Of Your Life	12/81	
Evergreen (From 'A Star Is Born')	2/77	5/77
The Main Event/Fight	7/79	
My Heart Belongs To Me	6/77	
❖ with Donna Summer No More Tears (Enough Is Enough)	11/79	11/79
People	6/64	
Stoney End	1/71	
The Way We Were	1/74	
Woman In Love	9/80	10/80
BARBRA & NEIL (US)		
You Don't Bring Me Flowers	11/78	12/78
Barbra STREISAND & Barry Gibb (US/UK)		
Guilty	12/80	
What Kind Of Fool	3/81	
STRING-A-LONGS (US)		
Wheels	2/61	3/61
Jud STRUNK (US)		
Daisy A Day	5/73	
STYLE COUNCIL (UK)		
Groovin'(You're The Best Thing)/Big Boss Groove		6/84
It Didn't Matter		1/87
The Lodgers		10/85
Long Hot Summer		8/83
Money Go Round (Pt.1)		6/83
My Ever Changing Moods		2/84
Shout To The Top		10/84
Solid Bond In Your Heart		11/83
Speak Like A Child		3/83
Walls Come Tumbling Down!		5/85
STYLISTICS (US)		
Betcha By Golly, Wow	4/72	
Break Up To Make Up	3/73	
Can't Give You Anything (But My Love)		8/75
Can't Help Falling In Love		5/76
Funky Weekend		3/76
I'm Stone In Love With You	12/72	11/72
Let's Put It All Together		11/74
Na Na Is The Saddest Word		12/75
Rockin' Roll Baby	12/73	2/74
Sing Baby Sing		5/75
16 Bars		9/76
Star On A TV Show		2/75
You Are Everything		12/71
You Make Me Feel Brand New	5/74	8/74
STYX (US)		
Babe	11/79	1/80
The Best Of Times	2/81	
Come Sail Away	12/77	
Don't Let It End	6/83	
Lady	3/75	
Mr. Roboto	3/83	
Show Me The Way	3/91	
Too Much Time On My Hands	5/81	
SUB SUB featuring Melanie Williams (UK)		
Ain't No Love (Ain't No Use)		4/93
SUEDE (UK)		
Animal Nitrate		3/93
SUGARHILL GANG (US)		
Rapper's Delight		12/79
SUGARLOAF (US)		
Green Eyed Lady	10/70	
SUGARLOAF/JERRY CORBETTA (US)		
Don't Call Us We'll Call You	3/75	
Donna SUMMER (US)		
Bad Girls	6/79	
Deep Down Inside		9/77
Dim All The Lights	10/79	
Heaven Knows	2/79	
Hot Stuff	5/79	6/79
I Don't Wanna Get Hurt		6/89
I Feel Love	10/77	7/77
I Love You		1/78
I Remember Yesterday		10/77
Last Dance	7/78	

	US Top 20 Ent	UK Top 20 Ent
Love Is In Control (Finger On The Trigger)	8/82	
Love To Love You Baby	1/76	2/76
Love's Unkind		12/77
MacArthur Park	10/78	10/78
On The Radio	2/80	
She Works Hard For The Money	7/83	
This Time I Know It's For Real	6/89	3/89
Unconditional Love		11/83
The Wanderer	10/80	
Donna SUMMER & Barbra Streisand (US)		
No More Tears (Enough Is Enough)	11/79	11/79
SUNNY (UK)		
Doctor's Orders		4/74
SUNNY & THE SUNGLOWS (US)		
Talk To Me	10/63	
SUPERTRAMP (UK)		
Breakfast In America		7/79
Dreamer	11/80	3/75
Goodbye Stranger	9/79	
It's Raining Again	12/82	
The Logical Song	5/79	4/79
Take The Long Way Home	11/79	
Diana Ross & The SUPREMES (US)		
★ Baby Love		9/74
I'm Livin' In Shame	2/69	5/69
In And Out Of Love	12/67	1/68
Love Child	11/68	1/69
Reflections	8/67	9/67
Someday We'll Be Together	12/69	1/70
Diana Ross & The SUPREMES & The Temptations (US)		
I'm Gonna Make You Love Me	12/68	2/69
SUPREMES (US)		
Automatically Sunshine		8/72
Baby Love	10/64	11/64
Back In My Arms Again	5/65	
Come See About Me	12/64	
Floy Joy		3/72
The Happening	4/67	6/67
I Hear A Symphony	11/65	
Love Is Here And Now You're Gone	2/67	
Love Is Like An Itching In My Heart	5/66	
My World Is Empty Without You	2/66	
Nathan Jones	6/71	9/71
Nothing But Heartaches	9/65	
Stoned Love	12/70	2/71
Stop! In The Name Of Love	3/65	4/65
Up The Ladder To The Roof	4/70	5/70
Where Did Our Love Go	8/64	9/64
You Can't Hurry Love	9/66	9/66
You Keep Me Hangin' On	11/66	12/66
SUPREMES & Four Tops (US)		
River Deep-Mountain High	1/71	7/71
AL B. SURE! (US)		
Nite And Day	7/88	
SURFACE (US)		
The First Time	1/91	
Shower Me With Your Love	8/89	
SURFARIS (US)		
Wipe Out	7/63	8/63
SURVIVOR (US)		
Burning Heart	12/85	2/86
Eye Of The Tiger	7/82	8/82
High On You	3/85	
I Can't Hold Back	12/84	
Is This Love	12/86	
The Search Is Over	6/85	
SUTHERLAND BROTHERS And Quiver (UK)		
Arms Of Mary		5/76
Billy SWAN (US)		
I Can Help	11/74	1/75
Patrick SWAYZE (with Wendy Fraser) (US)		
She's Like The Wind	2/88	
Keith SWEAT (US)		
I Want Her	3/88	
I'll Give All My Love To You	1/91	
Make You Sweat	8/90	
SWEET DREAMS (UK)		
Honey Honey		8/74
SWEET PEOPLE (F)		
Et Les Oiseaux Chantaient (And The Birds Were Singing)		10/80
SWEET SENSATION (US)		
If Wishes Came True	7/90	
Love Child	5/90	
SWEET SENSATION (UK)		

	US Top 20 Ent	UK Top 20 Ent
Purely By Coincidence		2/75
Sad Sweet Dreamer	3/75	10/74
SWEET (UK)		
Ballroom Blitz	9/75	9/73
Blockbuster		1/73
Co-Co		6/71
Fox On The Run	12/75	4/75
Funny Funny		4/71
Hell Raiser		5/73
Little Willy	4/73	7/72
Love Is Like Oxygen	5/78	2/78
Poppa Joe		3/72
The Six Teens		7/74
Teenage Rampage		1/74
Wig Wam Bam		9/72
SWING OUT SISTER (UK)		
Breakout	10/87	11/86
Surrender		1/87
SWINGING BLUE JEANS (UK)		
Good Golly Miss Molly		4/64
Hippy Hippy Shake		1/64
You're No Good		6/64
SWV (US)		
I'm So Into You	4/93	
Right Here (Human Nature)	8/93	8/93
Weak	5/93	
SYBIL (US)		
✤ with West End The Love I Lost		1/93
Walk On By		2/90
When I'm Good And Ready		4/93
SYLVERS (US)		
Boogie Fever	4/76	
Hot Line	12/76	
SYLVESTER (US)		
You Make Me Feel (Mighty Real)		10/78
SYLVIA (US)		
Nobody	11/82	
SYLVIA (US)		
Pillow Talk	5/73	
SYLVIA (Swe)		
Y Viva Espana		9/74
SYNDICATE OF SOUND (US)		
Little Girl	7/66	
SYREETA (US) See Billy Preston & Syreeta		
SYSTEM (US)		
Don't Disturb The Groove	6/87	
T-CONNECTION (US)		
Do What You Wanna Do		7/77
T. REX (UK)		
Bang A Gong (Get It On)	3/72	7/71
Children Of The Revolution		9/72
Debora/One Inch Rock		4/72
The Groover		6/73
Hot Love		3/71
I Love To Boogie		7/76
Jeepster		11/71
Metal Guru		5/72
Ride A White Swan		2/71
Solid Gold Easy Action		12/72
Teenage Dream		2/74
Telegram Sam		1/72
Truck On (Tyke)		12/73
20th Century Boy		3/73
★ 20th Century Boy		9/91
T99 (B)		
Anasthasia		5/91
TACO (H)		
Puttin' On The Ritz	8/83	
TAFFY (UK)		
I Love My Radio		2/87
TAG TEAM (US)		
Whoomp! (There It Is)	6/93	
TAKE THAT (UK)		
Babe		12/93
Could It Be Magic		12/92
It Only Takes A Minute		6/92
A Million Love Songs (EP)		10/92
Pray		7/93
Why Can't I Wake Up With You?		2/93
TAKE THAT featuring Lulu (UK)		
Relight My Fire		10/93
TALK TALK (UK)		
Today		9/82
TALKING HEADS (US)		

	US Top 20 Ent	UK Top 20 Ent
Burning Down The House	10/83	
Once In A Lifetime		3/81
Road To Nowhere		11/85
TAMS (US)		
Hey Girl Don't Bother Me		8/71
What Kind Of Fool (Do You Think I Am)	2/64	
TARRIERS (US)		
The Banana Boat Song	12/56	
✤ with Vince Martin Cindy, Oh Cindy	10/56	
TASTE OF HONEY (US)		
Boogie Oogie Oogie	8/78	7/78
Sukiyaki	5/81	
TAVARES (US)		
Don't Take Away The Music		10/76
Heaven Must Be Missing An Angel	9/76	7/76
It Only Takes A Minute	10/75	
More Than A Woman		5/78
Whodunit		5/77
Felice TAYLOR (US)		
I Feel Love Comin' On		11/67
James TAYLOR (US)		
Don't Let Me Be Lonely Tonight	1/73	
Fire And Rain	10/70	
Handy Man	8/77	
How Sweet It Is (To Be Loved By You)	8/75	
✤ with Carly Simon Mockingbird	3/74	
✤ with Art Garfunkel & Paul Simon Wonderful World	3/78	
You've Got A Friend	7/71	9/71
James TAYLOR & J. D. Souther (US)		
Her Town Too	4/81	
Johnnie TAYLOR (US)		
Disco Lady	3/76	
I Believe In You (You Believe In Me)	8/73	
Who's Making Love	11/68	
R. Dean TAYLOR (Can)		
Indiana Wants Me	10/70	5/71
There's A Ghost In My House		6/74
T-BONES (US)		
No Matter What Shape (Your Stomach's In)	1/66	
TEARDROP EXPLODES (UK)		
Reward		3/81
TEARS FOR FEARS (UK)		
Change		2/83
Everybody Wants To Rule The World	5/85	4/85
Everybody Wants To Run The World		6/86
Head Over Heels	10/85	7/85
Mad World		10/82
Pale Shelter		5/83
Shout	7/85	1/85
Sowing The Seeds Of Love	10/89	9/89
TECHNOTRONIC (B)		
Get Up! (Before The Night Is Over)	3/90	2/90
Megamix		10/90
Move That Body		6/91
Move This	8/92	
Pump Up The Jam	12/89	9/89
Rockin' Over The Beat		7/90
This Beat Is Technotronic		4/90
TEDDY BEARS (US)		
To Know Him, Is To Love Him	10/58	1/59
TEE SET (H)		
Ma Belle Amie	2/70	
TEEN QUEENS (US)		
Eddie My Love	3/56	
TEMPERANCE SEVEN (UK)		
Pasadena		6/61
You're Driving Me Crazy		4/61
Nino TEMPO & April Stevens (US)		
Deep Purple	10/63	
Whispering	1/64	
TEMPTATIONS (US)		
Ain't Too Proud To Beg	7/66	
All I Need	6/67	
Ball Of Confusion (That's What The World Is Today)	6/70	10/70
Beauty Is Only Skin Deep	9/66	
Cloud Nine	12/68	9/69
Get Ready		4/69
I Can't Get Next To You	9/69	2/70
I Could Never Love Another (After Loving You)	6/68	
(I Know) I'm Losing You	12/66	
✤ with The Supremes I'm Gonna Make You Love Me	12/68	2/69

	US Top 20 Ent	UK Top 20 Ent
I Wish It Would Rain	1/68	
Just My Imagination (Running Away With Me)	3/71	7/71
(Loneliness Made Me Realize) It's You That I Need	11/67	
Masterpiece	4/73	
My Girl	2/65	2/92
Papa Was A Rollin' Stone	11/72	
Psychedelic Shack	2/70	
Run Away Child, Running Wild	3/69	
Take A Look Around		5/72
The Way You Do The Things You Do	4/64	
You're My Everything	9/67	
10CC (UK)		
The Dean And I		9/73
Donna		10/72
Dreadlock Holiday		8/78
Good Morning Judge		5/77
I'm Mandy Fly Me		4/76
I'm Not In Love	7/75	6/75
Life Is A Minestone		4/75
Rubber Bullets		6/73
Things We Do For Love	3/77	1/77
Wall Street Shuffle		7/74
TEN CITY (US)		
That's The Way Love Is		2/89
TEN POLE TUDOR (UK)		
Swords Of A Thousand Men		5/81
TEN SHARP (H)		
You		4/92
TEN YEARS AFTER (UK)		
Love Like A Man		7/70
Tammi TERRELL (US) See Marvin Gaye & Tammi Terrell		
TESLA (US)		
Love Song	1/90	
Signs	3/91	
Joe TEX (US)		
Ain't Gonna Bump No More (With No Big Fat Woman)	6/77	5/77
Hold What You've Got	1/65	
I Gotcha	3/72	
Skinny Legs And All	12/67	
TEXAS (UK)		
I Don't Want A Lover		3/89
THEM (UK)		
Baby Please Don't Go		1/65
Here Comes The Night		4/65
THEN JERICO (UK)		
Big Area		2/89
THERAPY? (UK)		
Shortsharpshock (EP)		3/93
THEY MIGHT BE GIANTS (US)		
Birdhouse In Your Soul		3/90
THIN LIZZY (Ire/UK)		
The Boys Are Back In Town	7/76	7/76
Dancin' In The Moonlight (It's Caught Me In The Spotlight)		9/77
Don't Believe A Word		2/77
Killer On The Loose		10/80
Waiting For An Alibi		3/79
Whisky In The Jar		2/73
THIRD WORLD (J)		
Dancing On The Floor (Hooked On Love)		7/81
Now That We've Found Love		10/78
38 SPECIAL (US)		
Caught Up In You	6/82	
Second Chance	4/89	
B.J. THOMAS (US)		
(Hey Won't You Play) Another Somebody Done Somebody Wrong Song	4/75	
Hooked On A Feeling	1/69	
I Just Can't Help Believing	8/70	
I'm So Lonesome I Could Cry	3/66	
Raindrops Keep Fallin' On My Head	12/69	
Carla THOMAS (US)		
Gee Whiz (Look At His Eyes)	3/61	
Evelyn THOMAS (US)		
High Energy		6/84
Kenny THOMAS (UK)		
Best Of You		10/91
Thinking About Your Love		6/91
Nicky THOMAS (J)		
Love Of The Common People		7/70
Rufus THOMAS (US)		
Walking The Dog	11/63	

	US Top 20 Ent	UK Top 20 Ent
Timmy THOMAS (US)		
Why Can't We Live Together	1/73	4/73
THOMPSON TWINS (UK/NZ)		
Doctor! Doctor!	7/84	2/84
Hold Me Now	3/84	12/83
King For A Day	3/86	
Lay Your Hands On Me	11/85	
Love On Your Side		3/83
Sister Of Mercy		7/84
We Are Detective		5/83
You Take Me Up		4/84
Sue THOMPSON (US)		
James (Hold The Ladder Steady)	11/62	
Norman	1/62	
Sad Movies (Make Me Cry)	10/61	
Ali THOMSON (UK)		
Take A Little Rhythm	8/80	
Ken THORNE & His Orchestra (UK)		
Theme From 'The Legion's Last Patrol'		8/63
THREE DEGREES (US)		
Givin' Up Givin' In		11/78
My Simple Heart		12/79
The Runner		4/79
Take Good Care Of Yourself		5/75
✦ with MFSB TSOP (The Sound Of Philadelphia)	4/74	
When Will I See You Again	11/74	7/74
Women In Love		1/79
THREE DOG NIGHT (US)		
Black & White	9/72	
Easy To Be Hard	9/69	
Eli's Coming	12/69	
The Family Of Man	4/72	
Joy To The World	4/71	
Liar	8/71	
Mama Told Me (Not To Come)	6/70	9/70
Never Been To Spain	1/72	
An Old Fashioned Love Song	12/71	
One	6/69	
Shambala	6/73	
The Show Must Go On	4/74	
Johnny THUNDER (US)		
Loop De Loop	1/63	
THUNDERCLAP NEWMAN (UK)		
Something In The Air		6/69
Bobby THURSTON (US)		
Check Out The Groove		5/80
TIERRA (US)		
Together	2/81	
TIFFANY (US)		
All This Time	1/89	
Could've Been	1/88	3/88
I Saw Him Standing There	4/88	6/88
I Think We're Alone Now	10/87	1/88
TIGHT FIT (UK)		
Back To The Sixties		8/81
Fantasy Island		5/82
The Lion Sleeps Tonight		2/82
Tanita TIKARAM (UK)		
Good Tradition		8/88
Til TUESDAY (US)		
Voices Carry	6/85	
Johnny TILLOTSON (US)		
It Keeps Right On A-Hurtin'	6/62	
Poetry In Motion	10/60	12/60
Talk Back Trembling Lips	12/63	
Without You	9/61	
TIME (US)		
Jerk Out	8/90	
TIME FREQUENCY (UK)		
Real Love '93		11/93
TIMELORDS (UK) see KLF		
TIMEX SOCIAL CLUB (US)		
Rumors	8/86	
TIMMY T (US)		
One More Try	2/91	
TITANIC (N/UK)		
Sultana		10/71
TLC (US)		
Ain't Too Proud 2 Beg	4/92	6/92
Baby-Baby-Baby	7/92	
What About Your Friends	11/92	
TOAD THE WET SPROCKET (US)		
All I Want	9/92	
TOBY BEAU (US)		

	US Top 20 Ent	UK Top 20 Ent
My Angel Baby	8/78	
Art & Dotty TODD (US)		
Chanson D'amour (Song Of Love)	5/58	
TOGETHER (US)		
Hardcore Uproar		8/90
TOKENS (US)		
The Lion Sleeps Tonight	12/61	1/62
TOM TOM CLUB (US)		
Wordy Rappinghood		7/81
TOMMY TUTONE (US)		
867-5309/Jenny	4/82	
TONE LOC (US)		
Funky Cold Medina	4/89	
Wild Thing	1/89	
TONIGHT (UK)		
Drummer Man		2/78
TONY! TONI! TONE! (US)		
Anniversary	10/93	
Feels Good	11/90	
If I Had No Loot	7/93	
TOPOL (Isr)		
If I Were A Rich Man		7/67
Mel TORME (US)		
Coming Home Baby		1/63
Mountain Greenery		5/56
TORNADOS (UK)		
Globetrotter		1/63
The Ice Cream Man		6/63
Robot		4/63
Telstar	12/62	9/62
Mitchell TOROK (US)		
When Mexico Gave Up The Rumba		10/56
TOTO (US)		
Africa	12/82	2/83
Hold The Line	12/78	
I Won't Hold You Back	5/83	
I'll Be Over You	11/86	
Rosanna	6/82	
TOTO COELO (UK)		
I Eat Cannibals Pt. 1		8/82
TOTTENHAM HOTSPUR F.A. CUP FINAL SQUAD (UK)		
Ossie's Dream (Spurs Are On Their Way To Wembley)		5/81
TOURISTS (UK)		
I Only Want To Be With You		12/79
So Good To Be Back Home Again		3/80
Ed TOWNSEND (US)		
For Your Love	5/58	
Pete TOWNSHEND (UK)		
Let My Love Open The Door	8/80	
TOXIC TWO (US)		
Rave Generator		3/92
TOY DOLLS (UK)		
Nellie The Elephant		12/84
TOYAH (UK)		
Four From Toyah E.P.		3/81
Four More From Toyah E.P.		12/81
I Want To Be Free		5/81
Thunder In Mountains		10/81
TOYS (US)		
A Lovers Concerto	10/65	11/65
T'PAU (UK)		
China In Your Hand		11/87
Heart And Soul	7/87	9/87
Valentine		2/88
TRACIE (UK)		
The House That Jack Built		4/83
TRAFFIC (UK)		
Here We Go Round The Mulberry Bush		12/67
Hole In My Shoe		9/67
Paper Sun		6/67
TRAMMPS (US)		
Disco Inferno	5/78	
Hold Back The Night		11/75
TRANSVISION VAMP (UK)		
Baby I Don't Care		4/89
I Want Your Love		7/88
TRANS-X (Can)		
Living On Video		7/85
TRASHMEN (US)		
Surfin' Bird	1/64	
TRAVIS & BOB (US)		
Tell Him No	4/59	
John TRAVOLTA (US)		
Greased Lightning		12/78

	US Top 20 Ent	UK Top 20 Ent
Let Her In	7/76	
Sandy		10/78
John TRAVOLTA & Olivia Newton-John (US/UK)		
The Grease Megamix		12/90
Summer Nights	9/78	9/78
You're The One That I Want	4/78	6/78
TREMELOES (UK) also see Brian Poole		
(Call Me) Number One		11/69
Even The Bad Times Are Good	8/67	
Helule Helule		6/68
Here Comes My Baby	6/67	2/67
Me And My Life		10/70
My Little Lady		10/68
Silence Is Golden	8/67	5/67
Suddenly You Love Me		2/68
Jackie TRENT (UK)		
Where Are You Now (My Love)		5/65
Ralph TRESVANT (US)		
Sensitivity	12/90	
TRICKY DISCO (UK)		
Tricky Disco		8/90
TRIO (G)		
Da Da Da		7/82
TRIPLETS (US)		
You Don't Have To Go Home Tonight	5/91	
Kathy TROCCOLI (US)		
Everything Changes	4/92	
TROGGS (UK)		
Any Way That You Want Me		1/67
Give It To Me		3/67
I Can't Control Myself		10/66
Love Is All Around	5/68	11/67
Wild Thing	7/66	5/66
With A Girl Like You		7/66
Doris TROY (US)		
Just One Look	7/63	
Andrea TRUE CONNECTION (US)		
More, More, More (Pt. 1)	6/76	5/76
TUBES (US)		
She's A Beauty	6/83	
TUBEWAY ARMY (UK) See Gary Numan		
Tommy TUCKER (US)		
Hi-Heel Sneakers	3/64	
TUNE WEAVERS (US)		
Happy, Happy Birthday Baby	9/57	
Ike & Tina TURNER (US)		
Nutbush City Limits		10/73
Proud Mary	3/71	
River Deep Mountain High		6/66
Sammy TURNER (US)		
Lavender-Blue	7/59	
Spyder TURNER (US)		
Stand By Me	2/67	
Tina TURNER (US) also see Ike & Tina Turner		
The Best		9/89
Better Be Good To Me	11/84	
Disco Inferno		9/93
I Don't Wanna Fight	7/93	5/93
I Don't Wanna Lose You		12/89
✤ with Rod Stewart It Takes Two		12/90
✤ with Bryan Adams It's Only Love	1/86	
Let's Stay Together		12/83
Private Dancer	3/85	
Typical Male	10/86	
We Don't Need Another Hero		
(Thunderdome)	8/85	8/85
What You Get Is What You See	4/87	
What's Love Got To Do With It	7/84	7/84
TURTLES (US)		
Elenore	10/68	11/68
Happy Together	3/67	4/67
It Ain't Me Babe	9/65	
She'd Rather Be With Me	6/67	7/67
You Know What I Mean	9/67	
You Showed Me	2/69	
TV CAST (UK)		
Army Game		6/58
TWEETS (UK)		
The Birdie Song (Birdie Dance)		10/81
TWENTY 4 SEVEN featuring Captain Hollywood (US/G/H)		
I Can't Stand It		10/90
Dwight TWILLEY (US)		
Girls	4/84	
TWINKLE (UK)		
Terry		12/64

	US Top 20 Ent	UK Top 20 Ent
Conway TWITTY (US)		
Danny Boy	11/59	
It's Only Make Believe	10/58	11/58
Lonely Blue Boy	2/60	
Mona Lisa		8/59
2 IN A ROOM (US)		
Wiggle It	12/90	2/91
2 UNLIMITED (H)		
Faces		9/93
Get Ready For This		10/91
Magic Friend		8/92
No Limit		5/93
Tribal Dance		5/93
Twilight Zone		1/92
Workaholic		5/92
2PAC (US)		
I Get Around	9/93	
Keep Ya Head Up	11/93	
Bonnie TYLER (UK)		
Holding Out For A Hero		9/85
It's A Heartache	6/78	12/77
Lost In France		11/76
✤ with Shakin' Stevens A Rockin' Good Way		1/84
Total Eclipse Of The Heart	9/83	3/83
TYMES (US)		
Ms Grace		1/75
So Much In Love	7/63	
Wonderful! Wonderful!	9/63	
You Little Trustmaker	10/74	
TYPICALLY TROPICAL (UK)		
Barbados		7/75
TYRANNOSAURUS REX (UK) see T. Rex		
TYREE featuring Kool Rock Steady (US)		
Turn Up The Bass		3/89
UB40 (UK)		
Can't Help Falling In Love	6/93	5/93
Cherry Oh Baby		4/84
Don't Break My Heart		11/85
The Earth Dies Screaming/Dream A Lie		11/80
Here I Am (Come And Take Me)	6/91	
Higher Ground		8/93
Homely Girl		12/89
✤ with Robert Palmer I'll Be Your Baby Tonight		11/90
If It Happens Again		10/84
King/Food For Thought		4/80
Kingston Town		4/90
My Way Of Thinking/I Think It's Going To Rain		7/80
One In Ten		9/81
Please Don't Make Me Cry		11/83
Red Red Wine	10/88	9/83
Sing Our Own Song		7/86
The Way You Do The Things You Do	12/90	
UB40 & Chrissie Hynde (UK/US)		
Breakfast In Bed		7/88
I Got You Babe		8/85
UGLY KID JOE (US)		
Cat's In The Cradle	3/93	3/93
Everything About You	5/92	5/92
UK MIXMASTERS (UK)		
The Bare Necessities Megamix		12/91
Tracey ULLMAN (UK)		
Breakaway		4/83
Move Over Darling		12/83
They Don't Know	4/84	10/83
ULTRAVOX (UK)		
All Stood Still		6/81
Dancing With Tears In My Eyes		6/84
Hymn		12/82
Love's Great Adventure		11/84
The Thin Wall		9/81
Vienna		2/81
Piero UMILIANI (Ita)		
Mah Na Mah Na		5/77
UNDERCOVER (UK)		
Baker Street		8/92
Never Let Her Slip Away		11/92
UNDERTONES (UK)		
My Perfect Cousin		5/80
UNDISPUTED TRUTH (US)		
Smiling Faces Sometime	8/71	
UNION GAP (US) see Gary Puckett		

	US Top 20 Ent	UK Top 20 Ent
UNIT 4 PLUS 2 (UK)		
Concrete And Clay		3/65
You've Never Been In Love Like This Before		6/65
UPSETTERS (J)		
The Return Of Django		11/69
URBAN HYPE (UK)		
A Trip To Trumpton		7/92
URBAN COOKIE COLLECTIVE (UK)		
Feels Like Heaven		11/93
The Key The Secret		8/93
Midge URE (UK)		
If I Was		9/85
No Regrets		7/82
USA FOR AFRICA (US)		
We Are The World	4/85	4/85
USURA (Ita)		
Open Your Mind		1/93
UTAH SAINTS (UK)		
Believe In Me		5/93
Something Good		6/92
What Can You Do For Me		9/91
U2 (I)		
All I Want Is You		7/89
Angel Of Harlem	2/89	12/88
Desire	11/88	10/88
Even Better Than The Real Thing		6/92
The Fly		11/91
I Still Haven't Found What I'm Looking For	7/87	6/87
Mysterious Ways	1/92	
New Year's Day		2/83
One	5/92	
Pride (In The Name Of Love)		9/84
Stay (Faraway, So Close!)		12/93
The Unforgettable Fire		5/85
Where The Streets Have No Name	11/87	9/87
With Or Without You	4/87	3/87
U2 with B.B. King (I/US)		
When Love Comes To Town		4/89
Ricky VALANCE (UK)		
Tell Laura I Love Her		9/60
Jerry VALE (US)		
You Don't Know Me	9/56	
Ritchie VALENS (US)		
Donna	1/59	
Caterina VALENTE (F)		
The Breeze And I	4/55	8/55
Dickie VALENTINE (UK)		
A Blossom Fell		2/55
Christmas Alphabet		12/55
Christmas Island		12/56
Finger Of Suspicion		12/54
I Wonder		6/55
Mr. Sandman		1/55
One More Sunrise (Morgen)		11/59
Joe VALINO (US)		
Garden Of Eden	11/56	
Frankie VALLI (US) also see Four Seasons		
Can't Take My Eyes Off You	6/67	
Grease	7/78	9/78
My Eyes Adored You	2/75	3/75
Our Day Will Come	12/75	
Swearin' To God	7/75	
You're Ready Now		1/71
June VALLI (US)		
I Understand	7/54	
Leroy VAN DYKE (US)		
Walk On By	12/61	1/62
VAN HALEN (US/H)		
Dance The Night Away	7/79	
Finish What Ya Started	12/88	
I'll Wait	6/84	
Jump	2/84	3/84
(Oh) Pretty Woman	4/82	
Panama	8/84	
When It's Love	8/88	
Why Can't This Be Love	4/86	5/86
Luther VANDROSS (US)		
Don't Want To Be A Fool	10/91	
Here And Now	4/90	
Never Too Much		11/89
Power Of Love-Love Power	6/91	
Stop To Love	2/87	
Luther VANDROSS & Janet Jackson (US)		
The Best Things In Life Are Free	6/92	8/92

	US Top 20 Ent	UK Top 20 Ent
VANGELIS (Gre) also see Jon & Vangelis		
Chariots Of Fire	3/82	6/81
VANILLA FUDGE (US)		
(You Keep Me) Hangin' On	8/68	
VANILLA ICE (US)		
Ice Ice Baby	10/90	11/90
Play That Funky Music	1/91	2/91
VANITY FARE (UK)		
Early In The Morning	1/70	8/69
Hitchin' A Ride	6/70	
Gino VANNELLI (US)		
I Just Wanna Stop	11/78	
Living Inside Myself	4/81	
Randy VANWARMER (US)		
Just When I Needed You Most	5/79	9/79
VAPORS (UK)		
Turning Japanese		3/80
VARIOUS ARTISTS (UK)		
All Star Hit Parade		7/56
VARIOUS ARTISTS (UK)		
The Brits 1990		3/90
Frankie VAUGHAN (UK)		
Can't Get Along Without You/We're Not Alone		3/58
Garden Of Eden		1/57
Green Door		11/56
Happy Days And Lonely Nights		2/55
The Heart Of A Man		8/59
Heartless		5/54
Kewpie Doll		5/58
Kisses Sweeter Than Wine		1/58
Loop De Loop		2/63
Man On Fire/Wanderin' Eyes		10/57
There Must Be A Way		9/67
Tower Of Strength		11/61
Frankie VAUGHAN & The Kaye Sisters (UK)		
Come Softly To Me		5/59
Gotta Have Something In The Bank Frank		11/57
Malcolm VAUGHAN (UK)		
Chapel Of The Roses		5/57
Every Day Of My Life		7/55
More Than Ever (Come Prima)		10/58
My Special Angel		12/57
St. Therese Of The Roses		11/56
To Be Loved		4/58
Wait For Me		4/59
Sarah VAUGHAN (US)		
Broken-Hearted Melody	9/59	10/59
Make Yourself Comfortable	12/54	
Whatever Lola Wants	5/55	
Billy VAUGHN (US)		
Melody Of Love	1/55	
Sail Along Silvery Moon/Raunchy	1/58	
The Shifting Whispering Sands (Pts 1 & 2)	10/55	
Theme From 'The Threepenny Opera'		4/56
Bobby VEE (US)		
Charms	5/63	
Come Back When You Grow Up	9/67	
Devil Or Angel	10/60	
A Forever Kind Of Love		11/62
How Many Tears		9/61
More Than I Can Say		5/61
The Night Has A Thousand Eyes	1/63	2/63
Rubber Ball	1/61	2/61
Run To Him	12/61	1/62
Take Good Care Of My Baby	9/61	11/61
Suzanne VEGA (US)		
Luka	8/87	
❖ with DNA Tom's Diner	12/90	8/90
VENTURES (US)		
Hawaii Five-O	5/69	
Perfidia	12/60	12/60
Walk-Don't Run	8/60	9/60
Walk-Don't Run '64	8/64	
Billy VERA & The Beaters (US)		
At This Moment	1/87	
Larry VERNE (US)		
Mr. Custer	9/60	
Maria VIDAL (US)		
Body Rock		9/85
VILLAGE PEOPLE (US)		
Can't Stop The Music		9/80
In The Navy	4/79	3/79
Y.M.C.A.	12/78	12/78
★ Y.M.C.A.		12/93

	US Top 20 Ent	UK Top 20 Ent
VILLAGE STOMPERS (US)		
Washington Square	10/63	
Gene VINCENT & His Blue Caps (US)		
Be-Bop-A-Lula	7/56	
Lotta Lovin'/Wear My Ring	10/57	
Bobby VINTON (US)		
Blue On Blue	6/63	
Blue Velvet	9/63	10/90
Coming Home Soldier	1/67	
I Love How You Love Me	12/68	
Mr. Lonely	11/64	
My Heart Belongs To Only You	3/64	
My Melody Of Love	11/74	
Please Love Me Forever	11/67	
Rain Rain Go Away	10/62	
Roses Are Red (My Love)	6/62	8/62
Tell Me Why	6/64	
There I've Said It Again	12/63	
VIPERS SKIFFLE GROUP (UK)		
Cumberland Gap		4/57
Don't You Rock Me Daddy-O		2/57
VIRTUES (US)		
Guitar Boogie Shuffle	4/59	
VISAGE (UK)		
Damned Don't Cry		4/82
Fade To Grey		2/81
Mind Of A Toy		4/81
Night Train		7/82
VOGUES (US)		
Five O'Clock World	1/66	
My Special Angel	10/68	
Turn Around Look At Me	7/68	
You're The One	10/65	
VOICES THAT CARE (US)		
Voices That Care	4/91	
Adam WADE (US)		
As If I Didn't Know	8/61	
Take Good Care Of Her	4/61	
The Writing On The Wall	6/61	
WADSWORTH MANSION (US)		
Sweet Mary	2/71	
Jack WAGNER (US)		
All I Need	12/84	
WAH! (UK)		
The Story Of The Blues		1/83
John WAITE (US)		
Missing You	8/84	10/84
Johnny WAKELIN & The Kinshasa Band (UK)		
Black Superman (Muhammad Ali)		2/75
In Zaire		8/76
Walker BROTHERS (US)		
Another Tear Falls		10/66
Make It Easy On Yourself		9/65
My Ship Is Coming In		12/65
No Regrets		2/76
The Sun Ain't Gonna Shine Anymore	5/66	3/66
Jr. WALKER & The All Stars (US)		
(I'm A) Road Runner		5/69
Shotgun	3/65	
What Does It Take To Win Your Love	7/69	11/69
Scott WALKER (US)		
Joanna		5/68
Lights Of Cincinatti		7/69
Jerry WALLACE (US)		
How Time Flies	10/58	
Primrose Lane	10/59	
Joe WALSH (US)		
Life's Been Good	8/78	
Trevor WALTERS (J)		
Stuck On You		8/84
WANG CHUNG (UK)		
Everybody Have Fun Tonight	11/86	
Let's Go	3/87	
WAR (US)		
The Cisco Kid	4/73	
Gypsy Man	9/73	
Low Rider	11/75	2/76
Me And Baby Brother	1/74	
Slippin' Into Darkness	5/72	
❖ with Eric Burdon Spill The Wine	8/70	
Summer	9/76	
Why Can't We Be Friends?	7/75	
The World Is A Ghetto	1/73	
ANITA WARD (US)		

	US Top 20 Ent	UK Top 20 Ent
Ring My Bell	6/79	6/79
Billy WARD & His Dominoes (US)		
Stardust	8/57	9/57
Clifford T. WARD (UK)		
Gaye		7/73
Robin WARD (US)		
Wonderful Summer	12/63	
Jennifer WARNES (US)		
❖ with Bill Medley (I've Had) The Time Of My Life	11/87	11/87
★ with Bill Medley (I've Had) The Time Of My Life		1/91
Right Time Of The Night	4/77	
❖ with Joe Cocker Up Where We Belong	10/82	2/83
WARRANT (US)		
Cherry Pie	11/90	
Heaven	9/89	
I Saw Red	2/91	
Dionne WARWICK (US)		
All The Love In The World		1/83
Anyone Who Had A Heart	2/64	
Deja Vu	2/80	
Do You Know The Way To San Jose	5/68	6/68
Heartbreaker	12/82	11/82
I Say A Little Prayer	11/67	
I'll Never Fall In Love Again	1/70	
I'll Never Love This Way Again	8/79	
Message To Michael	5/66	
(Theme From) Valley Of The Dolls	2/68	
Then Came You	9/74	
This Girl's In Love With You	3/69	
Walk On By	5/64	5/64
DIONNE WARWICK & Friends (US/UK)		
That's What Friends Are For	12/85	
Dionne WARWICK & Jeffrey Osborne (US)		
Love Power	8/87	
WAS (NOT WAS) (US)		
Papa Was A Rolling Stone		6/90
Shake Your Head		7/92
Walk The Dinosaur	3/89	10/87
Dinah WASHINGTON (US)		
What A Difference A Day Makes	8/59	
Dinah WASHINGTON & Brook Benton (US)		
A Rockin' Good Way	6/60	
Baby (You Got What It Takes)	2/60	
Grover WASHINGTON JR. (US)		
Just The Two Of Us	3/81	
Keith WASHINGTON (US) See Kylie Minogue		
Sarah WASHINGTON (UK)		
I Will Always Love You		8/93
WATERBOYS (UK)		
The Whole Of The Moon		4/91
WATERFRONT (UK)		
Cry	6/89	
Dennis WATERMAN (UK)		
I Could Be So Good For You		11/80
Crystal WATERS (US)		
Gypsy Woman (She's Homeless)	6/91	5/91
Jody WATLEY (US)		
Don't You Want Me	12/87	
Everything	12/89	
Looking For A New Love	4/87	6/87
Real Love	4/89	
Some Kind Of Lover	4/88	
Jody WATLEY with Eric B & Rakim (US)		
Friends	8/89	
WAX (UK)		
Bridge To Your Heart		9/87
Jeff WAYNE (US)		
Eve Of The War (Ben Liebrand Remix)		12/89
Thomas WAYNE (US)		
Tragedy	3/59	
WE FIVE (US)		
You Were On My Mind	9/65	
WEATHER GIRLS (US)		
It's Raining Men		3/84
Jim WEATHERLY (US)		
The Need To Be	11/74	
Marti WEBB (UK)		
Always There		10/86
Ben		6/85
Take That Look Of Your Face		3/80
Joan WEBER (US)		
Let Me Go, Lover	12/54	
Fred WEDLOCK (UK)		

	US Top 20 Ent	UK Top 20 Ent
★ Reet Petite		12/86
Whispers (Gettin' Louder)	12/66	
(You Were Made For) All My Love	8/60	
Higher And Higher	9/67	6/69
★ Higher And Higher		7/87
Mari WILSON (UK)		
Just What I Always Wanted		10/82
Meri WILSON (US)		
Telephone Man		9/77
Nancy WILSON (US)		
(You Don't Know) How Glad I Am	8/64	
Kai WINDING (US)		
More	8/63	
WINGER (US)		
Miles Away	1/91	
Pete WINGFIELD (UK)		
Eighteen With A Bullet		7/75
WINGS (UK) see Paul McCartney		
WINSTONS (US)		
Color Him Father	7/69	
Edgar WINTER GROUP (US)		
Frankenstein	5/73	
Free Ride	10/73	
Hugo WINTERHALTER (US)		
The Little Shoemaker	7/54	
Hugo WINTERHALTER & Eddie Heywood (US)		
Canadian Sunset	8/56	
Ruby WINTERS (US)		
Come To Me		6/78
I Will		12/77
Steve WINWOOD (UK)		
Back In The High Life Again	8/87	
Don't You Know What The Night Can Do	10/88	
The Finer Things	4/87	
Higher Love	8/86	7/86
Holding On	1/89	
Roll With It	7/88	
Valerie	12/87	
While You See A Chance	3/81	
Norman WISDOM (UK)		
Don't Laugh At Me		2/54
Wisdom Of A Fool		3/57
Bill WITHERS (US)		
Ain't No Sunshine	9/71	
Lean On Me	6/72	
Lovely Day		1/78
★ Lovely Day		9/88
Use Me	9/72	
WIZZARD (UK)		
Angel Fingers		9/73
Are You Ready To Rock		1/75
Ball Park Incident		1/73
I Wish It Could Be Christmas Everyday		12/73
Rock 'n Roll Winter		5/74
See My Baby Jive		5/73
Peter WOLF (US)		
Lights Out	9/84	
WOMACK & WOMACK (US)		
Teardrops		9/88
Bobby WOMACK (US)		
Lookin' For A Love	4/74	
WOMBLES (UK)		
Banana Rock		7/74
Remember You're A Womble		4/74
The Wombling Song		2/74
Wombling Merry Christmas		12/74
WONDER STUFF (UK)		
✤ with Vic Reeves Dizzy		10/91
The Size Of A Cow		4/91
Welcome To The Cheap Seats (EP)		2/92
Stevie WONDER (US)		
Blowin' In The Wind	8/66	
Boogie On Reggae Woman	12/74	2/75
Do I Do	7/82	6/82
✤ with Paul McCartney Ebony And Ivory	4/82	4/82
Fingertips (Pt. 2)	7/63	
For Once In My Life	11/68	1/69
Go Home	1/86	
Happy Birthday		8/81
He's Misstra Know It All		5/74
Heaven Help Us All	11/70	
Higher Ground	9/73	
I Ain't Gonna Stand For It	2/81	1/81
I Just Called To Say I Love You	9/84	8/84
I Was Made To Love Her	7/67	8/67

	US Top 20 Ent	UK Top 20 Ent
I Wish	12/76	1/77
I'm Wondering	11/67	
If You Really Love Me	10/71	
Lately		3/81
Living For The City	12/73	
Master Blaster (Jammin')	11/80	9/80
My Cherie Amour	7/69	8/69
✤ with Julio Iglesias My Love		8/88
Never Had A Dream Come True		4/70
Part Time Lover	10/85	9/85
A Place In The Sun	12/66	
Send One Your Love	11/79	
Shoo-Be-Doo-Be-Doo-Da-Day	5/68	
Signed Sealed Delivered I'm Yours	7/70	8/70
Sir Duke	4/77	4/77
Superstition	1/73	2/73
That Girl	2/82	
Uptight (Everything's Alright)	2/66	
Yester-Me, Yester-You, Yesterday	11/69	11/69
You Are The Sunshine Of My Life	4/73	6/73
You Haven't Done Nothin	9/74	
WONDER WHO? (aka Four Seasons) (US)		
Don't Think Twice	12/65	
Brenton WOOD (US)		
Gimme Little Sign	10/67	2/68
Roy WOOD (UK)		
Forever		12/73
Going Down The Road		7/74
Oh What A Shame		6/75
Sheb WOOLEY (US)		
The Purple People Eater	6/58	7/58
WRECKX-N-EFFECT (US)		
Rump Shaker	11/92	
BETTY WRIGHT (US)		
Clean Up Woman	1/72	
Charles WRIGHT & The Watts 103rd Street Rhythm Band (US)		
Do Your Thing	4/69	
Express Yourself	10/70	
Gary WRIGHT (UK)		
Dream Weaver	2/76	
Love Is Alive	6/76	
Really Wanna Know You	9/81	
Ruby WRIGHT (US)		
Bimbo		4/54
WURZELS (UK)		
Combine Harvester (Brand New Key)		5/76
I Am A Cider Drinker (Paloma Blanca)		9/76
WWF SUPERSTARS (US)		
Slam Jam		12/92
Wrestlemania		4/93
Tammy WYNETTE (US/UK)		
D.I.V.O.R.C.E.		7/75
✤ with KLF Justified And Ancient	3/92	12/91
Stand By Your Man		5/75
Mark WYNTER (UK)		
Go Away Little Girl		1/63
It's Almost Tomorrow		11/63
Venus In Blue Jeans		10/62
XPANSIONS (UK)		
Move Your Body (Elevation)		3/91
XSCAPE (US)		
Just Kickin' It	10/93	
XTC (UK)		
Senses Working Overtime		2/82
Weird Al YANKOVIC (US)		
Eat It	4/84	
YARBROUGH & PEOPLES (US)		
Don't Stop The Music		1/81
Glenn YARBROUGH (US)		
Baby The Rain Must Fall	5/65	
YARDBIRDS (UK)		
Evil Hearted You/Still I'm Sad		10/65
For Your Love	6/65	4/65
Heart Full Of Soul	9/65	7/65
Over Under Sideways Down	8/66	6/66
Shapes Of Things	5/66	3/66
YAZOO (UK)		
Don't Go		7/82
Nobody's Diary		5/83
Only You		5/82
The Other Side Of Love		12/82
YAZZ (UK)		

	US Top 20 Ent	UK Top 20 Ent
Fine Time		2/89
Stand Up For Your Love Rights		11/88
Where Has All The Love Gone		5/89
YAZZ & The Plastic Population (UK)		
✤ with Coldcut Doctorin' The House		3/88
The Only Way Is Up		8/88
YELL! (UK)		
Instant Replay		2/90
YELLO (Swi)		
The Race		9/88
YELLOW DOG (UK)		
Just One More Night		2/78
YES (UK/SA)		
Owner Of A Lonely Heart	12/83	
Roundabout	4/72	
Wonderous Stories		9/77
YOUNG M.C. (US)		
Bust A Move	10/89	
YOUNG ONES (UK) See Cliff Richard & The Young Ones		
Faron YOUNG (US)		
Hello Walls	6/61	
It's Four In The Morning		8/72
Jimmy YOUNG (UK)		
Chain Gang		3/56
Little Things Mean A Lot		9/54
The Man From Laramie		9/55
More		10/56
Someone On Your Mind		1/56
Unchained Melody		5/55
John Paul YOUNG (Aus)		
Love Is In The Air	9/78	5/78
Karen YOUNG (US)		
Nobody's Child		10/69
Kathy YOUNG With The Innocents (US)		
A Thousand Stars	11/60	
Neil YOUNG (CAN)		
Heart Of Gold	3/72	4/72
Paul YOUNG (UK)		
Come Back And Stay		9/83
Everything Must Change		12/84
Everytime You Go Away	7/85	3/85
I'm Gonna Tear Your Playhouse Down	10/85	10/84
Love Of The Common People		11/83
Oh Girl	9/90	
✤ with Zucchero Senza Una Donna		5/91
Wherever I Lay My Hat (That's My Home)		7/83
Victor YOUNG (US)		
The High And The Mighty		8/54
YOUNG-HOLT UNLIMITED (US)		
Soulful Strut	1/69	
Sydney YOUNGBLOOD (US)		
If Only I Could		9/89
YOUNGBLOODS (US)		
Get Together	8/69	
YOUNG RASCALS (US) see Rascals		
Timi YURO (US)		
Hurt	8/61	
Helmut ZACHARIAS ORCHESTRA (G)		
Tokyo Melody		11/64
John ZACHERLE (US)		
Dinner With Drac (Part 1)	3/58	
ZAGER & EVANS (US)		
In The Year 2525 (Exordium & Terminus)	7/69	8/69
Michael ZAGER BAND (US)		
Let's All Chant		5/78
Georghe ZAMFIR (R)		
(Light Of Experience) Doina De Jale		9/76
Lena ZAVARONI (UK)		
Ma He's Making Eyes At Me		3/74
ZHANE (US)		
Hey Mr. D.J.	10/93	
ZOE (UK)		
Sunshine On A Rainy Day		8/91
ZOMBIES (UK)		
She's Not There	11/64	9/64
Tell Her No	2/65	
Time Of The Season	3/69	
ZUCCHERO/Paul Young (Ita/UK)		
Senza Una Donna (Without A Woman)		5/91
ZZ TOP (US)		
Gimme All Your Lovin'		11/84
Legs	7/84	
Sleeping Bag	11/85	
Viva Las Vegas		4/92

LISTINGS

BY TITLE

Title	Artist
Abacab	Genesis
Abba-Esque (EP)	Erasure
ABC	Jackson Five
Abracadabra	Steve Miller Band
Abraham Martin & John	Marvin Gaye
Abraham, Martin And John	Dion
Absolute Beginners	David Bowie
Absolute Beginners	Jam
Achy Breaky Heart	Billy Ray Cyrus
Action	Freddy Cannon
Activ 8 (Come With Me)	Altern 8
Addams Groove	Hammer
Addicted To Love	Robert Palmer
Adoration Waltz	David Whitfield
Adult Education	Daryl Hall & John Oates
Affair Of The Night	Rick Springfield
Africa	Toto
African Waltz	Johnny Dankworth
After All	Cher & Peter Cetera
After All	Frank And Walters
After The Love Has Gone	Earth, Wind & Fire
After The Lovin'	Engelbert Humperdinck
After The Rain	Nelson
Afternoon Delight	Starland Vocal Band
Agadoo	Black Lace
Again	Janet Jackson
Again And Again	Status Quo
Against All Odds (Take A Look At Me Now)	Phil Collins
Against The Wind	Bob Seger & The Silver Bullet Band
Ahab, The Arab	Ray Stevens
Ain't Gonna Bump No More (With No Big Fat Woman)	Joe Tex
Ain't Gonna Kiss Ya (E.P.)	Searchers
Ain't Got No - I Got Life	Nina Simone
Ain't It Fun	Guns N' Roses
Ain't Misbehavin'	Tommy Bruce & The Bruisers
Ain't No Doubt	Jimmy Nail
Ain't No Love (Ain't No Use)	Sub Sub Featuring Melanie Williams
Ain't No Mountain High Enough	Diana Ross
Ain't No Pleasing You	Chas & Dave
Ain't No Stoppin'	Enigma
Ain't No Stoppin' Us Now	McFadden & Whitehead
Ain't No Sunshine	Michael Jackson
Ain't No Sunshine	Bill Withers
Ain't No Way To Treat A Lady	Helen Reddy
Ain't No Woman (Like The One I've Got)	Four Tops
Ain't Nobody	Rufus & Chaka Khan
Ain't Nothin' But A Houseparty	Showstoppers
Ain't Nothing Goin' On But The Rent	Gwen Guthrie
Ain't Nothing Like The Real Thing	Marvin Gaye & Tammi Terrell
Ain't That A Shame	Pat Boone
Ain't That Funny	Jimmy Justice
Ain't That Peculiar	Marvin Gaye
Ain't Too Proud 2 Beg	TLC
Ain't Too Proud To Beg	Temptations
Air That I Breathe, The	Hollies
Airport	Motors
Al Di La	Emilio Pericoli
Albatross	Fleetwood Mac
Alfie	Cilla Black
Alice I Want You Just For Me	Full Force
Alive Again	Chicago
All Alone Am I	Brenda Lee
All Along The Watchtower	Jimi Hendrix Experience
All American Boy	Bobby Bare
Alive & Kicking	Simple Minds
All Around My Hat	Steeleye Span
All Around The World	Lisa Stansfield
All Because Of You	Geordie
All By Myself	Eric Carmen
All Cried Out	Lisa Lisa & Cult Jam With Full Force
All Cried Out	Alison Moyet
All Day And All Of The Night	Kinks
All Day And All Of The Night	Stranglers
All 4 Love	Color Me Badd
All For Love	Bryan Adams/Rod Stewart/Sting
All I Ask Of You	Cliff Richard
All I Ever Need Is You	Sonny & Cher
All I Have To Do Is Dream	Everly Brothers
All I Have To Do Is Dream	Bobbie Gentry & Glen Campbell
All I Know	Garfunkel
All I Need	Temptations
All I Need	Jack Wagner

Title	Artist
All I Need Is A Miracle	Mike + The Mechanics
All I Really Want To Do	Byrds
All I Really Want To Do	Cher
All I See Is You	Dusty Springfield
All I Wanna Do Is Make Love To You	Heart
All I Want	Toad The Wet Sprocket
All I Want For Christmas Is A Beatle	Dora Bryan
All I Want Is You	Roxy Music
All I Want Is You	U2
All Kinds Of Everything	Dana
All My Life	Linda Ronstadt (featuring Aaron Neville)
All My Love	Cliff Richard
All Night Long	Rainbow
All Night Long (All Night)	Lionel Richie
(All Of A Sudden) My Heart Sings	Paul Anka
All Of Me Loves All Of You	Bay City Rollers
All Of My Heart	ABC
All Of My Life	Diana Ross
All Or Nothing	Milli Vanilli
All Or Nothing	Small Faces
All Out Of Love	Air Supply
All Over The World	Electric Light Orchestra
All Right	Christopher Cross
All Right Now	Free
All She Wants Is	Duran Duran
All She Wants To Do Is Dance	Don Henley
All Shook Up	Elvis Presley
All Star Hit Parade	Various Artists
All Stood Still	Ultravox
All That She Wants	Ace Of Base
All The Love In The World	Dionne Warwick
All The Man That I Need	Whitney Houston
All The Things She Said	Simple Minds
All The Way	Frank Sinatra
All The Way From Memphis	Mott The Hoople
All The Young Dudes	Mott The Hoople
All This Time	Sting
All This Time	Tiffany
All Those Years Ago	George Harrison
All Through The Night	Cyndi Lauper
All Together Now	Farm
All You Need Is Love	Beatles
Allegheny Moon	Patti Page
Allentown	Billy Joel
Alley Cat	Bent Fabric
Alley-Oop	Dante & The Evergreens
Alley-Oop	Hollywood Argyles
Ally's Tartan Army	Andy Cameron
Almaz	Randy Crawford
Almost Paradise...Love Theme From Footloose	Mike Reno & Ann Wilson
Almost There	Andy Williams
Almost Unreal	Roxette
Alone	Petula Clark
Alone	Heart
Alone Again (Naturally)	Gilbert O'Sullivan
Alone At Last	Jackie Wilson
Alone Without You	King
Along Came Jones	Coasters
Along Comes A Woman	Chicago
Along Comes Mary	Association
Alphabet Street	Prince
Alright	Janet Jackson
Alright Alright Alright	Mungo Jerry
Also Sprach Zarathustra (2001)	Deodata
Alternate Title	Monkees
Alvin's Harmonica	Chipmunks
Always	Atlantic Starr
Always And Forever	Heatwave
Always Look On The Bright Side Of Life	Monty Python
Always On My Mind	Willie Nelson
Always On My Mind	Pet Shop Boys
Always On My Mind	Elvis Presley
Always There	Incognito Featuring Jocelyn Brown
Always There	Marti Webb
Always Yours	Gary Glitter
Am I That Easy To Forget	Engelbert Humperdinck
Amanda	Boston
Amanda	Stuart Gillies
Amateur Hour	Sparks
Amazing Grace	Judy Collins
Amazing Grace	Royal Scots Dragoon Guards
Amen	Impressions
America	Neil Diamond
America: What Time Is Love?	KLF
American Dream, An	Nitty Gritty Dirt Band

Title	Artist
Band On The Run	Paul McCartney & Wings
Bang A Gong (Get It On)	T. Rex
Bang Bang	B.A. Robertson
Bang Bang (My Baby Shot Me Down)	Cher
(Bang Zoom) Let's Go Go	Real Roxanne With Hitman Howie Tee
Bangin' Man	Slade
Bangla Desh	George Harrison
Bank Robber	Clash
Banks Of The Ohio	Olivia Newton-John
Banner Man	Blue Mink
Barbados	Typically Tropical
Barbara Ann	Beach Boys
Barbara Ann	Regents
Barcelona	Freddie Mercury & Montserrat Caballe
Bare Necessities Megamix, The	UK Mixmasters
Barefootin'	Robert Parker
Barracuda	Heart
Basketball Jones Feat Tyrone Shoelaces	Cheech & Chong
Batdance	Prince
Battle Hymn Of The Republic	Mormon Tabernacle Choir
Battle Of Kookamonga, The	Homer & Jethro
Battle Of New Orleans	Lonnie Donegan
Battle Of New Orleans, The	Johnny Horton
(Bazoom) I Need Your Lovin'	Cheers
Be Aggressive	Faith No More
Be Good To Yourself	Journey
Be Mine	Lance Fortune
Be My Baby	Vanessa Paradis
Be My Baby	Ronettes
Be My Girl	Jim Dale
Be My Guest	Fats Domino
Be Near Me	ABC
Be Quick Or Be Dead	Iron Maiden
Be Still My Beating Heart	Sting
Be Thankful For What You Got	William DeVaughn
Be True To Your School	Beach Boys
Be-Bop Baby	Ricky Nelson
Be-Bop-A-Lula	Gene Vincent & His Blue Caps
Beach Baby	First Class
Beach Boy Gold	Gidea Park
Beach Boys Medley, The	Beach Boys
Beast Of Burden	Rolling Stones
Beat Dis	Bomb The Bass
Beat Goes On, The	Sonny & Cher
Beat It	Michael Jackson
Beat Surrender	Jam
Beat The Clock	Sparks
Beatles Hits E.P.	Beatles
Beatles Movie Medley, The	Beatles
Beatnik Fly	Johnny & The Hurricanes
Beautiful Morning, A	Rascals
Beautiful Noise	Neil Diamond
Beauty And The Beast	Celine Dion & Peabo Bryson
Beauty Is Only Skin Deep	Temptations
Because	Dave Clark Five
Because I Love You (The Postman Song)	Stevie B
Because The Night	Patti Smith Group
Because They're Young	Duane Eddy
Bed Of Roses	Bon Jovi
Bed Sitter	Soft Cell
Beds Are Burning	Midnight Oil
Beep Beep	Playmates
Before The Next Teardrop Falls	Freddy Fender
Beg Steal Or Borrow	New Seekers
Begin The Beguine (Volver A Empezar)	Julio Iglesias
Beginnings	Chicago
Behind A Painted Smile	Isley Brothers
Behind Closed Doors	Charlie Rich
Behind The Groove	Teena Marie
Being Boiled	Human League
Being With You	Smokey Robinson
Belfast	Boney M
Belfast Child	Simple Minds
Believe In Me	Utah Saints
Believe What You Say	Ricky Nelson
Bell Bottom Blues	Alma Cogan
Bells, The	Originals
Ben	Michael Jackson
Ben	Marti Webb
Bend It	Dave Dee, Dozy, Beaky, Mick & Tich
Bend Me Shape Me	Amen Corner
Bend Me, Shape Me	American Breed
Bennie And The Jets	Elton John
Bernadette	Four Tops

Title	Artist
Best, The	Tina Turner
Best Disco In Town, The	Ritchie Family
Best Of Me, The	Cliff Richard
Best Of My Love	Eagles
Best Of My Love	Emotions
Best Of Times, The	Styx
Best Of You	Kenny Thomas
Best Thing That Ever Happened To Me	Gladys Knight & The Pips
Best Things In Life Are Free, The	Luther Vandross & Janet Jackson
Best Years Of Our Lives	Modern Romance
Betcha By Golly, Wow	Stylistics
Beth	Kiss
Bette Davis Eyes	Kim Carnes
Better Be Good To Me	Tina Turner
Better Days	Bruce Springsteen
Better Do It Salsa	Gibson Brothers
Better Love Next Time	Dr. Hook
Better The Devil You Know	Kylie Minogue
Betty, Betty, Betty	Lonnie Donegan
Beyond The Reef	Elvis Presley
Beyond The Sea	Bobby Darin
Beyond The Stars	David Whitfield
Bible Tells Me So, The	Don Cornell
Bicycle Race	Queen
Big Apple	Kajagoogoo
Big Area	Then Jerico
Big Bad John	Jimmy Dean
Big Boss Groove	Style Council
Big Eight	Judge Dread
Big Fun	Gap Band
Big Fun	Inner City
Big Girls Don't Cry	Four Seasons
Big Hunk O' Love	Elvis Presley
Big Hurt, The	Miss Toni Fisher
Big In Japan	Alphaville
Big Log	Robert Plant
Big Love	Fleetwood Mac
Big Man	Four Preps
Big Seven	Judge Dread
Big Ship	Cliff Richard
Big Shot	Billy Joel
Big Six	Judge Dread
Big Ten	Judge Dread
Big Time	Peter Gabriel
Big Yellow Taxi	Joni Mitchell
Biggest Part Of Me	Ambrosia
Billie Jean	Michael Jackson
Billy, Don't Be A Hero	Bo Donaldson & The Heywoods
Billy, Don't Be A Hero	Paper Lace
Bimbo	Ruby Wright
Bimbombey	Jimmie Rodgers
Bionic Santa	Chris Hill
Bird Dog	Everly Brothers
Bird Of Paradise	Snowy White
Birdhouse In Your Soul	They Might Be Giants
Birdie Song (Birdie Dance), The	Tweets
Birdland	Chubby Checker
Birds And The Bees, The	Jewel Akens
Bitch	Rolling Stones
Bitch Is Back, The	Elton John
Bits And Pieces	Dave Clark Five
Bitterest Pill (I Ever Had To Swallow), The	Jam
Black & White	Three Dog Night
Black And White	Greyhound
Black Betty	Ram Jam
Black Cat	Janet Jackson
Black Denim Trousers	Cheers
Black Dog	Led Zeppelin
Black Eyed Boys, The	Paper Lace
Black Hills Of Dakota	Doris Day
Black Is Black	Los Bravos
Black Is Black	La Belle Epoque
Black Magic Woman	Santana
Black Night	Deep Purple
Black Or White	Michael Jackson
Black Pearl	Sonny Charles & The Checkmates, Ltd.
Black Pearl	Horace Faith
Black Skin Blue Eyed Boys	Equals
Black Superman (Muhammad Ali)	Johnny Wakelin & The Kinshasa Band
Black Velvet	Alannah Myles
Black Velvet Band	Dubliners
Black Water	Doobie Brothers
Blackberry Way	Move

Title	Artist
Blame It On The Boogie	Big Fun
Blame It On The Boogie	Jacksons
Blame It On The Bossa Nova	Eydie Gormé
Blame It On The Pony Express	Johnny Johnson & The Bandwagon
Blame It On The Rain	Milli Vanilli
Blanket On The Ground	Billie Jo Spears
Blaze Of Glory	Jon Bon Jovi
Bless You	Tony Orlando
Blind Vision	Blancmange
Blinded By The Light	Manfred Mann's Earth Band
Blockbuster	Sweet
Bloodnok's Rock 'n' Roll Call	Goons
Blossom Fell, A	Nat 'King' Cole
Blossom Fell, A	Ronnie Hilton
Blossom Fell, A	Dickie Valentine
Blow The House Down	Living In A Box
Blow Your Mind	Jamiroquai
Blowin' In The Wind	Peter, Paul & Mary
Blowin' In The Wind	Stevie Wonder
Blowing Kisses In The Wind	Paula Abdul
Blowing Wild	Frankie Laine
Blue Angel	Roy Orbison
Blue Bayou	Roy Orbison
Blue Bayou	Linda Ronstadt
Blue Christmas	Elvis Presley
Blue Eyes	Elton John
Blue Eyes	Don Partridge
Blue Guitar	Justin Hayward & John Lodge
Blue Is The Colour	Chelsea F.C.
Blue Jean	David Bowie
Blue Monday	Fats Domino
Blue Monday	New Order
Blue Moon	Marcels
Blue Moon	Elvis Presley
Blue On Blue	Bobby Vinton
Blue Room	Orb
Blue Savannah	Erasure
Blue Star	Cyril Stapleton
Blue Suede Shoes	Carl Perkins
Blue Suede Shoes	Elvis Presley
Blue Velvet	Bobby Vinton
Blueberry Hill	Fats Domino
Bluebottle Blues	Goons
Bluer Than Blue	Michael Johnson
Bo Diddley	Buddy Holly
Boat That I Row, The	Lulu
Bobbie Sue	Oak Ridge Boys
Bobby Sox To Stockings	Frankie Avalon
Bobby's Girl	Marcie Blane
Bobby's Girl	Susan Maughan
Body And Soul	Mai Tai
Body Language	Queen
Body Rock	Maria Vidal
Body Talk	Imagination
Bohemian Rhapsody	Queen
Boll Weevil Song, The	Brook Benton
Boney M Megamix	Boney M
Bonnie Came Back	Duane Eddy
Bony Moronie	Larry Williams
Boogaloo Down Broadway	Fantastic Johnny C
Boogie Child	Bee Gees
Boogie Down	Eddie Kendricks
Boogie Fever	Sylvers
Boogie Nights	Heatwave
Boogie On Reggae Woman	Stevie Wonder
Boogie Oogie Oogie	Taste Of Honey
Boogie Wonderland	Earth, Wind & Fire With The Emotions
Boogie Woogie Bugle Boy	Bette Midler
Book, The	David Whitfield
Book Of Days	Enya
Book Of Love	Monotones
Book Of Love	Mudlarks
Boom Bang-A-Bang	Lulu
Boom! Shake The Room	Jazzy Jeff & Fresh Prince
Boops (Here To Go)	Sly And Robbie
Borderline	Madonna
Born A Woman	Sandy Posey
Born Free	Vic Reeves & The Roman Numerals
Born Free	Roger Williams
Born In The U.S.A.	Bruce Springsteen
Born To Be Alive	Patrick Hernandez
Born To Be My Baby	Bon Jovi
Born To Be Wild	Steppenwolf
Born To Be With You	Chordettes

Title	Artist
Born To Be With You	Dave Edmunds
Born Too Late	Poni-Tails
Born With A Smile On My Face	Stephanie De Sykes
Boss Drum	Shamen
Bossa Nova Baby	Elvis Presley
Both Sides Now	Judy Collins
Both Sides Of The Story	Phil Collins
Bottle Of Wine	Fireballs
Bouncer, The	Kicks Like A Mule
Boxer, The	Simon & Garfunkel
Boxer Beat	Joboxers
Boy From New York City	Darts
Boy From New York City, The	Ad Libs
Boy From New York City, The	Manhattan Transfer
Boy From Nowhere, A	Tom Jones
Boy Named Sue, A	Johnny Cash
Boy Without A Girl, A	Frankie Avalon
Boys	Kim Wilde
Boys Are Back In Town, The	Thin Lizzy
Boys Cry	Eden Kane
Boys Keep Swingin'	David Bowie
Boys Of Summer, The	Don Henley
Boys (Summertime Love)	Sabrina
Brand New Key	Melanie
Brand New Lover	Dead Or Alive
Brand New Me	Aretha Franklin
Brandy	Scott English
Brandy (You're A Fine Girl)	Looking Glass
Brass In Pocket	Pretenders
Brazil	Ritchie Family
Bread And Butter	Newbeats
Break Away	Beach Boys
Break Dance Party	Break Machine
Break It To Me Gently	Brenda Lee
Break It To Me Gently	Juice Newton
Break My Stride	Matthew Wilder
Break The Rules	Status Quo
Break Up To Make Up	Stylistics
Breakaway	Tracey Ullman
Breakdance	Irene Cara
Breakdown Dead Ahead	Boz Scaggs
Breakfast In America	Supertramp
Breakfast In Bed	UB40 & Chrissie Hynde
Breakin' Down The Walls Of Heartache	Johnny Johnson & The Bandwagon
Breakin' In A Brand New Broken Heart	Connie Francis
Breakin' My Heart (Pretty Brown Eyes)	Mint Condition
Breakin'...There's No Stopping Us	Ollie & Jerry
Breaking The Law	Judas Priest
Breaking Up Is Hard To Do	Partridge Family
Breaking Up Is Hard To Do	Neil Sedaka
Breakout	Swing Out Sister
Breakthru'	Queen
Breakup Song (They Don't Write 'Em), The	Greg Kihn Band
Breath Of Life	Erasure
Breathe Again	Toni Braxton
Breathless	Jerry Lee Lewis
Breeze And I, The	Caterina Valente
Brick House	Commodores
Bridge Over Troubled Water	Aretha Franklin
Bridge Over Troubled Water	Simon & Garfunkel
Bridge To Your Heart	Wax
Bridget The Midget (The Queen Of The Blues)	Ray Stevens
Bright Eyes	Art Garfunkel
Brilliant Disguise	Bruce Springsteen
Bring A Little Water Sylvie	Lonnie Donegan
Bring It On Home To Me	Animals
Bring It On Home To Me	Eddie Floyd
Bring It On Home To Me	Rod Stewart
Bring Me Edelweiss	Edelweiss
Bring The Boys Home	Freda Payne
Bring Your Daughter...To The Slaughter	Iron Maiden
Bringing On Back The Good Times	Love Affair
Bristol Stomp	Dovells
British Hustle	Hi Tension
Brits 1990, The	Various Artists
Broken Down Angel	Nazareth
Broken Hearted Me	Anne Murray
Broken-Hearted Melody	Sarah Vaughan
Broken Wings	Mr. Mister
Brontosaurus	Move
Brother Louie	Hot Chocolate
Brother Louie	Modern Talking
Brother Louie	Stories

Title	Artist
Brown Eyed Girl	Van Morrison
Brown Eyed Handsome Man	Buddy Holly
Brown Girl In The Ring	Boney M
Brown Sugar	Rolling Stones
Buddy	De La Soul
Buffalo Gals	Malcolm McLaren & The World's Famous Supreme Team
Buffalo Soldier	Bob Marley & The Wailers
Buffalo Stance	Neneh Cherry
Build Me Up Buttercup	Foundations
Build Your Love	Johnnie Ray
Bump, The	Kenny
Bungle In The Jungle	Jethro Tull
Buona Sera	Acker Bilk
Burlesque	Family
Burn It Up	Beatmasters With P.P. Arnold
Burning Bridges	Jack Scott
Burning Bridges (On And Off And On Again)	Status Quo
Burning Down The House	Talking Heads
Burning Heart	Survivor
Burning Love	Elvis Presley
Bus Stop	Hollies
Bust A Move	Young M.C.
Busted	Ray Charles
But I Do	Clarence 'Frogman' Henry
But You're Mine	Sonny & Cher
Butterfingers	Tommy Steele
Butterfly	Danyel Gerard
Butterfly	Charlie Gracie
Butterfly	Andy Williams
Buzz-Buzz-Buzz	Hollywood Flames
By The Light Of The Silvery Moon	Little Richard
Bye Bye Baby	Bay City Rollers
Bye, Bye, Baby (Baby Goodbye)	Four Seasons
Bye Bye Love	Everly Brothers
C Moon	Wings
Ca Plane Pour Moi	Plastic Bertrand
Cacharpaya (Andes Pumpsa Daesi)	Incantation
Calcutta	Lawrence Welk
Calendar Girl	Neil Sedaka
California Dreamin'	Mamas & The Papas
California Dreamin'	River City People
California Girls	Beach Boys
California Girls	David Lee Roth
California Man	Move
California Sun	Rivieras
Call Me	Blondie
Call Me	Aretha Franklin
Call Me	Go West
Call Me	Spagna
Call Me (Come Back Home)	Al Green
(Call Me) Number One	Tremeloes
Call On Me	Chicago
Call Rosie On The Phone	Guy Mitchell
Call To The Heart	Giuffria
Call Up The Groups	Barron Knights
Calling All The Heroes	It Bites
Calling Occupants Of Interplanetary Craft	Carpenters
Calling Your Name	Marilyn
Calypso	John Denver
Cambodia	Kim Wilde
Camouflage	Stan Ridgway
Can Can	Bad Manners
Can Can You Party	Jive Bunny & The Mastermixers
Can I Change My Mind	Tyrone Davis
Can I Play With Madness	Iron Maiden
Can I Take You Home Little Girl	Drifters
Can The Can	Suzi Quatro
Can We Talk	Tevin Campbell
Can You Do It	Geordie
Can You Feel It	Jacksons
Can You Feel The Force	Real Thing
(Can You) Feel The Passion	Blue Pearl
Can You Forgive Her?	Pet Shop Boys
Can't Be With You Tonight	Judy Boucher
Can't Buy Me Love	Beatles
Can't Fight This Feeling	REO Speedwagon
Can't Get Along Without You	Frankie Vaughan
Can't Get By Without You	Real Thing
Can't Get Enough	Bad Company
Can't Get Enough Of Your Love	Taylor Dayne
Can't Get Enough Of Your Love, Babe	Barry White
Can't Get It Out Of My Head	Electric Light Orchestra
Can't Get Used To Losing You	Beat

Title	Artist
Can't Get Used To Losing You	Andy Williams
Can't Give You Anything (But My Love)	Stylistics
Can't Help Falling In Love	Elvis Presley
Can't Help Falling In Love	Stylistics
Can't Help Falling In Love	Andy Williams
Can't Keep It In	Cat Stevens
Can't Let Go	Mariah Carey
(Can't Live Without Your) Love And Affection	Nelson
Can't Shake The Feeling	Big Fun
Can't Smile Without You	Barry Manilow
Can't Stand Losing You	Police
Can't Stay Away From You	Gloria Estefan & The Miami Sound Machine
Can't Stop	After 7
Can't Stop Dancin'	Captain & Tennille
Can't Stop Falling Into Love	Cheap Trick
Can't Stop The Music	Village People
Can't Stop This Thing We Started	Bryan Adams
Can't Take My Eyes Off You	Boystown Gang
Can't Take My Eyes Off You	Lettermen
Can't Take My Eyes Off You	Frankie Valli
Can't Take My Eyes Off You	Andy Williams
Can't Wait Another Minute	Five Star
Can't We Try	Dan Hill (duet with Vonda Shepard)
Can't You Hear My Heartbeat	Herman's Hermits
Can't You See That She's Mine	Dave Clark Five
Canadian Sunset	Andy Williams
Canadian Sunset	Hugo Winterhalter & Eddie Heywood
Candida	Dawn
Candle In The Wind	Elton John
Candle In The Wind (Live)	Elton John
Candy Girl	Four Seasons
Candy Girl	New Edition
Candy Man, The	Sammy Davis Jr.
Candy Man	Brian Poole & The Tremeloes
Cantina Band	Meco
Capstick Comes Home	Tony Capstick
Captain Beaky	Keith Michel
Captain Of Her Heart, The	Double
Captain Of Your Ship	Reperata & The Delrons
Car 67	Driver 67
Car Wash	Rose Royce
Cara Mia	Jay & The Americans
Cara Mia	David Whitfield
Caravan Of Love	Housemartins
Cardiac Arrest	Madness
Carefree Highway	Gordon Lightfoot
Careless Hands	Des O'Connor
Careless Whisper	George Michael
Caribbean Disco	Lobo
Caribbean Queen (No More Love On The Run)	Billy Ocean
Carnival Is Over, The	Seekers
Carolina Moon	Connie Francis
Caroline	Status Quo
Caroline (Live At The N.E.C.)	Status Quo
Carrie	Europe
Carrie	Cliff Richard
Carrie-Ann	Hollies
Carry On Wayward Son	Kansas
Carry The Blame	River City People
Cars	Gary Numan
Casanova	Coffee
Casanova	Levert
Cast Your Fate To The Wind	Sounds Orchestral
Castles In The Air	Don McLean
Cat Among The Pigeons	Bros
Cat Crept In, The	Mud
Cat's In The Cradle	Harry Chapin
Cat's In The Cradle	Ugly Kid Joe
Catch A Falling Star	Perry Como
Catch Me I'm Falling	Pretty Poison
Catch The Wind	Donovan
Catch Us If You Can	Dave Clark Five
Cathy's Clown	Everly Brothers
Caught Up In You	38 Special
Causing A Commotion	Madonna
C.C. Rider	Chuck Willis
Cecilia	Simon & Garfunkel
Celebration	Kool & The Gang
Centerfold	J. Geils Band
Certain Smile, A	Johnny Mathis
C'est La Vie	Robbie Nevil
Cha Cha Cha, The	Bobby Rydell
Chain Gang	Sam Cooke
Chain Gang	Jimmy Young

399

400

Title	Artist
Criticize	Alexander O'Neal
Crockett's Theme	Jan Hammer
Crocodile Rock	Elton John
Cross My Broken Heart	Jets
Cross My Broken Heart	Sinitta
Cross Over The Bridge	Patti Page
Crown, The	Gary Byrd & The GB Experience
Cruel Summer	Bananarama
Cruel To Be Kind	Nick Lowe
Cruisin'	Smokey Robinson
Cruising	Sinitta
Crumblin' Down	John Cougar Mellancamp
Crunch, The	Rah Band
Crush On You	Jets
Cry	Godley & Creme
Cry	Waterfront
Cry Baby	Garnet Mimms & The Enchanters
Cry For Help	Rick Astley
Cry Just A Little Bit	Shakin' Stevens
Cry Like A Baby	Box Tops
Cry Me A River	Joe Cocker
Cry Wolf	A-Ha
Cryin'	Aerosmith
Cryin'	Roy Orbison
Cryin' In The Rain	Everly Brothers
Crying	Don McLean
Crying Game, The	Dave Berry
Crying Game, The	Boy George
Crying In The Chapel	Lee Lawrence
Crying In The Chapel	Elvis Presley
Crying Laughing Loving Lying	Labi Siffre
Crying Over You	Ken Boothe
Crying Time	Ray Charles
Crystal Blue Persuasion	Tommy James & The Shondells
Cuba	Gibson Brothers
Cubik	808 State
Cuddle Me	Ronnie Gaylord
Cuddly Toy	Roachford
Cuff Of My Shirt	Guy Mitchell
Cult Of Personality	Living Colour
Cult Of Snap	Snap
Cum On Feel The Noize	Quiet Riot
Cum On Feel The Noize	Slade
Cumberland Gap	Lonnie Donegan
Cumberland Gap	Vipers Skiffle Group
Cupid	Sam Cooke
Cupid	Johnny Nash
Cupid-I've Loved You For A Long Time (Medley)	(Detroit) Spinners
Curly	Move
Curly Shuffle, The	Jump 'N The Saddle
Cut The Cake	Average White Band
Cutter, The	Echo & The Bunnymen
D-Days	Hazel O'Connor
Da Da Da	Trio
Da Doo Ron Ron	Shaun Cassidy
Da Doo Ron Ron	Crystals
Da Ya Think I'm Sexy	Rod Stewart
D-a-a-ance	Lambrettas
Daddy Cool	Boney M
Daddy Cool	Darts
Daddy Don't You Walk So Fast	Wayne Newton
Daddy-O	Fontane Sisters
Daddy's Home	Jermaine Jackson
Daddy's Home	Cliff Richard
Daddy's Home	Shep & The Limelites
Daisy A Day	Jud Strunk
Damn I Wish I Was Your Lover	Sophie B. Hawkins
Damned Don't Cry	Visage
Damned On 45	Captain Sensible
Dance Away	Roxy Music
Dance, Dance, Dance	Beach Boys
Dance, Dance, Dance (Yowsah, Yowsah, Yowsah)	Chic
Dance Little Lady Dance	Tina Charles
Dance On	Kathy Kirby
Dance On	Shadows
Dance On Little Girl	Paul Anka
Dance The Night Away	Van Halen
Dance To The Music	Sly & The Family Stone
Dance With Me	Peter Brown
Dance With Me	Orleans
Dance With Me Henry (Wallflower)	Georgia Gibbs
Dance With The Devil	Cozy Powell
(Dance With The) Guitar Man	Duane Eddy
Dance Yourself Dizzy	Liquid Gold
Dancin' In The Moonlight (It's Caught Me In The Spotlight)	Thin Lizzy
Dancin' Party	Chubby Checker
Dancin' Party	Showaddywaddy
Dancing Girls	Nik Kershaw
Dancing In The City	Marshall Hain
Dancing In The Dark	Bruce Springsteen
Dancing In The Moonlight	King Harvest
Dancing In The Street	Mick Jagger & David Bowie
Dancing In The Street	Martha (Reeves) & The Vandellas
Dancing Machine	Jackson Five
(Dancing) On A Saturday Night	Barry Blue
Dancing On The Ceiling	Lionel Richie
Dancing On The Floor (Hooked On Love)	Third World
Dancing Queen	Abba
Dancing Tight	Galaxy Featuring Phil Fearon
Dancing With Tears In My Eyes	Ultravox
Dancing With The Captain	Paul Nicholas
Dandelion	Rolling Stones
Dandy	Herman's Hermits
Dang Me	Roger Miller
Danger Games	Pinkees
Danger Zone	Kenny Loggins
Dangerous	Roxette
Daniel	Elton John
Danke Schoen	Wayne Newton
Danny Boy	Conway Twitty
Danny's Song	Anne Murray
Dare Me	Pointer Sisters
Dark Is The Night	Shakatak
Dark Lady	Cher
Dark Moon	Bonnie Guitar
Dark Moon	Gale Storm
Darlin'	Beach Boys
Darlin'	Frankie Miller
Darling Je Vous Aime Beaucoup	Nat 'King' Cole
Dat	Pluto Shervington
Daughter Of Darkness	Tom Jones
Davy's On The Road Again	Manfred Mann's Earth Band
Dawn (Go Away)	Four Seasons
Day After Day	Badfinger
Day Dreaming	Aretha Franklin
Day I Met Marie, The	Cliff Richard
Day The Rains Came, The	Jane Morgan
Day Trip To Bangor (Didn't We Have A Lovely Time)	Fiddler's Dram
Day Tripper	Beatles
Day Without Love, A	Love Affair
Daydream	Lovin' Spoonful
Daydream Believer	Monkees
Daydream Believer	Anne Murray
Daydreamer	David Cassidy
Days	Kinks
Days	Kirsty MacColl
Days Of Pearly Spencer, The	Marc Almond
Dazz	Brick
Dazzey Duks	Duice
De Do Do Do, De Da Da Da	Police
Dead End Street	Kinks
Dead Giveaway	Shalamar
Dead Man's Curve	Jan & Dean
Dead Or Alive	Lonnie Donegan
Dead Ringer For Love	Meat Loaf
Deadwood Stage	Doris Day
Dean And I, The	10cc
Dear Jessie	Madonna
Dear John	Status Quo
Dear Lady Twist	Gary U.S. Bonds
Dear Lonely Hearts	Nat 'King' Cole
Dear One	Larry Finnegan
Dear Prudence	Siouxsie & The Banshees
Death Of A Clown	Dave Davies
Debora	Tyrannosaurus Rex
December '63 (Oh What A Night)	Four Seasons
Deck Of Cards	Max Bygraves
Deck Of Cards	Wink Martindale
Dede Dinah	Frankie Avalon
Dedicated Follower Of Fashion	Kinks
Dedicated To The One I Love	Mamas & The Papas
Dedicated To The One I Love	Shirelles
Deep	East 17
Deep, Deep Trouble	Simpsons Featuring Bart & Homer
Deep Down Inside	Donna Summer
Deep Heat '89	Latino Rave
Deep Purple	Donny & Marie Osmond
Deep Purple	Nino Tempo & April Stevens
Deeper And Deeper	Madonna
Deeper Than The Night	Olivia Newton-John
Deeply Dippy	Right Said Fred
Deja Vu	Dionne Warwick
Delaware	Perry Como
Delilah	Sensational Alex Harvey Band
Delilah	Tom Jones
Delirious	Prince & The Revolution
Delta Dawn	Helen Reddy
Delta Lady	Joe Cocker
Denis	Blondie
Denise	Randy & The Rainbows
Der Kommissar	After The Fire
Desafinado	Stan Getz & Charlie Byrd
Desert Moon	Dennis Deyoung
Desiderata	Les Crane
Desire	Andy Gibb
Desire	U2
Desiree	Neil Diamond
Destiny	Johnnie Ray
Detroit City	Tom Jones
Deutscher Girls	Adam & The Ants
Devil Gate Drive	Suzi Quatro
Devil Inside	INXS
Devil Or Angel	Bobby Vee
Devil Went Down To Georgia, The	Charlie Daniels Band
Devil With A Blue Dress On & Good Golly Miss Molly	Mitch Ryder & The Detroit Wheels
Devil Woman	Cliff Richard
Devil Woman	Marty Robbins
Devil's Answer	Atomic Rooster
Devoted To You	Everly Brothers
Dial My Heart	Boys
Diamond Girl	Seals & Crofts
Diamonds	Herb Alpert
Diamonds	Jet Harris & Tony Meehan
Diamonds And Pearls	Prince & The New Power Generation
Diana	Paul Anka
Diane	Bachelors
Diary	Bread
Diary Of Horace Wimp, The	Electric Light Orchestra
Did It In A Minute	Daryl Hall & John Oates
Did You Ever	Nancy Sinatra & Lee Hazlewood
Did You Ever Have To Make Up Your Mind	Lovin' Spoonful
Didn't I (Blow Your Mind This Time)	Delfonics
Didn't I (Blow Your Mind)	New Kids On The Block
Didn't We Almost Have It All	Whitney Houston
Different Corner, A	George Michael
Different Drum	Stone Poneys
Different Strokes	Isotonik
Digging Your Scene	Blow Monkeys
Dim All The Lights	Donna Summer
Dim, Dim The Lights (I Want Some Atmosphere)	Bill Haley & His Comets
Dime And A Dollar	Guy Mitchell
Dinner With Drac (Part 1)	John Zacherle
Dippety Day	Father Abraham & The Smurfs
Dirty Cash	Adventures Of Stevie V
Dirty Diana	Michael Jackson
Dirty Laundry	Don Henley
Dirty Water	Standells
Dirty White Boy	Foreigner
Disappear	INXS
Disappointed	Electronic
D.I.S.C.O.	Ottawan
Disco Connection	Isaac Hayes
Disco Duck	Rick Dees & His Cast Of Idiots
Disco Inferno	Trammps
Disco Inferno	Tina Turner
Disco Lady	Johnnie Taylor
Disco Nights (Rock Freak)	G.Q.
Disco Queen	Hot Chocolate
Disco Stomp	Hamilton Bohannon
Distant Drums	Jim Reeves
Ditty	Paperboy
Divine Emotions	Narada
D.I.V.O.R.C.E.	Billy Connolly
D.I.V.O.R.C.E.	Tammy Wynette
Dixieland	Winifred Atwell
Dixie-Narco (EP)	Primal Scream
Dizzy	Vic Reeves & The Wonder Stuff
Dizzy	Tommy Roe
DJs Take Control	SL2

Title	Artist
Dream A Lie	UB40
Dream A Little Dream Of Me	Mama Cass
Dream Baby	Roy Orbison
Dream Is Still Alive, The	Wilson Phillips
Dream Lover	Bobby Darin
Dream On	Aerosmith
Dream Weaver	Gary Wright
Dream's A Dream, A	Soul II Soul
Dreamboat	Alma Cogan
Dreamer	Supertramp
Dreamin'	Johnny Burnette
Dreamin'	Vanessa Williams
Dreaming	Blondie
Dreaming	Orchestral Manoeuvres In The Dark
Dreaming	Cliff Richard
Dreamlover	Mariah Carey
Dreams	Fleetwood Mac
Dreams	Gabrielle
Dreams Can Tell A Lie	Nat 'King' Cole
Dreamtime	Daryl Hall
Dreams Of Children	Jam
Dress You Up	Madonna
Drift Away	Dobie Gray
Drinking Song	Mario Lanza
Drip Drop	Dion
Drive	Cars
Drive-In Saturday	David Bowie
Driven By You	Brian May
Drivin' My Life Away	Eddie Rabbitt
Driving In My Car	Madness
Drop The Boy	Bros
Drowning In Berlin	Mobiles
Drowning In The Sea Of Love	Joe Simon
Drummer Man	Tonight
Dub Be Good To Me	Beats International Featuring Lindy Layton
Duck, The	Jackie Lee
Dude (Looks Like A Lady)	Aerosmith
Dueling Banjos	Eric Weissberg & Steve Mandell
Duke Of Earl	Gene Chandler
Duke Of Earl	Darts
Dum Dum	Brenda Lee
Dungaree Doll	Eddie Fisher
Durham Town (The Leavin')	Roger Whittaker
Dust In The Wind	Kansas
Dyna-Mite	Mud
Dynamite	Jermaine Jackson
Dynomite	Bazuka
E=MC²	Big Audio Dynamite
Each Time You Break My Heart	Nick Kamen
Earache My Eye - Feat. Alice Bowie	Cheech & Chong
Early In The Morning	Vanity Fare
Earth Angel	Crew-Cuts
Earth Angel (Will You Be Mine)	Penguins
Earth Dies Screaming, The	UB40
Easier Said Than Done	Essex
Easier Said Than Done	Shakatak
Easy	Commodores
Easy Come, Easy Go	Bobby Sherman
Easy Going Me	Adam Faith
Easy Lover	Philip Bailey & Phil Collins
Easy Loving	Freddie Hart
Easy To Be Hard	Three Dog Night
Eat It	Weird Al Yankovic
Ebb Tide	Frank Chacksfield
Ebb Tide	Righteous Brothers
Ebeneezer Goode	Shamen
Ebony And Ivory	Paul McCartney & Stevie Wonder
Ebony Eyes	Everly Brothers
Ebony Eyes	Bob Welch
Echo Beach	Martha & The Muffins
Eddie My Love	Fontane Sisters
Eddie My Love	Teen Queens
Edelweiss	Vince Hill
Edge Of Heaven, The	Wham!
Edge Of Seventeen (Just Like The White Winged Dove)	Stevie Nicks
Egyptian Reggae	Jonathan Richman & The Modern Lovers
Eh Cumpari	Julius La Rosa
Eight Days A Week	Beatles
Eight Miles High	Byrds
867-5309	Tommy Tutone
18 And Life	Skid Row
Eighteen With A Bullet	Pete Wingfield

Title	Artist
18 Yellow Roses	Bobby Darin
Eighth Day	Hazel O'Connor
Einstein A Go-Go	Landscape
El Bimbo	Bimbo Jet
El Lute	Boney M
El Paso	Marty Robbins
Eleanor Rigby	Beatles
Elected	Alice Cooper
Election Day	Arcadia
Electric Avenue	Eddy Grant
Electric Blue	Icehouse
Electric Youth	Debbie Gibson
Elenore	Turtles
Elephant Stone	Stone Roses
Eli's Coming	Three Dog Night
Eloise	Damned
Eloise	Barry Ryan
Elusive Butterfly	Val Doonican
Elusive Butterfly	Bob Lind
Elvira	Oak Ridge Boys
Embarrassment	Madness
Emma	Hot Chocolate
Emotion	Samantha Sang
Emotional Rescue	Rolling Stones
Emotions	Mariah Carey
Emotions	Brenda Lee
Empty Garden (Hey Hey Johnny)	Elton John
Enchanted	Platters
Enchanted Sea, The	Islanders
End, The	Earl Grant
End Of Our Road, The	Gladys Knight & The Pips
End Of The Innocence, The	Don Henley
End Of The Road	Boyz II Men
End Of The World, The	Skeeter Davis
Endless Love	Diana Ross & Lionel Richie
Endless Sleep	Jody Reynolds
Endless Sleep	Marty Wilde
Endless Summer Nights	Richard Marx
Endlessly	Brook Benton
Engine Engine # 9	Roger Miller
Engine Number 9	Wilson Pickett
England Swings	Roger Miller
England We'll Fly The Flag	England World Cup Squad
English Country Garden	Jimmie Rodgers
Enjoy The Silence	Depeche Mode
Enjoy Yourself	Jacksons
Enola Gay	Orchestral Manoeuvres In The Dark
Enter Sandman	Metallica
Entertainer, The	Marvin Hamlisch
Epic	Faith No More
Eres Tu (Touch The Wind)	Mocedades
Ernie (The Fastest Milkman In The West)	Benny Hill
Erotica	Madonna
Escapade	Janet Jackson
Escape (The Pina Colada Song)	Rupert Holmes
Especially For You	Kylie Minogue & Jason Donovan
Et Les Oiseaux Chantaient (And The Birds Were Singing)	Sweet People
Eternal Flame	Bangles
Eton Rifles, The	Jam
European Female	Stranglers
Ev'ry Time We Say Goodbye	Simply Red
Ev'rybody's Twistin'	Frank Sinatra
Ev'rywhere	David Whitfield
Evapor 8	Altern 8
Eve Of Destruction	Barry McGuire
Eve Of The War (Ben Liebrand Remix)	Jeff Wayne
Even Better Than The Real Thing	U2
Even Now	Bob Seger & The Silver Bullet Band
Even The Bad Times Are Good	Tremeloes
Even The Nights Are Better	Air Supply
Ever Fallen In Love	Fine Young Cannibals
Evergreen (Love Theme From 'A Star Is Born')	Barbra Streisand
Everlasting Love	Carl Carlton
Everlasting Love	Howard Jones
Everlasting Love	Robert Knight
Everlasting Love	Love Affair
Everlasting Love, An	Andy Gibb
Evermore	Ruby Murray
Every Beat Of My Heart	Gladys Knight & The Pips
Every Beat Of My Heart	Rod Stewart
Every Breath You Take	Police
Every Day (I Love You More)	Jason Donovan
Every Day Hurts	Sad Cafe
Every Day Of My Life	Malcolm Vaughan

Title	Artist
Every Heartbeat	Amy Grant
Every Little Bit Hurts	Brenda Holloway
Every Little Kiss	Bruce Hornsby & The Range
Every Little Step	Bobby Brown
Every Little Thing She Does Is Magic	Police
Every Loser Wins	Nick Berry
Every 1's A Winner	Hot Chocolate
Every Rose Has Its Thorn	Poison
Every Time I Think Of You	Babys
Every Woman In The World	Air Supply
Everybody	Tommy Roe
Everybody Dance	Chic
Everybody Everybody	Black Box
Everybody Get Together	Dave Clark Five
Everybody Have Fun Tonight	Wang Chung
Everybody Hurts	REM
Everybody In The Place (EP)	Prodigy
Everybody Is A Star	Sly & The Family Stone
Everybody Knows	Dave Clark Five
Everybody Loves A Clown	Gary Lewis & The Playboys
Everybody Loves A Lover	Doris Day
Everybody Loves Me But You	Brenda Lee
Everybody Loves Somebody	Dean Martin
Everybody Needs Somebody To Love	Blues Brothers
Everybody Plays The Fool	Main Ingredient
Everybody Plays The Fool	Aaron Neville
Everybody Salsa	Modern Romance
Everybody Wants To Rule The World	Tears For Fears
Everybody Wants To Run The World	Tears For Fears
Everybody's Everything	Santana
Everybody's Free (To Feel Good)	Rozalla
Everybody's Gonna Be Happy	Kinks
Everybody's Got To Learn Sometime	Korgis
Everybody's Laughing	Phil Fearon & Galaxy
Everybody's Somebody's Fool	Connie Francis
Everybody's Talkin'	Nilsson
Everyday	Slade
Everyday Is Like Sunday	Morrissey
Everyday People	Sly & The Family Stone
Everyone's Gone To The Moon	Jonathan King
Everything	Jody Watley
Everything About You	Ugly Kid Joe
Everything Changes	Kathy Troccoli
Everything Counts	Depeche Mode
Everything I Am	Plastic Penny
(Everything I Do) I Do It For You	Bryan Adams
(Everything I Do) I Do It For You	Fatima Mansions
Everything I Own	Ken Boothe
Everything I Own	Boy George
Everything I Own	Bread
Everything Is Beautiful	Ray Stevens
Everything Must Change	Paul Young
Everything She Wants	Wham!
Everything That Touches You	Association
Everything Your Heart Desires	Daryl Hall & John Oates
Everything's Alright	Mojos
Everything's Tuesday	Chairmen Of The Board
Everytime You Go Away	Paul Young
Everywhere	Fleetwood Mac
Evil Hearted You	Yardbirds
Evil That Men Do, The	Iron Maiden
Evil Ways	Santana
Evil Woman	Electric Light Orchestra
Excerpt From A Teenage Opera	Keith West
Excitable	Amazulu
Exodus	Ferrante & Teicher
Experiments With Mice	Johnny Dankworth
Express	B.T. Express
Express	Dina Carroll
Express Yourself	Madonna
Express Yourself	Charles Wright & The Watts 103rd Street Rhythm Band
Expressway To Your Heart	Soul Survivors
Extended Play (E.P.)	Bryan Ferry
Exterminate!	Snap Featuring Niki Haris
Eye In The Sky	Alan Parsons Project
Eye Level	Simon Park Orchestra
Eye Of The Tiger	Survivor
Eyes Without A Face	Billy Idol
Fabulous	Charlie Gracie
Faces	2 Unlimited
Fade To Grey	Visage
Fading Like A Flower (Every Time You Leave)	Roxette
Fairytale	Dana
Fairytale	Pointer Sisters

Title	Artist	Title	Artist	Title	Artist
Fairytale Of New York	Pogues Featuring Kirsty MacColl	Fire	Prodigy	Forget Me Not	Kalin Twins
Faith	George Michael	Fire And Rain	James Taylor	Forget Me Not	Eden Kane
Faithful	Go West	Fire Brigade	Move	Forget Me Not	Martha & The Vandellas
Faithfully	Journey	Fire Lake	Bob Seger & The Silver Bullet Band	Forget Me Nots	Patrice Rushen
Fall In Love With You	Cliff Richard	Fireball	Deep Purple	Forgive My Heart	Nat 'King' Cole
Fallin' In Love	Hamilton, Joe Frank & Reynolds	First Cut Is The Deepest	Rod Stewart	Fort Worth Jail	Lonnie Donegan
Falling	Julee Cruise	First Of May	Bee Gees	Fortress Around Your Heart	Sting
Falling	Leblanc & Carr	First Time Ever I Saw Your Face, The	Roberta Flack	Fortunate Son	Creedence Clearwater Revival
Falling	Roy Orbison	First Time, The	Robin Beck	48 Crash	Suzi Quatro
Falling Apart At The Seams	Marmalade	First Time, The	Adam Faith	Forty Miles Of Bad Road	Duane Eddy
Fame	David Bowie	First Time, The	Surface	Four Bacharach & David Songs (EP)	Deacon Blue
Fame	Irene Cara	5-4-3-2-1	Manfred Mann	Four From Toyah E.P.	Toyah
Family Affair	Sly & The Family Stone	500 Miles Away From Home	Bobby Bare	Four Letter Word	Kim Wilde
Family Man	Daryl Hall & John Oates	Five Live (EP)	George Michael & Queen	Four More From Toyah E.P.	Toyah
Family Of Man, The	Three Dog Night	Five O'Clock World	Vogues	Four Walls	Jim Reeves
Fancy Pants	Kenny	5-7-0-5	City Boy	Fox On The Run	Manfred Mann
Fanfare For The Common Man	Emerson, Lake & Palmer	5-10-15-20 (25-30 Years Of Love)	Presidents	Fox On The Run	Sweet
Fanny (Be Tender With My Love)	Bee Gees	Flame, The	Cheap Trick	Frankenstein	Edgar Winter Group
Fantastic Day	Haircut 100	Flash	Queen	Frankie	Connie Francis
Fantasy	Black Box	Flashdance...What A Feeling	Irene Cara	Frankie	Sister Sledge
Fantasy	Earth, Wind & Fire	Flex	Mad Cobra	Frankie And Johnny	Sam Cooke
Fantasy Island	Tight Fit	F.L.M.	Mel & Kim	Freak Me	Silk
Far Far Away	Slade	Float On	Floaters	Freddie's Dead	Curtis Mayfield
Far From Over	Frank Stallone	Floral Dance, The	Brighouse And Rastrick Brass Band	Free	Deniece Williams
Farewell	Rod Stewart	Flowers In The Rain	Move	Free (E.P.)	Free
Farewell Is A Lonely Sound	Jimmy Ruffin	Flowers On The Wall	Statler Brothers	Free Fallin'	Tom Petty
Farewell My Summer Love	Michael Jackson	Fly, The	Chubby Checker	Free Ride	Edgar Winter Group
Fascinating Rhythm	Bass-O-Matic	Fly, The	U2	Free Your Mind	En Vogue
Fascination	Jane Morgan	Floy Joy	Supremes	Freebird	Will To Power
Fashion	David Bowie	Fly Away	John Denver	Freedom	Wham!
Fast Car	Tracy Chapman	Fly Like An Eagle	Steve Miller Band	Freedom Come Freedom Go	Fortunes
Fat Bottomed Girls	Queen	Fly Robin Fly	Silver Convention	Freedom '90	George Michael
Father Christmas Do Not Touch Me	Goodies	Flying Saucer (Parts 1 & 2), The	Buchanan & Goodman	Freeway Of Love	Aretha Franklin
Father Figure	George Michael	Fog On The Tyne (Revisited)	Gazza And Lindisfarne	Freeze-Frame	J. Geils Band
Fattie Bum-Bum	Carl Malcolm	Folk Singer, The	Tommy Roe	Freight Train	Chas McDevitt Skiffle Group
Favourite Shirts (Boy Meets Girl)	Haircut 100	Follow That Dream E.P.	Elvis Presley	French Kiss	Lil' Louis
F.B.I.	Shadows	Follow You Follow Me	Genesis	French Kissin' In The USA	Debbie Harry
Fear Of The Dark (Live)	Iron Maiden	Food For Thought	UB40	Fresh	Kool & The Gang
Feel Like Makin' Love	Bad Company	Fool # 1	Brenda Lee	Friday, I'm In Love	Cure
Feel Like Makin' Love	Roberta Flack	Fool (If You Think It's Over)	Chris Rea	Friday Night (Live Version)	Kids From 'Fame'
Feel Like Making Love	Pauline Henry	Fool Am I, A	Cilla Black	Friday On My Mind	Easybeats
Feel So Fine	Johnny Preston	Fool Never Learns, A	Andy Williams	Friend Or Foe	Adam Ant
Feel So High	Des'ree	Fool On The Hill, The	Sergio Mendes & Brasil '66	Friendly Persuasion	Pat Boone
Feel So Real	Steve Arrington	Fool Such As I, A	Elvis Presley	Friends	Arrival
Feel The Need In Me	Detroit Emeralds	Fool, The	Sanford Clark	Friends	Shalamar
Feelin' Stronger Every Day	Chicago	Fool To Cry	Rolling Stones	Friends	Amii Stewart
Feelings	Morris Albert	Fool's Gold	Stone Roses	Friends	Jody Watley With Eric B & Rakim
Feels Good	Tony! Toni! Tone!	Fooled Around And Fell In Love	Elvin Bishop	Friends And Lovers	Gloria Loring & Carl Anderson
(Feels Like) Heaven	Fiction Factory	Foolish Beat	Debbie Gibson	Friends And Neighbours	Max Bygraves &
Feels Like Heaven	Urban Cookie Collective	Foolish Little Girl	Shirelles		The Tanner Sisters
Feels Like I'm In Love	Kelly Marie	Fools Rush In	Rick Nelson	Friends And Neighbours	Billy Cotton & His Band
Feels Like The First Time	Foreigner	Foot Tapper	Shadows	Friggin' In The Riggin'	Sex Pistols
Feels So Good	Chuck Mangione	Footloose	Kenny Loggins	Frightened City	Shadows
Fernando	Abba	Footsee	Wigan's Chosen Few	From A Distance	Bette Midler
Ferry 'Cross The Mersey	Christians, Holly Johnson,	Footsteps	Steve Lawrence	From A Distance	Cliff Richard
	Paul McCartney, Gerry Marsden &	For All We Know	Shirley Bassey	From A Jack To A King	Ned Miller
	Stock Aitken Waterman	For All We Know	Carpenters	From A Window	Billy J. Kramer & The Dakotas
Ferry Across The Mersey	Gerry & The Pacemakers	For America	Red Box	From Here To Eternity	Frank Sinatra
Fever	Peggy Lee	For Once In My Life	Stevie Wonder	From Me To You	Beatles
Fever	Madonna	For The Good Times	Perry Como	From New York To L.A.	Patsy Gallant
Fever	McCoys	For The Good Times	Ray Price	From The Underworld	Herd
Fields Of Fire (400 Miles)	Big Country	For The Love Of Him	Bobbi Martin	From The Vine Came The Grape	Gaylords
Fifth Of Beethoven, A	Walter Murphy &	For The Love Of Money	O'Jays	From The Vine Came The Grape	Hilltoppers
	The Big Apple Band	For What It's Worth (Stop, Hey		Frozen Orange Juice	Peter Sarstedt
50 Ways To Leave Your Lover	Paul Simon	What's That Sound)	Buffalo Springfield	Full Metal Jacket (I Wanna Be Your	
59th Street Bridge Song		For Whom The Bell Tolls	Bee Gees	Drill Instructor)	Abigail Mead & Nigel Goulding
(Feelin' Groovy), The	Harpers Bizarre	For You	Rick Nelson	Fun, Fun, Fun	Beach Boys
Figaro	Brotherhood Of Man	For You Blue	Beatles	Funeral Pyre	Jam
Fight The Power Pt. 1	Isley Brothers	For Your Babies	Simply Red	Funkin' For Jamaica (N.Y.)	Tom Browne
Final Countdown, The	Europe	For Your Eyes Only	Sheena Easton	Funky Broadway	Wilson Pickett
Finally	Ce Ce Peniston	For Your Love	Ed Townsend	Funky Cold Medina	Tone Loc
Finchley Central	New Vaudeville Band	For Your Love	Yardbirds	Funky Gibbon	Goodies
Find Another Fool	Quarterflash	For Your Precious Love	Jerry Butler & The Impressions	Funky Moped	Jasper Carrott
Find My Love	Fairground Attraction	Forever	Kiss	Funky Street	Arthur Conley
Find The Time	Five Star	Forever	Little Dippers	Funky Town	Pseudo Echo
Fine Time	New Order	Forever	Roy Wood	Funky Weekend	Stylistics
Fine Time	Yazz	Forever & Ever	Slik	Funky Worm	Ohio Players
Finer Things, The	Steve Winwood	Forever Autumn	Justin Hayward	Funkytown	Lipps Inc.
Finger Of Suspicion	Dickie Valentine	Forever Kind Of Love, A	Bobby Vee	Funny	Joe Hinton
Finger Poppin' Time	Hank Ballard & The Midnighters	(Forever) Live And Die	Orchestral Manoeuvres In	Funny Face	Donna Fargo
Fingertips (Pt. 2)	Stevie Wonder		The Dark	Funny Familiar Forgotten Feelings	Tom Jones
Fings Ain't What They Used T'Be	Max Bygraves	Forever Love	Color Me Badd	Funny Funny	Sweet
Finish What Ya Started	Van Halen	Forever Young	Rod Stewart	Funny How Love Can Be	Ivy League
Fire	Crazy World Of Arthur Brown	Forever Your Girl	Paula Abdul	Funny Way Of Laughin'	Burl Ives
Fire	Ohio Players	Forget About You	Motors	Future Love (EP)	Seal
Fire	Pointer Sisters	Forget Him	Bobby Rydell		

Title	Artist
Gal With The Yaller Shoes	Michael Holliday
Galveston	Glen Campbell
Gambler	Madonna
Gamblin' Man	Lonnie Donegan
Game Of Love	Wayne Fontana & The Mindbenders
Games People Play	Alan Parsons Project
Games People Play	Joe South
Games Without Frontiers	Peter Gabriel
Gang That Sang 'Heart Of My Heart', The	Four Aces
Gangsta Lean	DRS
Gangsters	Specials
Garden Of Eden	Gary Miller
Garden Of Eden	Joe Valino
Garden Of Eden	Frankie Vaughan
Garden Party	Rick Nelson
Gasoline Alley Bred	Hollies
Gaye	Clifford T. Ward
Gee Baby	Peter Shelley
Gee Whiz (Look At His Eyes)	Carla Thomas
Gee Whiz It's You	Cliff Richard
Gemini Dream	Moody Blues
Geno	Dexy's Midnight Runners
Gentle On My Mind	Dean Martin
Georgia On My Mind	Ray Charles
Georgy Girl	Seekers
Geronimo	Shadows
Get A Job	Silhouettes
Get A Life	Soul II Soul
Get Away	Bobby Brown
Get Away	Georgie Fame
Get Back	Beatles With Billy Preston
Get Back	Rod Stewart
Get Closer	Seals & Crofts
Get Dancin'	Disco Tex & The Sex-O-Lettes
Get Down	Gene Chandler
Get Down	Gilbert O'Sullivan
Get Down And Get With It	Slade
Get Down, Get Down (Get On The Floor)	Joe Simon
Get Down On It	Kool & The Gang
Get Down Tonight	KC & The Sunshine Band
Get Here	Oleta Adams
Get It	Darts
Get It On (Bang A Gong)	T.Rex
Get It On (Bang A Gong)	Power Station
Get Lost	Eden Kane
Get Off	Foxy
Get Off Of My Cloud	Rolling Stones
Get On Up	Esquires
Get On Your Feet	Gloria Estefan
Get Outta My Dreams Get Into My Car	Billy Ocean
Get Ready	Rare Earth
Get Ready	Temptations
Get Ready For This	2 Unlimited
Get The Message	Electronic
Get Together	Youngbloods
Get Up And Boogie	Silver Convention
Get Up! (Before The Night Is Over)	Technotronic Featuring Ya Kid K
Getaway	Earth, Wind & Fire
Gett Off	Prince & The New Power Generation
Ghetto Child	(Detroit) Spinners
Ghetto Heaven	Family Stand
Ghost Town	Specials
Ghostbusters	Ray Parker Jr.
Ghosts	Japan
Giddy-Up-A-Ding-Dong	Freddie Bell & The Bellboys
Gigi	Billy Eckstine
Gilly Gilly Ossenfeffer Katzenellen Bogen By The Sea	Max Bygraves
Gimme All Your Lovin'	ZZ Top
Gimme Dat Ding	Pipkins
Gimme Gimme Gimme (A Man After Midnight)	Abba
Gimme Gimme Good Lovin'	Crazy Elephant
Gimme Hope Jo'anna	Eddy Grant
Gimme Little Sign	Brenton Wood
Gimme Some	Brendon
Gimme Some Lovin'	Spencer Davis Group
Gin House Blues	Amen Corner
Gina	Johnny Mathis
Ginger Bread	Frankie Avalon
Ginny Come Lately	Brian Hyland
Girl	St. Louis Union
Girl, A Girl, A	Eddie Fisher
Girl Can't Help It, The	Darts
Girl Can't Help It, The	Little Richard
Girl Crazy	Hot Chocolate

Title	Artist
Girl Don't Come	Sandie Shaw
Girl From Ipanema, The	Stan Getz & Astrud Gilberto
Girl I'm Gonna Miss You	Milli Vanilli
Girl Is Mine, The	Michael Jackson & Paul McCartney
Girl Like You, A	Young Rascals
Girl Like You, A	Cliff Richard
Girl Of My Best Friend	Elvis Presley
Girl Of My Dreams	Tony Brent
Girl Watcher	O'Kaysions
Girl You Know It's True	Milli Vanilli
Girl, You'll Be A Woman Soon	Neil Diamond
Girlfriend	Pebbles
Girlie Girlie	Sophia George
Girls	Moments And Whatnauts
Girls	Dwight Twilley
Girls Girls Girls	Motley Crue
Girls Girls Girls	Sailor
Girls Just Want To Have Fun	Cyndi Lauper
Girls Nite Out	Tyler Collins
Girls On Film	Duran Duran
Girls' School	Wings
Girls Talk	Dave Edmunds
Gitarzan	Ray Stevens
Give A Little Love	Aswad
Give A Little Love	Bay City Rollers
Give In To Me	Michael Jackson
Give It To Me	Troggs
Give It Up	KC & The Sunshine Band
Give Me Back My Heart	Dollar
Give Me Just A Little More Time	Chairmen Of The Board
Give Me Just A Little More Time	Kylie Minogue
Give Me Love (Give Me Peace On Earth)	George Harrison
Give Me The Night	George Benson
Give Me Your Heart Tonight	Shakin' Stevens
Give Me Your Word	Tennessee Ernie Ford
Give Peace A Chance	Plastic Ono Band
Givin' Up Givin' In	Three Degrees
Giving Him Something He Can Feel	En Vogue
Giving It All Away	Roger Daltrey
Giving It Up For Your Love	Delbert McClinton
Giving You The Benefit	Pebbles
Giving You The Best That I Got	Anita Baker
G.L.A.D.	Kim Appleby
Glad All Over	Dave Clark Five
Glad It's All Over	Captain Sensible
Glamorous Life, The	Sheila E
Glass Of Champagne	Sailor
Globetrotter	Tornados
Gloria	Laura Branigan
Gloria	Shadows Of Knight
Glory Days	Bruce Springsteen
Glory Of Love	Peter Cetera
Glow	Spandau Ballet
Go	Moby
Go All The Way	Raspberries
Go Away	Gloria Estefan
Go Away Little Girl	Steve Lawrence
Go Away Little Girl	Donny Osmond
Go Away Little Girl	Mark Wynter
Go (Before You Break My Heart)	Gigliola Cinquetti
Go Buddy Go	Stranglers
Go Home	Stevie Wonder
Go Jimmy Go	Jimmy Clanton
Go Now!	Moody Blues
Go On By	Alma Cogan
Go On With The Wedding	Patti Page
Go West	Pet Shop Boys
Go Wild In The Country	Bow Wow Wow
Go Your Own Way	Fleetwood Mac
God Gave Rock & Roll To You II	Kiss
God Only Knows	Beach Boys
God Save The Queen	Sex Pistols
Goin' Back	Dusty Springfield
Goin' Down	Greg Guidry
Goin' Out Of My Head	Lettermen
Goin' Out Of My Head	Little Anthony & The Imperials
Going Back To My Roots	FPI Project
Going Back To My Roots	Odyssey
Going Down The Road	Roy Wood
Going Home	Osmonds
Going In Circles	Friends Of Distinction
Going In With My Eyes Open	David Soul
Going Nowhere	Gabrielle
Going To A Go-Go	Miracles

Title	Artist
Going Underground	Jam
Going Up The Country	Canned Heat
Gold	Spandau Ballet
Gold	John Stewart
Golden Brown	Stranglers
Golden Years	David Bowie
Golden Years (E.P.), The	Motorhead
Goldfinger	Shirley Bassey
Gone	Ferlin Husky
Gonna Fly Now (Theme From 'Rocky')	Bill Conti
Gonna Get Along Without Ya Now	Patience & Prudence
Gonna Get Along Without You Now	Viola Wills
Gonna Make You A Star	David Essex
Gonna Make You An Offer You Can't Refuse	Jimmy Helms
Gonna Make You Sweat	C&C Music Factory Featuring Freedom Williams
Goo Goo Barabajagal (Love Is Hot)	Donovan & Jeff Beck Group
Good Enough	Bobby Brown
Good For Me	Amy Grant
Good Girls Don't	Knack
Good Golly Miss Molly	Swinging Blue Jeans
Good Golly, Miss Molly	Little Richard
Good Heart, A	Feargal Sharkey
Good Life	Inner City
Good Lovin'	Young Rascals
Good Luck Charm	Elvis Presley
Good Morning Freedom	Blue Mink
Good Morning Judge	10cc
Good Morning Starshine	Oliver
Good News	Sam Cooke
Good Old Rock 'n' Roll	Dave Clark Five
Good, The Bad & The Ugly, The	Hugo Montenegro & His Orchestra
Good Thing	Fine Young Cannibals
Good Thing	Paul Revere & The Raiders
Good Thing Going (We've Got A Good Thing Going)	Sugar Minott
Good Time Baby	Bobby Rydell
Good Times	Chic
Good Times	Sam Cooke
Good Times (Better Times)	Cliff Richard
Good Timin'	Jimmy Jones
Good Tradition	Tanita Tikaram
Good Vibrations	Beach Boys
Good Vibrations	Marky Mark & The Funky Bunch Featuring Loleatta Holloway
Good Year For The Roses, A	Elvis Costello
Goodbye	Mary Hopkin
Goodbye Baby	Jack Scott
Goodbye Cruel World	James Darren
Goodbye Girl	David Gates
Goodbye Jimmy, Goodbye	Kathy Linden
Goodbye Jimmy, Goodbye	Ruby Murray
Goodbye My Love	Glitter Band
Goodbye My Love	Searchers
Goodbye Sam Hello Samantha	Cliff Richard
Goodbye Stranger	Pepsi & Shirlie
Goodbye Stranger	Supertramp
Goodbye To Love	Carpenters
Goodbye Yellow Brick Road	Elton John
Goodness Gracious Me	Peter Sellers & Sophia Loren
Goodnight	Roy Orbison
Goodnight Girl	Wet Wet Wet
Goodnight Midnight	Clodagh Rodgers
Goodnight, Sweetheart, Goodnight	McGuire Sisters
Goodnight Tonight	Wings
Goodtime Charlie's Got The Blues	Danny O'Keefe
Goody Two Shoes	Adam Ant
Google Eye	Nashville Teens
Goonies 'R' Good Enough, The	Cyndi Lauper
Got A Hold On Me	Christine McVie
Got My Mind Set On You	George Harrison
Got To Be Certain	Kylie Minogue
Got To Be Real	Cheryl Lynn
Got To Be There	Michael Jackson
Got To Get	Rob 'n' Raz Featuring Leila K
Got To Get It	Culture Beat
Got To Get You Into My Life	Beatles
Got To Get You Into My Life	Cliff Bennett & The Rebel Rousers
Got To Get You Into My Life	Earth, Wind & Fire
Got To Give It Up (Pt.1)	Marvin Gaye
Got To Have Your Love	Mantronix Featuring Wondress
Gotta Go Home	Boney M

405

Title	Artist
Gotta Have Something In The Bank Frank	Frankie Vaughan & The Kaye Sisters
Gotta Pull Myself Together	Nolans
Gotta Travel On	Billy Grammer
Granada	Frankie Laine
Granada	Frank Sinatra
Grand Coolie Dam	Lonnie Donegan
Grand Piano	Mixmaster
Grandad	Clive Dunn
Grandma's Party	Paul Nicholas
Gravy (For My Mashed Potatoes)	Dee Dee Sharp
Grazin' In The Grass	Friends Of Distinction
Grazing In The Grass	Hugh Masekela
Grease	Frankie Valli
Grease Megamix, The	John Travolta/Olivia Newton-John
Greased Lightnin'	John Travolta
Great Balls Of Fire	Jerry Lee Lewis
Great Pretender, The	Freddie Mercury
Great Pretender, The	Jimmy Parkinson
Great Pretender, The	Platters
Greatest Love Of All	Whitney Houston
Green Door, The	Jim Lowe
Green Door	Shakin' Stevens
Green Door	Frankie Vaughan
Green Eyed Lady	Sugarloaf
Green Grass	Gary Lewis & The Playboys
Green Green Grass Of Home	Tom Jones
Green Leaves Of Summer, The	Kenny Ball
Green Manalishi (With The Two-Prong Crown), The	Fleetwood Mac
Green Onions	Booker T. & The M.G.'s
Green River	Creedence Clearwater Revival
Green Tambourine	Lemon Pipers
Greenfields	Brothers Four
Grey Day	Madness
Groove, The	Rodney Franklin
Groove Is In The Heart	Deee-Lite
Groove Line, The	Heatwave
Groove Me	King Floyd
Groover, The	T. Rex
Groovin'	Young Rascals
Groovin' With Mr. Bloe	Mr. Bloe
Groovin' (You're The Best Thing	Style Council
Groovy Kind Of Love	Phil Collins
Groovy Kind Of Love, A	Mindbenders
Groovy Situation	Gene Chandler
Groovy Train	Farm
Grow Some Funk Of Your Own	Elton John
G.T.O.	Ronny & The Daytonas
Guantanamera	Sandpipers
Gudbuy T'Jane	Slade
Guess Things Happen That Way	Johnny Cash
Guilty	Pearls
Guilty	Barbra Streisand & Barry Gibb
Guitar Boogie Shuffle	Virtues
Guitar Boogie Shuffle	Bert Weedon
Guitar Man	Bread
Guitar Tango	Shadows
Gum Drop	Crew-Cuts
Gurney Slade	Max Harris
Gypsy	Fleetwood Mac
Gypsy Man	War
Gypsy Woman	Brian Hyland
Gypsy Woman (She's Homeless)	Crystal Waters
Gypsys Tramps & Thieves	Cher
Ha Ha Said The Clown	Manfred Mann
Hair	Cowsills
Hajji Baba	Nat 'King' Cole
Half-Breed	Cher
Half Heaven-Half Heartache	Gene Pitney
Halfway Down The Stairs	Muppets
Halfway To Paradise	Billy Fury
Hallelujah	Milk & Honey
Hallelujah Freedom	Junior Campbell
Hand On Your Heart	Kylie Minogue
Handful Of Songs	Tommy Steele
Hands Off-She's Mine	Beat
Hands To Heaven	Breathe
Hands Up (Give Me Your Heart)	Ottawan
Handy Man	Jimmy Jones
Handy Man	James Taylor
Hang 'Em High	Booker T. & The M.G.'s
Hang On In There Baby	Johnny Bristol
Hang On In There Baby	Curiosity
Hang On Now	Kajagoogoo
Hang On Sloopy	Ramsey Lewis Trio
Hang On Sloopy	McCoys
Hang On To Your Love	Jason Donovan
Hangin' Tough	New Kids On The Block
Hanging On The Telephone	Blondie
Hanky Panky	Tommy James & The Shondells
Hanky Panky	Madonna
Happenin' All Over Again	Lonnie Gordon
Happening, The	Supremes
Happiest Girl In The Whole U.S.A., The	Donna Fargo
Happy Anniversary	Little River Band
Happy Birthday	Altered Images
Happy Birthday	Stevie Wonder
Happy Birthday, Sweet Sixteen	Neil Sedaka
Happy Days	Pratt & McClain
Happy Days And Lonely Nights	Ruby Murray
Happy Days And Lonely Nights	Frankie Vaughan
Happy-Go-Lucky-Me	Paul Evans
Happy, Happy Birthday Baby	Tune Weavers
Happy Hour	Housemartins
Happy Jack	Who
Happy Organ, The	Dave 'Baby' Cortez
H.A.P.P.Y. Radio	Edwin Starr
Happy Talk	Captain Sensible
Happy To Be On An Island In The Sun	Demis Roussos
Happy Together	Jason Donovan
Happy Together	Turtles
Happy Wanderer	Obernkirchen Children's Choir
Happy Wanderer	Stargazers
Happy Wanderer, The	Henri Rene
Happy Wanderer, The	Frank Weir
Happy Whistler, The	Don Robertson
Happy Xmas (War Is Over)	John & Yoko & The Plastic Ono Band
Harbor Lights	Platters
Hard Day's Night, A	Beatles
Hard Day's Night, A	Peter Sellers
Hard Habit To Break	Chicago
Hard Headed Woman	Elvis Presley
Hard Luck Woman	Kiss
Hard Rain's Gonna Fall, A	Bryan Ferry
Hard To Get	Giselle Mackenzie
Hard To Handle	Otis Redding
Hard To Say	Dan Fogelberg
Hard To Say I'm Sorry	Chicago
Hardcore Uproar	Together
Harden My Heart	Quarterflash
Harder I Try, The	Brother Beyond
Hare Krishna	Radha Krishna Temple
Harlem Shuffle	Bob & Earl
Harlem Shuffle	Rolling Stones
Harper Valley P.T.A.	Jeannie C. Riley
Harry Truman	Chicago
Harvest For The World	Christians
Harvest For The World	Isley Brothers
Hats Off To Larry	Del Shannon
Haunted House	Gene Simmons
Have A Drink On Me	Lonnie Donegan
Have I The Right?	Dead End Kids
Have I The Right?	Honeycombs
Have I Told You Lately	Rod Stewart
Have I Told You Lately That I Love You	Ricky Nelson
Have You Ever Been In Love	Leo Sayer
Have You Ever Needed Someone So Bad	Def Leppard
Have You Ever Seen The Rain	Creedence Clearwater Revival
Have You Never Been Mellow	Olivia Newton-John
Have You Seen Her	Chi-Lites
Have You Seen Her	M.C. Hammer
Have You Seen Your Mother Baby Standing In The Shadow?	Rolling Stones
Hawaii Five-O	Ventures
Hawaiian Wedding Song	Andy Williams
Hawkeye	Frankie Laine
Hazard	Richard Marx
Hazy Shade Of Winter	Bangles
Hazy Shade Of Winter, A	Simon & Garfunkel
He	Al Hibbler
He	McGuire Sisters
He Ain't Heavy, He's My Brother	Hollies
He Ain't No Competition	Brother Beyond
He Don't Love You (Like I Love You)	Tony Orlando & Dawn
He Will Break Your Heart	Jerry Butler
He'll Have To Go	Jim Reeves
He'll Have To Stay	Jeanne Black
He's A Rebel	Crystals
He's Gonna Step On You Again	John Kongos
He's Got No Love	Searchers
He's Got The Whole World (In His Hands)	Laurie London
He's In Town	Rockin' Berries
He's Mine	Platters
He's Misstra Know It All	Stevie Wonder
He's So Fine	Chiffons
He's So Shy	Pointer Sisters
He's Sure The Boy I Love	Crystals
He's The Greatest Dancer	Sister Sledge
Head Games	Foreigner
Head Over Heels	Go-Go's
Head Over Heels	Tears For Fears
Head To Toe	Lisa Lisa & Cult Jam
Headline News	Edwin Starr
Heal The World	Michael Jackson
Healing Hands	Elton John
Hear The Drummer (Get Wicked)	Chad Jackson
Heard It In A Love Song	Marshall Tucker Band
Heart	Max Bygraves
Heart	Eddie Fisher
Heart	Pet Shop Boys
Heart And Soul	Huey Lewis & The News
Heart And Soul	T'Pau
Heart Attack	Olivia Newton-John
Heart Full Of Soul	Yardbirds
Heart Of A Man, The	Frankie Vaughan
Heart Of A Teenage Girl	Craig Douglas
Heart Of Glass	Blondie
Heart Of Gold	Neil Young
Heart Of My Heart	Max Bygraves
Heart Of Rock 'n' Roll, The	Huey Lewis & The News
Heart Of Stone	Taylor Dayne
Heart Of Stone	Kenny
Heart On My Sleeve	Gallagher & Lyle
Heart-Shaped Box	Nirvana
Heart To Heart	Kenny Loggins
Heartache	Pepsi & Shirlie
Heartache Avenue	Maisonettes
Heartache Tonight	Eagles
Heartaches	Marcels
Heartaches By The Number	Guy Mitchell
Heartbeat	Nick Berry
Heartbeat	Don Johnson
Heartbeat	Ruby Murray
Heartbeat	Seduction
Heartbeat	Showaddywaddy
Heartbeat - It's A Lovebeat	DeFranco Family
Heartbreak Hotel	Elvis Presley
Heartbreaker	Dionne Warwick
Heartless	Frankie Vaughan
Heartlight	Neil Diamond
Hearts	Marty Balin
Hearts Of Stone	Charms
Hearts Of Stone	Fontane Sisters
Heat Is On, The	Glenn Frey
Heat Of The Moment	Asia
Heat Of The Night	Bryan Adams
Heat Wave	Martha & The Vandellas
Heat Wave	Linda Ronstadt
Heatseeker	AC/DC
Heaven	Bryan Adams
Heaven	Warrant
Heaven Help Me	Deon Estus
Heaven Help Us All	Stevie Wonder
Heaven In Your Eyes	Loverboy
Heaven Is A Place On Earth	Belinda Carlisle
Heaven Knows	Donna Summer
Heaven Knows I'm Miserable Now	Smiths
Heaven Must Be Missing An Angel	Tavares
Heaven Must Have Sent You	Elgins
Heaven Must Have Sent You	Bonnie Pointer
Heaven On The 7th Floor	Paul Nicholas
Helen Wheels	Paul McCartney & Wings
Hell Raiser	Sweet
Hello	Lionel Richie
Hello Again	Neil Diamond
Hello, Dolly!	Louis Armstrong
Hello Goodbye	Beatles
Hello Happiness	Drifters
Hello Hello I'm Back Again	Gary Glitter
Hello Hurray	Alice Cooper
Hello, I Love You	Doors
Hello It's Me	Todd Rundgren

Title	Artist
Hello Little Girl	Fourmost
Hello Mary Lou	Ricky Nelson
Hello Mudduh, Hello Fadduh	Allan Sherman
Hello Stranger	Yvonne Elliman
Hello Stranger	Barbara Lewis
Hello Susie	Amen Corner
Hello This Is Joannie (The Telephone Answering Machine Song)	Paul Evans
Hello (Turn Your Radio On)	Shakespears Sister
Hello Walls	Faron Young
Help	Bananarama/La Na Nee Nee Noo Noo
Help!	Beatles
Help Is On Its Way	Little River Band
Help Me	Joni Mitchell
Help Me Girl	Eric Burdon & The Animals
Help Me Make It Through The Night	John Holt
Help Me Make It Through The Night	Gladys Knight & The Pips
Help Me Make It Through The Night	Sammi Smith
Help Me, Rhonda	Beach Boys
Help Yourself	Tom Jones
Helule Helule	Tremeloes
Her Royal Majesty	James Darren
Her Town Too	James Taylor & J. D. Souther
Here	Tony Martin
Here And Now	Luther Vandross
Here Come The Nice	Small Faces
Here Comes My Baby	Tremeloes
Here Comes Summer	Jerry Keller
Here Comes That Feeling	Brenda Lee
Here Comes That Rainy Day Feeling Again	Fortunes
Here Comes The Judge	Shorty Long
Here Comes The Night	Them
Here Comes The Rain Again	Eurythmics
Here Comes The Sun	Steve Harley
Here Comes The Sun	Richie Havens
Here I Am (Come And Take Me)	Al Green
Here I Am (Come And Take Me)	UB40
Here I Am (Just When You Thought I Was Over You)	Air Supply
Here I Go Again	Archie Bell & The Drells
Here I Go Again	Hollies
Here I Go Again	Whitesnake
Here It Comes Again	Fortunes
Here We Are	Gloria Estefan
Here We Go	C&C Music Factory Featuring Freedom William & Zelma Davis
Here We Go	Stakka Bo
Here We Go Again	Ray Charles
Here We Go Again!	Portrait
Here We Go Round The Mulberry Bush	Traffic
Here You Come Again	Dolly Parton
Hernando's Hideaway	Archie Bleyer
Hernando's Hideaway	Johnston Brothers
Hernando's Hideaway	Johnnie Ray
Hero	Mariah Carey
Heroes And Villains	Beach Boys
Hersham Boys	Sham 69
Hey! Baby	Bruce Channel
Hey! Baby (They're Playing Our Song)	Buckinghams
Hey D.J. I Can't Dance To That Music You're Playing	Beatmasters Featuring Betty Boo
Hey Deanie	Shaun Cassidy
Hey Girl	Donny Osmond
Hey Girl	Small Faces
Hey, Girl	Freddie Scott
Hey Girl Don't Bother Me	Tams
Hey! Jealous Lover	Frank Sinatra
Hey Joe	Jimi Hendrix Experience
Hey Jude	Beatles
Hey Little Cobra	Rip Chords
Hey Little Girl	Major Lance
Hey Little Girl	Del Shannon
Hey Mr. D.J.	Zhane
Hey Music Lover	S'Express
Hey Nineteen	Steely Dan
Hey Paula	Paul & Paula
Hey Rock And Roll	Showaddywaddy
Hey There	Rosemary Clooney
Hey There	Sammy Davis Jr.
Hey There	Johnnie Ray
Hey There Lonely Girl	Eddie Holman
(Hey Won't You Play) Another Somebody Done Somebody Wrong Song	B.J. Thomas
(Hey You) The Rocksteady Crew	Rocksteady Crew
Hi-De-Ho	Blood Sweat & Tears
Hi-Fidelity	Kids From 'Fame'
Hi-Heel Sneakers	Tommy Tucker
Hi Ho Silver	Jim Diamond
Hi Tension	Hi Tension
Hi, Hi, Hi	Wings
Hi-Ho Silver Lining	Jeff Beck
Hi-Lili-Hi-Lo	Alan Price Set
Hide And Seek	Howard Jones
Hideaway	Dave Dee, Dozy, Beaky, Mick & Tich
High And The Mighty, The	Les Baxter
High And The Mighty, The	Leroy Holmes
High And The Mighty, The	Victor Young
High Class Baby	Cliff Richard
High Energy	Evelyn Thomas
High Enough	Damn Yankees
High Hopes	Frank Sinatra
High In The Sky	Amen Corner
High Life	Modern Romance
High On You	Survivor
High School Confidential	Jerry Lee Lewis
High Time	Paul Jones
Higher Ground	UB40
Higher Ground	Stevie Wonder
Higher Love	Steve Winwood
Him	Rupert Holmes
Him Or Me - What's It Gonna Be	Paul Revere & The Raiders
Hip Hop Hurray	Naughty By Nature
Hip To Be Square	Huey Lewis & The News
Hippy Hippy Shake	Swinging Blue Jeans
Hippychick	Soho
History	Mai Tai
Hit Me With Your Best Shot	Pat Benatar
Hit Me With Your Rhythm Stick	Ian Dury & The Blockheads
Hit That Perfect Beat	Bronski Beat
Hit The Road Jack	Ray Charles
Hitchin' A Ride	Vanity Fare
Hocus Pocus	Focus
Hold Back The Night	Trammps
Hold Her Tight	Osmonds
Hold Me	Fleetwood Mac
Hold Me	P.J. Proby
Hold Me	B.A. Robertson & Maggie Bell
Hold Me Close	David Essex
Hold Me In Your Arms	Rick Astley
Hold Me Now	Johnny Logan
Hold Me Now	Thompson Twins
Hold Me Thrill Me Kiss Me	Mel Carter
Hold Me Tight	Johnny Nash
Hold My Hand	Don Cornell
Hold On	En Vogue
Hold On	Santana
Hold On	Wilson Phillips
Hold On My Heart	Genesis
Hold On Tight	Electric Light Orchestra
Hold On To My Love	Jimmy Ruffin
Hold On To The Nights	Richard Marx
Hold The Line	Toto
Hold Tight	Dave Dee, Dozy, Beaky, Mick & Tich
Hold What You've Got	Joe Tex
Hold You Tight	Tara Kemp
Hold Your Head Up	Argent
Holding Back The Years	Simply Red
Holding On	Steve Winwood
Holding Out For A Hero	Bonnie Tyler
Hole Hearted	Extreme
Hole In My Shoe	neil
Hole In My Shoe	Traffic
Hole In The Ground	Bernard Cribbins
Holiday	Madonna
Holiday Rap	M.C. Miker 'G' & Deejay Sven
Holidays In The Sun	Sex Pistols
Holly Holy	Neil Diamond
Hollywood Nights	Bob Seger & The Silver Bullet Band
Hollywood Swinging	Kool & The Gang
Holy Cow	Lee Dorsey
Holy Smoke	Iron Maiden
Homburg	Procol Harum
Home Lovin' Man	Andy Williams
Homely Girl	Chi-Lites
Homely Girl	UB40
Homeward Bound	Simon & Garfunkel
Honaloochie Boogie	Mott The Hoople
Honey	Bobby Goldsboro
Honey Chile	Martha & The Vandellas
Honey Come Back	Glen Campbell
Honey Honey	Sweet Dreams
Honey I Need	Pretty Things
Honey-Babe	Art Mooney
Honeycomb	Jimmie Rodgers
Hong Kong Garden	Siouxsie & The Banshees
Honky Cat	Elton John
Honky Tonk (Parts 1 & 2)	Bill Doggett
Honky Tonk Women	Rolling Stones
Honolulu Lulu	Jan & Dean
Hooked On A Feeling	Blue Swede
Hooked On A Feeling	B.J. Thomas
Hooked On Classics	Royal Philharmonic Orchestra
Hooray For Hazel	Tommy Roe
Hooray Hooray It's A Holi-Holiday	Boney M
Hoots Mon	Lord Rockingham's XI
Hopeless	Andy Williams
Hopelessly Devoted To You	Olivia Newton-John
Horse, The	Cliff Nobles & Co.
Horse With No Name, A	America
Hot Blooded	Foreigner
Hot Child In The City	Nick Gilder
Hot Diggity	Michael Holliday
Hot Diggity (Dog Ziggity Boom)	Perry Como
Hot Fun In The Summertime	Sly & The Family Stone
Hot Girls In Love	Loverboy
Hot In The City	Billy Idol
Hot Line	Sylvers
Hot Love	T. Rex
Hot Pants (She Got To Use What She Got To Get What She Wants)	James Brown
Hot Pastrami	Dartells
Hot Rod Hearts	Robbie Dupree
Hot Rod Lincoln	Commander Cody & His Lost Planet Airmen
Hot Smoke & Sasafrass	Bubble Puppy
Hot Stuff	Donna Summer
Hot Tracks E.P.	Nazareth
Hotel California	Eagles
Hotel Happiness	Brook Benton
Hotlegs	Rod Stewart
Hound Dog	Elvis Presley
Hound Dog Man	Fabian
House Arrest	Krush
House Nation	House Master Boyz & The Rude Boy Of House
House Of Blue Lights, The	Chuck Miller
House Of Fun	Madness
House Of Love	East 17
House Of The Rising Sun	Animals
House Of The Rising Sun	Frijid Pink
House That Jack Built, The	Aretha Franklin
House That Jack Built, The	Alan Price Set
House That Jack Built, The	Tracie
House With Love In It, A	Vera Lynn
Housecall	Shabba Ranks Featuring Maxi Priest
How 'Bout Us	Champaign
How About That	Adam Faith
How Am I Supposed To Live Without You	Michael Bolton
How Am I Supposed To Live Without You	Laura Branigan
How Can I Be Sure	David Cassidy
How Can I Be Sure	Young Rascals
How Can I Ease The Pain	Lisa Fischer
How Can I Fall	Breathe
How Can I Love You More?	M People
How Can We Be Lovers	Michael Bolton
How Can You Expect To Be Taken Seriously	Pet Shop Boys
How Can You Mend A Broken Heart	Bee Gees
How Come	Ronnie Lane
How Deep Is Your Love	Bee Gees
How Do I Make You	Linda Ronstadt
How Do You Do It	Gerry & The Pacemakers
How Do You Do!	Roxette
How Do You Do?	Mouth & McNeal
How Do You Talk To An Angel	Heights
How Does That Grab You Darlin'	Nancy Sinatra
How Important Can It Be?	Joni James
How Long	Ace
How Many Tears	Bobby Vee
How Much I Feel	Ambrosia
How Much Love	Leo Sayer
How Soon	Henry Mancini & His Orchestra
How Sweet It Is (To Be Loved By You)	James Taylor

407

Title	Artist
How Sweet It Is To Be Loved By You	Marvin Gaye
How Time Flies	Jerry Wallace
How Will I Know	Whitney Houston
How You Gonna See Me Now	Alice Cooper
Howzat	Sherbet
Hubble Bubble Toil And Trouble	Manfred Mann
Hucklebuck, The	Chubby Checker
Hula Love	Buddy Knox
Human	Human League
Human Nature	Gary Clail On-U Sound System
Human Nature	Michael Jackson
Human Touch	Bruce Springsteen
Hummingbird	Les Paul & Mary Ford
Humpin' Around	Bobby Brown
Humpty Dance, The	Digital Underground
Hundred Pounds Of Clay, A	Craig Douglas
Hundred Pounds Of Clay, A	Gene McDaniels
Hungry	Paul Revere & The Raiders
Hungry Eyes	Eric Carmen
Hungry Heart	Bruce Springsteen
Hungry Like The Wolf	Duran Duran
Hunter Gets Captured By The Game, The	Marvelettes
Hunting High And Low	A-Ha
Hurdy Gurdy Man	Donovan
Hurry Up Harry	Sham 69
Hurt	Manhattans
Hurt	Timi Yuro
Hurt So Bad	Lettermen
Hurt So Bad	Little Anthony & The Imperials
Hurt So Bad	Linda Ronstadt
Hurt So Good	Susan Cadogan
Hurting Each Other	Carpenters
Hurts So Good	John Cougar
Hush	Deep Purple
Hush, Hush Sweet Charlotte	Patti Page
Hush Not A Word To Mary	John Rowles
Hustle, The	Van McCoy
Hustle! (To The Music...)	Funky Worm
Hymn	Ultravox
Hymn To Her	Pretenders
Hysteria	Def Leppard
I Adore Mi Amor	Color Me Badd
I Ain't Gonna Stand For It	Stevie Wonder
I Almost Lost My Mind	Pat Boone
I Am	Tony Bennett
I Am A Cider Drinker (Paloma Blanca)	Wurzels
I Am A Rock	Simon & Garfunkel
I Am ...I Said	Neil Diamond
I Am The Beat	Look
I Am Woman	Helen Reddy
I Apologise	P.J. Proby
I Beg Of You	Elvis Presley
I Beg Your Pardon	Kon Kan
I Believe	Bachelors
I Believe	EMF
I Believe In Father Christmas	Greg Lake
I Believe (In Love)	Hot Chocolate
I Believe In You (You Believe In Me)	Johnnie Taylor
I Believe There's Nothing Stronger Than Our Love	Paul Anka with Odia Coates
I Can Do It	Rubettes
I Can Dream About You	Dan Hartman
I Can Hear Music	Beach Boys
I Can Hear The Grass Grow	Move
I Can Help	Billy Swan
I Can Make You Feel Good	Shalamar
I Can Never Go Home Anymore	Shangri-Las
I Can Prove It	Phil Fearon
I Can See Clearly Now	Johnny Nash
I Can See For Miles	Who
I Can Take Or Leave Your Lovin'	Herman's Hermits
I Can't Control Myself	Troggs
I Can't Dance	Genesis
I Can't Explain	Who
I Can't Get Next To You	Temptations
(I Can't Get No) Satisfaction	Rolling Stones
I Can't Go For That (No Can Do)	Daryl Hall & John Oates
(I Can't Help) Falling In Love With You	UB40
I Can't Help It	Andy Gibb & Olivia Newton-John
I Can't Help Myself	Donnie Elbert
I Can't Help Myself	Four Tops
I Can't Hold Back	Survivor
I Can't Leave You Alone	George McCrae
I Can't Let Go	Hollies
I Can't Let Maggie Go	Honeybus

Title	Artist
I Can't Stand It	Eric Clapton
I Can't Stand It	Twenty 4 Seven Featuring Captain Hollywood
I Can't Stand It No More	Peter Frampton
I Can't Stand The Rain	Eruption
I Can't Stand Up For Falling Down	Elvis Costello
I Can't Stay Mad At You	Skeeter Davis
I Can't Stop	Osmonds
I Can't Stop Dancing	Archie Bell & The Drells
I Can't Stop Lovin' You	Don Gibson
I Can't Stop Lovin' You (Though I Try)	Leo Sayer
I Can't Stop Loving You	Ray Charles
I Can't Take The Power	Off-Shore
I Can't Tell A Waltz From A Tango	Alma Cogan
I Can't Tell The Bottom From The Top	Hollies
I Can't Tell You Why	Eagles
I Can't Wait	Stevie Nicks
I Can't Wait	Nu Shooz
I Can't Wait Another Minute	Hi-Five
I Close My Eyes And Count To Ten	Dusty Springfield
I Could Be Happy	Altered Images
I Could Be So Good For You	Dennis Waterman
I Could Easily Fall	Cliff Richard
I Could Never Love Another (After Loving You)	Temptations
I Could Never Take The Place Of Your Man	Prince
I Couldn't Live Without Your Love	Petula Clark
I Cried A Tear	Lavern Baker
I Cried For You	Ricky Stevens
I Did What I Did For Maria	Tony Christie
I Didn't Know I Loved You (Till I Saw You Rock'n'Roll)	Gary Glitter
I Didn't Mean To Turn You On	Robert Palmer
I Die:You Die	Gary Numan
I Dig Rock And Roll Music	Peter, Paul & Mary
I Do, I Do, I Do, I Do, I Do	Abba
I Don't Believe In If Anymore	Roger Whittaker
I Don't Blame You At All	Smokey Robinson & The Miracles
I Don't Care	Shakespears Sister
I Don't Have The Heart	James Ingram
I Don't Know Anybody Else	Black Box
I Don't Know How To Love Him	Helen Reddy
I Don't Know Why	Eden Kane
I Don't Like Mondays	Boomtown Rats
I Don't Like To Sleep Alone	Paul Anka with Odia Coates
I Don't Need You	Kenny Rogers
I Don't Think That Man Should Sleep Alone	Ray Parker Jr.
I Don't Wanna Cry	Mariah Carey
I Don't Wanna Dance	Eddy Grant
I Don't Wanna Fight	Tina Turner
I Don't Wanna Get Hurt	Donna Summer
I Don't Wanna Go On With You Like That	Elton John
I Don't Wanna Live Without Your Love	Chicago
I Don't Wanna Lose You	Kandidate
I Don't Wanna Lose You	Tina Turner
I Don't Want A Lover	Texas
I Don't Want Our Loving To Die	Herd
I Don't Want To Be A Hero	Johnny Hates Jazz
I Don't Want To Do Wrong	Gladys Knight & The Pips
I Don't Want To Live Without You	Foreigner
I Don't Want To Put A Hold On You	Berni Flint
I Don't Want To Talk About It	Everything But The Girl
I Don't Want To Talk About It	Rod Stewart
I Don't Want Your Love	Duran Duran
I Drove All Night	Cyndi Lauper
I Drove All Night	Roy Orbison
I Eat Cannibals Pt. 1	Toto Coelo
I Fall To Pieces	Patsy Cline
I Feel Fine	Beatles
I Feel For You	Chaka Khan
I Feel Free	Cream
I Feel Like A Bullet	Elton John
I Feel Like Buddy Holly	Alvin Stardust
I Feel Love	Bronski Beat & Marc Almond
I Feel Love	Donna Summer
I Feel Love Comin' On	Felice Taylor
I Feel So Bad	Elvis Presley
I Feel The Earth Move	Carole King
I Feel The Earth Move	Martika
I Feel You	Depeche Mode
I Fought The Law	Bobby Fuller Four
I Found Lovin'	Fatback Band
I Found Out The Hard Way	Four Pennies
I Found Someone	Cher

Title	Artist
I Get A Kick Out Of You	Gary Shearston
I Get A Little Sentimental Over You	New Seekers
I Get Around	Beach Boys
I Get Around	2Pac
I Get So Lonely	Four Knights
I Get The Sweetest Feeling	Jackie Wilson
I Get Weak	Belinda Carlisle
I Go Ape	Neil Sedaka
I Go Crazy	Paul Davis
I Go To Extremes	Billy Joel
I Go To Pieces	Peter & Gordon
I Go To Sleep	Pretenders
I Got A Feeling	Ricky Nelson
I Got A Man	Positive K
I Got A Name	Jim Croce
I Got Rhythm	Happenings
I Got Stung	Elvis Presley
I Got The Feelin'	James Brown
I Got You Babe	Sonny & Cher
I Got You Babe	UB40 & Chrissie Hynde
I Got You (I Feel Good)	James Brown
I Gotcha	Joe Tex
I Guess I'll Always Love You	Isley Brothers
I Guess That's Why They Call It The Blues	Elton John
I Had Too Much To Dream (Last Night)	Electric Prunes
I Hate Myself For Loving You	Joan Jett & The Blackhearts
I Have A Dream	Abba
I Have Nothing	Whitney Houston
I Haven't Stopped Dancing Yet	Pat & Mick
I Hear A Symphony	Supremes
I Hear You Knocking	Dave Edmunds
I Hear You Knocking	Gale Storm
I Hear You Now	Jon & Vangelis
I Heard A Rumour	Bananarama
I Heard It Through The Grapevine	Marvin Gaye
I Heard It Through The Grapevine	Gladys Knight & The Pips
I Honestly Love You	Olivia Newton-John
I Just Called To Say I Love You	Stevie Wonder
I Just Can't Help Believing	Elvis Presley
I Just Can't Help Believing	B.J. Thomas
I Just Can't Stop Loving You	Michael Jackson
(I Just) Died In Your Arms	Cutting Crew
I Just Don't Have The Heart	Cliff Richard
I Just Don't Know What To Do With Myself	Dusty Springfield
I Just Fall In Love Again	Anne Murray
I Just Wanna Stop	Gino Vannelli
I Just Want To Be Your Everything	Andy Gibb
I Just Want To Celebrate	Rare Earth
I Keep Forgettin' (Everytime You're Near)	Michael McDonald
I Knew You Were Waiting (For Me)	Aretha Franklin & George Michael
I Knew You When	Donny Osmond
I Knew You When	Billy Joe Royal
I Know	Perry Como
I Know	New Atlantic
I Know A Place	Petula Clark
I Know Him So Well	Elaine Paige & Barbara Dickson
(I Know) I'm Losing You	Rare Earth
(I Know) I'm Losing You	Temptations
I Know There's Something Going On	Frida
I Know What I Like	Huey Lewis & The News
I Know (You Don't Love Me No More)	Barbara George
I Like Dreamin'	Kenny Nolan
I Like It	Dino
I Like It	Gerry & The Pacemakers
I Like It Like That	Dave Clark Five
I Like It Like That (Pt.1)	Chris Kenner
I Like The Way (The Kissing Game)	Hi-Five
I Like Your Kind Of Love	Andy Williams
I Live For Your Love	Natalie Cole
I Lost My Heart To A Starship Trooper	Sarah Brightman & Hot Gossip
I Love	Tom T. Hall
I Love A Rainy Night	Eddie Rabbitt
I Love How You Love Me	Paris Sisters
I Love How You Love Me	Bobby Vinton
I Love Music (Pt. 1)	O'Jays
I Love My Radio	Taffy
I Love Rock 'n' Roll	Joan Jett & The Blackhearts
I Love The Night Life (Disco 'Round)	Alicia Bridges
I Love The Sound Of Breaking Glass	Nick Lowe
I Love The Way You Love	Marv Johnson

Title	Artist
I Love To Boogie	T. Rex
I Love To Love (But My Baby Loves To Dance)	Tina Charles
I Love You	Climax Blues Band
I Love You	People
I Love You	Cliff Richard
I Love You	Donna Summer
I Love You Baby	Paul Anka
I Love You Because	Al Martino
I Love You Because	Jim Reeves
I Love You Love Me Love	Gary Glitter
I Love You More And More Every Day	Al Martino
I Love You So Much It Hurts	Charlie Gracie
I Love Your Smile	Shanice
I Made It Through The Rain	Barry Manilow
I May Never Pass This Way Again	Perry Como
I May Never Pass This Way Again	Robert Earl
I Miss You	Klymaxx
I Missed Again	Phil Collins
I Must Be Seeing Things	Gene Pitney
I Need Love	L.L. Cool J
I Need You	America
I Need You	B.V.S.M.P.
I Need You Now	Eddie Fisher
I Need Your Love Tonight	Elvis Presley
I Need Your Lovin'	Alyson Williams
I Never Cry	Alice Cooper
I Never Loved A Man (The Way I Love You)	Aretha Franklin
I Only Have Eyes For You	Flamingos
I Only Have Eyes For You	Art Garfunkel
I Only Want To Be With You	Bay City Rollers
I Only Want To Be With You	Dusty Springfield
I Only Want To Be With You	Tourists
I Owe You Nothing	Bros
I Pretend	Des O'Connor
I Put A Spell On You	Alan Price Set
I Quit	Bros
I Ran (So Far Away)	Flock Of Seagulls
I Remember Elvis Presley (The King Is Dead)	Danny Mirror
I Remember Holding You	Boys Club
I Remember Yesterday	Donna Summer
I Remember You	Frank Ifield
I Remember You	Skid Row
I Saw Her Again	Mamas & The Papas
I Saw Him Standing There	Tiffany
I Saw Linda Yesterday	Dickey Lee
I Saw Mommy Kissing Santa Claus	Beverley Sisters
I Saw Mommy Kissing Santa Claus	Jimmy Boyd
I Saw Red	Warrant
I Saw The Light	Todd Rundgren
I Say A Little Prayer	Aretha Franklin
I Say A Little Prayer	Dionne Warwick
I Second That Emotion	Japan
I Second That Emotion	Smokey Robinson & The Miracles
I See A Star	Mouth & McNeal
I See The Moon	Stargazers
I Shot The Sheriff	Eric Clapton
I Should Be So Lucky	Kylie Minogue
I Should Have Known Better	Jim Diamond
I Shoulda Loved Ya	Narada Michael Walden
I Started A Joke	Bee Gees
I Still Believe	Ronnie Hilton
I Still Believe	Brenda K. Starr
I Still Believe In You	Cliff Richard
I Still Can't Get Over You	Ray Parker Jr.
I Still Haven't Found What I'm Looking For	Chimes
I Still Haven't Found What I'm Looking For	U2
I Surrender	Rainbow
I Thank You	Sam & Dave
I Think I Love You	Partridge Family
I Think It's Going To Rain	UB40
I Think It's Love	Jermaine Jackson
I Think Of You	Perry Como
I Think Of You	Merseybeats
I Think We're Alone Now	Tommy James & The Shondells
I Think We're Alone Now	Tiffany
I Touch Myself	Divinyls
I Understand	Freddie & The Dreamers
I Understand	June Valli
I Understand (Just How You Feel)	G-Clefs
I Understand Just How You Feel	Four Tunes
I Walk The Line	Johnny Cash
I Wanna Be A Cowboy	Boys Don't Cry
I Wanna Be Rich	Calloway
I Wanna Be Your Lover	Prince
I Wanna Be Your Man	Rolling Stones
I Wanna Dance Wit Choo'	Disco Tex & The Sex-O-Lettes
I Wanna Dance With Somebody (Who Loves Me)	Whitney Houston
I Wanna Do It With You	Barry Manilow
I Wanna Get Next To You	Rose Royce
(I Wanna Give You) Devotion	Nomad Featuring MC Mikee Freedom
I Wanna Go Back	Eddie Money
I Wanna Go Home	Lonnie Donegan
I Wanna Have Some Fun	Samantha Fox
I Wanna Love Him So Bad	Jelly Beans
I Wanna Love You	Jade
I Wanna Sex You Up	Color Me Badd
I Wanna Stay With You	Gallagher & Lyle
I Want A New Drug	Huey Lewis & The News
I Want Candy	Bow Wow Wow
I Want Candy	Strangeloves
I Want Her	Keith Sweat
I Want It All	Queen
I Want That Man	Deborah Harry
(I Want To Be) Elected	Mr. Bean & Smear Campaign
I Want To Be Free	Toyah
I Want To Be Wanted	Brenda Lee
I Want To Be Your Man	Roger
I Want To Break Free	Queen
I Want To Hold Your Hand	Beatles
I Want To Know What Love Is	Foreigner
I Want To Stay Here	Steve Lawrence & Eydie Gormé
I Want To Wake Up With You	Boris Gardiner
I Want To Walk You Home	Fats Domino
I Want You	Bob Dylan
I Want You	Marvin Gaye
I Want You Back	Bananarama
I Want You Back	Jackson Five
I Want You Back '88	Michael Jackson With The Jackson Five
I Want You, I Need You, I Love You	Elvis Presley
I Want You To Be My Girl	Frankie Lymon & The Teenagers
I Want You To Want Me	Cheap Trick
I Want Your Love	Chic
I Want Your Love	Transvision Vamp
I Want Your Lovin' (Just A Little Bit)	Curtis Hairston
I Want Your Sex	George Michael
I Want'a Do Something Freaky To You	Leon Haywood
I Was Born To Love You	Freddie Mercury
I Was Kaiser Bill's Batman	Whistling Jack Smith
I Was Made For Dancin'	Leif Garrett
I Was Made For Lovin' You	Kiss
I Was Made To Love Her	Stevie Wonder
I Was Only Joking	Rod Stewart
I (Who Have Nothing)	Shirley Bassey
I (Who Have Nothing)	Tom Jones
I Will	Billy Fury
I Will	Dean Martin
I Will	Ruby Winters
I Will Always Love You	Whitney Houston
I Will Always Love You	Sarah Washington
I Will Follow Him	Little Peggy March
I Will Return	Springwater
I Will Survive	Gloria Gaynor
I Wish	Stevie Wonder
I Wish It Could Be Christmas Everyday	Wizzard
I Wish It Would Rain	Faces
I Wish It Would Rain	Temptations
I Wish It Would Rain Down	Phil Collins
I Woke Up In Love This Morning	Partridge Family
I Won't Back Down	Tom Petty
I Won't Come In While He's There	Jim Reeves
I Won't Forget You	Poison
I Won't Forget You	Jim Reeves
I Won't Hold You Back	Toto
I Won't Last A Day Without You	Carpenters
I Won't Let The Sun Go Down On Me	Nik Kershaw
I Won't Let You Down	PhD
I Won't Run Away	Alvin Stardust
I Wonder	Dickie Valentine
I Wonder What She's Doing Tonight	Tommy Boyce & Bobby Hart
I Wonder Why	Showaddywaddy
I Wonder Why	Curtis Stigers
I Would Die 4 U	Prince & The Revolution
I Wouldn't Normally Do This Kind Of Thing	Pet Shop Boys
I Wouldn't Trade You For The World	Bachelors
I Write The Songs	Barry Manilow
I'd Die Without You	P.M. Dawn
I'd Do Anything For Love (But I Won't Do That)	Meat Loaf
I'd Like To Teach The World To Sing	Hillside Singers
I'd Like To Teach The World To Sing	New Seekers
I'd Love You To Want Me	Lobo
I'd Never Find Another You	Billy Fury
I'd Rather Go Blind	Chicken Shack
I'd Rather Jack	Reynolds Girls
I'd Really Love To See You Tonight	England Dan & John Ford Coley
I'd Wait A Million Years	Grass Roots
I'll Always Love You	Taylor Dayne
I'll Be Around	(Detroit) Spinners
I'll Be Back	Arnee & The Terminaters
I'll Be Doggone	Marvin Gaye
I'll Be Good To You	Brothers Johnson
I'll Be Home	Pat Boone
I'll Be Loving You (Forever)	New Kids On The Block
I'll Be Over You	Toto
I'll Be Satisfied	Shakin' Stevens
I'll Be There	Mariah Carey
I'll Be There	Damita Jo
I'll Be There	Escape Club
I'll Be There	Gerry & The Pacemakers
I'll Be There	Jackson Five
I'll Be There For You	Bon Jovi
I'll Be Your Baby Tonight	Robert Palmer & UB40
I'll Be Your Everything	Tommy Page
I'll Be Your Shelter	Taylor Dayne
I'll Come When You Call	Ruby Murray
I'll Find My Way Home	Jon & Vangelis
I'll Fly For You	Spandau Ballet
I'll Get By	Shirley Bassey
I'll Give All My Love To You	Keith Sweat
I'll Have To Say I Love You In A Song	Jim Croce
I'll Keep You Satisfied	Billy J. Kramer & The Dakotas
I'll Meet You At Midnight	Smokie
I'll Meet You Halfway	Partridge Family
I'll Never Dance Again	Bobby Rydell
I'll Never Fall In Love Again	Bobbie Gentry
I'll Never Fall In Love Again	Tom Jones
I'll Never Fall In Love Again	Dionne Warwick
I'll Never Find Another You	Seekers
I'll Never Get Over You	Johnny Kidd & The Pirates
I'll Never Get Over You (Getting Over Me)	Expose
I'll Never Love This Way Again	Dionne Warwick
I'll Never Stop Loving You	Doris Day
I'll Pick A Rose For My Rose	Marv Johnson
I'll Put You Together Again	Hot Chocolate
I'll Say Forever My Love	Jimmy Ruffin
I'll Stop At Nothing	Sandie Shaw
I'll Take You Home Again Kathleen	Slim Whitman
I'll Take You There	Staple Singers
I'll Tumble 4 Ya	Culture Club
I'll Wait	Van Halen
I'm A Believer	Monkees
I'm A Better Man	Engelbert Humperdinck
I'm A Boy	Who
I'm A Clown	David Cassidy
I'm A Fool To Care	Les Paul & Mary Ford
I'm A Man	Chicago
I'm A Man	Spencer Davis Group
(I'm A) Road Runner	Jr. Walker & The All Stars
I'm A Tiger	Lulu
I'm A Woman	Maria Muldaur
I'm A Wonderful Thing (Baby)	Kid Creole & The Coconuts
I'm Alive	Electric Light Orchestra
I'm Alive	Hollies
I'm Alright	Kenny Loggins
(I'm Always Touched By Your) Presence Dear	Blondie
I'm Comin' Home	Tom Jones
I'm Comin' Out	Diana Ross
I'm Crying	Animals
I'm Doing Fine Now	Pasadenas
I'm Easy	Keith Carradine
I'm Easy	Faith No More
I'm Every Woman	Whitney Houston
I'm Every Woman	Chaka Khan
I'm Falling	Bluebells

409

Title	Artist
I'm Free	Soup Dragons
I'm Goin' Down	Bruce Springsteen
I'm Gonna Be (500 Miles)	Proclaimers
I'm Gonna Be Strong	Gene Pitney
I'm Gonna Get Married	Lloyd Price
I'm Gonna Get Me A Gun	Cat Stevens
I'm Gonna Get You	Bizarre Inc
I'm Gonna Knock On Your Door	Eddie Hodges
I'm Gonna Knock On Your Door	Little Jimmy Osmond
I'm Gonna Love You Just A Little More Baby	Barry White
I'm Gonna Make You Love Me	Diana Ross & The Supremes & The Temptations
I'm Gonna Make You Mine	Lou Christie
I'm Gonna Run Away From You	Tami Lynn
I'm Gonna Sit Right Down And Write Myself A Letter	Billy Williams
I'm Gonna Tear Your Playhouse Down	Paul Young
I'm Henry VIII I Am	Herman's Hermits
I'm In Love Again	Fats Domino
I'm In The Mood For Dancing	Nolans
I'm In You	Peter Frampton
I'm Into Something Good	Herman's Hermits
I'm Just A Singer (In A Rock 'n' Roll Band)	Moody Blues
I'm Leaving It (All) Up To You	Donny & Marie Osmond
I'm Leaving It Up To You	Dale & Grace
I'm Livin' In Shame	Diana Ross & The Supremes
I'm Looking Out The Window	Cliff Richard
I'm Mandy Fly Me	10cc
I'm Not A Juvenile Delinquent	Frankie Lymon & The Teenagers
I'm Not Gonna Let It Bother Me Tonight	Atlanta Rhythm Section
I'm Not In Love	10cc
I'm Not In Love	Will To Power
I'm Not Lisa	Jessi Colter
I'm Not Scared	Eighth Wonder
I'm On Fire	5000 Volts
I'm On Fire	Bruce Springsteen
I'm Ready	Fats Domino
I'm Ready For Love	Martha & The Vandellas
I'm So Excited	Pointer Sisters
I'm So Into You	SWV
I'm So Lonesome I Could Cry	B.J. Thomas
I'm Sorry	John Denver
I'm Sorry	Brenda Lee
I'm Sorry	Platters
I'm Sorry I Made You Cry	Connie Francis
I'm Stickin' With You	Jimmy Bowen
I'm Still In Love With You	Al Green
I'm Still Standing	Elton John
I'm Still Waiting	Diana Ross
I'm Stone In Love With You	Johnny Mathis
I'm Stone In Love With You	Stylistics
I'm Telling You Now	Freddie & The Dreamers
I'm That Type Of Guy	L.L. Cool J
I'm The Leader Of The Gang (I Am)	Gary Glitter
I'm The Lonely One	Cliff Richard
I'm The One	Gerry & The Pacemakers
I'm The Urban Spaceman	Bonzo Dog Doo-Dah Band
I'm Too Sexy	Right Said Fred
I'm Walkin'	Fats Domino
I'm Walkin'	Ricky Nelson
I'm Walking Backwards For Christmas	Goons
I'm Wondering	Stevie Wonder
I'm Your Baby Tonight	Whitney Houston
I'm Your Boogie Man	KC & The Sunshine Band
I'm Your Man	Wham!
I'm Your Puppet	James & Bobby Purify
I'm Yours	Elvis Presley
I've Been A Bad Bad Boy	Paul Jones
I've Been In Love Before	Cutting Crew
I've Been Losing You	A-Ha
(I've Been) Searchin' So Long	Chicago
I've Been Thinking About You	Londonbeat
I've Done Everything For You	Rick Springfield
I've Found Someone Of My Own	Free Movement
I've Got Love On My Mind	Natalie Cole
I've Got News For You	Feargal Sharkey
I've Got The Music In Me	Kiki Dee
I've Got To Use My Imagination	Gladys Knight & The Pips
I've Got You Under My Skin	Four Seasons
I've Gotta Be Me	Sammy Davis Jr.
I've Gotta Get A Message To You	Bee Gees

Title	Artist
I've Had It	Bell Notes
(I've Had) The Time Of My Life	Bill Medley & Jennifer Warnes
I've Lost You	Elvis Presley
I've Never Been To Me	Charlene
I've Told Every Little Star	Linda Scott
I've Waited So Long	Anthony Newley
Ice Cream Man, The	Tornados
Ice Ice Baby	Vanilla Ice
Ice In The Sun	Status Quo
Idle Gossip	Perry Como
Idle On Parade (EP)	Anthony Newley
Iesha	Another Bad Creation
If	Bread
If	Janet Jackson
If	Telly Savalas
If Anyone Falls	Stevie Nicks
If Anyone Finds This I Love You	Ruby Murray
If Dreams Came True	Pat Boone
If Ever You're In My Arms Again	Peabo Bryson
If Every Day Was Like Christmas	Elvis Presley
If I Can Dream	Elvis Presley
If I Can't Have You	Yvonne Elliman
If I Can't Have You	Kim Wilde
If I Could	David Essex
If I Could Build My Whole World Around You	Marvin Gaye & Tammi Terrell
If I Could Reach You	Fifth Dimension
If I Could Turn Back Time	Cher
If I Didn't Care	David Cassidy
If I Ever Fall In Love	Shai
If I Give My Heart To You	Doris Day
If I Give My Heart To You	Denise Lor
If I Give My Heart To You	Joan Regan
If I Had A Hammer	Trini Lopez
If I Had A Hammer	Peter, Paul & Mary
If I Had No Loot	Tony! Toni! Tone!
If I Had Words	Scott Fitzgerald & Yvonne Keeley
If I May	Nat 'King' Cole
If I Only Had Time	John Rowles
If I Said You Had A Beautiful Body Would You Hold It Against Me	Bellamy Brothers
If I Was	Midge Ure
If I Were A Carpenter	Bobby Darin
If I Were A Carpenter	Four Tops
If I Were A Rich Man	Topol
If I Were Your Woman	Gladys Knight & The Pips
If It Happens Again	UB40
If It Isn't Love	New Edition
(If Loving You Is Wrong) I Don't Wanna Be Right	Luther Ingram
If Not For You	Olivia Newton-John
If Not You	Dr. Hook
If Only I Could	Sydney Youngblood
(If Paradise Is) Half As Nice	Amen Corner
If She Should Come To You	Anthony Newley
If The Kids Are United	Sham 69
If The Whole World Stopped Loving	Val Doonican
If This Is It	Huey Lewis & The News
If We Hold On Together	Diana Ross
If Wishes Came True	Sweet Sensation
If You Asked Me To	Celine Dion
If You Believe	Johnnie Ray
If You Can Want	Smokey Robinson & The Miracles
If You Can't Give Me Love	Suzi Quatro
If You Can't Stand The Heat	Bucks Fizz
If You Could Read My Mind	Gordon Lightfoot
If You Don't Know Me By Now	Harold Melvin & The Blue Notes
If You Don't Know Me By Now	Simply Red
If You Go Away	Terry Jacks
If You Go Away	New Kids On The Block
If You Gotta Go Go Now	Manfred Mann
If You Gotta Make A Fool Of Somebody	Freddie & The Dreamers
If You Know What I Mean	Neil Diamond
If You Leave	Orchestral Manoeuvres In The Dark
If You Leave Me Now	Chicago
If You Let Me Stay	Terence Trent D'Arby
(If You Let Me Make Love To You Then) Why Can't I Touch You	Ronnie Dyson
If You Love Me (Let Me Know)	Olivia Newton-John
If You Love Me (Really Love Me)	Kay Starr
If You Love Somebody Set Them Free	Sting
If You Really Love Me	Stevie Wonder
If You Think You Know How To Love Me	Smokey

Title	Artist
If You Wanna Be Happy	Jimmy Soul
If You Want Me To Stay	Sly & The Family Stone
If You Were Here With Me Now	Kylie Minogue & Keith Washington
If You're Lookin' For A Way Out	Odyssey
If You're Ready Come Go With Me	Staple Singers
Iko Iko	Belle Stars
Iko Iko	Natasha
Il Silenzio	Nini Rosso
Image Of A Girl	Safaris
Imaginary Lover	Atlanta Rhythm Section
Imagine	John Lennon
Impulsive	Wilson Phillips
In A Broken Dream	Python Lee Jackson
In All The Right Places	Lisa Stansfield
In America	Charlie Daniels Band
In And Out Of Love	Diana Ross & The Supremes
In Betweenies, The	Goodies
In Crowd, The	Bryan Ferry
"In" Crowd, The	Dobie Gray
"In" Crowd, The	Ramsey Lewis Trio
In Dreams	Roy Orbison
In Dulce Jubilo	Mike Oldfield
In For A Penny	Slade
In My Defence	Freddie Mercury
In My House	Mary Jane Girls
In My Little Corner Of The World	Anita Bryant
In My Own Time	Family
In Old Lisbon	Frank Chacksfield
In Private	Dusty Springfield
In Summer	Billy Fury
In The Air Tonight	Phil Collins
In The Army Now	Status Quo
In The Bad Bad Old Days	Foundations
In The Bush	Musique
In The Chapel In The Moonlight	Kitty Kallen
In The Closet	Michael Jackson
In The Country	Cliff Richard
In The Ghetto	Elvis Presley
In The Middle Of An Island	Tony Bennett
In The Middle Of Nowhere	Dusty Springfield
In The Midnight Hour	Wilson Pickett
In The Mood	Ernie Fields
In The Navy	Village People
In The Rain	Dramatics
In The Still Of The Night (I'll Remember)	Boyz II Men
In The Summertime	Mungo Jerry
In The Year 2525 (Exordium & Terminus)	Zager & Evans
In These Arms	Bon Jovi
In Thoughts Of You	Billy Fury
In Too Deep	Genesis
In Yer Face	808 State
In Your Eyes	George Benson
In Your Room	Bangles
In Zaire	Johnny Wakelin
Incense And Peppermints	Strawberry Alarm Clock
Incommunicado	Marillion
Independence	Lulu
Indian Giver	1910 Fruitgum Co
Indian Lake	Cowsills
Indian Love Call	Slim Whitman
Indian Reservation	Don Fardon
Indian Reservation (The Lament Of The Cherokee Reservation Indian)	Raiders
Indiana Wants Me	R. Dean Taylor
Infatuation	Rod Stewart
Infinite Dreams	Iron Maiden
Infinity	Guru Josh
Informer	Snow
Inner City Blues (Makes Me Wanna Holler)	Marvin Gaye
Innocent Man, An	Billy Joel
Innuendo	Queen
Insanity	Oceanic
Inside-Looking Out	Animals
Inside Out	Odyssey
Instant Karma (We All Shine On)	Lennon, Ono & The Plastic Ono Band
Instant Replay	Dan Hartman
Instant Replay	Yell!
Instinction	Spandau Ballet
International Bright Young Thing	Jesus Jones
International Jet Set	Specials
International Rescue	Fuzzbox
Into The Groove	Madonna
Into The Night	Benny Mardones

Title	Artist	Title	Artist	Title	Artist
Into The Valley	Skids	It's All In The Game	Tommy Edwards	Jack And Jill	Raydio
Intuition	Linx	It's All In The Game	Four Tops	Jack In The Box	Moments
Invincible (Theme From The Legend Of Billie Jean)	Pat Benatar	It's All In The Game	Cliff Richard	Jack In The Box	Clodagh Rodgers
		It's All Over	Cliff Richard	Jack Mix II	Mirage
Invisible Sun	Police	It's All Over Now	Rolling Stones	Jack Mix IV	Mirage
Invisible Touch	Genesis	It's All Right	Impressions	Jack O' Diamonds	Lonnie Donegan
Invisible Touch (Live)	Genesis	It's Almost Tomorrow	Dream Weavers	Jack That House Built, The	Jack 'n' Chill
I.O.U.	Freeez	It's Almost Tomorrow	Mark Wynter	Jack Your Body	Steve 'Silk' Hurley
Ire Feelings (Skanga)	Rupie Edwards	It's Alright	East 17	Jackie Blue	Ozark Mountain Daredevils
Irish Rover, The	Pogues & The Dubliners	It's Alright	Pet Shop Boys	Jackie Wilson Said	Dexy's Midnight Runners
Iron Lion Zion	Bob Marley & The Wailers	It's Alright (Baby's Coming Back)	Eurythmics	Jackson	Nancy Sinatra & Lee Hazlewood
Irresistible You	Bobby Darin	It's Been So Long	George McCrae	Jacob's Ladder	Huey Lewis & The News
Is It A Dream	Classix Nouveaux	It's Different For Girls	Joe Jackson	Jailhouse Rock	Elvis Presley
Is It Love	Mr. Mister	It's Ecstasy When You Lay Down Next To Me	Barry White	Jam	Michael Jackson
Is It Love You're After	Rose Royce			Jam Up Jelly Tight	Tommy Roe
Is That All There Is	Peggy Lee	It's For You	Cilla Black	Jamaica Farewell	Harry Belafonte
Is There Anybody Out There?	Bassheads	It's Four In The Morning	Faron Young	Jambalaya	Carpenters
Is There Something I Should Know	Duran Duran	It's Getting Better	Mama Cass	James (Hold The Ladder Steady)	Sue Thompson
Is This Love	Bob Marley & The Wailers	It's Going To Take Some Time	Carpenters	Jamie	Ray Parker Jr.
Is This Love	Alison Moyet	It's Gonna Be A Cold Cold Christmas	Dana	Jamming	Bob Marley & The Wailers
Is This Love	Survivor	It's Gonna Take A Miracle	Deniece Williams	Jane	Jefferson Starship
Is This Love	Whitesnake	It's Good News Week	Hedgehoppers Anonymous	Janie's Got A Gun	Aerosmith
Island Girl	Elton John	It's Impossible	Perry Como	January	Pilot
Island In The Sun	Harry Belafonte	It's In His Kiss	Linda Lewis	January February	Barbara Dickson
Island Of Dreams	Springfields	It's Just A Matter Of Time	Brook Benton	Japanese Boy	Aneka
Island Of Lost Souls	Blondie	(It's Just) The Way You Love Me	Paula Abdul	Jarrow Song	Alan Price
Islands In The Stream	Kenny Rogers & Dolly Parton	It's Late	Ricky Nelson	Java	Al Hirt
Isle Of Capri	Gaylords	It's Late	Shakin' Stevens	Jaws	Lalo Schifrin
Isn't It A Pity	George Harrison	It's My Life	Animals	Jazzman	Carole King
Isn't It Time	Babys	It's My Life	Dr. Alban	Je Ne Sais Pas Pourquoi	Kylie Minogue
Isn't Life Strange	Moody Blues	It's My Party	Lesley Gore	Je T'Aime (Moi Non Plus)	Judge Dread
Isn't She Lovely	David Parton	It's My Party	Dave Stewart & Barbara Gaskin	Je T'Aime...Moi Non Plus	Jane Birkin & Serge Gainsbourg
Israelites, The	Desmond Dekker & The Aces	It's My Turn	Diana Ross		
It Ain't Me Babe	Turtles	It's No Crime	Babyface	Jealous Guy	Roxy Music
It Ain't Over 'Til It's Over	Lenny Kravitz	It's Not Enough	Starship	Jealous Mind	Alvin Stardust
It Ain't What You Do It's The Way That You Do It	Fun Boy Three & Bananarama	It's Not For Me To Say	Johnny Mathis	Jealousy	Billy Fury
		It's Not Over ('Til It's Over)	Starship	Jean	Oliver
It Didn't Matter	Style Council	It's Not Unusual	Tom Jones	Jean Genie, The	David Bowie
It Doesn't Have To Be	Erasure	It's Now Or Never	Elvis Presley	Jeans On	David Dundas
It Doesn't Have To Be This Way	Blow Monkeys	It's Now Or Never	John Schneider	Jeepster	T. Rex
It Doesn't Matter Anymore	Buddy Holly	It's One Of Those Nights (Yes Love)	Partridge Family	Jennie Lee	Jan & Arnie
It Don't Come Easy	Ringo Starr	It's Only Love	Bryan Adams & Tina Turner	Jennifer Eccles	Hollies
It Don't Matter To Me	Bread	It's Only Love	Elvis Presley	Jennifer Juniper	Donovan
It Hurts So Much	Jim Reeves	It's Only Love	Simply Red	Jenny	Tommy Tutone
It Hurts To Be In Love	Gene Pitney	It's Only Make Believe	Glen Campbell	Jenny, Jenny	Little Richard
It Is Time To Get Funky	D. Mob Featuring LRS	It's Only Make Believe	Child	Jenny Take A Ride!	Mitch Ryder & The Detroit Wheels
It Isn't Right	Platters	It's Only Make Believe	Billy Fury	Jeopardy	Greg Kihn Band
It Keeps Rainin' (Tears From My Eyes)	Bitty McLean	It's Only Make Believe	Conway Twitty	Jericho	Prodigy
It Keeps Right On A-Hurtin'	Johnny Tillotson	It's Only Rock 'n Roll (But I Like It)	Rolling Stones	Jerk Out	Time
It May Be Winter Outside (But In My Heart It's Spring)	Love Unlimited	It's 'Orrible Being In Love (When You're 8 ½)	Claire & Friends	Jerk, The	Larks
				Jesamine	Casuals
It Mek	Desmond Dekker & The Aces	It's Over	Funk Masters	Jesse	Carly Simon
It Might As Well Rain Until September	Carole King	It's Over	Level 42	Jessie's Girl	Rick Springfield
It Must Be Him	Vikki Carr	It's Over	Roy Orbison	Jet	Paul McCartney & Wings
It Must Be Love	Madness	It's Raining	Darts	Jet Airliner	Steve Miller Band
It Must Be Love	Labi Siffre	It's Raining	Shakin' Stevens	Jig A Jig	East Of Eden
It Must Have Been Love	Roxette	It's Raining Again	Supertramp	Jilted	Teresa Brewer
It Never Rains In Southern California	Albert Hammond	It's Raining Men	Weather Girls	Jilted John	Jilted John
It Only Hurts For A Little While	Ames Brothers	It's So Easy	Linda Ronstadt	Jimmy Mack	Martha & The Vandellas
It Only Takes A Minute	One Hundred Ton & A Feather	It's So Easy	Andy Williams	Jingle Bell Rock	Max Bygraves
It Only Takes A Minute	Take That	It's So Hard To Say Goodbye To Yesterday	Boyz II Men	Jingle Bell Rock	Bobby Helms
It Only Takes A Minute	Tavares	It's Still Rock And Roll To Me	Billy Joel	Jingle Jangle	Archies
It Only Took A Minute	Joe Brown & The Bruvvers	It's The Same Old Song	Four Tops	Jive Talkin'	Bee Gees
It Should Have Been Me	Yvonne Fair	It's Time For Love	Chi-Lites	Jive Talkin'	Boogie Box High
It Started All Over Again	Brenda Lee	It's Time To Cry	Paul Anka	Joan Of Arc	Orchestral Manoeuvres In The Dark
It Started With A Kiss	Hot Chocolate	It's Too Late	Carole King	Joanna	Kool & The Gang
It Sure Brings Out The Love In Your Eyes	David Soul	It's Too Late	Quartz Introducing Dina Carroll	Joanna	Scott Walker
It Takes Two	Rod Stewart & Tina Turner	It's Too Soon To Know	Pat Boone	Joe Le Taxi	Vanessa Paradis
It Was A Good Day	Ice Cube	It's Too Soon To Know	Pat Boone	John And Julie	Eddie Calvert
It Was I	Skip & Flip	It's Up To You	Rick Nelson	John I'm Only Dancing	David Bowie
It Would Take A Strong Strong Man	Rick Astley	It's Wonderful	Jimmy Ruffin	John I'm Only Dancing (Again)	David Bowie
It'll Be Me	Cliff Richard	It's You	Freddie Starr	John Wayne Is Big Leggy	Haysi Fantayzee
It's A Fine Day	Opus III	It's You I Love	Fats Domino	Johnny Angel	Shelley Fabares
It's A Hard Life	Queen	It's Your Life	Smokie	Johnny B. Goode	Chuck Berry
It's A Heartache	Bonnie Tyler	It's Your Thing	Isley Brothers	Johnny Come Home	Fine Young Cannibals
It's A Love Thing	Whispers	Itchycoo Park	Small Faces	Johnny Get Angry	Joanie Sommers
It's A Man's Man's Man's World	James Brown	Itsy Bitsy Teenie Weenie Yellow Polka Dot Bikini	Brian Hyland	Johnny Reggae	Piglets
It's A Miracle	Culture Club			Johnny Remember Me	John Leyton
It's A Miracle	Barry Manilow	Itsy Bitsy Teeny Weeny Yellow Polka Dot Bikini	Bombalurina	Johnny Will	Pat Boone
It's A Mistake	Men At Work			Join Together	Who
It's A Shame	(Detroit) Spinners	Ivory Tower	Cathy Carr	Joker, The	Steve Miller Band
It's A Shame (My Sister)	Monie Love Featuring True Image	Ivory Tower	Charms	Jolene	Dolly Parton
		Ivy Rose	Perry Como	Jolly Green Giant, The	Kingsmen
It's A Sin	Pet Shop Boys			Journey To The Center Of The Mind	Amboy Dukes
It's A Sin To Tell A Lie	Gerry Monroe	Ja-Da	Johnny & The Hurricanes	Joy	Apollo 100
It's A Sin To Tell A Lie	Somethin' Smith & The Redheads	Jack & Diane	John Cougar	Joy	Soul II Soul

411

Title	Artist
Lay Down Sally	Eric Clapton
Lay Down Your Arms	Anne Shelton
Lay Lady Lay	Bob Dylan
Lay Your Hands On Me	Bon Jovi
Lay Your Hands On Me	Thompson Twins
Lay Your Love On Me	Racey
Layla	Eric Clapton
Layla	Derek & The Dominoes
Lazy River	Bobby Darin
Lazy Sunday	Small Faces
Le Freak	Chic
Lead Me On	Maxine Nightingale
Leader Of The Band	Dan Fogelberg
Leader Of The Pack	Shangri-Las
Lean On Me	Club Nouveau
Lean On Me	Mud
Lean On Me	Bill Withers
Lean On Me (Ah-Li-Ayo)	Red Box
Leaning On The Lamp Post	Herman's Hermits
Leap Up And Down (Wave Your Knickers In The Air)	St. Cecilia
Learnin' The Blues	Frank Sinatra
Leather And Lace	Stevie Nicks
Leave A Light On	Belinda Carlisle
Leave A Little Love	Lulu
Leave Me Alone	Michael Jackson
Leave Me Alone (Ruby Red Dress)	Helen Reddy
Leaving On A Jet Plane	Peter, Paul & Mary
Lebanon, The	Human League
Leeds United	Leeds United F.C.
Left Bank	Winifred Atwell
Left Right Out Of Your Heart	Patti Page
Left To My Own Devices	Pet Shop Boys
Legend Of Xanadu	Dave Dee, Dozy, Beaky, Mick & Tich
Legs	ZZ Top
Leroy	Jack Scott
Les Bicyclettes De Belsize	Engelbert Humperdinck
Lessons In Love	Level 42
Let 'Em In	Wings
Let Her In	John Travolta
Let It Be	Beatles
Let It Be	Ferry Aid
Let It Be Me	Jerry Butler & Betty Everett
Let It Be Me	Everly Brothers
Let It Out (Let It All Hang Out)	Hombres
Let It Rock	Rolling Stones
Let It Whip	Dazz Band
Let Me Be The One	Expose
Let Me Be The One	Shadows
Let Me Be There	Olivia Newton-John
Let Me Cry On Your Shoulder	Ken Dodd
Let Me Go, Lover	Kathy Kirby
Let Me Go, Lover	Dean Martin
Let Me Go, Lover	Ruby Murray
Let Me Go, Lover	Joan Weber
Let Me Go, Lover!	Teresa Brewer
Let Me In	Osmonds
Let Me In	Sensations
Let Me Love You Tonight	Pure Prairie League
Let Me Try Again	Tammy Jones
Let My Love Open The Door	Pete Townshend
Let The Four Winds Blow	Fats Domino
Let The Heartaches Begin	Long John Baldry
Let The Little Girl Dance	Billy Bland
Let The Music Play	Shannon
Let The Music Play	Barry White
Let The Sunshine In	Fifth Dimension
Let There Be Drums	Sandy Nelson
Let There Be Love	Nat 'King' Cole
Let There Be Love	Simple Minds
Let Your Love Flow	Bellamy Brothers
Let Your Yeah Be Yeah	Pioneers
Let's All Chant	Mick And Pat
Let's All Chant	Michael Zager Band
Let's Dance	David Bowie
Let's Dance	Chris Montez
Let's Dance	Chris Rea
Let's Do It Again	Staple Singers
Let's Get It On	Marvin Gaye
Let's Get It Up	AC/DC
Let's Get Rocked	Def Leppard
Let's Get Serious	Jermaine Jackson
Let's Get Together	Hayley Mills
Let's Get Together Again	Glitter Band
Let's Get Together No. 1	Big Ben Banjo Band
Let's Go	Cars

Title	Artist
Let's Go	Wang Chung
Let's Go All The Way	Sly Fox
Let's Go Crazy	Prince & The Revolution
Let's Go, Let's Go, Let's Go	Hank Ballard & The Midnighters
Let's Go Round Again Pt. 1	Average White Band
Let's Go To San Francisco	Flowerpot Men
Let's Groove	Earth, Wind & Fire
Let's Hang On	Darts
Let's Hang On!	Four Seasons
Let's Have A Ball	Winifred Atwell
Let's Have A Ding Dong	Winifred Atwell
Let's Have A Party	Winifred Atwell
Let's Have A Quiet Night In	David Soul
Let's Have Another Party	Winifred Atwell
Let's Hear It For The Boy	Deniece Williams
Let's Jump The Broomstick	Brenda Lee
Let's Live For Today	Grass Roots
Let's Lock The Door (And Throw Away The Key)	Jay & The Americans
Let's Party	Jive Bunny & The Mastermixers
Let's Pretend	Lulu
Let's Put It All Together	Stylistics
Let's Spend The Night Together	Rolling Stones
Let's Stay Together	Al Green
Let's Stay Together	Tina Turner
Let's Stick Together	Bryan Ferry
Let's Talk About Love	Helen Shapiro
Let's Talk About Sex	Salt-N-Pepa
Let's Think About Living	Bob Luman
Let's Try Again	New Kids On The Block
Let's Turkey Trot	Little Eva
Let's Twist Again	Chubby Checker
Let's Wait Awhile	Janet Jackson
Let's Work Together	Canned Heat
Letter, The	Box Tops
Letter, The	Joe Cocker
Letter From America	Proclaimers
Letter To You, A	Shakin' Stevens
LFO	LFO
Liar	Three Dog Night
Liar, Liar	Castaways
Licence To Kill	Gladys Knight
Lido Shuffle	Boz Scaggs
Liechtensteiner Polka	Will Glahe
Lies	Status Quo
Life	Haddaway
Life In A Northern Town	Dream Academy
Life In The Fast Lane	Eagles
Life Is A Highway	Tom Cochrane
Life Is A Long Song	Jethro Tull
Life Is A Minestone	10cc
Life Is A Rock (But The Radio Rolled Me)	Reunion
Life Is Too Short Girl	Sheer Elegance
Life On Mars	David Bowie
Life's Been Good	Joe Walsh
Lifeline	Spandau Ballet
Light My Fire	Doors
Light My Fire	Jose Feliciano
Light My Fire/137 Disco Heaven (Medley)	Amii Stewart
(Light Of Experience) Doina De Jale	Georghe Zamfir
Lightnin' Strikes	Lou Christie
Lights Of Cincinnati	Scott Walker
Lights Out	Peter Wolf
Lights Went Out In) Massachusetts, (The	Bee Gees
Like A Baby	Len Barry
Like A Prayer	Madonna
Like A Rock	Bob Seger & The Silver Bullet Band
Like A Rolling Stone	Bob Dylan
Like A Virgin	Madonna
Like Clockwork	Boomtown Rats
Like I Do	Maureen Evans
Like I've Never Been Gone	Billy Fury
Like Sister And Brother	Drifters
Like To Get To Know You Well	Howard Jones
Lil' Devil	Cult
Lil' Red Riding Hood	Sam The Sham & The Pharaohs
Lily The Pink	Scaffold
Lily Was Here	David A. Stewart Introducing Candy Dulfer
Limbo Rock	Chubby Checker
Linger	Cranberries
Lion Sleeps Tonight, The	Robert John
Lion Sleeps Tonight, The	Tight Fit
Lion Sleeps Tonight, The	Tokens
Lip Up Fatty	Bad Manners
Lipstick On Your Collar	Connie Francis

Title	Artist
Liquidator	Harry J. & The All Stars
Lisbon Antigua	Nelson Riddle
Listen People	Herman's Hermits
Listen To Me	Hollies
Listen To The Music	Doobie Brothers
Listen To What The Man Said	Wings
Listen To Your Heart	Roxette
Listen To Your Heart	Sonia
Little Arrows	Leapy Lee
Little Bird	Annie Lennox
Little Bit Me, A Little Bit You, A	Monkees
Little Bit More, A	Dr. Hook
Little Bit O' Soul	Music Explosion
Little Bit Of Love	Free
Little Bit Of Soap, A	Jarmels
Little Bit Of Soap, A	Showaddywaddy
Little Bitty Pretty One	Thurston Harris
Little Bitty Pretty One	Jackson Five
Little Bitty Tear, A	Burl Ives
Little Boy Sad	Johnny Burnette
Little Brown Jug	Glenn Miller
Little Children	Billy J. Kramer & The Dakotas
Little Darlin'	Diamonds
Little Devil	Neil Sedaka
Little Diane	Dion
Little Does She Know	Kursaal Flyers
Little Donkey	Beverley Sisters
Little Donkey	Nina & Frederick
Little Drummer Boy	Royal Scots Dragoon Guards
Little Drummer Boy	Harry Simeone Chorale
Little Drummer Boy, The	Beverley Sisters
Little Fluffy Clouds	Orb
Little Girl	Syndicate Of Sound
Little Green Apples	O.C. Smith
Little Honda	Hondells
Little In Love, A	Cliff Richard
Little Jeannie	Elton John
Little Lies	Fleetwood Mac
Little Love, A Little Kiss, A	Karl Denver
Little Love And Understanding, A	Gilbert Becaud
Little Loving, A	Fourmost
Little Man	Sonny & Cher
Little Miss Can't Be Wrong	Spin Doctors
Little Miss Lonely	Helen Shapiro
Little More Love, A	Olivia Newton-John
Little Old Lady (From Pasadena), The	Jan & Dean
Little Ole Man (Uptight-Everything's Alright)	Bill Cosby
Little Peace, A	Nicole
Little Red Corvette	Prince & The Revolution
Little Red Rooster	Sam Cooke
Little Red Rooster	Rolling Stones
Little Respect, A	Erasure
Little Shoemaker, The	Petula Clark
Little Shoemaker, The	Gaylords
Little Shoemaker, The	Frank Weir
Little Shoemaker, The	Hugo Winterhalter
Little Sister	Elvis Presley
Little Star	Elegants
Little Things	Dave Berry
Little Things	Bobby Goldsboro
Little Things Mean A Lot	Alma Cogan
Little Things Mean A Lot	Kitty Kallen
Little Things Mean A Lot	Jimmy Young
Little Time, A	Beautiful South
Little Town Flirt	Del Shannon
Little White Bull	Tommy Steele
Little Willy	Sweet
Little Woman	Bobby Sherman
Live And Learn	Joe Public
Live And Let Die	Guns N' Roses
Live And Let Die	Wings
Live In Trouble	Barron Knights
Live Is Life	Opus
Live It Up	Mental As Anything
Live To Tell	Madonna
Live Together	Lisa Stansfield
Live Your Life Be Free	Belinda Carlisle
Lively	Lonnie Donegan
Liverpool Lou	Scaffold
Livin' It Up (Friday Night)	Bell & James
Livin' On A Prayer	Bon Jovi
Livin' Thing	Electric Light Orchestra
Living After Midnight	Judas Priest
Living By Numbers	New Muzik
Living Daylights, The	A-Ha
Living Doll	Cliff Richard

413

Title	Artist
Living Doll	Cliff Richard & The Young Ones
Living For The City	Stevie Wonder
Living In A Box	Living In A Box
Living In America	James Brown
Living In Harmony	Cliff Richard
Living In Sin	Bon Jovi
Living In The Past	Jethro Tull
Living Inside Myself	Gino Vannelli
Living Next Door To Alice	Smokie
Living On My Own	Freddie Mercury
Living On The Ceiling	Blancmange
Living On The Front Line	Eddy Grant
Living On Video	Trans-X
Living Years, The	Mike + The Mechanics
L-L-Lucy	Mud
Lo Mucho Que Te Quiero (The More I Love You)	Rene & Rene
Loadsamoney (Doin' Up The House)	Harry Enfield
Loco In Acapulco	Four Tops
Loco-Motion, The	Grand Funk
Loco-Motion, The	Little Eva
Loco-Motion, The	Kylie Minogue
Locomotion	Orchestral Manoeuvres In The Dark
Loddy Lo	Chubby Checker
Lodgers, The	Style Council
Logical Song, The	Supertramp
Lola	Kinks
Lollipop	Chordettes
Lollipop	Mudlarks
London Calling	Clash
London Nights	London Boys
Lone Ranger, The	Quantum Jump
(Loneliness Made Me Realize) It's You That I Need	Temptations
Lonely	Acker Bilk
Lonely Blue Boy	Conway Twitty
Lonely Boy	Paul Anka
Lonely Boy	Andrew Gold
Lonely Boy	Donny Osmond
Lonely Bull, The	Herb Alpert
Lonely Days	Bee Gees
Lonely Night (Angel Face)	Captain & Tennille
Lonely Ol' Night	John Cougar Mellencamp
Lonely People	America
Lonely Pup (In A Christmas Shop)	Adam Faith
Lonely Street	Andy Williams
Lonely Teardrops	Jackie Wilson
Lonely Teenager	Dion
Lonely This Christmas	Mud
Lonesome	Adam Faith
Lonesome Loser	Little River Band
Lonesome Town	Ricky Nelson
Long And Winding Road, The	Beatles
Long As I Can See The Light	Creedence Clearwater Revival
Long Cool Woman (In A Black Dress)	Hollies
Long Haired Lover From Liverpool	Little Jimmy Osmond
Long Hot Summer	Style Council
Long Legged Woman Dressed In Black	Mungo Jerry
Long Live Love	Olivia Newton-John
Long Live Love	Sandie Shaw
Long Run, The	Eagles
Long Tall Glasses (I Can Dance)	Leo Sayer
Long Tall Sally	Little Richard
Long Train Runnin'	Doobie Brothers
Longer	Dan Fogelberg
Longest Time, The	Billy Joel
Longest Walk, The	Jaye P. Morgan
Longfellow Serenade	Neil Diamond
Look, The	Roxette
Look Around	Vince Hill
Look Away	Big Country
Look Away	Chicago
Look For A Star	Garry Mills
Look Homeward Angel	Johnnie Ray
Look In My Eyes	Chantels
Look In My Eyes Pretty Woman	Tony Orlando & Dawn
Look Of Love, The	Madonna
Look Of Love, The	Sergio Mendes & Brasil '66
Look Of Love, The	ABC
Look Through Any Window	Hollies
Look What They've Done To My Song Ma	New Seekers Featuring Eve Graham
Look What You Done For Me	Al Green
Look What You've Done To Me	Boz Scaggs

Title	Artist
Look Wot You Dun	Slade
Lookin' For A Love	Bobby Womack
Lookin' For Love	Johnny Lee
Lookin' Out My Back Door	Creedence Clearwater Revival
Lookin' Through The Eyes Of Love	Partridge Family
Lookin' Through The Windows	Jackson Five
Looking After Number One	Boomtown Rats
Looking Back	Nat 'King' Cole
Looking For A New Love	Jody Watley
Looking Through Patient Eyes	P.M. Dawn
Looking Through The Eyes Of Love	Gene Pitney
Looking Up	Michelle Gayle
Looks Like We Made It	Barry Manilow
Loop De Loop	Johnny Thunder
Loop De Loop	Frankie Vaughan
Loop Di Love	Shag
Lord's Prayer, The	Sister Janet Mead
Losing My Mind	Liza Minnelli
Losing My Religion	R.E.M.
Losing You	Brenda Lee
Losing You	Dusty Springfield
Lost In Emotion	Lisa Lisa & Cult Jam
Lost In France	Bonnie Tyler
Lost In Love	Air Supply
Lost In You	Rod Stewart
Lost In Your Eyes	Debbie Gibson
Lost John	Lonnie Donegan
Lost Without You Love	Bread
Lotta Love	Nicolette Larson
Lotta Lovin'	Gene Vincent & His Blue Caps
Louie Louie	Kingsmen
L-O-V-E (Love)	Al Green
Love Action (I Believe In Love)	Human League
Love And Affection	Joan Armatrading
Love & Kisses	Dannii Minogue
Love And Marriage	Frank Sinatra
Love & Pride	King
Love And Understanding	Cher
Love Bites	Def Leppard
Love Bizarre, A	Sheila E
Love Came To Me	Dion
Love (Can Make You Happy)	Mercy
Love Can't Turn Around	Farley 'Jackmaster' Funk
Love Cats, The	Cure
Love Changes (Everything)	Climie Fisher
Love Changes Everything	Michael Ball
Love Child	Diana Ross & The Supremes
Love Child	Sweet Sensation
Love Come Down	Evelyn King
Love Don't Live Here Anymore	Jimmy Nail
Love Don't Live Here Anymore	Rose Royce
Love Games	Belle & The Devotions
Love Grows (Where My Rosemary Goes)	Edison Lighthouse
Love Hangover	Diana Ross
Love Her Madly	Doors
Love Hit Me	Maxine Nightingale
Love Hurts	Jim Capaldi
Love Hurts	Nazareth
Love I Lost, The	West End Featuring Sybil
Love I Lost (Part 1), The	Harold Melvin & The Blue Notes
Love In An Elevator	Aerosmith
Love In The First Degree	Bananarama
Love In The Sun	Glitter Band
Love Is	Vanessa Williams & Brian McKnight
Love Is A Battlefield	Pat Benatar
Love Is A Hurtin' Thing	Lou Rawls
Love Is A Many-Splendored Thing	Four Aces
Love Is A Rose	Linda Ronstadt
Love Is A Stranger	Eurythmics
Love Is A Wonderful Thing	Michael Bolton
Love Is Alive	Gary Wright
Love Is All	Malcolm Roberts
Love Is All Around	Troggs
Love Is All We Need	Tommy Edwards
Love Is Blue	Paul Mauriat
Love Is Contagious	Taja Sevelle
Love Is Here And Now You're Gone	Supremes
Love Is In Control (Finger On The Trigger)	Donna Summer
Love Is In The Air	John Paul Young
Love Is Life	Hot Chocolate
Love Is Like A Violin	Ken Dodd
Love Is Like An Itching In My Heart	Supremes
Love Is Like Oxygen	Sweet

Title	Artist
Love Is On The Way	Saigon Kick
Love Is Strange	Everly Brothers
Love Is Strange	Mickey & Sylvia
Love Is Strange	Peaches & Herb
Love Is The Answer	England Dan & John Ford Coley
Love Is The Drug	Roxy Music
(Love Is) Thicker Than Water	Andy Gibb
Love Kills	Freddie Mercury
Love Letters	Ketty Lester
Love Letters	Alison Moyet
Love Letters	Elvis Presley
Love Letters In The Sand	Pat Boone
Love Like A Man	Ten Years After
Love Machine	Miracles
Love Makes The World Go Round	Perry Como
Love Makes The World Go Round	Deon Jackson
Love Makes Things Happen	Pebbles
Love Me	Yvonne Elliman
Love Me	Elvis Presley
Love Me As If There Were No Tomorrow	Nat 'King' Cole
Love Me Do	Beatles
Love Me For A Reason	Osmonds
Love Me Forever	Marion Ryan
Love Me Like I Love You	Bay City Rollers
Love Me Love My Dog	Peter Shelley
Love Me Or Leave Me	Sammy Davis Jr.
Love Me Tender	Elvis Presley
Love Me To Pieces	Jill Corey
Love Me Tonight	Tom Jones
Love Me Warm And Tender	Paul Anka
Love Me With All Your Heart	Ray Charles Singers
Love Missile F1-11	Sigue Sigue Sputnik
Love Of A Lifetime	Firehouse
Love Of My Life	Dooleys
Love Of The Common People	Nicky Thomas
Love Of The Common People	Paul Young
Love On A Mountain Top	Robert Knight
Love On A Two-Way Street	Moments
Love On The Rocks	Neil Diamond
Love On Your Side	Thompson Twins
Love Or Let Me Be Lonely	Friends Of Distinction
Love Overboard	Gladys Knight & The Pips
Love Plus One	Haircut 100
Love Potion Number Nine	Searchers
Love Power	Dionne Warwick & Jeffrey Osborne
Love Really Hurts Without You	Billy Ocean
Love Rears It's Ugly Head	Living Colour
Love Resurrection	Alison Moyet
Love Rollercoaster	Ohio Players
Love Shack	B-52's
Love So Right	Bee Gees
Love Somebody	Rick Springfield
Love Song	Cure
Love Song	Tesla
Love Song, A	Anne Murray
Love Song For A Vampire	Annie Lennox
Love Takes Time	Mariah Carey
Love Takes Time	Orleans
Love Theme From Romeo & Juliet	Henry Mancini & His Orchestra
Love Theme From 'The Thorn Birds'	Juan Martin
Love...Thy Will Be Done	Martika
Love To Hate You	Erasure
Love To Love You Baby	Donna Summer
Love Touch	Rod Stewart
Love Town	Booker Newberry III
Love Train	Holly Johnson
Love Train	O'Jays
Love Will Conquer All	Lionel Richie
Love Will Find A Way	Pablo Cruise
Love Will Keep Us Together	Captain & Tennille
Love Will Lead You Back	Taylor Dayne
Love Will Never Do (Without You)	Janet Jackson
Love Will Save The Day	Whitney Houston
Love Will Tear Us Apart	Joy Division
Love Will Turn You Around	Kenny Rogers
Love Won't Let Me Wait	Major Harris
Love Worth Waiting For, A	Shakin' Stevens
Love You Down	Ready For The World
Love You Inside Out	Bee Gees
Love You Save, The	Jackson Five
Love You So	Ron Holden
Love Zone	Billy Ocean
Love's Been A Little Bit Hard On Me	Juice Newton
Love's Been Good To Me	Frank Sinatra
Love's Gotta Hold On Me	Dollar

415

Title	Artist
Midnight In Moscow	Kenny Ball
Midnight Mary	Joey Powers
Midnight Rider	Paul Davidson
Midnight Train To Georgia	Gladys Knight & The Pips
Midnite Dynamos	Matchbox
Midnite Special	Paul Evans
Mighty Quinn	Manfred Mann
Miles Away	Winger
Milk And Alcohol	Dr. Feelgood
Million Love Songs, A	Take That
Million To One, A	Jimmy Charles
Mind Blowing Decisions	Heatwave
Mind Of A Toy	Visage
Minute By Minute	Doobie Brothers
Minute Of Your Time, A	Tom Jones
Minute You're Gone, The	Cliff Richard
Miracle	Jon Bon Jovi
Miracle	Whitney Houston
Miracles	Jefferson Starship
Mirage	Tommy James & The Shondells
Mirror In The Bathroom	Beat
Mirror Man	Human League
Mirror Mirror	Pinkerton's Assorted Colours
Mirror Mirror	Diana Ross
Mirror Mirror (Mon Amour)	Dollar
Misfit	Curiosity Killed The Cat
Misled	Kool & The Gang
Miss Ann	Little Richard
Miss Me Blind	Culture Club
Miss Sun	Boz Scaggs
Miss You	Rolling Stones
Miss You Like Crazy	Natalie Cole
Miss You Much	Janet Jackson
Miss You Nights	Cliff Richard
Missing You	Chris De Burgh
Missing You	Diana Ross
Missing You	John Waite
Missing You Now	Michael Bolton
Mission Bell	Donnie Brooks
Missionary Man	Eurythmics
Mississippi	Pussycat
Mrs. Brown You've Got A Lovely Daughter	Herman's Hermits
Mrs. Robinson	Simon & Garfunkel
Mrs. Robinson (E.P.)	Simon & Garfunkel
Mr. Big Stuff	Jean Knight
Mr. Blobby	Mr. Blobby
Mr. Blue	Fleetwoods
Mr. Blue	Mike Preston
Mr. Blue Sky	Electric Light Orchestra
Mr. Bojangles	Nitty Gritty Dirt Band
Mr. Custer	Charlie Drake
Mr. Custer	Larry Verne
Mr. Jaws	Dickie Goodman
Mr. Lee	Bobbettes
Mr. Lonely	Bobby Vinton
Mr. Loverman	Shabba Ranks
Mr. Roboto	Styx
Mr. Sandman	Chordettes
Mr. Sandman	Four Aces
Mr. Sandman	Dickie Valentine
Mr. Sleaze	Stock Aitken Waterman
Mr. Soft	Cockney Rebel
Mr. Tambourine Man	Byrds
Mr. Telephone Man	New Edition
Mr. Vain	Culture Beat
Mr. Wendal	Arrested Development
Mr. Wonderful	Peggy Lee
Mistletoe And Wine	Cliff Richard
Misty	Johnny Mathis
Misty	Ray Stevens
Misty Blue	Dorothy Moore
Misunderstanding	Genesis
Mixed Emotions	Rolling Stones
Mobile	Ray Burns
Mockingbird	Inez Foxx
Mockingbird	Carly Simon & James Taylor
Mockingbird Hill	Migil Five
Model, The	Kraftwerk
Modern Girl	Sheena Easton
Modern Love	David Bowie
Modern Woman	Billy Joel
Moments In Soul	JT And The Big Family
Moments To Remember	Four Lads
Mona	Craig McLachlan & Check 1-2
Mona Lisa	Conway Twitty
Monday Monday	Mamas & The Papas
Money	Flying Lizards
Money	Pink Floyd
Money For Nothing	Dire Straits
Money Go Round (Pt.1)	Style Council
Money Honey	Bay City Rollers
Money Money Money	Abba
Money's Too Tight (To Mention)	Simply Red
Monkey	George Michael
Monkey Spanner	Dave & Ansil Collins
Monkey Time, The	Major Lance
Monsieur Dupont	Sandie Shaw
Monster Mash	Bobby 'Boris' Pickett & The Crypt Kickers
Montego Bay	Amazulu
Montego Bay	Bobby Bloom
Monterey	Eric Burdon & The Animals
Montreux EP	Simply Red
Mony Mony	Billy Idol
Mony Mony	Tommy James & The Shondells
Moody Blue	Elvis Presley
Moody River	Pat Boone
Moon River	Jerry Butler
Moon River	Greyhound
Moon River	Henry Mancini
Moon River	Danny Williams
Moonglow And Theme From 'Picnic'	George Cates
Moonglow And Theme From 'Picnic'	Morris Stoloff
Moonlight Feels Right	Starbuck
Moonlight Gambler	Frankie Laine
Moonlight Serenade	Glenn Miller
Moonlight Shadow	Mike Oldfield
Moonlighting	Leo Sayer
Moonlighting ('Theme')	Al Jarreau
Moonshine Sally	Mud
More	Perry Como
More	Kai Winding
More	Jimmy Young
More And More	Captain Hollywood Project
More And More Party Pops	Russ Conway
More I See You, The	Chris Montez
More Like The Movies	Dr. Hook
More Love	Kim Carnes
More, More, More (Pt. 1)	Andrea True Connection
More Party Pops	Russ Conway
More Than A Feeling	Boston
More Than A Woman	Tavares
More Than Ever	Nelson
More Than Ever (Come Prima)	Malcolm Vaughan
More Than I Can Say	Leo Sayer
More Than I Can Say	Bobby Vee
More Than In Love	Kate Robbins & Beyond
More Than This	Roxy Music
More Than Words	Extreme
More Than Words Can Say	Alias
More Today Than Yesterday	Spiral Staircase
Morgen	Ivo Robic
Moritat (A Theme From 'The Three Penny Opera')	Dick Hyman
Mornin' Beautiful	Tony Orlando & Dawn
Morning	Val Doonican
Morning After (Song From The Poseidon Adventure), The	Maureen McGovern
Morning Has Broken	Cat Stevens
Morning Side Of The Mountain	Donny & Marie Osmond
Morning Train (9 To 5)	Sheena Easton
Morningtown Ride	Seekers
Most Beautiful Girl, The	Charlie Rich
Mother And Child Reunion	Paul Simon
Mother-In-Law	Ernie K-Doe
Mother Of Mine	Neil Reid
Mother Popcorn (You Got To Have A Mother For Me)	James Brown
Mothers Little Helper	Rolling Stones
Motor Biking	Chris Spedding
Motorcycle Mama	Sailcat
Motorhead Live	Motorhead
Motown Song, The	Rod Stewart
Motownphilly	Boyz II Men
Mouldy Old Dough	Lieutenant Pigeon
Mountain Greenery	Mel Torme
Mountain Of Love	Johnny Rivers
Mountain's High, The	Dick & Deedee
Move Any Mountain	Shamen
Move Away	Culture Club
Move Closer	Phyllis Nelson
Move It	Cliff Richard
Move Over Darling	Doris Day
Move Over Darling	Tracey Ullman
Move That Body	Technotronic Featuring Reggie
Move This	Technotronic Featuring Ya Kid K
Move Your Body (Elevation)	Xpansions
Movin'	Brass Construction
Moving On Up	M People
Mozart Symphony No. 40 In G Minor	Waldo De Los Rios
Ms Grace	Tymes
M.T.A.	Kingston Trio
Mule Skinner Blues	Fendermen
Mull Of Kintyre	Wings
Multiplication	Bobby Darin
Musclebound	Spandau Ballet
Muscles	Diana Ross
Music	John Miles
Music And Lights	Imagination
Music Box Dancer	Frank Mills
Music Of The Night, The	Michael Crawford
Music Of Torvill & Dean EP, The	Richard Hartley/Michael Reed Orchestra
Muskrat Love	Captain & Tennille
Muskrat Ramble	McGuire Sisters
Must Of Got Lost	J. Geils Band
Must To Avoid, A	Herman's Hermits
My Angel Baby	Toby Beau
My Arms Keep Missing You	Rick Astley
(My Baby Don't Love Me) No More	DeJohn Sisters
My Baby Just Cares For Me	Nina Simone
My Baby Loves Lovin'	White Plains
My Best Friend's Girl	Cars
My Bonnie Lassie	Ames Brothers
My Boomerang Won't Come Back	Charlie Drake
My Boy	Elvis Presley
My Boy Lollipop	Millie Small
My Boyfriend's Back	Angels
My Brother Jake	Free
My Bucket's Got A Hole In It	Ricky Nelson
My Camera Never Lies	Bucks Fizz
My Cherie Amour	Stevie Wonder
My Coo-Ca-Choo	Alvin Stardust
My Cup Runneth Over	Ed Ames
My Dad	Paul Peterson
My Destiny	Lionel Richie
My Ding-A-Ling	Chuck Berry
My Dixie Darling	Lonnie Donegan
My Empty Arms	Jackie Wilson
My Ever Changing Moods	Style Council
My Eyes Adored You	Frankie Valli
My Favourite Waste Of Time	Owen Paul
My Friend	Frankie Laine
My Friend Stan	Slade
My Friend The Sea	Petula Clark
My Generation	Who
My Girl	Madness
My Girl	Otis Redding
My Girl	Temptations
My Girl Bill	Jim Stafford
My Girl Josephine	Fats Domino
My Girl Lollipop (My Boy Lollipop)	Bad Manners
My Guy	Mary Wells
My Happiness	Connie Francis
My Heart Belongs To Me	Barbra Streisand
My Heart Belongs To Only You	Bobby Vinton
My Heart Can't Tell You No	Rod Stewart
My Heart Has A Mind Of Its Own	Connie Francis
My Heart Is An Open Book	Carl Dobkins Jr.
My Heart's Symphony	Gary Lewis & The Playboys
My Home Town	Paul Anka
My Hometown	Bruce Springsteen
My Kind Of Girl	Matt Monro
My Life	Billy Joel
My Little Lady	Tremeloes
My Little Town	Simon & Garfunkel
My Love	Petula Clark
My Love	Julio Iglesias (featuring Stevie Wonder)
My Love	Paul McCartney & Wings
My Love	Lionel Richie
My Love For You	Johnny Mathis
My Lovin' (You're Never Gonna Get It)	En Vogue
My Mammy	Happenings
My Maria	B.W. Stevenson
My Melody Of Love	Bobby Vinton
My Mind's Eye	Small Faces
My, My, My	Johnny Gill

Title	Artist	Title	Artist	Title	Artist
My Name Is Jack	Manfred Mann	Never Ending Story	Limahl	No Milk Today	Herman's Hermits
My Name Is Prince	Prince & The New Power Generation	Never Gonna Fall In Love Again	Eric Carmen	No More Heroes	Stranglers
My Oh My	Slade	Never Gonna Give You Up	Rick Astley	No More Lies	Michel'le
My Old Man's A Dustman	Lonnie Donegan	Never Gonna Give You Up	Musical Youth	No More Lonely Nights (Ballad)	Paul McCartney
My Old Piano	Diana Ross	Never Gonna Let You Go	Sergio Mendes	No More Mr. Nice Guy	Alice Cooper
My One Temptation	Mica Paris	Never Goodbye	Karl Denver	No More Tears (Enough Is Enough)	Donna Summer &
My Perfect Cousin	Undertones	Never Had A Dream Come True	Stevie Wonder		Barbra Streisand
My Personal Possession	Nat 'King' Cole	Never Knew Love Like This Before	Stephanie Mills	No More The Fool	Elkie Brooks
My Prayer	Gerry Monroe	Never Let Her Slip Away	Andrew Gold	No Myth	Michael Penn
My Prayer	Platters	Never Let Her Slip Away	Undercover	No No Song	Ringo Starr
My Prerogative	Bobby Brown	Never My Love	Association	No, Not Much!	Four Lads
My Pretty One	Cliff Richard	Never My Love	Blue Swede	No One But You	Billy Eckstine
My Resistance Is Low	Robin Sarstedt	Never My Love	Fifth Dimension	No One Can Make My Sunshine Smile	Everly Brothers
My Sentimental Friend	Herman's Hermits	Never Never	Assembly	No One Is Innocent	Sex Pistols
My September Love	David Whitfield	Never, Never Gonna Give Ya Up	Barry White	No One Is To Blame	Howard Jones
My Sharona	Knack	Never Never Land	Frank Weir	No Other Love	Ronnie Hilton
My Ship Is Coming In	Walker Brothers	Never Never Never	Shirley Bassey	No Particular Place To Go	Chuck Berry
My Simple Heart	Three Degrees	Never On Sunday	Chordettes	No Regrets	Midge Ure
My Son My Son	Vera Lynn	Never Surrender	Corey Hart	No Regrets	Walker Brothers
My Special Angel	Bobby Helms	Never Tear Us Apart	INXS	No Sleep Till Brooklyn	Beastie Boys
My Special Angel	Malcolm Vaughan	Never Too Late	Kylie Minogue	No Son Of Mine	Genesis
My Special Angel	Vogues	Never Too Much	Luther Vandross	No Sugar Tonight	Guess Who
My Sweet Lord	George Harrison	Never Trust A Stranger	Kim Wilde	No Tell Lover	Chicago
My Toot Toot	Denise La Salle	Never Turn Your Back On Mother Earth	Sparks	No Time	Guess Who
My True Love	Jack Scott	New Beginning (Mamba Seyra)	Bucks Fizz	No Woman No Cry	Bob Marley & The Wailers
My True Story	Jive Five	New England, A	Kirsty MacColl	Nobody	Sylvia
My Way	Elvis Presley	New Kid In Town	Eagles	Nobody But Me	Human Beinz
My Way	Sex Pistols	New Life	Depeche Mode	Nobody Does It Better	Carly Simon
My Way	Frank Sinatra	New Moon On Monday	Duran Duran	Nobody I Know	Peter & Gordon
My Way Of Thinking	UB40	New Orleans	Gary U.S. Bonds	Nobody Needs Your Love	Gene Pitney
My White Bicycle	Nazareth	New Sensation	INXS	Nobody Told Me	John Lennon
My Whole World Ended (The		New Song	Howard Jones	Nobody's Child	Karen Young
Moment You Left Me)	David Ruffin	New Year's Day	U2	Nobody's Darlin' But Mine	Frank Ifield
My Wish Came True	Elvis Presley	New York Groove	Ace Frehley	Nobody's Diary	Yazoo
My World Is Empty Without You	Supremes	New York Groove	Hello	Nobody's Fool	Cinderella
Mysterious Ways	U2	New York Mining Disaster 1941	Bee Gees	Nobody's Fool	Haircut 100
Mystery Song	Status Quo	Next Door To An Angel	Neil Sedaka	Nobody's Fool	Kenny Loggins
		Next Time I Fall, The	Peter Cetera & Amy Grant	Non Ho L'Eta Per Amarti	Gigliola Cinquetti
Na Na Hey Hey Kiss Him Goodbye	Bananarama	Next Time, The	Cliff Richard	Norman	Sue Thompson
Na Na Hey Hey Kiss Him Goodbye	Steam	Nice To Be With You	Gallery	North To Alaska	Johnny Horton
Na Na Is The Saddest Word	Stylistics	Night	Jackie Wilson	Northern Lights	Renaissance
Na Na Na	Cozy Powell	Night, The	Frankie Valli & Four Seasons	Not Fade Away	Rolling Stones
Nadia's Theme (The Young &		Night Birds	Shakatak	Not Me	Orlons
The Restless)	Barry DeVorzon & Perry Botkin	Night Chicago Died, The	Paper Lace	Not One Minute More	Della Reese
Nairobi	Tommy Steele	Night Fever	Bee Gees	Nothin' At All	Heart
Naked In The Rain	Blue Pearl	Night Games	Graham Bonnett	Nothin' But A Good Time	Poison
Name And Number	Curiosity	Night Has A Thousand Eyes, The	Bobby Vee	Nothin' My Love Can't Fix	Joey Lawrence
Name Game, The	Shirley Ellis	Night Moves	Bob Seger & The Silver Bullet Band	(Nothin' Serious) Just Buggin'	Whistle
Name Of The Game, The	Abba	Night Of Fear	Move	Nothing But Heartaches	Supremes
Nashville Cats	Lovin' Spoonful	Night Owl	Gerry Rafferty	Nothing Can Change This Love	Sam Cooke
Nasty	Janet Jackson	Night Owls, The	Little River Band	Nothing Can Divide Us	Jason Donovan
Nathan Jones	Supremes	Night The Lights Went Out		Nothing Comes Easy	Sandie Shaw
Native New Yorker	Odyssey	In Georgia, The	Vicki Lawrence	Nothing Compares 2 U	Sinead O'Connor
Natural Born Bugie	Humble Pie	Night They Drove Old Dixie Down, The	Joan Baez	Nothing Else Matters	Metallica
Natural High	Bloodstone	Night To Remember, A	Shalamar	Nothing Ever Happens	Del Amitri
Natural Sinner	Fair Weather	Night Train	Visage	Nothing From Nothing	Billy Preston
Natural Woman (You Make Me		Nightingale	Carole King	Nothing Rhymed	Gilbert O'Sullivan
Feel Like), A	Aretha Franklin	Nightmare On My Street, A	D.J. Jazzy Jeff &	Nothing's Gonna Change My	
Naughty Girls (Need Love Too)	Samantha Fox		The Fresh Prince	Love For You	Glenn Medeiros
Naughty Lady Of Shady Lane	Dean Martin	Nights Are Forever Without You	England Dan &	Nothing's Gonna Stop Me Now	Samantha Fox
Naughty Lady Of Shady Lane, The	Ames Brothers		John Ford Coley	Nothing's Gonna Stop Us Now	Starship
Navy Blue	Diane Renay	Nights On Broadway	Bee Gees	Notorious	Duran Duran
Neanderthal Man	Hotlegs	Nights On Broadway	Candi Staton	November Rain	Guns N' Roses
Near You	Roger Williams	Nightshift	Commodores	November Spawned A Monster	Morrissey
Need To Be, The	Jim Weatherly	Nikita	Elton John	Now I'm Here	Queen
Need You Tonight	INXS	Nine Times Out Of Ten	Cliff Richard	Now Is The Time	Jimmy James & The Vagabonds
Needles And Pins	Searchers	9 To 5	Dolly Parton	Now That We Found Love	Heavy D. & The Boyz
Needles And Pins	Smokie	9 To 5	Sheena Easton	Now That We've Found Love	Third World
Neither One Of Us (Wants To Be		19	Paul Hardcastle	Now Those Days Are Gone	Bucks Fizz
The First To Say Goodbye)	Gladys Knight & The Pips	1999	Prince & The Revolution	Nowhere Man	Beatles
Nel Blu Dipinto Di Blu (Volare)	Domenico Modugno	19th Nervous Breakdown	Rolling Stones	Nowhere To Run	Martha & The Vandellas
Nellie The Elephant	Toy Dolls	96 Tears	?(Question Mark) & The Mysterians	Nuff Vibes (EP)	Apache Indian
Nelson Mandela	Special AKA	98.6	Keith	No. 9 Dream	John Lennon
Nessun Dorma	Luciano Pavarotti	99 Luftballons (99 Red Balloons)	Nena	Numero Uno	Starlight
Neutron Dance	Pointer Sisters	Ninety-Nine Ways	Tab Hunter	Nut Rocker	B. Bumble & The Stingers
Never	Heart	Nite And Day	Al B. Sure!	Nutbush City Limits	Ike & Tina Turner
Never Be Anyone Else But You	Ricky Nelson	Nite Klub	Specials	Nuthin' But A "G" Thang	Dr. Dre
Never Be The Same	Christopher Cross	Nitty Gritty, The	Shirley Ellis	Nuttin' For Christmas	Barry Gordon
Never Been To Spain	Three Dog Night	No Arms Could Ever Hold You	Bachelors		
Never Can Say Goodbye	Communards	No Charge	J.J. Barrie	O Dio Mio	Annette
Never Can Say Goodbye	Gloria Gaynor	No Doubt About It	Hot Chocolate	O L'Amour	Dollar
Never Can Say Goodbye	Jackson Five	No Honestly	Lynsey De Paul	O Superman	Laurie Anderson
Never Do A Tango With An Eskimo	Alma Cogan	No Limit	2 Unlimited	Ob-La-Di Ob-La-Da	Marmalade
Never Ending Song Of Love	Delaney & Bonnie	No Matter How I Try	Gilbert O'Sullivan	Obsession	Animotion
	& Friends	No Matter What	Badfinger	Ode To Billie Joe	Bobbie Gentry
Never Ending Song Of Love	New Seekers	No Matter What Shape (Your Stomach's In)	T-Bones	Off The Wall	Michael Jackson

Title	Artist
Oh Babe What Would You Say	Hurricane Smith
Oh Boy	Brotherhood Of Man
Oh Boy	Mud
Oh, Boy!	Crickets
Oh Carol	Smokie
Oh! Carol	Neil Sedaka
Oh Carolina	Shaggy
Oh Diane	Fleetwood Mac
Oh Girl	Chi-Lites
Oh Girl	Paul Young
Oh Happy Day	Edwin Hawkins Singers
Oh How Happy	Shades Of Blue
Oh Julie	Crescendos
Oh Julie	Shakin' Stevens
Oh Lonesome Me	Craig Douglas
Oh Lonesome Me	Don Gibson
Oh Lori	Alessi
Oh, Mein Papa	Eddie Calvert
Oh My My	Ringo Starr
Oh! My Pa-Pa	Eddie Fisher
Oh No	Commodores
Oh No Not My Baby	Manfred Mann
Oh No Not My Baby	Rod Stewart
Oh Pretty Woman	Roy Orbison
(Oh) Pretty Woman	Van Halen
Oh Sheila	Ready For The World
Oh, Sherrie	Steve Perry
Oh Very Young	Cat Stevens
Oh Well	Fleetwood Mac
Oh What A Circus	David Essex
Oh What A Nite	Dells
Oh What A Shame	Roy Wood
Oh Woman Oh Why Oh Why	Paul McCartney
Oh Yeah (On The Radio)	Roxy Music
Oh Yes! You're Beautiful	Gary Glitter
Oh You Pretty Thing	Peter Noone
Ohio	Crosby, Stills, Nash & Young
O.K.	Rock Follies
O.K. Fred	Erroll Dunkley
Okay!	Dave Dee, Dozy, Beaky, Mick & Tich
Ol' Macdonald	Frank Sinatra
Ol' Rag Blues	Status Quo
Old Cape Cod	Patti Page
Old Days	Chicago
Old Fashioned Love Song, An	Three Dog Night
Old Lamplighter, The	Browns
Old Man Down The Road, The	John Fogerty
Old Rivers	Walter Brennan
Old Songs, The	Barry Manilow
Oldest Swinger In Town	Fred Wedlock
Ole Ola (Muhler Brasileira)	Rod Stewart
Oliver's Army	Elvis Costello
Olympic	808 State
On A Carousel	Hollies
On A Ragga Tip	SL2
On A Slow Boat To China	Emile Ford & The Checkmates
On And On	Stephen Bishop
On And On	Gladys Knight & The Pips
On Broadway	George Benson
On Broadway	Drifters
On Horseback	Mike Oldfield
On My Own	Patti Labelle & Michael McDonald
On My Radio	Selecter
On My Word	Cliff Richard
On Our Own	Bobby Brown
On The Beach	Cliff Richard
On The Dark Side	John Cafferty & The Beaver Brown Band
On The Inside (Theme 'Prisoner-Cell Block H')	Lynne Hamilton
On The Radio	Donna Summer
On The Rebound	Floyd Cramer
On The Road Again	Canned Heat
On The Street Where You Live	Vic Damone
On The Street Where You Live	David Whitfield
On The Wings Of Love	Jeffrey Osborne
On Top Of Spaghetti	Tom Glazer & The Do-Re-Mi Children's Chorus
On With The Motley	Harry Secombe
Once Bitten Twice Shy	Great White
Once Bitten Twice Shy	Vesta Williams
Once In A Lifetime	Talking Heads
Once In A While	Chimes
Once Upon A Dream	Billy Fury
Once Upon A Long Ago	Paul McCartney
Once You Get Started	Rufus

Title	Artist
One	Bee Gees
One	Three Dog Night
One	U2
One, The	Elton John
One And One Is One	Medicine Head
One And Only, The	Chesney Hawkes
One Bad Apple	Osmonds
One Broken Heart For Sale	Elvis Presley
One Day At A Time	Lena Martell
One Day I'll Fly Away	Randy Crawford
One Day In Your Life	Michael Jackson
One Fine Day	Chiffons
One Fine Day	Carole King
One Good Woman	Peter Cetera
One Heartbeat	Smokey Robinson
One Hell Of A Woman	Mac Davis
One Hundred Ways	Quincy Jones Featuring James Ingram
One I Love, The	R.E.M.
One In A Million You	Larry Graham
One In Ten	UB40
One Inch Rock	Tyrannosaurus Rex
One Kiss For Old Time's Sake	Ronnie Dove
One Last Cry	Brian McKnight
One Less Bell To Answer	Fifth Dimension
One Love	Bob Marley & The Wailers
One Love	Prodigy
One Love	Stone Roses
One Man Band	Leo Sayer
One Man Woman/One Woman Man	Paul Anka with Odia Coates
One Mint Julep	Ray Charles
One Moment In Time	Whitney Houston
One Monkey Don't Stop No Show (Pt. 1)	Honey Cone
One More Dance	Esther & Abi Ofarim
One More Night	Phil Collins
One More Sunrise (Morgen)	Dickie Valentine
One More Try	George Michael
One More Try	Timmy T
One Nation Under A Groove (Pt. 1)	Funkadelic
One Night	Elvis Presley
One Night In Bangkok	Murray Head
One Night In Heaven	M People
One Night Love Affair	Bryan Adams
10538 Overture	Electric Light Orchestra
One Of A Kind (Love Affair)	(Detroit) Spinners
One Of These Nights	Eagles
One Of Us	Abba
One On One	Daryl Hall & John Oates
One Shining Moment	Diana Ross
One Step Beyond	Madness
One Step Further	Bardo
One Step Up	Bruce Springsteen
One That You Love, The	Air Supply
One Thing Leads To Another	Fixx
One Toke Over The Line	Brewer And Shipley
One Track Mind	Bobby Lewis
1-2-3	Len Barry
1-2-3	Gloria Estefan & The Miami Sound Machine
One Two Three O'Leary	Des O'Connor
1 2 3 Red Light	1910 Fruitgum Co.
One Vision	Queen
One Way Love	Cliff Bennett & The Rebel Rousers
One Way Ticket	Eruption
One Who Really Loves You, The	Mary Wells
One You Love, The	Glenn Frey
Onion Song	Marvin Gaye & Tammi Terrell
Only Crying	Keith Marshall
Only Fools (Never Fall In Love)	Sonia
Only In My Dreams	Debbie Gibson
Only Living Boy In New Cross, The	Carter-Unstoppable Sex Machine
Only Love	Nana Mouskouri
Only Love Can Break A Heart	Gene Pitney
Only One I Know, The	Charlatans
Only One Woman	Marbles
Only Rhyme That Bites, The	MC Tunes Versus 808 State
Only Sixteen	Dr. Hook
Only Sixteen	Craig Douglas
Only The Lonely	Motels
Only The Lonely	Roy Orbison
Only The Strong Survive	Jerry Butler
Only The Young	Journey
Only Way Is Up, The	Yazz & The Plastic Population
Only Way Out, The	Cliff Richard

Title	Artist
Only When You Leave	Spandau Ballet
Only Women	Alice Cooper
Only Women Bleed	Julie Covington
Only Yesterday	Carpenters
Only You	Flying Pickets
Only You	Platters
Only You	Frank Pourcel's French Fiddles
Only You	Praise
Only You	Ringo Starr
Only You	Yazoo
Only You (And You Alone)	Hilltoppers
Only You Can	Fox
Ooh Baby Baby	Linda Ronstadt
O-O-O Child	Five Stairsteps
Ooh La La (I Can't Get Over You)	Perfect Gentlemen
Ooh La La La (Let's Go Dancing)	Kool & The Gang
Ooh To Be Ah	Kajagoogoo
Ooh-Wakka-Doo-Wakka-Day	Gilbert O'Sullivan
Ooh! What A Life	Gibson Brothers
Oop-Shoop	Crew-Cuts
Oops Up	Snap
Oops Upside Your Head	Gap Band
Open Arms	Journey
Open Letter To My Teenage Son, An	Victor Lundberg
Open Up Your Heart (And Let The Sunshine In)	Cowboy Church Sunday School
Open Your Heart	Human League
Open Your Heart	Madonna
Open Your Mind	Usura
O.P.P.	Naughty By Nature
Opportunities (Let's Make Lots Of Money)	Pet Shop Boys
Opposites Attract	Paula Abdul (duet With The Wild Pair)
Opus 17 (Don't You Worry 'Bout Me)	Four Seasons
Ordinary Day	Curiosity Killed The Cat
Ordinary World	Duran Duran
Orinoco Flow	Enya
Orville's Song	Keith Harris & Orville
Ossie's Dream (Spurs Are On Their Way To Wembley)	Tottenham Hotspur F.A. Cup Final Squad
Other Guy, The	Little River Band
Other Side Of Love, The	Yazoo
Other Woman, The	Ray Parker Jr.
Our Day Will Come	Ruby & The Romantics
Our Day Will Come	Frankie Valli
Our Favourite Melodies	Craig Douglas
Our House	Madness
Our Lips Are Sealed	Fun Boy Three
Our Love	Natalie Cole
(Our Love) Don't Throw It All Away	Andy Gibb
Our Winter Love	Bill Pursell
Out In The Fields	Gary Moore & Phil Lynott
Out Of Limits	Marketts
Out Of Space	Prodigy
Out Of The Blue	Debbie Gibson
Out Of Time	Chris Farlowe
Out Of Touch	Daryl Hall & John Oates
Outa-Space	Billy Preston
Over And Over	Dave Clark Five
Over And Over	Bobby Day
Over The Mountain; Across The Sea	Johnnie & Joe
Over Under Sideways Down	Yardbirds
Over You	Freddie & The Dreamers
Over You	Gary Puckett & The Union Gap
Over You	Roxy Music
Overkill	Men At Work
Owner Of A Lonely Heart	Yes
Oxygene Part IV	Jean-Michel Jarre
Oye Como Va	Santana
Pacific	808 State
Pac-Man Fever	Buckner & Garcia
Paint It, Black	Rolling Stones
Painter Man	Boney M
Pale Shelter	Tears For Fears
Palisades Park	Freddy Cannon
Paloma Blanca	George Baker Selection
Pamela Pamela	Wayne Fontana
Panama	Van Halen
Pandora's Box	Orchestral Manoeuvres In The Dark
Panic	Smiths
Papa Don't Preach	Madonna
Papa Loves Mambo	Perry Como
Papa Was A Rollin' Stone	Temptations
Papa Was A Rolling Stone	Was (Not Was)
Papa's Got A Brand New Bag	James Brown

Title	Artist
Put Your Love In Me	Hot Chocolate
Puttin' On The Ritz	Taco
Putting On The Style	Lonnie Donegan
Pyjamarama	Roxy Music
P.Y.T. (Pretty Young Thing)	Michael Jackson
Quadrophonia	Quadrophonia
Quarter To Three	Gary U.S. Bonds
Que Sera Mi Vida (If You Should Go)	Gibson Brothers
Queen Of Clubs	KC & The Sunshine Band
Queen Of Hearts	Dave Edmunds
Queen Of Hearts	Juice Newton
Queen Of The Hop	Bobby Darin
Queen Of The Night	Whitney Houston
Quentin's Theme (from TV Series 'Dark Shadows')	Charles Randolph Grean Sounde
Question	Moody Blues
Quicksand	Martha & The Vandellas
Quiereme Mucho (Yours)	Julio Iglesias
Quiet Village	Martin Denny
Rabbit	Chas & Dave
Race, The	Yello
Race Is On, The	Jack Jones
Race With The Devil	Gun
Radancer	Marmalade
Radar Love	Golden Earring
Radio Ga Ga	Queen
Rag Doll	Four Seasons
Ragamuffin Man	Manfred Mann
Rage Hard	Frankie Goes To Hollywood
Rags To Riches	Tony Bennett
Rags To Riches	Elvis Presley
Rags To Riches	David Whitfield
Ragtime Cowboy Joe	Chipmunks
Rain, The	Oran 'Juice' Jones
Rain	Madonna
Rain	Status Quo
Rain On The Roof	Lovin' Spoonful
Rain Or Shine	Five Star
Rain Rain Go Away	Bobby Vinton
Rain Rain Rain	Frankie Laine
Rain, The Park & Other Things, The	Cowsills
Rainbow	Russ Hamilton
Rainbow	Marmalade
Rainbow Valley	Love Affair
Raindrops	Dee Clark
Raindrops Keep Fallin' On My Head	Sacha Distel
Raindrops Keep Fallin' On My Head	B.J. Thomas
Rainy Day Women #12 & 35	Bob Dylan
Rainy Days And Mondays	Carpenters
Rainy Night In Georgia	Brook Benton
Ramblin' Man	Allman Brothers Band
Ramblin' Rose	Nat 'King' Cole
Ramona	Bachelors
Randy	Blue Mink
Ranking Full Stop	Beat
Rapper, The	Jaggerz
Rapper's Delight	Sugarhill Gang
Rapture	Blondie
Raspberry Beret	Prince & The Revolution
Rasputin	Boney M
Rat Race	Specials
Rat Trap	Boomtown Rats
Raunchy	Ernie Freeman
Raunchy	Bill Justis
Raunchy	Billy Vaughn
Rave Generator	Toxic Two
Rave On	Buddy Holly
Rawhide	Frankie Laine
Razzamatazz	Quincy Jones
Razzle Dazzle	Bill Haley & His Comets
Reach For The Stars	Shirley Bassey
Reach Out I'll Be There	Four Tops
Reach Out I'll Be There	Gloria Gaynor
Reach Out Of The Darkness	Friend And Lover
Ready Or Not	After 7
Ready To Take A Chance Again	Barry Manilow
Ready Willing And Able	Doris Day
Real Gone Kid	Deacon Blue
Real Love	Mary J. Blige
Real Love	Doobie Brothers
Real Love	Ruby Murray
Real Love	Jody Watley
Real Love '93	Time Frequency
Real Real Real	Jesus Jones
Real Thing, The	Jellybean Featuring Steven Dante
Really Saying Something	Bananarama With Funboy Three
Really Wanna Know You	Gary Wright
Reason To Believe	Rod Stewart
Reasons To Be Cheerful (Pt 3)	Ian Dury & The Blockheads
Rebel Rebel	David Bowie
Rebel-'Rouser	Duane Eddy
Rebel Yell	Billy Idol
Red Balloon	Dave Clark Five
Red Dress	Alvin Stardust
Red Light Spells Danger	Billy Ocean
Red Red Wine	UB40
Red River Rock	Johnny & The Hurricanes
Red Roses For A Blue Lady	Vic Dana
Red Roses For A Blue Lady	Bert Kaempfert
Red Rubber Ball	Cyrkle
Reeling In The Years	Steely Dan
Reet Petite	Jackie Wilson
Reflections	Diana Ross & The Supremes
Reflections Of My Life	Marmalade
Reflex, The	Duran Duran
Refugee	Tom Petty & The Heartbreakers
Reggae For It Now	Bill Lovelady
Reggae Tune	Andy Fairweather-Low
Regret	New Order
Relax	Frankie Goes To Hollywood
Release Me	Little Esther Phillips
Release Me	Wilson Phillips
Release Me (And Let Me Love Again)	Engelbert Humperdinck
Relight My Fire	Take That Featuring Lulu
Remember Me	Diana Ross
Remember Me This Way	Gary Glitter
Remember (Sha-La-La)	Bay City Rollers
Remember The Time	Michael Jackson
Remember (Walkin' In The Sand)	Shangri-Las
Remember You're A Womble	Wombles
Remember You're Mine	Pat Boone
Reminiscing	Little River Band
Renta Santa	Chris Hill
Requiem	London Boys
Rescue Me	Fontella Bass
Rescue Me	Madonna
Respect	Aretha Franklin
Respect Yourself	Staple Singers
Respect Yourself	Bruce Willis
Respectable	Mel & Kim
Rest In Peace	Extreme
Resurrection Shuffle	Ashton Gardner & Dyke
Return Of Django, The	Upsetters
Return Of The Los Palmas 7	Madness
Return To Me	Dean Martin
Return To Sender	Elvis Presley
Reunited	Peaches & Herb
Reveille Rock	Johnny & The Hurricanes
Reverend Mr. Black	Kingston Trio
Revolution	Arrested Development
Revolution	Beatles
Reward	Teardrop Explodes
Rhiannon (Will You Ever Win)	Fleetwood Mac
Rhinestone Cowboy	Glen Campbell
Rhythm Is A Dancer	Snap
Rhythm Is A Mystery	K-Klass
Rhythm Is Gonna Get You	Gloria Estefan & The Miami Sound Machine
Rhythm Nation	Janet Jackson
Rhythm Of My Heart	Rod Stewart
Rhythm Of The Night	DeBarge
Rhythm Of The Rain	Cascades
Rhythm Of The Rain	Jason Donovan
Rich Girl	Daryl Hall & John Oates
Rich In Paradise	FPI Project
Rico Suave	Gerardo
Ricochet	Teresa Brewer
Ricochet	Joan Regan
Riddle, The	Nik Kershaw
Ride	Dee Dee Sharp
Ride A White Swan	T. Rex
Ride Captain Ride	Blues Image
Ride Like The Wind	Christopher Cross
Ride Like The Wind	East Side Beat
Ride On Time	Black Box
Riders In The Sky	Ramrods
Riders In The Sky	Shadows
Riders On The Storm	Doors
Riding On A Train	Pasadenas
Right Back Where We Started From	Maxine Nightingale
Right Back Where We Started From	Sinitta
Right By Your Side	Eurythmics
Right Down The Line	Gerry Rafferty
Right Here (Human Nature)	SWV
Right Here, Right Now	Jesus Jones
Right Here Waiting	Richard Marx
Right Kind Of Love, The	Jeremy Jordan
Right On Track	Breakfast Club
Right Place Wrong Time	Dr. John
Right Said Fred	Bernard Cribbins
Right Thing, The	Simply Red
Right Time Of The Night	Jennifer Warnes
Rikki Don't Lose That Number	Steely Dan
Ring My Bell	Anita Ward
Ring Ring Ring (Ha Ha Hey)	De La Soul
Ringo	Lorne Greene
Rinky Dink	Dave 'Baby' Cortez
Rio	Duran Duran
Rip It Up	Bill Haley & His Comets
Rip It Up	Orange Juice
Rise	Herb Alpert
Rise	Public Image Ltd.
Rise & Fall Of Flingel Bunt, The	Shadows
Rise To The Occasion	Climie Fisher
Rising Sun	Medicine Head
River, The	Ken Dodd
River Deep Mountain High	Ike & Tina Turner
River Deep-Mountain High	Supremes & Four Tops
River Of Dreams, The	Billy Joel
Rivers Of Babylon	Boney M
Road To Hell (Pt. 2), The	Chris Rea
Road To Nowhere	Talking Heads
Roadrunner	Jonathan Richman & The Modern Lovers
Roam	B-52's
Robert De Niro's Waiting	Bananarama
Robin Hood	Dick James
Robin Hood	Gary Miller
Robot	Tornados
Robot Man	Connie Francis
Rock-A-Beatin' Boogie	Bill Haley & His Comets
Rock-A-Billy	Guy Mitchell
Rock-A-Bye Your Baby With A Dixie Melody	Jerry Lewis
Rock-A-Hula-Baby	Elvis Presley
Rock 'n' Roll	Status Quo
Rock 'n' Roll Ain't Noise Pollution	AC/DC
Rock And Roll All Nite (Live Version)	Kiss
Rock 'n' Roll Fantasy	Bad Company
Rock And Roll Heaven	Righteous Brothers
Rock 'n' Roll Is King	Electric Light Orchestra
Rock 'n' Roll Lady	Showaddywaddy
Rock And Roll Music	Beach Boys
Rock & Roll Music	Chuck Berry
Rock And Roll Part 2	Gary Glitter
Rock And Roll Waltz	Kay Starr
Rock 'n Roll Winter	Wizzard
R.O.C.K In The U.S.A. (A Salute To 60's Rock)	John Cougar Mellencamp
Rock Island Line	Lonnie Donegan
Rock Me	Steppenwolf
Rock Me Amadeus	Falco
Rock Me Baby	David Cassidy
Rock Me Gently	Andy Kim
Rock Me Tonite	Billy Squier
Rock'n Me	Steve Miller Band
Rock On	Michael Damian
Rock On	David Essex
Rock Steady	Aretha Franklin
Rock Steady	Whispers
Rock The Boat	Forrest
Rock The Boat	Hues Corporation
Rock The Casbah	Clash
Rock This Town	Stray Cats
Rock Wit'cha	Bobby Brown
Rock With You	Michael Jackson
Rock Your Baby	KWS
Rock Your Baby	George McCrae
Rockaria	Electric Light Orchestra
Rocket	Def Leppard
Rocket	Mud
Rocket Man	Elton John
Rocket Man (I Think It's Going To Be A Long Long Time)	Kate Bush

Title	Artist
Rocket 2 U	Jets
Rockford Files, The	Mike Post
Rockin' All Over The World	Status Quo
Rockin' Around The Christmas Tree	Brenda Lee
Rockin' Around The Christmas Tree	Mel & Kim
(Mel Smith & Kim Wilde)	
Rockin' Chair	Gwen McCrae
Rockin' Good Way, A	Shaky & Bonnie
Rockin' Good Way, A	Dinah Washington & Brook Benton
Rockin' Over The Beat	Technotronic Featuring Ya Kid K
Rockin' Pneumonia & The	
Boogie Woogie Flu	Johnny Rivers
Rock-In' Robin	Bobby Day
Rockin' Robin	Michael Jackson
Rockin' Roll Baby	Stylistics
Rockin' Through The Rye	Bill Haley & His Comets
Rocking Goose	Johnny & The Hurricanes
Rockit	Herbie Hancock
Rocky	Austin Roberts
Rocky Mountain High	John Denver
Rodrigo's Guitar Concerto	
De Aranjuez	Manuel & His Music Of The Mountains
Rok Da House	Beatmasters Featuring The Cookie Crew
Roll Away The Stone	Mott The Hoople
Roll Over Beethoven	Electric Light Orchestra
Roll Over Lay Down	Status Quo
Roll With It	Steve Winwood
Rollin' Stone	David Essex
Rolling Home	Status Quo
Romantic	Karyn White
Romeo	Petula Clark
Romeo	Dino
Romeo	Mr. Big
Romeo And Juliet	Dire Straits
Romeo's Tune	Steve Forbert
Roni	Bobby Brown
Ronnie	Four Seasons
Room At The Top	Adam Ant
Room In Your Heart	Living In A Box
Room To Move	Animotion
Rosanna	Toto
Rose, The	Bette Midler
Rose And A Baby Ruth, A	George Hamilton IV
Rose Garden	Lynn Anderson
Rose Garden	New World
Rose Has To Die, A	Dooleys
Rose Marie	Slim Whitman
Roses Are Red	Ronnie Carroll
Roses Are Red	Mac Band Featuring The McCampbell Brothers
Roses Are Red (My Love)	Bobby Vinton
Roses Of Picardy	Vince Hill
Rosetta	Fame And Price Together
Rosie	Don Partridge
Roulette	Russ Conway
Round And Round	Tevin Campbell
Round And Round	Perry Como
Round And Round	Jaki Graham
Round And Round	Ratt
Roundabout	Yes
Roussos Phenomenon E.P., The	Demis Roussos
Roxanne	Police
Royal Event	Russ Conway
Rub You The Right Way	Johnny Gill
Rubber Ball	Bobby Vee
Rubber Ball	Marty Wilde
Rubber Bullets	10cc
Rubber Duckie	Ernie
Rubberband Girl	Kate Bush
Rubberband Man, The	Spinners
Rubberneckin'	Elvis Presley
Ruby Baby	Dion
Ruby, Don't Take Your Love To Town	Kenny Rogers & The First Edition
Ruby Tuesday	Melanie
Ruby Tuesday	Rolling Stones
Ruby Tuesday	Rod Stewart
Rude Boys Outa Jail	Specials
Ruff In The Jungle Bizness	Prodigy
Rumors	Johnny Crawford
Rumors	Timex Social Club
Rump Shaker	Wreckx-N-Effect
Run Away Child, Running Wild	Temptations
Run, Baby Run (Back Into My Arms)	Newbeats
Run For Home	Lindisfarne
Run Joey Run	David Geddes
Run Run Run	Jo Jo Gunne
Run Runaway	Slade
Run Through The Jungle	Creedence Clearwater Revival
Run To Him	Bobby Vee
Run To Me	Bee Gees
Run To The Hills	Iron Maiden
Run To You	Bryan Adams
Run To You	Rage
Runaround Sue	Dion
Runaround Sue	Leif Garrett
Runaway	Jefferson Starship
Runaway	Del Shannon
Runaway Boys	Stray Cats
Runaway Train	Soul Asylum
Runner, The	Three Degrees
Runnin' On Empty	Jackson Browne
Running Bear	Johnny Preston
Running In The Family	Level 42
Running Scared	Roy Orbison
Running Up That Hill	Kate Bush
Running With The Night	Lionel Richie
Rupert	Jackie Lee
Rush Hour	Jane Wiedlin
Rush Rush	Paula Abdul
Russians	Sting
Sabre Dance	Love Sculpture
Sacred Emotion	Donny Osmond
Sacrifice	Elton John
Sad Eyes	Robert John
Sad Movies (Make Me Cry)	Sue Thompson
Sad Songs (Say So Much)	Elton John
Sad Sweet Dreamer	Sweet Sensation
Saddle Up	David Christie
Sadeness Part 1	Enigma
Safety Dance, The	Men Without Hats
Said I Love You....But I Lied	Michael Bolton
Sail Along Silvery Moon	Billy Vaughn
Sail On	Commodores
Sailing	Christopher Cross
Sailing	Rod Stewart
Sailing On The Seven Seas	Orchestral Manoeuvres In The Dark
Sailor	Petula Clark
Sailor	Anne Shelton
Sailor (Your Home Is The Sea)	Lolita
St. Elmo's Fire (Man In Motion)	John Parr
St. Therese Of The Roses	Malcolm Vaughan
St. Valentine's Day Massacre E.P.	Motörhead & Girlschool
Saints Rock 'n Roll, The	Bill Haley & His Comets
Sal's Got A Sugar Lip	Lonnie Donegan
Sally	Gerry Monroe
Sally Don't You Grieve	Lonnie Donegan
Sally G	Paul McCartney & Wings
Sally, Go 'Round The Roses	Jaynetts
Saltwater	Julian Lennon
Sam	Olivia Newton-John
Samantha	Kenny Ball
Same Old Lang Syne	Dan Fogelberg
Same Old Scene, The	Roxy Music
San Antonio Rose	Floyd Cramer
San Bernadino	Christie
San Franciscan Nights	Eric Burdon & The Animals
San Francisco (Be Sure To Wear Some Flowers In Your Hair)	Scott McKenzie
Sanctify Yourself	Simple Minds
Sandy	Larry Hall
Sandy	John Travolta
Santa Baby	Eartha Kitt
Santa Bring My Baby Back To Me	Elvis Presley
Santa Claus Is Comin' To Town	Bruce Springsteen
Santo Natale	David Whitfield
Sara	Fleetwood Mac
Sara	Starship
Sara Smile	Daryl Hall & John Oates
Sat In Your Lap	Kate Bush
Satisfied	Richard Marx
Saturday In The Park	Chicago
Saturday Love	Cherelle & Alexander O'Neal
Saturday Night	Bay City Rollers
Saturday Night At The Movies	Drifters
Saturday Night's Alright For Fighting	Elton John
Savage, The	Shadows
Save A Prayer	Duran Duran
Save It For Me	Four Seasons
Save Me	Dave Dee, Dozy, Beaky, Mick & Tich
Save Some Love	Keedy
Save The Best For Last	Vanessa Williams
Save The Last Dance For Me	Drifters
Save Your Heart For Me	Gary Lewis & The Playboys
Save Your Kisses For Me	Brotherhood Of Man
Save Your Love	Renee And Renato
Saved By The Bell	Robin Gibb
Saving All My Love For You	Whitney Houston
Saving Forever For You	Shanice
Saviour's Day	Cliff Richard
Say A Little Prayer	Bomb The Bass
Say, Has Anybody Seen My Sweet Gypsy Rose	Dawn Featuring Tony Orlando
Say Hello Wave Goodbye	Soft Cell
Say I Won't Be There	Springfields
Say I'm Your No. 1	Princess
Say It Again	Jermaine Stewart
Say It Isn't So	Daryl Hall & John Oates
Say It Loud-I'm Black And I'm Proud	James Brown
Say Say Say	Paul McCartney & Michael Jackson
Say Wonderful Things	Ronnie Carroll
Say You Don't Mind	Colin Blunstone
Say You Love Me	Fleetwood Mac
Say You, Say Me	Lionel Richie
Say You Will	Foreigner
Scarborough Fair	Sergio Mendes & Brasil '66
Scarborough Fair-Canticle	Simon & Garfunkel
Scarlet Ribbons	Browns
Scarlett O'Hara	Jet Harris & Tony Meehan
School Day	Chuck Berry
School Is Out	Gary U.S. Bonds
School Love	Barry Blue
School's Out	Alice Cooper
Scorpio	Dennis Coffey & The Detroit Guitar Band
Scotch On The Rocks	Band Of The Black Watch
Sea Cruise	Frankie Ford
Sea Of Love	Honeydrippers
Sea Of Love	Phil Phillips With The Twilights
Sea Of Love	Marty Wilde
Sealed With A Kiss	Jason Donovan
Sealed With A Kiss	Brian Hyland
Search Is Over, The	Survivor
Searchin'	Coasters
Searchin'	Hollies
Searchin' (I Gotta Find A Man)	Hazell Dean
Searching	Change
Seaside Shuffle	Terry Dactyl & The Dinosaurs
Seasons Change	Expose
Seasons In The Sun	Terry Jacks
Second Chance	Thirty Eight Special
Second Hand Love	Connie Francis
Second Time Around, The	Shalamar
Secret Agent Man	Johnny Rivers
Secret Love	Bee Gees
Secret Love	Doris Day
Secret Love	Kathy Kirby
Secret Lovers	Atlantic Starr
Secret Rendezvous	Karyn White
Secretly	Jimmie Rodgers
Secrets That You Keep, The	Mud
See Emily Play	Pink Floyd
See Me, Feel Me	Who
See My Baby Jive	Wizzard
See My Friend	Kinks
See Saw	Aretha Franklin
See See Rider	Eric Burdon & The Animals
See The Day	Dee C. Lee
See The Funny Little Clown	Bobby Goldsboro
See Those Eyes	Altered Images
See You	Depeche Mode
See You In September	Happenings
See You Later, Alligator	Bill Haley & His Comets
Self Control	Laura Branigan
Selfish One	Jackie Ross
Semi-Detached Surburban Mr.James	Manfred Mann
Send For Me	Nat 'King' Cole
Send In The Clowns	Judy Collins
Send Me Some Lovin'	Sam Cooke
Send One Your Love	Stevie Wonder
Sending All My Love	Linear
Senses Working Overtime	XTC
Sensitivity	Ralph Tresvant
Sentimental Lady	Bob Welch
Sentimental Street	Night Ranger
Sentinel	Mike Oldfield

421

Title	Artist
Senza Una Donna (Without A Woman)	Zucchero & Paul Young
Separate Lives	Phil Collins & Marilyn Martin
Separate Ways (Worlds Apart)	Journey
September	Earth, Wind & Fire
Serenade	Slim Whitman
Serious	Donna Allen
Serpentine Fire	Earth, Wind & Fire
Sesame's Treet	Smart E's
Set Adrift On Memory Bliss	P.M. Dawn
Set Me Free	Jaki Graham
Set Me Free	Kinks
Set The Night To Music	Roberta Flack With Maxi Priest
7	Prince & The New Power Generation
Seven Drunken Nights	Dubliners
747 (Strangers In The Night)	Saxon
Seven Little Girls Sitting In The Back Seat	Avons
Seven Little Girls Sitting In The Back Seat	Paul Evans & The Curls
Seven Rooms Of Gloom	Four Tops
Seven Seas Of Rhye	Queen
Seven Tears	Goombay Dance Band
7 Ways To Love	Cola Boy
7 Teen	Regents
Seventeen	Boyd Bennett & His Rockets
Seventeen	Fontane Sisters
Seventh Son	Johnny Rivers
Sexcrime (Nineteen Eighty Four)	Eurythmics
Sexual Healing	Marvin Gaye
Sexy Eyes	Dr. Hook
Sexy MF	Prince & The New Power Generation
Sh-Boom	Chords
Sh-Boom	Crew-Cuts
Sh-Boom	Stan Freberg
Sha La La	Manfred Mann
Sha La La La Lee	Small Faces
Sha-La-La (Make Me Happy)	Al Green
Shaddup You Face	Joe Dolce Music Theatre
Shadow Dancing	Andy Gibb
Shadow Waltz	Mantovani
Shadows Of The Night	Pat Benatar
Shake	Sam Cooke
Shake It	Ian Matthews
Shake It Down	Mud
Shake It Up	Cars
Shake, Rattle And Roll	Bill Haley & His Comets
(Shake, Shake, Shake) Shake Your Booty	KC & The Sunshine Band
Shake You Down	Gregory Abbott
Shake Your Body (Down To The Ground)	Jacksons
Shake Your Groove Thing	Peaches & Herb
Shake Your Head	Was (Not Was)
Shake Your Love	Debbie Gibson
Shakedown	Bob Seger & The Silver Bullet Band
Shakin' All Over	Johnny Kidd & The Pirates
Shakin' Stevens E.P., The	Shakin' Stevens
Shambala	Three Dog Night
Shame	Evelyn 'Champagne' King
Shame On The Moon	Bob Seger & The Silver Bullet Band
Shame Shame Shame	Shirley And Company
Shang-A-Lang	Bay City Rollers
Shangri-La	Robert Maxwell, His Harp & His Orchestra
Shannon	Henry Gross
Shapes Of Things	Yardbirds
Share The Land	Guess Who
Share Your Love	Kenny Rogers
Share Your Love With Me	Aretha Franklin
Sharing The Night Together	Dr. Hook
Shattered Dreams	Johnny Hates Jazz
Shazam	Duane Eddy
She	Charles Aznavour
She Ain't Worth It	Glenn Medeiros Featuring Bobby Brown
She Believes In Me	Kenny Rogers
She Blinded Me With Science	Thomas Dolby
She Bop	Cyndi Lauper
She Cried	Jay & The Americans
She Don't Let Nobody	Chaka Demus & Pliers
She Drives Me Crazy	Fine Young Cannibals
She Loves You	Beatles
She Makes My Day	Robert Palmer
She Means Nothing To Me	Phil Everly & Cliff Richard
She Wants To Dance With Me	Rick Astley
She Wears My Ring	Solomon King
She Works Hard For The Money	Donna Summer

Title	Artist
She'd Rather Be With Me	Turtles
She's A Beauty	Tubes
She's A Fool	Lesley Gore
She's A Lady	Tom Jones
She's A Woman	Beatles
She's About A Mover	Sir Douglas Quintet
She's Gone	Daryl Hall & John Oates
She's Got Claws	Gary Numan
She's In Love With You	Suzi Quatro
She's Just My Style	Gary Lewis & The Playboys
She's Leaving Home	Billy Bragg With Cara Tivey
She's Like The Wind	Patrick Swayze (with Wendy Fraser)
She's Not Just Another Woman	8th Day
She's Not There	Santana
She's Not There	Zombies
She's Not You	Elvis Presley
She's On It	Beastie Boys
She's Out Of My Life	Michael Jackson
She's Playing Hard To Get	Hi-Five
(She's) Sexy + 17	Stray Cats
She's So Modern	Boomtown Rats
Sheffield Grinder, The	Tony Capstick
Sheila	Tommy Roe
Sherry	Adrian Baker
Sherry	Four Seasons
Shifting, Whispering Sands, The	Rusty Draper
Shifting Whispering Sands (Pts 1 & 2), The	Billy Vaughn
Shindig	Shadows
Shine A Little Love	Electric Light Orchestra
Shinin' On	Grand Funk
Shining Star	Earth, Wind & Fire
Shining Star	Manhattans
Shiny Happy People	R.E.M
Ship Of Fools	Erasure
Ships	Barry Manilow
Shiralee	Tommy Steele
Shirley	Shakin' Stevens
Shocked	Kylie Minogue
Shoo-Be-Doo-Be-Doo-Da-Day	Stevie Wonder
Shoop	Salt-N-Pepa
Shoop Shoop Song (It's In His Kiss)	Betty Everett
Shoop Shoop Song (It's In His Kiss), The	Cher
Shop Around	Captain & Tennille
Shop Around	Miracles
Shoplifters Of The World Unite	Smiths
Short Fat Fannie	Larry Williams
Short People	Randy Newman
Short Shorts	Royal Teens
Shortsharpshock (EP)	Therapy?
Shotgun	Jr. Walker & The All Stars
Shotgun Wedding	Roy 'C'
Should I Do It	Pointer Sisters
Should've Known Better	Richard Marx
Shout	Louchie Lou & Michie One
Shout	Lulu
Shout	Tears For Fears
Shout (Pt. 1)	Joey Dee & The Starliters
Shout! Shout! (Knock Yourself Out)	Ernie Maresca
Shout To The Top	Style Council
Show, The	Doug E. Fresh & The Get Fresh Crew
Show And Tell	Al Wilson
Show Me Heaven	Maria McKee
Show Me Love	Robin S.
Show Me The Way	Peter Frampton
Show Me The Way	Styx
Show Me You're A Woman	Mud
Show Must Go On, The	Leo Sayer
Show Must Go On, The	Three Dog Night
Show You The Way To Go	Jacksons
Showdown	Electric Light Orchestra
Shower Me With Your Love	Surface
Showing Out (Get Fresh At The Weekend)	Mel & Kim
Shuffle, The	Van McCoy
Shut Up	Madness
Shy Boy	Bananarama
Sick Man Blues	Goodies
Side Saddle	Russ Conway
Side Show	Barry Biggs
Sideshow	Blue Magic
Sign 'O' The Times	Prince
Sign Of The Times	Belle Stars
Sign Of The Times, A	Petula Clark
Sign Your Name	Terence Trent D'Arby
Signed Sealed Delivered I'm Yours	Stevie Wonder

Title	Artist
Signs	Five Man Electrical Band
Signs	Tesla
Silence Is Golden	Tremeloes
Silent Lucidity	Queensryche
Silent Night	Bros
Silent Running (On Dangerous Ground)	Mike + The Mechanics
Silhouettes	Herman's Hermits
Silhouettes	Rays
Silhouettes	Cliff Richard
Silly Games	Janet Kay
Silly Love Songs	Paul McCartney
Silly Thing	Sex Pistols
Silver Dream Machine (Pt. 1)	David Essex
Silver Lady	David Soul
Silver Machine	Hawkwind
Silver Star	Four Seasons
Simon Says	1910 Fruitgum Co
Simon Smith & His Amazing Dancing Bear	Alan Price Set
Simon Templar	Splodgenessabounds
Simple Game	Four Tops
Simply Irresistible	Robert Palmer
Since I Don't Have You	Skyliners
Since I Fell For You	Lenny Welch
Since I Met You Baby	Ivory Joe Hunter
Since Yesterday	Strawberry Switchblade
Since You've Been Gone	Rainbow
Sincerely	McGuire Sisters
Sing	Carpenters
Sing A Song	Earth, Wind & Fire
Sing A Song Of Freedom	Cliff Richard
Sing Baby Sing	Stylistics
Sing It With Joe	Joe 'Mr. Piano' Henderson
Sing Little Birdie	Pearl Carr & Teddy Johnson
Sing Me	Brothers
Sing Our Own Song	UB40
Singin' In The Rain (Pt. 1)	Sheila B. Devotion
Singing Dogs (Medley), The	Singing Dogs
Singing The Blues	Guy Mitchell
Singing The Blues	Tommy Steele
Single Girl	Sandy Posey
Single Life	Cameo
Sink The Bismarck	Johnny Horton
Sippin' Soda	Guy Mitchell
Sir Duke	Stevie Wonder
Sister	Bros
Sister Christian	Night Ranger
Sister Golden Hair	America
Sister Jane	New World
Sister Of Mercy	Thompson Twins
Sisters Are Doin' It For Themselves	Eurythmics & Aretha Franklin
Sit Down	James
Sittin' In The Park	Georgie Fame
(Sittin' On) The Dock Of The Bay	Michael Bolton
(Sittin' On) The Dock Of The Bay	Otis Redding
Six Teens, The	Sweet
634-5789	Wilson Pickett
16 Bars	Stylistics
16 Candles	Crests
Sixteen Reasons	Connie Stevens
Sixteen Tons	Tennessee Ernie Ford
Sixteen Tons	Frankie Laine
'65 Love Affair	Paul Davis
Size Of A Cow, The	Wonder Stuff
Ska Train	Beatmasters
Skiing In The Snow	Wigan's Ovation
Skin Deep	Duke Ellington
Skin Deep	Ted Heath
Skin Tight	Ohio Players
Skinny Legs And All	Joe Tex
Skokiaan	Four Lads
Skokiaan	Ralph Marterie
Skweeze Me Pleeze Me	Slade
Sky High	Jigsaw
Skye Boat Song, The	Roger Whittaker & Des O'Connor
Slam	Onyx
Slam Jam	WWF Superstars
Slave To Love	Bryan Ferry
Slave To The Rhythm	Grace Jones
Slave To The Vibe	Aftershock
Sledgehammer	Peter Gabriel
Sleep	Little Willie John
Sleep Walk	Santo & Johnny
Sleeping Bag	ZZ Top

Title	Artist
Sleeping Satellite	Tasmin Archer
Sleepy Joe	Herman's Hermits
Sleepy Shores	Johnny Pearson Orchestra
Slightest Touch, The	Five Star
Slip Away	Clarence Carter
Slip Slidin' Away	Paul Simon
Slip Your Disc To This	Heatwave
Slippin' Into Darkness	War
Sloop John B	Beach Boys
Slow Down	John Miles
Slow Hand	Pointer Sisters
Slow It Down	East 17
Slow Twistin'	Chubby Checker
Smackwater Jack	Carole King
Small Town	John Cougar Mellencamp
Smalltown Boy	Bronski Beat
Smarty Pants	First Choice
Smells Like Teen Spirit	Nirvana
Smile	Nat 'King' Cole
Smile A Little Smile For Me	Flying Machine
Smiling Faces Sometime	Undisputed Truth
Smoke From A Distant Fire	Sanford/Townsend Band
Smoke Gets In Your Eyes	Platters
Smoke On The Water	Deep Purple
Smokie-Part 2	Bill Black's Combo
Smokin' In The Boys Room	Brownsville Station
Smokin' In The Boys Room	Motley Crue
Smooth Criminal	Michael Jackson
Smooth Operator	Sade
Smuggler's Blues	Glenn Frey
Smurf Song, The	Father Abraham & The Smurfs
Snap Mega Mix	Snap
Snap Your Fingers	Joe Henderson
Snooker Loopy	Matchroom Mob With Chas & Dave
Snookeroo	Ringo Starr
Snoopy Vs. The Red Baron	Hotshots
Snoopy Vs. The Red Baron	Royal Guardsmen
Snot Rap	Kenny Everett
Snow Coach	Russ Conway
Snowbird	Anne Murray
So Alive	Love And Rockets
So Close	Daryl Hall John Oates
So Cold The Night	Communards
So Do I	Kenny Ball
So Emotional	Whitney Houston
So Far Away	Carole King
So Fine	Fiestas
So Good To Be Back Home Again	Tourists
So Hard	Pet Shop Boys
So In To You	Atlanta Rhythm Section
So Lonely	Police
So Long Baby	Del Shannon
So Macho	Sinitta
So Many Ways	Brook Benton
So Much In Love	Tymes
So Rare	Jimmy Dorsey
So Sad (To Watch Good Love Go Bad)	Everly Brothers
So You Win Again	Hot Chocolate
Society's Child (Baby I've Been Thinking)	Janis Ian
Sock It To Me-Baby!	Mitch Ryder & The Detroit Wheels
Soft Summer Breeze	Eddie Heywood
Softly As I Leave You	Matt Monro
Softly Softly	Ruby Murray
Softly Whispering I Love You	Congregation
Soldier Blue	Buffy Sainte-Marie
Soldier Boy	Shirelles
Soldier Of Love	Donny Osmond
Soley Soley	Middle Of The Road
Solid	Ashford & Simpson
Solid Bond In Your Heart	Style Council
Solid Gold Easy Action	T. Rex
Solitaire	Laura Branigan
Solitaire	Andy Williams
Solsbury Hill	Peter Gabriel
Some Day	Frankie Laine
Some Enchanted Evening	Jay & The Americans
Some Girls	Racey
Some Guys Have All The Luck	Maxi Priest
Some Guys Have All The Luck	Rod Stewart
Some Kind-A Earthquake	Duane Eddy
Some Kind Of A Summer	David Cassidy
Some Kind Of Lover	Jody Watley
Some Kind Of Wonderful	Grand Funk
Some Like It Hot	Power Station
Some Of Your Lovin'	Dusty Springfield
Some People	Cliff Richard

Title	Artist
Somebody	Bryan Adams
Somebody Bad Stole De Wedding Bell	Eartha Kitt
Somebody Else's Guy	Jocelyn Brown
Somebody Help Me	Spencer Davis Group
(Somebody) Help Me Out	Beggar & Co
Somebody To Love	Jefferson Airplane
Somebody To Love	Queen
Somebody's Baby	Jackson Browne
Somebody's Been Sleeping	100 Proof Aged In Soul
Somebody's Knockin'	Terri Gibbs
Somebody's Watching Me	Rockwell
Someday	Mariah Carey
Someday	Glass Tiger
Someday	Ricky Nelson
Someday	Jodie Sands
Someday (I'm Coming Back)	Lisa Stansfield
Someday One Day	Seekers
Someday We'll Be Together	Diana Ross & The Supremes
Someday We're Gonna Love Again	Searchers
Someone	Johnny Mathis
Someone Could Lose A Heart Tonight	Eddie Rabbitt
Someone Else's Baby	Adam Faith
Someone Else's Roses	Joan Regan
Someone On Your Mind	Jimmy Young
Someone Saved My Life Tonight	Elton John
Someone Someone	Brian Poole & The Tremeloes
Someone's Looking At You	Boomtown Rats
Somethin' Stupid	Nancy & Frank Sinatra
Something	Shirley Bassey
Something	Beatles
Something 'Bout You Baby I Like	Status Quo
Something About You	Level 42
Something Better Change	Stranglers
Something Better To Do	Olivia Newton-John
Something Else	Sex Pistols
Something Good	Utah Saints
Something Got Me Started	Simply Red
Something Happened On The Way To Heaven	Phil Collins
Something Here In My Heart (Keeps A-Tellin' Me No)	Paper Dolls
Something In The Air	Thunderclap Newman
(Something Inside) So Strong	Labi Siffre
Something Old, Something New	Fantastics
Something So Strong	Crowded House
Something Tells Me (Something Is Gonna Happen Tonight)	Cilla Black
Something To Believe In	Poison
Something To Talk About	Bonnie Raitt
Something's Burning	Kenny Rogers & The First Edition
Something's Gotta Give	Sammy Davis Jr.
Something's Gotta Give	McGuire Sisters
Something's Gotten Hold Of My Heart	Marc Almond Featuring Gene Pitney
Something's Gotten Hold Of My Heart	Gene Pitney
Something's Happening	Herman's Hermits
Something's Wrong With Me	Austin Roberts
Sometimes	Erasure
Sometimes Love Just Ain't Enough	Patty Smyth With Don Henley
Sometimes When We Touch	Dan Hill
Somewhere	P.J. Proby
Somewhere In My Heart	Aztec Camera
Somewhere In The Night	Barry Manilow
Somewhere, My Love	Ray Conniff & The Singers
Somewhere Out There	Linda Ronstadt
Son-Of-A Preacher Man	Dusty Springfield
Son Of Hickory Hollers Tramp	O.C. Smith
Son Of My Father	Chicory Tip
Song For Guy	Elton John
Song For Love	Extreme
Song For Whoever	Beautiful South
Song Of Joy, A	Miguel Rios
Song Of The Dreamer	Eddie Fisher
Song Of The Dreamer	Johnnie Ray
Song Sung Blue	Neil Diamond
Songbird	Kenny G
Songs For Swinging Lovers (L.P.)	Frank Sinatra
Sooner Or Later	Grass Roots
Sorrow	David Bowie
Sorrow	Merseys
Sorry I'm A Lady	Baccara
Sorry (I Ran All The Way Home)	Impalas
Sorry Seems To Be The Hardest Word	Elton John
Sorry Suzanne	Hollies

Title	Artist
S.O.S.	Abba
Soul Man	Blues Brothers
Soul Man	Sam & Dave
Soulful Strut	Young-Holt Unlimited
Sound	James
Sound And Vision	David Bowie
Sound Of Silence, The	Bachelors
Sound Of The Suburbs	Members
Sounds Of Silence, The	Simon & Garfunkel
South Street	Orlons
Southern Freeez	Freeez
Southern Nights	Glen Campbell
Souvenir	Orchestral Manoeuvres In The Dark
Sowing The Seeds Of Love	Tears For Fears
Space Jungle, The	Adamski
Space Oddity	David Bowie
Space Race	Billy Preston
Spanish Eyes	Al Martino
Spanish Flea	Herb Alpert
Spanish Harlem	Aretha Franklin
Spanish Harlem	Ben E. King
Sparrow, The	Ramblers
Speak Like A Child	Style Council
Speak To Me Pretty	Brenda Lee
Speak To The Sky	Rick Springfield
Special Brew	Bad Manners
Special Lady	Ray, Goodman & Brown
Special Years, The	Val Doonican
Speedy Gonzales	Pat Boone
Spend The Night	Coolnotes
Spiders & Snakes	Jim Stafford
Spies Like Us	Paul McCartney
Spill The Wine	Eric Burdon & War
Spinning Wheel	Blood Sweat & Tears
Spirit In The Sky	Doctor & The Medics
Spirit In The Sky	Norman Greenbaum
Spirits In The Material World	Police
Splish Splash	Bobby Darin
Splish Splash	Charlie Drake
Spooky	Classics IV
Spot The Pigeon (E.P.)	Genesis
Squeeze Box	Who
S-S-S-Single Bed	Fox
Staccato's Theme	Elmer Bernstein
Stagger Lee	Lloyd Price
Stairway Of Love	Michael Holliday
Stairway To Heaven	Far Corporation
Stairway To Heaven	Rolf Harris
Stairway To Heaven	Neil Sedaka
Stand	R.E.M.
Stand And Deliver	Adam & The Ants
Stand Back	Stevie Nicks
Stand By Me	Ben E. King
Stand By Me	Spyder Turner
Stand By Your Man	Tammy Wynette
Stand Tall	Burton Cummings
Stand Up For Your Love Rights	Yazz
Standing In The Road	Blackfoot Sue
Standing In The Shadows Of Love	Four Tops
Standing On The Corner	Four Lads
Standing On The Corner	King Brothers
Star	Kiki Dee
Star	Erasure
Star On A TV Show	Stylistics
Star Trekkin'	Firm
Star Wars (Main Title)	London Symphony Orchestra
Star Wars Theme/Cantina Band	Meco
Stardust	David Essex
Stardust	Billy Ward & His Dominoes
Starmaker	Kids From 'Fame'
Starman	David Bowie
Starry Eyed	Michael Holliday
Stars	Simply Red
Stars On 45 (Medley)	Starsound (Stars On 45)
Stars On 45 (Vol 2)	Starsound
Stars Shine In Your Eyes	Ronnie Hilton
Start	Jam
Start Me Up	Rolling Stones
Start Movin' (In My Direction)	Sal Mineo
Starting Together	Su Pollard
State Of Shock	Jacksons
Stay	Jackson Browne
Stay	Eternal
Stay	Hollies
Stay	Shakespears Sister
Stay	Maurice Williams & The Zodiacs

423

Title	Artist
Stay Awhile	Bells
Stay Awhile	Dusty Springfield
Stay (Faraway, So Close)	U2
Stay In My Corner	Dells
Stay On These Roads	A-Ha
Stay Out Of My Life	Five Star
Stay The Night	Chicago
Stay With Me	Blue Mink
Stay With Me	Faces
Stayin' Alive	Bee Gees
Steal Away	Robbie Dupree
Steam	Peter Gabriel
Steam Heat	Patti Page
Step Back In Time	Kylie Minogue
Step By Step	Crests
Step By Step	New Kids On The Block
Step By Step	Eddie Rabbitt
Step By Step	Joe Simon
Step Inside Love	Cilla Black
Step It Up	Stereo MCs
Step Off (Pt. 1)	Grandmaster Melle Mel & The Furious Five
Step On	Happy Mondays
Steppin' Out	Joe Jackson
Steppin' Out (Gonna Boogie Tonight)	Tony Orlando & Dawn
Stereotype	Specials
Stewball	Lonnie Donegan
Stick It Out	Right Said Fred & Friends
Stick-Up	Honey Cone
Still	Bill Anderson
Still	Commodores
Still	Karl Denver
Still I'm Sad	Yardbirds
Still The One	Orleans
Still The Same	Bob Seger & The Silver Bullet Band
Still Water (Love)	Four Tops
Stir It Up	Johnny Nash
Stomp!	Brothers Johnson
Stone Love	Kool & The Gang
Stoned Love	Supremes
Stoned Soul Picnic	Fifth Dimension
Stones	Neil Diamond
Stoney End	Barbra Streisand
Stonk, The	Hale & Pace & The Stonkers
Stood Up	Ricky Nelson
Stool Pigeon	Kid Creole & The Coconuts
Stop	Sam Brown
Stop And Smell The Roses	Mac Davis
Stop And Think It Over	Dale & Grace
Stop Draggin' My Heart Around	Stevie Nicks with Tom Petty & The Heartbreakers
Stop Her On Sight (SOS)	Edwin Starr
Stop! In The Name Of Love	Supremes
Stop Me (If You've Heard It All Before)	Billy Ocean
Stop Stop Stop	Hollies
Stop The Cavalry	Jona Lewie
Stop To Love	Luther Vandross
Storm In A Teacup	Fortunes
Stormy	Classics IV
Story Of My Life	Gary Miller
Story Of My Life, The	Michael Holliday
Story Of The Blues, The	Wah!
Story Of Three Loves, The	Winifred Atwell
Story Of Tina	Ronnie Harris
Story Of Tina, The	Al Martino
Story Untold, A	Crew-Cuts
Stowaway	Barbara Lyon
Straight From The Heart	Bryan Adams
Straight On	Heart
Straight Up	Paula Abdul
Straighten Out	Stranglers
Stranded	Heart
Stranded In The Jungle	Cadets
Strange Band	Family
Strange Kind Of Woman	Deep Purple
Strange Lady In Town	Frankie Laine
Strange Little Girl	Stranglers
Strange Magic	Electric Light Orchestra
Strange Way	Firefall
Stranger, The	Shadows
Stranger In Paradise	Tony Bennett
Stranger In Paradise	Eddie Calvert
Stranger In Paradise	Four Aces
Stranger In Paradise	Tony Martin
Stranger On The Shore	Acker Bilk

Title	Artist
Strangers In The Night	Frank Sinatra
Strawberry Fair	Anthony Newley
Strawberry Fields Forever	Beatles
Strawberry Fields Forever	Candy Flip
Strawberry Letter 23	Brothers Johnson
Stray Cat Strut	Stray Cats
Streak, The	Ray Stevens
Street Dance	Break Machine
Street Life	Crusaders
Street Life	Roxy Music
Street Tuff	Rebel MC & Double Trouble
Streets Of London	Ralph McTell
Strike It Up	Black Box
Stripper, The	David Rose & His Orchestra
Stroll, The	Diamonds
Strollin'	Prince & The New Power Generation
Strut	Sheena Easton
Strut Your Funky Stuff	Frantique
Stuck In The Middle With You	Stealer's Wheel
Stuck On You	Elvis Presley
Stuck On You	Lionel Richie
Stuck On You	Trevor Walters
Stuck With You	Huey Lewis & The News
Stumblin' In	Suzi Quatro & Chris Norman
Stupid Cupid	Connie Francis
Stutter Rap (No Sleep 'til Bedtime)	Morris Minor & The Majors
Substitute	Clout
Substitute	Liquid Gold
Substitute	Who
Subterranean Homesick Blues	Bob Dylan
Suburbia	Pet Shop Boys
Success	Dannii Minogue
Such A Feeling	Bizarre Inc
Such A Night	Elvis Presley
Such A Night	Johnnie Ray
(Such An) Easy Question	Elvis Presley
Sucu-Sucu	Laurie Johnson
Suddenly	Angry Anderson
Suddenly	Billy Ocean
Suddenly Last Summer	Motels
Suddenly There's A Valley	Petula Clark
Suddenly There's A Valley	Gogi Grant
Suddenly There's A Valley	Lee Lawrence
Suddenly There's A Valley	Jo Stafford
Suddenly You Love Me	Tremeloes
Suedehead	Morrissey
Sugar And Spice	Searchers
Sugar Baby Love	Rubettes
Sugar Candy Kisses	Mac & Katie Kissoon
Sugar Daddy	Jackson Five
Sugar Me	Lynsey De Paul
Sugar Moon	Pat Boone
Sugar Shack	Jimmy Gilmer & The Fireballs
Sugar Sugar	Archies
Sugar Sugar	Sakkarin
Sugar Town	Nancy Sinatra
Sugar Walls	Sheena Easton
Sugartime	McGuire Sisters
Suicide Blonde	INXS
Sukiyaki	Kenny Ball
Sukiyaki	Kyu Sakamoto
Sukiyaki	Taste Of Honey
Sultana	Titanic
Sultans Of Swing	Dire Straits
Summer	War
Summer Breeze	Seals & Crofts
Summer Holiday	Cliff Richard
Summer In The City	Lovin' Spoonful
Summer Night City	Abba
Summer Nights	Marianne Faithfull
Summer Nights	John Travolta & Olivia Newton-John
Summer Of My Life	Simon May
Summer Of '69	Bryan Adams
Summer Rain	Johnny Rivers
Summer Set	Acker Bilk
Summer Song, A	Chad & Jeremy
Summer (The First Time)	Bobby Goldsboro
Summerlove Sensation	Bay City Rollers
Summertime	D.J. Jazzy Jeff & The Fresh Prince
Summertime	Billy Stewart
Summertime Blues	Blue Cheer
Summertime Blues	Eddie Cochran
Summertime City	Mike Batt
Sun Ain't Gonna Shine Anymore, The	Walker Brothers
Sun Always Shines On T.V., The	A-Ha

Title	Artist
Sun And The Rain, The	Madness
Sun Arise	Rolf Harris
Sun Goes Down (Living It Up), The	Level 42
Sunday Girl	Blondie
Sunday Will Never Be The Same	Spanky & Our Gang
Sundown	Gordon Lightfoot
Sunglasses At Night	Corey Hart
Sunny	Boney M
Sunny	Georgie Fame
Sunny	Bobby Hebb
Sunny Afternoon	Kinks
Sunshine	Jonathan Edwards
Sunshine After The Rain	Elkie Brooks
Sunshine Girl	Herman's Hermits
Sunshine Of Your Love	Cream
Sunshine Of Your Smile	Mike Berry
Sunshine On A Rainy Day	Zoe
Sunshine On My Shoulders	John Denver
Sunshine Superman	Donovan
Super Bad (Pts 1 & 2)	James Brown
Super Freak (Pt. 1)	Rick James
Super Trouper	Abba
Superfly	Curtis Mayfield
Superfly Guy	S'Express
Superman (Gioca Jouer)	Black Lace
Supermarioland	Ambassadors Of Funk Featuring MC Mario
Supernatural Thing Part 1	Ben E. King
Supernature	Cerrone
Superstar	Carpenters
Superstar	Murray Head
Superstition	Stevie Wonder
Superwoman	Karyn White
Sure Gonna Miss Her	Gary Lewis & The Playboys
Surf City	Jan & Dean
Surfer Girl	Beach Boys
Surfin' Bird	Trashmen
Surfin' Safari	Beach Boys
Surfin' U.S.A.	Beach Boys
Surrender	Elvis Presley
Surrender	Diana Ross
Surrender	Swing Out Sister
Surrender To Me	Ann Wilson & Robin Zander
Surround Yourself With Sorrow	Cilla Black
Susan	Buckinghams
Susie Darlin'	Robin Luke
Suspicion	Elvis Presley
Suspicion	Terry Stafford
Suspicious Minds	Fine Young Cannibals
Suspicious Minds	Elvis Presley
Sussudio	Phil Collins
Suzanne Beware Of The Devil	Dandy Livingstone
Suzie Q. (Pt. 1)	Creedence Clearwater Revival
Sway	Dean Martin
Sway	Bobby Rydell
Swayin' To The Music (Slow Dancin')	Johnny Rivers
Swearin' To God	Frankie Valli
Sweat (A La La La La Long)	Inner Circle
Swedish Rhapsody	Mantovani
Swedish Rhapsody	Ray Martin
Sweet And Gentle	Alan Dale
Sweet And Innocent	Donny Osmond
Sweet Blindness	Fifth Dimension
Sweet Caroline	Neil Diamond
Sweet Cherry Wine	Tommy James & The Shondells
Sweet Child O' Mine	Guns N' Roses
Sweet City Woman	Stampeders
Sweet Dream	Jethro Tull
Sweet Dreams	Air Supply
Sweet Dreams	Tommy McLain
Sweet Dreams (Are Made Of This)	Eurythmics
Sweet Freedom	Michael McDonald
Sweet Harmony	Beloved
Sweet Hitch-Hiker	Creedence Clearwater Revival
Sweet Home Alabama	Lynyrd Skynyrd
Sweet Inspiration	Johnny Johnson & The Bandwagon
Sweet Little Mystery	Wet Wet Wet
Sweet Little Sixteen	Chuck Berry
Sweet Love	Anita Baker
Sweet Love	Commodores
Sweet Mary	Wadsworth Mansion
Sweet Nothin's	Brenda Lee
Sweet Old Fashioned Girl, A	Teresa Brewer
Sweet Pea	Tommy Roe
Sweet Seasons	Carole King
Sweet Soul Music	Arthur Conley

424

Title	Artist	Title	Artist	Title	Artist
Sweet Surrender	John Denver	Teach Me Tonight	De Castro Sisters	That's All You Gotta Do	Brenda Lee
Sweet Surrender	Wet Wet Wet	Teacher	Jethro Tull	That's Amore	Dean Martin
(Sweet Sweet Baby) Since		Tear Fell, A	Teresa Brewer	That's How A Love Song Was Born	Ray Burns
You've Been Gone	Aretha Franklin	Teardrops	Shakin' Stevens	That's Life	Frank Sinatra
Sweet Talkin' Guy	Chiffons	Teardrops	Womack & Womack	That's Living (Alright)	Joe Fagin
Sweet Talkin' Woman	Electric Light Orchestra	Tears	Ken Dodd	That's My Home	Acker Bilk
Sweet Thing	Rufus Featuring Chaka Khan	Tears I Cried, The	Glitter Band	That's Old Fashioned (That's The	
Sweeter Than You	Ricky Nelson	Tears In Heaven	Eric Clapton	Way Love Should Be)	Everly Brothers
Sweetest Smile	Black	Tears Of A Clown	Beat	That's Rock 'n' Roll	Shaun Cassidy
Sweetest Taboo, The	Sade	Tears Of A Clown, The	Smokey Robinson &	That's The Way	Honeycombs
Sweetest Thing (I've Ever Known), The	Juice Newton		The Miracles	That's The Way (I Like It)	KC & The Sunshine Band
Sweetheart	Franke & The Knockouts	Tears On My Pillow	Little Anthony & The Imperials	That's The Way Boys Are	Lesley Gore
Sweets For My Sweet	Searchers	Tears On My Pillow	Kylie Minogue	That's The Way God Planned It	Billy Preston
Swing The Mood	Jive Bunny & The Mastermixers	Tears On My Pillow	Johnny Nash	That's The Way I've Always	
Swing Your Daddy	Jim Gilstrap	Tease Me	Chaka Demus & Pliers	Heard It Should Be	Carly Simon
Swingin' School	Bobby Rydell	Teddy Bear	Elvis Presley	That's The Way It Is	Mel & Kim
Swingin' Shepherd Blues	Ted Heath	Teddy Bear	Red Sovine	That's The Way Love Goes	Janet Jackson
Swinging On A Star	Big Dee Irwin	Teen-Age Crush	Tommy Sands	That's The Way Love Is	Marvin Gaye
Swiss Maid	Del Shannon	Teen Angel	Mark Dinning	That's The Way Love Is	Ten City
Swords Of A Thousand Men	Ten Pole Tudor	Teen Beat	Sandy Nelson	That's The Way Of The World	Earth, Wind & Fire
Sylvia	Focus	Teenage Dream	Marc Bolan & T. Rex	That's What Friends Are For	Dionne Warwick & Friends
Sylvia's Mother	Dr. Hook	Teenage Idol	Ricky Nelson	That's What Friends Are For	Deniece Williams
Synchronicity II	Police	Teenage Lament '74	Alice Cooper	That's What I Like	Jive Bunny & The Mastermixers
System Addict	Five Star	Teenage Prayer	Gale Storm	That's What Love Is For	Amy Grant
		Teenage Rampage	Sweet	That's What Love Will Do	Joe Brown & The Bruvvers
Tahiti (From Mutiny On The Bounty)	David Essex	Teenager In Love, A	Dion & The Belmonts	Theme For A Dream	Cliff Richard
Tainted Love	Soft Cell	Teenager In Love, A	Craig Douglas	Theme For Young Lovers	Shadows
Take A Chance On Me	Abba	Teenager In Love, A	Marty Wilde	Theme From 'A Summer Place'	Percy Faith
Take A Letter Maria	R.B. Greaves	Teenagers Romance, A	Ricky Nelson	Theme From 'Close Encounters	
Take A Little Rhythm	Ali Thomson	Telefone (Long Distance Love Affair)	Sheena Easton	Of The Third Kind'	John Williams
Take A Look Around	Temptations	Telegram Sam	T. Rex	Theme From Dixie	Duane Eddy
Take A Message To Mary	Everly Brothers	Telephone Line	Electric Light Orchestra	Theme From Doctor Kildare (Three	
Take Five	Dave Brubeck Quartet	Telephone Man	Meri Wilson	Stars Will Shine Tonight)	Richard Chamberlain
Take Good Care Of Her	Adam Wade	Tell Her About It	Billy Joel	Theme From 'Greatest American	
Take Good Care Of My Baby	Bobby Vee	Tell Her No	Zombies	Hero' (Believe It Or Not)	Joey Scarbury
Take Good Care Of Yourself	Three Degrees	Tell Him	Billie Davis	Theme From Harry's Game	Clannad
Take It Away	Paul McCartney	Tell Him	Exciters	Theme From Hill Street Blues, The	Mike Post Featuring
Take It Easy	Eagles	Tell Him	Hello		Larry Carlton
Take It Easy On Me	Little River Band	Tell Him No	Travis & Bob	Theme From Love Story	Henry Mancini & His Orchestra
Take It On The Run	REO Speedwagon	Tell It Like It Is	Heart	Theme From M*A*S*H (Suicide	
Take It To The Limit	Eagles	Tell It Like It Is	Aaron Neville	Is Painless)	Manic Street Preachers
Take Me Bak 'Ome	Slade	Tell It To My Heart	Taylor Dayne	Theme From M*A*S*H (Suicide Is Painless)	Mash
Take Me Home	Cher	Tell It To The Rain	Four Seasons	Theme From Mahogany (Do You	
Take Me Home	Phil Collins	Tell Laura I Love Her	Ray Peterson	Know Where You're Going To)	Diana Ross
Take Me Home, Country Roads	John Denver	Tell Laura I Love Her	Ricky Valance	Theme From New York New York	Frank Sinatra
Take Me Home Tonight	Eddie Money	Tell Me Something Good	Rufus	Theme From S'Express	S'Express
Take Me In Your Arms (Rock Me)	Doobie Brothers	Tell Me What He Said	Helen Shapiro	Theme From 'Shaft'	Isaac Hayes
Take Me To Heart	Quarterflash	Tell Me What You Want Me To Do	Tevin Campbell	Theme From S.W.A.T.	Rhythm Heritage
Take Me To The Mardi Gras	Paul Simon	Tell Me When	Applejacks	Theme From The Appartment	Ferrante & Teicher
Take Me To Your Heart	Rick Astley	Tell Me Why	Expose	Theme From 'The Legion's Last Patrol'	Ken Thorne &
Take Me With You	Prince & The Revolution	Tell Me Why	Elvis Presley		His Orchestra
Take My Advice	Kym Sims	Tell Me Why	Bobby Vinton	Theme From The Deer Hunter (Cavatina)	Shadows
Take My Breath Away	Berlin	Telstar	Tornados	Theme From 'The Three Penny Opera'	Louis Armstrong
Take On Me	A-Ha	Temma Harbour	Mary Hopkin	Theme From 'The Three Penny Opera'	
Take That Look Of Your Face	Marti Webb	Temple Of Love (1992)	Sisters Of Mercy	(Moritat), A	Richard Hayman & Jan August
Take That Situation	Nick Heyward	Temptation	Corina	Theme From 'The Threepenny Opera'	Billy Vaughn
Take The Long Way Home	Supertramp	Temptation	Everly Brothers	(Theme From) Valley Of The Dolls	Dionne Warwick
Take The Money And Run	Steve Miller Band	Temptation	Heaven 17	Theme Song From 'Song For A	
Take These Chains From My Heart	Ray Charles	Temptation Eyes	Grass Roots	Summer Night'	
Take This Heart	Richard Marx	Tender Love	Force M.D's	Themes From 'The Man With	
Take Time To Know Her	Percy Sledge	Tender Trap, The	Frank Sinatra	The Golden Arm'	Richard Maltby
Take Your Time	Mantronix Featuring Wondress	Tenderly	Nat 'King' Cole	Then Came You	Dionne Warwick
Take Your Time (Do It Right) (pt. 1)	S.O.S. Band	Tennessee	Arrested Development	Then He Kissed Me	Crystals
Takin' Care Of Business	Bachman-Turner Overdrive	Tennessee Wig Walk	Bonnie Lou	Then I Kissed Her	Beach Boys
Takin' It To The Streets	Doobie Brothers	Tequila	Champs	Then You Can Tell Me Goodbye	Casinos
Talk Back Trembling Lips	Johnny Tillotson	Terry	Twinkle	There Are More Questions Than Answers	Johnny Nash
Talk Dirty To Me	Poison	Tetris	Doctor Spin	There But For Fortune	Joan Baez
Talk Of The Town	Pretenders	Thank God I'm A Country Boy	John Denver	There Goes My Baby	Drifters
Talk Talk	Music Machine	Thank U Very Much	Scaffold	There Goes My Everything	Engelbert Humperdinck
Talk To Me	Stevie Nicks	Thank You (Falettinme Be Mice Elf Agin)	Sly &	There Goes My Everything	Elvis Presley
Talk To Me	Sunny & The Sunglows		The Family Stone	There Goes My First Love	Drifters
Talking About My Baby	Impressions	Thanks For The Memory (Wham		There I've Said It Again	Bobby Vinton
Talking In Your Sleep	Crystal Gayle	Bam Thank You Mam)	Slade	There Is A Mountain	Donovan
Talking In Your Sleep	Romantics	That Girl	Stevie Wonder	There It Is	Shalamar
Talking Loud And Clear	Orchestral Manoeuvres	That Girl Belongs To Yesterday	Gene Pitney	There Must Be A Reason	Frankie Laine
	In The Dark	That Lady	Isley Brothers	There Must Be A Way	Frankie Vaughan
Tall Paul	Annette	That Ole Devil Called Love	Alison Moyet	There Must Be An Angel	
Tallahassee Lassie	Freddy Cannon	That Same Old Feeling	Pickettywitch	(Playing With My Heart)	Eurythmics
Tallahassee Lassie	Tommy Steele	That Sounds Good To Me	Jive Bunny &	There There My Dear	Dexy's Midnight Runners
Tammy	Debbie Reynolds		The Mastermixers	There Won't Be Many Coming Home	Roy Orbison
Tap Turns On The Water	C.C.S.	That Sunday, That Summer	Nat 'King' Cole	There'll Be No Teardrops Tonight	Tony Bennett
Tarzan Boy	Baltimora	That Was Yesterday	Foreigner	There'll Be Sad Songs (To Make You Cry)	Billy Ocean
Taste Of Aggro, A	Barron Knights	That'll Be The Day	Crickets	There's A Ghost In My House	R. Dean Taylor
Taste Of Honey, A	Herb Alpert	That'll Be The Day	Linda Ronstadt	There's A Gold Mine In The Sky	Pat Boone
Taste Of Your Tears, The	King	That's All!	Genesis	There's A Heartache Following Me	Jim Reeves
Tea For Two Cha Cha	Tommy Dorsey Orchestra	That's All I Want From You	Jaye P. Morgan	There's A Kind Of Hush	Herman's Hermits

Title	Artist
There's A Kind Of Hush (All Over The World)	Carpenters
There's A Moon Out Tonight	Capris
There's A Whole Lot Of Loving	Guys & Dolls
(There's) Always Something There To Remind Me	Sandie Shaw
There's Always Something There To Remind Me	Naked Eyes
(There's) No Gettin' Over Me	Ronnie Milsap
There's No One Quite Like Grandma	St. Winifred's School Choir
There's No Other Way	Blur
There's The Girl	Heart
These Boots Are Made For Walkin'	Nancy Sinatra
These Dreams	Heart
These Eyes	Guess Who
They Don't Know	Tracey Ullman
They Just Can't Stop It The (Games People Play)	(Detroit) pinners
(They Long To Be) Close To You	Carpenters
They Were Doin' The Mambo	Vaughn Monroe
They're Coming To Take Me Away Ha-Haaa!	Napoleon XIV
Thieves In The Temple	Prince
Thin Wall, The	Ultravox
Thing Called Love, A	Johnny Cash
Things	Bobby Darin
Things Can Only Get Better	Howard Jones
Things That Make You Go Hmmmm....	C&C Music Factory Featuring Freedom Williams
Things We Do For Love	10cc
Think	Aretha Franklin
Think I'm In Love	Eddie Money
Think It Over	Crickets
Think Of Laura	Christopher Cross
Think Twice	Brook Benton
Thinking About Your Love	Kenny Thomas
Thinking Of You	Colour Field
Thinking Of You	Maureen
Thinking Of You	Sa-Fire
Thinking Of You	Sister Sledge
Third Rate Romance	Amazing Rhythm Aces
This Beat Is Technotronic	Technotronic Featuring MC Eric
This Corrosion	Sisters Of Mercy
This Could Be The Night	Loverboy
This Diamond Ring	Gary Lewis & The Playboys
This Door Swings Both Ways	Herman's Hermits
This Flight Tonight	Nazareth
This Girl Is A Woman Now	Gary Puckett & The Union Gap
This Girl's In Love With You	Dionne Warwick
This Golden Ring	Fortunes
This Guy's In Love With You	Herb Alpert
This House	Tracie Spencer
This Is It	Adam Faith
This Is It	Kenny Loggins
This Is It	Dannii Minogue
This Is It	Melba Moore
This Is My Song	Petula Clark
This Is My Song	Harry Secombe
This Is Not A Love Song	Public Image Ltd
This Is Tomorrow	Bryan Ferry
This Little Bird	Marianne Faithfull
This Little Girl	Gary U.S. Bonds
This Magic Moment	Jay & The Americans
This Masquerade	George Benson
This Old Heart Of Mine	Isley Brothers
This Old Heart Of Mine	Rod Stewart with Ronald Isley
This Ole House	Billie Anthony
This Ole House	Rosemary Clooney
This Ole House	Shakin' Stevens
This One's For The Children	New Kids On The Block
This Time	Troy Shondell
This Time I Know It's For Real	Donna Summer
This Time I'm In It For Love	Player
This Time (We'll Get It Right)	England World Cup Squad
This Town Ain't Big Enough For Both Of Us	Sparks
This Used To Be My Playground	Madonna
This Wheel's On Fire	Julie Driscoll, Brian Auger & The Trinity
This Will Be	Natalie Cole
Thorn In My Side	Eurythmics
Those Lazy-Hazy-Crazy Days Of Summer	Nat 'King' Cole

Title	Artist
Those Oldies But Goodies (Remind Me Of You)	Little Caesar & The Romans
Those Were The Days	Mary Hopkin
Thou Shalt Not Steal	Dick & Deedee
Thought I'd Died And Gone To Heaven	Bryan Adams
Thousand Stars, A	Kathy Young With The Innocents
3 A.M. Eternal	KLF Featuring The Children Of The Revolution
Three Bells, The	Browns
Three Coins In The Fountain	Tony Brent
Three Coins In The Fountain	Four Aces
Three Coins In The Fountain	Frank Sinatra
Three Little Pigs	Green Jelly
Three Nights A Week	Fats Domino
Three Stars	Tommy Dee
Three Steps To Heaven	Eddie Cochran
Three Steps To Heaven	Showaddywaddy
Three Times A Lady	Commodores
3 X 3 (E.P.)	Genesis
Thrill Is Gone, The	B.B. King
Thriller	Michael Jackson
Through The Barricades	Spandau Ballet
Through The Years	Kenny Rogers
Throw Down A Line	Cliff Richard
Throwing It All Away	Genesis
Thunder In Mountains	Toyah
Thunder Island	Jay Ferguson
Thunderbirds Are Go	FAB Featuring MC Parker
Ticket To Ride	Beatles
Tide Is High, The	Blondie
Tie A Yellow Ribbon Round The Old Oak Tree	Dawn
Tie Me Kangaroo Down, Sport	Rolf Harris
Tiger	Fabian
Tiger Feet	Mud
Tight Rope	Leon Russell
Tighten Up	Archie Bell & The Drells
Tighter, Tighter	Alive & Kicking
Tijuana Jail	Kingston Trio
('Til) I Kissed You	Everly Brothers
Till	Tom Jones
Till The End Of The Day	Kinks
Till Then	Hilltoppers
Till We Two Are One	Georgie Shaw
Time	Craig Douglas
Time	Alan Parsons Project
Time After Time	Cyndi Lauper
Time (Clock Of The Heart)	Culture Club
Time Drags By	Cliff Richard
Time Has Come, The	Adam Faith
Time Has Come Today	Chambers Brothers
Time In A Bottle	Jim Croce
Time Is On My Side	Rolling Stones
Time Is Tight	Booker T. & The M.G.'s
Time Is Time	Andy Gibb
Time, Love And Tenderness	Michael Bolton
Time Of The Season	Zombies
Time Passages	Al Stewart
Time To Make You Mine	Lisa Stansfield
Time Warp, The	Damian
Time Won't Let Me	Outsiders
Times Of Your Life	Paul Anka
Times They Are A-Changin'	Bob Dylan
Tin Man	America
Tin Soldier	Small Faces
Tina Marie	Perry Como
Tired Of Being Alone	Al Green
Tired Of Toein' The Line	Rocky Burnette
Tired Of Waiting For You	Kinks
To All The Girls I've Loved Before	Julio Iglesias & Willie Nelson
To Be A Lover	Billy Idol
To Be Loved	Malcolm Vaughan
To Be Or Not To Be	B.A. Robertson
To Be With You	Mr. Big
To Be With You Again	Level 42
To Cut A Long Story Short	Spandau Ballet
To Know Him, Is To Love Him	Teddy Bears
To Know You Is To Love You	Peter & Gordon
To Love Somebody	Michael Bolton
To Love Somebody	Nina Simone
To Love Somebody	Jimmy Somerville
To Sir With Love	Lulu
To Whom It Concerns	Chris Andrews
Tobacco Road	Nashville Teens
Toccata	Sky
Today	Talk Talk

Title	Artist
Together	Connie Francis
Together	P.J. Proby
Together	Tierra
Together Forever	Rick Astley
Together In Electric Dreams	Giorgio Moroder & Phil Oakey
Together We Are Beautiful	Fern Kinney
Tokoloshe Man	John Kongos
Tokyo Melody	Helmut Zacharias Orchestra
Tom Dooley	Lonnie Donegan
Tom Dooley	Kingston Trio
Tom Hark	Elias & His Zigzag Jive Flutes
Tom Hark	Piranhas
Tom Traubert's Blues (Waltzing Matilda)	Rod Stewart
Tom's Diner	DNA Featuring Suzanne Vega
Tomboy	Perry Como
Tomorrow	Johnny Brandon
Tomorrow	Sandie Shaw
Tomorrow Night	Atomic Rooster
Tomorrow's (Just Another Day)	Madness
Tom-Tom Turnaround	New World
Tonight	Ferrante & Teicher
Tonight	Kool & The Gang
Tonight	Move
Tonight	New Kids On The Block
Tonight	Rubettes
Tonight I Celebrate My Love	Peabo Bryson & Roberta Flack
Tonight I'm Yours (Don't Hurt Me)	Rod Stewart
Tonight She Comes	Cars
Tonight Tonight Tonight	Genesis
Tonight You Belong To Me	Patience & Prudence
Tonight's The Night (Gonna Be Alright)	Rod Stewart
Too Blind To See It	Kym Sims
Too Busy Thinking About My Baby	Marvin Gaye
Too Good To Be Forgotten	Amazulu
Too Good To Be Forgotten	Chi-Lites
Too Hot	Kool & The Gang
Too Hot To Handle	Heatwave
Too Late For Goodbyes	Julian Lennon
Too Late To Say Goodbye	Richard Marx
Too Late To Turn Back Now	Cornelius Brothers & Sister Rose
Too Many Broken Hearts	Jason Donovan
Too Many Rivers	Brenda Lee
Too Many Walls	Cathy Dennis
Too Much	Bros
Too Much	Elvis Presley
Too Much Heaven	Bee Gees
Too Much Love Will Kill You	Brian May
Too Much Time On My Hands	Styx
Too Much, Too Little, Too Late	Johnny Mathis & Deniece Williams
Too Much Too Young E.P	Specials
Too Nice To Talk To	Beat
Too Shy	Kajagoogoo
Too Soon To Know	Roy Orbison
Too Young	Donny Osmond
Too Young To Die	Jamiroquai
Too Young To Go Steady	Nat 'King' Cole
Toofunky	George Michael
Top Of The World	Carpenters
Topsy II	Cozy Cole
Torch	Soft Cell
Torn Between Two Lovers	Mary MacGregor
Tossin' And Turnin'	Bobby Lewis
Tossing And Turning	Ivy League
Total Eclipse Of The Heart	Bonnie Tyler
Total Mix, The	Black Box
Touch Me	Doors
Touch Me	49ers
Touch Me (All Night Long)	Cathy Dennis
Touch Me (I Want Your Body)	Samantha Fox
Touch Me In The Morning	Diana Ross
Touch Me Touch Me	Dave Dee, Dozy, Beaky, Mick & Tich
Touch Me When We're Dancing	Carpenters
Touch Of Grey	Grateful Dead
Touch Too Much, A	Arrows
Touchy!	A-Ha
Tougher Than The Rest	Bruce Springsteen
Tower Of Strength	Gene McDaniels
Tower Of Strength	Mission
Tower Of Strength	Frankie Vaughan
Town Called Malice	Jam

Title	Artist
Town Without Pity	Gene Pitney
Toy Balloons	Russ Conway
Toy Boy	Sinitta
Toy Soldiers	Martika
Traces	Classics IV
Tracks Of My Tears, The	Smokey Robinson & The Miracles
Tracks Of My Tears, The	Johnny Rivers
Tracy	Cuff Links
Tragedy	Bee Gees
Tragedy	Fleetwoods
Tragedy	Thomas Wayne
Trail Of The Lonesome Pine, The	Laurel & Hardy & The Avalon Boys
Train Of Thought	A-Ha
Trains And Boats And Planes	Burt Bacharach
Trains And Boats And Planes	Billy J. Kramer & The Dakotas
Tramp	Salt 'n' Pepa
Transfusion	Nervous Norvus
Trapped	Colonel Abrams
Trapped By A Thing Called Love	Denise La Salle
Travelin' Band	Creedence Clearwater Revival
Travelin' Man	Ricky Nelson
Travellin' Light	Cliff Richard
Treat Her Like A Lady	Cornelius Brothers & Sister Rose
Treat Her Right	Roy Head
Tribal Dance	2 Unlimited
Tribute (Right On)	Pasadenas
Tricky Disco	Tricky Disco
Trip To Trumpton, A	Urban Hype
Troglodyte (Cave Man)	Jimmy Castor Bunch
Trooper, The	Iron Maiden
Trouble	Lindsey Buckingham
Trouble Man	Marvin Gaye
Truck On (Tyke)	T. Rex
Trudie	Joe 'Mr. Piano' Henderson
True	Spandau Ballet
True Blue	Madonna
True Colors	Cyndi Lauper
True Faith	New Order
True Love	Bing Crosby & Grace Kelly
True Love	Glenn Frey
True Love	Elton John & Kiki Dee
True Love	Jane Powell
True Love Ways	Peter & Gordon
True Love Ways	Cliff Richard
Truly	Lionel Richie
Try It Baby	Marvin Gaye
Try To Remember	Gladys Knight & The Pips
Tryin' To Get The Feeling Again	Barry Manilow
Tryin' To Live My Life Without You	Bob Seger & The Silver Bullet Band
Tryin' To Love Two	William Bell
Trying To Hold On To My Woman	Lamont Dozier
TSOP (The Sound Of Philadelphia)	MFSB Featuring The Three Degrees
Tubular Bells	Mike Oldfield
Tuff Enuff	Fabulous Thunderbirds
Tulane	Steve Gibbons Band
Tulips From Amsterdam	Max Bygraves
Tumbling Dice	Rolling Stones
Tunnel Of Love	Bruce Springsteen
Tunnel Of Love, The	Fun Boy Three
Turn Around Look At Me	Vogues
Turn Back The Hands Of Time	Tyrone Davis
Turn It On Again	Genesis
Turn It Up	Conway Brothers
Turn Me Loose	Fabian
Turn The Beat Around	Vicki Sue Robinson
Turn The Music Up	Players Association
Turn To Stone	Electric Light Orchestra
Turn! Turn! Turn!	Byrds
Turn Up The Bass	Tyree Featuring Kool Rock Steady
Turn Your Love Around	George Benson
Turning Japanese	Vapors
Turtle Power	Partners In Kryme
Tusk	Fleetwood Mac
Tweedle Dee	Georgia Gibbs
Tweedle Dee	Little Jimmy Osmond
Tweedle Dee Tweedle Dum	Middle Of The Road
Twelfth Of Never, The	Johnny Mathis
Twelfth Of Never, The	Donny Osmond
Twelfth Of Never, The	Cliff Richard
20th Century Boy	T. Rex
Twenty Five Miles	Edwin Starr

Title	Artist
25 Or 6 To 4	Chicago
Twenty Four Hours From Tulsa	Gene Pitney
26 Miles	Four Preps
Twenty Tiny Fingers	Stargazers
Twilight Time	Platters
Twilight Zone	Golden Earring
Twilight Zone	2 Unlimited
Twine Time	Alvin Cash & The Crawlers
Twist, The	Chubby Checker
Twist & Shout	Deacon Blue
Twist And Shout	Beatles
Twist And Shout	Chaka Demus & Pliers/ Jack Radics/Taxi Gang
Twist And Shout	Brian Poole & The Tremeloes
Twist And Shout	Salt 'n' Pepa
Twist Of Fate	Olivia Newton-John
Twist, Twist Senora	Gary U.S. Bonds
Twist (Yo, Twist), The	Fat Boys & Chubby Checker
Twistin' The Night Away	Sam Cooke
Two Different Worlds	Ronnie Hilton
Two Faces Have I	Lou Christie
2-4-6-8 Motorway	Tom Robinson Band
Two Hearts	Pat Boone
Two Hearts	Phil Collins
Two Kinds Of Teardrops	Del Shannon
Two Little Boys	Rolf Harris
Two Lovers	Mary Wells
Two Occasions	Deele
Two Of Hearts	Stacey Q
Two Out Of Three Ain't Bad	Meat Loaf
Two Pints Of Lager And A Packet Of Crisps Please	Splodgenessabounds
Two Princes	Spin Doctors
Two Steps Behind	Def Leppard
Two To Make It Right	Seduction
Two Tribes	Frankie Goes To Hollywood
Typical Male	Tina Turner
U Can't Touch This	M.C. Hammer
U Got 2 Know	Cappella
U Got 2 Let The Music	Cappella
U Got The Look	Prince
Ugly Duckling, The	Mike Reid
Uh! Oh! Part 2	Nutty Squirrels
Uhh Ahh	Boyz II Men
Um Um Um Um Um Um	Wayne Fontana & The Mindbenders
Um, Um, Um, Um, Um, Um	Major Lance
Un Banc, Un Abre, Une Rue	Severine
Una Paloma Blanca	Jonathan King
Unbelievable	EMF
Unchain My Heart	Ray Charles
Unchained Melody	Les Baxter
Unchained Melody	Roy Hamilton
Unchained Melody	Al Hibbler
Unchained Melody	Righteous Brothers
Unchained Melody	Jimmy Young
Uncle Albert-Admiral Halsey	Paul & Linda McCartney
Unconditional Love	Donna Summer
Under Pressure	Queen & David Bowie
Under The Boardwalk	Drifters
Under The Boardwalk	Bruce Willis
Under The Bridge	Red Hot Chili Peppers
Under The Bridges Of Paris	Eartha Kitt
Under The Bridges Of Paris	Dean Martin
Under The Moon Of Love	Showaddywaddy
Under Your Thumb	Godley & Creme
Undercover Angel	Alan O'Day
Undercover Of The Night	Rolling Stones
Uneasy Rider	Charlie Daniels Band
Unforgettable	Natalie Cole
Unforgettable Fire, The	U2
Unicorn, The	Irish Rovers
Union City Blue	Blondie
Union Of The Snake	Duran Duran
United We Stand	Brotherhood Of Man
Unskinny Bop	Poison
Until It's Time For You To Go	Elvis Presley
Until You Come Back To Me (That's What I'm Gonna Do)	Aretha Franklin
Up Around The Bend	Creedence Clearwater Revival
Up On The Roof	Drifters
Up On The Roof	Kenny Lynch
Up The Junction	Squeeze
Up The Ladder To The Roof	Supremes
Up The Pool	Jethro Tull

Title	Artist
Up Up & Away	Fifth Dimension
Up Up And Away	Johnny Mann Singers
Up Where We Belong	Joe Cocker & Jennifer Warnes
Upside Down	Diana Ross
Uptight (Everything's Alright)	Stevie Wonder
Uptown	Crystals
Uptown Girl	Billy Joel
Uptown Top Ranking	Althia And Donna
Urgent	Foreigner
Use It Up And Wear It Out	Odyssey
Use Me	Bill Withers
Use Ta Be My Girl	O'Jays
Vacation	Connie Francis
Vacation	Go-Go's
Valentine	T'Pau
Valerie	Steve Winwood
Valleri	Monkees
Valley Of Tears	Fats Domino
Valley Road, The	Bruce Hornsby & The Range
Valotte	Julian Lennon
Vaya Con Dios	Les Paul & Mary Ford
Vehicle	Ides Of March
Veni Vidi Vici	Ronnie Hilton
Ventura Highway	America
Venus	Frankie Avalon
Venus	Bananarama
Venus	Don Pablo's Animals
Venus	Shocking Blue
Venus And Mars Rock Show	Wings
Venus In Blue Jeans	Jimmy Clanton
Venus In Blue Jeans	Mark Wynter
Very Special Love Song, A	Charlie Rich
Vibeology	Paula Abdul
Victim Of Love	Erasure
Victims	Culture Club
Victory	Kool & The Gang
Video Killed The Radio Star	Buggles
Vienna	Ultravox
Vienna Calling	Falco
View To Kill, A	Duran Duran
Village Of St. Bernadette, The	Andy Williams
Vincent	Don McLean
Virginia Plain	Roxy Music
Vision Of Love	Mariah Carey
Visions	Cliff Richard
Viva Bobbie Joe	Equals
Viva Las Vegas	Elvis Presley
Viva Las Vegas	ZZ Top
Vogue	Madonna
Voice In The Wilderness	Cliff Richard
Voices Carry	Til Tuesday
Voices That Care	Voices That Care
Volare	Marino Marini
Volare	Dean Martin
Volare	Bobby Rydell
Voodoo Chile	Jimi Hendrix Experience
Voodoo Ray E.P.	A Guy Called Gerald
Voulez Vous	Abba
Voyage Voyage	Desireless
Wah-Watusi, The	Orlons
Wait	Robert Howard & Kym Mazelle
Wait	White Lion
Wait For Me	Malcolm Vaughan
Waitin' In School	Ricky Nelson
Waiting For A Girl Like You	Foreigner
Waiting For A Star To Fall	Boy Meets Girl
Waiting For A Train	Flash And The Pan
Waiting For An Alibi	Thin Lizzy
Waiting For Love	Alias
Waiting On A Friend	Rolling Stones
Wake Me Up Before You Go-Go	Wham!
Wake The Town And Tell The People	Les Baxter
Wake Up Everybody (Pt. 1)	Harold Melvin & The Blue Notes
Wake Up Little Susie	Everly Brothers
Walk, The	Jimmy McCracklin
Walk A Mile In My Shoes	Joe South
Walk Away	Matt Monro
Walk Away From Love	David Ruffin
Walk Away Renee	Four Tops
Walk Away Renee	Left Banke
Walk Don't Run	John Barry Seven
Walk-Don't Run	Ventures
Walk-Don't Run '64	Ventures

427

429

Title	Artist
You'll Never Walk Alone	The Crowd
You'll Never Walk Alone	Gerry & The Pacemakers
You're A Lady	Peter Skellern
You're A Special Part Of Me	Marvin Gaye & Diana Ross
You're A Wonderful One	Marvin Gaye
You're All I Need To Get By	Marvin Gaye & Tammi Terrell
You're All That Matters To Me	Curtis Stigers
You're Breakin' My Heart	Keely Smith
You're Driving Me Crazy	Temperance Seven
You're Gonna Get Next To Me	Bo Kirkland & Ruth Davis
(You're) Having My Baby	Paul Anka with Odia Coates
You're History	Shakespear's Sister
You're In A Bad Way	Saint Etienne
You're In Love	Wilson Phillips
You're In My Heart	Rod Stewart
You're More Than A Number In My Little Red Book	Drifters
You're Moving Out Today	Carole Bayer Sager
You're My Best Friend	Queen
You're My Everything	Temptations
(You're My) Soul And Inspiration	Righteous Brothers
You're My World	Cilla Black
You're No Good	Linda Ronstadt
You're No Good	Swinging Blue Jeans
You're Not Alone	Chicago
You're Only Human (Second Wind)	Billy Joel
You're Only Lonely	J.D. Souther
You're Ready Now	Frankie Valli
You're Sixteen	Johnny Burnette
You're Sixteen	Ringo Starr
You're So Vain	Carly Simon
You're Such A Good Looking Woman	Joe Dolan
(You're The) Devil In Disguise	Elvis Presley
You're The First, The Last, My Everything	Barry White
You're The Inspiration	Chicago
You're The One	Vogues
You're The One That I Want	John Travolta & Olivia Newton-John
You're The Only Woman (You & I)	Ambrosia
You're The Reason	Bobby Edwards
You're The Reason I'm Living	Bobby Darin
You're The Voice	John Farnham
You've Got A Friend	James Taylor
You've Got Me Dangling On A String	Chairmen Of The Board
(You've Got) The Magic Touch	Platters
You've Got To Hide Your Love Away	Silkie
You've Got Your Troubles	Fortunes
You've Lost That Lovin' Feelin'	Cilla Black
You've Lost That Lovin' Feelin'	Righteous Brothers
You've Lost That Lovin' Feeling	Daryl Hall & John Oates
You've Made Me So Very Happy	Blood Sweat & Tears
You've Never Been In Love Like This Before	Unit 4 Plus 2
You've Really Got A Hold On Me	Miracles
Young And Foolish	Edmund Hockridge
Young At Heart	Bluebells
Young-At-Heart	Frank Sinatra
Young Blood	Coasters
Young Emotions	Ricky Nelson
Young Gifted And Black	Bob & Marcia
Young Girl	Union Gap Featuring Gary Puckett
Young Guns (Go For It)	Wham!
Young Hearts Run Free	Candi Staton
Young Love	Tab Hunter
Young Love	Sonny James
Young Love	Donny Osmond
Young Lovers	Paul & Paula
Young New Mexican Puppeteer, The	Tom Jones
Young Ones, The	Cliff Richard
Young Parisians	Adam & The Ants
Young Turks	Rod Stewart
Young World	Rick Nelson
Your Cheatin' Heart	Ray Charles
Your Love	Outfield
(Your Love Has Lifted Me) Higher And Higher	Rita Coolidge
(Your Love Keeps Lifting Me) Higher And Higher	Jackie Wilson
Your Love Is Driving Me Crazy	Sammy Hagar
Your Love Is King	Sade
Your Mama Don't Dance	Loggins & Messina
Your Mama Don't Dance	Poison
Your Precious Love	Marvin Gaye & Tammi Terrell
Your Song	Elton John
Your Wildest Dreams	Moody Blues
Yummy Yummy Yummy	Ohio Express
Zabadak	Dave Dee, Dozy, Beaky, Mick & Tich
Zambesi	Lou Busch
Zambesi	Eddie Calvert
Zip-A-Dee Doo-Dah	Bob B. Soxx & The Blue Jeans
Zoom	Fat Larry's Band
Zorba The Greek	Herb Alpert
Zorba's Dance	Marcello Minerbi

431